ESSENTIAL
AUSTRALIA

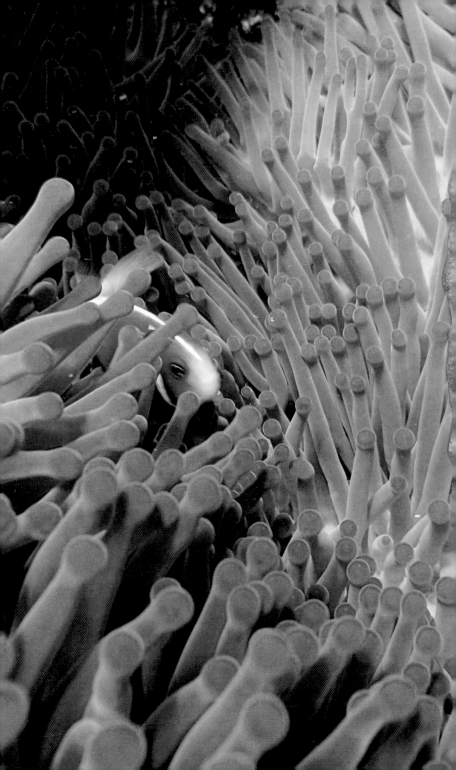

Welcome to Australia

A vast island continent, Australia teems with natural and cultural treasures. Relax on gorgeous beaches along the sprawling coastline, or plunge below the water in Queensland to explore the Great Barrier Reef. Nature enthusiasts revel in exciting adventures in the interior, from trekking around majestic Uluru to spotting wildlife in tropical rain forests. But there's more to life down under than outdoor activities. Cosmopolitan cities like Sydney and Melbourne entice with thriving dining and arts scenes, while world-class vineyards abound.

TOP REASONS TO GO

★ **Cool Cities:** Vibrant Sydney, artsy Melbourne, laidback Brisbane, far-flung Perth.

★ **Beaches:** From Bondi to the Gold Coast, stylish strands cater to all tastes.

★ **Food and Wine:** Mod Oz cuisine, top-notch whites and reds, and, of course, the barbie.

★ **Untamed Nature:** Adventures await in the Great Barrier Reef, the Outback, and Tasmania.

★ **Aboriginal Culture:** A rich heritage of music, art, and stories continues to thrive.

★ **Unique Wildlife:** From kangaroos to koalas, the wildlife here is sure to delight.

Contents

Fodor's Features

Contents

EXPERIENCE AUSTRALIA

26 ULTIMATE EXPERIENCES

Australia offers terrific experiences that should be on every traveler's list. Here are Fodor's top picks for a memorable trip.

1 Dive the Great Barrier Reef

The world's largest coral reef and one of the world's most spectacular natural attractions, the Great Barrier Reef can be explored on a day tour from Cairns or Port Douglas but is best experienced over a few days. Stay on the Whitsundays, snorkel and dive, and maybe even charter your own yacht or sailboat. *(Ch. 9)*

2 Shop For Aboriginal Art

Symbolic dot paintings and vibrant landscapes make beautiful souvenirs and reputable galleries and cooperatives now offer ethical shopping opportunities that also support Indigenous communities. *(Ch. 1)*

3 Marvel at the Big Prawn

A uniquely Australian penchant for giant food and animals has resulted in over 150 novelty structures across the country. The Big Prawn and the Big Banana are popular Queensland attractions. *(Ch. 8)*

4 Float in an Ocean Pool

Bermagui's Blue Pool is a natural ocean pool at the base of a cliff that is constantly refreshed with clear ocean water. Great for views and an invigorating swim. *(Ch. 4)*

5 Catch Footy Fever

Fast-paced Aussie Rules Football or Footy is the most popular sport in Australia. Go to a match (March to October), eat meat pies and sauce, and bond with locals. *(Ch. 5)*

6 Take an Epic Train Trip

Travel by train across Australia, through the majestic Blue Mountains and spectacular Nullarbor Plains, stopping at some of Australia's greatest sights along the way. *(Ch. 3)*

7 Aboriginal Culture

From Rock Art at Kakadu, Nourlangie Rock, and Ubirr to indigenous artists at work at Uluru, to understand Australia you need to visit its red heart. *(Ch. 11)*

8 Bungle Bungles

Hike this striking landscape of tiger-striped sandstone domes, through the towering walls of the narrow Echidna Chasm and to the natural amphitheatre of Cathedral Gorge. *(Ch. 11)*

9 Climb the Sydney Harbor Bridge

An iconic must-do, the 3.5-hour climb of the world's largest steel bridge rewards climbers with unbeatable 360-degree views of Sydney. *(Ch. 3)*

10 The Three Capes Track

This four-day bushwalk through rainforest, grasslands, and along steep bluffs takes you to the edge of the world, but with cabins and yoga mats along the way. *(Ch. 7)*

11 Kangaroo Island

One of the best places in Australia to see native wildlife up close, Kangaroo Island offers kangaroos aplenty as well as wild koalas, rare birds and seals, and black swans, too. *(Ch. 10)*

12 Parkes Observatory

Known for receiving the first images of the Apollo 11 moon landing, Parkes Observatory still offers some of the clearest skies and best star-spotting in Australia. *(Ch. 4)*

13 Feel the MONA Effect

Hobart's eclectic Museum of Old and New Art presents playful and provocative art in a subterranean, multi-tiered labyrinth cut into sandstone cliffs. *(Ch. 7)*

14 Hyams Beach

Located on the southern shores of Jervis Bay, Hyams Beach has clear, turquoise waters and pristine, bleached-white sands which have been recognized as the whitest sands in the world. *(Ch. 4)*

15 Sip Local Wine

The acclaimed Barossa wine region is home to prestigious winemakers including Penfolds and Henschke Cellars, as well as the popular labels Wolf Blass and Jacob's Creek. *(Ch. 10)*

16 Penguin Watch on Phillip Island

Watch the world's smallest species of penguin return home to their sandy burrows and see fur seals and koalas in their natural habits at this haven for wildlife. *(Ch. 6)*

17 Great Ocean Roadtrip

Enjoy expansive views of the Southern Ocean, pretty coastal towns, and temperate rainforests on an epic coastline drive from Melbourne to the 12 Apostles and beyond. *(Ch. 6)*

18 Sunset at Uluru

Walk Uluru's base trail before relaxing at a sunset viewing area to see this iconic sandstone monolith shift from ochre to orange to dark red. *(Ch. 11)*

19 Go Glamping

Secluded, luxurious safari tents with private decks and firepits in the stunning setting of Ikara-Flinders Ranges National Park bring you close to nature in style. *(Ch. 10)*

20 Surf School

Just north of Sydney, Newcastle boasts two world-class surfing beaches and multiple local surf schools. Beginners surf lessons usually run over three days. *(Ch. 3)*

21 Sail the Whitsundays

Bareboat through the waters of the idyllic Whitsunday islands and let the wind take you where it will, stopping only to swim, snorkel, or snooze. *(Ch. 9)*

22 Experience Cafe Culture

Melbourne is the epicenter of the nation's coffee obsession and you'll find a bewildering variety of caffeinated beverages in cute cafes tucked into its alleyways. *(Ch. 5)*

23 Coober Pedy

A "cool" stop halfway between Adelaide and Alice Springs, this small opal-mining town avoids desert heat with its unique subterranean residences, museum, bar, and hotel. *(Ch. 10)*

24 Turtle-Hatching

Ranger-led Turtle Encounters take place November to March at Mon Repos Conservation Park where thousands of baby turtles make a nightly dash from sandy nests to warm waters. *(Ch. 8)*

25 Litchfield National Park

A daytrip from Darwin, this park offers some of the best, and prettiest, swimming holes in the Top End including Buley Rockholes and Wangi and Florence Falls. *(Ch. 11)*

26 Fall in Love with a Quokka

Rottnest Island off the coast of Perth is home to a cat-sized marsupial (and social media star) with a cuddly appearance and a tendency to smile. *(Ch. 9)*

WHAT'S WHERE

1 Sydney. One of the most naturally beautiful cities in the world, Sydney blends beachside cool with corporate capitalism and Victorian-era colonial architecture. Arts, tourism, and business thrive around Sydney Harbour

2 New South Wales. Southeastern Australia displays most of the continent's rural and coastal variations: historic towns, mountains, dramatic beaches, and world-class vineyards.

3 Melbourne. Melbourne is Australia's most European city and a cultural melting pot; you can see that in its fantastic food and café scene.

4 Victoria. Rugged coastline, historic towns, wineries, fairy penguins, and national parks are reason enough to explore the Victorian countryside.

5 Tasmania. From Freycinet Peninsula to wild South West National Park, Tasmania's natural beauty testifies to Australia's topographic diversity. Don't miss the relics of the island's volatile days as a penal colony.

6 South East Queensland. Name your pleasure and you'll find it in Brisbane and sunny Queensland: nearly deserted beaches, lush rain forests, great restaurants, and easy access to family-friendly parks.

7 The Great Barrier Reef. Queensland's crown jewel is the 2,600-km-long (1,616-mile-long) Great Barrier Reef. More than 3,000 individual reefs and 900 islands make up this vast aquatic universe.

8 Adelaide and South Australia. Well-planned and picturesque Adelaide has many charms, including its famous biennial festival of the arts. Be sure to take a tour of the region's renowned wine country, and then unwind on a Murray River cruise.

9 The Outback. This region stuns with its diversity. In the country's vast, central desert region are Uluru and Kata Tjuta, monoliths of deep significance to the local Aboriginal people. Darwin is the gateway to World Heritage wetlands, monster cattle ranches, and rock art.

10 Perth and Western Australia. This is a remote, awe-inspiring region and the producer of much of Australia's mineral wealth. It includes the country's sunniest capital, Perth, and top-notch wine valleys.

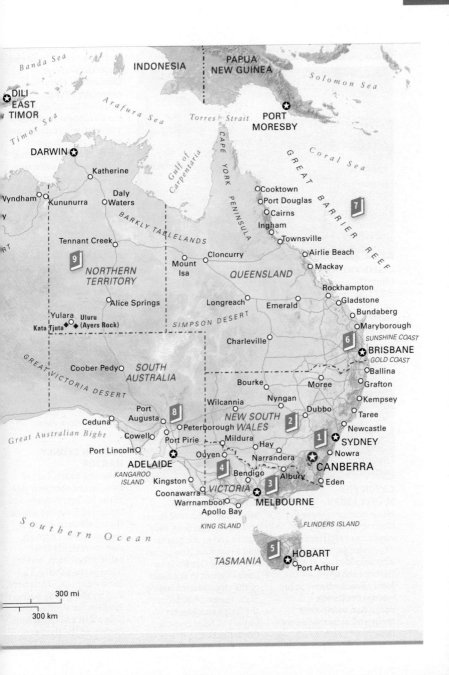

Ultimate Sydney

CLIMB THE HARBOUR BRIDGE

Climb the arches of one of the most famous bridges in the world for breathtaking views of one of the most iconic harbors in the world. The climb can be done by day or night and takes about 3 hours. Alternately, walk the bridge free of charge via the stairs on Cumberland Street.

CATCH THE MANLY FERRY

While most people use the historic Manly Ferry to commute to and from the city center, for visitors it offers glorious views of the Harbour and an escape to Manly Beach where you can wander the Corso's pedestrian strip before cooling off at one of Sydney's famed surf beaches.

THE ROYAL BOTANIC GARDEN

With over 70 acres of lawns and planted gardens, rare native and exotic plants, and a romantic rose garden, the Botanic Garden is an oasis of green in the heart of the city. Catch changing plant-themed exhibitions at the Calyx and The Art Gallery of NSW is in the Garden, too.

EAT AUSTRALIAN–CHINESE FOOD

Chinese food is the most popular cuisine in Australia and so if you want to eat like a local in Sydney, you'll want to visit Sydney's lively Chinatown, Australia's largest Chinatown. The area is especially alive on weekend mornings with the Cantonese tradition of yum cha, where diners are served from dozens of roaming trolleys bearing delights such as dim sum, roast duck, Singapore noodles, and steamed pork buns. Locals flock to Nine Dragons for all-day service.

TASTE AUTHENTIC SICILIAN GELATO

Founded in Darlinghurst in 2002, Gelato Messina has gained a cult following across Australia for its out–of–this–world flavors that change weekly (like baklava and matcha.) Made with milk from the Palumbo brothers' own dairy farm, Gelato Messina takes its name from their parents' hometown in Italy and continues the tradition with a modern twist.

SWIM IN SYDNEY HARBOR

Balmoral Beach, tucked away in the northern side of the harbor, is sandy and protected from the waves that crash on the rest of the coastline. There are also some shady trees behind the beach, making it the perfect spot for a family day out. While here, stop by the trendy Bathers' Pavilion for a coffee and grab a fish and chips from Bottom of the Harbour.

BONDI TO COOGEE COASTAL WALK

Bondi Beach, while beautiful, is often extremely crowed during the summer months. Fortunately, local favorites Tamarama, Bronte, and Coogee are all easily accessible via a four-mile clifftop walk that winds along the coast and offers stunning views, parks, bays, rock pools, and yes –beaches, on the way.

STROLL BARANGAROO

Sydney's coolest new neighborhood is an ongoing urban renewal project that runs along Sydney Harbour, offering a promenade open for walking and cycling, and trendy boutiques, cafes, and restaurants, most notably the three-level architectural gem, Barangaroo House.

BUSHWALK TO THE BEACH

Ku–ring–gai Chase National Park is only 15 miles north of the Sydney city center but feels a world away with rainforests, cliffs, mangroves, and hidden beaches. The Resolute Beach track is a classic two-mile trail that takes in Red Hands Cave which contains Aboriginal art made over 2000 years ago as well as engravings made by the Guringai people. The destination, Resolute Beach, is a secluded, sandy stretch with views of Barrenjoey Headland and Pittwater. A permit system is in effect between October and May so book early if your dates are limited.

SEE A SHOW AT THE OPERA HOUSE

Tucked under the unique sail design of this iconic sight are multiple venues that host everything from rap to musical theatre. The Australian Ballet, the Sydney Dance Company, and the Australian Opera Company are all regulars, and with over 40 shows a week performed in total.

Australia's Top Natural Wonders

LAKE HILLIER

This bubble-gum pink lake off the coast of Western Australia is not fully understood by scientists: the unique color is likely caused by high salinity combined with a specific bacteria, but unlike other pink lakes, Lake Hillier's waters remain bright all year round, even when bottled.

BLUE MOUNTAINS

This World Heritage area offers stunning scenery and dramatic valleys, canyons, and cliff faces carved by wind and water over millennia; Aboriginal engravings; excellent bushwalks; and some of the country's most diverse flora and fauna. Sunlight refracting off the fine oil mist from the world's most ecologically diverse tract of eucalypt forests gives the mountains their famous hue.

CRADLE MOUNTAIN

Part of the Tasmanian Wilderness World Heritage Area, the majestic Cradle Mountain looms over grasslands, rainforest, pines and beech trees, as well as gorgeous alpine lakes. To reach the summit is a full-day hike, and you might just encounter Tasmanian devils and echidnas along the way.

KAKADU NATIONAL PARK

Australia's largest national park is home to some of Australia's most significant Aboriginal rock art sites (Ubirr and Nourlangie); the rock pool made famous by the Crocodile Dundee movie; thousands of plant species and wildlife, and over thirty established bushwalk trails.

LORD HOWE ISLAND

In the Tasman Sea, between Australia and New Zealand, this secluded natural paradise is packed full of outdoor activities, thanks to a sheltered lagoon on one side and a pumping surf beach on the other. Almost half the island's native plants are endemic, including a cloud forest on the island's highest point, Mt Gower. Only 400 tourists are permitted to stay on the island at a time.

THE PINNACLES

Dutch explorers first though these pillars were the remains of an ancient city (if you look closely, you might be able to make out human-like figures among the thousands of ghostly limestone pillars), while others compare this bizarre Western Australian landscape to the surface of Mars.

DAINTREE RAINFOREST

The oldest tropical rainforest in the world, World Heritage-listed Daintree Rainforest is so beautiful that it served as the inspiration for the alien landscapes of Pandora in Avatar and so special that Sir David Attenborough declared it "the most extraordinary place on earth." Trek through lush jungles and discover ancient ferns and rare animals like tree-kangaroos and spotted quolls.

GREAT BARRIER REEF

This 2,600-km-long fragile natural wonder is the world's largest collection of reefs and the delicate and complex ecosystem it supports just off the coast of Queensland contains 300 types of coral and 1,500 fish species of every size and almost every conceivable color combination.

FLINDERS RANGES

With deep craters, rocky gorges, and weathered peaks, the 800-million-year-old rugged Flinders Ranges in South Australia's Outback form some of the most dramatic landscapes in the country. Favorite hiking trails include Mount Remarkable (with, you guessed it, remarkable views) and the huge natural amphitheater of Wilpena Pound. Look for the endangered Yellow-footed Rock Wallaby.

LAKE EYRE

About every eight years, Lake Eyre fills and blooms with wildflowers and waterbirds, but Australia's largest lake is usually dry, salty, and unbelievably vast. If you're not lucky enough to catch it full, the salt flats are impressive in themselves, as land and sky are difficult to separate.

Australia's Outdoor Adventures and Wildlife

SAIL THE WHITSUNDAYS (QLD)
Charter your own boat to skip the tourist spots and discover the Whitsundays at your own pace. Spend your days snorkeling crystal clear waters and your nights stargazing from the deck. If you don't feel confident bareboating, guided day and overnights trips are also available.

SHUCK OYSTERS IN COFFIN BAY (SA)
Wade offshore to a semi-submerged pontoon on top of a working oyster farm in South Australia's Coffin Bay, where you will learn how oysters grow and are farmed. Learn to properly shuck, and eat, Pacific and Angasi oysters while sipping a chilled glass of white wine.

BIKE DOWN SAND DUNES IN LORD HOWE ISLAND (NSW)
Feel the wind on your face as you race down the paper-white sand dunes of Lord Howe Island on a 400ccc quad bike. Bike 50-meter-high sand dunes—the largest moving dunes in the southern hemisphere—then head inland and explore the island's rugged bushland.

HOT AIR BALLOON OVER YARRA VALLEY (VIC)
Sip a glass of wine on a sunrise tour over Victoria's breathtaking Yarra Valley, one of Australia's most important and picturesque wine regions, and watch the sweeping valley transform into a spectacle of color, as the corridors of grape vines are bathed in pink light.

SURF AT BELLS BEACH (VIC)
Famous on the international surfing scene for its clean waves and consistent right-hander, this Victoria beach is home to the world's longest-running surf competition—the Rip Curl Pro Bells Beach—and the final scene of Point Break was also filmed here. If you're just a beginner, don't worry, the beach is suitable for all surfing levels.

CAVE DIVE ON THE LIMESTONE COAST (SA)
You'll feel like you're on another planet as you explore the mysterious landscape of South Australia's Limestone Coast, a region known for its water-filled caves and magical sinkholes. Popular spots include Kilsby Sinkhole, a shimmering crystal clear chamber located in the middle of a sheep paddock and Piccaninnie Ponds in Mount Gambier.

CAMP WITH KANGA-ROOS AT PEBBLY BEACH (NSW)
Seeing a kangaroo is at the top of most people's agendas when they come to Australia. At Pebbly Beach in Murramarang National

Park, you can go one better and camp alongside the beloved animal. This picturesque beach, surrounded by thousands of hectares of natural bushland, is famous for its swimming kangaroos. You'll see them sunbathing on the beach, grazing on the grass, and welcoming guests at the national park campsite.

DISCOVER THE RED CENTER (NT)

Immerse yourself in Australia's rich Indigenous history with a trip to the Red Centre in the Northern Territory. This extraordinary landscape of sweeping deserts, rocky gorges, and burnt-orange plains will pull you in with its magic and mystery. Listen to Dreamtime stories by a fire on a visit to Uluru, one of the most sacred Aboriginal sites. Be awed by the immense scope of the red-tinged Kings Canyon in Watarrka National Park. And cool off in still, secluded waterholes surrounded by soaring rocks and eucalyptus trees.

HIKE THE OVERLAND TRACK (TAS)

Considered one of the country's most famous trails, this track leads through the World Heritage–listed Cradle Mountain to Lake St. Claire, the deepest lake in Australia. You'll pass through eucalyptus forests, waterfalls, swimming holes, and breathtaking views of the mountain ranges. You might even come across an echidna, quoll, or wombat.

CANOE KATHERINE GORGE (NT)

Paddle slowly along a maze of sandstone waterways and take in rocky riverbanks teeming with native flora and fauna, rock art, waterfalls, and swimming holes. An overnight canoe tour allows you to travel farther upstream and reach the more remote, and stunning, gorges.

Australia's Best Beaches

TURQUOISE BAY

One of the best snorkeling spots in Western Australia, these appropriately turquoise waters are home to a marine wonderland. Prime snorkeling is at the northern end, near the seagrass area. At the south of the beach you can try drift snorkeling, letting the current carry you along the reef.

WHITEHAVEN BEACH

Located on Whitsunday Island in the Great Barrier Reef, this beach is a 7-km stretch of unspoiled, tropical paradise alongside turquoise waters. Because the sand is made almost entirely of silica–which gives it its milk-white color–it doesn't retain heat, meaning you can stroll barefoot.

MONKEY BEACH

Nestled on Great Keppel Island in the Great Barrier Reef, this secluded beach is a great way to explore the reef without the hustle and bustle of tourists. Think soft white sand, aqua marine water, and chirping tropical birds. Look out for kookaburras and the colorful rainbow lorikeets.

BONDI BEACH

No list of Australian beaches would be complete without Bondi, the beach that most defines Aussie beach culture. This sweeping one-kilometer stretch of white sand never fails to impress. T in the view from one of the coastal heads or enjoy the site from Bondi Baths, a saltwater swimming pool that's been a local landmark for a century.

BRONTE BEACH

This Sydney beach is the ideal spot to surf, swim and grab a quality cup of coffee. Bronte Beach has a more relaxed feel than its iconic neighbor Bondi and is great for all swimming levels. Young kids can play in the section of the beach protected by rocks, affectionately known as the Bogey Hole, surfers can enjoy the swell and for those who like to do laps, there is a 30-meter seawater pool nestled into the coast. The beach also has lots of green space for picnics and barbeques and if you walk further back, you'll even find a small waterfall.

HYAMS BEACH

Drive three hours south of Sydney to the world's whitest sands. Located on the southern shores of Jervis Bay, you can snorkel in the clear, turquoise waters, spot whales and dolphins on the horizon, follow walking trails through Booderee National Park, and glamp at Paperbark Camp.

LUCKY BAY

One of Australia's best-kept secrets, beautiful Lucky Bay is located in Cape Le

Grande National Park near Esperance in Western Australia and offers shimmering turquoise seas, blinding-white sands, and sunbathing kangaroos. Its remote location means you may be lucky enough to have it to yourself–well, you and the kangaroos.

NOOSA MAIN BEACH
Surrounded by tropical rainforest, Noosa is one of the few beach spots to offer the tranquility of a natural paradise with the perks of a cosmopolitan hub. You can eat organic ice cream while wading through the rippling blue waters, sip on a cocktail while watching the sun set, and sunbathe as colorful birds fly overhead.

PEBBLY BEACH
Say hi to cheerful kangaroos at this idyllic little beach in the Murramarang National Park in New South Wales. At Pebbly Beach you share the relaxing, golden sands with kangaroos, sea eagles and the odd goanna (an Australian monitor lizard). Take a stroll in the surrounding bushland that extends for 22 square kilometers and you'll likely find even more curious creatures. It's around three hours from Sydney and if you want to linger a while, there are lots of places to stay in picturesque Batemans Bay.

WINEGLASS BAY
With its snow-white sand, deep blue waters, soaring green mountains, and near perfect crescent shape, Wineglass Bay is a popular destination to pop the question but it is also a great place to enjoy sailing, fishing and sea kayaking. You'll probably meet a kangaroo or two on the beach.

PORT NOARLUNGA BEACH
Located south of Adelaide, this family-friendly beach has golden sand, calm waters, and a marine reserve that is home to more than 200 marine plant species and 60 fish species. Jump off the jetty right into a school of fish (or pop into the village for some fish and chips).

Australia's Top Indigenous Experiences

LORD'S KAKADU & ARNHEMLAND SAFARIS
Stay in a private camp in the middle of Kakadu where you are immersed in aboriginal culture and stunning scenery. Learn about bush tucker and playing the didgeridoo, and visit Nourlangie Rock and pristine billabongs and waterfalls.

K'GARI
"K'Gari," pronounced "gurri" and meaning "paradise" to the Aboriginal Butchulla people, is the traditional name of Fraser Island. Visitors can follow traditional pathways like the Fraser Island Great Walk, or take a 4WD tour of the island with Nomads Fraser Island to learn about the Butchulla people.

YIRIBANA GALLERY
At the heart of the Art Gallery of New South Wales, the Yiribana Gallery is devoted to Aboriginal and Torres Strait Islander art. The gallery showcases selections from a broad collection of works including key contemporary artists like Ian Abdulla and Bidjigal artist Esme Timbery.

MBANTUA FINE ART GALLERY AND CULTURAL MUSEUM
This fine art gallery with outposts in Darwin and Alice Springs, specializes in exhibiting and selling the works of Aboriginal artists. In addition to an extensive collection of paintings, both old and new, you'll find bowls, spears, shields and hair belts.

KOOMAL DREAMING TOUR
This three hour tour in Margaret River offers a guided bush walk to learn how to forage for native foods and medicines, a lunch featuring native ingredients, and a telling of Dreamtime-the period when Ancestral Spirits walked the earth and created life-in the depths of Ngilgi Cave.

BUSH TUCKER CUISINE
"Bush tucker", a wide assortment of native-derived ingredients that has been integral to the diet of the continent's indigenous peoples for tens of thousands of years is slowly making its way onto mainstream menus as Australians embrace the locavore concept. Look for ingredients such as lemon myrtle, quandong, lilli pillies, bush tomatoes, and native meats such as emu, wallaby, kangaroo, and crocodile. You can find bush-tucker at restaurants including The Kungkas Can Cook cafe in Alice Springs, The Tin Humpy in Sydney, and the Tali Wiru and Bush Tucker Journey experiences at Ayers Rock Resort at Uluru.

ULURU-KATA TJUTA NATIONAL PARK

Traditional owners believe this landscape was created at the beginning of time by ancestral beings and it remains a sacred place for the Anangu. It's a UNESCO World Heritage Site with a museum, both ancient rock art and contemporary Indigenous art, and walking trails.

WUKALINA WALK

The *wukalina* walk is a three night, four day Aboriginal owned and operated guided walk based in the stunning natural landscape of the Bay of Fires in Tasmania. Guests walk with *palawa* (Tasmanian Aboriginal) guides, encounter native wildlife, and learn about the area's history, and then stay in *palawa*-inspired domed huts and a Lighthouse Keepers Cottage. Traditional dinners include muttonbird, wallaby, and doughboys.

INGAN TOURS, QUEENSLAND

Aboriginal-owned and operated Ingan Tours brings travelers into the rainforest of the northern reaches of Queensland, home to the Jirrbal people, the only Aboriginal people who come from the rainforest. This is also the tribe of tour operator Dr. Ernie Grant, an Elder of the Jirrbal whose knowledge of topics like mythology and ethno-botany has helped to make Ingan's tours particularly precious. Take a kayak tour of Tully Gorge National Park to explore how the Jirrbal people knew and used the natural creeks and rivers.

BUNGLE BUNGLE TOUR

Bungle Bungle Guided Tours employs Aboriginal guides who share the cultural significance of the mountain range and the Aboriginal connection to the land. Learn about Bush Tucker, Aboriginal customs, and why Purnululu is World Heritage listed on guided day or overnight tours.

10 Things to Buy in Australia

ICONIC DESIGNERS
Some renowned high-end Australian designers to look for include Zimmermann, Collette Dinnigan, Alice McCall, Akira Isogawa, and Camilla and Marc. High street labels include Spell & The Gypsy Collective, Réalisation Par, Aje, and Nobody Denim.

AKUBRA HAT
A quintessential symbol of Australian working life, fourth-generation family-owned Akubra has been making its fur felt hats in NSW since 1874. While the brand carries more urban styles such as the trilby and fedora, it's the classic Bushman or Cattleman hats that you'll want to take home.

SWIMMERS
Known for its beautiful beaches and beach culture it makes sense that Australia is home to some of the best swimwear brands. Labels to look for include Seafolly, Matteau, Baku, Palm, and Zulu & Zephyr. The Bronte Surf Life Saving Club in Sydney sells swimwear along the promenade.

UGGS
PSA: the UGG brand is a U.S.-based company run by an Australian. "Ugg" is actually a generic term for sheepskin boots that have been made and worn Down Under since the 1930s. Avoid boots that pretend to be Aussie and are made in China and look for the Emu brand: their boots are made in Australia from local sheepskin.

VEGEMITE
Leaving Australia without a jar of Vegemite is like leaving Spain without olive oil or Switzerland without chocolate. Vegemite may not be to everyone's taste but few things are more iconically Australian—it is found in 90% of Aussie homes. Best enjoyed on toast (the staple Australian breakfast).

BEGA CHEESE
The friend in every Australian fridge, Bega cheese is based in Bega in NSW but its bitey cheddar cheese is found in supermarkets across the country. This is not a fancy impress-your-guests cheese—for that, buy Unicorn cheese from Nowra Farmhouse—but it's a real taste of Australia.

INDIGENOUS ART
If you are visiting the Red Centre, allow time to stop at an Aboriginal art center. There are three important ones in the Kimberleys—Warmun, Waringarri, and Mowanjum—and more scattered across Arnhem Land. If you're not heading inland you can find great works at the

Aboriginal-run gallery Boomalli in Sydney and Koolie Heritage Trust in Melbourne. The Ayers Rock Resort near Uluru has a number of galleries and artist programs, including live-in residencies, which allow visitors to have a personal connection with the art and artist.

KANGAROO JERKY

Kangaroo is a uniquely Australian meat that is a lean meat, and high in protein, iron, and zinc. It's also a great souvenir for your human and canine friends. Kangaroo jerky is easily available in grocery stores and at Duty Free.

BEAUTY PRODUCTS

With one of the harshest but also botanically diverse environments in the world it's no wonder Aussie beauty brands are some of the most innovative. Look for Sukin and Aesop skin care; Bondi Sands tanning products; Miranda Kerr's Kora Organics; and Kevin Murphy hair care. Melbourne-based Frank Body coffee scrubs and skincare kits have a cult-following. Also, pick up emu oil moisturizer, macadamia oil, and Lucas' Papaw Ointment. Hit up the supermarket or pharmacy for emu oil moisturizer, macadamia oil, and Lucas' Papaw Ointment which is perfect for chapped lips.

WINE

Whether it's a Shiraz from one of the top producers in the Barossa Valley, a Yarra Valley chardonnay, a Hunter Valley semillon, or a discovery from a lesser-known Margaret River label, you will want to bring wine home. Pack wine skins or have the winery ship for you.

What to Eat and Drink in Australia

QUANDONG
Also known as the "native peach" or "wild peach," quandongs have long been a staple in indigenous diets and mythology in the central desert and southern regions of Australia. These sweet, tart fruits are highly nutritious.

MORETON BAY BUGS
Also known as Bay lobster, Moreton Bay Bugs (named after the bay near Brisbane) are a sweet, lobster-like crustacean consumed on Australia's east coast a la blue crabs in Maryland or crawfish in New Orleans. Look for "Bugs" in seafood restaurants in Brisbane, Sydney, and Queensland.

LEMON-LIME AND BITTERS
Tangy, tasty, refreshing, and with a low alcohol content, few drinks quench a desert-thirst like a cold glass of lemon-lime and bitters. Made with soda water, lime cordial, and Angostura bitters it is consumed on a grand scale Down Under, be it bottled, canned, or homemade.

KANGAROO
Australia is perhaps the only country that eats its national icon. You'll find this lean meat in restaurants across Australia and in many supermarkets: look for kanga bangas (kangaroo sausages), steaks, and jerky. Aussies are encouraged to eat kangaroo meat to control a ballooning roo population.

AVO-TOAST
America has its pancakes, France has its croissants, and Australia has its avocado toast. Every self-respecting café has smashed avocado on toasted sourdough bread, often served with almond butter and citrus kurd or crumbled feta. Yes, it's overpriced, but it's not just toast, it's tradition!

TIM TAMS
With sales of about 35 million packs a year, Australia's national biscuit is made up of two layers of chocolate-malted biscuit, separated by a light chocolate filling and coated in melted chocolate. Tim Tam Slam: Bite off opposite corners of cookie and use as a straw to drink hot chocolate.

THE FLAT WHITE
The origins of this less-foamy cappuccinoesque drink, made with two shots of a sweet, concentrated espresso and heated, full-fat milk, is a touchy subject in Aussie-Kiwi relations, but it is agreed to be an essential ingredient in an afternoon of sightseeing, especially in Sydney or Melbourne.

HUNTER VALLEY SEMILLON

Like the Coonawarra region in South Australia or the Yarra Valley in Victoria, the Hunter Valley in New South Wales produces some of the country's most iconic labels. The climate is ideally suited to the semillon grape it's rare to find semillon unblended outside Australia. Look for producers like Tyrell's, Rothbury Estate, Pokolbin Estate, and McWilliams Mount Pleasant.

FERAL BREWING CO. BEER

While Australia is better known for its wine, it also has a burgeoning craft beer scene so maybe skip the cheesy Foster's and go Indie. One of the most notable is Feral Brewing Co, a Western-Australian independent brewery behind the pale ale Hop Hog and IBA Karma Citra.

WYNN'S BLACK LABEL CABERNET SAUVIGNON

Wynn's Coonawarra Estate began making wine in South Australia in the 1890s. The Black Label Cabernet Sauvignon is made from the top 20 per cent of fruit grown in Wynn's terra rossa vineyards. It's an icon of Australian wine and known as an affordable, excellent "must."

BARRAMUNDI

Barramundi is the Aboriginal name for a type of sea-bass that is native to Australia and the Indo-Pacific. It literally translates as "large-scaled silver fish". It's lean, packed with protein and Omega-3s, and sustainably farmed.

MEAT PIES

Have you even been to Australia if you didn't eat a meat pie? A flaky pastry package filled with diced or minced meat and gravy, and often cheese, mushrooms, and onions, too, the humble meat pie is known as Australia's national dish. Typically enjoyed smothered in ketchup at a Footy game.

Australia: What to Watch and Read Before You Go

MOVIE: *TRACKS*

This scenic and touching story follows one woman's near-impossible 2,000-mile walk from Alice Springs in the Northern Territory, to the coast of the Indian Ocean. The movie treks across the Gibson desert, past Ayers Rock, and through sacred indigenous grounds, with beautiful footage of wild Australia.

BOOK: *THE SONGLINES* BY BRUCE CHATWIN

Songlines catalogs Chatwin's travels to Alice Springs, in the Central Australian desert, where he studied aboriginal life past and present. While sometimes criticized for its colonialist-skewed observations, Chatwin's earnestness to understand the nature of man and man in nature shines through, and provides insight into the Australian landscape and the history of nomadic life.

BOOK: *THE SWAN BOOK BY ALEXIS WRIGHT*

Full of folkloric, surreal beauty and heartbreak, indigenous author and land activist Alexis Wright paints a vivid picture of Aboriginal people and landscape in the Gulf of Carpentaria. With a fantastical story of a young girl's experience in an imagined future Australia, Wright predicts the outcome of the long-standing, destructive treatment of indigenous people. The novel won literary acclaim and was short-listed for Australia's Miles Franklin Award.

BOOK: *A LONG WAY FROM HOME* BY PETER CAREY

Booker Prize–winning author Peter Carey tells the story of a spunky young woman and her neighbor on an improbable car trip around the unruly circumference of the continent. Along its way across the rugged Australian terrain, the narrative covers issues of race, and the troubled history of Aboriginal-white relations.

BOOK: *JOHNNO* BY DAVID MALOUF

The first novel of prolific Australian author David Malouf, Johnno is a loosely autobiographical story about childhood, friendship and memories, with the coastal city of Brisbane and its upper-class culture as a backdrop. It's a tender coming-of-age novel and a fair portrait of life in Brisbane and Queensland's Gold Coast.

BOOK: *PICNIC AT HANGING ROCK* BY JOAN LINDSAY

Lindsay's dramatic literary feat (recently turned into an Amazon Prime miniseries starring Natalie Dormer from Game of Thrones) is the haunting tale of a group of schoolgirls who mysteriously vanish while on a Valentines' Day picnic. The novel and its fictional premise have turned Hanging Rock (a geological formation North-West of Melbourne, with a real history as a sacred indigenous site) into a folkloric destination popular with tourists and local fans.

BOOK: *BIG LITTLE LIES* BY LIANE MORIARTY

Moriarty's grabbing and emotionally-charged novel is about female friendship, social politics, and the secrets and shame in the wealthy beach towns and private-school worlds of Australia's coast. Moriarty's depiction of the drama of elite suburban life inspired Nicole Kidman and Reese Witherspoon to star in (and executive produce) an HBO miniseries of the same name—though the setting for the show was moved to Monterey, California.

BOOK: *FOLLOW THE RABBIT-PROOF FENCE* BY DORIS PILKINGTON

In 1931, three young Aboriginal girls walked more than 1,600 km (1,000 miles) from the Moore River Native Settlement on the Western Coast, where they had been forced to live separated from their families, back home to the Jigalong community of Western Australia.

MOVIE: *THE SAPPHIRES*

Irish actor Chris O'Dowd leads a girl-band of Aboriginal Australians in the late '60s and and early '70s, as they travel to Vietnam to entertain the troops. The musical film is feel-good and funny, but touches on real issues of race, war, and human rights on both the Australian and world stage.

TV SERIES: *HOME AND AWAY*

Alan Bateman's long-running soap opera, filled with plenty of sex, drugs, and Australian beach drama, is widely popular throughout Australia and the United Kingdom. Filmed mostly in Sydney's Northern Beaches, the show is set in a fictional beachtown in New South Wales.

MOVIE: *A CRY IN THE DARK ("EVIL ANGELS" IN AUSTRALIA)*

To familiarize yourself with the long, press-ridden murder trial of Lindy Chamberlain (played here by Meryl Streep) is to understand a critical piece of Australian popular culture throughout the last few decades. In a sweep of popularity and controversy similar to the OJ Simpson trial in the states, Chamberlain's story captured Australian minds and television screens after her two-month old daughter went missing while the family was camping in Uluru, Central Australia. Lindy was convicted of murder, acquitted only after years spent appealing her case, swearing all along that she saw a wild dingo leave the tent where her little girl had been sleeping.

MOVIE: *THE ADVENTURES OF PRISCILLA, QUEEN OF THE DESERT*

In a wild roadtrip full of performance, personality, and diverse Australian walks of life, this comedic drama follows two drag queens and a transgender woman as they travel across the Australian outback in a tour bus named Priscilla. The 1994 film was a huge hit, and is celebrated for bringing a positive portrayal of LGBTQ people to mainstream Australian (and international) audiences.

MOVIE: *EMILY IN JAPAN: THE MAKING OF AN EXHIBITION*

This documentary follows aboriginal artist Emily Kame Kngwarreye (a native of Utopia, Central Australia), whose humble start to painting in her late 70s led to her becoming one of Australia's most prolific and highly regarded artists.

MOVIE: *ROGUE*

Worried there was a lack of giant killer crocodiles on this list? In this amped-up, JAWS-like horror/thriller, Australia's scariest predator is larger-than-life and hungry for humans. Between the animatronic, jaw-clamping thrills, big splashes, and narrow escapes, there are beautiful shots of Australia's Kakadu National Park.

MOVIE: *MURIEL'S WEDDING*

In PJ Hogan's 1994 romantic comedy, an ABBA-loving, wedding-crazed Toni Collette (nominated for a Golden Globe in her role as the adorable and bumbling Muriel Heslop) leaves life in her oppressive, cliquey beachtown to find herself (and maybe love) in big-city Sydney. A story more about friendship and self discovery than marriage, the movie is warm and quirky in a delightfully Australian way.

MOVIES: *MAD MAX* SERIES

George Miller's adventure franchise *(Mad Max, Mad Max 2, Mad Max Beyond Thunderdome,* and *Mad Max: Fury Road)* takes viewers on frenzied chases through a postapocalyptic Australian wasteland. The first three, starring a shockingly young Mel Gibson, were filmed in the 1980s in and around Melbourne. Scenes in 2015's *Mad Max: Fury Road* are actually of The Namib Desert, in Namibia and South Africa.

ABORIGIN
PAST

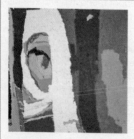

Today's Australian Aboriginals are guardians of the world's oldest living culture. Most experts agree that it was about 50,000 years ago (possibly as many as 80,000) when the continent's first inhabitants migrated south across a landmass that once connected Australia to Indonesia and Malaysia. These first Australians brought with them a wealth of stories, songs, tribal customs, and ceremonies—many of which are still practiced today.

By Sarah Gold

AL ART,
AND PRESENT

All Aboriginal ideology is based upon the creation period known as The Dreaming. During this primordial time, totemic ancestors (who were associated with particular animals, plants, and natural phenomena) lived on and journeyed across the earth. The legends of these ancestors—what they did, where they traveled, who they fought and loved—are considered sacred, and have been passed down among Aboriginal tribes for thousands of years. Though these stories are largely shared in secret rituals, they have also been documented through the creation of unique, highly symbolic artworks.

This is why Aboriginal art, despite traditional beginnings as rock carvings and ochre paintings on bark, now hang in some of the world's finest museums. These works aren't just beautiful; they're also profound cultural artifacts—and a window into humanity's oldest surviving civilization.

(top right) Nourlangie Rock, Kakadu;
(top left) Art by Emily Kame Kngwarreye;
(bottom left) Work from Papunya Tula;
(bottom right) Maningrida Art and Culture, Darwin

EARLY ABORIGINAL ART

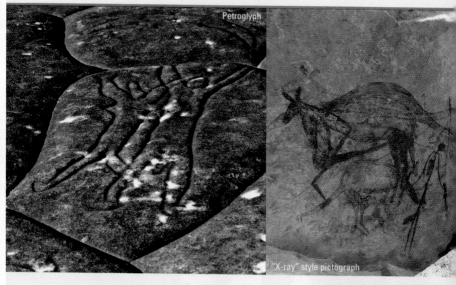

Petroglyph

"X-ray" style pictograph

While dot paintings are the most widely recognized Aboriginal artworks today, they're only the latest incarnation of a creative legacy that stretches back thousands of years. The achievements of Australia's earliest artists can still be seen—etched right onto the sacred landscapes that inspired them.

PETROGLYPHS

The earliest Aboriginal artworks were petroglyphs—engravings carved into flat rock surfaces or faces of cliffs (most likely using pointed stones or shards of shell). Some surviving etchings show lines and circles similar to those in modern-day paintings; others depict animals, fish, birds, and human or spirit figures. The oldest known engravings on the continent, at Pilbara in Western Australia and Olary in South Australia, are estimated to be 40,000 years old. Perhaps the most visited, though, are those in Ku-rin-gai Chase National Park, less than an hour's drive north of Sydney.

PROTECTING ROCK-ART SITES

Given the centuries of weathering they've endured, it's remarkable that so many ancient rock art sites remain intact. In many places, the longevity of the artworks can be attributed to local Aboriginal tribes, who consider it a sacred responsibility to preserve and repaint fading images. Help preservation efforts by staying on marked paths, not touching the artwork, and taking a tour of the site with an indigenous guide.

Freehand pictograph

Stencil painting

PICTOGRAPHS

Other early Aboriginal artists chose to paint images rather than etch them. Using ochres and mineral pigments, and employing sticks, feathers, and their own fingers as brushes, these ancient painters chose sheltered spots—like the insides of caves and canyons—for their mural-like images. Protection from the elements allowed many of these ancient rock paintings to survive; today they're still found all over Australia.

REGIONAL STYLES

The styles of painting varied by region. In the Northern Territory, in Arnhem Land and what is now Kakadu National Park, early Aboriginals painted "X-ray" portraits of humans and animals with their skeletons and internal organs clearly displayed. The Kimberley and Burrup Peninsula in Western Australia are rich repositories of elegant freehand paintings portraying human, animal, and ancestral Dreaming figures. And Queensland, especially the area that is now Carnarvon National Park, is known for its stencil paintings, in which the artists sprayed paint from their mouths.

EARTH TONES (LITERALLY)

Early Aboriginal artists used the earth to make pigments. Red, yellow, and brown were made from mineral-rich clays. Black was created with charcoal or charred tree bark; white from crushed gypsum rock; and grey from ashes left over from cooking fires. Modern artists may mix their pigments with oil or acrylic, but the traditional palette remains the same.

DECIPHERING "DOT PAINTINGS"

An artist uses a small, straight stick dipped in paint to create a dot painting. Ancient symbols and intricate dot motifs combine to create powerful works of art.

To a visitor wandering through a gallery, Aboriginal artwork can seem deceptively simple. Many traditional paintings feature basic designs—wavy lines, concentric circles—comprised of myriad tiny dots. They look as though they were created with the end of a paint-covered stick (and indeed, most were).

But the swirling motifs in these "dot paintings" aren't just abstractions—they're visual representations of ancestral legends.

According to Aboriginal beliefs, as the ancestors lived their lives during the Dreaming, they also gave shape to the landscape. In each spot where the ancestor shot an arrow, danced, or gave birth, an enduring mark was left on the topography: a hill, a ravine, a rock spire. As they conjured these geographical features, they sang out their names—composing singing maps of the territory they covered. Each is known as a "songline," and they crisscross the entire continent.

Now thousands of years old, these songs are still memorized and sung by many of today's Aboriginal peoples. Songlines are the basis of all indigenous traditions and tribal laws; learning and teaching the songs are considered sacred—and very secret—duties. Over many centuries, however, artists have revealed parts of the songlines through the symbology of dot paintings.

The symbols may seem cryptic, but many are recurring and give clues to the ancestral stories they depict. Shapes punctuating dot paintings usually correspond to landmarks: bodies of water, rock formations, campsites, or resting places. The lines that surround the shapes and connect them represent the tracks of the ancestors as they moved from place to place. Each dot painting is, in effect, a sacred walking map that plots an ancestor's journey.

COMMON SYMBOLS IN ABORIGINAL ART

woman

emu tracks

four women sitting around a campfire

ants, fruits, flowers, or eggs

well or main campsite

water, fire, smoke, lightning, or bushfire

holes, clouds, or nests

Honey ant

Coolamon (wooden dish)

kangaroo tracks

star

meeting place

traveling paths or heavy rain

running water connecting two waterholes

man

Witchetty grub

possum tracks

boomerang

snake

spear

cloud, rainbow, sandhill, or cliff

people sitting

THE DAWNING OF ABORIGINAL ART APPRECIATION

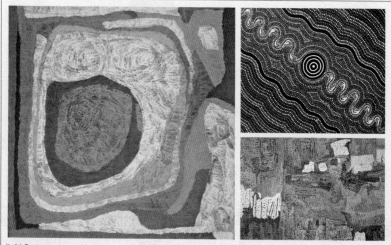

(left) Contemporary painting done in earth tones by a member of the Papunya Tula Artists collective; (top right) artwork from the Warlukurlangu Artists Aboriginal Corporation; (bottom right) Papunya Tula artwork.

IN THE BEGINNING . . .

It took a long time for Aboriginal art to gain the recognition it enjoys today. Australia's first European colonists, who began arriving in the late 18th century, saw the complex indigenous cultures it encountered as primitive, and believed that, as "nomads," Aboriginals had no claim to the land. Consequently, expansion into tribal lands went unchecked; during the 19th and early 20th centuries, most Aboriginals were forced onto white-owned cattle stations and missionary outposts.

Aboriginal land rights weren't formally acknowledged until 1976, when the first legislation was passed granting claim of title to natives with "traditional association" to the land. This watershed decision (called the Aboriginal Land Rights Act) allowed for the establishment of tribal land councils, which—in partnership with the Australian government—today manage many of the country's national parks and sacred ancient sites.

BREAKING GROUND

The growing awareness of Aboriginal heritage brought with it an increased interest in indigenous art. Before the 1970s, there had been only one celebrated Aboriginal artist in Australia—Albert Namatjira, who grew up on a Lutheran mission in Hermannsburg (in what is now the Northern Territory). In the 1930s, Namatjira studied under a white Australian artist and learned to paint sophisticated watercolor landscapes. Though these had almost nothing in common with traditional indigenous artworks, they won Namatjira enormous fame (by the 1950s, he was listed in *Who's Who*) which reinforced an idea that was

Curators often provide relevant historical context.

already burgeoning in the country: that Aboriginal creativity should receive the same attention and scholarship as non-Aboriginal forms of art.

ABORIGINAL ART CENTERS

Perhaps the single most significant event in modern Aboriginal art history occurred in 1973, with the formation of the Aboriginal Arts Board. The advent of this agency, as part of the government-funded Australia Council for the Arts, heralded a new level of respect for indigenous art. Its aim was to establish a standardized support system for Aboriginal artists through grant money.

But early board members (who came from both European and Aboriginal backgrounds) found this to be another challenge. Aboriginal artists were scattered all over the continent, many of them in isolated, far-flung camps surrounded by vast desert or impenetrable rainforests. How was the organization to find these artists, decide which of them deserved funds, and then dispense those funds in an organized way?

The solution was to set up art centers at specific Aboriginal communities around the country—helmed by

Renowned artist David Malangi, Central Arnhem Land

art-industry specialists who could both cultivate connections with local artists and manage their nuts-and-bolts requirements (like arranging for deliveries of art supplies, and for transport of finished artworks to exhibitors and buyers).

The plan worked, and is still working. There are some 50 Aboriginal art centers in Australia today (most in the Northern Territory and Western Australia), and they collectively represent more than a thousand artists. These centers are the conduit by which most modern Aboriginal works get to art dealers—and then on to galleries, museums, auction houses, and private collectors.

PAPUNYA TULA

Brenda Nungarrayi Lynch, well-known Western Desert artist

The founding members of the Aboriginal Arts Board were inspired by the example of a particular Northern Territory desert settlement, Papunya Tula. Here, with the help of a white Australian art teacher, residents had begun to create and then sell "Dreaming paintings" (what are known today as dot paintings) to nearby galleries. By 1972, the community had established its own thriving and successful art collective, Papunya Tula Artists.

Today Papunya Tula Artists (which has never been government-subsidized) is the most famous Aboriginal art center in the country. The highly acclaimed dot paintings of its artists have hung in New York's Metropolitan Museum of Art and Paris's Musée du Quai Branly; their annual dollar sales are in the millions.

ABORIGINAL ART TODAY

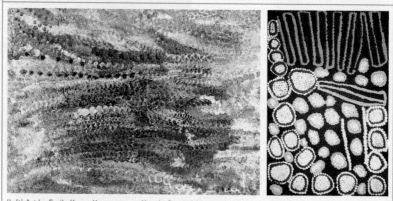

(left) Art by Emily Kame Kngwarreye, Utopia Central Australia; (right) Papunya Tula

Over the past 30 years, the art world's regard for Aboriginal works has skyrocketed—not just in Australia, but all over the world. Ancient etchings and modern dot paintings now hang in museums from London's British to the Chicago Art Institute; gallerists and art dealers vie to represent rising Aboriginal art stars; and many artists who got their start at art centers in the 1980s (such as Dorothy Napangardi, Michael Nelson Tjakamarra, and Paddy Stewart Tjapaljarri) are near-celebrities today. A few of these pioneers of the modern Aboriginal art movement (like Rover Thomas and David Malangi) were in their seventies and eighties by the time their canvases began decorating exhibit halls and commanding six-figure auction bids.

Some of Australia's most celebrated Aboriginal artists, though, never got to see just how popular their work became. Clifford "Possum" Tjapaltjarri, for example, whose painting *Warlugulong* sold at a Sotheby's auction in 2007 for $2.4 million—the highest price ever paid for a piece of Aboriginal art—died five years beforehand. And Emily Kame Kngwarreye died in 1996, a dozen years before the National Museum of Australia mounted a huge solo exhibition of her work.

The new generation of Aboriginal artists faces its own set of obstacles. The appetite among art dealers for a steady supply of works to sell has led some of them to cut exploitative deals directly with artists (rather than working through the relative safety net of art centers). Other opportunists have mass-produced paintings and then sold them as "authentic"—thus tainting the integrity of the real Aboriginal art market.

But even these problems, unsavory though they are, can be seen from a certain angle as signs of positive change. It was only decades ago, after all, that the phrase "Aboriginal artist" seemed oxymoronic for many Australians. Today, those "primitive" assemblages of lines, circles, and dots account for almost 75 percent of the country's art sales. They have, in effect, helped put Australia on the map.

Today, symbols might be just half the story: colors can range from calm and subdued to bright and vibrant.

TIPS FOR WHERE AND HOW TO BUY ART

The most easily accessible sources for buying Aboriginal art are galleries. When considering a purchase, ascertain the art's authenticity and ethicality. The Australian Indigenous Art Trade Association recommends asking:

■ Is the artwork documented with a certificate of authenticity from a reputable source, or by photos of the artist with the art?

■ How did the artwork get to the gallery? Is the artist represented by a recognized art center, cooperative, or respected dealer?

■ Is it clear that the artist was treated fairly and paid a fair price for putting the artwork on the market?

MUSEUM AND GALLERY COLLECTIONS

Australia has hundreds of galleries and museums at least partially devoted to Aboriginal artworks. Here are some of the best:

PERMANENT COLLECTIONS

The Australian Museum, Sydney
australianmuseum.net.au

The National Gallery of Australia, Canberra
nga.gov.au

Queensland Art Gallery, Brisbane
www.qagoma.qld.gov.au

National Gallery of Victoria, Melbourne
www.ngv.vic.gov.au

ROTATING EXHIBITIONS

Aboriginal Fine Arts Gallery, Darwin
www.aaia.com.au

Gallery Gabrielle Pizzi, Melbourne

www.gabriellepizzi.com.au

Australia Today

GOVERNMENT

Australia is a constitutional monarchy, and the Queen of England is Australia's Queen as well. Her only role under the constitution, however, is to appoint her representative in Australia, the Governor-General, which she does on advice from Australia's Prime Minister. In 1975 the Governor-General caused a political crisis when he sacked the Prime Minister and his government and installed the opposition minority as caretaker until new elections could be held. The Governor-General retains that power, but his or her duties are primarily ceremonial. Australia's government is elected for three-year terms, with no limit on how many terms a Prime Minister can serve. Controversially, Australia has had six Prime Ministers between 2010 and 2018. Voting is compulsory for all citizens 18 years and older, and failure to vote can result in a fine.

ECONOMY

Australia is a major exporter of wheat and wool, iron-ore and gold, liquefied natural gas and coal. The major industries are mining, industrial and transport equipment, energy and utilities, agriculture, finance, and healthcare. The services sector dominates the domestic economy.

Abundant natural assets and massive government spending initially softened the impact of the global financial crisis that started in 2008. Demand for Australia's commodities from China and India has dipped, and mining has slowed. These developments have led to a slowdown in the country's economic growth.

TOURISM

On- and offshore wonders, unique wildlife, beach culture, indigenous history, and multicultural cuisines help maintain Australia's multibillion-dollar tourism industry. The major challenges are keeping Australia on travelers' radars as other countries gain popularity, and protecting the most fragile attractions. Climate change has already affected the Great Barrier Reef, a World Heritage site on most visitors' must-see lists, and programs are in place to try to minimize the impact of rising sea temperatures and nearby mining sites. Contentious logging of old-growth forests for pulp, particularly in Tasmania, continues, and the opening of new mines rarely fits comfortably with conservation and cultural issues.

RELIGION

Australia's first settlers were predominantly English, Irish, and Scottish Christians. Now, almost two-thirds of Australians call themselves Christians (52%), with Islam a distant second (2.6%), and Buddhism third (2.4%); however, almost a third of the population (30%) ticked "no religion" on the 2016 census. Active church worship has declined over recent decades, and many religions struggle to attract members.

LITERATURE

Life Down Under has bred contemporary writers who speak with distinctly Australian voices. Tim Winton's book Breath brilliantly evokes the power of surfing and the angst of adolescence, while Kate Grenville's acclaimed The Secret River explores Australia's brutal colonial past and its effect on indigenous people. Look out for award-winning authors Alexis Wright, Kim Scott, Richard Flanagan, Michelle de Kretser, Christos Tsiolkas, David Malouf, and Helen Garner, among others. Morris Gleitzman and Andy Griffiths write (mostly) laugh-out-loud books for children and the young at heart.

Chapter 2

TRAVEL SMART
AUSTRALIA

Updated by
Molly McLaughlin

★ **CAPITAL:**
Canberra

POPULATION:
24.6 million

LANGUAGE:
English; multiple Indigenous
languages

$ **CURRENCY:**
Australian dollar

☎ **COUNTRY CODE:**
61

⚠ **EMERGENCIES:**
000

🚗 **DRIVING:**
On the left

⚡ **ELECTRICITY:**
240 volts, 50 cycles alternat-
ing current (AC). Wall outlets
take slanted three-prong
plugs and plugs with two flat
prongs set in a V.

🕐 **TIME:**
15 hours ahead of New York

🌐 **WEB RESOURCES:**
www.australia.com

*www.australiangeographic.
com.au*

www.traveller.com.au

INDONESIA

AUSTRALIA

Canberra

NEW
ZEALAND

What You Need to Know Before You Visit Australia

AUSTRALIA IS BIGGER THAN YOU THINK IT IS

Australia is about the same size in terms of land mass as the continental U.S. However, the population density is around seven people per square mile compared to 92 people per square mile in the States, so you can drive for hours without seeing even a gas station. For first-time visitors, it usually makes the most sense to travel the East Coast (via Brisbane, Sydney, and Melbourne) first and then venture into the interior or fly up north.

YOU NEED A VISA

Visitors to Australia need and Electronic Travel Authority (ETA), a type of electronic visa, to enter the country for short-term tourism or business stays. Citizens of the United States and Canada can apply online (⊕ *www.eta.homeaffairs.gov.au/ETAS3/etas*; visas cost $15 USD and the average processing time is less than one day. ⚠ **Be sure your visa details match your passport exactly or you may be refused entry upon arrival.**

AUSTRALIAN CUSTOMS IS VERY STRICT AND VERY UNSMILING

Gruff manners. Unfriendly faces. Nothing says "Welcome to Australia" like sniffing dogs and rude customs agents. While the Border Force Officials represent the Australian government, they do not represent the Australian people who are generally warm, friendly, and generous in spirit. With that in mind, just follow their instructions, fill out the forms, and don't dare try to sneak anything in: if the dogs don't sniff out your guilty conscience, the agents will.

WITH THAT IN MIND, PACK MINDFULLY!

Australian customs officials are tasked with an important job: making sure no unexpected plants or animals get into the country that could upset the delicate ecosystem. The insects, spiders, and micro-organisms that might have snuck into your backpack, hidden in the dirt on your hiking boots cozied intothose bamboo placemats you bought in Bali, are all unwanted critters in Australia.

If your visit to Australia is part of a larger international itinerary (lucky you), consider all purchases on the way. Check the Border Force's website for a list of what must be declared or avoided entirely. Also, be sure to carefully clean hiking or camping equipment before you travel.

ABORIGINAL PEOPLE HAVE LIVED IN AUSTRALIA FOR MORE THAN 50,000 YEARS

Aboriginal and Torres Strait Islander people have lived in Australia for tens of thousands of years and retain a strong connection to their traditional lands. The continent's first peoples come from many groups with rich and diverse cultures, with more than 250 distinct languages spoken in the pre-colonial era and more than 100 still in use today.

THE OUTBACK IS NOT A REAL PLACE

If you tell an Australian you're going to the Outback, they'll likely ask you to be a bit more specific. Alongside "the bush," which connotes more substantial vegetation, the phrase "the Outback" is used by some city slickers to refer to basically the whole interior of the continent.

You could be visiting Uluru in the Red Centre (which, by the way, is almost 300 miles from Alice Springs). You could be exploring the rugged Top End stretching south from Darwin. Or, you could be driving across one of Australia's many deserts or the arid Nullarbor Plain. Whichever outback destination you choose, it's bound to be an unforgettable adventure (just make sure to take a good look at the map before you decide).

YOU'RE GOING TO NEED TO HIRE A CAR

Due to Australia's low population density, public transportation outside of capital cities is woeful. If you want to travel independently anywhere other than the East Coast, a hire car is almost essential as buses can be indirect and infrequent and intercity trains are almost nonexistent. Domestic flights can be an option, but they are often the more expensive route (again, with the exception of the East Coast). Australia's vastness lends itself to roadtrips, and a car is the best way to discover natural beauty off the beaten track.

YOU DON'T NEED TO TIP

Thanks to a high minimum wage (around US$13 for an unskilled worker), tipping is completely optional in Australia and usually reserved for exceptional service. Australians rarely tip in cafés or casual restaurants, and at fine-dining restaurants it is common to leave a 10% tip or simply round up the bill for a big group.

THE CAPITAL CITY ISN'T SYDNEY OR MELBOURNE

When the separate colonies became the federation of Australia in 1901, the newly created nation needed a capital. After strong competition between Sydney and Melbourne, a site roughly in between the two was chosen in 1908. Often referred to as a big country town, over the past decade Canberra has evolved into a creative, green city with a high standard of living.

THE SUN IS DANGEROUS HERE BUT SO IS YOUR SUNSCREEN

While many of the world's most popular sun spots are enacting bans on coral reef-harming sunscreens, Australia has yet to act … but it is just a matter of time. Be proactive: look for mineral-based sunscreens with zinc oxide and/or titanium dioxide and avoid formulas with oxybenzone and octinoxate.

AUSTRALIA HAS RAIN FORESTS AND MOUNTAINS AS WELL AS DESERTS AND BEACHES

Such a large geographic area across changing climatic zones means there's a bunch of different ecosystems to explore in Australia. Ever heard of the Daintree Rainforest? Well, it's the oldest continuously surviving tropical rain forest in the world. At the other extreme, the picturesque Mount Feathertop is part of the Australian Alps and is covered in snow for half the year. All this and more coexists Down Under.

SOME OF THE BEST FOOD IN AUSTRALIA ISN'T "AUSTRALIAN"

When you picture Australian food, the first thing that comes to mind is probably a sausage on the barbecue. Other staples include meat pies, Vegemite, and fairy bread (a concoction of white bread and butter covered in sprinkles). All that meat and sugar, while understandable in the context of British settlement of an arid continent, can be a bit uninspiring, so foodies should experiment with local Vietnamese, Chinese, Greek, and Ethiopian for a real kick.

BONDI IS NOT AUSTRALIA'S BEST BEACH

Aussies avoid Bondi like the plague and you should, too. On weekends or during the summer school holidays, it is impossible to find a patch of sand not occupied by a sunburned British backpacker, and prices at the bars and cafés reflect its status as a tourist hot spot. In Sydney, head to Bronte or Manly for your beach fix, or blow the city off all together and head up the north coast where hundreds of pristine sandy beaches await with not a tacky souvenir shop in sight.

Getting Here and Around

Australia is divided into six states and two territories—Northern Territory (NT) and Australian Capital Territory (ACT)—similar to the District of Columbia. Tasmania, the smallest state, is an island off mainland Australia's southeast point.

✈ Air Travel

Qantas is Australia's flagship carrier. It operates direct flights to Sydney from New York, Dallas, San Francisco, and Los Angeles, and from Los Angeles to Melbourne and Brisbane. Because Pacific-route flights from the United States to Australia cross the international date line, you lose a day, but regain it on the journey home. Flight time is usually around 20 hours.

Australia's large distances mean that flying is often the locals' favorite way of getting from one city to another. On routes between popular destinations like Sydney, Melbourne, and Brisbane there are often several flights each hour, although tickets don't come cheap during peak season.

⛵ Boat Travel

Organized boat tours from the Queensland mainland are the only way to visit the Great Barrier Reef. The Great Barrier Reef Marine Park Authority website has helpful advice on how to choose a tour operator and lists which companies are ecotourism-certified.

The daily ferries *Spirit of Tasmania I* and *II* take 10 hours to connect Melbourne with Devonport on Tasmania's north coast. Make reservations as early as possible, particularly during the busy December and January school holidays.

🚌 Bus Travel

Bus travel in Australia is comfortable and well organized. Australia's national bus network is run by Greyhound Australia (no connection to Greyhound in the United States), which serves far more destinations than any plane or train services. Murrays Coaches is another affordable option for travel between Canberra and the East Coast. However, Australia is a vast continent, and bus travel requires plenty of time.

🚗 Car Travel

Driving is generally easy in Australia, once you adjust to traveling on the left side of the road and the prevalence of roundabouts. When you're preparing a driving itinerary, it's vital to bear in mind the huge distances involved and calculate travel time and stopovers accordingly.

Most rental companies in Australia accept driving licenses from other countries, including the United States, provided that the information on the license is clear and in English. Otherwise, an International Driver's Permit is required (but they'll still want to see your regular license, too). Rental companies have varying policies and charges for unusual trips, such as lengthy cross-state expeditions around the Top End and Western Australia. Ask about additional mileage, fuel, and insurance charges if you're planning to cover a lot of ground.

Gas is known in Australia as "petrol." Self-service petrol stations are plentiful near major cities and in rural towns. In really out-of-the-way places, carrying a spare petrol can is a good idea, as smaller petrol stations often close at night and on Sunday, though in major cities and

From	To	Distance	Main Highway Names
Sydney	Melbourne	873 km (542 miles)/1,043 km (648 miles)	Hume/Princes
Sydney	Brisbane	982 km (610 miles)	Pacific
Brisbane	Cairns	1,699 km (1,056 miles)	Bruce
Melbourne	Adelaide	732 km (455 miles) /912 km (567 miles)	Dukes/Pacific
Adelaide	Perth	2,716 km (1,688 miles)	Eyre and Great Eastern
Adelaide	Alice Springs	1,544 km (959 miles)	Stuart
Alice Springs	Darwin	1,503 km (934 miles)	Stuart
Darwin	Cairns	2,885 km (1,793 miles)	Bruce, Flinders, Barkley, and Stuart

on main highways there are plenty of stations open round the clock.

Intercity highways are usually in good condition, but more remote roads can often be unpaved or full of potholes and are better suited to a 4WD. Animals—kangaroos and livestock, primarily—are common causes of road accidents in rural Australia, especially at dusk and dawn, so make sure to keep an eye out.

Always carry plenty of water with you and don't count on your cell phone working in the middle of nowhere. The Australian Automobile Association has a branch in each state and it's affiliated with AAA worldwide, with reciprocal services to American members, including emergency road service.

🚢 Cruise Ship Travel

Cruises along the Great Barrier Reef and between the Whitsunday Islands are popular, as well as across the Top End and between Brisbane and Sydney. Other routes connect Australia's East Coast with New Zealand and the Pacific.

🚕 Taxi Travel

Taxis are available in cities and major towns throughout Australia, especially outside airports, bus stations, and train stations. In other areas hailing a taxi on the street is practically unheard of, so call ahead to avoid long wait times.

🚆 Train Travel

Australia has a network of long-distance trains providing first- and economy-class service along the east and south coasts, across the south of the country from Sydney to Perth, and through the middle of the country between Adelaide and Darwin.

Most long-distance trains are operated by various state-government-owned enterprises. The luxurious exceptions to the rule are the *Ghan, Indian Pacific,* and *Overland,* all run by the private company Great Southern Rail.

Before You Go

🌐 Passports and Visas

All U.S. citizens require a valid passport to enter Australia for stays of any length, plus the relevant visa. Your passport should be valid for at least three months after your planned departure from Australia and must have at least two empty pages for arrival and departure stamps.

For tourist stays of 90 days or less, U.S. citizens can apply for an Electronic Travel Authority (E.T.A.). The E.T.A. is valid for one year and permits the visa holder to enter Australia for multiple stays of three months or less each time. You can apply online via the Department of Home Affairs website and the cost is US$15. If all your details are correct, the visa should be granted within 24 hours.

🖊 Immunizations

There are no immunizations required to enter Australia. However, all travelers should confirm they are up to date with routine vaccinations. Cases of dengue fever have occurred in Far North Queensland, so you should speak to your doctor if you are planning to visit that area.

🗽 US Embassy/Consulate

There are U.S. consulates in Melbourne, Perth, and Sydney and the U.S. Embassy in Canberra. The Embassy and consulates can offer a variety of services to U.S. citizens, including legal and medical assistance, passport and citizenship services, voting, emergency financial assistance, and emergency services in the unlikely event of arrest, death, serious injury, or crime.

Enroll in STEP (Smart Traveler Enrollment Program) before your departure for easy access to information and so you can be contacted in an emergency. Consulates can be reached by phone, mail, or email; find the relevant details online.

📅 When to Go

Australia's climate can be broadly divided into north and south. Most travelers choosing to avoid the south's winters (July to August) and the north's summers (December to February).

The East Coast can be visited all year round, with high season over summer (especially school holidays in December and January) and low season over winter. Spring and fall are ideal times to visit. However, the tropical north (including Darwin and the Great Barrier Reef) experiences a heavy rainy season in summer which both slows the flow of tourists and often means lower prices.

Much of Western Australia, South Australia, the Northern Territory, and interior New South Wales can be uncomfortably hot during summer, especially if you're planning on making the most of the great outdoors. Of course, nights in the Outback can also get very chilly. Again, fall and spring are the perfect compromise.

"Stinger season," when there is a high risk of jellyfish in northern Queensland, runs from October to May, when beaches will often be signposted with the risk level. More than 30 popular beaches north of Banny Point are protected by a visible enclosure to keep out the majority of stingers. Wet suits or other protective clothing are also recommended during this time of year.

Essentials

🛏 Lodging

Australia operates a rating system of one to five stars. Five-star hotels include on-site dining options, concierge and valet services, a business center, and, of course, very luxurious rooms. Four stars denote an exceptional property that just doesn't have all the extras needed for five. Three stars means quality fittings and service.

Judging from the huge number of short-term rental properties in Australia, many locals prefer doing their own thing to being in a hotel and it's easy for you to do likewise. Serviced apartments and peer-to-peer accommodation options are plentiful in Australia for those who'd rather avoid the big hotel chains. Homestays in rural and regional areas are another great way to experience the real Australia.

Airbnb has also emerged as a popular type of accommodation in Australia. Here you'll find houses and apartments as well as properties off the beaten track, including farm stays, rain-forest retreats, and houseboats, often with a much more intimate feel and at significantly lower prices than traditional establishments.

🍴 Dining

Fresh ingredients, friendly service, innovative flavor combinations, and great value for your money mean that eating out Down Under is usually a pleasant experience. Australia's British heritage is evident in the hearty food served in pubs, roadhouses, and country hotels. It all seems to taste much better than food in Britain, though. On the other hand, its proximity to Asia brings delicious and authentic cuisine from all over the region.

PAYING
At most restaurants you ask for the bill at the end of the meal. At sandwich bars, burger joints, takeout spots, and some cafés, you pay up front. Visa and Master-Card are widely accepted in all but the simplest eateries, but American Express cards may not be accepted or may incur an additional fee.

RESERVATIONS AND DRESS
Regardless of where you are, it's a good idea to make a reservation if you can. In some places (Sydney, for example) it's expected. For popular restaurants, book as far ahead as you can (often 30 days), and reconfirm as soon as you arrive. (Large parties should always call ahead to check the reservations policy.) Formal dress codes are rare, although at fine-dining establishments in Sydney and Melbourne a jacket and tie are expected.

🏛 Customs and Duties

Australian customs regulations are unlike any other. Australia is free from many pests and diseases endemic in other places, and it wants to stay that way. Customs procedures are very thorough, and it can take up to an hour to clear them.

All animals are subject to quarantine and many foodstuffs and natural products are forbidden. If in doubt, declare something—the worst-case scenario is that it will be taken from you, without a fine.

➕ Health

Sunburn and sunstroke are the greatest health hazards when visiting Australia. Stay out of the sun in the middle of the day (the hottest hours are generally 11 am–2 pm) and, regardless of whether

Essentials

you normally burn, follow the locals' example and slather on the sunscreen. Dehydration is another concern, especially in the Outback. It's easy to avoid: carry plenty of water and drink it often.

Some of the world's deadliest creatures call Australia home. The chances of running into one are low, particularly in urban areas, but wherever you go, pay close heed to any warnings given by hotel staff, tour operators, lifeguards, or locals in general. The best advice is to always be cautious, and double-check the situation at each stop with the appropriate authority.

Australian coastal waters are also home to strong currents known as "rips." Pay close attention to the flags raised on beaches, and only swim in areas patrolled by lifeguards. If you get caught in a rip, the standard advice is never to swim against it, as you rapidly become exhausted. Instead, try to relax and float parallel to the shore: eventually the current will subside and you will be able to swim back to the shore, albeit farther down the coast.

⊙ Packing

A light sweater or jacket will keep you comfy in autumn, but winter in the southern states demands a heavier coat—ideally a raincoat with a zip-out lining. On the other hand, summer can be sweltering, so light shirts and breezy pants are in order. Sydney is famously temperate, whereas Melbourne is known to experience four seasons in one day.

Wherever you are, your accessories of choice are high-quality sunglasses and a hat with a brim—the sun is strong and dangerous.

Carry insect repellent and avoid lotions or perfume in the tropics, as they attract mosquitoes and other insects. Flies are a consistent annoyance in rural and regional areas.

You should pack sturdy walking boots if you're planning any bushwalking, otherwise sneakers or flats are fine for sightseeing. Flip-flops are confusingly referred to as thongs down under, and are popular in casual settings.

Whether you're hitting the beach, a river, a waterhole or simply the hotel pool, cooling off is Australia's favorite pastime. Variously referred to as togs, bathers, or swimmers around the country, a swimsuit is essential all year round.

⊙ Tours

ABORIGINAL ART

Aboriginal Travel

SPECIAL-INTEREST | This agency has several Aboriginal art tours, including a five-day collectors tour and shorter rock-art tours. ☎ 08/8234–8324 ⊕ www.aboriginaltravel. com ✉ From A$69.

Adventure Tours Australia

SPECIAL-INTEREST | This company runs a host of both long and short trips, many of which are Aboriginal-culture centric, particularly the three-day Rock the Centre tour of Uluru and surroundings. ☎ 1300/654604 in Australia, 03/8102–7800 outside Australia ⊕ www.adventuretours.com.au ✉ From A$110.

Palya Art Tours

SPECIAL-INTEREST | Pilot and art lover Helen Read flies you and guides you on Palya Art Tours' small-group trips through remote indigenous communities in northwestern Australia. ⊕ www.palya.com.au ✉ From $8800.

CULTURE

National Geographic Expeditions

SPECIAL-INTEREST | Local experts lead National Geographic's extensive Australia expeditions, which take in the Great Barrier Reef and Uluru, but that knowledge doesn't come cheap, nor does the private air transport they use. ☎ 888/966–8687 in U.S. ⊕ www.nationalgeographicexpeditions.com ✉ From $7990.

SEIT Outback Australia

SPECIAL-INTEREST | Join SEIT to experience small-group tours and workshops in Central Australia, working in partnership with Aboriginal communities and operators. ☎ 08/8956–3156 ⊕ www.seitoutbackaustralia.com.au ✉ From A$92.

Smithsonian Journeys

SPECIAL-INTEREST | Learning is the focus of Smithsonian Journeys' small-group tours, led by university professors. Their 22-day Splendors of Australia and New Zealand tour covers the best of Australia—and much of New Zealand, too. ☎ 855/338–8687 ⊕ www.smithsonianjourneys.org ✉ From $9057.

DIVING

Daintree Air Services

SPECIAL-INTEREST | Local flightseeing company Daintree Air Services' Ultimate Dive package includes 18 dives in nine days. The Great Barrier Reef, Coral Sea, and a wreck dive are included. ☎ 1800/246206 in Australia, 07/4034–9300 outside Australia ⊕ www.daintreeair.com.au ✉ From A$160.

Diversion Dive Travel

SPECIAL-INTEREST | Working with dive operators around Australia, Diversion connects you with Australia's diving hotspots including the Great Barrier Reef, Christmas Island, and the south and west Australian coasts. ☎ 1800/607913 within Australia, 07/4039–0200 outside Australia ⊕ www.diversiondivetravel.com.au ✉ From A$630.

ECO-TOURS AND SAFARIS

Northern Experience Eco Tours

SPECIAL-INTEREST | Experience the beauty of North Queensland's World Heritage-listed Wet Tropics Rain forests and the Atherton Tablelands with this family-owned, eco-tour operator. Trips include swimming in waterfalls, a lake cruise, visiting national parks, Aboriginal Dreamtime education and stories, as well as plentiful encounters with local flora and fauna. ☎ 07/4058–0268 ⊕ www.northern-experience.com.au ✉ From A$125.

Sacred Earth Safaris

SPECIAL-INTEREST | This family-operated tour company specializes in 4WD tours through remote and Top End Australia, including the Kakadu and Kimberley frontiers, the Nullarbor Plain, the Flinders Ranges, Kangaroo Island, and Pilbara. ☎ 0415/692–855 ⊕ www.sacredearthsafaris.com.au ✉ From A$645.

Wayoutback Australian Safaris

SPECIAL-INTEREST | This tour company employs certified eco-tour operators who run camping and accommodated safaris, as well as Desert Walks, throughout Australia, with a strong focus on Aboriginal culture. ☎ 1300/551510 in Australia, 08/8952–4324 outside Australia ⊕ www.wayoutback.com.au ✉ From A$375.

FOOD AND WINE

Adelaide's Top Food and Wine Tours

SPECIAL-INTEREST | Eat and drink your way around the famous vineyards and providores of The Barossa Valley, McLaren Vale, Clare Valley, and Adelaide Hills on these personalized, small-group tours. ☎ 08/8386–0888 ⊕ www.topfoodandwinetours.com.au ✉ From A$55.

Great Itineraries

First Timer's Itinerary: Sydney, the Great Barrier Reef, Uluru

This classic 10-day journey takes in three of Australia's most natural treasures, including the Blue Mountains, the Great Barrier Reef, and Uluru.

DAYS 1–2: EXPLORING SYDNEY

On your first day in Australia's largest city, visit the world-renowned **Sydney Opera House,** stopping for lunch at the Opera Bar with its sweeping views of the cityscape and Harbour Bridge. In the afternoon, take a guided walking tour through the historic **Rocks** area beyond **Circular Quay.** After some much-needed rest, start the second day with a harbor cruise. You can enjoy the best vantage points for seeing this spectacular city and its magnificent waterfront setting. In the afternoon, head over to **Sydney Harbour Bridge,** where a trek up the stairs of the South East Pylon rewards you with an unbeatable harbor panorama.

DAY 3: DAY TRIP TO THE BLUE MOUNTAINS

Leave Sydney in the morning on a day trip to the Blue Mountains, approximately one hour away by car or bus. Head for **Katoomba** at the peak of the Blue Mountains National Park, where the **Three Sisters** await, an unusual rock formation representing three sisters who were turned to stone according to Aboriginal legend. Head to neighboring **Scenic World** and choose the scenic skyway, walkway, railway, or cableway to experience the majesty of the Jamison Valley. On your way back, make a small detour in the pretty garden village of **Leura,** with its many fine coffee shops, restaurants, and galleries. Return to Sydney for dinner and stay the night there.

DAY 4: WINE TOUR OF THE HUNTER VALLEY

Take an organized day trip from Sydney to the **Hunter Valley Wine Region,** 150 km (93 miles) north of Sydney, and spend the day experiencing a selection of more than 150 wineries and cellar doors. Discover the region's finest Shiraz or Chardonnay and taste some of the freshest produce and best cheeses that Australia has to offer. Return to Sydney at night for dinner.

DAY 5: FLIGHT TO CAIRNS

Fly to Cairns, a tropical city nestled in North Queensland and the gateway to the Great Barrier Reef. Relax after your three-hour flight from Sydney with a visit to the **Cairns Tropical Zoo** to cuddle a koala. At night, take in the atmosphere by strolling along the **Esplanade,** or beat the heat by taking a dip in the pristine **Cairns Lagoon.**

DAY 6: KURANDA VILLAGE AND TJAPUKAI ABORIGINAL CULTURAL PARK

Take a full-day tour of nearby **Kuranda** village and the surrounding rain forest. Experience one of Australia's most scenic rail journeys, the **Skyrail Rainforest Cableway,** for a bird's-eye view over the forest. After lunch, head to the **Tjapukai Aboriginal Cultural Park** to watch traditional Aboriginal dances and listen to music and informational talks—perhaps even try your hand at throwing a boomerang or playing the didgeridoo!

DAY 7: CRUISE TO THE GREAT BARRIER REEF

Book a full-day cruise from Cairns to the **Great Barrier Reef** and get up close and personal with the abundant sea life of the world's largest coral reef system. With some of the best snorkeling and diving on the planet, nothing beats getting in the water and swimming with groupers, clown fish, and rays. Then revel in the

Map labels:

INDIAN OCEAN

Gulf of Carpentaria

Coral Sea

NORTHERN TERRITORY

Kuranda Village and Tjapukai Aboriginal Cultural Park

Great Barrier Reef

Cairns

Uluru (Ayers Rock)

QUEENSLAND

WESTERN AUSTRALIA

SOUTH AUSTRALIA

NEW SOUTH WALES

Hunter Valley

Blue Mountains

Sydney

VICTORIA

SOUTHERN OCEAN

TASMANIA

fact you're experiencing one of the seven wonders of the natural world firsthand.

DAYS 8–9: TWO DAYS IN ULURU

Rise and shine early to catch the three-hour flight inland to the physical and spiritual heart of Australia: World Heritage–listed **Uluru,** the iconic symbol of the Australian Outback. Once you arrive and check in at Ayers Rock Resort, book a seat at the **Sounds of Silence** dinner, where you can feast on a barbecue buffet of kangaroo, crocodile, and barramundi and marvel at the immense desert sky.

Wake up before dawn the next morning to catch the majestic sunrise over Uluru (Ayers Rock). See the magnificence of Uluru as its surface changes color with the rising sun, from pink to blood-red to mauve throughout the day. Afterward, walk around Uluru's base with a guide and learn about how this sacred site was created by spirit ancestors in the Dreamtime. In the afternoon, sign up for a tour of **Kata Tjuta** (the Olgas), the nearby rock domes over which you can watch the sun set.

DAY 10: BACK TO SYDNEY

Once you return to Sydney, take the short ferry ride to **Taronga Zoo** and stroll around the zoo's harborside location, spying kangaroos, koalas, and other animal natives.

Tips

■ If driving around Sydney, avoid traveling at peak times. Either leave early or head off later, once the commuter traffic has died down.

■ Cairns has a wide range of hotels and resorts to suit any budget— a romantic getaway, weekend escape, or family vacation. It's worth booking ahead and finding somewhere central to the city.

■ When visiting the Great Barrier Reef for a dive or snorkel experience, the best time of year is in the winter months when marine stingers aren't present in the water and there is less need for a protective wet suit.

If you have time, a short bus or train ride to the world-famous Bondi Beach is in order for a taste of Sydney's much heralded beach life. Spend early evening at the Bondi Icebergs club, where you can enjoy a glass of Australian wine while gazing out over the picturesque southern end of the beach.

Great Itineraries

The Southern Experience: Melbourne, Tasmania, Kangaroo Island

Taking in the best of the south of the country, this 11-day trip combines Australia's second-largest city, Melbourne, and the surrounding region with the great Tasmanian outdoors and South Australia's Kangaroo Island.

DAYS 1–2: MELBOURNE

Start off in Australia's cultural capital, **Melbourne,** with its world-class shopping and thriving arts scene. No visit to Melbourne is complete without a freshly made espresso. Some of the best are on **Degraves Street,** directly off Flinders. Sit down at one of the RMB Café Bar's outdoor tables and enjoy delicious eggs Benedict with your coffee. Jump on the free city circle tram to get an overview of the city. It offers good hop-on, hop-off transportation for visitors and locals alike.

DAY 3: YARRA VALLEY WINE REGION

Leave the sights and sounds of Melbourne for a day of wine tasting at the **Yarra Valley.** It's within easy driving distance of the city, but your best bet is to go with a winery tour, which often provide transfers from the CBD. These generally include visits to four or five wineries and lunch. Return to Melbourne for dinner.

DAY 4: MELBOURNE AND PHILLIP ISLAND

Explore the farther reaches of the city by visiting the trendy suburbs of **Richmond, St Kilda, Fitzroy,** or **Prahran.** All offer great café and shopping strips with a more laid-back feel than in downtown Melbourne. Take an evening tour to nearby **Phillip Island** to see the **Little Penguin Parade,** when the world's smallest penguins come ashore after a day's fishing.

DAYS 5–6: HOBART

Fly direct from Melbourne to **Hobart** (one-hour flight) to explore Tasmania, Australia's natural state. In the harbor capital, sate your Tasmanian appetite with a mix of history and contemporary art and culture. Start at **Salamanca Place** on the harbor-front and browse the galleries, art studios, cafés, and restaurants lining the quaint waterfront in original 19th-century warehouses. Then make your way up the hill to Battery Point and wander streets where grand colonial houses face out over the Derwent River. The **Museum of Old and New Art (MONA)** is a must-see for art lovers and visitors alike, and is only a 15-minute drive (or 25-minute ferry ride) from the center of Hobart.

DAY 7: PORT ARTHUR

Hire a car and make the 90-minute drive to **Port Arthur** on the Tasman Peninsula or join the cruise from Hobart to Port Arthur aboard the MV Marana, which takes approximately 2½ hours. Experience Australia's most intact convict site with more than 30 buildings, ruins, and restored homes. Hop on board a short cruise to the **Isle of the Dead** to join a guided tour of the settlement's island burial ground and learn about the lives of the people who lived in Port Arthur. On your return to Hobart, grab a bite to eat at Salamanca Place and enjoy some art, crafts, music, and theater at the Salamanca Arts Centre.

DAY 8: BACK TO MELBOURNE

Fly back to Melbourne in the morning, and then it's time for shopping. A great place to start is at the **Queen Victoria Market** on Elizabeth Street, a shopping institution that showcases a wide range of quality food, clothing, jewelry, new-age products, and souvenirs. For

more upmarket items, head to **Emporium Melbourne, QV Retail,** or **Melbourne GPO.** If you're feeling shopped out, take a trip to the **Eureka Skydeck 88** for impressive and expansive views of the city from the Southern Hemisphere's highest viewing platform.

DAY 9: THE DANDENONG RANGES

You've tried the Yarra Valley but haven't yet explored the Dandenong Ranges, a tranquil region of towering rain forests and quaint mountain villages, just a short half-hour drive or one-hour train ride from Melbourne city (disembark at Hurstbridge, Lilydale, or Belgrave station, where you'll find connecting buses). You can hike through the **Dandenong Ranges National Park** and enjoy incredible views of Melbourne's skyline from the Skyhigh, perched on top of Mt. Dandenong. Afterward, explore your creative interests among the shops, galleries, and tearooms of nearby Olinda, Belgrave, and Sassafras. Overnight at one of the many quaint B&Bs nestled in the mountains, or make the brief journey back to Melbourne.

DAYS 10–11: KANGAROO ISLAND

Visiting the southern tip of Australia wouldn't be complete without a trip to **Kangaroo Island,** Australia's third-largest island. The island is a pristine wilderness located southwest of Adelaide and home to some of the largest untouched populations of native Australian animals. Take the short flight to **Adelaide** from Melbourne and then a further flight or ferry ride across to the Island. **Sealink Ferries** offers a range of single- and multi-day tours and accommodation packages, showcasing the best of the region's wildlife, coastline, and specialty food and wine.

If adventure is your thing, Kangaroo Helicopters offers a Heli Experience and Scenic Flight or, for wildlife enthusiasts, options include guided tours within the Seal Bay or Kelly Hill Conservation Parks. Fly via Adelaide back to Melbourne or on to the next stage of your journey.

Great Itineraries

Road Trip: From Sydney to Brisbane

Drive along one of the most glorious and seductive stretches of land in northern New South Wales. It's a big trip—1,100 km (687 miles)—so allow a minimum of seven days if you decide to drive the entire route.

DAY 1: SYDNEY TO POKOLBIN, 175 KM (109 MILES)

Start the journey heading north out of Sydney, with the famed Harbour Bridge in your rearview mirror. Take the Sydney–Newcastle (F3) Freeway about 75 km (47 miles) north to the Peats Ridge Road exit, and wind through the forested hills to Wollombi, a delightful town founded in 1820. Browse the antiques shops, sandstone courthouse, and museum. Next, head northeast to Cessnock and Pokolbin, the hub of the Lower Hunter, and spend the day tasting—and buying—fine wines and artisanal cheeses. Know that Australia has a strict 0.5 blood alcohol limit when driving. Be sure to choose a designated driver or, better yet, take one of our recommended wine-tasting tours.

DAY 2: POKOLBIN TO PORT MACQUARIE, 271 KM (168 MILES)

Get up early with the birds and drive east via Cessnock to the Pacific Highway. Turn north for the long drive to Port Macquarie, Australia's third-oldest settlement. Have a well-earned lunch break in the café at Sea Acres Rainforest Centre and then stroll the elevated boardwalk—or take a guided tour—through centuries-old cabbage tree palms. Make a quick visit to the Koala Hospital in Port Macquarie for feeding time (3 pm), and then head into town for a lazy afternoon on a beach. The most pressing question is: Which of the 13 regional beaches should you laze on?

DAY 3: PORT MACQUARIE TO COFFS, 260 KM (162½ MILES)

After a rest and an alfresco breakfast, resume driving up the Pacific Highway. Leave the highway 140 km (88 miles) north at the exit to Bellingen, one of the prettiest towns on the New South Wales north coast. It's a nice place to stop for lunch and a quick peek into a few galleries. Continue inland up onto the Dorrigo Plateau. Dorrigo National Park is one of about 50 reserves and parks within the World Heritage–listed Gondwana Rainforests of Australia. Stopping into the Dorrigo Rainforest Centre to learn about the area is gratifying, as is the forest canopy Skywalk. Back in your car, drive on to Dorrigo town and turn right onto the winding, partly unpaved, but scenic road to Corumba and Coffs Harbour. Now you've earned a two-night stay in Coffs.

DAY 4: COFFS, NO DRIVING

Scuba dive on the Solitary Isles? White-water raft the Nymboida River? Or kick back on a beach? However you spend your day, don't miss an evening stroll to Muttonbird Island from Coffs Harbour marina. From September to April you can watch muttonbirds (or shearwaters) returning to their burrows. When the whales are about, it's also a good humpback viewing spot.

DAY 5: COFFS TO BYRON BAY, 247 KM (154 MILES)

Drive north again, past Coffs Harbour's landmark Big Banana and up the coast to Byron Bay.

There is just too much to do in Byron: kayak with dolphins; dive with gray nurse sharks; go beachcombing and swimming; tread the Cape Byron Walking Track; or tour the lighthouse atop Cape Byron, which is mainland Australia's easternmost point. It's best to decide over lunch at open-air Byron Bay Beach Café, a local legend. When the sun sets, wash

Brisbane ✪
GOLD COAST
QUEENSLAND
Mt. Warning ◆ ○ **Murwillumbah**
Byron Bay ○

SOLITARY ISLANDS

Dorrigo ○
Dorrigo National Park ◆ ○ ○ **Coffs**
Bellingen ○

○ **Port Macquarie**
◆ **Sea Acres Rainforest Centre**

NEW SOUTH
WALES

Pokolbin ○
Wollombi ○ ○ **Cessnock**

✪ **Sydney**

off the salt and head out for some great seafood and then overnight in Byron Bay—there's everything from hostels to high-end villas.

DAY 6: BYRON BAY TO MURWILLUMBAH, 53 KM (33 MILES)

Catch up on the Byron Bay you missed yesterday before driving north to Murwillumbah and its remarkable natural landmark. Wollumbin (Mt. Warning) is the 3,800-foot magma chamber of an extinct shield volcano. From the top, on a clear day, there is a 360-degree view of one of the world's largest calderas, with mountainous rims on three sides and the Tweed River running through its eroded east rim. Climb this mountain (four hours round-trip), then reward yourself with a night at Crystal Creek Rainforest Retreat (bookings essential).

DAY 7: MURWILLUMBAH TO BRISBANE, 50 KM (31 MILES)

Relaxed and reinvigorated, you should make your way over the New South Wales border to Queensland and Australia's most developed stretch of coastline. With Brisbane just 90 minutes' drive farther north, you can spend as much or as little time as you want on the Gold Coast. Visit theme parks; toss dice at the casino; ride waves in gorgeous sunshine. Don't miss feeding the lorikeets at Currumbin Wildlife Sanctuary before Brisbane beckons.

Great Itineraries

Road Trip: Great Ocean Road

Arguably one of the country's most spectacular drives, the iconic Great Ocean Road hugs the windswept, rugged coastline just west of Melbourne. Allow six days for this 900-km (562-mile) road trip and be prepared to enjoy some of Victoria's best.

DAY 1: MELBOURNE TO APOLLO BAY, 187 KM (117 MILES)

Having escaped Melbourne, drive down the Princes Freeway for about 75 km (47 miles) to the Torquay/Great Ocean Road turnoff. A quarter hour more at the wheel brings you to Torquay, Australia's premier surfing and windsurfing resort town. On your way out of town, detour to Bell's Beach, the setting for Australia's principal surfing competition each Easter. The renowned Great Ocean Road officially starts 30 km (19 miles) beyond Bell's Beach, but the dramatic splendor of Victoria's southwest coast reveals itself sooner.

Stop in Lorne, at the foot of the lush Otway Ranges, for lunch. Once you're back on the road, slow down and enjoy it. The winding Great Ocean Road is narrow; don't pass unless you can see far ahead. There are designated pull-over areas where you can safely enjoy the vista.

Drive the 45 km (28 miles) to Apollo Bay for dinner and the night.

DAY 2: APOLLO BAY TO PORT FAIRY, 234 KM (146 MILES)

The 91-km (57-mile) Great Ocean Walk starts just west of Apollo Bay in Marengo. Here the Great Ocean Road heads inland. Stay on the main road to Lavers Hill; then detour about 17 km (11 miles) east to the Otway Fly. This 1,969-foot-long elevated treetop walk takes you up into the rain-forest canopy for a bird's-eye view of giant myrtle beech, blackwood, and mighty mountain ash. Backtrack to Lavers Hill and the Great Ocean Road. The road's most famous landmarks lie along a 32-km (20-mile) stretch of coast within Port Campbell National Park.

First stop is the Twelve Apostles—there are now only eight of these offshore limestone stacks, but who's counting? Take a helicopter flight for a jaw-dropping view of the coast. Next stop is Loch Ard Gorge, named after the iron-hulled clipper that hit a reef and sank here in 1878. Loch Ard is a natural gallery of sea sculpture. Don't stay in your car if the sun doesn't show, though. Only when a howling wind is roughing up the Southern Ocean will you fully appreciate why this is called the Shipwreck Coast. Leaving the Great Ocean Road now, drive to the maritime village of Port Fairy for the night. In whale season (June–November), divert to Logan's Beach, in Warrnambool, where southern right cows and calves often loll just off the beach.

DAY 3: PORT FAIRY TO HALLS GAP, 146 KM (91 MILES)

Take a leisurely postbreakfast promenade around Port Fairy, Victoria's second-oldest town and widely considered to be its prettiest. Then backtrack 7 km (4½ miles) to the Penshurst/Dunkeld Road and drive 74 km (46 miles) north to Dunkeld, on the edge of the Grampians National Park. Stop for lunch before undertaking the 60-km (37-mile) drive to Halls Gap, the main accommodation base. Be sure to slow down and enjoy one of the most picturesque drives in the Grampians; pull in at the Brambuk Cultural Centre, just before Halls Gap, and learn about the park's rich Aboriginal history.

Check into your Halls Gap accommodation for two nights.

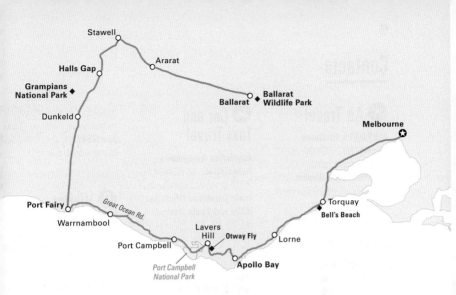

DAY 4: GRAMPIANS NATIONAL PARK, NO DRIVING

Spend a day exploring on foot. Walks of varied grades showcase the Grampians' extraordinary geology; don't miss the Pinnacle Walk, just out of Halls Gap, the valley and ranges view from Chatauqua Peak, and Hollow Mountain in the park's north.

DAY 5: HALLS GAP TO BALLARAT, 140 KM (88 MILES)

Drive out of Halls Gap to Ararat, on the Western Highway, and follow the highway east to the famous gold town of Ballarat. Spend the rest of the morning among the gold-rush-era Victorian architecture on Sturt and Lydiard streets. Visit the Ballarat Fine Art Gallery, if only to see the tattered remains of the Southern Cross flag that the rebels flew during the 1854 Eureka uprising over mine license fees. Spend the afternoon at Sovereign Hill, where you can pan for gold, ride a horse-drawn stagecoach, and stick your teeth together with old-fashioned candy.

DAY 6: BALLARAT TO MELBOURNE, 111 KM (69 MILES)

Have encounters with saltwater crocodiles, snakes, wombats, kangaroos, and other Australian fauna at Ballarat Wildlife Park. After that, continue your journey or head back to Melbourne.

Tips

■ Unleaded petrol, diesel, and LPG are available at gas stations in major centers; however, LPG is rare in small country towns.

■ There is a petrol price cycle in Victoria; try to fill up on Tuesday and Wednesday, and avoid buying fuel on Friday.

■ Choosing accommodation as you go gives you flexibility in when and where you stop. For peace of mind, though, you might prefer to prebook.

■ Fixed speed radars are used on Victoria's major freeways, and fines are high. Stick to the speed limits.

■ Watch for animals straying onto the road, especially on rural roads near sunset and sunrise.

Contacts

✈ Air Travel

AIRPORTS Brisbane Airport. ☎ 07/3406–3000 ⊕ www.bne.com. au. **Melbourne Airport.** ☎ 03/9297–1600 ⊕ www. melbourneairport. com.au. **Sydney Airport.** ☎ 02/9667–9111 ⊕ www. sydneyairport.com.au.

AIRLINES Qantas. ☎ 1800/227–4500 in U.S., 13–1313 in Australia ⊕ www.qantas.com.au.

⛴ Boat and Ferry Travel

Great Barrier Reef Marine Park Authority. ☎ 07/4750–0700 ⊕ www.gbrmpa. gov.au. **Spirit of Tasmania.** ☎ 1800/634906 ⊕ www. spiritoftasmania.com.au.

🚌 Bus Travel

Greyhound Australia. ☎ 1300/473946 ⊕ www. greyhound.com.au. **Murrays Coaches .** ☎ 13–2251 ⊕ www.murrays.com.au. **Public Transport Victoria.** ☎ 3/9662–2505 ⊕ www. ptv.vic.gov.au. **Transport NSW.** ☎ 2/4907–7501 ⊕ transportnsw.info.

🚕 Car and Taxi Travel

Australian Automobile Association. ☎ 02/6247–7311 ⊕ www.aaa.asn.au. **Taxis Combined (Victoria, NSW and South Australia).** ☎ 13–2227 ⊕ www. taxiscombined.com.au.

🇺🇸 Embassy

CANBERRA U.S. Embassy. ✉ Moonah Pl., Yarralumla, Canberra ☎ 02/6214–5600 ⊕ au.usembassy.gov/ embassy-consulates/ canberra.

PERTH U.S. Consulate. ✉ 16 St. George's Tce., Perth ☎ 08/6144–5100 ⊕ au.usembassy.gov/ embassy-consulates/ perth.

SYDNEY U.S. Consulate. ✉ MLC Centre, 19–29 Martin Pl., Level 10, Sydney ☎ 300/139–399 ⊕ au.usembassy.gov/ embassy-consulates/ sydney.

🚆 Train Travel

Public Transport Victoria ☎ 3/9662–2505 ⊕ www. ptv.vic.gov.au.

Rail Australia. ☎ 1800/872467 in Australia, 07/3235–1122

outside Australia ⊕ www railaustralia.com.au. **Transport NSW.** ☎ 2/4907–750 ⊕ transportnsw.info.

📍 Visitor Information

Canberra ☎ +61 2/6205–0044 ⊕ visitcanberra. com.au

National Parks ☎ 1800/803772 ⊕ www. environment.gov.au

New South Wales ☎ 1800/067676 ⊕ www. visitnsw.com

Northern Territory ☎ 1300/138886 ⊕ northernterritory.com

Queensland ☎ +61 7/3535 3535 ⊕ teq.queensland. com

South Australia ☎ 1300/588140 ⊕ southaustralia.com

Tasmania ☎ +61 3/6238–4222 ⊕ www.discovertasmania.com.au

Victoria ☎ +61 3/9658–9658 ⊕ www.visitvictoria. com

Western Australia ☎ +61 8/9483–1111 ⊕ www. westernaustralia.com

Chapter 3

SYDNEY

Updated by Amy
Nelmes Bissett

👁 Sights	🍴 Restaurants	🛏 Hotels	🛍 Shopping	🍸 Nightlife
★★★★☆	★★★★★	★★★★★	★★★☆☆	★★★☆☆

WELCOME TO SYDNEY

TOP REASONS TO GO

★ **A Harbor Sail:** Take a ferry, sail a yacht, or paddle a kayak, but make sure you get out into Sydney Harbour. It's a glorious sight. Check out the Sydney Harbour section for tours of the harbor by boat.

★ **A Night at the Opera:** From rock to rap, theater to tap dancing, there's always something interesting happening at the world's most famous playhouse.

★ **Exquisite Dining:** Sydney restaurants are among the finest eateries in the world. Don't miss out on the fresh seafood and top-notch Mod Oz and Asian cuisines.

★ **Glorious Beaches:** Sydneysiders are besotted by the beach, and you'll be, too. With 100 to choose from, you can watch surfers ride the waves or paddle around the calmer waters of a sheltered harbor beach.

★ **National Parks and Wildlife:** Sydney's untamed beauty is close at hand. See native birds and colorful wildflowers just a few miles from the city.

Sydney is built around its huge harbor. The city center and main attractions are on the south shore. Harbour Bridge connects The Rocks on the south side with Milsons Point on the north side. Greater Sydney is vast, some 80 km (50 miles) from north to south and 70 km (43 miles) from east to west; however, the city center is relatively small. From the Opera House and Circular Quay the city stretches south for about 3 km (2 miles), and east to west for about 2 km (1 mile). Beyond the harbor, the city center is essentially a business and shopping precinct, with colonial and modern buildings. The restaurant and nightlife suburbs of Darlinghurst, Surry Hills, and Potts Point flank the city's eastern and southern edges.

1 Sydney Harbour. This spectacular waterway has a 240-km (149-mile) shoreline of bays, headlands, and quiet beaches. It's the city's jewel.

2 The Rocks. Sydney's oldest area, The Rocks, is full of restored 19th-century warehouses and pubs with great views of the famous bridge.

3 Domain and Macquarie Street. This stately quarter of town contains Parliament House, formal gardens, and the Domain, where concerts are staged.

4 The Opera House and the Royal Botanic Gardens. The white "sails" of the Opera House dominate the harbor; the neighboring Royal Botanic Gardens are an oasis on the harbor's edge.

5 Darling Harbour and Barangaroo. A former goods yard on the city's western edge, Darling Harbour now houses museums, the aquarium, restaurants, and hotels while neighboring Barangaroo is a newly opened precinct with waterfront restaurants, bars, and stores.

6 Sydney City Center. Dominated by 880-foot Sydney Tower, the city center is packed with historic and modern shopping arcades.

7 Inner Sydney and the Eastern Suburbs. A few miles east of the city you'll find palatial harborside homes, beaches, and café-culture, bohemian-chic enclaves.

8 Greater Sydney. National parks, beautiful beaches, and relics of Sydney's colonial past can all be explored within an hour of the city center.

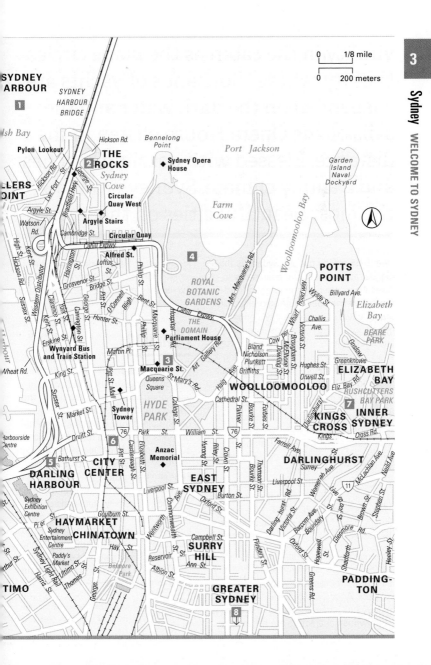

0 1/8 mile

0 200 meters

SYDNEY HARBOUR

1

SYDNEY HARBOUR BRIDGE

lsh Bay

Pylon Lookout

Hickson Rd.

Bennelong Point

Port Jackson

Garden Island Naval Dockyard

THE ROCKS

2

Sydney Cove

Sydney Opera House

LLERS OINT

Circular Quay West

Argyle St.

Argyle Stairs

Watson Rd.

Cambridge St.

Circular Quay

Farm Cove

Woolloomooloo Bay

4

POTTS POINT

Billyard Ave.

High St.

Kent St.

Sussex St.

Cahill Expwy.

Alfred St.

Loftus St.

ROYAL BOTANIC GARDENS

Mrs. Macquarie's Rd.

Wylde St.

Challis Ave.

Elizabeth Bay

BEARE PARK

Harrington St.

Grosvenor St.

Bridge St.

George St.

Pitt St.

O'Connell

Bligh

Phillip St.

Macquarie St.

Hospital Rd.

THE DOMAIN

Cowper Wharf Roadway

Onslow

Greenknowe Ave.

Clarence St.

Kent St.

Carrington St.

Hunter St.

Parliament House

Bland

McElhone St.

Brougham St.

Victoria St.

Hughes St.

ELIZABETH BAY

Erskine St.

York St.

Wynard Bus and Train Station

Martin Pl.

Bligh St.

Phillip St.

Macquarie St.

Art Gallery Rd.

Nicholson Plunkett

Dowling St.

Orwell St.

RUSHCUTTERS BAY PARK

Wheat Rd.

King St.

Sussex St.

3

Macquarie St.

Griffiths

WOOLLOOMOOLOO

Eliz. Bay Rd.

7

INNER SYDNEY

Queens Square

St. Mary's Rd.

Haig Ave.

Forbes St.

KINGS CROSS

Market St.

Sydney Tower

HYDE PARK

College St.

Cathedral St.

Palmer St.

Bourke St.

Kings Cross Rd.

Harbourside Centre

Druitt St.

6

Park St.

76

William St.

Crown St.

76

Farrell Ave.

DARLINGHURST

Bathurst St.

5

CITY CENTER

Castlereagh St.

Elizabeth St.

Anzac Memorial

EAST SYDNEY

Riley St.

Yurong St.

Thomson St.

Bourke St.

Liverpool St.

Surrey

Womerah Ave.

McLachlan Ave.

Neild Ave.

DARLING HARBOUR

Sydney Exhibition Centre

Pier St.

HAYMARKET

Liverpool St.

Oxford St.

Burton St.

Darling hurst Rd.

Victoria St.

Live Pool St.

Bacom Ave.

Brown St.

Stephen St.

11

Goulburn St.

Sydney Entertainment Centre

CHINATOWN

Wentworth Ave.

Commonwealth St.

Campbell St.

Flinders St.

Boundary St.

Glenmore Rd.

Hopewell

Shadforth

Heeley St.

Hay St.

SURRY HILL

PADDING-TON

TIMO

Paddy's Market

Ultimo

Thomas St.

Belmore Park

Reservoir St.

Ann St.

Albion St.

Harris St.

Sydney Light Rail

George St.

GREATER SYDNEY

Oxford St.

Greens Rd.

8

Sydney belongs to the exclusive club of cities that generate excitement. At the end of a marathon flight there's renewed vitality in the cabin as the plane circles the city, where thousands of yachts are suspended on the dark water and the sails of the Opera House glisten in the distance. Blessed with dazzling beaches and a sunny climate, Sydney is among the most beautiful cities on the planet.

With 5.64 million people, Sydney is the biggest and most cosmopolitan city in Australia. A wave of immigration from the 1950s has seen the Anglo-Irish immigrants who made up the city's original population joined by Italians, Greeks, Turks, Lebanese, Chinese, Vietnamese, Thais, and Indonesians. This intermingling has created a cultural vibrancy and energy—and a culinary repertoire—that was missing only a generation ago.

Sydneysiders embrace their harbor with a passion. Indented with numerous bays and beaches, Sydney Harbour is the presiding icon for the city, and urban Australia. Captain Arthur Phillip, commander of the 11-ship First Fleet, wrote in his diary when he first set eyes on the harbor on January 26, 1788: "We had the satisfaction of finding the finest harbor in the world."

Although a visit to Sydney is an essential part of an Australian experience, the city is no more representative of Australia than Los Angeles is of the United States. Sydney has joined the ranks of the great cities whose characters are essentially international. What Sydney offers is style, sophistication, and great looks—an exhilarating prelude to the continent at its back door.

Planning

WHEN TO GO

The best times to visit Sydney are in late spring and early fall (autumn). The spring months of October and November are pleasantly warm, although the ocean is slightly cool for swimming. The summer months of December through February are typically hot and humid, February being the most humid. In the early autumn months of March and April weather is typically stable and comfortable, outdoor city life is still in full swing, and the ocean is at its warmest. Even the coolest winter months of July and August typically stay mild and sunny, with average daily maximum temperatures in the low 60s.

PLANNING YOUR TIME

You really need three days in Sydney to see the essential city center, while six days would give you time to explore the beaches and inner suburbs.

Start with an afternoon **Harbour Express Cruise** for some of the best views of the city. Follow with a tour of **The Rocks,** the nation's birthplace, and take a sunset walk up onto the **Sydney Harbour Bridge.** The following day, take a tour of the famous **Sydney Opera House** and a stroll through the **Royal Botanic Gardens** to visit **Mrs. Macquarie's Chair** for a wonderful view of the harbor icons. Spend some time exploring the city center and another spectacular panorama from the top of **Sydney Tower.** Include a walk around Macquarie Street, a living reminder of Sydney's colonial history, and, if you have time, the contrasting experience of futuristic Darling Harbour, with its museums and aquarium, and colorful, aromatic **Chinatown.** Barangaroo, the city's trendy new multimillion-dollar harbor-front development is a must visit. You'll find a range of restaurants, lots of activity and people-watching, and plenty of shopping options.

On your third day make your way to **Bondi,** Australia's most famous beach, and if the weather is kind follow the clifftop walking path to Coogee Beach. The next day catch the ferry to **Manly** to visit its beach and the historic Quarantine Station. From here, take an afternoon bus tour to the northern beaches, or return to the city to shop or visit museums and galleries. Options for the last day include a trip to the **Blue Mountains** west of the city or a wildlife park such as **WILD LIFE Sydney Zoo** at Darling Harbour or **Taronga Zoo,** on the north side of the harbor.

GETTING HERE AND AROUND
AIR TRAVEL

Sydney's main airport is Kingsford–Smith International, 8 km (5 miles) south of the city. Kingsford–Smith's international (T1) and domestic terminals (T2 and T3) are 3 km (2 miles) apart. To get from one to the other, take a taxi for about A$22, use the complimentary Airport Shuttle Bus (called the TBus; it takes 10 minutes), or take the Airport Link train, A$6.40, which takes two minutes. Destination New South Wales has two information counters in the arrival level of the international terminal. One provides free maps and brochures and handles general inquiries. The other books accommodations and tours, and sells travel insurance. Both counters are open daily from approximately 6 am to 11 pm. You can convert your money to Australian currency at the Travelex offices in both the arrival and departure areas.

AIRPORT TRANSFERS

Airport Link rail travels to the city center in 15 minutes. A one-way fare is A$18.70. Taxis are available outside the terminal buildings. Fares are about A$45 to A$55 to city and Kings Cross hotels. There are a couple of shuttle-bus services from the airport that drop passenger at hotels in the city center, Kings Cross, and Darling Harbour for around A$15 to A$17 one-way and A$28 round-trip. ■TIP➔ **Passengers with only a little luggage can save money by taking the state government run bus No. 400, to Bondi Junction.** The fare is a mere A$5 for the hour-long bus ride, and is ideal for those staying at nearby Bondi Beach.

BUS TRAVEL

Bus travel in Sydney is slow due to congested streets and the undulating terrain. Fares are calculated in sections; the minimum section fare (A$3.80) applies to trips in the inner-city area, such as between Circular Quay and Kings Cross, or from Bondi Junction railway station to Bondi Beach. Bus information can be found at ⊕ *www.sydneybuses.info.*

CAR TRAVEL

With the assistance of a good road map you shouldn't have too many problems driving in and out of Sydney, thanks to the decent freeway system. However, driving a car around Sydney is not recommended because of congestion and lack of parking space. If you decide to drive a rental car, it costs between A$75 and A$85 per day. Local operator Bayswater Car Rental has cars from as little as A$25 per day (on a seven-day rental plan) for a one-year-old vehicle. Camper-vans that sleep two people can be hired from operator Jucy Rentals for A$75 a day and A$130 in the January peak season.

CRUISE TRAVEL
There are two cruise ship terminals in Sydney. The Overseas Passenger Terminal (OPT) is on the western side of Circular Quay in the heart of The Rocks; White Bay Cruise Terminal is in Rozelle, 6 km (4 miles) west of the city center. There is a taxi stand near the White Bay terminal, and it's best way to get into the city center for sightseeing, as the nearest public bus stop is around 3 km (2 miles) away—a taxi ride to the city costs around A$20, A$50 to the airport.

TAXI TRAVEL
Taxis charge A$2.19 per km (½ mile), plus a flag fall (hiring charge) of A$3.60. Extra charges apply to baggage weighing more than 55 pounds, telephone bookings, and Harbour Bridge and tunnel tolls. Fares are 20% higher between 10 pm and 6 am, when the numeral "2" will be displayed in the tariff indicator on the meter, plus an additional A$2.50 flag fall surcharge. ■TIP➔ **Uber isn't allowed into Sydney's airport for pickups but can be used for drop-offs.**

TRAM AND TRAIN TRAVEL
The Sydney Light Rail is an efficient link between Central Station, Darling Harbour, the Star City casino/entertainment complex, Sydney fish markets, and two inner western suburbs. The modern trams operate at 10- to 30-minute intervals 24 hours a day. One-way tickets are A$3.80. The main terminal for long-distance, intercity, and Sydney suburban trains is Central Station. There are a number of good-value train passes including the

Discovery Pass, which at A$275 (for one month) allows unlimited travel between Sydney, Canberra, Melbourne, and Brisbane. Sydney's suburban train network, City Rail, links the city with dozens of suburbs as well as Blue Mountains and South Coast towns. Tickets start from A$4 one-way and are sold at all City Rail stations. Off-peak day return tickets are the best option.

DISCOUNTS AND DEALS
To save money on admissions into attractions, the best option is **The Sydney Pass** (⊕ *seesydneypass.iventurecard.com*), which gets you into 40 Sydney sights and attractions, including the Opera House, Sydney Aquarium, and harbor cruises. Several different cards are available, including four-, five-, and seven-day choices. Prices start at A$109 for a pass with entry to three attractions.

NSW Transport operates all of the Sydney trains, buses, and ferries and the best way to travel on these is with an Opal card (it's similar to Oyster in London or Octopus in Hong Kong). Buses in Sydney no longer sell individual tickets so you will need an Opal card to travel. Opal cards can be bought at the airport or from most newsagents throughout the city (from A$10). To top up, there are machines at newsagents, train stations, wharves, and light rail stops. You can also refill your card online at ⊕ *www.opal. com.au*. To use your card, ■TIP➔ **Tap your Opal card on the reader when getting on but be sure to tap off, too, or you will be charged for the full route,.**

RESTAURANTS
Sydney is blessed with excellent dining. Its 4,000-plus restaurants range from ultrahip and expensive celebrity chef venues overlooking the harbor to uber-cool eateries in the fringe suburbs of Darlinghurst and Surry Hills to neighborhood Italian and Asian joints loved by locals.

HOTELS

The Sydney hotel sector is the strongest in Australia with consistent occupancy levels in the mid to high 80% range and average rates growing sharply. In recent years, the city has seen an influx of new hotels, including the much-anticipated $A900-million Sofitel Darling Harbour, as well as a variety of unique boutique properties in heritage buildings in the city suburbs of Surry Hills, Darlinghurst, and Kinds Cross/Potts Point.

Hotel reviews have been shortened. For full information, visit Fodors.com.

What It Costs in Australian Dollars			
$	$$	$$$	$$$$
RESTAURANTS			
under A$36	A$36–A$45	A$46–A$65	over A$65
HOTELS			
under A$201	A$201–A$300	A$301–A$450	over A$450

TOURS

SIGHTSEEING TOURS

Big Bus Sydney

BUS TOURS | FAMILY | This fleet of brightly colored double-decker buses (with open tops) follows two routes: the Sydney route has 25 stops, and the Bondi and Bays has 10 stops. Both trips take 90 minutes. Sydney trips depart Circular Quay at 8:30 am daily (last bus departs at 7:30 pm); the Bondi bus departs Eddy Avenue, Central Station at 9 am daily (last bus at 7:30 pm). ■TIP➔ These days the operators are adding the Bondi and Bays trip at no extra charge—meaning the two trips will cost A$40 if taken in a 24-hour period, which is good value, and A$60 if taken over a 48-hour period. ⊠ *Sydney* ☎ *02/9567–8400* ⊕ *www.bigbustours. com* ✉ *From A$40.*

Mount 'n Beach Safaris

BUS TOURS | This operator runs tours to the Blue Mountains and minicoaches around Sydney and the Hunter Valley,

from A$125. The company's most popular tour, The Blue Mountains Hike The World Heritage, provides the opportunity to see koalas and kangaroos, have morning tea in the bush, and explore the highlights of the Blue Mountains. ⊠ *68 Whiting St., Artarmon* ☎ *02/9972–0899* ⊕ *www. mountnbeachsafaris.com.au* ✉ *From A$125.*

Oz Jet Boating

BOAT TOURS | These bright red boats are the most distinctive of the jet boats operating on Sydney Harbour. The bow is painted with huge white teeth to resemble a shark. The 30-minute rides, at 75 kph (47 mph), zip past the Opera House, Harbour Bridge, and Clark and Shark islands, and perform 270-degree spins. Despite passengers being issued hooded raincoats, they always get wet. At least two trips run every day (at noon and 3) and more on the weekends and in summertime. Rides are A$85, and occasional discounts (for Internet bookings) are offered in the winter and spring. ⊠ *Sydney Harbour, Circular Quay, Eastern Pontoon, Sydney Harbour* ☎ *02/9808–3700* ⊕ *www.ozjetboating. com.au* ✉ *From A$85.*

SPECIAL-INTEREST TOURS

Aboriginal Heritage Tour

SPECIAL-INTEREST | The Aboriginal Heritage Tour (A$41) is a tour of the Royal Botanic Gardens' display of plants that were growing before Europeans arrived on Sydney's shores in 1788. The tour, which operates Wednesday, Friday, and Saturday at 10 am (1½ hours duration), is led by an Aboriginal guide who explains the plants and their uses and bush foods. ⊠ *Royal Botanic Gardens, Mrs. Macquaries Rd., Circular Quay* ⊹ *Tours depart from info booth outside Garden Shop at Palm Grove Centre* ☎ *02/9231–8111* ⊕ *www.rbgsyd.nsw.gov.au/whatson/aboriginal-heritage-tour* ✉ *From A$41.*

Bass and Flinders Cruises

SPECIAL-INTEREST | You can go whale-watching from Sydney Harbour with Bass and Flinders Cruises. Boats leave from Darling Harbour or Circular Quay mid-May to early December, venturing a few miles outside Sydney Heads. Two-, three-, and four-hour cruises are available, and tours start from A$79, although online discounts are often available. ⊠ *Cockle Bay Marina, Darling Harbour* ☎ *02/9583–1199* ⊕ *www.bass-flinders.com.au* ✉ *From A$79.*

Bonza Bikes

SPECIAL-INTEREST | Bonza Bikes lets you see the best Sydney sights without having to worry about heavy traffic. The half-day Classic Sydney Tour cruises past the Opera House, winds around the harbor, and cycles through the Royal Botanic Gardens. A bike and helmet are included on all tours. ⊠ *30 Harrington St., The Rocks* ☎ *02/9247–8800* ⊕ *www.bonzabiketours.com* ✉ *From A$129.*

★ BridgeClimb

SPECIAL-INTEREST | This unique tour affords the ultimate view of the harbor and city center from Sydney Harbour Bridge. The hugely popular tours take 3½ hours and start at A$168, with sunrise, day, sunset, and nighttime tours available. They are all worth doing, but for sheer romance, the night tour is hard to beat. An option for those on a budget or with a fear of heights is the 90-minute BridgeClimb Sampler, which takes climbers within the bridge's inner arch to a point around halfway to the top. Prices are higher during the peak season December 25–January 14 inclusive. ⊠ *5 Cumberland St., The Rocks* ☎ *02/8274–7784* ⊕ *www.bridgeclimb.com* ✉ *From A$168.*

★ Sydney Pub Tours

WALKING TOURS | This tour lets visitors drink in Sydney's history at five historic—and unique—pubs in The Rocks, and dine on some unusual pizzas during a 3½-hour jaunt. Operated by locals with a passion for handcrafted beers, the walking tour sets off from the Mercantile Hotel at 6:30 pm. It is designed for those who want to learn more about The Rocks' fascinating history (rather than party-types). The tour guide regales folks with tales of 19th-century rum smuggling and the quirky characteristics of each watering hole. There's a visit to one of the cellars, which is normally off-limits to the public. Adventurous diners might like to order the kangaroo or even crocodile pizza at the Australian Heritage Hotel. Non–beer drinkers are offered wine or a soft drink at each pub. ⊠ *Mercantile Hotel, 25 George St., The Rocks* ☎ *02/4058–3990* ⊕ *www.daves.com.au* ✉ *A$125.*

Sydney Seaplanes

SPECIAL-INTEREST | A flight on Sydney Seaplanes is a wonderful way to see Sydney's sights and soar over beaches. Short flights taking in the harbor, Bondi Beach and all the way up to the Northern Beaches, including the picture-perfect Palm Beach. The on-site restaurant serves breakfast and lunch with views of the seaplaces taking off from Rose Bay. It's also a fully licensed premises offering cocktails and champagne. ⊠ *1 Vickery Ave., Rose Bay* ☎ *02/9388–1978, 1300/732752* ⊕ *www.seaplanes.com.au* ✉ *From A$285.*

SYDNEY BY BOAT
Aboriginal Culture Cruise

HISTORIC SITE | Former Sydney tugboat the *Mari Nawi* is owned by the Tribal Warrior Association, an organization committed to empowering disadvantaged Aboriginal people. They operate cultural cruises year-round, showing passengers the sights and telling stories associated with tribes including the Eora, Cadigal, and Wangal, who inhabited areas around Sydney Harbour. After departing from Circular Quay, the cruises head to Clark Island for a traditional welcoming ceremony and dance performance. Back on board, passengers are shown cultural landmarks, fishing spots, and ancient rock carvings. The two-hour cruises cost A$60 per person and depart Saturdays April–September at 1 pm and October–March at 3 pm. The cruise departs from Eastern Pontoon, Circular Quay. ⊠ *Eastern Pontoon, Circular Quay, Sydney Harbour* ☎ *02/9699–3491* ⊕ *www.tribalwarrior.org* 🖃 *From $A60.*

★ Captain Cook Cruises
BOAT TOURS | The best introduction to Sydney Harbour is Captain Cook's two-hour Harbour Story Cruise (A$45), which follows the southern shore to Watsons Bay, crosses to the north shore to explore Middle Harbour, and returns to Circular Quay. Other options include breakfast, lunch, and dinner cruises; and the popular 24-hour Hop-on-Hop-Off ferry service (A$45) to nine stops around the harbor. ☎ *02/9206–1111* ⊕ *www.captaincook.com.au* 🖃 *From A$45.*

Fantasea Yellow Water Taxis
BOAT TOURS | A fun, fast, but somewhat expensive way to get around is by water taxi. (Circular Quay to Manly, for example, costs A$215 for four people, and A$10 for each extra person.) One company, Aussie Water Taxis, runs a taxi shuttle between Darling Harbour and the Opera House for A$20 one-way. Minitours of the harbor in these little yellow taxi boats begin at A$34 per person for 45 minutes. ⊠ *Cockle Bay Wharf, Darling Harbour* ☎ *02/9211–7730* ⊕ *yellowwatertaxis.com.au* 🖃 *From $20.*

★ Manly Ferry
BOAT TOURS | There is no finer introduction to the city than a trip aboard one of the commuter ferries that ply Sydney Harbour. The hub of the ferry system is Circular Quay, and ferries dock at the almost 30 wharves around the harbor between about 6 am and 11:30 pm. One of the most popular sightseeing trips is the Manly Ferry, a 30-minute journey from Circular Quay that provides glimpses of harborside mansions and the sandstone cliffs and bushland along the north shore. The one-way Manly Ferry fare is A$7.60, and the Manly Fast Ferry, operated by a private company (⊕ *www.manlyfastferry. com.au*), costs A$9.10 one-way. ⊠ *Wharf 2, Circular Quay* ☎ *13–1500* ⊕ *www. transportnsw.info* 🖃 *From A$8.*

WALKING TOURS
Ghost Tours
WALKING TOURS | The Rocks' dark alleyways can be scary, and The Rocks Ghost Tours make sure people are suitably spooked, as the guides, dressed in long black cloaks and carrying lanterns, regale them with stories of the murders and other nasty goings-on in the early days of the colony. Tours depart nightly at 6:45 (April–September) and 7:45 (October–March) from Cadmans Cottage. ⊠ *Cadmans Cottage, George St. at Argyle St., Circular Quay* ☎ *02/9241–1283* ⊕ *www. ghosttours.com.au* 🖃 *A$45.*

Rocks Walking Tours
WALKING TOURS | Discover Sydney's first European settlement, with an emphasis on the buildings and personalities of the convict period on tours with this operator. The 1½-hour tours leave daily at 10:30 and 1:30. ⊠ *Clocktower Sq., Argyle St. at Harrington St., Shop 4a, The Rocks* ☎ *02/9247–6678* ⊕ *www.rockswalkingtours.com.au* 🖃 *$A32.*

VISITOR INFORMATION
There are information kiosks at locations throughout the city, including Circular Quay (Alfred and Pitt streets), Martin Place (at Elizabeth Street), and Town Hall (at George and Bathurst streets).

The Sydney Visitor Centre is the major source of information for Sydney and New South Wales. There are two locations: The Rocks and Darling Harbour.

CONTACTS Sydney Visitor Centre. ⊠ *Level 2, The Rocks Centre, Argyle St. at Playfair St., The Rocks* ☎ *02/8273–0000, 1800/067676* ⊕ *www.therocks.com.*

Sydney Harbour

On a bright sunny day there's no more magical sight than glistening Sydney Harbour. The white sails of the Opera House are matched by the dozens of sailing boats skimming across the blue expanse. It's both a hive of activity and blissfully peaceful: It's easy to get away from the bustle in one of this area's many remote little corners. Explore by taking a ferry, walking across the bridge, or hiking around its native bushland edges. But whatever you do, get up close and enjoy the view.

GETTING HERE AND AROUND

Sydney is well served by public transport. Buses travel from a base in Circular Quay through the city center to the inner suburbs of Kings Cross, Darlinghurst, and Surry Hills and to the eastern suburb beaches. Trains travel from Central Station through the city on a circle line (calling at Circular Quay and Town Hall), out to Bondi Junction, over the bridge to the north shore and out to the west. Ferries leave Circular Quay for Manly, Balmain, Darling Harbour, and other suburbs, while the free 555 shuttle bus does a circuit through the city, calling at the main sights.

◉ Sights

Admiralty House

HOUSE | The Sydney residence of the governor-general, the Queen's representative in Australia, this impressive residence is occasionally open for inspection and can be viewed (from the water) during harbor cruises. ⊠ Kirribilli Ave., Kirribilli ⊕ Both Kirribilli and Admiralty House are at harbor end of Kirribilli Ave.; to get there take ferry from Circular Quay to either Kirribilli Wharf or Milson's Point Wharf, or take train from Town Hall to Milson's Point Station. The No. 267 bus does a loop from McMahon's Point to North Sydney via Kirribilli. There is no public access to either of these grand houses.

Fort Denison

ARCHAEOLOGICAL SITE | For a brief time in the early days of the colony, convicts who committed petty offenses were kept on this harbor island, where they existed on such a meager diet that the island was named Pinchgut. Fortification of the island was completed in 1857, when fears of Russian expansion in the Pacific spurred the government on. Today the firing of the fort's cannon doesn't signal imminent invasion, but merely the hour—one o'clock. New South Wales National Parks and Wildlife Service runs half-hour tours at Fort Denison. Purchase tickets (from $A37.50) from either the NSW National Parks office (☎ 1300/072757) or at Captain Cook Cruises' booth at Jetty 6, Circular Quay; the ferries depart for the island from 10:30 am to 4 pm daily from Jetty 6. ⊠ Circular Quay, Alfred St., Jetty 6, Sydney Harbour ☎ 1300/072757 ⊕ www.nationalparks.nsw.gov.au or www.fortdenison.com.au ☞ Tours from A$38.

Garden Island

ISLAND | Although it's still known as an "island," this promontory was connected with the mainland in 1942. During the 1941–45 War of the Pacific (WWII and a number of preceding conflicts), Australia's largest naval base and dockyard was a frontline port for Allied ships. Part of the naval base is now open to the public. Access, seven days a week, to the site is via ferry from Circular Quay (take the Watsons Bay ferry). Visitors can view the museum and picnic on the hill. The Naval Historical Society runs tours to the "secure" section of Garden Island but these must be booked well in advance. The 90-minute tours (A$20) run every Thursday and include morning tea and a video. ⊠ Garden Island ⊕ Take ferry from Circular Quay to Watsons Bay and ask to be let off at Garden Island. No buses go directly to Garden Island.

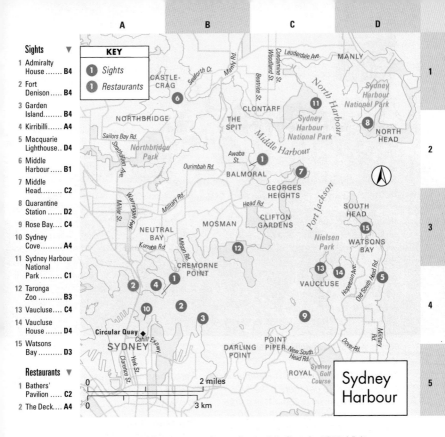

KEY

1 Sights

1 Restaurants

Sydney Harbour

☎ 02/9359–2243 ⊕ www.navyhistory.org.au.

Kirribilli

NEIGHBORHOOD | Residences in this attractive suburb opposite the city and Opera House have million-dollar views—and prices to match. Two of Sydney's most important mansions stand here. The more modest of the two is **Kirribilli House,** the official Sydney home of the prime minister, which, along with Admiralty House, is open to the public once a year, usually around May. ⊠ *Kirribilli.*

Macquarie Lighthouse

LIGHTHOUSE | When the sun shines, the 15-minute cliff-top stroll along South Head Walkway between The Gap and the Macquarie Lighthouse affords some of Sydney's most inspiring views. Convict-architect Francis Greenway (jailed for forgery) designed the original lighthouse here, Australia's first, in 1818. Visitors climb the 100 stairs to the top of the lighthouse on guided tours (20 minutes duration; A\$5) that are run every two months by the Sydney Harbour Federation Trust. Call or check the website for dates and bookings. ⊠ *Old South Head Rd., Vaucluse* ✛ *To reach Watsons Bay either take ferry from Circular Quay or Bus 324 or 325 from Circular Quay. Bus 324 goes past lighthouse* ☎ *02/8969–2100* ⊕ *www.harbourtrust.gov.au.*

Middle Harbour

BODY OF WATER | Except for the yachts moored in the sandy coves, the upper reaches of Middle Harbour are almost exactly as they were when the first Europeans set eyes on Port Jackson more than 200 years ago. Tucked away in idyllic bushland are tranquil suburbs just a short drive from the city. ⊠ *Middle Harbour*

Giraffes at the Sydney's world-class Taronga Zoo

⚓ *The focal point of Middle Harbour is Spit Bridge. To get there, take train from either Central or Town Hall station to Milson's Point then take Bus 229 to Spit Bridge. From Spit Bridge walk to Manly and view most of beautiful Middle Harbour.*

Middle Head

MILITARY SITE | Despite its benign appearance today, Sydney Harbour once bristled with armaments. In the mid-19th century, faced with expansionist European powers hungry for new colonies, the authorities erected artillery positions on the headlands to guard harbor approaches. One of Sydney's newest open spaces, Headland Park, has opened on a former military base. A walking track winds past fortifications, tunnels, and heritage buildings, several of which are now used as cafés, including the Tea Room Gunners' Barracks. ⊠ *1200 Middle Head Rd., Mosman ⚓ Several buses travel from central Sydney to Mosman, Balmoral, and Chowder Bay, which are all suburbs within Middle Head area and close to Headland*

Park. They include Buses 244, 245, 246, and 247 ☏ *02/8969–2100 Harbour Trust* ⊕ *www.harbourtrust.gov.au* ✉ *Free.*

Quarantine Station

ARCHAEOLOGICAL SITE | From the 1830s onward, ship passengers who arrived with contagious diseases were isolated on this outpost in the shadow of North Head until pronounced free of illness. You can access the station as part of a guided tour, and now stay overnight in the four-star hotel and cottage accommodation known as Q Station; there are also two waterfront restaurants. There are day tours and five different evening ghost tours (the station reputedly has its fair share of specters) that depart from the visitor center at the Quarantine Station, and a "ghostly sleep-over" for those who want to spent the night in reputedly haunted rooms. Reservations are essential. ■TIP→ **Visitors can also visit the site without taking a tour, however, if you want to dine, you must make prior restaurant reservations.** ⊠ *North Head, North Head Scenic Dr., Manly ⚓ Take ferry to*

Manly from Circular Quay, then Bus 135 to site. Or catch Q Station's complimentary bus shuttle opposite Manly Wharf ☎ 02/9466–1500, 02/9466–1551 tour bookings ⊕ www.qstation.com.au ⌨ Tours from A$18.

Rose Bay

BEACH—SIGHT | This large bay, the biggest of Sydney Harbour's 66 bays, was once a base for the Qantas flying boats that provided the only passenger air service between Australia and America and Europe. The last flying boat departed from Rose Bay in the 1960s, but the "airstrip" is still used by floatplanes on scenic flights connecting Sydney with the Hawkesbury River and the central coast. It's a popular place for joggers, who pound the pavement of New South Head Road, which runs along the bay. ⊠ New South Head Rd., Rose Bay ⚓ Take Bus 325 from Circular Quay, or take ferry to Watsons Bay (it stops at Rose Bay).

★ Sydney Cove

BODY OF WATER | Sydney Harbour is spotted with many coves, but perhaps the most famous is Sydney Cove, an inlet better known as Circular Quay. With the Sydney Opera House and Bennelong Point, offering stunning restaurants and incredible views to the east, the Rocks to the west, and Harbour Bridge looming over it all, this spot really captures the essence of the city of Sydney. A walkway loops around the cove and is busy no matter what time of day. ⊠ Sydney Cove ⚓ Take train from Central or Town Hall to Circular Quay railway station; or take any number of buses to Circular Quay from all over Sydney. Ferries travel to Circular Quay from many different parts of Sydney, including north side of harbor, Rose Bay, Balmain, and Parramatta. Circular Quay is right in middle of Sydney Cove.

★ Sydney Harbour National Park

ISLAND | This massive park is made up of 958 acres of separate foreshores and islands, most of them on the north side of the harbor. To see the best areas,

put on your walking shoes and head out on the many well-marked trails. The Hermitage Foreshore Walk skirts through bushland around Vaucluse's Nielsen Park. On the north side of the harbor, Bradleys Head and Chowder Head Walk is a 5-km (3-mile) stroll that starts from Taronga Zoo Wharf. The most inspiring trail is the 9½-km (6-mile) Manly Scenic Walkway, which joins the Spit Bridge with Manly by meandering along sandstone headlands, small beaches, and pockets of rain forest, and past Aboriginal sites and the historic Grotto Point Lighthouse. You can take day tours of two harbor islands, Fort Denison and Goat Island, which have interesting colonial history and buildings. Call The New South Wales National Parks and Wildlife Service for tickets. You can also visit Shark Island (off Rose Bay) on a cruise with Captain Cook Cruises (A$20) departing daily from Jetty 6 at Circular Quay. ⊠ Jetty 6, Alfred St., The Rocks ☎ 1300/072757 ⊕ www.nationalparks.nsw.gov.au.

Taronga Zoo

ZOO | FAMILY | Sydney's zoo, in a natural bush area on the harbor's north shore, houses an extensive collection of Australian fauna, including everybody's favorite marsupial, the koala. The zoo has taken great care to create spacious enclosures that simulate natural habitats. The hillside setting is steep in parts, and a complete tour can be tiring, but you can use the map distributed free at the entrance gate to plan a leisurely route. The views of the harbor are stunning. Use of children's strollers (the basic model) is free. The best way to get here from the city is by ferry from Circular Quay or Darling Harbour. From Taronga Wharf a bus or the cable car will take you up the hill to the main entrance. The ZooPass, a combined ferry–zoo ticket (A$57) is available at Circular Quay. You can also stay overnight at the zoo in what's billed as the "wildest slumber party in town." The "Roar and Snore" program includes a night tour, two behind-the-scenes tours, drinks,

The boardwalk around Sydney Cove on a typical sunny day

dinner, breakfast, and luxury tent accommodation at A$288 per adult on weeknights and A$320 per adult on Friday/Saturday. Other special programs include being a "Keeper for a Day." ⊠ *Bradleys Head Rd., Mosman* ☎ *02/9969–2777* ⊕ *www.taronga.org.au* ✉ *A$47.*

Vaucluse

TOWN | The palatial homes in this glamorous harbor suburb provide a glimpse of Sydney's high society. The small beaches at Nielsen Park and Parsley Bay are safe for swimming and provide wonderful views. Both beaches are packed with families in summer. ⊠ *Vaucluse.*

Vaucluse House

HOUSE | The suburb takes its name from the 1803 Vaucluse House, one of Sydney's most illustrious remaining historic mansions. The 15-room Gothic Revival house and its lush gardens, managed by Sydney Living Museums (previously called Historic Houses Trust), are open to the public. The tea rooms, built in the style of an Edwardian conservatory, are popular spots for lunch and afternoon tea on weekends. Events are regularly held at the "House" including vintage Sundays (where visitors can picnic in the grounds and dress up in costumes from various eras, such as Victorian and Edwardian) and Christmas-carol singing. ⊠ *Wentworth Rd., Vaucluse* ⊹ *Take Bus 325 from Circular Quay bus stand* ☎ *02/9388-7922* ⊕ *www.vauclusehousetearooms.com.au* ✉ *A$12.*

★ Watsons Bay

BEACH—SIGHT | Established as a military base and fishing settlement in the colony's early years, Watsons Bay is a charming suburb, with a popular waterfront pub, that has held on to its village ambience despite the exorbitant prices paid for tiny cottages here. Unlike Watsons Bay's tranquil harbor side, the side that faces the ocean is dramatic and tortured, with the raging sea dashing against the sheer, 200-foot sandstone cliffs of The Gap. ⊠ *Military Rd., Watsons Bay.*

Beaches

Balmoral Beach

BEACH—SIGHT | This 800-yard-long beach—among the best of the inner-harbor beaches—is in one of Sydney's most exclusive northern suburbs. There's no surf, but it's a great place to learn to windsurf (sailboard rentals are available). The Esplanade, which runs along the beachfront, has a handful of upscale restaurants, as well as several snack bars and cafés that serve award-winning fish-and-chips. In summer you can catch performances of Bard on the Beach. You could easily combine a trip to Balmoral with a visit to Taronga Zoo. To reach Balmoral, take the ferry from Circular Quay to Taronga Zoo and then board Bus 238. Or take Bus 247 from the city (near Wynyard Station) to Mosman and then walk down Raglan Street hill to the Esplanade, the main street running along Balmoral Beach. **Amenities:** food and drink; showers; toilets. **Best for:** swimming; walking; windsurfing. ⊠ *Raglan St., Balmoral.*

Camp Cove

BEACH—SIGHT | Just inside South Head, this crescent beach is where Sydney's fashionable people come to watch and be seen. The gentle slope and calm water make it a safe playground for children. A shop at the northern end of the beach sells salad rolls and fresh fruit juices. The grassy hill at the southern end of the beach has a plaque to commemorate the spot where Captain Arthur Phillip, the commander of the First Fleet, first set foot inside Port Jackson. Parking is limited, and keep in mind it's a long walk to the beach. Dive company Abyss (☎ *02/9588–9662*) operates an easy dive off the beach here. Take Bus 324 or 325 from Circular Quay to Watsons Bay and walk along Cliff Street. **Amenities:** food and drink; toilets. **Best for:** solitude; sunset; swimming. ⊠ *Cliff St., Watsons Bay.*

Need A Break? 🍴

Tea Room Gunners Barracks. Housed in a beautiful sandstone building that served a number of military purposes for more than 130 years, the Tea Room Gunners Barracks has breathtaking views of the harbor and the surrounding gardens and bushland. Their traditional afternoon tea (A\$50) is a great way to relax after exploring the armaments of Middle Head. ⊠ *202 Suakin Dr., Mosman* ☎ *02/8962–5900* ⊕ *www.gunnersbarracks.com.au.*

Lady Jane

BEACH—SIGHT | Officially called Lady Bay, Lady Jane is the most accessible of the nude beaches around Sydney. It's also a popular part of Sydney's gay scene. Only a couple of hundred yards long and backed by a stone wall, the beach has safe swimming with no surf. From Camp Cove, follow the path north and then descend the short, steep ladder leading down the cliff face to the beach. Take Bus 234 or 325 from Circular Quay to Watsons Bay. From there walk along Cliff Street toward Camp Cove. **Amenities:** toilets. **Best for:** nudists; solitude; swimming. ⊠ *Cliff St., Watsons Bay.*

Nielsen Park

BEACH—SIGHT | By Sydney standards, this beach at the end of the Vaucluse Peninsula is small, but behind the sand is a large, shady park that's ideal for picnics. The headlands at either end of the beach are especially popular for their magnificent views across the harbor. The beach is protected by a semicircular net, so don't be deterred by the beach's correct name, Shark Beach. The casual café is open daily and sells drinks, snacks, and meals; there is also a more upscale restaurant open for lunch daily. Parking is often difficult on weekends. Historic Greycliffe House—built in 1840 and now used as National Park offices—is in the park, while the more elaborate and stately Vaucluse House is a 10-minute walk away. Take Bus 325 from Circular Quay. **Amenities:** food and drink; showers; toilets. **Best for:** swimming; walking. ✉ *Greycliffe Ave., off Vaucluse Rd., Vaucluse.*

🍴 Restaurants

★ Bathers' Pavilion

$$$ | **AUSTRALIAN** | Balmoral Beach is blessed. Not only does it have an inviting sandy beach and great water views, but it also has one of the best eating strips north of the Harbour Bridge. **Known for:** great views; casual dining at the café; wood-fired pizzas. [$] *Average main: A$50* ✉ *4 The Esplanade, Balmoral* ☎ *02/9969-5050* 🌐 *www.batherspavilion.com.au.*

The Deck

$ | **MODERN AUSTRALIAN** | If you've wanted to know just what's inside that giant face on the north side of the harbor under the bridge, well this is your chance. The Deck is located in a swanky refurbished space just as you step through the giant mouth of Luna Park, Sydney's long-established fun park. **Known for:** Opera-House views; lively cocktail bar; great sharing plates. [$] *Average main: A$34* ✉ *Luna Park, 1 Olympic Dr., Milsons Point* ☎ *02/9033-7670* 🌐 *www.thedecksydney.com.au* ⏲ *Closed Mon. and Tues. No dinner Sun.*

🍸 Nightlife

BARS AND DANCE CLUBS

The Oaks

BREWPUBS/BEER GARDENS | For a northern Sydney landmark, The Oaks encapsulates the very best of the modern pub. The immensely popular watering hole, named after the huge oak tree in the center of the large beer garden, is big and boisterous. The pub has a restaurant and several bars with varying levels of sophistication. It's packed on Friday and Saturday nights. ✉ *118 Military Rd., Neutral Bay* ☎ *02/9953-5515* 🌐 *www.oakshotel.com.au.*

🎫 Performing Arts

BALLET, OPERA, AND CLASSICAL MUSIC

★ Sydney Opera House

CONCERTS | This venue showcases all the performing arts in its five theaters, one of which is devoted to opera. The Australian Ballet, the Sydney Dance Company, and the Australian Opera Company also call the Opera House home. The complex includes two stages for theater and the 2,700-seat Concert Hall, where the Sydney Symphony Orchestra and the Australian Chamber Orchestra perform. The box office is open Monday to Saturday 9–8:30 and until 5 on Sunday. ✉ *Bennelong Point, Circular Quay* ☎ *02/9250-7777* 🌐 *www.sydneyoperahouse.com.*

DANCE

★ Bangarra Dance Theatre

DANCE | An acclaimed Aboriginal modern dance company, Bangarra Dance Theatre celebrated its 25th anniversary in 2015. The company stages dramatic productions based on contemporary Aboriginal social themes. The performances are described as a fusion of contemporary dance and storytelling; some will have you transfixed by the sheer energy, lighting, and special effects. ✉ *Pier 4, 15 Hickson Rd., Walsh Bay* ☎ *02/9251-5333* 🌐 *www.bangarra.com.au.*

Sydney Dance Company

DANCE | Sydney Dance Company is an innovative contemporary dance troupe with an international reputation. Spanish choreographer Rafael Bonachela is the artistic director. The company performs in Sydney at the Wharf Theatre, the Sydney Opera House, and the new Sydney Theatre and also runs casual drop-in dance classes for A$22: see the website for class schedules. ✉ *The Wharf, Pier 4, Hickson Rd., Walsh Bay* ☎ *02/9221-4811* 🌐 *www.sydneydancecompany.com.*

THEATER

★ Wharf Theatre

THEATER | Wharf Theatre, on a redeveloped wharf in the shadow of Harbour Bridge, is the headquarters of the Sydney Theatre Company (STC), one of Australia's most original and highly regarded performance groups. Contemporary British and American plays and the latest shows from leading Australian playwrights such as David Williamson and Nick Enright are the main attractions. The company also performs at the Sydney Opera House and at the new Sydney Theatre just a few doors away, located opposite Pier 6/7 at No. 22 Hickson Road. ⊠ *Pier 4, Hickson Rd., Walsh Bay* ☎ *02/9250–1777* ⊕ *sydneytheatre.com.au.*

The Rocks

The Rocks is the birthplace not just of Sydney, but of modern Australia. Here the 11 ships of the First Fleet, the first of England's 800-plus ships carrying convicts to the penal colony, dropped anchor in 1788. This stubby peninsula enclosing the western side of Sydney Cove became known simply as The Rocks.

Most of the architecture here dates from the Victorian era, by which time Sydney had become a thriving port. Warehouses lining the waterfront were backed by a row of tradesmen's shops, banks, and taverns, and above them, ascending Observatory Hill, rose a tangled mass of alleyways lined with the cottages of seamen and wharf laborers.

Today The Rocks is a hot spot of cafés, restaurants, and quaint boutiques, and it's one of the city's most popular destinations. And because it's Sydney's most historic area, the old architecture has been beautifully maintained.

GETTING HERE AND AROUND

You can take the train or any number of buses to Circular Quay and then walk to The Rocks. From Bondi and Paddington, take the 380, 382, or 333 bus to Circular Quay via Elizabeth Street. From Clovelly, take the 339 bus all the way to The Rocks, via Central Station. Once there, the best way to get around is on foot—there are quite a few sandstone steps and narrow alleyways to navigate, and your feet are your best friends.

◉ Sights

Argyle Cut

HISTORIC SITE | Argyle Street, which links Argyle Place and George Street, is dominated by the Argyle Cut and its massive walls. In the days before the Cut (tunnel) was made, the sandstone ridge here was a major barrier to traffic crossing between Circular Quay and Millers Point. In 1843 convict work gangs hacked at the sandstone with hand tools for 2½ years before the project was abandoned due to lack of progress. Work restarted in 1857, when drills, explosives, and paid labor completed the job. On the lower side of the Cut an archway leads to the **Argyle Stairs,** which begin the climb from Argyle Street up to the Sydney Harbour Bridge walkway. There's a spectacular view from the South East Pylon. ⊠ *Argyle Pl., Millers Point.*

Argyle Place

HOUSE | With all the traditional requirements of an English green—a pub at one end, a church at the other, and grass in between—this charming enclave in the suburb of Millers Point is unusual for Sydney. Argyle Place is lined with 19th-century houses and cottages on its northern side and overlooked by Observatory Hill to the south. ⊠ *Argyle Pl., Millers Point.*

Cadman's Cottage

HISTORIC SITE | Sydney's oldest building, completed in 1816, has a history that outweighs its modest dimensions. John Cadman was a convict who was sentenced for life to New South Wales for stealing a horse. He later became superintendent of government boats, a

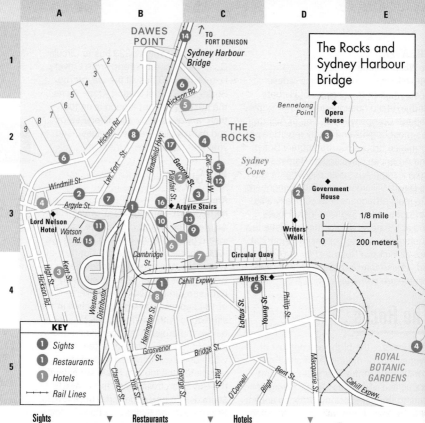

The Rocks and Sydney Harbour Bridge

KEY
- ① Sights
- ① Restaurants
- ① Hotels
- ┼─┼─┼ Rail Lines

Exploring The Rocks on Foot

Begin at Circular Quay, the lively waterfront ferry terminal, and walk west toward Harbour Bridge, passing the Museum of Contemporary Art, and climb the few stairs into George Street. Pass the historic Fortune of War pub, then as you round the corner head down the sandstone stairs on the right to **Campbell's Cove** and its warehouses. The waterfront restaurants and cafés are pleasant spots for a drink or meal. Continue along Hickson Road toward the Sydney Harbour Bridge until you are directly beneath the bridge's massive girders. Walk under the bridge to **Dawes Point Park** for excellent views of the harbor, including the Opera House and the small island of Fort Denison.

Now turn your back on the bridge and walk south and west, via Lower Fort Street. Explore Argyle Place and continue walking south, past the **Sydney Observatory.** While you're in the neighborhood, be sure to pick up brochures and city information at the **Sydney Visitor Centre at The Rocks,** on the corner of Argyle and Playfair streets. Turn right at **Nurses Walk,** another of the area's historic and atmospheric backstreets, then left into Surgeons Court, and left again onto George Street. On the left is the handsome sandstone facade of the former Rocks Police Station, now a crafts gallery. From this point, Circular Quay is only a short walk away.

position that entitled him to live in the upper story of this house. The water once practically lapped at Cadman's doorstep, and the original seawall still stands at the front of the house. The small extension on the side of the cottage was built to lock up the oars of Cadman's boats, since oars would have been a necessity for any convict attempting to escape by sea. The cottage can only be viewed from the outside. ⊠ *110 George St., The Rocks* ☎ *02/9337–5511* ⊕ *www.environment. nsw.gov.au.*

Campbell's Cove
LIGHTHOUSE | Robert Campbell was a Scottish merchant who is sometimes referred to as the "father of Australian commerce." Campbell broke the stranglehold that the British East India Company exercised over seal and whale products, which were New South Wales's only exports in those early days. The cove's atmospheric sandstone **Campbell's Storehouse,** built from 1838 onward, now houses waterside restaurants. The pulleys that were used to hoist cargoes

still hang on the upper level of the warehouses. The cove is also the mooring for Sydney's fully operational tall ships, which conduct theme cruises around the harbor. ⊠ *Campbell's Storehouse, 7–27 Circular Quay West, The Rocks.*

Customs House
BUILDING | The last surviving example of the elegant sandstone buildings that once ringed Circular Quay, this former customs house now features an amazing model of Sydney under a glass floor. You can walk over the city's skyscrapers, all of which are illuminated by fiber-optic lights. The Customs House has an excellent two-level library, art galleries, and ground-floor bar. The rooftop Café Sydney, the standout in the clutch of restaurants and cafés in this late-19th-century structure, overlooks Sydney Cove. The building stands close to the site where the British flag was first raised on the shores of Sydney Cove in 1788. ⊠ *Customs House Sq., 31 Alfred St., Circular Quay* ☎ *02/9242–8551* ⊕ *www. sydneycustomshouse.com.au.*

Dawes Point Park

VIEWPOINT | The wonderful views of the harbor (and since the 1930s, the Harbour Bridge) have made this park and its location noteworthy for centuries. Named for William Dawes, a First Fleet marine officer and astronomer who established the colony's first basic observatory nearby in 1788, this park was also once the site of a fortification known as Dawes Battery. The cannons on the hillside pointing toward the Opera House came from the ships of the First Fleet. ⊠ *Hickson Rd., The Rocks.*

Holy Trinity Garrison Church

RELIGIOUS SITE | FAMILY | Every morning, redcoats would march to this 1840 Argyle Place church from Dawes Point Battery (now Dawes Point Park), and it became commonly known as the Garrison Church, although now officially called the Church Hill Anglican. As the regimental plaques and colors around the walls testify, the church still retains a close military association. Sunday services are held at 9:30 am and 4 pm. ⊠ *Argyle Pl., Argyle St. at Lower Fort St., The Rocks* ☎ *02/9247–1071.*

Lower Fort Street

NEIGHBORHOOD | At one time the handsome Georgian houses along this street, originally a rough track leading from the Dawes Point Battery to Observatory Hill, were among the best addresses in Sydney. Elaborate wrought-iron lacework still graces many of the facades. ⊠ *Lower Fort St., The Rocks.*

Museum of Contemporary Art

MUSEUM | This ponderous art deco building houses one of Australia's most important collections of modern art, as well as two significant collections of Aboriginal art, a sculpture garden, and continually changing temporary exhibits. Free tours, talks, and hands-on art workshops are conducted regularly. ⊠ *140 George St., The Rocks* ☎ *02/9245–2400* ⊕ *www.mca. com.au* 🖼 *Free.*

Nurses Walk

HISTORIC SITE | Cutting across the site of the colony's first hospital, Nurses Walk acquired its name at a time when "Sydney" and "sickness" were synonymous. Many of the 736 convicts who survived the voyage from Portsmouth, England, aboard the First Fleet's 11 ships arrived suffering from dysentery, smallpox, scurvy, and typhoid. A few days after he landed at Sydney Cove, Governor Phillip established a tent hospital to care for the worst cases. ⊠ *Between Harrington and George Sts., The Rocks* ⊕ *www.therocks. com.*

Observatory Hill

CITY PARK | The city's highest point, at 145 feet, was known originally as Windmill Hill, since the colony's first windmill occupied this breezy spot. Its purpose was to grind grain for flour, but soon after it was built the canvas sails were stolen, the machinery was damaged in a storm, and the foundations cracked. The signal station at the top of the hill was built in 1848. This later became an astronomical observatory. This is a great place for a picnic with a view. ⊠ *Upper Fort St., The Rocks.*

Overseas Passenger Terminal

COMMERCIAL CENTER | Busy Circular Quay West is dominated by this multilevel steel-and-glass port terminal, which is often used by visiting cruise ships. There are several excellent waterfront restaurants in the terminal, all with magnificent harbor views. Even if you're not dining in the terminal, it's worth taking the escalator to the upper deck for a good view of the harbor and Opera House. ⊠ *Circular Quay West, The Rocks* ⊕ *www.therocks. com.*

Suez Canal

NEIGHBORHOOD | So narrow that two people can't walk abreast, this alley acquired its name before drains were installed, when rainwater would pour down its funnel-like passageway and gush across George Street. Lanes such as this were once the haunt of the notorious late-19th-century Rocks gangs, when robbery was rife in the area. ✉ *Harrington St. at George St., The Rocks* ⊕ *www. therocks.com.*

★ **Sydney Harbour Bridge**

VIEWPOINT | Despite its nickname "the coat hanger," the bridge has a fond place in all Sydneysiders' hearts. Its opening on March 19, 1932 (during the height of the Great Depression), lifted the spirits of citizens and provided some very unexpected theater. As NSW Premier Jack Lang waited to cut the ribbon, Captain Francis de Groot, a member of the paramilitary New Guard, galloped up on his horse, drew his sword, and slashed the ribbon first.

There are several ways to experience the bridge and its spectacular views. One way is through the South East Pylon. To reach this city-side pylon of the Sydney Harbour Bridge, walk along the bridge's pedestrian pathway. Access is from stairs on Cumberland Street, The Rocks (near BridgeClimb). This structure houses a display on the bridge's construction, and you can climb the 200 steps to the lookout and its unbeatable harbor panorama.

A second (more expensive) way is through the BridgeClimb tour. Not for those afraid of heights, the BridgeClimb tour takes you on a guided walking tour to the very top of Harbour Bridge, 439 feet above sea level. The cost is A$293 per person for a night climb midweek and A$303 for a day climb, with slightly higher prices on weekends.

The third option is to walk to the midpoint of the bridge to take in the views free of charge, but be sure to take the eastern footpath, which overlooks the Sydney Opera House. Access is via the stairs on Cumberland Street (near the BridgeClimb meeting point) and close to the Shangri-La Hotel. ✉ *Cumberland St., The Rocks.*

Sydney Observatory

OBSERVATORY | **FAMILY** | Originally a signaling station for communicating with ships anchored in the harbor, this handsome building on top of Observatory Hill is now an astronomy museum. During evening observatory shows you can tour the building, watch videos, and get a close-up view of the universe through a 16-inch mirror telescope. The digital Sydney Planetarium showcases the virtual night sky to just 20 visitors at a time in a small theater. Reservations are required for the evening shows only. ✉ *Watson Rd., Millers Point* ☎ *02/9921–3485* ⊕ *www.maas. museum/sydney-observatory* ⎙ *Museum free, shows from A$10; Sydney Planetarium A$10.*

Sydney Visitor Centre at the Rocks

INFO CENTER | Known as The Rocks Centre, this ultramodern space is packed with free maps and brochures, and the friendly staff dispenses valuable information and will book tours, hotel rooms, and bus travel. It's near the popular Löwenbräu Keller, where many tourists gather for a beer. ✉ *The Rocks Centre, Argyle St. at Playfair St., The Rocks* ☎ *02/9240–8788, 1800/067676* ⊕ *www. therocks.com.*

Upper George Street

MARKET | The restored warehouses and Victorian terrace houses that line this part of George Street make this a charming section of the Rocks. The covered **Rocks Market** takes place here on weekends and it's a great spot to find aboriginal art, trinkets, and anitiques. ✉ *George St., The Rocks.*

🍴 Restaurants

Altitude

$$$$ | **MODERN AUSTRALIAN** | The lure of this decadent restaurant high above Sydney Harbour on the 36th floor of the luxurious Shangri-La Hotel, is the view through the floor-to-ceiling windows, but the Mod Oz dishes presented with a strong European

influence are equally impressive. The produce hails from local farmers, and highlight dishes include Blue Mountain quail with caramelized butternut pumpkin emulsion. **Known for:** stylish dining; locally sourced produce; high-end prices. Ⓢ *Average main: A$73* ✉ *Shangri-La Hotel, 176 Cumberland St., level 36, The Rocks* ☎ *02/9250–6123* ⊕ *www.36levelsabove. com.au/altitude* ⊘ *Closed Sun. No lunch.*

★ Aria

$$$$ | AUSTRALIAN | With windows overlooking the Opera House and Harbour Bridge, Aria could easily rest on the laurels of its location. Instead, celebrity chef Matthew Moran creates a menu of extraordinary dishes that may be your best meal down under. **Known for:** foodie favorite; seafood like Skull Island prawns and surf clams and eel; incredible views of the harbor. Ⓢ *Average main: A$145* ✉ *1 Macquarie St., Circular Quay* ☎ *02/9240–2255* ⊕ *www.ariarestaurant. com* ⊘ *No lunch weekends* 🎩 *Jacket required.*

★ Bennelong

$$$$ | AUSTRALIAN | One of Australia's most renowned chefs, Peter Gilmore, oversees the kitchen at possibly the most superbly situated dining room in town. Tucked into the side of the Opera House, the restaurant affords views of Sydney Harbour Bridge and the city lights. **Known for:** incredible views; high-end dining experience; Opera House–shaped pavlova. Ⓢ *Average main: A$135* ✉ *Bennelong Point, Sydney Opera House, Circular Quay* ☎ *02/9240–8000* ⊕ *www.bennelong.com.au* ⊘ *No lunch Sat.* 🎩 *Jacket required.*

Botanic Gardens Restaurant

$ | AUSTRALIAN | With wide verandas providing tranquil views over the gardens, the sound of birdsong filling the air, and a menu that changes seasonally and may include starters such as kangaroo tenderloin tartare, Botanic Gardens Restaurant is a lovely place to have lunch during the week or brunch on the weekend. The

Art and Angst

If you like a bit of controversy with your culture, head to the Art Gallery of New South Wales to view the finalists in the annual **Archibald Prize** (⊕ *www. thearchibaldprize.com.au*). Each year since 1921, the competition has attracted plenty of drama as everyone debates the merits of the winners. Prizes are announced in early March, and the exhibition hangs until mid-May.

downstairs café serves lighter fare and is open daily from 8:30 am to 4 (and later in summer). **Known for:** pretty Botanic Gardens setting; weekend brunch spot; great coffee. Ⓢ *Average main: A$25* ✉ *Royal Botanic Gardens, Mrs. Macquarie's Rd., Royal Botanic Gardens* ☎ *1300/558980* ⊘ *No dinner.*

★ Quay

$$$$ | MODERN AUSTRALIAN | Quay has been Sydney's top restaurant for 30 years and it's still going strong with chef Peter Gilmore's experimental Mod Oz cuisine created with seasonal, local produce. Menu highlights include the smoked pig jowl with clams and shiitake mushrooms and the southern crab with greenlip abalone, but it's the White Coral dessert, a dramatic finale with white chocolate ganache filled with feijoa ice cream and coconut cream, that keeps this place booked-out for lunch and dinner most days. **Known for:** experimental cuisine; White Coral dessert; harbor views. Ⓢ *Average main: A$210* ✉ *West Circular Quay, Overseas Passenger Terminal, upper level, The Rocks* ☎ *02/9251–5600* ⊕ *www. quay.com.au* ⊘ *No lunch Mon.–Thurs.*

Walsh Bay Kitchen

$ | ASIAN FUSION | Found inside the Roslyn Packer Theatre, the Walsh Bay Kitchen offers Asian fusion fare like crumbed

Building Sydney

Descended from Scottish clan chieftains, Governor Lachlan Macquarie was an accomplished soldier and a man of vision. Macquarie, who was in office from 1810 to 1821, was the first governor to foresee a role for New South Wales as a free society rather than an open prison. He laid the foundations for that society by establishing a plan for the city, constructing significant public buildings, and advocating that reformed convicts be readmitted to society.

Macquarie's policies of equality may seem perfectly reasonable today, but in the early 19th century they marked him as a radical. When his vision of a free society threatened to blur distinctions between soldiers, settlers, and convicts, Macquarie was forced to resign. He was later buried on his Scottish estate, his gravestone inscribed with the words "the Father of Australia."

Macquarie's grand plans for the construction of Sydney might have come to nothing had it not been for Francis Greenway. Trained as an architect in England, where he was convicted of forgery and sentenced to 14 years in New South Wales, Greenway received a ticket of prison leave from Macquarie in 1814 and set to work transforming Sydney. Over the next few years he designed lighthouses, hospitals, convict barracks, and many other government buildings, several of which remain to bear witness to his simple but elegant eye. Greenway was eventually even depicted on one side of the old A$10 notes, which went out of circulation early in the 1990s. Only in Australia, perhaps, would a convicted forger occupy pride of place on the currency.

Wagyu beef cheek with zucchini jam, lemon, and mustard butter and duck for two, which comes with Asian greens and an apple cinnamon sauce. It gets busy here before a show, due in part to the fact that the food here is so much cheaper than at neighboring restaurants, with $52 for two courses and a glass of wine. **Known for:** pretheater dinner; buzzy atmosphere; affordable for the area. [$] *Average main: A$34* ✉ *Roslyn Packer Theatre Walsh Bay, 22 Hickson Rd., Walsh Bay* ☎ *02/9250–1777* 🌐 *www.walshbaykitchen.com.au.*

Hotels

★ Harbour Rocks Hotel
$$$ | **HOTEL** | Formerly a wool-storage facility, this four-story hotel is an Accor MGallery property, which is a select portfolio of distinctive and individual hotels in Australia. **Pros:** great location near harbor; ultrastylish; unique courtyard in the city. **Cons:** heritage rooms could be larger; Wi-Fi is an additional charge; no pool. [$] *Rooms from: A$340* ✉ *34 Harrington St., The Rocks* ☎ *02/8220–9999* 🌐 *www.harbourrocks.com.au* 🛏 *59 rooms* 🍴 *Free breakfast.*

Holiday Inn Old Sydney
$$ | **HOTEL** | Even though it's been around for a few decades, this hotel with its low-key facade is still a bit of a secret. **Pros:** fantastic location near harbor; good value; top-story pool. **Cons:** still has a dated look; street-facing rooms very noisy; bathrooms need a renovation. [$] *Rooms from: A$240* ✉ *55 George St., The Rocks* ☎ *02/9255–1800* 🌐 *www.holidayinn.com* 🛏 *174 rooms* 🍴 *No meals.*

★ The Langham Sydney

$$$ | **HOTEL** | More English country manor than inner-city hotel, this gorgeous property feels like a decadent, luxurious sanctuary. **Pros:** sumptuous Venetian- and Asian-inspired decor; excellent in-house restaurant; afternoon tea. **Cons:** lack of views; a bit isolated; expensive. [$] *Rooms from: A$450* ✉ *89–113 Kent St., The Rocks* ☎ *02/9256–2222* 🌐 *www.sydney.langhamhotels.com.au* 🛏 *100 rooms* 🍴 *Free breakfast.*

Lord Nelson Brewery Hotel

$$ | **B&B/INN** | If your idea of heaven is sleeping above a pub that brews its own boutique beers (or ales, as they're rightly called), this is the place. **Pros:** great location near harbor; fun pub; cheap rates; free Wi-Fi. **Cons:** may be noisy on weekend nights; some rooms are small; limited breakfast options. [$] *Rooms from: A$210* ✉ *19 Kent St., The Rocks* ☎ *02/9251–4044* 🌐 *www.lord-nelsonbrewery.com* 🛏 *9 rooms* 🍴 *Free breakfast.*

★ Park Hyatt Sydney

$$$$ | **HOTEL** | A multimillion-dollar total rebuild, which included the addition of an entire top floor, has seen the iconic Park Hyatt Sydney reemerge as Sydney's best address. **Pros:** fantastic location; gorgeous views; superior dining options. **Cons:** a distance from the CBD; expensive; very quiet. [$] *Rooms from: A$850* ✉ *7 Hickson Rd., The Rocks* ☎ *02/9241–1234* 🌐 *www.hyatt.com/en-US/hotel/australia/park-hyatt-sydney/sydph* 🛏 *155 rooms* 🍴 *No meals.*

Rendezvous Hotel Sydney The Rocks

$$ | **HOTEL** | Situated in the heart of the historic Rocks precinct, the lodging has a boutique-hotel style. **Pros:** great location; good value; spacious rooms. **Cons:** simply appointed rooms; no restaurant or bar; discreet street entrance can be difficult to find. [$] *Rooms from: A$250* ✉ *75 Harrington St., The Rocks* ☎ *02/9251–6711* 🌐 *www.tfehotels.com/brands/rendezvous-hotels/rendezvous-hotel-sydney-the-rocks* 🛏 *68 rooms* 🍴 *No meals.*

The Russell

$$ | **HOTEL** | For charm, character, and central location, it's hard to beat this ornate Victorian hotel. **Pros:** location; personal service; warm ambience; includes breakfast. **Cons:** not all rooms have en suite bathrooms; near a pub and busy area, so can be noisy; bit dated. [$] *Rooms from: A$250* ✉ *143A George St., The Rocks* ☎ *02/9241–3543* 🌐 *www.therussell.com.au* 🛏 *50 rooms* 🍴 *Free breakfast.*

★ Shangri-La Hotel Sydney

$$$ | **HOTEL** | Towering above Walsh Bay from its prime position alongside the Sydney Harbour Bridge, this sleek hotel is *the* place for a room with a bird's-eye view. **Pros:** breathtaking views; soothing ambience; great in-house restaurant. **Cons:** impersonal and busy feel at times; expensive; low-level rooms have limited views. [$] *Rooms from: A$350* ✉ *176 Cumberland St., The Rocks* ☎ *02/9250–6000* 🌐 *www.shangri-la.com* 🛏 *565 rooms* 🍴 *No meals.*

🍸 Nightlife

BARS AND DANCE CLUBS

Blu Bar on 36

WINE BARS—NIGHTLIFE | Blu Bar on 36 has a stellar view! Situated on the 36th floor of the Shangri-La Hotel, this is a sophisticated place to relax after work or enjoy a late-night drink while taking in the sweeping views of Sydney Harbour and the Opera House. Get here early (just after 5 pm) for a ringside seat. ✉ *Shangri-La Hotel, 176 Cumberland St., The Rocks* ☎ *02/9250–6000* 🌐 *www.shangri-la.com.*

Hacienda

BARS/PUBS | Set above Circular Quay in the Quay Grand Sydney Harbour, this cocktail bar offers incredible views with outstanding tipples. Rum cocktails are the specialty drink of choice. On the weekends, this place comes alive in the afternoon for sundowners. During the week, it's a bit more of a relaxed crowd, enjoying a predinner drink in a more chilled atmosphere than the nearby Opera Bar, which is always packed, day and night. Arrive early and also enjoy some Latin American small bites, including the buttermilk-fried-chicken tortilla. ⊠ *61 Macquarie St., Circular Quay* ☎ *2/9256–4000* ⊕ *haciendasydney.com. au.*

★ **Opera Bar**

BARS/PUBS | Perched beneath the concourse of the Opera House and at eye level with Sydney Harbour, Opera Bar has the best location in all of Sydney. Cozy up for a drink in the enclosed bar area or grab a waterside umbrella table and take in the glimmering skyline. Live music plays under the stars nightly from either 5:30 or 8 pm on weeknights, and from 2 pm on weekends. The bar has a full menu, though the attraction here is the scenery, not the cuisine. ⊠ *Sydney Opera House, Circular Quay* ☎ *02/9247–1666* ⊕ *operabar.com.au.*

PUBS WITH MUSIC
Mercantile Hotel

MUSIC CLUBS | In the shadow of Harbour Bridge, Mercantile Hotel is Irish and very proud of it. Fiddles, drums, and pipes rise above the clamor in the bar, and lilting accents rejoice in song seven nights a week from 8:30 pm until late and on weekends from 3 pm. ⊠ *25 George St., The Rocks* ☎ *02/9247–3570* ⊕ *www. themercantilehotel.com.au.*

🛍 Shopping

MARKETS
★ **The Rocks Market**

OUTDOOR/FLEA/GREEN MARKETS | This sprawling covered bazaar transforms the upper end of George Street into a multicultural collage of music, food, arts, crafts, and entertainment. It's open weekends 10–5. Be sure to check out the new Rocks Foodies Market with delicious fare, on Friday 9–3. ⊠ *Upper George St., near Argyle St., The Rocks* ⊕ *www.therocks.com/things-to-do/ the-rocks-markets.*

Domain and Macquarie Street

Some of Sydney's most notable Victorian-era public buildings, as well as one of its finest parks, can be found in this area. In contrast to the simple, utilitarian stone convict cottages of The Rocks, these buildings were constructed at a time when Sydney was experiencing a long period of prosperity thanks to the gold rushes of the mid-19th century and an agricultural boom. The sandstone just below the surface of many coastal areas proved an ideal building material—easily honed into the ornamentation so fashionable during the Victorian era. Macquarie Street is Sydney's most elegant boulevard. It was shaped by Governor Macquarie, who planned the transformation of the cart track leading to Sydney Cove into a stylish street of dwellings and government buildings. An occasional modern high-rise breaks up the streetscape, but many of the 19th-century architectural delights here escaped demolition.

GETTING HERE AND AROUND
The area is served by two train stations—Martin Place and St. James—but they are not on the same line. You can catch trains to both stations from Central and Town Hall. St. James is right next to Hyde Park, and Martin Place has an exit on Macquarie Street. From Macquarie Street it's a short walk to the Domain via the passageway that cuts through Sydney Hospital. A number of buses (including the 380/382 and 333 from Bondi Beach and 555 free shuttle) travel along Elizabeth Street.

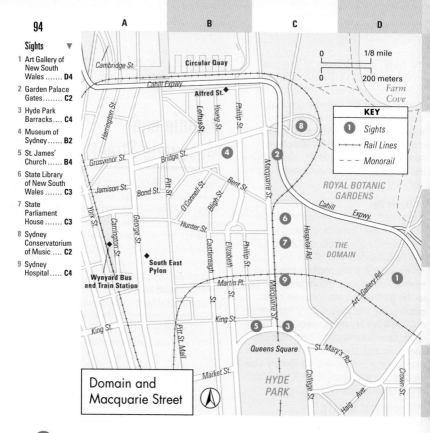

Domain and Macquarie Street

◉ Sights

★ Art Gallery of New South Wales

MUSEUM VILLAGE | Apart from Canberra's National Gallery, this is the best place to explore the evolution of European-influenced Australian art, as well as the distinctly different concepts that underlie Aboriginal art. All the major Australian artists of the last two centuries are represented in this impressive collection. The entrance level, where large windows frame spectacular views of the harbor, exhibits 20th-century art. Below, in the gallery's major extensions, the Yiribana Gallery displays one of the nation's most comprehensive collections of Aboriginal and Torres Strait Islander art. There are monthly free audio tours and free talks. ✉ Art Gallery Rd., The Domain ☎ 02/9225–1700, 1800/679278 ⊕ www. artgallery.nsw.gov.au ⛁ Free; fee for special exhibits.

Hyde Park Barracks

JAIL | Before Governor Macquarie arrived, convicts were left to roam freely at night. Macquarie was determined to establish law and order, and in 1819 he commissioned convict-architect Francis Greenway to design this restrained, classically Georgian-style building. Today the Barracks houses compelling exhibits that explore behind the scenes of the prison. For example, a surprising number of relics from this period were preserved by rats, which carried away scraps of clothing and other artifacts for their nests beneath the floorboards. A room on the top floor is strung with hammocks, exactly as it was when the building housed convicts. The barracks are part of the Sydney Living Museums collection of

12 historic buildings. ✉ *Queens Sq., Macquarie St., The Domain* ☎ *02/8239–2311* ⊕ *www.sydneylivingmuseums.com.au* ☜ *A$12.*

Garden Palace Gates

MEMORIAL | These gates are all that remain of the Garden Palace, a massive glass pavilion that was erected for the Sydney International Exhibition of 1879 and destroyed by fire three years later. On the arch above the gates is a depiction of the Garden Palace's dome. Stone pillars on either side of the gates are engraved with Australian wildflowers. ✉ *Macquarie St., between Bridge and Bent Sts., The Domain.*

Museum of Sydney

MUSEUM | This museum built on the site of the original Government House documents Sydney's early period of European colonization. Aboriginal culture, convict society, and the gradual transformation of the settlement at Sydney Cove are woven into an evocative portrayal of life in the country's early days. A glass floor in the lobby reveals the foundations of the original structure. One of the most intriguing exhibits, however, is outside (and free): the striking Edge of the Trees sculpture, where Koori (Aboriginal) voices recite Sydney place names as you walk around and through the collection of 29 wood, iron, and sandstone pillars. ✉ *Bridge St. at Phillip St., The Domain* ☎ *02/9251–5988* ⊕ *www.sydneylivingmuseums.com.au* ☜ *A$15.*

St. James' Church

ARTS VENUE | Begun in 1819, the colonial Georgian–style St. James' is the oldest surviving church in the City of Sydney, and another fine Francis Greenway design. Now lost among the skyscrapers, the church's tall spire once served as a landmark for ships entering the harbor. Plaques commemorating Australian explorers and administrators cover the interior walls. Half-hour lunchtime concerts are presented every Wednesday from late February to late December at

Need A Break? 🍴

Rooftop Cafe Australian Museum. Found on the top floor of the Australian Museum, this hidden gem offers incredible sweeping views of Sydney's cityscape and harbor, as well as a lengthy wine list and a wide menu ranging from simple sandwiches and salads to a hearty lamb ragout. ✉ *1 William St., Darlinghurst NSW 2010, The Domain* ☎ *02/9320–6000* ⊕ *www.australianmuseum.net.au/food-and-dining.*

1:15. ✉ *Queens Sq., 173 King St., Hyde Park* ☎ *02/8227–1300* ⊕ *www.sjks.org.au.*

State Library of New South Wales

LIBRARY | This large complex is based around the Mitchell and Dixson libraries, which make up the world's largest collection of Australiana. Enter the foyer through the classical portico to see one of the earliest maps of Australia, a copy in marble mosaic of a map made by Abel Tasman, the Dutch navigator, in the mid-17th century. Through the glass doors lies the vast Mitchell Library reading room, but you need a reader's ticket (establishing that you are pursuing legitimate research) to enter. You can, however, take a free escorted history and heritage tour weekdays at 10:30 am. The library continuously runs free exhibitions, and the opulent Shakespeare Room is open to the public Tuesday 10–4. ✉ *Macquarie St., between Royal Botanic Gardens and Parliament House, The Domain* ☎ *02/9273–1414* ⊕ *www.sl.nsw.gov.au.*

State Parliament House

GOVERNMENT BUILDING | The simple facade and shady verandas of this Greenway-designed 1816 building, formerly the Rum Hospital, typify Australian colonial architecture. From 1829, two rooms of the old hospital were used for meetings of the

Sydney has enough museums and art galleries to appeal to just about every taste.

executive and legislative councils, which had been set up to advise the governor. These advisory bodies grew in power until New South Wales became self-governing in the 1840s, at which time Parliament occupied the entire building.

State Parliament generally sits between mid-February and late May, and again between mid-September and late November. You can visit the public gallery and watch democracy in action. When parliament is not sitting, you can take a free escorted tour (they are conducted on the first Thursday of the month at 1 pm) or walk around at your leisure. You must reserve ahead for tours and to sit in the public gallery. ⊠ *6 Macquarie St., The Domain* ☎ *02/9230–2111* ⊕ *www. parliament.nsw.gov.au.*

Sydney Conservatorium of Music
ARTS VENUE | Providing artistic development for talented young musicians, this institution hosts lunchtime concerts (entry by small donation) and free student performances throughout the year and other musical events. Guided tours

take place every Wednesday at 11 am and 2 pm and Saturday at 10 am and 1 pm, with tickets to be purchased online or by phone in advance (A$25). The conservatory's turreted building was originally the stables for nearby Government House. The construction cost caused a storm among Governor Macquarie's superiors in London, and eventually helped bring about the downfall of both Macquarie and the building's architect, Francis Greenway. ⊠ *Bridge St. at Macquarie St., The Domain* ☎ *02/9351–1222* ⊕ *music.sydney.edu.au* ⊠ *A$25.*

Sydney Hospital
HOSPITAL—SIGHT | Completed in 1894 to replace the main Rum Hospital building, which had stood on the site since 1811, this institution provided an infinitely better medical option. By all accounts, admission to the Rum Hospital was only slightly preferable to death itself. Convict nurses stole patients' food, and abler patients stole from the weaker. The kitchen sometimes doubled as a mortuary,

and the table was occasionally used for operations.

In front of the hospital is a bronze figure of a boar. This is *Il Porcellino*, a copy of a statue that stands in Florence, Italy. According to the inscription, if you make a donation in the coin box and rub the boar's nose, "you will be endowed with good luck." Sydney citizens seem to be a superstitious bunch, because the boar's nose is very shiny indeed. ⊠ *8 Macquarie St., The Domain* ☎ *02/9382–7111.*

The Opera House and the Royal Botanic Gardens

Bordering Sydney Cove, Farm Cove, and Woolloomooloo Bay, this section of Sydney includes the iconic Sydney Opera House, as well as extensive and delightful harborside gardens and parks.

The colony's first farm was established here in 1788, and the botanical gardens were laid out in 1816. The most dramatic change to the area occurred in 1959, however, when ground was broken on the site for the Sydney Opera House at Bennelong Point. This promontory was originally a small island, then the site of 1819 Fort Macquarie, later a tram depot, and finally the Opera House, one of the world's most striking modern buildings. The area's evolution is an eloquent metaphor for Sydney's own transformation.

GETTING HERE AND AROUND
The best way to get to the Opera House is to take one of the many ferries, buses, or trains that go to Circular Quay and then walk the pedestrian concourse. Some buses travel down Macquarie Street to the Opera House, which involves a slightly shorter walk. To get to the Royal Botanic Gardens, take the CityRail suburban train from the Town Hall, Central, or Bondi Junction station to Martin Place station, exit on the Macquarie Street side, and walk a few hundred yards.

◉ Sights

Andrew (Boy) Charlton Pool
SPORTS VENUE | FAMILY | This heated saltwater eight-lane swimming pool overlooking the navy ships tied up at Garden Island has become a local favorite. There's also a covered splash pool for younger children. Complementing its stunning location is a radical design in glass and steel. The pools also have a chic terrace café above Woolloomooloo Bay, serving breakfast and lunch. There's a kiosk for smoothies and fresh coconuts. It's open from September 1 until April 30. ⊠ *1c Mrs. Macquaries Rd., The Domain* ☎ *02/9358–6686* ⊕ *www. abcpool.org* ⊠ *A$7.*

Farm Cove
BODY OF WATER | The shallow bay east of the Opera House is called Farm Cove. The original convict-settlers established their first gardens on this bay's shores. The enterprise was not a success: the soil was too sandy for agriculture, and most of the crops fell victim to pests, marauding animals, and hungry convicts. The long seawall was constructed from the 1840s onward to enclose the previously swampy foreshore. The area is now home to the Royal Botanic Gardens, a wonderful place to escape the city bustle. ⊠ *Sydney* ✢ *Enter Botanic Gardens through gates near Opera House and in Macquarie St. From Opera House, turn right and walk along harbor foreshore (seawall is on your left, Botanic Gardens on your right). To enter Macquarie St. gates, take train to Martin Pl. railway station, exit station, turn left, and walk few hundred yards down Macquarie St.*

Mrs. Macquarie's Chair
MEMORIAL | During the early 1800s, Elizabeth Macquarie often sat on the point in the Domain at the east side of Farm Cove, at the rock where a seat has been

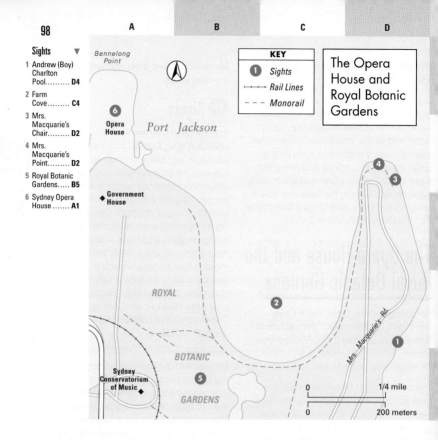

hewn in her name. The views across the harbor are sensational. ⊠ *Mrs. Macquaries Rd., Royal Botanic Gardens.*

Mrs. Macquarie's Point

VIEWPOINT | The inspiring views from this point, to the east of Bennelong Point (site of the Opera House), combine with the shady lawns to make this a popular place for picnics. The views are best at dusk, when the setting sun silhouettes the Opera House and the Harbour Bridge. ⊠ *Mrs. Macquaries Rd., Royal Botanic Gardens.*

★ Royal Botanic Gardens

GARDEN | More than 80 acres of sweeping green lawns, groves of indigenous and exotic trees, duck ponds, greenhouses, and some 45,124 types of plants—many of them in bloom—grace these gardens. The elegant property, which attracts strollers and botany enthusiasts from all

over the country, is a far cry today from what it once was: a failed attempt by convicts of the First Fleet to establish a farm. Though their early attempts at agriculture were disastrous, the efforts of these first settlers are acknowledged in the Pioneer Garden, a sunken garden built in their memory. Among the many other feature gardens on the property are the Palm Grove—home to some of the oldest trees in Sydney, the Begonia Garden, and the Rare and Threatened Plants Garden. Not to be missed is a cutting from the famous Wollemi Pine, a plant thought to be extinct until it was discovered in a secluded gully in the Wollemi National Park in the Blue Mountains in 1994. Plants throughout the gardens have various blooming cycles, so no matter what time of year you visit, there are sure to be plenty of flowers. The gardens include striking sculptures and hundreds of species of birds. There are spectacular views over the harbor and the Opera House from the garden's sea wall and two lovely restaurants are open for lunch and snacks. ■TIP➜ For those who don't want to walk, the ChooChoo Express toylike train offers a 25-minute ride through the gardens, making four stops (A$10). ✉ Mrs. Macquaries Rd., The Domain ☎ 02/9231–8111 ⊕ www.rbgsyd.nsw.gov.au or www.choochoo.com.au 🎟 Free.

★ **Sydney Opera House**

ARTS VENUE | One of the most iconic and recognizable buildings in the world, and listed as a World Heritage site in 2007, the Sydney Opera House is a multivenue performing arts center and a unique architectural sight that wows more than 8 million visitors annually. While it sits pretty and worry-free today, this famous landmark had a long and troubled backstory. What should have taken Danish architect Joern Utzon four years and A$7 million to complete when commissioned in 1959, in fact took 15 years, A$102 million, and an additional team of Australian architects. Although you can access the building throughout the day and early evening, all you really get to see is the main foyer area, which is less than inspiring. To see the best of "the house" join one of the guided tours, which include the one-hour Sydney Opera House Tour, departing daily from the lower forecourt level between 9 and 5; the two-hour backstage tour, departing daily at 7 am. Or book in to see many of the shows running in its five theaters. ✉ 2 Macquarie St., Circular Quay ☎ 02/9250–7111, 02/9250–7250 tour bookings ⊕ www.sydneyoperahouse.com 🎟 Tours from A$40.

Darling Harbour and Barangaroo

Until the mid-1980s this horseshoe-shape bay on the city center's western edge was a wasteland of disused docks and railway yards. Then, in an explosive burst of activity the whole area was redeveloped and opened in time for Australia's bicentenary in 1988. Now there's plenty to take in at the Darling Harbour complex: the National Maritime Museum, SEA LIFE Sydney Aquarium, WILD LIFE Sydney Zoo, and the gleaming Exhibition Centre, whose masts and spars recall the square-riggers that once berthed here. At the harbor's center is a large park shaded by palm trees. To the right, is Barangaroo Reserve, Sydney's latest harbor playground, with world class eateries and stunning walks. Waterways and fountains lace the complex together.

GETTING HERE AND AROUND

Take the train to either Town Hall or Central Station. From Town Hall it's a short walk down Druitt Street; from Central you walk through Haymarket and Chinatown. The Light Rail tram (A$3.80 one-way) connects Central Station with Darling Harbour and The Star casino a little farther to the west.

◉ Sights

Australian National Maritime Museum

MUSEUM | **FAMILY** | The six galleries of this soaring, futuristic building tell the story of Australia and the sea. In addition to figureheads, model ships, and brassy nautical hardware, there are antique racing yachts and the jet-powered Spirit of Australia, current holder of the world water speed record, set in 1978. The USA Gallery displays objects from such major U.S. collections as the Smithsonian Institution, and was dedicated by President George Bush Sr. on New Year's Day 1992. An outdoor section

The Sydney Opera House at night, viewed from The Rocks side of Circular Quay

showcases numerous vessels moored at the museum's wharves, including the HMAS *Vampire,* a retired Royal Australian Navy destroyer, and the historic tall ship the *James Craig.* You can also climb to the top of the 1874 Bowling Green lighthouse. ⊠ *Maritime Heritage Centre, 2 Murray St., Wharf 7, Darling Harbour* ☏ *02/9298–3777* ⊕ *www.anmm.gov.au* ☞ *Free.*

★ Barangaroo Reserve

CITY PARK | Barangaroo is Sydney's newest shopping and eating precinct, an ongoing redevelopment of the an old wharf area once known as "The Hungry Mile," between Walsh Bay and The Rocks and a fast favorite with locals because of its central location, easy access, and multiofferings. The harbor front is punctuated with all levels of dining, from high-end to trendy burger bars, and in the newly cobbled streets that run behind them, toward the CBD, there's a maze of fashion boutiques. There's also a boardwalk that currently links Barangaroo to its neighbours, with Darling Harbour to its south and Walsh Bay and the Harbour Bridge to its north. The park's name, Barangaroo Precinct, honors the powerful companion of Benelong, the Indigenous man known to the first European settlers, whose name was given to the point on the other side of the city where the Opera House stands. Barangaroo was an outspoken woman who advocated against the colonization of Sydney. Learn more about the origins of the Barangaroo Precinct and the 6-hectacre headland that surrounds it on a daily Aboriginal culture tour ($36.50), leaving at 10.30 am. Barangaroo will be completed in 2021 and will include a new hotel and casino. ⊠ *Millers Point* ⊕ *www.barangaroo.com.*

Chinatown

NEIGHBORHOOD | Bounded by George Street, Goulburn Street, and Paddy's Market, Chinatown takes your senses on a galloping tour of the Orient. Within this compact grid are aromatic restaurants, traditional apothecaries, Chinese grocers, clothing boutiques, and shops selling Asian-made electronics. The best way to get a sense of the area is to take a stroll along Dixon Street, now a pedestrian mall with a Chinese Lion Gate at either end. Sydney's Chinese community was first established here in the 1800s, in the aftermath of the gold rush that originally drew many Chinese immigrants to Australia. For the next few years the area will be getting a major face-lift that will include new lighting, artwork, and more pedestrian walkways. Most Sydneysiders come here regularly to dine, especially on weekends for dim sum (called *yum cha*). ⊠ *Dixon St., Haymarket.*

Chinese Garden of Friendship

GARDEN | Chinese prospectors came to the Australian goldfields as far back as the 1850s, and the nation's long and enduring links with China are symbolized by the Chinese Garden of Friendship, the largest garden of its kind outside China. Designed by Chinese landscape architects, the garden includes bridges, lakes, waterfalls, sculptures, and Cantonese-style pavilions—the perfect place for a refreshing cup of tea from the café. Free 35-minute guided tours run daily. ⊠ *38 Harbour St., Darling Harbour* ☎ *02/9240–8888* ⊕ *www.darlingharbour. com* ☜ *A$6* ☞ *Tours run daily 10:30 and 2:30 Oct.–Apr., noon May–Sept.*

Cockle Bay Wharf

MARINA | Fueling Sydney's addiction to fine food, most of this sprawling waterfront complex, on the city side of Darling Harbour, is dedicated to gastronomy, as well as a few bars and nightclubs. If you have a boat you can dock at the marina—and avoid the hassle of parking a car in one of the city's most congested centers. ⊠ *201 Sussex St., Darling Harbour* ☎ *02/9269–9800* ⊕ *www.cocklebaywharf.com.au.*

Madame Tussauds Sydney

MUSEUM | Hugh Jackman as Wolverine, songstress Kylie Minogue, and Olympic champion Cathy Freeman are among the contingent of Australian wax figures at the Madame Tussauds Sydney, the only version of the well-known museum in Australia. Located between SEA LIFE Sydney Aquarium and WILD LIFE Sydney Zoo at Darling Harbour, the museum has nine interactive themed areas where patrons can, for example, jump on a surfboard with world champion female surfer Layne Beachley or sing in the band with legendary Aussie rocker Jimmy Barnes. The 70 figures are grouped in themes such as world leaders, cultural icons, and music and film stars. ■ **TIP**→ **Save more than A$12 on the "walk up" price by buying single-entry tickets or combination tickets (which include any of four other attractions) online.** ⊠ *Aquarium Wharf, near Wheat St., Darling Harbour* ☎ *02/8251–7800* ⊕ *www.madametussauds.com.au/sydney/en* ☜ *A$40.*

The Playground

PARK—SPORTS-OUTDOORS | **FAMILY** | Found just a short walk from Darling Harbour is Darling Quarter, a bustling cultural precinct set around a large open space, punctuated by manicured gardens and surrounded by restaurants that specialize in alfresco dining. At the heart of this area is The Playground, an ever-popular spot for families and those needing a five-minute break from touring on foot. The park offers an intricate water play area for children, with jets of water illuminated by colorful rays of light. This spot really comes to life on a sunny Sydney day, when you will find live music and cultural events on the green, including yoga for all ages every Friday. ⊠ *1–25 Harbour St., Darling Harbour* ⊕ *www. darlingquarter.com.*

Powerhouse Museum

MUSEUM | **FAMILY** | Learning the principles of science is a painless process with this museum's stimulating, interactive displays ideal for all ages. Exhibits in the former 1890s electricity station that once powered Sydney's trams include a whole floor of working steam engines, space modules, airplanes suspended from the ceiling, state-of-the-art computer

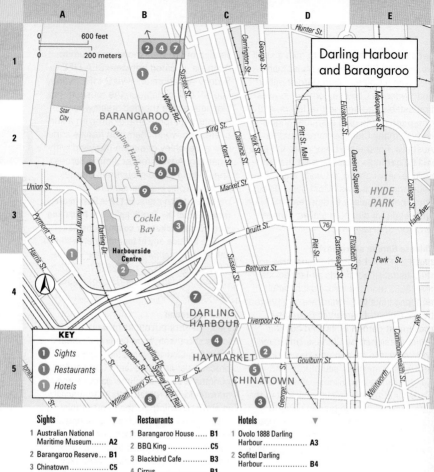

Darling Harbour and Barangaroo

KEY

- **1** Sights
- **1** Restaurants
- **1** Hotels

Sights ▼

1 Australian National
   Maritime Museum...... **A2**
2 Barangaroo Reserve... **B1**
3 Chinatown................. **C5**
4 Chinese Garden
   of Friendship **C5**
5 Cockle Bay Wharf **B3**
6 Madame Tussauds
   Sydney................... **B2**
7 The Playground **C4**
8 Powerhouse
   Museum **B5**
9 Pyrmont
   Bridge.................... **B3**
10 SEA LIFE Sydney
   Aquarium **B2**
11 WILD LIFE
   Sydney Zoo............. **B2**

Restaurants ▼

1 Barangaroo House **B1**
2 BBQ King **C5**
3 Blackbird Cafe **B3**
4 Cirrus..................... **B1**
5 Golden Century **C5**
6 The Malaya.............. **B2**
7 12-Micron................ **B1**

Hotels ▼

1 Ovolo 1888 Darling
   Harbour.................. **A3**
2 Sofitel Darling
   Harbour.................. **B4**

Off The Beaten Path 👁

Sydney Fish Market. Second in size only to Tokyo's giant Tsukiji fish market, Sydney's is a showcase for the riches of Australia's seas. An easy 10-minute walk from Darling Harbour (and with its own stop on the Metro Light Rail network), the market is a great place to sample sushi, oysters, octopus, spicy Thai and Chinese fish dishes, and fish-and-chips at the waterfront cafés overlooking the fishing fleet. Behind the scenes guided tours, including the auction, begin at 6:40 am and run until 8:30 am on Monday, Wednesday, Thursday, and Friday ($A45). They also offer cooking classes. Call ahead for advance reservations or book on the website. ⊠ Pyrmont Bridge Rd., at Bank St., Pyrmont West ☎ 02/9004–1100 ⊕ www.sydneyfishmarket.com.au.

gadgetry, and a 1930s art deco–style movie-theater auditorium. The museum also stages many excellent exhibitions that are not science-based on everything from fashion and crochet and jewelry to computer games. ⊠ 500 Harris St., Ultimo, Darling Harbour ☎ 02/9217–0111 ⊕ www.powerhousemuseum.com ☑ A$15.

Pyrmont Bridge

BRIDGE/TUNNEL | Dating from 1902, this is the world's oldest electrically operated swing-span bridge. The structure once carried motor traffic, but it's now a walkway that links Darling Harbour's western side with Cockle Bay on the east. The center span still swings open to allow tall-masted ships into Cockle Bay, which sits at the bottom of the horseshoe-shape shore. ⊠ Darling Harbour.

SEA LIFE Sydney Aquarium

ZOO | FAMILY | Bay of Rays and Shark Valley are among 14 themed areas at SEA LIFE Sydney Aquarium at Darling Harbour. Home to some 13,000 creatures, the huge aquarium also has two of only five dugongs (large, rare marine mammal similar to a manatee) mainly found off the coast of northern Australia) that are on display anywhere in the world. The Sydney Harbour exhibit shows you what's underneath Sydney's huge expanse of water, while the new open coral tank is dazzlingly colorful. Fish and mammal feedings take place throughout the day, along with talks on some of these amazing creatures. A behind-the-scenes tour is a good value at A$18 over the online admission price. The aquarium is part of the Merlin Entertainments group and good combination ticket deals are available for the company's other attractions that include WILD LIFE Sydney Zoo, the new Madame Tussauds (both located next door to the Aquarium), and the Sydney Tower Eye (A$63). ■ TIP➔ **Buy tickets online to save around A$12 on single-entry and various combo deals.** ⊠ Aquarium Pier, 1–5 Wheat Rd., Darling Harbour ☎ 1800/199657 ⊕ www.sydneyaquarium. com.au ☑ A$40.

WILD LIFE Sydney Zoo

ZOO | FAMILY | This recently renamed Sydney attraction brings thousands of Australian animals right to the heart of Sydney. Kangaroos, koalas, and dozens of other species come together under the one huge roof—in nine separate habitats—next door to the SEA LIFE Sydney Aquarium and the new Madame Tussauds. All three attractions are run by the same operator, Merlin Entertainments, and all are able to be visited on one combination ticket. In Devil's Den you'll see the famed Tasmanian devils; in Wallaby Cliffs there are yellow-footed wallabies and hairy-nosed wombats, while you can walk among the eastern grey kangaroos and agile wallabies with their joeys and the spiky echidnas in Kangaroo Walkabout. Watch out for Rex, the 16-foot saltwater crocodile in the Kakadu Gorge habitat. A popular spot is Gum Tree Alley where you'll meet koalas, while the endangered (and very cute) Greater Bilby is in the Nightfall nocturnal zone. ■ TIP→ **The best deals for stand-alone tickets or combination tickets with other Merlin Entertainment attractions are online. There are savings of around A$12 for a single ticket, while the current combo ticket is A$69.** ⊠ *Aquarium Pier, Wheat Rd., Darling Harbour* ☎ *1800/206158* ⊕ *www.wildlifesydney.com.au* ⌑ *A$44.*

🍴 Restaurants

★ Barangaroo House

$$ | **AUSTRALIAN** | Sitting at the edge of newly completed Barangaroo like an elegant stack of wide, plant-filled bowls clad in charred timber, this three-level spaceship has a seating capacity of 900 people and a variety of spaces for casual and fine dining. The House Bar at the pedestrian promenade level offers craft beers and share plates, like barramundi bites; In the middle is Bea, a sprawling fine-dining restaurant with elevated Australian fare and both indoor and outdoor dining; the buzzy rooftop bar, Smoke, has good views across the harbor. **Known for:** excellent design; Bea's whole roast duck from the Southern Highlands; lively rooftop bar. $ *Average main: A$45* ⊠ *35 Barangaroo Ave., Sydney* ☎ *02/8587–5400* ⊕ *www.barangaroohouse.com.au.*

BBQ King

$ | **CHINESE** | You can find better basic Chinese food elsewhere in town, but for duck and pork, barbecue-loving Sydneysiders know that this is the place to come. The poultry hanging in the window are the only decoration at this small Chinatown staple, where the food is so fresh you can almost hear it clucking—make sure you sample the duck pancakes. **Known for:** duck pancakes;

late-night feed; quick turnaround. $ *Average main: A$33* ⊠ *18–20 Goulburn St., Haymarket* ☎ *02/9267–2586.*

Blackbird Café

$ | **AUSTRALIAN** |**FAMILY** | Blackbird Café is great place to take a break while exploring Darling Harbour. The weekday lunch specials are all under A$20 and a good value. **Known for:** family-friendly; great value; balcony with views. $ *Average main: A$20* ⊠ *Cockle Bay Wharf, 201 Sussex St., balcony level, Darling Harbour* ☎ *02/9283–7385* ⊕ *www.blackbirdcafe.com.au.*

★ Cirrus

$$ | **AUSTRALIAN** | It's named after a cloud, but with its floor-to-ceiling-windows looking out on Cockle Bay, timber fencing (both on the floor and strung in different lengths from the ceiling) akin to what you might see in sand dunes, a suspended/flying vintage speed boat named Alvin, and perhaps the best and freshest seafood offerings in Sydney, Cirrus may as well be named for the sea it floats above. The A$95 five-course, degustation-style menu is very popular but the seafood platter of oysters, fat Skull Island prawns, strawberry clams, ocean bugs, and pippies with seaweed mayo ponzu and red-wine vinaigrette is a must. **Known for:** five-course menu; seafood platter; views of the harbor. $ *Average main: A$44* ⊠ *23 Barangaroo Ave., Sydney* ☎ *02/9220–0111* ⊕ *www.cirrusdining.com.au.*

Golden Century

$ | **CHINESE** | For two hours—or as long as it takes for you to consume delicately steamed prawns, luscious mud crab with ginger and shallots, and *pipis* (triangular clams) with black-bean sauce—you might as well be in Hong Kong. This place is heaven for seafood lovers, with wall-to-wall fish tanks filled with crab, lobster, abalone, and schools of barramundi, parrot fish, and coral trout. **Known for:** large range of seafood; late-night dining; lengthy queue. $ *Average main:*

A\$30 ✉ 393–399 Sussex St., Haymarket ☎ 02/9212–3901 ⊕ www.goldencentury.com.au.

The Malaya

\$ | **MALAYSIAN** | The cocktails (all A\$18.50) are legendary, the view is captivating, and the food, a traditional Chinese/Malay fusion, is extraordinary. After 50 years in the business (first opened in 1963), in different venues around Sydney, this modern Asian restaurant still does a roaring trade. **Known for:** great views; beef Rendang; Szechuan eggplant. \$ *Average main: A\$30* ✉ *King Street Wharf, 39 Lime St., Darling Harbour* ☎ *02/9279–1170* ⊕ *www.themalaya.com.au* ☽ *No lunch Sun.*

12-Micron

\$\$\$ | **AUSTRALIAN** | Head chef Justin Wise's focus here is celebrating the elements of air, land, and sea in a menu that celebrates local farmers and fine Australian wines. Menu highlights include the pork bowl with black pudding and riberries and lamb neck with potato and broad beans. **Known for:** superior wine pairing; dessert bar; tasting menu. \$ *Average main: A\$55* ✉ *Tower 1, 100 Barangaroo Ave., level 2, Sydney* ☎ *02/8322–2075* ⊕ *12micron.com.au* ☽ *No lunch Mon.*

🛏 Hotels

Ovolo 1888 Darling Harbour

\$ | **HOTEL** | This former wool warehouse has been turned into one of Sydney's most cutting-edge designer hotels. **Pros:** contemporary and cool design; close to Darling Harbour and the city center; free Wi-Fi and free phone calls (in Australia). **Cons:** small rooms; some rooms next to busy road. \$ *Rooms from: A\$300* ✉ *139 Murray St., Darling Harbour* ☎ *02/8586–1888* ⊕ *www.ovolohotels.com.au/ovolo1888darlingharbour* ⇱ *90 rooms* ⦿ *Free breakfast.*

Sofitel Darling Harbour

\$\$\$ | **HOTEL** |**FAMILY** | When it comes to views, it doesn't get much better than the Sofitel Darling Harbour, especially from the top floor, where the floor-to-ceiling windows offer sweeping vistas of the beaches in the Eastern Suburbs. **Pros:** incredible views in all rooms; central location; quality finishes. **Cons:** Wi-Fi isn't free; no train nearby; busy lobby. \$ *Rooms from: A\$420* ✉ *12 Darling Dr., Darling Harbour* ☎ *02/8388–8888* ⊕ *www.accorhotels.com* ⇱ *590 rooms* ⦿ *Free Breakfast.*

🍸 Nightlife

BARS AND DANCE CLUBS

Bungalow 8

BARS/PUBS | With its primo waterside location at the northern end of King Street Wharf, and famous mussels from its open kitchen, Bungalow 8 invites a night of posing and partying. This is the place to be seen bobbing your head to the spinning of several ultracool resident DJs. ✉ *King St. Wharf, 3 Lime St., Darling Harbour* ☎ *02/8322–2006.*

Marquee - The Star Sydney

DANCE CLUBS | Nightclubbers are heading to Marquee—on the top level of the relaunched casino and entertainment complex, The Star Sydney—to dance the night away. The huge nightclub heaves with 1,500 twentysomethings who take to the dance floors in the Main Room and the smaller Boom Box, or chill out in the opulent Library bar. R&B artists and local and international DJs perform on weekends, with tickets from A\$10 if you get in before 11 pm. When it's time to cool down, there are great outdoor balconies overlooking the city and Darling Harbour. ✉ *80 Pyrmont St., Darling Harbour* ☎ *02/9657–7737* ⊕ *www.marqueesydney.com* ⇱ *A\$35.*

🎭 Performing Arts

Sydney Lyric

DANCE | At The Star casino and entertainment complex, Sydney Lyric is one of the city's most spectacular performing-arts venues. Despite its size, there's no better place to watch big-budget musicals. Every seat in the lavishly spacious, 2,000-seat theater is a good one. ⊠ *20–80 Pyrmont St., Pyrmont, Darling Harbour* ☎ *02/9505–3600 tickets* ⊕ *sydneylyric.com.au.*

🛍 Shopping

MARKETS

Paddy's Market

OUTDOOR/FLEA/GREEN MARKETS | Paddy's Market is a huge fresh produce and flea market held under the Market City complex near the Sydney Entertainment Centre in the Chinatown precinct. There has been a market on this site since 1834, and much of the historic exterior remains. The Metro Light Rail stops at the door. ⊠ *9–13 Hay St., Haymarket* ⊕ *www.paddysmarkets.com.au.*

Sydney City Center

Shopping is the main reason to visit Sydney's city center, but there are several buildings and other places of interest among the office blocks, department stores, and shopping centers.

GETTING HERE AND AROUND

Buses from the eastern suburbs run along Elizabeth Street on the western side of Hyde Park; buses from the inner western suburbs such as Balmain travel to and from the Queen Victoria Building. The main train stations are Town Hall and Martin Place, while Hyde Park is served by both St. James and Museum Station on the City Circle rail line. The free shuttle bus (No. 555) completes a circuit around the city center, stopping at the main attractions.

👁 Sights

Anzac Memorial

MEMORIAL | In the southern section of Hyde Park (near Liverpool Street) stands the 1934 art deco Anzac Memorial, a tribute to the Australians who died in military service during World War I, when the acronym ANZAC (Australian and New Zealand Army Corps) was coined. The 120,000 gold stars inside the dome represent each man and woman of New South Wales who served. The lower level exhibits war-related photographs, and a beautiful, poignant sculpture of an ANZAC soldier and shield. ⊠ *Hyde Park* ☎ *02/8262–2900.*

Australian Museum

MUSEUM | **FAMILY** | The strength of this natural history museum, a well-respected academic institution, is its collection of plants, animals, geological specimens, and cultural artifacts from the Asia-Pacific region. Particularly notable are the collections of artifacts from Papua New Guinea and from Australia's Aboriginal peoples. One of the most popular exhibits is "Dinosaurs" on Level 2, containing 10 complete skeletons, eight life-size models, and interactive displays, while "Surviving Australia" (about Australian animals) and "Indigenous Australia" are the most popular with overseas visitors. There are behind-the-scenes tours (A\$98), an excellent shop, and a lively café. ⊠ *6 College St., near William St., Hyde Park* ☎ *02/9320–6000* ⊕ *www.australianmuseum.net.au* 🎦 *A\$15* ☞ *Free guided tours daily, usually at 11 and 2 although subject to change.*

Hyde Park

NATIONAL/STATE PARK | Declared public land by Governor Phillip in 1792 and used for the colony's earliest cricket matches and horse races, this area was turned into a park in 1810. The gardens are formal, with fountains, statuary, and tree-lined walks, and its tranquil lawns are popular with office workers at lunchtime. The park has two sections, with Park Street (a traffic street) dividing the two halves. Several events, such as the Night Noodle Markets (open-air Asian food markets) in October, are held in the park.

✉ *Elizabeth, College, and Park Sts., Hyde Park* ⊕ *www.cityofsydney.nsw.gov.au.*

Marble Bar

HOTEL—SIGHT | Stop in at the Marble Bar to experience a masterpiece of Victorian extravagance. The 1890 bar was formerly in another building that was constructed on the profits of the horse-racing track, thus establishing the link between gambling and majestic public architecture that has its modern-day parallel in the Sydney Opera House. Threatened with demolition in the 1970s, the whole bar was moved—marble arches, color-glass ceiling, elaborately carved woodwork, paintings of voluptuous nudes, and all—to its present site in the basement of the Hilton Sydney Hotel. There is live music most weekends. ✉ *Hilton Sydney, 488 George St., City Center* ☎ *02/9265–6026* ⊕ *www.marblebarsydney.com.au.*

Martin Place

COMMERCIAL CENTER | Sydney's largest pedestrian precinct, flanked by banks, offices, and shopping centers, is the hub of the central business district. There are some grand buildings here—including the beautifully refurbished Commonwealth Bank and the 1870s Venetian Renaissance–style General Post Office building with its 230-foot clock tower (now a Westin hotel). Toward the George Street end of the plaza the simple 1929 cenotaph war memorial commemorates Australians who died in World War I. ✉ *Between Macquarie and George Sts., City Center* ⊕ *www.cityofsydney.nsw.gov.au.*

Queen Victoria Building (QVB)

STORE/MALL | Originally the city's produce market, this huge 1898 sandstone structure was handsomely restored with sweeping staircases, enormous stained-glass windows, and the 1-ton Royal Clock, which hangs from the glass roof. The clock chimes the hour from 9 am to 9 pm with four tableaux: the second shows Queen Elizabeth I knighting Sir Frances Drake; the last ends with an

executioner chopping off King Charles I's head. The complex includes more than 200 boutiques and restaurants including the lovely Tea Room on level 3. Boutiques on the upper floors are generally more upscale. Guided tours cost A$15 and depart Tuesday, Thursday, and Saturday at 11:30 am; bookings are essential. ✉ *455 George St., City Center* ☎ *02/9264–9209* ⊕ *www.qvb.com.au.*

St. Andrew's Cathedral

RELIGIOUS SITE | The foundation stone for Sydney's Gothic Revival Anglican cathedral—the country's oldest—was laid in 1819, although the original architect, Francis Greenway, fell from grace soon after work began. Edmund Blacket, Sydney's most illustrious church architect, was responsible for its final design and completion—a whopping 50 years later in 1868. Notable features of the sandstone construction include ornamental windows depicting Jesus's life and a great east window with images relating to St. Andrew. ✉ *George St. at Bathurst St., next to Town Hall, City Center* ☎ *02/9265–1661* ⊕ *www.sydneycathedral.com.*

St. Mary's Cathedral

RELIGIOUS SITE | The first St. Mary's was built here in 1821, but fire destroyed the chapel. Work on the present cathedral began in 1868. The spires weren't added until 2000, however. St. Mary's has some particularly fine stained-glass windows and a terrazzo floor in the crypt, where exhibitions are often held. The cathedral's large rose window was imported from England. Separate tours take in the cathedral, the crypt, and the bell tower. Free guided tours depart after Sunday mass. ✉ *College St. at Cathedral St., Hyde Park* ☎ *02/9220–0400* ⊕ *www.stmaryscathedral.org.au* ✉ *Tours free.*

★ Sydney Tower

VIEWPOINT | Short of taking a scenic flight, a visit to the top of this 309-meter (1,000 foot) golden-turret-topped spike is the best way to see Sydney's spectacular

Sydney City Center

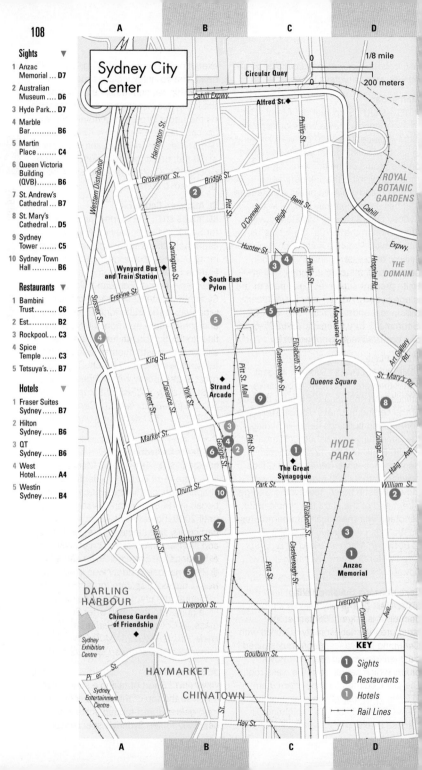

Circular Quay

Alfred St. ◆

Cahill Expwy.

ROYAL
BOTANIC
GARDENS

Harrington St.

Grosvenor St.

Bridge St.

Pitt St.

O'Connell

Bligh

Bent St.

Cahill

Expwy.

THE
DOMAIN

Western Distributor

Carrington St.

Hunter St.

Phillip St.

Hospital Rd.

Wynyard Bus
and Train Station ◆

◆ South East
Pylon

Erskine St.

Sussex St.

Martin Pl.

Macquarie St.

Art Gallery Rd.

King St.

Elizabeth St.

Castlereagh St.

Queens Square

St. Mary's Rd.

Clarence St.

York St.

Kent St.

◆ Strand
Arcade

Pitt St. Mall

Market St.

George St.

Pitt St.

HYDE
PARK

College St.

Haig Ave.

Druitt St.

Park St.

The Great
Synagogue ◆

William St.

DARLING
HARBOUR

Bathurst St.

Sussex St.

Liverpool St.

Pitt St.

Castlereagh St.

Elizabeth St.

Anzac
Memorial

Liverpool St.

Commonw

Ave.

Chinese Garden
of Friendship ◆

Sydney
Exhibition
Centre

Pi er St.

Sydney
Entertainment
Centre

HAYMARKET

CHINATOWN

Goulburn St.

Hay St.

1/8 mile

200 meters

KEY

1 *Sights*

1 *Restaurants*

1 *Hotels*

———— *Rail Lines*

ayout. This is the city's tallest building, and the views from its indoor observation deck encompass the entire Sydney metropolitan area. You can often see as far as the Blue Mountains, more than 80 km (50 miles) away. You can view it all from the Sydney Tower Eye Observation Deck 820 feet above the city streets. The building houses two restaurants in the turret. ✉ *100 Market St., between Pitt and Castlereagh Sts., City Center* ☎ *02/9333–9222* 🌐 *www.sydneytower-eye.com.au* 🎫 *Observation deck A$28, cheaper tickets available online.*

Sydney Town Hall
GOVERNMENT BUILDING | Sydney's Town Hall—an elaborate sandstone structure—is one of the city's most ornate Victorian buildings. A centerpiece of the building is the massive 8,000-pipe Grand Organ, one of the world's most powerful, which is used for lunchtime concerts. Tours, conducted by the "Friends of Town Hall" for A$5, can be booked through the website. Mingle with locals on the marble steps of the front entrance. ✉ *483 George St., City Center* ☎ *02/9265–9198 general inquiries* 🌐 *www.cityofsydney.nsw.gov.au* 🎫 *Free.*

🍴 Restaurants

Bambini Trust
$$ | ITALIAN | It's hidden behind huge black doors in one of the city's historic sandstone buildings, but once you're inside you'd swear you were in Paris. Dark-wood paneling, black-and-white photographs, and mirrors bearing the day's specials in flowing script lend a bistro feel. **Known for:** great location; outdoor dining options; open late. [$] *Average main: A$38* ✉ *185 Elizabeth St., City Center* ☎ *02/9283–7098* 🌐 *www.bambini-trust.com.au* 🕒 *Closed Sun. No breakfast or lunch Sat.*

Est
$$$$ | MODERN AUSTRALIAN | This elegant, pillared dining room is the perfect setting for showing off chef Peter Doyle's modern, light touch with Mod Oz cuisine. Menu highlights include the prawn tartare and the aged pork loin with rhubarb, mostarda, and cabbage. **Known for:** delicious seafood dishes; tasting menu; interesting ice-cream desserts. [$] *Average main: A$105* ✉ *Establishment Hotel, 252 George St., City Center* ☎ *02/9114–7312* 🌐 *www.merivale.com.au/est* 🕒 *Closed Sun. No lunch Sat.*

★ **Rockpool**
$$$$ | MODERN AUSTRALIAN | A meal at Rockpool is a crash course in what Mod Oz cooking is all about, conducted in a glamorous, long dining room with a catwalk-like ramp. Chefs Neil Perry and Corey Costelloe weave Thai, Chinese, Mediterranean, and Middle Eastern influences into their repertoire with effortless flair and originality. **Known for:** date tart; wide caviar selection; dramatic interiors. [$] *Average main: A$185* ✉ *11 Bridge St., City Center* ☎ *02/8099–7077* 🌐 *www.rockpool.com* 🕒 *Closed Sun. No lunch Sat.* 👔 *Jacket required.*

Spice Temple
$$ | CHINESE | The culinary focus of this chic basement eatery—another of the restaurants owned by Neil Perry of Rockpool fame—is regional China. There are dishes from far-flung Yunnan, Hunan, and Sichuan provinces, and as the names suggests, they all have a kick. **Known for:** trendy; great atmosphere; extensive cocktail list. [$] *Average main: A$40* ✉ *10 Bligh St., City Center* ☎ *02/8078–1888* 🌐 *www.rockpool.com/spicetemplesydney* 🕒 *Closed Sun. No lunch Sat.*

★ **Tetsuya's**
$$$$ | MODERN AUSTRALIAN | It's worth getting on the waiting list—there's *always* a waiting list—to sample the unique blend of Western and Japanese-French flavors crafted by Sydney's most applauded chef, Tetsuya Wakuda. The serene, expansive dining room's unobtrusive Japanese aesthetic leaves the food as the true highlight. **Known for:** incredible Japanese

The fountain in Hyde Park with the Australian Museum in the background

fare; degustation meals; quiet atmosphere. [$] *Average main: A$220* ✉ *529 Kent St., City Center* ☎ *02/9267–2900* 🌐 *www.tetsuyas.com* 🕑 *Closed Sun. and Mon. No lunch Tues.–Fri.*

Hotels

Fraser Suites Sydney

$$ | HOTEL | This serviced-apartment hotel is one of Sydney's swankiest places to stay. **Pros:** cutting-edge design; well priced for longer stays; free Wi-Fi throughout. **Cons:** minimalist design may not be to everyone's taste; no balconies; impersonal due to size. [$] *Rooms from: A$250* ✉ *488 Kent St., City Center* ☎ *02/8823–8888* 🌐 *sydney.frasershospitality.com* 🛏 *201 rooms* 🍴 *No meals.*

Hilton Sydney

$$ | HOTEL | At this landmark hotel in downtown Sydney you enter a spacious, light-filled lobby displaying a stunning four-story sculpture. **Pros:** excellent service; lavishly appointed rooms; hip bar. **Cons:** impersonal and busy; no views; located on busy street. [$] *Rooms from: A$270* ✉ *488 George St., City Center* ☎ *02/9266–2000* 🌐 *www.hiltonsydney.com.au* 🛏 *577 rooms* 🍴 *No meals.*

QT Sydney

$$$ | HOTEL | This hotel is the answer for those seeking color and quirkiness, teamed with style and super-efficient service. **Pros:** great location; catchy design; stylish bars; historic restored building. **Cons:** funkiness may not be to all tastes; super-soft beds; no pool or balconies. [$] *Rooms from: A$330* ✉ *49 Market St., at George St., City Center* ☎ *02/8262–0000* 🌐 *www.qtsydney.com.au* 🛏 *200 rooms* 🍴 *No meals.*

West Hotel

$$$ | HOTEL | Situated in a perfect little pocket of Sydney between Darling Harbour, Barangaroo Reserve, and the city center, in a jewel-like building of glass panels that capture and reflect light, West Hotel offers modern, elegant rooms with luxurious finishes in marble, brass, velvets, and gem tones, and a central atrium filled with greenery. **Pros:**

excellent location for exploring; elegant, comfortable base; exceptional bar and dining options. **Cons:** Wi-Fi fee; inconsistent service; no swimming pool. $ *Rooms from: A$305* ⊠ *65 Sussex St., City Center* ☎ *02/8297–6500* ⚲ *182 rooms* ⦿ *Free Breakfast.*

Westin Sydney

$$$ | **HOTEL** | The Westin hotel chain is renowned for its heavenly beds—in Sydney it has heavenly service, too. **Pros:** in-room entertainment systems; great service; free Wi-Fi in public areas. **Cons:** slightly corporate feel; Wi-Fi extra for multiple devices; rooms feel dated. $ *Rooms from: A$430* ⊠ *1 Martin Pl., City Center* ☎ *02/8223–1111* ⊕ *www.westin.com/sydney* ⚲ *416 rooms* ⦿ *No meals.*

▼ Nightlife

BARS AND DANCE CLUBS

★ The Arthouse Hotel

BARS/PUBS | A former School of the Arts building, The Arthouse Hotel has been renovated into a modern, belle epoque–style hot spot, with four bars and a restaurant spread over three cavernous floors. Art is the focus here, whether it's visual—life-drawing classes are given on Monday, a burlesque drawing class biweekly on Tuesday—aural, or edible, and there is a full-time curator dedicated to programming music, events, and exhibitions. ⊠ *275 Pitt St., City Center* ☎ *02/9284–1200* ⊕ *www.thearthousehotel.com.au.*

★ Bambini Wine Room

WINE BARS—NIGHTLIFE | Bambini Wine Room is a sparkling little jewel box encased in marble-clad walls and topped with lovely chandeliers. You can sip cocktails (A$17) and any number of fine wines late into the night and feast on affordable bar snacks. ⊠ *185 Elizabeth St., City Center* ☎ *02/9283–7098* ⊙ *Closed Sun.*

Hemmesphere

BARS/PUBS | One of a string of swanky venues in the area, Hemmesphere is still drawing a hip crowd more than a decade after it first opened. Named for Justin Hemmes, son of iconic 1970s fashion designers Jon and Merivale Hemmes, this is where Sydney's hippest pay homage to cocktail culture from low, leather divans. The mood is elegant and sleek, and so are the well-dressed guests, who often include whichever glitterati happen to be in town. It's on the fourth level of the Establishment Hotel complex and draws those seeking an escape from the rowdy action downstairs. ⊠ *252 George St., level 4, City Center* ☎ *02/9714–7313* ⊕ *merivale.com.au/hemmesphere* ⊙ *Closed Sun.*

Ivy

BARS/PUBS | This multilevel complex of bars, pubs, and eateries is in an ultrahip George Street complex. Cocktails are great but expensive, and the crowd varies depending on the night. If you don't fancy this bar, then there's the decadent Pool bar on the top floor, where if you get there early you can recline in your own cabana overlooking the swimming pool. Also on-site are the Den (a lavish bar with chaise longue furniture, chandeliers, and cigar menu), the casual Royal George pub, and the Ash Street Cellar bistro. ⊠ *330 George St., City Center* ☎ *02/9240–8100* ⊕ *merivale.com.au/ivy* ⊙ *Closed Sun.*

Lobo Plantation

BARS/PUBS | This Cuban-themed bar is a hit in Sydney. Patrons love the palm trees, the cane furniture, and the wall lined with Cuban bank notes. Cocktails (from around A$18) have a 1950s theme so you could try an Esther Williams, a Nuclear Daiquiri, or a Message in a Bottle, which comes with its own miniature bottle, or go all out and take a one-hour "rum flight," sipping your way through seven different rums (from A$60; bookings essential). The affordable bar menu, which runs from tamales to black bean stew and pork crackling, helps soak up the alcohol. ⊠ *209 Clarence St.,* basement, City Center ☎ 02/9240–3000 ⊕ www.thelobo.com.au ⊗ Closed Sun.

Marble Bar

PIANO BARS/LOUNGES | Stop in at the Marble Bar to experience a masterpiece of Victorian extravagance. The 1890 bar was formerly in another building that was constructed on the profits of the horse-racing track, thus establishing the link between gambling and majestic public architecture that has its modern-day parallel in the Sydney Opera House. Threatened with demolition in the 1970s, the whole bar was moved—marble arches, color-glass ceiling, elaborately carved woodwork, paintings of voluptuous nudes, and all—to its present site in the basement of the Hilton Sydney Hotel. There is live music most weekends. ⊠ Hilton Sydney, 488 George St., City Center ☎ 02/9265–6026 ⊕ www.marblebarsydney.com.au.

★ O Bar and Dining

PIANO BARS/LOUNGES | This is the place to come at sunset for the view, tapas, and cocktails—and the '70s kitsch of a revolving restaurant. Located on level 47 of the Australia Square building, O Bar has floor-to-ceiling windows, so no matter which seat you have, the view is great, and constantly changing. It's perfect for a predinner drink, or dinner, too. It's open daily from 5 pm and Friday lunch. ⊠ Australia Sq., 264 George St., level 47, City Center ☎ 02/9247–0777 ⊕ obardining.com.au.

🎭 Performing Arts

THEATER
Belvoir Street Theatre

THEATER | Belvoir Street Theatre has two stages that host innovative and challenging political and social drama. The smaller downstairs space showcases a lineup of brave new Australian drama. The theater is a 10-minute walk from Central Station. ⊠ 25 Belvoir St., Surry Hills ☎ 02/9699–3444 ⊕ www.belvoir.com.au.

Capitol Theatre

CONCERTS | This century-old city landmark was refurbished with such modern refinements as fiber-optic ceiling lights that twinkle in time to the music. The 2,000-seat theater specializes in Broadway blockbusters, such as The Lion King and Mary Poppins, and also hosts pop and rock concerts. Guided behind-the-scenes tours are available (A$38.50); bookings are essential. ⊠ 13 Campbell St., Haymarket ☎ 02/9320–5000 ⊕ www.capitoltheatre.com.au.

SBW Stables Theatre

THEATER | This small 120-seat venue is home of the Griffin Theatre Company, which specializes in new Australian writing. ⊠ 10 Nimrod St., Kings Cross ☎ 02/9361–3817 ⊕ www.griffintheatre.com.au.

★ State Theatre

CONCERTS | State Theatre is the grande dame of Sydney theaters. It operates as a cinema in June each year, when it hosts the two-week-long Sydney Film Festival; at other times this beautiful space hosts local and international performers. Built in 1929 and restored to its full-blown opulence, the theater has a vaulted ceiling, mosaic floors, marble columns and statues, and brass and bronze doors. A highlight of the magnificent theater is the 20,000-piece chandelier that is supposedly the world's second largest, which Robin Williams once likened to "one of Imelda Marcos's earrings." Even if you don't see a show here, it's worth popping into the lobby for a look around, or join a guided tour to get a good look at the theater's many treasures (A$25.50). ⊠ 49 Market St., City Center ☎ 02/9373–6655 ⊕ www.statetheatre.com.au ⊂ Guided tours Mon.–Wed. 10 am and 1 pm.

📖 Shopping

BOOKS

Ariel Booksellers

BOOKS/STATIONERY | This is a large, bright browser's delight, and the place to go for literature, pop culture, avant garde, and art books. They also hold book readings and other literary events. ⊠ 98 Oxford St., City Center ⊕ www.arielbooks.com. au.

Dymocks

BOOKS/STATIONERY | This big, bustling bookstore is packed to its gallery-level coffee shop and is the place to go for all literary needs. ⊠ 424 George St., City Center ☎ 02/9235–0155 ⊕ www. dymocks.com.au.

CLOTHING

Country Road

CLOTHING | The fashion here stands somewhere between Ralph Lauren and Timberland, with an all-Australian assembly of classic, countrified his 'n' hers, plus an ever-expanding variety of soft furnishings in cotton and linen for the rustic retreat. You'll find Country Road clothes in most department stores, but the biggest range is here in this flagship store. ⊠ 142–144 Pitt St., City Center ☎ 02/9394–1818 ⊕ www.countryroad.com.au.

★ Paddy Pallin

SPECIALTY STORES | This should be the first stop for serious bush adventurers heading for wild Australia and beyond. Maps, books, and mounds of gear are tailored especially for the Australian outdoors. ⊠ 507 Kent St., City Center ☎ 02/9264–2685 ⊕ www.paddypallin.com.au.

★ R. M. Williams

SPECIALTY STORES | The place to go for riding boots, Akubra hats, Drizabone raincoats, and moleskin trousers—the type of clothes worn by Hugh Jackman and Nicole Kidman in the movie Australia. ⊠ 389 George St., City Center ☎ 02/9262–2228 ⊕ www.rmwilliams. com.au.

A Sea of Talent 🎟

Sculpture by the Sea. A steel whale's tail sticking out of the ocean and retro kettles cunningly disguised as penguins strapped to a huge rock being lashed by waves are some of the imaginative artworks that have wowed visitors to the annual show called Sculpture by the Sea. Since 1996, artists have positioned more than 100 sculptures on and under rocky outcrops and on hilltops along the much-trodden Bondi-to-Bronte Coastal Walk. This free exhibition runs for two weeks beginning in late October. ⊠ Bondi-to-Bronte Coastal Walk, Bondi Beach ⊕ www.sculpturebythesea.com.

DEPARTMENT STORES AND SHOPPING CENTERS

★ David Jones

DEPARTMENT STORES | The city's largest department store maintains a reputation for excellent service and high-quality goods. Clothing by many of Australia's finest designers is on display here, and the store also sells its own fashion label at reasonable prices. ⊠ Elizabeth St. at Market St., City Center ☎ 02/9266–5544 ⊕ www.davidjones.com.au.

Myer

DEPARTMENT STORES | Buy clothing and accessories by Australian and international designers at this department store opposite the Queen Victoria Building. ⊠ George St. at Market St., City Center ☎ 02/9238–9111 ⊕ www.myer.com.au.

Pitt Street Mall

SHOPPING CENTERS/MALLS | The heart of Sydney's shopping area includes the Mid-City Centre, the huge Westfield Sydney Shopping Centre, Skygarden, Myer, and the charming and historic Strand Arcade—five multilevel shopping plazas crammed with more than 500 shops, from mainstream clothing stores to designer boutiques. ■TIP→ **Just a short walk away is the iconic David Jones store on Elizabeth Street.** ✉ *182 Pitt St., City Center ✛ Between King and Market Sts.*

★ Queen Victoria Building

SHOPPING CENTERS/MALLS | This is a splendid Victorian-era building with more than 200 boutiques, cafés, and antiques shops. The building is open 24 hours, so you can window-shop even after the stores have closed. Guided history tours, which run 45 minutes, cost A$15 and depart 11:30 am Tuesday, Thursday, and Saturday. Book at the concierge on the ground floor. ✉ *George, York, Market, and Druitt Sts., City Center* ☎ *02/9265–6800* ⊕ *www.qvb.com.au.*

★ Strand Arcade

SHOPPING CENTERS/MALLS | This ornate three-story shopping arcade built in 1891 runs between George Street and Pitt Street Mall and is one of Sydney's most elegant shopping strips. Beautiful Victorian-era floor tiles, magnificent cedar staircases, and charmingly old-fashioned shopfronts help make the shopping here refreshingly chain-store free. The upstairs galleries are home to high-end Australian fashion designers and jewelers, while the ground floor has a charming mix of cozy speciality tea and cake shops, beauty and gift stores, and fashion boutiques. Strand Hatters is the best men's hat store in the city and the place to buy an Akubra or Fedora. The arcade is bookended by two of the country's iconic chocolate stores—Haigh's Chocolates at George Street and Koko Black on Pitt Street—and both are virtually irresistible. ✉ *412–414 George St., Sydney* ☎ *02/9265–6800* ⊕ *www. strandarcade.com.au.*

JEWELRY AND ACCESSORIES

Dinosaur Designs

SPECIALTY STORES | This fun store sells luminous bowls, plates, and vases, as well as fanciful jewelry crafted from resin and Perspex in eye-popping colors. There's another location at 339 Oxford Street in Paddington. ✉ *Strand Arcade, George St., Shop 77, City Center* ☎ *02/9223–2953* ⊕ *www.dinosaurde-signs.com.au.*

The National Opal Collection

JEWELRY/ACCESSORIES | This is the only Sydney opal retailer with total ownership of its entire production process—mines, workshops, and showroom—making prices very competitive. In the Pitt Street showroom, you can prearrange to see artisans at work cutting and polishing the stones or visit the on-site museum and learn about the process of opal development and opalized fossils. ✉ *60 Pitt St., City Center* ☎ *02/9247–6344* ⊕ *www. nationalopal.com.*

Paspaley Pearls

JEWELRY/ACCESSORIES | The jewelers here order their exquisite material from pearl farms near the remote Western Australia town of Broome. Prices start high and head for the stratosphere, but if you're serious about a high-quality pearl, this gallery requires a visit. ✉ *Paspaley Bldg., 2 Martin Pl., City Center* ☎ *02/9232–7633* ⊕ *www.paspaleypearls.com.*

Percy Marks Fine Gems

JEWELRY/ACCESSORIES | Here you'll find an outstanding collection of high-quality Australian gemstones, including dazzling black opals, pink diamonds, and pearls from Broome. ✉ *70 Casterleigh St., City Center* ☎ *02/9233–1355* ⊕ *www.percy-marks.com.au.*

Rox Gems and Jewellery

JEWELRY/ACCESSORIES | Come here for serious one-off designs at the cutting edge of lapidary chic. ✉ *Shop 31, Strand Arcade, George St., City Center* ☎ *02/9232–7828* ⊕ *www.rox.com.au.*

MUSIC

Birdland Records

SPECIALTY STORES | This institution for music lovers has an especially strong selection of jazz, blues, African, and Latin American music in multiple formats, including vinyl and super audio CDs, as well as an authoritative staff ready to lend some assistance. ⊠ *Dymocks Bldg., Level 4, 428 George St., City Center* ☎ *02/9231–1188* ⊕ *www.birdland.com. au.*

Inner City and the Eastern Suburbs

Sydney's inner city and eastern suburbs are truly the people's domain. They are the hip zones of Sydney featuring the foodie precincts as well as some of the most expensive real estate, great shopping, and the most accessible beaches. Architecture ranges from the mansions of the colonial aristocracy and the humble laborers' cottages of the same period to the modernized terrace houses of Paddington, one of Sydney's most charming and most desirable suburbs. A good way to explore the area is to take the Bondi & Bays Explorer bus that stops at 10 sites including Bondi Beach, Double Bay, Paddington, and Rose Bay.

GETTING HERE AND AROUND
The inner city and eastern suburbs are well served by buses, although the journey out to the eastern suburbs beaches can be quite long at rush hour. Most depart from Circular Quay (Alfred Street). Travel to Paddington and Bondi is on Nos. 380, 333, and 382; and to Watsons Bay and Vaucluse (via Double Bay and Rose Bay) on Nos. 323, 324, and 325. Buses 380, 382, and 333 travel along Oxford Street, the main artery of the alternative (and gay) neighborhood of Darlinghurst. It is quicker to take the train to Edgecliff or Bondi Junction stations to connect with buses traveling to many of the eastern suburbs including Coogee and Clovelly. A ferry operates between Circular Quay and Watsons Bay, calling at Garden Island, Darling Point, Double Bay, and Rose Bay. It is an easy walk to Darlinghurst and Surry Hills from the city center, while Kings Cross has its own

train station, just one stop from the city center.

⊙ Sights

Centennial Park
CITY PARK | More than 500 acres of palm-lined avenues, groves of Moreton Bay figs, paperbark tree–fringed lakes, and cycling and horse-riding tracks make this a popular park and Sydney's favorite workout circuit. In the early 1800s the marshy land at the lower end provided Sydney with its fresh water. The park was proclaimed in 1888, the centenary of Australia's founding as a colony. The Centennial Park Café is often crowded on weekends, but a mobile canteen between the lakes in the middle of the park serves snacks and espresso. Bikes and blades can be rented from the nearby Clovelly Road outlets, on the eastern side of the park. The Moonlight Cinema screens movies during the summer months. ⊠ *Oxford St., at Centennial Ave., Centennial Park* ☎ *02/9339–6699* ⊕ *www.centennialparklands.com.au.*

Elizabeth Bay
NEIGHBORHOOD | Much of this densely populated but still-charming harborside suburb was originally part of the extensive Elizabeth Bay House grounds. Wrought-iron balconies and French doors on some of the older apartment blocks give the area a Mediterranean flavor. During the 1920s and 1930s this was a fashionably bohemian quarter, and it remains a favorite among artists and writers. ⊠ *Elizabeth Bay Rd., Elizabeth Bay.*

Elizabeth Bay House
HOUSE | This 1835–39 mansion was regarded in its heyday as the "finest house in the colony." It retains little of its original furniture, although the rooms have been restored in Georgian style. The most striking feature is an oval-shaped salon with a winding staircase, naturally lighted by glass panels in the domed roof. The view from the

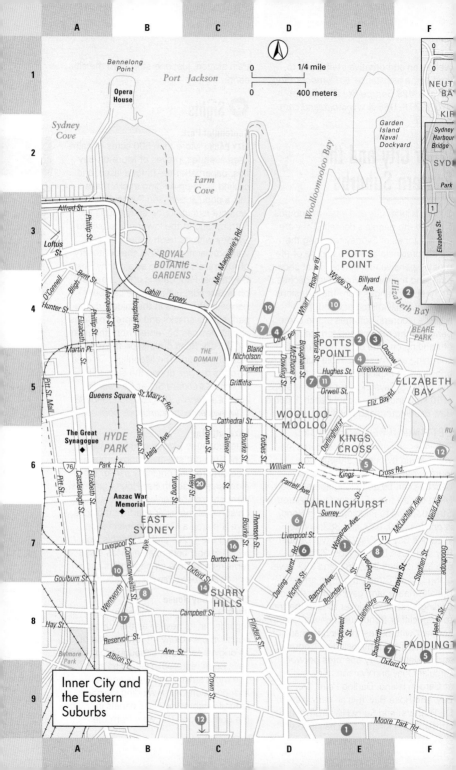

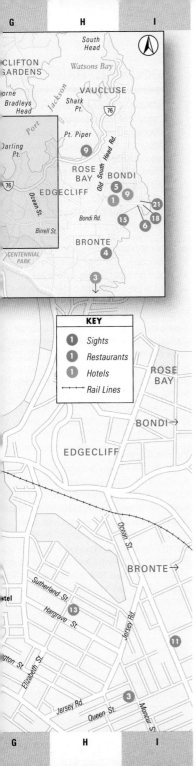

Sights ▼

1. Centennial Park..........**E9**
2. Elizabeth Bay.............**F4**
3. Elizabeth Bay House **E5**
4. Henry's Café
   de Wheels...............**D4**
5. Paddington **F9**
6. Sydney Jewish
   Museum **D7**
7. Victoria Barracks........**E8**

Restaurants ▼

1. bills **E7**
2. Billy Kwong...............**E4**
3. Bistro Moncur.............**I9**
4. Bronte Belo..............**H3**
5. Brown Sugar..............**I2**
6. The Bucket List **I3**
7. The Butler **D5**
8. Buon Ricordo.............**E7**
9. Catalina Restaurant **H2**
10. Chin Chin Sydney **B8**
11. Chiswick..................**I8**
12. Four ate Five.............**C9**
13. Four in Hand.............**H8**
14. The Goods................**C8**
15. Icebergs Dining Room
    and Bar **I3**
16. Joe's Table...............**C7**
17. Longrain **B8**
18. North Bondi Fish..........**I3**
19. Otto Ristorante **D4**
20. Red Lantern on Riley ...**C6**
21. Sean's Panaroma.........**I3**

Hotels ▼

1. Adina Apartment Hotel
   Bondi Beach **H3**
2. Arts Hotel Sydney **D8**
3. Crowne Plaza
   Coogee Beach **H4**
4. De Vere Hotel **E5**
5. Hotel 59 & Cafe **E6**
6. Medusa **D7**
7. Ovolo
   Woolloomooloo **D4**
8. Paramount House
   Hotel......................**B8**
9. QT Bondi...................**I3**
10. Simpsons of
    Potts Point...............**E4**
11. Spicers Potts Point **E5**
12. Vibe Hotel
    Rushcutters **F6**

3

Sydney INNER CITY AND THE EASTERN SUBURBS

KEY

- ① Sights
- ① Restaurants
- ① Hotels
- ⊢—— Rail Lines

front-facing windows across Elizabeth Bay is stunning. A variety of soirees and talks are held in the house throughout the year. ⊠ *7 Onslow Ave., Elizabeth Bay* ☎ *02/9356–3022* ⊕ *sydneyliving-museums.com.au/elizabeth-bay-house* ⊠ *A$12.*

Harry's Café de Wheels

RESTAURANT—SIGHT | The attraction of this all-day dockyard food stall is not so much the delectable meat pies and coffee served as the clientele. Famous opera singers, actors, and international rock stars have been spotted here rubbing shoulders with shift workers and taxi drivers. This "pie cart" has been a Sydney institution since 1945, when the late Harry "Tiger" Edwards set up his van to serve sailors from the nearby Garden Island base. Drop in any time from 8:30 am (9 am on weekends) until the wee hours for a Tiger Pie, made with mushy peas, mashed potatoes, and gravy. Harry's now has nine other locations in Sydney. ⊠ *1 Cowper Wharf Rd., Wool-loomooloo* ☎ *02/9357–3074* ⊕ *www.harryscafedewheels.com.au.*

Paddington

HISTORIC SITE | Most of this suburb's elegant two-story terrace houses were built during the 1880s, when the colony experienced a long period of economic growth following the gold rushes that began in the 1860s. The balconies are trimmed with decorative wrought iron, sometimes known as Paddington lace, which initially came from England and later from Australian foundries. Rebuilt and repainted, the now-stylish Paddington terrace houses give the area its characteristic village-like charm. The Oxford Street shopping strip is full of upscale and funky boutiques, cafés, and several good pubs. ⊠ *Oxford St., between Boundary and Queen Sts., Paddington.*

Sydney Jewish Museum

MUSEUM | Artifacts, interactive displays, and audiovisual displays chronicle the history of Australian Jews and

Need A Break? 🍴

Royal Hotel. The Royal Hotel is an enjoyable Victorian pub with leather couches and stained-glass windows. It's a good place to stop for something cool to drink. The top floor has a balcony restaurant that's popular on sunny afternoons. ⊠ *237 Glenmore Rd., Paddington* ☎ *02/9331–2604* ⊕ *royalhotel.com.au.*

commemorate the 6 million killed in the Holocaust. Exhibits are brilliantly arranged on eight levels, which lead upward in chronological order, from the handful of Jews who arrived with the First Fleet in 1788 to the 30,000 concentration-camp survivors who came after World War II—one of the largest populations of Holocaust survivors to be found anywhere. A free 40-minute guided tour starts at noon on Monday, Wednesday, Friday, and Sunday. ⊠ *148 Darlinghurst Rd., Darlinghurst* ☎ *02/9360–7999* ⊕ *www.sydneyjewishmuseum.com.au* ⊠ *A$15.*

Victoria Barracks

MILITARY SITE | If you're curious about the Australian military, you'll enjoy the free tours of this Regency-style barracks (built from 1841), which take place every Thursday at 10 am sharp. The tour includes entry to the Army Museum of New South Wales, which has exhibits covering Australia's military history from the days of the Rum Corps to the Malayan conflict of the 1950s. ⊠ *Oxford St., at Oatley Rd., Paddington* ☎ *02/8335–5330* ⊕ *www.armymuseumnsw.com.au* ⊠ *Tours free, museum A$2.*

🏖 Beaches

★ Bondi Beach

BEACH—SIGHT | Wide, wonderful Bondi (pronounced *bon*-dye) is the most famous and most crowded of all Sydney

Surf school at Bondi Beach

beaches. It has something for just about everyone, and the droves that flock here on a sunny day give it a bustling, carnival atmosphere unmatched by any other Sydney beach. Facilities include toilets, open-air showers for rinsing sandy feet and salty bodies, and a kiosk on the beach that rents out sun lounges, beach umbrellas, and even swimsuits. Cafés, ice-cream outlets, restaurants, and boutiques line Campbell Parade, which runs behind the beach. But despite its popularity, it's also a dangerous beach, with an estimated 30 swimmers saved by the seven lifeguards who man this spot every day, even in winter. Families tend to prefer the calmer waters of the northern end of the beach. Surfing is popular at the south end, where a path winds along the sea-sculpted cliffs to Tamarama and Bronte beaches. Take Bus 380, 382, or 333 all the way from Circular Quay, or take the train from the city to Bondi Junction and then board Bus 380, 381, 382, or 333. **Amenities:** food and drink; lifeguards; parking (fee); showers; toilets; water sports. **Best for:** partiers;

sunrise; surfing; swimming; walking. ✉ *Campbell Parade, Bondi Beach.*

★ **Bronte Beach**

BEACH—SIGHT | FAMILY | If you want an ocean beach that's close to the city and has a terrific setting, with both sand and grassy areas, this one is hard to beat. A wooded park of palm trees and Norfolk Island pines surrounds Bronte. The park includes a playground and sheltered picnic tables, and excellent cafés are in the immediate area. The breakers can be fierce, but swimming is safe in the sea pool at the southern end of the beach. Take Bus 378 from Central Station, or take the train from the city to Bondi Junction and then board Bus 378. Bus 362 runs between Bondi and Coogee beaches, stopping at Bronte Beach and Tamarama on the weekends only. **Amenities:** food and drink; lifeguard; showers; toilets. **Best for:** sunrise; surfing; walking. ✉ *Bronte Rd., Bronte.*

Clovelly

BEACH—SIGHT | FAMILY | Even on the roughest day it's safe to swim at the end of this long, keyhole-shape inlet, which makes it a popular family beach. There are toilet facilities, a kiosk, and a café. This is also a popular snorkeling spot that usually teems with tropical fish, including a huge blue groper, which has called this enclave home for more than a decade. Take Bus 339 from Argyle Street, Millers Point (the Rocks), Wynyard, or Central Station; or a train from the city to Bondi Junction, then board Bus 360. **Amenities:** food and drink; lifeguards; parking (fee); showers; toilets. **Best for:** snorkeling; sunrise; swimming. ✉ *Clovelly Rd., Clovelly.*

Coogee

BEACH—SIGHT | **FAMILY** | A reef protects this lively beach (pronounced *kuh*-jee), creating slightly calmer swimming conditions than those found at its neighbors. For smaller children, the southern end offers a small enclosed pool, or keep following the coastal path, and there's a small women's-only natural pool that costs just 20 cents entry. The grassy headland overlooking the beach has an excellent children's playground. Cafés in the shopping precinct at the back of the beach sell ice cream, pizza, and the ingredients for picnics Take Bus 373 or 374 from Circular Quay or Bus 372 from Central Station. **Amenities:** food and drink; lifeguards; parking (fee); showers; toilets. **Best for:** sunrise; swimming; walking. ✉ *Coogee Bay Rd. at Arden St., Coogee.*

Tamarama

BEACH—SIGHT | This small, fashionable beach—aka "Glam-a-rama"—is one of Sydney's prettiest, but the rocky headlands that squeeze close to the sand on either side make it less than ideal for swimming. The sea is often hazardous here, and surfing is prohibited. A café in the small park behind the beach sells sandwiches, fresh juices, and fruit whips. Take the train from the city to Bondi Junction and then board Bus 360 or 361, or walk for 10 minutes along the cliff path from the south end of Bondi Beach. **Amenities:** food and drink; lifeguard; showers; toilets. **Best for:** sunrise; surfing ✉ *Tamarama Marine Dr., Tamarama.*

🍴 Restaurants

DARLINGHURST

★ bills

$ | **CAFÉ** | Named after celebrity chef and cookbook author Bill Granger, this sunny corner café is so addictive it should come with a health warning. It's a favorite hangout of everyone from local nurses to semi-disguised rock stars, and you never know who you might be sitting next to at the newspaper-strewn communal table. **Known for:** ricotto hotcakes; buzzy atmosphere; great service. [$] *Average main: A$25* ✉ *433 Liverpool St., Darlinghurst* ☎ *02/9360–9631* 🌐 *www.bills.com.au* 🕐 *No dinner.*

The Goods

$ | **CAFÉ** | Griddle pan dishes are the draw at this friendly, and slightly noisy, organic café and food store on the city fringe. Served in cast-iron skillets and topped with two baked eggs, the griddle choices include creamed corn with chorizo or their own home-cured smoky bacon. **Known for:** lively atmosphere; great weekend spot; great coffee. [$] *Average main: A$20* ✉ *253 Crown St., Darlinghurst* ☎ *02/9357–6690* 🕐 *No dinner.*

Joe's Table

$ | **VIETNAMESE** | A lot of care goes into the creations in this popular South East Asian spot: the pork hock is braised for four hours each night before being pressed and then tossed with homemade chilli jam, while coconut milk is smoked overnight and then churned into ice-cream in the morning. As delicious and affordable as the sandwiches and dumplings are, be sure to save space for this true star of the show, which is served enveloped in smoke under a glass dome and topped with tender young coconut shavings and a simple pinch of salt. **Known for:** smoking coconut ice cream; jumbo lunch sandwiches;

delicious South East Asian fare. $ *Average main: A$20* ✉ *1/28 Kings La., Darlinghurst, Darlinghurst* ☎ *02/8385–7110.*

KINGS CROSS AND POTTS POINT

★ Billy Kwong

$$ | CHINESE | Locals rub shoulders while eating no-fuss Chinese food at TV chef Kylie Kwong's trendy restaurant. Kwong prepares the kind of food her family cooks, with Grandma providing not just the inspiration but also the recipes. **Known for:** trendy eatery; buzzy on weekends; superior Asian fare. $ *Average main: A$38* ✉ *1/28 Macleay St., Elizabeth Bay* ☎ *02/9332–3300* ⊕ *billykwong. au* ⊙ *No lunch.*

The Butler

$ | LATIN AMERICAN | Tucked away on a pretty backstreet in Potts Point, this restaurant is packed with the beautiful people on the weekend soaking in its buzzy atmosphere, sweeping vistas of Sydney's cityscape, extensive cocktail list, and excellent menu. Prebook a table on the balcony as they go quickly, and then pick a few sharing plates. **Known for:** buzzy atmosphere; great small plates; great views. $ *Average main: A$35* ✉ *123 Victoria St., Potts Point* ☎ *02/8354–0742.*

Red Lantern on Riley

$$ | VIETNAMESE | Owned by Vietnamese TV chef Luke Nguyen, this restaurant is popular with his legions of TV fans. Diners should always start with the country's great export, rice paper rolls. **Known for:** relaxed atmosphere; full tasting menu; great cocktail list. $ *Average main: A$45* ✉ *60 Riley St., Darlinghurst* ☎ *02/9698–4355* ⊕ *www.redlantern.com.au* ⊙ *No lunch Sat.–Wed.*

WOOLLOOMOOLOO

Otto Ristorante

$$ | ITALIAN | Few restaurants have the magnetic pull of Otto, a place where radio shock jocks sit side by side with fashion-magazine editors and confirmed foodies. Yes, it's a scene, but fortunately one with good Italian food prepared by chef Richard Ptacnik. **Known for:** great waterfront location; buzzy weekend atmosphere; incredible pasta. $ *Average main: A$44* ✉ *Wharf at Woolloomooloo, Area 8, 6 Cowper Wharf Rd., Eastern Suburbs* ☎ *02/9368–7488* ⊕ *www.ottoristorante.com.au.*

PADDINGTON

Buon Ricordo

$$$ | ITALIAN | Walking into this happy, bubbly place is like turning up at a private party in the backstreets of Naples. Host, chef, and surrogate uncle Armando Percuoco invests classic Neapolitan and Tuscan techniques with inventive personal touches to produce such dishes as the thinly sliced kingfish with gin and orange, truffled egg pasta, and scampi with saffron sauce and black-ink risotto. **Known for:** friendly staff; great service; stand-out menu. $ *Average main: A$48* ✉ *108 Boundary St., Paddington* ☎ *02/9360–6729* ⊕ *www.buonricordo. com.au* ⊙ *Closed Sun. and Mon. No lunch Tues.–Thurs.*

Four in Hand

$$ | AUSTRALIAN | At this cute, popular little pub in Paddington, chef Colin Fassnidge (an Irishman who emerged as the most controversial guest judge on Australian TV cooking show *My Kitchen Rules*) has been wowing patrons for years with his shared dish for two of slow-braised lamb shoulder with kipfler potatoes, baby carrots, and salsa verde. His whole suckling pig is also a popular Sunday long-lunch treat. **Known for:** relaxed dining; pub-style atmosphere; boozy Sundays. $ *Average main: A$39* ✉ *105 Sutherland St., Paddington* ☎ *02/9326–2254* ⊕ *www.fourinhand. com.au* ⊙ *Closed Mon.*

WOOLLAHRA

Bistro Moncur

$$ | FRENCH | This bistro in the Woollahra Hotel spills over with happy-go-lucky

Continued on page 130

3

Sydney INNER CITY AND THE EASTERN SUBURBS

Australia's
Modern
Cuisine

It may be referred to as the land down under, but the culinary movement that's sweeping Australia means this country has come out on top. Modern Australian cuisine has transformed the land of Vegemite sandwiches and shrimp-on-the-barbie into a culinary Promised Land with local flavors, organic produce, and bountiful seafood, fashioned by chefs who remain unburdened by restrictive traditions.

Australia is fast proving to be one of the most exciting destinations in the world for food lovers. With its stunning natural bounty, multicultural inspirations, and young culinary innovators, it ticks off all the requisite foodie boxes.

In Sydney, chefs are dishing up new twists on various traditions, creating a Modern Australian (Mod Oz) cuisine with its own compelling style. Traditional bush tucker, for example, has been transformed from a means of survival into a gourmet experience. Spicy Asian flavors have been borrowed from the country's neighbors to the north, and homage has been paid to the precision and customs brought by Australia's early European settlers.

The diversity of the modern Australian culinary movement also means that it is more than just flavors: it's an experience. And one that can be obtained from the award-winning luxury restaurant down to the small Thai-style canteens, pubs, and outdoor cafés.

While purists might argue that Mod Oz cuisine is little more than a plagiarism of flavors and cultures, others will acknowledge it as unadulterated fare with a fascinating history of its very own. Either way, it still offers a dining experience that's unique from anywhere else in the world.

MENU DECODER

Barbie: barbeque | Snags: sausages | Chook: chicken | Vegemite: salty yeast spread | Lamington: small chocolate sponge cake with coconut | Pavlova: meringue dessert topped with cream and fruit | Floater: meat pie with mushy peas and gravy | Damper: simple bread cooked on a campfire | Sanga: sandwich | Cuppa: cup of tea | Tucker: food | Chips: French fries | Tomato sauce: ketchup | Muddy: mud crab | Prawn: shrimp

Seared tuna with avocado, cilantro, and black sesame seeds, topped with caviar

BUSH TUCKER

Bush Tucker fond; Tropical rainforest fruits on paper bark

BACK THEN

Native Australian plants and animals have played a vital role in the diets of the Aboriginal people for more than 50,000 years. Generally referred to as bush tucker, these native fruits, nuts, seeds, vegetables, meats, and fish are harvested around the country—from arid deserts to coastal areas and tropical rainforests.

Once little more than a means of survival, today they're touted as gourmet ingredients. And you certainly don't need to go "walkabout" to find them.

RIGHT NOW

Bush tucker has undergone much transformation over the decades, experiencing a renaissance in recent years. Heavily influenced by multicultural cooking techniques, game meats such as emu and wallaby have been elevated from bush-stew ingredients to perfectly seared cuts of meat garnished with seasonal herbs and vegetables. Kangaroo is making its way into stir-fries and curries, while crocodile—once cooked over coals on the campfire—is now served as carpaccio, tempura, or curry, among the many preparations. Seafood, like rock lobster and barramundi, can be found in humble fish-and-chip shops and top-notch eateries.

Of course, bush tucker isn't just about the protein. Native spices, wild fruits, and indigenous nuts have found favor in countless culinary applications. Lemon myrtle leaves lend a lemony flavor to baked goods and savory dishes. Alpine pepper, a crushed herb, gives foods a fiery zing. Quandong is a wild plum-like fruit with subtle apricot flavor. It once was dried as a portable energy source but now is made into jams and pie fillings. Kakadu plums are made into "super" juices with enormous vitamin C content. Bush tomatoes also have become popular in jams and sauces, and are available in

Witchetty grub

Tandoori kangaroo

INDIGENOUS MEATS

CAMEL: With some one million camels in Australia, camel is fast being served up on many menus, though most are in the Northern Territory. The meat is often compared to mutton and has a similar taste and texture to beef.

CROCODILE: This meat may be fish-like in texture and appearance, but it tastes similar to chicken. The most popular cut is the tail, however legs and meat from the body are also consumed. Crocodile is growing in popularity because of its delicate flavor and versatility. It is often fried and grilled, but may be served raw in carpaccio or sushi rolls.

EMU: Although it's fowl, emu meat is similar in texture and flavor to beef with a light flavor and slight gamey tones on the palate. The meat is high in iron and very low in fat and cholesterol. Typical cuts include rump, strip loin, and oyster filet. It may be served pan-seared or lightly grilled.

KANGAROO: A dark red meat, it is extremely lean with only about 2% fat. The filet or rump is best eaten rare to medium rare, and is typically seared, barbecued, or stir-fried. Young kangaroo meat tastes like beef, while aged cuts take on a gamier flavor.

WALLABY: A cousin to the kangaroo, this meat has a somewhat milder flavor. It is a rich burgundy color and is best prepared with simple, delicate cooking styles, such as barbecuing or pan frying.

WITCHETTY GRUB: The larvae of ghost moths, these grubs are eaten raw or barbecued. People describe the taste as similar to egg, with the texture of a prawn.

supermarkets. Native nuts include the bunya nut, which is chestnut-like with pine notes, the shells of which are used for smoking meat. Macadamia nuts, meanwhile, are among the country's biggest exports.

WHERE TO FIND IT

Despite the presence of numerous bush ingredients in Sydney restaurants, the modern bush tucker dining experience is more prominent in the northern parts of the country. You are most likely to find dishes such as kangaroo, and occasionally crocodile, on the menu of restaurants in the city's main tourist precincts of The Rocks and Circular Quay.

In Queensland and the Northern Territory, you'll find full degustation menus combining local meats and seafood with native herbs, spices, and berries. Some even offer tasting tours of their kitchen gardens where you can sample popular flavors like lemon myrtle, tarragon, and hibiscus flower straight from the bush.

Simple meal of grilled camel with vegetables

UPDATED EUROPEAN FARE

Seafood Salad

BACK THEN

Although the foundation of Mod Oz cuisine stems from the arrival of early British settlers, the food scene has certainly steamed ahead since the days of boiled beef and damper.

The real progression of modern Australian food came after World War II, when European immigrants brought a new wave of cooking to the country. It was the French and Italians who really opened the eyes of Australians with their distinguished flavors, commitment to freshness, and masterful culinary techniques. They also laid the foundations for some of the finest vineyards and cheese makers in the country.

RIGHT NOW

Though small, there are still degrees of British influence in modern Australian cooking, albeit slightly updated. The quintessential English meat pie is now filled with ingredients such as Murray cod, lamb, bush tomato, and kangaroo. Traditional Sunday roasts and fish-and-chips spring up in pubs and cafes, but often with a twist. And tea is still a staple on the breakfast table with a true Aussie favorite, Vegemite on toast.

Poaching, roasting, and braising are now popular methods to cook everything from reef fish and yabbies to lamb, suckling pig, and rabbit. Omelettes, cassoulets, and soufflés as well as pasta, risotto, and gnocchi are very well suited to the country's prize-winning meats, vegetables, and seafood. And the rigorous use of garlic, saffron, basil, and tarragon is common in many kitchens.

Greeks, Germans, and Spaniards have also greatly influenced dining, with tapas bars, tavernas, and schnitzel houses well represented throughout the country. Middle Eastern and North African flavors are also beginning to leave their marks.

Even casual pubs are updating dishes to reflect ethnic influences

Aussie meat pie

AUSTRALIA'S NATURAL BOUNTY

CHEESE FRUIT: Grown in tropical areas, this fruit high in vitamin C has long been used for medicinal purposes. It's eaten while still green since it has a distinct rotting cheese smell when ripe. Leaves can also be eaten raw or cooked.

ILLAWARRA PLUMS: Usually used in jams and chutneys or as a rich sauce to accompany kangaroo, venison, or emu. High in antioxidants, they have a subtle plum flavor with a hint of pine.

LEMON MYRTLE: A native tree with a citrus fragrance and flavor. Leaves can be used fresh or dried and ground in sweet and savory styles of cooking.

MACADAMIA NUTS: Known as Kindal Kindal by native Australians, the macadamia is a round white nut with a hard brown shell and creamy flavor.

MUNTRIES: Small berry-like fruit that have a distinct apple flavor. Also known as emu apples, they can be eaten fresh in salads or added to desserts.

PAPER BARK: Papery leaves from the Mellaluca tree, used to cook meat and seafood.

QUANDONG: A bright red fruit similar to a native peach. It's commonly used to make jams and sauces.

WARRIGAL GREENS: A herb-like vegetable with a flavor similar to spinach. They must be well cooked to eliminate their toxic oxalate content.

WATTLESEED: Also known as acacia seeds. They have a nutty to coffee-like flavor and are very high in protein. Often ground down and used in baking.

and local products. It's not unusual to see items like spicy chorizo pizza and Peking Duck pizza on their menus.

Another hallmark of Mod Oz cuisine—and one that parallels America's current culinary trends—is its fascination with seasonal vegetables and organic meats. Specialist farms raising free-range poultry and livestock have become extremely popular with many restaurants throughout the country. Menus often cite an ingredient's producer, i.e. "Blackmore's wagyu bresaola," and also note whether ingredients are "pasture-raised" or "locally grown."

The "paddock to plate" philosophy is getting more attention from top restaurateurs. This means a restaurant aims to source its produce from farmers and producers within their community, ensuring transport miles stay low while food is fresh and region-specific. Some establishments go a step further by growing and harvesting produce on-site in their own kitchen gardens.

Meringue topped with fresh fruit

ASIAN FUSION

Thai-style kangaroo curry

BACK THEN

Much has changed in the way of Asian food in Australia. Sixty years ago sushi didn't exist in the vocabulary, now there are Japanese restaurants on almost every street.

The Gold Rush of the mid-19th century brought an influx of Chinese immigrants to Australia, prompting Asian cuisine's humble beginnings here. Thai, Vietnamese, Indian, Malaysian, and Japanese migrants followed in various waves in the 20th century. Before long, a cuisine that had started out in family-run restaurants in the outer suburbs of Sydney had become a burgeoning new trend. And by the late 1990s the children of the first wave of immigrants had formed the new guard.

RIGHT NOW

Traditional Chinese, Thai, and Japanese restaurants are very popular in Australia. But Asian fusion restaurants are leading the charge in creating Australia-specific taste innovations. Asian fusion cuisine combines the traditional flavors of Thai, Chinese, Japanese, and Vietnamese cooking, using local Australian ingredients and Western culinary techniques. Chic contemporary interiors, often with long communal tables and shared dishes, are the latest trend. Robust herbs such as mint and coriander, fiery chili, zesty black vinegar, ginger, and pickled vegetables are core ingredients, often wok-fried with fresh Australian ingredients such as Barossa Valley chicken, Thirlmere duck, or Bangalow pork.

Leading the charge is world-renowned, Sydney-based chef Tetsuya Wakuda. His signature dish, a confit of Petuna Tasmanian Ocean Trout with konbu, apple, daikon, and wasabi is a prime example of Asian fusion, uniquely blending French techniques with his Japanese heritage and excellent Australian products.

Yet, smaller modern canteen-style eateries are also serving up

Red chile peppers

Rock Lobsters

LOCAL FISH AND SEAFOOD

ABALONE: A large sea snail with an edible muscular foot. It has a firm, rubbery texture with a very delicate flavor and can retail for about $100 per kilogram. Abalone are often seared or fried.

BALMAIN OR MORETON BAY BUGS: A smaller relative of the rock lobster with a short tail, flat head, and bug-like eyes. They have a sweet taste and a medium texture. A favorite served cold in salads and seafood platters, or split down the middle and grilled.

BARRAMUNDI: A member of the perch family, it's a highly versatile fish with a medium to firm flesh and white to light pink tones. Native to Australia, it lives in both fresh and salt waters and is farmed as well as caught in the wild.

ROCK LOBSTERS: A spiny lobster with long antennae and no claws. The four main types—eastern, southern, western, and tropical—each offer slightly different flavours and textures. The tropical are excellent as sashimi, while the eastern, southern and western lend themselves to baking and barbecue.

SYDNEY ROCK OYSTERS: Despite their name, these bivalves are commonly found throughout the east coast. They're prized for their distinct rich and creamy flavor, and are smaller in size than Pacific oysters. Try eating them raw with a squirt of lemon.

YABBIES: A fresh-water crayfish with firm white flesh and a sweeter taste than rock lobster. Small in size, they can be tricky to eat but are worth the effort. They're often cooked simply in a pot of salted, boiling water.

contemporary Asian fare that provides excellent quality at a fraction of the price. It's in these bustling restaurants that flavors and dishes such as shucked oyster with chili and galangal vinaigrette, roasted duck in coconut curry, wagyu-beef hotpot, soft-shell crab with chili jam, and green curry of barramundi bounce off their plates.

While the majority of Asian fusion food in Australia relies heavily on light cooking styles and fresh ingredients, clay pot cooking as well as heavier-style Malaysian and Indian curries, such as rendang and vindaloo made with local lamb and beef, are also becoming popular.

Asian influences have also made their mark on traditional seafood restaurants, where ginger, lime, coriander, and chili add extra zing to alfresco menus. Exquisite dishes include Japanese-inspired butter-grilled scallops, steamed mussels in Thai-style coconut broth, or ocean trout grilled with garlic, soy, and chili.

Salad of yabby tails

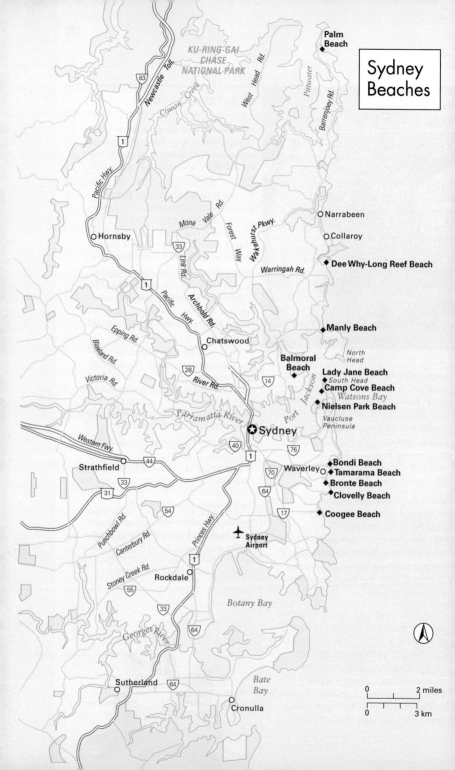

Palm Beach

KU-RING-GAI CHASE NATIONAL PARK

Newcastle Toll

Cowan Creek

West Head Rd.

Pittwater

Barrenjoey Rd.

83

1

Pacific Hwy.

Mona Vale Rd.

Forest Way

Wakehurst Pkwy.

O Narrabeen

Hornsby

O Collaroy

33

Warringah Rd.

◆ **Dee Why-Long Reef Beach**

Link Rd.

Pacific Hwy.

Archbold Rd.

1

Epping Rd.

Blaxland Rd.

Victoria Rd.

Chatswood

River Rd.

28

◆ **Manly Beach**

North Head

Balmoral Beach

14

Lady Jane Beach
◆ *South Head*
Camp Cove Beach
Watsons Bay
◆ **Nielsen Park Beach**

Parramatta River

Port Jackson

Vaucluse Peninsula

★ Sydney

40

76

Western Fwy.

44

Strathfield

Waverley ○

70

◆**Bondi Beach**
◆ **Tamarama Beach**
◆ **Bronte Beach**
◆**Clovelly Beach**

31

33

54

64

◆ **Coogee Beach**

17

Punchbowl Rd.

Canterbury Rd.

Princes Hwy.

✈ Sydney Airport

Stoney Creek Rd.

Rockdale

1

55

Botany Bay

33

64

Georges River

Sutherland

64

Bate Bay

Cronulla

Sydney Beaches

0 ——— 2 miles
0 ——— 3 km

›atrons—mostly locals from around the eafy suburb of Woollahra—who have ›een coming back for more than 20 ›ears now. The best dishes are inspired akes on Parisian fare, like the grilled Sirloin Café de Paris, French onion soufflé ;ratin, and port sausages with potato ›uree and Lyonnaise onions, although he signature dish you must try is the nuch-loved, twice-cooked soufflé. **Known or:** great atmosphere; friendly staff; :aters to a long lunch. [$] *Average main: A$42* ✉ *Woollahra Hotel, 116 Queen St., Noollahra* ☎ *02/9327–9713* 🌐 *woollahra-otel.com.au.*

:hiswick

| **MODERN AUSTRALIAN** | Few central Syd-ıey restaurants have access to their own ıomegrown produce, but here in trendy ınd leafy Woollahra—just a few kilome-ers east of the city—is an all-white and efreshingly bright restaurant surrounded ›y formal gardens and a large kitchen jarden. Chiswick is all about stylish :asual dining using the freshest of pro-luce and a wonderful place to linger over long lunch on a sunny day. **Known for:** ıearty meals; lively atmosphere; great vine list. [$] *Average main: A$34* ✉ *65 Ocean St., Woollahra* ☎ *02/8388–8688* 🌐 *www.chiswickrestaurant.com.au.*

SURRY HILLS

:hin Chin Sydney

:$$ | **ASIAN** | For a long time, those vanting to experience Chin Chin had to ıead to Melbourne. But in 2016, a sister estaurant finally opened its doors in Sur-y Hills, and it has since elbowed its way o epicurean cult status among foodies. **Known for:** superior Southeast Asian food; ›uzzy atmosphere; cult following so ›acked on weekends. [$] *Average main: A$50* ✉ *69 Commonwealth St., Surry Hills* ☎ *02/9281–3322* 🌐 *www.chinchin-restaurant.com.au/sydney.*

Four ate Five

$ | **CAFÉ** | This buzzy little café serves some of the best breakfasts in Surry Hills, which is really saying something as there is plenty of stiff competition in this part of town. Come here for the house-made muesli and organic yogurt or fuel up with the 485—egg, hummus, feta, pilpelchuma chili paste, Israeli pickles, and red cabbage salad on a bagel or pret-zel—and wash it down with some ginger turmeric kombucha. **Known for:** espresso coffee; desserts; relaxed atmosphere. [$] *Average main: A$16* ✉ *485 Crown St., Surry Hills* ☎ *02/9698–6485* 🌐 *fourate-five.com* 🕒 *No dinner.*

★ Longrain

$$ | **THAI** | It's always a fun night at this fashionable post-industrial Thai eatery because you never know who you'll end up meeting at the large communal table. The generous-size innovative mains—some say the best Thai food in town—are designed to be shared. **Known for:** trendy eatery; great service; extensive cocktail list. [$] *Average main: A$36* ✉ *85 Commonwealth St., Surry Hills* ☎ *02/9280–2888* 🌐 *www.longrain.com* 🕒 *No lunch Sat.–Thurs.*

BONDI BEACH

Bronte Belo

$ | **BRAZILIAN** | One of eight or nine eateries in the buzzy café strip opposite Bronte Beach, this is a great place to refuel after the Bondi-to-Bronte clifftop walk. All share the same postcard-perfect view, but Bello is worth seeking out for its consistently good coffee and spicy sticky chai. **Known for:** relaxed dining experience; brilliant breakfast spot; gets busy. [$] *Average main: A$23* ✉ *469 Bronte Rd., Bronte* ☎ *02/9369–5673* 🌐 *brontebelo.com.*

Brown Sugar

$ | **MODERN AUSTRALIAN** | You have to seek out this Bondi Beach restaurant, as it's situated several hundred feet back from the beach. You'll quickly find out, how-ever, why locals love this place: organic, seasonal, handcrafted food. **Known for:** wholesome food; focus on health; great location near beach. $ *Average main: A\$35* ⊠ *106 Curlewis St., Bondi Beach* ☎ *02/9130–1566* ⊕ *www.brownsugarbondi.com.au* ⊘ *Closed Mon. No breakfast or lunch Tues.–Thurs.*

The Bucket List

$ | SEAFOOD |FAMILY | In the famous buttercup-yellow Bondi Pavilion, this beachfront restaurant has broad appeal—there are gatherings of families having brunch; lunchers enjoying the spectacular views; twentysomethings in for an early evening cocktail at the swanky bar; and couples tucking into seafood under the stars. A bucket of Australian tiger prawns are there to be shared; larger dishes include fish-and-chips, hake, and fish burger with fries. **Known for:** lively day and night; casual feeds; beachfront location. $ *Average main: A\$29* ⊠ *Bondi Pavillion, Shop 1, Queen Elizabeth Dr., Bondi Beach* ☎ *02/9365–4122* ⊕ *www.thebucketlistbondi.com* ⊘ *No dinner Mon. and Tues.* ☞ *No bookings taken for outside areas.*

Catalina Restaurant

$$$ | SEAFOOD | This harbor-front restaurant occupies the site of the old "airport" (back in the days when the fastest way to get to England was by flying boat), and has ringside views of the harbor and Shark Island. Patrons can watch modern seaplanes take off and land just meters away while dining on fine seafood. **Known for:** formal dining; special occasions; incredible views. $ *Average main: A\$48* ⊠ *Lyne Park, New South Head Rd., Rose Bay* ☎ *02/9371–0555* ⊕ *www.catalinarosebay.com.au* ⊘ *No dinner Sun.*

★ Icebergs Dining Room and Bar

$$$ | ITALIAN | The fashionable and famous (including celebrities like Mick Jagger and Paris Hilton) just adore perching like seagulls over the swimming pool at the south end of Australia's most famous beach. It is one of the must-visit restaurants in Sydney, for both the sensational view and the exquisite food. **Known for:** Bondi institution; amazing views of Bondi and the beach; superior food and drinks.

$ *Average main: A\$48* ⊠ *1 Notts Ave., Bondi Beach* ☎ *02/9365–9000* ⊕ *idrb.com* ⊘ *Closed Mon.*

North Bondi Fish

$ | AUSTRALIAN | Celeb-chef Matt Moran's much-celebrated beachfront fish-and-chips offering is so much more than just standard fish-and-chips. It's located under the North Bondi RSL and attracts a devoted and lively clientele. **Known for:** busy and popular spot; oceanfront location; fun atmosphere. $ *Average main: A\$35* ⊠ *120 Ramsgate Ave., Sydney* ☎ *02/9130–2155* ⊕ *www.northbondifish.com.au.*

Sean's Panaroma

$$ | AUSTRALIAN | North Bondi Beach wouldn't be the same without Sean's Panaroma ("Sean's" to locals), perched on a slight rise a stone's throw from the famous beach. It's been there since the mid-1990s and owner Sean Moran loads his menu with fresh produce grown on his farm in the Blue Mountains, aptly named "Farm Panaroma." Dishes change regularly and are only featured on a black board: they may include baked blue-eye fish with roasted cauliflower, or a ravioli of zucchini, mozzarella, and lemons. **Known for:** great seafood dishes; average service; great atmosphere. $ *Average main: A\$45* ⊠ *270 Campbell Parade, Bondi Beach* ☎ *02/9365–4924* ⊕ *www.seanspanaroma.co* ⊘ *No dinner Sun.–Tues. No lunch Mon.–Thurs.*

🛏 Hotels

PADDINGTON

Arts Hotel Sydney

$ | HOTEL | On a quiet stretch in the trendy shopping precinct of Paddington, this small, friendly, family-run hotel has simple accommodations at an outstanding price. **Pros:** great value; personal service; warm feel. **Cons:** simply appointed rooms; dated interiors throughout; limited breakfast options. $ *Rooms from: A\$185* ⊠ *21 Oxford St., Paddington* ☎ *02/9361–0211*

🌐 *www.artshotel.com.au* 🛏 *64 rooms* 🍴 *No meals.*

DARLINGHURST

Medusa

$$$ | **HOTEL** | If you're tired of the standard travelers' rooms, this renovated Victorian terrace house may be just the tonic. **Pros:** good location; flashy design; warm service; kichenettes in every room; entry to off-site pool and gym; pet-friendly. **Cons:** urban location may get noisy; not much privacy due to small size; funky interiors might not be to everyone's taste. [$] *Rooms from: A$310* ✉ *267 Darlinghurst Rd., Darlinghurst* ☎ *02/9331–1000* 🌐 *www.medusa.com.au* 🛏 *18 rooms* 🍴 *No meals.*

KINGS CROSS

Hotel 59 & Cafe

$ | **B&B/INN** | In its character as well as its dimensions, this friendly B&B on a quiet part of a bar- and club-lined street is reminiscent of a European *pensione.* Simple, tastefully outfitted rooms come with high-quality beds and linens, as well as wooden blinds over the windows. **Pros:** comfortable rooms; free Wi-Fi and a cooked breakfast. **Cons:** simply appointed; half-hour to the city center; interiors look dated. [$] *Rooms from: A$135* ✉ *59 Bayswater Rd., Kings Cross* ☎ *02/9360–5900* 🌐 *www.hotel59.com.au* 🛏 *9 rooms* 🍴 *Free breakfast.*

SURRY HILLS

★ Paramount House Hotel

$$$ | **HOTEL** | Set in Sydney's trendy dining and drinking hot spot of Surry Hills and sharing the former headquarters of Paramount Pictures with the Golden Age Cinema and Bar, Paramount Coffee Project, a rooftop recreation center, and a co-working office space, Paramanount House Hotel's loft-like rooms with plant-filled balconies is the coolest place to stay and play in Sydney. **Pros:** stylish design throughout; superior cocktails, coffee, and cinema on-site; close to dining and nightlife. **Cons:** reception is through busy café; no on-site dining option yet; no nearby rail. [$] *Rooms from: A$350* ✉ *80 Commonwealth St., Surry Hills* ☎ *2/9211–1222* 🌐 *paramounthousehotel.com* 🛏 *29 rooms* 🍴 *No meals.*

POTTS POINT

De Vere Hotel

$ | **HOTEL** | "Simply comfortable and affordable" is the slogan at this 1920s-style hotel at the leafy end of Potts Point, and it's hard to disagree on either count. **Pros:** good value; spacious rooms; friendly staff. **Cons:** breakfast, although available on-site, is no longer included in rate. [$] *Rooms from: A$127* ✉ *44–46 Macleay St., Potts Point* ☎ *02/9358–1211* 🌐 *www.devere.com.au* 🛏 *118 rooms* 🍴 *No meals.*

★ Simpsons of Potts Point

$$ | **HOTEL** | This luxurious boutique hotel is the gem of inner Sydney. **Pros:** friendly, elegant, and cozy; free Wi-Fi and use of computers; limited free parking. **Cons:** no elevator; 20-minute walk to city center; can get noisy due to location. [$] *Rooms from: A$255* ✉ *8 Challis Ave., Potts Point* ☎ *02/9356–2199* 🌐 *www.simpsonshotel.com.au* 🛏 *11 rooms, 1 suite* 🍴 *Free breakfast.*

★ Spicers Potts Point

$$$ | **B&B/INN** | Set over three adjoining Victorian terraces on a tree-lined street close to Kings Cross and Potts Points, Spicers Potts Point combines heritage charm with modern elegance for a cool and calming retreat right in the middle of things. **Pros:** modern, elegant design; inner-city sanctuary; convenient to the Harbour and CBD. **Cons:** street parking; not family-friendly; no gym or restaurant on-site. [$] *Rooms from: A$400* ✉ *122 Victoria St., Sydney* ☎ *1300/525442* 🌐 *www.spicerspottspoint.com* 🛏 *20 rooms* 🍴 *No meals.*

RUSHCUTTERS BAY
Vibe Hotel Rushcutters
$$ | HOTEL | This good-value hotel fronting a lovely harborside park is a more peaceful alternative to staying in Kings Cross, but still within walking distance of the restaurants and bars of the buzzy nightlife strip. **Pros:** bayside location; quieter alternative to Kings Cross; good value. **Cons:** small rooms; 50-minute walk into the city. $ *Rooms from: A$187* ✉ *100 Bayswater Rd., Potts Point* ☎ *02/8353–8988* ⊕ *www.tfehotels.com* ⇨ *245 rooms* ❄ *No meals.*

WOOLLOOMOOLOO
Ovolo Woolloomooloo
$$$$ | HOTEL | This ultrahip hotel occupies a former wool shipping shed that includes authentic structures of the former wharf (pulleys, giant trusses, and brontosaurus-like machinery), a great location (a stone's throw from the Opera House), and the chance to be on the harbor but in a quieter location. **Pros:** large bathrooms, high-end tech; trendy bar, trendier location. **Cons:** a bit of walk into the city; foyer is freezing in the winter; breakfast is an expensive add-on. $ *Rooms from: A$459* ✉ *Wharf at Woolloomooloo, 6 Cowper Wharf Rd., Woolloomooloo* ☎ *02/9331–9000* ⊕ *www.ovolohotels.com.au/ovolowoolloomooloo* ⇨ *136 rooms* ❄ *No meals.*

BONDI BEACH
Adina Apartment Hotel Bondi Beach
$$$ | HOTEL | This hotel apartment complex, several hundred feet from Bondi Beach, includes more than a dozen restaurants, bars, and stores. **Pros:** great location; spacious apartments; part of a trendy complex. **Cons:** fee for parking. $ *Rooms from: A$349* ✉ *69–73 Hall St., Bondi Beach* ☎ *02/9300–4800* ⊕ *www.adinahotels.com.au* ⇨ *111 rooms* ❄ *No meals.*

QT Bondi
$$$ | HOTEL | Boutique hotel meets cool apartment, QT Bondi is for the modern traveler who cares less about spas, gyms, and room service, and more about a great location, creative design, and considered home-away-from-home amenities (which at QT Bondi means everything from kitchenettes with dishwashers and washing machines to shoehorns and beachbags). **Pros:** close to beach and great cafés and restaurants; kitchenettes; quirky, cool design. **Cons:** can be noisy; no swimming pool; no restaurant on-site. $ *Rooms from: A$410* ✉ *6 Beach Rd., Bondi Beach* ☎ *2/8362–3900* ⊕ *www.qthotelsandresorts.com* ⇨ *69 rooms* ❄ *No meals.*

COOGEE
Crowne Plaza Coogee Beach
$$$ | HOTEL | Live like a local at Coogee Beach, which is just as gorgeous as nearby Bondi, but without the crowds. **Pros:** great location; some rooms have balconies with ocean views; good value for beachfront accommodations. **Cons:** fee for parking; incredibly busy foyer; rooms a little dated. $ *Rooms from: A$345* ✉ *242 Arden St., Coogee* ☎ *02/9315–7600* ⊕ *www.crowneplazacoogee.com.au* ⇨ *209 rooms* ❄ *No meals.*

🍸 Nightlife

BARS AND DANCE CLUBS
Beach Road Hotel
BARS/PUBS | This Bondi institution is famous for its Sunday Sessions, when locals come to enjoy a barbecue, drink, and dance in the outdoor courtyard. There's music every night in summer (except Monday), good affordable food, and a A$20 roast with all the trimmings on Sunday night. ✉ *71 Beach Rd., Bondi Beach* ☎ *02/9130–7247* ⊕ *www.beachroadbondi.com.au.*

★ Eau de Vie
BARS/PUBS | You might have to seek them out but there are quite a few speakeasy-style bars sprinkled around Sydney. Eau de Vie, at the rear of the trendy Kirketon Hotel in Darlinghurst, perfectly fits

he bill, especially with its cocktail menu. 's designed as a journey through the heater, with a "Shakespeare" touching n a yuzu mule with vodka, honey, and uzu curd (A$20). There's also the "Carhen" cocktail from a Night At The Opera, vith gin, sherry, and rosemary poured ver crushed ice. Drinks are a little ricey, but the bar staff and the patrons re friendly and the jazz-infused music akes the pain out of the bill. There's a bar nack menu, too. ⊠ *229 Darlinghurst Rd., Darlinghurst* ☎ *02/8646-4930* ⊕ *www. audevie.com.au.*

COMEDY CLUBS

he Comedy Store

COMEDY CLUBS | The city's oldest comedy lub is in a plush 300-seat theater in he Entertainment Quarter, which most eople still refer to as Fox Studios (its ormer name). The difficult-to-find theater s at the rear of the complex, close to the arking lot. Shows are Thursday–Saturday t 8:30 pm, and admission is usually round A$30. ⊠ *Entertainment Quarter, 22 Lang Rd., Bldg. 207, Centennial Park* ☎ *02/9357-1419* ⊕ *www.comedystore. com.au.*

GAY AND LESBIAN BARS AND CLUBS

Most of the city's gay and lesbian venues re along Oxford Street, in Darlinghurst. The free *Sydney Star Observer*, available long Oxford Street, has a roundup of Sydney's gay and lesbian goings-on, or heck the magazine's website (⊕ *www. starobserver.com.au*). A monthly free magazine, *Lesbians on the Loose* ⊕ *www.lotl.com*), lists events for women.,

ARQ

BARS/PUBS | Sydney's biggest, best-looking, and funkiest gay nightclub, ARQ ttracts a clean-cut crowd who like to whip off their shirts as soon as they hear he beat. (Some women head here, too.) There are multiple dance floors, a bar, nd plenty of chrome and sparkly lighting. It's open from 9 pm until whenever

Have A Gay Old Time

If you're in Sydney in late February and early March, you'll think the whole city has gone gay. The Sydney Gay and Lesbian Mardi Gras parade, which began as a gay rights protest march in 1978, is one of Australia's major events. Dozens of floats covered with buff dancers make their way from College Street, near St. Mary's Cathedral, up Oxford Street to Taylor's Square. Thousands of spectators watch this amazing party parade.

Thursday through Sunday; a Thursday night drag contest is free and so is entry on a Friday night, while shows have a cover charge ranging from A$15 to A$25 (and sometimes a little more). ⊠ *16 Flinders St., Darlinghurst* ☎ *02/9380–8700* ⊕ *www.arqsydney.com.au.*

Stonewall Hotel

MUSIC CLUBS | Set over three floors, with drag acts, DJs, and incredible dancers putting on shows throughout the evening until the early hours of the morning, the Stonewall is *the* place to get your dance on. While the drinks are cheap, the service is slow, so pack your patience. Admission varies depending on the time of arrival. Get in before midnight and it's free, unless there's an extra-special show on that night. ⊠ *175 Oxford St., Darlinghurst* ☎ *2/9360–1963* ⊕ *stonewallhotel. com.*

PUBS WITH MUSIC

Harold Park Hotel

BARS/PUBS | This is a great comedy venue that also serves up excellent jazz, pop, rock, and blues performances on Sunday afternoon, often featuring artists playing in Australia's top world music and blues festivals when they are in town. Often the performances are free. Comedy nights (around A$10 to A$15 for a performance) are held on Tuesday and Friday at 8 pm; international comedy stars have been known to drop into the pub when they're in town (and do a spot of stand-up). ⊠ *70A Ross St., Glebe* ☎ *02/9660–4745.*

Unity Hall Hotel

BARS/PUBS | This quaint pub in the left-of-center suburb of Balmain declares itself the "spiritual home of jazz and live music for the past 40 years." Its resident jazz band has been playing there since 1970, and you can hear them for free each Sunday at 4 pm (except for the first Sunday of the month, when another jazz band takes their place). A variety of live music including pop, rock, swing, and blues is also on the bill. Music cranks up on Friday and Saturday night from 9 pm. The pub attracts a friendly, unpretentious crowd and supports up-and-coming bands. ⊠ *292 Darling St., Balmain* ☎ *02/9810–1331* ⊕ *www.unityhallhotel. com.au.*

🛍 Shopping

ART AND CRAFT GALLERIES

Cooee Aboriginal Art

ART GALLERIES | This gallery, open Tuesday–Saturday 10–5, exhibits and sells high-end Aboriginal paintings, sculptures, and limited-edition prints. It's a five-minute walk from Bondi Beach. ⊠ *31 Lamrock Ave., Bondi Beach* ☎ *02/9300–9233* ⊕ *www.cooeeart.com.au.*

BOOKS

Gertrude & Alice Café Bookshop

BOOKS/STATIONERY | Need something to read on Bondi Beach? Take a stroll to Gertrude & Alice Café Bookshop, named in honor of lovers Gertrude Stein and Alice B. Toklas. Always buzzing with people, it's a great place to sip coffee or chai lattes, or have lunch while perusing the mostly secondhand books. ⊠ *46 Hall St., Bondi Beach* ☎ *02/9130–5155.*

CLOTHING

Belinda

CLOTHING | This is where Sydney's female fashionistas go when there's a dress-up occasion looming. From her namesake store that scores high marks for innovation and imagination, former model Belinda Seper sells nothing but the very latest designs off the catwalks. ⊠ *8 Transvaal Ave., Double Bay* ☎ *02/9328–6288* ⊕ *www.belinda.com.au.*

Scanlan & Theodore

CLOTHING | This is the Sydney outlet for one of Melbourne's most distinguished fashion houses. Designs take their cues from Europe, with superbly tailored women's knitwear, suits, and stylishly glamorous evening wear. ⊠ *Bay St., Double Bay, Paddington* ☎ *02/9328–4886* ⊕ *www.scanlantheodore.com.*

DEPARTMENT STORES AND SHOPPING CENTERS

Oxford Street

SHOPPING CENTERS/MALLS | Nicknamed the "Style Mile," Paddington's main artery, from South Dowling Street east to Queen Street, Woollahra, is dressed to thrill. Lined with boutiques, home-furnishings stores, and cafés, it's a perfect venue for watching the never-ending fashion parade. Take Bus No. 380, 382, or 333 from Circular Quay. ⊠ *Oxford St., Paddington.*

MARKETS

★ Bondi Markets

OUTDOOR/FLEA/GREEN MARKETS | This relaxed and friendly beachside market at Bondi is the place to go for clothes—vintage or by up-and-coming designers—plus handmade jewelry, organic cosmetics, art, retro furniture, and secondhand goods. Look closely at the faces in the crowd, you'll often find visiting celebrities lurking behind messy bed hair and dark glasses. The markets are on every Sunday 10–4. ⊠ *Bondi Beach Public School, Campbell Parade, Bondi Beach* ☎ *02/9315–7011* ⊕ *www.bondimarkets. com.au.*

Aboriginal artwork is a visual representation of ancestral stories from "The Dreaming."

★ Paddington Markets

OUTDOOR/FLEA/GREEN MARKETS | About 200 stalls crammed with clothing, plants, crafts, jewelry, and souvenirs fill this busy churchyard market (sometimes called Paddington Bazaar). Distinctly New Age and highly fashion-conscious, the market is an outlet for a handful of avant-garde clothing designers. Go early as it can get very crowded. ⊠ *Paddington Uniting Church, 395 Oxford St., Paddington* ☎ *02/9331–2923* ⊕ *www.paddingtonmarkets.com.au.*

🏃 Activities

AUSTRALIAN RULES FOOTBALL

Sydney Cricket Ground

FOOTBALL | A fast, demanding game in which the ball can be kicked or punched between teams of 22 players, Australian Rules Football has won a major audience in Sydney, even though the city has only one professional team—the Sydney Swans—compared to the dozen that play in Melbourne—the home of the sport. Sydney Cricket Ground (SCG) hosts games April to September. ⊠ *Centennial Park, Moore Park Rd., Paddington* ☎ *02/9360–6601* ⊕ *www.sydneycricketground.com.au.*

BICYCLING

Sydney's favorite cycling track is Centennial Park's Grand Parade, a 3¾-km (2¼-mile) cycle circuit around the perimeter of this grand, gracious eastern suburbs park.

Centennial Park Cycles

BICYCLING | Rent bicycles here for around A$25 per hour, A$75 per day. There is an additional location inside Centennial Park on Grand Drive. ⊠ *50 Clovelly Rd., Randwick* ☎ *02/9398–5027* ⊕ *www.cyclehire.com.au.*

Sydney Bike Sharing

BICYCLING | **FAMILY** | There are 2,500 dockless bikes around the city, which can be located and activated via a smartphone app (⊕ *www.reddygo.com.au*). ⊠ *City Center* ☎ *02/9265–9333* ⊕ *www.cityofsydney.nsw.gov.*

Sydney Sports 101

Given its climate and its taste for the great outdoors, it's no surprise that Sydney is addicted to sports. In the cooler months rugby league dominates the sporting scene, although these days the Sydney Swans, the city's flag bearer in the national Australian Rules Football (AFL) competition, attract far bigger crowds. In summer cricket is the major spectator sport, and nothing arouses more passion than international test cricket games—especially when Australia plays against England, the traditional enemy. Sydney is well equipped with athletic facilities, from golf courses to tennis courts, and water sports come naturally on one of the world's greatest harbors.

Ticketek. This is the place to buy tickets for major sports events: the telephone line is notorious for being constantly busy, so try online first. ✉ *Sydney* ☎ *13–2849* ⊕ *premier.ticketek. com.au.*

au/explore/getting-around/cycling/ dockless-bike-sharing.

BOATING AND SAILING
EastSail
BOATING | Rent bareboat sailing and motored yachts from this operator for A$295 per half day (four hours); a manned yacht costs around A$1,865 for four hours and includes the skipper. It also conducts sailing schools. ✉ *D'Albora Marina, New Beach Rd., Rushcutters Bay, Eastern Suburbs* ☎ *02/9327–1166* ⊕ *www.eastsail.com.au.*

★ Sydney Harbour Kayaks
BOATING | Sydney Harbour Kayaks rents one- and two-person kayaks. The location beside Spit Bridge has calm water for novices, as well as several beaches and idyllic coves. Prices per hour start from A$20 for a one-person kayak and A$40 for a double. Guided four-hour tours depart every Saturday and Sunday at 8:30 am (A$125 per person). Novices can take part in three-hour free lessons (A$50 for kayak hire). ✉ *81 Parriwi Rd., Mosman* ☎ *02/9969–4590* ⊕ *www.sydneyharbourkayaks.com.au.*

CRICKET
Cricket is Sydney's summer sport, and it's often played in parks throughout the nation. For Australians the pinnacle of excitement is the Ashes, when the national cricket team takes the field against England. It happens every other summer, and the two nations take turns hosting the event. Cricket season runs from October through March.

Sydney Cricket Ground
CRICKET | International and interstate games are played at the Sydney Cricket Ground (commonly called the SCG). ✉ *Centennial Park, Moore Park Rd., Paddington* ☎ *02/9360–6601* ⊕ *www.scgt. nsw.gov.au.*

RUGBY LEAGUE
Sydney Football Stadium
RUGBY | Known locally as football (or footy), rugby league is Sydney's winter addiction. This is a fast, gutsy, physical game that bears some similarities to North American football, although the action is more constant and the ball cannot be passed forward. The season falls between March and September. Sydney Football Stadium (now known by its corporate sponsorship name of

Allianz Stadium) is the home ground of the Sydney Roosters. Other games are played at ANZ Stadium (Sydney Olympic Park) and stadiums throughout the suburbs. ⊠ *Centennial Park, Moore Park Rd., Paddington* ☎ *02/9360–6601* ⊕ *www. scgt.nsw.gov.au.*

SCUBA DIVING
Pro Dive

SCUBA DIVING | Pro Dive is a PADI operator conducting courses and shore- or boat-diving excursions around the harbor and city beaches. Some of the best dive spots—with coral, rock walls, and lots of colorful fish—are close to the eastern suburb beaches of Clovelly and Coogee. The company also has a center in Manly. A four-hour boat dive with a guide costs around A$109, including rental equipment; a learn-to-dive course is A199. Check the website for specials. ⊠ *27 Alfreda St., Coogee* ☎ *02/9665–6363* ⊕ *www.prodive.com.au.*

SURFING
Lets Go Surfing

SURFING | This is a complete surfing resource for anyone who wants to hang five with confidence. Lessons are available for all ages and you can rent or buy boards and wet suits. The two-hour beginner surfer lesson, in a small group, is A$95. ⊠ *128 Ramsgate Ave., North Bondi* ☎ *02/9365–1800* ⊕ *www.letsgo-surfing.com.au.*

Rip Curl

SURFING | This store has a huge variety of boards and surfing supplies, including cool clothes. It's right at Bondi Beach. ⊠ *82 Campbell Parade, Bondi Beach* ☎ *02/9130–2660* ⊕ *www.ripcurl.com.au.*

Surfection Bondi Beach

SURFING | Here is every surfer's idea of retail heaven: surfboards and cool clothing all housed in one huge sparkling store. ⊠ *31 Hall St., Bondi Beach* ☎ *02/9130–1051.*

Greater Sydney

The Greater Sydney area has numerous attractions that can be easily reached by public transport. These include historic townships, the Sydney 2000 Olympics site, national parks where you can explore and enjoy the Australian bush, and wildlife and theme parks that appeal to children.

Other points of interest are the northside beaches, particularly Manly, and the historic city of Parramatta, founded in 1788 and 26 km (16 miles) to the west; and the magnificent Hawkesbury River, which winds its way around the city's western and northern borders. The waterside suburb of Balmain has pubs and restaurants, an atmospheric Saturday flea market, and backstreets full of character.

GETTING HERE AND AROUND
Trains travel from Central Station to Parramatta daily, and directly to Sydney Olympic Park on weekdays. To reach Olympic Park on weekends, take the train to Lidcombe and then change trains for the short ride to Olympic Park station. The RiverCat ferry travels from Circular Quay to Parramatta, calling at Sydney Olympic Park on the way. Trains depart from Central Station for the Hawkesbury River (alight at Hawkesbury River station in the town of Brooklyn). They also travel to the Royal National Park (alight at Engadine or Heathcote stations, or Loftus, where a tram travels from the station to the park on Sunday only).

TIMING
Each of the sights here could easily fill the better part of a day. If you're short on time, try a tour company that combines visits within a particular area—for example, a day trip west to the Olympic Games site, Featherdale Wildlife Park, and the Blue Mountains.

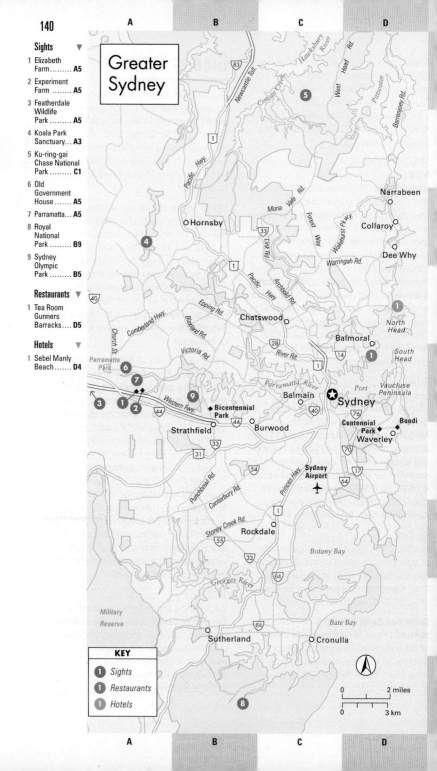

Greater Sydney

Sights

Elizabeth Farm

HOUSE | The oldest European building in Australia, Elizabeth Farm was built by John and Elizabeth Macarthur in 1793. With its simple but elegant lines and long, shady verandas, the house became a template for Australian farmhouses that survives to the present day. It was here, too, that the merino sheep industry began, since the Macarthurs were the first to introduce the tough Spanish breed to Australia. Although John Macarthur has traditionally been credited as the father of Australia's wool industry, it was Elizabeth who largely ran the farm while her husband pursued his official and more-lucrative unofficial duties as an officer in the colony's Rum Corps. Inside are personal objects of the Macarthur family, as well as a re-creation of their furnishings. Free tours are at 11, noon, 1, and 2 each day. ⊠ *70 Alice St., Rosehill* ☎ *02/9635–9488* ⊕ *sydneylivingmuseums.com.au/elizabeth-farm* ⊠ *A$8.*

Experiment Farm

MUSEUM | The site of the first private land grant in Australia, Experiment Farm was settled in 1789 by James Ruse, a former convict who was given 1½ acres by Governor Phillip on condition that he become self-sufficient—a vital experiment if the colony was to survive. Luckily for Phillip, his gamble paid off. The bungalow, with its wide verandas, was built by colonial surgeon John Harris in the 1830s; it contains a fine collection of Australian colonial furniture, and the cellar now houses an exhibition on the life and work of James Ruse. The surrounding ornamental garden is most beautiful in early summer, when the floral perfumes are strongest. ⊠ *9 Ruse St., Harris Park* ☎ *02/9635–5655* ⊕ *www.nationaltrust. org.au* ⊠ *From A$9.*

Featherdale Wildlife Park

ZOO | **FAMILY** | This is the place to see kangaroos, dingoes, wallabies, and echidnas (and even feed some of them) in native bush settings 40 km (25 miles) west of Sydney. The daily crocodile feeding sessions are very popular. Take the train to Blacktown Station and then board the 725 bus for the park. ■**TIP**→ **The park is on the way to the Blue Mountains.** ⊠ *217 Kildare Rd., Doonside* ☎ *02/9622–1644* ⊕ *www.featherdale.com.au* ⊠ *A$32.*

Koala Park Sanctuary

ZOO | **FAMILY** | At this private park in Sydney's northern outskirts you can feed a kangaroo or get close to a koala. (Koala presentations are daily at 10:20, 11:45, 2, and 3.) The sanctuary also has dingoes, wombats, emus, penguins, and wallaroos. There are sheep-shearing and boomerang-throwing demonstrations. ⊠ *84 Castle Hill Rd., West Pennant Hills* ☎ *02/9484–3141* ⊕ *koalapark-sanctuary. com.au* ⊠ *A$28.*

Ku-ring-gai Chase National Park

NATIONAL/STATE PARK | Nature hikes here lead past rock engravings and paintings by the Guringai Aboriginal tribe, the area's original inhabitants for whom the park is named. Created in the 1890s, the park mixes large stands of eucalyptus trees with moist, rain-forest-filled gullies where swamp wallabies, possums, goannas, and other creatures roam. The delightful trails are mostly easy or moderate, including the compelling 3-km (2-mile) Garigal Aboriginal Heritage Walk at West Head, which takes in ancient rock-art sites. From Mt. Ku-ring-gai train station you can walk the 3-km (2-mile) Ku-ring-gai Track to Appletree Bay, while the 30-minute, wheelchair-accessible Discovery Trail is an excellent introduction to the region's flora and fauna. Leaflets on all of the walks are available at the park's entry stations and from the Wildlife Shop at Bobbin Head. ⊠ *Ku-ring-gai Chase National Park, Bobbin Head Rd., Mount Colah* ☎ *02/9472–8949* ⊕ *www. nationalparks.nsw.gov.au* ⊠ *A$12 per vehicle, per day.*

Old Government House

GOVERNMENT BUILDING | On the bank of the Parramatta River, Old Government House (which was the country residence of Sydney's 10 early governors) is Australia's oldest surviving public building, and the World Heritage–listed building is a notable work from the Georgian period. Built by governors John Hunter and Lachlan Macquarie, the building has been faithfully restored in keeping with its origins, and contains the nation's most significant collection of early Australian furniture. In the 260-acre parkland surrounding the house are Governor Brisbane's bathhouse and observatory and the Government House Dairy. The house is often home to special exhibitions. ✉ *Inside Parramatta Park, Parramatta ✛ Pitt St. entrance* ☎ *02/9635–8149* ⊕ *www. nationaltrust.org.au* ⌛ *A$16.*

Parramatta

TOWN | This bustling satellite city 26 km (16 miles) west of Sydney is one of Australia's most historic precincts. Its origins as a European settlement are purely agrarian. The sandy, rocky soil around Sydney Cove was too poor to feed the fledgling colony, so Governor Phillip looked to the banks of the Parramatta River for the rich alluvial soil they needed. In 1789, just a year after the first convicts-cum-settlers arrived, Phillip established Rosehill, an area set aside for agriculture. The community developed as its agricultural successes grew, and several important buildings survive as outstanding examples of the period. The two-hour self-guided Harris Park Heritage Walk, which departs from the RiverCat Ferry Terminal, connects the key historic sites and buildings. The ferry departs at frequent intervals from Sydney's Circular Quay, and is a relaxing, scenic alternative to the drive or train ride from the city. A free shuttle bus travels in a loop around Parramatta. ■ **TIP→ A good place to start discovering Parramatta is the Heritage Centre at 346A Church Street.** ✉ *Parramatta* ⊕ *www.discoverparramatta.com.*

Royal National Park

NATIONAL/STATE PARK | Established in 1879 on the coast south of Sydney, the Royal has the distinction of being the first national park in Australia and the second in the world, after Yellowstone National Park in the United States. Several walking tracks traverse the grounds, most of them requiring little or no hiking experience. The Lady Carrington Walk, a 10-km (6-mile) trek, is a self-guided tour that crosses 15 creeks and passes several historic sites. Other tracks take you along the coast past beautiful wildflower displays and through patches of rain forest. You can canoe the Port Hacking River upstream from the Audley Causeway; rentals are available at the Audley boat shed on the river. The Illawarra train line, from Central Station, stops at Loftus, Engadine, Heathcote, Waterfall, and Otford stations, where most of the park's walking tracks begin. There are three campsites in the park. ✉ *Royal National Park, Sydney ✛ Royal National Park Visitor Centre, 35 km (22 miles) south of Sydney via Princes Hwy. to Farnell Ave., south of Loftus, or McKell Ave. at Waterfall* ☎ *02/9542–0648 visitor center, 02/9542–0648 campsite reservations* ⊕ *www.nationalparks.nsw.gov. au* ⌛ *A$12 per vehicle per day, overnight camping from A$10; booking required.*

Sydney Olympic Park

SPORTS VENUE | FAMILY | The center of the 2000 Olympic and Paralympic Games lies 14 km (8½ miles) west of the city center. Sprawling across 1,900 acres on the shores of Homebush Bay, the site is a series of majestic stadiums, arenas, and accommodation complexes. Among the park's sports facilities are an aquatic center, archery range, tennis center, and the centerpiece: the 85,000-seat ANZ Olympic Stadium. Since the conclusion of the 2000 Games it has been used for major sporting events like the 2003 Rugby World Cup and concerts for international acts including The Rolling Stones. The Explore interactive stadium

A bird's-eye view of the boats in Parramatta River

tour, costing A$28.50 per person, takes you behind the scenes to sit in the media room and have your photo taken on the winners' dais. The Gantry Tour (A$49) also includes a trip to the gantry (where the sound equipment and spotlights are kept, 140 feet above the stadium). Don't miss the adjacent Bicentennial Park, made up of 247 acres of swamps, lakes, and parks dotted with picnic grounds and bike trails. The most scenic and relaxing way to get to Sydney Olympic Park is to take the RiverCat from Circular Quay to Homebush Bay. You can also take a train from Central Station, Sydney, to Olympic Park. ⊠ 1 Herb Elliot Ave., Homebush Bay ☎ 02/9714–7888 ⊕ www. sydneyolympicpark.com.au ⊕ www. anzstadium.com.au.

🌀 Beaches

Dee Why–Long Reef

BEACH—SIGHT | Separated from Dee Why by a narrow channel, Long Reef Beach is remoter and much quieter than its southern neighbor. However, Dee Why has better surfing conditions, a big sea pool, and several good restaurants. To get here, take Bus 136 from Manly. **Amenities:** food and drink; lifeguard; parking (fee); showers; toilets. **Best for:** swimming; walking. ⊠ The Strand, Dee Why.

★ Manly Beach

BEACH—SIGHT | The Bondi Beach of the north shore, Manly caters to everyone except those who want to get away from it all. On sunny days Sydneysiders, school groups, and travelers from around the world crowd the 2-km-long (1-mile-long) sweep of white sand and take to the waves to swim and ride boards. The beach is well equipped with changing and toilet facilities and lockers. The promenade that runs between the Norfolk Island pines is great for people-watching and rollerblading. Cafés, souvenir shops, and ice-cream parlors line the nearby shopping area, the Corso. Manly also has several nonbeach attractions, including Oceanworld, an aquarium about 200 yards from the ferry wharf. The ferry ride from the city makes a day at Manly feel more like a holiday than just an excursion to the beach. Take a ferry or the Manly Fast Ferry from Circular Quay. From the dock at Manly the beach is a 10-minute walk. The visitor center is located on the Forecourt of Manly Wharf. The Novotel Sydney Pacific Hotel and the Sebel Manly Beach Hotel are two upscale properties located on the beachfront. **Amenities:** food and drink; lifeguards; parking (fee); showers; toilets. **Best for:** sunrise; surfing; swimming; walking. ⊠ *Steyne St., Manly* ⊕ *www.hellomanly.com.au.*

★ **Palm Beach**

BEACH—SIGHT | The golden sands of Palm Beach glitter as much as the bejeweled residents of the stylish nearby village. The beach is on one side of the peninsula separating the large inlet of Pittwater from the Pacific Ocean. Bathers can easily cross from the ocean side to Pittwater's calm waters. You can take a circular ferry trip around this waterway from the wharf on the Pittwater side. The view from the lighthouse at the northern end of the beach is well worth the walk. Shops and cafés sell light snacks and meals. North Palm Beach is only patrolled by lifeguards in summer (December to February). Take Bus 190 or L90 from Wynyard bus station. **Amenities:** food and drink; lifeguards; showers; toilets. **Best for:** surfing; swimming. ⊠ *Ocean Rd., Palm Beach.*

🍴 Restaurants

Tea Room Gunners Barracks

$$$ | **AUSTRALIAN** | Housed in a beautiful sandstone building that served a number of military purposes for more than 130 years, the Tea Room Gunners Barracks has breathtaking views of the harbor and the surrounding gardens and bushland. Their traditional afternoon tea (A$50) is a great way to relax after exploring the armaments of Middle Head. **Known for:** beautiful desserts; idylic views; stunning grounds. $ *Average main: A$50* ⊠ *202*

Run for Your Life

Pack your jogging shoes for the biggest footrace in the country. **City to Surf** (⊕ *city2surf.com.au*) attracts more than 50,000 people each August—some taking it very seriously, others donning a gorilla suit or fairy outfit. The race starts at Hyde Park and winds through the eastern suburbs 14 km (9 miles) to Bondi Beach, via the notorious "Heartbreak Hill" at Rose Bay. For some reason, it never seems to rain on the second Sunday in August.

Suakin Dr., Mosman ☎ *02/8962–5900* ⊕ *www.gunnersbarracks.com.au.*

🛏 Hotels

Sebel Manly Beach

$$ | **HOTEL** | Right on the beachfront of beautiful Manly, this boutique hotel is a mixture of studios and one- and two-bedroom suites, all with private balconies; the more-spacious accommodations have hot tubs, kitchenettes, and high-tech goodies. **Pros:** beachside locale; well-appointed rooms. **Cons:** busy place; expect crowds in summer; no Wi-Fi in rooms. $ *Rooms from: A$280* ⊠ *8–13 S. Steyne, Manly* ☎ *02/9977–8866* ⊕ *www. thesebelmanlybeach.com.au* ⟲ *83 rooms* ⊙ *No meals.*

🏃 Activities

SCUBA DIVING

Dive Centre Manly

SCUBA DIVING | Located at the popular northern Sydney beach, Dive Centre Manly runs all-inclusive shore dives each day, which let you see weedy sea dragons and other sea creatures. PADI certification courses are also available.

Sydneysiders have more than 30 beaches to choose from.

The cost for a shore dive is A$245. ⊠ *10 Belgrave St., Manly* ☎ *02/9977–4355* ⊕ *www.divesydney.com.au.*

SURFING
Manly Surf School

SURFING | This company conducts courses for adults and children, and provides all equipment, including wet suits. Adults can join a two-hour group lesson (four per day) for A$70. Private instruction costs A$110 per hour. Stand-up paddling (on a board) lessons are also available, and are held on the calm waters of Balmoral and Narrabeen lakes. ⊠ *North Steyne Surf Club, North Steyne, Manly Beach, Manly* ☎ *02/9932–7000* ⊕ *www. manlysurfschool.com.*

WINDSURFING
Balmoral Water Sports Center

WINDSURFING | Balmoral Water Sports Center runs classes from its base at this north-side harbor beach. Private windsurfing lessons are A$135 per hour. Stand-up paddleboards and kayaks can be rented out for A$30 and A$25 per hour respectively. ⊠ *The Esplanade, Balmoral* ☎ *02/9960–5344* ⊕ *www.sailingschool. com.au.*

Rose Bay Aquatic Hire

WINDSURFING | Rose Bay Aquatic Hire offers kayaks and paddleboards at A$25 an hour. Whatever mode of transport chosen, an hour or two on Sydney's beautiful harbor is time well spent. ⊠ *1 Vickery Ave., Rose Bay* ☎ *0416/239543, 0416/123339* ⊕ *www.rosebayaquatichire. com.*

🛍 Shopping

ART AND CRAFT GALLERIES
Kate Owen Gallery + Studio

ART GALLERIES | This gallery showcases quality indigenous art over three levels in Rozelle, a suburb about 15 minutes west of the city center. Take the M50 or M52 bus from the bus station behind the Queen Victoria Building; alight at the corner of Victoria Road and Darling Street. ⊠ *680 Darling St., at Victoria Rd., Rozelle* ☎ *02/9555–5283* ⊕ *www.kateowengallery.com.*

DEPARTMENT STORES AND SHOPPING CENTERS
Birkenhead Point
SHOPPING CENTERS/MALLS | A factory outlet with more than 100 clothing, shoe, and housewares stores on the western shores of Iron Cove, about 7 km (4 miles) west of Sydney, Birkenhead Point is a great place to shop for discounted labels including Alannah Hill, Witchery, Bendon (Elle Macpherson's lingerie range), Rip Curl, and David Jones warehouse. Take Bus 504, 506, 518, or the M52 from Druitt Street near Town Hall station and also Circular Quay. Water taxis depart from the site for Circular Quay and Darling Harbour. ⊠ *Roseby St., near Iron Cove Bridge, Drummoyne* ☎ *02/9182–8800* ⊕ *www.birkenheadpoint.com.au.*

MARKETS
Balmain Market
OUTDOOR/FLEA/GREEN MARKETS | In a leafy churchyard less than 5 km (3 miles) from the city, Balmain Market has a rustic quality that makes it a refreshing change from city-center shopping. Crafts, handmade furniture, plants, bread, toys, tarot readings, and massages are among the offerings at the 140-odd stalls. Inside the church hall you can buy international snacks. Take Bus No. 442 from the Queen Victoria Building in York Street. ⊠ *St. Andrew's Church, Darling St., Balmain* ☎ *04/1104–7655* ⊕ *www.balmainmarket.com.au.*

Glebe Markets
OUTDOOR/FLEA/GREEN MARKETS | Handmade and secondhand are the order of the day at this colorful market at the top end of Glebe Point Road. One of the best markets for lovers of all things vintage, Glebe also hosts live music on the lawn and good food stalls as well. The markets are open every Saturday 10–4. ⊠ *Glebe Public School, Derby Pl. at Glebe Point Rd., Glebe* ⊕ *www.glebemarkets.com.au.*

Chapter 4

NEW SOUTH WALES

4

Updated by Amy
Nelmes Bissett

◉ Sights	🍴 Restaurants	🛏 Hotels	🛍 Shopping	🍸 Nightlife
★★★★★	★★★★☆	★★★★☆	★★★☆☆	★★★☆☆

WELCOME TO NEW SOUTH WALES

TOP REASONS TO GO

★ **Getting in Touch with Nature:** Exotic birds are prolific in the Blue Mountains and North Coast and South Coast regions.

★ **The Great Australian Bite:** There are lots of fine restaurants in the Hunter Valley and in the North Coast towns of Coffs Harbour and Byron Bay. Seafood and world-famous oysters in the South Coast is a must.

★ **Outdoor Adventure:** The region's mountains and national parks offer opportunities for walks and hikes, horseback riding, rappelling, canyoning, and rock climbing.

★ **World-Class Wineries:** The Hunter Valley has an international reputation for producing excellent Chardonnay, Shiraz, and a dry Sémillon.

★ **Deserted Beaches:** The coastline has some of the most beautiful white-sand beaches in the country. Most of them are wonderfully undeveloped and crowd-free, with hardly a skyscraper in sight.

Despite being Australia's most populous state, the rich variety of landscapes is the biggest selling point. The Blue Mountains, a World Heritage Site, lie approximately 100 km (60 miles) to the west of Sydney; the Hunter Valley is about 160 km (100 miles) or two hours north of Sydney. The North Coast and South Coast are exactly where their name suggests, while Lord Howe Island is offshore, 700 km (435 miles) northeast of Sydney.

1 Wentworth Falls. A charming village with some of the finest scenery and bushwalks in the Blue Mountains.

2 Leura. One of the prettiest town centers in the Blue Mountains.

3 Katoomba. Amazing viewpoints and a scenic railway, walkway, and skyway.

4 Blackheath. Great hiking trails and trendy dining.

5 Mount Victoria. A popular base for activities

6 Pokolbin and Nearby. Home to some of Australia's best-known wine labels.

7 Newcastle. Beautiful beaches and ocean baths.

8 Port Macquarie. Pristine rivers, lakes, and beaches.

9 Bellingen. A relaxing getaway and great base for exploring.

10 Coffs Harbour. A popular vacation spot with great beaches.

11 Byron Bay. Gorgeous beaches, breathtaking bushwalks, and lively town.

12 Lord Howe Island. Island paradise with vivid coral reefs, sheltered beaches, great trails, and famous twin peaks.

13 Berry. Popular weekend escape from Sydney with good dining and relaxing vibe.

14 Jervis Bay. Some of the most pristine white-sand beaches in all of th Australia, if not the world.

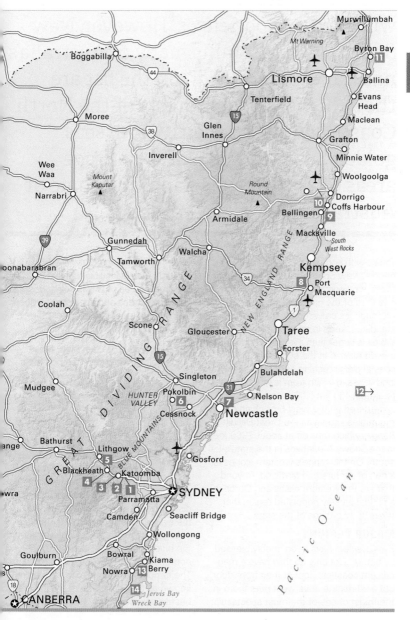

For many travelers Sydney is New South Wales, and they look to the other, less-populous states for Australia's famous wilderness experiences. However, New South Wales contains many of Australia's natural wonders. High on the list are the subtropical rain forests of the North Coast, lush river valleys, warm seas, golden beaches, the World Heritage areas of Lord Howe Island, and some of Australia's finest vineyards.

Today, with approximately 7.54 million people, New South Wales is Australia's most populous state—it's home to about one-third of the nation's population. Although it's crowded by Australian standards, keep in mind that New South Wales is larger than every U.S. state except Alaska. In the state's east, a coastal plain reaching north to Queensland varies in width from less than a mile to almost 160 km (100 miles). This plain is bordered on the west by a chain of low mountains known as the Great Dividing Range, which tops off at about 7,300 feet in the Snowy Mountains in the state's far south. On this range's western slopes is a belt of pasture and farmland. Beyond that are the western plains and Outback, an arid, sparsely populated region that takes up two-thirds of the state.

MAJOR REGIONS

Sydneysiders have been doubly blessed by nature. Not only do they have a magnificent coastline right at their front door, but a 90-minute drive west puts them in the midst of one of the most spectacular

wilderness areas in Australia—World Heritage **Blue Mountains National Park.** This rippling sea of hills is covered by tall eucalyptus trees and dissected by deep river valleys—the area is perfect terrain for hiking and adventure activities.

Standing 3,500-plus feet high, these "mountains" were once the bed of an ancient sea. Gradually the sedimentary rock was uplifted until it formed a high plateau, which was etched by eons of wind and water into the wonderland of cliffs, caves, and canyons that exists today. Now the richly forested hills, crisp mountain air, cool-climate gardens, vast sandstone chasms, and little towns of timber and stone are supreme examples of Australia's diversity. The mountains' distinctive blue coloring is caused by the evaporation of oil from the dense eucalyptus forests. This disperses light in the blue colors of the spectrum, a phenomenon known as Rayleigh Scattering. The famous sandstone rock formations known as the Three Sisters are the area's best-known attraction. **Wentworth Falls** is home to the most stunning natural falls in the mountains. The prettiest of mountain towns, **Leura**, offers a dazzling 19-km (12-mile) journey along Cliff Drive skirts the rim of the valley—often only yards from the cliff edge—providing truly spectacular Blue Mountains views.

To almost everyone in Sydney, **the Hunter Valley** conjures up visions of one thing: wine. The Hunter is the largest grape-growing area in the state, with more than 120 wineries producing excellent varieties. The Hunter is divided into seven subregions, each with its own unique character. The hub is the **Pokolbin/Rothbury** region, where many of the large operations are found, along with several boutique wineries.

The Hunter Valley covers an area of almost 25,103 square km (9,692 square miles), stretching from the town of Gosford north of Sydney to 177 km (110 miles) farther north along the coast, and almost 300 km (186 miles) inland. The meandering waterway that gives this valley its name is also one of the most extensive river systems in the state.

The North Coast is one of the most glorious and seductive stretches of terrain in Australia, stretching almost 680 km (422 miles) from Newcastle up to the Queensland border. An almost continuous line of beaches defines the coast, with the Great Dividing Range rising to the west the farther you travel north. These natural borders frame a succession of rolling green pasturelands, mossy rain forests, towns dotted by red-roof houses, and waterfalls that tumble in glistening arcs from the escarpment. A journey along the coast leads through several rich agricultural districts, beginning with grazing country in the south and moving into plantations of bananas, sugarcane, mangoes, avocados, and macadamia nuts. Dorrigo National Park, outside Bellingen, and Muttonbird Island, in Coffs Harbour, are two parks good for getting your

feet on some native soil and for seeing unusual birdlife.

The tie that binds the North Coast is the Pacific Highway, but despite its name, this highway rarely affords glimpses of the Pacific Ocean. You can drive the entire length of the North Coast in a single day, but allow at least three—or, better still, a week—to properly sample some of its attractions.

Visitors have always had a magical pull to NSW's North Coast but for Sydneysiders, it has always been about the region's **South Coast.** There's an understated beauty here, with miles-upon-miles of rolling green hills rolling alongside the country's most idyllic beaches. From Sydney to the Victoria border, it's a seven-hour drive over 546 km (339 miles) but most just dip their toes into the vast riches southern NSW has to offer by heading to **Berry,** a rural country town just three hours south of the city, before continuing to **Jervis Bay,** a truly majestic beach town that boasts to having the world's whitest sand.

Planning

WHEN TO GO

For visitors from the northern hemisphere the Australian summer (approximately December–February) has great pull. The best times to visit the Hunter Valley are during the February–March grape harvest season and the June Hunter Food and Wine Festival. The spring flower celebration, Floriade, lasts from mid-September to mid-October. The North Coast and South Coast resort regions are often booked solid between Christmas and the first half of January, but autumn and spring are good times to visit.

PLANNING YOUR TIME

It's wise to decide in advance whether you'd like to cover a lot of ground quickly or choose one or two places to linger a while. If you have less than four days, stick close to Sydney. In a busy four- to seven-day period you could visit the Blue Mountains and the Hunter Valley as well.

Start with a visit to the **Blue Mountains.** You could arrange a round-trip itinerary from Sydney in a fairly hectic day or, preferably, spend a night in **Katoomba, Blackheath,** or **Leura** and make it a two-day excursion. Return to Sydney, and then head north to the **Hunter Valley.** A two-day/one-night driving visit here allows you enough time to see the main sights and spend time touring the wineries before traveling back to Sydney on the second day.

If you have more time in the region, continue to the North Coast. In three days of driving you won't likely get much farther than **Coffs Harbour** (with overnights there and in **Port Macquarie**), and this requires rushing it, but it's possible to fly back to Sydney from Coffs. Alternatively, travel south with a pit-stop at the historical village of Berry before traveling to Jervis Bay, which is a four-hour drive from Sydney and offers 20 km of some of the country's most pristine beaches.

GETTING HERE AND AROUND
AIR TRAVEL
New South Wales is peppered with airports, so flying is the easiest way to get around if you're traveling long distances. You can score the best fares during the quieter seasons. From Sydney, REX (Regional Express) Airlines services Ballina and Lismore (both about 30 minutes from Byron Bay). Qantas flies into Port Macquarie, Coffs Harbour, and Lord Howe Island; its low-cost subsidiary Jetstar flies into Ballina, while Virgin Australia goes to Newcastle, Canberra, Port Macquarie, Ballina, and Coffs Harbour.

AIRLINE CONTACTS Jetstar. ☎ *13–1538* ⊕ *www.jetstar.com.* **Qantas Airways.** ☎ *13–1313* ⊕ *www.qantas.com.au.* **REX Airlines.** ☎ *13–1713* ⊕ *www.rex.com.*

au. **Virgin Australia.** ☎ *13–6789* ⊕ *www.virginaustralia.com.*

CAR RENTAL
Hiring your own car is the most convenient way of getting around the region, especially the South Coast. The scenic Blue Mountains and Hunter Valley routes and attractions are outside the towns, so having your own set of wheels is helpful. When visiting the wine country, be aware that Australia has very strict rules against drunk driving and there are many tours available that show the best the region has to offer, with a few even departing from Sydney. Most towns have major car-rental companies. You can pick up a car at one point and drop off at another for an extra fee.

TRAIN TRAVEL
As in the States, most people drive here, so train services aren't great and can often cost more than other options. It is possible to travel by train to the Blue Mountains with the Sydney Trains (aka CityRail) commuter network. NSW Train-Link (aka CountryLink) connects Sydney to towns in the Hunter Valley and along the North Coast. The South Coast's Jervis Bay can not be reached by train; it's quicker and more convenient to drive.

TRAIN INFORMATION NSW TrainLink. ☎ *13–2232, 02/4907–7501* ⊕ *www.nswtrainlink.info.* **Sydney Trains.** ☎ *13–1500* ⊕ *www.sydneytrains.info.*

RESTAURANTS
Dining varies dramatically throughout New South Wales, from superb city-standard restaurants to average country-town fare. As popular weekend retreats for Sydneysiders, the Blue Mountains have a number of fine restaurants and cozy tea rooms that are perfect for light meals. In the Hunter Valley several excellent restaurants show off the region's fine wines. Unsurprisingly, seafood dominates on the North Coast and the South Coast, and again, thanks to holidaying Sydneysiders with high

standards, you should be able to tuck into some memorable meals.

HOTELS

Accommodations include everything from run-of-the-mill motels and remote wilderness lodges to historic, cliff-perched properties and expansive seaside resorts. Rates are often much lower on weekdays, particularly in the Blue Mountains and the Hunter Valley, as traffic from Sydney is heavier on weekends. The North Coast and the South Coast is popular during summer and Easter school holidays, so book as far ahead as possible. *Hotel reviews have been shortened. For full information, visit Fodors.com.*

What It Costs In Australian dollars			
$	**$$**	**$$$**	**$$$$**
RESTAURANTS			
under A$21	A$21–A$35	A$36–A$50	over A$50
HOTELS			
under A$151	A$151–A$200	A$201–A$300	over A$300

Wentworth Falls

95 km (59 miles) west of Sydney.

This attractive township is home to the Blue Mountains' most stunning natural waterfalls and bush walking trails. The Falls themselves straddle the highway, but most points of interest and views of the Jamison Valley and Blue Mountains National Park are a short way south.

GETTING HERE AND AROUND

From Sydney, head west onto Parramatta Road, then take the M4, following signs to the Blue Mountains. You'll pay a toll at the end of the motorway. It's also easy to catch a train to Wentworth Falls; the journey from Sydney Central Station takes 1¾ hours, with trains leaving roughly every hour. The Blue Mountains

Bus Company (☏ *02/4751–1077* ⊕ *www.bmbc.com.au*) connects towns within the region with Routes 685 and 695, connecting Wentworth Falls to Leura and Katoomba.

⊙ Sights

Norman Lindsay Gallery and Museum

HOUSE | If driving from Sydney, be sure to stop at the National Trust–listed Norman Lindsay Gallery and Museum, dedicated to the Australian artist and writer. Considered one of the cultural highlights of the Blue Mountains, Lindsay lived in this house during the latter part of his life until he died in 1969. Lindsay is best known for his paintings, etchings, and drawings (many of voluptuous nudes), but he also built model boats, sculpted, and wrote poetry and children's books, among which *The Magic Pudding* has become an Australian classic. The delightful landscaped gardens contain several of Lindsay's sculptures, and you can also take a short but scenic bushwalk beyond the garden or take refreshments in the café. Daily tours of Lindsay's studios run from 10:30 am to 2:30 pm and are included in the price, while dedicated art fans can stay in the cottage on the grounds for A$175 a night midweek or A$220 a night Friday, Saturday, and Sunday. ⊠ *14 Norman Lindsay Crescent, Faulconbridge* ☏ *02/4751–1067* ⊕ *www.normanlindsay.com.au* 🎟 *A$17.*

🍴 Restaurants

Conservation Hut

$ | **AUSTRALIAN** | From its prime spot in Blue Mountains National Park, on a cliff overlooking the Jamison Valley, this spacious, mud-brick bistro serves simple, savory fare. Lovely brunch dishes include herbed mushrooms with a poached egg and roasted tomatoes on toast. For lunch, dig into hearty soups, beef pies, or goats cheese tartlet. Be sure to save room for the dessert cakes. An open balcony is a delight on warm days, and a fire blazes in the cooler months. A hiking trail from the bistro leads down into the Valley of the Waters, one of the splendors of the mountains. It's a wonderful pre- or postmeal walk. **Known for:** views; hearty meals; great brunch spot. $ *Average main: A$18* ✉ *88 Fletcher St.* ☎ *02/4757–3827* ⊘ *No dinner.*

2773

$$ | **MODERN AUSTRALIAN** | In Glenbrook, one of the first Blue Mountains towns you'll reach coming from Sydney, this is a great place for breakfast or a relaxing lunch before continuing to Wentworth Falls, about a 30-minute drive west. Dinner, served Thursday through Saturday, includes dishes like salt and pepper lamb cutlets and organic meats from the Lithgow Valley (on the other side of the mountains). The best value is the A$36 Plank, featuring a little bit of just about everything on the menu. 2773 serves only fair-trade tea, coffee, and chocolate and uses many organically grown ingredients and locally sourced beer and wine. Live music on Sunday afternoon is a great way to enjoy the weekend. Kids love meeting the pigs out the back. **Known for:** organic farm-to-table menu; fair-trade coffee; relaxing atmosphere. $ *Average main: A$28* ✉ *19 Ross St., Glenbrook* ☎ *02/4739–5908* ⊕ *www.2773glenbrook.com.au* ⊘ *No dinner Mon.–Wed. and Sun.*

🏃 Activities

HIKING

Falls Reserve

HIKING/WALKING | From a lookout in Falls Reserve, south of the town of Wentworth Falls, you can take in magnificent views both out across the Jamison Valley to the Kings Tableland and of the 935-foot-high **Wentworth Falls** themselves. To find the best view of the falls, follow the trail that crosses the stream and zigzags down the sheer cliff face, signposted "national pass." If you continue, the trail cuts back

across the base of the falls and along a narrow ledge to the delightful Valley of the Waters, where it ascends to the top of the cliffs, emerging at the Conservation Hut. The complete circuit takes at least three hours and is a moderately difficult walk. ✉ *End of Falls Rd.*

Leura

5 km (3 miles) west of Wentworth Falls.

Leura, the prettiest and chicest of the mountain towns, is bordered by bush and lined with excellent cafés, restaurants, and gift shops. From the south end of the main street (the Mall), the road continues past superb local gardens as it winds down to the massive cliffs overlooking the Jamison Valley. The dazzling 19-km (12-mile) journey along Cliff Drive skirts the rim of the valley—often only yards from the cliff edge—providing truly spectacular Blue Mountains views.

GETTING HERE AND AROUND

The train station at Leura is one stop beyond Wentworth Falls, and the station is walking distance from all the town's shops and galleries. By car, Leura is a few kilometers west of Wentworth Falls on the Great Western Highway. Alternatively, catch a Blue Mountains Bus Company bus—Routes 685 and 695 connect the town with Wentworth Falls and Katoomba.

👁 Sights

Everglades Historic House and Gardens

GARDEN | Everglades Gardens, a National Trust–listed, cool-climate arboretum and nature reserve established in the 1930s, is one of the best public gardens in the Blue Mountains region. This former home of a Belgian industrialist is surrounded by 13 acres of native bushland and exotic flora, a rhododendron garden, an alpine plant area, and formal European-style terraces. The views of the Jamison Valley are magnificent. ⊠ *37 Everglades Ave.* ☎ *02/4784–1938* ⊕ *www.nationaltrust. org.au/places/everglades-house-gardens* 🎫 *A$13.*

Leuralla

HOUSE | FAMILY | This imposing 1911 mansion still belongs to the family of Dr. H. V. ("Doc") Evatt (1894–1965), the first president of the General Assembly of the United Nations and later the leader of the Australian Labor Party. A 19th-century Australian art collection and a small museum dedicated to Dr. Evatt are inside the home. Baby boomers and their children (and grandchildren) will love the collection in the New South Wales Toy and Railway Museum, which is both inside the house and in the gardens. The museum is comprised of an extensive collection of railway memorabilia, antique curios from yesteryear (including lots of dolls depicting *Alice in Wonderland* scenes), and exhibitions on iconic dolls like Barbie. Directly across the street from the mansion are the Leuralla Public Gardens (entry A$2), with spectacular views of the Jamison Valley. ⊠ *36 Olympian Parade* ☎ *02/4784–1169* ⊕ *www. toyandrailwaymuseum.com.au* 🎫 *A$15; gardens only A$10.*

Sublime Point Lookout

VIEWPOINT | This viewpoint just outside Leura lives up to its name with a great view of the Jamison Valley and the generally spectacular Blue Mountains scenery. It's a quiet vantage point that provides a different perspective from that of the famous **Three Sisters** lookout at nearby Katoomba. ⊠ *Sublime Point Rd.*

🍴 Restaurants

★ Leura Garage

$$ | EUROPEAN | This buzzy eatery housed in an old garage opposite the railway station in Leura serves top-notch food in a delightfully informal setting. Dishes are designed to share and although they might sound simple in name, they

Bloomin' Beautiful

Leura Garden Festival. When spring is in the air in the mountains, one of the most beautiful places to be is Leura. Dozens of cherry blossoms line the main street, and private gardens are open for viewing. Make a date for the weeklong Leura Garden Festival in early October. The gardens are adorned with the work of local artists keen to win the annual art prize. A village fair caps off the celebrations. One ticket (A$25) buys entrance to all the gardens on show. ⊠ *Leura* ☎ *0431/095279* ⊕ *www.leuragardens-festival.com.au.*

are simply astounding—the burrata (a handmade ball of mozzarella cheese with fresh tomato) will make you swoon when you cut into it and the soft center oozes out onto the plate. The menu changes seasonally, but longtime favorites include the salted anchovy pizza with potato and confit garlic, and pork meatballs from the nearby Lithgow Valley. Most of the produce is local and all of the wine is sourced from nearby Mudgee or Orange district. One of the few places in the mountains, other than traditional cafés, to have all-day dining, the restaurant is also a great value, with a two-person, six-course tasting menu for just A$59 per person. **Known for:** fresh menu that regularly changes; trendy eatery; buzzy atmosphere. $ *Average main: A$25* ⊠ *84 Railway Parade* ☎ *02/4784–3391* ⊕ *leuragarage.com.au.*

★ Silk's Brasserie

$$$ | AUSTRALIAN | Thanks to its Sydney-standard food, wine, and service, Silk's still rates as one of the finest Blue Mountains restaurants after more than 20 years. The menu here changes

seasonally, but popular dishes include the pan-seared scallops with tomato confit, asparagus, pancetta, and a chicory-watercress salad with honey-mustard-seed dressing, and the main course pork tenderloin with black pudding and caramelised cider jus. A favorite dessert is the warm bittersweet chocolate fondant with pistachio ice cream and orange syrup. The restaurant is housed in a Federation-era building, and in colder months a log fire warms the century-old simple but elegant interior, where yellow ocher walls reach from black-and-white checkerboard floor to sky-high ceiling. **Known for:** fine dining; epicurean institution; sophisticated experience. $ *Average main: A$37* ✉ *128 The Mall* ☎ *02/4784–2534* ⊕ *www. silksleura.com.*

🛏 Hotels

Bygone Beautys Cottages
$$ | **B&B/INN** | These two country cottages, at Wentworth Falls and in the nearby village of Bullaburra, provide self-contained accommodations for couples, families, or small groups. **Pros:** antiques collectors love the connected tea room; romantic setting; wood-burning fireplaces. **Cons:** old-world design isn't for everyone; bathrooms can be chilly in winter; distance from the Blue Mountains. $ *Rooms from: A$195* ✉ *Grose St. at Megalong St.* ☎ *02/4784–3117* ⊕ *www. bygonebeautys.com.au* ⤳ *2 cottages* ⊚ *Free Breakfast.*

Fairmont Resort Blue Mountains MGallery by Sofitel
$$$ | **HOTEL** | Perched on a cliff, the Fairmont Hotel offers a sweeping vista of the valley below and you'll want to wake up early to see the Blue Mountains creak to life with birds breaking into their morning chorus. **Pros:** incredible views; luxury spa; cascading swimming pools. **Cons:** can be overrun with families; not rustic nor luxurious; property a little tired in places. $ *Rooms from: A$280* ✉ *1 Sublime Point Rd.* ☎ *02/4785–0000* ⊕ *www.*

fairmontresort.com.au/accommodation ⤳ *222 rooms* ⊚ *No meals.*

🛍 Shopping

Josophan's
FOOD/CANDY | This gorgeous chocolate boutique in Leura's main shopping street has fast become *the* place to stop for luscious handmade chocolates and drinking chocolate. You can also take part in classes (how does making chocolate truffles sound?) and take away lovely gift boxes of sweets. For a light snack and yummy chocolate desserts, walk across the road to Cafe Madeline (*187a The Mall*), which is also owned by Josophan's proprietor and chocolatier Jodie Van der Velden. ✉ *132 The Mall* ☎ *02/4784–2031* ⊕ *www. josophans.com.au.*

Katoomba

2 km (1 mile) west of Leura.

The largest and busiest town in the Blue Mountains, Katoomba developed in the early 1840s as a coal-mining settlement, turning its attention to tourism later in the 19th century. The town center on Katoomba Street has shops, restaurants, and cafés, but the marvels at the lower end of town are an even greater draw.

GETTING HERE AND AROUND
Katoomba is just a few minutes' drive from Leura on the Great Western Highway. A train station connects the town with the rest of the region, as does the Blue Mountains Bus Company. A$50 buys a day's access to the red double-decker Explorer buses that travel around Katoomba and Leura stopping at 29 places (⊕ *www.explorerbus.com.au*).

TOURS
Blue Mountains Adventure Company
ADVENTURE TOURS | The well-established Blue Mountains Adventure Company runs abseiling (rappelling), rock-climbing, canyoning, bushwalking, and

mountain-biking trips. Lunch, snacks, and all the equipment are generally included. Introductory and intermediate canyoning tours go to such places as Empress Falls or Serendipity Canyon. ⊠ *84A Bathurst Rd.* ☎ *02/4782–1271* ⊕ *www.bmac.com. au* ⊠ *From A$220.*

High n Wild
ADVENTURE TOURS | This outfitter conducts rappelling, canyoning, rock-climbing, and mountain-biking tours throughout the year. Half-day rappelling trips cost A$135; one-day trips are A$175; combination rappelling and canyoning tours cost A$225. The company's office is based at the YHA youth hostel, a short walk from the station. ⊠ *207 Katoomba St.* ☎ *02/4782–6224* ⊕ *www.high-n-wild. com.au* ⊠ *From A$135.*

VISITOR INFORMATION
CONTACTS Blue Mountains Visitor Information Centre. ⊠ *Echo Point Rd.* ☎ *1300/653408* ⊕ *www.bluemountainscitytourism.com.au.*

◉ Sights

Blue Mountains Chocolate Company
STORE/MALL | If you have a sweet tooth, try this artisan chocolate shop. Here you can watch chocolate being made and taste it for free. There are 60 different varieties of handmade chocolates, as well as hot chocolate (perfect for chilly mountain days) and homemade ice cream (chocolate, of course) for those sultry summer days. ⊠ *176 Lurline St.* ☎ *02/4782–7071* ⊕ *www.bluemountainschocolate.com.au.*

★ Echo Point
VIEWPOINT | Overlooking the densely forested Jamison Valley and three soaring sandstone pillars, this lofty promontory has the best views around Katoomba. The formations—called the Three Sisters—take their name from an Aboriginal legend that relates how a trio of siblings was turned to stone by their witch-doctor father to save them from the clutches of

---

Artist Haven 🎟

The Blue Mountains harbor a wealth of talent. You'll find artists, writers, composers, and performers living in this vibrant cultural community. Check out the galleries, browse in the bookshops, or pop into a café or pub to catch some good music.

Blue Mountains Music Festival. Held over a weekend every March (in the middle of the month) in beautiful Katoomba, this Music Festival of Folk, Blues, and Roots showcases artists from around the world and across Australia in intimate and relaxed settings. ⊕ *www.bmff.org. au.*

---

a mythical monster. The area was once a seabed that rose over a long period and subsequently eroded, leaving behind tall formations of sedimentary rock. From Echo Point—where the visitor center is located—you can clearly see the horizontal sandstone bedding in the landscape. There is a wide viewing area as well as the start of walks that take you closer to the Sisters. At night the Sisters are illuminated by floodlights. There are cafés and a visitor information center near the site. ⊠ *Echo Point Rd., off Katoomba St.*

★ Scenic World
TOUR—SIGHT | **FAMILY** | Thrill-seekers can choose their own adventure on the Scenic Railway, whose trains descend 1,000 feet down the mountainside—the seats allow passengers to adjust the incline angle from 52 to a hair-raising 64 degrees. The railway is one of three attractions at Scenic World, which has carried more than 25 million passengers to the valley floor since it opened in 1945. Once at the base, visitors can hike on easy trails through the rain forest or make the 20-minute hike to Cableway, a

huge cable car that whisks passengers back up the mountain. You can also hike back up, but it's a steep, strenuous climb. The third attraction is Scenic Skyway, a glass-enclosed and-floored cabin that travels from one cliff to another, some 920 feet above the ravines below. The A$37 day pass provides unlimited rides on all three attractions. ✉ *Cliff Dr., at Violet St.* ☎ *02/4780–0200* 🌐 *www.scenicworld.com.au* 🎟 *From A$37.*

🍴 Restaurants

Darley's Restaurant
$$$$ | AUSTRALIAN | Found in Lilianfels Blue Mountains Resort & Spa, Darley's focuses on fine dining in a sophisticated setting that exudes old-school charm, with the walls covered in framed photos showing how the Blue Mountains have transformed over the years. The scallop silk and caviar as a starter is a crowd pleaser. Then for main, the 16-hour Wagyu onglet with wasabi and sprouts has been hailed as a culinary masterpiece. The drunken chocolate cake with vinegar mousse is a celebrated finale to a rich epicurean journey. Two courses are A$95. Three courses are A$125. **Known for:** high-end dining; 16-hour Wagyu onglet with wasabi and sprouts; weekend tables booked far in advance. [$] *Average main: A$95* ✉ *Lilianfels Ave., Katoomba* ☎ *02/4780–1200* 🌐 *www.darleysrestaurant.com.au.*

Palette Dining
$$ | CONTEMPORARY | Housed over two floors, Palette is a restaurant with two distinct personalities: downstairs caters to those wanting quick bites and a few drinks while upstairs offers fancier fare and delicious NSW wines. But at the heart of both is locally sourced produce from the Blue Mountains region. The pork belly with candied jalapeños is a delicious starter. The lamb shoulder with molasses is a must-try for the main. And for dessert, the focus here is on old-school puddings, like a quince upside-down cake. **Known for:** locally sourced ingredients; trendy vibe; lamb shoulder with molasses. [$] *Average main: A$32* ✉ *92 Bathurst Rd., Katoomba* ☎ *02/4782–9530* 🌐 *www.palettedining.com* ⏲ *Closed Mon.–Wed.*

🛏 Hotels

The Carrington
$$$$ | HOTEL | Established in 1880, this is one of the grande dames of the Blue Mountains, a Victorian-era relic that, in its heyday, was considered one of the four great hotels of the British Empire. **Pros:** drinks on their veranda are a pleasant way to end the day; breakfast included; free Wi-Fi in rooms. **Cons:** the newer rooms lack character; some rooms have shared bathrooms; very quiet outside of the weekend. [$] *Rooms from: A$309* ✉ *15–47 Katoomba St.* ☎ *02/4782–1111* 🌐 *www.thecarrington.com.au* 🛏 *115 rooms* 🍴 *Free Breakfast.*

Echoes Boutique Hotel & Restaurant
$$$$ | HOTEL | Perched on the edge of the Jamison Valley, this stylish boutique hotel has one of the best views in the Blue Mountains. **Pros:** spectacular views from the terrace; slick, contemporary design; brilliant restaurant. **Cons:** little pricey; isolated location ; small. [$] *Rooms from: A$525* ✉ *3 Lilianfels Ave.* ☎ *02/4782–1966* 🌐 *www.echoeshotel.com.au* 🛏 *14 rooms* 🍴 *Free Breakfast.*

★ Hydro Majestic Blue Mountains
$$$ | HOTEL | This iconic and much-loved cliff-top hotel in Medlow Bath recaptured its former art deco splendor when it reopened a few years ago and is once again a destination hotel. **Pros:** most rooms have amazing views; heritage glamour and living history; delightful high tea. **Cons:** rooms are small; expensive; packed on weekends. [$] *Rooms from: A$269* ✉ *Great Western Hwy., Medlow Bath* ☎ *02/4782–6885* 🌐 *www.hydromajestic.com.au* 🛏 *57 rooms* 🍴 *No meals.*

Great Hikes in Katoomba

Echo Point to Scenic Railway

In the 1930s, the **Giant Staircase** was hewn out of the cliff by teams of park rangers. The top of the steps are the **Three Sisters Lookout** and the walk down is very steep and narrow in places. It's difficult going but the views make it all worthwhile. Look out for the encouraging halfway sign. At the bottom, keep your eyes peeled for echidnas, brush-tailed and ring-tail possums, bandicoots, quolls, and grey-headed flying foxes. If you're keen for more exertion once you've reached the Railway, take the **Furber Steps.** It's a challenging but rewarding track that has great views of **Katoomba Falls** and **Mt. Solitary** across the valley.

Prince Henry Cliff Walk

If you prefer to hike in the mountains rather than along the forest floor, you'll enjoy this section of the Cliff Walk with superb vistas across the valley. From the Leura Cascades picnic area on Cliff Drive, the trail descends beside Leura Falls creek toward **Bridal Veil Falls.** Be sure to slow down and take in the great views over the **Leura Forest.** Continue on Prince Henry Drive; at **Tarpeian Rock** you can see Mt. Solitary. Keep going uphill toward Olympian Rock and Elysian Rock. From here, follow the cliff line to **Millamurra** and **Tallawarra Lookouts.** The last part of the climb to the **Three Sisters** is perhaps the most challenging but also the most rewarding. Take a few minutes and savor the sweeping views of the valley.

★ Lilianfels Blue Mountains Resort & Spa
$$$ | **HOTEL** | Teetering close to the brink f Echo Point, this glamorous boutique otel adds a keen sense of manor-house tyle to the standard Blue Mountains uesthouse experience. **Pros:** luxurious nd restful bathrooms; friendly five-star ervice; lovely drawing room with views. **ons:** 19th-century style is not for every-ne; restaurant is very expensive; can el impersonal. [$] *Rooms from: A$475* *5–19 Lilianfels Ave., at Panorama Dr.* *02/4780–1200* 🌐 *www.lilianfels.com.* *u* *Reservations essential* *85 rooms* *Free Breakfast.*

★ Lurline House
| **B&B/INN** | This historic little B&B is guably the town's best. **Pros:** rooms ave four-poster beds; warm and elcoming; manicured gardens. **Cons:** ounger trendsetters might find the place ot to their taste; not for those who e private hotel stays. [$] *Rooms from: A$140* ✉ *122 Lurline St.* ☎ *02/4782–4609* 🌐 *www.lurlinehouse.com.au* 🛏 *8 rooms* 🍴 *Free Breakfast.*

Mountain Heritage Hotel & Spa
$$$$ | **HOTEL** | This hotel overlooking the Jamison Valley is steeped in history: it served as a "coffee palace" during the temperance movement, a rest-and-relaxation establishment for the British navy during World War II, and a religious retreat in the 1970s. **Pros:** friendly service; manicured gardens; public areas are charming with great valley views. **Cons:** furniture is a little dated; some rooms are small; not in walking distance to anything. [$] *Rooms from: A$330* ✉ *Apex St. at Lovel St.* ☎ *02/4782–2155* 🌐 *www.mountainheritage.com.au* 🛏 *37 rooms, 4 suites* 🍴 *Free Breakfast.*

Activities

A good hiking brochure can be picked up at Blue Mountains Visitor Centre at Echo Point, which lists walks varying in length from a half hour to three days.

ECO-TOURS

Tread Lightly Eco Tours

HIKING/WALKING | This eco-minded company operates small-group tours of Blue Mountains National Park and guided day and night walks, as well as four-wheel-drive tours and breakfast trips to view wildlife. Half- and full-day walking tours take in such areas as Fern Bower, Blue Gum Forest, and the Ruined Castle. ✉ *100 Great Western Hwy., Medlow Bath* ☎ *04/1497–6752* ⊕ *www.treadlightly.com.au* ✉ *From A$145.*

HIKING

Blue Mountains Guides

HIKING/WALKING | Single-day, overnight, and three-day walks are available through this guiding company. The half-day Grand Canyon Walk near Blackheath (A$165) is a great way to experience the rain forest if time is short. A four-wheel-drive trip, which includes breakfast with wild kangaroos, is another good choice. ✉ *33 Portland Rd., Medlow Bath* ☎ *04/1415–2185* ⊕ *www.bluemountainsguides.com.au* ✉ *From A$145.*

Blue Mountains Walkabout

HIKING/WALKING | Experience the Blue Mountains from an Aboriginal perspective on this outfitter's challenging one-day walks, which follow a traditional walkabout song line. Indigenous guides take you on a 7-km (4½-mile) off-track walk through rain forests, while giving some background on Aboriginal culture. You'll also taste bush tucker (food). The walk involves some scrambling, so you need to be fit. The tours depart from Faulconbridge Railway Station (near Springwood, in the lower Blue Mountains), about a 30-minute drive east of Katoomba.

✉ *Springwood* ☎ *0408/433822* ⊕ *www.bluemountainswalkabout.com* ✉ *A$95.*

Blackheath

12 km (7½ miles) north of Katoomba.

Magnificent easterly views over the Grose Valley—which has outstanding hiking trails—delightful gardens, good restaurants, and antiques shops head the list of reasons to visit the village of Blackheath, at the 3,495-foot summit of the Blue Mountains.

GETTING HERE AND AROUND

Blackheath is an easy drive north from Katoomba, traveling on the Great Western Highway, passing Medlow Bath on the way. There's also a train station on the Blue Mountains line, and the town is also serviced by Blue Mountains Bus Company on Route 698 between Katoomba and Mount Victoria.

VISITOR INFORMATION

CONTACTS Blue Mountains Heritage Centre. ✉ *Govetts Leap Rd. at Mel Ave.* ☎ *02/4787–8877* ⊕ *www.nationalparks.nsw.gov.au.*

Sights

Govetts Leap Lookout

VIEWPOINT | Blackheath's most famous view is from the Govetts Leap Lookout, with its striking panorama of the Grose Valley and Bridal Veil Falls. Govett was a surveyor who mapped this region extensively in the 1830s. This lookout is the start or finish of several excellent bushwalks. Brochures are available at the Blue Mountains Heritage Centre. ✉ *End of Govett's Leap Rd.* ⊕ *www.nationalparks.nsw.gov.au.*

Trains, Planes and Automobiles

STORE/MALL | **FAMILY** | Children and adults will enjoy a browse around this store that bills itself as the best antique toy

Great Hikes in Blackheath

Grand Canyon Walk

From the parking lot at Evans Lookout, 4.5 km (2.8 miles) from Blackheath, follow the Grand Canyon signs as the path zigzags down the hillside, and the vegetation becomes more like a rain forest. The trail takes you down into the canyon and over a creek. It winds past a few overhanging rocks, then starts a steep decline toward a sandy overhang called the **Rotunda.** After a break here, follow the signs to **Evans Lookout,** which leads you through a tunnel and past two waterfalls. You eventually reach the 33-foot **Beauchamp Falls** in the center of the creek. From here head up through a gap in the cliffs, weaving through boulders, again following signs to Evans Lookout. From Evans Lookout, you can follow a 6.5-km (4-mile) cliffside walk to **Pulpit Rock** along the Cliff Top Track. The entire loop is 6 km (3.75 miles) and takes around 3½ hours.

Perrys Lookdown to Blue Gum Forest

This is a hard, but rewarding, four-hour walk. From the Perry Lookdown parking lot (turn east into Hat Hill Road from the Great Western Highway at Blackheath), follow the signs pointing out the trail down the hill to **Perrys Lookdown.** You'll have fine views over the **Grose Valley** with its sheer sandstone cliffs with the **Blue Gum Forest** below. Next, head down the hill and do a quick detour to **Docker's Lookout** with its view of Mt. Banks to the north. Head back following the Perrys Lookdown-Blue Gum Forest walk signs. The descent to Blue Gum Forest will take about 90 minutes. Once you've explored the forest floor and its dense canopy, head back up the steep track to Perrys Lookdown.

hop in the world. ⊠ *50 Govetts Leap Rd.* *02/4787–7974* ⊕ *www.antiquetoys.* *om.au.*

🍴 Restaurants

⭐ Cinnabar Kitchen

$ | **WINE BAR** | The newest kid on the culinary block, this lively wine bar–style eatery has attracted quite a bit of hype, and the attention of Sydney-based foodies who have been arriving each weekend in droves, since its opening in early 2018. It's so popular, in fact, the restaurant is now demanding a $48 minimum spend from each diner on the weekend. A truly unusual move for a Blue Mountains eatery but with dishes like the sizzling Jamaican spiced prawns for a main and the wild scallop tartare for a starter, worth it. **Known for:** trendy spot; $48 minimum spend from each diner on the weekend; Jamaican spiced prawns. $ *Average main: A$28* ⊠ *246 Great Western Hwy.* ☎ *02/4787–7269* ⊕ *www. cinnabar.kitchen* ⊙ *Closed Sun.–Tues.*

🛏 Hotels

Jemby Rinjah Eco Lodge

$$$ | **B&B/INN** | Designed for urbanites seeking a wilderness experience, these rustic, self-contained wooden cabins and lodges are set deep in the bush. **Pros:** private and tranquil; hearty and healthy mountain fare at the restaurant; incredible native birds. **Cons:** some might find the eco-toilet disconcerting; the

Off The Beaten Path

Mount Tomah Botanic Garden. This is the cool-climate branch of Sydney's Royal Botanic Gardens (30 km [19 miles] northeast of Mount Victoria). The garden is 3,280 feet above sea level, and is a spectacular setting for native and imported plants. You'll find beautiful rhododendrons and European deciduous trees, as well as plants that evolved in isolation for millions of years in the Gondwana Forest. The famous Wollemi Pine (once thought to be extinct) is also here. There are picnic grounds, a café with views of the ranges, and a daily guided tour at 11:30 am. Admission is free. ⊠ *Bells Line of Rd., Mount Tomah* 🕾 *02/4567–3000* ⊕ *www.mounttomah-botanicgarden.com.au.*

lodges can be booked out by groups, who can get noisy; minimum two-night stay. Ⓢ *Rooms from: A$240* ⊠ *336 Evans Lookout Rd.* 🕾 *02/4787–7622* ⊕ *www. jemby.com.au* 🛏 *13 rooms* ⊺◎⊺ *No meals.*

🏃 Activities

HIKING
Auswalk

HIKING/WALKING | This environmentally conscious company, which also leads walks in other parts of Australia, has three-day guided hiking tours through the region, staying at historic inns along the way, with all meals and admission to some local attractions included. The seven-day walk is A$1,595 per person (double occupancy). The owners advise that you be in reasonable shape before starting. 🕾 *03/9597–9767* ⊕ *www.aus-walk.com.au* 🍽 *From A$1225.*

HORSEBACK RIDING
Megalong Australian Heritage Centre

HORSEBACK RIDING | This rural farm in a deep mountain valley off the Great Western Highway is the place to saddle up and explore the many mountain and valley trails. Both adults and children can go horseback riding around the farm's 2,000 acres, with prices ranging from A$50 for an hour's wilderness ride to A$95 for the most popular two-hour ride to A$395 for a full-day ride with breakfast and lunch. ⊠ *993 Megalong Rd., Megalong* ⊹ *15 km (9 miles) south of Blackheath* 🕾 *02/4787–8188* ⊕ *www.megalongcc. com.au* 🍽 *From A$50.*

Mount Victoria

7 km (4½ miles) northwest of Blackheath.

The settlement of Mount Victoria is the highest point in the Blue Mountains, and there's a Rip Van Winkle air about it—drowsy and only just awake in an unfamiliar world. A walk around the village reveals many atmospheric houses, stores, a charming old post office, and a stately old hotel with the patina of time spelled out in the fading paint of these buildings. Mount Victoria is at the far side of the mountains at the western limit of this region, and the village serves as a good jumping-off point for a couple of out-of-the-way attractions.

GETTING HERE AND AROUND
Mount Victoria is an easy drive north of Blackheath on the Great Western Highway, and it's also on the main Blue Mountains railway line linking Sydney with Lithgow. The 698V bus route connects the village with Katoomba, but only on weekdays.

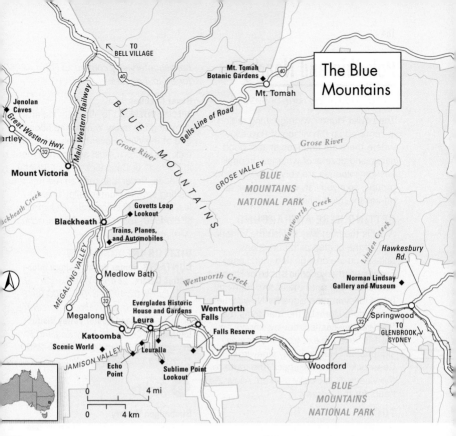

The Blue Mountains

TO BELL VILLAGE

Mt. Tomah Botanic Gardens

Mt. Tomah

Jenolan Caves

Great Western Hwy.

Hartley

Main Western Railway

BLUE MOUNTAINS

Bells Line of Road

Grose River

Grose River

Mount Victoria

GROSE VALLEY

BLUE MOUNTAINS NATIONAL PARK

Creek

Blackheath Creek

Govetts Leap Lookout

Blackheath

Trains, Planes, and Automobiles

MEGALONG VALLEY

Medlow Bath

Wentworth Creek

Linden Creek

Hawkesbury Rd.

Norman Lindsay Gallery and Museum

Everglades Historic House and Gardens

Wentworth Falls

Megalong

Leura

Katoomba

Falls Reserve

Springwood

TO GLENBROOK SYDNEY

Scenic World

Leuralla

JAMISON VALLEY

Echo Point

Sublime Point Lookout

Woodford

BLUE MOUNTAINS NATIONAL PARK

0   4 mi

0   4 km

◉ Sights

★ Jenolan Caves

CAVE | FAMILY | Stalactites, stalagmites, columns, and lacelike rock on multiple levels fill the fascinating Jenolan Caves, a labyrinth of vast limestone caverns sculpted by underground rivers. There are as many as 320 caves in the Jenolan area. Two caves (Nettles Cave and Devil's Coachhouse) near the surface can be explored on your own, but a guide is required to reach the most intriguing formations. Standard tours lead through the most popular caves—many say that Orient Cave is the most spectacular, while the more rigorous adventure tours last up to seven hours. The one- to two-hour walks depart every 15 to 30 minutes, on weekends less frequently. Prices range from A$42 for a standard tour to A$220 for the full-day Mammoth Cave Adventure Tour where you squeeze through ancient passageways—it includes a bit of rappelling and is not for the claustrophobic. Concerts and murder mystery nights are also held in this spooky environment. Cave House, on the same site, is a nostalgic retreat and has been providing lodging since 1887. To get here, follow the Great Western Highway north out of Mount Victoria, then after Hartley, turn southwest toward Hampton. ⊠ *4655 Jenolan Caves Rd., Jenolan Caves* ⊹ *59 km (37 miles) southwest of Mount Victoria* ☎ *1300/763311* ⊕ *www.jenolancaves. org.au* ⌑ *From A$42.*

Pokolbin and Nearby

163 km (100 miles) north of Sydney.

The Lower Hunter wine-growing region is centered on the village of Pokolbin, where there are antiques shops, good cafés, and dozens of wineries. In peak season, wineries are very busy with tour groups, so if you can visit midweek or off-season, all the better.

GETTING HERE AND AROUND

A car is the best way to visit the wineries and off-the-beaten-path attractions unless you are on a guided tour. Leave Sydney via the Harbour Bridge or Harbour Tunnel and get onto the Pacific Highway (keep following the signs for Newcastle). Just before Hornsby the road joins the Sydney–Newcastle Freeway, known as the M1. Take the exit from the freeway signposted "Hunter Valley vineyards via Cessnock." From Cessnock, the route to the vineyards is clearly marked. Allow 2½ hours for the journey.

TOURS

Any tour of the area's vineyards should begin at Pokolbin's **Hunter Valley Wine Country Visitors Information Centre,** which has free maps of the vineyards, brochures, and a handy visitor's guide.

AAT Kings

SPECIAL-INTEREST | From Sydney, AAT Kings operates a daylong wine-tasting bus tour of the Hunter Valley and another to Hunter Valley Gardens. Buses collect passengers from city hotels from 7 am. ☏ *1300/228546* ⊕ *www.aatkings.com.au* ✉ *From A$240.*

Heidi's Hunter Valley

SPECIAL-INTEREST | Local operator Heidi's Hunter Valley operates personalized day tours to the wineries and restaurants in a sleek four-wheel-drive vehicle. Heidi Duckworth, who worked for the Hunter Valley Wine Tourism organization for 12 years, knows all the best places in the valley. ☏ *0408/623136* ⊕ *www.*

heidishuntervalley.com.au ✉ *From A$250 for up to 4 guests.*

Rover Coaches

SPECIAL-INTEREST | To avoid driving after sampling too many wines, hop aboard one of the Wine Rover buses, which will pick you up from most accommodations in Pokolbin or Cessnock to visit several wineries. Rover also runs an Ale Trail tour, visiting several Hunter Valley breweries. ⊠ *231–233 Vincent St., Cessnock* ☏ *02/4990–1699* ⊕ *www.rovercoaches. com.au* ✉ *From A$55.*

VISITOR INFORMATION

CONTACTS Hunter Valley Visitors Information Centre. ⊠ *455 Wine Country Dr., Pokolbin* ☏ *02/4993–6700, 1300/6948–6837* ⊕ *www.huntervalleyvisitorcentre. com.au.* **Maitland Hunter Valley Visitor Information Centre.** ⊠ *New England Hwy. at High St., Maitland* ☏ *02/4931–2800* ⊕ *www.mymaitland.com.au.*

◉ Sights

Bimbadgen Winery

WINERY/DISTILLERY | This winery is particularly well-known for its very popular Day on the Green concerts, which are held several times between October and March. Artists have included Tom Jones and Leonard Cohen. Beyond the shows, the winery also produces some very good wines—try the signature Chardonnay or Sémillon. It is also home to one of the Hunter's best restaurants, Esca, which has fantastic views across the vineyards towards the Brokenback Mountains. To take full advantage of the views, you could also prebook a picnic (A$100), which comes with deli meats, cheeses, fresh bread, and a bottle of the winery's best. The restaurant serves lunch every day and dinner Wednesday through Saturday. The cellar door is open daily for tastings. ⊠ *790 McDonalds Rd., Pokolbin* ☏ *02/4998–4650 cellar door, 02/4998–4666 restaurant* ⊕ *www. bimbadgen.com.au.*

Continued on page 175

HIKING THE BLUE MOUNTAINS

Kanangra Falls

Head west of Sydney along the M4, or simply hop a bus or train, and within an hour you'll be on a gradual climb along a traditional Aboriginal pathway into the heart of the Blue Mountains—a sandstone plateau formed 150 million years ago that tops out at 3,600 feet. Dramatic valleys, canyons, and cliff faces to the north and south of the main road have been carved by wind and water over millennia. And the blue? That's light refracting off the fine oil mist from the world's most ecologically diverse tract of eucalypt forest.

(top) Looking out over the Jamison Valley.

A WORLD HERITAGE WONDERLAND

Part of the Greater Blue Mountains World Heritage Area, Blue Mountains National Park encompasses 2,678 sq km (1,034 sq ft) of prime hiking country. Most tracks skirt the cliff edges or run along the bottom of the canyons; paths that connect the two levels are often at points along the cliff that offer breathtaking panoramas of the Jamison, Megalong, or Grose Valleys.

While the geological landscape is worth the trip alone, the flora and fauna are some of the country's most unique. Within just a few square miles, the world's widest variety of eucalypts in one contiguous forest have evolved to thrive in everything from open scrub plains to dense valley rainforests. The Wollami pine, a tree that grew alongside dinosaurs, can only be found in a few small areas here. Then there are the rare or threatened creatures like the Blue Mountains water skink, the yellow-bellied glider, and the long-nosed potoroo. It seems only fitting that both Charles Darwin and John Muir visited here. In 1932 it became one of the first formally protected tracts of land in Australia.

Towns dot the main highway through the Blue Mountains, but Katoomba is the unofficial capital, fully outfitted with resources for visitors and the starting point for some of the most iconic walks. Less-bustling Black-heath, minutes up the road from Katoomba, has our favorite eco-lodges and is closest to the best walks of the Grose Valley. You can get a feel for the region on a day trip from Sydney, but if your schedule permits, stay a night (or three) to fit in a few different hikes.

HIKING LITE: THREE WAYS TO SEE THE JAMISON VALLEY WITHOUT BREAKING A SWEAT

Scenic Skyway

SCENIC CABLEWAY

Less crowded than the Scenic Railway, the world's steepest cable car feels gentle in comparison. The enclosed gondola glides between the valley floor and the cliff rim with views of the Three Sisters.

SCENIC SKYWAY

This Swiss-style, glass-bottom cable car takes you on a 720 m (1/2 mi) long journey 270 m (886 ft) above the gorge for great 360 degree views across the Jamison Valley, the Ka-toomba Falls, and the famous Three Sisters.

KATOOMBA SCENIC RAILWAY

An incline of 52 degrees makes this former coal-haul railway the world's steepest. Grab a seat in the front. Be prepared for lines at peak visiting times. The railway runs every 10 minutes until 4:50 pm.

Claustral Canyon

BLUE MOUNTAIN TRAIL OVERVIEW

Lookout at Echo Point

KATOOMBA-ECHO POINT	TRAIL TIPS	HIGHLIGHTS
ECHO POINT TO SCENIC RAILWAY: This may not be a long walk, but thanks to the 900 steps of the Giant Staircase, don't underestimate it.	This route is very popular, especially on weekends, so set off early. Be aware that the last railway and cable car up leave at 4:50 pm. If you miss them, you'll have to walk.	• Expansive views across the Jamison Valley and beautiful forest vistas. • Brings you right up against the Three Sisters. • Scenic Railway boarding area is at the end of the trail, so you don't have to walk back up.
PRINCE HENRY CLIFF WALK: Start at the Leura Cascades picnic area and head up the mountain to Echo Point. This is a tough hike and not for the faint of heart.	Olympian Rock and Elysian Rock are perfect spots to picnic.	• Thanks to the level of difficulty, you'll be able to escape the crowds at Katoomba. • Spot lyre birds, kookaburras, and glossy black cockatoos.
BLACKHEATH	TRAIL TIPS	HIGHLIGHTS
GRAND CANYON WALK: Possible for anyone who's reasonably fit (though there are some steps) and well worth the effort.	A great choice for hot days: the canyon's cool temperatures will come as welcome relief.	• A winding path through lush vegetation and around plummeting waterfalls. • Spectacular views of gorges, forest, and cliff lines at Evans lookout.
PERRY'S LOOKDOWN TO BLUE GUM FOREST: This track starts at Perry's Lookdown parking lot, 9 km (5.5 mi) northeast of Blackheath, and takes you down a steep track into the lovely Blue Gum Forest.	Stop by the Heritage Centre in nearby Blackheath for excellent information on historic sites and hiking trips.	• Experience for yourself why the ecologically unique Blue Gum Forest attracted conservationists' attention in Australia. • You might spot possums, gliders, bandicoots, brown antechinuses, and swamp wallabies.
GLENBROOK	TRAIL TIPS	HIGHLIGHTS
RED HANDS CAVE TRACK: This moderately difficult circuit walk goes up the Red Hands Creek Valley along a creek and through the rainforest.	It's best to park at the Visitors Centre on Bruce Road and then walk for 10 minutes following the signs to the Glenbrook causeway, as there is no easy parking at the causeway itself.	• Bring your binoculars, because there are many birdwatching opportunities. • See the Blue Mountains' most sacred Aboriginal site, Red Hands Cave. The cave is named after the displays of Aboriginal hand stencils on its walls.

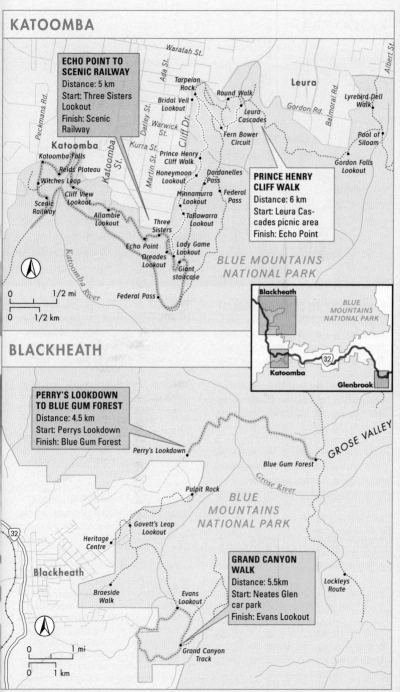

KATOOMBA

ECHO POINT TO SCENIC RAILWAY
Distance: 5 km
Start: Three Sisters Lookout
Finish: Scenic Railway

PRINCE HENRY CLIFF WALK
Distance: 6 km
Start: Leura Cascades picnic area
Finish: Echo Point

Waratah St.

Tarpeian Rock

Round Walk

Leura

Lyrebird Dell Walk

Bridal Veil Lookout

Leura Cascades

Gordon Rd.

Ada St.

Fern Bower Circuit

Pool of Siloam

Peckmans Rd.

Darley St.

Warwick St.

Cliff Dr.

Kurra St.

Katoomba

Katoomba Falls

Reids Plateau

Witches Leap

Cliff View Lookout

Scenic Railway

Allambie Lookout

Prince Henry Cliff Walk

Honeymoon Lookout

Minnamurra Lookout

Tallawarra Lookout

Three Sisters

Echo Point

Oreades Lookout

Giant staircase

Lady Game Lookout

Dardanelles Pass

Federal Pass

Martin St.

Katoomba St.

Gordon Falls Lookout

Albert St.

Balmoral Rd.

BLUE MOUNTAINS NATIONAL PARK

Katoomba River

Federal Pass

0 — 1/2 mi
0 — 1/2 km

BLACKHEATH

PERRY'S LOOKDOWN TO BLUE GUM FOREST
Distance: 4.5 km
Start: Perrys Lookdown
Finish: Blue Gum Forest

Perry's Lookdown

Blue Gum Forest

GROSE VALLEY

Grose River

Pulpit Rock

BLUE MOUNTAINS NATIONAL PARK

Govett's Leap Lookout

32

Heritage Centre

Blackheath

Braeside Walk

Evans Lookout

GRAND CANYON WALK
Distance: 5.5km
Start: Neates Glen car park
Finish: Evans Lookout

Lockleys Route

Grand Canyon Track

0 — 1 mi
0 — 1 km

Blackheath

BLUE MOUNTAINS NATIONAL PARK

Katoomba

32

Glenbrook

KATOOMBA

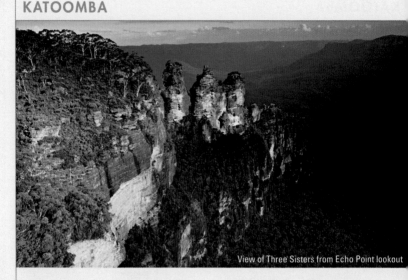

View of Three Sisters from Echo Point lookout

ECHO POINT TO SCENIC RAILWAY

In the 1930s, the **Giant Staircase** was hewn out of the cliff by teams of park rangers. The top of the steps are near **Three Sisters Lookout** and the walk down is very steep and narrow in places. It's difficult going but the views make it all worthwhile. Look out for the encouraging half way sign. At the bottom, keep your eyes peeled for echidnas, brushtailed and ring-tail possums, bandicoots, quolls, and grey-headed flying foxes. If you're keen for more exertion once you've reached the Railway, take the **Furber Steps**. It's a challenging but rewarding track that offers great views of **Katoomba Falls** and **Mt. Solitary** across the valley.

PRINCE HENRY CLIFF WALK

If you prefer to hike in the mountains rather than along the forest floor, you'll enjoy this section of the Cliff Walk with its superb vistas across the valley. From the picnic area, the trail descends beside Leura Cascades creek towards **Bridal Veil lookout**. Be sure to slow down and take in the great views over the **Leura Forest**. Continue on Prince Henry Drive; at **Tarpeian Rock** you can see Mt.

Solitary. Keep going uphill towards Olympian Rock and Elysian Rock. From here, follow the cliff line to **Millamurra** and **Tallawarra Lookouts**. The last part of the climb to the **Three Sisters** is perhaps the most challenging but also the most rewarding. Take a few minutes and savor the sweeping views of the valley.

QUICK BITES/SUPERMARKETS FOR PICNIC GOODIES

You can stock up at either Coles or ALDI supermarkets in Katoomba or Woolworths supermarket in Leura. Scenic World has two restaurants. For gourmet treats visit Carrington Cellars at the rear of the Carrington Hotel, or stop at Brown's Siding Store & Café at Medlow Bath for breakfast, lunch, and goodies.

STAY HERE IF:

On weekends tour buses descend on the town, but once they've headed back to Sydney, the place isn't over-run with vistors. Katoomba has a very relaxed feel helped in no small part by a small hippy community. It also has plenty of nice old pubs and cafés, cute vintage shops, and rural versions of big department stores.

BLACKHEATH

Mount Hay, Grose Valley

GRAND CANYON WALK

From the parking lot, 4.5 km (2.8 mi) from Blackheath, follow the Grand Canyon track signs as the path zig-zags down the hillside and the vegetation becomes more like a rainforest. The trail takes you down into the canyon and over a creek. It winds past a few overhanging rocks, then starts a steep decline towards a sandy overhang called the **Rotunda**. After a break here, follow the signs to **Evans Lookout**, which will lead you through a tunnel and past two waterfalls. You eventually reach the 10-meter-tall (33 ft) **Beauchamp Falls** in the center of the creek. From here head up through a gap in the cliffs, weaving through boulders, again following signs to Evans Lookout. From Evans Lookout, you can do a 6.5 km (4 mi) Cliffside walk to **Pulpit Rock** along the Cliff Top Track.

PERRYS LOOKDOWN TO BLUE GUM FOREST

From the parking lot, follow the signs pointing out the trail down the hill to **Perrys Lookdown**. You'll have fine views over the **Grose Valley** with its sheer sandstone cliffs with the Blue Gum Forest below. Next, head down the hill and do a quick detour to **Docker's Lookout** with its view of Mt. Banks to the north. Head back following the Perrys Lookdown–Blue Gum Forest walk signs. The descent to **Blue Gum Forest** will take about 90 minutes. Once you've explored the forest floor and its dense canopy, head back up the steep track to Perrys Lookdown.

QUICK BITES/SUPERMARKETS FOR PICNIC GOODIES

Blackheath has something of a gourmet reputation. A particular highlight is **Ashcrafts** (18 Govetts Leap Rd.). There's also a small IGA supermarket.

STAY HERE IF:

Blackheath is smaller and less-visited than Katoomba, but the old weatherboard houses give it a similar feel. There's also enough quirky shops and quaint cafes and restaurants to keep it entertaining. Several Sydney restaurateurs relocated here, so there's a breadth of excellent dining venues.

GLENBROOK

Glenbrook Gorge

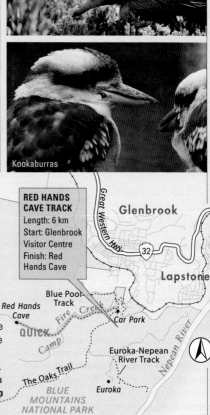

An echidna

Kookaburras

RED HANDS CAVE TRACK

Red Hands Cave has some well pre-served Aboriginal hand stencillings. The stencils are behind Plexiglas (called Perspex here) to protect them from graffiti. There are a few good placards explaining the history and describing the artifacts found in the area. The walk starts on the southern side of the causeway, and after about 2 km (1.2 mi) of gentle steps down the gully, the well-defined track forks: take the right-hand path just after a large rocky outcrop near the edge of a gully. ■ TIP → **Take care near the edge, there's a significant dropoff.** Up the hill near **Camp Fire Creek**, keep an eye out for axe grinding grooves (oval-shaped inden-tations in sandstone outcrops that Aboriginal peoples used to shape and sharpen stone axes). The trail passes through several types of forest, includ-ing dry eucalypt forest, so there's a good variety of birds in the area. Watch for echidnas in the open forest and chestnut-rumped heathwrens and rock warblers in the sandstone area near the Red Hands Cave.

RED HANDS CAVE TRACK
Length: 6 km
Start: Glenbrook Visitor Centre
Finish: Red Hands Cave

Great Western HWY

Glenbrook

32

Lapstone

Blue Pool Track

Red Hands Cave

Fire Creek

Car Park

QUICK

Camp

Nepean River

Euroka-Nepean River Track

The Oaks Trail

BLUE MOUNTAINS NATIONAL PARK

Euroka

BITES/SUPERMARKETS FOR PICNIC GOODIES

Glenbrook doesn't have the same variety of food and lodging options as Katoomba and Blackheath, but there's a small supermarket on Park Street. Ross Street has a few nice cafes; check out **Mash Café's** delicious breakfasts.

Binnorie Dairy

STORE/MALL | Drop by this cheesemaker at Tuscany Wine Estate to sample and buy Simon Gough's irresistible, handcrafted soft cow and goat cheeses made from locally sourced milk. You'd be hard-pressed to find a tastier marinated feta outside Greece—or even in it. ✉ *Tuscany Wine Estate, Hermitage Rd. at Mistletoe La., Pokolbin* ☎ *02/4998–6660* ⊕ *www. binnorie.com.au.*

Briar Ridge Vineyard

WINERY/DISTILLERY | In a delightful rural corner of the Mount View region, this is one of the Hunter Valley's most prestigious small wineries. It produces a limited selection of sought-after reds, whites, and sparkling wines. The Sémillon, Chardonnay, Shiraz, and intense Cabernet Sauvignon are highly recommended. The vineyard is on the southern periphery of the Lower Hunter vineyards, about a five-minute drive from Pokolbin. ✉ *593 Mt. View Rd., Mount View* ☎ *02/4990–3670* ⊕ *www.briarridge.com.au.*

★ Hunter Valley Gardens

GARDEN | FAMILY | Garden lovers and those who admire beauty in general should flock to the Hunter Valley Gardens, in the heart of the Pokolbin wine-growing district. The 12 separate gardens occupy 50 acres and include European formal gardens, a Chinese Moongate garden, and a delightful children's storybook garden featuring characters such as the Mad Hatter and Jack and Jill. The gardens have a dazzling Christmas lights display each year; the park is open at night during the holiday season (mid-November–late January) from 6 to 10. The adjacent complex houses restaurants, a popular pub, a hotel, a cute wedding chapel, the underground **Hunter Cellars,** and a selection of boutiques selling gifts as well as wonderful chocolates and fudge. ✉ *2090 Broke Rd., Pokolbin* ☎ *02/4998–4000* ⊕ *www.huntervalleygardens.com.au* 💳 *A$30.*

Lindeman's Ben Ean Winery

WINERY/DISTILLERY | This has been one of the largest and most prestigious winemakers in the country since the early 1900s. In addition to its Hunter Valley vineyards, the company owns property in South Australia and Victoria, and numerous outstanding wines from these vineyards can be sampled in the tasting room. Try the Shiraz, Sémillon, or Chardonnay. The winery has its own museum, displaying vintage winemaking equipment; the 1843 Harvest Cafe; and two picnic areas, one near the parking lot and the other next to the willow trees around the dam. ✉ *McDonalds Rd., just south of DeBeyers Rd., Pokolbin* ☎ *02/4993–3705* ⊕ *www.benean.com.au.*

Margan Family Winegrowers

WINERY/DISTILLERY | A leading light in the new wave of Hunter winemakers, Margan Family Winegrowers produces some of the valley's best small-volume wines. Try their full-bodied Verdelho, rosé-style Saignée Shiraz, and Certain Views Cabernet Sauvignon. A riper-than-most Sémillon is the flagship. Many items on the fine-dining lunch menu in the restaurant are sourced from the chef's vegetable and herb garden on-site, along with fresh eggs. Tasting plates are a great way to sample many of the dishes, such as pancetta-wrapped quail. ✉ *1238 Milbrodale Rd., Broke* ☎ *02/6579–1317 cellar door* ⊕ *www.margan.com.au.*

Matilda Bay Brewhouse Hunter Valley

WINERY/DISTILLERY | There are 12 craft beers produced in this boutique brewery, including the brewer's acclaimed "three-hop" beers: premium lager, premium light lager, and pilsner, along with its alcoholic ginger beer. You can order a chef's beer tasting "paddle" with small glasses of each, complete with tasting notes. Soak up the alcohol with fish-and-chips, meatballs, pizzas, and other light fare, and there's live music most days. It's part of a large complex that includes the resort, a wine school, cooking school, candy making classes, day spa, horseback riding, and Segway tours. ✉ *Hermitage Rd. at Mistletoe La., Pokolbin* ☎ *02/4998–7829* ⊕ *www.hunterresort.com.au.*

McGuigan Wines

WINERY/DISTILLERY | Adjoining the Hunter Valley Gardens is the cellar-door complex of McGuigan Wines, one of the most well-known wine labels in the Hunter Valley. Here you can taste and buy wines, such as Vineyard Select and Personal Reserve labels, that are not available in suburban wine shops. Winery tours depart at noon every day. While you're there try some of the superb cheeses at the adjacent **Hunter Valley Cheese Company**—look out for the washed-rind Hunter Valley Gold and the deliciously marinated soft cows'-milk cheese. You can also see the cheeses being made by hand. There is a cheese talk daily at 11. ✉ *Broke Rd. at McDonalds Rd., Pokolbin* ☎ *02/4998–4111* ⊕ *www.mcguiganwines.com.au.*

McWilliams Mount Pleasant Estate

WINERY/DISTILLERY | At this estate, part of Australia's biggest family-owned wine company, chief winemaker Jim Chatto (only the fourth since the winery was founded in 1921) continues the tradition of producing classic Hunter wines. The flagship Maurice O'Shea Shiraz and Chardonnay, and the celebrated Elizabeth Sémillon, are among the wines that can be sampled in the huge cellar door. ✉ *401 Marrowbone Rd., Pokolbin* ☎ *02/4998–7505* ⊕ *www.mountpleasantwines.com.au* ⊑ *Tours A$5, tastings free.*

★ Roche Estate

WINERY/DISTILLERY | You can't miss this ultramodern facility in the heart of Pokolbin. This futuristic winery is a joint venture between two leading Hunter Valley families: the Roches (owners of Hunter Valley Gardens) and the McGuigans, who have made wine for four generations. The winery is best known for its Pinot Gris; however, you can sample a wide variety, including Sémillon,

Sauvignon Blanc, Chardonnay, and Shiraz in the stylish tasting room. There's also a Goldfish Wine Bar and Oishii, an on-site fine-dining Japanese-Thai restaurant. If you can, stop in at the winery's branch of the Hunter Valley Smelly Cheese Shop. In the summer the winery hosts major concerts in its 10,000-seat amphitheater—past performers have included Elton John, Rod Stewart, and the Beach Boys. ✉ *Broke Rd. at McDonalds Rd., Pokolbin* ☎ *02/4998–4098 cellar door* ⊕ *www.rocheestate.com.au.*

Tyrrell's Wines

WINERY/DISTILLERY | Founded in 1858, Tyrrell's Wines is one of the Hunter Valley's oldest family-owned vineyards. This venerable establishment crafts a wide selection of wines, and was the first to produce Chardonnay commercially in Australia. Its famous Vat 47 Chardonnay is still a winner. Enjoy the experience of sampling fine wines in the rustic tasting room, or take a picnic lunch to a site overlooking the valley. Guided tours (A$5) are given daily at 10:30. ✉ *1838 Broke Rd., Pokolbin* ☎ *02/4993–7028* ⊕ *www.tyrrells.com.au.*

🍴 Restaurants

★ Bistro Molines

$$$ | FRENCH | Local French-born celebrity chef Robert Molines, who used to run Roberts Restaurant, has a restaurant on the grounds of the lovely Tallavera vineyard, which has one of the best views in the valley. Make sure you nab a table on or near the veranda. Food isn't overly complicated or styled, which fits nicely with the relaxed (but professional) service. The twice-roasted Hunter duckling on braised cabbage is delicious, while seafood fans love the Jewfish with jamon consomme. Those who want a nap after a long lunch, or don't want to drive home, might want to book into the two-bedroom cottage (operated by Robert and his wife Sally) that's just a stroll from the restaurant. **Known for:** incredible

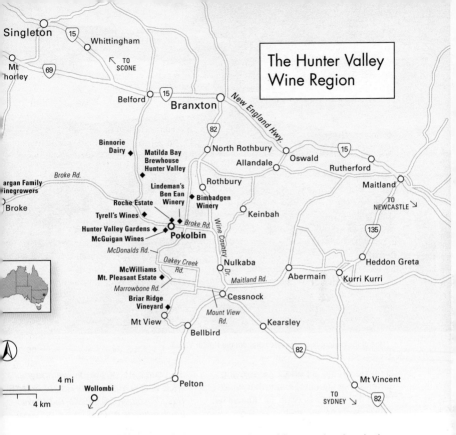

The Hunter Valley Wine Region

...iews; overnight accommodation if ...eeded; must-visit cellar door. [$] *Average main: A$42* ☒ *Tallavera Grove, 749 Mount View Rd., Mount View* ☎ *02/4990–9553* ⊕ *www.bistromolines.com.au* ⊘ *Closed ...ues. and Wed. No dinner Mon. and ...hurs.*

...afe Enzo

$ | **CAFÉ** | This breakfast and lunch café is ...t Peppers Creek Village, a charming little ...hopping and dining enclave in Pokolbin ...vith a village green atmosphere. Housed ...a sandstone building, with a lovely ...ttached sun-drenched courtyard over-...ooking a fountain, this is a great spot for ... hearty lunch after a visit to neighboring ...David Hooks winery and the clothing and ...ntiques shops. Meals are substantial ...nd may include handmade linguine with ...ger prawns and fresh chili or zucchini ...nd corn fritters with beetroot-cured

Atlantic salmon. It's a popular place in the warmer months, and even breakfast can be booked out on weekends. **Known for:** rustic fare; seafood specials; very busy. [$] *Average main: A$30* ☒ *Peppers Creek Village, Broke Rd. at Ekerts Rd., Pokolbin* ☎ *02/4998–7233* ⊕ *www.enzohuntervalley.com.au* ⊘ *No dinner.*

Circa 1876

$$$$ | **MODERN AUSTRALIAN** | This restaurant in grapevine-covered, 1876-built Pepper Tree Cottage wins the ambience award hands down. The seasonal Mod Oz menu draws inspiration from regional recipes of France and Italy and applies it to local game, seafood, beef, and lamb. A good choice is the chef speciality cherry glazed duck breast or the curry myrtle smoke emu fillet. Opt for the A$75 two-course menu or splurge on the A$120 five-course Chefs Tasting Menu. The cozy

One of the hundreds of vineyards that dot the Hunter Valley

fireside lounge is perfect for enjoying after-dinner liqueurs, or another wine from the extensive wine list. **Known for:** European vineyard feel; special occasion; stunning interiors. [$] *Average main: A$75* ✉ *64 Halls Rd., Pokolbin* ☎ *02/4998–4999* 🌐 *convent.com.au.*

Il Cacciatore

$$ | **ITALIAN** | Serving up a vast selection of northern Italian specialties, the outdoor terrace at Il Cacciatore is the perfect place for a leisurely weekend lunch. The exterior is classic Australian, with a veranda overlooking the vineyards. Once you step inside, your senses will be overwhelmed by the wonderful aromas wafting from the kitchen. Italian favorites crowd this menu: try the hearty Aged Hunter beef fillet served on Gorgonzola potato rösti with baby spinach and Nebbiolo jus, or one of their innovative pizzas. Make sure you leave plenty of room for the long list of *dolci* (desserts), too. An extensive list of local and imported wines complements the menu. **Known for:** vineyard setting; Northern Italian menu; boutique hotel onsite. [$] *Average main: A$35* ✉ *609 McDonalds Rd., at Gillard Rds., Pokolbin* ☎ *02/4998–7639* 🕒 *No lunch weekdays.*

Leaves & Fishes

$$$$ | **ASIAN FUSION** | A rustic boathouse-style café with a deck that projects over a fish-stocked dam and a lovely garden, this is the place to savor delicious seafood with an Asian twist, and share antipasto dishes. Fish comes straight from farm to plate, and wines are from local vineyards. You could start with the roasted Harvery Bay scallops or the soft shell crap with Singaporean chilli. Those who are not fans of seafood can tuck into the crispy chicken cutlets roasted in harissa. Desserts from the specials board might include steamed fig and ginger pudding. Reservations are recommended, especially on weekends, and it's a two-course minimum (A$68) at both lunch and dinner. There is also boathouse-style accommodation on the property, ideal for couples. **Known for:** idyllic surroundings; popular spot; great

eafood. $ _Average main: A$68_ ✉ _737_
ovedale Rd., Lovedale ☎ _02/4930–7400_
⊕ _www.leavesandfishes.com.au_
⊘ _Closed Mon.–Wed. No dinner Thurs._
nd Sun.

🛏 Hotels

arriages Boutique Hotel
$$ | **B&B/INN** | On 36 acres at the end of
quiet country lane, this rustic-looking
ut winsome guesthouse, set on a small
ineyard, is all about privacy. **Pros:** roman-
c in winter with roaring fireplaces in
ome rooms; lovely verandas overlooking
he grounds; private. **Cons:** no children
llowed; wedding groups sometimes
ook out most of the place; isolated.
$ _Rooms from: A$275_ ✉ _112 Halls Rd.,_
Pokolbin ☎ _02/4998–7591_ ⊕ _www._
hecarriages.com.au ⇌ _10 rooms_ ⦿ _Free_
Breakfast.

edars Mount View
$$$ | **B&B/INN** | This property nestled in
he hills above the valley might tempt
ou to forget about wine tasting for a
ew days. **Pros:** private and luxurious;
athrooms have decadent sunken
vhirlpool baths; luxury toiletries. **Cons:**
ocation a bit too remote for some; no
oom service; no pool. $ _Rooms from:_
_A$485_ ✉ _60 Mitchells Rd., Mount View_
☎ _02/4990–9009_ ⊕ _www.cedars.com.au_
⇌ _4 villas, 1 cottage_ ⦿ _Free Breakfast._

he Cooperage Bed and Breakfast
$$ | **B&B/INN** | This lovely B&B is in the
eart of Kelman Vineyards Estate, a
vorking vineyard with a cellar door just
stone's throw from the rooms. **Pros:**
ig comfy beds; guesthouse rooms
ave private decks; free Wi-Fi. **Cons:** not
uitable for children under 10; can be
ooked out months ahead; decor not to
veryone's taste. $ _Rooms from: A$278_
☒ _41 Kelman Vineyards, off Oakey Creek_
Rd., Pokolbin ☎ _02/4990–1232_ ⊕ _www._
untervalleycooperage.com ⇌ _5 rooms_
⦿ _Free Breakfast._

Mercure Resort Hunter Valley Gardens
$$$ | **HOTEL** | This good-value hotel is hard
to beat when it comes to location: it's
next door to the Hunter Valley Gardens
and boutiques and within walking distance to half a dozen wineries, including
Roche and Hope estates, which both
host big-name musicians such as Elton
John and Fleetwood Mac at regular concert events. **Pros:** great location; walking
distance to major wineries; rooms have
balconies or terraces. **Cons:** can get busy
with conference groups; more business
hotel than resort in style; not really country rustic inside. $ _Rooms from: A$250_
✉ _2090 Broke Rd., Pokolbin_ ☎ _02/4998–
2000_ ⊕ _www.mercurehuntervalley.com.
au_ ⇌ _72 rooms_ ⦿ _No meals._

Peppers Convent
$$$ | **B&B/INN** | This former convent, built
in 1909 and transported 605 km (375
miles) from its original home in western
New South Wales, is ideal for those
who love traditional guesthouses. **Pros:**
romantic and secluded; balconies are a
superb place to watch the sunset. **Cons:**
standard rooms are on the small side; a
bit noisy; busy on weekends. $ _Rooms
from: A$300_ ✉ _88 Halls Rd., Pokolbin_
☎ _02/4998–4999_ ⊕ _www.peppers.com.
au_ ⇌ _17 rooms_ ⦿ _No meals._

🏃 Activities

BICYCLING
Hunter Valley Cycling
BICYCLING | Your bike, helmet, and a map
of the area will be delivered to your hotel
door by owner Mark or one of his friendly
staff. Half-day rentals are A$25, and
full-day costs A$35. ✉ _266 De Beyers
Rd., Pokolbin_ ☎ _0418/281480_ ⊕ _www.
huntervalleycycling.com.au._

HELICOPTER TOURS
Slattery Helicopter Charter
TOUR—SPORTS | Soaring over a patchwork
of wineries and the dramatic Brokenback
Range is a thrilling experience—and
can be a relatively inexpensive one (as

helicopter rides go) with flights starting at A$135 per person for eight minutes, although you can splurge A$500 for a one-hour flight to the beaches of Newcastle and the Central Coast. All flights require a minimum of two people. ⊠ *230 Old Maitland Rd., Hexham* ☎ *0408/649696* ⊕ *www.slatteryhelicopters.com.au* ✈ *From A$135.*

HORSEBACK RIDING

Hunter Valley Horse Riding and Adventures

HORSEBACK RIDING | These friendly folks welcome equestrians of all levels and ages and have a nice selection of guided rides around the valley, from a one-hour ride to the popular sunset ride (A$80), when you're most likely to see wildlife. ⊠ *288 Talga Rd., Rothbury* ☎ *02/4930–7111* ⊕ *www.huntervalleyhorseriding.com.au* ✈ *From $A60.*

HOT-AIR BALLOONING

★ **Balloon Aloft Hunter Valley**

BALLOONING | It's an early start to the day, but drifting above the vineyards at sunrise in a hot air balloon is an absolutely magical way to see the Hunter Valley. Balloon Aloft has been operating since the late '70s and runs hour-long sunrise flights, which culminate with a celebratory Champagne breakfast at Petersons Winery. ⊠ *Wine Country Dr., Pokolbin* ⊹ *Meet at Petersons Champagne House* ☎ *02/4991–1955, 1300/723279* ⊕ *www.balloonaloft.com* ✈ *From A$269.*

Newcastle

160 km (100 miles) north of Sydney.

Once known as the Steel City, today Newcastle is one of Australia's hippest cities. It's flanked by the Pacific Ocean and six beaches on its eastern side and a harbor on its west side. Gentrification began when the steel mills closed in 1999. Nowadays the old wharves and warehouses form part of the lively riverside Honeysuckle precinct, which buzzes with hotels, cafés, and restaurants.

Wollombi ⊙

Wollombi. Nothing seems to have changed in the atmospheric town of Wollombi, 24 km (15 miles) southwest of Cessnock, since the days when the Cobb & Co. stagecoaches rumbled through town. Founded in 1820, Wollombi was the overnight stop for the coaches on the second day of the journey from Sydney along the convict-built Great Northern Road—at that time the only route north. The town is full of delightful old sandstone buildings and antiques shops, and there's also a museum in the old courthouse with 19th-century clothing and bushranger memorabilia. ⊕ *www.visitwollombi.com.au.*

GETTING HERE AND AROUND

This city of about 550,000 is easy to navigate, as the harbor area and city center are just 3 km (2 miles) from the beaches and buses run between them. Hunter Street—the main artery—runs parallel to the harbor, and it's only a five-minute walk from harbor to downtown. Trains from Sydney stop at Hamilton and Broadmeadow, and shuttle buses take you into the city center. Buses also travel from Hunter Street to Darby Street, the main shopping and dining area.

⊙ Sights

Fort Scratchley

BUILDING | This was one of several forts built on headlands along Australia's shore in the mid-to-late 19th century to defend the colony against a possible Russian attack. Built in 1882, its guns had never been fired in anger until June 8, 1942, when the fort returned fire from Japanese submarines in a little-known World War II confrontation called "the shelling of Newcastle"—the city sustained 34 hells but neither damage nor loss of life. he fort, situated on Flagstaff Hill in Newastle's east end (not far from the railway tation), was occupied by the Australian rmy until 1972, after which it became a istoric site. Although admission is free, tour of the fort's tunnels is A$12.50, nd a tunnel and fort tour is A$16. Tours in from 10:30, with the last one at 2:30. *Nobby's Rd.* ⊕ *www.fortscratchley. rg.au.*

Merewether Baths

OOL | The largest ocean baths (swiming pools) in the southern hemisphere, Merewether Baths are a Newcastle con perfect for swimming and splashing ll year round. Opened in 1935 at one f the city's six fabulous beaches, they omprise two pools, with one suitable or children. Complete with barbecues nd picnic tables, the baths are the ideal lace for a family outing. ■TIP→ **The aths are patrolled by lifeguards during he summer months only, from around late eptember to late April.** ⊠ *Henderson Parade* ⊠ *Free.*

Newcastle Museum

MUSEUM | FAMILY | In the former headquarters of the Great Northern Railway, right n Newcastle Harbour, this museum ells the story of the city's coal mining nd steel production. Visitors can don a ard hat to witness the Fire and Earth xhibition, which re-creates life in a steel nill complete with furnaces, theatrical Irama, and interactive displays that shed ght on the workers' challenging lives. Jewcastle's other faces are captured vith exhibits on Aboriginal history, the orgeous beaches, and the earthquake hat struck the city in 1989. A popular Iraw for kids, the Supernova Hands-on icience Centre explains how a heavy car s lifted, a tornado occurs, and magnetic elds work. ⊠ *Workshop Way* ☎ *02/4974– 400* ⊕ *www.newcastlemuseum.com. u* ⊠ *Free.*

Nobby's Lighthouse

LIGHTHOUSE | A Newcastle landmark, Nobby's Lighthouse (on Nobby's Headland) was the third to be built in New South Wales when it opened in 1854. It's at the end of a long narrow spit (a longshore drift) and is accessed by a nearly 1-km (½-mile) path. Before it was converted to electricity in 1935, the original 20,000-candle light was tended by three keepers. The grounds of the lighthouse, and one of the lightkeeper's cottages, are open Sunday 10–4. It's a terrific vantage point for avid photographers. ⊠ *Nobby's Headland* ⊕ *www.newcastle.nsw.gov.au* ⊠ *Free.*

🍴 Restaurants

Estabar Newcastle Beach

$ | CAFÉ | Perched right on Newcastle Beach, Estabar is known for its great coffee, organic foods, superb Spanish hot chocolate drinks, and wonderful gelato. Open all day from breakfast until sundown, it's a small space with little tables and a short menu, but it draws a big local following. Breakfast favorites are the porridge with poached fruits and brown sugar on the side, and the homemade baked beans; lunchtime salads include lentil, walnut, and feta. The views over Newcastle Beach, the closest one to the downtown area, are also delectable at any time and if you are lucky, you may see whales offshore in winter months. **Known for:** great coffee; views over Newcastle Beach; local hotspot. $ *Average main: A$17* ⊠ *61 Shortland Esplanade, at Ocean St.* ☎ *02/4927–1222* ⊗ *No dinner.*

The Landing Bar & Kitchen

$$ | MODERN AUSTRALIAN | Enjoy the passing parade of tugboats and tankers coming and going in Newcastle Harbour from this buzzy bar and restaurant on the Honeysuckle strip. Locals come here for casual catch-ups over cocktails, pizzas, and shared plates on the deck, but the serious foodies head inside for the larger Mod Oz plates, mostly designed

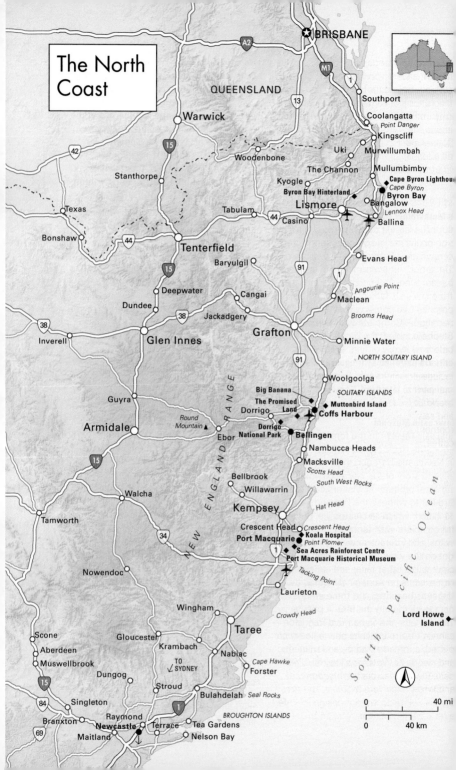

The North Coast

BRISBANE

QUEENSLAND

Warwick

Woodenbone

Stanthorpe

Texas

Bonshaw

Tenterfield

Baryulgil

Deepwater

Dundee

Inverell

Glen Innes

Cangai

Jackadgery

Guyra

Armidale

Round Mountain ▲

Ebor

Bellbrook

Willawarrin

Kempsey

Walcha

Tamworth

Nowendoc

Wingham

Scone

Aberdeen

Gloucester

Krambach

Muswellbrook

Nabiac

Dungog

Singleton

Stroud

Bulahdelah

Branxton

Raymond Terrace

Newcastle

Maitland

Tea Gardens

Nelson Bay

Southport

Coolangatta

Point Danger

Kingscliff

Uki

Murwillumbah

The Channon

Mullumbimby

Kyogle

Cape Byron Lighthouse

Byron Bay Hinterland

Cape Byron

Byron Bay

Lismore

Bangalow

Casino

Lennox Head

Tabulam

Ballina

Evans Head

Angourie Point

Maclean

Brooms Head

Grafton

Minnie Water

NORTH SOLITARY ISLAND

Woolgoolga

SOLITARY ISLANDS

Big Banana

The Promised Land

Muttonbird Island

Dorrigo

Coffs Harbour

Dorrigo National Park

Bellingen

Nambucca Heads

Macksville

Scotts Head

South West Rocks

Hat Head

Crescent Head

Crescent Head

Koala Hospital

Port Macquarie

Point Plomer

Sea Acres Rainforest Centre

Port Macquarie Historical Museum

Tacking Point

Laurieton

Crowdy Head

Lord Howe Island

Taree

NEW ENGLAND RANGE

Cape Hawke

Forster

Seal Rocks

BROUGHTON ISLANDS

South Pacific Ocean

0   40 mi

0   40 km

to share. The restaurant is famous for its charcuterie board and other dishes featuring locally grown meats, but the fish is just as good, especially the calamari fritters. **Known for:** relaxed atmosphere; sundowners; cheap eats. $ *Average main: A$28* ✉ *1 Honeysuckle Dr.* ☎ *02/4927–1722* ⊕ *thelanding.com.au* ⊘ *Closed Mon. and Tues.*

Merewether Surfhouse
$$ | **MODERN AUSTRALIAN** | Opened on the site of the Merewether Beach's original surfhouse (a lifeguard station), this stunning three-story venue has fantastic ocean views from all three of its eateries. The ground floor café, pizza, and gelato bar are steps from the beach, while the top-level restaurant has expansive panoramas and is open for lunch and dinner. You might begin with the local Port Stephens oysters with shallot vinegar before moving on to house-smoked trout or hand-rolled gnochi for main. Desserts include the mouthwatering salted caramel parfait. The café is open for all-day breakfast and lunch daily, offering burgers and salads. **Known for:** always fun environment; different types of cuisine; good coffee. $ *Average main: A$30* ✉ *Henderson Parade* ☎ *02/4918–0000* ⊕ *www.surfhouse.com.au* ⊘ *Closed Mon. and Tues.; no dinner Sun.*

Rustica
$$ | **MEDITERRANEAN** | Meaning "rural" in Italian, this lushly decorated restaurant with stunning views over Newcastle Beach is one of the rising stars in the city's expanding dining scene. The restaurant serves cuisine inspired by the Mediterranean, from the shores of northern Africa to the foothills of Tuscany. The seasonal menu has featured Moroccan vegetable and chickpea tagine with pistachio, pan-roasted pork medallions, and slow-roasted lamb shoulder, and desserts such as orange blossom pavlova and white-chocolate mousse. The rich, Spanish-inspired interior design includes a retro Mediterranean map on the wall, brass sculptures, and a tiled bar adorned with a bull's head, while the outdoor look is pure Australian beach culture. **Known for:** stunning views; Moroccan vegetable and chickpea tagine; popular local spot. $ *Average main: A$32* ✉ *2/1 King St.* ☎ *02/4929–3333* ⊕ *www.rustica.com.au* ⊘ *No lunch Mon.–Wed. No dinner Sun.*

Scratchleys on the Wharf
$$ | **MODERN AUSTRALIAN** | This swank establishment is as close as Newcastle comes to having an iconic restaurant. Enclosed on three sides by glass and perched over the harbor on the busy esplanade, Scratchley's opened not long after the Honeysuckle precinct transformed Newcastle into a hip and happening place more than a decade ago. The restaurant has one of the best views in Newcastle and an extensive menu to please all-comers. Starters include seafood chowder, oysters, and prawn salad, while several dishes—king prawn linguine, and prawn satay with spicy peanut sauce—are available in either starter or main sizes. Non–seafood fans have steaks, lamb cutlets, and corn-fed chicken breast dishes to consider, and a range of vegetarian options and Hunter Valley cheeses to sustain them. **Known for:** incredible seafood; great views; romantic. $ *Average main: A$32* ✉ *200 Wharf Rd.* ☎ *02/4929–1111* ⊕ *www.scratchleys.com.au*

★ Subo Newcastle
$$$$ | **MODERN AUSTRALIAN** | A bright, intimate star in Newcastle's dining scene, Subo has quickly become the hot spot in town and is often booked out weeks ahead. A stylish bistro in the central business district, Subo serves an A$95 five-course tasting plate that changes every six weeks and might include prawn carpaccio and foie gras, confit of chicken wings with blackened corn, Wagyu beef with smoked leeks, and chocolate-orange mousse with rum-and–orange syrup cake. **Known for:** stylish and trendy; extensive cocktail list; must-have

desserts. [$] *Average main: A$95* ✉ *551d Hunter St.* ☎ *02/4023–4048* ⏲ *Closed Mon. and Tues.*

Hotels

Brezza Bell B&B

$$ | **B&B/INN** | This lovely timber cottage with a white-picket fence is the ideal place for a quiet, romantic escape near the beach, a girls' weekend away, or a safe and friendly overnight when traveling solo. **Pros:** home-cooking at its best; posh amenities. **Cons:** just two rooms; limited facilities. [$] *Rooms from: A$195* ✉ *1 Rown Crescent* ☎ *02/4963–3812* 🌐 *www.brezzabella.com.au* 🛏 *2 rooms* 🍴 *Breakfast.*

Ibis Newcastle

$$ | **HOTEL** | Set about a kilometer from Newcastle's downtown, the Ibis is a value-priced chain hotel with parking and a restaurant. **Pros:** good location; good price. **Cons:** not on beach or waterfront; expensive in-room Wi-Fi; small rooms with very small bathrooms. [$] *Rooms from: A$159* ✉ *700 Hunter St.* ☎ *02/4925–2266* 🌐 *www.ibis.com* 🛏 *97 rooms* 🍴 *No meals.*

Novotel Newcastle Beach

$$$ | **HOTEL** |**FAMILY** | Just a few minutes' walk from the east end of the beach, Novotel has sweeping views of the ocean and of the city. **Pros:** spacious rooms; great location; free parking. **Cons:** Wi-Fi isn't free; no balconies; breakfast is additional. [$] *Rooms from: A$276* ✉ *5 King St.* ☎ *2/4032–3700* 🌐 *www.accorhotels.com/gb/hotel-8771-novotel-newcastle-beach/index.shtml* 🛏 *88 rooms* 🍴 *No meals.*

Rydges Newcastle

$$$ | **HOTEL** | Newcastle's most upscale hotel, the Rydges Newcastle, formerly known as the Crowne Plaza, is in the trendy Honeysuckle Precinct and has the best location of any hotel in town. **Pros:** great location; free Wi-Fi. **Cons:** parking is expensive. [$] *Rooms from: A$245* ✉ *Merewether St. at Wharf St.* ☎ *02/4907–5000* 🌐 *www.ihg.com* 🛏 *175 rooms* 🍴 *No meals.*

Activities

BICYCLING

Spinway Newcastle

BICYCLING | Interbike's swipe-and-ride bicycle rental is a great way to get around Newcastle. Rent bikes for an hour, half-, or full day using your credit card at one of the two bike rental terminals on Honeysuckle Drive. There's a handy basket at the back for any bags and you can pick up a free helmet and lock at the either the Maritime Centre or the Crowne Plaza Hotel, where the two terminals are located. ✉ *3 Honeysuckle Dr.* 🌐 *www.interbike.com.au* 🎟 *From A$11 per hr.*

KAYAKING

Newcastle Kayak Tours

KAYAKING | As the world's largest export coal port, Newcastle has a genuine working harbor. It's fascinating to watch the huge freighters as they line up beyond the harbor in the open sea, come through the heads, fill up with coal, and depart. Since the steelworks closed down in 1999, the harbor has opened up to visitors and is lined with smart apartments, hotels, and restaurants. For a close-up look at the giant ships and smaller boats, hop into a kayak for a guided excursion with Newcastle Kayak Tours. The two-hour (A$50) blue tour is the easiest and most popular—it begins at Dog Beach (so named because dogs are allowed), skirts past Queen's Wharf, and then meanders up Throsby Creek and past Newcastle Marina. Limited to 12 paddlers, the tour takes in all the highlights, and you may even be fortunate enough to spot dolphins. Longer and more challenging tours are also available. ✉ *Newcastle* ☎ *0432/913318* 🌐 *www.newcastlekayaktours.com.au* 🎟 *From A$50* ⏲ *Tours run in summer only.*

Port Macquarie

390 km (243 miles) northeast of Sydney.

Port Macquarie was founded as a convict settlement in 1821 and is the third-oldest settlement in Australia. Set at the mouth of the Hastings River, the town was chosen for its isolation to serve as an open jail for prisoners convicted of second offenses in New South Wales. By the 1830s the pace of settlement was so brisk that the town was no longer isolated, and its usefulness as a jail had ended.

Today's Port Macquarie has few reminders of its convict past and is flourishing as a vacation area. With its pristine rivers and lakes and 13 regional beaches, including beautiful Town Beach and Shelley Beach, which both have sheltered swimming, it's a great place to get into water sports, catch a fish for dinner, and watch migrating humpback whales in season, usually May to August and September to November.

GETTING HERE AND AROUND

It's a five-hour drive from Sydney heading north on the Pacific Highway. Greyhound and Premier Motor Service run coaches from Sydney Central Station. NSW TrainLink trains operate three services daily between Sydney and the North Coast, though there is no direct train to Port Macquarie. Passengers depart at Wauchope station and then take a bus to Port Macquarie (a 20-minute journey). Timetables are available at the Greater Port Macquarie Visitor Centre or online. Qantas and Virgin Australia have flights from Sydney; Virgin Australia also flies to and from Brisbane.

VISITOR INFORMATION

CONTACTS Visitor Information Centre.
☒ *The Glasshouse, Clarence St. at Hay St.* ☎ *02/6581–8000, 1300/303155* ⊕ *www.portmacquarieinfo.com.au.*

Thar she blows! ◉

Whales travel up and down the New South Wales coast by the hundreds, so book a whale-watching cruise to catch all the action at close range. Southern right whales and humpbacks travel up from Antarctica from May to August and down again from September to November. Dolphins can be seen almost any time of the year—you never know when an agile pair will shoot through a wave or bob up near your boat.

◉ Sights

★ Koala Hospital

ZOO | FAMILY | Operated by the Koala Preservation Society of New South Wales, the town's Koala Hospital is both a worthy cause and a popular attraction. The Port Macquarie region is home to many of these extremely appealing marsupials, and the hospital cares for 250 to 300 sick and injured koalas each year. The staff is passionate about their furry patients and happy to tell you about the care the animals receive. You can walk around the grounds to view the recuperating animals; you can even adopt one (but you can't take it home). Try to visit during feeding times at 8 in the morning or 3 in the afternoon. There are guided tours daily at 3. ☒ *Macquarie Nature Reserve, Lord St.* ☎ *02/6584–1522* ⊕ *www.koala-hospital.org.au* ☒ *Donation requested.*

Port Macquarie Historical Museum

MUSEUM | Housed in a two-story convict-built house dating from 1836, this eclectic museum displays period costumes, memorabilia from World Wars I and II, farm implements, antique clocks and watches, and relics from the town's convict days. ☒ *22 Clarence St.*

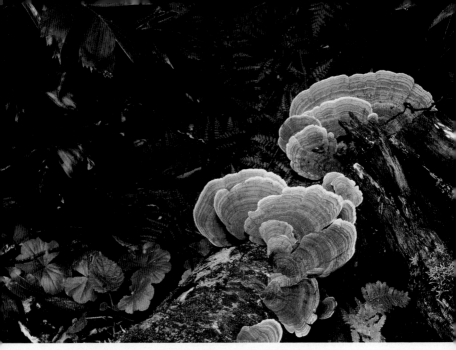

Orange fungi growing on the Rainforest Tree at Dorrigo National Park

☎ 02/6583–1108 ⊕ www.portmuseum. org.au 🎫 A$7.

★ Sea Acres Rainforest Centre
NATIONAL/STATE PARK | This interpretive center comprises 178 pristine acres of coastal rain forest on the southern side of Port Macquarie. There are more than 170 plant species here, including 300-year-old cabbage-tree palms, as well as native mammals, reptiles, and prolific birdlife. An elevated boardwalk allows you to stroll through the lush environ- ment without disturbing the vegetation. The center has informative guided tours, as well as a gift shop and a pleasant rain-forest café, a lovely place for a bite to eat while listening to the birdsong. ✉ Pacific Dr., near Shelley Beach Rd. ☎ 02/6582–3355 ⊕ www.nationalparks. nsw.gov.au 🎫 Free.

St. Thomas Church
RELIGIOUS SITE | This 1828 church, the country's fifth-oldest house of worship, was built by convicts using local cedar and stone blocks cemented together with powdered seashells. ✉ Hay St. at William St. ☎ 02/6584–1033.

🍴 Restaurants

The Boathouse Bar & Restaurant
$$ | AUSTRALIAN |FAMILY | With views of moored yachts and tropical gardens, there's a real vacation vibe to this eatery. There are espresso coffees available at breakfast and espresso martinis at night, with live bands playing on the weekend as rowdy tables pop champagne bottles. The menu is heavy on seafood with the seared squid salad as a superior starter. For main, the fish of the day is always a winner. Or for meat lovers, the glazed pork belly with fennel and cabbage slaw is delicious. There are also classic Aussie desserts, like pavlova with fresh fruits, but really, this is the place to enjoy a few cocktails into the night instead. **Known for:** buzzy atmosphere; sundowner cocktails; fun Sunday afternoons. $ Average main: A$32 ✉ 20 Park St. ☎ 02/6589–5100 ⊕ www.rydges.com/accommodation/

*port-macquarie-nsw/sails-port-macquarie/
eat-drink-port-macquarie/.*

The Corner

$$ | AUSTRALIAN | This stylish, contemporary café packs in the crowds, thanks to its fabulously tasty meals, though you may need to exercise a little patience, as service can be a bit slow at times. Try the Corner Breakfast (A$22), which has everything from eggs the way you like them to hamhock-braised beans. Return for dinner to sample the chicken Wellington with grilled asparagus and pea puree. As the name suggests, it sits on a corner and is part of the Macquarie Waters Hotel & Apartments complex. **Known for:** great brunch; buzzy atmosphere; slow service. $ *Average main: A$33* ⊠ *Clarence St. at Munster St.* ☎ *02/6583–3300* ⊕ *www.cornerrestaurant.com.au* ⊙ *No dinner Sun.*

★ The Stunned Mullet

$$$ | MODERN AUSTRALIAN | Opposite Town Beach, Port Macquarie's best restaurant also has the best views, but don't let that distract you from the food. With so much sea in front of you it's only natural that the menu also features lots of seafood—all of it sustainably line caught or farmed—but other dishes worth trying, if they are on the menu when you visit, include the venison with tamarillo and juniper berry or the confit duck leg. Desserts are equally show-stopping with salty crème caramel with spice rum jelly. The wine list is suitably impressive. **Known for:** incredible views; superior seafood; extensive dessert menu with wine pairing. $ *Average main: A$39* ⊠ *24 William St.* ☎ *02/6584–7757* ⊕ *thestunnedmullet.com.au.*

 Hotels

Beachcomber Resort

$$$ | RESORT | This self-catering resort opposite Town Beach is a great option if you are staying for a few days or traveling with a family. **Pros:** well-maintained

barbecue area; great location opposite the beach; swimming pool with kids' wading pool. **Cons:** no elevators; design a bit dated and tired; can be noisy during peak time. $ *Rooms from: A$205* ⊠ *54 William St.* ☎ *02/6584–1881, 1800/001320* ⊕ *www.beachcomberresort.com.au* ⊅ *39 rooms* ⊙ *No meals.*

Ibis STYLE Port Macquarie

$$$ | HOTEL | Although the building dates from the late 1960s—when its sawtooth shape was considered very stylish—it's filled with up-to-the-minute amenities: designer furnishings, luxurious linens, marble bathrooms, and private balconies with ocean and river views. **Pros:** a good continental breakfast is brought to your room; toasters in rooms; beautiful breakfast room on the top floor with ocean views; free Wi-Fi. **Cons:** some street noise; a few rooms overlook car park. $ *Rooms from: A$285* ⊠ *1 Stewart St.* ☎ *02/6583–1200* ⊕ *www.accorhotels.com* ⊅ *45 rooms* ⊙ *No meals.*

★ The Observatory

$$$ | HOTEL | The most stylish digs in Port Macquarie are just a short walk across leafy parkland to the city's main beach. **Pros:** close to beach; great restaurants; pool. **Cons:** packed with families in summer; can be impersonal due to size; communal areas a little dated. $ *Rooms from: A$220* ⊠ *40 William St.* ☎ *02/6586–8000* ⊕ *www.observatory.net.au* ⊅ *81 rooms, 2 penthouses* ⊙ *No meals.*

🏃 Activities

Unsurprisingly, most of the outdoor activities in this area revolve around the town's crystal clear waters.

FISHING
Ocean Star

FISHING | Deep-sea anglers will enjoy the daylong trips on this 40-foot custom Randel charting boat. Typical catches include snapper, pearl perch, dolphin fish, and grouper. If you have cooking facilities, the crew is happy to clean, ice, and pack your

Trial Bay Gaol

Trial Bay Gaol. Trial Bay Gaol, a jail dating from the 1870s, occupies a dramatic position on the cliffs overlooking the seaside village of South West Rocks, 100 km (62 miles) north of Port Macquarie. The building, now partly in ruins, was used to teach useful skills to the prisoners who constructed it, but the project proved too expensive and was abandoned in 1903. During World War I the building served as an internment camp for some 500 Germans. It's free to walk around the outside of the ruins and visit the beach; the A$11 admission includes entry to a small museum. To get there, travel north through Kempsey and turn off to South West Rocks and follow the signs. The Trial Bay Kiosk Restaurant is a wonderful spot for lunch with a glass of wine while enjoying the stunning views across the bay—the fresh local seafood is always superb—but it's also open for breakfast (daily) and dinner on Friday and Saturday. ✉ *Arakoon National Park, Cardwell St., South West Rocks* ☎ *02/6566–6168* ⊕ *www. nationalparks.nsw.gov.au* ✎ *A$11.*

catch. ✉ *Town Wharf, 74 Clarence St.* ☎ *0416/240877* ⊕ *www.portmacquariefishingcharters.com.au.*

HORSEBACK RIDING
Bellrowan Valley Horseriding
HORSEBACK RIDING | Thirty minutes' drive inland from Port Macquarie, Bellrowan welcomes experts and beginners with short trail rides and overnight treks. The two-day Great Aussie Pub Ride ends the day's ride in some of the region's most interesting pubs and costs A$120 with all meals and accommodation. A two-hour trail ride is A$110. ✉ *Crows Rd., Beechwood* ☎ *02/6587–5227* ⊕ *www. bellrowanvalley.com.au* ✎ *From A$75.*

SURFING
Port Macquarie Surf School
SURFING | Head back to school and learn to ride the waves from some very competent coaches, all of whom are fully accredited, licensed, and insured with Surfing Australia. There are daily group lessons (A$45 for two hours), or you can opt for one-on-one tutoring (A$85 per hour). Surfboards, wet suits, rash vests, and sunscreen are provided. ✉ *46 Pacific Dr.* ☎ *02/6584–7733* ⊕ *www.portmacquariesurfschool.com.au* ✎ *From A$45.*

WHALE-WATCHING
Port Cruise Adventures
WHALE-WATCHING | Majestic humpback whales migrate past Port Macquarie nonstop from May to the end of November, and Port Cruise Adventures gets you up close with great-value cruises (A$60) for up to two hours, depending on how far off-shore the whales are. The company also has both long and short cruises to see local bottlenose dolphins, which can be spotted year-round. ✉ *Short St. Wharf* ☎ *02/65838811* ⊕ *portjet.com.au* ✎ *From A$20.*

Bellingen

210 km (130 miles) north of Port Macquarie, 520 km (323 miles) from Sydney.

In a river valley a few miles off the Pacific Highway, artsy Bellingen is one of the prettiest towns along the coast. Many of Bellingen's buildings have been classified by the National Trust, and the museum, cafés, galleries, and crafts outlets are favorite hangouts for artists, craft workers, and writers. You'll find food, entertainment, and 250 stalls at the community markets that take place on the third Sunday of every month.

GETTING HERE AND AROUND

It's a seven-hour drive from Sydney along the Pacific Highway, but the town is just 30 minutes from Coffs Harbour and its airport. NSW TrainLink trains run from Sydney to Brisbane twice daily, stopping at Urunga, 10 km (6 miles) away. Both Greyhound and Premier Motor Service also run buses between Sydney and Urunga. From Urunga, either catch a taxi or a local Busways bus to Bellingen—though the bus is quite infrequent. There is also a Busways bus service from Coffs Harbour to Bellingen.

VISITOR INFORMATION

CONTACTS Waterfall Way Visitor Centre. ✉ *29–31 Hyde St.* ☎ *02/6655–1522, 1800/705735* 🌐 *www.visitnsw.com/visitor-information-centres/waterfall-way-visitor-centre-bellingen.*

Sights

★ Dorrigo National Park

NATIONAL/STATE PARK | From Bellingen a meandering and spectacular road leads inland to Dorrigo and then travels back east eventually reaching the Pacific Highway, close to Coffs Harbour. This circular scenic route, beginning along the Bellinger River, climbs more than 1,000 feet up the heavily wooded escarpment to the Dorrigo Plateau. At the top of the plateau is Dorrigo National Park, a small but outstanding subtropical rain forest that is included on the World Heritage list. Signposts along the main road indicate walking trails. The Satinbird Stroll is a short rain forest walk, and the 6-km (4-mile) Cedar Falls Walk leads to the most spectacular of the park's many waterfalls, but the most dramatic of all is the free Skywalk lookout, a 230-foot boardwalk above the canopy that has panoramic views out to the coast. The national park is approximately 31 km (19 miles) from Bellingen. ✉ *Dorrigo Rainforest Centre, Dome Rd., Dorrigo* ☎ *02/6657–2309* 🌐 *www.nationalparks.nsw.gov.au* 🎫 *A$2 donation to visit Rainforest Centre.*

Dorrigo Rainforest Centre

NATIONAL/STATE PARK | The excellent Dorrigo Rainforest Centre, open daily 9–4:30, has a good display on the natural heritage of the park and a small café that serves good coffee. From here you can walk out high over the forest canopy along the **Skywalk** boardwalk. ☎ *02/6657–2309* 🌐 *www.dorrigo.com.*

Hotels

Koompartoo Retreat

$$ | **B&B/INN** | These self-contained hardwood cottages on a hillside overlooking Bellingen are superb examples of local craftsmanship, particularly in their use of timbers from surrounding forests. **Pros:** from the chalet verandas you can see kookaburras and black cockatoos; each cottage has a small library. **Cons:** no wheelchair access; heating is noisy. [$] *Rooms from: A$195* ✉ *Rawson St. at Dudley St.* ☎ *0457/678746* 🌐 *www.koompartoo.com.au* 🛏 *4 cottages* 🍴 *No meals.*

Activities

HORSEBACK RIDING

Valery Trails

HORSEBACK RIDING | **FAMILY** | This large equestrian center is 10 km (6 miles) from Bellingen on the edge of Bongil Bongil National Park. They have 45 horses, and a variety of treks through the local rain forests. Choose from the popular two-hour rides (A$65), breakfast and afternoon barbecue rides, and a two-day ride to Bellingen to stay in the Federal Hotel for (A$450). ✉ *758 Valery Rd., Valery* ☎ *02/6653–4301* 🌐 *www.valerytrails.com.au* 🎫 *From A$65.*

The Promised Land

The Promised Land. If you have an hour to spare (and a set of wheels), cross the river at Bellingen and take an 18-km (11-mile) excursion on the Bellingen–Gleniffer Road to the village of Gleniffer. This tranquil, rambling journey leads through farmlands and wooded valleys and across the evocatively named Never Never River to—believe it or not—the Promised Land, a peaceful, pastoral region with spots for picnics and swimming. Author

Peter Carey once lived in this vicinity, and the river and its surroundings provided the backdrop for his novel *Oscar and Lucinda*.

Promised Land Retreat. If you want to stay overnight in the area, the three chalets at the 100-acre Promised Land Retreat are lovely self-contained sanctuaries. ✉ *934 Promised Land Rd., Bellingen* ☏ *02/6655–9578* ⊕ *www. promisedlandretreat.com.au* ✉ *From A$250 per night.*

Coffs Harbour

35 km (22 miles) northeast of Bellingen via the Pacific Hwy., 103 km (64 miles) from Bellingen via the inland scenic route along the Dorrigo Plateau, 534 km (320 miles) from Sydney.

The area surrounding Coffs Harbour is the state's "banana belt," where long, neat rows of banana palms cover the hillsides. Set at the foot of steep green hills, the town has great beaches and a mild climate. This idyllic combination has made it one of the most popular vacation spots along the coast. Coffs is also a convenient halfway point on the 1,000-km (620-mile) journey between Sydney and Brisbane.

GETTING HERE AND AROUND
Coffs Harbour is a comfortable 7½-hour drive from Sydney and a 6-hour drive from Brisbane. Regular Greyhound and Premier Buses connect the town to Sydney. There is a train station with daily NSW TrainLink services to and from Sydney and Brisbane. And the local airport, 6 km (4 miles) from the central Ocean Parade, is served by Qantas,

Virgin Australia, and Tigerair. For more information, contact the visitor center, which is open 9–5 daily.

AIRPORT INFORMATION Coffs Harbour Airport. ✉ *Hogbin Dr.* ☏ *02/6648–4767* ⊕ *www.coffsharbourairport.com.*

VISITOR INFORMATION
CONTACTS Coffs Coast Visitors Information Centre. ✉ *253 Pacific Hwy.* ☏ *02/6652–4366* ⊕ *www.coffscoast.com.au.*

◉ Sights

★ The Big Banana
AMUSEMENT PARK/WATER PARK | FAMILY
| Just north of the city, impossible to miss, is the Big Banana—the symbol of Coffs Harbour. This monumental piece of kitsch has stood at the site since 1964. It welcomes visitors to the Big Banana complex, which takes a fascinating look at the past, present, and future of horticulture. There's a multimedia display called "World of Bananas" and a walkway that meanders through the banana plantations and banana packing shed. The park is fantastic for kids and has varied rides all with different prices, including toboggan rides (A$7), a

waterslide (A$19.50 for 90 minutes), an ice-skating rink (A$16.50), and laser tag (A$9.90). There's a café on the premises, as well as the Banana Barn, which sells the park's own jams, pickles, fresh tropical fruit, and frozen chocolate-covered bananas on a stick. ⊠ *351 Pacific Hwy.* ☎ *02/6652–4355* ⊕ *www.bigbanana.com* ▭ *Entry to Big Banana free; rides and tours extra.*

Dolphin Marine Magic

ZOO | FAMILY | Near the port in Coffs Harbour, the Dolphin Marine Magic aquarium includes colorful reef fish, turtles, seals, penguins, baby crocodiles, and dolphins. Shows take place daily at 10 and 1, and visitors are advised to arrive 30 minutes earlier to get a good seat and receive free "dolphin kisses" from the cute critters before each show. Children may help feed and "shake hands" with dolphins, as well as interact with the seals. You can swim, pat, and play ball with the dolphins and seals in special group encounters if you book in advance. These sessions vary in price depending on time of year—during peak holiday season, seal encounters cost A$220 per person and dolphin encounters run around A$370 per person. The company's official name is Dolphin Marine Magic but many of the locals still call it by its old name, the Pet Porpoise Pool. ⊠ *65 Orlando St., beside Coffs Creek* ☎ *02/6659–1900* ⊕ *www.dolphinmarinemagic.com.au* ▭ *A$38.*

Muttonbird Island

NATIONAL/STATE PARK | The town has a lively and attractive harbor in the shelter of Muttonbird Island, and a stroll out to this nature reserve is delightful in the evening. To get here, follow the signs to the Coffs Harbour Jetty, then park near the marina. A wide path leads out along the breakwater and up the slope of the island. The trail is steep, but the views from the top are worth the effort. The island is named after the muttonbirds (also known as shearwaters) that nest here between September and April.

Between June and September Muttonbird Island is also a good spot for viewing migrating humpback whales. ⊠ *Coffs Harbour* ⊕ *www.nationalparks.nsw.gov.au.*

🍴 Restaurants

★ Fishermen's Co-op

$ | SEAFOOD | Fish-and-chips don't come any fresher than those served at the fishermen's co-op near the breakwall on the northern side of the harbor in Coffs—everything on the menu is straight off the trawler. Although most of the retail space is given to sales of fresh seafood, you can buy freshly cooked (grilled, battered, or crumbed) fish-and-chips here, as well as calamari, fish cocktails, and salads. There are a few tables on a covered deck out front, but the best place to eat is perched on a rock on the nearby breakwall, staring out to sea. **Known for:** cheap eat; relaxed dining; great at lunchtime. $ *Average main: A$15* ⊠ *69 Marina Dr.* ☎ *02/6652–2811* ⊕ *coffsfishcoop.com.au.*

Shearwater Restaurant

$$ | ECLECTIC | This waterfront restaurant with views of Coffs Creek (which is spotlighted at night—look for stingrays swimming by) is open for breakfast, lunch, and dinner, and leaves no culinary stone unturned in its search for novel flavors. The menu in the open-air dining room includes lunch dishes like prawn and scallop red curry. If you want a table on the deck in summer, book ahead. Service is friendly and attentive. **Known for:** great service; extensive menu; busy on weekends. $ *Average main: A$32* ⊠ *The Promenade, 321 Harbour Dr.* ☎ *02/6651–6053* ⊕ *www.shearwaterrestaurant.com.au* ⊗ *No dinner Sun.–Tues.*

🛏 Hotels

BreakFree Aanuka Beach Resort

$$ | RESORT |FAMILY | Teak furniture and antiques collected from Indonesia and the South Pacific fill the accommodations at this resort, which sits amid palms, frangipani, and hibiscus. **Pros:** brilliant setting in a private beachfront cove; great value for families; home away from home. **Cons:** some rooms need updating; kid-phobes might not appreciate all the families; a little isolated. $ *Rooms from: A$186* ⊠ *11 Firman Dr.* ☎ *02/6652–7555* ⊕ *www.aanukabeachresort.com.au* ⇆ *27 studios, 39 suites, 12 villas* ❖❘ *Free Breakfast*.

Smugglers on the Beach

$$$$ | **RESORT** | Five minutes' drive north of Coffs Harbour's busy city center is this small resort with just 16 self-contained one- to three-bedroom apartments, some with hot tubs, spread out among tropical gardens. **Pros:** resort has fishing equipment and a barbecue, so you can catch your dinner; beautiful beachside location; good deals if staying for more than five nights. **Cons:** two-night minimum, checkout is at 9:30 am; isolated. $ *Rooms from: A$310* ⊠ *36 Sandy Beach Rd.* ☎ *02/6653–6166* ⊕ *www.smugglers. com.au* ⇆ *16 apartments* ❖❘ *No meals*.

🏃 Activities

SCUBA DIVING

The warm seas around Coffs Harbour make this particular part of the coast, with its moray eels, manta rays, turtles, and gray nurse sharks, a scuba diver's favorite. Best are the Solitary Islands, 7 km–21 km (4½ miles–13 miles) offshore.

Jetty Dive Centre

SCUBA DIVING | This outfitter rents gear, schedules scuba and snorkeling trips, and hosts certification classes. A double-dive trip costs A$125; a one-day learn-to-dive course is A$249. There are also whale- and dolphin-watching cruises from June to October from A$59. ⊠ *398 Harbour Dr.* ☎ *02/6651–1611* ⊕ *www. jettydive.com.au*.

WHITE-WATER RAFTING
Wildwater Adventures

WHITE-WATER RAFTING | This highly regarded company conducts half-day, one-day, and two-day rafting trips down the Nymboida River. Trips begin from Bonville, 14 km (9 miles) south of Coffs Harbour on the Pacific Highway, but pickups from the Coffs Harbour and Bellingen region can be arranged. Half-day trips are A$80, one-day trips are A$185, and two-day trips cost A$430 per person including snacks and meals. Overnight trips feature camping on the river bank, breakfast, and dinner. ⊠ *16 Prince St.* ☎ *042/876498* ⊕ *www.coffscentral.com/wildwater* ⊠ *From A$80*.

Byron Bay

247 km (154 miles) north of Coffs Harbour, 772 km (480 miles) north of Sydney.

Byron Bay is the easternmost point on the Australian mainland, and perhaps earns Australia its nickname the "Lucky Country." Fabulous beaches, storms that spin rainbows across the mountains behind the town, and a sunny, relaxed and somewhat hippy style cast a spell over practically everyone who visits. For many years Byron Bay lured surfers with abundant sunshine, perfect waves on Watego's Beach, and tolerant locals who allowed them to sleep on the sand. These days a more upscale crowd frequents Byron Bay.

Byron Bay is also one of the must-sees on the backpacker circuit, and the town has a youthful energy that fuels late-night partying. There are many art galleries and crafts shops, a great food scene, and numerous adventure tours. The town is at its liveliest on the first Sunday of each month, when Butler Street becomes a bustling market.

The waters surrounding Byron Bay offer top conditions for water sports.

GETTING HERE AND AROUND

Byron is the North Coast's most popular destination, and is well served by buses and trains from Sydney and Coffs Harbour. If driving, the journey takes 11 hours from Sydney and 3½ hours from Coffs Harbour. The closest airports are at Ballina and Lismore, both a 30-minute drive away. Virgin Australia, Jetstar, and REX fly to Ballina; REX also flies from Sydney to Lismore. All the usual car companies are there, or you can get a taxi into Byron or take a Ballina-Byron shuttle bus (operated by Byron Easy Bus) for A$20 one-way.

AIRPORT SHUTTLE Byron Easy Bus.
☎ *02/6685–7447* ⊕ *www.byronbayshuttle.com.au.*

VISITOR INFORMATION

CONTACTS Byron Visitor Centre. ✉ *Old Station Master's Cottage, 80 Jonson St.* ☎ *02/6680–8558* ⊕ *www.visitbyronbay.com.*

◉ Sights

★ Byron Bay Hinterland

SCENIC DRIVE | Undulating green hills that once boasted a thriving dairy industry are dotted with charming villages and small organic farms growing avocados, coffee, fruits, and macadamia nuts. The best way to discover this gorgeous part of the world—nicknamed the Rainbow Region—is to grab a map and just drive. From Byron, take the road toward the regional town of Lismore for about 15 km (9 miles) to the pretty village of **Bangalow.** Walk along the lovely main street lined with 19th-century storefronts. Carefully follow your map and wind your way northwest for about 20 km (13 miles) to **Federal.** Meander, via the cute towns of **Rosebank** and **Dunoon,** to **The Channon,** where on the second Sunday of every month you'll find a wonderful market with dozens of stalls and entertainment. ✉ *Byron Bay* ⊕ *www.tropicalnsw.com.au.*

Cape Byron Lighthouse

LIGHTHOUSE | The most powerful beacon on the Australian coastline, Cape Byron Lighthouse dominates the southern end of the beach at Byron Bay and attracts huge numbers of visitors, who want to tick standing at Australia's most easterly point off their bucket list. You can tour the lighthouse (no children under five) daily from 10 am, with the last tour departing at 3 pm. The tours are led by volunteers, and while there's no entry charge, a donation is appreciated. Whale-watching is popular between June and September, when migrating humpback whales come close to shore. Dolphins swim in these waters year-round, and you can often see pods of them from the cape. You can stay in either of the two six-person assistant lightkeeper's cottages for A$360 a night in low season; prices rise from mid-December to late January and a two-week period over Easter (book well in advance during this period). There's a three-night minimum stay. ⊠ *Lighthouse Rd.* ☎ *02/6620–9300* ⊕ *www.byronbaylighthouse.com* ⊠ *Free, suggested donation for tours.*

Cape Byron Walking Track

TRAIL | This popular trail circumnavigates a 150-acre reserve, passes through grasslands and rain forest, and has sensational seas views as you circle the peninsula and the lighthouse. From several vantage points along the track you may spot dolphins in the waters below. The track begins east of the town on Lighthouse Road. ⊠ *Off Lighthouse Rd.* ⊕ *www. nationalparks.nsw.gov.au.*

🏖 Beaches

Several superb beaches lie in the vicinity of Byron Bay. In front of the town, Main Beach provides safe swimming, and Clarkes Beach, closer to the cape, has better surf. The most famous surfing beach, however, is Wategos', the only entirely north-facing beach in the state. To the south of the lighthouse Tallow Beach extends for 6 km (4 miles) to a rocky stretch of coastline around Broken Head, which has a number of small sandy coves. Beyond Broken Head is lonely Seven Mile Beach. Topless sunbathing is popular on many Byron Bay beaches.

Main Beach

BEACH—SIGHT | As the name suggests Main Beach is right in the heart of Byron Bay, across the road from the much-loved Beach Hotel (a popular pub that has good restaurants and accommodation). It stretches southward for some 3 km (2 miles) where its name changes to Clarkes Beach and then The Pass, the latter a legendary surfing spot. Always busy in the summer months, the beach is most easily reached on foot from the town center. There's a sea wall and swimming pool at the northern end, and about 300 feet offshore lies the wreck of the *Tassie II,* a small ammunition supply boat that sunk around the end of World War II. Swimmers should always swim beside the flags as rips and currents can make this beach hazardous at times—an average of about nine swimmers annually require rescue. There are barbecues and picnic tables in the leafy park flanking the beach. **Amenities:** food and drink; lifeguards (summer only); showers; toilets. **Best for:** snorkeling; swimming; walking. ⊠ *Jonson St. at Bay St.*

Watego's Beach

BEACH—SIGHT | Named for a farming family who grew bananas and vegetables in the hinterland (now a residential area) just behind the beach, Watego's is a lovely 2,000-foot strip of golden sand backed by pandanus palms. It's sheltered from the winds and popular with all comers. If you fancy a walk, you can reach the beach from the city center via the 4-km (2½-mile) Cape Byron Track. Otherwise, drive here and look for parking in the lot or on the street (it can be challenging during busy times). Coin-operated barbecues and picnic tables make this a perfect spot for do-it-yourself lunching, all in the shadow of the majestic Cape Byron Lighthouse, which looms over the beach. The upscale boutique hotel, Rae's of Watego's, is nearby. **Amenities:** lifeguards (summer only); parking (fee); toilets. **Best for:** swimming; sunrise. ✉ *Marine Parade, off Palm Valley Dr.*

🍴 Restaurants

Beach Byron Bay

$$ | **CAFÉ** | A Byron Bay legend, this open-air café is a perfect place to sit in the morning sun and watch the waves. Breakfast runs the gamut from wholesome (award-winning locally produced Brookfarm Macadamia muesli with yogurt and banana) to hearty (corned-beef hash, sautéed spinach, fried egg with béarnaise sauce). For lunch, try the king prawns with chili and garlic or the potato gnochi with ossobuco. The café is open for cocktails and dinner during the summer months of December and January and has an attached takeout section for those who want to have light meals on the run. Reservations are recommended during the summer. **Known for:** perfect for day and night; great coffee; fresh fare. [$] *Average main: A$32* ✉ *Clarkes Beach, Near parking lot at end of Lawson St.* ☎ *1300/583766* 🌐 *www.beachbyronbay.com.au* 🕓 *No dinner Feb.–Nov.*

★ **Fig Tree Restaurant & Rooms**

$$$$ | **AUSTRALIAN** | In this century-old farmhouse with distant views of Byron Bay the draw is upmarket Mod Oz cuisine blending Asian and Mediterranean flavors. Produce fresh from the owners' farm is featured in the weekly seven-course menu (A$120),along with locally produced Bangalow duck, Bangalow pork belly, and Binna Burra sirloin steak. As the name suggests, the restaurant also has accommodations: the Dairy and the Sunrise House, two cottages with wonderful views, can both sleep up to eight people; prices are from A$600 a night in the holiday season of Christmas, January and Easter with a minimum stay of three nights. The restaurant and rooms are 5 km (3 miles) inland from Byron Bay at Ewingsdale. **Known for:** big with weddings so check on weekends; incredible grounds with native plants; local produce. [$] *Average main: A$75* ✉ *4 Sunrise La., Ewingsdale* ☎ *02/6684–7273* 🌐 *www.figtreerestaurant.com.au* 🕓 *Closed Mon.–Wed. No dinner Sun. No lunch Thurs.–Sat.*

Three Blue Ducks

$$ | **AUSTRALIAN** |**FAMILY** | Found at The Farm, a working property near the main entry point into Byron Bay, Three Blue Ducks is the sister restaurant to the hugely successful Sydney eatery of the same name. This is the perfect spot for breakfast or lunch, with the coffee counter always heaving. The farm-to-table movement is in full flow within this barn-style restaurant, with everything on the menu grown or butchered on-site. And nothing goes to waste here, with the chefs creating innovative dishes that ensure all parts of plant and animal are used. The chicken liver parfait is a must try and their take on a simple beef burger is really a culinary delight. It's probably best to weave through the farm after feasting, just so you feel a little less guilty about eating the many cows', pigs', and chickens' friends. **Known for:** rustic restaurant; sustainable menu; farm-to-table fare. [$] *Average main: A$24* ✉ *11 Ewingsdale* ☎ *02/6684–7795* 🌐 *www.threeblueducks.com/byron.*

🛏 Hotels

Byron Bay Beach Bure

$$$$ | **B&B/INN** | Three luxury bures—the Fijian word for cabin—may be only 650 feet from the city center, but the lush, peaceful setting makes it feel like a private oasis. **Pros:** perfect for a romantic getaway; two elevated bures have beach views. **Cons:** can book up early. [$] *Rooms from: A$380* ✉ *36 Lawson*

St. ☎ *02/6680–8483* 🛏 *3 bures* 🍴 *Free Breakfast.*

★ Elements of Byron Bay

$$$$ | **RESORT** |**FAMILY** | Since opening in 2016, the $190-million Elements of Byron Bay has been an instant success in Bryon Bay thanks to high-end technology and finishes and an open and free-flowing design that pulls the surrounding rain forest in. **Pros:** beach and rain-forest location; huge adults-only pool; rain forest-facing terraces with fireplaces and lounges. **Cons:** a little distance from Byron; solar train to Byron Bay is not free; breakfast is extra. [$] *Rooms from: A$520* ✉ *144 Bayshore Dr.* ☎ *2/6639–1500* 🌐 *elementsofbyron.com.au* 🛏 *68 villas* 🍴 *No meals.*

Julian's Apartments

$$$ | **B&B/INN** | These studio apartments just opposite Clarkes Beach are neat, spacious, and well equipped. **Pros:** perfect for families (cots and baby supplies can be rented); this is the quiet end of Byron Bay town; close to beach. **Cons:** taxi, or hike into town, required; popular, so book early; has seen better days. [$] *Rooms from: A$240* ✉ *124 Lighthouse Rd.* ☎ *02/6680–9697* 🌐 *www.julians-byronbay.com* 🛏 *11 apartments* 🍴 *No meals.*

Rae's on Wategos

$$$$ | **B&B/INN** | A high-design boutique hotel, Rae's luxurious Mediterranean-style villa surrounded by a tropical garden offers individually decorated rooms with an eclectic mix of antiques, Indonesian art, Moroccan tables, and fine furnishings. **Pros:** perfect for a romantic break; superb food and spa; rooms have fireplaces and private terraces. **Cons:** have to take a taxi to town; breakfast is pricey; minimum two-night stay on weekends. [$] *Rooms from: A$550* ✉ *Watego's Beach, 8 Marine Parade* ☎ *02/6685–5366* 🌐 *raesonwategos.com* 🛏 *7 suites* 🍴 *No meals.*

🍸 Nightlife

For a small town, Byron rocks by night. Fire dancing—where bare-chested men dance with flaming torches—is a local specialty. Bars and clubs are generally open until about 2 am on weekends and midnight on weekdays.

Arts Factory Village

GATHERING PLACES | Head to this legendary complex—also known as the Piggery—to catch a movie at the Pighouse Flicks, grab a bite, have a beer brewed at the on-site Byron Bay Brewery, or see a live band at the Buddha Bar. A Nomads backpackers lodge is attached to the venue, so expect a lively crowd especially at the weekly talent show. ✉ *1 Skinners Shoot Rd., at Gordon St.* ☎ *02/6685–7709* 🌐 *www.pighouseflicks.com.au.*

Beach Bar

BARS/PUBS | This lounge in the iconic Beach Hotel often hosts live bands. ✉ *Bay St. at Jonson St.* ☎ *02/6685–6402* 🌐 *www.beachhotel.com.au.*

Hotel Great Northern

MUSIC CLUBS | Bands perform most evenings at this old-school pub. ✉ *Jonson St. at Byron St.* ☎ *02/6685–6454* 🌐 *www.thenorthern.com.au.*

Railway Friendly Bar

MUSIC CLUBS | Live music rocks this pub, known locally as The Rails, every night; it's built on the old railway station site. ✉ *Jonson St. Railway Station* ☎ *02/6685–7662* 🌐 *www.therailsbyronbay.com.*

🛍 Shopping

Byron Bay is one of the state's arts-and-crafts centers, with many innovative and high-quality articles for sale, such as leather goods, offbeat designer clothing, essential oils, natural cosmetics, and ironware. The community market, held on the first Sunday of every month, fills the Butler Street reserve with more than

300 stalls selling art, crafts, and local produce.

Byron Bay Hat Co.

CLOTHING | This local shopping institution carries great hats and bags perfect for the beach. ✉ *4 Jonson St.* ☎ *02/6685–8357* ⊕ *byronbayhatcompany.com.*

🏃 Activities

KAYAKING

Go Sea Kayak

KAYAKING | Owned and operated by local surf lifesavers (volunteer lifeguards), this new company runs three-hour kayak tours in two-person kayaks that venture out into the open ocean in search of viewing bottlenose dolphins, sea turtles, and even whales in the season. Guides weave in local Aboriginal history and point out the sights. ✉ *Apex Park, Opposite 56 Lawson St.* ☎ *0416/222344* ⊕ *www.goseakayakbyronbay.com.au* ✉ *From A$75.*

SCUBA DIVING

The best local diving is at Julian Rocks Marine Reserve, some 3 km (2 miles) offshore, where the confluence of warm and cold currents supports a profusion of marine life and is one of the few sites south of the Great Barrier Reef where you can snorkel with both tropical fish and deep-water animals from the Southern Ocean.

Byron Bay Dive Centre

SCUBA DIVING | This dive center runs snorkeling and scuba-diving trips for all levels of experience, plus gear rental and instruction. The five-hour introductory diving course costs A$160; a single dive with all equipment and guide and some 50 minutes of diving near Julian Rocks costs A$99. A 60-minute snorkel trip, complete with wet suit, is A$67. ✉ *9 Marvel St.* ☎ *02/6685–8333* ⊕ *www. byronbaydivecentre.com.au* ✉ *From A$60.*

Sundive

SCUBA DIVING | This PADI dive center has courses for all level of divers, as well as boat dives and snorkel trips. The first dive, with all equipment, is A$110; snorkeling trips are available, too. ✉ *9–11 Middleton St.* ☎ *02/6685–7755* ⊕ *www. sundive.com.au* ✉ *From A$70.*

Lord Howe Island

Fringed by the world's southernmost coral reef as well as gorgeous, sheltered beaches, dominated by two dramatic peaks, and inhabited by just around 400 permanent residents—Lord Howe Island is a secluded slice of paradise that lies about 600 km (370 miles) east of mainland Australia. As a UNESCO World Heritage island, it welcomes just 400 visitors at any time, so it never feels overcrowded. It's a great place for a digital detox—there is no mobile phone coverage anywhere on the island and Internet access is patchy at best. Most visitors rent bicycles and spend their time snorkeling in the lagoon, hand-feeding fish, hiking, and bird-watching, while hardy types climb the summit of 875-meter (2,870-foot) Mt. Gower for sensational views.

GETTING HERE AND AROUND

Qantas subsidiary Qantas Link flies to Lord Howe Island from Sydney, Brisbane, and Port Macquarie. The flight from Sydney is 1 hour and 50 minutes. Flights from the other destinations are 10 minutes or so shorter. As Qantas is the only carrier, and only 400 tourists can visit the island, fares can be quite high—typically more than A$600 one-way. The most economical way to travel to Lord Howe is with an air-and-hotel package deal.

Just 10 km (6 miles) long and with a width varying from 1,000 feet to 2 km (1 mile), crescent-shape Lord Howe Island is compact and easy to navigate. The lagoon hugs the western shore of the

En Route

Fifty-three km (33 miles) northwest of Byron Bay is the towering, conical **Mt. Warning**, a 3,800-foot extinct volcano that dominates the pleasant town of Murwillumbah. Its radical shape can be seen from miles away, including the beaches at Byron.

A well-marked **walking track** winds up Mt. Warning, which is a World Heritage national park, from the Breakfast Creek parking area at its base. The 4½-km (2½-mile) track climbs steadily through fern forest and buttressed trees where you can often see native brush turkeys and pademelons (small wallaby-like marsupials). The last 650 feet of the ascent is a strenuous scramble up a steep rock face using chain-link handrails. The local Aboriginal name for the mountain is Wollumbin, which means "cloud catcher," and the metal walkways on the summit are sometimes shrouded in clouds. On a clear day, however, there are fabulous 360-degree views of the massive caldera, one of the largest in the world: national parks crown the southern, western, and northern rims, and the Tweed River flows seaward through the eroded eastern wall. Many people undertake the Mt. Warning ascent before dawn, so they can catch the first rays of light falling on mainland Australia.

island. The town, known as Old Settlement, is midway along the lagoon, and most accommodations are within an easy cycle ride or walk from there. The airport is slightly south of the town, and the two volcanic peaks—Mt. Lidgbird and Mt. Gower—dominate the island's southeast extremity.

Beaches

★ Ned's Beach

BEACH—SIGHT | FAMILY | This beautiful beach on the northeast side of the island is a mecca for fish because fishing bans protect them here. Brightly colored tropical creatures, such as parrot fish and their less-spectacular mullet mates (which are occasionally chased by a harmless reef shark), swim up to shore and greet visitors at the daily 4 pm fish feed. However, visitors can also feed them at other times—you can buy fish food to toss to them from a beach kiosk. This feeding frenzy is fun to watch. Bring snorkel gear to explore the coral a little farther out, or bring a picnic and relax on this beach that's one of the cleanest in Australia. The beach is an easy drive, cycle, or walk from town and the northern hotels. **Amenities:** none. **Best for:** snorkeling; sunrise; swimming; walking. ⊠ *Ned's Beach Rd., Ned's Beach* ⊕ *www. lordhoweisland.info.*

Restaurants

★ Arajilla

$$$$ | MODERN AUSTRALIAN | Dining at Arajilla Retreat at least once during a stay on Lord Howe Island is a must. The cuisine, which changes daily, uses fish straight from the ocean and lovely homegrown vegetables. Begin with a drink at the cozy bar, decked out just a little like a gentlemen's club with leather armchairs, and then take a seat at the restaurant with its white walls and one dramatic burgundy-color feature wall. The three-course menu changes often: recent choices have included baby beetroot salad with goat cheese and toasted almonds; a grilled kingfish with potato rosti, asparagus, and egg-yolk ravioli for

Did You Know?

Masked boobies, brown noddies, providence petrels, red-tailed topic birds, and sooty terns will be more than just the cute names of feathered friends after a few days on LHI (as the locals call Lord Howe Island). The skies are full of birds gliding and swooping on the warm currents, while at ground level Lord Howe wood hens will be picking at your feet. It's a bird-lover's paradise.

main; and grilled Mediterranean vegetables with polenta chips and Parmesan cheese. Desserts are irresistible and may include black sticky rice with lychee sorbet, toasted coconut, and kaffir lime. **Known for:** fresh and quality produce; healthy; sophisticated dining. $ Average main: A$95 ✉ Lagoon Rd., Old Settlement Beach ☎ 1800/063928 ⊕ www.arajilla.com.au ⊙ Only dinner open to nonguests.

Greenback's Eatery

$$ | SEAFOOD | Named after a Lord Howe Island fishing vessel, Greenback's Eatery naturally specializes in fresh fish. This casual spot, basically a veranda attached to boat owner Dave Gardiner's house, is open only on Monday and Thursday night (from 6:30), and the only choice on the menu is the catch of the day, but at least you know it's superfresh. You can bring your own wine or beer, although it is licensed. It's small and popular with locals, so book ahead. Dave also sells fresh sashimi packs to take away. **Known for:** BYO alcohol; fun on weekends; fresh produce. $ Average main: A$30 ✉ Middle Beach, 2 Skyline Dr. ☎ 02/6563–2208 ⊕ www.fishlordhowe.com.au 🚫 No credit cards ⊙ Closed Fri.–Wed. No lunch.

★ Lord Howe Golf Club

$$ | AUSTRALIAN | This is a fine place to socialize with the locals and tourists and enjoy some honest, unpretentious food. The on-site Sunset Bar & Grill is open for dinner on Thursday, Friday, and Sunday, and the menu includes a variety of roasts (such as roast chicken or lamb), steak with garlic butter, schnitzel, fish, and salads, plus pizza on Sunday nights. Friday night is the "big night out" on the island, when almost everyone turns up for the sunset barbecue—try the barbecue kingfish and grab an ice-cold beer. Desserts include what appears to be the island staple—sticky-date pudding—and ice cream. It's best to come early to take in the view over the golf links and the lagoon beyond. Sunday morning only,

breakfast is served. **Known for:** the place to go on a Friday and Saturday; relaxed dining; friendly staff. $ Average main: A$25 ✉ Lord Howe Island ☎ 02/6563–2179 ⊕ www.lordhowegolf.com.au ⊙ Closed Mon., Wed., Thurs., and Sat. No lunch.

Pinetrees Lodge

$$$$ | ECLECTIC | For four generations Pinetrees has been opening its doors to visitors, and staff have certainly honed the art of hospitality. Pop into the lagoon-front lodge for a buffet lunch of assorted salads with the dish of the day, or drop in for dinner; the local kingfish is always a highlight. Don't miss the signature "fish fry " buffet with kingfish sashimi and sushi followed by a battered kingfish and chips. The five-course menu changes daily, but you can usually expect sushi, soup, fresh fish, lamb, and beef prepared with homegrown herbs and vegetables, followed by delicious desserts. Afternoon tea is also available. **Known for:** signature fish fry buffet; afternoon tea; local institution. $ Average main: A$65 ✉ Pinetrees Lodge, Lagoon Rd. ☎ 02/6563–2177 ⊕ www.pinetrees.com.au.

🛏 Hotels

★ Arajilla Lord Howe Island

$$$$ | RESORT | One of the most luxurious accommodations on Lord Howe, Arajilla Retreat contains 10 spacious suites and two two-bedroom suites. **Pros:** exclusive and secluded; rates include all meals, minibar, and predinner drinks; free bike use. **Cons:** expensive; interiors might not be to everyone's taste. $ Rooms from: A$700 ✉ Old Settlement Beach, Lagoon Rd. ☎ 02/6563–2002 ⊕ www.arajilla.com.au 🛏 12 suites ❚⊙❙ All-inclusive.

Capella Lodge

$$$$ | B&B/INN | In the shadow of Mt. Gower, Capella Lodge is Lord Howe Island's most posh lodging. **Pros:** great location; fantastic views; pure luxury; rates include breakfast, dinner, and

drinks. **Cons:** steep rates; isolated; some rooms small. $ *Rooms from: A$750* ✉ *Lagoon Rd.* ☎ *02/9918–4355* ⊕ *www. lordhowe.com* ➪ *9 suites* ⦿ *Free Breakfast.*

Ocean View Apartments

$$ | **HOTEL** | If you want to get the low-down on Lord Howe Island history, take a room at this apartment complex owned and operated by fifth- and sixth-genera-tion descendants of the island's original settlers, T. B. and Mary Wilson. **Pros:** great location with easy walk into town; kitchenettes; saltwater swimming pool. **Cons:** dated furnishings. $ *Rooms from: A$180* ✉ *Ocean View Dr., Old Settlement Beach* ☎ *02/6563–2041* ⊕ *oceanview-lordhoweisland.com.au* ➪ *16 apartments* ⦿ *No meals.*

Pinetrees Lodge

$$$$ | **HOTEL** | Right on Lagoon Beach and a short walk from the popular bowling club, the Pinetrees Lodge has a terrific location and is the largest accommoda-tion on Lord Howe Island—with motel rooms, suites, and garden cottages. **Pros:** great amenities; excellent location; good five-night packages available online. **Cons:** can be noisy with families in peak times; can feel a bit like living in other guests' pockets. $ *Rooms from: A$790* ✉ *Lagoon Rd.* ☎ *02/9262–6585* ⊕ *www. pinetrees.com.au* ➪ *34 rooms, 4 suites* ⦿ *All-inclusive.*

☩ Activities

BIRD-WATCHING

Lord Howe Island Birdwatching

BIRD WATCHING | Lord Howe Island is home to 14 species of seabirds, which breed there in the hundreds and swoop and dive over the two bulbous peaks, Mt. Gower and Mt. Lidgbird. A good viewing spot that's also easier to climb are the Malabar cliffs, on the northeast corner of the island. Here from September to May, you'll see red-tailed tropic birds perform-ing their courting rituals. This is also the

time that shearwaters (also known as mutton birds) return to the island daily at dusk, making for an extraordinary avian spectacle. One of the rarest birds, the Providence petrel, returns to the island to nest in winter (June to August), while sooty terns are also a regular sight at Ned's Beach and the Northern Hills between September and January. The island also hosts more than 130 species of permanent and migratory birds, such as the flightless Lord Howe Island woodhen. Author and naturalist **Ian Hutton** (⊕ *lordhowe-tours.com.au*) conducts nature tours and seabird cruises. ✉ *Lord Howe Island.*

DIVING AND SNORKELING

Lord Howe Island Marine Park

DIVING/SNORKELING | UNESCO World Heritage lists Lord Howe Island's beautiful lagoon, which is sheltered by the world's southernmost coral reef, stretching for some 6 km (4 miles) along the western coast. Contained within Lord Howe Island Marine Park, the lagoon harbors some 500 species of fish and 90 species of coral. There are several ways to explore the lagoon and the coral-filled beaches of the eastern coast, which are only about 3 km (2 miles)—by glass-bot-tom boat, snorkeling, or scuba diving. Ned's Beach, the site of the island's fish-frenzy, is perfect for snorkelers. Another great spot is the wreck of the ship *The Favourite,* at North Bay, the lagoon's northernmost point. Divers have more than 50 sites to choose from, rang-ing from shallow resort dives near the beach, to spectacular trenches, caves, and volcanic drop-offs. Experienced divers love the waters around Ball's Pyramid, which abound with kingfish and Galapagos sharks up to 14 feet long. ■ **TIP** ➔ **If you don't bring your own snorke-ling gear, you can rent it from local resorts.** ✉ *Lord Howe Island Visitor Center, Mid-dle Rd. at Lagoon Rd.* ☎ *02/6563–2114* ⊕ *www.lordhoweisland.info.*

FISHING
Fishing at Ball's Pyramid

FISHING | Towering some 1,800 feet above the ocean, Ball's Pyramid is a unique rock stack and one of the world's tallest monoliths in water. Located 23 km (14 miles) south of Lord Howe Island, it's part of the pristine Lord Howe Island Marine Park, in which commercial fishing is banned and huge species of fish abound, making it a top destination for sportfishing. The boat trip to Ball's Pyramid takes 75 minutes and is a perfect way to soak up stunning views back toward the island before you start reeling in the catch. Several dedicated fishing charter operators, including Blue Billie (a fifth-generation family of fishermen), run tours to the pyramid, offering half- and full-day expeditions with rates starting from around A$200 per person. ⊠ *Lord Howe Island Marine Park* ⊕ *www.lordhoweisland.info.*

HIKING
★ Mt. Gower

HIKING/WALKING | The larger of the two volcanic peaks located at the southern end of Lord Howe Island, Mt. Gower rises 875 meters (2,870 feet) above sea level. The hike to the summit is arduous and can only be undertaken with a guide. Covering a distance of about 14 km (9 miles) round-trip and taking about 8½ hours to complete, it's a wonderful experience and affords sensational views across the island, the reef, and out to Ball's Pyramid, 23 km (14 miles) away. Along the way, guides point out rare plants and birdlife. Fifth-generation islander Jack Shick, of Lord Howe Island Tours, is a highly experienced guide and takes tours twice a week (Monday and Thursday); the cost is about A$70 per person. ⊠ *Lord Howe Island* ☎ *02/6563–2218 Jack Shick* ⊕ *www.lordhoweisland-tours.net* ◱ *A$70.*

Berry

142 km (88 miles) South from Sydney.

For the past decade, Sydneysiders have decamped to Berry for a weekend away from the city. There's something incredibly relaxing about this small country village, surrounded by countryside and a short distance from the ocean. And while it might be small in size, with only 2,500 locals calling this spot home, it sure packs a punch, with award-winning restaurants, boutique shops and stunning walking tracks. There's also an abundance of antiques shops that line the main high street. It's the perfect one-night pit stop before winding further down the South Coast.

GETTING HERE AND AROUND

To get to Berry, the only viable way is to drive. There's no train service and the bus from Sydney has many changes and is an arduous task that's not really time- or cost-effective. Once there, the village itself is easy to navigate on foot, running just a short 1 km (½ mile) in length.

◉ Sights

Berry Museum

BUILDING | **FAMILY** | This cute little museum features an extensive collection of artifacts, memorabilia, photographs, and records donated by the local community to provide a great introduction to Berry's local history and its agricultural roots. Kids love the "Please Do Touch" room. ⊠ *135 Queen St.* ☎ *02 /4464–3097* ⊕ *www.berryhistory.org.au.*

Boat Harbour Rock Pool

HOT SPRINGS | **FAMILY** | In the hotter months, locals all head out to this lesser-known swimming spot in Gerringong, found on the coast, to cool down. It's about 1 km (½ miles) from the main high street that runs through Berry. Just follow the directions to Gerringong and you'll soon find the boat ramp that runs close to the pool. It's a small pool that once lived its life as a local swim spot for women only. But today, anyone is welcome and it's an especially great spot for young children. There's no charge but also no facilities. Best time to go is at high tide as it can get a little shallow during low tide. ✉ *Gerringong.*

🍴 Restaurants

Berry Sourdough Cafe

$ | AUSTRALIAN |FAMILY | Set on a back lane just off Queen Street, this rustic eatery has become a bit of an institution: no one goes to Berry and skips breakfast at Berry Sourdough Cafe (hence the long line on weekends).The coffee is superior and the breakfast option is popular. There's a working bakery on-site, so if the wait to get a seat is too long then grab one of their homemade sausage rolls or meat pies and a coffee for the road. There are also many different varieties of bread available, with sourdough naturally being the most celebrated. **Known for:** sourdough bread; flaky sausage rolls and pies; zucchini flower and buffalo feta omelet with avocado. [$] *Average main: A$20* ✉ *23 Prince Alfred St.* ☎ *02/4464–1617* 🌐 *berrysourdoughcafe.com.au.*

★ The Famous Berry Donut Van

$ | AUSTRALIAN | For the last 55 years, The Famous Berry Donut Van has been just that, a famous must-visit spot for those visiting Berry. The quality of their cinnamon doughnuts is unrivaled. They are made-to-order so are always piping hot. Collin and Shirley London toured the doughnut van around Australia in the 1960s but once they arrived in Berry, they decided it was home. Best bit? They're open every day from 9 am until 6 pm, come summer or winter. **Known for:** cinnamon doughnuts; made-to-order doughnuts; local institution. [$] *Average main: A$5* ✉ *73 Queen St.* ☎ *04/2331–9413.*

Silos Estate

$$ | AUSTRALIAN | This swank estate ticks all the boxes. The restaurant offers farm-style fare in a rustic environment, with share plates, like the overflowing charcutterie, available at lunch and a two-course dining menu in the evening (A$60). The menu is meat heavy but there are a few veggie options. The star of the show here is one of them, zucchini flowers stuffed with ricotta and goat's curd, drizzled with honey. This dish matches perfectly with the cellar's other star, its Semillon. But there's no need to rush into the restaurant. There's wine tasting at the cellar door, which can also be enjoyed before visiting the art gallery. There'a also an on-site bed-and-breakfast available, starting at A$225 a night, offering a cottage-style stay. **Known for:** casual dining and share plates; hit with arty types; must-visit cellar door. [$] *Average main: A$35* ✉ *Princes Hwy.* ☎ *02/4448–6082* 🌐 *thesilos.com* 🕓 *Closed Mon.–Wed. No dinner Sun.*

SOUTH on albany

$$ | AUSTRALIAN | This casual but elegant restaurant is always busy and that's truly down to the menu being packed with seasonal and local fare. Each dish is a taste sensation but arrives looking so pretty that you'll want to stare in awe for a while. That's thanks to co-owner Sonia Greig's background in food styling. For starters, it's a crime not to order the oysters. It's a deep understanding that the oysters from the South Coast are the best in Australia. And then for main, the roasted pork cutlet with parsnip puree, broccolini, lentils and fennel jam and cider jus. Always leave room for dessert here, with the white chocolate mousse, lime curd, hazelnut and cocoa meringue being a memory maker. **Known for:** trendy; busy, so prebook; incredible desserts. [$] *Average main: A$30* ✉ *3/65 Queen St.* ☎ *2/4464–2005* 🌐 *southonalbany.com* 🕓 *Closed Mon. and Tues. No lunch Wed.–Fri.*

Hotels

Raintree B&B
$$$$ | B&B/INN | Nestled in the rain forest just south of Berry, the outstanding Raintree is a secluded retreat that fully immerses guests in nature. **Pros:** peaceful nature setting; spacious guest rooms; luxurious retreat. **Cons:** out of town; incredibly quiet; hot breakfast is extra. [$] *Rooms from: A$620* ✉ *160 Red Cedar La.* ☎ *04/3824–1150* 🌐 *www.raintreebnb.com.au* 🛏 *8 rooms* 🍴 *No meals.*

Jervis Bay

Jervis Bay is 197km (122 miles) from Sydney.

Jervis Bay is the name of both the oceanic bay and the village that surrounds it, and it is the unrivalled white-sand oasis of the South Coast, found in the Shoalhaven region about four hours south of Sydney and an hour south of Berry. The bay is nine times bigger than Sydney Harbour and is, in fact, the deepest bay in Australia. Here you'll find 22 km (14 miles) of the most pristine white-sand beaches the country has to offer.

GETTING HERE AND AROUND

Jervis Bay is a comfortable four-hour drive from Sydney, winding through the many small country towns along the way. The views over Kiama, about halfway down the coast is a true breathtaking moment. The easiest way to adventure through the South Coast is by car. There's no train service and there's no direct bus service.

VISITOR INFORMATION

CONTACTS Visitor Information. ✉ *Dent St. at Woollamia Rd.* ☎ *02/4441–5999.*

Sights

★ **Booderee National Park**
NATIONAL/STATE PARK | Booderee is the Aboriginal word meaning "bay of plenty" and there really is plenty to see and do at this incredibly beautiful National park, located at the southernmost part of Jervis Bay. Camping sites are available throughout the park. Cave Beach has on-site showers and a small walk down to a vast beach that's a safe spot for swimming. Green Patch Beach is a good location for snorkelers with its bounty of interesting fish on its tranquil shores. The historic Cape St George Lighthouse is the perfect location for whale- and bird-watching. ✉ *Jervis Bay Rd.* ☎ *02/4443–0977* 🌐 *parksaustralia.gov.au/booderee.*

Point Perpendicular Lighthouse
LIGHTHOUSE | FAMILY | This modest white lighthouse may be decommissioned but its scenic approach, winding through natural scrub and a spattering of colorful wildflowers, and unrivalled views and whale-watching on Jervis Bay make it a must visit if you are nearby. Built in 1898 with a concrete-block construction that was a first at the time, Point Perpendicular Lighthouse was a working lighthouse until 1993. The best time to visit is at sunrise when the skies swirl with purples and pinks. You'll often see dolphins playing in the waters below the dramatic cliff's edge. ✉ *Lighthouse Rd., Beecreoft Peninsula, Lot 51.*

Beaches

Chinamans Beach
BEACH—SIGHT | Just north of Hyams Beach, this smaller beach has the same enviable white sands and incredible clear waters minus the crowds. During high season, it's worth heading to this quieter spot to enjoy all that Jervis Bay has to offer. The water is safe for swimming and the coastal path that runs along it

takes you to Greenfield Beach. **Amenities:** toilets. **Best for:** swimming; water sports. ✉ *Aster St.*

Greenfield Beach

BEACH—SIGHT | Set in Jervis Bay National Park, Greenfield Beach offers powdery white sands, access to walking trails and an abundance of wildlife including kangaroos and wallabies, and it's a safe swimming spot, even for those with little experience in the sea. **Amenities:** showers; toilets; barbecue. **Best for:** swimming; picnics. ✉ *Cyrus St.*

★ Hyams Beach

BEACH—SIGHT | **FAMILY** | Of the 22 km (14 miles) of beautiful beaches that Jervis Bay has to offer, Hyams Beach is the most famous. The white sands are apparently the whitest in the world (per Guinness World Records), and while such hype can often lead to disappointment, this beach lives up to expectations. The sands are magnificently white, the waters are crystal clear turquoise, and the combination is paradise found. In the summer months, it can get a little busy here but nothing like the Sydney beaches. In the spring and autumn months, there's a little more room to breathe. **Amenities:** showers; toilets; café. **Best for:** swimming; water sports. ✉ *Cyrus St.*

🍴 Restaurants

★ Gunyah

$$$ | **AUSTRIAN** | Set in the remarkable Paperbark Camp glamping spot filled with high-end tree houses that are available for two-night minimum stays on the weekend, this restaurant is a romantic and warmly-lit tree house for grown-ups. The menu is a set, three-course affair (A$70). Soft, slow-cooked teriyaki lamb is often on the ever-changing menu, with chocolate cake, crème anglaise, and rhubarb compote for dessert. **Known for:** great for a special occasion; advance reservations; very romantic. $ *Average*

main: A$70 ✉ *Paperbark Camp, 571 Woollamia Rd.* ☎ *02/4441–7299* ⊕ *www.paperbarkcamp.com.au.*

Hyams Beach Cafe and General Store

$ | **AUSTRALIAN** | Manned by a dog named Albert, and frequented by locals who declare it serves the best burger in town, this beach-vibe café has exactly what's needed after a full day of activities in Jervis Bay. On weekend nights, there's a three-course dinner menu, featuring locally caught seafood. The Parisian dessert chef creates perfect sweet delights, like salted caramel-chocolate tarts and delicate lemon meringue. **Known for:** meat-heavy menu; hearty, unfussy meals; delightful desserts. $ *Average main: A$20* ✉ *Hyams Beach, 76 Cyrus St.* ☎ *02/4443–3874* ⊕ *www.hyamsbeachcafe.com.au.*

Wildginger

$$$ | **THAI** | The chef here cut his teeth at one of Sydney's top Thai restaurants so it's no surprise that this Thai-inspired, Asian-fusion restaurant is one of the most popular spots in the area. The banquet option is very popular, allowing you to try a mix of the many dishes available here. For A$39 (banquet for one person), there's cod and trout fishcakes, veal mousse dim sum, and steamed ocean perch in Penang Malaysian, to name a few. Entrée highlights include the three-hour braised beef cheeks in southern-style green curry and the whole shallow-fried barramundi. **Known for:** seafood specialties; banquet tasting menu; three-hour braised beef cheeks in southern-style green curry. $ *Average main: A$40* ✉ *42 Owen St.* ☎ *02/4441–5577* ⊕ *www.wild-ginger.com.au.*

🛏 Hotels

★ Hyams Beach Seaside Cottages

$$ | **RENTAL** | Built in the 1920s by a group of fisherman who wanted to be close to the water, these pint-sized, one-bedroom

cottages painted in baby blue, pink, and yellow will appeal to tiny-home fans. **Pros:** beachfront location; amazing views; unique experience. **Cons:** book out fast; no breakfast; can feel a little small. [$] *Rooms from: A$200* ✉ *55/53 Cyrus St.* ☎ *0412/029096* 🌐 *www.hyamsbeachseasidecottages.com.au* 🛏 *7 cottages* 🍴 *No meals.*

Jervis Bay Holiday Park

$$ | **RESORT** | The name might suggest a caravan park, but don't be fooled: Jervis Bay has fantastically finished villas along the waterfront, with a balcony and patio with either pool views or river views. **Pros:** lots of amenities; great for families; waterfront views. **Cons:** can be noisy; not on the beach; a short drive into Jervis. [$] *Rooms from: A$180* ✉ *785 Woollamia Rd.* ☎ *02/4441–5046* 🌐 *jervisbayholidaypark.com.au* 🛏 *12 rooms* 🍴 *No meals.*

Activities

Jervis Bay Stand Up Paddle

CANOEING/ROWING/SKULLING | Jervis Bay is the perfect place to go paddleboarding, and for beginners, there's a daily stand-up class with tour (reservations are essential). ✉ *1/2 Erina Rd.* ☎ *0403/354716* 🌐 *www.jervisbaystanduppaddle.com.au.*

Sea Kayak Jervis Bay

CANOEING/ROWING/SKULLING | Guide Tracy Gibson has plenty of funny tales to tell about the area in between helpful guidance to get more power from your paddle. ✉ *2/3 Snapper Rd.* ☎ *0418/649082* 🌐 *www.seakayakjervisbay.com.au.*

Chapter 5

MELBOURNE

5

Updated by
Molly McLaughlin

◉ Sights	🍴 Restaurants	🛏 Hotels	🛍 Shopping	🍸 Nightlife
★★★★★	★★★★★	★★★☆☆	★★★★☆	★★★★★

WELCOME TO MELBOURNE

TOP REASONS TO GO

★ **Fabulous Markets:** Melbourne has nearly a dozen major markets. The huge Queen Victoria Market has more than 1,000 stalls.

★ **International Cuisine:** Melbourne's dining scene is a vast smorgasbord of cuisines.

★ **Sizzling Nightlife:** Melbourne's nightlife centers on King Street and Flinders Lane, with dozens of retro-style bars and clubs. The city's famous live music scene can be viewed in historic pubs in Fitzroy, Collingwood, and Brunswick.

★ **Sports Galore:** Melburnians, like Aussies in general, do love a good match. The Melbourne Cup horse race in November brings the entire city to a standstill. The same is true of Australian Rules Football.

★ **Arts and Culture:** Melbourne is renowned for its rich and lively arts scene. Live performances range from small, experimental theater productions to international comedy, fashion, and theater festivals.

The Yarra River cuts through the city center; the main business district is on the northern side, the southern side has arts, entertainment, and restaurant precincts. Several exclusive suburbs hug the southeastern shore of the bay. The Yarra Valley wineries and the Dandenong Ranges are an hour's drive to the east. The beaches and vineyards of the Mornington Peninsula are a 90-minute drive south.

1 City Center. The place to be for arts, funky back alleys, shopping, and Australia's best food. Explore the Southgate development, the arts district around the National Gallery of Victoria, and the King's Domain.

2 Richmond. Heaven for foodies and fashionistas in need of retail therapy. Come here for a new wardrobe, a Vietnamese soup kitchen, a Korean barbecue, a Laotian banquet, or a Thai hole-in-the-wall.

3 East Melbourne. The harmonious streetscapes in this historic enclave of Victorian houses, which date from the boom following the gold rushes of the 1850s, are a great excuse for a stroll.

4 South Melbourne. This leafy, charming suburb is home to South Melbourne Market and a thriving café scene.

5 St. Kilda. Dozens of alfresco restaurants overflow into the streets, and the cafés and bars are buzzing with young fashionistas.

6 Fitzroy. Come here if you're looking for an Afghan camel bag, a secondhand paperback, or live music and a beer in a backstreet beer garden.

7 Brunswick. Melbourne's eclectic and multicultural heart with Mediterranean and Middle Eastern markets, craft coffee shops, and a lively nightlife scene.

8 Carlton. Known for its beautiful old town houses, authentic Italian food, and proximity to the city center, this lively suburb is also home to Carlton Garden, which houses the modern Melbourne Museum.

9 South Yarra and Prahran. Two neighboring suburbs south of Melbourne, both crammed with bars, cafés, and great shopping.

10 Brighton. Colorful bathing boxes and a pretty beach and town are the draw here.

Consistently rated among the "world's most livable cities" in quality-of-life surveys, Melbourne is built on a coastal plain at the top of the giant horseshoe of Port Phillip Bay. The city center is an orderly grid of streets where the state parliament, banks, multinational corporations, and splendid Victorian buildings that sprang up in the wake of the gold rush still stand. This is Melbourne's heart, which you can explore at a leisurely pace in a couple of days.

In Southbank, one of the newer precincts south of the city center, the sprawling Crown Melbourne entertainment complex and the Southgate Centre's bars, restaurants, and shops have refocused Melbourne's vision on the Yarra River. Once a blighted stretch of factories and run-down warehouses, the southern bank of the river is now a vibrant, exciting part of the city, and the river itself is finally taking its rightful place in Melbourne's psyche.

Just a hop away, Federation Square—with its host of restaurants, galleries, and museums—has become a civic hub for both Melburnians and visitors. A subtler city icon, its "laneways" thread the city center between major streets and are home to fascinating bars, cafés, shops, and art galleries.

Melbourne's inner suburbs have a character all their own. Stroll along the Esplanade in St. Kilda, amble past the elegant houses of East Melbourne, enjoy the shops and cafés of Fitzroy or Carlton, rub shoulders with locals at the Queen Victoria Market, nip into the Windsor for afternoon tea, or rent a canoe at Studley Park to paddle along one of the prettiest stretches of the Yarra—and you may discover Melbourne's soul as well as its heart.

Planning

WHEN TO GO

Melbourne and Victoria are at their most beautiful in autumn, from March to May. Days are crisp, and the foliage in parks and gardens is glorious. Melbourne winters can be gloomy, although the vild seas and leaden skies from June to August provide a suitable backdrop for the dramatic coastal scenery of the Great Ocean Road. By September the weather begins to clear, and the football finals are on. Book early to visit Melbourne during the Spring Racing Carnival and the Melbourne International Festival (late October/early November) and during mid-January when the Australian Open tennis tournament is staged.

PLANNING YOUR TIME

The free City Circle Tram is an easy hop-on/hop-off way to see many of the city's sights in a short time without exhausting yourself. The Parliament House tram stop goes to the Princess Theatre, the grand Windsor Hotel, Parliament House, the "Paris End" of Collins Street, and St. Patrick's Cathedral. Get off at Flinders Street to take a peek at the infamous *Chloe* painting in Young and Jackson's pub, and then walk over the Princes Bridge. There you can stroll the banks of the Yarra, looking back at Federation Square, before checking out the restaurants, shops, and the casino in the Southbank precinct. A trip to the Eureka Skydeck, the southern hemisphere's highest viewing platform, puts the city into perspective, and from there you can decide whether to head northeast to Fitzroy for an amble along groovy Brunswick Street, or north to Carlton to immerse yourself in Little Italy.

You might squeeze in a bit more exploring at the Treasury Gardens and Captain Cook's Cottage in the adjoining Fitzroy Gardens, or meet the sharks at the Melbourne Aquarium, opposite Southbank. On your second day, stroll through the Royal Botanic Gardens and see the Shrine of Remembrance. Afterward, take a tram along St. Kilda Road to the hip Acland Street area, in the suburb of St. Kilda, for dinner. On Day 3, tour Chapel Street's shops, restaurants, and bars.

If you have additional time, head east to the Yarra Valley for an organized winery tour or ride on the Puffing Billy steam train, which leaves from Belgrave and travels through the fern gullies and forests of the Dandenong Ranges. On the way back, stop at a teahouse in Belgrave or Olinda and browse the curio stores. If possible, take an evening excursion to Phillip Island for the endearing Penguin Parade at sunset. A trip to the Mornington Peninsula wineries and Arthurs Seat, just 90 minutes south of Melbourne, is another great day out.

GETTING HERE AND AROUND

Melbourne is most easily reached by plane, as it's hours by car from the nearest big city. International airlines flying into Melbourne include Air New Zealand, United, Singapore Airlines, Emirates, Etihad, Thai Airways, Malaysia Airlines, Virgin Australia, and Qantas. ■TIP➔ **Make sure to check which airport your flight arrives into, as Avalon is a 40-minute drive southwest of the city but Tullamarine is much closer.**

BUS AND TRAM TRAVEL

To use public transportation in Melbourne, you need a ticket called a Myki (a stored-value smart card). It can be purchased (A$6 for the card itself) at 7-Eleven stores, train stations, vending machines at major tram stops, and the Melbourne Visitors Hub at Town Hall. Each time you enter a train station, or hop on a tram or bus, you must touch the Myki card to a validator. The standard two-hour fare of A$4.30 is activated the first time you touch on, and you can change between any bus, tram, or train during this period. Daily travel is capped at two, two-hour fares (A$8.60), at which point you can travel as much as you like without extra charge. Trams run until midnight (1 am on Friday and Saturday) and can be hailed wherever you see a green-and-white tram-stop sign.

CAR TRAVEL

Melbourne's regimented layout makes it easy to negotiate by car, but two unusual rules apply because of the tram traffic. At intersections in the city center, trams should be passed by swinging to the far left before turning right (known as the "hook turn"); and when a tram stops to allow passengers to disembark across a roadway to the curb, the cars behind it also must stop. Motorists using various tollways have 72 hours to pay the toll after using the highway. To pay by credit card, call ☎ *132–629*. Alternatively, you can buy passes online. A weekend pass is around A$17.50.

CRUISE TRAVEL TO MELBOURNE

Cruise ships stopping in Melbourne dock in Port Melbourne at Station Pier. Tour buses, taxis, and a shuttle bus can collect visitors, and the terminus of tram 109 is just beyond the start of the pier. Frequent trams take passengers from here directly to the city center. The area around Station Pier has numerous restaurants and attractive water views. The lively entertainment and dining hub of St. Kilda is a pleasant 5-km (3-mile) walk southeast from here, alongside attractive bay beaches.

TRAIN TRAVEL

The main entrance to Southern Cross Railway Station is at Spencer and Little Collins streets. From here the statewide V/Line rail company sells tickets for 11-hour rail trips to Sydney, as well as services to many regional centers in Victoria. V/Line buses connect with the trains to provide transport to coastal towns; take the train to Geelong to connect with a bus to Lorne, Apollo Bay, and Port Campbell, or travel by train to Warrnambool and take a bus to Port Fairy.

RESTAURANTS

Melbourne teems with top-quality restaurants, particularly in St. Kilda, South Yarra, Fitzroy, and Southbank. Lygon Street is still a favorite with those who love great coffee, pasta, and Italian bakeries, while the city center also has many back alleys (known as "laneways") containing popular cafés that serve meals as well as good coffee (a Melbourne trademark). Reservations are generally advised

(though not possible for some places). Although most places are licensed to sell alcohol, the few that aren't usually allow you to bring your own. Many places serve food throughout the day, but lunch menus usually operate noon–2:30 pm, and dinner is usually served 7–10:30 pm. Tipping is not customary in Australia, but if you receive good service a 10% tip is welcome. Note there may be a corkage fee in restaurants, which allows you to bring in your own alcoholic drinks.

HOTELS

Staying in the heart of Melbourne, on Collins or Flinders streets and their nearby laneways, or at Southbank, is ideal for those who like dining and shopping. Another fashionable area, a little out of town, is South Yarra, which has excellent shopping. Wherever you stay, make sure you're near a tram or train line. *Hotel reviews have been shortened. For full information, visit Fodors.com.*

What It Costs in Australian Dollars			
$	$$	$$$	$$$$
RESTAURANTS			
under A$21	A$21–A$35	A$36–A$50	over A$50
HOTELS			
under A$151	A$151–A$200	A$201–A$300	over A$300

TOURS

The free City Circle tram operates every 12 minutes from 10 to 9 Thursday–Saturday and 10–6 Sunday–Wednesday around the edge of the Central Business District and Docklands, with stops on Flinders, La Trobe, Victoria, and Spring streets, and Harbour Esplanade. Look for the burgundy-and-cream trams. Metropolitan buses operate daily until around 9 pm to all suburbs, while the NightRider bus service runs between 2 am and 5 am on Saturday and 2 am and 6 am on Sunday.

AAT Kings

GUIDED TOURS | This tour agency runs a half-day Magnificent Melbourne tour (A$71) that explores historical sights, gardens, and the iconic Melbourne Cricket Ground. The company also organizes longer tours outside Melbourne. ✉ Federation Sq., Flinders St. at Russell St., City Center ☎ 1300/228546 ⊕ aatkings.com ☞ From A$71.

Chocoholic Tours

SPECIAL-INTEREST | FAMILY | Chocoholic Tours runs tours of Melbourne for chocolate lovers on Wednesday, Friday, and weekends, including the Melbourne Lanes and Arcades Chocolate Walking Tour, which offers 10 tastings scattered throughout the city's famous backstreets The Yarra Valley Chocolate and Winery Tour is another popular option, taking tourists on a unique journey through Victoria's produce. Other tours are available, including private ones. Bookings are essential. ✉ Block Arcade, 282 Collins St., City Center ☎ 13/0091–5566 ⊕ www.chocoholictours.com.au ☞ From A$49.

Golden Mile Heritage Walk

WALKING TOURS | Hidden Secrets Tours runs guided walks of Melbourne's Golden Mile Heritage Trail, visiting the city's architectural and historic sites. The 2½-hour tours depart daily at 10 am from Federation Square and finish at the Melbourne Town Hall on weekdays and the Melbourne Museum on weekends. ✉ Melbourne ☎ 03/9663–3358 ☞ From A$49.

Gray Line

BUS TOURS | Explore Melbourne and its environs on Gray Line's guided bus and boat tours. The Melbourne Morning City Tour visits the city center's main attractions and some of the surrounding parks. The four-hour tour departs daily at 8:10 am. ✉ Federation Sq., Flinders St. at Russell St., City Center ☎ 1300/858687 ⊕ www.grayline.com.au ☞ From A$71.

Melbourne's Best Tours

BUS TOURS | The tour company runs half-day tours around Melbourne as well as taking visitors farther afield on three- and four-day treks. ✉ Federation Sq., Flinders St. at Russell St., City Center ☎ 1300/958416 ⊕ www.melbournetours.com.au ☞ From A$70.

Melbourne Greeters

WALKING TOURS | The Melbourne Greeter service, a Melbourne Visitor Hub program, provides a free orientation walking tour at 9:30 am daily, guided by a knowledgeable local volunteer. Tours are available in languages other than English. Book tours 24 hours ahead, and depart from the Melbourne Visitor Hub at Town Hall. ✉ Town Hall, Little Collins St. at Swanston St., City Center ☎ 03/9658–9658 weekdays, 03/9658–9942 weekends ⊕ www.melbourne.vic.gov.au/greeter ☞ Free.

Melbourne River Cruises

BOAT TOURS | One of the best ways to see Melbourne is from the deck of a boat on the Yarra River. Melbourne River Cruises' fleet of modern, glass-enclosed boats operate one- and two-hour Yarra River cruises daily (A$25 and A$35, respectively), traversing either west through the commercial heart of the city or east through the parks and gardens, or a combination of the two. Cruises run roughly every hour from 11 to 3, depending on weather and tide conditions. Tours depart from Southgate Berth 3. ✉ Vault 11, Banana Alley, 367 Flinders St., City Center ☎ 03/8610–2600 ⊕ www.melbcruises.com.au ☞ From A$25.

Queen Victoria Market Food Tour

SPECIAL-INTEREST | The two-hour, guided Ultimate Foodie tour is conducted at Queen Victoria Market, where you'll taste your way around the market while learning some of its history. This tour runs Tuesday, Thursday, and twice on Saturday and makes the most of seasonal, local produce. ✉ Queen Victoria Market, Queen St. at Elizabeth St., City Center

☎ *03/9320–5822* ⊕ *www.qvm.com.au* 🎫 *A$69.*

VISITOR INFORMATION

The Melbourne Visitor Hub at Town Hall provides touring details in multiple languages. Large-screen videos and touch screens add to the experience, and permanent displays follow the city's history. Daily newspapers are available, and there's access to the Melbourne website (⊕ *www.visitmelbourne.com*). The center is open daily 9–6. The Best of Victoria Booking Service here can help if you're looking for accommodations. It also has cheap Internet access.

City Ambassadors, who provide information, can be identified by their bright red uniforms and found mainly along Swanston Street.

A free bus route map is available from the Melbourne Visitor Hub.

CONTACTS
City of Melbourne Ambassadors Program
City Ambassadors—usually mature men and women easily spotted by their red uniforms—are volunteers for the City of Melbourne and rove the central retail area providing directions and information for people needing their assistance (Monday–Saturday 10–4, Sunday 11:30–3). ✉ *City Center* ☎ *03/9658–9658.*

Melbourne Visitor Hub
Find information and booking services at the information center, open daily 9–6. ✉ *Town Hall, Little Collins St. at Swanston St., City Center* ☎ *03/9658–9658* ⊕ *www.visitmelbourne.com.*

City Center

The City Center (CBD) is designed in a grid formation, with myriad alleyways twisting between them, often containing restaurants, galleries, and bars. The CBD is bounded by Spring Street in the east, Victoria Street to the north, Flinders Street to the South, and Spencer Street to the West. The Federation Square area, opposite the Flinders Street Station, is considered the CBD's heart and is an ideal starting point. The most popular shopping areas are the elegant eastern end of Collins Street and the busy pedestrian mall of Bourke Street. Spring Street holds many of the city's historic buildings from the mid-1800s.

GETTING HERE AND AROUND

Melbourne and its suburbs are well served by trams, trains, and buses. The free City Circle tram is perfect for sightseeing, but often crowded. Trams run east–west and north–south across the city, and travel to the popular St. Kilda and Docklands. The Metro train network operates a City Loop service with stops at Flinders Street, Parliament, Flagstaff, Melbourne Central, and Southern Cross stations, where you'll find connections with a network of trains to outer areas, including the Dandenong Ranges.

◉ Sights

★ The Arts Centre

ARTS VENUE | Melbourne's most important cultural landmark is the venue for performances by the Australian Ballet, Opera Australia, Melbourne Theatre Company, and Melbourne Symphony Orchestra. It encompasses Hamer Hall, the Arts Centre complex, the original National Gallery of Victoria, and the outdoor Sidney Myer Music Bowl. A 60-minute tour of the five floors of the complex, plus the current gallery exhibition and refreshment at the café, takes place Monday to Saturday at 11 am. On Sunday a 90-minute backstage tour begins at 11 am. Neither tour is suitable for children under 12 and both must be booked in advance. At night, look for the center's spire, which creates a magical spectacle with brilliant fiber-optic cables. ✉ *100 St. Kilda Rd., City Center* ☎ *03/9281–8000, 1300/182183 bookings* ⊕ *www.artscentremelbourne.com.au* 🎫 *Tours A$20.*

Block Arcade

STORE/MALL | Melbourne's most elegant 19th-century shopping arcade dates from the 1880s, when "Marvelous Melbourne" was flush with the prosperity of the gold rushes. A century later, renovations scraped back the grime to reveal a magnificent mosaic floor. Tours (A$15) operate on Tuesday and Thursday at 11 am and 1 pm; reservations are essential. ⊠ *282 Collins St., City Center* ☎ *03/9654–5244* ✉ *$A15.*

Cook's Cottage

MEMORIAL | Once the on-leave residence of the Pacific navigator Captain James Cook, this modest two-story home, built in 1755 by Cook senior, was transported stone by stone from Great Ayton in Yorkshire, England, and rebuilt in the lush Fitzroy Gardens in 1934. It's believed that Cook lived in the cottage between his many voyages. The interior is simple, a suitable domestic realm for a man who spent much of his life in cramped quarters aboard sailing ships. ⊠ *Fitzroy Gardens, Lansdowne St. at Wellington Parade, City Center* ☎ *03/9658–9658* ✉ *A$7.*

Eureka Skydeck

VIEWPOINT | Named after the goldfields uprising of 1854, the Eureka Tower which houses the 88th-level Eureka Skydeck) is the highest public vantage point in the southern hemisphere. The funky-shape blue-glass building with an impressive gold cap is the place to get a bird's-eye view of Melbourne and overcome your fear of heights, especially on the Skydeck. An enclosed all-glass cube, known as the Edge (A$12 additional charge), projects 3 meters (9.84 feet) out from the viewing platform—here you can stand, seemingly suspended, over the city on a clear glass floor. ⊠ *7 Riverside Quay, City Center* ☎ *03/9693–8888* ⊕ *www.eurekaskydeck.com.au* ✉ *A$23.*

Federation Square

PLAZA | Encompassing a whole city block, the bold, abstract-style landmark was

Exploring the Theaters

Melburnians love their theater, and major shows often open in Melbourne first. If you want to take in Broadway or West End–style theater in grand surroundings, check out what's playing at the Regent and the Princess. Both are owned by Marriner Theatres, which lovingly restored the Regent for its reopening in the mid-1990s. For performances, check out ⊕ *www. marrinertheatres.com.au.*

designed to be Melbourne's official meeting place, with a variety of attractions and restaurants within it. The square incorporates the second branch of the National Gallery of Victoria (Ian Potter Centre), which exhibits only Australian art, as well as the Australian Centre for the Moving Image; the Deakin Edge amphitheater, a contemporary music and theater performance venue; and the Koorie Heritage Trust, which runs exhibitions, programs, and tours relating to Aboriginal Melbourne. Regular events are held in the square and along the path beside the Yarra River. Crowds often gather to watch events on the giant "Fed TV" in the center of the square. ⊠ *Flinders St., between Swanston and Russell Sts., City Center* ☎ *03/9655–1900* ⊕ *www. fedsquare.com* ✉ *Free.*

Fitzroy Gardens

NATIONAL/STATE PARK | FAMILY | This 65-acre expanse of European trees, manicured lawns, garden beds, statuary, and sweeping walks is Melbourne's most popular central park. Among its highlights is the **Avenue of Elms,** a majestic stand of 130-year-old trees that is one of the few in the world that has not been devastated by Dutch elm disease. ⊠ *Lansdowne*

St. at Wellington Parade, City Center ⊕ *www.fitzroygardens.com* ☒ *Free.*

Flinders Street Station

TRANSPORTATION SITE (AIRPORT/BUS/FERRY/TRAIN) | Much more than just a train station, Flinders Street Station is a Melbourne icon and a popular meeting place. The term "meet me under the clocks" is widely known and used, indicating the timepieces on the front of this grand Edwardian hub of Melbourne's suburban rail network. When it was proposed to replace them with television screens, an uproar ensued. Today there are both clocks and screens. ☒ *Flinders St. and St. Kilda Rd., City Center.*

The Hotel Windsor

HOTEL—SIGHT | Not just a grand hotel, the Windsor is home to one of Melbourne's proudest institutions—the ritual of afternoon tea (A$75 midweek), which is served noon–2 pm, and 2:30–4:30 from Wednesday to Friday. An even more indulgent dessert buffet (A$99), complete with chocolate fountain and other goodies, is added on weekends. Although the Grand Ball Room—a Belle Époque extravaganza with a gilded ceiling and seven glass cupolas—is reserved for private functions, occasionally afternoon tea is served there, so it's best to call first to check. ☒ *111 Spring St., City Center* ☎ *03/9633–6000* ⊕ *www. thewindsor.com.au.*

★ Ian Potter Centre: NGV Australia

MUSEUM | The Australian art collection of the National Gallery of Victoria hangs on the walls of this gallery. Covering the 19th and 20th centuries, it includes paintings from the famous Heidelberg school, such as Frederick McCubbin's *Lost* and Tom Roberts' *Shearing the Rams.* Other displays include textiles, sculpture, and photography. A gallery highlight is the indigenous collection, which changes every six months and includes both traditional and contemporary art. ☒ *The Atrium, Federation Sq., Flinders St. at Russell St., City Center* ☎ *03/8620–2222*

⊕ *www.ngv.vic.gov.au* ☒ *Free; special exhibitions have varying ticket prices.*

National Gallery of Victoria International

MUSEUM | This massive, moat-encircled, bluestone-and-concrete edifice houses works from renowned international painters, including Picasso, Renoir, and Van Gogh. It also hosts international blockbuster exhibitions that require tickets. In the Great Hall, it's considered perfectly reasonable to stretch out on the floor in order to properly appreciate the stained glass ceiling by Leonard French. A second branch of the National Gallery, in Federation Square in the city center, exhibits only Australian art. ☒ *180 St. Kilda Rd., City Center* ☎ *03/8620–0222* ⊕ *www.ngv.vic.gov.au* ☒ *Free.*

Old Melbourne Gaol

JAIL | This blue-stone building, the city's first jail, is now a museum that has three tiers of cells with catwalks around the upper levels and is rumored to be haunted. Its most famous inmate was the notorious bushranger Ned Kelly, who was hanged here in 1880. The Hangman's night tours (reservations essential) are a popular, if macabre, facet of Melbourne nightlife. ☒ *Russell St., between LaTrobe and Victoria Sts., City Center* ☎ *03/9656–9889* ⊕ *www.oldmelbournegaol.com.au* ☒ *From A$28.*

Royal Arcade

PUBLIC ART | Opened in 1870, this is the country's oldest shopping arcade, and despite alterations it retains an airy, graceful elegance that often transfixes passersby. Walk about 30 feet into the arcade to see the statues of Gog and Magog, the mythical monsters that toll the hour on either side of **Gaunt's Clock.** ☒ *335 Bourke St., City Center* ☎ *04/3889–1212* ⊕ *www.royalarcade. com.au.*

St. Patrick's Cathedral

RELIGIOUS SITE | Construction of the Gothic Revival building began in 1858 and took 82 years to finish. Ireland supplied

Australia with many of its early immigrants, especially during the Irish potato famine in the mid-19th century. A statue of the Irish patriot Daniel O'Connell stands in the courtyard. ⊠ *Cathedral Pl., City Center* ☎ *03/9662–2233* ⊕ *www. cam.org.au/cathedral.*

St. Paul's Cathedral

RELIGIOUS SITE | This 1892 headquarters of Melbourne's Anglican faith is one of the most important works of William Butterfield, a leader of the Gothic Revival style in England. In 2006 the cathedral underwent a massive restoration. Outside is a statue of Matthew Flinders, the first seaman to circumnavigate Australia, between 1801 and 1803. ⊠ *Flinders St. at Swanston St., City Center* ☎ *03/9653–4333* ⊕ *www.cathedral.org.au.*

SEA LIFE Melbourne Aquarium

ZOO | **FAMILY** | Become part of the action as you stroll through a transparent tunnel surrounded by water and the denizens of the deep on the prowl. Or press your nose to the glass in the Antarctica exhibition and watch King and Gentoo penguins waddling around on ice and darting through water. You can also don snow gear and sit among the penguins. If you're feeling brave, do a shark dive—they're held daily, include scuba equipment, and are led by an instructor. The aquamarine building illuminates a previously dismal section of Yarra River bank, opposite Crown Casino. ⊠ *Flinders St. at King St., City Center* ☎ *03/9620–0999, 1800/026576* ⊕ *www.melbourneaquarium.com.au* ☞ *Entry A$42; shark dives A$299; Penguin Passport A$149.*

Southgate

PROMENADE | On the river's edge next to the Arts Centre, Southgate is a prime spot for lingering—designer shops, classy restaurants, bars, and casual eating places help locals and visitors while away the hours. The promenade links with the forecourt of Crown Casino and its hotels. ⊠ *Maffra St., at City Rd.,*

City Center ☎ *03/9686–1000* ⊕ *www. southgatemelbourne.com.au.*

State Library of Victoria

LIBRARY | On a rise behind lawns and heroic statuary, this handsome 1853 building was constructed during the goldrush boom and houses more than 1½ million volumes as well as bushranger Ned Kelly's famous armor. Large reading areas—including the splendid domed reading room up the grand staircase—make this a comfortable place for browsing, and three galleries display works from the library's Pictures Collection. ⊠ *328 Swanston St. , at La Trobe St., City Center* ☎ *03/8664–7000* ⊕ *www.slv.vic. gov.au* ☞ *Free.*

Young and Jackson Hotel

HOTEL—SIGHT | Pubs are not generally known for their artwork, but climb the steps to the top-floor bar here to see *Chloe,* a painting that has scandalized and titillated Melburnians for many decades. The larger-than-life nude, painted by George Lefebvre in Paris in 1875, has adorned the walls of Young and Jackson's Hotel (which now specializes in Australian craft beers) since 1909. ⊠ *1 Swanston St., opposite Flinders St. Station, City Center* ☎ *03/9650–3884* ⊕ *www.young-andjacksons.com.au.*

🍴 Restaurants

Becco

$$$ | **ITALIAN** | Every city center needs a place like this, with a drop-in bar and lively dining room. At lunchtime no-time-to-dawdle business types tuck into Italian classics, while those with a sweet tooth will go weak at the knees over a decadent tiramisu. Things get a little moodier at night, when a Campari and soda at the bar is an almost compulsory precursor to dinner. **Known for:** great service; gnocchi osso bucco; Macchiato cocktail. **$** *Average main: A$39* ⊠ *11–25 Crossley St., City Center* ☎ *03/9663–3000* ⊕ *www.*

becco.com.au ⊘ *Closed Sun. No lunch Sat.*

Chin Chin

$$ | **ASIAN** | Shared plates of Asian dishes form the basis of Chin Chin's popular menu. Modeled on hawker-style dining, the restaurant only takes reservations for groups of 10 or more, so you may have a short wait for a table. Come for an early or late lunch to avoid the rush, or kill some time at the attached Go Go Bar. **Known for:** kingfish sashimi; Feed Me menu; sophisticated curries. $ *Average main: A$28* ⊠ *125 Flinders La., City Center* ☎ *03/8663–2000* ⊕ *www. chinchinrestaurant.com.au* ⊟ *No credit cards.*

ezard

$$$ | **MODERN AUSTRALIAN** | Chef Teage Ezard's adventurous—and often exhilarating—take on fusion pushes the boundaries between Eastern and Western flavors. As with all upscale restaurants these days, there's an eight-course tasting menu (A$185 per person, vegetarian and vegan options available) featuring mouthwatering steamed scallop dumplings with aged hon mirin dressing. On weekdays an à la carte option is offered, but on weekends the choice is between either the tasting menu or the fixed-price three-course menu. **Known for:** inspired seafood; Ezard 45 weekday lunch set menu (A$45); indulgent dessert. $ *Average main: A$50* ⊠ *Adelphi Hotel, 187 Flinders La., City Center* ☎ *03/9639–6811* ⊕ *www.ezard.com.au* ⊘ *Closed Sun. No lunch Sat.*

Flower Drum

$$$ | **CANTONESE** | Superb Cantonese cuisine is the hallmark of one of Australia's truly great Chinese restaurants, which is still receiving awards after opening in 1975. The restrained elegance of the design, deftness of the service, and intelligence of the wine list puts most other restaurants to shame. Those in the know don't order from the menu at all but simply ask the waiter to bring the specials,

King's Domain Gardens ◉

This expansive stretch of parkland includes Queen Victoria Gardens, Alexandra Gardens, the Shrine of Remembrance, the Pioneer Women's Garden, the Sidney Myer Music Bowl, and the Royal Botanic Gardens. The temple-style **Shrine of Remembrance** is designed so that a beam of sunlight passes over the Stone of Remembrance in the Inner Shrine at 11 am on Remembrance Day—the 11th day of the 11th month, when in 1918 the armistice marking the end of World War I was declared.

which often changes between lunch and dinner with the arrival of produce fresh from suppliers. **Known for:** roast duck; retro decor; double-boiled almond soup. $ *Average main: A$40* ⊠ *17 Market La., City Center* ☎ *03/9662–3655* ⊕ *flowerdrum.melbourne* ⊘ *No lunch Sun.*

Grossi Florentino

$$$$ | **ITALIAN** | Since 1928, dining at Florentino has meant experiencing the pinnacle of Melbourne hospitality. After taking a seat in the famous mural room, with its huge chandeliers, wooden panels, and Florentine murals, you can sample dishes like suckling pig, and spanner crab risotto. At lunch, the upstairs restaurant serves two courses for A$65; the three-course dinner menu is A$150. The five-course tasting menu, called the Gran Tour (A$180), is also a popular option. Downstairs, the Grill has more business-like fare, while the Cellar Bar is perfect for a glass of wine and pasta of the day. **Known for:** food and wine pairings; romantic atmosphere; quality ingredients. $ *Average main: A$65* ⊠ *80 Bourke St., City Center* ☎ *03/9662–1811* ⊕ *www. grossiflorentino.com* ⊘ *Closed Sun.*

The picturesque Yarra River is lined with picnic spots, fishing jettys, and bike paths.

Hanabishi

$$$ | **JAPANESE** | Touted as the city's best Japanese restaurant, Hanabishi sits in slightly seedy King Street, an area known for its bars, club venues, and occasionally unsavory clientele. With wooden floors, blue walls, and traditional ceramic serving trays, Hanabishi is the playground of Osakan chef Akio Soga, whose seasonal menu includes such gems as abalone sashimi and aburi salmon. There are long lists of hot and chilled sake and wines, ranging from reasonable to pricey. **Known for:** bento boxes; vegetarian menu; Wagyu beef. [$] *Average main: A$40* ✉ *187 King St., City Center* ☎ *03/9670–1167* 🌐 *www.hanabishi.com.au* 🕓 *Closed Sun. No lunch Sat.*

★ **HuTong Dumpling Bar**

$$ | **CHINESE** | The name means "alleyway" and in a sea of dumpling houses in Melbourne, down this little alleyway, you'll find the best of them all. The boiled pork dumplings are popular (A$14.20 for 12), though the panfried variations of pork, chicken, prawn, and chives hold up well, too. The staff is highly trained, and if the space on the ground floor is too snug, ask to go upstairs where there's room to breathe. Bookings are essential, but if you're feeling lucky, arrive at 11:30 am on the dot to try for a table—there will probably be a line of hopefuls already. **Known for:** wantons with hot chilli sauce; bustling atmosphere; extensive menu. [$] *Average main: A$26* ✉ *14–16 Market La., City Center* ☎ *03/9650–8128* 🌐 *www.hutong.com.au.*

Krimper

$ | **AUSTRALIAN** | Designed to showcase the building's warehouse origins, Krimper's design is rough-hewn but warm. Hidden away among former motorcycle repair shops and a burgeoning dining street, Krimper serves innovative food, excellent coffee, and hot chocolate from local company, Mork. Breakfast includes Australian classic Avo on Toast, lunches include a lamb shank and fish of the day. **Known for:** great coffee; trendy vibe; classic breakfast with a twist. [$] *Average main: A$19* ✉ *20 Guildford La., City*

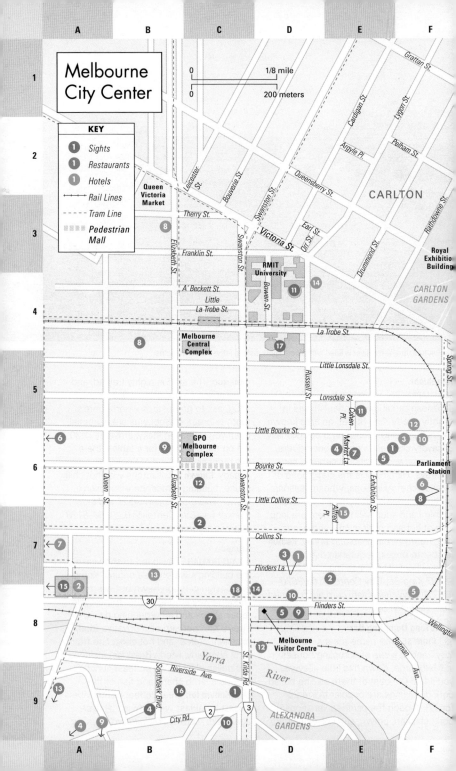

Melbourne
City Center

0   1/8 mile
0   200 meters

KEY

- ① Sights
- ① Restaurants
- ① Hotels
- Rail Lines
- Tram Line
- Pedestrian Mall

Queen Victoria Market

Therry St.

Franklin St.

A' Beckett St.

Little La Trobe St.

Lancaster St.

Bouverie St.

Swanston St.

Victoria St.

Earl St.

Drummond St.

Rathdowne St.

Grattan St.

Cardigan St.

Lygon St.

Pelham St.

Argyle Pl.

Queensberry St.

CARLTON

Royal Exhibitio Building

CARLTON GARDENS

Elizabeth St.

⑧

RMIT University

Bowen St.

⑪ ⑭

La Trobe St.

⑰

Melbourne Central Complex

⑧

Little Lonsdale St.

Russell St.

Spring St.

Lonsdale St.

Cohen Pl.

⑪

⑫

⑥

⑨

GPO Melbourne Complex

Little Bourke St.

Market La.

④ ⑦

① ③ ⑩

⑤

⑫

Bourke St.

Parliament Station

⑥

⑧

Queen St.

Elizabeth St.

⑫

Swanston St.

Little Collins St.

Alfred Pl.

⑮

Exhibition St.

⑦

②

Collins St.

③ ①

Flinders La.

②

⑤

⑬

⑮ ②

⑱

⑭

⑩

⑤ ⑨

Flinders St.

⑤

30

⑦

◆

Melbourne Visitor Centre

⑫

Wellingto

Batman Ave.

Yarra

River

Southbank Blvd.

Riverside Ave.

St. Kilda Rd.

⑬

⑯

①

②

③

ALEXANDRA GARDENS

④

⑨

City Rd.

④

⑩

Sights ▼

Restaurants ▼

Hotels ▼

Center ☎ 03/9043–8844 🌐 www.krimper.com.au.

The Little Mule Cafe

$ | **AUSTRALIAN** | Melburnians love to head out for breakfast, and Little Mule is one of many popular laneway cafés satisfying the hunger. Excellent coffee is teamed with simple meals made in the tiny, open kitchen. Look for the fresh cookies and make your own dream breakfast with the flexible mix-and-match menu. **Known for:** quirky decor; fresh bagels; homemade staples. [$] *Average main: A$13 ✉ 19 Somerset Pl., City Center ☎ 03/9670–4904 🌐 business.google.com/website/thelittlemulecafe 🕓 Closed Sun.*

MoVida Next Door

$ | **SPANISH** | As the name suggests, this popular Spanish tapas restaurant is next door to something—in this case the grown-up parent restaurant called MoVida. This is the casual little sister (or daughter) for those who don't want to linger too long over their dinner. Dishes range from tapas (from A$4.20 to A$8.50), like chorizo-filled Catalan potato bomb with spicy sauce, to *racion* (bigger plates ranging from A$9 to A$28). Finish the meal off with *churros con chocolate* (Spanish fried dough served with a hot, thick chocolate drink). If you're after a bigger meal, book table space at MoVida next door. Both eateries are owned by Frank Camorra, a big name in the Melbourne dining scene. **Known for:** large specials menu; friendly service; great for groups. [$] *Average main: A$17 ✉ 1 Hosier La., City Center ☎ 03/9663–3038 🌐 www.movida.com.au 🕓 Closed Mon. No lunch Tues.–Thurs.*

Seamstress Restaurant & Bar

$$ | **MODERN ASIAN** | This bar-restaurant occupies a heritage-listed four-story building that has housed an undergarment manufacturer, a 1930s sweatshop, a brothel, and even a Buddhist temple (but not at the same time). Tasty Asian dishes, in small, medium, and large portions, are designed to be shared. Everything is served in an atmospheric brick-walled first-floor dining area decorated with swaths of fabric and sewing machines; the wine selection is stored in battered metal luggage lockers. **Known for:** generous banquets; $45 three-course set lunch; red duck curry. [$] *Average main: A$34 ✉ 113 Lonsdale St., City Center ☎ 03/9663–6363 🌐 www.seamstress.com.au 🕓 Closed Sun. No lunch Sat.*

Taxi Kitchen

$$$ | **MODERN AUSTRALIAN** | Occupying an innovatively designed steel-and-glass space above Federation Square, Taxi boasts both extraordinary food and spectacular views over Melbourne. East meets West on a menu that combines Japanese flavors—tempura prawn tails with yuzu and nori salt—with such European-inspired fare as slow-roasted lamb shoulder with root vegetables and jus. There is also an impressive list of new- and old-world wines. To taste some of Australia's best craft beers, have a premeal drink at the Transport Bar on the ground floor. **Known for:** six-course tasting; unbeatable views; rare seared kangaroo. [$] *Average main: A$45 ✉ Level 1, Transport Hotel, Federation Sq., Flinders St. at St. Kilda Rd., City Center ☎ 03/9654–8808 🌐 www.taxikitchen.com.au.*

Wayside Inn

$$$ | **STEAKHOUSE** | Another addition to the city's gastropubs, this fully renovated historic building is a pleasant walk from bustling Southbank. The menu concentrates on high-quality aged cuts of steak from rural Victoria and Tasmania (A$32–A$140), but the wood-fired pizza is also popular. There's an impressive local craft beer list, knowledgeable staff, and a comfortable beer garden that round out the awesome experience. **Known for:** locally sourced ingredients; outdoor seating; Black Angus burger. [$] *Average main A$42 ✉ 446 City Rd., South Melbourne ☎ 03/9682–9119 🌐 www.waysideinn.com.au 🕓 Closed Sun.*

Hotels

The Adelphi

$$$$ | HOTEL | This "dessert hotel" focuses on sweet treats in its rooms and Om Nom kitchen dessert bar. **Pros:** hip laneway location; free Wi-Fi; unlimited movies and free bar fridge snacks. **Cons:** design a bit too edgy for some; occasional late-night street noise; sweet tooth is a must. $ *Rooms from: A$435* ⊠ *187 Flinders La., City Center* ☎ *03/8080–8888* ⊕ *www.adelphi.com.au* ⮑ *33 rooms, 1 suite* ⦿ *No meals.*

Best Western Melbourne

$$ | HOTEL | This 114-room hotel with a serious dash of industrial chic (exposed brick walls and black, brown, and red minimalist decor) is just the sort of lodging you'd expect in hip central Melbourne. **Pros:** hip, but homey; good value; near Southern Cross Station for intercity arrivals. **Cons:** industrial design may not be to everyone's liking; a little removed from restaurants in the city center; some rooms lack views. $ *Rooms from: A$166* ⊠ *16 Spencer St., City Center* ☎ *03/9621–3333, 0396/213333* ⊕ *www. bestwesternmelbourne.com.au* ⮑ *114 rooms* ⦿ *No meals.*

Crossley Hotel

$$ | HOTEL | There's an unexpected sense of space and lots of light in this compact boutique hotel half a block from Chinatown. **Pros:** great location; good restaurant; reasonable price. **Cons:** sparse but functional rooms; outdated bathrooms; street noise. $ *Rooms from: A$159* ⊠ *51 Little Bourke St., City Center* ☎ *03/9639–1639* ⮑ *84 rooms, 4 apartments* ⦿ *Free breakfast.*

Crown Metropol

$$$ | HOTEL | Crown Casino's newest hotel may be huge (it has 665 rooms, making it one of the country's biggest), but it still retains an elegant boutique-type feel. **Pros:** professional service; great pool; extensive dining options. **Cons:** casino area might not appeal to all; impersonal feel; vertiginous views. $ *Rooms from: A$268* ⊠ *8 Whiteman St., City Center* ☎ *03/9292–6211* ⊕ *www.crownmetropol-melbourne.com.au* ⮑ *632 rooms, 33 apartments* ⦿ *Free breakfast.*

Hotel Lindrum

$$$ | HOTEL | Housed in the Heritage-listed Lindrum family billiards center, a short walk from Federation Square, this is one of Melbourne's savviest boutique properties. **Pros:** warm feel; exceptional service; full in-room entertainment systems. **Cons:** on busy thoroughfare; small restaurant and bar; some may find the traditional decor outdated. $ *Rooms from: A$265* ⊠ *26 Flinders St., City Center* ☎ *03/9668–1111* ⊕ *www.hotellindrum. com.au* ⮑ *59 rooms* ⦿ *Free breakfast.*

The Hotel Windsor

$$$ | HOTEL | Built in 1883, this aristocrat of Melbourne hotels combines Victorian-era character with modern comforts, and is a must for history lovers. **Pros:** elegant heritage feel; central location; high tea. **Cons:** heritage rooms decor may be too "old world" for some; some rooms lack views; basic breakfast. $ *Rooms from: A$219* ⊠ *111 Spring St., City Center* ☎ *03/9633–6000* ⊕ *www.thehotelwindsor.com.au* ⮑ *160 rooms, 20 suites* ⦿ *Free breakfast.*

InterContinental Melbourne The Rialto

$$$ | HOTEL | Tucked behind one of Melbourne's most iconic Gothic facades, The Rialto is a five-star luxury hotel designed by William Pitt, the architect behind many Melbourne landmarks. **Pros:** spectacular, historic facade; great bar and club lounge; convenient location. **Cons:** slightly corporate feel; fee for in-room Wi-Fi; outdated entertainment system. $ *Rooms from: A$212* ⊠ *495 Collins St., City Center* ☎ *03/8627–1400* ⊕ *www. melbourne.intercontinental.com* ⮑ *244 rooms, 9 suites* ⦿ *No meals.*

Jasper Hotel

$$ | HOTEL | A former YWCA, the Jasper has undergone a radical face-lift,

Melbourne's restaurant scene is a global potpourri of ethnic influences.

redesigned and polished to a shine. **Pros:** close to the Victoria Markets; lovely courtyard; free Wi-Fi. **Cons:** may be noisy in the morning, being near the markets; neutral decor; slightly removed from city center. *Rooms from: A$159 ✉ 489 Elizabeth St., City Center ☎ 03/8327–2777, 1800/468359 🌐 www.jasperhotel.com.au 80 rooms, 10 suites No meals.*

Middle Park Hotel
$ | HOTEL | In the picturesque suburb of Middle Park, toward the lively St. Kilda area, this 25-room hotel has been stylishly designed by renowned local architects Six Degrees, giving the 125-year-old building new life. **Pros:** historic surroundings; warm service; sophisticated decor. **Cons:** might be too far from city for some; small rooms in a historic building; no elevator. *Rooms from: A$121 ✉ 102 Canterbury Rd., City Center ☎ 03/9690–1958 🌐 middleparkhotel.com.au 23 rooms, 1 suite, 1 apartment Free breakfast.*

Ovolo Laneways
$$$ | HOTEL | Much effort has gone into making this 43-room boutique hotel uniquely stylish and comfortable, including its laneway location, which is ideal for those who want to be in the heart of the action. **Pros:** latest entertainment technology in the rooms; central location; free Wi-Fi. **Cons:** area can be noisy late at night; small lobby; no restaurant. *Rooms from: A$206 ✉ 19 Little Bourke St., City Center ☎ 03/8692–0777 🌐 www.ovolohotels.com 43 rooms Free breakfast.*

★ Park Hyatt Melbourne
$$$$ | HOTEL | Set right next to Fitzroy Gardens and opposite St. Patrick's Cathedral, this is one of Melbourne's most elegant hotels. **Pros:** lavish appointments; world-class service; free Wi-Fi in rooms. **Cons:** a little removed from the city center; slightly corporate atmosphere; breakfast buffet is underwhelming. *Rooms from: A$310 ✉ 1 Parliament Sq., City Center ☎ 03/9224–1234 🌐 www.hyatt.com/en-US/hotel/australia/park-hyatt-melbourne/melph 216 rooms, 24 suites Free breakfast.*

uest Gordon Place

$ | **HOTEL** | This National Trust–listed 1884 odging house is one of the most interesting and comfortable apartment hotels n the city. **Pros:** modern apartment-style amenities; great location; independent iving. **Cons:** homey feel; no carpark; ome may find the furnishings slightly lated. $ *Rooms from: A$170* ✉ *24 Little Bourke St., City Center* ☎ *1800/334033* ⊕ *www.questapartments.com.au/properties/vic/melbourne/quest-gordon-place* ⇨ *54 apartments* ¶❍ *No meals.*

he Sebel Melbourne Flinders Lane

$$$ | **HOTEL** | The smallest of the city's upscale hotels, the Sebel has a central ocation and a mix of lovely one- and wo-bedroom suites, which sleep four o eight people. **Pros:** elegant design; wanky feel; ideal location. **Cons:** not for he budget-conscious; no restaurant; ooms book out quickly. $ *Rooms from: A$319* ✉ *321 Flinders La., City Center* ☎ *03/9629–4088* ⊕ *www.accorhotels. om* ⇨ *58 suites* ¶❍ *No meals.*

pace Hotel

| **HOTEL** | Located just minutes from bustling Lygon Street, Carlton Gardens, and Queen Victoria Market, this family-run venue targets budget travelers who like a bit more comfort. **Pros:** central location; great value; easy to meet other travelers. **Cons:** can get noisy with lively patrons; shared facilities; slightly outdated rooms. $ *Rooms from: A$119* ✉ *380 Russell St., City Center* ☎ *03/9662–3888* ⊕ *spacehotel.com.au* ⇨ *128 rooms* ¶❍ *No meals.*

tamford Plaza Melbourne

$$ | **HOTEL** | Diamond-faceted glass elevators carry guests from the marble obby of this "Paris-end," all-suite hotel o rooms decorated with plush, rich ued velvets and art deco–ish crystal amps. **Pros:** lush decor; great restaurant; entral location. **Cons:** might not appeal to overs of contemporary decor; breakfast ot included; slightly dated in-room entertainment system. $ *Rooms from: A$251* ✉ *111 Little Collins St., City Center* ☎ *03/9659–1000* ⊕ *www.stamford.com. au* ⇨ *283 rooms* ¶❍ *Free breakfast.*

▼ Nightlife

BARS

The Atrium Bar on 35

BARS/PUBS | This cocktail bar on the 35th floor of the Sofitel Melbourne on Collins has spectacular views. ✉ *25 Collins St., City Center* ☎ *03/9653–0000* ⊕ *www. sofitel-melbourne.com.*

Cookie

BARS/PUBS | Located in a lofty warehouse-style space with exposed ceiling pipes and a balcony, Cookie focuses on domestic and international craft beer and great Thai food. ✉ *Curtin House, 252 Swanston St., 1st fl., City Center* ☎ *03/9663–7660* ⊕ *cookie.net.au.*

Embla

WINE BARS—NIGHTLIFE | Welcoming but still sophisticated, Embla is a throwback to and an improvement on Melbourne's original small bar scene. An accessible but often obscure wine list is accompanied by wholesome snacks from the wood-fired oven that are cooked to perfection. ✉ *122 Russell St., City Center* ☎ *03/9654–5923.*

Gin Palace

BARS/PUBS | Reminiscent of Hollywood's golden era, Gin Palace has more than enough types of martinis to satisfy any taste. ✉ *10 Russell Pl., off Bourke St., City Center* ☎ *03/9654–0533* ⊕ *www. ginpalace.com.au.*

Melbourne Supper Club

BARS/PUBS | Age-buffed leather sofas, cigars, and an exhaustive wine list characterize the classy Melbourne Supper Club. ✉ *161 Spring St., 1st fl., City Center* ☎ *03/9654–6300.*

Mitre Tavern

BARS/PUBS | One of the oldest pubs in town, locals love the unpretentious vibe, and U.K.-like surrounding. It's especially popular with nine-to-fivers who like an after-work beer. ⊠ *5 Bank Pl., City Center* ☎ *03/9670–5644* ⊕ *www.mitretavern. com.au.*

Ms Collins

BARS/PUBS | A bar from Tuesday to Saturday, with food designed by some of Melbourne's top chefs, Ms Collins turns Latin American on Thursday and R&B club on Friday night. ⊠ *425 Collins St., City Center* ☎ *03/8614–2222* ⊕ *www. mscollins.com.au.*

Section 8

BARS/PUBS | Located in a car park, and housed in a shipping container, Section 8 is a reliably trendy bar, popular with the artsy student crowd. ⊠ *27–29 Tattersalls La., City Center* ☎ *0430/291–588* ⊕ *www.section8.com.au.*

COMEDY CLUBS
Comic's Lounge

COMEDY CLUBS | This comedy club is a good place for a laugh. ⊠ *26 Errol St., North Melbourne* ☎ *03/9348–9488* ⊕ *thecomicslounge.com.au.*

MUSIC CLUBS
Cherry Bar

MUSIC CLUBS | This small and intimate rock 'n' roll bar is located on AC/DC Lane. The address alone says it all. ⊠ *AC/DC La., City Center* ☎ *03/9639–8122* ⊕ *www. cherrybar.com.au.*

Max Watt's House of Music

MUSIC CLUBS | This popular venue is known for live local and lesser-known international rock bands, and as a stand-up venue during the International Comedy Festival. ⊠ *125 Swanston St., City Center* ☎ *1300/843–443 tickets* ⊕ *maxwatts.com.au.*

🎭 Performing Arts

MUSIC AND DANCE
Australian Ballet

DANCE | In the 2,000-seat State Theatre at the Arts Centre, the Australian Ballet stages six programs annually, and presents visiting celebrity dancers from

A Funny Night Out

Melburnians love a laugh, and the annual Melbourne International Comedy Festival is a great opportunity to enjoy top Australian and international comedians. The month-long event takes place in the Melbourne Town Hall and venues across town, with free events in open spaces. In addition to hosting comedy stars, the festival seeks out new talent and culminates with the Raw Comedy award for the best new Australian stand-up performer. If you're in town in April, you won't be laughing if you miss it. ⊕ *www. comedyfestival.com.au.*

around the world. ⊠ *The Arts Centre, 100 St. Kilda Rd., Southbank* ☎ *1300/182183, 136–100 Ticketmaster* ⊕ *www.australianballet.com.au.*

Melbourne Symphony Orchestra

MUSIC | The Melbourne Symphony Orchestra performs year-round in the 2,600-seat Hamer Hall. ⊠ *The Arts Centre, 100 St. Kilda Rd., Southbank* ☎ *1300/182183* ⊕ *www.mso.com.au.*

Sidney Myer Music Bowl

MUSIC | Open-air concerts take place December through March at the Sidney Myer Music Bowl. ⊠ *King's Domain, near Swan St. Bridge, City Center* ☎ *136–100 Ticketmaster.*

THEATER
Comedy Theatre

THEATER | Revues and plays are staged at the Comedy Theatre, which along with the Princess, Regent, and Forum theaters is owned by the Marriner Group and uses the same telephone numbers. ⊠ *240 Exhibition St., City Center* ☎ *03/9299–9800, 1300/111011 tickets* ⊕ *www.marrinergroup.com.au.*

Melbourne is known for its robust live theater scene.

ortyfivedownstairs

ABARET | Cutting-edge independent theater, cabaret acts, and exhibitions are featured here. ⊠ *45 Flinders La., City Center* ☎ *03/9662–9966* ⊕ *www. ortyfivedownstairs.com.*

Malftix

THEATER | This ticket booth in the Melbourne Town Hall sells tickets to theater attractions at half price on performance days. It's open Monday 10–2, Tuesday–Thursday 11–6, Friday 11–6:30, and Saturday 10–4. Phone for information about shows on sale (recorded message), or see listings on the website. Sales are cash only, and only from the booth. The booth also sells tickets for bus tours. ⊠ *Melbourne Town Hall, Swanston St. at Collins St., City Center* ☎ *03/9650–9420* ⊕ *www.halftixmelbourne.com.*

Regent Theatre

THEATER | An ornate 1920s building, the Regent originally opened to screen movies but nowadays presents mainstream productions, including *The Lion King* and Andrew Lloyd Webber's *Cats.* ⊠ *191*

Collins St., City Center ☎ *03/9299–9800, 1300/111011 box office* ⊕ *www.marriner-group.com.au.*

⬭ Shopping

BOOKS
Books for Cooks
BOOKS/STATIONERY | A fantastic array of cookbooks stock the shelves of Books for Cooks, including many from local chefs. Located at the Queen Victoria Market, the shop's only steps from plenty of fresh produce, meat, and fish to support any sudden inspirations. ⊠ *Queen Victoria Market, Queen St., City Center* ☎ *03/8415–1415* ⊕ *www. booksforcooks.com.au.*

SHOPPING CENTERS
Block Arcade
SHOPPING CENTERS/MALLS | An elegant 19th-century shopping plaza with mosaic-tile floors, Block Arcade contains the venerable Hopetoun Tea Rooms, the French Jewel Box, Dafel Dolls and Bears, Basement Discs, Gewurzhaus, and

Australian By Design. ⊠ *282 Collins St., City Center* ☎ *03/9654–5244* ⊕ *theblock. com.au.*

Bourke Street Mall

SHOPPING CENTERS/MALLS | Once the busiest east–west thoroughfare in the city, Bourke Street Mall is a pedestrian-only zone—but watch out for those trams! Two of the city's biggest department stores are here; an essential part of growing up in Melbourne is being taken to Myer at Christmas to see the window displays. ⊠ *Bourke St., City Center.*

Bridge Road

SHOPPING CENTERS/MALLS | In Richmond, east of the city, Bridge Road is a popular shopping strip for women's retail fashion that caters to all budgets. ⊠ *Bridge Rd., Richmond* ⊕ *www.bridgerd.com.au.*

David Jones

DEPARTMENT STORES | This big, upmarket department store has a large array of luxury brands for both men and women. ⊠ *310 Bourke St., between Elizabeth and Swanston Sts., City Center* ☎ *03/9643–2222.*

Emporium Melbourne

SHOPPING CENTERS/MALLS | Many international brands established their first Australian outlets at this major shopping mall in the city center. The mall is filled with fashion, technology, food, and art outlets, and joined via aboveground walkways to the Myer and David Jones department stores and Melbourne Central shopping center. Stores include Michael Kors and Victoria's Secret. ⊠ *Lonsdale St., City Center* ☎ *03/8609–8221* ⊕ *emporium-melbourne.com.au.*

Flinders Lane

SHOPPING CENTERS/MALLS | Dotted with chic boutiques, many of them selling merchandise by up-and-coming Australian designers, Flinders Lane will keep fashionistas happy. Between Swanston and Elizabeth streets, look for Cathedral Arcade, home to vintage and designer stores, in the bottom of the Nicholas Building. The lift leads to an eclectic collection of tiny shops full of unique fashion and accessories. ⊠ *Flinders La., City Center.*

Little Collins Street

SHOPPING CENTERS/MALLS | A precinct of stores frequented by shoppers with perhaps more money than sense, Little Collins Street is still worth a visit. In between frock shops you'll find musty stores selling classic film posters, antique and estate jewelry, and Australian opals. At the eastern end of **Collins Street,** beyond the cream-and-red Romanesque facade of St. Michael's Uniting Church, is the **Paris End,** a name coined by Melburnians to identify the elegance of its fashionable shops as well as its general hauteur. Here you find big-name international designer clothing, bags, and jewelry. ⊠ *Little Collins St., City Center.*

Melbourne Central

SHOPPING CENTERS/MALLS | Here you'll find a dizzying complex huge enough to enclose an 1880s redbrick shot tower (once used to make bullets) in its atrium. ⊠ *300 Lonsdale St., City Center* ☎ *03/9922–1122* ⊕ *www.melbournecentral.com.au.*

Myer

SHOPPING CENTERS/MALLS | Myer is one of the country's largest department stores, carrying a myriad of both casual and luxury brands for men and women. ⊠ *314–336 Bourke St., between Elizabeth and Swanston Sts., City Center* ☎ *03/9661–1111.*

Royal Arcade

SHOPPING CENTERS/MALLS | Built in 1846, this is Melbourne's oldest shopping plaza. It remains a lovely place to browse and is home to the splendid Gaunt's Clock, which tolls away the hours. ⊠ *355 Bourke St., City Center* ⊕ *www.royalarcade.com.au.*

Southgate

SHOPPING CENTERS/MALLS | The shops and eateries at this spectacular riverside ocation are a short walk from both the ity center, across the Ponyfish Island pedestrian bridge, and the Arts Center. There's outdoor seating next to the Southbank promenade. ⊠ *4 Southbank Promenade, City Center* ☎ *03/9686–1000* ⊕ *www.southgatemelbourne.com.au.*

JEWELRY

Craft Victoria

JEWELRY/ACCESSORIES | Craft Victoria fosters creativity with seminars and exhibits, and has a top-notch selection of Australian pottery, textile works, and jewelry. ⊠ *Watson Pl., Flinders La., City Center* ☎ *03/9650–7775* ⊕ *www.craft.org.au.*

MARKETS

★ Queen Victoria Market

OUTDOOR/FLEA/GREEN MARKETS | This market has buzzed with food and bargain shoppers since 1878. With more than 1,000 mostly open-air stalls, this sprawling, spirited bazaar is the city's prime produce outlet—many Melburnians come here to buy strawberries, fresh flowers, imported cheeses, meat, and eye-bright fresh fish. On Sunday there is less food and more great deals on jeans, T-shirts, and souvenirs. ⊠ *Elizabeth St. at Victoria St., City Center* ☎ *03/9320–5822* ⊕ *www. qvm.com.au.*

SHOES AND LEATHER GOODS

Roberts and Hassett

SHOES/LUGGAGE/LEATHER GOODS | If you're looking for something special in leather goods, bespoke shoemakers Roberts and Hassett sell handmade shoes, belts, satchels, and wallets made mostly from kangaroo leather. Much of their leather is sourced from Greenhalgh Tannery, which specializes in tanning with wattle tree bark. The business operates out of the "Gentleman's Outfitter," Captains of Industry, which also has a café, a barbershop, and a jeweler. ⊠ *Captains of Industry, 2 Somerset Pl., Levels 1/2, City Center* ✛ *Off Little Bourke St.* ☎ *03/9670–4405* ⊕ *roberts-hassett.com. au.*

🏃 Activities

BICYCLING

Bicycle Network

BICYCLING | This company can provide advice on cycling in Melbourne and Victoria, including information about the road rules in relation to cyclists. The office sells some maps and books for cycling tours. Its website has trail maps. ⊠ *4/246 Bourke St., City Center* ☎ *03/8376–8888* ⊕ *www.bicyclenetwork.com.au.*

Real Melbourne Bike Tours

BICYCLING | The daily bike tours offered by this company promise to show the best of Melbourne. The four-hour rides (which depart at 10 am) include coffee and cakes in Little Italy and lunch. The company also rents bicycles for A$15 per hours (A$40 per day) and electric bikes from A$40 for two hours (A$80 per day), and provides a map of five top rides, with suggestions of where to eat and drink. It's on the edge of the Yarra River just near Princes Bridge and Federation Square. ⊠ *Vault 14, Federation Sq., City Center* ✛ *On riverbank level, near Princes Walk* ☎ *0417/339–203* ⊕ *www.rentabike. net.au* 💰 *From A$110.*

TENNIS

Melbourne Park Tennis Centre

TENNIS | This center has 24 outdoor and 8 hard indoor Plexicushion courts, plus 8 Italian Clay Courts. Play is canceled during the Australian Open in January. ⊠ *Batman Ave., City Center* ☎ *1300/836647* ⊕ *www.mopt.com.au* 💰 *Court hire from A$30/hr.*

Richmond

Home of Victoria Street—Melbourne's "little Vietnam"—and the lively discount shopping stretch of Bridge Road, Richmond is 2 km (1 mile) east of the city center (take Tram 48 or 75 from Flinders Street for Bridge Road, or Tram 109 from Collins Street for Victoria Street). If you're looking for a new wardrobe, a Vietnamese soup kitchen, a Korean barbecue, a Laotian banquet, or a Thai hole-in-the-wall, this is the place to come.

GETTING HERE AND AROUND

Several tram lines connect central Melbourne with Richmond. Take Tram 70 from Flinders Street Station to Swan Street, Richmond, or take Tram 109 from Collins Street to Victoria Street. Trams 48 and 75 take you from Flinders Street to Bridge Road, while Tram 78 travels along Chapel Street (in South Yarra) north through the heart of Richmond. Trains connect Flinders Street Station with several useful local stations: Richmond, East Richmond and Burnley (for Swan Street), West Richmond (for Bridge Road), and North Richmond (for Victoria Street). If driving, or even walking, proceed east along Flinders Street, which becomes Wellington Parade, past the prominent Melbourne Cricket Ground, then cross Hoddle Street.

Sights

Bridge Road

NEIGHBORHOOD | Once a run-down area of Richmond, this street is now a bargain shopper's paradise. It's packed with clothing shops, cafés, and factory outlets selling leather goods, shoes, and gourmet foods. Take Tram 48 or 75 from the city. ✉ *Bridge Rd., Richmond* 🌐 *www.bridgerd.com.au.*

Victoria Street

NEIGHBORHOOD | One of Melbourne's most popular "eat streets," this 2-km (1-mile) stretch has restaurants ranging from simple canteens to tablecloth-and-candlelight dining spots. The street also features Vietnamese grocers, kitchenware stores, several art galleries, and several chichi drinking spots. Once a year at Tet, Vietnamese New Year (in January and February but the exact date varies from year to year), the street comes to life with a day-long Lunar Festival, with dragon dances, music, and more food! ✉ *Victoria St., Richmond.*

Waltzing Matilda

Shopping mixes with history and a touch of patriotism at Melbourne Central shopping center. The main attraction is the historic brick shot tower, rising 165 feet above the center and encased in a glass cone. Built in 1890, the shot tower was used to make "shot" or bullets. Also suspended from the roof is a huge fob-watch that plays a musical rendition of "Waltzing Matilda." You'll find this mall on the corner of La Trobe and Swanston streets.

Restaurants

★ I Love Pho

$ | **VIETNAMESE** | Tucking into a steaming bowl of *phở* (traditional noodle soup) at this Victoria Street restaurant is like channeling the backstreets of Hanoi and Saigon. Each order comes with a piled plate of Vietnamese mint, bean shoots, and lemon wedges, and there are bottles of chili paste and fish sauce on every mock-marble plastic table. Vegetarian phở is also available. This restaurant is crowded with Vietnamese and other *phở* lovers on weekends, so you often have to line up on the footpath, but turnover is fast so it's never long before you are seated and eating some of Melbourne's best—and cheapest—food. I Love Pho also has an outlet at the Melbourne Emporium food hall in the city center. **Known for:** best phở in town; rice-paper rolls; friendly service. [$] *Average main: A$10* ✉ *264 Victoria St. Richmond* ☎ *03/9427–7749* 🌐 *pholove.com.au.*

Richmond Hill Café and Larder

$$ | CAFÉ | Opened by iconic Australian cook Stephanie Alexander, this bright and buzzy café–cum–produce store is a local mainstay. The bistro fare brims with wonderful flavors, from house-made dips and charcuterie boards to seasonal salads, seafood, and burgers. Desserts are mouthwateringly simple and impossible to resist. It's so popular you might have to wait briefly if you haven't booked a table. After you've eaten, pick up some marvelous cheese and country-style bread from the adjoining cheese room and grocery. **Known for:** grilled cheese toast; all-day breakfast; charcuterie boards to share. ⓢ *Average main: A$25* ✉ *48–50 Bridge Rd., Richmond* ☎ *03/9421–2808* ⊕ *www.rhcl.com.au* ☾ *No dinner.*

Hotels

Richmond Hill Hotel

$ | HOTEL | Just a short ride from the city center (on the No. 70 tram), this inexpensive boutique hotel occupies a garden-fronted 1918 mansion. **Pros:** city-fringe location; friendly service; historic charm. **Cons:** somewhat spartan digs; a bit mazelike; front rooms get peak-hour traffic noise. ⓢ *Rooms from: A$99* ✉ *353 Church St., Richmond* ☎ *03/9428–6501, 1800/801618* ⊕ *www.richmondhillhotel. com.au* ⇌ *42 rooms* ⦿ *Free breakfast.*

ⓨ Nightlife

MUSIC CLUBS

Corner Hotel

MUSIC CLUBS | The Corner Hotel has alternative, reggae, rock, blues, and jazz acts with an emphasis on homegrown bands. Tasty pub meals can be had on the rooftop for a pre-gig dinner. ✉ *57 Swan St., Richmond* ☎ *03/9427–7300 bar, 1300/724867 tickets* ⊕ *cornerhotel.com.*

East Melbourne

The harmonious streetscapes in this historic enclave of Victorian houses, which date from the boom following the gold rushes of the 1850s, make East Melbourne a great neighborhood for a stroll.

GETTING HERE AND AROUND

East Melbourne's attractions are an easy walk from the city center. The Free City Circle tram travels along Spring Street, stopping at Parliament House and the Old Treasury building. The free, red-color Melbourne Visitor Shuttle bus also does a loop and stops at the Sports Precinct, which is a short walk from the MCG and Fitzroy Gardens. Trams 48 and 75 travel along Flinders Street and Wellington Parade to East Melbourne sights: Fitzroy Gardens is on the north side of Wellington Parade, and the MCG is on the south side.

⊙ Sights

Melbourne Cricket Ground (MCG)

SPORTS VENUE | A tour of this complex is essential for an understanding of Melbourne's sporting obsession. You can get the stories behind it all at the National Sports Museum. The site is a pleasant 10-minute walk from the city center or a tram ride (Nos. 48 and 75) to Jolimont Station. ✉ *Jolimont Terr., East Melbourne* ☎ *03/9657–8888* ⊕ *www.mcg.org.au* 🎫 *A$25.*

🛏 Hotels

Baden Powell Hotel

$ | HOTEL | One of the best ways to experience Melbourne's historic pubs is to stay inside one, and the well-appointed Baden Powell Hotel is an ideal fit. **Pros:** good location for sport and nightlife; great value; quality restaurant downstairs. **Cons:** strict check-in times; can be noisy on weekends; infrequent housekeeping. ⓢ *Rooms from: A$100* ✉ *61 Victoria*

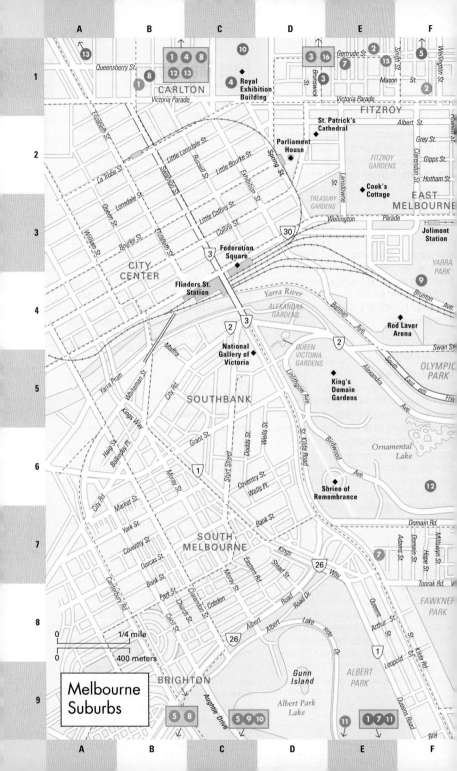

Melbourne Suburbs

Sights ▼

1 Acland Street **E9**
2 Bridge Road **H3**
3 Brunswick Street **D1**
4 Carlton Gardens **C1**
5 CERES Community Environment Park **F1**
6 Chapel Street **I8**
7 Luna Park **E9**
8 Lygon Street **B1**
9 Melbourne Cricket Ground (MCG) **F4**
10 Melbourne Museum **C1**
11 Rippon Lea **E9**
12 Royal Botanic Gardens **F6**
13 Sydney Road **A1**
14 Victoria Street **I1**

Restaurants ▼

1 Abla's **B1**
2 Añada **E1**
3 Babka **D1**
4 Brunetti **B1**
5 Café di Stasio **C9**
6 Caffe e Cucina **I8**
7 Charcoal Lane **E1**
8 D.O.C **B1**
9 Dog's Bar **C9**
10 Donovan's **C9**
11 Fitzrovia **E9**
12 400 Gradi **B1**
13 Hellenic Republic **B1**
14 I Love Pho **I1**
15 Ladro **E1**
16 Lune Croissanterie **D1**
17 Richmond Hill Café and Larder **H3**

Hotels ▼

1 Arrow On Swanston.... **B1**
2 Baden Powell Hotel **F1**
3 The Como Melbourne **I7**
4 The Lyall Hotel and Spa **H7**
5 The Prince **B9**
6 Richmond Hill Hotel **I4**
7 Royce Hotel **E7**
8 Tolarno Hotel **B9**

KEY

① Sights
① Restaurants
① Hotels
Rail Lines
Tram Line

Parade, Collingwood ☎ 03/9486–0811 ⊕ www.badenpowellhotel.com.au ⇌ 11 rooms ⦿ No meals.

⛹ Activities

CRICKET

Melbourne Cricket Ground

CRICKET | All big international and inter-state cricket matches in Victoria are played at the Melbourne Cricket Ground from October to March. The stadium has lights for night games and can accommodate 100,000 people. Tickets are available at the gate or through Ticketek. ✉ Yarra Park, Brunton Ave., Richmond ☎ 03/9657–8867 stadium, 132–849 Ticketek ⊕ www.mcg.org.au.

GOLF

Yarra Bend Golf Course

GOLF | FAMILY | Despite being just 4 km (2½ miles) northeast from the city, this challenging course seems a world away, due to long length and surrounding parkland. Ten thousand bats have also made it their home on the back 9. A golf range is ideal to practice your game before the round. The course even has a 36-hole adventure mini golf course (A$23), suitable for children and adults. ✉ Yarra Bend Rd., Fairfield ☎ 03/9481–3729 ⊕ www.yarrabendgolf.com ✐ Weekdays: 18 holes A$40, 9 holes A$29; weekends: 18 and 9 holes, up to A$46 ⅄ 18 holes, 6056 yards, par 70.

TENNIS

★ Australian Open

TENNIS | The Australian Open, held in January, is one of the world's four Grand Slam tournaments. You can buy tickets at the event or from Ticketek. ✉ Batman Ave., Melbourne ☎ 03/9039–9407 tickets ⊕ www.australianopen.com.

Powlett Reserve Tennis Centre

TENNIS | This center has five synthetic-grass outdoor courts. ✉ Powlett Reserve, Albert St., East Melbourne ☎ 03/9417–6511 ⊕ powlettreservetennis-centre.com ✐ Court hire from A$25/hr.

A Day at the Races ⛹

The usually serene atmosphere of Albert Park is turned into motorhead heaven every March, when Melbourne stages the Australian Grand Prix. It's the opening event of the Formula One season, with four full-throttle days of excitement on and off the track. Drivers scream around Albert Park Lake to the delight of fans and the horror of some nearby residents. Albert Park is 3 km (2 miles) south of the city center. ⊕ www.grandprix.com.au.

South Melbourne

With leafy streets and heritage buildings restored to house chic boutiques, cafés, and restaurants, South Melbourne is one of Melbourne's oldest, and most charming, suburbs. The highlight here is the bustling South Melbourne Market but in the warmer seasons the area's shops, bars, cafes, and restaurants spill out onto the streets between Southbank and the grassy expanses of Albert Park.

🎭 Performing Arts

MUSIC AND DANCE

Opera Australia

OPERA | Opera Australia has regular seasons, often with performances by world-renowned stars. The length and time of seasons vary, but all performances take place within the Arts Centre. ✉ Fawkner St. at Fanning St., Southbank ☎ 03/9685–3777, 03/9685–3700 box office ⊕ opera.org.au ✐ From A$60.

THEATER

Melbourne Theatre Company

THEATER | Australia's oldest professional theater company stages up to 12 productions per year in various venues around the city, including the Southbank Theatre and the Arts Centre in St. Kilda Road. ✉ *Southbank Theatre, 140 Southbank Blvd., Southbank* ☎ *03/8688–0800 box office* ⊕ *www.mtc.com.au.*

Playbox at the CUB Malthouse Company
THEATER | The city's second-largest company, the **Malthouse Theatre**, stages about 10 new or contemporary productions a year. The CUB Malthouse is a flexible theater space designed for drama, dance, and circus performances. ✉ *113 Sturt St., Southbank* ☎ *03/9685–5111* ⊕ *www. malthousetheatre.com.au.*

🛍 Shopping

SHOPPING CENTERS
South Wharf
OUTLET/DISCOUNT STORES | This shopping precinct near the Exhibition Centre and the Polly Woodside historic ship hosts riverside restaurants and cafés in heritage sheds, along with discount outlet shopping of brands like Billabong, Kathmandu, Sass & Bide, and Tigerlilly Swimwear. ✉ *South Wharf Promenade, Southbank* ⊕ *southwharf.com.au.*

MARKETS
★ South Melbourne Market
OUTDOOR/FLEA/GREEN MARKETS | Established in 1867, South Melbourne Market is Melbourne's second-oldest market. You'll find a huge selection of fresh produce and foodstuffs (the Dim Sims are famous). ✉ *Cecil St. at Coventry St., South Melbourne* ☎ *03/9209–6295* ⊕ *www.southmelbournemarket.com.au.*

St. Kilda

Most nights of the week, the streets of this Victorian seaside suburb come alive with visitors, and its many restaurants, cafés, and bars buzz with energy. The holiday atmosphere continues on Sunday at open-air markets on the beach, while the tree-lined promenade and pier extending into Port Phillip Bay are perfect for strolling and people-watching. The quaintly named St. Kilda Sea Baths (now a modern swimming pool–spa complex) are housed in a turn-of-the-20th-century building. Although no one wanted to live there in the 1970s and '80s, St. Kilda is now a very smart address. Many visitors choose to stay here and hop on a tram to the city center.

GETTING HERE AND AROUND
Several trams travel to St. Kilda from central Melbourne. Trams 96 (from Bourke Street) and 12 (from Collins Street) head east–west through the city center, then go all the way south to St. Kilda. Tram 16 runs to St. Kilda from Melbourne University along Swanston Street, as does Tram 3A at weekends. A good place to board these latter two trams is the stop between Flinders Street Station and Federation Square. It's a pleasant ride down St. Kilda Road into Fitzroy Street and past the bay.

👁 Sights

Acland Street
NEIGHBORHOOD | An alphabet soup of Chinese, French, Italian, and Lebanese eateries—along with a fantastic array of cake shops—lines the sidewalk of St. Kilda's ultra-hip restaurant row. The street faces Luna Park. ✉ *Acland St., between Barkly St. and Shakespeare Grove, St. Kilda.*

Luna Park
AMUSEMENT PARK/WATER PARK | A much-photographed Melbourne landmark, the park's entrance is a huge, gaping mouth, swallowing visitors whole and delivering them into a world of ghost trains, pirate ships, and carousels. Built in 1912, the **Scenic Railway** is the park's most popular ride. It's said to be the oldest continually operating roller coaster in the world. The railway is less roller coaster and more a relaxed loop-the-loop,

The groovy cafés of St. Kilda

with stunning views of Port Phillip Bay between each dip and turn. Luna Park is a five-minute stroll southeast of St. Kilda. ✉ *Lower Esplanade, St. Kilda* ☎ *03/9525–5033, 1300/888272* ⊕ *www.lunapark. com.au* 🖃 *A$2 entry, rides from A$11.*

🏖 Beaches

St. Kilda Beach

BEACH—SIGHT | While there is no surf to speak of, this half-mile stretch of sand still remains one of the country's liveliest beaches as it's close to bars, restaurants, and hotels. While most people like to hang out on the sand, windsurfing, sailing, rollerblading, and beach volleyball are other popular activities. Two iconic landmarks—St. Kilda Baths and St. Kilda Pier—are close by and give visitors something to do on those blistering hot summer afternoons. The Sunday foreshore market is just minutes away as well. **Amenities:** food and drink; parking (fee); toilets. **Best for:** partiers; swimming; windsurfing. ✉ *Marine Parade, St. Kilda.*

🍽 Restaurants

Café di Stasio

$$$ | **ITALIAN** | This upscale bistro treads a very fine line between mannered elegance and decadence. A sleek marble bar and modishly ravaged walls contribute to the sense that you've stepped into a scene from *La Dolce Vita*. Happily, the restaurant is as serious about its food as its sense of style. Crisply roasted duck is now a local legend, and the pasta is always al dente. A seasonal lunch special (two courses with wine and coffee) for A$40 is a great value if you're nearby. For an informal drink before your meal, an adjoining bar has local wines and a snack menu. **Known for:** expert staff; long lunches; crayfish omelet. 🖫 *Average main: A$39* ✉ *31 Fitzroy St., St. Kilda* ☎ *03/9525–3999.*

Dog's Bar

$$ | **MEDITERRANEAN** | With its blazing fires, artfully smoky walls, and striking, art deco–ish wrought-iron ceiling lights, this three-decade-old restaurant has a lived-in, neighborly look. The food is good, its Australian wine is taken very seriously, and the kitchen is open until late each night. **Known for:** live music; shared plates; local favorite. $ *Average main: A$22* ✉ *54 Acland St., St. Kilda* ☎ *03/9593–9535* ⊕ *www.dogsbar.com. au.*

Donovan's

$$$ | **AUSTRALIAN** | Grab a window table at this very popular bayside restaurant (housed in the former 1920s bathing pavilion), and enjoy wide-open views of St. Kilda beach and its passing parade of in-line skaters, skateboarders, dog walkers, and ice-cream lickers. Owners Kevin and Gail Donovan are such natural hosts you may feel like bunking down on the plush cushions near the cozy fireplace. **Known for:** top-notch seafood; ocean views; extensive wine list. $ *Average main: A$48* ✉ *40 Jacka Blvd., St. Kilda* ☎ *03/9534–8221* ⊕ *www.donovans.com. au.*

Fitzrovia

$$$ | **MODERN AUSTRALIAN** | With a philosophy of celebrating local produce, Fitzrovia is known for fresh flavors with a European twist. The building, one of Melbourne's historical mansions overlooking Albert Park, is suitably grand while the food is hearty and sophisticated. Upmarket all-day dining and friendly service give the café a welcoming attitude. **Known for:** vegetarian-friendly dishes; Door-Stop sandwich (bacon, mozzarella, and pear relish); laid-back lunches. $ *Average main: A$30* ✉ *2/155 Fitzroy St., St. Kilda* ☎ *03/9537–0001* ⊕ *www.fitzrovia.com.au* ☾ *No dinner Sun.–Tues.*

 ## Hotels

The Prince

$$ | **HOTEL** | Cutting-edge design, contemporary artworks and sculptural furniture, and spare yet inviting luxury make this boutique hotel perfect for aficionados of unfussy elegance. **Pros:** super

Golfing

Sandringham Golf Club. Five minutes from the beach, Sandringham Golf Course is one of the better public courses, and one of several in Melbourne's renowned (coastal) Sand Belt. Located opposite the Royal Melbourne Golf Club, Sandringham is an 18-hole, par-72 course. A licensed café also operates on-site. Book online for discounted rates. ✉ *Cheltenham Rd., Sandringham* ☎ *03/9598–3590* ⊕ *www. sandringham.golf* ☑ *Weekdays: 18 holes A$43, 9 holes A$29; weekends: 18 holes A$44, 9 holes A$31* ⅃. *18 holes, 6174 yards, par 72.*

comfortable rooms; gallery feel; great location. **Cons:** the modern shapes and neutral hues might not appeal to some; hotel can be noisy due to functions; no free parking. $ *Rooms from: A$189* ✉ *2 Acland St., St. Kilda* ☎ *03/9536–1111* ⊕ *www.theprince.com.au* ⬎ *39 rooms* ⅠⓄⅠ *Free breakfast.*

Tolarno Hotel

$$ | **HOTEL** | Set in the heart of St. Kilda's café, bar, and club precinct, Tolarno Hotel was once owned by artists who ran a gallery out of the space, and it still has an idiosyncratic artistic bent. **Pros:** great restaurant; cool vibe; heart-of-breezy–St. Kilda location. **Cons:** area can have a dubious crowd; can be noisy late at night; no elevator. $ *Rooms from: A$185* ✉ *42 Fitzroy St., St. Kilda* ☎ *03/9537–0200* ⊕ *www.hoteltolarno.com.au* ⬎ *32 rooms, 5 suites* ⅠⓄⅠ *No meals.*

Nightlife

BARS
★ Esplanade Hotel

BARS/PUBS | Not only is this hallowed live music venue a great place to see local bands, but the Esplanade, or "Espy," is a historic pub—built in 1878—listed with the National Trust. ✉ *11 Upper Esplanade, St. Kilda* ☎ *03/9639–4000* ⊕ *www.hotelesplanade.com.au.*

CONCERT VENUE
Palais Theatre
MUSIC CLUBS | This theater features film, music festival openings, and concerts by Australian and international acts such as the Soweto Gospel Choir and Joe Bonamassa. ✉ *Lower Esplanade, St. Kilda* ☎ *03/8537–7677, 136–100 Ticketmaster* ⊕ *palaistheatre.com.au.*

MUSIC CLUBS
Prince of Wales
MUSIC CLUBS | For rock and roll, punk, and grunge, head to the Prince Bandroom at the Prince of Wales, which attracts a straight and gay crowd. Ticket prices vary widely, depending on the gig. ✉ *29 Fitzroy St., St. Kilda* ☎ *03/9636–1111* ⊕ *princebandroom.com.au.*

🎭 Performing Arts

THEATER
Theatre Works
THEATER | This theater concentrates on contemporary Australian plays. ✉ *14 Acland St., St. Kilda* ☎ *03/9534–3388* ⊕ *www.theatreworks.org.au.*

🛍 Shopping

MARKETS
The Esplanade Market St. Kilda
OUTDOOR/FLEA/GREEN MARKETS | Open since 1970, this market started as an outlet for local artists. Today, it has up to 200 stalls selling contemporary paintings, crafts, pottery, jewelry, and homemade gifts. It's open every Sunday from 10 to 5 from October to April and 10 to 4 in the colder months. ✉ *Upper Esplanade, St. Kilda* ☎ *03/9209–6634* ⊕ *www.stkildaesplanademarket.com.au.*

Australian Rules Football ⚽

This fast, vigorous game, played between teams of 18, is one of four kinds of football Down Under. Aussies also play Rugby League, Rugby Union, and soccer, but Australian Rules, widely known as "footy," is the one to which Victoria, South Australia, the Northern Territory, and Western Australia subscribe. The ball can be kicked or punched in any direction, but never thrown. Players make spectacular leaps vying to catch ("mark") a kicked ball before it touches the ground, for which they earn a free kick.

🏃 Activities

AUSTRALIAN RULES FOOTBALL
★ **Melbourne Cricket Ground**
FOOTBALL | The Melbourne Cricket Ground is the prime venue for AFL games and is also home to the National Sports Museum. ✉ *Brunton Ave., Yarra Park* ☎ *03/9657–8867* ⊕ *www.mcg.org.au.*

HORSE RACING
Champions: Thoroughbred Racing Gallery
HORSE RACING/SHOW | Horse-racing information, displays, and a mini-shrine to Australia's most famous race house, Phar Lap, take center stage at this gallery in the National Sports Museum. ✉ *Melbourne Cricket Ground, Brunton Ave., Gate 3, Yarra Park* ☎ *03/9657–8879* ⊕ *www.nsm.org.au* 💰 *A$30.*

KITEBOARDING
The Zu Boardsports
WATER SPORTS | The Zu Boardsports runs kiteboarding lessons at St. Kilda. Private lessons are A$189 for two hours ✉ *330 Beaconsfield Parade, at Pier Rd., St. Kilda*

☎ *03/9525–5655* 🌐 *www.thezu.com.au* 🎟 *A$189 per 2-hr lesson.*

Fitzroy

Melbourne's bohemian quarter is 2 km (1 mile) northeast of the city center. If you're looking for an Afghan camel bag or a secondhand paperback, or perhaps to hear some tunes while sipping a pint in a backstreet beer garden, Fitzroy is the place. Take Tram 11 or 86 from the city.

GETTING HERE AND AROUND

Fitzroy is an easy place to access, both from the city and nearby suburbs. From the city, take the No. 11 from Collins Street. It will take you all the way up Brunswick Street. From Bourke Street, hop on the No. 86 tram for a ride to Gertrude Street.

Sights

Brunswick Street

NEIGHBORHOOD | Along with Lygon Street in nearby Carlton, Brunswick Street is one of Melbourne's favorite places to dine. You might want to step into a simple kebab shop serving tender meats for less than A$12, or opt for dinner at one of the stylish, highly regarded bar-restaurants. The street also has many galleries, bookstores, bars, arts-and-crafts shops, and clothes shops (vintage fashion is a feature). ✉ *Brunswick St., between Alexandra and Victoria Parades, Fitzroy.*

Restaurants

★ Añada

$$ | **SPANISH** | A chalkboard on the exposed brick wall lists eight dry and six sweet sherries to start (or finish), and there are Spanish and Portuguese wines to accompany your selection of tapas and *raciones* (larger shared plates). Seated at a table or on a stool at the bar, begin with anchovy tapa, and go on to the authentic paella. Just leave room for dessert; the churros and chocolate are sinful. If you really can't decide, a dessert tasting plate for two absolves you of making a decision. **Known for:** obscure meats; local produce; shared plates. [$] *Average main: A$25* ✉ *197 Gertrude St., Fitzroy* ☎ *03/9415–6101* 🌐 *anada.com.au* 🕓 *No lunch weekdays.*

Babka

$ | **CAFÉ** | Food lovers in the know are often found loitering at this tiny, bustling café. Try the excellent pastries, fresh-baked breads, or more substantial offerings like the Russian borscht (beetroot and cabbage soup) or *menemen*—scrambled eggs with chili, mint, tomato, and a sprinkling of feta cheese. It's an all-day brunch-style café, and there are often lines, so be prepared to wait for a table. **Known for:** incredible sandwiches; freshly baked bread; bustling atmosphere. [$] *Average main: A$13* ✉ *358 Brunswick St., Fitzroy* ☎ *03/9416–0091* 🕓 *Closed Mon. No dinner.*

Charcoal Lane

$$ | **AUSTRALIAN** | Charcoal Lane is a social enterprise restaurant providing vulnerable young people with an opportunity to transform their lives by gaining a traineeship in the restaurant business. The inventive menu includes many Australian bushland ingredients, and the dishes have an Aboriginal influence. Named after a song by acclaimed Aboriginal singer/songwriter Archie Roach, it is housed in the former health service community center, dubbed Charcoal Lane by the many Aboriginal people, who for decades would drop in and swap stories and wisdom. They might include starters of roasted emu fillet or a wild food tasting plate of native produce. Mains include wallaby wrapped in Parma ham and pumpkin and wattleseed gnocchi. Desserts also have a "bush tucker" influence. **Known for:** feel-good dining; native meats; chic decor. [$] *Average main: A$35* ✉ *136 Gertrude St., Fitzroy* ☎ *03/9235–9200* 🌐 *www.charcoallane.com.au* 🕓 *Closed Sun. and Mon.*

Ladro

$$ | **ITALIAN** | A local favorite, this stellar Italian bistro emphasizes flavor over starchy linen and stuffy attitude. Here, lamb rump is scented with garlic and parsley and slow-roasted to impossible tenderness, and the service is as upbeat as the wine list. Delicious wood-fired pizzas, that some insist are the best in the city, are yet another reason to visit this suburban gem (thankfully, it's only a short walk from the city). The Ladro family also includes Ladro TAP, an environmentally sustainable Italian eatery in Greville St Prahran. Vegan and gluten-free options are available. **Known for:** sustainability initiatives; puttanesca pizza; cannoli specials. [$] *Average main: A$26* ✉ *224 Gertrude St., Fitzroy* ☎ *03/9415–7575* 🌐 *ladro.com.au* 🕒 *No lunch Mon.–Sat.*

Lune Croissanterie

$ | **BAKERY** | Locals and tourists alike can be found queueing outside Lune each morning for the city's most beloved croissants, in experimental flavors that may include pumpkin pie and Persian love cake. Inside a Brutalist concrete warehouse, croissants and cruffins fly out of the oven and into the hands of eager customers until there are none left. The pastries are best consumed with Lune's excellent coffee. A city outpost is located at 161 Collins Street. **Known for:** world-famous croissant flavors; exclusive atmosphere; long queues. [$] *Average main: A$6* ✉ *119 Rose St., Fitzroy* ☎ *03/9419–2320* 🌐 *www.lunecroissanterie.com* 🕒 *Closed Tues. and Wed.*

🍸 Nightlife

BARS

The Everleigh

PIANO BARS/LOUNGES | One of the city's best cocktail bars, the Everleigh also makes a perfect spot for couples, with dark lighting and soft tunes. ✉ *150–156 Gertrude St., upstairs, Fitzroy* ☎ *03/9416–2229* 🌐 *www.theeverleigh.com.*

Polly

BARS/PUBS | Mix with colorful and quirky clientele in an equally fun 1920s design with red-velvet lounges, gilt mirrors, and chandeliers. Also enjoy a traditional or contemporary cocktail—there are 55 concoctions to choose from. ✉ *401 Brunswick St., Fitzroy* ☎ *03/9417–0880* 🌐 *www.pollybar.com.au.*

MUSIC CLUBS

The Night Cat

MUSIC CLUBS | Bands and DJs play Afro-Cuban and disco dance music here Thursday to Saturday evening, and the Latin big band on Sunday night is legendary. ✉ *141 Johnston St., Fitzroy* ☎ *03/9417–0090* 🌐 *www.thenightcat.com.au.*

The Rainbow

BARS/PUBS | Most nights of the week, for the past few decades, this great pub, located down a backstreet, has been showcasing local acts. There's also a great range of craft beers available, which you can enjoy in the beer garden during the warmer months. ✉ *27 St. David St., Fitzroy* ☎ *03/9419–4193* 🌐 *therainbow.com.au.*

🛍 Shopping

ART AND CRAFT GALLERIES

Gallery Gabrielle Pizzi

GIFTS/SOUVENIRS | The gallery shows and sells the work of established and new Aboriginal artists from the communities of Balgo Hills, Papunya, Maningrida, Turkey Creek (Warmun), the Tiwi Islands, and others in the Central Desert, Top End, and Kimberley regions. Visits are by appointment only. ✉ *77 Flinders La., Fitzroy* ☎ *03/9654–2944* 🌐 *www.gabriellepizzi.com.au.*

BOOKS

Brunswick Street Bookstore

BOOKS/STATIONERY | Brunswick Street Bookstore specializes in art, design, and architecture publications, but also stocks modern Australian literature. ✉ *305 Brunswick St., Fitzroy* ☎ *03/9416–1030.*

CLOTHING

The Social Studio

CLOTHING | This nonprofit store provides work experience, employment, and passageways for refugee youth. Limited-edition women's fashion designs are made using only reclaimed materials sourced from the local fashion industry. ✉ *128 Smith St., Collingwood* ☎ *03/9417–2143* ⊕ *www.thesocialstudio.org.*

SHOPPING CENTERS

Brunswick Street

SHOPPING CENTERS/MALLS | Northeast of the city in Fitzroy, Brunswick Street has hip and grungy restaurants, coffee shops, gift stores, and clothing outlets selling the latest look. ✉ *Brunswick St., Fitzroy.*

Smith Street

SHOPPING NEIGHBORHOODS | Perhaps Melbourne's hippest street, this colorful strip is dotted with bars, restaurants, and many vintage-style clothing shops. Toward the northern end are clothing factory outlets. ✉ *Smith St., Fitzroy.*

Brunswick

Just 4 km (2 miles) north of the city center, Brunswick is Melbourne's multicultural heart. Here Middle Eastern spice shops sit next to avant-garde galleries, Egyptian supermarkets, Turkish tile shops, Japanese yakitori eateries, Lebanese bakeries, Indian haberdasheries, and secondhand bookstores. Take Tram 19 from the city.

GETTING HERE AND AROUND

Tram 19 travels from Flinders Street Station in the city along Elizabeth Street and Brunswick's main thoroughfare, Sydney Road. You can also catch a train to Brunswick; take the Upfield Railway Line from Flinders Street Station and alight at either Jewell, Brunswick, or Anstey stations—they're all in Brunswick.

Off To The Races

Flemington Race Course. Australia's premier racecourse, 3 km (2 miles) outside the city, is home to the Melbourne Cup each November. ✉ *448 Epsom Rd., Flemington* ☎ *1300/727–575* ⊕ *www.flemington. com.au* ⌅ *From A$31 on race day.*

◉ Sights

CERES Community Environment Park

LOCAL INTEREST | FAMILY | On the banks of the Merri Creek in East Brunswick, this award-winning sustainability center is home to a permaculture and bushfood nursery. Buy local produce and crafts here, eat at the Merri Table Cafe, and explore the green technology displays. ✉ *45 Roberts St., at Stewart St., Brunswick East* ☎ *03/9389–0100* ⊕ *ceres.org. au* ⌅ *Free.*

Sydney Road

NEIGHBORHOOD | Cultures collide on Sydney Road as Arabic mingles with French, Hindi does battle with Bengali, and the muezzin's call to prayer argues with Lebanese pop music. Scents intoxicate and colors beguile. Cafés serving everything from pastries to *tagines* (Moroccan stews) to Turkish delight sit shoulder-to-shoulder along the roadside with quirky record shops, antiques auction houses, and Bollywood video stores. ✉ *Sydney Rd., between Brunswick Rd. and Bell St., Brunswick.*

🍽 Restaurants

400 Gradi

$$ | ITALIAN | This is the place for authentic Italian pizza: chef Johnny Di Francesco trained in Naples to make pizza to the Associazione Verace Pizza Napoletana rules. Besides pizza, the restaurant

serves excellent pasta and other Italian dishes in a buzzing section of Lygon Street. There are also iterations in Essendon, Southbank, and the Yarra Valley and an aptly titled gelato spinoff, Zero Gradi, in Brunswick. **Known for:** Margherita pizza; house-made gelato; slick decor. [$] *Average main: A$30* ✉ *99 Lygon St., Brunswick East* ☎ *03/9380–2320* 🌐 *www.400gradi.com.au.*

Hellenic Republic

$$ | MODERN GREEK | Owned by well-known TV chef George Calombaris, Hellenic Republic pays homage to Calombaris's Greek heritage, creating a lively taverna type setting with a focus on communal food. We suggest the Masa Menu (A$55), which consists of numerous courses including meat from the omnipresent spit, whose mouthwatering scent envelopes the room upon entering. Naturally the friendly staff will try to entice you into having a sip of ouzo, and since everyone else seems to be doing it, we suggest you do, too. There are also Hellenic Republic locations in Williamstown, Brighton, and Kew. **Known for:** slow-roasted meat; incredible spanakopita; friendly service. [$] *Average main: A$30* ✉ *434 Lygon St., Brunswick East* ☎ *03/9381–1222* 🌐 *hellenicrepublic.com.au* 🕓 *No lunch Mon.–Thurs.*

Nightlife

BARS

Alehouse Project

BARS/PUBS | Regarded as having one of the best beer lists in the city, this local favorite also has an excellent menu, matched especially to the beers on offer. Head to the beer garden out back in the warmer months. ✉ *98 Lygon St., Brunswick East* ☎ *03/9387–1218* 🌐 *www.thealehouseproject.com.au.*

Retreat Hotel

BARS/PUBS | This expansive pub has local bands performing most nights of the week. It also has one of the city's best beer gardens. ✉ *280 Sydney Rd., Brunswick* ☎ *03/9380–4090* 🌐 *retreathotelbrunswick.com.au.*

Union Hotel

BARS/PUBS | This family-friendly pub showcases local music on weekends. The atmosphere is always friendly and welcoming. ✉ *109 Union St., Brunswick West* ☎ *03/9388–2235* 🌐 *unionhotelbrunswick.com.au.*

MUSIC CLUBS

Spotted Mallard

MUSIC CLUBS | In addition hosting live bands, this venue also has trivia nights and serves a range of microbrewery beers. ✉ *314 Sydney Rd., Brunswick* ☎ *03/9380–8818* 🌐 *www.spottedmallard.com.*

Carlton

To see the best of Carlton's Victorian-era architecture, walk along Drummond Street, with its rows of gracious terrace houses (notably Rosaville at No. 46, Medley Hall at No. 48, and Lothian Terrace at No. 175), and Canning Street, which has a mix of workers' cottages and grander properties.

GETTING HERE AND AROUND

Carlton is served by the many Swanston Street tram routes that terminate at Melbourne University (located in Parkville, just west of Carlton). Tram 1 extends north beyond the university, turning into the top end of Lygon Street. Alternatively, catch a bus (No. 200 or 207) from Lonsdale Street to Carlton.

Sights

Carlton Gardens

GARDEN | Forty acres of tree-lined paths, artificial lakes, and flower beds in this English-style 19th-century park are the backdrop for the outstanding Melbourne Museum, and the World Heritage–listed Royal Exhibition Building, erected in

1880. ✉ *Victoria Parade, at Nicholson, Carlton, and Rathdowne Sts., Carlton.*

Lygon Street

NEIGHBORHOOD | Known as Melbourne's Little Italy, Lygon Street is a perfect example of the city's multiculturalism: where once you'd have seen only Italian restaurants, there are now Thai, Malay, Caribbean, and Greek eateries. The city's famous café culture was also born here, with the arrival of Melbourne's first espresso machine at one of the street's Italian-owned cafés in the 1950s. ✉ *Lygon St., between Victoria and Alexandra Parades, Carlton.*

Melbourne Museum

MUSEUM | **FAMILY** | A spectacular, postmodern building (in Carlton Gardens) houses displays of the varied cultures around Australia and the Pacific Islands. The Bunjilaka Aboriginal Cultural Center explores the traditions of the country's Aboriginal groups, while the Australia Gallery focuses on Victoria's heritage (and includes the preserved body of Australia's greatest racehorse, Phar Lap). There's plenty for kids, too, with the wooded Forest Gallery, Children's Gallery (housed in what looks like a giant Rubik's Cube), Mind and Body Gallery, and Science and Life Gallery. The museum regularly hosts touring blockbuster exhibitions (additional fee). ✉ *Carlton Gardens, 11 Nicholson St., Carlton* ☎ *131–102 local, 03/8341–7777 international* 🌐 *museumsvictoria.com.au/melbournemuseum* 🎫 *A$15.*

🍴 Restaurants

Abla's

$$ | **LEBANESE** | Matriarch Abla Amad has been re-creating the much-loved family recipes from her homeland of Lebanon since 1979. This intimate restaurant resembles a lounge room of a family house, which with Abla walking around talking to diners, adds to the feeling of being looked after. Bookings are recommended and you can BYO wine. **Known for:** chicken and rice; homemade baklawa; 12-course banquet. [$] *Average main: A$30* ✉ *109 Elgin St., Carlton* ☎ *03/9347–0006* 🌐 *www.ablas.com.au* 🕓 *No lunch Sat.–Wed.*

Brunetti

$$ | **CAFÉ** | First opened in 1974, this iconic Romanesque bakery has moved around Carlton on several occasions, and the masses have followed. Its biggest undertaking is in the heart of Lygon Street and still filled with perfect biscotti, mouthwatering cakes, and great service. In addition to an expanded lunch menu, a wood-fire oven—specially imported from Italy—makes pizzas, and you can finish it all off with a perfect espresso or a thick European-style hot chocolate with a *cornetto con crema* (custard-filled croissant). Enjoy the same tempting delights at branches in Flinders Lane and Myer department store in Bourke Street. **Known for:** chocolate eclairs; decadent cake display; Italian-style espresso. [$] *Average main: A$23* ✉ *380 Lygon St., Carlton* ☎ *03/9347–2801* 🌐 *www.brunetti.com.au.*

D.O.C.

$$ | **ITALIAN** | A major player in Melbourne's pizza wars, D.O.C. has perfected the art of using fresh, simple ingredients to create something special. The real treats lie in their pizza of the day. One with Ubriaco Amarone cheese, Romana artichokes, smoked toasted almonds, radicchio, and shaved Parmesan might be on offer, or perhaps another with Petrilli passata, garlic, artisan stracciatella, Cantabrico anchovies, and basil (around A$25). Whatever is in season or comes in, they will use. A chocolate pizza is at the ready for those with a sweet tooth. They also have a delicatessen around the corner (*330 Lygon St.*), which could be a good option for a packed lunch, and there's another location in the picturesque seaside town of Mornington. **Known for:** pizza specials; mozzarella degustation; passionate service.

$ *Average main: A$25* ✉ *295 Drummond St., Carlton* ☎ *03/9347–2998* ⊕ *www. docgroup.net.*

🛏 Hotels

Arrow on Swanston

$ | **HOTEL** | Location and great value make up for the limited space in this CBD-edge hotel. **Pros:** easy walk to eateries and CBD attractions; budget-friendly; amenities suitable for longer stays. **Cons:** limited space; plain decor; only basic housekeeping. $ *Rooms from: A$110* ✉ *488 Swanston St., Carlton* ☎ *03/9225– 9000* ⊕ *www.arrowonswanston.com. au* 🛏 *47 rooms, 38 apartments* 🍽 *No meals.*

🛍 Shopping

BOOKS

Readings

BOOKS/STATIONERY | An independent retailer with an exceptional range of books, magazines, and CDs, Readings is a Melbourne institution. The Carlton store has operated since 1969, and there are now four suburban branches and another shop in the State Library in the city center. ✉ *309 Lygon St., Carlton* ☎ *03/9347–6633* ⊕ *www.readings.com. au.*

South Yarra and Prahran

One of the most chic and fashion-conscious areas to be on any given day (or night) is in South Yarra–Prahran. The area is chock-full of bars, eateries, and upscale boutiques.

GETTING HERE AND AROUND

Several trams, including Nos. 6, 72, and 78, travel to either South Yarra or Prahran or both. No. 6 comes down St. Kilda Road from Flinders Street Station and turns into High Street, Prahran. Tram 78 travels down Chapel Street from Richmond. You can also catch a train to both South Yarra and Prahran; take the Sandringham Line from Flinders Street Station.

👁 Sights

★ Chapel Street

NEIGHBORHOOD | The heart of the trendy South Yarra–Prahran area, this long road is packed with pubs, bars, notable restaurants, and upscale boutiques—more than 1,000 shops can be found within the precinct. Australian icons like Dinosaur Designs and Scanlan Theodore showcase their original work at the fashion-conscious, upscale Toorak Road end of the street (nearest to the city). Walk south along Chapel Street to Greville Street and visit a small lane of hip bars, clothing boutiques, and record stores. Past Greville Street, at the south end of Chapel Street, it's hipper, with cafés and vintage shops. ✉ *Chapel St., between Toorak and Dandenong Rds., Prahran* ☎ *03/9529– 6331* ⊕ *www.chapelstreet.com.au.*

Rippon Lea

HOUSE | Construction of Rippon Lea, a sprawling polychrome brick mansion built in the Romanesque style, began in the late 1860s. By the time it was completed in 1903, the original 15-room house had expanded into a 33-room mansion. Notable architectural features include a grotto, a tower that overlooks a lake, and humpback bridges. There is also a fernery and an orchard with more than 100 varieties of heritage apples and pears. Access to the house is for exhibitions or, between exhibitions, by guided tour only, but a self-guided tour of the grounds only is available. To get here, take a Sandringham line train from Flinders Street Station; it's a 15-minute ride south of the city center. ✉ *192 Hotham St., Elsternwick* ☎ *03/9523–6095* ⊕ *www. ripponleaestate.com.au* 🎫 *House and garden: A$15.*

Off The Beaten Path

Melbourne Zoo. Verdant gardens and open-environment animal enclosures are hallmarks of this world-renowned zoo, which is 4 km (2½ miles) north of the city center. A lion park, reptile house, and butterfly pavilion, where more than 1,000 butterflies flutter through the rain-forest setting, are on-site, as is a simulated African rain forest where a group of Western Lowland gorillas lives. The spectacular Trail of the Elephants, home of five Asiatic elephants, has a village, tropical gardens, and a swimming pool. The orangutan sanctuary and baboon outlook are other highlights. It's possible to stay overnight with the Roar 'n' Snore package (A$205 per adult) and enjoy dinner, supper, breakfast, close encounters with animals, and a behind-the-scenes look at the zoo's operations. ⊠ Elliott Ave., Parkville ☎ 03/9285–9300, 1300/966784 reservations ⊕ www.zoo.org.au ☜ A$37.

Royal Botanic Gardens

GARDEN | FAMILY | Within its 100 acres are 12,000 species of native and imported plants and trees, sweeping lawns, and ornamental lakes populated with ducks and swans that love to be fed. The Children's Garden is a fun and interactive place for kids to explore. Summer brings alfresco performances of classic plays, usually Shakespeare, and children's classics like Wind in the Willows, as well as the popular Moonlight Cinema series. The present design and layout were the brainchild of W.R. Guilfoyle, curator and director of the gardens from 1873 to 1910. ⊠ Birdwood Ave., South Yarra ☎ 03/9252–2300 ⊕ www.rbg.vic.gov.au ☜ Free.

🍴 Restaurants

Caffe e Cucina

$$ | ITALIAN | If you're looking for a quintessential Italian dining experience in a place where it's easy to imagine yourself back in the old country, this is it. Fashionable, look-at-me types flock here for coffee and pastries downstairs, or more-leisurely meals upstairs in the warm, woody dining room. Try the melt-in-your-mouth gnocchi, or calamari Sant' Andrea (lightly floured and shallow fried).

Known for: decadent tiramisu; knowledgeable staff; traditional menu. $ Average main: A$35 ⊠ 581 Chapel St., South Yarra ☎ 03/9827–4139 ⊕ caffeecucina.com.au.

🛏 Hotels

The Como Melbourne

$$$ | HOTEL | With its opulent and funky modern furnishings, this luxury hotel is as popular with business travelers as it is with visiting artists and musicians. **Pros:** lavishly appointed rooms; great shopping and restaurants nearby; great service. **Cons:** outside the city center; breakfast not included; parking not included. $ Rooms from: A$254 ⊠ 630 Chapel St., South Yarra ☎ 03/9825–2222 ⊕ www.comomelbourne.com.au ☞ 107 rooms ⏴ Free breakfast.

The Lyall Hotel and Spa

$$$ | HOTEL | The spacious one- and two-bedroom suites at this exclusive hotel make an art form of understated elegance, and they come with all the luxuries: CD and DVD players, velour bathrobes and slippers, gourmet mini-bars, and a pillow "menu." The in-house spa administers a full range of massages, facials, and body treatments (try the organic green tea exfoliation). **Pros:** an extravagant spa; 24-hour bistro; 24-hour

gym. **Cons:** outside city center; some rooms lack views; location may be too quiet for some. $ *Rooms from: A$272* ✉ *14 Murphy St., South Yarra* ☎ *03/9868–8222, 1800/388234* ⊕ *www.thelyall.com* ⇨ *40 rooms* ⏻ *Free breakfast.*

Royce Hotel
$$$ | HOTEL | Natural light bathes the rooms in this elegant, 1920s-style hotel, in a former Rolls-Royce showroom. **Pros:** old-fashioned charm; lavish appointments, including hot tubs in some rooms; near parks and Botanic Gardens. **Cons:** some rooms have bland views; outside the city center; basic breakfast. $ *Rooms from: A$229* ✉ *379 St. Kilda Rd., South Yarra* ☎ *03/9677–9900, 1800/820909* ⊕ *www.roycehotels.com. au* ⇨ *100 rooms* ⏻ *Free breakfast.*

 Nightlife

BARS
Revolver Upstairs
BARS/PUBS | This bar caters predominantly to young partygoers, with early-morning recovery sessions—a time for revelers around town to keep on partying—that are especially popular. ✉ *229 Chapel St., Prahran* ☎ *03/9521–5985* ⊕ *revolverupstairs.com.au.*

 Activities

GOLF
Albert Park Golf Course
GOLF | Four kilometers (2½ miles) south of the city, Albert Park Golf Course is an 18-hole, par-72 course beside Albert Park Lake, where the Formula 1 Grand Prix is held in March. Clubs, buggies, and carts can be hired at the course. Golf lessons for everyone from beginners to advanced players, starting at A$65 for a half-hour lesson for a single player. ✉ *Queens Rd., Albert Park* ☎ *03/9510–5588* ⊕ *www. albertparkgolf.com.au* ⛳ *Weekdays: 18 holes A$36, 9 holes A$26; weekends: 18 holes A$41, 9 holes A$26* ⛳ *18 holes, 6280 yards, par 72.*

TENNIS
Fawkner Park Tennis Centre
TENNIS | Play tennis here on six synthetic-grass outdoor courts. ✉ *Fawkner Park, Toorak Rd. W, South Yarra* ☎ *03/9820–0611* ⊕ *www.fawknerparktenniscentre. com* ⛳ *Court hire from A$19/hr weekends, A$28/hr weekdays.*

🛍 Shopping

ART
Signed and Numbered
ART GALLERIES | Melbourne is famous for its street art, and this purveyor of limited-edition prints sells work by well-known local street artists like Ghostpatrol and Kaff-eine, as well as other national and international artists. ✉ *Greville Print Shop, 153 Greville St., South Yarra* ☎ *03/9193–1687* ⊕ *signedandnumbered. com.au.*

CLOTHING
Eco D
CLOTHING | International and Australian designers mix and mingle here, so you can find local fashion icons like Cable Melbourne, LIFEwithBIRD, and Camilla and Marc here. There are also boutiques in Prahran, South Yarra, Brighton, and Hawthorn. ✉ *1064 High St., Windsor* ☎ *03/9500–0004* ⊕ *shop.ecod.com.au.*

SHOPPING CENTERS
Chapel Street
SHOPPING CENTERS/MALLS | This street is where you can find some of the ritziest boutiques in Melbourne, as well as cafés, art galleries, bars, and restaurants. ✉ *Chapel St., between Toorak and Dandenong Rds., Prahran.*

High Street
SHOPPING CENTERS/MALLS | Located between the suburbs of Prahran and Armadale, to the east of Chapel Street, High Street has the best collection of antiques shops in Australia. ✉ *High St., between Chapel St. and Orrong Rd., Prahran.*

Melbourne Bicycling 101

Melbourne and its environs contain more than 100 km (62 miles) of bike paths, including scenic routes along the Yarra River and Port Phillip Bay. The Beach Road Trail extends 19 km (12 miles) around Port Phillip Bay from Elwood Beach to Sandringham. The new Docklands area of Melbourne can be cycled around—start on the Southbank Promenade, travel west, and then cross over the new Webb Street to Docklands Park and Harbour Esplanade; you can join the Main Yarra Trail bicycle route at the mouth of the Yarra River, just north of the West Gate Bridge or at Southbank. You can then follow the Yarra River for 35 km (22 miles) until it meets up with the Mullum Mullum Creek Trail in Templestowe in Melbourne's eastern suburbs. Information on paths can be found on the websites for each council area, or via VicRoads (⊕ www.vicroads. vic.gov.au). Bicycle Network can also give some advice.

The City of Melbourne has a bike share scheme around the city. Hire begins at A\$3 for half an hour, but daily and weekly hire is also available. See ⊕ www.melbournebikeshare.com. au for the details. Note that under Australian law, all cyclists must wear helmets.

The Jam Factory
SHOPPING CENTERS/MALLS | This historic redbrick brewery-turned-factory complex houses cinemas, fashion, food, and gift shops. ⊠ 500 Chapel St., South Yarra ☎ 03/9860–8500 ⊕ www.thejamfactory. com.au.

JEWELRY
Dinosaur Designs
JEWELRY/ACCESSORIES | This shop sells a range of luminous bowls and vases, and funky resin and silver jewelry. ⊠ 562 Chapel St., South Yarra ☎ 03/9827–2600 ⊕ www.dinosaurdesigns.com.au.

MARKETS
Camberwell Sunday Market
OUTDOOR/FLEA/GREEN MARKETS | A popular haunt for seekers of the old and odd, this market, about 6 km (4 miles) northeast of Chapel Street, South Yarra, has more than 300 stalls selling antiques, preloved clothing, books, and knickknacks. Food vans provide sustenance. ⊠ Station St., Camberwell ⊕ camberwellsundaymarket. org.

Chapel Street Bazaar
OUTDOOR/FLEA/GREEN MARKETS | Everything from estate jewelry and stylish second-hand clothes to porcelain and curios is on sale at these wooden cubicles and glass-fronted counters. ⊠ 217–223 Chapel St., Prahran ☎ 03/9529–1727 ⊕ www. chapelstreet.com.au.

Prahran Market
OUTDOOR/FLEA/GREEN MARKETS | A fantastic, mouthwatering array imported from all over the world is available at this food market. The free Hidden Gems tour runs the first and second Saturdays of each month. ⊠ 163 Commercial Rd., South Yarra ☎ 03/8290–8220 ⊕ www.prahran-market.com.au.

MUSIC
Greville Records
MUSIC STORES | A Melbourne music institution, Greville Records carries rare releases in rock, alternative, and vinyl. ⊠ 152 Greville St., Prahran ☎ 03/9510–3012 ⊕ www.grevillerecords.com.au.

Brighton

One of Melbourne's most iconic tourist destinations, Brighton boasts a beautiful and scenic beach with a line of 90 colorful bathing boxes, which date back to about the 1900s.

⊙ Beaches

★ Middle Brighton Beach

BEACH—SIGHT | Most commonly known for its colorful and culturally significant bathing boxes, which were built more than a century ago in response to very Victorian ideas of morality and seaside bathing, Brighton Beach is also ideal for families since its location in a cove means that it's protected from the wind. Perfect for those looking for a quieter spot to bathe than St. Kilda Beach, the Middle Brighton Baths is a nice place to view the boats and have a bite to eat. Good views of the bathing boxes and Melbourne's skyline can be enjoyed from the gardens at Green Point. **Amenities:** parking (fee); toilets. **Best for:** solitude; swimming. ⊠ Esplanade, Brighton.

⊛ Activities

GOLF

Brighton Public Golf Course

GOLF | The 18-hole, par-67 Brighton Public Golf Course has lovely scenery, with trees and wetlands, but is quite busy on weekends and midweek mornings. The first nine holes are considered less challenging than the last nine. Club rental is available for A$20, and carts are available for A$42. The course allows unlimited playing after 4 pm in winter and after 5:30 pm in summer in its Twilight Golf Specials (A$15). ⊠ 230 Dendy St., Brighton ☎ 03/9592–1388 ⊕ www.brightongolf-course.com.au ☜ 18 holes A$35, 9 holes A$25 ⸯ. 18 holes, 5335 yards, par 67.

SIDE TRIPS FROM MELBOURNE AND GREATER VICTORIA

6

Updated by
Belinda Jackson

◉ Sights	🍴 Restaurants	🛏 Hotels	🛍 Shopping	🍸 Nightlife
★★★★★	★★★★★	★★★★☆	★☆☆☆☆	★☆☆☆☆

WELCOME TO SIDE TRIPS FROM MELBOURNE AND GREATER VICTORIA

TOP REASONS TO GO

★ **The Amazing Outdoors:** Victoria has outstanding national parks. Bushwalking, canoeing, fishing, rafting, and horse riding are all on the menu.

★ **Golden Country:** You can still pan for gold—and find it—in rivers northwest of Melbourne. But the gold-rush era's most attractive remnants are beautiful 19th-century towns constructed from its riches.

★ **Wonderful Wineries:** You'll find hundreds of wineries across the state, particularly in the Yarra Valley, Rutherglen, and on the Mornington Peninsula.

★ **Unique Wildlife:** With parrots in Sherbrooke, Phillip Island's penguin parade, and platypuses and dingoes at the Healesville Sanctuary, Victoria teems with native fauna.

★ **Foodie Heaven:** Victoria has a reputation for excellent local produce and wine. Even in rural towns, cafés and restaurants focus on fresh seasonal items.

The Yarra Valley wineries and the Dandenong Ranges are an hour's drive east of Melbourne, while the beaches and vineyards of the Mornington Peninsula are an hour's drive south of the city. The Great Ocean Road begins at Torquay, southwest of Melbourne, and continues along the Southern Ocean coast to Portland, a distance of about 350 km (220 miles). The Goldfields are between one and two hours northwest of Melbourne. The Grampians and the Murray River region and its wineries are about a three-hour drive north to northeast of the city.

1 Yarra Valley and Healesville. Small towns with good cafés and shops, and a good base for travel to Yarra Valley wineries and the Dandenongs Region.

2 The Dandenong Ranges. Winding roads connect national parks and walking trails.

3 Mornington Peninsula. Seaside villages, pretty beaches, and wall-to-wall wineries.

4 Phillip Island. Breathtaking natural beauty and the famous penguin parade.

5 Queenscliff. A seaside town and popular detour on the drive to the start of the Great Ocean Road.

6 Lorne. A lively, holiday town on the Great Ocean Road.

7 Apollo Bay. A quieter town on Great Ocean Road and base for nearby National Parks.

8 Port Campbell National Park. Home to

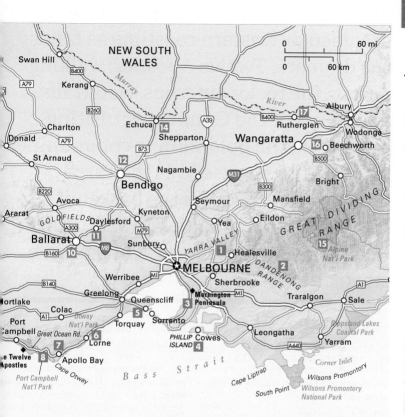

some of the most famous geological formations in Australia.

9 Port Fairy. The state's prettiest village.

10 Ballarat. A former Gold town with impressive museums and Victorian architecture.

11 Daylesford and Hepburn Springs. Known for natural springs and spas.

12 Bendigo. Bustling small city with historic mines and great galleries and wineries.

13 Grampians National Park. Stunning mountain scenery, great bushwalks, and Aboriginal rock art sites.

14 Echuca. An historic Murray River town with a large paddle steamer fleet.

15 Alpine National Park. Gorgeous alpine scenery, grasys plains, and lots of outdoor activities.

16 Beechworth. A town with Ned Kelly associations and within easy reach of national parks.

17 Rutherglen. The source of Australia's finest fortified wines.

Without venturing too far from the Melbourne city limits, you can indulge in all sorts of pastimes—exploring the spectacular western coastline as far as the dramatic Twelve Apostles; walking among the rocky outcrops, waterfalls, and fauna of the Grampians; visiting historic inland gold-mining communities; toasting the sunrise over the Yarra Valley vineyards from the basket of a hot-air balloon; or taking in a Murray River sunset from the deck of a paddle steamer.

Sweeping landscapes are quilted together in this compact state. Many of the state's best sights are within a day's drive of Melbourne. Go further afield and you can experience the high-country solitude of Alpine National Park.

MAJOR REGIONS

Victoria's relatively compact size makes the state's principal attractions appealingly easy to reach, and the state's excellent road system makes driving the best option. There are a handful of enticing destinations within a 60- to 90-minute drive of the city. Victoria is blessed with 22 distinct wine regions (and around 600 cellar doors, where you can try and buy the product). **The Yarra Valley,** 65 km (40 miles) east of Melbourne, is Victoria's oldest wine region and a pleasant place to spend a day on an organized tour. About 35 km (22 miles) south of the Yarra Valley is Olinda, a cute village at the heart of the **Dandenong Ranges.** This area of beautifully forested hills and valleys is a favorite weekend escape for Melburnians. **The Mornington Peninsula** is famous for its wineries and beaches, while **Phillip Island,** just off the Mornington Peninsula, is famous for its nightly Penguin Parade. On the western shore of Port Phillip Bay, the Bellarine Peninsula also has a burgeoning winery industry, but it's the grand 19th-century hotels of **Queenscliff** that most attract day-trippers.

The **Great Ocean Road,** which snakes along Victoria's rugged and windswept southwestern coast, is arguably Australia's most spectacular coastal drive. The road, built by returned soldiers after World War I along majestic cliffs, occasionally dips down to sea level. Here, in championship surfing country, some of the world's finest waves pound mile after mile of uninhabited, golden, sandy beaches and rocky headlands. Although the route is officially deemed to be 243 km (152 miles), and runs between the towns of Torquay in the east and Allansford (near Warnambool) in the west, most people think of it as the much longer route that continues farther west to Port Fairy, Portland and to the South Australian border, and inland to small towns such as Colac. Its many twists and turns and wonderful sights along the way take many hours to explore. Allow time to stop in the attractive towns of **Lorne** and **Apollo Bay,** and to explore **Port Campbell National Park** and **Port Fairy.**

Victoria was changed forever in the early 1850s by the discovery of gold in the center of the state. News of fantastic gold deposits caused immigrants from every corner of the world to pour into Victoria's **Gold Country** to seek their fortunes as "diggers"—a name that has become synonymous with Australians ever since. Few miners became wealthy from their searches, however. The real money was made by those supplying goods and services to the thousands who had succumbed to gold fever. Gold towns like **Ballarat** and **Bendigo** sprang up like mushrooms to accommodate these fortune seekers, and prospered until the gold rush receded. Afterward, they became ghost towns or turned to agriculture to survive. However, many beautiful buildings were constructed from the spoils of gold, and these gracious old public buildings and grand hotels survive today and make a visit to Bendigo and Ballarat a pleasure for those who love classic architecture. Between Ballarat and other historic gold towns to the north are the twin hot spots of **Daylesford and Hepburn Springs**—which together constitute the spa capital of Australia.

The Grampians. Encompassing a series of rugged sandstone ranges covered with native bushland, **Grampians National Park** is a wilderness area three hours from the heart of Melbourne. Spectacular rock formations including the Balconies, the Pinnacle, and the Fortress can be visited via walking trails. The Wonderland Range forms a wall behind the township of Halls Gap, which is a popular hangout for kangaroos.

Murray River Region. The mighty Murray River forms the border between Victoria and New South Wales, and is an aquatic playground. Houseboats, speedboats, and old paddle wheelers share the river, and golf courses, farms, historic towns like **Echuca,** and stands of majestic eucalyptus trees hug its banks. Wineries produce internationally acclaimed fortified wines and full-bodied reds.

Victoria's dramatic **High Country** is just under the NSW-Victorian border, and includes the state's main ski resorts and **Alpine National Park.** In spring and fall, some of the prettiest drives are along its mountain roads, including the C522, dubbed the Snow Road for its winter parade of skiiers and snowboarders heading up to the ski resorts around Mt. Hotham and Falls Creek. Slow down to enjoy the drive between gorgeously picturesque villages such as Chiltern and **Beechworth,** photograph rustic tobacco kilns set against snowy peaks, and keep an eye out for roadside shops and cafés selling delicious local produce, as the High Country enjoys a revival thanks to food, wine, and adventure-loving travelers. Steeped in history and natural beauty, the High Country region is a gourmet foodies' heaven known for its fruit, olives, honey, and cheeses, and is also a renowned wine region. Victoria exports more than A$200 million worth of wine annually, and this region's muscats and ports are legendary. The **Rutherglen** area, in particular, produces the country's finest fortified wines (dessert wines or "stickies").

Planning

WHEN TO GO

Victoria is at its most beautiful in fall, March through May, when days are crisp, sunny, and clear and the foliage in parks and gardens is glorious. Winter, with its wild seas and leaden skies, stretches June through August in this region, providing a suitable backdrop for the dramatic coastal scenery. It's dry and sunny in the northeast, however, thanks to the cloud-blocking bulk of the Great Dividing Range. Northeast summers, December through February, are extremely hot, so it's best to travel here and through the Gold Country in spring (September through November) and fall.

PLANNING YOUR TIME

From Melbourne, head for the town of Belgrave. Here you can ride the Puffing Billy train through the fern gullies and forests of the Dandenongs. In the afternoon, travel to Phillip Island for the endearing sunset penguin parade. Stay the night, and on the third morning meander along the coastal roads of the Mornington Peninsula through such stately towns as Sorrento and Portsea. Stop at a beach, or lunch at a winery before returning to Melbourne that afternoon.

If you have more time to spend in the area, make your way west from Melbourne, stopping at Queenscliff on the Bellarine Peninsula, before setting off down the Great Ocean Road. (If you are starting from the Mornington Peninsula, you take the Sorrento-Queenscliff car and passenger ferry, which crosses Port Phillip Bay in 45 minutes.) The Great Ocean Road is one of the world's finest scenic drives, with stops at some irresistible beaches. Overnight in Lorne, beneath the Otway Ranges, then drive west to Port Campbell Marine National Park. Here you can view the 12 Apostles rock formations and stroll along the beach. Continue to Port Fairy for the night, making sure that you check out the wonderful Bay of Islands and Bay of Martyrs rock stacks (in the sea) along the way. On Day 4 wander along the banks of Port Fairy's Moyne River and amble around Griffiths Island. You can then drive northeast to the Goldfields center of Ballarat. That evening, explore the town's 19th-century streetscapes, then catch the sound-and-light show at Sovereign Hill. Spend the night here, and in the morning head to the wineries and spas around Daylesford and Hepburn Springs before returning to Melbourne.

GETTING HERE AND AROUND

The best way to explore Victoria is by car. The state's road system is excellent, with clearly marked highways linking the Great Ocean Road to the Mornington Peninsula and Wilson's Promontory, the Yarra Valley, and the Murray River region. Distances are not as extreme as in other states. Many scenic places (Bendigo, Ballarat, Beechworth, and Echuca, for instance) are less than three hours from Melbourne; the vineyards of the Yarra Valley and the Mornington Peninsula are an easy 90-minute drive. Buses and trains, which cost less but take more time, also run between most regional centers.

RESTAURANTS

Chefs in Victoria take pride in their trendsetting preparations of fresh local produce. International flavors are found in both casual and upscale spots: some of the best bargains can be found in local cafés, and several of the state's top restaurants are located in small country towns. On Sundays, be sure to join in the Victorian tradition of an all-day "brekky."

HOTELS

Lodgings in Victoria include grand country hotels, simple roadside motels, secluded bushland or seaside cabins, friendly bed-and-breakfasts, backpacker hostels, and "glamping" (glamorous camping). Although you don't find many sprawling resorts in this state, most of the grand old mansions and country homes have air-conditioning, home-cooked meals, and free parking. Rates are usually reduced after school and national holidays. The state government's tourism board (⊕ www.visitvictoria.com) has a list of Victoria's's accommodations to help you plan. *Hotel reviews have been shortened. For full information, visit Fodors.com.*

What It Costs in Australian Dollars

	$	$$	$$$	$$$$
RESTAURANTS				
	under A$21	A$21–A$35	A$36–A$50	over A$50
HOTELS				
	under A$151	A$151–A$200	A$201–A$300	over A$300

Yarra Valley and Healesville

65 km (40 miles) northeast of Melbourne.

★ The Yarra Valley spreads eastward from Melbourne's suburban fringe, and is a popular area with both locals and international visitors. Because Melburnians often use the valley for weekend breaks, the best time to visit is on working weekdays when the crowds are thinner. The small, attractive towns are dotted with good cafés, restaurants, and shops; in the rolling countryside between them you'll find numerous fine wineries that have excellent restaurants with impressive food and views.

Healesville is a good base for travel to Yarra Valley wineries and the Dandenongs region, as it's an easy drive from both. This pleasant town with a tree-shaded main street is also home to the Healesville Sanctuary, an open-plan zoo that showcases all manner of Australian native wildlife. Two popular areas within Yarra Ranges National Park—Badger Weir

Walk and Maroondah Reservoir—are ideal for bushwalking and picnics.

GETTING HERE AND AROUND

Healesville, on the eastern side of the Yarra Valley, is 65 km (40 miles) from Melbourne. Take the Eastern Freeway (M3) from Melbourne to its junction with the Maroondah Highway (B360) and follow the signs to Lilydale and on to Healesville. Trains, operated by Metro, travel from central Melbourne to Lilydale, and McKenzie's buses connect Lilydale with Yarra Glen and Healesville via Route 685. It's advisable to have a car to explore the wineries, or take a half- or full-day tour. Most tours will pick you up at your hotel.

CONTACTS McKenzie's Tourist Services. ☎ 03/5962–5088 ⊕ www.mckenzies. com.au. **Metro.** ☎ 1800/800007 ⊕ www. ptv.vic.gov.au.

TOURS

Several companies operate winery tours from Melbourne or the Yarra Valley itself. Tours generally include visits to four to five wineries and lunch.

Swans on Doongalla Horse Drawn Carriages

SPECIAL-INTEREST | Daily from 11 to 4, visit four wineries in horse-drawn carriages along St. Huberts Road for a minimum of four people. A light lunch is served at Yering Farm winery. The meeting place is St. Huberts Winery. ☎ 03/9762–1910, 0419/877093 ⊕ www.swansondoongalla. com.au ⊠ From A$150.

Wine Tours Victoria

SPECIAL-INTEREST | These full-day tours depart from Melbourne to visit four to five wineries in either the Yarra Valley, Mornington Peninsula, Mt. Macedon, or Bellaraine Peninsula wine regions. Includes a two-course lunch with wine at one of the cellar doors. ☎ 03/5428–8500, 1800/946386 toll-free in Australia ⊕ www.winetours.com.au ⊠ From A$180.

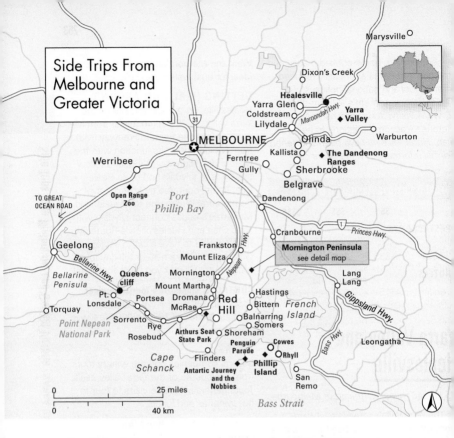

Side Trips From Melbourne and Greater Victoria

Yarra Valley Railway

TRAIN TOURS | Rail enthusiasts can still enjoy the tracks even though regular passenger train services to Healesville ceased in 1980. You can travel along part of the track in railmotors (all-in-one motor and carriage) operated by the Yarra Valley Railway. The railmotors travel from Healesville through picturesque country, over Watts River, under bridges, and through the historic Tarrawarra brick tunnel and back again—a round trip of about 8 km (5 miles) that takes about 45 minutes. Trains depart every hour, on the hour, 10–4 Sundays and public holidays, with extra services in school holidays. ✉ *Healesville-Kinglake Rd., Healesville* ☎ *03/5962–2490 reservations* ⊕ *www. yvr.com.au* ✇ *From A$18.*

Yarra Valley Transfers

PERSONAL GUIDES | Design your own bespoke cellar door tour with this company, which also offers airport transfers and tours to other Victorian wine regions ☎ *1800/146706* ⊕ *www.yarravalleytransfers.com.au* ✇ *Day tours from A$250.*

Zoobus

BUS TOURS | The Zoobus runs a daily return bus service from Melbourne city center to Healseville Sanctuary. It also sells bus and entry ticket packages, and offers private tour guides. ☎ *0455/054545* ⊕ *www.zoobus.com.au* ✇ *Fares from A$43.*

VISITOR INFORMATION

CONTACTS Yarra Valley Visitor Information ☎ *03/8739–8000* ⊕ *www.visityarravalley.com.au.*

Sights

The Yarra Valley is known for its wonderful produce—fruit, vegetables, herbs, bread, and cheeses—on sale at the monthly regional farmers' markets, including one at Yering Station (see listing below).

De Bortoli

WINERY/DISTILLERY | A family winery for three generations, De Bortoli was established (in New South Wales) in 1928, four years after the founder Vittorio De Bortoli and his wife Giuseppina migrated to Australia from northern Italy. Today, this Yarra Valley winery specializes in Chardonnay, Pinot Noir, and Riesling, along with a changing array of less-famous wines including Gamays, Pinot Blanc, and Sangiovese. Wine tastings cost A$5, which includes the famous Noble One, De Bortoli's most awarded wine since its release in 1982. The restaurant, which has stunning views of the surrounding vines, landscaped gardens, and mountains, serves Northern Italian dishes using Yarra Valley produce; on Saturdays the fixed-price two-course lunch is A$60 a head and the three-course option on weekends is A$75. The on-site cheese shop also matures and stocks artisan cheeses, which they will happily match with their wines. Trophy Room cheese and wine tastings for a minimum of four people include De Bertoli classics and cost A$32.50 a person. ⊠ 58 Pinnacle La., Dixon's Creek ☎ 03/5965–2271 ⊕ www.debortoliyarra.com.au.

★ Domaine Chandon

WINERY/DISTILLERY | Established by French Champagne house Moet et Chandon, this vineyard has one of the most spectacular settings in the Yarra Valley; its Chandon tasting bar has enormous floor-to-ceiling windows providing fantastic views over the vineyards and the Yarra Ranges. Apart from sparkling wines, the winery produces Shiraz, Pinot Noir, Meunier, and Chardonnay. Take

---

Wine and Song

Catch a little jazz at lunch or spend the whole day watching great performances by local and international headline acts. From opera to rock, Victoria's wineries provide an array of entertainment for music connoisseurs in summer, so check out the events with local tourist offices. Make sure you book early for the popular Day on the Green concert series held at Rochford Wines in the Yarra Valley, Mt. Duneed Estate near Geelong, All Saints Winery in Rutherglen, and Mitchelton Wines in Nagambie. ⊕ www.adayonthegreen.com.au

---

a free self-guided tour of the winery's history and production methods from 10:30 to 4:30 daily, or sign up for a A$125 wine discovery class on Sunday with a maximum of 12 people (bookings essential) to get a closer look at wine appreciation. Charcuterie boards, tapas, and mains (A$11–A$40) are served in the Restaurant from noon–4 daily, and in the more casual Lounge Bar 11–4 daily. Each dish has a recommended accompanying wine (from A$11 a glass), or choose the two-course set lunch with wine (A$65, minimum two people). Selections include panfried snapper, pipis, and sea vegetables with the 2014 Chandon Yarra Valley Curvée. ⊠ 727 Maroondah Hwy., Coldstream ☎ 03/9738–9200 ⊕ www.chandon.com.au.

Healesville Sanctuary

NATURE PRESERVE | **FAMILY** | Come face-to-face with wedge-tailed eagles, grumpy wombats, nimble sugar gliders, and shy platypuses at Healesville Sanctuary, a lovely, leafy, native wildlife sanctuary. Don't miss the twice-daily Spirits of the Sky show, during which raptors and parrots fly close overhead; and the daily Tales from Platypus Creek session, which features Australia's most unusual critter. You can pat a dingo or admire a koala on a Close-Up Encounter (A$20 extra), and for A$182 you can join a platypus in the water via the Wade with the Platypus option. Another highlight is the Land of Parrots aviary, where you can feed and interact with colorful birds. You can also view the animal hospital to see wildlife recovering from injury or illness. The Future Vets play space lets kids—and their parents—dress up as vets and role-play caring for animals. Take a break and refuel at the zoo's three cafés, including the largest, Sanctuary Harvest café, which serves full meals made with Yarra Valley's seasonal produce. ✉ *Badger Creek Rd., Healesville* ☎ *03/5957–2800, 1300/966784* 🌐 *www.zoo.org.au* 🎫 *A$37.*

Rochford Wines

WINERY/DISTILLERY | This winery occupies a striking-looking property; its cellar door building crafted almost entirely of glass overlooks the vineyards and rolling green paddocks. The family-owned winery produces renowned Pinot Noir and Chardonnay, and in recent years, has become the most happening place in the Yarra Valley—its huge amphitheater plays host to international and local performers during the annual A Day on the Green concert series (acts have included Alicia Keys and Elton John). The wine-tasting bar is open daily 9–5 and Isabella's restaurant serves French Mediterranean meals and light platters 11:30–4, seven days a week, and pizzeria 400 Gradi is open for lunch and dinner on weekends and lunch only on Monday. ✉ *878 Maroondah Hwy., Coldstream* ☎ *03/5957–3333* 🌐 *www.rochfordwines.com.au.*

Yering Station

WINERY/DISTILLERY | Victoria's first vineyard still has plenty of rustic charm, and it's a delightful place to eat, drink, and stay. An 1859 redbrick building is home to the busy cellar door, where you can taste its renowned Pinot Noirs and Shiraz Viogniers, or take a guided tasting, from A$10. The property's architectural and gastronomical pièce de résistance is the winery building, which houses the Wine Bar Restaurant ($$$). It's a sweeping, hand-hewn stone building with floor-to-ceiling windows overlooking spectacular valley scenery. Yering hosts an annual sculpture exhibition from October to December, and a farmers' market takes place on the third Sunday of the month. ✉ *38 Melba Hwy., Yarra Glen* ☎ *03/9730–0100* 🌐 *www.yering.com.*

🍴 Restaurants

Innocent Bystander

$$ | **PIZZA** | Despite the lofty modern steel and glass interior, this spacious contemporary restaurant in the town of Healesville has a warm, welcoming feel, and serves excellent food. It also hosts a winery's cellar door, along with a gourmet food shop and bakery. **Known for:** variety of pizzas; local wine and beer; reservations required on weekends. [$] *Average main: A$24* ✉ *316 Maroondah Hwy., Healesville* ☎ *03/5999–9222* 🌐 *www.innocentbystander.com.au.*

Stones of the Yarra Valley

$$$$ | **MODERN AUSTRALIAN** | Housed in an old weather-beaten barn that has been beautifully restored, Stones of the Yarra Valley is set amid vines and apple orchards and surrounded by century-old oak trees with views of the Yarra Ranges The Barn is a great place for weekend lunches (Saturday serves two courses for A$60 or three for A$75, Sunday's La Famiglia share table costs $75), and the Stables restaurant also serves weekend lunch and a five- or seven-course chef's tasting dinner on Friday and Saturday (A$95 or A$125). **Known for:** beautiful setting; weekend lunch; boutique guesthouse next door. [$] *Average main: A$60* ✉ *14 St. Huberts Rd., Coldstream* ☎ *03/8727–3000* 🌐 *stonesoftheyarravalley.com.*

Just a short drive from Melbourne is the captivating beauty of the Yarra Valley." —photo by lisargold, odors.com member

★ TarraWarra Estate

$$ | **AUSTRALIAN** | Turning off a country lane, TarraWarra Estate is a series of bold architectural statements: step through a hobbit-like door set into the green hills of its subterranean cellar door to taste the flagship chardonnays and Pinot Noir (open 11–5). Then wander between towering sculptures to the sunny restaurant for innovative Australian cuisine inspired by the bountiful kitchen gardens, set on the estate of nearly a thousand rolling acres of vines (serving noon–3). **Known for:** plant-based cuisines with a strong vegan focus; contemporary art, sculpture, and architecture. $ Average main: A$38 ⊠ 311 Healesville-Yarra Glen Rd., Healesville ☎ 03/5957–3510 ⊕ www. tarrawarra.com.au or www.twma.com.au ⊘ Closed Mon.

🛏 Hotels

Balgownie Estate Vineyard Resort and Spa

$$$ | **HOTEL** | This resort has it all—stylish suites and apartment-style accommodations overlooking the Yarra Valley and Dandenong Ranges, plus a ton of other amenities. **Pros:** excellent facilities; on-site cellar door; great day spa. **Cons:** holds conferences, so may get busy at times; service inconsistent; showing some wear and tear. $ Rooms from: A$320 ⊠ 1309 Melba Hwy., at Gulf Rd., Yarra Glen ☎ 03/9730–0700 ⊕ www. balgownieestate.com.au ➪ 15 rooms, 55 spa suites ◦◦ Free breakfast.

Chateau Yering

$$$$ | **HOTEL** | Once an 1860s homestead, whose grounds later became the Yarra Valley's first vineyard, this luxury hotel features opulent suites that have antique furniture and deep claw-foot or spa bathtubs. **Pros:** grand living; excellent dining options; beautiful setting and valley views. **Cons:** high tea is a little disappointing; needs some updates; service inconsistent. $ Rooms from: A$395 ⊠ 42 Melba Hwy., Yarra Glen ☎ 03/9237–3333, 1800/237333 ⊕ www.chateauyering.com. au ➪ 32 rooms ◦◦ Free breakfast.

Healesville Hotel

$ | **HOTEL** | This famous local lodge in a restored 1910 pub has seven colorful, modern upstairs rooms with high ceilings, tall windows, and genteel touches such as handmade soaps. **Pros:** funky accommodation; great food; historic hotel. **Cons:** limited facilities; shared bathrooms within the main building. [$] *Rooms from: A$130* ✉ *256 Maroondah Hwy., Healesville* ☎ *03/5962–4002* 🌐 *www.yarravalleyharvest.com.au* 🛏 *7 rooms, 1 house* 🍴 *No meals.*

Shopping

Four Pillars

WINE/SPIRITS | The bellwether of Australia's craft gin movement, Four Pillars' industrial-style distillery bustles with admirers: its Navy Strength Gin has won best its class at the world Gin Masters four years running. Pop in for a tasting paddle of gins and a light snack and watch the distillers at work behind a glass window, or go deeper with a tour of the distillery. Like what you taste? All its standard gins and limited-edition gins (such as the Christmas gin, available from November), as well as its preferred tonic waters, are available for purchase, along with stylish cookbooks and chic drinking paraphernalia. ✉ *2a Lilydale Rd., Healesville* ☎ *800/374446* 🌐 *www.fourpillarsgin.com.au.*

Yarra Valley Chocolaterie

FOOD/CANDY | **FAMILY** | Resident European chocolatiers create a vast array of high-quality treats in all shapes and styles—more than 300 of them, in fact—at this artisan chocolate and ice-cream maker. Many items include locally grown ingredients such as rosemary and lavender, and there's a bush tucker range of chocolates incorporating native plant products such as lemon myrtle, jindilli nut, and wattleseed. They even have a range of beauty products, if the adults want an excuse to smear chocolate-inspired goodness all over their faces. The Chocolaterie has year-round events including kids' chocolate-making classes. It also has outposts on the Mornington Peninsula and Great Ocean Road. ■ **TIP→ The on-site café ($) has a beautiful view over hilly green farmland and is a great place to eat chocolate and made-on-the-premises ice cream, and also serves light meals; we also suggest you buy a selection of chocolates to enjoy later.** ✉ *35 Old Healesville Rd., Yarra Glen* ☎ *03/9730–2777* 🌐 *www.yvci.com.au.*

Activities

There are plenty of opportunities to get out in the fresh air in the Yarra Valley. Those with cash to spare can go ballooning; others may just like to walk or ride a bike along the trails or play a round of golf. Wine tasting is a given.

BALLOONING

Global Ballooning

BALLOONING | This hot-air ballooning operation runs flights over the Yarra Valley. Take off at dawn and drift peacefully over the vineyards for an hour. For A$30 extra, enjoy a breakfast with sparkling wine after the flight at Balgownie Estate. Check the website for accommodation packages. ☎ *1800/627661* 🌐 *www.globalballooning.com.au* 🎟 *From A$405.*

BIKING

Yarra Valley Cycles

BICYCLING | Rent all types of bikes—including mountain, electric, road, and kids' bikes—and compulsory helmet from A$42 a day and Yarra Valley Cycles will steer you to the best cycling routes in the valley. It offers a one-way pickup service for an additional A$15 on the popular, (mostly) flat 38-km (24-mile) Warburton Rail Trail. ✉ *108 Main St., Lilydale* ✥ *Across road from Lilydale Railway Station* ☎ *03/9735–1483* 🌐 *www.yarravalleybikehire.com.*

BUSHWALKING

Yarra Ranges National Park

HIKING/WALKING | About 80 km (50 miles) east of Melbourne, this nearly 200,000-acre national park extending north of the Yarra River has plenty to keep your legs busy. Cross a 1,148-foot-long elevated walkway (known as the Rainforest Gallery) to see 400-year-old Mountain Ash and Myrtle Beech trees, trek all or a section of the 29-km (18-mile) O'Shannassy Aqueduct Trail, or climb the lookout tower at the peak of Mt. Donna Buang. Afterward, unpack lunch at one of several picnic areas, which can be reached by car. ⊠ *Yarra Ranges National Park* ☎ *13–1963, 03/8427–2002* ⊕ *www. parkweb.vic.gov.au.*

GOLF

Warburton Golf Club

GOLF | This gem of a course is hidden among the Yarra Ranges. For A$30 for 18 holes on weekends (A$24 on weekdays), you can golf over meandering streams and bushland blooming with wildflowers. Although it's a semiprivate club, visitors are very welcome to come and play 9 or 18 holes if they call and book in advance. Rental clubs are available (A$7) if you didn't pack your own. The course is hilly and golf carts can be hired for A$40. Warburton is 30 km (19 miles) southeast of Healesville. ⊠ *17 Dammans Rd., Warburton* ☎ *03/5966–2306* ⊕ *www.war-burtongolf.com.au* ⊠ *18 holes: weekdays A$24, weekends A$30; 9 holes: A$18/A$21* ⅄ *18 holes, 5925 yards, par 69.*

The Dandenong Ranges

Melburnians come to the beautiful Dandenong Ranges, also known simply as the Dandenongs, for a breath of fresh air, especially in fall when the deciduous trees turn golden and in spring when the public gardens explode into color with tulip, daffodil, azalea, and rhododendron blooms. At Mt. Dandenong, the highest point (2,077 feet), a scenic lookout known as SkyHigh Mt. Dandenong affords spectacular views over Melbourne and the bay beyond. Dandenong Ranges National Park, which encompasses five smaller parks, including Sherbrooke Forest and Ferntree Gully, has dozens of walking trails.

The many villages (which include Olinda, Sassafras, Kalorama, Sherbrooke, and Kallista) have curio shops, art galleries, food emporiums, cafés, and restaurants, and are dotted with lovely B&Bs. Visitors should be aware that the Dandenong Ranges and the high point of Mt. Dandenong are completely different from Dandenong, an outer suburb of Melbourne (30 km [19 miles] southeast of downtown and on the Pakenham railway line).

GETTING HERE AND AROUND

Motorists can either take the Yarra Valley route *(see above)*, turn off at Lilydale, and head south to Montrose and on to Olinda, or take the Eastern Freeway or M3 (a toll applies) and exit at the Ringwood Bypass (State Route 62), which becomes the Mt. Dandenong Road and on to Olinda. Trains travel from Flinders Street Station to Belgrave on the Belgrave line. This town is on the southern edge of the Dandenongs and is the home of the steam train called *Puffing Billy.* Other towns on the same railway line are Ferntree Gully and Upper Ferntree Gully.

Bus 688 runs from Upper Ferntree Gully Station through the trees to Sassafras and Olinda, then passes William Ricketts Sanctuary; while Bus 694 links Belgrave Station to the Mt. Dandenong Lookout, via the villages of Sherbrooke, Sassafras, and Olinda. Alternatively, take the train from Flinders Street Station to Croydon (on the Lilydale line), then take the 688 bus south to William Ricketts Sanctuary and Olinda.

TOURS

Gray Line

SPECIAL-INTEREST | This operator runs day tours to about a dozen destinations near Melbourne, including a half-day to the steam-powered Puffing Billy train, which can be combined with visits to wineries or Healesville Sanctuary. ⊠ *Federation Sq., Flinders St. at Russell St., City Center* ☎ *1300/858687* ⊕ *www.grayline. com.au* ⌨ *From A$101.*

Melbourne's Best Day Tours

SPECIAL-INTEREST | This tour company takes visitors to major sights in the region, including the 12 Apostles, Sovereign Hill, and Mt. Buller, among others. Combine a full-day visit to the penguin parade on Phillip Island with lunch at a winery. ⊠ *Federation Sq., Flinders St. at Russell St., City Center* ☎ *1300/130550* ⊕ *www.melbournetours.com.au* ⌨ *From A$110.*

VISITOR INFORMATION

Dandenong Ranges Information

Find brochures and maps, and get tips for places to see from its website or the information carousels at the major tourist sites. ⊠ *Upper Ferntree Gully* ☎ *03/8739–8000* ⊕ *www.visitdandenongranges. com.au.*

◉ Sights

Cloudehill Gardens & Nursery

GARDEN | These glorious gardens are divided into 25 "garden rooms" that include the Maple Court, the Azalea Steps, and century-year-old European beech trees. They were first established in the late 1890s as commercial and cut-flower gardens by the Woolrich family. The gardens are dotted with artworks by local artists and the Diggers Garden Shop hosts workshops, as well as selling plants and books. A central terraced area, with manicured hedges and a sculpture of a huge vase, is stunning, as is the view across the mountain ranges from the garden café. The café serves breakfast, lunch, and afternoon tea daily, with some ingredients coming from its own kitchen garden. A popular dish is the "Chatter Platter" for two, with a selection of cheeses, dips, garlic prawns, and salad (A$50). ⊠ *89 Olinda-Monbulk Rd., Olinda* ☎ *03/9751–1009* ⊕ *www. cloudehill.com.au* ⌨ *A$10.*

★ Dandenong Ranges Botanic Garden

GARDEN | The expansive gardens contain the largest collection of rhododendrons in the southern hemisphere, with around 15,000 rhododendrons, and thousands more azaleas and camellias; the garden's premier season is spring, when they put on a show of spectacular white, mauve, yellow, and pink blooms. Several miles of walking trails lead to vistas over the Yarra Valley, and the gardens are a short stroll from Olinda village. For a perfect afternoon, combine your visit with tea and scones in the park's garden's café or back down in the village. ⊠ *The Georgian Rd., Olinda* ☎ *13–1963* ⊕ *parks.vic.gov. au* ⌨ *Free.*

George Tindale Memorial Garden

GARDEN | Azaleas, camellias, and hydrangeas spill down the hillsides in this 6-acre, English-style garden. While at its most colorful in spring, when the flowers are in bloom, and in autumn, when the trees turn gold and yellow, it is also beautiful in winter with a touch of snow. It's located just 8 km (5 miles) north of Belgrave in the little forest settlement of Sherbrooke, where whipbird calls echo through the trees. ⊠ *33 Sherbrooke Rd., Sherbrook* ☎ *13–1963* ⊕ *parks.vic.gov.au* ⌨ *Free.*

Puffing Billy

TRANSPORTATION SITE (AIRPORT/BUS/FERRY/TRAIN) | FAMILY | This gleaming narrow-gauge steam train, based 46 km (28 miles) from Healesville in the town of Belgrave, runs on a line originally built in the early 1900s to open up the Dandenong Ranges to 20th-century pioneers. It's a great way to see the foothill landscapes. Daily trips between Belgrave and

All aboard the *Puffing Billy* steam train

Emerald Lake pass through picturesque forests and over spectacular wooden trestle bridges. The 13-km (8-mile) trip takes an hour; it's another hour if you continue to the historic town of Gembrook. There are also lunch and dinner trips, plus special music and children's events. ✉ *1 Old Monbulk Rd., Belgrave* ☎ *03/9757–0700* ⊕ *www.puffingbilly. com.au* ✉ *From A$36.*

SkyHigh Mount Dandenong
VIEWPOINT | **FAMILY** | This lookout at the top of Mt. Dandenong has breathtaking views over Melbourne to the Mornington Peninsula and Port Phillip Bay. You can picnic or barbecue on the grounds, eat at the bistro (breakfast, lunch and dinner), or stroll along the pleasant English Garden Walk while the kids get lost in the hedge maze (additional entry fee). Other fun attractions include a Wishing Tree and the Giant's Chair. Bistro open for breakfast, lunch, and dinner daily. On Sundays, book ahead for its popular roast lunch and afternoon teas. ✉ *26 Observatory Rd., Mt. Dandenong* ☎ *03/9751–0443*

⊕ *www.skyhighmtdandenong.com.au* ✉ *A$7 per car; maze A$6.*

★ William Ricketts Sanctuary
GARDEN | Fern gardens, moss-covered rocks, waterfalls, towering mountain ash, and 92 kiln-fired sculptures of Aborigines and Australian native animals fill this 4-acre property on Mt. Dandenong. William Ricketts, who established the sanctuary in the 1930s, meant it to stand as an embodiment of his philosophy: that people must act as custodians of the natural environment as Australia's Aborigines have for many millennia. Take an audio tour around the gardens (A$5) or download the podcast (free). ✉ *1402 Mt. Dandenong Tourist Rd., Mt. Dandenong* ☎ *13–1963 Parks Victoria* ⊕ *parkweb.vic. gov.au* ✉ *Free.*

🍴 Restaurants

Olinda has a handful of good restaurants and cafés, and many specialty boutique stores selling curios and gifts. It's a short drive from here to the Dandenong

Ranges Botanical Garden, Olinda Falls picnic grounds, Cloudehill Gardens, and various hiking trails.

Miss Marple's Tea Room

$ | **CAFÉ** | This determinedly old-fashioned and charming establishment is modeled after an English tea room and is renowned for its afternoon teas. Named after the famous Agatha Christie detective, this place is a holdout from the era when the Dandenong Ranges were visited by genteel folk looking for polite conversation over a civilized cup of tea. **Known for:** afternoon tea; long lines on weekends; scones with jam and cream. [$] *Average main: A$17* ✉ *382 Mt. Dandenong Tourist Rd., Sassafras* ☎ *03/9755–1610* 🌐 *www.missmarplestearoom.com.*

Ranges

$$ | **EUROPEAN** | This popular café-restaurant, right in the heart of Olinda, buzzes all day and is the perfect place for a snack or meal after browsing the adjacent curio shops or gardens. It's open daily for breakfast, lunch, and morning and afternoon tea. **Known for:** lively spot; daily savory pies; afternoon tea. [$] *Average main: A$25* ✉ *5 Olinda-Monbulk Rd., Olinda* ☎ *03/9751–2133* 🌐 *www.ranges.com.au* 🕒 *No dinner Sun. and Mon.*

Ripe Cafe

$$ | **AUSTRALIAN** | With crackling open fires in winter and a covered deck for summer grazing, this buzzy cottage café-cum-providore is the perfect place for a heart-warming casual lunch or afternoon tea. The menu changes daily, but may include baguettes, fish, or pasta, with a focus on vegan, vegetarian, and gluten-free choices. **Known for:** home-baked cakes; locally made relishes and condiments for sale; coffee and dessert only after 4 pm. [$] *Average main: A$22* ✉ *376 Mt. Dandenong Tourist Rd., Sassafras* ☎ *03/9755–2100* 🌐 *ripecafesassafras.com* 🕒 *No dinner.*

Hotels

Olinda is the main village in the Dandenong Ranges region and a good base for exploring the area. It's actually two villages (Lower and Upper Olinda, though Lower Olinda is better known by the name of the peak it sits beneath, Mt. Dandenong). The two are connected by Monash Avenue, along which you'll find a lot of the town's B&Bs and self-catering cottages.

Varra Ranges Getaways

$$$ | **RENTAL** | Curl up with a book in front of the open fire in a charming 1880s cottage, or take over a sprawling house on 10 acres of landscaped gardens—there are 28 properties in this group, ranging from one-bedroom cottages to a four-bedroom house. **Pros:** historic properties. **Cons:** two-night minimum stay on weekends. [$] *Rooms from: A$295* ✉ *361 Mt. Dandenong Tourist Rd., Sassafras* ☎ *03/9751–2464, 1300/488448* 🌐 *www.valleyrangesgetaways.com.au* 🛏 *28 cottages and houses* 🍴 *Free breakfast.*

Activities

HIKING

Dandenong Ranges National Park

HIKING/WALKING | Several reserves, including the Sherbrooke Forest—home to Sherbrooke Falls—make up this beautiful leafy and hilly national park. Trails include the Olinda Forest Trail (from Mt. Dandenong to Kallista), the Western Trail from the top of Mt. Dandenong to Ferntree Gully, the Sherbrooke Loop, and the Tourist Track from Sassafras to Emerald. Brochures and a trail map are available on the park's website. ✉ *Dandenong Ranges, Olinda* ☎ *13–1963* 🌐 *www.parks.vic.gov.au.*

Mornington Peninsula

The Mornington Peninsula circles the southeastern half of Port Phillip Bay. A much larger piece of land than it first appears, the peninsula is lapped by water on three sides, with 192 km (121 miles) of coastline, and measures about 65 km (40 miles) by 35 km (22 miles). Along the bay's coast is a string of seaside villages stretching from the larger towns of Frankston and Mornington to the summer holiday towns of Mount Martha, Rosebud, and Rye, with upmarket Sorrento and Portsea at its tip. On the Western Port Bay side, the smaller settlements of Flinders, Somers, and Hastings have quieter beaches without the crowds.

Together with Main Ridge and Merricks, Red Hill is one of the state's premium producers of cool-climate wines, particularly Pinot Noir and Chardonnay. The majority of the peninsula's 60 wineries are clustered around Red Hill and Red Hill South; however, there are another dozen or more dotted around areas farther north, including Moorooduc, Dromana, and Merricks. For an afternoon of fine wine, excellent seafood, and spectacular coastal views, plan a route that winds between vineyards. Red Hill has a busy produce-and-crafts market, which has been operating for decades and shows no signs of abating. It's held on the first Saturday morning of each month from September to May. A good website for getting all the lowdown on peninsula wineries is ⊕ *www.visitmorningtonvineyards.com.*

Sorrento is one of the region's prettiest beach towns and one of the most popular day-tripper spots on the peninsula. It's also the peninsula's oldest settlement, and thus is dotted with numerous historic buildings and National Trust sites (among them the Collins Settlement Historical Site, which marks the first settlement site at Sullivan Bay; and the Nepean Historical Society Museum, with its displays of Aboriginal artifacts and settlers' tools). In summer the town transforms from a sleepy seaside village into a hectic holiday hot spot. Sorrento Back Beach, with its rock pools and cliff-side trails, is one of the most popular hangouts.

Perfect Picnics 🍴

The Dandenongs are heaven for fresh-air freaks, flower fanatics, and foodies. Pick up some goodies at Olinda's Saturday morning market and work up an appetite taking the 2 km (1½-mile) loop walk to Sherbrooke Falls from O'Donohue Picnic Ground. Ask the tourist office about other great walks and picnic spots.

GETTING HERE AND AROUND

Renting a car in Melbourne is the most practical way of seeing the Mornington Peninsula. The simplest way is via the tolled M1 and M3 freeways, so you won't pass a single traffic light or roundabout on your way) until Frankston. From here, pick up the Mornington Peninsula Freeway (M11), which continues south to the various bay-side towns. Otherwise, and drive south along the Nepean Highway and at Frankston take the Frankston-Moorooduc Highway or stay on the Nepean Highway—eventually they both merge into the M11. A train runs from Flinders Street Station to Frankston. At Frankston, connect with a diesel-train service to towns on the east of the peninsula including Hastings, Bittern, Point Crib, and Stony Point. Buses also run from Frankston to the bay-side towns; the No. 781 bus goes to Mornington and Mount Martha and the No. 782 and 783 buses travel to Hastings and Flinders on the Western Port side.

Ferries run passenger services to Phillip Island and French Island from Stony Point, and a car and passenger ferry services Queenscliff and Sorrento. A shuttle bus runs from Melbourne Airport to Frankston and the Mornington Peninsula.

TRANSPORTATION

SkyBus - Peninsula Express

Ride from Melbourne Airport's Terminal 4 (T4) to Rosebud on the Mornington Peninsula with 16 stops along the bay including Frankston and Mordialloc train station. One-way fares range from A$22 to A$55. The buses have free Wi-Fi, no prebooking required. ☎ *1300/759287* ⊕ *www.skybus.com.au.*

Sorrento-Queenscliff Ferry

This car and passenger ferry crosses Port Phillip Bay, sailing between Sorrento (Mornington Peninsula) and Queenscliff (Bellarine Peninsula), departing every hour on the hour 7 am–6 pm, later in peak holiday season. One-way fares are A$12 (foot passenger), and a car costs from A$65, plus fares for any passengers. ☎ *03/5257–5400* ⊕ *www.searoad. com.au.*

Western Port Ferries

Cross from Stony Point (on the eastern side of the Mornington Peninsula) to Phillip Island and French Island and back again on this foot ferry (bicycles permitted A$4 extra, one-way). Parking is available, and trains run to the Stony Point terminus. An adult one-way ferry fare is A$13. ☎ *03/5257–4565* ⊕ *www. westernportferries.com.au.*

WINERY TOURS

Amour of the Grape

SPECIAL-INTEREST | Choose a personal tour to create your own itinerary or a set winery tour for groups of two to seven passengers. A day's outing includes tastings at four or five preselected cellar doors, and a gourmet lunch and a glass of wine at a boutique winery café. Golf tours and spa packages are also available. ☎ *0414/704801* ⊕ *www.*

amourofthegrape.com.au ✉ *A$160 per person Mornington Peninsula pickup; central Melbourne pickup A$275 per person (for 2 people).*

VISITOR INFORMATION

Mornington Peninsula Visitor Information Centre

Besides brochures and travel advice, you can book accommodation and some tours from the center. ✉ *359B Point Nepean Rd., Dromana* ☎ *03/5950–1579, 1800/804009 toll-free* ⊕ *www.visitmorningtonpeninsula.org.*

◉ Sights

Arthurs Seat State Park

NATIONAL/STATE PARK | FAMILY | Sweeping views of the surrounding countryside can be seen from this park, taking in Port Phillip Bay, Port Phillip Heads, and—on a clear day—the city skyline, the You Yangs, and Mt. Macedon. The mountain, which gives Arthurs Seat State Park its name, is the highest point on the Mornington Peninsula and named after Arthurs Seat in Edinburgh. A marked scenic drive snakes its way up to the summit, and walking tracks meander through the park's stands of eucalyptus. Seawinds, a public garden established by a local gardener in the 1940s, also forms part of the park and is a 10-minute walk or about 500 yards away. The road from Mornington is open at all times, so you can enjoy the spectacular mountaintop view by day or at night to see the lights. ✉ *Arthurs Seat Rd., Arthur's Seat* ☎ *13–1963* ⊕ *www. parks.vic.gov.au* ✉ *Free.*

★ Arthur's Seat Eagle

SCENIC DRIVE | FAMILY | There's been a chairlift climbing up to Arthur's Seat since 1960, now the new Eagle's gondolas take 14 minutes to drift slowly above the eucalyptus forests up to Arthur's Seat, at 314 meters (1,030 feet) above sea level. The gondolas are surprisingly quiet, so you'll hear the birdcall among the trees: keep an eye out for the wedge-tailed eagle, after which the Eagle chairlift is named. You can travel one way or return, starting from either the base station, or down from the summit station at Arthur's Seat. It's not a mountain, but the peak affords magnificent views back to Melbourne and across Port Phillip Bay. Take coffee or lunch at the café at the top before your return journey. There is plenty of parking at the base, as well as a small café, but limited parking at the peak, and the entire facility is wheelchair-friend-ly. From the summit, take the 1.8-km (1.1-mile) circuit walk, which passes several scenic viewing points. ⊠ *Base station, 1085 Arthurs Seat Rd., Dromana* ☎ *03/5978–0600* ⊕ *www.aseagle.com.au* ⊠ *From $18.*

Crittenden Estate

WINERY/DISTILLERY | One of the region's most picturesque wineries with a lovely lakeside setting, Crittenden Estate produces Chardonnay, Pinot Noir, Pinot Grigio, and some Spanish and Italian styles. The flagship Crittenden Estate Pinot Noir and Chardonnay are made from vines that are among the oldest on the peninsula. The cellar door is open for tastings daily, and winery tours can be arranged by appointment. The restaurant, Stillwater at Crittenden ($$$), is lovely year-round, and when the weather is fine, diners sit out on a terrace under shady umbrellas while enjoying views over the lake. It is open weekends for dinner and daily for lunch, except in winter when it closes Monday and Tuesday. Want to lin-ger awhile? The estate has three stylish overwater bungalows, a minute's amble along the lake's edge from the cellar door and restaurant. ⊠ *25 Harrisons Rd., Dromana* ☎ *03/5981–9555 restaurant, 03/5987–3800 cellar door, 0400/339995 accommodations* ⊕ *www.crittenden-wines.com.au or www.lakesidevillas. com.au.*

★ Point Leo Estate

ART GALLERIES—ARTS | The once private estate of one of the wealthiest men in Australia, Point Leo Estate opened to the public in late 2017 with a fine dining restaurant and winery experience set against dramatic coastal views and enhanced by an ambitious collection of more than 50 large-scale contemporary international and local works dotted along winding paths. Download the audio walk app from Point Leo's website before you visit and plan to spend an entire afternoon exploring. If all that sculpture gets you thirsty, take a break for a wine tasting at the cellar door (or take a glass on your walk). If you can plan ahead, make a reservation at Laura, considered Victoria's top restaurant, or at the bistro next door, Pt. Leo Estate Dining Room. ⊠ *3649 Frankston-Flinders Rd., Merricks* ☎ *03/5989–9011* ⊕ *www.ptleoestate. com.au* ⊠ *$16 for wine tasting and sculpture park entry.*

Red Hill Estate

WINERY/DISTILLERY | This winery, which has won numerous medals for its Chardonnay, Pinot Noir, and Shiraz, has an equally impressive view. Not only are there sweeping vistas over the 23-acre vineyard, but the magnificent waters of Western Port are spread out in the distance. On clear days you can see as far as Phillip Island as you wander around the gardens. The award-winning cuisine and fabulous floor-to-ceiling windows make **Max's Restaurant** (*$$$; No dinner Sunday–Thursday*) the perfect place to while away at least half the day. Order from the à la carte menu (mains A$42) or its three-course lunches, A$80, or A$105 with matching wines for each course, available daily. Dinner is served on Friday and Saturday nights. You can also book a room in the rustic Max's Retreat (from A$220 a night). Although it may be a little chilly, winter is a good time to visit, as several events are staged, including art shows and the region's Winter Wine Weekend in June. ⊠ *53 Shoreham Rd., Red Hill South* ☎ *03/5989–2838 cellar door, 03/5931–0177 restaurant* ⊕ *www.*

Continued on page 274

6

Side Trips from Melbourne and Greater Victoria   **MORNINGTON PENINSULA**

In recent decades Australia has emerged as an international wine powerhouse. The country's varied climate has proven favorable for growing high-quality grapes, and winemakers now produce some of the world's best Shiraz (Syrah) wines, as well as acclaimed Pinot Noirs and Rieslings. Wine sales currently contribute about $5.5 billion to the country's economy, and Australia is the third largest supplier to the United States behind France and Italy.

Touring wineries here is easy, as most properties have tasting rooms with regular hours. Whether you're sipping in situ at a winery or tasting wines at a shop in Sydney, here's how to get the most from your wine experience.

By Erica Watson

(top) Pinot noir grapes (right) Vineyard in One Tree Hill, South Australia

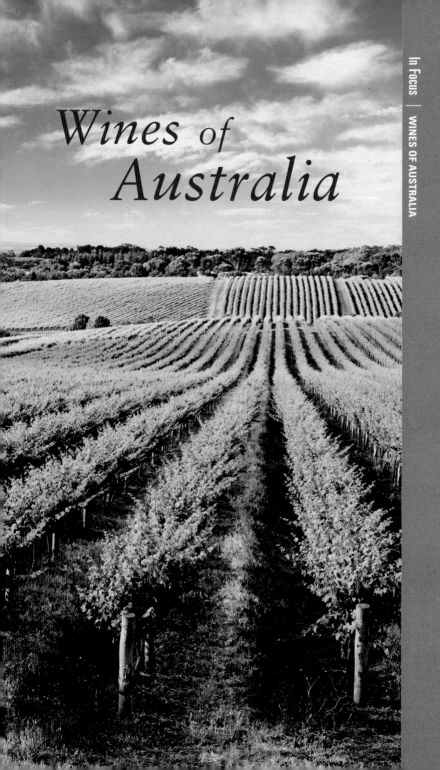

Wines of *Australia*

WINE TRENDS: THEN AND NOW

(top left) Wine bottles await labels, (bottom left) Hunter Valley vista, (right) tasting in Barossa Valley

Although the first grapes in Australia arrived with British settlers in 1787, it really wasn't until the mid 1960s that a more refined tradition of wine making began to take hold. Prior to 1960, Australia's wine repertoire extended little beyond sherry and port, but after WWII, an influx of European immigrants, notably from Germany and Italy, opened the country's eyes to new tastes and production methods.

Australia now produces many classic varietals at prices from A$10 to A$40,000 (for a 1951 Penfolds Grange Hermitage, made by Australian pioneer Max Schubert). There are more than 60 wine regions dotted across the country and many of the smaller producers in lesser-known areas are beginning to flourish.

Although the industry has experienced rapid growth, it hasn't been without its problems. The health of the global economy, international competition, global warming, disease, drought, and bushfire have each presented challenges along the way.

These days, Australian vintners are known for combining old traditions with new ideas and technical innovations. While oak barrels are still widely used, stainless steel and plastic tanks are now recognized as suitable fermentation and storage methods. Screw caps, introduced more than a decade ago, are becoming more popular with winemakers and consumers.

The industry's latest trends also include a growing interest in environmental sustainability, with organic and biodynamic wines appearing from numerous producers. The internet has revolutionized business, giving even the smallest vintners access to an international stage.

Like well-cellared wine, the palate of modern Australia is continually maturing. Whether your taste is for robust reds from Coonawarra and Barossa or the delicate and versatile whites of the Hunter Valley and Margaret River, Australia's winemakers are producing beautiful wines perfect to enjoy now or later.

AUSTRALIA'S DOMINANT VARIETALS

REDS

SHIRAZ

Australia's classic varietal. A full-bodied wine that, in hot areas, makes an earthy expression with softer acidity. Cooler regions produce a leaner, peppery style.

CABERNET SAUVIGNON

Dark red with blackcurrant and black cherry flavors, often with firm tannins and more acidity than Shiraz.

MERLOT

Intensely purple colored, full-bodied wine characterized by moderate tannins, aromas of plum, and a velvety mouth-feel.

PINOT NOIR

Lighter-bodied with gentle tannins and fruity aromas of red berries.

WHITES

CHARDONNAY

Full-bodied wine that is often high in alcohol and low in acidity. Most Australian versions are oaked.

RIESLING

Lighter-bodied wines with citrus and honey notes. Most are unoaked and dry or slightly off-dry.

SAUVIGNON BLANC

Makes crisp, dry wines with high acid and aromas of peach and lime.

SEMILLON

Light-bodied wines that have crisp acidity and complex flavors, including herbs, nuts, and honey.

WHITE BLENDS

Chardonnay-Semillon and Sauvignon Blanc-Semillon blends are popular. Semillon adds bright notes.

WINE TOURING TIPS

Large vintners like Rosemount, McGuigan Wines, Jacobs Creek, Yalumba, and Wolf Blass are well equipped for visitors and many offer vineyard tours, as well as restaurants or cafes. Some require appointments.

Many boutique producers also have "cellar doors,"

a.k.a. tasting rooms, open seven days a week, but it is advisable to check their websites for details. The average tastings cost around A$10 to A$15 for a flight of up to five different styles. Some include cheese, cracker, and fruit plates.

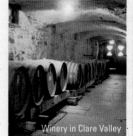
Winery in Clare Valley

AUSSIE WINE REGIONS

SOUTH AUSTRALIA

Barossa Valley

❶ BAROSSA VALLEY

The country's best-known wine region, Barossa Valley has more than 550 grape growers, including some fifth- and sixth-generation families. Shiraz is highly celebrated, particularly the lauded Penfolds Grange. Cabernet Sauvignon, Grenache, Merlot, Riesling, Semillon, and Chardonnay are all well suited to Barossa's temperate climate, which is slightly cooler on its peaks and in neighboring Eden Valley. Big producers Jacobs Creek and Wolf Blass both have visitors centers with modern tasting rooms and restaurants. For a history lesson, take a tour at Langmeil Winery. An impressive property is Yalumba, with a stone winery and clock tower. So, too, is the well-established Peter Lehmann Estate on the banks of the North Para River.

❷ ADELAIDE HILLS

For world-class Chardonnays, Sauvignon Blancs, Rieslings, and sparkling wines, look to the Adelaide Hills. Just 25 minutes from the center of Adelaide, this high-altitude region, amid Mount Lofty and down through the Piccadilly Valley, has nurtured elegantly refined white wines. The cooler climate also means that it's one of South Australia's leading producers of the temperamental Pinot Noir. There are about 25 cellars that offer tastings, including Petaluma Cellar, well known for its sparkling wines, Rieslings, and Chardonnays as well as its modern Bridgewater Mill restaurant. To try Italian varietals, head to Chain of Ponds. For excellent Sauvignon Blanc, stop into Shaw and Smith's 46-hectare estate.

Adelaide Hills

❸ MCLAREN VALE

Situated in the Fleurieu Peninsula region, McLaren Vale is an easy 40-minute trip south of Adelaide. Uniquely located by the coast, it's regarded as one of the more unpretentious regions thanks to laid-back beach lifestyle, passionate vintners, and family-owned wineries. This fusion of ideals, together with its warm climate, has most likely sparked its interest in experimenting with more exotic varieties such as Tempranillo, Zinfandel, and Mourvedre, as well as Viognier and Sangiovese. There are more than 60 cellar tasting rooms, ranging from the large producers such as Rosemount Estate and Tintara Winery to boutique producers such as Wirra Wirra, D'Arenberg, and Gemtree, each offering sales and wine flights that include the chance to sample local foods.

Hunter Valley

4 LIMESTONE COAST

Coonawarra's long ripening season coupled with the region's "terra rossa" soil atop rich limestone beds is responsible for some of Australia's most famed wines, notably full-bodied reds. Often described as the Bordeaux of Australia, Coonawarra is a top spot for Cabernet Sauvignon, Cabernet blends, and spicy Shiraz. And they don't come any better than at places like Penley, Katnook Estate, Holick, and Wynns Coonawarra Estate. Sixty kilometers to the north is Padthaway. While reds still prevail, the region's slightly warmer climate produces fruity Chardonnay and enjoyable Sauvignon Blanc, Verdelho, and Riesling. Built from limestone in 1882, the historic Padthaway Estate provides the perfect backdrop to sample some of the region's finest. Stonehaven and Henry's Drive are also worth a visit.

VICTORIA
5 YARRA VALLEY

Close proximity to Melbourne makes the Yarra an easy choice if your touring time is limited. A cool climate and diverse mix of volcanic and clay soils have allowed Chardonnay and Pinot Noir to flourish. Other notable varieties here include Viognier, Gewürztraminer, Pinot Gris, and Sauvignon Blanc, as well as Malbec, Sangiovese, and Nebbiolo. Sparkling wine is also a winner and Domaine Chandon is a magnificent spot to enjoy some perfect bubbly. For a laidback experience, Lillydale is also a good choice. But upping the style stakes is the magnificent Yering Station with its modern Australian restaurant and gallery space. Elsewhere, De Bortoli sells delicious top-end wines.

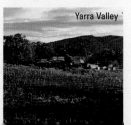

Yarra Valley

NEW SOUTH WALES
6 HUNTER VALLEY

Despite being a producer of award-winning Chardonnay, Verdelho, and Shiraz, it's the honeyed Semillon, which can mature for up to two decades, that Hunter Valley does best. Split into upper and lower regions, it has more that 150 years of winemaking up its sleeve and 120 cellar doors. It's safe to say the Hunter knows how to entertain. From large-scale music concerts at Bimbadgen Estate and Tempus Two to the annual Jazz in the Vines event and other small food and wine festivals year-round, the region is constantly buzzing. Pokolbin, Broke, Wollombi, Lovedale, Rothbury and Mt View are the main areas to sample the regions best offerings. Autumn is an excellent time to visit.

AUSSIE WINE REGIONS

Margaret River

WESTERN AUSTRALIA

7 MARGARET RIVER REGION With the first vines planted in 1967, Margaret River might be one of the country's younger wine areas but that hasn't stopped it from producing exception-ally high quality vintages. Cool breezes from the Indian Ocean and a steady, Mediterranean-style climate offer perfect conditions for developing complex styles of Chardonnay and minty-toned Cabernet Sauvignons. Shiraz, Merlot, Semillon, Sauvignon Blanc, and Chenin Blanc also thrive. Although the area produces about 20% of Australia's premium wines, it only accounts for about 3% of the nation's grapes. Try the West Australian Marron—or crayfish—with a crisp glass of Leeuwin Estate chardonnay. Cape Mentelle and Evans & Tate are also among the region's highlights, with many of their special releases sold only through their cellar doors.

READING THE LABEL

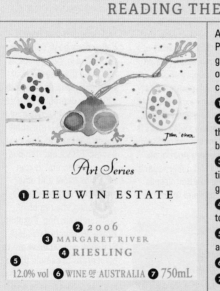

Art Series

1 LEEUWIN ESTATE

2 2006
3 MARGARET RIVER
4 RIESLING
5
12.0% vol **6** WINE OF AUSTRALIA **7** 750mL

According to Australia's Label Integrity Program, when a wine label states re-gion, grape variety, or vintage, then 85% of the wine contained in the bottle must come from that region, variety, or vintage.

1 The producer of the wine.

2 The vintage year, meaning the year the grapes were picked, crushed, and bottled.

3 Australian GIs, or Geographic Indica-tions, identify the region where the wine grapes were grown.

4 The varietal, or type of grapes used to make the wine.

5 The wine in this bottle contains 12% alcohol content by volume.

6 The wine's country of origin.

7 The volume of wine in the bottle.

MORE TASTING OPPORTUNITIES

Wine tasting at Mitchell Winery, Clare Valley

SIPPING IN SHOPS AND BARS

Even when you're not ensconced in the country's lush vineyards, high-quality wine isn't far away. The capital cities serve as a gateway for many of the wine country's top tastes.

In Sydney, try wine bars like the **Ivy's Ash Street Cellar**, **Glass Brasserie** wine bar at the Hilton Hotel and the **Gazebo Wine Garden** in Elizabeth Bay. **The Australian Wine Centre** in Circular Quay offers private tastings (with prior notice) and the **Ultimo Wine Centre** has free tastings each Saturday.

Heading south, visit Melbourne's **Prince Wine Store** at one of its three locations. Or soak up the atmosphere at **The Melbourne Supper Club** or **Melbourne Wine Room**. The bar of the award-winning **Press Club** restaurant also has an excellent Australian and international selection.

Apothecary 1878 on Adelaide's Hindley Street and **The Wine Underground**, just a few blocks away, both have a cosmopolitan ambience. Smaller vineyards are well represented at the city's **East End Cellars**.

In Perth, wine and dine alfresco at **Must Winebar** in Highgate. And **Amphoras Bar** in West Perth also has a long list of the country's best wines by the glass and bottle. No visit would be complete without heading to East Fremantle's **Wine Store**, for regular tastings and an extensive range of bottles. It also has an online store.

WINE FESTIVALS

Festivals offer chance to interact with the winemakers as well as sample local produce, especially cheese, fruit, and seafood. **The Barossa Vintage Festival** is one of the largest and longest running wine events in South Australia. Held in April each year it has everything from rare wine auctions to family friendly events. Other notables are **Adelaide's Tasting Australia** (April), **Coonawarra After Dark Weekend** (April), and **McLaren Vale Sea and Vines Festival** (June). In Western Australia, the **Margaret River Gourmet Escape** (April) celebrates culinary and winemaking talents.

RESEARCH & PLANNING

A little planning will allow you to make the perfect choices when it comes to deciding which regions to visit and where to taste. The websites of Australia's tourism commissions are filled with helpful planning informations. Not only do they offer winery information but also options for tours, accommodation and other sights to see while in the area. These include ⊕ *www.visitvictoria.com*, ⊕ *www.southaustralia. com*, *www.winecountry. com.au*, ⊕ *www.westernaustralia.com*

Once on the ground, visitors centers such as the **Margaret River Wine Centre, Adelaide's National Wine Centre of Australia, and Hunter Valley Wine Country Tourism** can offer sound advice, especially on the best varietals and history of the regions.

Barossa Vintage Festival

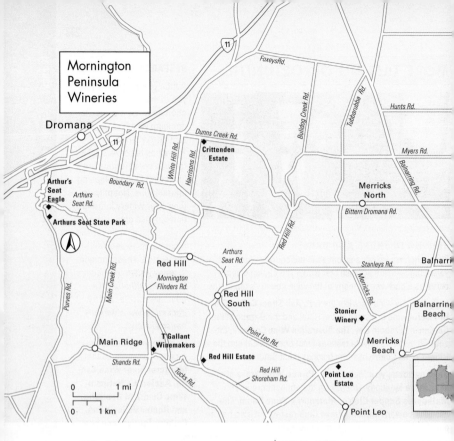

Mornington Peninsula Wineries

redhillestate.com.au or www.maxsrestaurant.com.au.

Stonier Winery

WINERY/DISTILLERY | This preeminent Mornington Peninsula producer of wines uses grapes from the region's oldest vines. The establishment specializes in Chardonnay and Pinot Noir (from vines first planted in 1978 and 1982, respectively) and also makes a sparkling Chardonnay & Pinot Noir. Although there's no restaurant, platters of local Red Hill cheeses accompany the daily tastings. If time permits, visitors may be invited on an informal tour of the fermentation and barrel rooms. Several events take place during the year, such as the dedicated Sparkling day in December. ⊠ *2 Thompsons La., Merricks* ☎ *03/5989–8300* ⊕ *www.stonier.com.au.*

★ T'Gallant Winemakers

WINERY/DISTILLERY | Home to the peninsula's first Pinot Grigio vines, this popular Italian-themed winery also contains a restaurant. T'Gallant produces excellent Pinot Noir, Prosecco, and Pinot Gris. If you're an art lover as well as an wine far you'll also admire the beautiful artwork on its bottle labels. The on-site pizza bar is always buzzing and the food is exceptional, with dishes made from local ingredients, including items from the house herb garden. Tuck into a signature Italian wood-fired pizza or a chocolate ganache brownie paired with its pink Moscato. Open seven days a week, there's live music every weekend at lunchtime. Their annual winter Mushrooms in May festiva is very popular and bookings are essential. ⊠ *1385 Mornington–Flinders Rd., Main Ridge* ☎ *03/5931–1300* ⊕ *www.tgallant.com.au.*

Be Amazed

Victorians do love their mazes, and you'll find these quaint English-garden features dotted around the Mornington Peninsula. There are topiary and sculptured mazes, mystery lawn puzzles, and big garden chess sets.

Ashcombe Maze & Lavender Gardens. Check out the world's first circular rose maze, a Cypress-hedge maze, a lavender labyrinth, and a "legendary" Great Gnome Hunt at this attraction, handily located east of T'Gallant Winery. Open 9–5 daily. ✉ *15 Shoreham Rd., Shoreham* ☎ *03/5989–8387* 🌐 *www.ashcombemaze.com.au* 🎟 *A$19.*

Enchanted Maze Garden. Find your way through a traditional hedge maze or test your navigational skills in the indoor 3-D maze at this delightful attraction. The property also has "tree surfing," in which participants make their way through an aboveground obstacle course and a 200-meter (655-foot) zipline. ✉ *55 Purves Rd., Arthur's Seat* ☎ *03/5981–8449* 🌐 *www.enchantedmaze.com.au* 🎟 *From A$30.*

Beaches

Rosebud Beach

BEACH—SIGHT | Backing onto the suburb of Rosebud, this popular beach has been rated one of the safest in Victoria. The white-sand flats extend a long way offshore and sand bars keep the area protected for swimming, while trees provide natural shade. The beach reserve includes a jetty (from which many locals fish), boat ramp, and camping ground. A picnic and barbecue area and adventure playground make the beach a hit with families, and the nearby Bay Trail walking and cycling track is popular. Accommodation around here tends to be motels and cottages for rent. **Amenities:** food and drink; lifeguards; parking (free); restrooms; showers. **Best for:** swimming; walking. ✉ *Point Nepean Rd., end of Jetty Rd., Rosebud.*

Restaurants

Cellar & Pantry

$ | **DELI** | Busy produce store-cum-deli, this is the perfect place to pick up the makings of a picnic lunch or a dinner in self-contained accommodation. It is packed full of crusty loaves, cured and fresh meats, fruits and vegetables, aromatic cheeses, olives, relishes and chutneys, and countless other goodies. **Known for:** picnic supplies; local wines and coffee; veranda seating. [$] *Average main: A$11* ✉ *141 Shoreham Rd., Red Hill South* ☎ *03/5989–2411* 🌐 *www.cellar-andpantry.com.au.*

★ Laura

$$$$ | **AUSTRALIAN** | Named for the Jaume Plensa sculpture of a girl's head, which is in full view of the best tables, this award-winning new restaurant sits at the heart of a $40-million-plus sculpture park and its set menus celebrate the peninsula's bounty: its dairy and vineyards, its farms and fish. The decor is calm and elegant with leather-wrapped tables and neutral, soothing shades that do not distract from the stunning setting, and the four-, five-, and six-course degustation menus are tight, creative, and special; the only stress is with the wait list for reservations. **Known for:** modern fine-dining; lion's mane mushrooms from a nearby Mornington farm; elegant setting and views. [$] *Average main: A$120* ✉ *3649 Frankston - Flinders Rd., Merricks*

☎ 03/5989–9011 ⊕ www.ptleoestate.
com.au.

★ **Montalto Vineyard & Olive Grove**
$$$ | **AUSTRALIAN** | Overlooking a vineyard
of rolling green hills, this restaurant has
an à la carte weekday menu, as well as
a five- or six-course tasting menu which
changes regularly, based on available
local produce. The wine list borrows from
the best of the estate's vintages, as well
as classic wines from other regions.
Known for: beautiful setting; picnic
hampers in summer; sculpture gardens
and bird-watching. $ Average main:
A$44 ✉ 33 Shoreham Rd., Red Hill South
☎ 03/5989–8412 ⊕ www.montalto.com.
au ☺ No dinner Sun.–Thurs.

🛏 Hotels

Hotel Sorrento
$$ | **HOTEL** | Built in 1871, this historic
hotel has attractive rooms with exposed
limestone walls, stylish interiors, and
water views. **Pros:** great location; impressive views from some rooms. $ Rooms
from: A$180 ✉ 15 Hotham Rd., Sorrento
☎ 03/5984–8000 ⊕ www.hotelsorrento.
com.au 🛏 31 rooms, 6 apartments ◯ No
meals.

★ **Lakeside Villas at Crittenden Estate**
$$$$ | **B&B/INN** | Wine and dine to your
heart's content, then amble home to a
stylish overwater bungalow on a tranquil
lake. **Pros:** beautiful setting; free wine
tastings; breakfast hamper with eggs,
bacon, and local museli. **Cons:** nearby
Stillwater Restaurant is open for dinner
only on Friday and Saturday; limited
availability. $ Rooms from: A$320 ✉ 25
Harrisons Rd., Dromana ☎ 03/5987–3275
⊕ www.lakesidevillas.com.au 🛏 3 villas
◯ Free breakfast.

★ **Lindenderry at Red Hill**
$$$$ | **HOTEL** | A stalwart of 30 years on the
peninsula, Lindenderry's recent multimillion-dollar makeover sees the boutique
hotel channel a stylish country house,
with generously sized rooms, each

Precious Resource 👁

Victoria has weathered major
droughts, and Australians are very
conscious about the probability of
another dry stretch. As a result,
signs are displayed in many places,
including hotels, suggesting water-
saving measures. Do as the locals do
and use water carefully wherever
you can.

with doors leading out to Mediterranean-style terraces or gardens overlooking
a landscape of Australian bushland and
manicured vines. **Pros:** beautiful setting
on 30-acre estate; spacious rooms with
a chic, muted palette; short walk to Red
Hill markets and other wineries. **Cons:** no
natural light in the bathrooms. $ Rooms
from: A$320 ✉ 142 Arthurs Seat Rd., Red
Hill South ☎ 03/5989–2933 ⊕ www.lanc-
emore.com.au/lindenderry 🛏 40 rooms
◯ Free breakfast.

🏃 Activities

DIVING AND SNORKELING
Bayplay Adventure Tours
DIVING/SNORKELING | This adventure tour
company runs a variety of activities,
including diving, snorkeling, bike riding,
and sea kayaking. You can explore colonies of weedy seadragons, dive through
an octopus's garden, or feel the wash
when dolphins leap over your kayak.
Dives start from A$68, while a three-hour
sea kayaking tour to a dolphin sanctuary
costs A$99 per person. ✉ 3755 Port
Nepean Rd., Portsea ☎ 03/5984–0888
⊕ www.bayplay.com.au.

HIKING
The Mornington Peninsula is a memorable walking destination. There are walks
for all levels of fitness and interest, from
cliff-top strolls to the ultimate 26-km

(16-mile) Two Bays Walking Track. Stop in at the visitor information center at Dromana or Sorrento to see what walking maps they have on hand, or contact Parks Victoria, the government body that manages the state's national parks.

Arthurs Seat State Park: There is a one-hour circuit walk to Kings Falls, otherwise the relaxing Seawinds Gardens walk is less than a mile in length and takes only about half an hour.

Bushrangers Bay Walk: An exhilarating 6-km (4-mile) return walk along Western Port begins at Cape Schanck Lighthouse and winds past basalt cliffs and Bushranger Bay, to finish at Main Creek.

Coppin's Track: A pleasant 3-km (2-mile) round-trip walk that stretches from Sorrento ocean beach (or Back Beach as it's known) to Jubilee Point along the Bass Strait coastline.

Two Bays Walking Track: A hardcore 26-km (16-mile) walking track that links Dromana, on Port Phillip Bay, with Cape Schanck on Western Port Bay.

Parks Victoria
HIKING/WALKING | This government agency manages all of Victoria's national parks. Its informative website includes park descriptions and trail maps that can be downloaded, as well as information on safety considerations, special events, and park attractions. ☎ 13–1963 ⊕ www. parks.vic.gov.au.

HORSEBACK RIDING
Ace-Hi Beach Rides
HORSEBACK RIDING | FAMILY | Catering to both beginners and experienced riders, Ace-Hi has horse and pony rides on weekends and during school holidays (which includes the December to January summer vacation). One-hour scenic rides traverse the 200-acre property, while the Forest and Bush'n'Beach rides go farther afield. Short and simple pony rides give the under-sixes some fun as well. ⊠ 810 Boneo Rd., Cape Schanck

☎ 03/5988–6262 ⊕ www.ace-hi.com.au ⊠ From A$79 per hr.

🛍 Shopping
SPAS
⭐ **Peninsula Hot Springs**
FITNESS/HEALTH CLUBS | Set among tranquil bushland, this fabulous bathing experience sees more than 20 natural thermal mineral water pools ranging from deliciously steamy to truly chilling plunge pools. Inspired by bathing traditions and rituals from around the world, you'll find Japanese bathing experiences, a Moroccan hammam, body clay painting, treatments using indigenous ingredients, and the Fire & Ice experience, which includes an ice cave and Deep Freeze going as low as –25 degrees, before getting toasty in the 50-degree wet and dry saunas. Some sections are family friendly, while the Spa Dreaming center and private bathing areas are for bathers over 16 years. Budget for a half day of dipping, perhaps enjoy a massage or facial in the private spa sanctuary, and lunch in the on-site café. Wildly popular on summer weekends, the best time to visit is midweek mornings. Winter bathing is a special experience, when mist and steam intermingle. Basic bathing packages start from A$25, and A$75 for private bathing experiences. ⊠ Springs La., Fingal, Mornington ☎ 03/5950–8777 ⊕ www.peninsulahotsprings.com.

Phillip Island

124 km (77 miles) southeast of Melbourne.

South of Melbourne and just off the Mornington Peninsula, Phillip Island has long been a playground for Victorians. Amid the striking coastal landscapes and bushland interior live more than 200 bird species, wallabies, and native flora. The perennial highlight, however, is the famous Penguin Parade, in which the little birds march ashore each evening to the delight of onlookers.

Take a walk along the extensive board-walks that cover the coastal cliffs, visit the blowhole, and view the silvergull rookery. Short-tailed shearwaters (also known as mutton birds) arrive on Phillip Island around the last week of September after a 12,000-km (7,450-mile) migration from the Aleutian Islands, near Alaska, where they'll return in April. Further out, Seal Rocks host Australia's largest colony of fur seals; up to 20,000 creatures bask on the rocky platforms and cavort in the water here year round. Boat tours cruise past these playful creatures.

GETTING HERE AND AROUND

To reach the island from Melbourne, take the Princes Freeway (M1) south-east to the South Gippsland Highway (M420), and follow this to the Bass Highway (A420). The bridge at San Remo crosses over to Phillip Island. V/Line runs combined train and bus service directly to Cowes, or a train to Stony Point on the Mornington Peninsula, where a daily passenger ferry runs to Phillip Island and French Island.

TRANSPORTATION
V/Line

This combination train and bus service goes from Southern Cross Station to Cowes (with change at Dandenong or Koo Wee Rup railway stations), a journey of 2½ to 3½ hours. You can also get the V/Line train from suburban Frankston to Stony Point, and take the ferry to Cowes. ☎ 1800/800007 ⊕ www.vline.com.au.

Western Port Ferries

Cross from Stony Point (on the eastern side of the Mornington Peninsula) to Phillip Island and French Island and back again on this foot ferry (bicycles permitted A$4 extra, one-way). Park for A$2 or get to the terminus via train. Parking is available, and trains from Melbourne run to the Stony Point terminus. An adult one-way ferry fare is A$13. ☎ 03/5257–4565 ⊕ www.westernportferries.com.au.

TOURS
Gray Line

GUIDED TOURS | This operator runs various day tours of the penguin parade, often combined with other sights, including Seal Rocks or Moonlit Sanctuary in the Yarra Valley. ☎ 1300/858687 ⊕ www.grayline.com.au ⌦ From A$143.

Melbourne's Best Day Tours

GUIDED TOURS | **FAMILY** | Take a day tour to see the penguin parade, or sign up for the full Phillip Island Wildlife and Penguin Experience, which includes pelican feeding and a visit to the Koala Conservation Centre. ☎ 1300/130550 ⊕ www.melbournetours.com.au ⌦ From A$125.

Wildlife Coast Cruises

SPECIAL-INTEREST | This operator runs two-hour cruises from Cowes Jetty to the Nobbies and Seal Rocks, spending 30–40 minutes viewing the seal colony. Full-day and half-day cruises run daily all year round, including a twilight bay cruise. Its whale-watching cruises run from June to November, and it also operates one-hour trips to Cape Woolamai. ✉ 13 The Esplanade, Cowes ☎ 1300/763739 ⊕ www.wildlifecoastcruises.com.au ⌦ From A$28.

VISITOR INFORMATION
Phillip Island Visitor Information Centre

Along with brochures and advice, the center has an accommodation booking service and sells tickets for attractions on the island, including the Penguin Parade, cruises, and local festivals and events. ✉ 895 Phillip Island Rd., Newhaven ☎ 1300/366422 ⊕ www.visitphillipisland.com.

Sights

Antarctic Journey and The Nobbies

NATURE PRESERVE | **FAMILY** | Phillip Island's marine wildlife attraction is just 3 km (1 mile) from the Penguin Parade, perched on the very edge of Point Grant on the island's far west end. It's an ultramodern interpretative center, with an interactive, multimedia Antarctic Journey, which includes a freezing "chill zone." Outside, a series of wooden boardwalks wind around the rocky headland to the nearby blowhole, with fantastic views of Nobbies headland and Seal Rocks beyond it. ✉ *1320 Ventnor Rd.* ☎ *03/5951–2800* ⊕ *www.penguins.org.au/attractions/the-nobbies* ⊟ *A$18.*

Cowes

TOWN | The seaside town of Cowes is the hub of Phillip Island; the pier is where you can board sightseeing cruises and the passenger ferry that travels across Western Port to French Island and Stony Point on the Mornington Peninsula. It has a lively café scene and several quality gift shops interspersed with the traditionally cheaper tourist fare. Restaurant and hotel bookings are essential in the busy summer months. ✉ *Cowes.*

Koala Conservation Centre

NATURE PRESERVE | **FAMILY** | At this excellent wildlife center you can stroll along treetop-high boardwalks and view koalas in their natural habitat. At the visitor center, learn some fascinating things about the cute furry creatures—such as how they sleep 21 hours a day. It is located just a short drive from the tourist information center at Newhaven; follow the signs along Phillip Island Tourist Road. ✉ *1810 Phillip Island Rd., Cowes* ☎ *03/5952–1610* ⊕ *www.penguins.org.au/attractions/koala-conservation-centre* ⊟ *A$13.*

★ Penguin Parade

ISLAND | **FAMILY** | Phillip Island's main draw is the nightly parade of little penguins, also called fairy penguins, waddling from the sea to their burrows in nearby dunes. The parade of miniature penguins attracts onlookers year-round and crowds on summer weekends and holidays. There are several ways to view the Penguin Parade: general admission,

with viewing from concrete bleachers; the Penguin Plus experience, which puts you on a smaller viewing platform that is closer to the action. There's even a small underground section to watch the penguins as they go to their nests. The Guided Ranger Tour puts you on the sand with a ranger, while the VIP Tour gets you into a private, elevated "Skybox" overlooking the beach. The Ultimate Adventure Tour, for private groups, includes headphones and night-vision equipment and a secluded spot on a separate beach. The spectacle begins at around sunset each night; booking ahead is essential in summer and during public holidays. Wear closed shoes and warm clothing—even in summer—and rain protection gear. Make sure to arrive an hour before the tour begins. ✉ *1019 Ventnor Rd.* ☎ *03/5951–2800* ⊕ *www.penguins.org.au* ⊟ *From A$27.*

Rhyll

TOWN | Quieter than Cowes, Rhyll is a charming fishing village on the eastern side of Phillip Island. You can rent a boat from the dock or take a sightseeing cruise from the pier. The local wetlands are full of resident and migratory birds, and a mangrove boardwalk leads to Conservation Hill and the Koala Conservation Centre. ✉ *Rhyll.*

🏖 Beaches

Cape Woolamai Surf Beach

BEACH—SIGHT | Phillip Island's only surf lifesaving club is based on this long, exposed stretch of prime surfing beach, recognised as a National Surfing Reserve. The hazardous 4.2-km (2.6-mile) beach has strong undertows, so it's for experienced surfers and swimmers only, and only between the safety flags when lifeguards are on patrol, from December to mid-April: check the surf lifesaving club's website for patrol times. Walkers can take in the views here on a ramble to The Pinnacles. The Woolamai Beach Road runs off Phillip Island Road and is 14 km (9 miles) from Cowes. The nearest accommodation is generally cottage-style; Black Dolphin has a luxury penthouse and a cottage on the Cape, on Corona Road. **Amenities**: food and drink; lifeguards; parking (free); restrooms; showers. **Best for:** surfing; swimming; walking. ✉ *Woolamai Beach Rd., Cape Woolamai* 🌐 *www.woolamaibeach.asn.au.*

Kitty Miller Bay

BEACH—SIGHT | Regarded as one of Australia's best beaches, this south-facing beach provides excellent swimming and snorkeling, and a walking trail to view the remains of the wreck of the SS *Speke* at low tide. Sheltered by Watts Point and Kennon Head, the curved beach has low waves, with undertows only appearing when the waves whip up at high tide, which is the best time for surfing. There's not much shade and no kiosk, so bring water, food, and sunscreen with you. The beach is at the intersection with Watts Road. From Cowes, go either via Ventnor Road to Back Beach Road, or via Phillip Island Road and Back Beach Road, turning onto Kitty Miller Road. The beach is around 10 km (6 miles) from Cowes. The low-key nature of Phillip Island and the remote nature of the beach means that accommodation is usually B&B-style. Try the Kitty Miller Bay B&B on Watts Road. **Amenities:** parking (free). **Best for:** snorkeling; surfing; swimming; walking. ✉ *Kitty Miller Rd.*

🍴 Restaurants

Harry's on the Esplanade

$$$ | **ECLECTIC** | Spilling onto an upstairs terrace above the main Cowes beach, Harry's is a Phillip Island institution. Its menu, which changes regularly, draws heavily on seafood bought fresh from local trawlers, along with locally raised beef and lamb. **Known for:** fresh seafood; Australian wines; homemade bread and pastries. [$] *Average main: A$38* ✉ *17 The Esplanade, upper level, Cowes* ☎ *03/5952–6226* 🌐 *www.harrysrestaurant.com.au* 🕒 *Closed Mon.*

🛏 Hotels

Glen Isla House

$$$ | **B&B/INN** | A beautiful, safe swimming beach is right at the doorstep of this luxurious B&B, which contains six individually themed rooms. **Pros:** gorgeous furnishings; on a pristine beach; short drive to penguins. **Cons:** the heritage style may be too traditional for some. [$] *Rooms from: A$255* ✉ *230 Church St., Cowes* ☎ *03/5952–1882* 🌐 *www.glenisla.com* 🔑 *6 rooms, 1 suite, 1 cottage* 🍽 *No meals.*

🏃 Activities

AUTO-RACING

Phillip Island Grand Prix Circuit

AUTO RACING | **FAMILY** | The island has had a long involvement with motor sports: the first Australian Grand Prix was run on its local, unpaved roads back in 1928, before a circuit was built in the 1950s. The track was completely redeveloped in the 1980s, and in 1989 hosted the first Australian Motorcycle Grand Prix. The circuit holds regular races as well as big-ticket events, such as the MotoGP in October and Superbike World Championships in February. Speed freaks can buckle up for hot laps in a racing car (from A$360 for three laps) driven by a professional driver year round (dates and times vary, see website), or drive a go-kart (A$35 for 10 minutes) around a scale replica of the actual track. There are 60-minute guided walking tours of the track daily at 2 pm (subject to availability), a 45-meter slot car Grand Prix Circuit replica racing track; and a museum showcasing the island's motor racing history. ✉ *Back Beach Rd.* ☎ *03/5952–9400* 🌐 *www.phillipislandcircuit.com.au* 🎫 *Tours A$25; museum A$18; slot cars A$8.*

HIKING

Walking Tracks on Phillip Island

HIKING/WALKING | Walking tracks and viewing platforms around Phillip Island have splendid views, with routes to suit all fitness levels. The Cape Woolamai trail at the island's eastern tip is a reminder of the island's volcanic past, and the Bush to Bay Trail can be broken down into sections. Churchill Island has several good walking tracks, and there are great views from the boardwalks around the Nobbies. For information on all the good walking trails, visit the Phillip Island Visitor Information Centre at Newhaven, the small town you encounter as you come across the bridge from the mainland. ✉ *Phillip Island Visitor Information Centre, 895 Phillip Island Rd., Newhaven.*

WATER SPORTS

Outthere Outdoor Activities

WATER SPORTS | These knowledgeable folk have been teaching people to surf, snorkel, kayak, and ride bodyboards for 15 years. Lessons are held on Phillip Island and Wilson's Promontory. A two-hour group surfing lesson costs from A$65 per person. There are also kayak and biking tours, guided bushwalks, and equipment for rent. Contact Outthere to confirm the meeting points. ✉ *Newhaven* ☎ *0412/852291* ⊕ *www.outthere.net.au.*

Queenscliff

103 km (64 miles) southwest of Melbourne.

In the late 19th century, Queenscliff, on the Bellarine Peninsula, was a favorite weekend destination for well-to-do Melburnians, who traveled by paddle steamer or train to stay at the area's grand hotels, some of which are still in business today. Be sure to check out Fort Queenscliff, another landmark from bygone days. Good restaurants and quiet charm are also traits of Queenscliff. The playground of families during the day and

En Route 👁

From Queenscliff, follow Great Ocean Road signs for 45 km (28 miles) to **Torquay,** Australia's premier surfing and windsurfing resort, and Bell's Beach, famous for its Easter surfing contests and its October international windsurfing competitions. The Great Ocean Road, a positively magnificent coastal drive, officially begins at Torquay. The seaside towns of Anglesea, Aireys Inlet, and Fairhaven are other good warm-weather swimming spots.

dog walkers come dusk, Queenscliff is a restful alternative to the resort towns of Sorrento and Portsea on the other side of the bay. At the end of November, the annual Queenscliff Music Festival (⊕ *www.qmf.net.au*) draws thousands of visitors to town.

GETTING HERE AND AROUND

The lovely coastal village of Queenscliff and nearby smaller sibling Point Lonsdale make for a worthy—and well-signposted—detour on the drive from Melbourne to the start of the Great Ocean Road.

It's about a 60- to 90-minute drive from Melbourne to Geelong via the Princes Freeway (M1), then to Queenscliff via the Bellarine Highway (B110). Trains run from Melbourne's Southern Cross Station to Geelong, where buses (Nos. 75 and 76) continue on to Queenscliff. The Queenscliff–Sorrento Ferry departs on the hour (in both directions) from 7 am to 6 pm and to 7 pm in the summer months. The journey takes 40 minutes and costs A$10 for pedestrians, A$69 for cars including two passengers in the high season.

It's easy to walk around Queenscliff's main attractions; ask at the visitor center in Hesse Street for maps.

TRANSPORTATION

Bellarine Railway

This narrow-gauge tourist train runs the 16 km (10 miles) between the towns of Queenscliff and Drysdale several times a week. On Saturday, and occasional Friday nights, between August and May, the popular Blues Train (🌐 *www.thebluestrain.com.au*) mixes dinner with live blues entertainment; tickets cost A$118 per person. For gourmands, the route becomes a moveable feast, with the restaurant train offering a four-hour fine dining journey with a six-course degustation during the first week of the month, as well as every second Thursday, on the Q Train (🌐 *www.theqtrain.com.au*). Tickets from $119 per person. ✉ *Queenscliff Railway Station, 20 Symonds St.* ☎ *03/5258–2069* 🌐 *bellarinerailway.com.au.*

Port Phillip Ferries

This passenger-only ferry service sails two return services daily between Docklands, in the heart of Melbourne city, to the town of Portarlington, on the northern side of the Bellarine Peninsula, 28 km (17 miles) from Geelong. (A$14.50 one-way.) ☎ *03/9514–8959* 🌐 *www.portphillipferries.com.au.*

Queenscliff–Sorrento Ferry

This car and passenger ferry travels between these two towns on opposite sides of the Port Phillip Bay, sailing between Sorrento (Mornington Peninsula) and Queenscliff (Bellarine Peninsula), departing every hour, on the hour from 7 to 6, later in peak holiday season. One-way adult fares are A$12 (foot passenger), and a car costs A$65 one-way, plus fares for any passengers. ✉ *Queenscliff* ☎ *03/5258–3244* 🌐 *www.searoad.com.au.*

V/Line

Catch a V/Line train to Geelong, and connect to a local bus to Queenscliff. ☎ *1800/800007* 🌐 *www.vline.com.au.*

Light Up Your Trip

There are seven historic lighthouses of varying shapes and sizes on the coast—from Point Lonsdale in the east to Portland in the west. Don't miss the tall red-capped white **Split Point Lighthouse** at Aireys Inlet, while **Cape Otway Lighthouse**, the oldest on mainland Australia, marks the point where the Southern Ocean and Bass Strait collide. Farther west at Portland is majestic **Cape Nelson Lighthouse.** Guided tours are available, and you can also arrange to sleep in a lighthouse.

VISITOR INFORMATION

Queenscliff Visitor Information Centre

Get tips and brochures from this center's staff, plus advice about finding local accommodations. ✉ *55 Hesse St.* ☎ *03/5258–4843, 1300/884843* 🌐 *www.queenscliff.com.au.*

Hotels

Vue Grand Hotel

$$$ | HOTEL | Built in 1881, this stylish hotel blends old-world elegance with modern touches in its recently restored grand premises. **Pros:** grand experience; wonderful dining room. **Cons:** not on the seaside. $ *Rooms from: A$250* ✉ *46 Hesse St.* ☎ *03/5258–1544* 🌐 *www.vuegrand.com.au* 🛏 *29 rooms, 3 suites* 🍴 *Free breakfast.*

Lorne

148 km (92 miles) southwest of Melbourne, 95 km (59 miles) southwest of Queenscliff, 50 km (31 miles) southwest of Torquay.

Located between sweeping Loutit Bay and the Great Otway National Park, pretty Lorne is one of the most popular towns on the Great Ocean Road, with a definite surf-and-holiday feel. It's the site of both a wild celebration every New Year's Eve and the popular Pier-to-Pub Swim held on the first weekend in January. Some people make their reservations a year or more in advance. It's also the starting point for the Great Ocean Road Running Festival held each May (the footrace ends in Apollo Bay). The town has a lively café and pub scene, as well as several upscale restaurants, trendy boutiques, and a day spa.

GETTING HERE AND AROUND

You really need a car to get to Lorne and other Great Ocean Road towns; the next best option is to take an organized tour. Public transport is available, but it's a long process: take the V/Line train to Geelong, then transfer to a bus to Apollo Bay, which stops at Lorne (about five hours). If driving, take the Princes Highway west from Melbourne across the Westgate Bridge to Geelong. From there, follow signs along the Surf Coast Highway to Torquay, where you'll connect with the Great Ocean Road.

VISITOR INFORMATION

Lorne Visitor Information Centre
Open daily 9–5, the center provides maps and information, as well as discounts on some tickets and tours. The Great Ocean Road Heritage Centre is also located here. ✉ *15 Mountjoy Parade* ☎ *03/5289–1152, 1300/891152* 🌐 *www.lovelorne.com.au.*

Beaches

Lorne Beach
BEACH—SIGHT | This stretch of the Victorian coast is sometimes called The Shipwreck Coast, with reputedly up to 700 ships at rest offshore. Lorne itself has a shipwreck plaque walk along the foreshore, giving the history of local disasters and near-misses dating from 1854. The Lorne Surf Life Saving Club patrols the southern end of popular Lorne Beach, which runs south from the Erskine River for 1.2 km (¾ mile). Care must be taken when the waves are high as the undertow and rips can be dangerous: swim in the patrolled areas between the flags. The beach has parking for 250 cars, a lookout, shade trees and shelters, barbecue and play areas, and a cycle track. The Lorne Beach Pavilion has a swimming pool, large playground, outdoor trampoline, and skate park as well. A camping ground and caravan park are also near the beach. Parking is available at the junction of Bay Street, Mountjoy Parade, and the Great Ocean Road, or along the Great Ocean Road itself. Other entrances to the beach are via **Grove Street** or **William Street**. The Mantra Lorne resort, with 12 acres of gardens and a range of rooms and apartments, is directly on the beach. **Amenities:** food and drink; lifeguards; parking (free); restrooms; showers. **Best for:** surfing; swimming; walking. ✉ *Great Ocean Rd., at Bay St.*

Restaurants

★ Brae
$$$ | **AUSTRALIAN** | Up in the hinterland above the Great Ocean Road, in a village at a crossroads, sits one of Australia's most celebrated restaurants. Chef Dan Hunter's Brae serves a daily set menu renowned for its fine organic fare, much drawn from its own farm, which surrounds the dining room, the rest from ethical, sustainable suppliers of the highest quality. **Known for:** destination dining; organic fare from its own farm; six guest rooms on-site in high demand. [$] *Average main: A$275* ✉ *4285 Cape Otway Rd., Birregurra* ☎ *03/5236–2226* 🌐 *www.braerestaurant.com* 🕒 *Closed Tues. and Wed.*

Marks
$$ | **SEAFOOD** | Fresh seafood—from fried calamari to roasted flathead—is the draw

at this Lorne institution, which has been going strong since 1989. The design is "funky seaside," with bright walls, blue chairs, and a smattering of local art and sculpture for sale. **Known for:** catch of the day; oysters; chocolate mousse. $ *Average main: A$34* ✉ *122 Mountjoy Parade* ☎ *03/5289–2787* 🌐 *www.marksrestaurant.com.au* 🕑 *Closed Sun. and Mon. and in July and Aug. No lunch Sun.–Thurs.*

Hotels

Mantra Lorne
$$$ | RESORT | You can fall asleep listening to waves rolling ashore at this huge complex on 12 acres near the water's edge in Lorne. **Pros:** close to the beach; lots of facilities. **Cons:** superbusy in summer holidays; 10 am checkout. $ *Rooms from: A$244* ✉ *Mountjoy Parade* ☎ *03/5228–9777* 🌐 *www.mantralorne.com.au* 🛏 *142 rooms, 135 apartments* 🍴 *Free breakfast.*

Activities

HIKING

The Great Ocean Road and the "Surf Coast" section of it around Torquay, Lorne, and Aireys Inlet have fantastic walks providing great cliff-top views, while inland a little way there are waterfalls and picnic grounds to explore.

The 30-km (19-mile) Surf Coast Walk, which begins near Jan Juc car park (1 mile west of Torquay) and ends around Moggs Creek Picnic Area at Aireys, can be done in short segments.

Inland is the vast Great Otway National Park, which has many picturesque walks, including the 12-km (7½-mile) walk from Aireys Inlet to Distillery Creek, which can be quite strenuous. There are 10 waterfalls within 10 km (6 miles) from Lorne, including short, easier walks to Erskine Falls and Sheoak Falls (see 🌐 *www.lovelorne.com.au*). The Torquay and Lorne visitor centers have trail maps.

Apollo Bay

45 km (28 miles) west of Lorne.

A small attractive town on a wide curving bay, Apollo Bay is midway on the great Ocean Road. There are many places to eat and plenty of opportunities for aquatic activities. It's most popular as a base to explore the famous rock formations of the 12 Apostles Marine National Park, and the greenery of Great Otway National Park.

GETTING HERE AND AROUND

Driving is the most convenient way to get here. Otherwise take the combined V/Line train-bus option, which involves riding a train from Melbourne's Southern Cross Station to Geelong and then a bus along the Great Ocean Road to Apollo Bay, via Lorne and other Surf Coast towns.

Beaches

Apollo Bay Beach
BEACH—SIGHT | At 195 km (121 miles) from Melbourne, you'll find one of Victoria's most popular holiday beaches. Protected by a working fishing harbor and Point Bunbury, the waves are gentler toward the southern end of the bay: care must be taken with an undertow that gets stronger as you go north. The local surf lifesaving club patrols between flags at the southern end. The 3-km (almost 2-mile) beach runs parallel to the Great Ocean Road (also called Collingwood St. within the town), and there's a reserve with shady trees, a barbeque, playground and a picnic area near the main shopping area. Behind the street is a row of shops and cafés, and on most Saturdays, the Apollo Bay market sees stall holders lining the foreshore path to sell local produce and crafts. Behind the town, the green hills of the Otways provide a change of scenery. Walk up the pathway to Marriners Lookout for idyllic views, though a sunken steamship lurks

Sea kayaking in Apollo Bay

beneath the waters. If you want to get closer to the sea, Apollo Bay Surf and Kayak runs kayaking tours to see the local seal colony, as well as providing surfing and paddleboarding lessons. The Seaview Motel and Apartments are near the beach, and some rooms have balconies looking over the view. **Amenities:** food and drink; lifeguards (in summer); parking (free); restrooms; showers. **Best for:** surfing; swimming; walking. ✉ *Great Ocean Rd.*

Hotels

Beachfront Motel

$$ | **HOTEL** | You couldn't hope for better placement at this seaside town accommodation, which is located near beaches and shops. **Pros:** convenient location. **Cons:** there may be some noise from the adjacent main road. [$] *Rooms from: A$190* ✉ *163 Great Ocean Rd.* ☎ *03/5237–6666* 🌐 *www.beachfrontmotel.com.au* 🛏 *10 rooms* 🍴 *No meals.*

★ **Chris's Beacon Point Restaurant and Villas**

$$$ | **HOTEL** | Set high in the Otway Ranges overlooking the Great Ocean Road and the sea, this is a wonderful place to dine or bed down for the night. **Pros:** sensational views. **Cons:** steep walk to some rooms. [$] *Rooms from: A$265* ✉ *280 Skenes Creek Rd.* ✥ *Take Skenes Creek Rd. turnoff about 3 km (2 miles) from Apollo Bay and wind up hill to Beacon Point* ☎ *03/5237–6411* 🌐 *www.chriss.com.au* 🛏 *4 villas, 5 studios* 🍴 *Free breakfast.*

Port Campbell National Park

283 km (75 miles) southwest of Melbourne via the Great Ocean Rd., 90 km (56 miles) west of Apollo Bay, 135 km (83 miles) west of Lorne.

It is possible to visit Port Campbell National Park on an organized day trip

En Route

Otway Fly Treetop Adventures. A spectacular 1,969-foot-long elevated treetop walk allows you to stroll a steel walkway above the rain-forest canopy. One section is springboard-cantilevered, and gently bounces as you pass over Young's Creek. For a faster thrill, take its 30-meter (99-foot) zipline. The entrance is about an hour's drive and 70 km (43 miles) from Lorne. To get there, follow the Great Ocean Road until it joins Skenes Creek Road, then take Forrest-Apollo Bay Road to Beech Forest Road, then Colac-Lavers Hill Road until you reach the signed turnoff to Phillips Track. From the Fly, you'll see the tops of giant myrtle beech, blackwood, and mountain ash trees, as well as spectacular views of the surrounding region. ✉ *360 Phillips Track* ☎ *03/5235–9200, 1800/300477* ⊕ *www.otwayflytreetopadventures. com.au* ✎ *A$25.*

from Melbourne, but better to stay overnight at one of the nearby towns and explore the region at your leisure. Port Campbell township is a logical place to base yourself, with a range of accommodation and dining options. The 30-km (19-mile) coastal drive is crammed with amazing sea sculptures, and you'll be stopping in the car parks along the way to get out and walk along the boardwalks to viewing platforms and steps that lead down to the coast.

GETTING HERE AND AROUND

The scenic route to Port Campbell National Park (which is actually a few miles east of the town of Port Campbell) is via the Great Ocean Road from Torquay, via Lorne and Apollo Bay. A car is the best way to go. A shorter drive is via the Princes Highway (M1) from Melbourne to Warrnambool, then the Great Ocean Road east to Port Campbell. A V/Line train operates to Warrnambool, and then a bus can be taken to Port Campbell. The journey takes about five hours.

TRANSPORTATION V/Line.
☎ *1800/800007* ⊕ *www.vline.com.au.*

VISITOR INFORMATION

Port Campbell Visitor Information Centre
Offers free hire of binoculars, telescopes, anemometers (for measuring wind speed), GPS units, digital cameras, and compasses. Open daily 9–5. ✉ *26 Morris St., Port Campbell* ☎ *1300/137255* ⊕ *www.visit12apostles.com.au.*

◉ Sights

★ Port Campbell National Park

NATIONAL/STATE PARK | Stretching some 30 km (19 miles) along Victoria's southeastern coastline, Port Campbell National Park is the site of some of the most famous and most beautiful geological formations in Australia. The ferocious Southern Ocean has gnawed at the limestone cliffs along this coast for eons, creating a sort of badlands-by-the-sea, where strangely shaped formations stand offshore amid the surf. The most famous of these formations is the 12 Apostles, as much a symbol for Victoria as the Sydney Opera House is for New South Wales (the name has always been a misnomer, as there were originally only nine of these stone columns—or sea stacks as they are correctly termed. Collapses in 2005 and 2009 mean that eight remain). If you happen to be visiting the 12 Apostles just after sunset, you're likely to see bands of little penguins returning to their burrows on the beach. There's a population of around 3,000 of these cute creatures in the area.

Loch Ard Gorge, named after the iron-hulled clipper that wrecked on the shores of nearby Mutton Bird Island in 1878, is another spectacular place to walk. Four of the *Loch Ard*'s victims are buried in a nearby cemetery, while a sign by the gorge tells the story of the ship and its crew. This stretch of coast is often called the Shipwreck Coast for the hundreds of vessels that have met untimely ends in the treacherous waters. The Historic Shipwreck Trail, with landmarks describing 25 of the disasters, stretches from Moonlight Head to Port Fairy.

Spectacular all year round, it is busiest in the warmer months, November to April, so expect to share key sights with many other visitors. This is also the best time to witness the boisterous birdlife on nearby Mutton Bird Island. Toward nightfall, hundreds of hawks and kites circle the island in search of baby mutton birds emerging from their protective burrows. The birds of prey beat a hasty retreat at the sight of thousands of adult shearwaters approaching with food for their chicks as the last light fades from the sky. Other amazing sea stacks and stone formations farther west along the Great Ocean Road are also not to be missed. These include the Grotto, London Bridge (now an arch after an earlier collapse), and the spectacular Bay of Islands and Bay of Martyrs.

A self-guided, 1½-hour Discovery Walk begins near Port Campbell Beach, where it's safe to swim. The pounding surf and undertow are treacherous at other nearby beaches. ✉ *Port Campbell National Park, Port Campbell.*

En Route

Warrnambool. About 66 km (41 miles) west of Port Campbell, Warrnambool is Victoria's southern right whale nursery. Platforms at Logan's Beach, about 3 km (2 miles) east of the city, provide views of an amazing marine show from June to September. Whales return to this beach every year to calve, with the females and young staying close to the shore and the males playing about 150 yards out to sea. ✉ *Warrnambool* ⊕ *www.flagstaffhill. com.*

🍴 Restaurants

Waves

$$ | AUSTRALIAN | A relaxed main street eatery with a spacious sundeck and friendly staff, open for breakfast from 8 am, there are daily fish and soup specials, and Devonshire teas with fresh scones. **Known for:** casual dining; simple, hearty meals; tea and scones. ⑤ *Average main: A$30* ✉ *29 Lord St., Port Campbell* ☎ *03/5598–6111* ⊕ *www.wavesport-campbell.com.au.*

🛏 Hotels

Daysy Hill Country Cottages

$$ | RENTAL | Set in manicured gardens with lavender-lined walkways, these five attractive sandstone-and-cedar cottages look over the Newfield Valley. **Pros:** good price; good location. **Cons:** limited facilities. ⑤ *Rooms from: A$200* ✉ *2585 Cobden-Port Campbell Rd., Port Campbell* ☎ *03/5598–6226* ⊕ *www.daysyhill-cottages.com.au* � *5 cottages, 3 cabins* ❏ *No meals.*

Southern Ocean Villas

$$$ | RENTAL | Ideally situated on the edge of Port Campbell National Park,

Loch Ard Gorge in Port Campbell National Park, Great Ocean Road

within short walking distance of the town center and beach, these villas are stylishly furnished and fitted with polished wood floors, picture windows, and high ceilings. **Pros:** good location near Twelve Apostles. **Cons:** located in sleepy town; difficult to find. $ *Rooms from: A$280* ⊠ *2 McCue St., Port Campbell* ☎ *03/5598–4200* ⊕ *www.southernocean-villas.com* ⇆ *20 villas* ⦿ *No meals.*

🏃 Activities

DIVING

The 12 Apostles Marine National Park and the nearby Arches Marine Sanctuary both provide fantastic diving opportunities. Local wrecks that can be explored with experienced guides include the *Napier* at Port Campbell, the famous *Loch Ard* (off Muttonbird Island), the *Schomberg* at Peterborough, and the *Fiji* near Moonlight Head. All wrecks are protected by federal law, and are not to be disturbed in any way. *(See Port Campbell boat charters in Tours, above.)*

HIKING

The Port Campbell National Park area, which is home to the 12 Apostles, Loch Ard George, and other amazing landforms, has many good walks. Most are along wooden boardwalks; some also include steep stairs down to the beach. The Visitor Centre at Port Campbell has all the details.

Inland from Port Campbell is the Camperdown-Timboon Rail Trail (also known as the Coast to Crater Rail Trail). It passes by lakes and streams and open volcanic plains. It is suitable for walkers and mountain bikers. The 36-km (22-mile) trail has good signage. Ask at the tourist offices for details.

Port Fairy

377 km (215 miles) southwest of Melbourne via the Great Ocean Rd.; it is shorter if you take the Princes Hwy. (M1).

Port Fairy is widely considered to be the state's prettiest village. The second-oldest town in Victoria, it was originally known as Belfast, and there are indeed echoes of Ireland in the landscape and architecture. More than 50 of the cottages and sturdy bluestone buildings that line the banks of the River Moyne have been classified as landmarks by the National Trust, and few towns repay a leisurely stroll so richly. Huge Norfolk Island pines line many of the streets, particularly Gipps Street, and the town is dotted with good cafés, pubs, and art galleries.

The town still thrives as the base for a fishing fleet, and as host to the Port Fairy Folk Festival, one of Australia's most famous musical events, held every March. The town has a large colony of short-tailed shearwaters that nest on Griffiths Island. Amazingly, these birds travel here from the Aleutian Islands near Alaska, always arriving within three days of September 22. You can take a 45-minute walk around the island on marked trails to the historic lighthouse.

GETTING HERE AND AROUND
The most convenient form of transport is by car; the 377-km (234-mile) trip along the Great Ocean Road from Melbourne takes about 6½ hours, and it's advisable to break up the journey, as there's so much to see along the way. It's a shorter trip if you take the Princes Highway (M1).

TRANSPORTATION
V/Line
Travel from Melbourne's Southern Cross Station to Warrnambool (3½ hours) on V/Line trains, and then make the short distance (29 km [18 miles]) on V/Line buses to Port Fairy. ☎ 1800/800007 ⊕ www.vline.com.au.

VISITOR INFORMATION
Port Fairy Visitor Information Centre
The center provides maps and information, can help plan itineraries, and advises on accommodation and tours.

Open 9–5 daily. ✉ Railway Pl., Bank St. ☎ 1300/656564 ⊕ www.portfairyaustralia.com.au.

◉ Sights

Port Fairy Historical Society
MUSEUM | The historical society's museum contains relics from the 19th-century whaling days, when Port Fairy was a whaling station with one of the largest ports in Victoria. It also highlights the stories of the many ships that have come to grief along this dangerous coast. ✉ Old Courthouse, 30 Gipps St. ☎ 03/5568–2263 ⊕ www.historicalsociety.port-fairy.com ⛋ A$5.

Tower Hill State Game Reserve
NATURE PRESERVE | This reserve is packed with native Australian animals in their natural state. The Worn Gundidj Visitor Centre in the reserve conducts cultural interpretative walks. Take its one-hour personalized bush and nature walk to learn about indigenous lifestyles, bush food, and medicine, and hear about the local inhabitants, which include emus, sugar gliders, koalas, kangaroos, birds, and reptiles. The standard tour is A$25.50; also ask about the availability of other occasional specialist tours, including twilight visits. Parks Victoria's website also has a map of the reserve and self-guided walking trails. ✉ Tower Hill State Game Reserve, Princes Hwy., between Port Fairy and Warrnambool, Tower Hill ☎ 13–1963 Parks Victoria, 03/5561–5315 Tower Hill Tours ⊕ parks.vic.gov.au ☞ See www.towerhill.org.au for tour information.

🍴 Restaurants

Time & Tide
$$$$ | CAFÉ | "High Tea by the High Sea" is the menu highlight of this luscious café, which has an appetite-stimulating Southern Ocean view. Take a seat on a high-backed chair and indulge in three tiers of savory tarts, finger sandwiches,

brownies, filled meringues, and more, including tea or coffee. **Known for:** savory tarts; grand high tea; books up fast. [$] *Average main: A$59* ✉ *21 Thistle Pl.* ☎ *03/5568–2134* 🌐 *www.timeandtide-hightea.com* 🕓 *Closed Mon. and Tues. No dinner.*

Hotels

Merrijig Inn

$ | **B&B/INN** | One of Victoria's oldest inns, this beautifully restored 1841 Georgian-style building overlooks Port Fairy's working wharf from King George Square. **Pros:** cute and cozy; great food. **Cons:** upstairs rooms have character, but they're small. [$] *Rooms from: A$150* ✉ *1 Campbell St.* ☎ *03/5568–2324* 🌐 *www.merrijiginn.com* 🛏 *8 rooms* 🍴 *Free breakfast.*

★ **Oscars Waterfront Boutique Hotel**

$$$$ | **B&B/INN** | Overlooking the waterfront and a marina of yachts, this hotel gives French provincial style an Australian edge. **Pros:** fantastic location; great breakfasts. **Cons:** town is dead in the off-season. [$] *Rooms from: A$325* ✉ *41B Gipps St.* ☎ *03/5568–3022* 🌐 *www.oscarswaterfront.com* 🛏 *7 rooms* 🍴 *Free breakfast.*

Activities

HIKING

There are several walks around Port Fairy that highlight the town's historical aspects and the area's great beauty. Pick up a Historic Walks map from the visitor center and follow a trail past some 30 beautiful buildings; it takes about an hour. The Port Fairy Maritime & Shipwreck Heritage Walk is a 2-km (1-mile) trail that passes the sites of several shipwrecks: the barque *Socrates,* which was battered by huge seas in 1843; the barque *Lydia,* which was wrecked off the coast in 1847; the schooner *Thistle,* which went down in 1837; and the brigantine *Essington,* which sank while moored at Port Fairy in 1852. Other historic attractions en route include the town port, the lifeboat station, riverside warehouses, cannons and gun emplacements at Battery Hill, and Griffiths Island Lighthouse. The walk is well marked.

Ten minutes or 14 km (9 miles) east of Port Fairy is Tower Hill State Game Reserve, nested in an extinct volcano. There are several walking trails and plenty of chances to see emus and kangaroos. About 40 minutes northeast is Mount Eccles National Park, another extinct volcano. Here there are four walks, including one to the crater rim and lava caves.

Ballarat

116 km (73 miles) northwest of Melbourne.

In the local Aboriginal language, the name Ballarat means "resting place." In pre-gold-rush days, nearby Lake Wendouree provided the area with a plentiful supply of food. Once the gold boom hit, however, the town became much less restful; in 1854 Ballarat was the scene of the Battle of the Eureka Stockade, a skirmish that took place between miners and authorities over gold license fees that miners were forced to pay, though they had no vote. More than 30 men died in the battle. Today their flag—the Southern Cross—is a symbol of Australia's egalitarian spirit and can be viewed in the Eureka Centre.

Despite the harsh times, fortunes made from the mines (and from the miners) resulted in the grand Victorian architecture on Sturt and Lydiard streets—note the post office, the town hall, Craig's Royal Hotel, and Her Majesty's Theatre. The Old Colonists' Hall and the Mining Exchange (at 16 and 8 Lydiard Street, respectively) now house shops and cafés. The visitor center has a self-guided heritage walk.

Great Ocean Road Tours

AAT Kings. This operator has a seven-day tour from Melbourne to Adelaide that travels the length of the Great Ocean Road and also includes visits to Mt. Gambier and Kangaroo Island. ✉ *Melbourne Day Tours, Federation Sq., at Flinders and Russell Sts., City Center* ☎ *1300/228546* ⊕ *www.aatkings.com.au* ✉ *From A$2925.*

Adventure Tours Australia. Find adventure on three-day tours to both the Great Ocean Road and the Grampians National Park (A$125 each) and on to Adelaide (A$450), and the four-day tour (A$850) includes an overnight stay on Kangaroo Island in South Australia. Some meals are included. Young backpackers are the target market, but anyone can join the tours, and there's a choice between dorm accommodation and singles or doubles. ☎ *1300/654604* ⊕ *www.adventuretours.com.au* ✉ *From A$450.*

Auswalk. This tour company runs guided and self-guided Great Ocean Walk tours ranging from four to eight days. The tidy four-day guided walk journeys from Blanket Bay to the 12 Apostles, taking in Wreck Beach and Loch Ard Gorge, with a stay at the 19th-century Cape Otway light station. Walkers carry a day pack only; a support vehicle carries the luggage by car from hotel (or B&B) to hotel. ☎ *03/9597–9767* ⊕ *www.auswalk.com.au* ✉ *From $A1695.*

Great Ocean Road Adventure Tours. GORATS, as this operator's called, runs mountain-bike and canoeing tours across the region. Many tours run to the town of Forrest, considered a mountain-bike mecca, and numerous trails in the area showcase the natural beauty of the Otway Ranges. Flat-water canoe tours on the Barwon, Anglesea, and Aire rivers are also available. ☎ *0417/576973* ⊕ *www.gorats.com.au* ✉ *From A$85 (2-hr bike tour).*

Split Point Lighthouse tours. Explore the majestic, and still operational, Split Point Lighthouse at Aireys Inlet, also known as the White Queen. You can see her for miles as you approach this section of the Great Ocean Road west of Anglesea—just look for the huge white tower with the red cap—and the views from the top are amazing. The 45-minute tours operate year-round, weather permitting, but bookings are required on weekdays. ✉ *Split Point lighthouse, Federal St., Aireys Inlet* ☎ *1800/174045* ⊕ *www.splitpointlighthouse.com.au* ✉ *From A$14.*

Spring Creek Horse Rides. Ride through beautiful Otway National Park on horseback for a leisurely hour or two. ✉ *245 Portreath Rd., Bellbrae* ☎ *0423/456922 mobile* ⊕ *www.springcreekhorserides.com.au* ✉ *From A$50.*

12 Apostles Helicopters. One exciting way to appreciate the awesome force of the Southern Ocean and this amazing natural sculpture park is by helicopter. Fifteen-minute flights take in the 12 Apostles and Loch Ard Gorge; longer flights travel farther up the coast to the west and inland. ✉ *12 Apostles Information Centre, Great Ocean Rd., at Booringa Rd., Port Campbell* ☎ *03/5598–8283* ⊕ *www.12apostleshelicopters.com.au* ✉ *From A$145.*

GETTING HERE AND AROUND

It's an easy 90-minute drive to Ballarat along the Western Highway (M8) from Melbourne. The road, however, is the main artery between Melbourne and Adelaide, and many huge trucks also use the road. Take care and drive within the speed limit. From Ballarat you can easily drive north to the spa-country towns of Daylesford–Hepburn Springs and Bendigo on the Midland Highway. The city itself is well signposted. The city center is built around a well-planned grid and has ample parking. Local bus services run from Sturt Street, the main thoroughfare, to most of Ballarat's attractions.

TRANSPORTATION
V/Line

Take trains between Ballarat and Melbourne, and buses from Ballarat to other Gold Country destinations such as Daylesford and Bendigo. ☎ *1800/800007* ⊕ *www.vline.com.au.*

VISITOR INFORMATION
Ballarat Visitor Information Centre

Located in Town Hall, this useful bureau gives advice and sells the Ballarat Pass (three attractions A$101, four attractions A$112), which includes entry to multiple local sights. ✉ *225 Sturt St.* ☎ *1800/446633* ⊕ *www.visitballarat.com.au.*

◉ Sights

Art Gallery of Ballarat

MUSEUM | This impressive art museum has a large collection of Australian art, from 19th-century works to contemporary pieces. Keep an eye out for its paintings by landscape artist Eugene von Guerard, who captured Ballarat as it appeared in the raucous early gold rush days. ✉ *40 Lydiard St.* ☎ *03/5320–5858* ⊕ *www.artgalleryofballarat.com.au.*

Ballarat Botanical Gardens

GARDEN | On the shores of Lake Wendouree, the Ballarat Botanical Gardens are identifiable by the brilliant blooms

Ballarat Trails 🏃

The 55-km (34-mile) Ballarat-Skipton Rail Trail cuts through open paddocks, eucalypt forests, native grasslands, and bush alive with native birds and wildflowers, and passes the former Chinese settlement at Nintingbool.

The Yarrowee River Trail is a 17-km (10-mile) walking and biking trail that passes through bird-rich reserves, gold mining heritage sites, and wetlands as well as the city center. It connects with other trails along the four tributaries of the Yarrowee River.

and classical statuary. At the rear of the gardens, the Conservatory hosts events during the town's Begonia Festival held each March, with other events taking place near the lake. ✉ *Gillies St. N at Lake Gardens Ave.* ☎ *03/5320–5135* ⊕ *www.ballaratbotanicalgardens.com.au.*

Ballarat Wildlife Park

NATURE PRESERVE | FAMILY | All sorts of native animals, including kangaroos and emus (which roam free), saltwater crocodiles, snakes, Tasmanian devils, wombats, tree kangaroos, and echidnas can be found at this wildlife sanctuary. Daily tours of the park are led at 11, with a koala show at 2 and a wombat show at 2:30. Sunday at 3 is "crunch time," when Crunch the crocodile gets a feed. If you're also hungry, the park has a café and picnic areas. ✉ *Fussel St. at York St., Ballarat East* ☎ *03/5333–5933* ⊕ *www.wildlifepark.com.au* ☞ *A$35.*

★ Eureka Centre

HISTORIC SITE | The Eureka Centre stands on the site of the 1854 Eureka Stockade revolt, in which gold miners staged an armed rebellion against police corruption and for the establishment of democracy in Victoria. The museum brings history to

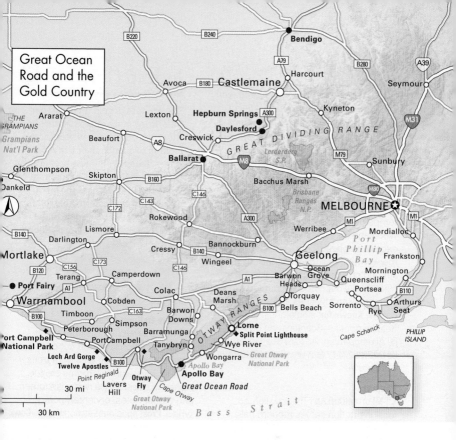

Great Ocean Road and the Gold Country

life via impressive interactive technology. Visitors learn about democracy around the world and can admire the tattered but beautiful remains of the original Eureka Flag, which flew above the site of the battle. A simple on-site café serves coffee and cake. ✉ *102 Stawell St. S* ☎ *03/5333–0333* ⊕ *www.ballarat.vic.gov. au* ☞ *A$12.*

★ Sovereign Hill

HISTORIC SITE | FAMILY | Built on the site of the former Sovereign Hill Quartz Mining Company's mines, this replica town provides an authentic look at life, work, and play during Ballarat's gold rush era. Highlights of the main street include a hotel, blacksmith's shop, bakery, and post office—all perfectly preserved relics of their time. You can have your photo taken in period costumes, take a mineshaft tour, pan for gold (and find some), ride in a stagecoach, or head to the "lolly shop" to taste old-fashioned candy. Return at night for "Aura," a 90-minute sound-and-light spectacular that tells the story of the Eureka uprising. Your entry ticket gets you two days' entrance into the town and also into the **Gold Museum,** across Bradshaw Street, which displays an extensive collection of nuggets from the Ballarat diggings. ✉ *Bradshaw St.* ☎ *03/5337–1199* ⊕ *www.sovereignhill. com.au* ☞ *From A$53.*

🍽 Restaurants

The Forge

$$ | PIZZA | FAMILY | This former industrial building now houses a pizzeria that serves top-notch wood-fired pizzas in a big dining room with long timber tables, wooden beams, and exposed brick walls. The pizzas are excellent, with light crusts and tasty toppings; try the Volcano (hot salami, chili pepper, Gorgonzola, feta, olives, and anchovies) for an entrée with a zing. **Known for:** industrial-cool decor and setting; Volcano pizza; pizza-strips with dip appetizer. $ *Average main: A$21* ✉ *14 Armstrong St. N* ☎ *03/5337–6635* ⊕ *www.theforgepizzeria.com.au.*

★ FIKA

$ | CAFÉ | Taking its name from the Swedish word for coffee break, this sleek contemporary café decked out with blonde wood and industrial light fittings serves excellent coffee. There's also a light meal menu with a healthy twist, including almond chia pudding for breakfast and a freekah salad for lunch—counterbalanced with steak sandwiches and single-origin coffee. **Known for:** single-origin coffee; healthy options; Scandinavian design. $ *Average main: A$10* ✉ *36a Doveton St.* ☎ *0427/527447* ⊕ *www.fikacoffeebrewers.com.au.*

L'Espresso

$ | MEDITERRANEAN | This low-lighted local institution serves modern Italian classics for breakfast and lunch daily, with specials like linguini alla Bolognese; or a risotto with beets, walnuts, and goat cheese. The corn fritters with salmon are a great way to start the day, as is the classic Aussie breakfast dish of smashed avocado with feta cheese and poached eggs. **Known for:** Italian classics; smashed avo and feta cheese; music CDs for sale. $ *Average main: A$17* ✉ *417 Sturt St.* ☎ *03/5333–1789.*

Hotels

The Ansonia

$ | HOTEL | Built in the 1870s as professional offices, this building now houses an excellent boutique hotel. **Pros:** cozy; arty; free parking. **Cons:** rooms opening onto the atrium lack privacy. $ *Rooms from: A$150* ✉ *32 Lydiard St.* ☎ *03/5332–4678* ⊕ *www.theansoniaonlydiard.com.*

Liquid Gold 👁

The promise of gold "in them thar hills" drew mobs of prospectors in the 1850s, but today's visitors aren't looking to quench their thirst for riches. Ballarat's climate produces great Pinot Noir and Chardonnay, while the Grampians is the birthplace of Great Western, Australia's first and best-known sparkling wine. The Pyrenees region is known for its classic Shiraz.

au ⬏ *16 rooms, 3 apartments* ⊙ *Free breakfast.*

Mercure Ballarat Hotel

$$ | HOTEL | FAMILY | This single-story accommodation is spread out over a large property dotted with gum trees next to Sovereign Hill; rooms are furnished in classic style, with dark green and timber notes, or contemporary white. **Pros:** spacious; atmospheric. **Cons:** about 2½ km (1½ miles) from the city center. $ *Rooms from: A$168* ✉ *613 Main Rd.* ☎ *03/5327–1200* ⊕ *www.mercureballarat.com.au* ⬏ *88 rooms, 9 apartments* ⊙ *No meals.*

Daylesford and Hepburn Springs

109 km (68 miles) northwest of Melbourne, 45 km (28 miles) northeast of Ballarat.

Nestled in the slopes of the Great Dividing Range, Daylesford and its nearby twin, Hepburn Springs, are a spa-lover's paradise. The water table here is naturally aerated with carbon dioxide and rich in soluble mineral salts, making it ideal for indulging in mineral baths and other rejuvenating treatments. The natural springs were first noted during the gold rush, and Swiss-Italian immigrants established a spa at Hepburn Springs in 1875. There are now about 70 natural springs in the area. The best time to visit the area is autumn, when the deciduous trees turn bronze and you can finish up a relaxing day next to an open fire with a glass of local red.

GETTING HERE AND AROUND

The twin towns of Daylesford and Hepburn Springs are easily reached by car from Melbourne. Take the Western Highway (M8) to Ballarat, then take the Midland Highway for another 40 km (25 miles) to Daylesford (via Creswick). Hepburn Springs is a mile or two from Daylesford. V/Line operates trains from Southern Cross Station, Melbourne, to Ballarat or Woodend (near Mount Macedon), and V/Line buses connect with the trains to take passengers to Daylesford.

TRANSPORTATION

V/Line

Trains operate from Southern Cross Station in Melbourne to Ballarat or Woodend (near Mount Macedon), where buses connect to Daylesford. ☎ *1800/800007* 🌐 *www.vline.com.au.*

VISITOR INFORMATION

Daylesford Regional Visitor Information Centre

This helpful office can give advice about local attractions and accommodations. ✉ *98 Vincent St., Daylesford* ☎ *1800/454891* 🌐 *www.visithepburnshire.com.au.*

Sights

★ Bromley & Co

MUSEUM | This impressive art gallery displays the stylish, contemporary work of David Bromley—one of Australia's top contemporary artists—along with other artists. The narrow shopfront belies a fascinating interior, with art pieces scattered down the long, narrow interior, to spaces upstairs, and out to a garden. ✉ *45a Vincent St., Daylesford* ☎ *03/5348–3979* 🌐 *www.bromleyandco.com.*

Convent Gallery

ARTS VENUE | Perched on a hillside overlooking Daylesford, this gallery occupies a former 19th-century nunnery that has been restored to its lovely Victorian-era state. It houses three levels of fine art and a nun-related museum, and occasionally stages live arts performances. At the front of the gallery is Bad Habits, a sunny café that serves light lunches and snacks, while Altar Bar is a hip place for a drink. The second-story penthouse suite is the ultimate in decadence, with its own hydrotherapy bath and a boudoir-style bedroom ($$$). For groups, the 1920s Monastiraki guesthouse lets you sleep among yet more art from the Convent's owner, Tina Banitska, which displays a wicked sense of humour ($$$). ✉ *Hill St. at Daly St., Daylesford* ☎ *03/5348–3211* 🌐 *www.theconvent.com.au* 🎟 *A$5.*

Mineral Springs Reserve

HOT SPRINGS | Above the Hepburn Bathhouse and Spa, a path winds past a series of mineral springs in this 74-acre reserve, created in 1865. Each spring has a slightly different chemical composition—and a significantly different taste. You can bring empty bottles and fill them for free with the mineral water of your choice. The reserve includes walking trails, playgrounds, and a café. ✉ *Mineral Springs Reserve, Hepburn Springs.*

Hotels

★ The Dudley Boutique Hotel

$$$$ | **B&B/INN** | This fine example of timber Edwardian-style architecture sits behind a neat hedge and picket gate on the main street of Hepburn Springs. **Pros:** tranquil garden setting; great heritage character. **Cons:** limited number of rooms may limit available booking dates. [$] *Rooms from: A$549* ✉ *101 Main Rd., Hepburn Springs* ☎ *03/5348–3033*

🌐 *www.thedudley.com.au* 🛏 *7 rooms* 🍴 *Free breakfast.*

★ **Lake House**

$$$$ | **HOTEL** | Featuring one of Australia's best restaurants, this rambling lakeside hotel adds a distinct glamor to spa country. A day spa administers some treatments specifically for men and expectant mothers, as well as those for couples, along with the more-traditional pampering. **Pros:** renowned food; tranquil garden setting; tree house hot tubs with lagoon views. **Cons:** two-night minimum stay on weekends; some suites don't have views; service can be inconsistent. [$] *Rooms from: A$329* ✉ *King St., Daylesford* ☎ *03/5348–3329* 🌐 *www.lakehouse.com.au* 🛏 *33 rooms* 🍴 *All-inclusive.*

Shopping

SPAS

★ **Hepburn Bathhouse & Spa**

SPA/BEAUTY | A destination for relaxation and wellness since the 19th century, this facility is the centerpiece of Australia's premier spa destination, and one of the largest and most spectacular spas in the country. The complex encompasses the original Edwardian Bathhouse (circa 1895), which houses private mineral baths and more than 20 wet-and-dry treatment rooms, and a stunning, contemporary building, where you find the public bathhouse and the private sanctuary area. Patrons can buy two-hour passes for the bathhouse or the sanctuary. The bathhouse includes a relaxation mineral pool and a spa pool (A$42 Tuesday–Thursday and A$52 Friday–Monday), while the sanctuary has underwater spa couches (for the ultimate in hydrotherapy), an aroma steam room, and a salt therapy pool. There is also the day spa area, where you can choose from a long list of therapies, including body wraps and polishes, facials, and other treatments using the mineral waters. Products used in the spa include a Hepburn Collection range specifically designed for Hepburn Bathhouse & Spa. ✉ *1 Mineral Springs Crescent, Hepburn Springs* ☎ *03/5321–6000* 🌐 *www.hepburnbathhouse.com.*

Bendigo

150 km (93 miles) northwest of Melbourne, 92 km (57 miles) south of Echuca.

Gold was discovered in the Bendigo district in 1851, and it skyrocketed as the richest city in the world until 1900. The city's magnificent public buildings bear witness to the richness of its mines. Today Bendigo has reinvented itself as a cultural destination, with distinguished buildings lining both sides of Pall Mall in the city center. These include the Shamrock Hotel, the Old Post Office, and the Bendigo Town Hall, all majestic examples of late-Victorian architecture. Although these glorious relics of a golden age dominate the landscape, the city is far from old-fashioned. You'll also find a lively café and restaurant scene, 30 boutique wineries, some of which can be visited on organized winery tours, and a strong arts scene led by one of the best regional art galleries in Australia.

GETTING HERE AND AROUND

To reach Bendigo, take the Calder Highway northwest from Melbourne; the trip takes about 1 hour and 40 minutes. V/Line operates trains to Bendigo from Melbourne's Southern Cross Station, a journey of about two hours. There's also an airport bus running from Melbourne Airport to Bendigo.

TRANSPORTATION

Bendigo Airport Service

This coach service runs daily between Melbourne Tullamarine Airport and Bendigo, with stops along the way. Bookings are essential, and online bookings can be made up to three hours before departure. A one-way ticket costs $47. ✉ *Platform*

2, Bendigo Railway Station, Bendigo
☎ *03/5444–3939* ⊕ *www.bendigoairport-service.com.au.*

V/Line

There are up to 20 train services a day from Melbourne's Southern Cross Station to Bendigo, a journey of about two hours. V/Line buses also travel between Bendigo and Daylesford, and on to Ballarat. ☎ *1800/800007* ⊕ *www.vline.com.au.*

TOURS

Food Fossicking Tour

WALKING TOURS | The food scene in Bendigo has improved greatly in recent years, and this weekly walking tour highlights the best of the city's eating. Departing from the Bendigo Visitor Centre, the tour visits a chocolate shop, a sourdough bakery, and a whole-foods emporium, among other stops. In addition, you'll hear directly from the makers and taste samples along the way. ⊠ *Bendigo Visitor Centre, 51 Pall Mall* ☎ *1800/813153* ⊕ *www.bendigotourism.com* 🖃 *A$75* ⌖ *Departs 10 am Sat.*

Vintage Talking Tram

BUS TOURS | A good introduction to Bendigo is a tour aboard this hop-on, hop-off streetcar, which includes a taped commentary on the town's history. The half-hourly tram runs on an 8-km (5-mile) circuit between the Central Deborah Gold Mine and the Joss House temple, making six stops at historic sites. ⊠ *Bendigo* ☎ *03/5442–2821* ⊕ *www.bendigotramways.com* 🖃 *From A$18.*

VISITOR INFORMATION

Bendigo Visitor Centre

Book accommodations, as well as tickets for tours and attractions here. There are two interesting free art galleries attached to the center. You can also purchase gold prospecting maps and get advice on prospecting licenses and equipment rental. ⊠ *51 Pall Mall* ☎ *03/5434–6060, 1800/813153* ⊕ *www.bendigotourism.com.au.*

⊙ Sights

★ Bendigo Art Gallery

MUSEUM | A notable collection of contemporary Australian painting can be found in this beautiful gallery, including the work of Rupert Bunny, Emily Kame Kngwarreye, and Arthur Boyd. The gallery also has some significant 19th-century French realist and impressionist works, bequeathed by a local surgeon. International exhibitions are regularly hosted. There are free guided tours every day at 11 am and 2 pm. ⊠ *42 View St.* ☎ *03/5434–6088* ⊕ *www.bendigoartgallery.com.au* 🖃 *Entry to permanent exhibition free; touring exhibitions cost from A$10.*

Bendigo Pottery

HISTORIC SITE | Australia's oldest working pottery workshop turns out distinctive brown-and-cream style pieces that many Australians have in their kitchens. Founded in 1858, the historic workshop hosts demonstrations. You can even get your hands dirty creating your own clay piece during an affordable wheel-throwing lesson (bookings essential during school holidays); there's also a clay play area for small children. Impressive beehive brick kilns, which you can step inside, are star exhibits in the museum. It's 6½ km (4 miles) northeast of Bendigo on the way to Echuca. ⊠ *146 Midland Hwy., Epsom* ☎ *03/5448–4404* ⊕ *www.bendigopottery.com.au* 🖃 *Free, museum A$8, wheel-throwing lessons from A$20.*

★ Central Deborah Gold Mine

FACTORY | FAMILY | This historic mine, with a 1,665-foot shaft, yielded almost a ton of gold before it closed in 1954. Aboveground you can pan for gold, see the old stamper battery, and climb up the poppet head, but the thrill of mining is felt belowground. Three underground tours explore different mine levels; on the Mine Experience you descend 200 feet to widened tunnels, while the Underground Adventure puts you another

78 feet deeper. Nine Levels of Darkness is the ultimate adventure here; over 3½ hours you sign on as a "new chum" and ride a tiny cage lift 748 feet down to dripping original tunnels, where you work a drill, "set" explosives, and climb ladders. Open 9–4:30 daily (last tour at 3). ✉ *76 Violet St.* ☎ *03/5443–8255* 🌐 *www.central-deborah.com* 🎟 *A$7 (aboveground only); self-guided tours (including entry) from A$32.*

Golden Dragon Museum

MUSEUM | The Chinese community's important role in Bendigo life, past and present, is explored within this museum. Its centerpieces are the century-old Loong imperial ceremonial dragon and the Sun Loong imperial dragon, which, at more than 106 yards in length, is said to be the world's longest. When carried in procession, the body alone requires 52 carriers and 52 relievers, and more to carry the head, neck and tail; the head alone weighs 64 pounds. Also on display are other ceremonial objects, costumes, and historic artifacts. The lovely Yi Yuan Gardens, opposite, with ponds and bridges, are part of the museum and close at 4:30. ✉ *1–11 Bridge St.* ☎ *03/5441–5044* 🌐 *www.goldendragonmuseum.org* 🎟 *A$12* 🕒 *Closed Mon.*

Joss House

RELIGIOUS SITE | An active place of worship on the outskirts of the city, this small Chinese temple was built during the gold rush days by Chinese miners. At the height of the boom in the 1850s and 1860s, about a quarter of Bendigo's miners were Chinese. These men were usually dispatched from villages on the Chinese mainland, and they were expected to work hard and return as quickly as possible with their fortunes. Sadly, tensions with white miners were a feature of that era, along with anti-Chinese riots. Luckily this attractive element of their presence, built in 1871, has endured from those turbulent times. Open daily 11–3. ✉ *3 Finn St.* ☎ *03/5442–1685* 🌐 *www.bendigojosshouse.com* 🎟 *A$7.*

🍴 Restaurants

★ The Woodhouse

$$ | **STEAKHOUSE** | This excellent restaurant in a former blacksmith's workshop serves quality, locally sourced food in a casual dining environment. The atmospheric interior has exposed brick walls and timber beams, with a wood-fired pizza oven visible at one end of the bar. **Known for:** wood-fired pizza; nice setting; craft beers. [$] *Average main: A$33* ✉ *101 Williamson St.* ☎ *03/5443–8671* 🌐 *www.thewoodhouse.com.au* 🕒 *Closed Sun. and Mon.*

🛏 Hotels

Hotel Shamrock

$ | **HOTEL** | The lodgings at this landmark Victorian hotel in the city center range from traditional guest rooms to spacious suites. **Pros:** historic gold-era building; central location. **Cons:** limited facilities. [$] *Rooms from: A$150* ✉ *Pall Mall, at Williamson St.* ☎ *03/5443–0333* 🌐 *www.hotelshamrock.com.au* 🛏 *36 rooms and suites* 🍽 *Free breakfast.*

★ Quest Schaller Hotel Bendigo

$ | **HOTEL** | Named after Australian artist Mark Schaller, this property is a cutting-edge addition to the Bendigo accommodation scene. **Pros:** stylish design; lively lobby; walking distance to the city center. **Cons:** small rooms; queen beds are the largest size available. [$] *Rooms from: A$149* ✉ *Lucan St., at Bayne St.* ☎ *03/4433–6100* 🌐 *www.questapartments.com.au* 🛏 *120 rooms* 🍽 *No meals.*

🏃 Activities

BIKING

There are some great bike trails and four self-guided winery cycle tours ranging in length from 21 to 50 km (13 to 31 miles).

The Mandurang Valley Wine Trail is the shortest and leads to the Chateau Dore Winery and Lynnevale Estate. You can also cycle along the O'Keefe Rail Trail and the Bendigo Bushland Trail; maps and brochures are available at the visitor center.

Moroni's Bikes

BICYCLING | This long-established company rents out bikes and also invites cyclists to join in its thrice-weekly social road rides. The rides depart every Tuesday and Thursday mornings from 6, and Sunday from 8, from its premises. They range from 35 km up to 60 km (21.5–37 miles) for fitter folk. Contact the store for details of weekly rides for more experienced cyclists and mountain bikers. ✉ *104 Mitchell St.* ☎ *03/5443–9644* ⊕ *www. moronisbikes.com.au* 🖃 *Bike rental A$40 per day.*

HIKING AND WALKING

There are many excellent self-guided walks around Bendigo, and trails interconnect with the popular biking trails. You can do your own themed walk following in the gold-rush trail or admiring the city's grand old buildings. Popular bushland walks include One Tree Hill, Wildflower Drive, and the Old Tom Mine Walk in the Greater Bendigo National Park. The visitor center on Pall Mall has maps and brochures, as does its website.

HORSEBACK RIDING
Ironbark Riding Centre

HORSEBACK RIDING | Stroll or canter through the beautiful Ironstone Reserve and the Whipstick section of the Greater Bendigo National Park, only a few minutes from Bendigo, on trail rides from half an hour to a full day. Owner Phillip Gahan also gives riding lessons. ✉ *189 Watson St.* ☎ *03/5436–1565* ⊕ *www. bwc.com.au/ironbark* 🖃 *Rides from A$35.*

Gold Country Tours ◉

AAT Kings. The Sovereign Hill Gold Rush coach tour visits the gold rush-era historical reenactment village within Ballarat. ✉ *Melbourne Day Tours, Federation Sq., at Flinders and Russell Sts., City Center* ☎ *1300/228546* ⊕ *www. aatkings.com.au* 🖃 *A$169.*

Gray Line. This operator runs four day tours to the historical reenactment town, Sovereign Hill. ✉ *Federation Sq. E, at Flinders and Russell Sts., City Center* ☎ *1300/858687* ⊕ *www.grayline.com.au* 🖃 *From A$162.*

Grampians National Park

260 km (162 miles) west of Melbourne, 100 km (62 miles) north of Hamilton.

Bushwalking is by far the most popular activity in the national park. Some of the best walks include Mackenzie Falls, the walk to Mt. Abrupt (or Mt. Murdadjoog in the Aboriginal language), the Hollow Mountain walk, and another to Silverband Falls. Even if you're not a big walker you can still see many of the best-known rock formations. Elephant Hide, the Balconies, the Pinnacle, and the Fortress are only a short walk from a car park. Canoeing is another great way to get away from the crowds and experience the lakes and rivers of the Grampians.

The most popular attractions of the central Grampians region can be visited in one day. However, if you want to visit the fascinating Brambuk Aboriginal Cultural Centre and take in a few wineries, allow yourself another day or two. From the town of Halls Gap it's a 15-km (9-mile)

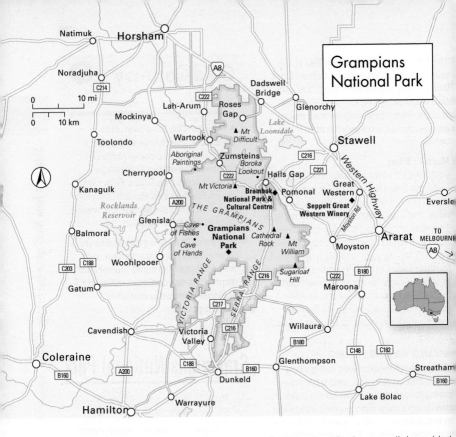

drive (plus a 100-yard walk from the car park) to the spectacular Boroka Lookout.

GETTING HERE AND AROUND

Halls Gap (the base town for the Grampians National Park) is reached via Ballarat and Ararat on the Western Highway (Highway 8). The town is 260 km (162 miles) northwest of Melbourne, 97 km (60 miles) northeast of Hamilton, and 140 km (87 miles) west of Ballarat. V/Line operates trains to Ballarat from Melbourne. V/Line buses connect with the trains to take passengers to Halls Gap. For timetables and fares, contact V/Line.

TOURS

Hangin' Out

ADVENTURE TOURS | For those who love experiencing the great outdoors from different angles, Hangin' Out runs rock climbing and abseiling tours to suit beginners and more experienced climbers; they also have an all-day guided adventure walk (A$140, minimum four people) from Mt. Stapylton to Hollow Mountain in the north of the Grampians. A four-hour taste of real rock climbing and rappelling costs A$85 (minimum two people); a full-day introduction to the rope sports is A$140. Private guided single- and multipitch climbs can be arranged. ☎ 0407/684831 ⊕ www.hanginout.com.au.

VISITOR INFORMATION

Halls Gap Visitor Information Centre

The center stocks the usual brochures and gives advice on sights and accommodations. ⊠ 117 Grampians Rd., Halls Gap ☎ 1800/065599 ⊕ www.visitgrampians.com.au.

tawell and Grampians Visitor Information entre

he center provides information on local ights and accommodations. It operates ut of the Stawell Gift Hall of Fame ıuseum. The Gift began in Easter 1878 nd is now Australia's oldest and richest hort-distance running race. ✉ *8 Main t., Stawell* ☎ *1800/330080* 🌐 *www. isitgrampians.com.au.*

Sights

rambuk National Park & Cultural Centre

USEUM | Owned and operated by boriginal people, this park and center rovide a unique living history of indig- nous culture in this part of Victoria. isplays of artwork, weapons, clothes, nd tools give a glimpse into the life of oori people (Aboriginal people of south- astern Australia). A film screened in the reaming Theatre describes the Creation gends of the Grampians mountains. ducational programs, including boo- erang throwing, painting, and didgeri- oo workshops, are presented daily and ıere is a bush tucker discovery walk and sting most days. Ceremonial music and ances are performed weekly. Visitors an learn the significance of paintings nearby Bunjil's Shelter on the Bunjil eation tour, conducted on weekdays at 30 am. ✉ *277 Grampians Tourist Rd., alls Gap* ☎ *03/8427–2311* 🌐 *www.bram- ık.com.au* 🎫 *Free; films and activities $6, bush discovery walks A$9, Bunjil eation Tour A$70.*

Grampians National Park

ATIONAL/STATE PARK | Comprising four ountain ranges—Mt. Difficult, Mt. illiam, Serra, and Victoria—the impres- ve Grampians National Park spills over 2,000 acres. Its rugged peaks, tower- g trees, waterfalls, creeks, and plethora wildlife attract bushwalkers, rock mbers, and nature lovers. Spectacular ldflowers carpet the region in spring, hile a number of significant Aboriginal ck art sites make it an ideal place to learn about Victoria's indigenous history. The township of Halls Creek (population 600) sits within the national park, and with its 10,000 tourist beds it becomes quite a busy place in summer and at Easter. If you're staying in a self-catering accommodation, it's wise to stock up on groceries and wine in the big towns of Ballarat, Ararat, Hamilton, or Horsham, since prices at the Halls Gap general store are inflated. One of the most pictur- esque drives in the park is the 60 km (37 miles) stretch from Halls Gap to Dunkeld.

Some areas in the park can be affected by fire and flood from year to year, so check with Parks Victoria for current road and camping conditions. ✉ *Grampi- ans National Park, Halls Gap* ☎ *131963* 🌐 *parks.vic.gov.au.*

Restaurants

Kookaburra Hotel

$$ | **AUSTRALIAN** | In the heart of Halls Gap, this is one of the town's best dining options and serves an imaginative range of dishes. The restaurant and bar provides a casual, gastropub experience, with signature dishes like the spinach crepe, baked duckling, blackened bar- ramundi, and the kangaroo fillet. **Known for:** spinach crepe; regional wines; gets busy, so book ahead. [$] *Average main: A$33* ✉ *125 Grampian Rd., Halls Gap* ☎ *03/5356–4222* 🌐 *www.kookaburra- hotel.com.au* 🕒 *Closed Mon. No lunch Tues.–Fri.*

★ **Royal Mail Hotel**

$$$ | **MODERN AUSTRALIAN** | Expansive views of the southern Grampians peaks compete with the extraordinary food plat- ed up at the only hotel in the tiny town of Dunkeld, 64 km (40 miles) south of Halls Gap. The menu changes daily depending on the harvest from the kitchen gardens, specializing in organic and heirloom vegetables. **Known for:** mountain views; produce sourced from on-site gardens and farm; cozy accommodations on-site.

Off The Beaten Path

Seppelt Great Western Winery. This old winery is also one of Australia's most famous, the name Great Western being associated with a long-lived sparkling wine and known for its the Salinger and Fleur de Lys ranges as well as a sparkling Shiraz and various table wines. Beneath the winery is a 3-km (2-mile) underground labyrinth of tunnels, known as the Drives, dating back to 1868 and originally built by gold miners. This is where the best sparkling wines are kept. You can take a day tour of these tunnels and the nearby shaft house and taste 20 Seppelt wines, or enjoy a barbecue and evening tour. Packages to tour and dine in the Drives, including cheese platters, two or three courses, and wine tastings, are also available from A$120 per person. The barbecue and dining options require a minimum of 15 people. ✉ *36 Cemetery Rd., Great Western* ☎ *03/5361–2239* 🌐 *www.seppelt.com.au* 🎟 *Cellar door free; tours from A$15.*

$ *Average main: A$46* ✉ *98 Parker St., Dunkeld* ☎ *03/5577–2241* 🌐 *www.royal-mail.com.au* ☞ *Sat. dinner degustation only.*

Hotels

★Boroka Downs

$$$$ | **HOTEL** | On 100 acres of bush, scrub, and grassland, bordering the Grampians National Park, Boroka's five villas are nothing short of spectacular. **Pros:** floor-to-ceiling windows frame mountain views; nature setting; eco-friendly but luxurious. **Cons:** pricey; two-night minimum stay; three-night stay in peak periods. $ *Rooms from: A$900* ✉ *51 Birdswing Rd., Halls Gap* ☎ *03/5356–6243* 🌐 *www.borokadowns.com.au* 🛏 *5 villas* 🍴 *Free breakfast.*

Activities

CANOEING

Absolute Outdoors

CANOEING/ROWING/SKULLING | If you want to experience the Grampians wilderness via its serene lakes, a half-day canoeing trip with this company that operates from a shop that sells outdoor equipment in Halls Gap may be the answer. It hosts outings on Lake Bellfield, a little to the southeast of the township. It also runs rock climbing, abseiling, and mountain bike adventures within the park. ✉ *105 Main Rd. (aka Grampians Rd.), Halls Gap* ☎ *03/5356–4556, 1300/526258* 🌐 *www.absoluteoutdoors.com.au* 🎟 *From A$60 for 2½-hr canoeing tour.*

HIKING

Auswalk

HIKING/WALKING | This long-established walking tour specialist operates guided and self-guided, seven-night, inn-to-inn hikes following the new Grampians Peak Trail from Mount Zero to Dunkeld. Luggage is transported between accommodation stops (which are more luxurious on the self-guided walk). Maps and other information are provided for self-guided walkers, and only two participants are needed for a tour to take place. The terrain of the walk is graded "moderate" for up to 85% of the walk, with about 15% rated strenuous. Wildlife, particularly kangaroos and wallabies, is abundant and wildflowers festoon the park from August to November. Self-guided trips run year-round, although you may want to avoid wet, chilly July. ☎ *03/9597–976*

itting on edge of Boroka Lookout in the Grampians National Park

www.auswalk.com.au ✉ From A$2695
er person, self-guided.

Echuca

*06 km (128 miles) north of Melbourne,
94 km (120 miles) west of Rutherglen,
2 km (57 miles) north of Bendigo.*

he name Echuca comes from a local
boriginal word meaning "meeting of
he waters," a reference to the town's
ocation at the confluence of the Murray,
ampaspe, and Goulburn rivers. In the
econd half of the 19th century Echuca
as Australia's largest inland port. Many
eminders of Echuca's colorful heyday
emain in the restored paddle steamers,
arges, and historic hotels, and in the
ed Gum Works, the town's sawmill,
ow a working museum.

ETTING HERE AND AROUND

chuca is a three-hour drive from Mel-
ourne, reached most directly by the
orthern Highway (Highway B75). V/Line
ains take 3½ hours to reach Echuca

from Melbourne's Southern Cross Station
once or twice a day; at other times trains
connect at Bendigo or Murchison East
with bus services to Echuca.

VISITOR INFORMATION

Echuca Visitor Information Centre
The center can book accommodations
and activities, as well as provide information on the region. ✉ *Old Pump Station,
2 Heygarth St.* ☎ *1800/039043* ⊕ *www.
echucamoama.com.*

◉ Sights

★ Historic River Precinct

HISTORIC SITE | The inland river port of
Echuca is a heritage town, home to a
large paddle steamer fleet and its historic
wharf. Among the vessels docked at the
wharf is the PS *Adelaide* (built in 1866),
the world's oldest operating wood-
en-hulled paddle steamer. Other historic
buildings include the **Bridge Hotel**, built
by ex-convict Henry Hopwood and the
"father of Echuca," who had the foresight
to establish a punt, and then to build

a bridge at this commercially strategic point on the river. The **Star Hotel**, built in the 1860s, has an underground bar and escape tunnel, which was used by after-hours drinkers in the 19th century to evade the police. The **Port of Echuca Discovery Centre** is now open and full of historical displays. It's also a booking office, where you can get tickets to paddle steamer cruises and other historic sights, plus a spooky Port After Dark tour (A$19.50) and a Pubs of the Port tour on Saturday nights (A$28). The center itself runs daily tours (A$14) covering its displays and the recently revitalized wharf areas (warehouses, old railroad tracks, and riverboats included), and the Star Hotel.

One-hour river excursions are a refreshing treat at the end of a hot summer's day. Step aboard the historic *Pevensey*, and the *Alexander Arbuthnot* (🌐 *www.echucapaddlesteamers.net.au*) or the *Canberra* and *Emmylou* (🌐 *www.murrayriverpaddlesteamers.com.au*), a 19th-century-style boat built in 1980–82 for a television series (Murray River Paddle Steamers). The paddle wheelers depart at least twice daily: check with the tourism office. A one-hour cruise on the PS *Emmylou* costs A$29.50. ✉ *74 Murray Esplanade* ☎ *03/5481–0500, 1300/942737* 🌐 *www.portofechuca.org.au.*

Hotels

PS Emmylou

$$$$ | **B&B/INN** | Departing from Echuca around sunset, the world's only wood-fired cruising paddle steamer chugs down the Murray River on cruises ranging from two hours to three nights, sailing through ancient wetlands, stopping to visit wineries, sites of Aboriginal cultural significance, and the 1860s Perricoota Station homestead. **Pros:** fabulous sense of history; lots of birdlife; lovely scenery. **Cons:** limited facilities; some rooms better than others. [$] *Rooms from: A$310* ✉ *57 Murray Esplanade* ☎ *03/5482–5244* 🌐 *www.murrayrivercruises.com.au* ⏰ *Closed June–Aug.* 🛏 *9 rooms* 🍴 *No meals.*

Activities

BOATING

Murray River Houseboats

BOATING | A popular pursuit on the Murray is to rent a houseboat and drift slowly down the river, and this operator's top-tier vessels are five-star floating experiences with Jacuzzis, state-of-the-art kitchens, and the latest appliances. They can sleep from two to 12 people and be rented from three days to a week and longer. There are six boats for rent. Prices start from A$1,790 for three nights in the peak late-December/January period, for two to seven people. ✉ *Riverboat Dock* ☎ *03/5480–2343* 🌐 *www.murrayriverhouseboats.com.au.*

CANOEING

River Country Adventours

BOATING | If you want to canoe up a lazy river—the Goulburn, which is a tributary of the Murray—you can arrange for a half- or full-day guided safari with this tour company. ✉ *Kyabram* ☎ *03/5852–2736, 0428/585227 mobile* 🌐 *www.adventours.com.au* 🎟 *From A$75 per person.*

Alpine National Park

323 km (200 miles) northeast of Melbourne, 40–50 km (25–31 miles) south t southeast of Mt. Buffalo.

The Alpine National Park stretches from central Gippsland in Victoria, all the way to the New South Wales border where it adjoins Kosciuszko National Park. Within the park are some of Australia's most stunning alpine landscapes, including mountain peaks, escarpments, and grassy high plains.

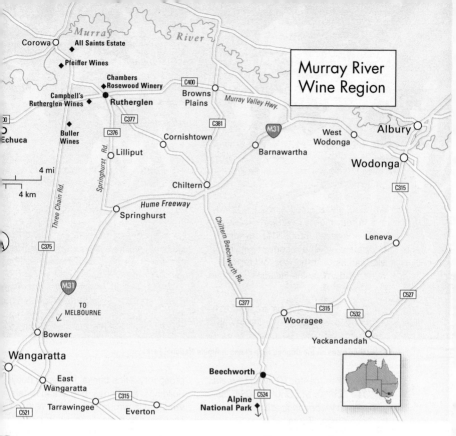

Murray River
Wine Region

Sights

Alpine National Park

NATIONAL/STATE PARK | This national park covers three loosely connected areas in eastern Victoria, which follow the peaks of the Great Dividing Range. One of these areas, formerly Bogong National Park, contains some of the highest mountains on the continent. As such, it a wintertime destination for skiers who flock to the resorts at Falls Creek, Mt. otham, and Dinner Plain.

he land around here is rich in history. ogong is an Aboriginal word for "big oth," and it was to Mt. Bogong that oorigines came each year after the inter thaw in search of bogong moths, nsidered a delicacy. Aborigines were ventually displaced by cattle ranchers ho brought their cattle here to graze.

The main townships in the area are Bright and Mount Beauty, both of which have visitor information centers. ⊠ *Alpine National Park* ☎ *13–1963* ⊕ *parks.vic.gov. au.*

Restaurants

Reed & Co. Distillery

$$ | **AUSTRALIAN** | A bright restaurant and café, the real reason to pop in is Reed & Co's artisanal gin, The Remedy—employing such Australian botanicals as eucalyptus and pine—for a quality afternoon G&T or gin cocktail. Its bar snacks and restaurant menu also go deep into Australian territory, with a wallaby tartare, steak from Tasmania's Cape Grim, cod from the Buffalo-Murray River, all cooked over redgum-fueled fire. **Known for:** artisanal Remedy Gin; seasonal ingredients from other small Australian producers;

Snow Gum trees on the Bogong High Plains in Alpine National Park

on-site coffee roaster. [$] *Average main: A$30* ✉ *15 Wills St., Bright* ☎ *03/5750–1304* 🌐 *www.reedandcodistillery.com* 🕒 *Closed Tues.–Thurs.*

Sixpence Coffee

$ | **CAFÉ** | Coffee aficionados make a beeline for here for house-roasted coffee and sensational pastries. Open Tuesday–Friday 8–3, Saturday 8–2. **Known for:** small-batch coffee roastery; delicious pastries; beans to go. [$] *Average main: A$5* ✉ *15 Wills St., Bright* ☎ *0423/262386* 🌐 *www.sixpencecoffee.com.au* 🕒 *Closed Sun. and Mon.*

Beechworth

271 km (168 miles) northeast of Melbourne, 96 km (60 miles) northwest of Alpine National Park, 44 km (26 miles) south of Rutherglen.

One of the prettiest towns in Victoria, Beechworth flourished during the gold rush. When gold ran out, the town of 30,000 was left with all the trappings of prosperity—fine banks, imposing public buildings, breweries, parks, and hotels wrapped in wrought iron—but with scarcely two nuggets to rub together. However, poverty protected the town from such modern improvements as aluminum window frames, and many historic treasures that might have been destroyed in the name of progress have been retained.

GETTING HERE AND AROUND

Beechworth and Rutherglen are on opposite sides of the Hume Freeway, the main Sydney–Melbourne artery. The 44-km (26-mile) Rutherglen-Beechworth Road (C377) connects both towns. Beechworth is about a three-hour drive from Melbourne, four hours from Canberra and six hours from Sydney. Beechworth can also be reached by taking a train from Melbourne's Southern Cross Station to Wangaratta, then changing to a bus service to the town; it's about a 3½-hour journey.

Ned Kelly

The English have Robin Hood, the Americans Jesse James. Australians have Ned Kelly, an Irish-descended working-class youth whose struggles against police injustice and governmental indifference made him a legend (though whether he was a hero or villain can still be a hot topic of conversation). The best way to learn about this local legend is to visit the town of Beechworth, where a Ned Kelly Guided Walking Tour departs from the visitor information center every day at 1:15 pm (A$15, includes entrance to several attractions). You'll see the courthouse where he was tried and the jail where he was imprisoned during his many scrapes with the law. The Burke Museum displays one of his death masks, made shortly after he was hanged at Old Melbourne Gaol. If you long to hear more, visit Glenrowan (40 km [25 miles] southwest of Beechworth), the scene of his famous "last stand" in 1880. It was here that Kelly, clad in his legendary iron armor, walked alone down the main street, fending off police bullets. He was finally shot in the leg, arrested, and hung in Old Melbourne Gaol. A huge statue, and a sound-and-light show that has received rather mixed reviews, commemorate Australia's most infamous outlaw.

VISITOR INFORMATION

Beechworth Tourist Information Centre

The center can book accommodations and tours as well as providing information on local attractions. It sells the Beechworth Heritage Pass, which gives entrance to the Burke Museum, the Kelly Vault, the Historic Courthouse and the Telegraph Station, and lets you join the Echoes of History and the Ned Kelly walking tours, which depart daily. The pass, valid for seven days, costs A$15. ✉ Old Town Hall, 103 Ford St. ☎ 03/5728–8065, 1300/366321 ⊕ www.explorebeechworth.com.au.

👁 Sights

Billson's Breweries

MUSEUM | The 1920s temperance movement helped to turn this brewery's focus to the brewing of nonalcoholic cordials. The cordials are produced using old-time recipes and seasonal flavors, such as Sicilian blood orange, using the area's natural spring water. You'll find a display of antique brewing equipment, worldwide beer labels, and rare bottles. On the same site is the Beechworth Carriage Museum, a collection of 20 horse-drawn vehicles and Australian Light Horse Infantry memorabilia from World War I. Tastings are free. Open daily 10–5. ✉ 29 Last St. ☎ 03/5728–1304, 1800/990098 ⊕ www.billsons.com.au ✉ Free.

Burke Museum

MUSEUM | This 160-year-old museum takes its name from Robert O'Hara Burke who, with William Wills, became one of the first white explorers to cross Australia from south to north in 1861. Burke served as superintendent of police in Beechworth from 1856 to 1859. Not surprisingly, the small area dedicated to Burke is overshadowed by the Ned Kelly collection, held in a separate vault here. You can see his death mask (several were made at the time of his death), replicas of the Kelly Gang's armor, and some memorabilia that give insight into the man and his misdeeds. The museum also displays a reconstructed streetscape of Beechworth in the 1880s. ✉ Loch St. ☎ 03/5728–8067 ⊕ www.burkemuseum.com.au ✉ A$15 for the Beechworth

The mighty Murray River is the lifeblood of the region

Heritage Pass, which includes 4 historic sites and 2 guided walks.

Ford Street

NEIGHBORHOOD | A stroll along Ford Street is the best way to absorb the historic character and charm of Beechworth. Between fabulous cafés, homewares shops, and the town's signature Beechworth Honey business (stop in for free tastings and to sample their honey-based hand creams), the distinguished buildings are **Tanswell's Commercial Hotel,** the **Town Hall,** and the **Courthouse.** It was in the latter that the committal hearing for the famous bushranger Ned Kelly took place in August 1880. His feisty mother, Ellen Kelly, was also sentenced to three years in jail at this court. The town bustles on Saturday mornings, especially when the excellent farmers' market is held on the grounds of the Christ Church Anglican Church, on the first Saturday of the month. ✉ *Ford St.* 🌐 *www.explorebeechworth.com.au.*

🍴 Restaurants

Beechworth Ice Creamery

$ | CAFÉ | FAMILY | On a hot summer's day, after a bike ride on the Rail Trail, pull up for a handmade sorbet from this family business, which has been making its sorbets in the back kitchen for 18 years. There is a standard list of 22 flavors, but the real winners are those blended with seasonal, locally grown fruits: the raspberry sorbet is a firm favorite. **Known for:** local institution; seasonal sorbets; gluten-, egg-, and dairy-free sorbets. [$] *Average main: A$6* ✉ *3 Camp St.* ☎ *03/5728–1330.*

★ Bridge Road Brewers

$ | PIZZA | FAMILY | Taste great craft beer and eat amazing pizza at this busy brewer, one of eight craft breweries of the High Country Brewery Trail. Tucked down a little lane off the main street, choose a picnic table beneath the umbrellas and listen to a folk band while you share a quality pizza or burger made with local produce. **Known for:** award-winning brews; family friendly; convenient to rail trail. **$** *Average main: A$20* ✉ *Old Coach House Brewers La., 50 Ford St.* ☎ *03/5728–2703* ⊕ *www.bridgeroad-brewers.com.au.*

★ Provenance

$$$$ | JAPANESE FUSION | Set in an ornate old bank which dates to 1856, this feted restaurant sees classic Australian ingredients such as kangaroo or local goat presented with Japanese preparation and accoutrements. There is a strong showing of sake on the drinks menu, which is curated by Chef Ryan's winemaker-sommelier wife, Jeanette Henderson, who also ensures almost every other wine is from the Beechworth region. **Known for:** local ingredients with Japanese twist; sake; stylish accommodations on-site. **$** *Average main: A$75* ✉ *86 Ford St.* ☎ *03/5728–1786* ⊕ *www.theprovenance. com.au* ⊙ *Closed Mon. and Tues. No dinner Sun.*

🏃 Activities

BICYCLING

The area from the Murray River to the mountains of northeast Victoria is ideal for cyclists of all persuasions, including casual pedalers and mountain bike enthusiasts.

Murray to Mountains Rail Trail

BICYCLING | A 98-km (61-mile) paved trail stretches from Wangaratta to Bright, with a branch line to Beechworth and recent extensions to Milawa. Bicycle rentals are available at Wangaratta, Beechworth, Bright, and Myrtleford. A trail map is available from the visitor centers at each of these towns, and can also be downloaded from the trail website. ✉ *100 Murphy St.* ☎ *1800/801065 Wangaratta Visitor Information Centre* ⊕ *www.murraytomountains.com.au.*

HIKING

There are several national parks within easy reach of Beechworth: Chiltern–Mt. Pilot National Park, Beechworth Historic

En Route 👁

Mt. Buffalo National Park. A perfect day trip from Bright, the park is full of fascinating granite formations, waterfalls, and animal and plant life. There are many more miles of walking tracks than you're likely to cover. The 2½-km (1½-mile) Gorge Walk is particularly scenic. Lake Cantani has swimming and a camping area in summer, while in winter, the snow-covered park becomes a playground for skiers and tobogganers. ✉ *Mt. Buffalo, Rutherglen* ✛ *The park is 42 km (26 miles) west of Bright* ☎ *13–1963* ⊕ *parks.vic.gov.au.*

Park, Mount Buffalo National Park, Mount Granya State Park, and Warby-Ovens National Park. The Beechworth visitor center and Parks Victoria have information on bushwalks. The town of Beechworth is the perfect place to get out and about and stretch your legs while admiring late 19th-century architecture. You can pick up a copy of "Echoes of History," a self-guided walking tour of the town from the visitor information center.

Parks Victoria

HIKING/WALKING | This government organization has information on Victoria's National Parks and walking trails. ☎ *13–1963* ⊕ *www.parks.vic.gov.au.*

Rutherglen

274 km (170 miles) northeast of Melbourne, 40 km (25 miles) northwest of Beechworth.

The surrounding red-loam soil signifies the beginning of the Rutherglen wine district, the source of Australia's finest fortified wines. If the term conjures up visions of cloying Ports, you're in for a surprise. In his authoritative *Australian Wine Compendium*, James Halliday says, "Like Narcissus drowning in his own reflection, one can lose oneself in the aroma of a great old muscat."

The main event in the region is Tastes of Rutherglen, held over two consecutive weekends in March ⊕ *www.tastesofruth-erglen.com.au*. The festival is a celebration of food, wine, and music—in particular jazz, folk, and country. Events are held in town and at all surrounding wineries. Another popular day in the vineyards is the Rutherglen Winery Walkabout held in June, when wine, food, and music are again on the menu ⊕ *www.winerywalka-bout.com.au*.

GETTING HERE AND AROUND

See Beechworth above. Rutherglen is 274 km (170 miles) north of Melbourne, about a 3½- to 4-hour drive along the Hume Freeway. V/Line train and bus services also come to Rutherglen.

TRANSPORTATION
V/Line

This train and bus service operates daily on V/Line from Melbourne's Southern Cross Station via Seymour and Wanga-ratta, a journey of about 3 hours and 25 minutes. ☎ *1800/800007* ⊕ *www.ptv.vic. gov.au*.

TOURS
Rutherglen Bus and Tour

BUS TOURS | Rutherglen Bus and Tour has winery tours for a minimum of six people, with visits to five to six wineries on half-day tours and eight to nine estates on day tours. Half-day tours cost A$40 per person, and day tours cost from A$55 per person (with pickup from Rutherglen accommodations only, though pickups from other towns can be arranged for A$15 per person). ☎ *0417/328774* ⊕ *www.rutherglenbu-sandtour.com* ⧆ *From A$40*.

En Route

Yackandandah. This cute small town, 23 km (14 miles) northeast of Beech-worth, shot to fame after the release of the lighthearted comedy *Strange Bedfellows*, starring Paul Hogan. The town's pretty historic buildings (including the two pubs, the post office, and the bank) were used as settings, and many of the town's 700 residents were movie extras. The town (Yack, to its friends), isn't looking to the past: it aims to be a carbon-neutral town by 2022. ⊠ *Yackandandah* ⊕ *www.explorey-ackandandah.com.au*.

VISITOR INFORMATION
Rutherglen Wine Experience and Visitor Information Centre

The friendly tourism office stocks local produce including olives and oils and has a good selection of Rutherglen wines for sale, along with the usual services. Book accommodations through them, buy tickets to events, or rent bicycles from A$25 for a half day to cycle the flat rail trail amid the vineyards. ⊠ *57 Main St.* ☎ *1800/622871* ⊕ *www.exploreruther-glen.com.au*.

Sights

All Saints Estate

WINERY/DISTILLERY | In business since 1864, this winery has a splendid, turreted castle that was built in the 1880s with capacious storage areas for its product. The old bottling hall and cellar have been revamped as a cheese tasting room, and a corrugated iron former Chinese dormitory is the property's third heritage-listed building, which you can visit to see in its original state—bunks and all—on guided tours of the winery. Tours are conducted at 11 am on weekends; book in advance. The winery produces Muscat and

Muscadelle from 60-year-old vines, and a range of crisp whites and full-bodied reds. The on-site Indigo Food Company providore sells regional cheeses and condiments ideal for a lavish picnic hamper. The menu at the Terrace restaurant—considered the best in the region—changes seasonally; desserts are excellent, especially when combined with a formidable northeast fortified wine. The cellar door and cheese room are open daily; the restaurant is open for lunch from Wednesday to Sunday and for dinner on Saturday only. The winery hosts a huge A Day on the Green music festival each February (⊕ www.adayonthegreen.com. au). ⊠ All Saints Rd., Wahgunyah ⊹ 9 km (5½ miles) northeast of Rutherglen ☎ 02/6035–2222, 1800/021621 ⊕ www. allsaintswine.com.au ➰ Free.

★ Buller Wines

WINERY/DISTILLERY | Established by Reginald Langdon Buller in 1921, this Rutherglen winery produces delicious fortified wines and gutsy, full-bodied reds, the flagship being its Shiraz. As the old Shiraz vines are not irrigated, the annual yields are low, but the fruit produced has intense flavor, which winemaker Dave Whyte crafts into wines of great depth and elegance. Tastings and sales are at the cellar door, free, or pay A$4 for tastings of its 50-year-old Muscats. The winery is also home to the very smart restaurant, Ripe, where chef Gavin Swalwell cruises his extensive gardens for produce to match Buller's wines on a sophisticated menu with good vegetarian options. ⊠ 2804 Federation Way ☎ 02/6032–9660 ⊕ www.bullerwines. com.au ➰ Free.

Campbell's Rutherglen Wines

WINERY/DISTILLERY | Wines have been made here by five generations of the Campbell family, dating back to 1870. Brothers Colin and Malcolm Campbell, the winemaker and viticulturist respectively, have been at the helm for the past 40 years. Famed for its award-winning

Rentals 🛏

Bright Escapes. Find your home in Bright, from a luxury couples retreats to a family-friendly spot or a property set right on the Rail Trail, catering for Bright's keen cycling scene. ⊠ Shop 5, 6 Anderson St., Bright ☎ 1300/551117 ⊕ www. brightescapes.com.au ⊗ Closed Sun. ⥩ 101 properties ⦿ No meals.

Bobbie Burns Shiraz and Merchant Prince Rare Rutherglen Muscat, the property covers a picturesque 160 acres. You can wander freely through the winery on a self-guided tour and taste wines at the cellar door, including rare and aged vintages. Vintage Reserve wines are available only at the cellar door. Private tastings and guided tours can be booked. The winery does not have a restaurant but sells baskets of local gourmet goodies. The winery also takes part in the annual Tastes of Rutherglen wine festival, when food and music are on the agenda. ⊠ 4603 Murray Valley Hwy. ⊹ 3 km (2 miles) west of Rutherglen ☎ 02/6033–6000, 1800/359458 ⊕ www. campbellswines.com.au ➰ Free.

Chambers Rosewood Winery

WINERY/DISTILLERY | Established in the 1850s, this is one of Australia's heavyweight producers of fortified wines. Stephen Chambers's Muscats are legendary, with blending stocks that go back more than a century. Stephen runs a very relaxed winery, which is genuinely rustic, being just a few corrugated iron sheds in an off-the-beaten-track road. The cellar door is renowned for great value and plenty of tastings; you can take home reasonably priced red and white wine and a full range of fortified wines—from the clean-skin variety (no-label stock) to big two-liter flagons. There's no restaurant, just a cellar door, which also sells homemade jams and condiments.

✉ *Barkley St., off Corowa Rd.* ☎ *02/6032–8641* 🌐 *www.chambersrosewood.com.au* 🎫 *Free.*

Pfeiffer Wines

WINERY/DISTILLERY | Since its first vines were planted in 1895, this winery has made exceptional fortified wines such as Topaque and Muscat, and varietal wines, including Shiraz and Durif. It also has one of the few Australian plantings of Gamay, the classic French grape used to make Beaujolais. At this small rustic winery you can preorder (with at least 24 hours' notice) picnic baskets for each season stuffed with gourmet products, cake, and a glass of table wine for A$115 for two, including plates and cutlery. Vegetarian baskets, and little children's hamper are A$12.50 per child. Cheese platters (A$30) are available any time. Winemaker Jen Pfeiffer also makes an aperitif called Pfeiffer Seriously Pink, which makes a cheeky wine cocktail. ✉ *167 Distillery Rd., Wahgunyah* ✥ *9 km (5½ miles) northwest of Rutherglen* ☎ *02/6033–2805* 🌐 *www.pfeifferwinesrutherglen.com.au* 🎫 *Free.*

Hotels

★ Mount Ophir Estate

$$$$ | **RENTAL** | **FAMILY** | Impossibly romantic, the Tower at Mount Ophir Estate was built in 1903, part of a French provincial style winery in an unmistakably Australian landscape. **Pros:** impeccable design and styling; magnificent historical buildings; unique accommodations. **Cons:** requires a car; steep staircases in the Tower suit agile adults only; two-night minimum in the Tower. [$] *Rooms from: A$550* ✉ *168 Stillards La.* ☎ *02/6035–2222* 🌐 *www.mountophirestate.com.au* 🛏 *5 cottages, 1 tower* 🍴 *No meals.*

Tuileries

$$$ | **HOTEL** | Incorporating a vineyard, olive groves, and a renowned restaurant, this accommodation feels like an exclusive retreat. **Pros:** beautifully appointed suites; tranquil vineyard and garden setting; set beside Rutherglen Estates' exciting indigenous art gallery. **Cons:** next to no nightlife in Rutherglen. [$] *Rooms from: A$225* ✉ *13 Drummond St.* ☎ *02/6032–9033* 🌐 *www.tuileries-rutherglen.com.au* 🛏 *16 rooms* 🍴 *Free breakfast.*

Chapter 7

TASMANIA

Updated by
Dan Broun

⊙ Sights	🍴 Restaurants	🛏 Hotels	🛍 Shopping	🍸 Nightlife
★★★★☆	★★★★☆	★★★☆☆	★☆☆☆☆	★★☆☆☆

WELCOME TO TASMANIA

TOP REASONS TO GO

★ **Beautiful Walks:** Tasmania has some of Australia's best walking terrain. Stunning walks of varying lengths can be experienced all over the state.

★ **Colonial Homes and Cottages:** Many of the Georgian mansions and charming cottages from Tasmania's early days as a colony are lovely lodging options.

★ **Tassie Tastes:** Hungry Tasmanians and tourists alike are well served, thanks to the state's beautiful produce and excellent wine.

★ **Stunning Capital:** Hobart, nestled beneath kunanyi/Mt. Wellington and hugging the Derwent Estuary, has long attracted lovers of nature and the arts.

★ **Living History:** The World Heritage–listed Port Arthur Historic Site is Australia's most famous penal settlement.

1 Hobart. A historic walkable little city with cool cafes, bars, and MONA.

2 The Huon Valley. Known for sandy beaches and Hastings Caves and Thermal springs.

3 Richmond. Popular Colonial village with antique stores, cafes, and excellent vineyards.

4 Port Arthur and the Tasman Peninsula. A large historical park, a fascinating convict past, and Tasi Devils.

5 East-Coast Resorts. Beautiful coastal scenery, stunning beaches, and little fishing towns.

6 Freycinet National Park. Renowned among adventure seekers and those who appreciate stunning scenery.

7 Launceton. Pleasant parks, historic mansions, and the Tamar Valley Wine Route.

8 Devonport and Nearby. A base for exploring the beautiful northwest region.

9 Stanley. A pretty village with the Nut, Tasmania's version of Uluru.

10 Cradle Mountain-Lake St. Clair National Park. Alpine scenery and popular hiking trails.

Wild and dramatic landscapes, empty white beaches, unique art and music festivals, and heavenly food and wine—Tasmania's charms have been overlooked for too long by international travelers. Hikers have always known about the island's wilderness trails, which lead you through magical forests and a diversity of national parks. More recently gourmands have discovered Tassie's superb local produce, making it a world-class gourmet destination, too.

Tasmania's attractions encompass the historic, the healthy, and the hedonistic. Although Tasmania now is an unspoiled reminder of a simpler, slower lifestyle away from the rat race, its bloody history is never far from the surface. Today, walking through the lovely grounds in Port Arthur, the notorious penal colony, or the unhurried streets of Australia's smallest capital city, Hobart, with its profusion of Georgian buildings, it's difficult to picture Tasmania as a land of turmoil and tragedy. But the near genocide of the Aboriginal population, who are thought to have crossed into Tasmania approximately 36,000 years ago, is a dark stain on the island's memory.

In many ways Tasmania is still untamed, making it a hiker's delight. The island's 19 national parks encompass impenetrable rain forests and wild rivers that cut through chains of untracked mountains. The coastlines are scalloped with endless desolate beaches—some pristine white,

fronting serene turquoise bays, and some rugged and rocky, facing churning, choppy seas.

These beautiful surroundings form part of Tasmania's newest claim to fame as a gourmet haven. Thanks to the island's many microclimates, you can grow or harvest virtually anything from superb dairy produce to wonderful meat, and its clear seas abound in wonderful seafood. Oenophiles have also discovered the island's cool climate wines, and the island's wine routes are worth a slow meander.

MAJOR REGIONS

Perhaps Australia's most beautiful state capital, the compact city of **Hobart** has a vibrant culture with beautifully preserved colonial architecture in genteel surroundings. **Side trips from Hobart** include short drives to some of Tasmania's most scenic and historic places, including **the Huon Valley** with its Hastings Caves and

Thermal Springs, the charming colonial village of **Richmond**, and **Port Arthur and the Tasman Peninsula** with its historical park and Tasmanian Devil Conservation Park. You can take these side trips in a day but if you can, stay a night or two to experience their delights at a leisurely pace.

The east coast enjoys Tasmania's mildest climate, pristine beaches, and excellent fishing spots. The stretches of white sand along **Freycinet National Park and East Coast Resorts** are often so deserted that you can pretend you're Robinson Crusoe. The **East Coast Resorts** and towns in this region are quiet but historically interesting; in Louisville, for example, you can catch a ferry to the Maria Island National Park, which was a whaling station and penal settlement in the mid-19th century. Farther north, the town of Swansea has numerous stone colonial buildings that have been restored as hotels and restaurants, as well as the unusual Spiky Bridge (so named because of its vertically placed sandstone "spikes") and the convict-built Three Arch Bridge, both of which date from 1845. The jewel of the eastern coast is **Freycinet National Park,** renowned among adventure seekers and those who appreciate stunning scenery. The spectacular granite peaks of the Hazards and the idyllic protected beach at Wineglass Bay have been dazzling visitors to this peninsula since it became a park in 1916. Tasmania's second-biggest city, **Launceton,** is a pleasant place to while away time, thanks to its attractive parks and historic colonial mansions.

Tasmania's **Northwest** region is one of the most beautiful and least explored areas of the state. For its sheer range of landscapes, from jagged mountain contours to ancient rain forests and alpine heathlands in the **Cradle Mountain** area alone, the northwest can't be matched. The region's beauty saw it designated the Tasmanian Wilderness World Heritage Area, protecting one of the last true wilderness regions on Earth. These regions are a major draw for hikers and sightseers. The port town of **Devonport** is worth a visit as is the town of **Stanley,** one of the prettiest towns in Tasmania. The western side of the northwest tip of Tasmania bears the full force of the roaring forties winds coming across the Indian Ocean, and this part of Tasmania contains some of the island's most dramatic scenery. Mining was a major industry a century ago, and although some mines still operate, the townships have a rather forlorn look.

Planning

WHEN TO GO

Cold weather–phobes beware: Tasmanian winters can draw freezing blasts from the Antarctic, so this is not the season to explore the highlands or wilderness areas, unless, of course, you like a little snow play. It's wiser in the colder months to investigate the many art galleries or enjoy the cozy interiors of colonial cottages and the open fireplaces of welcoming pubs.

Summer can be hot—bushfires do occasionally occur—but temperatures tend to be lower than on the Australian mainland.

The best seasons to visit are autumn, summer, and spring; early autumn is beautiful, with deciduous trees in full color and still conditions. Spring, with its splashes of pastel wildflowers and mild weather, is equally lovely. Tassie really comes alive in summer, when it's warm enough to swim at the many gorgeous beaches, the fresh summer produce is bountiful, and the lavender farms are in bloom.

Tasmania is a relaxing island with few crowds, except during the mid-December to mid-February school holiday period and at the end of the annual Sydney-to-Hobart yacht race just after Christmas, but you can always find a secluded beach or nature walk even at peak tourist season.

Most attractions and sights are open year-round.

PLANNING YOUR TIME

If you have limited time in Tasmania, spend your first morning in Hobart, where you can stroll around the docks, Salamanca Place, and Battery Point, and have some fish-and-chips from the harbor's floating chippies. After lunch, drive to Richmond and explore its 19th-century streetscape, then stay in a local bed-and-breakfast. On the second day head for Port Arthur, and spend the morning exploring the fascinating former penal colony. Spend the afternoon taking in the dramatic scenery of the Tasman Peninsula, noting the bizarre Tessellated Pavement and Tasman Arch blowhole near Eaglehawk Neck, or take the four-hour return walk to the spectacular Cape Huay. Return to Hobart for the night, then on the third morning take a leisurely drive around the scenic Huon Valley. On return to Hobart, finish your tour with a trip to the summit of kunanyi/Mt. Wellington or a wander around the amazing Museum of Old and New Art (MONA).

If you have more time, continue on to Freycinet National Park. Climb the steep path to the outlook over Wineglass Bay, then descend to the sands for a picnic and swim. Stay two nights in the park, then meander back through the east-coast wine regions. Return to the capital, topping off the day with city views from kunanyi/Mt. Wellington.

GETTING HERE AND AROUND

Tasmania is compact—the drive from Hobart in the south to the northern city of Launceston takes little more than two hours. The easiest way to see the state is by car, as you can plan a somewhat circular route around the island. Begin in Hobart or Launceston, where car rentals are available from the airport and city agencies, or in Devonport if you arrive on the ferry from Melbourne. Allow plenty of time for stops along the way, as there are some fabulous sights to be seen. Bring a sturdy pair of shoes and warm clothing for impromptu mountain and seaside walks; you'll most often have huge patches of forest and long expanses of white beaches all to yourself.

In some cases the street addresses for attractions may not include building numbers (in other words, only the name of the street will be given). Don't worry—this just means either that the street is short and the attractions are clearly visible or that signposts will clearly lead you there.

If you are exploring several national parks in the space of a few weeks or months it is recommended to buy a Holiday Vehicle Pass that is valid for two months for A\$60 per vehicle in the National Parks of Tasmania.

AIR TRAVEL

Hobart International Airport is 22 km (14 miles) east of Hobart, one hour by air from Melbourne or two hours from Sydney. Although most interstate flights connect through Melbourne, Qantas, Jetstar, and Virgin Australia also run direct flights to other mainland cities. Launceston airport is at Western Junction, 16 km (10 miles) south of central Launceston. It's served by Jetstar, Tiger Airways, and Virgin Australia.

On the island, King Island Airlines, Regional Express Airlines(REX) or Sharp Airlines can get you to the northwest and King or Flinders Islands. Tickets can be booked through the airlines or through the Tasmanian Travel and Information Centre. Skybus has an airport shuttle service for A\$18.50 per person between the airport and city hotels. Metered taxis are available at the stand in front of the terminal. The fare to downtown Hobart is approximately A\$45.

CAR TRAVEL

Port Arthur is an easy 90-minute drive from Hobart via the Arthur Highway. A private vehicle is essential if you want to explore parts of the Tasman Peninsula

eyond the historic settlement. A vehicle
s absolutely essential on the west coast.
he road from Hobart travels through the
Derwent Valley and past lovely historic
owns before rising to the plateau of
entral Tasmania. Many of the roads in
vestern Tasmania are twisty and even
npaved in the more remote areas, but
vo-wheel drive is sufficient for most
ouring. Be prepared for sudden weather
hanges: snow in the summertime is not
ncommon in the highest areas. Lake
t. Clair is 173 km (107 miles) northwest
f Hobart, and can be reached via the
yell Highway, or from Launceston via
eloraine or Poatina. Cradle Mountain is
5 km (53 miles) south of Devonport, and
an be reached by car via Claude Road
om Sheffield or via Wilmot. Both lead
0 km (19 miles) along Route C132 to
radle Valley.

ESTAURANTS

lthough there are elegant dining
otions in the larger towns—especially
obart—most eateries serve meals
a casual setting. Fiercely proud of
eir local produce, Tasmania's res-
urateurs have packed their menus
ith homegrown seafood, beef, lamb,
nd cheeses, washed down with their
mous cold-climate wines or craft beers.
asmanian wine is nearly unknown in the
est of the world, however the secret is
ut, with Tasmanian pinots and sparkling
ine wowing wine judges around the
orld. The Tasmanian whiskey scene is
so thriving with boutique distilleries
merging all the time.

OTELS

he hospitality industry is thriving in
asmania, so in popular areas you'll find
wide range of accommodation options,
om inexpensive motels to genteel
&Bs, rustic lodges to luxury hotels.
lost hotels will have air-conditioning,
ut bed-and-breakfast lodgings often do
ot. Apart from a few hotels right in the
ain city center, most Hobart accommo-
ations have free parking. No smoking

is allowed inside any Tasmanian public
building. *Hotel reviews have been shortened. For full information, visit Fodors.
com.*

What It Costs in Australian Dollars			
$	**$$**	**$$$**	**$$$$**
RESTAURANTS			
under A$21	A$21–A$35	A$36–A$50	over A$50
HOTELS			
under A$151	A$151–A$200	A$201–A$300	over A$300

Hobart

Straddling the Derwent River at the foot
of kunanyi/Mt. Wellington's forested
slopes, Hobart was founded as a penal
settlement in 1803. It's the second-oldest city in the Australia after Sydney, and
it certainly rivals its mainland counterpart
as Australia's most beautiful state capital.
Close-set colonial brick-and-sandstone
shops and homes line the narrow, quiet
streets, creating a genteel setting for
this historic city of 240,000. Life revolves
around the River Derwent and its port,
one of the deepest harbors in the world.
Here warehouses that once stored
Hobart's major exports of fruit, wool,
corn, and products from the city's former
whaling fleet still stand alongside the
wharf today.

Hobart sparkles between Christmas and
New Year—summer Down Under—during the annual Sydney-to-Hobart yacht
race. The event dominates conversations
among Hobart's citizens, who descend
on Constitution Dock to welcome
the yachts and join in the boisterous
festivities of the crews. The New Year
also coincides with the Taste of Tasmania
Festival, when the dockside area comes
alive with the best of Tasmanian food and
wine on offer in numerous cafés, bars,
and waterfront stalls. In recent years, the

eclectic Museum of Old and New Art (MONA) has invigorated Hobart's cultural life. The "MONA effect" has triggered a mini-explosion of cool, new places to eat, drink, and play. The Dark Mofo festival in the dead of winter now attracts tens of thousands to a hedonistic celebration of all things dark and dangerous. Otherwise, Hobart is a placid city whose nightlife is largely confined to excellent restaurants, jazz clubs, and whiskey bars.

GETTING HERE AND AROUND
Hobart, being teeny-tiny, is eminently walkable; once you're in the city center, no attraction is more than 15 minutes' walk away, apart from the Cascade Brewery and the Museum of Old and New Art (MONA). Because of the many one-way streets, it's best to park a car and leave it for the day as you explore. If you prefer two wheels to two legs, you can hire trendy electric bicycles from Hobart Bike Hire on Brooke Street for A$45 for the day. There are also open-topped double-decker buses with a hop-on, hop-off ticket, valid for 24 hours, available for A$35.

VISITOR INFORMATION
CONTACTS Tasmanian Travel and Information Centre. ⊠ *20 Davey St., at Elizabeth St., Hobart Waterfront* ☎ *03/6238–4222* ⊕ *www.hobarttravelcentre.com.au.*

◉ Sights

★ Brooke Street Pier
MARINA | The busy waterfront at Brooke Street Pier is the city's key departure point for harbor cruises. Newly renovated, the translucent building has an excellent cocktail bar and restaurant as well as plenty of tourist information and a trading space for Tasmanian artisans. ⊠ *Franklin Wharf* ⊕ *www.brookestreetpier.com.*

Cascade Brewery
WINERY/DISTILLERY | This is Australia's oldest and most picturesque brewery, producing fine Tasmanian beers since 1824. You can see its inner workings on

Off The Beaten Path ◉

Bonorong Wildlife Sanctuary. About 25 km (16 miles) north of Hobart on the highway toward Launceston, this sanctuary hosts a diverse selection of Australian species—many of which have been rescued—including koalas, wombats, quolls, and the adorable Tasmanian devil. The private dusk tours are highly recommended and provide a rare opportunity to experience Tassie's beautiful nocturnal animals at their most active. ⊠ *593 Briggs Rd., Brighton* ☎ *03/6268–1184* ⊕ *www. bonorong.com.au* ⊠ *A$30, dusk tours A$160.*

the 90-minute tours, which require lots of walking and climbing, but you're rewarded with three free drinks at the end. Note that appropriate attire (long pants and closed-toe shoes only) is required, and tour reservations are essential. It's a 30-minute walk from the city center, or buses leave from Franklin Square every 35 minutes from 9:15 am. ⊠ *140 Cascade Rd., South Hobart* ☎ *03/6224–1117* ⊕ *www.cascadebreweryco.com.au* ⊠ *A$30.*

Constitution Dock
MARINA | Yachts competing in the annual Sydney-to-Hobart race moor at this colorful marina dock from the end of December through the first week of January. Buildings fronting the dock are century-old reminders of Hobart's trading history. Nearby Hunter Street is the original spot where British ships anchored at the time of colonization. There's a multitude of eateries, none better than the fish punts on the wharf. ⊠ *Argyle St at Davey St., Hobart Waterfront* ⊠ *Free.*

Maritime Museum of Tasmania

MUSEUM | FAMILY | The old state library building houses one of the best maritime collections in Australia, including figureheads, whaling implements, models, and photographs dating from as far back as 1804. It's a small museum though, so don't plan on spending more than an hour. Upstairs the Carnegie Gallery has rotating exhibitions in a magnificent space. ⊠ Carnegie Bldg., Argyle St. at Davey St., Hobart Waterfront ☎ 03/6234–1427 ⊕ www.maritimetas.org ⊠ A$10.

★ Museum of Old and New Art (MONA)

ARTS VENUE | Australia's largest privately funded museum is home to a diverse array of exhibits from Tasmanian millionaire David Walsh's private collection. The unusual collection contains more than 400 often provocative pieces, including Sidney Nolan's Snake—an impressive mural made of more than 1,500 individual paintings—and Wim Delvoye's Cloaca Professional, an interesting contraption that transforms food into excrement. Each year, the museum also hosts the Mona Foma festival, Tasmania's largest contemporary music festival. MONA's two-week winter festival, Dark Mofo, celebrates the dark through large-scale public art, food, music, and light. Sometimes compared with Bilbao's Guggenheim Museum, MONA has an eclectic mix of antiquities and contemporary art. The unusual building itself is set into cliffs on the Berriedale peninsula, and visitors to the museum use touch-screen devices to learn about the exhibits as they wander around. To reach MONA, it's a 15-minute drive, or you can take the MONA-ROMA minibus from the Hobart waterfront or airport. There is also the MONA fast catamaran from the Hobart waterfront. ⊠ 651–655 Main Rd., Berriedale ☎ 03/6277–9900 ⊕ www.mona. net.au ⊠ A$28 ⊘ Closed Tues.

Narryna Heritage Museum

MUSEUM | Exhibits in this gracious old Georgian town house, surrounded by a lovely rose-filled garden, depict the life of Tasmania's upper-class pioneers. Of particular interest are the collections of colonial furniture, clothes, paintings, and photos. ⊠ 103 Hampden Rd., Battery Point ☎ 03/6234–2791 ⊕ www.narryna. com.au ⊠ A$10.

Penitentiary Chapel Historic Site

BUILDING | "The Tench," as it was known by its inhabitants, was the prisoners' barracks for Hobart Town. The buildings, only a short walk from Hobart's CBD, vividly portray Tasmania's penal, judicial, and religious heritage in their courtrooms, old cells, and underground tunnels. If you want to get spooked, come for the nighttime ghost tour (reservations necessary). ⊠ Brisbane St. at Campbell St., City Center ☎ 03/6231–0911 ⊕ nationaltrust-tas.rezdy.com ⊠ From A$20.

Royal Tasmanian Botanical Gardens

GARDEN | FAMILY | The largest area of open land in Hobart, these well-tended gardens are rarely crowded and provide a welcome relief from the city. Plants from all over the world are here—more than 6,000 exotic and native species in all. The collection of Tasmania's unique native flora is especially impressive. The café serves wholesome meals with some produce grown on-site. ⊠ Lower Domain Rd., Queen's Domain ☎ 03/6236–3075 ⊕ www.rtbg.tas.gov.au ⊠ Free.

★ Salamanca Place

NEIGHBORHOOD | Many of the warehouses once used by whalers from ships docking at Salamanca Place have been converted into delightful craft shops, art galleries, and restaurants. At the boisterous Saturday market, which attracts all elements of Tasmanian society, from hippies to the well-heeled, dealers in Tasmanian arts and crafts, fresh produce, clothing, rare books, and much more display their wares between 8:30 and 3. Keep an eye open for items made from beautiful Tasmanian timber, particularly Huon pine. ⊠ Salamanca Pl., Hobart Waterfront ⊕ www.salamanca.com.au.

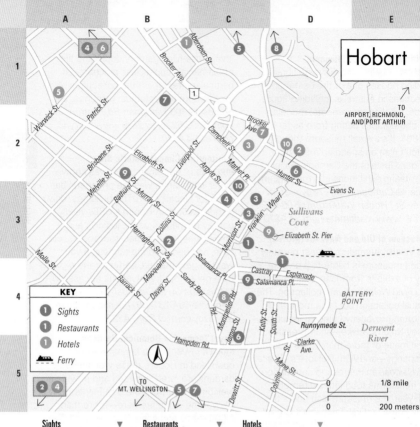

Hobart

TO AIRPORT, RICHMOND, AND PORT ARTHUR

Sullivans Cove

Elizabeth St. Pier

Castray Esplanade

Salamanca Pl.

BATTERY POINT

Runnymede St.

Derwent River

Clarke Ave.

TO MT. WELLINGTON

0   1/8 mile

0   200 meters

KEY

- Sights
- Restaurants
- Hotels
- Ferry

★ Tasmanian Museum and Art Gallery

MUSEUM | Housed in a series of coloni-al-era buildings overlooking Constitution Dock, this art and artifact gallery is a good starting point for uncovering Tasmania's rich history. With one of Australia's largest and most diverse collections it's a great place in Hobart to learn about the island's Aboriginal culture and unique wildlife. There are free guided tours Wednesday to Sunday at 11, 1, and 2. ⊠ Dunn Pl., Hobart Waterfront 🕾 03/6165–7000 ⊕ www.tmag.tas.gov. au 🖃 Free.

🔱 Beaches

Hobart, which is surrounded by water, has a number of spectacular sandy beaches, most of them close to the city center or Derwent estuary.

Cornelian Bay Beach

BEACH—SIGHT | Just five minutes' drive from Hobart's city center, this safe and quiet beach lies immediately north of the Queen's Domain urban parkland. Assorted sailing boats sit offshore in Cornelian Bay, while a popular trail, the Queen's Walk, runs directly behind the beach. The Cornelian Bay trail is popular among the locals. Charming Heritage-list-ed boathouses, picnic sites, a children's playground, and barbecues line the shore. The waterfront-facing Cornelian Bay Boathouse Restaurant is known for creative locally caught seafood and fresh Tasmanian produce. **Amenities:** food and drink; parking (free). **Best for:** solitude; walking. ⊠ Cornelian Bay, Queen's Domain.

Seven Mile Beach

BEACH—SIGHT | One of Hobart's favorite beaches, this long, sandy stretch of sand is less than a 20-minute drive outside of Hobart, close to the airport. It is both isolated and stunning to look at, although it can be noisy with planes taking off and landing nearby. Considered a great family beach, it's rarely crowded and ideal for

kunanyi/ Mt. Wellington

kunanyi is the Tasmanian Aboriginal name for Mt. Wellington, the ever-present behemoth that hovers over Hobart. The Mountain, as most locals refer to it, is a place for recreation and wonder for Hobartians. There are a multitude of walking tracks from the city to the summit. Other tracks are designed specifically for mountain biking. kunanyi/ Mt. Wellington is clad in mixed forest types, dozens of creeks and waterfalls, giant boulder fields, and an alpine moorland. You can hire a bike to ride back down.

long walks along sand that's peppered with many unusual shells. The small surrounding community includes a playgrounds, golf courses, and restaurants. Seven Mile Beach Cabin and Caravan Park is set within a beautiful beach alongside the beach. There are numerous day-use areas—No. 1 has unsheltered tables and a lawn area suitable for picnicking. **Amenities:** food and drink; parking (free); showers; toilets. **Best for:** solitude; swimming; walking. ⊠ Seven Mile Beach.

🍴 Restaurants

Constitution Dock is the perfect place for yacht-watching, as well as gobbling fresh fish-and-chips from one of the punts (floating fish-and-chips shops) moored on the water. Ask for the daily specials, such as local blue grenadier or trevally, which cost A$7–A$16, or go for some freshly shucked oysters. The city's main restaurant areas include the docks and the streets around Salamanca Place.

★ Blue Eye Seafood Restaurant

$$$ | SEAFOOD |FAMILY | Located on Castray Esplanade opposite Princes Wharf, Blue

Eye offers up a wide variety of fresh Tasmanian seafood, cooked to perfection. The BBQ Pirates Bay octopus is a highlight, as is the mixed grill, washed down with a cool Tasmanian craft beer. **Known for:** BBQ Pirates Bay octopus; Bruny Island oysters; local craft beers. [$] *Average main: A$38* ✉ *1 Castray Esplanade, Battery Point* ☎ *03/6223–5297* 🌐 *www.blueeye.net.au.*

★ Fico

$$$ | ITALIAN | Describing itself as "a neo bistro blurring the lines between fine dining and a traditional bistro," Fico is helmed by two young, creative chefs who offer fresh thinking, strong technique, and modern Italian cuisine with a distinctly Tasi flavor. The food is locally sourced and all food suppliers, from cabbages to pigeon, sea urchin to sheep, are proudly touted. **Known for:** modern Italian; tasting menu; expertly roasted pigeon. [$] *Average main: A$45* ✉ *151 Macquarie St., City Center* ☎ *03/6245–3391* 🌐 *www.ficofico.net.*

★ Frank Restaurant

$$ | ARGENTINE | South American food culture has inspired the menu of this eclectic but sophisticated eatery on Hobart's waterfront. Blending fresh Tasmanian produce with centuries of South American flavor refinement, Frank is a lively spot for a reason. **Known for:** South American–influenced menu; waterfront location; eclectic decor. [$] *Average main: A$24* ✉ *1 Franklin Wharf, Hobart Waterfront* ☎ *03/6231–5005* 🌐 *www.frankrestaurant.com.au.*

Lebrina

$$$ | AUSTRALIAN | Elegant surroundings in an 1840 brick colonial home inspire classic Tasmanian cooking in Hobart's most formal dining room. The best of the island's fresh produce is well utilized in such dishes as the twice-cooked soufflé of Pyengana cheddar, or the line-caught, Pedra Branca hapuku fillet. **Known for:** special-occasion restaurant; private-home setting; delicious desserts. [$] *Average main: A$50* ✉ *155 New Town Rd., New Town* ☎ *03/6228–7775* 🌐 *lebrina.com* ⏲ *Closed Sun. and Mon. No lunch.*

Me Wah

$$$ | CHINESE | FAMILY | Featuring a superb range of wines from around the world, this sumptuously decorated Sandy Bay eatery rivals many of the better Chinese restaurants in Sydney and Melbourne. There is a broad menu, ranging from the pricey "candy heart" dried abalone to traditional favorites, such as Me Wah's delicious steamed dumplings; there's even a banquet option. **Known for:** steamed dumplings; broad menu; traditional Cantonese tea service. [$] *Average main: A$45* ✉ *16 Magnet Ct., Sandy Bay* ☎ *03/6223–3688* 🌐 *www.mewah.com.au* ⏲ *Closed Mon.*

Peacock and Jones

$$$ | AUSTRALIAN | Tucked away in the sandstone buildings of Hunter Street, Peacock and Jones offers intimate fine dining in a contemporary-art-filled space. The stars of the show are the highest-quality Tasmanian produce and an enticing wine list. **Known for:** seasonal produce; contemporary art; romantic vibe. [$] *Average main: A$40* ✉ *25 Hunter St., Hobart Waterfront* ☎ *03/6210–7700* 🌐 *peacockandjones.com.au.*

The Point Revolving Restaurant

$$$$ | MODERN AUSTRALIAN | This revolving restaurant atop one of Hobart's tallest buildings (it's also home to the city's casino) has breathtaking views, and the food is equally rewarding. The Rannoch Farm quail breast is a wonderful starter; for a main course, try the Cape Grim Scotch fillet served with Cygnet gourmet mushrooms, bone marrow, cocktail onions, and parsley. **Known for:** great views; French-inspired menu; casino in building. [$] *Average main: A$55* ✉ *Wrest Point Hotel, 410 Sandy Bay Rd., Sandy Bay* ☎ *03/6221–1888* 🌐 *www.wrestpoint.com.au/restaurant/point-revolving-restaurant* ⏲ *Closed Mon. No lunch Sat.–Thurs.*

Continued on page 3

FOLLOWING THE
CONVICT TRAIL

For many, Tasmania conjures up grim images of chain-ganged prisoners: British convicts banished from the motherland to languish on a distant island in a faraway colony.

Its humble (and brutal) beginning as a penal colony is a point of pride for many Australians. It's no small feat that a colony comprised of, among others, poor Irish, Scottish, and Welsh convicts—many imprisoned for crimes as petty as stealing a loaf of bread—were able to build what is now Australia. It epitomizes a toughness of character that Australians prize. Many here can accurately trace their lineage back to the incarcerated. Kevin Rudd, the country's former Prime Minister, is himself descended from six convicts, including Mary Wade, the youngest female prisoner transported to Australia at the age of 11.

Tasmania has a number of remarkably well-preserved convict sites, most of which are set on the isolated Tasman Peninsula, some 75 km (47 mi) southeast of Hobart. Here, the region's beautifully rugged landscape belies the horrors of the past. Exploring Tasmania's convict heritage and the dramatic beauty of the island are two sides of the same coin. The region's isolation, impenetrable rain forests, and sheer cliffs falling into the sea made it a perfect island prison. By following signs on what's called the Convict Trail, you'll go home with provocative insight into what life was like for the almost 75,000 souls sent to Tasmania between 1803 and 1853.

by Helena Iveson

The rugged and beautiful Tasmanian Coast.

TASMANIA'S CONVICT PAST

Port Arthur Historic Site

"It is impossible to convey, in words, any idea of the hideous phantasmagoria of shifting limbs and faces which moved through the evil-smelling twilight of this terrible prison-house. Callot might have drawn it, Dante might have suggested it, but a minute attempt to describe its horrors would but disgust. There are depths in humanity which one cannot explore, as there are mephitic caverns into which one dare not penetrate."

—Marcus Clarke's description of Port Arthur's Separate Prison in his famous novel *For the Term of his Natural Life.*

They came in chains to this hostile island, where the seasons were all the wrong way around and the sights and smells were unfamiliar. In the 50 years following the establishment of the first settlement in Tasmania (Van Diemen's Land) in 1803, 57,909 male and 13,392 female prisoners were sent to the island. From 1830 on, many ended up at the newly built penal settlement at Port Arthur, where the slightest infraction would be punished by 100 lashes or weeks of solitary confinement on a diet of bread and water. Life was spent in chains, breaking up rocks or doing other menial tasks—all meant to keep criminal tendencies at bay.

The location of the settlement on the Tasman Peninsula was ideal for a prison. Joined to the rest of the island by a narrow neck of land with steep cliffs pounded by surging surf, it was easy to isolate and guard with half-starved dogs on the infamous dogline. Even though convicts were sentenced for a specific number of years, conditions were so brutal that even a few years could become a life sentence. With no chance of escape, some prisoners saw suicide as the only way out.

As the number of prisoners increased, more buildings went up. In time, the penal colony became a self-sufficient industrial center where prisoners sawed timber, built ships, laid bricks, cut stone, and made tiles, shoes, iron castings, and clothing.

A sculpture representing the infamous dogline at Eaglehawk Neck, Tasman Peninsula

HOW TO EXPLORE

GETTING HERE
To fully experience the trail, you'll need a car. It's possible to get to Port Arthur via operators such as Tassielink, but you can't access the whole trail by public transportation.

From Hobart head north to the well-preserved village of Richmond before continuing southeast on the Arthur Highway (A9) to the small town of Sorell. Not far from here is the infamous Eaglehawk neck, marking the start of the Tasman Peninsula. The Convict Trail runs in a circle around the peninsula, with signs clearly marking the many sites along the way.

TIMING
Port Arthur is 120 km (75 mi) or an hour and a half away from Hobart, but will take longer if you intend on making stops at Richmond and Sorell (which you should).

This trip can be done in one long day, but if you want to thoroughly explore the Tasman Peninsula, allow for two or three days. The Convict Trail booklet is available from visitor information centers across Tasmania and details the key sites and attractions along the route.

Richmond Bridge and Church

EXPLORING
It's easy to forget that Port Arthur wasn't an isolated settlement. The whole of the Tasman Peninsula was part of a larger penal colony, so, for the full experience, don't overlook the smaller sights. There are plenty of cafés and accommodations along the way, so take your time.

STUNNING VIEWS
Don't miss the vistas at the Tasman National Park Lookout. The walk along dramatic sea cliffs, which are among the highest and most spectacular in Australia, is easy and rewarding. The views of Pirates Bay, Cape Hauy, and the two islands just off the coast called The Lanterns are spectacular.

EN ROUTE
Take a break at the famous Sorell Fruit Farm where from November to May it's pick-you-own-berry season (✉ 174 Pawleena Road, Sorell ☎ 03/6265–2744 ⊕ www.sorellfruitfarm.com ☉ Oct., Mar., Apr., and May 10–4; Nov., Dec., Jan., and Feb. 8:30–5).

Isle of the Dead

TOURING THE CONVICT TRAIL

It's hard to absorb this disturbing story of human suffering. Around 73,000 convicts were transported here, and about 1 in 5 served time in Port Arthur, on Tasmania's southernmost tip.

Stone bridge at Richmond

❶ RICHMOND BRIDGE. Australia's oldest bridge was built by convict labor in 1825 and is a lasting symbol of the island's convict heritage. Don't miss the village's gaol, which predates Port Arthur by five years.

❷ SORELL. This early settlement is where bloody bushranger battles were fought in the colony's formative years. Bushrangers were actually

Sorell Berry Farm

outlaws who lived in the bush. A walk around the town reveals some interesting heritage buildings; there are also plenty of antiques shops and cafes to keep you occupied.

❸ THE DOGLINE. Statues of snarling hounds represent the dogs that prevented the convicts from escaping and mark the infamous dogline along the narrow strip of land linking the Tasman Peninsula with the rest of Tasmania.

Old wooden jetty in Norfolk Bay

❹ NORFOLK BAY. This is the site of a human-powered tramway. Goods were unloaded from ships at the Convict Station and then transported to Port Arthur by a tram dragged by convicts across the peninsula. This saved the ship a dangerous journey across the peninsula's stormy bays.

❺ PORT ARTHUR. Walking among the peaceful ruins and quiet gardens, it's difficult to imagine that this place was hell-on-earth for the convicts. When the settlement closed in 1877, the area was renamed Carnarvon in an attempt to disconnect the land from the horrors associated with its former name. However, in 1927 it was reinstated as Port Arthur and opened to a public keen to embrace this aspect of the Australian story.

TRAIL MARKERS

The Convict Trail is marked with a broad arrow symbol that was stamped on convict-made goods. It's framed in yellow to reference the color of convict clothing.

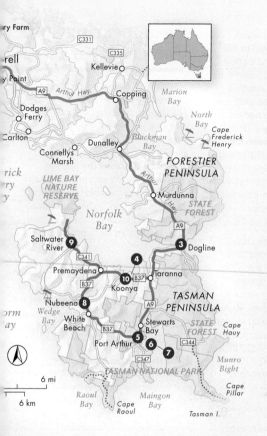

Sandstone church at Port Arthur

❼ ISLE OF THE DEAD CONVICT CEMETERY. A small island in the harbor near Port Arthur is the final resting place for about a thousand people, most of them convicts and ex-convict paupers who were buried mostly in unmarked graves.

❽ NUBEENA was established as an outstation of Port Arthur and for many years was an important convict farming community. It was also the sight of a semaphore station, used to raise the alarm if a convict made a bid for freedom.

❾ SALTWATER RIVER. Exploring the abandoned mines reveals the terrible conditions in which the convicts suffered: restored tiny underground cells, totally without light and filled with fetid air give horrifying insight.

❿ KOONYA. The probation station here was once an important convict outpost known as the Cascades. It operated between 1843 and 1846 and you'll find a few isolated houses and a well-restored penitentiary that once held 400 men, at least a quarter of them in chains.

❻ POINT PUER BOYS PRISON. More than 3,000 boys, some as young as age nine, passed through here from 1834 to 1849. Located just across the harbor from the main Port Arthur settlement, this was the first jail in the British Empire built exclusively for juvenile male convicts. But just because they were young doesn't mean they were spared from hard labor like stone-cutting and construction. The prison was also infamous for its stern discipline—solitary confinement, days at a time on a

The Penitentiary Block

tread wheel, and whipping were standard punishments for even a trivial breach of the rules.

Syra
$ | **MIDDLE EASTERN** |**FAMILY** | A simple and unpretentious venue tucked in the back of Salamanca Square, and a short stroll from the waterfront and Salamanca Place, Syra's Middle Eastern–inspired menu is designed to be shared with your fellow diners. Let the kitchen "feed you" four dishes to share for $50 per person, or five for $65. **Known for:** Middle Eastern food; family-style dining; chef's choice dishes. [$] *Average main: A$20* ✉ *8 Salamanca Sq., Battery Point* ☎ *03/6287–6286* 🌐 *www.syrarestaurant.com.au* 🕒 *No lunch Mon.–Thurs.*

Urban Greek
$$ | **GREEK FUSION** | Urban Greek combines the flavors of the old world with antipodean audacity, all set in a modern space. The variety of seating options includes communal benches, tables for groups, or kitchen-bar placement. **Known for:** traditional Greek cuisine with modern Australian twist; affordable eats; communal seating. [$] *Average main: A$30* ✉ *103 Murray St., North Hobart* ☎ *03/6109–4712* 🌐 *www.urbangreekhobart.com.*

Hotels

Hobart has some lovely lodgings in old, historic houses and cottages, most of which have been beautifully restored. If you're seeking more modern conveniences, there are plenty of newer hotels, too.

Corinda's Cottages
$$$$ | **B&B/INN** | This complex comprises a charming residence built in the 1880s for Alfred Crisp, a wealthy timber merchant who later became Lord Mayor of Hobart, as well as three lovingly restored outbuildings in which each of the accommodations are located—these include a gardener's residence, servants' quarters, and coach house. **Pros:** wonderfully restored historic accommodation; generous buffet breakfast; walking distance to CBD and waterfront. **Cons:** no leisure facilities; steep steps in the Gardener's Cottage. [$] *Rooms from: A$445* ✉ *17 Glebe St., Glebe* ☎ *03/6234–1590* 🌐 *www.corindacollection.com.au/corindas-cottages* 🛏 *3 cottages* 🍴 *Free breakfast.*

Disappearing Devils

Tasmanian devils are becoming extremely rare because of a deadly cancer devastating the devil population—in 2009 they were officially listed on the endangered species list. Experts estimate that 70% to 80% of the population has already succumbed, and unless a cure is found the species faces extinction. To help research donations can be made to the Save the Tasmanian Devil program.

★ **The Henry Jones Art Hotel**
$$$ | **HOTEL** | Arguably one of Australia's best hotels, right on the Hobart waterfront, this row of historic warehouses and a former jam factory have been transformed into a sensational, art-theme hotel, where the work of Tasmania's finest contemporary artists is displayed. **Pros:** incredible art collection; stunning rooms worth lingering in; excellent location. **Cons:** excellent breakfast is A$35; tours, restaurants, cocktail bar are all pricey; some rooms look into atrium so no natural light. [$] *Rooms from: A$280* ✉ *25 Hunter St., City Center* ☎ *03/6210–7700* 🌐 *www.thehenryjones.com* 🛏 *56 rooms* 🍴 *No meals.*

Hotel Grand Chancellor
$$$ | **HOTEL** | Across the street from the old wharves and steps from some of the most exciting restaurants in Hobart, this imposing glass-and-stone building offers sumptuous accommodation in one of the city's best locations. **Pros:** steps

away from the city's museums; offers familiar chain comforts. **Cons:** some traffic noise; stark lobby; fee for parking. $ *Rooms from: A$265* ✉ *1 Davey St., Hobart Waterfront* ☎ *03/6235–4535, 1800/753379* ⊕ *www.ghihotels.com* ⌐ *244 rooms* ⦿ *No meals.*

★ Islington Hotel

$$$$ | **HOTEL** | Built in 1847, this elegant Regency mansion was converted to a five-star luxury boutique hotel and is now one of the finest urban lodgings in Australia. **Pros:** fully tailored hospitality experience; sophisticated service from staff; free parking. **Cons:** 20-minute walk to city center; only accommodates children 15 years and over. $ *Rooms from: A$445* ✉ *321 Davey St., South Hobart* ☎ *03/6220–2123* ⊕ *www.islingtonhotel. com* ⌐ *11 rooms* ⦿ *Free breakfast.*

Lodge on Elizabeth

$$ | **HOTEL** | This opulent grand manor, convict-built in 1829 and home over the years to many Hobart notables, is within walking distance of the city center, but far enough removed to feel like a sanctuary. **Pros:** hearty continental buffet breakfast; convenient option for groups; many local entertainment options. **Cons:** a few bedrooms are on the small side; some street noise. $ *Rooms from: A$200* ✉ *249 Elizabeth St., City Center* ☎ *03/6231–3830* ⊕ *www.thelodge.com.au* ⌐ *14 rooms, 1 cottage* ⦿ *Free breakfast.*

★ MONA Pavilions

$$$$ | **HOTEL** | These eight high-style pavilions are easily Tasmania's most cutting-edge accommodations—the pavillions are on the grounds of Tasmania's world-class experimental art museum, the Museum of Old and New Art (MONA). **Pros:** stunning setting and views; individually themed rooms with featured art; private museum tours. **Cons:** high-tech features can be confusing; limited availability; restaurant closed Tuesday. $ *Rooms from: A$600* ✉ *655 Main Rd., Berriedale* ☎ *03/6277–9900*

⊕ *mona.net.au/stay/mona-pavilions* ⌐ *8 chalets* ⦿ *Free breakfast.*

Old Woolstore Apartment Hotel

$$$ | **HOTEL** | **FAMILY** | With a mix of standard rooms as well studios and one- and two-bedroom apartments, this property just a block from Hobart's iconic waterfront occupies one of the city's oldest and most historic buildings, the Roberts Limited Woolstore. **Pros:** central location; complimentary parking; historic ambience. **Cons:** small balconies; confusing drive-in entrance; busy neighborhood. $ *Rooms from: A$250* ✉ *1 Macquarie St., City Center* ☎ *1800/814676, 03/6235–5355* ⊕ *www.oldwoolstore. com.au* ⌐ *59 rooms, 177 apartments, 6 suites* ⦿ *No meals.*

Salamanca Inn

$$$ | **B&B/INN** | **FAMILY** | These elegant, self-contained apartments blend in well with the surrounding historic district and are perfect for families, as they have queen-size beds, modern kitchens, and free laundry facilities. **Pros:** in the heart of the restaurant and shopping district; excellent reception staff; spotlessly clean. **Cons:** some roads around the hotel are blocked off during the Saturday markets; Wi-Fi in the rooms can be slow. $ *Rooms from: A$269* ✉ *10 Gladstone St., Battery Point* ☎ *03/6223–3300, 1800/030944* ⊕ *www.salamancainn.com. au* ⌐ *60 suites* ⦿ *No meals.*

Somerset on the Pier

$$$ | **RENTAL** | **FAMILY** | On one of Hobart's historic piers, this all-suites complex is only a five-minute walk from the city, Salamanca Place, and many popular restaurants and nightspots. **Pros:** lovely views of the harbor; family-friendly yet also suits business travelers; close to everything. **Cons:** stuffy bathrooms; some restaurant noise is audible on weekends. $ *Rooms from: A$225* ✉ *Elizabeth St. Pier, Hobart Waterfront* ☎ *03/6220–6600, 1800/620462* ⊕ *www.somerset.com* ⌐ *54 apartments* ⦿ *No meals.*

Sullivans Cove Apartments

$$$$ | RENTAL |FAMILY | This is an impressive collection of 47 handsome, self-catered apartments and penthouses spread across five waterfront precincts in Hobart. **Pros:** close to Salamanca Place shops and waterfront; stunning interiors; wide selection of apartment styles. **Cons:** need to book early to reserve; some noise from adjoining businesses in waterfront precincts. $ *Rooms from: A$410* ✉ *Sullivans Cove Apartments & Check-in, 5/19a Hunter St., Hobart Waterfront* ☎ *03/6234–5063* ⊕ *www.sullivanscoveapartments.com.au* ⇱ *47 apartments* ⦿ *No meals.*

Nightlife

Although Hobart has the only true nightlife scene in Tasmania, it's extremely tame compared to what's in Melbourne and Sydney. There are few dance clubs, and evenings out tend to revolve around a bottle of excellent local wine.

BARS AND DANCE CLUBS

Cargo Bar Pizza Lounge

BARS/PUBS | This beautifully furnished bar has inviting booth-style seats toward the back—a peaceful refuge during the busy dinner hour. Note the generous wine selection, with plenty of notable beers and spirits, too, and the tasty pizzas. In winter, sit outside under a heater and catch one of the occasional live acoustic performances. On the weekends after dinner service the DJs move in and the place starts to jump. ✉ *51 Salamanca Pl., Battery Point* ☎ *03/6223–7788* ⊕ *www.cargobarsalamanca.com.au.*

★ The Glass House

BARS/PUBS | One of Hobart's newest and best-placed venues, The Glass House brings a collection of the most enticing cocktails and delicious food together in a unique translucent floating facility with impressive views of the Derwent. This venue is also the home pier for the ferry service to and from MONA and provides the perfect place to wind down after a day of sensory extension. ✉ *Brooke St. Pier, Hobart Waterfront* ☎ *03/6223–1032* ⊕ *www.theglass.house.*

★ Preachers

BREWPUBS/BEER GARDENS | This cute and cozy Heritage-listed cottage hides Hobart's best beer garden in its backyard, along with a full-size bus. Warm in winter, bright and breezy in summer, with good food, a great relaxed vibe, and a selection of local craft beers and ciders—Preachers ticks all the boxes. ✉ *5 Knopwood St., Battery Point* ☎ *03/6223–3621.*

Republic Bar and Cafe

BARS/PUBS | FAMILY | The cool kids head to this raucous, art deco pub warmed by roaring log fires to watch nightly live music, including plenty of top Tasmanian and touring bands. The food on offer is excellent and good value. ✉ *299 Elizabeth St., North Hobart* ☎ *03/6234–6954* ⊕ *www.republicbar.com.*

★ Room For A Pony

CAFES—NIGHTLIFE | FAMILY | By day an alfresco restaurant offering café fare, and by night a bar and beer garden with shareable snacks and live music, this cool, converted gas station is a flexible and light-filled hot spot with bespoke wood furniture and room for several ponies. The name is a tongue-in-cheek reference to a British '90s sitcom, *Keeping Up Appearances,* and the space is appropriately friendly with touches of quirk and humor. ✉ *338 Elizabeth St., North Hobart* ☎ *03/6231–0508* ⊕ *www.roomforapony.com.au.*

★ Shambles Brewery

BREWPUBS/BEER GARDENS | Nestled between Hobart's CBD and the café strip of North Hobart, Shambles occupies a fond place in Hobartians' hearts for it's excellent beer (brewed on-site), its relaxed, urbane atmosphere, and long benches for large groups or smaller nooks for a more intimate experience. Give their Dirty Copper amber ale a try. ⊠ *222 Elizabeth St., North Hobart* ☏ *03/6289–5639* ⊕ *www.shamblesbrewery.com.au.*

T42

CAFES—NIGHTLIFE | FAMILY | Officially called Tavern 42 Degrees South, this lively waterfront spot is popular for both dining and drinking—it's something of a Hobart institution. Patrons have the choice of sitting inside or out, noshing on tapas, sipping wine, and looking out over the harbor. The T42 house breakfast is a great kick-start to a day of exploring Hobart. ⊠ *Elizabeth St. Pier, Hobart Waterfront* ☏ *03/6224–7742* ⊕ *www.tav42.com.au.*

LIVE MUSIC
Federation Concert Hall

MUSIC | The permanent home of the acclaimed Tasmanian Symphony Orchestra, this 1,100-seat tiered auditorium welcomes touring musicians and speakers and is adjacent to the Hotel Grand Chancellor. The acoustics here are excellent. ⊠ *1 Davey St., Hobart Waterfront* ☏ *03/6235–4535* ⊕ *www.tso.com.au.*

THEATER
Theatre Royal

THEATER | This 1834 architectural gem with portraits of composers painted on its magnificent dome stages classic and contemporary plays by Australian and international playwrights. The 2018/19 renovation and development of the site will see extra theaters added to the precinct. ⊠ *29 Campbell St., Hobart Waterfront* ☏ *03/6233–2299* ⊕ *www.theatreroyal.com.au.*

🛍 Shopping

Tasmanian artisans and craftspeople work with diverse materials to fashion unusual pottery, metalwork, and wool garments. Items made from regional timber, including myrtle, sassafras, and Huon pine, are popular. The wonderful scenery around the island is an inspiration for numerous artists.

Along the Hobart waterfront at Salamanca Place are a large number of shops that sell arts and crafts. On Saturday (between 8 and 3) the area turns into a giant market, where still more local artists join produce growers, bric-a-brac sellers, and itinerant musicians to sell their wares.

Art Mob

ART GALLERIES | Set close to the waterfront by the Henry Jones Art Hotel, Art Mob exhibits and sells a wide range of local Tasmanian Aboriginal art and crafts, including jewelry, from many communities and artists. The collection includes rare necklaces and exquisite baskets as well as fine prints and paintings by noted Aboriginal artists. ⊠ *29 Hunter St., City Center* ☏ *03/6236–9200* ⊕ *www.artmob.com.au.*

Gallery Salamanca

CRAFTS | This retail shop and gallery specializes in high-quality products made in Tasmania, including ceramics, glass, jewelry, sculpture, and textiles. The mission here is showcase the talents of Tasmania's emerging and established artists. Located within the Salamanca Arts Centre just off Salamanca Place, the gallery represents more than 90 artisans. ⊠ *65 Salamanca Pl., Battery Point* ☏ *03/6223–5022* ⊕ *www.gallerysalamanca.com.au.*

Handmark Gallery

ART GALLERIES | Featuring the work of some of Tasmania's finest artists, this gallery is one of the gems of Salamanca Place. Inside you'll find Hobart's best wooden jewelry boxes as well as art deco jewelry and pottery, paintings, works on paper, and sculpture. The gallery also runs a number of exhibitions each year in conjunction with its sister gallery in Evandale, Northern Tasmania. Some of the exhibiting artists here have gone on to show at national and international galleries. The works of Tasmanian Aboriginal elder Lola Greeno are a very special feature. ⊠ *77 Salamanca Pl.,*

Battery Point ☎ *03/6223–7895* ⊕ *www. handmark.com.au.*

Red Parka

CERAMICS/GLASSWARE | A funky shopfront for local artists working across varied disciplines, you will find ceramics, textiles, books, and many other treasures. Often with a local twist, featuring native flora and fauna or made from local materials, this is a must for the souvenir hunter. ⊠ *22 Criterion St., City Center* ⊕ *redparka.com.au.*

★ **Wild Island Shop**

ART GALLERIES | This gallery and shop sells environmental art, cards, calendars, diaries, jewelry, clothing and ceramics, all made in Australia and all supporting the Australian environment. Regular exhibitions feature local artists who use the Tasmanian wilderness as their inspiration. ⊠ *The Galleria, 8/33 Salamanca Pl., Battery Point* ☎ *03/6224–0220* ⊕ *www. wildislandtas.com.au.*

⚙ Activities

Hobartians are an outdoorsy lot who make the most of the city's waterfront location by fishing, cruising, and sailing or heading inland to kunanyi/Mt. Wellington to explore the many trails that start there.

BICYCLING

Crank-e Electric Mountain Bike Hire

BICYCLING | Crank-e Electric Mountain Bike Hire offers the perfect options for tackling the more challenging trails around Hobart or on kunanyi/Mt Wellington. With electric and nonpowered bikes available, the challenging North-South Track will be a breeze. ⊠ *93 Harrington St.* ☎ *0408/176758* ⊕ *www.islandcycletours.com.*

Hobart Bike Hire

BICYCLING | FAMILY | This conveniently located outfitter for renting bikes makes for a fun way to get around the city, particularly via the old railway lines along the western bank of the Derwent River.

In addition to pedal bikes for adults and kids, tandem bikes and automatic electric bikes are available. ⊠ *1a Brooke St., Hobart Waterfront* ☎ *0447/556189* ⊕ *www.hobartbikehire.com.au* 🖄 *From A$25 daily.*

Spoke Bike Hire

BICYCLING | Conveniently located adjacent to the Hobart Cenotaph, an easy ride along a bike path will take you to Cornelian Bay and on to MONA. Spoke is a short walk from the city center. ⊠ *Regatta Grounds, Queen's Domain* ☎ *03/6232–4848* ⊕ *spokebikehire.com.au* 🖄 *From A$15 hourly.*

BOAT TOURS

Hobart Historic Cruises

BOAT TOURS | FAMILY | The distinctively bright red *Spirit of Hobart* runs enjoyable and affordable cruises with several options for sightseeing or lunch and dinner. ⊠ *Murray St. Pier, Hobart Waterfront* ☎ *03/6200–9074* ⊕ *www.hobarthistoriccruises.com.au* 🖄 *From A$28.*

★ **Pennicott Wilderness Journeys**

BOAT TOURS | FAMILY | From Hobart, this operator runs a range of cruises, including a 2½-hour trip that explores Hobart's waterways, a full-day seafood-focused tour on which you cruise down to Bruny Island, taste oysters shucked straight from the water, and watch your guide dive for abalone and sea urchin. You can also choose to drive yourself to Adventure Bay on Bruny Island (the Bruny Island Ferry can take any size vehicle) and join a three-hour wilderness cruise, where you can spot seals and, if you're lucky, dolphins and whales. ⊠ *Constitution Dock Bridge, Franklin Wharf, Hobart Waterfront* ☎ *03/6234–4270* ⊕ *www.pennicottjourneys.com.au* 🖄 *From A$125.*

Peppermint Bay Cruises

BOATING | FAMILY | This catamaran races through the majestic waterways of the Derwent River and the D'Entrecasteaux Channel to Peppermint Bay at Woodbridge and provides a fantastic way to spy some of Tasmania's epic wildlife. And it is abundant, from sea eagles and falcons soaring above the weathered cliffs to pods of dolphins swimming alongside the boat. Underwater cameras explore kelp forests and salmon in the floating fish farms. ⊠ *Brooke St. Pier, Sulivans Cove, Hobart Waterfront* ☎ *1300/137919* ⊕ *www.peppermintbay.com.au* ✉ *From A$78*.

FISHING

Tasmania's well-stocked lakes and streams are among the world's best for trout fishing. The season runs from August through May, and licensed trips can be arranged through the Tasmanian Travel and Information Centre.

Several professional fishing guides are based on the island. For information on these guides, as well as related tours, accommodations, and sea charters, check out ⊕ *www.troutguidestasmania. com.au* or inquire at the Tasmanian Travel and Information Centre for a professional guide in the area you are visiting.

Mr Flathead

FISHING | If you fancy taking to the ocean to explore local fishing hot spots, check with this company that runs half- and full-day family-friendly tours on which you'll find scores of flathead, whiting, and salmon. All rods, reels, and equipment are supplied. ⊠ *Dodges Ferry boat ramp, Tiger Head Rd., Dodges Ferry* ☎ *0439/617200* ⊕ *www.mrflathead.com. au* ✉ *$A150 ½ day*.

Rod & Fly Tasmania

FISHING | Tasmania is home to some world-class fishing, and if you'd like to catch some local trout in the region's wonderfully clear rivers and highland lakes, this friendly operator is a good choice for setting up an outing, with more than 30 years of experience. ⊠ *35 Misty Hill Rd., Mountain River* ☎ *03/6266–4480, 0408/469771* ⊕ *www. rodandfly.com.au*.

GOLF

There are about 80 golf courses around Tasmania, and visitors are welcome to play on many of them. Greens fees range from A$10 for 9 holes at the smaller country courses all the way up to A$80 for 18 holes at the more exclusive, larger clubs. Accessibility may vary (for example, some courses may require that you be introduced by a member), so it's always best to check first by phoning ahead.

There are several excellent golf courses within the Hobart area.

Claremont Golf Club

GOLF | Situated on a stunning peninsula jutting into the River Derwent and within close proximity of Hobart and its surroundings, this is the only public 18-hole golf club situated in the northern suburbs of the city. ⊠ *1 Bournville Crescent* ☎ *03/6249–1000* ⊕ *www.claremontgolf. com.au* ✉ *A$50* ⛳ *18 holes, 5747 yards, par 69*.

★ **Ratho Farm Golf Links**

GOLF | This quirky 9-hole layout, about 75 km (47 miles) north of Hobart in the village of Bothwell, was established in 1822, making it the oldest golf course outside Scotland, where the sport originated—it's part of a working farm. Ratho also has a welcoming, warm homestead with dining, bar facilities, and 16 attractive en suite rooms in lovingly restored old farm buildings. ⊠ *2122 Highland Lakes Rd., Bothwell* ☎ *03/6259–5628* ⊕ *www.rathofarm.com* ✉ *A$15 for 9 holes, A$40 for 18 holes* ⛳ *18 holes, 5660 yards, par 70*.

HIKING

Pick up a Mt. Wellington Walk Map from the tourist office on Elizabeth Street in Hobart to make the most out of the park that towers over Hobart. Although shops around town stock outdoor equipment, you should bring your own gear if you're planning any serious bushwalking. There are hundreds of walking tracks in

The extremely popular Saturday Salamanca Market

Wellington Park and sneakers are adequate for most trails and along beaches, however some of the walks cross exposed alpine environments where the weather can change from bad to worse very quickly; prepare accordingly. A car is necessary to access several of the trails around the Wellington Range.

Tasmanian Hikes

HIKING/WALKING | Go hiking with this guide company—you can choose from a range of breathtaking hikes. A nine-day South Coast trek starts in Hobart and explores the wild southern shoreline, but they conduct a range of other wilderness walks throughout Tasmania and some shorter options close to Hobart. ☎ 0400/882742 ⊕ www.tasmanianhikes. com.au.

WALKING TOURS
Hobart Historic Tours

HIKING/WALKING | This tour company leads history walks through old Hobart, around the waterfront and maritime precinct, and to historic pubs. ✉ Hobart Travel Centre, Davey St. at Elizabeth St., Hobart Waterfront ☎ 03/6234–5550 ⊕ www. hobarthistorictours.com.au ✍ From A$33.

YACHTING
If the annual Sydney-to-Hobart race has inspired you to find your sea legs, you're in the right place.

★ Hobart Yachts

BOATING | Hobart yachts run a range of cruises, from three-hour twilight sailings on the River Derwent to weeklong charters up the East Coast or to Port Davey. ✉ Hobart Waterfront ☎ 0438/399477 ⊕ www.hobartyachts.com.au.

The Huon Valley

40 km (25 miles) south of Hobart.

★ En route to the vast wilderness of South West National Park is the tranquil Huon Valley. Sheltered coasts and sandy beaches are pocketed with thick forests and small farms. William Bligh planted the first apple tree here, founding one of the region's major industries. Salmon and trout caught fresh from churning blue rivers are also delicious regional delicacies.

The valley is also famous for the Huon pine, much of which has been logged over the decades. The trees that remain are strictly protected, so other local timbers are used by the region's craftspeople.

◉ Sights

Hastings Caves and Thermal Springs

HOT SPRINGS | Spectacular cave formations and thermal pools amid a fern glade await at the Hastings Caves and Thermal Springs. The caves are about 125 km (78 miles) south of Hobart, past Huonville and Dover. You can take a tour of the chambers, or just relax at the well-equipped picnic areas and make use of the thermal pool. The route to the site is well marked from the town of Dover. Hours vary seasonally, so check ahead. ⊠ *754 Hastings Caves Rd., Hastings* ☏ *03/6298–3209* ⊕ *www.parks.tas.gov. au* ⌲ *A$24.*

Tahune AirWalk Tasmania

BRIDGE/TUNNEL | **FAMILY** | Beyond Geeveston, the cantilevered, 1,880-foot-long Tahune AirWalk rises to 150 feet above the forest floor, providing a stunning panorama of the Huon and Picton rivers and the Hartz Mountains. The best views are from the platform at the end of the walkway, and if you have time, follow one of the trails that lead from the center through the surrounding forests. If one day isn't enough you can stay the night on-site in the reasonably priced Tahune Lodge or in a self-contained cabin. There's also a shop and a café with free Wi-Fi. ⊠ *Arve Rd., Geeveston* ☏ *03/6251–3903* ⊕ *tahuneairwalk.com. au* ⌲ *A$30.*

★ Willie Smith's Apple Shed

FARM/RANCH | En route to Huonville, this museum, cider house, and café showcases the best of the local product.

It's housed in a former apple-packing shed and is a remarkable time capsule, depicting the lives of the early Huon Valley settlers. Over the years this venue has evolved to offer regular events, great food, and even better cider. The Sunday Session is a great way to end a weekend in the valley. ⊠ *2064 Huon Hwy., Grove* ☏ *03/6266–4345* ⊕ *www.williesmiths. com.au* ⌲ *Free.*

⊕ Beaches

Cockle Creek

BEACH—SIGHT | Cockle Creek is the southernmost "town" in Australia. It consists of a campground, a rangers station and a campground, but also a series of stunning beaches. The neighboring hamlet of Catamaran is similarly dotted with picturesque bays and beaches, surrounded by forests and mountains. French explorers landed here before English settlement and aspects of that history can be explored also. There are walking tracks including the awe inspiring Lion Rock at South Cape Bay. **Amenities:** campgrounds; toilets. **Best for:** hiking; kayaking; swimming. ⊠ *Cockle Creek Rd., Hastings* ⊕ *www.parks.tas.gov.au/ file.aspx?id=19219.*

Kingston Beach

BEACH—SIGHT | This is the first main swimming beach southwest of Hobart—it's less than 30 minutes' drive from the Huon Valley. The beach sits in front of the fairly developed town of Kingston, on the Derwent River at the mouth of Browns Rivulet. Shopping and housing sit behind and to the south of the beach, and a narrow reserve, picnic area, and playground back the sand. Kingston Beach is patrolled by the local Surf Life Saving Club; however, you should still keep clear of any boating activity in the south corner—the waters are quite deep directly off the beach. **Amenities:** food and drink; lifeguards; parking (free); showers; toilets. **Best for:** surfing; swimming;

walking. ✉ *Beach Rd. at Osbourne Esplanade, Kingston Beach.*

🍴 Restaurants

Home Hill Winery Restaurant

$$ | **AUSTRALIAN** | Large plate-glass windows open to the Home Hill winery's endless hillside vineyards at this boutique vineyard, cellar door, and restaurant—a true Tasmanian country retreat. The seasonal menu features many local producers. **Known for:** pretty setting; slow-cooked lamb shoulder; morning and afternoon tea. [$] *Average main: A$35* ✉ *38 Nairn St., Ranelagh* ☎ *03/6258–1120* 🌐 *homehillwines.com.au.*

🛏 Hotels

★ Herons Rise Vineyard

$$ | **B&B/INN** | Mornings in any of the vineyard's three self-contained cottages are bucolic and gorgeous; you'll wake to glorious water views out over the flower gardens, where you might see rabbits nibbling while you soak up the tranquillity of this peaceful environment. **Pros:** peaceful surroundings; beautiful views of the Tasman Sea and rural landscape; convenient to Bruny Island. **Cons:** no leisure facilities; smoke from fireplaces might be a problem for some; breakfast not included (but bountiful provisions available). [$] *Rooms from: A$170* ✉ *Saddle Rd., Kettering* ☎ *0412/152164* 🌐 *www.heronsrise.com.au* 🛏 *2 cottages* 🍴 *Free breakfast.*

Off the Path

From the village of Kettering 25 km (16 miles) south of Hobart, a vehicle ferry crosses the narrow D'Entrecasteaux Channel to reach Bruny Island. Names here reflect the influence of the French explorers who sailed through this region in the 1770s and '80s. Bruny Island has many charms, including Australia's southernmost winery, the world-famous Bruny Island Cheesery, numerous walking tracks, and a remarkable mob of albino wallabies. The Bruny Island ferry runs daily; check 🌐 *www.sealinkbrunyisland.com.au* for booking details.

Richmond

24 km (15 miles) northeast of Hobart.

★ Twenty minutes' drive from Hobart and a century behind the big city, this colonial village in the Coal River valley is a major tourist magnet. Visitors stroll and browse through the craft shops, antiques stores, and cafés along the main street. Richmond is also home to a number of vineyards, all of which produce excellent cool-climate wines.

🍴 Restaurants

Ashmore on Bridge Street

$ | **CAFÉ** |**FAMILY** | Once you've perused all of Richmond's cute shops and historic sights, be sure to recharge in this surprisingly trendy café with an open roaring fire and a friendly owner. The creamy scrambled eggs on sourdough toast with Tasmanian cold-smoked salmon and house relish is delicious for breakfast, and in the afternoon the huge and delectable Devonshire teas will have you sighing with pleasure. **Known for:** Devonshire tea; cozy setting; great breakfasts. [$] *Average main: A$20* ✉ *34 Bridge St.* ☎ *03/6260–2238.*

★ Frogmore Creek

$$ | **AUSTRALIAN** | Wine tasting and an art gallery complement this unpretentious but upscale restaurant with floor-to-ceiling windows looking out to views over the vineyards of Frogmore Creek and Barilla Bay. In the restaurant creative yet simple dishes make choosing a meal difficult, seasonal and local is the mantra.

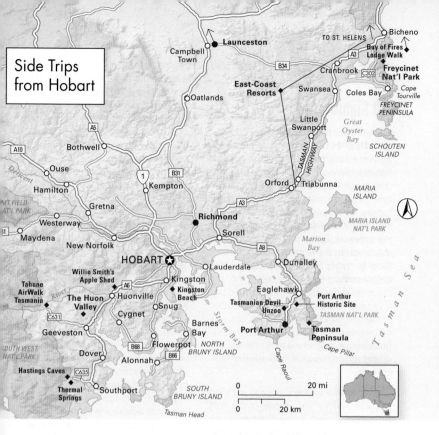

Launceston

Campbell Town

East-Coast Resorts

Oatlands

TO ST. HELENS

Bicheno

Bay of Fires Lodge Walk

Freycinet Nat'l Park

Cranbrook

Swansea

Coles Bay

Cape Tourville

FREYCINET PENINSULA

Little Swanport

Great Oyster Bay

SCHOUTEN ISLAND

Bothwell

Ouse

Hamilton

Kempton

Orford

Triabunna

MARIA ISLAND

MARIA ISLAND NAT'L PARK

Gretna

Richmond

Sorell

Marion Bay

Westerway

Maydena

New Norfolk

HOBART

Lauderdale

Dunalley

Willie Smith's Apple Shed

Kingston

Tahune AirWalk Tasmania

The Huon Valley

Huonville

Kingston Beach

Snug

Eaglehawk

Port Arthur Historic Site

Tasmanian Devil Unzoo

TASMAN NAT'L PARK

Cygnet

Barnes Bay

Port Arthur

Tasman Peninsula

Geeveston

Flowerpot

NORTH BRUNY ISLAND

Cape Pillar

SOUTH WEST NAT'L PARK

Dover

Alonnah

Hastings Caves

Thermal Springs

Southport

SOUTH BRUNY ISLAND

Tasman Head

Cape Raoul

Tasman Sea

Storm Bay

0   20 mi

0   20 km

Known for: vineyard views; tapas-style menu; fresh oysters. $ *Average main: A$35* ⊠ *699 Richmond Rd., Cambridge* ☎ *03/6274–5844* ⊕ *www.frogmorecreek. com.au* ⊗ *No dinner.*

🛏 Hotels

Riversdale Estate

$ | **B&B/INN** | This working estate produces sumptuous wines from its 40 hectares of vines but also add an authentic farm-stay feel. **Pros:** peaceful setting; French Provincial decor; family-friendly. **Cons:** working vineyard, so there can be equipment noise; restaurant is disappointing; service can be inconsistent. $ *Rooms from: A$150* ⊠ *222 Denholms Rd., Cambridge* ☎ *03/6248–5555* ⊕ *riversdalees- tate.com.au* ➡ *7 cottages* ⊗ *No meals.*

Port Arthur and the Tasman Peninsula

102 km (63 miles) southeast of Hobart.

When Governor George Arthur, lieutenant-governor of Van Diemen's Land (now Tasmania), was looking for a site to dump his worst convict offenders in 1830, the Tasman Peninsula was a natural choice. Joined to the rest of Tasmania only by the narrow Eaglehawk Neck, the spit was easy to isolate and guard. Between 1830 and 1877, more than 12,000 convicts served sentences at Port Arthur in Britain's equivalent of Devil's Island. Dogs patrolled the narrow causeway, and guards spread rumors that sharks infested the waters. Reminders of those dark days remain in some of the area names—Dauntless Point, Stinking Point, Isle of the Dead.

👁 Sights

★ Port Arthur Historic Site

HISTORIC SITE | FAMILY | This property, formerly the grounds of the Port Arthur Penal Settlement, is now a lovely—and quite large—historical park with a fascinating convict past central to Tasmania's history. Be prepared to do some walking between widely scattered sites. Begin at the excellent visitor center, which introduces you to the experience by "sentencing, transporting, and assigning" you before you set foot in the colony. Most of the original buildings were damaged by bushfires in 1895 and 1897, shortly after the settlement was abandoned, but you can still see the beautiful church, round guardhouse, commandant's residence, model prison, hospital, and government cottages.

The old **lunatic asylum** is now an excellent museum, with a scale model of the Port Arthur settlement, a video history, and a collection of tools, leg irons, and chains. Along with a walking tour of the grounds and entrance to the museum, admission includes a harbor cruise, of which there are eight scheduled daily in summer. There's a separate twice-daily cruise to and tour of the **Isle of the Dead,** which sits in the middle of the bay. It's estimated that 1,769 convicts and 180 others are buried here, mostly in communal pits. Ghost tours (reservations are essential) leave the visitor center at dusk and last about 90 minutes. Buy your tickets at the site, or at the Brooke Street Pier, at Franklin Wharf in Hobart. ⊠ *Arthur Hwy., Port Arthur* ☎ *1800/659101* ⊕ *www. portarthur.org.au* 🚢 *From A$39.*

Tasmanian Devil Unzoo

NATURE PRESERVE | FAMILY | This "unzoo" offers a four-in-one wildlife nature experience that combines up-close animal encounters, wildlife adventures, a Tasmanian native garden, and original art. It is also the best place to come face to face with real live Tasmanian devils. Spot these burrowing carnivorous marsupials (about the size of a small dog), as well as quolls, boobooks (small, spotted brown owls), masked owls, eagles, and other native fauna. The philosophy of the "unzoo" is to challenge the way native animals are presented to the public. ⊠ *5990 Port Arthur Hwy., Taranna* ✢ *11 km (7 miles) north of Port Arthur* ☎ *1800/641641* ⊕ *tasmaniandevilunzoo. com.au* 🚢 *A$36.*

🏖 Beaches

White Beach

BEACH—SIGHT | FAMILY | It's less than a 10-minute drive from the historic former penal colony of Port Arthur to the pristine white sands of beautiful White Beach, a wild, unspoiled, crescent-shape beach often named one of the most beautiful beaches in Australia. The breathtaking views from the beach are among the most beautiful in all of Tasmania, stretching as far as the eye can see across Wedge Bay to Storm Bay and then beyond to the Hartz Mountains. The local trails are worth exploring, not far from the usually deserted 3-km (2-mile) beach, although world-class diving is also available at Eaglehawk Neck and decent surfing at Roaring Beach. White Beach Tourist Park fronts directly onto the beach, and the general area has a number of cafés and restaurants offering excellent local Tasmanian cuisine. **Amenities:** food and drink; parking (free); toilets. **Best for:** snorkeling; solitude; sunrise; sunset; surfing; swimming; walking. ⊠ *White Beach Rd., Port Arthur.*

🍴 Restaurants

1830

$$$ | AUSTRALIAN |FAMILY | Feast on wonderfully fresh Tasmanian seafood and game in the heart of the Port Arthur

Historic buildings from Tasmania's convict past can be seen in Port Arthur

Historic Site at this small but lovely restaurant. Standout appetizers include the area's local oysters. **Known for:** pretour dinner; fresh oysters; a tad overpriced. $ *Average main: A$38* ⊠ *Port Arthur Historic Site, Port Arthur* ☎ *03/6251–2310, 1800/659101* ⊕ *www.portarthur.org.au.*

🛏 Hotels

Stewarts Bay Lodge

$$ | B&B/INN | Less than five minutes' drive from the Port Arthur Historic Site, this cabin park is located on the edge of a gorgeous bay with white sandy beach ringed by tall eucalypt forest. **Pros:** natural setting; private beach is stunning; good on-site restaurant. **Cons:** marked difference between cabin styles; booked up far in advance in peak season; on-site restaurant is only dining option. $ *Rooms from: A$200* ⊠ *6955 Arthur Hwy., Port Arthur* ☎ *03/6250–2888* ⊕ *stewartsbay-lodge.com.au* ⇌ *19 cabins, 21 chalets* ⊚| *No meals.*

East-Coast Resorts

★ From Hobart, the east-coast Tasman Highway travels cross-country to Orford, then passes through beautiful coastal scenery with spectacular white-sand beaches, usually completely deserted, before reaching Swansea. Bicheno, just north of Freycinet National Park, and St. Helens, which is farther north, are both fishing and holiday towns with quiet, sheltered harbors.

◉ Sights

★ Bay of Fires Lodge Walk

BEACH—SIGHT | Taking the four-day guided Bay of Fires Walk along the coast north of St. Helens is a wonderful way to enjoy the rugged beauty and tranquility of the coast. The walk, which is about 27 km (18 miles) long, winds along the edge of Mt. William National Park and allows you to visit stunning beaches, heathlands, Aboriginal sites, and peppermint forests, where a profusion of plant and animal life flourishes. During part of the relatively easy walk you'll stay at an ecologically sound campsite, which is as luxurious as it can get, with timber floors and kitchen facilities, and two nights at the dramatic, remote, and ecologically sustainable **Bay of Fires Lodge.** All meals and most beverages are provided, as well as return transfers between Launceston and the walk base, two qualified guides, a backpack and jacket, National Park pass, and optional kayaking day. ⊠ *Bay of Fires* ☎ *03/6392–2211* ⊕ *www.taswalk- ingco.com.au/bay-of-fires-lodge-walk* 🖃 *A$2395.*

Beaches

Bicheno Beach

BEACH—SIGHT | FAMILY | Extending 650 feet along the southern shore of Waubs Bay, this gentle beach is in the heart of pretty Bicheno. A secondary north-facing beach sits on the western side of the bay. Rounded granite rocks border and separate the two beaches. There is a car park and toilet facilities at the middle of the beach where Beach Street meets the sand, while the town itself sits on the slopes at the south end. A popular shoreline walking track follows the rocky coast around the headland. If the swell is up, be sure to look for the blowhole. **Amenities:** food and drink; parking (free); toilets. **Best for:** surfing; swimming; walk- ing. ⊠ *Bicheno.*

Friendly Beaches

BEACH—SIGHT | FAMILY | Contained within the boundaries of the Freycinet Nation- al Park, this long, sweeping, beautiful beach is accessed from Coles Bay Road, 9 km (6 miles) south of the turnoff on the Tasman Highway. Enjoy going barefoot as the sand is extremely soft, fine, and bright as a result of its high silicon content. The signature orange lichen encrusted granite boulders contrasts beautifully against the white sand and turquoise water. The waves are excellent for surfers, but there are strong rip and

tidal currents, so exercise care. Start at the small parking area, take the short stroll to the beach, and bring water and sunscreen, as there are no nearby facili- ties. **Amenities:** parking (free); toilets. **Best for:** solitude; surfing; swimming; walking. ⊠ *Coles Bay Rd., Coles Bay.*

Hotels

★ Avalon Coastal Retreat

$$$$ | RENTAL | This gorgeous three-bed- room house is the ultimate in exclusivity: it sits entirely alone on Tasmania's east coast, with just the occasional passing white-bellied sea eagle for company. **Pros:** unadulterated privacy; gorgeous views; fully stocked. **Cons:** expensive; three-night minimum stay; limited avail- ability. Ⓢ *Rooms from: A$900* ⊠ *11922 Tasman Hwy., Swansea* ☎ *1300/361136 Australia, 428/250399 international* ⊕ *www.avalonretreats.com.au/coastal* 🛏 *1 3-bedroom house* ⓧ *Free breakfast.*

Diamond Island Resort

$$$ | RESORT | Direct access to a deserted beach, island walks, and penguin-viewing platforms are among the draws of this peaceful hideaway 1½ km (1 mile) north of Bicheno and overlooking the Tasman Sea. Twelve two-bedroom duplexes are nestled within 7 acres of landscaped gar- dens; there are also 14 smaller one-bed- room units. **Pros:** minutes from a superb beach; kitchenettes in all units. **Cons:** not great value for what you get. Ⓢ *Rooms from: A$240* ⊠ *69 Tasman Hwy., Bicheno* ☎ *03/6375–0100, 1800/030299* ⊕ *www. diamondisland.com.au* 🛏 *27 rooms* ⓧ *Free breakfast.*

Eastcoaster

$$ | RESORT |FAMILY | This seaside complex in the town of Louisville is a great jump- ing-off point for exploring Maria Island National Park; the resort's catamaran, the *Eastcoaster Express,* makes three or four trips a day to the island. **Pros:** family-friendly resort; inexpensive and unpretentious; leisure facilities. **Cons:**

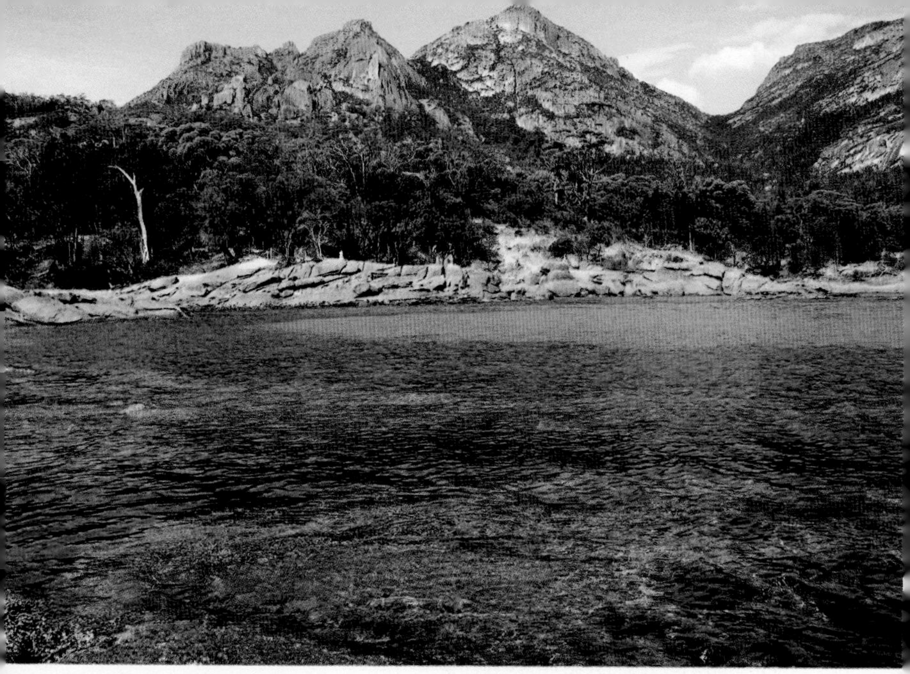

We had driven from Friendly Beach further into the Park when we came across this beautiful area." —
hoto by Gary Ott, Fodors.com member

omewhat dated design. $ *Rooms rom: A$180* ✉ *1 Louisville Rd., Orford* ☎ *03/6257–1172* 🌐 *eastcoasterresort. om.au* 🛏 *48 rooms, 8 cabins, 30 caravan sites* 🍴 *No meals.*

amptons on the Bay

$$ | **HOTEL** | These seven water-facing abins have dramatic views over Great Dyster Bay and the Freycinet Peninsula hrough full-length windows in living and edroom areas. **Pros:** friendly property nanager; incredible views over the cean; 10-minute drive to Swansea's res-aurants. **Cons:** barbecue area is between abins 5 and 6, which could impact rivacy; no Wi-Fi in rooms; no on-site ining. $ *Rooms from: A$260* ✉ *12164 asman Hwy., Swansea* ☎ *0417/481777* 🌐 *www.hamptonsonthebay.com.au* 🛏 *6 -bedroom cabins, 1 2-bedroom cabin, 3-bedroom house* 🍴 *No meals* 💳 *No redit cards.*

leredith House and Mews

$ | **B&B/INN** | Exquisite red-cedar urnishings and antiques decorate this rand 1853 refurbished residence in the center of Swansea. **Pros:** excellent service from affable hosts; superb freshly cooked breakfasts; authentic colonial-era building. **Cons:** books up well in advance. $ *Rooms from: A$200* ✉ *15 Noyes St., Swansea* ☎ *03/6257–8119* 🌐 *www.meredith-house.com.au* 🛏 *11 rooms* 🍴 *Free breakfast.*

Wagners Cottages

$$$ | **B&B/INN** | These four charming stone cottages, two of which date from the 1850s, sit amid rambling gardens not far from the water; they're decorated with country antique–style furniture, and each has a fireplace and hot tub. **Pros:** open fires are a treat in winter; cozy feel to rooms. **Cons:** not ideal for children; no leisure facilities. $ *Rooms from: A$225* ✉ *13182 Tasman Hwy., near Francis St., Swansea* ⊕ *3 km (2 miles) south of town* ☎ *03/6257–8494* 🌐 *www.wagnerscottages.com* 🛏 *4 cottages* 🍴 *Free breakfast.*

⚐ Activities

AIR TOURS

Freycinet Air

TOUR—SPORTS | This company flies from the Friendly Beaches Airfield, located 18 km (11 miles) north of Coles Bay, and has scenic flights with unparalleled views of Wineglass Bay, the Hazards, and the Peninsula. Freycinet Air offer a range of flights in fixed-wing planes and helicopters. Prices start at A$145 per person (two-person minimum) for a 30-minute flight. ⊠ *Friendly Beaches Airfield, Rosny Park* ☎ *03/6375–1694* ⊕ *www.freycinetair.com.au* ☎ *From A$145.*

CRUISES

★ Wineglass Bay Cruises

BOATING | FAMILY | Another way to experience the wonders of the Freycinet Peninsula is on a scenic cruise on the *Schouten Passage II* with Wineglass Bay Cruises. Guides endeavor to show you whales, dolphins, seals, white-bellied sea eagles, and albatrosses on the four-hour tour—you'll also experience stunning scenery and a rare, intimate perspective on an extraordinary Tasmanian location. Tour prices include lunch, and drinks can be purchased from the fully licensed bar, with an indulgent upper deck option in the Sky Lounge providing all drinks and freshly shucked oysters in the fare. ⊠ *Jetty, Jetty Rd., Coles Bay* ☎ *03/6257–0355* ⊕ *www.wineglassbaycruises.com* ☎ *From A$150* ⊗ *Closed June–Aug.*

HIKING

Freycinet Experience Walk

HIKING/WALKING | Get to the heart of this stunning area with a four-day exploration of the Freycinet Peninsula. A boat ferries you to Schouten Island where the group climbs Bear Hill or explores the beaches; the following day it delivers you to the secluded Bryan's Beach for a walk to the famous Wineglass Bay. Day 3 provides another highlight, Bluestone Bay and Whitewater Wall. Each evening is spent wining and dining at Freycinet Lodge, a welcome luxury after the exertions of the day. ⊠ *Coles Bay* ☎ *03/6223–7565* ⊕ *www.freycinet.com.au.*

KAYAKING

Freycinet is Tasmania's premier sea-kayaking destination, and it's possible to do guided tours or hire your own kayak and cruise around at your own pace.

★ Freycinet Adventures

KAYAKING | FAMILY | Providing a memorable way to explore the spectacular coastline at a leisurely pace, this family-run company runs half-day kayaking tours around the peninsula, as well as two day trips. Along the way guides point out local marine life, such as sea eagles. Tour packages aim at all skill levels. ⊠ *2 Freycinet Dr., Coles Bay* ☎ *03/6257–0500* ⊕ *www.freycinetadventures.com.au* ☎ *From A$105.*

WILDLIFE WATCHING

Bicheno Penguin Tours

WILDLIFE-WATCHING | FAMILY | At Bicheno, a very popular tour is the nightly hour-long vigil to see the penguins emerge from the water and clamber up to their nesting area. The daily tours begin at dusk, and penguin numbers often exceed 50. It's a magical opportunity to view these creatures up-close. ⊠ *70 Burgess St., Bicheno* ☎ *03/6375–1333* ⊕ *www.bichenopenguintours.com.au* ☎ *A$40.*

Freycinet National Park

238 km (149 miles) north of Port Arthur, 214 km (133 miles) southwest of Launceston, 206 km (128 miles) northeast of Hobart.

The road onto the Freycinet Peninsula ends just past the township of Coles Bay, from that point the Freycinet National Park begins and covers 24,700 acres.

ESSENTIALS

Freycinet National Park Offices

Parks passes are required for entering all Tasmanian national parks; they can be purchased here or at Service Tasmania offices. ✉ *Coles Bay Rd., Coles Bay* ☎ *03/6256–7000* 🌐 *www.parks.tas.gov.au.*

Sights

★ Freycinet National Park

NATURE PRESERVE | FAMILY | Highlights of the dramatic scenery here include the mountain-size granite formations known as the **Hazards.** On the ocean side of the peninsula there are also sheer cliffs that drop into the deep-blue ocean; views from the lighthouse at Cape Tourville are unforgettable. A series of tiny coves, one called Honeymoon Bay, provide a quieter perspective on the Great Oyster Bay side. **Wineglass Bay,** a perfect crescent of dazzling white sand, is best viewed from the lookout platform, about a 30-minute walk up a gentle hill from the parking lot; if you're feeling energetic, though, the view from the top of Mt. Amos, one of the Hazards, is worth the effort. A round-trip walk from the parking lot to Wineglass Bay takes about 2½ hours, and there are longer hiking options in the park. The park's many trails are well signposted. Daily entry to the park costs A$12 per person and A$24 per vehicle. ✉ *Coles Bay Rd., Coles Bay* ☎ *03/6256–7000* 🌐 *www.parks.tas.gov.au.*

Beaches

Nine Mile Beach

BEACH—SIGHT | FAMILY | A stone's throw from the historic town of Swansea, this long, sweeping beach is a favorite for swimming, fishing, and simply soaking up the views and peaceful surroundings—visitors enjoy uninterrupted views across Great Oyster Bay to Schouten Island, The Hazards, and the Freycinet Peninsula. Dangerous rips can be a concern here—take care, especially near the sand bar. The western end of the beach has a variety of lodgings and holiday rentals. Great Swanport lagoon and wetlands form the back side of the beach. There's parking for about 100 cars in the lot. **Amenities:** parking (free). **Best for:** solitude; surfing; swimming; walking. ✉ *Dolphin Sands Rd., Swansea.*

Hotels

Edge of the Bay

$$$ | RENTAL | The outstanding views from these modern, minimalist-style water-view suites and cottages set along 27 acres of untouched wilderness stretch for miles across Great Oyster Bay to the Hazards. **Pros:** animals wander freely around the resort; idyllic setting. **Cons:** two-night minimum; no breakfast is served but breakfast baskets can be ordered. [$] *Rooms from: A$295* ✉ *2308 Main Rd., Coles Bay* ☎ *03/6257–0102* 🌐 *www.edgeofthebay.com.au* 🛏 *14 suites, 7 cottages* 🍴 *No meals.*

Freycinet Lodge

$$$$ | RENTAL | With cabin-style accommodation scattered through the densely wooded forest overlooking Great Oyster Bay, this cushy eco-lodge has a remote setting that allows for an intimate connection with the surrounding scenic environment. **Pros:** superb food in fine-dining restaurant; perfect for getting away from it all; proximity to the national park. **Cons:** utilitarian furniture for the price; only the premier spa cabin has a TV; rooms can be on the cold side. [$] *Rooms from: A$379* ✉ *Freycinet National Park, Coles Bay Rd., Coles Bay* ☎ *03/6256–7222* 🌐 *www.freycinetlodge.com.au* 🛏 *60 cabins* 🍴 *Free breakfast.*

★ Saffire Freycinet

$$$$ | RESORT | Blame it on jaw-dropping views of Great Oyster Bay and the Hazards Mountains that frame the resort, or the eco-friendly space-age architecture fit for the likes of James Bond—a far-flung luxe getaway doesn't get much better than this. **Pros:** views from every inch of the property; comfy, modern suites; great excursions; all-inclusive

The Midlands

You can speed between Hobart and Launceston on the 200-km (124-mile) Highway 1 (Midlands Highway, also known as the Heritage Highway) in less than 2½ hours. Doing so, however, means bypassing one of Tasmania's most charmingly lovely pastoral regions and rural villages.

Heading north from Hobart, the first community you'll encounter (it's about 85 km [53 miles] outside the city) is the Georgian town of **Oatlands**, set on the shore of Lake Dulverton. Built in the 1820s as a garrison for the local farming community, the town still retains many original buildings that were built from the glorious golden sandstone of the region. There are also some fine old churches and a wind-powered mill that produces the finest stone-ground flour which you can sample in its best form at the local bakery.

The quaint village of **Ross**, about 55 km (34 miles) northeast of Oatlands, also has some wonderful historic buildings dating from the mid-19th century. The town's most iconic landmark, though, is the 1836 Ross Bridge, whose graceful sandstone arches are adorned with decorative carving.

A short detour from the Midlands Highway will bring you to **Longford** (it's 72 km [45 miles] northwest of Ross). Settled in 1813, Longford was one of northern Tasmania's first towns, and is now a National Trust historic site. Of particular early historic interest here is Christ Church, built in 1839. Although it's only open on Sunday, the church has a beautiful west window that is regarded as one of the country's finest. Nearby Woolmers Estate is a fascinating property to explore and book a stay at.

There are a number of other **historic villages** in the vicinity of Longford that are worth a visit. Hadspen, Carrick, Hagley, Perth, and Evandale are all within a short 25-km (16-mile) radius of the town, and all have their own special charms. Near Evandale on the road toward Nile, Clarendon House is one of the great Georgian houses of Australia, restored by the National Trust.

Spending the night in one of the towns along the Midlands Highway will let you more fully indulge in the historic-charm experience; many of the lodgings in the region occupy beautiful old buildings. Perhaps most impressive of all is **Brickendon** (☎ 03/6391–1383, 03/6391–1251 ⊕ www. brickendon.com.au) in Longford, whose restored cottages have antique tubs, fireplaces, and private gardens. The compound is a true colonial village, with a chapel, a trout lake, and more than 20 National Trust–classified buildings.

rates. **Cons:** extremely remote (transfers are not included); one restaurant; very pricey. $ *Rooms from: A$2200 ⊠ Coles Bay Rd., Freycinet Peninsula, Coles Bay* ☎ *03/6256–7888* ⊕ *www.saffire-freycinet.com.au* ⇨ *20 suites* ⧉ *Free breakfast.*

Launceston

200 km (124 miles) north of Hobart.

Nestled in a fertile agricultural basin where the South Esk and North Esk rivers join to form the Tamar, the city of

Launceston (pronounced *Lon*-sess-tun), or Lonie to locals, is the commercial center of Tasmania's northern region. Many unusual markets and shops are concentrated downtown (unlike Hobart, which has most of its stores in the historic center, set apart from the commercial district).

Launceston is far from bustling, and has a notable number of pleasant parks, late-19th-century homes, historic mansions, and private gardens. The sumptuous countryside that surrounds the city—rolling farmland and the rich loam of English-looking landscapes—set off by the South Esk River meandering through towering gorges, is also appealing.

◉ Sights

Cataract Gorge
BODY OF WATER | FAMILY | Almost in the heart of the city, the South Esk River flows through the stunningly beautiful Cataract Gorge on its way toward the Tamar River. A 1-km (½-mile) path leads along the face of the precipices to the **Cliff Gardens Reserve,** where there are picnic tables, a swimming pool, and a restaurant. Take the chairlift in the first basin for a thrilling aerial view of the gorge—at just over 900 feet, it's the longest single span in the world. Self-guided nature trails wind through the park, and it's a great place for a picnic. ⊠ *Basin Rd.* ☏ *03/6331–5915* ⊕ *www.launcestoncataractgorge.com.au* ⊠ *Gorge free, chairlift from A$13.*

Franklin House
HISTORIC SITE | FAMILY | Built in 1838 by noted a local businessman and brewer, who had once been a convict, this fine late-Georgian house is notable for its beautiful cedar architecture and collection of period English furniture, clocks, and fine china. The tea room serves light meals and refreshments and often hosts special events such as garden parties or High Tea. ⊠ *413 Hobart Rd.,*

Franklin Village ☏ *03/6344–7824* ⊕ *www. nationaltrust.org.au/places/franklin-house* ⊠ *A$10.*

James Boag Brewery Experience
WINERY/DISTILLERY | Since 1881, this operation has been brewing some of Australia's finest beer in an imposing brick building, in which weekday brewery tours are run. Visitors learn the entire process, from brewhouse to packaging, and end with beer tastings (plus a cheese platter if you book the more expensive option). Bookings are essential. ⊠ *39 William St.* ☏ *03/6332–6300* ⊕ *www.jamesboag. com.au/agegate* ⊠ *Tour A$33.*

Queen Victoria Museum and Art Gallery
MUSEUM | FAMILY | Opened in 1891, the gallery presents fascinating insights into the city's history, including the rich Aboriginal and colonial past. There's also a large natural-history collection of stuffed birds and animals (including the now-extinct thylacine, or Tasmanian tiger). Regular tours and history talks are a great way to dig a little deeper into the museum's collection. ⊠ *2 Invermay Rd.* ☏ *03/6323–3777* ⊕ *www.qvmag.tas.gov. au* ⊠ *Free.*

★ Tamar Valley Wine Route
SCENIC DRIVE | Along both sides of the Tamar River north of Launceston, the soil and cool weather are perfect for grape growing. Here in the Tamar Valley wine region, some of the outstanding varieties grown include Pinot Noir, Riesling, and Pinot Grigio; the sparkling wines produced here are world-leading. A map of the route, available for download at their website, will help you to plan your visit. Noteworthy stops along the route are Pipers Brook Vineyard, Joseph Cromy, Holm Oak, Holyman wines at Stoney Rise, Clover Hill, and The Jansz Wine Room. ⊠ *Launceston* ⊕ *www.tamarvalleywineroute.com.au.*

Restaurants

Hallam's Waterfront

$$$ | SEAFOOD | The menu at this restaurant with a fabulous location by the Tamar River highlights fresh local seafood, mainly from the East Coast. Try such dishes as Cape Grim porterhouse steak with crispy sweet potato and pepper jus, or seafood (it might be prawns, scallops, mussels, clams, or fish). $ *Average main: A$40* ⊠ *13 Park St.* ☎ *03/6334–0554* ⊕ *www.hallamswaterfront.com.au* ⊘ *Closed Sun.*

Jailhouse Grill

$$ | STEAKHOUSE |FAMILY | If you have to go to jail, this is the place to do it—in a 130-year-old historic building where you'll dine on succulent grass-fed beef, typically of the Angus or Hereford breed. Despite being furnished with chains and bars, it was never actually a place for incarceration, so relax and feast on prime beef cuts (or fish and chicken), and an all-you-can-eat salad bar. **Known for:** epic salad bar; excellent selection of Australian wines; busy, so can be hard to get a table. $ *Average main: A$35* ⊠ *32 Wellington St.* ☎ *03/6331–0466* ⊕ *www.jailhousegrill.com.au* ⊘ *No lunch Mon.–Wed.*

★ Stillwater

$$$ | AUSTRALIAN | Part of Ritchie's Mill—a beautifully restored 1830s flour mill beside the Tamar River—this much-lauded restaurant and Launceston institution, serves wonderfully creative seafood dishes, usually with an Asian twist, such as the confit of Macquarie Harbour ocean trout with wasabi mash, trout crackle, and citrus and flying fish roe emulsion. The five-course tasting menu includes wine pairings from the great selection of Tasmanian wines. **Known for:** fish of the day; five-course tasting menu; wine bar and gallery on premises, too. $ *Average main: A$45* ⊠ *Ritchie's Mill, 2 Bridge Rd.* ☎ *03/6331–4153* ⊕ *www.stillwater.com.au* ⊘ *No dinner Sun. and Mon.*

Hotels

Alice's Cottages

$$$ | B&B/INN | Constructed from the remains of three 1840s buildings, this delightful B&B is full of whimsical touches. **Pros:** perfect for a romantic getaway, especially the "boudoir"-themed room; spa bathrooms are luxurious and decadent. **Cons:** not child-friendly. $ *Rooms from: A$210* ⊠ *129 Balfour St.* ☎ *03/6334–2231* ⊕ *www.alicescottages. com.au* ⊃ *8 cottages* ⦿ *Free breakfast.*

Country Club Tasmania

$$ | RESORT | At this luxury property on the outskirts of Launceston you can choose between resort rooms and one- to three-bedroom villas, some of which have fully equipped kitchens. **Pros:** impressive and classy rooms; plenty of entertainment on-site from gambling to golf; great location. **Cons:** 10-minute drive from the town; casino can get rowdy on a Friday night; feels a bit dated. $ *Rooms from: A$190* ⊠ *Country Club Ave., Prospect Vale* ☎ *1800/635344* ⊕ *www. countryclubtasmania.com.au* ⚲ *A$30 for 9 holes, A$45 for 18 holes* ⊃ *102 rooms* ⦿ *No meals.*

Hotel Grand Chancellor

$$ | HOTEL | This modern six-story building in the city center has large rooms that blend classic if slightly bland furnishings with modern conveniences. **Pros:** central location; check-in is a breeze. **Cons:** rooms look faded compared to the lobby. $ *Rooms from: A$190* ⊠ *29 Cameron St* ☎ *03/6334–3434, 1800/753379* ⊕ *www. grandchancellorhotels.com* ⊃ *165 rooms, 7 suites* ⦿ *No meals.*

Old Bakery Inn

$ | B&B/INN | History comes alive at this colonial complex made up of a converted stable, the former baker's cottage, and the old bakery. **Pros:** quaint and sensitively restored rooms; great value; walking distance to downtown Launceston. **Cons:** some noise from busy road; breakfast ends at 9 am sharp. $ *Rooms* *from: A$120* ✉ *York St.* ☎ *03/6331–7900, 1800/641264* 🌐 *www.oldbakeryinn.com.au* 🛏 *24 rooms* 🍴 *Free breakfast.*

Peppers Seaport Hotel

$$$ | **HOTEL** | Superbly situated on the Tamar riverfront, this popular urban-chic hotel is part of the Seaport Dock area and is shaped like a ship. **Pros:** lovely waterfront views from some rooms; immaculate lobby and service; free Wi-Fi. **Cons:** parking costs extra; the waterfront scene isn't very lively. $ *Rooms from: A$260* ✉ *28 Seaport Blvd.* ☎ *03/6345–3333* 🌐 *www.peppers.com.au* 🛏 *60 rooms* 🍴 *No meals.*

TwoFourTwo

$$$ | **RENTAL** | Three contemporary apartments and a town house built within a historic Launceston property have all modern conveniences, including espresso machines and iPod docks, plus the wonderful timber design work of Alan Livermore, one of the owners. **Pros:** rooms are stylish and well laid out; personal touches like fresh flowers and a thoughtfully stocked in-room wine selection. **Cons:** no leisure facilities. $ *Rooms from: A$230* ✉ *242 Charles St.* ☎ *03/6331–9242* 🌐 *www.twofourtwo.com.au* 🛏 *4 apartments* 🍴 *No meals.*

Nightlife

The local *Examiner* is the best source of information on local nightlife and entertainment, but be warned: no one goes to Launceston to party.

★ Saint John

BREWPUBS/BEER GARDENS | The Saint John craft brewery and bar joins a proliferation of trendy tea rooms, cafés, and bars to solidify Launceston's evolution to hipster status. Try their beers on tap and bar snacks. ✉ *133 Saint John St.* ☎ *03/6333–0340* 🌐 *saintjohncraftbeer.com.au.*

Shopping

Launceston is a convenient place for a little shopping, with most stores central on George Street and in nearby Yorktown Mall.

Aspire Adventure Equipment

SPORTING GOODS | This outdoor adventure store is the perfect place to stock up on all the things you will need for a camping trip around Tasmania or if you just need an emergency sweater to survive the Tassie winter. The staff are extremely knowledgeable, and this store stocks a wide variety of quality equipment. ✉ *136 York St.* ☎ *03/6331–8708* 🌐 *www.aspire-adventureequipment.com.au.*

Design Centre of Tasmania

ART GALLERIES | Carrying beautiful items made from Tasmanian wood, this studio carries custom-designed furniture and locally crafted pottery, glass, and woolen clothing. It's also known for its inspiring contemporary art exhibitions and design collections. The center often has an artist in residence and is just a short walk from the city center. ✉ *Brisbane St.* ☎ *03/6331–5506* 🌐 *www.designtasmania.com.au.*

Sheep's Back

CLOTHING | This shop is a true Launceston icon—it sells beautifully made woolen products, such as sweaters, blankets, underwear and the ever-popular UGG boot. ✉ *53 George St.* ☎ *03/6331–2539* 🌐 *www.thesheepsback.com.au.*

Activities

There are plenty of opportunities to spot wildlife, fish, or birds in the lovely countryside surrounding Launceston and the Tamar Valley.

BIRD-WATCHING

Tamar Island Wetlands

BIRD WATCHING | **FAMILY** | This bird sanctuary on the banks of the Tamar River just outside Launceston is the ideal place to see purple swamp hens and black swans from boardwalks over the wetlands while scanning the sky for white-breasted sea eagles or forest ravens. Cape Barren Geese have been known to visit on occasion. ⊠ *West Tamar Hwy., Riverside* ☎ *03/6327–3964* ⊕ *www.parks.tas.gov. au* ✉ *Free.*

RIVER CRUISES

Tamar River Cruises

BOATING | FAMILY | This company conducts relaxing trips on the Tamar, past many wineries and into Cataract Gorge. The *Tamar Odyssey* catamaran, which has an upper and lower deck and spacious lounges is used for the longer cruises, while the gorgeous, old-fashioned *Lady Launceston* takes visitors on the shorter Cataract Gorge cruises. Prices vary depending on the cruise chosen. ⊠ *Home Point Cruise Terminal, Home Point Parade* ☎ *03/6334–9900* ⊕ *www. tamarrivercruises.com.au* ✉ *From A$33.*

WALKING

Launceston Historic Walks

HIKING/WALKING | FAMILY | This professional outfit conducts a leisurely one-hour sightseeing stroll through the historic heart of the city. The guided walks leave from the 1842 Gallery and present an engaging look at Launceston's charming architecture and the city's colorful past. ⊠ *Cimitiere St.* ☎ *03/6331–2213* ⊕ *www.1842.com.au/launceston-historic-walks* ✉ *A$15.*

WILDLIFE-WATCHING

Pepperbush Adventures

WILDLIFE-WATCHING | FAMILY | This husband-and-wife team runs tours out of Scottsdale, but the majority of tours depart from Launceston and cover Tasmania's northeast, looking at local wildlife in its natural habitat. The full-day Quoll Patrol takes you to view the "bandit of the Bush," as well as wallabies, platypuses, and, if you're lucky, some devils. Trout fishing and full-day wine tasting tours are also available, as well as several multiday excursions, including a six-day

experience that visits the Bay of Fires on the northeast coast and the Tarkine, the greatest expanse of cool temperate rain forest in Australia. ⊠ *65 King St.* ⊕ *www. tasmanianwildlifetours.com.au* ✉ *From A$215.*

ZIP LINING

★ **Hollybank Treetops Adventure**

TOUR—SPORTS | FAMILY | Just 15 minutes' drive northeast of Launceston, this popular attraction that's especially appealing to kids, or kids at heart, offers three-hour zip-lining tours through a verdant forest canopy high above the Pipers River. ⊠ *66 Hollybank Rd., Underwood* ☎ *03/6395–1390* ⊕ *www.treetopsadventure.com.au* ✉ *From A$125.*

Devonport and Nearby

89 km (55 miles) northwest of Launceston, 289 km (179 miles) northwest of Hobart.

In the middle of the North Coast, Devonport is the Tasmanian port where ferries from Melbourne dock. Visitors often dash off to other parts of Tasmania without realizing that the town and its surroundings have many interesting attractions.

◉ Sights

Ashgrove Farm Cheese Factory

RESTAURANT—SIGHT | FAMILY | This dairy makes delicious English-style cheeses like cheddar, Lancashire, and Cheshire, and is an inviting place to learn about cheese production, sample some of the tasty products, and browse through other locally produced goods, like jams, olive oils, and honey. Tours are available, and no advance notice is needed for individuals or small groups. The café serves great snacks, too. ⊠ *6173 Bass Hwy., Elizabeth Town* ☎ *03/6368–1105* ⊕ *www.ashgrove-cheese.com.au* ✉ *Free.*

Bass Strait Maritime Centre

MUSEUM | FAMILY | This interpretive center highlights the natural history of the Bass Strait and its many islands as well as showing exhibits that explore Devonport's development into a port city, the area's rich naval past, and the arrival and settlement of the early Europeans. Regular exhibitions feature different aspects of Tasmania's rich maritime history. ✉ *6 Gloucester Ave., Devonport* ☎ *03/6424–7100* 🌐 *www.bassstraitmaritimecentre.com.au* 🎟 *A$10.*

Don River Railway

TRANSPORTATION SITE (AIRPORT/BUS/FERRY/TRAIN) | FAMILY | This re-creation of an early-20th-century passenger railway with working steam and diesel engines takes a glorious 30-minute journey along the banks of the Don River. The route, which leads through native vegetation and affords lovely water views, is well worth the price. The train departs from the restored railway station, where there's a large collection of vintage engines, carriages, and wagons. ✉ *Forth Rd., Devonport* ☎ *03/6424–6335* 🌐 *www.donriverrailway.com.au* 🎟 *A$19.*

House of Anvers

STORE/MALL | FAMILY | South from Devonport along the Bass Highway toward Launceston, the House of Anvers specializes in making exquisite chocolates—and you can watch the confectionery staff as they mold and dip different truffles, pralines, and fudges. (If your mouth starts to water, hit the on-site café for a yummy chocolate dessert or hot cocoa.) They also provide an online store if you can't fit all the sweet delicacies in your suitcase. ✉ *9025 Bass Hwy., Latrobe* ☎ *03/6426–2958* 🌐 *www.anvers-chocolate.com.au* 🎟 *Free.*

Sheffield

PUBLIC ART | FAMILY | In the small village of Sheffield, 32 km (20 miles) south of Devonport, with the ever-present Mt. Roland overlooking the valley, more than 50 murals painted on the exterior walls of local buildings depict scenes of local history. This village is worth a special detour; its cafés and galleries are interesting, and it's the perfect rest point on the way to Cradle Mountain. ✉ *Sheffield* ☎ *03/6491–1061* 🌐 *www.sheffieldtasmania.com.au.*

Tiagarra Aboriginal Culture Centre and Museum

INFO CENTER | Tasmania's Aboriginal culture is being revitalised through regular cultural events. On display is artworks and a series of reproduced Aboriginal huts. Among the exhibits are many cultural artifacts including beautiful Aboriginal rock engravings, which were discovered on the nearby Mersey Bluff headland in 1929 and subsequently collected here for protection. Tours must be arranged in advanced. ✉ *Mersey Bluff, Devonport* 🌐 *tiagarra.weebly.com.*

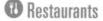

🍴 Restaurants

Pedro's

$$ | SEAFOOD |FAMILY | Despite the Spanish-sounding name, there's nothing Latin or Iberian about the menu at this unusually situated restaurant overhanging the water at the wharf in Ulverstone. A local institution, you can expect seafood caught fresh and cooked up daily in this restaurant on the edge of the Leven River. [$] *Average main: A$30* ✉ *Wharf Rd., Ulverstone* ☎ *03/6425–6663 restaurant, 03/6425–5181 take-out counter* 🌐 *www.pedrostherestaurant.com.au.*

🛏 Hotels

Westella House

$ | B&B/INN | This charming 1885 homestead has stunning sea views, wood-burning fireplaces, handcrafted banisters and mantels, and antique furnishings that can't fail to draw you into the cozy setting. **Pros:** lovely gazebo in the garden to sit in and enjoy the views; complimentary sherry goes down well in winter; hosts are very welcoming. **Cons:** far from any restaurants or shops; a little dated; showing wear and tear. $ *Rooms from: A$140* ✉ *68 Westella Dr., Ulverstone* ☎ *03/6425–6222* ⊕ *www.westella.com* ➥ *3 rooms* ⚫ *Free breakfast.*

Stanley

140 km (87 miles) northwest of Devonport, 400 km (248 miles) northwest of Hobart.

Stanley is one of the prettiest villages in Tasmania, and a must for anyone traveling in the northwest. A gathering of historic cottages at the foot of the Nut, Tasmania's version of Uluru (Ayers Rock), it's filled with friendly tea rooms, interesting shops, and old country inns.

👁 Sights

Highfield Historic Site

HISTORIC SITE | FAMILY | At this atmospheric site you can explore the town's history at the fully restored Regency house and grounds where Van Diemen's Land Company, who settled the estate in 1824, once stood. Day tours are self-guided, but guides in period costumes are on hand to answer any questions. Views over the town and surrounding areas make the trip to Highfield worthwhile. ✉ *Green Hills Rd.* ☎ *03/6458–1100* ⊕ *www.historic-highfield.com.au* ➥ *A$12.*

The Nut

NATURE SITE | FAMILY | This sheer volcanic plug that's some 12½ million years old rears up right behind the village—it's almost totally surrounded by the sea. You can ride a chairlift to the top of the 500-foot-high headland, where the views are breathtaking; or, you can make the 20-minute trek on a footpath leading to the summit, where walking trails lead in all directions. It's a stunning place to view birdlife and the whole northwest coastline. ✉ *Browns Rd.* ☎ *03/6458–1286* ➥ *Chairlift A$11.*

🏖 Beaches

Godfreys Beach

BEACH—SIGHT | FAMILY | Just north of the Nut is Stanley's curving Godfreys Beach, at which you can detect how elements of the region have formed by volcanic activity—note the basalt rock formations. The 1-km (½-mile) beach is largely protected from the region's strong westerly winds, which can lead to waves of 3 feet or higher. A favorite location for serious photographers, this is also a lovely stretch of sand for strolling, but it's a bit chilly for swimming. You can park at the lot near town, at the south end of the sand, where you'll also find a playground. **Amenities:** parking (free); showers; toilets. **Best for:** solitude; walking. ✉ *Green Hill Rd.*

🍽 Restaurants

Beachside Retreat West Inlet

$$ | B&B/INN |FAMILY | These unique, environmentally friendly cabins are located directly on waterfront sand dune overlooking the sea with kilometers of absolutely private beach frontage. **Pros:** guests with special needs are well catered to; breathtaking views from cabins. **Cons:** two-night minimum; limited food availability on-site. $ *Rooms from: A$200* ✉ *253 Stanley Hwy.* ☎ *03/6458–1350* ⊕ *www.beachsideretreat.com* ➥ *4 cabins* ⚫ *No meals.*

Stanley's on the Bay

$$ | AUSTRALIAN | Set on the waterfront in the fully restored old Bond Store, this unpretentious restaurant specializes in succulent steaks and freshly cooked seafood. Try the eye fillet of beef—Australian terminology for the top-quality beef cut—topped with prawns, scallops, and fish fillets, served in a creamy white-wine sauce. $ *Average main: A$30* ✉ *15 Wharf Rd.* ☎ *03/6458–1404* ⊕ *www.stanleyvillage.com.au* ⊙ *Closed Sun. and July and Aug. No lunch.*

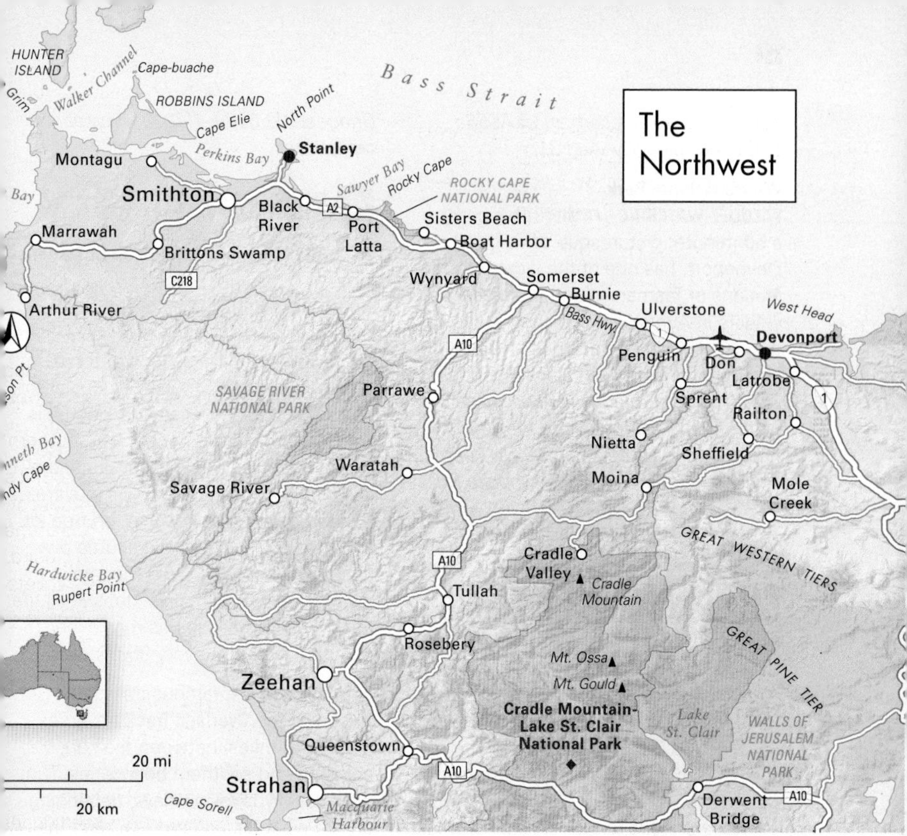

Hotels

★ Tarkine Wilderness Lodge
$$$ | **B&B/INN** | This superb country lodge sits atop a grassy rise amid ancient rain forest. **Pros:** ancient rain forest on the property; wildlife experiences; friendly hosts. **Cons:** some distance to any services. [$] *Rooms from: A$410* ✉ *Newhaven Track, Meunna* ☎ *03/6445–0184* 🌐 *tarkinelodge.com.au* 🛏 *3 rooms* 🍴 *Free Breakfast.*

Activities

FISHING

Murray's Day Out
FISHING | The exuberant owner of this tour service takes guests out on a full day's fishing expedition, providing everything necessary, including lunch and refreshments, and imparting his fantastic knowledge of Tasmania. Some of his recommended common fishing spots include Stanley Wharf, Beauty Point, and Garden Island. Murray also runs personalized shopping and scenic day tours, overnight trips, and other customized excursions. ✉ *2/15–19 King St., Devonport* ☎ *03/6424–2439* 🌐 *www.murraysdayout.com.au* 🎫 *From A$150.*

WILDLIFE WATCHING

Stanley Seal Cruises
WILDLIFE-WATCHING | **FAMILY** | Twice a day (except in winter), the motor cruiser *Sylvia C* leads passengers on 75-minute journeys from Stanley's dock to Bull Rock, where they view delightful Australian fur seals basking on the Bass Strait rocks. Southern right whales are also sometimes spotted in the waters near the Nut. ✉ *Dockside, Wharf Rd.* ☎ *0419/550134* 🌐 *www.*

stanleysealcruises.com.au ✉ *A\$55* ⊘ *Closed mid-May–Aug 31.*

Wing's Wildlife Park

WILDLIFE-WATCHING | FAMILY | This park, a 50-minute, picturesque drive from Devonport, has one of the larger collections of Tasmanian and international wildlife in Australia, which as well as all the usual suspects includes an aquatic section where you can view albino rainbow trout and Atlantic salmon. Excellent guided tours can be tailored to your interests and an on-site café will keep your hunger sated. ✉ *137 Winduss Rd., Gunns Plains* ☎ *03/6429–1151* ⊕ *www. wingswildlife.com.au* ✉ *A\$22.*

Cradle Mountain–Lake St. Clair National Park

173 km (107 miles) northwest of Hobart to Lake St. Clair at the southern end of the park, 85 km (53 miles) southwest of Devonport, 181 km (113 miles) from Launceston, 155 km (97 miles) northeast from Strahan to Cradle Mountain at the northern end of the park.

This expansive, remote park contains some of the most spectacular alpine scenery and mountain trails in Australia. Popular with hikers of all abilities, the park has several high peaks, including Mt. Ossa, the highest in Tasmania (more than 5,300 feet).

ESSENTIALS

Cradle Mountain Visitor Centre

All national parks in Tasmania require a pass. These can be bought at the visitor center along with souvenirs and light meals. ✉ *4057 Cradle Mountain Rd., Cradle Mountain* ☎ *03/6492–1110* ⊕ *www. parks.tas.gov.au.*

Lake St. Clair Visitor Centre

Ferry tickets, national parks passes, and much more can be purchased here. ✉ *Lake St. Clair National Park, Derwent*

Bridge ☎ *03/6289–1172* ⊕ *www.parks. tas.gov.au.*

⊙ Sights

★ **Cradle Mountain–Lake St. Clair National Park**

MOUNTAIN—SIGHT | FAMILY | The Cradle Mountain section of the park lies in the north. The southern section of the park, centered on Lake St. Clair, is popular for boating and hiking. Many walking trails lead from the settlement at the southern end of the lake, which is surrounded by low hills and dense forest. Visitors are advised to park their cars in the free lot and then make use of the shuttle bus that runs from the Cradle Mountain Visitor Centre and makes stops at all the trails. In summer the bus runs every 15 minutes, in winter every 30 minutes.

One of the most famous trails in Australia, the **Overland Track** traverses 65 km (40 miles) between the park's northern and southern boundaries. The walk usually takes six days, depending on the weather, and on clear days the mountain scenery seems to stretch forever. Hikers are charged A\$200 to do the Overland during peak walking season (October to May), and Tasmania's Parks and Wildlife Service has provided several basic sleeping huts that are available on a first-come, first-served basis. Because space in the huts is limited, hikers are advised to bring their own tents. If you prefer to do the walk in comfort, you can use well-equipped, heated private structures managed by Cradle Mountain Huts. ✉ *Cradle Mountain–Lake St. Clair National Park, Cradle Mountain* ☎ *03/6492–1110* ⊕ *www.parks.tas.gov.au/index.aspx- ?base=3297* ✉ *A\$17 per person.*

🛏 Hotels

Cradle Mountain Hotel

\$\$ | RESORT | Five minutes' drive from the entrance to the national park is this upmarket lodge, complete with rooms

Looking out across Cradle Mountain–Lake St. Clair National Park

that face the woods and have perching posts for local birds. **Pros:** delicious meals in fine dining restaurant; on-site art gallery; tours from the door. **Cons:** can be packed with corporate events. $ *Rooms from: A$200 ⊠ 3718 Cradle Mountain Rd., Cradle Mountain ☎ 03/6492–1404 ⊕ www.cradlemountainhotel.com.au ⇥ 60 rooms ◯ No meals.*

Discovery Holiday Parks, Cradle Mountain

$ | RENTAL | FAMILY | Near the forest at the northern edge of the park, Discovery Holiday Parks is the best budget accommodation in the area, with campgrounds, RV sites, four-bed bunkhouses with cooking facilities, and self-contained cabins with kitchens. **Pros:** family-friendly and good-value accommodation; free Internet. **Cons:** reception closes early; most expensive spa cabins are pricey; Wi-Fi doesn't reach most cabins. $ *Rooms from: A$130 ⊠ 3832 Cradle Mountain Rd., Cradle Mountain ☎ 03/6492–1395 ⊕ www.discoveryholidayparks.com. au ⇥ 38 unpowered sites, 10 powered*

sites, 75 bunkhouse beds, 36 cabins ◯ No meals.

★ Peppers Cradle Mountain Lodge

$$$ | RESORT | FAMILY | This charming lodge with its collection of wood cabins dotted around the wilderness of Cradle Mountain Valley is a firm favorite with park visitors. **Pros:** good range of food options; fireplaces are a hit in winter; great spa. **Cons:** no room service; no TVs; Internet restricted to the lobby. $ *Rooms from: A$270 ⊠ 4038 Cradle Mountain Rd., Cradle Mountain ☎ 1300/806192 ⊕ www. cradlemountainlodge.com.au ⇥ 58 rooms, 28 suites ◯ Free breakfast.*

🏃 Activities

AIR TOURS
Cradle Mountain Helicopters

TOUR—SPORTS | FAMILY | The views are magnificent on this company's scenic helicopter flights from Cradle Mountain village to the country's deepest gorge, Fury Gorge, and then on to picture-post-card Dove Lake, set against epic Cradle

Mountain itself. The panoramas over the rugged Tasmanian landscape are breathtaking. ⊠ *Cradle Mountain* ☎ *03/6492–1132* ⊕ *www.cradlemountainhelicopters.com.au* ✉ *From A$250.*

HIKING
Cradle Mountain Canyons
WATER SPORTS | Canyoning is the most exciting way to experience the World Heritage wilderness at Cradle Mountain. Launch yourself off waterfalls, abseil down cliffs, and shoot through nature's waterslides under the guidance and encouragement of your guides. Be prepared to get wet and a little chilly. ⊠ *3845 Cradle Mountain Rd., Cradle Mountain* ☎ *1300/032384* ⊕ *cradlemountaincanyons.com.au.*

Cradle Mountain Coaches
HIKING/WALKING | This Devonport-based company provides bus transport to Cradle Mountain, Lake St. Clair, Walls of Jerusalem, Frenchmans Cap, and many other popular bushwalking destinations. ⊠ *283 Port Sorell Rd., Wesley Vale* ☎ *03/6427–7626* ⊕ *www.cradlemountaincoaches.com.au.*

HORSEBACK RIDING
Cradle Country Adventures
HORSEBACK RIDING | **FAMILY** | Choose from half-day, full-day, and multiday horse rides through stunning natural vistas—available packages are suitable for both novices and experienced riders. All equipment, guides, and transfers are included. ⊠ *Cradle Mountain* ☎ *1300/656069* ⊕ *www.cradleadventures.com.au* ✉ *From A$120.*

Chapter 8

SOUTH EAST QUEENSLAND

8

Updated by
Melissa Fagan

👁 Sights	🍴 Restaurants	🛏 Hotels	🛍 Shopping	🍸 Nightlife
★★★★★	★★★★☆	★★★★☆	★★★☆☆	★★★☆☆

WELCOME TO SOUTH EAST QUEENSLAND

TOP REASONS TO GO

★ **Getting Wild:** Reefs teeming with fish, rays and turtles; pristine rain forests filled with rare birds and reptiles; unspoiled beaches and islands; meandering rivers and dramatic gorges; and of course, kangaroos and koalas.

★ **Slowing Down:** Queensland has a relaxed and welcoming vibe, even at the upmarket hotels and fine-dining restaurants.

★ **Going Local:** From Indigenous-themed tours, to wineries, microbreweries, local produce-driven restaurants, and a thriving local music scene, the region is ripe with homegrown goodness.

★ **Being Forever Young:** The Gold Coast's theme parks provide endless thrills; the region is also an outdoor adventure-lover's playground, with some of the world's best surf breaks, diving, hiking, and more.

★ **Savoring the Arts:** Brisbane's renowned Gallery of Modern Art (GoMA), performance centers, galleries and art spaces are innovative, edgy, and world-class.

1 Brisbane. Queensland's lively capital.

2 Southern Downs. Home to Queensland's best viticultultural regions.

3 Coomera and Oxenford. These northern Gold Coast suburbs are all about theme parks.

4 Southport and Main Beach. Boat, bike, and surf along this natural peninsula.

5 Surfers Paradise and Broadbeach. A stunning stretch of beach with great surfing.

6 Burleigh Heads and Beyond. Popular foodie and surf destination and great wildlife parks.

7 Gold Coast Hinterland. Superb national parks and nature reserves.

8 Noosa. Stylish resort town.

9 Peregian and Coolum. A great base for exploring the Sunshine Coast.

10 Maroochydore. Popular beach town with great beaches.

11 Mooloolaba. Cute town wth a lively Esplanade.

12 Caloundra. Nine beaches from family-friendly to surfer-friendly.

13 Glass House Mountains Area. Home to famous Australia Zoo.

14 Montville. Artsy mountain village.

15 Maleny. Eclectic rural village with scenic reserve.

16 Yandina, Eumundi, and Cooroy. Famous markets, restaurants, and a ginger factory.

17 Lady Elliot Island. The closest Great Barrier Reef island to Brisbane.

18 Lady Musgrave Island. Some of the best diving and snorkeling in Queensland.

19 Heron Island. Leisurely island, great for snorkeling and scuba diving.

20 Great Keppel Island. Palm-fringed beaches, great hiking, and unspoiled coral.

21 K'Gari (Fraser) Island. Unique island with multi-color sand cliffs, rainforest, whale-watching, and Aboriginal sites.

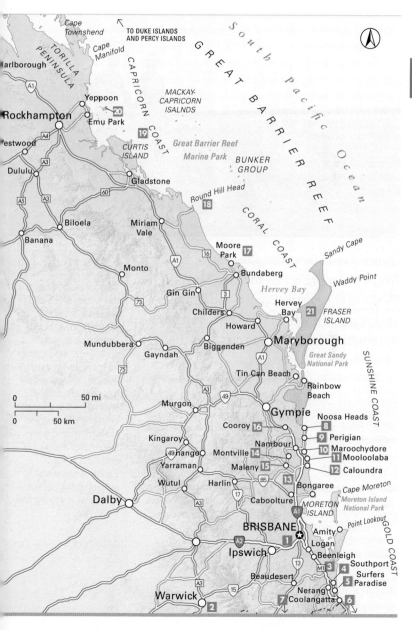

SUNSHINE COAST'S TOP BEACHES

Queensland's Sunshine Coast stretches from Caloundra in the south to Noosa Heads in the north. Along it you'll find everything from family-friendly beaches to thundering surf breaks to pretty sheltered coves ideal for snorkeling.

The Sunshine Coast is less developed than its southern counterpart, the Gold Coast. Although it has its share of shops, cafés, and resorts, there are still dozens of clean, uncrowded beaches where you can sunbathe, stroll, cast a line, or jump in the unspoiled waters to swim, snorkel, and surf.

Some beaches are perfect for water sports such as sailing, windsurfing, kayaking, or wakeboarding. Others are known for their reliable surf breaks. You'll find secluded rocky coves where you can "fossick" (Australian for beachcomb) among rock pools, or don a mask and snorkel to come face-to-face with colorful fish, rays, sea stars, and squid. There are also safe, lifeguard-patrolled swimming beaches with playgrounds, skate parks, kiosks, changing rooms, and picnic facilities ideal for families.

WHEN TO GO

The Sunshine Coast has sunny skies and year-round balmy temperatures, but beaches can get crowded during school holidays and at peak season, and prices are higher. Crowds are smaller and the weather is still summery in November and early December and March and April (except Easter week when school is out). January and February bring the most rain.

SUNSHINE BEACH

Lovely Sunshine Beach, the last easterly facing beach before Noosa, is patrolled year-round. Beach breaks, reliable swell, a rocky headland sheltering it from winds, and clear, glassy water make Sunshine popular with surfers. When northeasterlies blow, surf the northern pocket. Fish off the beach year-round for dart, bream, and flathead, or cast a long line into deep water to hook numerous seasonal species. Use covered picnic areas, barbecues, toilets, and parking.

MOOLOOLABA BEACH

This super-safe, family-friendly swimming beach is patrolled year-round, and has just enough swell to make it fun. Surfers might want to check out the left-hand break that sometimes forms off the rocks at the northern end. There are shady picnic areas with barbecues, playgrounds, showers, toilets, public phones, exercise areas, and parking—as well as the local meeting point, the Loo with a View. Stroll south along the coastal path to the river mouth and rock wall (off which you can fish, year-round, for bream); north to Alexandra Headland for views of the bay; or along Mooloolaba Esplanade, lined with casual eateries and boutiques.

COOLUM BEACH

Coolum Beach is a popular choice for families, boasting a surf club, skate park, playgrounds, changing rooms, toilets, kiosks, shorefront parks, and picnic areas. A long, white-sand beach, Coolum is patrolled year-round, and has a nice beach break and some decent waves off the headland. Fish from the beach in the evening for grouper, tailor, bream, and dart; catch bream around the headland, especially in winter. Walk south along the boardwalk to the headland park for magnificent coastal views, or north to quieter Peregian Beach with its patrolled surf, playground, and adjacent Environmental Park.

SAFETY

Most popular Sunshine Coast beaches are patrolled by lifeguards in school holiday and peak periods and on weekends throughout the warmer months. On some Sunshine Coast beaches, sandbanks, strong currents, and riptides make surf conditions challenging. Even on patrolled beaches, swimming unaccompanied is not recommended.

Swim between the red-and-yellow flags, and follow lifeguards' directives. Locals are often the best sources of advice on where and when to dive in.

Sharks are rarely a problem; however, lifeguards keep watch and issue warnings if they're sighted. A more constant hazard is the harsh Queensland sun: apply SPF50-plus sunscreen at regular intervals. Get information on local beaches at ⊕ *coastalwatch.com*, and surf reports on Surf Life Saving Queensland's website, ⊕ *www.lifesaving.com.au*. Contact SLSQ Lifesaving at ☎ *07/3846–8000*.

COASTAL AND WILDERNESS WALKS

South East Queensland lays claim to some of the world's most superb wilderness areas, and the best way to explore them is on foot. Behind the Gold and Sunshine coasts are national parks, forests, and nature reserves dense with trails and walkways. Several also trace scenic sections of the coastline.

Coastal trails wind along the beachfront, trace rain-forest-clad headlands, and meander through waterfront reserves from the Gold Coast to the national parkland north of Noosa.

A string of national parks and wilderness areas connects the Gold and Sunshine Coast hinterlands, with trails of varying lengths and degrees of difficulty. Walkers are rewarded with memorable sights: dramatic waterfalls and pristine pools, tracts of ancient rain forest, and glow-worm caves; wildflowers, wildlife, and exceptional views, some stretching as far as the coast.

SAFETY

For bushwalking you'll need sturdy shoes with grip, a hat, sunscreen, insect repellent, wet- and cold-weather gear, drinking water, food, camping equipment and permits (if overnighting), and a map and compass. Leech-proof yourself by wearing long socks over your pant legs and carrying a lighter to burn off any hitchhikers. Let others know your planned route and timing, even for day hikes.

QUEENSLAND'S GREAT WALKS

If your schedule allows it, tackle one of Queensland's Great Walks. A A$10-million state government initiative, the Great Walks aim to allow visitors of all ages and of average fitness to explore significant wilderness areas in a safe, eco-sensitive way.

A standout is the 54-km (34-mile) Gold Coast Hinterland Great Walk, linking the species-rich, Gondwana Rainforests of Australia World Heritage Area of Lamington and Springbrook plateaus via the glorious Numinbah Valley. En route, you'll traverse ancient volcanic terrain and pristine rain forest, passing torrential streams and waterfalls and 3,000-year-old hoop pines. Allow three days for the full walk, camping at designated sites en route, or trek just one section.

The Sunshine Coast Hinterland Great Walk, a 58-km (36-mile) hike traversing the Blackall Range northwest of Brisbane, includes sections of Kondalilla and Mapleton Falls national parks, Maleny Forest Reserve, and Delicia Road Conservation Park. The four- to six-day hike takes you past waterfalls and through open eucalypt and lush subtropical rain forest teeming with native birds, reptiles, and frogs.

The Cooloola Great Walk meanders through Great Sandy National Park north of Noosa. A 90-km (55-mile) network of graded walking tracks passes the spectacular multihue sand dunes of Rainbow Beach, and includes walks of varying distances and difficulty across a range of conditions.

Fraser Island Great Walk rewards hikers with exceptional scenery—wide, white-sand beaches, pristine deep-blue lakes, rain-forest tracts, and plenty of birds, reptiles, wallabies, and dingoes.

SHORTER OPTIONS

Coastal Trails. Compact Burleigh Head National Park, midway between Surfer's Paradise and Coolangatta, includes coastal rain forest and heath that's home to wallabies, koalas, lizards, snakes, and brush turkeys. Trek the 2.3-km (1.43-mile) Rainforest Circuit for excellent views, or the shadier, shorter, 1.2-km (0.75-mile) Oceanview Walk. Noosa National Park offers a range of options, from the 1.1-km (0.7-mile) return Palm Grove walk to the 10.8-km return Coastal Walk, which takes you around bush-covered headlands and pristine bays.

Hinterland Trails. Mt. Tamborine, Springwood, Witches Falls-Joalah, and Lamington national parks in the Gold Coast hinterland are all ideal for exploring on foot. Several wilderness retreats in the region include guided bushwalks as part of the package. West of the Sunshine Coast, short scenic walking trails in Kondallilla National Park take you past waterfalls, boulder-strewn streams, and lush rain forest.

The sunny climes of South East Queensland attracts everyone from families, partygoers, nature-lovers, to escapists. Whether you want to surf or soak in the Pacific Ocean, enjoy fresh cuisine with local flourishes, sip from your favorite cocktail or microbrewed beer, chill out at a health retreat, hike through subtropical rain forests, or join seabirds and turtles on a pristine coral isle—it's all here.

Local license plates deem Queensland "The Sunshine State"—a laid-back stretch of beaches and sun where many Australians head for their vacations. The state has actively promoted tourism, and areas such as the Gold Coast, an hour south of Brisbane, and the Sunshine Coast, a roughly equivalent distance north of the capital, offer high-rise hotels, nightclubs, trendy bars, markets and cafés, shopping precincts, and a variety of water-based activities. These thriving coastal strips are the major attraction of southern Queensland for Australians and foreign tourists alike—along with a scattering of islands, notably Fraser Island, off Hervey Bay, and the Mackay-Capricorn islands lying on the southern end of the Great Barrier Reef.

Queensland is a vibrant and cosmopolitan place to visit, and while elsewhere in Australia, Queenslanders may have a reputation for being parochial and even backwards, the state—especially the South East—is home to an increasingly diverse population. Still, as with many regions blessed with abundant sunshine, the lifestyle here is relaxed.

MAJOR REGIONS

Brisbane. Queensland's capital city is a breezily cheerful, increasingly sophisticated city with cultural attractions, great restaurants, nightlife, and galleries all centered on the city's sprawling river. If the Brisbane cityscape gives you a thirst for pastoral rolling hills—and fabulous wine—you're in luck, because some of Queensland's best viticultural regions like **Southern Downs** lie within a two-hour drive of the city

The Gold Coast. An hour's drive south of Brisbane, Queensland's first coastal resort has a bit of everything—from the high-rise glitz of Surfers Paradise to the retro holiday vibes of Burleigh, action-packed theme parks, upmarket eateries, hidden bars and hectic clubs. Take a surf lesson on some of world's best-known breaks, walk down to the beach and curl your toes in the sand, or for something different drive west and spend a day (or several) exploring towns like **Coomera and Oxenford, Southport and Main Beach,** and **Broadbeach,** and the lush **Gold Coast Hinterland.**

The Sunshine Coast is a 60-km (37-mile) stretch of white-sand beaches, inlets, lakes, and mountains that begins at the Glass House Mountains, an hour's drive north of Brisbane, and extends to Rainbow Beach in the north. Kenilworth is its inland extreme, 40 km (25 miles) from the ocean. For the most part, the Sunshine Coast is less developed than its southern cousin, the Gold Coast. Although there are plenty of stylish restaurants and luxurious hotels, this coast is best loved for its national parks, secluded coves, and relaxed beachside towns like **Noosa, Peregian and Coolum, Maroochydore, Mooloolaba,** and **Caloundra.**

The Sunshine Coast Hinterland, extending from the Glass House Mountains just northwest of Brisbane to Eumundi and Yandina, west of the northern Sunshine Coast town of Noosa, is ideal terrain for day-trippers. Tracts of subtropical rain forest and mountainous areas linked by scenic drives and walking trails are interspersed with charming hillside villages, their main streets lined with cafés, galleries, gift shops, and guesthouses. Here you'll also find thriving markets; renowned restaurants and cooking schools; ginger, nut, and pineapple farms; theme and wildlife parks; and luxury B&Bs. The Hinterland's southerly extent is the nine distinctive conical outcrops of the **Glass House Mountains**—the eroded remnants of ancient volcanoes—rising dramatically from a flattish landscape 45 km (27 miles) northwest of Brisbane. Meander north through the mountains to reach the arty village of **Maleny** and the quaint, European-style **Montville.** Continue north to the towns of **Yandina, Eumundi, and Cooroy,** where among other treasures, you'll find much-lauded restaurant Spirit House and the Ginger Factory, and thriving markets.

Despite its name, **the Mackay–Capricorn Islands,** a group of islands lying offshore between Bundaberg and Rockhampton, is closer to the southern half of Queensland than it is to the city of Mackay. They comprise the section of the Great Barrier Reef known as Capricorn Marine Park, which stretches for 140 km (87 miles) and cuts through the Tropic of Capricorn, **Heron Island** being the closest point. **Heron, Wilson, Lady Musgrave, Lady Elliot, and Great Keppel islands** are great for wildlife: turtles use several of the islands as breeding grounds; seabirds nest here; and humpback whales pass through on their migration to Antarctica each spring—generally between July and October.

A gigantic sand island off Hervey Bay, **Fraser Island** is paradise for the active visitor. What it lacks in luxe amenities it makes up for in scenery: miles of white-sand beaches, deep-blue lakes, and bushland bristling with wildlife—including some of the world's most purebred dingoes.

Planning

WHEN TO GO

Temperatures average 15.6°C (60°F) between May and September with chillier nights, and 20°C (68°F) to 29°C (80°F) December to February. From December through March, expect high humidity and periods of heavy rain. Temperatures run slightly cooler inland. Sea- and reef-side Queensland tends to fill up from mid-December through January and can also be heavily booked in July, September, and throughout Easter. There's no daylight saving time in the state.

PLANNING YOUR TIME

If you're after a quick, Miami Beach–style holiday, fly into Brisbane and head straight for the glitzy Gold Coast, overnighting in Surfers Paradise. You could end the spree with a final night and morning in nearby Lamington National Park, renowned for its subtropical wilderness and birdlife.

If you have a bit more time, do three days on shore and two days on the reef. Stay a night in Brisbane, then head to the Sunshine Coast for a hike in the Glasshouse Mountains on the way to Noosa Heads. When you've had your fill of beaches and surf, take a leisurely drive through the Sunshine Coast's lovely hinterland villages for quaint shops and cafés and stunning natural scenery. Then make your way north to Bundaberg or Gladstone for a flight to Lady Elliot, Heron, or Wilson islands to wildlife-watch, dive, and snorkel; or a ferry to Fraser Island, off Hervey Bay, where you can swim in pristine lakes, 4WD along beaches stretching 80 km (50 miles), and see wild dingoes.

GETTING HERE AND AROUND
AIR TRAVEL
Qantas (⊕ www.qantas.com.au), Virgin Australia (⊕ www.virginaustralia.com), and a number of other carriers fly direct from U.S. cities to Australian capitals and regional tourist hubs. Qantas, Virgin Australia, and Jetstar (⊕ www.jetstar.com.au) link several regional centers throughout Queensland. Budget carrier Tigerair (⊕ www.tigerair.com.au) also covers most major centers, including Cairns and the Whitsunday Coast.

BOAT TRAVEL
Ferries and charter boats ply the waters between the South East Queensland mainland and its various islands and offshore resorts. Most make daily or more frequent return trips; some carry vehicles as well as passengers.

BUS TRAVEL
Buses service most major towns and tourist areas around South East Queensland, and are reliable and affordable—though on many routes it's as cheap, and faster, to fly. During holiday periods on popular routes buses are often heavily booked; buy tickets in advance, and don't expect to stretch out, even on overnight services. Tourist offices can advise which companies go where.

CAR TRAVEL
Traveling outside of cities is often simplest and most comfortable by car. Roads are generally good, but signage varies in clarity; study maps and work out highway exits in advance (although most hire cars will have GPS installed). Be prepared for heavy traffic between Brisbane and the Gold and Sunshine coasts in peak periods. Expect temporary road closures and detours after heavy rains. Roads are narrow and winding in some parts of the hinterlands. You'll need a 4X4 to get around Fraser Island, the sand islands of Moreton Bay, and some national park roads and Outback tracks. You can rent a small runabout from about A$25 per day; a decent touring car from about A$30 a day, an SUV or four-wheel drive from $35 a day, and a passenger van from about A$80 per day (based on a weekly rental period). Gas costs vary, and tend to be pricier away from major towns and highways.

TRAIN TRAVEL
Frequent trains service routes between the capital and the Gold and Sunshine coasts, though transfers are required to major beach resorts. The Queensland Rail network links regional towns and tourist centers, and is a scenic way to travel (though on longer routes it's often cheaper to fly). The *Sunlander* and high-speed *Tilt Train* ply the coast between Brisbane and Rockhampton or Cairns, servicing towns that act as launching pads for island resorts.

RESTAURANTS
South East Queensland has come into its own as a foodie hub. Cosmopolitan Brisbane boasts its share of modern Australian, Mediterranean, and Asian-influenced menus capitalizing on fresh regional produce, as well as local wines and local microbrew beers. The cuisine at many of Queensland's high-end resorts

now rivals the standards of big-city fine-dining. Open-air market-style dining is available year-round in Brisbane, and increasingly, on the coasts—featuring food trucks, live music, and a convivial atmosphere. Coastal tourist towns are full of casual open-air restaurants that take advantage of the tropical climate—an increasing number of them helmed by city-class chefs. If you're on the road, an old-fashioned pub meal is more than satisfying and a great way to get to know the locals.

HOTELS

Accommodations in this region run the gamut from rain-forest lodges, boutique hotels, Outback pubs, backpacker hostels, and colonial "Queenslander" bed-and-breakfasts—beautiful timber houses built high on stilts, with wraparound verandas and character windows—to deluxe beachside resorts and big-city hotels. The luxury resorts are clustered around the major tourist areas of the Gold and Sunshine coasts and nearby islands such as Heron and Wilson. In smaller coastal towns, accommodation is mostly in motels, apartments, and B&Bs. There is a range of eco-friendly accommodation options, which utilize green technologies such as renewable energy and water conservation systems to minimize their impact on the environs. Many of Queensland's island resorts fall into this category. *Hotel reviews have been shortened. For full information, visit Fodors.com.*

What It Costs in Australian Dollars			
$	$$	$$$	$$$$
RESTAURANTS			
under A$21	A$21–A$35	A$36–A$50	over A$50
HOTELS			
under A$151	A$151–A$200	A$201–A$300	over A$300

TOURS

Guided day tours are a simple way to see Brisbane if your schedule is tight. View the city's many attractions from the comfort of a chauffeured coach, with a driver giving insider information. Buses are also great for covering the relatively short distances between Brisbane and nearly all of the mainland attractions. Within an hour or two you can be taste-testing your way through the Tambourine or Scenic Rim wineries, or making friends with local wildlife—feeding dolphins, whale-watching, or having your photo taken with a koala!

Most day tours include admission to sights, refreshments, and on full-day tours, lunch, as well as commentary en route and time to explore.

JPT Tour Group

SPECIAL-INTEREST | Also known as Australian Day Tours, this company conducts transfers, half-, full-, and multiday tours across popular sites in Brisbane, Moreton Island, the Gold and Sunshine coasts, Fraser Island, and more. ✉ *2 Elkhorn Ave., Shop 18, Surfers Paradise* ☎ *07/5630–1602 outside Australia, 1300/781362* ⊕ *www.daytours.com.au* ✉ *From A$60.*

Queensland Day Tours

SPECIAL-INTEREST | This group runs day tours to some of South East Queensland's most popular beach and hinterland destinations, including the Gold Coast; Springbrook; Mt. Tamborine; and Fraser, Moreton, and Stradbroke Islands. Tour options include wildlife encounters, whale and dolphin watching, wine tastings, and more. ☎ *0488/332257* ⊕ *www.qdtours.com.au* ✉ *From A$79.*

Brisbane

Called Meanjin by the local Jagera and Turrbal people, the city of Brisbane was first occupied by white settlers in 1824 as a penal colony. Today the city sprawls out along the wide, meandering Brisbane River (Maiwar). Many beautiful timber Queenslander homes, built in the 1800s, still dot the riverbanks and inner suburbs, and in spring the city's numerous parks erupt in a riot of colorful jacaranda, poinciana, and bougainvillea blossoms. Today the Queensland capital is one of Australia's most up-and-coming cities: glittering high-rises mark its polished business center, slick fashion boutiques, restaurants, and start-up businesses abound, and numerous outdoor attractions beckon. In summer, the city swelters with high daytime temperatures and stifling humidity—which may explain the ongoing popularity of air-conditioned cinemas. Wear SPF 50-plus sunscreen and a broad-brimmed hat outdoors, even on overcast days.

Brisbane's inner suburbs, a 5- to 10-minute drive or 15- to 20-minute walk from the city center, have a mix of intriguing eateries, funky waterholes and quiet accommodations. Fortitude Valley combines Chinatown with a cosmopolitan mix of clubs, cafés, and boutiques. Spring Hill has several high-quality hotels, and Paddington, New Farm, Petrie Terrace, West End, and Woolloongabba feature an eclectic mix of restaurants, bars and markets. Brisbane is also a convenient base for trips to the Sunshine and Gold coasts, the mountainous hinterlands, and the Moreton Bay islands.

GETTING HERE AND AROUND
AIR TRAVEL
Brisbane is Queensland's major transit hub. Qantas, Virgin Australia, Jetstar, and Tigerair fly to all Australian capital cities and many regional hubs around Queensland, including the Gold, Sunshine, and Whitsunday coasts.

Brisbane International Airport is 9 km (5½ miles) from the city center. Con-x-ion operates a bus service to meet all flights and drops passengers door to door at major hotels throughout Brisbane and the Gold Coast. The one-way fare is A$15 to Brisbane, A$41 to Gold Coast hotels, with cheaper deals available for families.

Airtrain has rail services to stations throughout Brisbane and the Gold Coast. The one-way fare is A$18.50 per person, or A$35 for a round-trip from the airport to the city (discounts apply for groups and tickets purchased online). Trains depart up to four times an hour, taking 20 minutes to reach the city center. Kids (5–14 years) travel free. Taxis to downtown Brisbane cost A$35 to A$50, depending on time of day.

CONTACTS Brisbane Airtrain. ☎ 07/3216–3308, 1800/119091 ⊕ www.airtrain.com.au . **Brisbane International Airport.** ✉ Airport Dr., Brisbane Airport ☎ 07/3406–3000 ⊕ www.bne.com.au.

BOAT AND FERRY TRAVEL
CityCat boats and City Ferries dock at 25 points along the Brisbane River from Hamilton to St. Lucia, running every 15 minutes or more for most of the day (the last service is at 11:45 pm). There is also a peak-hour SpeedyCat express service with limited stops. The ferries are terrific for a quick survey of the Brisbane waterfront, from the city skyline to luxury homes and beautiful parkland. If you're staying within the CBD and South Bank, try the free CityHopper ferry, which runs every 30 minutes between 6 am and midnight every day.

CONTACTS CityCat ferries. ☎ 13–1230 ⊕ www.translink.com.au.

BUS TRAVEL
Greyhound Australia, the country's only nationwide bus line, travels to around 1,100 destinations. Bus stops are well signposted, and vehicles usually run on schedule. It's 1,716 km (1,064 miles), a 30-hour journey, between Brisbane and Cairns. Book in person at Greyhound's Roma Street office, by phone, or online. Purchase point-to-point tickets or flexible passes that allow multiple stops. Most buses are also equipped with USB ports and Wi-Fi.

Crisps Coaches operates a morning and afternoon service from Brisbane to the Southern Downs and towns to the city's south and west. TransLink's help line and website can help you find bus lines that run to your destination.

CONTACTS Con-x-ion. ☎ *1300/266946* ⊕ *www.con-x-ion.com* . **Crisps Coaches.** ⊠ *78 Grafton St., Warwick* ☎ *07/4661–8333* ⊕ *www.crisps.com.au* **Greyhound Australia—Brisbane Travel Center.** ⊠ *Brisbane Transit Centre, Level 3, 151–171 Roma St., City Center* ☎ *7/3736–2601, 1300/473946* ⊕ *www.greyhound.com.au* **TransLink.** ☎ *13–1230* ⊕ *www.translink. com.au.*

RENTAL CAR TRAVEL

Most major car rental companies have offices in Brisbane, including Avis, Thrifty, Budget, and Hertz. Four-wheel-drive vehicles, motor homes, and camper vans (sleeping two to six people) are available from Britz, and Maui Rentals. If you're heading north along the coast or northwest into the bush, you can rent in Brisbane and drop off in Cairns or other towns. One-way rental fees usually apply.

Brisbane is 1,002 km (621 miles) from Sydney, a 12-hour drive along the Pacific Highway (Highway 1). Another route follows Highway 1 to Newcastle, then heads inland on the New England Highway (Highway 15). Either drive can be made in a long day, although two days or more are recommended for ample time to rest and sightsee.

CONTACTS Britz Australia Campervan Hire and Car Rentals. ⊠ *21 Industry Ct., Eagle Farm* ☎ *07/3868–1248, 1300/738087* ⊕ *www.britz.com.au.* **Maui Australia Motorhome Rentals and Car Hire.** ⊠ *21 Industry Ct., Eagle Farm* ☎ *07/3868–1248, 1800/827821* ⊕ *www.maui.com. au.*

TAXI TRAVEL

Taxis are metered and relatively inexpensive. They are usually available at designated taxi stands outside hotels, downtown, and at Brisbane Transit and Roma Street stations, although it is often best to phone for one. Ride-sharing service Uber is also available to anyone with the smartphone app. Fares are often cheaper than traditional taxis.

CONTACTS Black and White Cabs. ☎ *13–3222* ⊕ *www.blackandwhitecabs. com.au.* **Uber.** ⊕ *www.uber.com/cities/ brisbane.* **Yellow Cab Co.** ☎ *13–1924* ⊕ *www.yellowcab.com.au.*

TRAIN TRAVEL

CountryLink trains make the 14-hour journey between Sydney and Brisbane. Rail services from Brisbane city and airport to the Gold Coast run regularly from 5:30 am until midnight. The *Spirit of Queensland* makes the 24-hour trip along the state's coast from Brisbane to Cairns five times a week, with stops at Mackay, Townsville, the Whitsunday coast, and more. All trains include the option of luxurious RailBed carriages with convertible lie-down bed seats, personal entertainment systems, and meals. The speedy, state-of-the-art *Tilt Train* runs from Brisbane to Bundaberg and Brisbane to Rockhampton six days a week, passing through various regional centers along the way.

Other long-distance passenger trains from Brisbane include the *Westlander,* to and from Charleville (twice weekly); and the *Spirit of the Outback,* to and from Longreach, via Rockhampton (twice weekly). Trains depart from Roma Street Station.

CONTACTS Queensland Rail Travel. ⊠ *Brisbane Central Travel Center, 305 Edward St.* ☎ *07/3072–2222, 1300/131–722* ⊕ *www.queenslandrail.com.au.*

TOURS

At the Brisbane Visitor Information and Booking Center, pick up a self-guided Brisbane CityWalk map (also available from tourist information offices and online), as well as brochures and maps

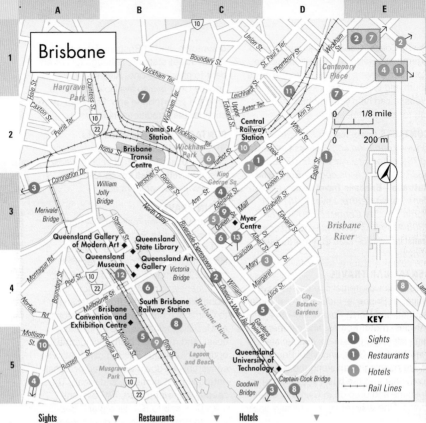

Brisbane

KEY
- ① Sights
- ① Restaurants
- ① Hotels
- ┼┼┼ Rail Lines

Sights ▼

1 Anzac Square and the Shrine of Remembrance **C2**

2 The Commissariat Store Museum **C4**

3 Lone Pine Koala Sanctuary..............**A3**

4 Museum of Brisbane....**C3**

5 Parliament House........**C4**

6 Queensland Cultural Centre....................**B4**

7 Roma Street Parkland **B2**

8 South Bank Parklands................**B4**

Restaurants ▼

1 Blackbird Bar and Grill..................**D2**

2 Breakfast Creek Hotel...**E1**

3 Cafe O-Mai **D5**

4 Caravanserai............**A5**

5 The Charming Squire...**B5**

6 Donna Chang............**C3**

7 e'cco **D1**

8 Enoteca 1889 ....**D5**

9 Felix For Goodness **C3**

10 The Gunshop Café......**A5**

11 Happy Boy................**D1**

12 Julius Pizzeria............**B4**

13 Pancake Manor..........**C3**

Hotels ▼

1 Adina Apartment Hotel Brisbane **C2**

2 The Calile **E1**

3 Capri by Fraser...........**D4**

4 Edward Lodge............**E1**

5 Next Hotel Brisbane.....**C3**

6 Ovolo Incholm............**C2**

7 Ovolo The Valley **E1**

8 The Point Brisbane **E4**

9 Rydges South Bank.....**B5**

10 Sofitel Brisbane Central **C2**

11 Spicers Balfour **E1**

detailing other designated Brisbane walking trails.

Blackcard Cultural Tours

WALKING TOURS | FAMILY | Explore Meeanjin (Brisbane) with knowledge-able Aboriginal tour guides. Discover Aboriginal history, art, and bush tucker on 90-minute or three-hour walking tours. ⊠ *Southbank* ☎ *07/3899–8153* ⊕ *www. theblackcard.com.au/tours.*

★ Brisbane Greeters

WALKING TOURS | FAMILY | Discover Bris-bane through the eyes of the friendly Brisbane Greeters, a complimentary walking tour service staffed by passion-ate volunteer tour guides. "Greeters' Choice" tours depart daily at 10 am from Brisbane City Hall, and can be booked up to three hours in advance. Or with seven days' notice, you can design your own "Your Choice" tour. Available in more than 20 different languages. ⊠ *Brisbane City Hall, King George Sq. entrance, City Center* ☎ *07/3006–6290* ⊕ *www.visitbris-bane.com.au/brisbane-greeters.*

JPT Tours

BUS TOURS | JPT Tours (also known as Australian Day Tours) conducts half- and full-day tours of Brisbane, Moreton Island, Fraser Island, Springbrook Nation-al Park, Mt. Tamborine, Byron Bay, and northwards to Australia Zoo in Beerwah, with options to include meals and attrac-tions. Check online to view current rates, last-minute specials, and promotions. ⊠ *2 Elkhorn Ave., Shop 18, Surfers Paradise* ☎ *07/5630–1602, 1300/781362* ⊕ *www. jpttours.com* 🖃 *From A$89.*

Kookaburra Showboat Cruises

BOAT TOURS | Enjoy a full-day of sightsee-ing, lunch, dinner, or high tea on a paddle wheeler cruise along the Brisbane River. Lunch cruises include scenic and historic commentary; live entertainment and dancing are highlights of dinner cruises. ⊠ *Eagle St. Pier, 45 Eagle St., City Center* ☎ *07/3221–1300* ⊕ *www.kookaburrariver-queens.com* 🖃 *From A$49.*

River City Cruises

BOAT TOURS | FAMILY | Daily sightseeing tours through and around South Bank, the City Center, and Kangaroo Point cliffs, including morning and afternoon tea options. Tours depart from Jetty A at South Bank Parklands, in front of the Wheel of Brisbane. ⊠ *Jetty A, South Bank Parklands* ☎ *0428/278473* ⊕ *www. rivercitycruises.com.au* 🖃 *From A$29.*

Story Bridge Adventure Climb

SPECIAL-INTEREST | Energetic visitors might want to scale Brisbane's Story Bridge for a 360-degree views of the city and beyond. Regular departures during the day, at dawn, twilight, and at night. Express Climb and Climb & Abseil options also available. ⊠ *170 Main St., Kangaroo Point* ☎ *07/3188–9070* ⊕ *www. storybridgeadventureclimb.com.au* 🖃 *From A$119.*

VISITOR INFORMATION

CONTACTS Brisbane Visitor Information and Booking Center. ⊠ *The Regent, 167 Queen St. Mall, Queen St., City Center* ☎ *07/3403–8888* ⊕ *www.brisbane.qld. gov.au.*

◉ Sights

Brisbane's city-center landmarks—a mix of Victorian, Edwardian, and slick contem-porary architecture—are best explored on foot. Most lie within the triangle formed by Ann Street and the bends of the Bris-bane River. ∎TIP→ **Streets running toward the river are named after female British royalty; those parallel to the river after male royalty.** The well-tended South Bank pre-cinct has riverfront parklands and cultural centers, alfresco cafés, a man-made beach, and weekend markets. Upriver, the quiet, leafy suburb of Fig Tree Pocket is home to Australia's best-known koala sanctuary.

Anzac Square and the Shrine of Remembrance

HISTORIC SITE | Paths stretch across manicured lawns toward the Doric Greek

Revival shrine made of Queensland sandstone. An eternal flame burns here for Australian soldiers who died in World War I. In the Shrine of Remembrance, a subsurface crypt stores soil samples from key battlefields. On April 25, Anzac Day, a moving dawn service is held here in remembrance of Australia's fallen soldiers. ⊠ *Adelaide St., between Edward and Creek Sts., City Center* ⌷ *Free.*

The Commissariat Store Museum

HISTORIC SITE | Convict-built in 1829 on the site of the city's original timber wharf, this was Brisbane's first stone building. It has served as a customs house, storehouse, and immigrants' shelter, and is currently the headquarters of The Royal Historical Society of Queensland. The RHSQ library and Commissariat Store museum is open to visitors Tuesday to Friday, and holds exhibitions, historical documents, manuscripts, and artifacts dating back to Brisbane's early colonial days. Group tours of the museum are welcome. ⊠ *115 William St., City Center* ☎ *07/3221–4198* ⊕ *www.commissariat-store.org.au* ⌷ *A$7.*

★ **Lone Pine Koala Sanctuary**

NATURE PRESERVE | FAMILY | Founded in 1927, Queensland's most famous fauna park is recognized by the *Guinness Book of World Records* as the world's first and largest koala sanctuary. As well as more than 130 koalas, you'll find emus, wombats, crocodiles, bats, platypuses, and lorikeets. You can hand-feed baby kangaroos, have a snake wrapped around you, or have your photo taken next to a koala. There are sheepdog shows, regular bird feedings, and animal presentations. Intimate encounters and behind-the-scenes tours can also be arranged for small groups. For an extra special visit, book a combo ticket (from A$78) via Mirimar Cruises (⊕ *http://mirimarcruises.com.au)* and travel to Lone Pine along the Brisbane River. ⊠ *708 Jesmond Rd., Fig Tree Pocket* ☎ *07/3378–1366 Lone Pine*

Sanctuary, 0412/749426 Mirimar Cruises ⊕ *www.koala.net* ⌷ *A$36.*

★ **Museum of Brisbane**

CLOCK | FAMILY | Housed in City Hall in the center of Brisbane City, the museum offers a rotating schedule of innovative and interactive exhibitions throughout the year that celebrate the city, its people, culture, and history. There are also a range of free tours including a daily Museum highlights tour at noon, and self-guided Museum Tours and Clock Tower Tours every 15 minutes 10:15 am–4:45 pm. Free except for special exhibitions or programs. ⊠ *City Hall, Level 3, 64 Adelaide St., City Center* ☎ *07/3339–0800* ⊕ *www.museumofbrisbane.com.au.*

Parliament House

GARDEN | Opened in 1868, this splendid, stone-clad, French Renaissance building with a Mount Isa copper roof earned its colonial designer a meager 200-guinea (A$440) fee. The interior is fitted with polished timber, brass, and frosted and engraved glass. Free half-hour tours run on weekday afternoons, depending on demand. High Tea is served in the elegant Strangers' Dining Room from 10:30 am to noon the first Friday of every month (A$45 per person). The adjacent, kid-friendly City Botanic Gardens have native and exotic plants and theme areas, including the Bamboo Grove and Weeping Fig Avenue, along with sculptures, ponds, and an on-site café. ⊠ *George St. at Alice St., City Center* ☎ *07/3553–6000* ⊕ *www.parliament.qld.gov.au* ⌷ *Free.*

★ **Queensland Cultural Centre**

ARTS VENUE | On the southern bank of the Brisbane River, you'll find a variety of world-class facilities nestled together among landscaped lawns and cafés. The world-famous Gallery of Modern Art (GoMA) with its ever-changing exhibitions and events is a must-visit, as is the equally impressive Queensland Art Gallery, Queensland Museum, and Sciencentre. The State Library of Queensland

one Pine Koala Sanctuary, Brisbane

as a host of free, interactive children's ctivities and the Queensland Performing rts Centre (QPAC) bustles with concerts nd stage shows. There's also a host of estaurants, cafés, gift and book shops, a cketing agent (in QPAC), public-access omputer terminals, and various public paces. Regular special events and festials are also held in front of the Cultural entre, particularly on weekends. Green abs (modern rickshaws) are a fun and nique way to get around and sightsee this area. Starting at the Wheel of risbane adjacent QPAC, they'll ferry pasengers anywhere between West End nd Fortitude Valley. ⊠ Melbourne St. at rey St., South Bank, South Brisbane ⓘ 07/3840–7303 galleries, 07/3840–7555 useum and Sciencentre, 07/3840–7666 tate Library, 07/3840–7444 QPAC www.qagoma.qld.gov.au ⊠ Free xcluding Sciencentre and certain GoMA xhibitions).

ɔma Street Parkland

ARDEN | FAMILY | The world's largest ιbtropical garden within a city is a gentle mix of forest paths, floral displays, and structured plantings surrounding a fish-stocked lake. Highlights include the Lilly Pilly Garden, with native evergreen rain forest plants, interesting children's play areas, and the friendly resident birds and lizards. Free hour-long guided garden tours begin daily at 11 am and 1 pm. From Wednesday to Sunday, hop on the Parkland Explorer, a trackless train that gives guests a full tour of the gardens for a gold coin donation. Self-guided tour maps are available at the Roma Street Parkland Information Hub, The Sound Society is a monthly live music event, from 9 am to midday on a Sunday. ⊠ 1 Parkland Blvd., City Center ☎ 1300/137468 ⊕ www.visitbrisbane. com.au/roma-street-parkland-and-spring-hill ⊠ Free.

★ South Bank Parklands

MARKET | FAMILY | This vibrant community space on the banks of the Brisbane River includes parklands, shops, hotels, a maritime museum, walking and cycling paths, a sprawling man-made beach, a stunning

Modern sculpture at the Queensland Cultural Centre, South Bank, Brisbane

Nepalese pagoda, and excellent city views. The weekend Collective Markets is the place to discover handmade goods, live entertainers, buskers, artists, and emerging designers. Almost every week you'll find a new festival or event lighting up the Cultural Forecourt. Nearby Grey Street is lined with trendy shops and cafés, as well as contemporary international restaurants, bars, and a cinema. The Wheel of Brisbane (A$21), a giant Ferris wheel at the northern entrance of South Bank, has some of the most spectacular views of the city. South Bank Parklands stretches along the riverbank south of the Queensland Cultural Centre. ✉ Grey St., south of Melbourne St. ☎ 07/3156–6366 Parklands, 07/3844–3464 Wheel of Brisbane, 07/3844–5361 Maritime Museum ⊕ www.visitbrisbane. com.au/south-bank 🚇 Parklands free, museum A$16.

🍴 Restaurants

Brisbane offers a wide range of dining options, from casual eateries to cutting-edge fine dining. Top chefs have decamped to Brisbane's best eateries and are busy putting put a fresh subtropical spin on Modern Australian, pan-Asian, and Mediterranean cuisine.

Imaginative dishes capitalize on abundant regional produce: fine fresh seafood—notably the local delicacy, the Moreton Bay bug (a sweet-fleshed crustacean)—premium steak, Darling Downs lamb, cheeses, macadamia nuts, avocados, olives, and fruit, matched with fine regional wines.

Most of the city's hip cafés, bars, and smart fine dining establishments are clustered in the CBD, South Bank, West End, Fortitude Valley, New Farm, Teneriffe, and Petrie Terrace; you'll also find some excellent eateries around the suburbs, particularly Rosalie, Paddington, Milton, Ascot and Woolloongabba. For terrific fresh seafood, head for Brisbane ayside suburbs, such as Manly, Red-liffe, and Sandgate.

ypically, dining ambience is relaxed, eating is alfresco, and well-mannered hildren are welcomed. Given its year-ound temperate climate, open-air night narket dining is increasingly popular.

lackbird Bar and Grill

$$ | **AUSTRALIAN** | With its prime riverfront ocation at Eagle Street Pier, overlooking he Story Bridge, floor-to-ceiling windows nd designer interiors inspired by the reat Gatsby, Blackbird is a great place or a special night out. With a focus on ustainable, locally sourced produce, nenu highlights include sumptuous hellfish platters, as well as a choice of 0 varieties of steak and local fish cooked o perfection on an open wood-fired grill. **nown for:** steaks cooked on a wood-red grill; sustainably sourced seafood; verside location with views. [$] *Average nain: A$45* ✉ *Riverside Center, 123 agle St., City Center* ☎ *07/3229–1200* 🌐 *www.blackbirdbrisbane.com.au.*

reakfast Creek Hotel

$$ | **AUSTRALIAN** | Perched on the wharf t Breakfast Creek, this iconic, her-age-listed hotel is renowned for its reezy tropical beer garden and superb ademark steaks. Nonsteak eaters also ave plenty of options, including vege-rian dishes, salads, and fresh seafood. **nown for:** classic pub food; historic archi-ecture; iconic location. [$] *Average main: $38* ✉ *2 Kingsford Smith Dr., Albion* ☎ *07/3262–5988* 🌐 *www.breakfastcreek-otel.com.*

Cafe O Mai

| **VIETNAMESE** | This family-run café on risbane's southside is always busy, erving dishes that combine traditional etnamese flavours and techniques ith local ingredients, great coffee, esserts and fresh juices. Baguettes e baked in-house daily, and specialties e pork sausages and spring rolls are andmade in-store. **Known for:** handmade pork sausages; freshly squeezed juices; authentic pho. [$] *Average main: A$16* ✉ *15 Cracknell Rd., South Brisbane* ☎ *07/3255–9778* 🌐 *www.cafeomai.com.au.*

Caravanserai

$$ | **TURKISH** | Decked out in traditional woven kilims and Mediterranean lanterns, this ambient Turkish restaurant is a treat for the senses, with its rich, generously portioned servings of contemporary Middle Eastern fare served among cozy nooks of candlelit tables and breezy views over West End. **Known for:** authentic Turkish atmosphere; sultan's banquet; river views from back veranda. [$] *Average main: A$30* ✉ *1–3 Dornoch Terr., West End* ☎ *07/3217–2617* 🌐 *www.caravanserairestaurant.com.au* ⏲ *Closed Mon.*

The Charming Squire

$$ | **MODERN AUSTRALIAN** | Named after legendary convict brewmaster James Squire, this stylish new brewery and restaurant in South Bank's cultural precinct boasts a large, open-plan bar area—featuring sweeping ceilings, polished concrete flooring, repurposed timber, and trendy copper accents. Enjoy local beef, lamb, and pork slow-cooked on the Iron Bark coal pit, alongside traditional pub favorites like fish-and-chips, burgers, pizza, salads, and antipasto-style share plates. **Known for:** Australian pub cuisine; wide selection of craft beers and ciders; slow cooking on the Iron Bark coal pit. [$] *Average main: A$30* ✉ *133 Grey St., Southbank* ☎ *07/3077–7254* 🌐 *www.thecharmingsquire.com.au* ☞ *Bookings recommended, especially on weekends.*

★ Donna Chang

$$ | **CHINESE** | An exciting addition to Brisbane's dining scene, this modern Chinese restaurant offers delicious, fresh food and a wonderful wine list amid the grandeur of a renovated 1920s bank. Beneath soaring ceilings and chandeliers, choose from a menu that includes traditional favourites (with a focus on spice)

and more adventurous combinations like Moreton Bay bugs with salted duck egg and fermented chilli. **Known for:** modern Chinese menu; stunning heritage setting; fine dining without the fuss. [$] *Average main: A$35* ✉ *171 George St., Shop 3, Brisbane* ☎ *07/3243–4888* 🌐 *www.donnachang.com.au.*

★ e'cco

$$$ | MEDITERRANEAN | Beloved Brisbane institution e'cco closed its doors in 2017 and reemerged in 2018 in a similar contemporary bistro setting in Newstead but with a more relaxed vibe, and serving the same innovative fare to a loyal following. The menu consists of seasonally changing Mediterranean and Asian-inspired Mod Oz dishes, with a focus on fresh, local ingredients. **Known for:** celebrated chef; visually appealing food with bold flavors; tasting menu with wine pairings. [$] *Average main: A$45* ✉ *63 Skyring Terr., New Farm* ☎ *07/3831–8344* 🌐 *www.eccobistro.com* ⏲ *Closed Sun. and Mon.*

★ Enoteca 1889

$$$ | ITALIAN | Specializing in "vera cucina Romana" (real Roman food), this award-winning Italian restaurant in Woollangabba's antique quarter is well worth crossing the Brisbane River for. The menu favors simplicity over complexity: elegant starters like lightly fried zucchini flowers stuffed with cheese and anchovies, freshly made pasta or fish of the day for main, tiramisu or pannacotta for dessert. **Known for:** traditional Roman fare in suitably romantic surroundings; seasonal four-course set menu; historic 1889 Moreton Rubber building. [$] *Average main: A$40* ✉ *10–12 Logan Rd., Woolloongabba* ☎ *07/3392–4315* 🌐 *www.1889enoteca.com.au* ⏲ *No lunch Sat., no dinner Sun., closed Mon.*

★ Felix for Goodness

$ | AUSTRALIAN | Hidden away in Burnett Lane just off Queen Street, Felix for Goodness dishes up delectable made-from-scratch breakfasts, lunches, snacks and cakes (with an emphasis on organic) since 2014. In terms of decor, think exposed brick and concrete, natural light, and clean lines. **Known for:** rustic, homemade goodness; all-day brunch; extensive range of gluten-free and vegetarian options. [$] *Average main: A$20* ✉ *50 Burnett La., City Center* ✣ *Restaurant is at mezzanine level, through a narrow doorway and up a set of stairs* ☎ *07/3161–7966* 🌐 *felixforgoodness.com* ⏲ *No dinner and closed Sun.*

The Gunshop Café

$ | CAFÉ | Named after its previous life as an actual gun shop, this trendy West End café is the place to go for breakfast and brunch on weekends. Unfinished brick walls where guns once hung set the stage for an eclectic Mod Oz menu, flavorsome Merlo coffee, and spicy chai tea with honey from the café's own rooftop bees. **Known for:** potato-feta hash cakes with spinach, house-dried tomato, and herbed sour cream; flourless chocolate fudge cake; breakfast until 3 pm. [$] *Average main: A$20* ✉ *53 Mollison St., West End* ☎ *07/3844–2241* 🌐 *www.thegunshopcafe.com* ⏲ *No dinner.*

Happy Boy

$ | CHINESE | With its minimal decor and open-air fairy-lit deck, this bustling little wine bar and eatery in Fortitude Valley is not your average Chinese restaurant. Locals and foodies alike flock to experience its delicious, regional Chinese fare. **Known for:** innovative Chinese food; weekend brunch from 9 am; extensive, sommelier-selected wine list. [$] *Average main: A$20* ✉ *East St., between Ann and Wickham Sts., Fortitude Valley* ☎ *0413/246890* 🌐 *www.happyboy.com.au* ⏲ *Closed Mon. No brunch Tues.–Fri.*

★ Julius Pizzeria

$$ | PIZZA | FAMILY | Ideally positioned for a quick pre- or posttheater dinner, this always-busy pizzeria combines breezy yet attentive service with low-fuss dining—and delicious Italian food. Pizzas feature crisp wood-fired bases, with a variety of Rosse (tomato sauce–based) and ianche (without sauce) toppings that ollow the less-is-more approach. **Known or:** open kitchen featuring a wood-fired ven; friendly but efficient service; Bamini menu for children. $ *Average main: A$23* ✉ *77 Grey St., South Brisbane* ☎ *07/3844–2655* ⊕ *juliuspizzeria.com.au* ⏱ *Closed Mon.*

ancake Manor

| **CAFÉ** |**FAMILY** | Housed inside the hisoric, heritage-listed St. Luke's Cathedral, his elegant 24-hour pancake parlor is Brisbane institution. Guests can take seat in one of the Manor's converted hurch pew booths and chow down on tempting menu of snacks, breakfasts, alads, steaks, and sweets beneath the uilding's grand redbrick arches. **Known or:** heritage building; grilled bananas in reamy butterscotch sauce; kid-friendly ining. $ *Average main: A$16* ✉ *18 Charotte St., City Center* ☎ *07/3221–6433* ⊕ *www.pancakemanor.com.au.*

🛏 Hotels

nner-city Brisbane is home to an ver-growing array of luxury and designer otels, boutique accommodations, and martly serviced apartments. Many have ood-value packages and seasonal and st-minute specials. Jump online for the est deals.

dina Apartment Hotel Brisbane

 | **HOTEL** | With its central, riverside cation opposite Queen Street's Myer uilding, this apartment hotel in a renoated 1920s bank building offers a range f well-equipped rooms from studios ith kitchenette to three-bedroom partments with sweeping river or city ews. **Pros:** excellent location; combines eritage charm with modern amenities; xternal rooms feature balcony. **Cons:** ternal rooms can be dark; free Wi-Fi nly 1 MBS (extra for high-speed); inteor design is stylish and functional but cks flair. $ *Rooms from: A$152* ✉ *171 eorge St., City Center* ☎ *07/3155–1000*

⊕ *www.adinahotels.com/en/apartments/ brisbane* ⤳ *220 rooms* ⏱ *No meals.*

★ The Calile

$$$$ | **HOTEL** | More Byron than Brisbane, the Calile offers a luxury resort-like experience in the heart of inner-city Brisbane, with James Street's designer boutiques and restaurants at your doorstep. **Pros:** vacation vibes in an urban setting; large outdoor pool; understated sophistication. **Cons:** a little out of the city center; limited free Wi-Fi; breakfast extra. $ *Rooms from: A$327* ✉ *48 James St., Fortitude Valley* ☎ *07/3607–5888* ⊕ *www.thecalilehotel.com* ⤳ *175 rooms* ⏱ *No meals.*

Capri by Fraser

$$$ | **HOTEL** | Contemporary design meets superior comfort at this newly completed, health-focused hotel, perfectly positioned between the Queen Street Mall and the Botanic Gardens in CBD. **Pros:** great service and location; free, fast Wi-Fi; quality, healthy buffet breakfast. **Cons:** pricey parking; clean and comfortable but minimal atmosphere; rooms on the small side. $ *Rooms from: A$208* ✉ *80 Albert St., City Center* ☎ *07/3013–0088* ⊕ *brisbane.capribyfraser.com* ⤳ *239 rooms* ⏱ *Free Breakfast.*

Edward Lodge

$ | **B&B/INN** | This charming, inner-suburban, art deco B&B is set among Asian-style tropical gardens and close to cafés and restaurants, New Farm Park, Brisbane Powerhouse, and the CityCat ferry. **Pros:** guest kitchen and laundry; vibrant area; free continental breakfast. **Cons:** 15-minute walk from the city; no room service; no pool. $ *Rooms from: A$145* ✉ *75 Sydney St., New Farm* ☎ *07/3358–2680, 07/3358–3583* ⊕ *www. edwardlodge.com.au* ⤳ *9 rooms, 1 apartment* ⏱ *Free Breakfast.*

★ Next Hotel Brisbane

$$ | **HOTEL** | Modern technology is the order of the day at this state-of-the-art, high-tech, high-rise hotel, merging innovative, plush design and an unbeatable

location on the Queen Street Mall. **Pros:** clean, comfortable and quiet; central location; free unlimited Wi-Fi, movies, and minibar items. **Cons:** limited parking; technology may be off-putting to some; on-site dining is expensive—better options nearby. [$] *Rooms from: A$189* ✉ *72 Queen St., City Center* ☎ *07/3222–3222* 🌐 *www.nexthotels.com/next/brisbane* 🛏 *304 rooms* 🍴 *Free Breakfast.*

Ovolo Incholm

$$ | **HOTEL** | This delightful art deco hotel in inner-city Spring Hill has received an Ovolo face-lift—all the old-world glamour remains, including the original elevator, but public spaces have been tastefully and artistically remodeled, and rooms upgraded. **Pros:** old-world charm meets modern comfort; personalized service and lots of freebies; free continental breakfast (direct bookings only) includes barista coffee. **Cons:** no pool; '80s music in public areas can get a bit much; hot breakfast is an additional charge. [$] *Rooms from: A$178* ✉ *73 Wickham Terr., Brisbane* ☎ *07/3226–8888* 🌐 *www.ovolohotels.com.au/ovoloinchcolm* 🛏 *50 rooms* 🍴 *Free Breakfast.*

Ovolo The Valley

$$ | **HOTEL** | Following a refurb that embraces the Valley's quirky history while adding a funky sophistication and all the latest tech touches, Fortitude Valley's Emporium has reopened as Ovolo The Valley. **Pros:** superb design and facilities; close to nightlife; rooftop pool with views. **Cons:** outside the city center; expensive parking; can be noisy—ask for a room away from street. [$] *Rooms from: A$169* ✉ *1000 Ann St., Fortitude Valley* ☎ *07/3253–6999* 🌐 *thevalleybrisbane.com.au* 🛏 *103 rooms* 🍴 *Free Breakfast.*

The Point Brisbane

$$ | **HOTEL** | Across the river from central Brisbane, this modern hotel on picturesque Kangaroo Point has great city skyline and river views from each balcony. **Pros:** terrific on-site facilities; free parking; wheelchair-accessible rooms. **Cons:** a 20-minute walk to the city; free Wi-Fi but can be slow; rooms on freeway side of hotel may be noisy. [$] *Rooms from: A$175* ✉ *21 Lambert St., Kangaroo Point* ☎ *07/3240–0888, 1800/088388* 🌐 *www.thepointbrisbane.com.au* 🛏 *201 rooms* 🍴 *Free Breakfast.*

Rydges South Bank

$$ | **HOTEL** |**FAMILY** | Surrounded by Brisbane's famous South Bank Parklands and Cultural Precinct, within walking distance of numerous attractions, this tasteful, well-maintained hotel is an excellent choice if location's your focus. **Pros:** lively location; excellent restaurant and facilities; riverside rooms feature great city views. **Cons:** steep fees for parking; not all rooms have balconies so be sure to request one; pool is on the small side. [$] *Rooms from: A$189* ✉ *9 Glenelg St., at Grey St., South Brisbane* ☎ *07/3364–0800* 🌐 *www.rydges.com/southbank* 🛏 *304 rooms* 🍴 *No meals.*

Sofitel Brisbane Central

$$$ | **HOTEL** | This decadent, French-flavored hotel is a quiet and classy choice in a central location. **Pros:** prompt, pleasant service; luxurious rooms and facilities; superb buffet breakfast. **Cons:** pricey meals and minibar; expensive Wi-Fi and parking; compact bathrooms. [$] *Rooms from: A$261* ✉ *249 Turbot St., City Center* ☎ *07/3835–4444* 🌐 *www.sofitelbrisbane.com.au* 🛏 *433 rooms* 🍴 *Free Breakfast.*

★ **Spicers Balfour**

$$$ | **HOTEL** | A distinctly local experience perfect for weary travelers looking for a home away from home, this elegant boutique hotel has nine suites housed inside a traditional Queenslander mansion, complete with flowing verandas, tropical gardens, and breezy river views. **Pros:** attentive and personalized service; close to public transport and ferry; free Wi-Fi, parking, and à la carte breakfast included in rate. **Cons:** outside the city center; off-street parking is limited; some rooms on the small side. [$] *Rooms from: A$25*

✉ *37 Balfour St., New Farm* ☎ *07/3358–8888* ⊕ *www.spicersgroup.com.au* ⇆ *17 rooms* ⦿*| Free Breakfast.*

ⓨ Nightlife

You'll find a range of nightlife options throughout Brisbane, from sophisticated riverfront cocktail bars, to hidden laneway bars, suburban microbreweries, live music venues, and traditional pubs. Many bars in the city center close at midnight; after that all the action is on Caxton Street and Fortitude Valley, which can get raucous in the wee hours. Local licensing laws require all patrons to present photo identification for entry after 10 pm, so if you're looking for a late night drink be sure to carry your passport. For up-to-date information visit ⊕ *www.visitbrisbane.com.au/things-to-do/nightlife.*

BARS

Cloudland

WINE BARS—NIGHTLIFE | An "urban oasis" with fanciful design, a retractable glass roof, and street-front waterfall flowing over its contemporary architectural facade, Cloudland restaurant and nightclub woos well-heeled locals and tourists alike with an extensive drinks menu, cut-above food, and an exciting, expensive ambience. ✉ *641 Ann St., Fortitude Valley* ☎ *07/3872–6600* ⊕ *www.cloudland.tv.*

Cru Bar + Cellar

WINE BARS—NIGHTLIFE | Sleek and sophisticated, Cru Bar + Cellar has leather ottomans, a long onyx bar, circa-1800 French chandeliers, and a fine-wine-loving clientele. Cru's huge cellar houses hundreds of top Australian vintages, to drink on-site or later; the cocktail menu is also extensive and impressive. Cheese tasting plates are available all day. It's a good ideal to book in advance for dinner. ✉ *James St. Market, 22 James St., Fortitude Valley* ☎ *07/3252–2400* ⊕ *www.crubar.com.*

★ Lefty's Old Time Music Hall

BARS/PUBS | This award-winning saloon-style bar on bustling Caxton Street mixes old-school American charm with modern craft brews and a hefty range of spirits (including more than 100 rye whiskies). Decked out in vintage taxidermy and moody chandeliers, the retro Americana vibe continues with the Southern-themed bar food, including po'boys, corn dogs, and popcorn shrimp and the latest addition, Ben's burgers. A rollicking mix of country and rockabilly tunes burst from the stage and speakers. ✉ *15 Caxton St., Petrie Terrace* ⊕ *www.leftysoldtimemusichall.com* ☞ *Closed Mon. and Tues.*

CASINOS

Treasury Casino & Hotel

CASINOS | With a "neat and tidy" dress code geared to securing an upscale clientele, The Treasury is a European-style casino with three levels of gaming beneath a stunning four-story atrium. Beneath a seduction of light and color, the facility comes alive at night with more than 80 gaming tables and more than 1,300 machines, as well as six restaurants and six bars. It's open 24 hours but you will need photo identification for entry after 10 pm. ✉ *130 William St., City Center* ☎ *07/3306–8888* ⊕ *www.treasurybrisbane.com.au.*

🎭 Performing Arts

The Saturday edition of the *Courier–Mail* newspaper (⊕ *www.couriermail.com.au*) lists live gigs and concerts, ballet, opera, theater, jazz, and other events in its Life section, while Friday's *CM2* insert has a comprehensive entertainment guide for the weekend ahead. *The Weekend Edition* (⊕ *www.theweekendedition.com.au*) has suburb-by-suburb listings of Brisbane's best cafés, restaurants, shopping, and nightlife spots, as well as weekly updates on new events and establishments around the city. Alternately, visit *Brisbane Art* (⊕ *www.bneart.*

com) for up-to-date listings of arts events and galleries around the city.

ARTS CENTERS

Brisbane Powerhouse

ARTS CENTERS | Housed in a grand, former coal power station, the Heritage-listed Brisbane Powerhouse hosts frequent, often-free, art exhibitions, live performances, and children's events in its flexible 200- and 400-seat theaters. Cafés, restaurants, bikeways, boardwalks, and picnic areas complement the spacious, contemporary riverside hub, which also adjoins beautiful New Farm Park. A recent renovation added a new café-bar, a roof terrace, and enlarged theater spaces. ⊠ *119 Lamington St., New Farm* ☎ *07/3358–8600 box office, 07/3358–8622 reception* ⊕ *www.brisbanepowerhouse.org.*

⚡ Activities

Brisbane offers a host of outdoor activities. You kayak or paddleboard on the Brisbane River, and numerous scenic bushwalking, climbing, and rappelling sites lie less than 90 minutes by car from Brisbane. Government-run Outdoors Queensland (QORF) (⊕ *www.qorf.org.au*) gives regional information and lists businesses offering adventure activities from hiking to horse riding.

BICYCLING

An extensive network of bicycle paths crisscrosses Brisbane. One of the best paths follows the level and impeccably maintained Bicentennial Bikeway southeast along the Brisbane River, across the Goodwill Bridge, then along to South Bank Parklands or Kangaroo Point cliffs. The Kurilpa Bridge and Go Between Bridge are also both cyclist-friendly ways to cross the river between the city and South Brisbane. The city's famous Riverwalk gives cyclists and pedestrians a scenic route from New Farm to the CBD.

Bike Obsession

BICYCLING | Rent bikes here from A$25 for two hours. Pick yours up nearby the Brisbane Botanic Gardens or arrange to have the bike dropped off at CBD hotels. Books, maps, and cycling advice are also available. ⊠ *133 Mary St., City Center* ☎ *07/3221–7228* ⊕ *www.bikeobsession.com.au/bike-hire.*

Cycling Brisbane

BICYCLING | This Brisbane City Council website provides safety tips and information on cycling as an online interactive map and downloadable maps of the city's bikeway network. You'll also find information on the CityCycle network, which has bikes available from 150 designated points around the inner city. ⊠ *Brisbane* ⊕ *www.cyclingbrisbane.com.au.*

GOLF

St. Lucia Golf Links and Golf World

GOLF | One of Brisbane's oldest golf courses, St. Lucia Golf Links and Golf World is an 18-hole, par-70, pay-and-play course open to visitors. Work up an appetite on the fairways, then dine on-site at the Hillstone clubhouse's Hundred Acre Bar, overlooking the 18th green. ⊠ *Indooroopilly Rd., at Carawa St., St. Lucia* ☎ *07/3403–2556 golf course, 07/3870–3433 Hillstone Clubhouse* ⊕ *www.hillstonestlucia.com.au* 🏌 *From $A24 (9 holes), $A37 (18 holes)* 🏌 *18 holes, 5917 yards, par 69.*

MULTISPORT OUTFITTERS

Riverlife Adventure Centre

CLIMBING/MOUNTAINEERING | FAMILY | A one-stop-shop for adventure in the inner city, Riverlife runs guided rock-climbing and abseiling sessions off Kangaroo Point cliffs, cycling and Segway tours around Brisbane attractions, day and night kayaking and stand-up paddleboarding trips on the Brisbane River (followed by barbecue dinner and seafood options). The Mirrabooka Aboriginal Cultural Experience includes a traditional performance by the Yuggera Aboriginal Dancers and hands-on instruction in fire-starting, instrument playing, boomerang throwing, and painting. The center also rents bicycles, rollerblades, kick bikes, and scooters. ✉ *Naval Stores, Lower River Terr., Kangaroo Point* ☎ *07/3891–5766* ⊕ *www.riverlife.com.au* ✉ *From A$20.*

WATER SPORTS
Moreton Bay

WATER SPORTS | A half-hour's drive east of Brisbane city brings you to Moreton Bay, stretching 125 km (78 miles) from the Gold Coast to the Sunshine Coast. A number of operators based in Brisbane's bayside suburbs—Manly, Redcliffe, Sandgate—run sailing, diving, sightseeing, and whale- and dolphin-watching trips around the Bay, and trips to its various islands. Some cruises include tours of St. Helena Island's historic prison ruins; others visit Moreton Island, where you can toboggan down massive white sand dunes. ✉ *Moreton Island National Park* ⊕ *www.moretonbay.qld.gov.au.*

Moreton Bay Escapes

WATER SPORTS | FAMILY | This operator runs tours and charters around Moreton Island National Park that includes 4WD driving, snorkeling, kayaking, body-boarding, hiking, and sand-boarding. Tailored excursions incorporate bird-watching, fishing, swimming with dolphins, and more. Admission includes ferry trip, park entry fees, and meals. ✉ *Brisbane* ☎ *1300/559355* ⊕ *www.moretonbayescapes.com.au* ✉ *From A$129.*

🛍 Shopping

For more information on shopping in Brisbane, visit ⊕ *www.visitbrisbane.com.au/things-to-do/shopping.*

ANTIQUES
Camp Hill Antique Center and Tart Cafe

ANTIQUES/COLLECTIBLES | The old Woollangabba Antiques Center has moved to a new location in a refurbished 1950s cinema, but the retro vibes continue with 70-plus stalls, an on-site tart café, and everything from fine china, collectibles,

Earth's Fastest Moving Island 👁

Moreton Island lies just 35 km (20 miles) offshore. This 38-km-long (23-mile-long) mass is shifting at an estimated 3¼ feet a year toward the Queensland coast. Attractions include tobogganing down sand dunes, bird-watching, dolphin spotting, water sports, and cetacean- and dugong-watching. Camping within Moreton Island National Park is possible (A$5.95 per person permit; information available at ⊕ *parks.des.qld.gov.au/parks/moreton-island/camping.html*).

and the kitschiest of curiosities, to clothing, records, prints, paintings, home wares, games, and a vast collection of Australiana. Open weekdays 9–5 and weekends 7–5. ✉ *545 Old Cleveland Rd., Brisbane* ☎ *07/3392–1114* ⊕ *www.camphillantiquecentre.com.*

Empire Revival

ANTIQUES/COLLECTIBLES | Located in a converted theater, Empire Revival (formerly Paddington Antique Centre) is brimming with antiques, furniture, collectibles, various bric-a-brac as well as colorful vintage clothing. Around 50 dealers operate within the center, alongside an on-site café. It's open daily 10–5, closing an hour earlier on Sunday. ✉ *167 Latrobe Terr., Paddington* ☎ *07/3369–8088* ⊕ *www.empirerevival.com.au.*

AUSTRALIAN PRODUCTS
Woollongabba Art Gallery

LOCAL SPECIALTIES | The gallery represents indigenous and contemporary artists. Works cost between A$50 and A$10,000, and come with certificates of authenticity. It's open Tuesday–Friday 9–6 and Saturday 9–3, with regular exhibitions. ✉ *613 Stanley St., Woolloon-gabba* ☎ *07/3891–5551* ⊕ *www.wag. com.au.*

MALLS AND ARCADES
Brisbane Arcade
SHOPPING CENTERS/MALLS | Heritage-listed Brisbane Arcade, circa 1923, joins Queen Street Mall and Adelaide Street and houses designer boutiques, jewelry shops, and upscale gift, art, and antiques stores. ✉ *160 Queen St. Mall, City Center* ☎ *07/3831–2711* ⊕ *www.brisbanearcade. com.au.*

James Street
SHOPPING NEIGHBORHOODS | This new upmarket lifestyle precinct in Fortitude Valley has an ever-growing array of local fashion, homewares, jewelry, and design stores, alongside trendy cafés and bars. ✉ *James St., Fortitude Valley* ☎ *07/3850–0111* ⊕ *www.jamesst.com.au.*

MacArthur Central
SHOPPING CENTERS/MALLS | Historic MacArthur Central, the WWII headquarters of U.S. General Douglas MacArthur, houses boutiques and specialty shops, a food court, and a museum. Located at the bottom of the Queen Street Mall, the streets surrounding the center also feature a range of high-end fashion boutiques including Louis Vuitton, Hermès, and Tiffany & Co. The MacArthur Museum is open to the public Tuesday, Thursday, and Sunday 10–3. ✉ *201 Edward St., City Center* ☎ *07/3211–7052 museum* ⊕ *www.mmb.org.au.*

Queen Street Mall
SHOPPING CENTERS/MALLS | FAMILY | Fun and lively Queen Street Mall is nearly a third of a mile long, and incorporates 700 retailers and five major shopping centers, including the Myer Centre, Wintergarden, and Queens Plaza, as well as two large department stores, Myer and David Jones. There are also four arcades: historic Tattersall's Arcade and MacArthur Central, Heritage-listed Brisbane Arcade, and Broadway on the Mall, all housing designer boutiques and a range of specialty stores. On weekends, free entertainment and performances can often be found on the Mall's two open stages. ✉ *Queen St., City Center* ☎ *07/3006–6200* ⊕ *www.visitbrisbane. com.au/the-city/things-to-do/shopping/ queen-street-mall.*

MARKETS
Brisbane Powerhouse Farmers Market
OUTDOOR/FLEA/GREEN MARKETS | The Brisbane Powerhouse hosts a local produce farmers' market from 6 am to noon every Saturday. Enjoy a fresh, leisurely breakfast on the lawn by the river, and afterward, stroll through nearby New Farm Park. ✉ *119 Lamington St., New Farm* ☎ *07/3358–8600* ⊕ *www. janpowersfarmersmarkets.com.au/ powerhouse-farmers-markets.*

The Collective Market South Bank
OUTDOOR/FLEA/GREEN MARKETS | South Bank Parklands hosts a weekend Collective Market, showcasing high-quality and emerging designer clothing, accessories, artwork, craft, food, and music. It runs Friday 5–9, Saturday 10–9, and Sunday 9–4 in Stanley Street Plaza. ✉ *Grey St., At Stanley St. Plaza, City Center* ☎ *07/3844–2440* ⊕ *www.collectivemarkets.com.au.*

Eat Street Markets
OUTDOOR/FLEA/GREEN MARKETS | FAMILY | Located on a revamped shipping wharf at riverside Hamilton, this bustling interactive market gives visitors a taste of Brisbane's best street food from more than 60 funky shipping container "restaurants." Open Friday and Saturday evening 4 pm–10 pm and Sunday 10 am–3 pm, there's also a regular line up of live music and entertainment, and hip wares from local artists and makers. Entry costs A$3. ✉ *Macarthur Ave., Brisbane* ☎ *07/3358–2500* ⊕ *www.eatstreetmarkets.com* ⊘ *Closed Mon.–Thurs.*

Riverside Markets
OUTDOOR/FLEA/GREEN MARKETS | FAMILY | This eclectic arts-and-crafts bazaar

State library, Queensland Cultural Centre

in Brisbane's Botanic Gardens sells everything from pressed flowers to hand-painted didgeridoos and homemade treats and clothing. It's open Sunday 8–3. ✉ *City Botanic Gardens, Alice St. at Albert St., City Center* ☎ *07/3870–2807* ⊕ *www.theriversidemarkets.com.au* ⊙ *Closed Mon.–Sat.*

OUTDOOR GEAR OUTFITTERS
Paddy Pallin

SPORTING GOODS | With stores throughout Australia, Paddy Pallin sells quality outdoor and travel gear, including hats, footwear, clothing, backpacks, and equipment. On staff are dedicated bushwalkers, rock climbers, and travelers. ✉ *120 Wickham St., Fortitude Valley* ☎ *07/3839–3811* ⊕ *www.paddypallin.com.au.*

Southern Downs

From Brisbane, the Granite Belt is 225 km (140 miles) west, Mt. Tamborine is 62 km (39 miles) southwest, and Scenic Rim wineries are around 135 km (85 miles) southwest.

Drive two hours west on the Cunningham Highway and you'll reach the Southern Downs, where spring brings the scent of peach and apple blossoms and fall finds the region's 50-plus vineyards, concentrated around Stanthorpe, ripe for harvest. Winter is ideal for wine-country excursions, with clear days and tastings by fireplace by night. This area, extending from Cunninghams Gap in the east to Goondiwindi in the west, Allora in the north to Wallangarra in the south, is known as the Granite Belt.

The local Italian community pioneered viticulture here, planting the first Shiraz grapes in 1965. Today the Granite Belt is the state's largest wine region, with nearly 2,000 acres under vines and more than 50 cellar doors (wine tasting rooms), most attached to family-run and boutique wineries. Thanks to its altitude (2,500–4,000 feet above sea level) and decomposed-granite soils, the region enjoys unique growing and ripening conditions, enabling the production of outstanding, full-bodied reds and extra-crisp whites.

Just over an hour's drive southwest of Brisbane, inland from the Gold Coast, you'll find the world's largest caldera and one of the state's most exciting emerging wine regions: the Scenic Rim. The region's rich volcanic soils, first planted with vines in the late 19th century, now produce fine red and white varieties. On the region's easterly edge, you'll find a dozen wineries and a distillery within a compact area around Mt. Tamborine.

GETTING HERE AND AROUND
Driving yourself is an option but may not be the best idea if you plan to skip the spit bucket on your tasting stops. However, for the self-guiders out there, the Granite Belt and Scenic Rim tourism boards provide downloadable maps. Find Granite Belt winery and walking trails at ⊕ www.granitebeltwinecountry.com.au, and Scenic Rim winery and trail maps at ⊕ www.visitscenicrim.com.au.

Arguably, the safest way to sample the offerings of the region's wineries is via guided tour. More than half a dozen companies run tours of wineries in the Scenic Rim and Mt. Tamborine areas, but some require groups of at least six people.

TOURS
Cork 'n Fork Winery Tours
SPECIAL-INTEREST | Family-run Cork 'n Fork Winery Tours runs daily and overnight viticultural tours for couples and small groups to Mt. Tamborine and the Scenic Rim. Their popular full-day tour includes hotel pickups from the Gold Coast or Brisbane, lunch, and five winery visits with guided tastings. ☎ 0415/454313 ⊕ corknforktours.com ✉ From A$140.

Filippo's Tours
SPECIAL-INTEREST | This popular operator runs an assortment of specialist food, wine, and brewery tours across the Granite Belt, with departures from both Stanthorpe and Brisbane. Small, customized, group tours are also available.

☎ 1800 /020383 ⊕ www.filippostours.com.au ✉ From A$110.

Granite Highlands Maxi Tours
SPECIAL-INTEREST | This local operator runs half-day, full-day, and weekend tours of Granite Belt wineries, specializing in the verdant vineyards of Stanthorpe. Departing Brisbane and various regional centers, most tours also include meals, sightseeing, and local attractions. ✉ Stanthorpe ☎ 07/4681–3969, 1800/852969 ⊕ www.maxitours.com.au ✉ From A$85.

⊙ Sights

Ballandean Estate Wines
HISTORIC SITE | Just south of Glen Aplin is the town of Ballandean, home to award-winning Ballandean Estate Wines, the oldest family-owned and-operated vineyard and winery in Queensland. The first grapes were grown on the Granite Belt site in 1931, and the tasting room is the original brick shed built in 1950. The Barrel Room Cafe behind it—with massive, 125-year-old wooden barrels lining one wall—serves modern Italian cuisine, showcasing local produce and quality coffee (lunch Wednesday–Monday, dinner Thursday–Sunday). There are free 45-minute tours of the facility daily at 11 am. ✉ 354 Sundown Rd., Ballandean ☎ 07/4684–1226 ⊕ www.ballandeanestate.com ✉ Free.

Girraween National Park
FOREST | FAMILY | One of the most popular parks in southeast Queensland—meaning "place of flowers"—sits at the end of the New England Tableland, a stepped plateau area with elevations ranging from 1,968 to 4,921 feet. The 17 km (11 miles) of walking tracks, most starting near the information center and picnic area, wind past granite outcrops, giant boulders, eucalyptus forests, and spectacular wildflowers in spring. Along the way you might encounter kangaroos, echidnas, brush-tailed possums, and turquoise parrots. To camp, you'll need a permit from

the NPRSR (🌐 *www.qld.gov.au/camping*). ✉ *Ballandean* ✥ *11 km (7 miles) north of Wallangarra or 26 km (16 miles) south of Stanthorpe, off New England Hwy.* ☎ *07/4684–5157* 🌐 *www.nprsr.qld.gov.au/parks/girraween.*

Sirromet Wines at Mount Cotton

RESTAURANT—SIGHT | Queensland's largest winery sits midway between Brisbane and the Gold Coast. Sirromet's much-lauded wines—distinctive reds, crisp whites, and some terrific blended varieties—can be sampled at their impressive cellar door, alongside coffee and cake, Devonshire tea, and lunchtime platters (bookings required). Additional dining options are Restaurant Lurleen's and The Tuscan Terrace. ✉ *850–938 Mount Cotton Rd., Mount Cotton* ☎ *07/3206–2999* 🌐 *www.sirromet.com* 🎟 *Tastings from A$5; guided tours from A$20.*

Hotels

Spicers Peak Lodge

$$$$ | **RESORT** | This luxurious, all-inclusive mountain retreat offers a range of lavishly appointed suites, most with stone fireplaces, and all with views and complimentary minibars. **Pros:** world-class restaurant with terrific wine list; thoughtful, impeccable service; stunning, serene location. **Cons:** all-inclusive package pricey; no public transport to lodge; two-night minimum stay on weekends. [$] *Rooms from: A$999* ✉ *Wilkinsons Rd., Maryvale* ☎ *1300/198386* 🌐 *www.spicersretreats.com/spicers-peak-lodge* 🛏 *12 suites* 🍴 *All-inclusive.*

★ **Vineyard Cottages and Café**

$$$ | **B&B/INN** | Built around a turn-of-the-20th-century church that's now the Vineyard Cafe and restaurant, this popular property boasts seven period-style cottages set amid 2 acres of manicured gardens, only two blocks from Ballandean village. **Pros:** warm ambience with excellent food and wine; close to top wineries; disabled friendly. **Cons:** 20 minutes to Stanthorpe; some road noise—request a cottage in back to avoid; free Wi-Fi in public areas only. [$] *Rooms from: A$245* ✉ *New England Hwy., near Bents Rd., Ballandean* ☎ *07/4684–1270* 🌐 *www.vineyardcottages.com.au* 🛏 *4 cottages, 3 suites* 🍴 *No meals.*

Coomera and Oxenford

48–51 km (30–32 miles) south of Brisbane.

The biggest draws of these two northern Gold Coast suburbs are their family-oriented theme parks—Dreamworld, Warner Bros. Movie World, Wet 'n' Wild Water World, Paradise Country, the Australian Outback Spectacular, and WhiteWater World. The sprawling complexes have many attractions: each takes about a day for a leisurely visit. An array of ticketing options are available, including multiday and multipark passes. For more information visit 🌐 *themeparks.com.au* or 🌐 *www.dreamworld.com.au*

Sights

Australian Outback Spectacular

AMUSEMENT PARK/WATER PARK | **FAMILY** | The Australian Outback Spectacular lets visitors experience "the heart and soul of the Australian Outback." The evening show features state-of-the-art visual effects and performances from top local stunt riders, interactive team racing, and live country and orchestral music. Guests get a hearty, three-course dinner and complimentary drinks during the 90-minute, A$23-million production, plus a souvenir stockman's hat. There is also a matinee performance some Sundays. ✉ *Pacific Motorway, Oxenford* ☎ *13–3386 bookings and information* 🌐 *outbackspectacular.com.au* 🎟 *From A$100.*

Dreamworld

AMUSEMENT PARK/WATER PARK | FAMILY | At Coomera's Dreamworld, the main draw is the "big nine": high-tech thrill rides including the aptly named Giant Drop, a nearly 400-foot vertical plummet akin to skydiving; the nine-story, 360-degree pendulum swing of Claw; and Tail Spin, a soaring mini airplane adventure. Animal lovers will enjoy Tiger Island where Bengal tigers and their gorgeous cubs swim and play, Koala Country, and the conservation-focused on-site Wildlife Sanctuary (including crocs). There are also Family Rides, a range of rides for young children, pools and waterslides of Whitewater World, and Corroboree, an interactive celebration of Aboriginal and Torres Strait Island heritage and culture. Make the most of your day by signing up for Q4U virtual queueing on your smartphone (from A$30), which saves you from waiting in line for popular rides. Purchase tickets online for discounts and specials. ⊠ *1 Dreamworld Pkwy., Coomera* ☎ *07/5588–1111, 1800/073300* ⊕ *www.dreamworld.com.au* ✉ *Entry (includes Dreamworld and Whitewater World) from A$85* ⊘ *Closed Christmas Day and Anzac Day (Apr. 25).*

Paradise Country

AMUSEMENT PARK/WATER PARK | FAMILY | Billed as "an authentic Australian farm experience," the park appeals to families with wildlife tours, animal feedings, koala cuddling, sheep shearing, boomerang throwing, and displays of horsemanship. Meanwhile, adults can book a private wine tasting session. You can also stay overnight in an on-site tent or your own motor home. The park is directly behind the Australian Outback Spectacular. Car parking spaces are limited. ⊠ *Pacific Motorway, Oxenford* ☎ *13–3386, 07/5519–6200* ⊕ *paradisecountry.com.au* ✉ *From A$27* ⊘ *Closed Anzac Day (Apr. 25) and Christmas Day.*

Warner Bros. Movie World

AMUSEMENT PARK/WATER PARK | FAMILY | Mixingold Hollywood ambience with live character shows, interactive adventures, and thrill rides for young and old, Warner Bros offers something for everyone. Rides include the Batman-themed 1.4 km DC Rivals HyperCoaster—the Southern Hemisphere's longest, fastest (at 115 km/hr) and highest (at 61.6 meters). With a large portion of its area now covered by a 43,055-square-foot roof, this park is a smart choice in bad weather. It's adjacent to Australian Outback Spectacular. ⊠ *Pacific Motorway, Oxenford* ☎ *13–3386* ⊕ *www.movieworld.com.au* ✉ *From A$89* ⊘ *Closed Anzac Day (Apr. 25) and Christmas Day.*

Wet 'n' Wild Water World

AMUSEMENT PARK/WATER PARK | FAMILY | Oxenford's Wet 'n' Wild Water World boasts magnificent, adrenaline-pumping water slides including a tandem, entwined-tube and family-friendly slides; a wave pool; and the Surfrider that simulates the sensation of surfing the world's biggest waves. Kids love Buccaneer Bay, a pirate-themed aquatic playground with multiple levels, and the new Wet 'n' Wild Junior area, featuring another eight kid-friendly slides, including mini versions of the park's most popular thrill rides. Select pools and slides are heated May through September, when days are often still sunny and warm. The park is ½ km (¼ mile) down the Pacific Highway from Warner Bros. Movie World. ⊠ *Pacific Hwy., Oxenford* ☎ *13–3386* ⊕ *www. wetnwild.com.au* ✉ *From A$74.*

Southport and Main Beach

16 km (10 miles) southeast of Oxenford.

South of Oxenford, look for the turnoff to the Spit, a natural peninsula that stretches 4 km (2½ miles) north, almost to the tip of South Stradbroke Island. Seaworld Drive runs the full length of the Spit, from Mariner's Cove (a popular covered area with affordable restaurants and fast-food outlets) to a nature reserve. This narrow peninsula is bordered by the Pacific Ocean to the east and the calm waters of the Broadwater (a long lagoon) to the west. Two of the Gold Coast's most opulent hotels face each other across Seaworld Drive and are connected to Marina Mirage, arguably the most elegant shopping precinct on the Gold Coast. An assortment of adventure sports operators can also be found in this area, including jet boating and skiing, helicopter flights, fishing charters, electric bike rentals, surf schools, and sailing lessons.

🍴 Restaurants

Misono Japanese Steakhouse
$$$$ | JAPANESE |FAMILY | Run by charismatic chefs, who clearly love to please a crowd, this popular Teppanyaki restaurant is as much about the spectacle of their meal as the quality ingredients and perfectly executed flavors. Try the succulent fillet steak with teriyaki chicken, traditional tofu and hibachi vegetables, or salmon and lobster tail. **Known for:** largest Teppanyaki restaurant in Australia; deluxe seafood and Wagyu banquets; signature cocktails. $ *Average main: A$65* ⊠ *Marriott Hotel, Level 3, 158 Ferny Ave., Surfers Paradise* ☎ *07/5592–9770* ⊙ *No lunch.*

Omeros Bros Seafood Restaurant
$$$ | SEAFOOD | This iconic seafood restaurant perched on the waterfront at the lovely Marina Mirage center has dishes spanning the seafood spectrum—from Bouillabaisse and classic surf-and-turf to local barramundi, lobster, oysters, mud crab, and Moreton Bay bugs. This is also a tempting selection of meat, vegetarian, and pasta dishes, and an extensive dessert menu and wine list. **Known for:** spectacular waterfront views and sunsets; excellent service; fresh local seafood. $ *Average main: A$38* ⊠ *Marina Mirage, Seaworld Dr., Shop 55/74, Southport* ☎ *07/5591–7222* ⊕ *www.omerosbros. com.*

🛏 Hotels

Palazzo Versace
$$$$ | HOTEL | The famous Italian fashion house lent its flair to this expansive, opulent waterfront hotel—the first of its kind in the world. **Pros:** five-star service and dining; palm-fringed 206-foot-long lagoon pool; all rooms include a spa bath. **Cons:** pricey; opulent style may not be to all tastes; still an icon, but may have seen better days. $ *Rooms from: A$499* ⊠ *94 Seaworld Dr., adjoining Marina Mirage, Southport* ☎ *07/5509–8000* ⊕ *www.palazzoversace.com* 🛏 *200 rooms* ⎸⊘⎸ *Free Breakfast.*

🏃 Activities

BOAT TOURS
★ Paradise Jet Boating
ADVENTURE TOURS | FAMILY | The thrill-seekers' way to sightsee, these high-speed jet boats rocket through the Gold Coast's scenic beaches and waterways, treating passengers to 360-degree spins, high-speed drifting, and other exciting maneuvers along the way. ⊠ *Mariners Cove Marina, 60 Seaworld Dr., Shop 7B, Southport* ☎ *07/5526–3089, 1300/538262* ⊕ *www.paradisejetboating. com.au* 🎫 *From A$64.*

CYCLING
Gold Coast Bike Tours
BICYCLING | For an active experience this group runs personalized tours along the region's stunning coastline. The most

popular option takes you on a loop from Surfers Paradise through Main Beach to The Spit, then back past Seaworld and Marina Mirage, taking 2½ hours. Book tours in advance. Bike rental also available and includes delivery, pickup, helmet, and lock. ☎ *0490 /446176* 🎫 *Guided tours from A$120. Bike rental from A$30.*

SURFING

Get Wet Surf School

SURFING | Get Wet Surf School holds twice-daily group lessons (up to six students per coach) at a sheltered, crowd-free beach off the Spit, just north of Surfers Paradise, as well as lessons outside park hours in the controlled environment of WhiteWater World's large wave pool (heated in winter). They also host private lessons and multiday surf tours. ✉ *Seaworld Dr., Main Beach, Southport* ☎ *1800/438938* 🌐 *www.getwetsurf.com* 🎫 *From A$65.*

Shopping

Marina Mirage Gold Coast

SHOPPING CENTERS/MALLS | The sleek Marina Mirage Gold Coast features 80-plus stores, including high-end gift and homewares, jewelry, and designer fashion boutiques like Christensen Copenhagen and Calvin Klein, along with famous Australian brands, fine waterfront restaurants, beauty salons and day spas, and marina facilities. On Saturday morning (7 am–noon), buy fresh gourmet produce at the Marina Mirage Gourmet Farmers' Markets. ✉ *74 Seaworld Dr., Main Beach, Southport* 🌐 *www.marinamirage.com.au.*

Surfers Paradise and Broadbeach

5 km (3 miles) south of Southport.

Before the Gold Coast existed as a tourism entity, there was Surfers Paradise: a stunning 3-km (2-mile) stretch of beach with great surf, 5 km (3 miles) south of Southport. Now a strip of high-rises, it's still a vibrant beachside town, with plentiful shopping options and an emergent arts and fine-dining culture (check out the 4217 for some of the region's up and coming artisans and providores (🌐 *www.the4217.com*). For stunning 360-degree views of the entire coast and hinterland, venture up to the SkyPoint observation deck and Seventy7 Café + Bar located on the 77th floor of Surfers' famous Q1 Tower, the tallest building in the southern hemisphere. For the latest on events, nightlife, new eateries and more visit 🌐 *www.surfersparadise.com.*

Two miles further south, Broadbeach is one of the most popular areas on the Gold Coast, especially with locals. It's also home to some great cafés, trendy nightspots, and the mega-shopping mall Pacific Fair. For up-to-date information visit 🌐 *broadbeachgc.com*

Hotels

★ Peppers Soul

$$$$ | **HOTEL** |**FAMILY** | With its central location right on Cavill Ave. and across the road from a patrolled beach, the 77-story Peppers Soul offers some of the most stunning views on the Gold Coast. **Pros:** all rooms have ocean views; breakfast is a cut above; central Surfers Paradise location. **Cons:** due to number of floors, elevator can be slow from higher floors; can get hectic during school holidays; not a good choice for those with vertigo. [$] *Rooms from: A$365* ✉ *8 The Esplanade, Surfers Paradise* ☎ *07/5635–5700* 🌐 *www.soulsurfersparadise.com.au* 🛏 *287 rooms* 🍴 *No meals.*

QT Gold Coast

$$$ | **HOTEL** | One of Queensland's most popular destination hotels, this vibrant retro-meets-modern resort boasts 360-degree views of the beach and hinterland, on-site restaurants and bars, and enough quirk and energy to make it stand brightly apart. **Pros:** lively atmosphere and design; excellent on-site dining and bar options; close to beach. **Cons:** design getting a little tired; parking costs A$8 per night; area can be noisy at night (ask for a room on a higher level). $ *Rooms from: A$229 ⊠ 7 Staghorn Ave., Surfers Paradise* ☎ *07/5584–1200* ⊕ *www.qtgoldcoast.com.au* ⇌ *297 rooms* ⍟ *No meals.*

The Star Gold Coast

$$$$ | RESORT | This massive, glitzy resort in Broadbeach houses The Star Grand and The Darling hotels: the former offering tasteful rooms with a calming palette and the latter, spacious suites and penthouses designed with decadence in mind. **Pros:** modern, luxury furnishings and facilities; close to shopping centers; free parking for guests. **Cons:** 15-minute walk to the beach; no complimentary water in rooms; pool at The Star Grand is on the small side. $ *Rooms from: A$302 ⊠ Broadbeach Island, Casino Dr., off Gold Coast Hwy.* ☎ *07/5592–8100* ⊕ *www.star.com.au/goldcoast* ⇌ *The Star Grand: 596 rooms; The Darling: 56 suites* ⍟ *Free Breakfast.*

The Wave Resort

$$$ | RESORT | This ultramodern high-rise apartment resort is one of Broadbeach's most luxurious. **Pros:** free parking, unlimited Wi-Fi, and Foxtel Platinum cable TV package; helpful staff; well-maintained and soundproofed rooms. **Cons:** minimum three-night (or, in peak periods, five-night) stay; fully self-contained: no meal plans and in-room provisions not replenished; checkout is 10 am. $ *Rooms from: A$252 ⊠ 89–91 Surf Parade* ☎ *07/5555–9200* ⊕ *www.thewaveresort.com.au* ⇌ *118 apartments* ⍟ *No meals.*

⊜ Shopping

★ Pacific Fair

SHOPPING CENTERS/MALLS | A sprawling indoor/outdoor shopping hub, Pacific Fair is Queensland's largest mall, featuring Myer and David Jones department stores, major retailers, and more than 400 specialty stores and services (including travel agencies, fashion outlets, and sports and outdoor gear). For a breather, head to the landscaped grounds with restaurants and cafés dotted around sparkling pools and water features, a children's park, and village green, or take in a movie at the 12-screen cinema complex. ⊠ *Hooker Blvd., at Gold Coast Hwy., opposite The Star Casino and Hotel* ⊕ *www.pacificfair.com.au* ⊙ *Closed Anzac Day (Apr. 25) and Christmas Day.*

Surfers Paradise Beachfront Markets

OUTDOOR/FLEA/GREEN MARKETS | Thrice weekly—Wednesday, Friday, and Sunday night—crowds flock to haggle for handmade crafts and gifts at the busy Surfers Paradise Beachfront Markets. More than 100 market stalls line the beachfront from 4 pm. ⊠ *The Esplanade, between Hanlan St. and Elkhorn Ave., Surfers Paradise.*

Burleigh Heads and Beyond

At the southern end of the Gold Coast, between Broadbeach and the New South Wales border, you'll find a burgeoning strip of funky restaurants, bars and cafés, high-rise apartment blocks sitting jeek-by-jowl alongside old-school seaside shacks and motels, and some of the world's most renowned surf breaks. Foodies will feel well at home; many of the Gold Coast's best restaurants are to be found here. Families will love Currumbin Wildlife Sanctuary, and the calm waters of Tallebudgera Beach. Hotel accommodation is limited—you're more likely to find holiday apartment rentals. For all the latest information about Burleigh Heads visit ⊕ *www.burleightourism.com.au.* For the beaches beyond Burleigh, including Currumbin, Coolangatta, and Rainbow Bay go to ⊕ *www.southerngoldcoast.com.au.*

Sights

★ Currumbin Wildlife Sanctuary

NATURE PRESERVE | FAMILY | A Gold Coast institution and perhaps the most ecologically minded wildlife facility in the region, Currumbin Wildlife Sanctuary is a 70-acre, not-for-profit National Trust Reserve featuring more than 60 koalas and an on-site wildlife hospital. Established in 1947 as a lorikeet sanctuary, it now shelters a wide variety of Australian species, including kangaroos, crocodiles, wombats, dingoes, Tasmanian devils, echidnas, emus, and rare birds. There are more than 10 daily animal feedings, shows, and performances, friendly 'roos (often with joeys in their pouches!) love to be petted and hand-fed, and the fleet of young koalas make for perfect cuddle and photo opportunities. Con-x-ion provides a paid shuttle service from Broadbeach and Surfers Paradise (🌐 *www.con-x-ion.com).* All revenue goes toward Currumbin's work protecting, treating, and rehabilitating local wildlife. **■ TIP→ Tickets are much cheaper if bought online in advance, especially in low season.** ✉ *28 Tomewin St., off Gold Coast Hwy., Currumbin* ✥ *14 km (8½ miles) south of Broadbeach* ☎ *07/5534–1266, 1300/886511* 🌐 *currumbinsanctuary.com.au* 🎫 *From A$50* 🕒 *Closed Anzac Day (Apr. 25) and Christmas Day.*

David Fleay Wildlife Park

NATURE PRESERVE | FAMILY | Located in the town of Burleigh Heads—7 km (4½ miles) south of Broadbeach—and named for an Australian wildlife naturalist, the park features a daily program of ranger-led walks and presentations, a boardwalk trail, and picnic facilities. See koalas, kangaroos, dingoes, platypuses, and crocodiles, grouped together in separate zones according to their natural habitat, or discover threatened species and the elusive platypus in the state-of-the-art nocturnal house. There's also a café and a gift shop. **■ TIP→ Daily presentations are included in the ticket price; the platypus feeding at 10:30 am is a must-see.** ✉ *Tallebudgera Creek Rd., near W. Burleigh Rd., Burleigh Heads* ☎ *07/5579–2051* 🌐 *www.npsr.qld.gov.au/parks/david-fleay* 🎫 *From A$23* 🕒 *Closed Anzac Day (Apr. 25) morning, Christmas Day.*

Restaurants

The Collective

$$ | CONTEMPORARY | FAMILY | This market-style collaboration has been at the forefront of a new wave of dining establishments hitting the Gold Coast since 2016. With five kitchens operating under the one roof, patrons can choose from contemporary Australian, Mexican, Italian, Asian, or American-inspired cuisines, in this airy, light-filled space. **Known for:** huge variety of dishes including gluten-free and vegetarian options; rooftop bar perfect for sunset drinks; fun, noisy vibe. [$] *Average main: A$25* ✉ *1128 Gold Coast Hwy.* ☎ *07/5534–6707* 🌐 *www.thecollectivepalmbeach.com.au.*

The Fish House

$$$ | SEAFOOD | The name says it all: The Fish House is the place to go for fresh seafood and fine dining (and wining) in a beachfront location. From its daily-changing menu featuring the finest Australian seafood to its 20-page drinks list, including an impressive array of wines by the glass, this Burleigh Heads icon has all the ingredients for a memorable lunch or dinner. **Known for:** chef's selection Menu of the Day degustation with optional caviar and wine-matching; wines carefully chosen to match seafood-driven menu; stunning oceanfront location. [$] *Average main: A$48* ✉ *50 Goodwin Terr., Burleigh Heads* ☎ *07/5535–7725* 🌐 *thefishhouse.com.au.*

Hotels

★ Bon Sol

$$$$ | RENTAL | Featuring interior styling by Anna Spiro, responsible for the makeover of Cabarita's Halcyon House, these unassuming 1960s two-bedroom apartments—currently two in total—offer a completely different Gold Coast experience. **Pros:** unlike anywhere else on the Gold Coast; in the heart of groovy Burleigh Heads; luxe fittings, designer interiors, and personalized service. **Cons:** expensive; minimum three-night stay; not suitable for children under 13. *$ Rooms from: A$690 ✉ 44 The Esplanade, Burleigh Heads ☎ 0499/114162 🌐 bonsol.com.au 🛏 2 apartments 🍴 No meals.*

Activities

SURFING

★ Walkin on Water

SURFING | FAMILY | Learn to surf amid the pristine beach and point breaks of Greenmount and Coolangatta. Walkin' on Water offers group beginner lessons and private lessons daily, as well as a SurfGroms program especially for kids. Board and rashvest are included in the price, as is a wet suit if you need one. Two-hour group lessons from A$50 per person. ✉ *Marine Parade, in carpark opposite Greenmount Surf Club* ☎ *0418/780311* 🌐 *www.walkinonwater.com.*

Gold Coast Hinterland

No visit to the Gold Coast would be complete without an excursion to the region's verdant hinterland. The natural grandeur of the area lies in dramatic contrast to the human-made excesses of the coastal strip. The Gold Coast Hinterland's superb national parks and nature reserves protect magnificent waterfalls, natural rock pools, mountain lookouts with expansive views of the surrounding terrain and coast, and an array of wildlife. Walking trails traverse rain forest dense with ancient trees. Among the parks lie boutique wineries and quaint villages where a high-rise is anything over one story. The parks form part of a unique, ancient geological region known as the Scenic Rim: a chain of mountains running parallel to the coast through southeast Queensland and northern New South Wales. Because it rises to 3,000 feet above sea level, some parts of the hinterland are 4°C–6°C (7°F–11°F) cooler than the coast.

GETTING HERE AND AROUND

The Hinterland's main areas—Tamborine Mountain, Lamington National Park, and Springbrook—can be reached from the Pacific Highway or via Beaudesert from Brisbane, and are a 30- to 40-minute drive inland from the Gold Coast. To reach Tamborine, around 80 km (50 miles) south of Brisbane and 36 km (24 miles) from Southport, take Exit 57 off the Pacific Motorway to the Oxenford–Tamborine Road; or take Exit 71 off the Pacific Motorway, the Nerang–Beaudesert Road, to Canungra. From Canungra, follow the signs to Tamborine, 4 km (2½ miles) along Tamborine Mountain Road. The Gold Coast Hinterland is ideal for touring by car: rent a vehicle, arm yourself with local maps, fill the tank, and take to the hills.

TOURS

Araucaria Ecotours

ECOTOURISM | Departing Brisbane, this eco-certified company runs single and multiday guided tours of Mt. Tamborine and the Scenic Rim, taking in its rich diversity of wildlife and habitat. Travel options include camping, bird-watching, glowworm cave tours, wine tasting, and more. ☎ *07/5544–1283* 🌐 *www.learnaboutwildlife.com* 🎟 *From A$209.*

JPT Tour Group

ECOTOURISM | This tour company (also known as Australian Day Tours) picks up passengers from Gold Coast hotels and the Brisbane Transit Centre daily at 8:45 am and travels via Tamborine Mountain to the Hinterland and O'Reilly's Rainforest Retreat, before returning to the Gold Coast at 5 pm (Brisbane at 6 pm). Tour highlights include the Mt. Tamborine

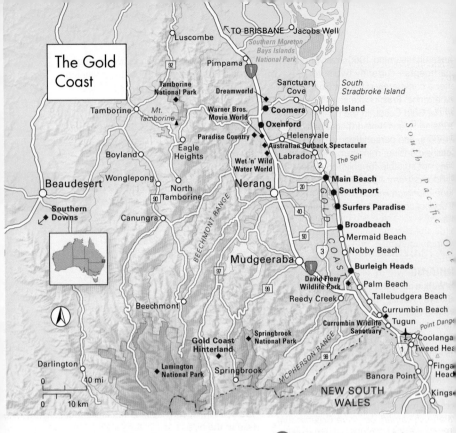

The Gold Coast

TO BRISBANE — Jacobs Well
Luscombe
Southern Moreton
Bays Islands
National Park
Pimpama
92
Tamborine
National Park
Dreamworld
Sanctuary
Cove
South
Stradbroke Island
Tamborine
Mt.
Tamborine
Warner Bros.
Movie World
Coomera
Hope Island
Oxenford
Paradise Country
Helensvale
Eagle
Heights
Australian Outback Spectacular
Boyland
Labrador
Wet 'n' Wild
Water World
The Spit
2
Wonglepong
Beaudesert
North
Tamborine
Nerang
20
Main Beach
Southport
90
Southern
Downs
Canungra
40
Surfers Paradise
Broadbeach
50
Mermaid Beach
97
3
Nobby Beach
Mudgeeraba
Burleigh Heads
99
David Fleay
Wildlife Park
Palm Beach
Beechmont
Reedy Creek
Tallebudgera Beach
Currumbin Beach
Currumbin Wildlife
Sanctuary
Tugun
Point Danger
Springbrook
National Park
Coolanga
Gold Coast
Hinterland
98
Tweed Hea
Darlington
Lamington
National Park
Springbrook
Banora Point
Finga
Head
0   10 mi
NEW SOUTH
WALES
Kings
0   10 km

South Pacific Oce

GOLD COAST

BEECHMONT RANGE

MCPHERSON RANGE

Gallery Walk, and lunch with optional
bird-feeding at O'Reilly's. The company
also runs nightly tours and guided walks
through local Hinterland caves, which,
when the sun is down, light up spectac-
ularly with populations of glowworms.
✉ *9 Trickett St., Shop 6, Surfers Paradise*
☏ *1300/781362, 07/5630–1602* ⊕ *www.
jpttours.com* ✉ *From A$110 (adults),
A$70 (children).*

Southern Cross Day Tours

GUIDED TOURS | Keeping a good distance
from the crowds, this father and son
team leads expeditions to the natural
wonders of the area, including several
national parks, plus wildlife spotting and
cultural activities along the way. ✉ *3078
Surfers Paradise Blvd., Surfers Paradise*
☏ *1300/762665* ⊕ *southerncrossday-
tours.com.au* ✉ *From A$68.*

◉ Sights

★ Lamington National Park

BODY OF WATER | Part of the Gondwana
Rainforests of Australia World Heritage
Area, beautiful Lamington National Park
is a lush, subtropical-temperate zone
that shelters abundant and highly diverse
plant and animal life. Forming part of
the largest subtropical rain forest in the
world, find Antarctic beech trees dating
back more than 3,000 years, as well as
waterfalls, mountain pools, breathtaking
views, bright wildflowers, and more than
160 native bird species. The Park is laced
with 160 km (100 miles) of bushwalking
tracks, ranging from 1.2 km (¾ mile) to
54 km (34 miles), with campsites along
the way. All park camping areas require
nightly permits (A$6.55 per person, or
A$26.20 per family per night), obtained
in advance. ✉ *Binna Burra* ☏ *13–7468*

⊕ *findapark.npsr.qld.gov.au/parks/laming-ton* ✉ *Free.*

Springbrook National Park

BODY OF WATER | The peaks of Springbrook National Park rise to around 3,000 feet, dominating the skyline west of the Gold Coast. The World Heritage–listed park has four regions: scenic Springbrook plateau, Mt. Cougal, Natural Bridge, and Numinbah. Highlights include waterfalls and cascades, Jurassic-Age hoop pines, ancient rain forest, and abundant native birds and wildlife. Thanks to steep, winding roads and longish distances between sections, it takes at least a full day to explore this large park. It's about 30 km (19 miles) from the tiny hamlet of Springbrook to Natural Bridge—a waterfall that cascades through a cavern roof into an icy pool, which is home to Australia's largest glowworm colony. Several waterfalls, including the area's largest, Purling Brook Falls, can be reached via a steepish 4-km (2½-mile) path (allow 5 minutes for each half-mile). The 54-km Gold Coast Hinterland Great Walk extends from the Settlement campground to Green Mountains campsite in Tamborine National Park. For those short on time or energy, the lookout near the parking lot has beautiful waterfall views. Camping is permitted only in designated private campgrounds. ✉ *Springbrook* ☎ *13–7468* ⊕ *www.explorespringbrook. com* ✉ *Free.*

Tamborine National Park

FOREST | More than 20 million years ago, volcanic eruptions created rugged landscapes, while fertile volcanic soils produced the luxuriant tracts of rain forest that make up the enchanting Tamborine National Park. It's worth spending at least a day or two here. Apart from the natural environment, there are wineries, lodges, restaurants, and the famed Gallery Walk, a 1-km-long (½-mile-long) street lined with art galleries. Some of the simplest (under two hours) and best trails here are the Cedar Creek Falls Track with waterfall

views, Palm Grove Rainforest Circuit, and Macdonald Rainforest Circuit, a quieter walk popular with bird-watchers. Start your visit with a stop at Tamborine Mountain Visitor Information Centre (open 9:30 am to 3:30 pm weekdays and until 4 pm weekends), and don't forget to stop by the local Botanic Gardens for a rest and a picnic. ✉ *Main Western Rd., Mt. Tamborine* ☎ *07/5545–3200 information center* ⊕ *visittamborinemountain.com. au* ✉ *Free.*

🛏 Hotels

Binna Burra Mountain Lodge & Campsite

$ | B&B/INN |FAMILY | At the doorstep of Lamington National Park, this historic, eco-certified, back-to-basics mountain lodge and campground is a birdwatcher's paradise, with sweeping views across Heritage-listed rain forest and more than 160 km (99 miles) of walking trails. **Pros:** beautiful setting, views, and wildlife; old-fashioned, communal atmosphere; great choice for families. **Cons:** buffet-style, communal dining may be off-putting for some; mountain lodge in need of refurbishment; while rooms are heated, the area can be cold and damp in winter. ⑤ *Rooms from: A$112* ✉ *Binna Burra Rd., via Beechmont, Lamington National Park* ☎ *07/5533–3622, 1300/246622* ⊕ *www.binnaburralodge. com.au* ⇝ *35 cabins (9 with shared bath), 3 studios, 5 apartments* ⊘ *No meals.*

★ Gwinganna Lifestyle Retreat

$$$$ | ALL-INCLUSIVE | Gwinganna means lookout in the local Yugambeh language, and true to its name, this 500-acre property sits high on a plateau in the Tallebudgera Valley, with views out to the ocean—just 60 minutes from Brisbane Airport. **Pros:** tranquil location with spectacular views, conveniently located to major centers; award-winning spa and unique experiences including equine therapy; simple, yet delicious cuisine with focus on in-season, fresh organic ingredients. **Cons:** set arrival dates apply; communal vibe and meals may be off-putting for some; no alcohol or caffeine, except for some weekend programs. $ *Rooms from: A$1045* ✉ *192 Syndicate Rd.* ☎ *1800/219272, 07/5589–5000* ⊕ *www.gwinganna.com* ➥ *60 rooms* ⦿ *All-inclusive.*

O'Reilly's Rainforest Retreat, Villas & Lost World Spa

$$ | **RESORT** |**FAMILY** | One thousand meters (3,280 feet) above sea level and immersed in the subtropical rain forests of World Heritage–listed Lamington National Park, the eco-certified O'Reilly's Rainforest Retreat boasts a range of accommodation options, from simple garden and mountain view rooms, to one- and two-bedroom canopy suites, and luxury, multiroom mountain villas (complete with balcony Jacuzzis). **Pros:** breathtaking location; luxurious Lost World Spa and infinity pool both feature stunning mountain views; proximity to abundant birdlife and wildlife including kangaroos. **Cons:** long drive up mountain—use a coach or transfer service if you're not confident on Australian roads; Wi-Fi available in public areas but can be slow; restaurant meals are expensive. $ *Rooms from: A$157* ✉ *Lamington National Park Rd., Canungra* ☎ *07/5544–0644, 1800/688722* ⊕ *www.oreillys.com. au* ➥ *120 rooms* ⦿ *Free Breakfast.*

Pethers Rainforest Retreat

$$$$ | **RESORT** | Set on 12 acres of privately owned rain forest, this secluded, couples-only resort comprises 10 spacious tree houses with timber floors, French doors opening onto verandas, fireplaces, hot tubs, and open-plan interiors furnished with Asian antiques. **Pros:** luxurious appointments; glorious environs; complimentary Wi-Fi, parking, and breakfast. **Cons:** no on-site dinner Sunday to Wednesday; limited mobile phone coverage; breakfast could be more substantial. $ *Rooms from: A$325* ✉ *28B Geissmann St., North Tamborine*

☎ *07/5545–4577* ⊕ *www.pethers.com.au* ➥ *10 tree houses* ⦿ *Free Breakfast.*

⊙ Activities

HIKING

Bushwalking is a popular pastime in the national parks and nature reserves of the Gold Coast Hinterland, where an extensive network of well-maintained scenic trails caters to recreational walkers, serious hikers, campers, and wildlife lovers. The region's many protected wilderness tracts, including World Heritage–listed Gondwana Rainforests of Australia (within Springbook National Park), contain hundreds of well-marked trails that vary from easy half-hour strolls to steep half-day hikes and multiday treks. Most Hinterland walks offer spectacular views and sights.

However, conditions can be challenging and changeable, so before setting out on longer hikes, get suitably equipped. Download local trail maps and detailed park info from the Queensland Parks and Forests website or regional visitor information offices, and follow the guidelines

When walking, wear sturdy shoes, sunscreen, and protective gear; carry maps and a compass; and pack drinking water, emergency food supplies, and a well-charged mobile phone. If possible, walk in a group, especially on long hikes. Check local weather conditions with the Bureau of Meteorology and trail conditions on the Parks and Forests website before you go.

If exploring the national parks by car, check road conditions with the RACQ's website and be sure you have local maps, good tires, sound brakes, water, and a full tank of gas before setting out.

CONTACTS Department of Environment and Science, Parks and Forests Portfolio. ☎ *13–7468 camping permits and information* ⊕ *www.npsr.qld.gov.au.* **Royal**

uke's Bluff Lookout on O'Reilly's Plateau, Lamington National Park

Automobile Club of Queensland (RACQ).
☎ 1300/888449 ⊕ www.racq.com.au.

Noosa

*29 km (24 miles) northeast of Nambour,
17 km (11 miles) north of Coolum, 140
km (87 miles) north of Brisbane.*

Set along the calm waters of Laguna
Bay at the northern tip of the Sunshine
Coast, Noosa is one of Australia's most
stylish resort areas. Until the mid-1980s
the town consisted of little more than a
few shacks—then surfers discovered the
spectacular waves that curl around the
sheltering headland of Noosa National
Park. Today Noosa is an enticing mix
of surf, sand, and sophistication, with
a serious reputation for distinctive,
always-evolving cuisine. Views along the
trail from Laguna Lookout to the top of
the headland north of Main Street take in
miles of magnificent beaches, ocean, and
dense vegetation.

 Sights

Teewah Coloured Sands

NATURE SITE | About 3 km (2 miles)
northeast of Noosa Heads you'll find
the Teewah Coloured Sands, an area of
multicolor dunes created in the Ice Age
by natural chemicals in the soil. Teewah's
sands stretch inland from the beach to a
distance of about 17 km (11 miles); some
of the 72 distinctly hued sands even form
cliffs rising to 600 feet. A four-wheel-
drive vehicle is essential for exploring this
area and interesting sites to the north,
such as Cooloola National Park—home to
1,300-plus species of plants, 700 native
animals, and 44% of Australia's bird
species—and Great Sandy National Park.
Access is by ferry across the Noosa River
at Tewantin.

Tour operators run day trips via cruise
boat and four-wheel drive that take in
these sights; some include visits to
Fraser Island, north of Rainbow Beach.
You can also explore the area on foot.
One of Queensland's latest Great Walks

Main beach in Byron Bay, Queensland's Gold Coast

winds through Cooloola National Park. ⊠ *Noosa Heads.*

🏖 Beaches

Noosa Main Beach

BEACH—SIGHT | FAMILY | With gentle waves and year-round lifeguard patrol, Noosa's Main Beach is a perfect swimming spot, ideal for families or those who aren't confident in the bigger swells. The beach backs onto leafy Hastings Street with its bustle of upmarket cafés, bars, restaurants, and shopping spots. For a quieter scene, adventure around the corner to **Noosa Spit**, a popular picnic spot and off-leash dog beach. **Amenities:** food and drink; lifeguards; parking; showers; toilets. **Best for:** sunrise; sunset; swimming; walking. ⊠ *Hastings St., Noosa Heads* ⊕ *www.visitnoosa.com.au.*

★ Sunshine Beach

BEACH—SIGHT | Incorporating 16 km (10 miles) of beachfront that stretches north to Noosa national park, lovely Sunshine Beach is patrolled year-round. Beach breaks, reliable swell, a rocky headland sheltering it from winds, and clear, glassy water make Sunshine popular with surfers. End a long day of swimming with a beer or a meal at The Sunshine Beach Surf Club. **Amenities:** food and drink; lifeguards; parking; showers; toilets. **Best for:** sunrise; sunset; surfing; swimming; walking. ⊠ *Belmore Terr., Sunshine Beach.*

🍴 Restaurants

Bistro C

$$$ | MODERN AUSTRALIAN | Spectacular views of the bay from the open dining area make a stunning backdrop for this fashionable restaurant's Mod Oz cuisine. The fresh, tropical menu highlights local seafood, though landlubbers can partake of several meat and vegetarian dishes (think lamb rump, caramelized pork belly, duck confit, or risotto verde). **Known for:** award-winning cuisine including signature calamari and seafood spaghetti served in a pan; Noosa beachfront location; special tapas and drinks menu pm to 5 pm daily. $ *Average main: A$37* ✉ *49 Hastings St., on Beach Complex, Noosa Heads* ☎ *07/5447–2855* ⊕ *www. bistroc.com.au.*

Ricky's River Bar + Restaurant

$$$ | MODERN AUSTRALIAN | A dining room overlooking the Noosa River makes this picturesque restaurant the perfect spot for a relaxed lunch or a romantic dinner. The menu features "modern Noosa cuisine," which mingles Mediterranean flavors beautifully with Australian ingredients. **Known for:** stunning Noosa riverfront location; tasting menu with matching wines; delicious dessert cocktails. $ *Average main: A$42* ✉ *Noosa Wharf, Quamby Pl., Noosa Heads* ☎ *07/5447–2455* ⊕ *www.rickys.com.au.*

 ## Hotels

Sofitel Noosa Pacific Resort

$$$$ | RESORT | Facing fashionable Hastings Street on one side, the river on the other, this former Sheraton property remains the place to stay in Noosa. **Pros:** close to beach and shops; beautiful pool area; spacious, well-kept rooms. **Cons:** pricey; pool can get busy during school holidays; free Wi-Fi only if room booked through hotel's website. $ *Rooms from: A$314* ✉ *14–16 Hastings St., Noosa Heads* ☎ *07/5449–4888* ⊕ *www.sofitel-noosapacificresort.com.au* 🛏 *176 rooms* ⑩ *No meals.*

 ## Activities

RIVER CRUISING
Noosa Everglades Discovery

BOATING | Eco-accredited Noosa Everglades Discovery runs half- and full-day river cruises and guided canoe trips through the glassy waters of the Noosa Everglades. ✉ *Noosa Everglades, 204 Lake Flat Rd., Noosaville* ☎ *07/5449–0393* ⊕ *www.thediscoverygroup.com.au* ✉ *From A$79.*

Hope Island 👁

This isn't your average island. Like several Gold Coast islands, it is actually a mile or two inland and circled by the Coomera River and a series of canals. The resort has a marina full of luxury launches and yachts, two golf courses, a swanky hotel, beautiful condos, and upscale restaurants, nightclubs, and shops. Stop by if you're passing through for a glimpse into jet-set culture, Queensland style.

Hope Island is accessed via bridges from the west or east. Route 4, also known as the Oxenford–Southport Road, passes straight through.

SURFING
Go Ride a Wave

SURFING | This operator rents equipment and runs surfing lessons for beginners in the sheltered warmth of Noosa Heads Beach. Book in advance to secure two-hour beginner, group, or private lessons, with surfboard, wet suit, and all other equipment included in the fee (A$72). Discounts apply for multiple lessons. ✉ *On beach, Hastings St., near Haul St., Noosa Heads* ☎ *1300/132441* ⊕ *www. goriadeawave.com.au.*

Peregian and Coolum

Peregian is 11 km (7 miles) south of Noosa, with Coolum 17 km (11 miles) south of Noosa and 25 km (16 miles) northeast of Nambour.

At the center of the Sunshine Coast, Coolum makes an ideal base for exploring the countryside. It has one of the finest beaches in the region, a growing reputation for good food and quality accommodations, and all the services you might need: banks with

ATMs, medical centers, gas stations, pharmacies, supermarkets, gyms, beauty salons, and day spas—even a beachfront playground, kiosk, and skate park. Ten minutes north of Coolum is Peregian, a quaint little seaside town with numerous fashionable shops, eateries, and facilities, a string of stunning beaches, and a local produce and crafts market on the first and third Sunday of the month.

Beaches

★ Coolum Beach

BEACH—SIGHT | **FAMILY** | A popular choice for families, beautiful **Coolum Beach** boasts a surf club, skate park, playgrounds, change rooms, toilets, kiosk, shorefront parks, and well-maintained picnic areas. A long, white-sand beach, Coolum is patrolled year-round and has a nice beach break and some decent, uncrowded waves off the headland. Walk south along the boardwalk to the headland park for magnificent coastal views, or north to quieter **Peregian Beach** with its patrolled surf, playground, and adjacent Environmental Park. **Amenities:** food and drink; lifeguards; parking; showers; toilets. **Best for:** sunset; surfing; swimming; walking. ✉ *David Low Way, Coolum* 🌐 *www.visitsunshinecoast.com.au.*

Restaurants

Coolum Surf Club

$$ | **AUSTRALIAN** | **FAMILY** | This lively oceanfront restaurant serves fresh seafood and simple, pub-style fare in its large dining room overlooking Coolum Beach. Reasonable prices, rotating meal specials, live entertainment, and a friendly, casual atmosphere ensure it is always well attended by locals and visitors alike. **Known for:** only surf club in Australia with a wood-fired chargrill; ultimate brekky tower—big breakfast for 2–4 people; casual dining with a spectacular oceanfront setting. [$] *Average main: A$24* ✉ *1775–1779 David Low Way, Coolum* ☎ *07/5446–1148* 🌐 *www.coolumsurfclub.com.*

★ Pitchfork

$$ | **MODERN AUSTRALIAN** | Positioned within the café and shopping strip along Peregian Beach, this contemporary seaside bistro entices crowds with its imaginative, subtropical Mod Oz cuisine and modern, rustic styling. Highlights include the lightly fried stuffed zucchini flowers or baby squid to start, and the Hervey Bay scallop fusilli with smoked pancetta for main. **Known for:** rotating seasonal menu including extensive gluten-free and vegetarian options; kid-friendly minimeal menu; entire menu available for takeout. [$] *Average main: A$35* ✉ *5/4 Kingfisher Dr., Peregian Beach* ☎ *07/5471–3697* 🕒 *Closed Mon.*

Hotels

Coolum Seaside Holiday Apartments

$$ | **RENTAL** | **FAMILY** | These sleek and spacious self-contained studios and one- to four-bedroom apartments are just around the corner from Coolum's restaurants, shops, and beach. **Pros:** good on-site facilities; complimentary Wi-Fi, cable TV, and parking; central to beach and restaurants. **Cons:** dated design in some units; minimum two-night stay; about a 10-minute walk to the beach. [$] *Rooms from: A$190* ✉ *6–8 Perry St., Coolum* ☎ *07/5455–7200, 1800/809062* 🌐 *www.coolumseaside.com* 🛏 *44 apartments* 🍴 *No meals.*

Activities

SURFING

Coolum Surf School

SURFING | Run by an expert surfer and local lifeguard, Coolum Surf School runs two-hour group and 90-minute private lessons, as well as board and gear hire. You'll find it north of Coolum Surf Lifesaving Club, next to the skate park. ✉ *Coolum Boardriders Clubhouse, Tickle Park, David Low Way, Coolum*

☎ *0438/731503* 🌐 *www.coolumsurf-school.com.au* 🎫 *Classes from $60 (prices include gear).*

Maroochydore

18 km (11 miles) south of Coolum, 18 km (11 miles) east of Nambour.

Maroochydore, at the mouth of the Maroochy River, has been a popular beach resort town for years, and has its fair share of high-rise towers. Its draw is excellent surfing and swimming beaches.

Beaches

Alexandra Headland

BEACH—SIGHT | FAMILY | South of Maroochydoore's main beach and just north of Mooloolaba, Alexandra Headland offers a reliable surf break in moderate to high swell. The beach is patrolled year-round, but swimmers need to take care to avoid the headland rocks at the southern end of the beach where there is often a strong rip. A shady park, barbecue and picnic area, kiosk, playground, skate park, and walking and cycling tracks color the foreshore, with many alfresco cafés and restaurants also nearby. **Amenities:** food and drink; lifeguards; parking; showers; toilets. **Best for:** sunset; surfing; swimming; walking. ✉ *Alexandra Parade, Alexandra Headland* 🌐 *www.visitsunshinecoast.com.au.*

Maroochydore Beach

BEACH—SIGHT | FAMILY | Patrolled year-round by one of Queensland's oldest surf lifesaving clubs, rips are common along this strip, so stay in the central area between the red-and-yellow flags. A busy walking and cycling track runs adjacent to the beachfront, connecting visitors to both Cotton Tree and Alexandra Headland. A few minutes north is Maroochy River, a popular fishing spot and water sports activities hub. As with almost all Sunshine Coast beaches, an array of shops, cafés, and eateries line the esplanade. **Amenities:** food and drink; lifeguards; parking; showers; toilets; water sports. **Best for:** sunset; surfing; swimming; walking. ✉ *Alexandra Parade* 🌐 *www.visitsunshinecoast.com.au.*

Restaurants

Raw Energy

$ | CAFÉ | Keep your fuel up for long days of swimming and surfing with a stop at Raw Energy, where freshly made smoothies and juices, hearty burgers and wraps, and fair trade coffee will give you just the boost you need. So successful that it sparked a chain, here you'll find light-and-healthy fare including protein- and superfood-packed smoothies; seasonal, locally flavored fruit, veggie and green juices; and an array of burgers stacked sky-high with fresh ingredients. **Known for:** healthy energy bowls and smoothies; all-day breakfast; free-range and locally grown produce. [$] *Average main: A$15* ✉ *20 Memorial Ave.* ☎ *07/5443–7322* 🌐 *www.rawenergy.com.au.*

Hotels

The Sebel Maroochydore

$$$ | RENTAL | FAMILY | Each spacious one- or two-bedroom apartment in this stylish, view-rich, 15-level hotel has a curved feature wall and full gourmet kitchen bristling with modern European appliances, and most have separate media rooms. **Pros:** 25-meter (82-foot) pool and separate kids pool; hot tub in every room; free parking. **Cons:** noise from pool area and traffic at night; beach is across a four-lane road; nonmembers incur charge for Wi-Fi. [$] *Rooms from: A$259* ✉ *20 Aerodrome Rd.* ☎ *07/5479–8000* 🌐 *www.thesebel.com/queensland/the-sebel-maroochydore* 🛏 *28 apartments* 🍴 *No meals.*

Mooloolaba

5 km (3 miles) south of Maroochydore.

Mooloolaba stretches along a lovely beach and riverbank, both an easy walk from town. The Esplanade has many casual cafés, upscale restaurants, and fashionable shops. Head to the town outskirts for picnic spots and prime coastal views.

Sights

SEA LIFE Sunshine Coast

ZOO | **FAMILY** | This all-weather sea life sanctuary has back-to-back marine presentations, including stingray feedings, guided shark tours, and seal and otter shows, all accompanied by informative talks. Eleven themed zones spread over three levels, including Australia's largest and most interactive jellyfish display, a seahorse sanctuary, and a famous underwater tunnel that gets you face-to-face with the majestic creatures of the deep. A souvenir shop and a café are also on-site, as well as a three-level indoor playground for kids. The aquarium is part of Mooloolaba's Wharf Complex, which features a marina, restaurants, and a tavern. **■TIP→ Save up by booking a fully-flexible ticket valid for up to 12 months online in advance.** ✉ *10 Parkyn Parade, The Wharf* ☎ *07/5458–6280* 🌐 *www.underwaterworld.com.au* 🎟 *A$39* 🕒 *Closed Anzac Day (Apr. 25), Christmas Day.*

Beaches

★ Mooloolaba Beach

BEACH—SIGHT | **FAMILY** | A super-safe, family-friendly swimming beach, Mooloolaba Beach is patrolled year-round and has just enough swell to make it fun. Surfers might want to check out the left-hand break that sometimes forms off the rocks at the northern end. There are shady picnic areas with barbecues, playgrounds, and exercise areas—as well as the local meeting point, the Loo with a View. Stroll south along the coastal path to the river mouth and rock wall (off which you can fish, year-round, for bream); north to Alexandra Headland for views of the bay; or along Mooloolaba Esplanade, lined with casual eateries and boutiques. **Amenities:** food and drink; lifeguards; parking; showers; toilets. **Best for:** sunrise; sunset; swimming; walking. ✉ *Beach Terr.* 🌐 *www.visitsunshinecoast.com.au.*

Restaurants

Bella Venezia Italian Restaurant & Bar

$$$ | **ITALIAN** | A large mural of Venice, simple wooden tables, and terra-cotta floor tiles decorate this popular restaurant in an arcade off the Esplanade. You can eat in or take out traditional and modern Italian cuisine including an extensive selection of pizza, pasta, and risotto, as well as wine and cocktails. **Known for:** Sunshine Coast's longest-established restaurant; pasta made from scratch in-house; modern spin on Italian classics. [$] *Average main: A$37* ✉ *95 The Esplanade* ☎ *07/5444–5844* 🌐 *www.bellav.com.au.*

Hotels

Mantra Sirocco

$$$$ | **RENTAL** | Located across the road from the beach and surrounded by trendy restaurants and cafés, this popular, upscale apartment complex on Mooloolaba's main drag has spacious, self-contained two- and three-bedroom apartments, an impressive pool and Jacuzzi area, and a large fitness center. **Pros:** fantastic views from big balconies; in-room Jacuzzis; free parking. **Cons:** minimum two-night stay; Wi-Fi costs extra; interiors in need of updating. [$] *Rooms from: A$335* ✉ *59–75 The Esplanade* ☎ *07/5444–1400, 1800/811454 reservations* 🌐 *www.mantrasirocco.com.au* 🔑 *43 apartments* 🍴 *No meals.*

Caloundra

29 km (18 miles) south of Maroochydore, 63 km (39 miles) south of Noosa, 91 km (56 miles) north of Brisbane.

This unassuming southern seaside town is a bit of a hidden gem. Popular with families, Caloundra has nine beaches of its own, which include everything from placid wading beaches (King's Beach and Bulcock Beach are best for families) to bays with thundering surf, such as Dicky, Buddina, and Wurtulla beaches.

⛱ Beaches

Bulcock Beach

BEACH—SIGHT | Flanked by a timber boardwalk with stunning views across the coastline, Bulcock Beach is one of Caloundra's most popular surfing spots. Surf the break off Deepwater Point, or enjoy boogie-boarding or bodysurfing in the swell closer to shore. Rips can form through the channel, so stay between the flags and only swim when the beach is patrolled (September–May). Head across the road for cafés, restaurants, shops, and a place to cool off. **Amenities:** lifeguards; parking; toilets. **Best for:** sunrise; sunset; surfing; walking. ⊠ *The Esplanade.*

★ King's Beach

BEACH—SIGHT | FAMILY | With rockpools, water fountains, an oceanfront saltwater swimming pool, and gentle, patrolled swimming areas, it's no surprise that festive King's Beach is one of the Sunshine Coast's most popular choices for families. The region's closest beach to Brisbane, it also attracts plenty of surfers chasing the breaks toward the beach edges. **Amenities:** food and drink; lifeguards; parking; showers; toilets. **Best for:** sunset; surfing; swimming; walking. ⊠ *Ormond Terr.*

🍴 Restaurants

Alfie's Mooo Char & Bar

$$ | AUSTRALIAN | Owned by legendary (and now retired) Queensland Rugby League footballer Allen "Alfie" Langer, this airy, steak-centric restaurant has an ideal setting right on Bulcock Beach, overlooking the sheltered inlet known as Pumicestone Passage. The design is light and bright, and there's both indoor and outdoor dining. **Known for:** chargrilled steaks cooked to order; range of fresh seafood platters; excellent location overlooking the Caloundra Esplanade. $ *Average main: A$35* ⊠ *The Esplanade at Otranto Ave.* ☎ *07/5492–8155* ⊕ *www.alfies.net.au.*

🛏 Hotels

★ Rolling Surf Resort

$$$ | RESORT | The stunning white sands of Kings Beach front this modern, airy resort comprised of well-equipped one- to three-bedroom oceanfront and poolside apartments enveloped in tropical gardens. **Pros:** huge pool; right on the beach; free parking. **Cons:** two-night minimum stay in high season; steep charge for extra towels, toiletries, etc.; limited complimentary Wi-Fi. $ *Rooms from: A$240* ⊠ *10 Levuka Ave., Kings Beach* ☎ *07/5491–9777, 1800/775559* ⊕ *www.rollingsurfresort.com.au* ⇄ *66 apartments* ⦿ *No meals.*

🏃 Activities

SURFING

★ Caloundra Surf School

SURFING | FAMILY | The only operator with exclusive permits to operate in three of Caloundra's beaches, Caloundra Surf School specializes in private and group sessions. Owner-operator John takes a no-nonsense, safety-first approach to introduce you to the thrill of surfing in Caloundra's gentle surf. Surfboard and bodyboard hire also available. ⊠ *Caloundra* ☎ *0413/381010.*

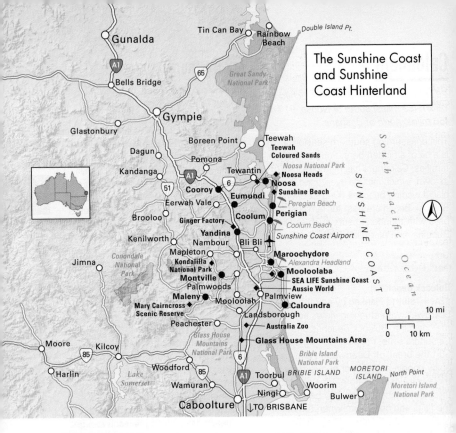

Glass House Mountains Area

35 km (22 miles) north of Brisbane on Bruce Hwy. to the Glass House Mountains Rd. exit; 4 km (2½ miles) south of Beerwah.

More than 20 million years old, the Glass House Mountains consist of nine conical outcrops—the eroded remnants of volcanoes—that rise dramatically from a flattish landscape northwest of Brisbane. Get a great view of the mountains from Glass House Mountains Lookout. Access is 10 km (6 miles) from the village via Glass House Mountains Tourist Route. The lookout is also the starting point for a scenic 25-minute walk. Several longer walks begin from nearby vantage points, such as Mt. Beerburrum and Wild Horse Mountain Lookout.

👁 Sights

Aussie World

AMUSEMENT PARK/WATER PARK | FAMILY | The Sunshine Coast's colorful Aussie World amusement park features several games rooms, a hall for "Funnybone Flicks," and a bustling fairground with 30-plus rides, including bumper cars, a retro merry-go-round, Ferris wheel, roller coaster, log ride, minigolf—even a sideshow alley. Admission is cheap, the "old school" carnival vibe is fun and friendly, and the park is far less crowded than its Gold Coast equivalents. An eclectic range of specialty stores are also housed within the complex, as well as the iconic Aussie World Pub (formerly Ettamogah Pub): a quirky, much-photographed watering hole full of kitsch Australiana and classic Aussie pub meals. ✉ *73 Frizzo Rd., Palmview* ☎ *07/5494–5444* 🌐 *www.aussieworld.com.au* 🎫 *From A$40.*

★ **Australia Zoo**

ZOO | FAMILY | Made famous by the late Steve Irwin, this popular, 110-acre park is home to all manner of Australian animals: koalas, kangaroos, wallabies, dingoes, Tasmanian devils, snakes, wombats, lizards—and, naturally, crocodiles. There are also otters, lemurs, tigers, red pandas, and a giant rain forest aviary. Daily shows feature crocs, birds of prey, koalas, and more. There are also plenty of extras that let you get up close and personal with the residents, including petting and hand-feeding red pandas (A$79), getting cozy with cheetahs (A$69–A$150) and rhinos (A$79), cuddling a koala (A$39), or partaking in an Outback-style camel ride (A$79). Get around the park on foot or try the free hop-on, hop-off mini-trains. Private guided tours and Segway adventures (A$60) are also available. ✉ *1638 Steve Irwin Way, Beerwah* ✣ *5 km (3 miles) north of Glass House Mountains* ☎ *07/5436–2000* 🌐 *www.australiazoo.com.au* 🎫 *From A$59* ⏲ *Closed Christmas Day.*

Montville

16 km (10 miles) northwest of Forest Glen.

This charming mountain village, settled in 1887, is known as the creative heart of the Sunshine Coast, as many artists live here. There are panoramic views of the coast from the main street, a charming mix of Tudor, Irish, and English cottages constructed of log or stone; Bavarian and Swiss houses; quaint B&Bs; and old Queenslander homes. Shops are a browser's delight, full of curiosities and locally made crafts, while galleries showcase more serious pieces by local artists.

Sights

Kondalilla National Park

BODY OF WATER | FAMILY | With its swimming hole, 295-foot waterfall, picnic grounds, and walking trails, Kondalilla National Park is a popular local attraction. Three bushwalks begin near the grassy picnic area: Picnic Creek Circuit, Rock Pools Walk, and the Kondalilla Falls Circuit. They're all rated easy to moderate and range from 2 km (1 mile) to 5 km (3 miles) in length. The **Sunshine Coast Hinterland Great Walk** (58 km [34 miles]) is accessible from the Falls Loop track, and links with parks farther north. Download maps from the Queensland Government Parks and Forests website. Camping is not permitted within the park. ✉ *Kondalilla Falls Rd., off Montville–Mapleton Rd., near Flaxton* ☎ *13/5494–3983* 🌐 *www.npsr.qld.gov.au* 🎫 *Free.*

Restaurants

★ **Altitude**

$$$ | AUSTRALIAN | Helmed by head chef Nick Stapleton (Gordita, Brisbane), with stunning 180-degree view from across the range to the coast, Altitude combines low-key fine dining with straight-up delicious food—and wines to match. The interior is modern, with a bush-inspired palette. **Known for:** two- and three-course lunch menu (A$33 or A$38) is excellent value; casual fine dining with stunning views; innovative menu that combines local produce with pan-cultural flavors. [$] *Average main: 37* ✉ *94–96 Main St.* ☎ *07/5478–5889* 🌐 *altitudeonmontville.com.au* ☞ *Courtesy bus to local accommodations available 5:30 pm–9:30 pm.*

Montville Café Bar Grill

$$ | AUSTRALIAN | Twinkling with fairy lights by night and window-box blooms by day, this friendly, "ye olde English"–style family pub on Montville's main street provides a free courtesy bus to and from local accommodations every evening. Start with the salt-and-pepper

Fishing at Bulcock Beach, Caloundra, Sunshine Coast

calamari, and work your way up to a generous Darling Downs eye fillet, with a quality range of Australian wines to accompany. **Known for:** live entertainment on weekends; convivial pub atmosphere; local institution. [$] *Average main: A$30* ✉ *Main St.* ☎ *07/5278–5535* 🌐 *www.montvillepub.com.au.*

Hotels

★ Narrows Escape Rainforest Retreat

$$$$ | **B&B/INN** | In a fecund valley on the Montville outskirts, this tranquil, couples-only retreat features six self-contained, generously appointed cottages nestled deep in the Hinterland Rain forest. **Pros:** beautiful, peaceful setting; excellent service; no children or large groups. **Cons:** a little way out of town; secluded bushland setting—no views; most pavilions have queen-size beds. [$] *Rooms from: A$415* ✉ *78 Narrows Rd.* ☎ *07/5478–5000* 🌐 *www.narrowsescape.com.au* 🛏 *6 cottages* 🍴 *Free Breakfast.*

The Spotted Chook & Amelie's Petite Maison

$$$ | **B&B/INN** | **FAMILY** | Just over a mile from Montville, this whimsical, French-provincial-style B&B feels a world away with its picturesque country gardens and sweeping views over Obi Obi Gorge. **Pros:** warm and welcoming ambience; delicious French-style country breakfasts included in rate; wheelchair-friendly cottage, ramps, and walkways. **Cons:** two-night minimum stay on weekends; Wi-Fi only in public areas; books up quickly in wedding season. [$] *Rooms from: A$295* ✉ *176 Western Ave.* ☎ *07/5442–9242* 🌐 *www.spottedchook.com.au* 🛏 *4 suites, 1 cottage* 🍴 *Free Breakfast.*

Treetops Montville

$$$ | **B&B/INN** | Convenient to beautiful Kondalilla Falls, these cutting-edge-design tree houses perched on an escarpment are the ideal location for a romantic escape. **Pros:** stunning views; peaceful setting; close to town and walking tracks. **Cons:** minimum two-night stay on weekends; no Wi-Fi in rooms; limited phone reception. $ *Rooms from: A$260 ✉ 4 Cynthia Hunt Dr., off Konda-lilla Falls Rd., Flaxton* ☎ *07/5478–6618, 1800/087330* ⊕ *www.treetopsmontville. com.au* ↻ *4 tree houses, 4 cabins* ❍ *Free Breakfast.*

Maleny

14 km (8½ miles) west of Montville.

The Hinterland village of Maleny is a lively mix of rural life, the arts, wineries, cafés, and cooperative ventures. First settled around 1880, eclectic Maleny is now a popular tourist center with a strong community spirit, as well as a working dairy town.

◉ Sights

Mary Cairncross Scenic Reserve

INFO CENTER | One of the area's most popular picnic spots, Mary Cairncross Reserve is 5 km (3 miles) southeast of Maleny at the intersection of the Landsborough–Maleny Road and Mountain View Road. The 130 acres of subtropical rain forest shelter an array of wildlife that includes bandicoots, goannas, echidnas, wallabies—and even pythons. There are two easy walks and a A$4.7-million Rain-forest Discovery Center offers interactive displays, as well as sensory experiences and exhibits. Eat in the café (serving fair-trade coffee and homemade cakes) or at picnic tables for magnificent views of the Glass House Mountains. ✉ *148 Mountain View Rd.* ☎ *07/5429–6122* ⊕ *www. mary-cairncross.com.au.*

🍴 Restaurants

Maple 3 Café

$ | **CAFÉ** | This local favorite changes its menu daily, but there are always fresh salads, focaccias, pastas, and plenty of dessert options. Come in for breakfast or brunch, grab a sandwich and a huge

slice of homemade cake, and head down to Lake Baroon for a picnic. **Known for:** local institution with great coffee and hearty breakfasts; dessert selection, including cheesecake and Maleny "mud pie"; three resident water dragons that sit by the tables, very much at home. $ *Average main: A$19 ✉ 3 Maple St.* ☎ *07/5499–9177* ⊕ *www.facebook.com/ maple3cafe.*

Hotels

Blue Summit Cottages

$$$ | **B&B/INN** | With four luxurious cottages and a grand house that sleeps up to 14, all on a view-rich mountaintop property set among 10 acres of immaculate gardens and rolling hills, this is the perfect place to get away from it all. **Pros:** breathtaking location; complete privacy and serenity; free Wi-Fi and cable TV. **Cons:** a 10-minute drive to town; books out quickly in high season; weekends can be expensive—book midweek for better deals. $ *Rooms from: A$300 ✉ 547 Maleny-Kenilworth Rd.* ☎ *07/5435–8410* ⊕ *www.bluesummitcottages.com.au* ↻ *3 cottages, 1 house* ❍ *Free Breakfast.*

Maleny Tropical Retreat

$$$ | **B&B/INN** | At the end of a steep driveway, ensconced in a misty rain-forest valley, lies this romantic B&B retreat. **Pros:** top location and service; quality cooked breakfast; large DVD and games library. **Cons:** higher rates and two-night minimum stay on weekends; patchy phone reception and Wi-Fi in some villas and cottages; interiors in some rooms could do with a refresh. $ *Rooms from: A$250 ✉ 540 Maleny–Montville Rd.* ☎ *07/5435–2113* ⊕ *www.malenytropicalretreat.com* ↻ *9 rooms* ❍ *Free Breakfast.*

Yandina, Eumundi, and Cooroy

Yandina is 110 km (68 miles) north of Brisbane on the Bruce Hwy., Eumundi is 12 km (7½ miles) north of Yandina.

Yandina and Eumundi, just 12 km (7½ miles) apart, are home to some of the most iconic attractions in the area. Don't miss the Ginger Factory in Yandina, where you can learn—and eat—lots while enjoying the mini-amusement-park-like attractions; or stop in at the tranquil Spirit House for a meal, cooking class, or cocktail at the Hong Sa Bar. The Eumundi Market (on Wednesday and Saturday) is also a must.

Sights

★ Eumundi Market

LOCAL INTEREST | FAMILY | The big attraction of this area is the twice-weekly Eumundi Market—the best and largest street market on the Sunshine Coast. More than 600 stall-holders gather along Memorial Drive in the picturesque town of Eumundi to sell arts, crafts, clothing, accessories, and fresh and gourmet produce. Buses run to Eumundi from Noosa and other Sunshine Coast towns on market days, when the town swells to near-cosmopolitan proportions. Live musicians, poets, and masseurs keep the crowd relaxed. ✉ *80 Memorial Dr., Eumundi* ☎ *07/5442–7106* 🌐 *www.eumundimarkets.com.au.*

The Ginger Factory

AMUSEMENT PARK/WATER PARK | FAMILY | This legendary Queensland establishment goes far beyond its original factory-door sale of ginger. You can still take a 40-minute guided tour of the world's only publicly accessible ginger processing plant. A café and shop sell ginger in all forms—incorporated into jams, cookies, chocolates, ice cream, wine, and herbal products. There's also a train trip and a boat ride, a miniature rain forest for kids, a live beehive tour that includes a honey tasting, and plenty of shops to browse. Just up the road, you'll find the beautiful Yandina Historic House. ✉ *50 Pioneer Rd., Yandina* ☎ *07/5447–8431, 1800/067686* 🌐 *www.gingerfactory.com.au* 🎟 *Free entry; tours, demos, and rides from A$8.*

Restaurants

Maison de Provence

$ | BISTRO | The charming Maison de Provence is one part patisserie and one part French homewares shop. Find light meals like quiches, baguettes, and the delectable pastries and cakes, including tarte aux fruits, eclairs, and brioche. **Known for:** tempting range of chocolates and macarons made on the premises; traditional hot chocolate made with real chocolate flakes; out-of-the-way hidden gem. [$] *Average main: A$17* ✉ *9/13 Garnet St., Cooroy* ☎ *07/5472–0077* 🕒 *Closed Mon.*

★ Spirit House

$$$ | MODERN ASIAN | This iconic Yandina restaurant does a remarkable job re-creating contemporary Thai cuisine on Queensland soil. The menu, designed around plates to share, changes seasonally, with most ingredients sourced locally. **Known for:** signature whole crispy fish with tamarind-chili sauce; contemporary Thai food in a serene garden setting; knowledgeable, friendly service—all staff spend time in Thailand as part of their training. [$] *Average main: A$39* ✉ *20 Ninderry Rd., Yandina* ☎ *07/5446–8977* 🌐 *www.spirithouse.com.au* 🕒 *No dinner Sun.–Tues.*

Lady Elliot Island

80 km (50 miles) off the Queensland coast.

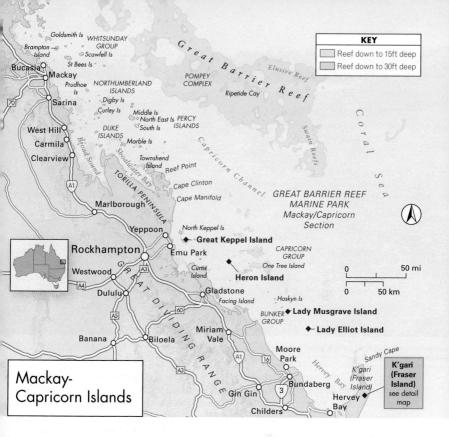

The map shows the Mackay-Capricorn Islands region.

KEY
- Reef down to 15ft deep
- Reef down to 30ft deep

Goldsmith Is, WHITSUNDAY GROUP, Brampton Island, Scawfell Is, St Bees Is, Bucasia, Mackay, Prudhoe Is, NORTHUMBERLAND ISLANDS, POMPEY COMPLEX, Elusive Reef, Sarina, Digby Is, Curley Is, Middle Is, North East Is, PERCY ISLANDS, South Is, Ripetide Cay, West Hill, DUKE ISLANDS, Carmila, Marble Is, Clearview, Townshend Island, Reef Point, Shoalwater Bay, Cape Clinton, Marlborough, TORILLA PENINSULA, Broad Sound, Cape Manifold, North Keppel Is, GREAT BARRIER REEF MARINE PARK, Mackay/Capricorn Section, Coral Sea, Swain Reefs, Capricorn Channel, Yeppoon, Great Keppel Island, CAPRICORN GROUP, Rockhampton, Emu Park, Curtis Island, One Tree Island, Heron Island, Westwood, GREAT DIVIDING RANGE, Dululu, Gladstone, Facing Island, Hoskyn Is, BUNKER GROUP, Banana, Biloela, Miriam Vale, Lady Musgrave Island, Lady Elliot Island, Moore Park, Sandy Cape, Hervey Bay, K'gari (Fraser Island), K'gari (Fraser Island) see detail map, Gin Gin, Bundaberg, Hervey Bay, Childers

Great Barrier Reef

0 — 50 mi
0 — 50 km

Mackay-Capricorn Islands

The closest Great Barrier Reef island to Brisbane, Lady Elliot Island is a highly protected coral cay approximately 85 km (53 miles) northeast of Bundaberg. The 111-acre island is a sanctuary for more than 1,200 species of marine life, which—along with its crystal clear waters and healthy coral—make it one of the top snorkeling and diving destinations on the reef.

GETTING HERE AND AROUND

Lady Elliot is the only Barrier Reef coral cay with its own airstrip. There is no boat access, but small chartered aircraft transfers are available from Bundaberg (30 minutes), Hervey Bay (40 minutes), Brisbane (80 minutes), and the Gold Coast (100 minutes). Plane size varies from 9-seater Britten Norman Islander to 19-seater Twin Otter. Strict luggage limits for both hand and checked baggage

allow 15 kilograms (33 pounds) per person for overnight guests. Excess luggage charges apply.

You can day-trip to Lady Elliot, too. The cost includes scenic flight, buffet lunch, reef walking, glass-bottom boat ride, snorkeling, and island tour. Tours require a minimum of two passengers.

AIRLINES Seair Pacific. ☎ 07/5599–4509, 1300/473247 ⊕ www.seairpacific.com. au.

◉ Sights

★ Lady Elliot Island

ISLAND | One of just six island resorts actually on the reef, Lady Elliot Island is a high-level Marine National Park Zone. Wildlife here easily outnumbers the guests (a maximum of 150 overnight guests and 100 day visitors are permitted

Lady Elliot Island is a highly protected coral cay

at any one time)—and that reality is underscored by the ammoniacal odor of hundreds of nesting seabirds and, in season, the sounds and sights of them courting, mating, and nesting.

Divers enjoy the easy access to the reef and the variety of diving sites around Lady Elliot. Fringed on all sides by coral reefs and blessed with a stunning white-sand, coral-strewn shore and bright azure waters, this oval isle seems to have been made for diving. There's a busy dive shop and a reef education center with marine-theme exhibits (plus an educational video library—great for rainy days). Inclement weather and choppy waves can lead to canceled dives and washed-out underwater visibility. When the waters are calm, you'll see turtles, morays, sharks, rays, and millions of tropical fish. Many divers visit Lady Elliot specifically to encounter the resident population of manta rays that feed off the coral.

From October to April, Lady Elliot becomes a busy breeding ground for crested and bridled terns, silver gulls, lesser frigate birds, and the rare red-tailed tropic bird. Between November and March, green and loggerhead turtles emerge from the water to lay their eggs; hatching takes place after January. During the hatching season, staff biologists host guided turtle-watching night hikes. From about July through October, pods of humpback whales are visible from the beachfront restaurant.

Lady Elliot is one of the few islands in the area where camping—albeit modified—is part of the resort, and a back-to-basics, eco-friendly philosophy dominates the accommodations. ⊠ *Lady Elliot Island* ⊕ *www.ladyelliot.com.au.*

🛏 Hotels

Lady Elliot Island Eco Resort
$$$$ | RESORT |FAMILY | All accommodation on the island is provided by Lady Elliot Island Eco Resort, where you'll feel more like a marine biologist at an island field camp than a tourist enjoying a luxury resort. **Pros:** eco-friendly and

unbeatable proximity to nature; plenty of activities; hearty meals. **Cons:** no Wi-Fi, TV, or phone reception in rooms; limited leisure options for rainy, nondiving days; minimum three-night stay over holidays. [$] *Rooms from: A$310* ✉ *Lady Elliot Island* ☎ *07/5536–3644 head office, 07/4156–4444 resort* 🌐 *www.ladyelliot.com.au* 🛏 *43 rooms* 🍴 *Free Breakfast.*

Lady Musgrave Island

40 km (25 nautical miles) north of Lady Elliot Island, 96 km (53 nautical miles) northeast of Bundaberg.

This island sits at the southern end of the Great Barrier Reef Marine Park, about 40 km (25 miles) north of Lady Elliot Island and 96 km (60 miles) northeast of Bundaberg. The cay, part of Capricornia Cays National Park, has a 2,945-acre surrounding reef, about one-third of which is a massive yet calm lagoon, a true coral cay of 39.5 acres. Like nearby Lady Elliot Island, it has some of the best diving and snorkeling in Queensland.

From October through April the island is a bird and turtle rookery, with black noddies, wedge-tailed shearwaters, bridled terns, more timid black-naped and roseate terns, and green and loggerhead turtles. There's also an abundance of flora, including casuarina and pisonia trees.

There is no permanent accommodation on the island; however, it is possible to camp at certain times of the year. Permits are required and there is a limit of 40 campers at any time. While there are a range of options for day trips to the island, campers are able to fully immerse themselves in the experience of living simply on a coral cay, amid the myriad sea life.

GETTING HERE AND AROUND

Lady Musgrave Barrier Reef Cruises

BOAT TOURS | Get out to the reef in 75 minutes and enjoy more than five hours on the reef, including a buffet lunch and a 90-minute stopover on the Outer Reef with this cruise company. From a pontoon in the vast deep-water coral lagoon off Lady Musgrave Island, you can snorkel, view 350 varieties of colorful live coral and 1,300 species of tropical fish year-round from a submersible or glass-bottom boat, take a guided island walk, see migrating whales in season, swim with turtles, or do some scuba diving or reef fishing before the boat cruises back to the mainland in the afternoon. Reef fishing and scuba diving are extra (for novice and certified divers, with or without gear). Cruises depart daily from the Town of 1770 at 8:30 am (board from 8 am). The day trip, including most extras, is A$210 per person (including an A$10 reef tax); campers staying on-island pay A$400 return. Lady Musgrave Barrier Reef Cruises also ferries campers to the island. Baggage is limited to 12 cubic feet per person, as space on board is tight. Campers must have a permit at time of boarding (A$5.95 per person, per night). In low season and bad weather, ring ahead to make sure the boat is leaving as scheduled. ✉ *Town of 1770 Marina, Captain Cook Dr., Seventeen Seventy* ☎ *07/4974–9227* 🌐 *www.lmcruises.com.au* 🎟 *A$190.*

Lady Musgrave Experience

BOAT TOURS | **FAMILY** | The Lady Musgrave Experience operates transfers and day tours from Bundaberg, a four-hour drive from Brisbane, aboard a three-level, high-speed luxury catamaran. It takes approximately 2½ hours to reach Lady Musgrave Island, and the full day tour includes morning tea and lunch, and activities include snorkeling, glass-bottom boat tours, and guided island walks. With a resident marine biologist on hand to answer all your questions about the Great Barrier Reef and its marine life, tours are educational and eco-conscious, as well as being a great day out. Tour price is A$218 (adults) and A$118 (children). Scuba diving is A$110 per dive. Return transfers for campers also available: A$440. ✉ *15–17 Marina Dr.* ☎ *07/4151–5225* ⊕ *ladymusgraveexperience.com.au.*

VISITOR INFORMATION
CONTACT Capricornia Cays National Park. ⊕ *findapark.npsr.qld.gov.au/parks/capricornia-cays.*

🏃 Activities

At the resort dive shop you can rent equipment and arrange dive courses to more than a dozen excellent sites, including Lighthouse Bommie, home to a 40-strong manta ray colony, and the Blow Hole and Hiro's Cave. Refresher pool dives, a shore snorkeling trip, and guided reef, nature, and historical walks are free for resort guests. Off-boat snorkeling and glass-bottom boat rides are A$36 for adults or A$22 for children. Boat dives and night dives range A$75–A$100, but all guests are entitled to one complimentary combined tour during their stay. Open-water certification courses cost A$650; "Discover Scuba Diving" short courses are A$195; and referral courses, available to those who've completed the classroom and pool portions of a certification course prior to arrival, are A$480.

Diving here is weather-dependent, so plan accordingly if you intend to do a dive course over multiple days. Special five-night packages, including buffet breakfast and dinner, a glass-bottom boat tour, snorkeling tours, and reef tax, start at A$740 per person. Flights are extra. Several other special deals and packages are available.

Heron Island

72 km (45 miles) northeast of the mainland port of Gladstone.

Most resort islands lie well inside the shelter of the distant reef, but Heron Island, some 72 km (45 miles) northeast of the mainland port of Gladstone, is actually part of the reef. The waters off this 40-acre island are spectacular, teeming with fish and coral, and ideal for snorkeling and scuba diving. The water is generally clearest in June and July and cloudiest during the rainy season, January and February. Heron Island operates on "island time"—an hour ahead of Australian Eastern Standard Time—and at its own leisurely pace. You won't find much in the way of nightlife, as the island's single resort accepts a cozy maximum of 250 people—and there are no day-trippers. But these might be reasons why you decide to come here.

GETTING HERE AND AROUND
Once in Gladstone, passengers can board the high-speed, 112-foot Heron Islander from the city's marina. The launch makes the two-hour run to Heron Island from Gladstone, on the Queensland coast, for A$64 one-way, departing at 2 pm daily and arriving at 4:30 pm. The return boat departs from Heron Island for the mainland at 10 am EST (9 am island time) and arrives at 12:30 pm. This can be a rough journey: take ginger or antinausea medicine a half hour before departure. A courtesy shuttle bus transfers guests from Gladstone Airport, leaving at 12:40 pm daily, and meets all afternoon boats. (Fly to Gladstone from Brisbane, Mackay, Rockhampton, Townsville, and Cairns with Qantas or Virgin Australia.) You can also arrange transfers to and from Gladstone Station; get here on Queensland Rail's fast *Tilt Train* or *Spirit of Queensland* from the north or south (⊕ *www.queenslandrail.com.au*).

Scuba diving off Heron Island

Australia by Seaplane
If you're short on time, Australia by Seaplane makes scenic, 25-minute flights to Heron Island from Gladstone from A$349 one-way, operating daily (except Christmas Day, Boxing Day, and New Year's Day). The baggage restriction is 33 pounds per person, with soft suitcases preferred. Lockup facilities for excess baggage are provided free. ✉ *Heron Island* ☎ *1800/875343, 0419/669575* 🌐 *www.australiabyseaplane.com.au.*

Marine Helicopter Charter
Daily transfers to Heron Island with Marine Helicopter Charter take 30 minutes each way and include expert commentary from your pilot. Baggage allowance is 33 pounds per person with soft luggage preferred. Adult tickets are A$449 each way if you book a return ticket. Single one-way tickets are A$530. ✉ *Heron Island* ☎ *07/4978–0129* 🌐 *www.heronislandhelicopters.com.*

🛏 Hotels

Heron Island Resort
$$$$ | **RESORT** | Set among palm trees and connected by sand paths, this secluded, eco-certified resort has a range of accommodation types, from the deluxe Beach House with private outdoor shower and beach boardwalk to the comparatively compact, garden-level Turtle Rooms. **Pros:** lots of activities; eco-friendly; under-12s stay and eat free (most packages). **Cons:** no mobile phone coverage; Wi-Fi is limited and costs extra; no TVs in rooms. [$] *Rooms from: A$347* ✉ *Heron Island* ☎ *1300/731551* 🌐 *www.heronisland.com* 🛏 *109 rooms* 🍴 *Free Breakfast.*

🏃 Activities

You can book snorkeling, scuba diving, and fishing excursions as well as turtle-watching tours and sunset cruises through Heron Island Marine Centre & Dive Shop. Snorkeling lessons are free, refresher dive courses from A$10. Snorkeling trips are A$50.

DIVING

Various diving options include a resort diving course for beginners, including training and one guided dive, for A$200 (subsequent dives, A$160). For certified divers it's A$75 per dive, and just A$55 per dive upward of five dives. Night dives, including light stick and flashlight, are A$100. Three-, five-, and seven-night dive packages include multiple dives throughout Heron and Wistari reefs, as well as accommodation, breakfast, buffet lunch, dinner, and all tanks and weights. Price is upon application. Half- and full-day dive boat charters are also available.

For all dives, prebooking is essential, and gear costs you extra. Children under 8 aren't permitted on snorkeling trips, under-12s can't go diving, and under-14s must be accompanied by an adult (and if diving, must be certified).

FISHING

Heron Island Marine Centre & Dive Shop
DIVING/SNORKELING | In addition to diving, snorkeling, and semisubmersible trips (A$50), Heron Island Marine Centre & Dive Shop runs three-hour fishing trips (A$180) and half-day (A$920) guided reef-fishing charters for up to 10 passengers, with gear, tackle, and optional stops for snorkeling. Toast the sunset on an hour-long wine-and-cheese cruise (A$60) or book a charter cruise for up to eight people (A$600–A$800). ✉ *Heron Island* ☎ *07/4972–9055* ⊕ *www.heronisland. com.*

SNORKELING AND SEMISUBMERSIBLE

Nondivers wanting to explore their underwater environs can take a half-day snorkeling tour of Heron and Wistari reefs, or an hour-long, naturalist-guided semisubmersible tour. Guided reef and birdlife walks, movies under the stars, and visits to the island's Marine Research Station are free.

Great Keppel Island

40 km (25 miles) from the Great Barrier Reef.

Positioned at the southern end of the Great Barrier Reef near the Tropic of Capricorn, idyllic Great Keppel Island boasts crystal clear waters, palm-fringed white sand beaches, scenic hiking trails, and some of the most diverse and unspoiled coral on the reef. The 593-acre island is also home to a rich diversity of flora and fauna, including more than 90 species of birds.

GETTING HERE AND AROUND
AIR TRAVEL

Low-cost carrier Virgin Australia flies to Rockhampton from Brisbane, with connections to all major Australian cities. Qantas has direct flights to Rockhampton from Brisbane, Townsville, and Mackay, connecting to other capitals.

AIRLINES Peace Aviation. ☎ *07/4927– 4355, 0429/616758* ⊕ *www.peaceaviation.com.* **Qantas.** ☎ *13–1313* ⊕ *www. qantas.com.au.* **Virgin Australia.** ☎ *13– 6789* ⊕ *www.virginaustralia.com.*

BOAT AND FERRY TRAVEL
Freedom Fast Cats
These ferries transfer guests to the island from Pier 1 at Rosslyn Bay Harbour, near Yeppoon (across the bay from the marina). Departures are early- to mid-morning (check schedules) daily, and return trips back to the mainland are early- to mid-afternoon. The cost is A$45 per adult, round-trip (A$30 for early crossing). Glass bottom boat tours (A$78 per adult) and various cruise packages are also available. Depending on the time of your flight arrival, you may need to stay overnight in Rockhampton or Yeppoon before and after your island stay. ✉ *Great Keppel Island* ☎ *07/4933–6888* ⊕ *www. freedomfastcats.com.*

Keppel Bay Marina

Keppel Bay Marina runs day cruises to secluded coves and beaches: choose a romantic sunset cruise (A$50) or a full-day cruise including snorkeling, fishing, beachcombing, and a full buffet lunch on board (A$115). Three-day adventure cruises (including accommodation), as well as private charters, are also available by request. ✉ *Great Keppel Island* ☎ *07/4933–6244* ⊕ *www.keppelbaymarina.com.au.*

● Sights

Great Keppel Island

BEACH—SIGHT | Although Great Keppel is large, at 8 km (5 miles) by 11 km (7 miles), it lies 40 km (25 miles) from the Great Barrier Reef, which makes for a long trip from the mainland. There's lots to do, with walking trails, 17 stunning safe swimming beaches, excellent coral gardens in many sheltered coves, plenty of friendly local wildlife, and dozens of beach and water-sports activities available. An abundance of bushwalking tracks allows visitors to explore the island's interior and access secluded beaches. The island has a marina and an airstrip, and a number of places to stay, including Great Keppel Island Holiday Village. ✉ *Great Keppel Island.*

⊨ Hotels

Great Keppel Island Holiday Village

$$ | RENTAL |FAMILY | Surrounded by stunning beaches and untouched bush, this is a modest, quiet alternative for travelers looking to get back to basics and enjoy the environs the "old-fashioned" way. **Pros:** beautiful and peaceful location; relaxed and friendly atmosphere; great value. **Cons:** patchy mobile phone coverage; no Wi-Fi or TV (except in Keppel House); some design getting quite dated. $ *Rooms from: A$200* ✉ *Great Keppel Island* ☎ *07/4939–8655, 1800/537735*

⊕ *www.gkiholidayvillage.com.au* ⇆ *44 rooms* ¶Ⓞ *No meals.*

☺ Activities

WATER SPORTS
Keppel Water Sports

WATER SPORTS | Based at the water-sports hut on Fisherman's Beach, this operator runs guided kayak and motorized canoe trips, and water taxi drop-offs to and pickups from surrounding beaches and islands. They also rent out water-sports equipment, including kayaks and paddleboards, and have banana and tube rides. ✉ *Fisherman's Beach* ⊕ *www.gkiholidayvillage.com.au.*

K'gari (Fraser Island)

200 km (125 miles) north of Brisbane

K'gari (Fraser Island), at 1,014 square km (391 square miles), is the largest of Queensland's islands and the most unusual. K'gari is the world's largest sand island—instead of coral reefs and coconut palms, it has wildflower-dotted meadows; 100-plus freshwater lakes; dense, tall stands of rain forest; towering dunes; sculpted, multicolor sand cliffs; up to 40,000 migratory shorebirds; and rare and endangered species including dugongs, turtles, Illidge's ant-blue butterfly, and eastern curlews—a lineup that won the island a place on UNESCO's World Heritage list.

The island has Aboriginal sites dating back more than a millennium. The surf fishing is legendary, and humpback whales and their calves winter in Hervey Bay between May and September.

Hervey Bay is the name given to the expanse of water between K'gari and the Queensland coast, and to four nearby coastal towns—Urangan, Pialba, Scarness, and Torquay—that have merged into a single settlement. Hervey Bay and Rainbow Beach are the main jumping-off

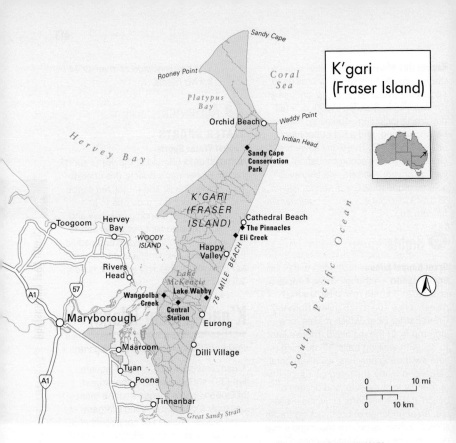

points for offshore excursions. (Maps and road signs usually refer to individual town names.)

GETTING HERE AND AROUND
AIR TRAVEL
Several direct air services on Jetstar, Qantas, and Virgin Australia connect Sydney and Fraser Coast (Hervey Bay) Airport. Bay 2 Dore shuttle buses link the airport to Urangan, meeting flights upon request.

AIRPORT CONTACT Fraser Coast (Hervey Bay) Airport. ✉ *Don Adams Dr., Hervey Bay* ☎ *07/4194–8100* ⊕ *www.fraser-coastairport.com.au.*

SHUTTLE Bay 2 Dore Airport Shuttle. ☎ *07/4125–3983, 0417/637447* ⊕ *www. bay2dore.com.au.*

BOAT AND FERRY TRAVEL
Numerous vehicular ferries service Fraser Island from Rainbow Beach and Hervey Bay. Manta Ray Fraser Island Barges runs a regular service from 6 am to 5:30 pm between Inskip Point, near Rainbow Beach, and Hook Point at the island's southern end. The company's two to three barges make up to 40 round-trips daily, so if you miss one barge, the next will be along soon. Buy tickets online (recommended) or as you board.

Fraser Island Barges' *Fraser Venture* makes the half-hour trip between River Heads, 20 minutes' drive south of Hervey Bay, and Wanggoolba Creek, opposite Eurong Bay Resort on the island's west coast, three times a day. The Kingfisher Bay Passenger and Vehicle Ferry also connects River Heads with Kingfisher

Bay Resort in 50 minutes up to six times a day.

BOAT AND FERRY CONTACTS Fraser Island Barges. ☎ *07/4194–9300, 1800/227437* ⊕ *www.fraserislandferry. com.au.* **Kingfisher Bay Ferry.** ☎ *07/4194– 9300, 1800/227437* ⊕ *www.kingfisher- bay.com/getting-here/fraser-island-ferry. html/* **Manta Ray Fraser Island Barges.** ☎ *07/5486–3935, 0418/872599* ⊕ *www. mantarayfraserislandbarge.com.au.*

CAR AND BUGGY TRAVEL
K'gari's east coast favors two Australian passions: beaches and vehicles. Unrestricted access has made this coast a giant sandbox for four-wheel-drive vehicles, busiest in school-holiday periods.

The southernmost tip of K'gari is just more than 200 km (125 miles) north of Brisbane. The simplest access is via barge from Rainbow Beach or Hervey Bay, 90 km (56 miles) farther north. For Rainbow Beach, take the Bruce Highway toward Gympie, then follow signs to Rainbow Beach. For Hervey Bay, head to Maryborough, then follow the signs to River Heads.

Every vehicle entering the island by barge from the mainland must have a one-month Vehicle Access Permit (A$51.60). To obtain these and island camping permits (A$6.55 per person, per night), contact QPWS ⊕ *www.nprsr.qld.gov.au.*

You can rent four-wheel-drive vehicles from Aussie Trax 4WD Hire at Kingfisher Bay Resort and Village for upward of A$91 per person per day, or from various rental companies at Urangan and Hervey Bay Airport for considerably less.

Four-wheel-drive rentals may be cheaper on the mainland, but factoring in the ferry ticket makes rental on-island a viable option. Most commodities, including gas, are pricier on-island.

Wet weather and sandy surfaces can make island driving challenging and hazardous. Consult QPWS's website

Getting Help 👁

While there is a permanent paramedic on the island, K'gari does not have a resident doctor. Emergency medical assistance can be obtained at the ranger stations in Eurong, Waddy Point, and Dundubara, but these have variable hours—if no answer, phone the base station at Nambour on the mainland. Kingfisher Bay Resort has first-aid facilities and resident nursing staff.

for detailed information on safe driving and local hazards. Basic mechanical assistance and tow-truck services are available from Eurong. Orchid Beach has emergency towing only. If you can't get the mechanical assistance you need, phone Eurong Police.

CAR RENTAL Budget Car Rental. ⊠ *Hervey Bay Airport, Airport Terminal, Hervey Bay* ☎ *07/4125–6906* ⊕ *www.budget.com.au.*

ESSENTIALS
VEHICLE PERMITS Queensland National Parks and Wildlife Service. ☎ *13–7468 info and permits* ⊕ *www.npsr.qld.gov.au.*

VISITOR INFORMATION Hervey Bay Visitor Information Centre. ⊠ *227 Maryborough-Hervey Bay Rd., Hervey Bay* ☎ *1800/811728* ⊕ *www.visitfrasercoast. com.*

TOURS
Air Fraser Island
AIR EXCURSIONS | Air Fraser Island runs day trips, transfers, and scenic and whale-watching flights (in season) from Hervey Bay, using the pristine beaches of Fraser Island as its landing strip. Overnight packages, including 4WD rentals, are also available. ⊠ *Fraser Island* ☎ *07/4125–3600* ⊕ *www.airfraserisland. com.au* 🚗 *From A$100.*

Fraser Explorer Tours

ADVENTURE TOURS | This group operates one- and two-day 4WD tours across World Heritage-Listed Fraser Island, taking in its pristine beaches and colored sands, fresh water lakes, verdant forests, and abundant marine life. Departing both Hervey Bay and Rainbow Beach, tours include barge transfers, meals, National Park fees, and audio guides in various languages. ⊠ *1 Eastern St.* ☎ *07/4194–9222, 1800/678431* ⊕ *www.fraserexplorertours.com.au* ✉ *From A$210.*

★ **Nomads Fraser Island**

GUIDED TOURS | Take a two- or three-day 4WD tour of the island led by experienced, local guides. ECO-certified Nomads Fraser Island Tours share the incredible natural attractions of the island while also providing a background on the legends, stories, and beliefs of the Butchulla people. Enjoy bushwalks, swims, and food and lodging while also learning which sites on the island were used for Butchulla ceremonies, rituals, gatherings, child birth, fishing, and disputes. ⊠ *Fraser Island* ☎ *07/3041–3256* ⊕ *nomadsfraserisland.com.*

◉ Sights

Highlights of a drive along the east coast, which is known as Seventy-Five Mile Beach for its sheer distance, include **Eli Creek,** a great freshwater swimming hole. North of this popular spot lies the rusting hulk of the *Maheno,* half buried in the sand, a roost for seagulls and a prime hunting ground for anglers when the tailor are running. Once a luxury passenger steamship that operated between Australia and New Zealand (and served as a hospital ship during World War I), it was wrecked during a cyclone in 1935 as it was being towed to Japan to be sold for scrap metal. North of the wreck are the **Pinnacles**—dramatic, deep-red cliff formations. About 20 km (12 miles) south of Eli Creek, and surrounded by massive

sand-blow (or dune), is **Lake Wabby,** the deepest of the island's lakes.

Note that swimming in the ocean off the island is not recommended because of the rough conditions and sharks that hunt close to shore. Stick to the inland lakes.

K'gari (Fraser Island), Sandy Cape Conservation Park

NATIONAL/STATE PARK | This park covers the top third of K'gari. Beaches around Indian Head are known for their shell middens—shell heaps that were left behind after Aboriginal feasting. The head's name is another kind of relic: Captain James Cook saw Aborigines standing on the headland as he sailed past, and he therefore named the area after inhabitants he believed to be "Indians." Farther north, past Waddy Point, is one of K'gari's most magnificent variations on sand: wind and time have created enormous dunes. Nearby at Orchid Beach are a series of bubbling craters known as the Champagne Pools. ⊠ *Fraser Island* ☎ *13–7468* ⊕ *www.npsr.qld.gov.au/parks/fraser.*

Wanggoolba Creek

BODY OF WATER | A boardwalk heads south from Central Station to Wanggoolba Creek, a favorite spot for photographers. The little stream snakes through a green palm forest, trickling over a bed of white sand between clumps of rare angiopteris fern. The 1 km (½-mile) circuit takes 30 minutes to an hour. ⊠ *Fraser Island.*

⌨ Hotels

★ **Kingfisher Bay Resort**

$$$ | **RESORT** | **FAMILY** | This stylish, high-tech marriage of glass, stainless steel, dark timber, and corrugated iron nestles in tree-covered dunes on the island's west coast. **Pros:** terrific facilities, tours, and activities; eco-friendly; excellent location. **Cons:** many rooms in need of updating; west-coast beaches unsuitable for 4WD vehicles; charge for Wi-Fi.

Camping on Fraser Island 🛏️

The Queensland Parks and Wildlife Service manages the island and maintains ranger bases at Dundubara and Eurong. You can pitch a tent anywhere you don't see a "no camping" sign; there are four main public campgrounds—Central Station, Dundubara, Lake Boomanjin, and Waddy Point—though all sites on the Island require you to book your permit in advance. These campgrounds have fenced sites to protect from dingoes (advised if you have kids under 14), toilet blocks, drinking water, hot

showers (some coin-operated), gas grills, phones, and other amenities. There are also smaller designated camping areas along Fraser Island's Great Walk, and a number of established beach campsites, all run by The Queensland Parks and Wildlife Service. They have toilet blocks, picnic tables, and walking trails. Most lack drinking water, so bring plenty with you. Because the entire island is a World Heritage site, permits for camping (A$6.55 per person, per night) are required.

$ Rooms from: A$269 ✉ North White Cliffs, 75 Mile Beach ☎ 07/4120–3333, 1800/072555 ⊕ www.kingfisherbay.com ⇥ 260 rooms, 184 beds in lodges (for 18–35s) ⍥ No meals.

🏃 Activities

FISHING
Hervey Bay Fishing Charters
FISHING | This family-run business caters to all levels of experience with its half- and full-day fishing trips through the waters off Fraser Island. Morning tea, lunch, refreshments, bait, tackle, and fish cleaning is all included. Private and overnight charters are also available upon request. ✉ 51 Tristania Crescent, Urangan ☎ 07/4125–3958, 0427/621623 ⊕ www.herveybayfishingcharters.com.au ✉ From A$150.

Offshore fishing, K'gari (Fraser Island)
FISHING | All freshwater fish are protected on Fraser Island, so you can't fish in lakes or streams, but just offshore is one of Australia's richest, most diverse fishing areas, with whiting, flathead, trevally, red emperor, snapper, sea perch, coronation trout, cod, and, in summer, mackerel,

cobia, amberjack, and more. This is partly due to the diversity of habitat; choose between estuary, surf beach, reef, sport, and game fishing. On reef-fishing trips dolphins are commonly sighted, as are whales in season.

When angling off Fraser Island beaches and jetties, follow QPWS guidelines. To discourage dingoes and other undesirable visitors, clean fish away from campsites and dispose of scraps carefully (bury fish scraps at least a foot below the tide line). Some beaches are closed to fishing during August and September, and bag and size limits apply to some species; for details, go to ⊕ www.npsr.qld.gov.au. ✉ Fraser Island ⊕ www.nprsr.qld.gov.au.

HIKING
Central Station
HIKING/WALKING | The island's excellent network of walking trails converges at Central Station, a former logging camp at the center of the island. Services here are limited to a map board, parking lot, and campground. It's a promising place for spotting dingoes. Comparative isolation has meant that K'gari's dingoes are the most purebred in Australia. They're

also wild animals, so remember: don't feed them, watch from a distance, don't walk alone after dark, store food and dispose of rubbish carefully, and keep a close eye on children, especially between late afternoon and early morning.

Most of the island's well-marked trails are sandy tracks. Guides advise wearing sturdy shoes, wearing sunscreen, and carrying first-aid supplies and drinking water on all walks. ⊠ *Central Station.*

Pile Valley

HIKING/WALKING | One trail from Central Station leads through rain forest—growing, incredibly enough, straight out of the sand—to Pile Valley, which has a stand of giant satinay trees. Allow two hours to walk the full 4½-km (2¼-mile) circuit. ⊠ *Fraser Island.*

SWIMMING
Lake McKenzie

SWIMMING | The center of Fraser Island is a quiet, natural garden of paperbark swamps, giant satinay and brush box forests, wildflower heaths, and 40 freshwater lakes. The spectacularly clear Lake McKenzie, ringed by a beach of incandescent white sand, is arguably the most stunning of the lakes and is the perfect place for a refreshing swim, day or night. ⊠ *Lake McKenzie.*

THE GREAT BARRIER REEF

Updated by
Skye Gilkeson

Sights	Restaurants	Hotels	Shopping	Nightlife
★★★★★	★★★★★	★★★★★	★★★☆☆	★★★★☆

WELCOME TO THE GREAT BARRIER REEF

TOP REASONS TO GO

★ **Reef Explorations:** There are thousands of spectacular dive sites scattered along the coral spine of the Great Barrier Reef.

★ **Wildlife Watching:** Flora and fauna on the islands themselves can be fascinating: rain forests, hills and rocky areas, and postcard-perfect beaches provide diverse habitat.

★ **Cultural Immersion:** The Kuku Yalanji people have lived in the area between Port Douglas and Cookdown for millennia. A highlight of visiting the region is experiencing this unique landscape from the perspective of its traditional owners.

★ **Ancient Rain Forest:** The UNESCO World Heritage–listed Daintree rain forest is a rich and ancient ecosystem in which you'll find sustainable resorts, jungle zip lines, and deserted beaches.

★ **Outback Adventures:** West of Port Douglas lie vast tracts of savannah dotted with termite mounds and teeming with kangaroos, wallabies, reptiles, and birds.

A map linking all of northern Queensland's coastal ports and offshore resorts from the Whitsundays north to Lizard Island would look like a lace-up boot 1,600 km (1,000 miles) long. However, you'd only see less than half the reef, which extends south to Lady Elliot Island and as far north as the near-roadless wilderness of Cape York and the shores of Papua New Guinea.

1 Cairns. A "tourist-town" and perfect base for exploring the Great Barrier Reef.

2 Palm Cove. A beachside suburb of Cairns and idyllic base for exploring Northern Queensland.

3 Port Douglas. It's all about rainforest and reef here as well as Four Mile Beach and a lively yet laidback little town.

4 Mossman. A sugarcane town at the foot of the mountains and stop off on the way to Mossman Gorge and Daintree.

5 Cape Tribulation. The activities and accommodations base for the spectacular Daintree National Park.

6 Cooktown. At the edge of wilderness, with pristine beaches, magical views, and nearby Aboriginal rock art sites.

7 Airlie Beach. A lively town and the gateway to the Whitsunday Islands and the Great Barrier Reef.

8 Long Island. Mostly national parkland with great trails, excellent snorkeling, and some peaceful retreats.

9 Hamilton Island. Buzzing with activity but also offering beautiful beaches and views.

10 Orpheus Island. A national park and a true Great Barrier Reef island with unspoiled beaches and reefs.

11 Bedarra Island. A tiny and quiet island with dense rain forest and luxe hotel resort.

12 Fitzroy Island. A popular day trip from Cairns with extensive fringing coral reef and access to water activities.

13 Lizard Island. Excellent walking trails, spectacular views, and luxe beachfront accommodations.

14 Townsville. A lively coastal city with turn-of-the-20th-century colonial structures.

15 Magnetic Island. Twenty-three island beaches, nine offshore shipwrecks, and a haven for wildlife.

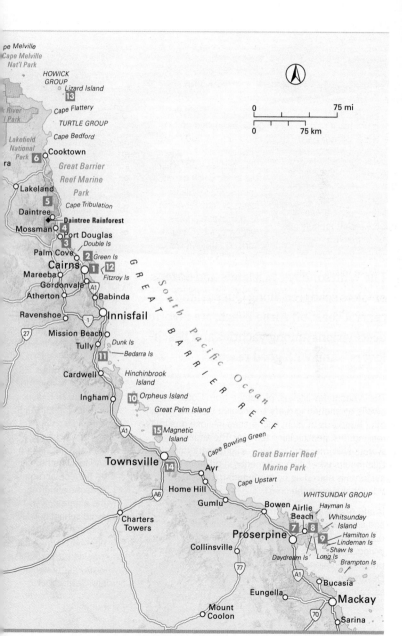

SAILING THE WHITSUNDAY ISLANDS

The Whitsundays, 74 islands and dozens of islets scattered along Queensland's central coast off Airlie Beach, are favorite destinations among yachties and beach-lovers—and with good reason.

The Whitsunday islands, protected from Coral Sea swells by sheltering reefs and cooled by trade winds, offer hundreds of yacht anchorages in close proximity, making this ideal cruising territory. The aquamarine waters shimmer and sparkle—a light-scattering effect that results when fine sediment run-off from river systems is stirred up by the 3- to 5-meter (10- to 16-foot) tides that sweep the coast.

Island resorts offer safe moorings for passing yachts, and an array of water sports and facilities. Farther out, on the Barrier Reef, you'll find fine snorkeling, diving, and fishing sites. Most Whitsunday Islands are unspoiled national parks; just a few—Hayman, Hamilton, Daydream, and South Long—have resorts.

WHEN TO GO

With a climate moderated by cooling trade winds, the Whitsundays are typically balmy year-round, though summer days can sometimes exceed 100°F. Over winter (June through August) it's warm and sunny by day and cool at night. Spring and fall weather can be perfect, and these seasons are often the quietest, if you avoid school holidays. Migrating southern right and humpback whales traverse these waters between July and September.

WHERE CAN I FIND …

Underwater adventure? Most Whitsunday resorts have dedicated dive shops offering scuba and snorkeling lessons and rental gear; all either run or can organize day trips to dive and snorkeling spots nearby. Highlights include Hardy Reef and the iconic Heart Reef, where a purpose-built pontoon floats in sheltered waters teeming with tropical fish, turtles, and rays. Not keen to get wet? Take a semisubmersible coral-viewing tour, guided reef walk, or scenic heli-flight. Sheltered coves and coral-fringed beaches around many Whitsunday islands also offer good snorkeling.

Luxury? At Qualia, Hamilton Island's most lavish accommodation, sleek suites have infinity pools and alfresco areas, artfully lighted after dark, and fine food and wine brought in from Hamilton's best restaurants. Bedarra, Orpheus, and Lizard Island resorts serve up gourmet meals and exclusive accommodations.

Family-friendliness? Daydream and Hamilton islands have dedicated kids' clubs, playgrounds, and myriad kid-at-heart features and activities. At Fitzroy Island Resort, children's activity programs mean parents can relax or join in the fun, while nature-based activities on Lizard Island are great for older kids.

White beaches? Whitehaven Beach on Whitehaven Island, the largest of Queensland's tropical Whitsunday Islands, offers those quintessential bleach-white, pure silica sands contrasting against aquamarine waters that vacation dreams are made of. Get here by seaplane or boat from Airlie Beach or charter your own yacht and drop anchor here for a few days.

TOP REASONS TO GO

Aquatic Playground
This is a snorkelers' and divers' paradise and one of the world's top sailing and cruising areas. It's also great for kayaking, windsurfing, and paragliding—and most resorts include the use of nonmotorized water sports equipment in their rates.

Tropical Paradise
Enjoy a mild climate and warm, clear waters whatever the season, plus beautiful fine white-sand beaches.

Gourmet Destination
Several Whitsunday and Barrier Reef island resorts offer cuisine to rival that of high-end city establishments. Island-resort food runs the gamut from four-star gourmet fare to regional cuisine presented with site-specific twists.

Resort Variety
You can divide your time easily between luxurious, leisurely resorts (such as Elysian Retreat on South Long Island) and an activity-oriented isle (such as Hamilton).

OUTDOOR ADVENTURES IN DAINTREE

Cape Tribulation, Daintree National Park is an ecological wonderland. Here you can see several of the world's most ancient plants and some of Australia's rarest creatures, protected by the Daintree's traditional owners, the Eastern Kuku Yalanji, for thousands of years.

A two-hour drive north of Cairns, Daintree is the oldest tropical rainforest in the world. The park extends over approximately 22,000 acres, although the entire Wet Tropics region—which stretches from Townsville to Cooktown and covers 1,200 square km (463 square miles)—was declared a UNESCO World Heritage site in 1988. Within it, experts have identified several species of angiosperms, the most primitive flowering plants in existence, many of which are found nowhere else on the planet. Stand in awe under the branches of the Zamia Fern, which has an underground trunk system evolved in defense against dinosaurs.

WHEN TO GO

Sunny days, comfortably cool nights, no stingers in the ocean and mud-free rain forest: "the Dry" season is the most pleasant time to visit.

"The Wet"—roughly November through April—can be wonderful, too: foliage is lush and buds turn to hothouse blooms. Drawbacks include occasional flash flooding and high humidity.

Spring and late fall can be a good compromise: the weather—and the water—are typically warm and clear, and activities are less heavily booked.

A SACRED SITE

Its traditional custodians are the Eastern Kuku Yalanji, a peaceable people who've been coexisting with and subsisting on the forest's abundant flora and fauna for tens of thousands of years. Designating five rather than four seasons in a year, the Eastern Kuku Yalanji used changes in weather and growth cycles to guide hunting and foraging expeditions into the rain forest: when the *jun jun* (blue ginger) came into fruit, they'd catch *diwan* (Australian brush-turkey); when *jilngan* (mat grass) flowered, they'd collect *jarruka* (orange-footed scrubfowl) eggs; and year-round, they'd track tree-dwelling animals—*yawa* (possum), *kambi* (flying fox), and *murral* (tree kangaroo). Even today, members of the Kuku Yalanji can tell you which local plants can be eaten, used as medicines, and made into utensils, weapons, and shelter.

The Daintree's indigenous inhabitants believe many of the area's natural sites have spiritual significance, attributing particular power to Wundu (Thornton Peak), Manjal Dimbi (Mt. Demi), Wurrmbu (The Bluff), and Kulki (Cape Tribulation). Dozens of spots in the rain forest—waterfalls, crags, peaks, and creeks—are deemed by the Kuku Yalanji to have spiritual, healing, or regenerative powers. Take a walk with one of the area's traditional custodians to get an intimate, intriguing perspective on this extraordinary terrain.

Various indigenous-guided tours and experiences in the Daintree area focus on bush tucker and medicines, wildlife and hunting techniques, culture, history, and ritual. A waterhole just behind Daintree Eco Lodge & Spa is deemed a site of special significance for women: a dip in its healing waters is a female-only ritual.

TOP REASONS TO GO

Animals. Watch for the rare Bennett's tree kangaroo, believed to have evolved from possums; the endangered, spotted-tailed quoll, a marsupial carnivore; a giant white-tailed rat (prone to raiding campsites); and the Daintree River ringtail possum, found only around Thornton Peak and the upper reaches of the Daintree and Mossman rivers.

Birds. Daintree National Park shelters hundreds of bird species: azure kingfishers swoop on crabs in the creeks, white-rumped swiftlets dart above the canopy. The pied imperial pigeon flies south from Papua New Guinea to breed here—as does the glorious buff-breasted paradise kingfisher, distinguished by its orange underbelly, blue wings, and long white tail. Year-round, you'll see orange-footed scrubfowl foraging or building gigantic leaf-litter nest-mounds. If you're very lucky, you might even spot the 6-foot-tall, flightless southern cassowary.

A maze of 3,000 individual reefs and 900 islands stretching for 2,300 km (1,429 miles), the Great Barrier Reef is among the world's most spectacular natural attractions. Known as Australia's "Blue Outback," the reef is a haven for thousands of species of marine creatures as well as turtles and birds. Most visitors explore this section of Australia from one of the dozen-plus resorts strung along the coasts of islands in the southern half of the marine park, most of them in or north of the Whitsunday Islands group. Although most Barrier Reef islands are closer to the mainland than they are to the spectacular outer reef, all island resorts offer (or can organize) boat excursions to various outer-reef sites.

The Great Barrier Reef system began to form approximately 6,000–8,000 years ago, say marine scientists. It's composed of individual reefs and islands, which lie to the east of the Coral Sea and extend south into the Pacific Ocean. Most of the reef is about 65 km (40 miles) off the Queensland coast, although some parts extend as far as 300 km (186 miles) offshore. Altogether, it covers an area bigger than Great Britain, forming the largest living feature on Earth and the only one visible from space. The reef was established as a marine park in 1975, and the United Nations designated the Great Barrier Reef a World Heritage site in 1981. Strict legislation was enacted in 2004, prohibiting fishing along most of the reef—a further attempt to protect the underwater treasures of this vast, delicate ecosystem. Any visitor over the age of four must pay a A$6.50 per day Environmental Management Charge ("reef tax") to support ongoing efforts to preserve the reef.

MAJOR REGIONS

A laid-back tropical tourist hub built around a busy marina and swimming lagoon, **Cairns** bristles with hotels, tour agencies, dive-cruise boats, and travelers en route to the rain forest and reef. It has some fine retail stores and markets, plus an extensive waterfront park and entertainment precinct.

Along the pristine coastline **north of Cairns** the Captain Cook Highway runs from Cairns to **Mossman,** a relatively civilized stretch punctuated by charming villages and tourist towns, including **Palm Cove,** with its European Riviera ambience, and bustling **Port Douglas,** with its sparkling marina, sprawling resorts, and hip café scene. North of the Daintree River, wildlife parks and sunny coastal villages fade into sensationally wild terrain. UNESCO World Heritage–listed wilderness extends to **Cape Tribulation** and beyond. If you came to Australia seeking high-octane sun, pristine coral cays, steamy jungles filled with exotic birdcalls and riotous vegetation, and a languid beachcomber lifestyle, head for the coast between Daintree and Cooktown, a frontier destination that tacks two days onto your itinerary. Here you'll find few services but some terrific, eco-friendly rain-forest retreats.

Discovered in 1770 by Captain James Cook of the HMS *Endeavour,* the glorious **Whitsunday Islands**—a group of 74 islands situated within 161 km (100 miles) of each other and around 50 km (31 miles) from Shute Harbour, just off the mid-north-Queensland coast—today lure holidaymakers with world-class water sports, sheltered yacht anchorages, and resorts catering to every taste. The Whitsundays are a favorite sailing destination and an easy-access base

from which to explore the midsection of the Great Barrier Reef. Only a few of the islands have resorts; others serve as destinations for day trips, beach time, and bushwalks, or simply as backdrop at scenic moorings. Shute Harbor is the principal mainland departure point, but **Airlie Beach,** the closest mainland town, buzzes with backpackers, who flock to its man-made lagoon, markets, bars, and budget digs. Well-heeled travelers might prefer the boutique retreats and resorts that hug the hillsides above the main drag. Islands include **Hamilton Island** and **Long Island.** Note that Cyclone Debbie did extensive damage to the islands in 2017. They underwent complete reconstruction and some, including Hayman Island, will reopen in mid-2019.

North Coast Islands. The upscale, eco-conscious boutique resort on **Orpheus Island** and **Bedarra Island,** off Ingham and Mission Beach, are tailored to foodies and honeymooners, reclusive VIPs, and nature-loving travelers. **Fitzroy Island** and **Lizard Island,** off Cairns, offer ready access to world-class dive and game-fishing sites

Townsville and Magnetic Island. Regional city **Townsville** has gracious heritage buildings, excellent museums and marine centers, and a well-maintained waterfront with a man-made swimming lagoon. Townsville, along with adjacent twin city Thuringowa make up Australia's largest tropical city, with a combined population of just under 200,000. It's the commercial capital of the north, and a major center for education, scientific research, and defense. Spread along the banks of Ross Creek and around the pink granite outcrop of Castle Hill, Townsville is a pleasant city of palm-fringed malls, historic colonial buildings, extensive parkland, and gardens. It's also the stepping-off point for offshore **Magnetic Island,** a popular holiday spot, with high-end and budget accommodations and an array of aquatic activities, including sea kayaking and scuba diving.

Planning

WHEN TO GO

The bulk of the Great Barrier Reef islands lie north of the tropic of Capricorn in a monsoonal climate zone. In the hot, wet season (roughly December through April), expect tropical downpours that can limit outdoor activities and mar underwater visibility.

The warm days, clear skies, and pleasantly cool nights of the dry season, especially June through August, are ideal for traveling around and above Cairns. In the Whitsundays, some winter days may be too cool for swimming and nights can be chilly (pack a sweater and long pants).

The islands are warm, even in winter; during the summer months, temperatures regularly top 35°C (95°F), and the farther north you go, the hotter it gets. The water temperature is mild to cool year-round; however, in jellyfish season (typically, November through May), you'll need to wear a full-body stinger suit to swim anywhere but within patrolled, netted areas.

PLANNING YOUR TIME

Most visitors to the Great Barrier Reef combine stays on one or more islands with time in Queensland's coastal towns and national parks. With a week or more, you could stay at two very different Barrier Reef island resorts: perhaps at an activities-packed Whitsundays resort and one of the more remote northerly islands, allowing a day or two to travel between them. If you want to resort-hop, opt for the Whitsundays, where island resorts lie in relatively close proximity and are well serviced by water and air transport.

If you have limited time, take a boat from Cairns or Port Douglas to a pontoon on the outer reef for a day on the water. A helicopter flight back to the mainland will give you an exhilarating aerial view of the reef and its islands. Alternatively, catch an early boat from Cairns to Fitzroy Island or from Shute Harbour to Daydream Island. Spend a couple of hours snorkeling, take a walk around, then relax on a quiet beach or in the resort bar.

GETTING HERE AND AROUND
AIR TRAVEL
Jetstar, Virgin Australia, and Qantas have daily direct flights linking capital cities around Australia to Cairns Airport (which also handles international flights). These airlines also have flights to Townsville, Whitsundays Coast (Proserpine), Hamilton Island, and Mackay airports, linking with east-coast capitals and major regional cities throughout Queensland. From these hubs, regular boat and charter air services are available to most of the Great Barrier Reef resorts. Generally, island charter flights are timed to connect with domestic flights, but double-check. *For information about reaching the islands, see Getting Here and Around under each island's heading.*

CONTACTS Airport Connections. ✉ *14 Comport St., Cairns* ☎ *07/4049–2244* ⊕ *www.tnqshuttle.com.* **Cairns Airport.** ✉ *Airport Ave., Cairns Airport, Cairns QLD 4870, Aeroglen* ☎ *07/4080–6703* ⊕ *www.cairnsairport.com.au.*

BOAT TRAVEL
Usually, island launches are timed to connect with charter flights from island or mainland airports, but do ask. Crossings can be choppy; take ginger tablets for motion sickness ahead of time. If you're based on the mainland or in a hurry, many operators run day trips out to the reef and resort islands.

Several operators provide skipper-yourself (bareboat) and crewed charters to explore the Whitsundays. Almost all have five-day minimum charter periods; most offer discounts for multiday hires and optional extras such as catering. Packages start from around A$1,200 per person, per night, but can be several times that on crewed or luxury vessels.

BUS TRAVEL

Long-distance buses are an economical but often cramped way to travel along the North Queensland coast; don't expect to get much sleep on board. Shuttle buses transfer visitors from regional airports, Cairns, and beaches and towns to as far north as Cape Tribulation. They link airports, railway stations, and local towns to island ferry services departing from Mission Beach, Airlie Beach, and Shute Harbour. Hotel pickups are usually available; call ahead to confirm.

CAR TRAVEL

If you're visiting several North Queensland destinations, it may be simplest to drive. Most popular North Queensland routes are paved, though roads may be flooded in the wet season. A 4WD vehicle is advised. Leave extra time if you're crossing the Daintree River or driving between Port Douglas and Cairns—peak-season traffic and roadwork may create congestion. If you're heading farther north, fill up with gas at or before Wonga Beach, and carry water, tools, and supplies. Past this point, services are infrequent, and gas and goods can be pricey.

RESTAURANTS

Typically, restaurants on Barrier Reef islands are part of each island's main resort, so many resorts' rates include some or all meals. Some larger resorts have a range of restaurants, with formal dining rooms, outdoor barbecues, and seafood buffets; some have premium dining options for which you pay extra. On the mainland you'll find plenty of casual, open-air restaurants, serving mainly Modern Australian–style meals that showcase seafood and regional produce. With a few notable exceptions, Cairns, Palm Cove, and Port Douglas are your best bets for upscale dining.

HOTELS

Most inhabited islands have just one main resort, typically offering a range of lodging types and prices. Choose island destinations based on your budget and the kind of vacation you want—active or relaxed, sociable or quiet, or a mix. Offerings range from luxurious enclaves with upscale facilities (Lizard, Orpheus, Bedarra, Hayman islands) to small, eco-focused retreats (Long Island) to activity-packed, family-friendly resorts (Long, Daydream islands and Fitzroy islands). The more rustic, remote resorts may lack modern conveniences such as telephones, televisions, and Internet access. Even on some Barrier Reef resorts close to the mainland, Internet connections can be slow and mobile phone coverage limited or nonexistent, and critters may infiltrate your room. *Hotel reviews have been shortened. For full information, visit Fodors.com.*

What It Costs in Australian Dollars

	$	$$	$$$	$$$$
RESTAURANTS				
	under A$36	A$36–A$45	A$46–A$65	over A$65
HOTELS				
	under A$201	A$201–A$300	A$301–A$450	over A$450

HEALTH AND SAFETY

You'll find large, well-equipped hospitals in Cairns, Townsville, and Mackay; doctors and medical centers in Port Douglas and Airlie Beach, and nearby towns. Emergency services are scarce between the Daintree River and Cooktown. Island resort front-desk staff typically handle emergencies and can summon doctors and aerial ambulance services. Remote islands have "flying doctor" kits and Hamilton Island has its own doctors.

Avoid midday rays, even in winter, and wear a hat and SPF15-plus sunscreen to prevent sunburn. Rehydrate often and take it easy in the heat.

Avoid touching coral: it is easily damaged, and can cut and sting. Clean cuts thoroughly, scrubbing with a brush and flushing the affected area with saline solution. Toxic and stinging jellyfish frequent waters off the mainland and some Barrier Reef islands over the warmer months. Avoid the ocean at these times, unless you're wearing a stinger suit. If in doubt, ask a local.

Mosquitoes, midges, and leeches can be a problem in wet summer months. Wear insect repellent to avoid being bitten; check extremities, especially between your toes, after walking in damp, forested areas, and remove leeches by applying a flame or salt.

Estuarine crocodiles live in rivers and coastal waters along the North Queensland coast and on some Barrier Reef islands. Don't swim where crocs live (ask a local), especially in breeding season, September to April—and never dangle your limbs over the sides of boats.

Cairns

Tourism is the lifeblood of Cairns (pronounced *Caans*). The city makes a good base for exploring the wild top half of Queensland, and international travelers use it as a jumping-off point for activities such as scuba diving and snorkeling trips to the Barrier Reef, as well as boating, fishing, parasailing, scenic flights, and rain-forest treks.

It's a tough environment, with intense heat and fierce wildlife. Along with wallabies and gray kangaroos in the savanna and tree kangaroos in the rain forest, you'll find stealthy saltwater crocodiles, venomous snakes, and jellyfish so deadly they put the region's stunning beaches off-limits to swimmers for nearly half the year. Yet despite this formidable setting,

Cairns and tropical North Queensland are far from intimidating places. The people are warm and friendly, the sights spectacular, and—at the right time of year—the beachside lounging is world-class.

GETTING HERE AND AROUND
AIR TRAVEL
Cairns Airport is a major international gateway, and a connection point for flights to other parts of Queensland, including Townsville, Mackay, Rockhampton, Hamilton Island, and the Northern Territory, as well as all Australia's capital cities.

Airport Connections runs coaches between Cairns International Airport and town—an 8-km (5-mile) trip that takes about 10 minutes and costs A$18. All seats must be prebooked. The company also services Cairns's northern beaches, Palm Cove, Port Douglas, Silky Oaks Lodge (near Mossman), and Daintree Village (A$25 to A$70). Port Douglas–based Exemplar Chauffeured Coaches and Limousines provides services direct from the airport to Cairns CBD (A$16), Palm Cove (A$24), and Port Douglas (A$44), just over an hour's drive north of Cairns, by coach or limousine. Sun Palm Transport is the only shuttle company that takes walk-up business with a desk at Cairns airport and costs about A$15 to the CBD. Private taxis and Uber also operate from Cairns airport.

CAR TRAVEL
Between Brisbane and Cairns, the Bruce Highway rarely touches the coast. Unless you're planning to stop off en route or explore the Great Green Way, fly or take the *Spirit of Queensland* (⊕ *www. queenslandrailtravel.com.au*) train to Cairns, renting a vehicle on arrival. Avis, Budget, Hertz, Enterprise, Thrifty, and Europcar all have rental cars and four-wheel-drive vehicles available.

TRAIN TRAVEL

Trains arrive at Cairns Railway Station in the city center. The *Spirit of Queensland* takes 24 hours to make the 1,681-km (1,045-mile) journey between Brisbane and Cairns but is a comfortable ride, whether you're in a reclining Premium Economy seat or on one of the state-of-the-art RailBed seats, which convert to pod-like beds (premium economy A$369; RailBed A$519, includes three meals). The *Savannahlander* links Cairns and Forsayth, taking up to four days (with overnight stops en route) to traverse the 425 km (264 miles) of varying terrain including rain forest, savanna land, and arid Outback (A$840–A$1,690, accommodation and tours included). You can also take shorter segments of all these journeys.

TRAIN INFORMATION Cairns Railway Station. ⊠ *Bunda St., between Spence and Scott Sts., CBD* ☎ *07/4036–9250* ⊕ *www.queenslandrailtravel.com.au.*

TOURS

★ **Adventure North Australia: Daintree Dreaming Day Tour**

ADVENTURE TOURS | On Adventure North's Daintree Dreaming Day Tours, you can explore Cooya Beach and coastal mangroves, World Heritage–listed Daintree rain-forest trails, and Mossman Gorge with the area's traditional owners. ⊠ *36 Aplin St.* ☎ *07/4028–3376* ⊕ *www.adventurenorthaustralia.com* ⊠ *From A$255.*

BTS Tours

SPECIAL-INTEREST | **FAMILY** | BTS Tours runs various trips out of Cairns and Port Douglas, including a popular full-day Daintree tour and half-day Mossman Gorge trip. The Daintree itinerary includes a croc-spotting river cruise, canoeing, swimming in rain-forest pools, guided walks, and a barbecue lunch (A$165–A$175). Take the 90-minute Kuku Yalanji–guided tour of the Mossman Gorge, including rain-forest walk, bush tea, and free time to swim and sightsee (an additional A$104). ⊠ *53–61 Macrossan St.,*

ATM Logistics

It's better to change money before arriving on any resort island as rates are generally more favorable on the mainland and it's not always offered on the island.

Shop 8, Port Douglas ☎ *07/4099–5665* ⊕ *www.btstours.com.au* ⊠ *From A$29.*

Coral Expeditions

BOAT TOURS | **FAMILY** | This established operator's comfortable expedition-style ships take no more than 50 passengers on three-, four-, and seven-day live-aboard trips, departing Cairns twice a week. Exclusive outer Barrier Reef moorings mean you see more of the marine life. Stops at Lizard, Dunk, and Fitzroy islands as well as Coral Expedition own idyllic island, Pelorus, allow you ample time to relax and explore. Friendly crew, dive guides, and an onboard marine biologist ensure scuba novices are up to speed and snorkelers are catered to. The per-person fare includes a glass-bottom coral-viewing tour, complimentary scuba skills sessions, snorkeling gear, twin-berth accommodation, all meals, and most activities. ⊠ *Coral Expeditions head office, 24 Redden St., Portsmith* ☎ *07/4040–9999, 1800/079545 toll-free in Australia* ⊕ *www.coralexpeditions.com* ⊠ *From A$1740.*

Down Under Tours

SPECIAL-INTEREST | **FAMILY** | Eco-certified Down Under Tours makes half- and full-day trips and four-wheel-drive excursions, as well as reef trips, river cruises, white-water rafting, bungee jumping, and hot-air ballooning adventures, most departing from Cairns. Popular guided half- and full-day excursions take in the attractions of Kuranda, Hartley's Crocodile Adventures, and Mossman Gorge, the Daintree, and Cape Tribulation. ✉ *26 Redden St., CBD* ☎ *07/4035–5566* ⊕ *www.downundertours.com* ✉ *From A$84.*

Heritage 4WD Safari Tours - Wilderness Challenge

ADVENTURE TOURS | FAMILY | Advanced eco–certified Heritage Tours-Wilderness Challenge runs nine-day Gulf Savannah tours departing Cairns (A$3,795 per person, twin-share, or A$4,595 sole use), and seven-day fly/drive to 12-day overland trips to Cape York Peninsula during the dry season, May through early October. Two popular seven-day, fly/drive tours between Cairns and Cape York start at A$3,500 twin-share, or A$4,595 sole use. On all tours, you get to stand on top of mainland Australia and all are accommodated. All tours have a maximum of 25 guests and are accompanied by a senior guide. ✉ *21 Salter Close* ☎ *07/4054– 7750, 1800/775533* ⊕ *www.heritage- tours.com.au* ✉ *From A$2449.*

Kuku Yalanji Cultural Habitat Tours

SPECIAL-INTEREST | The Eastern Kuku Yalanji people have called the Daintree area home for tens of thousands of years, and have an intimate understanding of the terrain. Today, the Kubirri Warra brothers pass on a little of that boundless ancestral wisdom on two-hour beach, mudflat, and mangrove walks (daily, 9:30 am and 1:30 pm, A$90) with Adventure North's Kuku Yalanji Cultural Habitat Tours. Learn techniques for throwing spears, tracking coastal food sources, and much more from your knowledgeable, skillful guides. A medium to high level of fitness is required. Transfers between the Port Douglas area and Cooya Beach, a 25-minute drive north, are A$30. ☎ *07/4098– 3437* ⊕ *www.kycht.com.au* ✉ *A$90.*

★ Ocean Spirit Cruises

BOAT TOURS | FAMILY | Long-established Ocean Spirit Cruises runs full-day tours to glorious Michaelmas Cay, a remote Great Barrier Reef sand isle encircled by fish-and turtle-filled coral gardens. It's

also a protected sanctuary for migratory seabirds. Cruise out to the cay on *Ocean Spirit*, a 105-foot luxury sailing catamaran, for four hours of snorkeling, semisubmersible coral-viewing tours, and marine biologist presentations, with a full buffet lunch, morning and afternoon tea, snorkeling gear, and reef tax included in the A$212.50 per person cost. *Ocean Spirit* departs daily from Cairns Reef Fleet Terminal. Transfers from Cairns and the Northern Beaches are available from $A28. ✉ *Reef Fleet Terminal, 1 Spence St., Office 3, Level 1, CBD* ☎ *07/4044– 9944* ⊕ *www.oceanspirit.com.au.*

⊙ Sights

Cosmopolitan Cairns, the unofficial capital of Far North Queensland, is Australia's 15th-largest city, with a burgeoning population pushing 164,536—double that when you include the thriving hinterland. Once a sleepy tropical town sprawled around Trinity Bay and Inlet, the city has expanded hugely in recent decades, and now extends north to Ellis Beach, west to the Atherton Tablelands, and south along the Great Green Way as far as Edmonton.

Kuranda Experience ⊙

Tropical Kuranda offers several nature-oriented attractions, including the Australian Butterfly Sanctuary, Birdworld Kuranda, and Kuranda Koala Gardens. See these sites individually, visit on a Kuranda Wildlife Experience pass (A$49.50), which gives entry to all three, or buy a return Skyrail & Kuranda Wildlife Experience package that includes return Skyrail tickets (from A$129).

Australian Butterfly Sanctuary

NATURE PRESERVE | More than 1,200 tropical butterflies—including dozens of the electric-blue Ulysses species and Australia's largest butterfly, the green-and-gold Cairns Birdwing—flutter within a compact rain-forest aviary, alighting on foliage, interpretative signage, and feeding stations. About 60 butterflies are released into the aviary each day, ensuring the colorful spectacle continues. Free half-hour guided tours of the aviary and caterpillar breeding area are full of fascinating tidbits. ⊠ *8 Rob Veivers Dr., Kuranda* ☎ *07/4093–7575* ⊕ *www. australianbutterflies.com* 🖅 *From A$20 entry and guided tour.*

★ Birdworld Kuranda

NATURE PRESERVE | One of your best chances to see the endangered Southern cassowary, a prehistoric emu-like bird, is at Birdworld Kuranda. It's home to hundreds of colorful birds from nearly 60 species, more than 20 of them native to vanishing rain-forest areas—walking and flying freely in a gigantic aviary. Many of them are tame enough to perch on your shoulders. Wear a hat and sleeved shirt: birds' claws are scratchy. ⊠ *Kuranda Heritage Village , Rob Vievers Dr., Kuranda* ☎ *07/4093–9188* ⊕ *www.birdworldkuranda.com* 🖅 *From A$18.*

Cairns Art Gallery

MUSEUM | FAMILY | Occupying the impressive former Public Office Building constructed in the 1930s, Cairns Art Gallery houses a hodgepodge of local, national, international, and indigenous artworks, including a fine collection of Australian photography, in its wood-paneled rooms. The shop stocks high-quality Australian giftware, toys, jewelry, prints, books, and cards. Prebook a 45-minute guided tour; there are also kids' programs, classes, talks, and workshops. ⊠ *City Place, Shields St. at Abbott St., CBD* ☎ *07/4046–4800* ⊕ *www.cairnsartgallery. com.au* 🖅 *Free.*

★ The Esplanade

PROMENADE | Fronting Cairns Harbour, this busy boardwalk and recreational zone is the focal point of life in Cairns. Along the walk you'll encounter shady trees and public art, picnic and barbecue facilities, a large saltwater swimming lagoon, volleyball courts, an imaginative kids' playground, a state-of-the-art skate plaza, and areas for fitness, markets, and live entertainment. A shallow, 4,800-square-meter (51,667-square-foot) filtered saltwater lagoon swimming pool with a sandy shore, decking, and shelters, patrolled by lifeguards year-round, provides free, convenient relief from the often sticky air. Along the street opposite and along the marina at the boardwalk's southern end, you'll find hotels, shops, galleries, bars, and eateries. ⊠ *Between Spence and Upward Sts., CBD* ☎ *1300/692247 Cairns City Council* ⊕ *www.cairnsesplanade.com* 🖅 *Free.*

Kuranda Scenic Railway

SCENIC DRIVE | The historic Kuranda Scenic Railway makes a 110-minute ascent through rain forest and 15 hand-hewn tunnels to pretty Kuranda village, gateway to the Atherton Tableland. Book a simple Heritage Class seat; get a cool towel and souvenir pack; or splurge on a Gold Class ticket with fine local food and wine, table service, swanky decor, and a souvenir guide. Several tour packages are available, from full-day rain-forest safaris, and visits to local Aboriginal centers and wildlife parks to simple round-trips combining rail and cable-car journeys. ⊠ *Cairns Railway Station, Bunda St., CBD* ☎ *07/4036–9333, 1800/577245* ⊕ *www. ksr.com.au* 🖅 *From A$50.*

★ Reef Teach

COLLEGE | FAMILY | Knowledgeable marine biologists and conservationists give entertaining talks and multimedia presentations, usually to packed houses, about everything Great Barrier Reef–related, from sea turtles' sleep cycles to coral-killing starfish. Expect to learn more

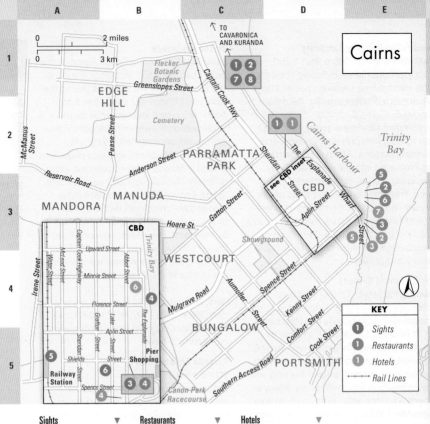

Cairs

Sights ▼

1 Australian Butterfly
Sanctuary.................**C1**
2 Birdworld Kuranda **C1**
3 Cairns Art Gallery.......**B5**
4 The Esplanade **B4**
5 Kuranda Scenic
Railway **A5**
6 Reef Teach **B5**
7 Skyforest Rainforest
Cableway.................**C1**
8 Tjapukai Aboriginal
Cultural Park **C1**

Restaurants ▼

1 Bayleaf Balinese
Restaurant...............**D2**
2 M Yogo....................**E3**
3 Ochre Restaurant........**E3**
4 Perrotta's at the
Gallery **B5**
5 Salt House...............**E3**
6 Waterbar & Grill
Steakhouse..............**E3**

Hotels ▼

1 Bay Village
Tropical Retreat
& Apartments **D2**
2 Cairns Harbour Lights
Hotel......................**E3**
3 Hilton Cairns.............**E3**
4 Pullman Cairns
International.............**B5**
5 Pullman Reef
Hotel Casino.............**E3**
6 Riley, a Crystalbrook
Collection Resort **B4**
7 Shangri-La Hotel,
The Marina **E3**

Scenic Drive: The Great Green Way 👁

Babinda Boulders. About an hour's drive from Cairns, Babinda Boulders is a popular swimming hole—and a sacred Aboriginal site. It's 7 km (5 miles) inland on The Boulders Road from the town of Babinda, accessible via the Bruce Highway about 60 km (37 miles) south of Cairns. You can also hike to the boulders, taking the 19-km (12-mile) **Goldfield Track (Wooroonooran National Park)** that starts in Goldsborough Valley, southwest of Cairns, and ends in Babinda Boulders car park. ⊠ *Babinda Information Centre, 1 Munro St., at Bruce Hwy., Babinda* ☎ *07/4067–1008 info center* ⊕ *www.babindainfocentre.com.au.*

Great Green Way. A scenic section of the Bruce Highway locals call the Great Green Way links Cairns with Townsville, taking you through sugarcane, papaya, and banana plantations, past white-sand beaches and an island-dotted ocean. The 348-km (216-mile) drive takes about 4½ hours. Allow time to explore towns, parks, and rainforest tracts along the way. ⊠ *Bruce Hwy., between Cairns and Townsville.*

Paronella Park. A sprawling Spanish-style castle and gardens grace this offbeat National Trust site in the Mena Creek Falls rain forest. Explore the park on a self-guided botanical walk or 45-minute guided tour, enjoy Devonshire tea on the café's deck, buy local crafts, and cool off under a 40-foot waterfall. On hour-long flashlight-lit evening tours starting nightly at 6:15, you might spot eels, water dragons, fireflies, and glowworms. Allow at least three hours to explore. ⊠ *1671 Japoonvale Rd. (Old Bruce Hwy.), Mena Creek* ☎ *07/4065–0000* ⊕ *www.paronellapark.com.au* 🎟 *A$46.*

Tully Gorge National Park. In the wettest zone of the Wet Tropics World Heritage area, the mighty Tully River is a magnet for white-water rafters, while the gorge's scenic, often mist-shrouded trails suit walkers of all levels. Access Tully Gorge National Park via the town of Tully, 141 km (88 miles) or about two hours' drive south of Cairns, then continue for 54 km (34 miles)—approximately 40 minutes—along Jarra Creek and Cardstone roads to Kareeya Hydroelectric Station parking lot and viewing platform. Other excellent vantage points are the Tully Falls lookout, 24 km (15 miles) south of Ravenshoe, and the Flip Wilson and Frank Roberts lookouts. ⊠ *Tully Falls Rd., Koombooloomba* ☎ *07/4068–2288 Tully visitor information, 13–7468 Parks camping permits and general inquiries* ⊕ *www.nprsr.qld.gov.au/parks/tully-gorge.*

Wooroonooran National Park. Extending south of Gordonvale to the Palmerston Highway near Innisfail, this is one of the most densely vegetated areas in Australia. Rain forest rules—from the lowland tropical variety to the stunted growth on Mt. Bartle Frere—at 5,287 feet, the highest point in Queensland. Walking tracks range from the stroll-in-the-park Tchupala Falls and Josephine Falls circuits (30 minutes each) to the challenging Walshs Pyramid track, just south of Cairns, and the gruelling two-day Bartle Frere trail. You may camp throughout the park with permits. ⊠ *Josephine Falls Rd.* ☎ *07/4067–1008 Babinda Information Centre* ⊕ *www.nprsr.qld.gov.au/parks/wooroonooran.*

than you thought possible about the reef's evolution and the diverse inhabitants of this delicate marine ecosystem. The attached Marine Shop sells an array of reef-themed merchandise: T-shirts, DVDs, books, field guides, and souvenirs. Sign up for a Reef Teach seat by midday. ⊠ *Mainstreet Arcade, Level 2, CBD* ✛ *Between Lake and Grafton Sts.* ☎ *07/4031–7794* ⊕ *www.reefteach.com.au* ✉ *A$23* ⊘ *Closed Tues., Thurs., weekends.*

★ **Skyrail Rainforest Cableway**
TRANSPORTATION SITE (AIRPORT/BUS/FERRY/TRAIN) | FAMILY | From the Skyrail terminal just north of Cairns, take a six-person cable car on a breathtaking 7½-km (5-mile) journey across pristine, World Heritage–listed rain-forest canopy to the highland village of Kuranda, where you can visit local wildlife parks and shop for local crafts and Aboriginal art. At two stations along the way, you can hop off and explore (the Skyrail ticket price includes a short ranger-guided rain-forest tour at Red Peak, and there's an info center and lookout at Barron Falls). Upgrade your ticket to the glass floor Diamond View Gondola for an even better view. The cableway base station is 15 km (9 miles) north of Cairns. Many visitors take the Scenic Railway to Kuranda, the cableway on the return trip. ⊠ *6 Skyrail Dr., Smithfield* ☎ *07/4038–5555* ⊕ *www.skyrail.com.au* ✉ *From A$53.*

Tjapukai Aboriginal Cultural Park
MUSEUM VILLAGE | FAMILY | At the base of the Skyrail Rainforest Cableway, this park offers many opportunities to learn about indigenous Djabugay people through exhilarating dance performances, hands-on workshops in traditional fire-making, spear and boomerang throwing, arts and crafts, didgeridoo lessons, and talks on bush tucker and natural medicines. You can buy Aboriginal artworks, artifacts, and instruments (including didgeridoos) at the retail gallery on-site; café fare, buffet lunches, and dinners are also available. One of Australia's most informative

Beaches

Because Cairns lacks city beaches, most people head out to the reef to swim and snorkel. North of the airport, neighboring areas including **Machans Beach, Holloways Beach, Yorkey's Knob, Trinity Beach,** and **Clifton Beach** are perfect for swimming from June through September and sometimes even October; check local weather reports. Avoid the ocean at other times, however, when deadly box jellyfish (marine stingers) and invisible-to-the-eye Irukandji jellyfish float in the waters along the coast.

cultural attractions, it's also one of the few that returns profits to the indigenous community. Ticket options include Tjapukai by Day and Tjapukai by Night, the latter a nightly four-course buffet dinner/performance package. ⊠ *Cairns Western Arterial Rd., next to Skyrail terminal, Cavaronica* ✛ *15 km (9 miles) north of Cairns* ☎ *07/4042–9999* ⊕ *www.tjapukai.com.au* ✉ *From A$62. Transfers from A$28.*

Restaurants

★ **Bayleaf Balinese Restaurant**
$ | INDONESIAN | Dining in the open-sided restaurant or alfresco under the light of tiki torches, you can enjoy some of the most delicious, innovative cuisine in North Queensland. Choose from an expansive menu that combines traditional Balinese spices and recipes with native Australian ingredients, such as the crocodile satay and mouthwatering *be celeng base manis* (pork in sweet soy sauce). **Known for:** traditional rijsttafel feast for two (includes rice with lots of curries, salads, fish dishes, stews, pickle sides, and, if you can squeeze them in, desserts); award-winning wine list and

The Skyrail Rainforest Cableway outside Cairns

long, tropically themed cocktail menu; local favorite. $ *Average main: A$29* ⊠ *Bay Village Tropical Retreat, 227 Lake St. , at Gatton St., CBD* ☎ *07/4047–7955* ⊕ *www.bayleafrestaurant.com.au* ⊙ *No lunch Sat.–Mon.*

★ Ochre Restaurant

$$ | AUSTRALIAN |FAMILY | Local seafood and native and seasonal ingredients take top billing at this upscale yet relaxed Cairns institution that specializes in bush dining. Try the popular Australian antipasto platter: 'roo terrine, emu carpaccio, and smoked crocodile, with fine Antipodean wines to match. **Known for:** Australian game; gluten-free and vegetarian options; signature dessert— wattle-seed pavlova with Davidson plum sorbet and macadamia biscotti. $ *Average main: A$38* ⊠ *6/1 Marlin Parade, CBD* ☎ *07/4051–0100* ⊕ *ochrerestaurant. com.au.*

Perrotta's at the Gallery

$ | MODERN AUSTRALIAN |FAMILY | This outdoor café and wine bar at Cairns Art Gallery serves sumptuous breakfasts as well as lunch and dinner. Lunch fare features a signature duck salad, gourmet sandwiches, and heartier meals, while dinner options include Italian and Modern Australian dishes: antipasto, burgers, pasta, and pizza. **Known for:** central location; road menu; smoothies. $ *Average main: A$25* ⊠ *Gallery Deck, Cairns Art Gallery, 38 Abbott St., at Shield St., CBD* ☎ *07/4031–5899* ⊕ *www.perrottasatg. com.*

M Yogo

$ | MODERN FRENCH | Offering refined dining in relaxed environs, Chef Masa puts a deft, modern-Japanese spin on classic French dishes at this restaurant that occupies a prime pier-front position. The food is as inspiring as the marina, inlet, and mountain views, and the waitstaff can help you select the perfect match from a well-chosen Antipodean wine list. **Known for:** set-price lunch specials are a good value; fresh seafood platter; award-winning. $ *Average main: A$32* ⊠ *Pier Shopping , Shop G9 Pierpoint Rd.*

☎ *07/4051–0522* 🌐 *www.matureyogo.com.*

Salt House

$$ | **MODERN AUSTRALIAN** | Blessed with mountain and ocean views and located in prime position at the Cairns Marina, Salt House serves Modern Australian fare in casual chic environs. A carefully considered menu includes standouts such as the seafood taster, Kangaroo carpaccio, and a mouthwatering selection of local cuts of meat cooked on the custom Argentinian grill. **Known for:** A$20 lunch special; seafood tasting plate; stunning waterside location. [$] *Average main: A$39* ✉ *Marina Point , 6/2 Pierpoint Rd., CBD* ☎ *07/4041–7733* 🌐 *salthouse.com.au.*

Waterbar & Grill Steakhouse

$$ | **STEAKHOUSE** | At this busy waterfront eatery, you can gaze at Cairns's bustling marina while chowing down on a locally sourced, chargrilled steak, which come in all cuts and sizes, with thick fries on the side. There's also a nice selection of barbecued lamb ribs, burgers, seafood, and lighter lunch fare, such as pita wraps and salads. **Known for:** pork ribs; good cocktail menu; prime waterfront location. [$] *Average main: A$39* ✉ *Pier Shopping Centre, Pier Point Rd., Shop G1A, CBD* ☎ *07/4031–1199* 🌐 *www.waterbarandgrill.com.au.*

Hotels

Bay Village Tropical Retreat & Apartments

$ | **RESORT** |**FAMILY** | The sociable public areas at this family-friendly complex include a lovely lagoon pool, an Internet area, a guest laundry, and the terrific Bayleaf Balinese Restaurant & Bar. The main complex offers simple but spacious double, family, and studio rooms, some with balconies. **Pros:** excellent restaurant on-site; clean, generously sized rooms; a lovely central courtyard with pool, surrounded by tropical gardens. **Cons:** pool area and ground-floor rooms can be noisy; standard rooms lack ambient lighting and all but simple amenities; no elevator access to second floor. [$] *Rooms from: A$135* ✉ *227 Lake St. at Gatton St., CBD* ☎ *07/4051–4622* 🌐 *www.bayvillage.com.au* 🛏 *81 rooms* 🍴 *No meals.*

Cairns Harbour Lights Hotel

$ | **HOTEL** | The hotel rooms and one- and two-bedroom apartments at this hotel on Cairns's waterfront are a two-minute stroll to Reef Fleet Terminal, making them ideal for early-morning reef trips. **Pros:** terrific central location; good on-site dining options; great inlet views. **Cons:** fees for parking and Wi-Fi; pool small, and can be chilly in cooler months; lacks personality and feels a little corporate. [$] *Rooms from: A$179* ✉ *1 Marlin Parade* ☎ *07/4057–0800* 🌐 *www.cairnsharbourlightshotel.com.au* 🛏 *84 rooms* 🍴 *No meals* ☞ *Takeout available from Dundee's on ground floor.*

★ **Hilton Cairns**

$$ | **HOTEL** | This attractive hotel has an enviable location near the waterfront, a flotilla of services, and classy on-site drinking and dining options. **Pros:** modern rooms with comfortable beds; free Wi-Fi for Hilton members; friendly, helpful service. **Cons:** pricey Internet access for non-Hilton members; steep fees for parking; large tour groups can create crowds in public areas. [$] *Rooms from: A$229* ✉ *34 Esplanade* ☎ *07/4050–2000* 🌐 *www3.hilton.com* 🛏 *262 rooms* 🍴 *No meals.*

Pullman Cairns International

$$ | **HOTEL** | This practicality-meets-luxury hotel near Cairns's waterfront has an impressive three-story lobby, an elegant day spa, and rooms and suites with furnished balconies. **Pros:** central location; good on-site services and facilities; comfortable beds. **Cons:** clean but rooms need updating; fees for parking; dated furnishings in rooms. [$] *Rooms from: A$218* ✉ *17 Abbot St., at Spence St., CBD* ☎ *07/4031–1300* 🌐 *www.*

Off The Beaten Path

Undara Experience. This extraordinary complex on the edge of Undara Volcanic National Park, 275 km (171 miles) or a four-hour scenic drive or rail trip from Cairns, supplies the complete Outback experience: bush breakfasts, campfire activities, lava-tube tours, and guided evening wildlife walks, plus a range of distinctive accommodation. Vintage railway cars have been converted into comfortable (if compact), fan-cooled motel rooms with their own en suites. You can also stay in a modern, air-conditioned "Pioneer Hut" with private veranda, fridge, and bathroom (A$190 per night in high season), in a safari tent; or at a powered or unpowered site with shared amenities. One-night "budget" self-drive packages that incorporate tours, campfire activities, and swag-tent accommodation cost A$110 per person in high season, A$167 per person with meals; or from A$259 to A$309 per person with swankier accommodation. Two-night packages including meals, rail-carriage or Pioneer Hut accommodation, and tours range from A$405 to A$471 per person in high season. Other packages include transfers to and from Cairns via coach or on heritage train *The Savannahlander*. Drink and dine on-site at Fettler's Iron Pot Bistro; breakfast at the Ringer's Camp. ✉ *Undara Volcanic Park, Savannah Way, Mt. Surprise* ☎ *07/4097–1900, 1800/990992* ⊕ *www.undara.com.au.*

pullmancairnsinternational.com.au 🛏 *321 rooms* ⦿ *No meals.*

★ **Pullman Reef Hotel Casino**

$$$ | HOTEL | Part of a lively entertainment complex in the heart of Cairns, this high-end hotel has spacious rooms and suites—as well as several restaurants and bars, a theater, a casino, an outdoor swimming pool, and a small wildlife sanctuary and ropes course in its rooftop dome. **Pros:** several on-site entertainment and dining options; helpful, high-end service; generously sized rooms. **Cons:** chilly pool; casino on-site; large, busy complex, lacks intimate feel. Ⓢ *Rooms from: A$341* ✉ *35–41 Wharf St., CBD* ☎ *07/4030–8888* ⊕ *www.pullmanhotels. com* 🛏 *128 rooms* ⦿ *No meals.*

Riley, a Crystalbrook Collection Resort

$$ | HOTEL | This modern, contemporary property on the Cairns Esplanade is in the heart of the city, and rooms come with a view of Cairns, the resort, or the sea. **Pros:** great, central location; complimentary parking; Cairns' highest rooftop bar. **Cons:** suited for younger market; some oddly shaped rooms in the tower; public access to bars, pool, and restaurant. Ⓢ *Rooms from: A$209* ✉ *131–141 Esplanade* ☎ *1300/002050 reservations* ⊕ *www.crystalbrookcollection.com/riley* 🛏 *311 rooms* ⦿ *No meals.*

Shangri-La Hotel, The Marina

$$$ | HOTEL | With chic modern decor in blues and blue-grays reflecting the waterfront location and buzzing on-site bars and eateries, this marina-side resort is among Cairns's hippest. **Pros:** great views; free Wi-Fi; proximity to the marina. **Cons:** lower-floor pier-side rooms above the bar can be noisy; Horizon Club breakfast can be underwhelming; guests have to pay for parking. Ⓢ *Rooms from: A$330* ✉ *Pierpoint Rd., CBD* ☎ *07/4031–1411, 1800/222448* ⊕ *www.shangri-la. com/cairns/shangrila* 🛏 *184 rooms* ⦿ *No meals.*

⏱ Nightlife

Cairns's Esplanade and the CBD streets leading off it come alive at night, with most restaurants serving until late, and wine or a cold beer is a staple with evening meals. Several rowdy pubs catering to backpackers and younger travelers line the central section of City Place; a few bars and hotel venues manage to be upscale while remaining true to the city's easygoing spirit. Unless noted, bars are open nightly and there's no cover charge.

Bar36

MUSIC CLUBS | Popular with visitors and locals alike, this sleek bar-lounge off the main foyer of Pullman Reef Hotel Casino has live bands (including big-name acts) Tuesday through Sunday. Get a table early and enjoy a quiet drink and some tapas before the crowds pile in. ⌧ *Pullmanpullmann Reef Hotel Casino, 35–41 Wharf St., ground-fl. foyer, CBD* ☎ *07/4030–8888* ⊕ *www.reefcasino. com.au/venue/bar36.*

The Conservatory Bar

WINE BARS—NIGHTLIFE | Faux-brick-lined walls and a glorious wood-topped bar create a relaxed vibe at this discreet watering hole. It serves fine Australian wines, classic cocktails, and customized "grazing boards" to a sophisticated, largely local crowd. A long, well chosen wine list has plenty of fine Aussie vintages by the glass. Sit in air-conditioned comfort or on the shady patio and chill out to jazz while you tipple and graze. There's live music on Friday and weekend evenings. ⌧ *The Conservatory Laneway, 12–14 Lake St.* ☎ *0429 /322293, 0431/858137* ⊕ *www.theconservatory-bar.com.au.*

Hemingway's Brewery

BREWPUBS/BEER GARDENS | Located on the water in the Cruise Liner Terminal, Hemingway's Brewery is in a historic building, has a relaxed vibe, and there's plenty of room for families or groups to spread out. Enjoy Trinity Inlet views over one of the 20 beers on tap (10 of which are brewed in house). There is also a simple food menu featuring local produce served in sliders, tacos, burgers, and salads for those who want something to pair with their pale ale. It's a fun venue with lovely views and good beers. ⌧ *Cairns Wharf, 4 Wharf St., CBD* ☎ *07/4099–6663* ⊕ *www.hemingwaysbrewery.com/ cairns-wharf.*

The Pier Bar

WINE BARS—NIGHTLIFE | A prime waterside location and a big, breezy deck draw an upbeat, mixed crowd to The Pier Bar. They flock here for wood-fired pizzas, well-priced drinks, and laid-back Sunday sessions with live music and DJs. The bar gets noisier, younger, and more crowded as the night wears on, but service is friendly and food is palatable, even when the bar's jam-packed. ⌧ *The Pier Shopping Centre, 1 Pierpoint Rd.* ☎ *07/4031–4677* ⊕ *www.thepierbar.com.au.*

⭐ Performing Arts

The Precinct

ARTS CENTERS | The Precinct combines two performing arts spaces including the Cairns Performing Arts Centre and the Munro Martin Parklands. Munro Martin Parklands hosts audiences in its open-air amphitheatre surrounded by lush tropical gardens, while the CPAC features two indoor theatres. Each showcases local and international talent performing across many genres from dance to theater, ballet, music, and comedy. ⌧ *9–11 Florence St.* ☎ *07/4050–7777* ⊕ *www. cairns.qld.gov.au/council/major-projects/ the-precinct.*

★ Tanks Arts Centre

ARTS CENTERS | FAMILY | This vibrant arts center is housed in a trio of repurposed World War II–era oil storage tanks in Cairns's lush Flecker Botanic Gardens, 4 km (2 miles) north of the Cairns city center. It has become a vital creative hub for the region, showcasing everything from dance and theater troupes to local folk, blues, jazz, and indigenous artists. The Centre hosts a colorful arts and food market, with live music and free kids' activities, on the last Sunday of the month from April to November. ✉ *46 Collins Ave., Edge Hill* ☎ *07/4032–6600* ⊕ *www.tanksartscentre.com* ✉ *Galleries free, venue ticket prices vary* ⊙ *Closed weekends, except last Sun. of the month.*

🛍 Shopping

Cairns Central

SHOPPING CENTERS/MALLS | Adjacent to Cairns Railway Station, Cairns Central houses 180-plus specialty stores, a supermarket, department stores, a food court, several coffee shops, and a cinema complex. Strollers are available to rent. It also has the only free parking in Cairns CBD: three hours' free Monday through Saturday, and all day Sunday. ✉ *McLeod St. at Spence St., CBD* ☎ *07/4041–4111* ⊕ *www.cairnscentral.com.au.*

Cairns Night Markets

OUTDOOR/FLEA/GREEN MARKETS | **FAMILY** | If you're looking for bargain beachwear, local jewelry, art and crafts, a massage, a meal, a coffee, or souvenirs, The Cairns Night Markets, open daily 5 to 11 pm, are the place to go. Bring cash—several of the 70-plus merchants charge additional fees for credit cards. ✉ *71–75 The Esplanade, at Aplin St., CBD* ☎ *01/4051–7666* ⊕ *www.nightmarkets.com.au.*

Rusty's Markets

OUTDOOR/FLEA/GREEN MARKETS | **FAMILY** | Cairns's iconic weekend "street" market, Rusty's attracts 180-plus stallholders, who peddle everything from fresh tropical produce to art and crafts, jewelry, clothing, natural health and skin-care products, and food. The market is covered, offering a pleasant respite from the sun. Take advantage of two hours' free parking in Gilligan's/Rusty's carpark, above Rusty's on Sheridan Street.

Cairns Night Markets 🍴

The food court in the lively, inexpensive Cairns Night Markets between Shield and Spence streets (✉ *71–75 The Esplanade,* ⊕ *www. nightmarkets.com.au*) offers something for every palate, from Korean barbecue to sweet-and-sour chicken, sushi, Thai, and Italian. You can also max out on desserts, with outlets offering crepes, waffles, churros, gelato, ice cream, and Italian-style coffee. The food court's open daily from 10 am to 11 pm; the night markets, 5 to 11 pm. ■ **TIP→ Most food stalls accept credit cards, but bring cash just in case.**

✉ *57–89 Grafton St., CBD* ☎ *07/4040–2705, 0438/753460 market manager Justin Welch* ⊕ *www.rustysmarkets.com. au.*

Tusa Dive Shop

SPORTING GOODS | This store stocks a wide range of big-name dive gear as well as stinger and wet suits, swimwear, kids' gear, and accessories such as snorkels and sunscreen. ✉ *The Esplanade, at Shields St., CBD* ☎ *07/4047–9120* ⊕ *www.tusadive.com.*

🏃 Activities

It's no surprise that lots of tours out of Cairns focus on the Great Barrier Reef. Half-day snorkeling, diving, and fishing trips out of Cairns, most departing from the Reef Fleet Terminal, start from around A$100; full-day trips start from about A$250. Scuba dives and gear generally cost extra. Typically you'll pay an additional admin fee that includes the A$6.50 per person, per day Environmental Management Charge (EMC) or "reef tax," and you may also be hit with a Port

Authority charge of around A$8.50 per person, per day.

Ask a few pertinent questions before booking diving tours: dive trips vary in size, and some cater specifically to, say, sightseers; others to experienced divers. If you're a beginner or Open Water diver, ensure that you book excursions that visit suitable dive sites, with certified staff on hand to assist you.

Cairns is also a great base for adventure activities and horse riding on the Atherton Tableland, ballooning over the Mareeba Valley, and day tours to the UNESCO World Heritage–listed Daintree rain forest. The offices of adventure-tour companies, tourist offices and booking agents are concentrated around the Esplanade.

Cairns Marlin Marina
MARINA | This floating marina's 261 berths bristle with charter fishing, diving, and private vessels, including superyachts up to 60 meters (197 feet) long. At the Reef Fleet Terminal off Marlin Wharf, you'll find tour offices, shops, cafés, and Wi-Fi connectivity. Big-game fishing is a big business here; fish weighing more than 1,000 pounds have been caught in the waters off the reef. Most of the dive boats and catamarans that ply the Great Barrier Reef dock here or at nearby Trinity Wharf. ⊠ 1 Spence St., CBD ☎ 07/4052–3866 ⊕ www.portsnorth.com.au/marina.

Deep Sea Divers Den
DIVING/SNORKELING | Long-established, PADI-five-star-rated Deep Sea Divers Den has a roaming permit that allows its guides to visit any part of the Great Barrier Reef, including 17 exclusive moorings on the reef's outer edge frequented by turtles, rays, and colorful reef fish. Open water and advanced PADI dive courses include live-aboard trips. Daily transfers take divers out to luxury live-aboard vessel, OceanQuest, which operates around the Norman, Saxon, and Hastings Reefs. Guests can book in to

stay on OceanQuest for as many nights as they like. Day trips include up to three dives or snorkeling opportunities; gear and lunch is included in the price, but reef tax (A$20) and photos cost extra. ⊠ 319 Draper St., CBD ☎ 07/4046–7333 ⊕ www.diversden.com.au ☎ From A$180.

★ Mike Ball Dive Expeditions
DIVING/SNORKELING | Mike Ball, an enthusiastic American who's been diving the Great Barrier Reef since 1969, runs multiday, multidive trips along the Queensland coastline on which novice divers are given expert guidance and experienced divers get to set their own bottom times and dive their own plans. Custom-built, twin-hulled live-aboard boats loaded with top-end gear, serious divers, and qualified chefs depart twice-weekly to visit renowned dive sites and spot minke whales and sharks. Dive courses cost extra, but there are several available, and the quality of instruction is high. ⊠ 3 Abbott St., CBD ☎ 07/4053–0500, 0407/146834 ⊕ www.mikeball.com ☎ From A$1987, with standard gear rental fees from A$44 per day; personal guides from A$50 per dive.

★ Ocean Spirit Cruises
DIVING/SNORKELING | FAMILY | This operator offers daily trips on its sleek sailing catamaran that include four hours at Michaelmas Cay on the Great Barrier Reef, a marine biologist presentation, snorkeling gear, guided snorkeling, a fish-feeding demonstration, a semisubmersible tour, morning and afternoon tea, a buffet lunch, and a glass of wine on the return journey. Reef and port charges are an extra A$6.50. If you're a beginner, have mobility issues, or aren't a strong swimmer, this might be the best operator for you. ⊠ Reef Fleet Terminal, 1 Spence St., CBD ☎ 07/4044–9944 ⊕ www.oceanspirit.com.au ☎ From A$213.

Pro Dive Cairns
DIVING/SNORKELING | This Advanced Ecotourism–certified operator runs multiday,

live-aboard trips on its custom-built dive boat, and offers PADI-five-star-accredited courses at its state-of-the-art training facility in Cairns. Three-day, two-night live-aboard trips take a maximum of 32 divers and snorkelers to Outer Barrier Reef, where they can dive ecologically diverse sites with optimal visibility. Trips include accommodation in serviced twin or double cabins, equipment, transfers, and an initial guided orientation on the first dive. ⊠ *Pro Dive Cairns Training Centre, 116 Spence St., CBD* ☏ *07/4031–5255* ⊕ *www.prodivecairns.com* ⊠ *A$865 for 3-day/2-night live-aboard trip.*

★ **Raging Thunder Adventures**

TOUR—SPORTS | FAMILY | This operator has various adventure packages: snorkel and kayak around the Barrier Reef's Fitzroy Island; glide over the Mareeba Valley or Atherton Tablelands in a hot-air balloon; or white-water raft through the hinterland's rugged gorges. ⊠ *59–63 The Esplanade, CBD* ☏ *07/4030–7990* ⊕ *www. ragingthunder.com.au* ⊠ *From A$79.*

RnR White Water Rafting

TOUR—SPORTS | FAMILY | This operator runs white-water rafting expeditions for adults on the Barron, North Johnstone, and Tully rivers. They also offer snorkeling trips, ATV adventure tours, balloon rides, and packages combining a half-day's Barron River rafting with a half-day on Fitzroy Island. All gear and safety equipment is provided. ⊠ *52 Fearnley St., CBD* ☏ *07/4030–7944* ⊕ *www.raft.com.au* ⊠ *From A$109.*

★ **Tusa Dive**

DIVING/SNORKELING | FAMILY | Among Cairns's best dive boats are the custom-built fast cats run by Tusa Dive, a PADI-, SSI-, and Advanced Ecotourism–accredited outfit that whisks passengers out to two sites on the Great Barrier Reef. Get dive briefs and info en route, along with continual refreshments including a big lunch. In the water, people of all experience levels can dive or snorkel under the watchful gaze of well-trained guides. ⊠ *Shield St., at The Esplanade, CBD* ☏ *07/4047–9100* ⊕ *www.tusadive. com* ⊠ *From A$215.*

Palm Cove

23 km (14 miles) north of Cairns.

A 35-minute drive north of Cairns, Palm Cove is one of Queensland's jewels: an idyllic, albeit pricey, base from which to explore the far north. It's a quiet place, sought out by those in the know for its magnificent trees, calm waters, exceptionally clean beach, and excellent restaurants.

Prime time for visiting the far north is May through September, when daily maximum temperatures average around 27°C (80°F) and the water is comfortably warm. During the wet season, November through April, expect rain, humidity, and lots of bugs. Highly poisonous box and Irukandji jellyfish make the coastline unsafe for swimming from October through May, but "jellies" hardly ever drift out as far as the reefs, so you're safe to get wet there.

GETTING HERE AND AROUND

Getting here from Cairns is a cinch: by car, follow the signs from the city center to Captain Cook Highway, then head north, taking the Palm Cove turnoff after about 25 km (16 miles). Regular shuttle buses service Palm Cove from the airport, Cairns, and Port Douglas, farther north. Around this compact beach area, though, most people walk or cycle.

◉ Sights

A charming beachside village that sprawls back toward the highway, Palm Cove is navigated easily on foot. Many of the best accommodations, bars, and eateries are strung along the oceanfront strip of Williams Esplanade, fronting what has been dubbed Australia's cleanest beach. At its far north end, a five-minute

Palm Cove is one of many pristine beaches along the tropical Queensland coast

stroll from the "village," there's a jetty and a small marina.

Hartley's Crocodile Adventures

ZOO | **FAMILY** | Hartley's houses thousands of crocodiles as well as koalas, wallabies, quolls, snakes, lizards, southern cassowaries, and tropical birds in natural environs, accessible via boardwalks and boat tours. A lagoon cruise, on which keepers feed big crocs at close range, is included in your entry price. There are daily cassowary, wallaby, quoll, and koala feedings, croc and snake shows, and croc farm tours. Most thrilling is the Big Croc Experience, held daily at 10:30 and 1 (book 24 hours ahead). It's your chance to handle squirming baby crocs and pole-feed gigantic ones, and includes a guided tour and commemorative photo. The Gondwana Grill showcases local delicacies, including crocodile, of course. If you don't feel like driving, **Down Under Tours** (🌐 *www.downundertours.com/wildlife-experiences/hartleys-crocodile-adventures-pm*), **Tropical Horizons Tours** (🌐 *tropicalhorizonstours.com.au*), and several other operators include Hartley's on their day-tour itineraries. ✉ *Captain Cook Hwy., Wangetti* ☎ *07/4055–3576* 🌐 *www.crocodileadventures.com* 🎫 *Entry from A$41.*

🍴 Restaurants

Beach Almond Beach House

$$ | **SEAFOOD** | This low-key eatery's simple beach-shack setting on Palm Cove's seafront underplays the freshness and flavor of its Modern Asian food. The small but satisfying menu is full of fresh spins on favorite dishes from around Southeast Asia, and seafood is the specialty here. **Known for:** signature dishes include whole Singaporean chill mud crab and a lavish two-person seafood platter; butter prawns; Asian fusion menu. [$] *Average main: A$39* ✉ *145 Williams Esplanade* ☎ *07/4059–1908, 0488/145147* 🌐 *www.beachalmond.com.*

Lime & Pepper Restaurant

$$ | **INTERNATIONAL** | European flair meets great local produce at this upscale

beachfront restaurant and bar. Lime & Pepper mixes fresh seafood, tropical fruits, and bush-tucker ingredients, such as native finger limes and Davidson plums, in innovative dishes, with a worthy wine list and tropical cocktails. **Known for:** poolside dining; tasting plate; modern Australian menu plus kids menu. $ *Average main: A$39* ⊠ *Peppers Beach Club & Spa, 123 Williams Esplanade* ☎ *07/4059–9200* ⊕ *www.limepepper. com.au.*

★ **NuNu Restaurant**

$$$ | **MODERN AUSTRALIAN** | Sexy suede lounges, intimate banquettes, and unbroken views of the Coral Sea make lingering easy at this Palm Cove eatery with the region's best and freshest produce. Select tapas-style tasting plates, such as baby barramundi, or wok-fried north Queensland mud crab with chili tamarind, sweet pork, and market greens. **Known for:** whey-poached reef fish; four- or seven-course tasting menu (A$89/ A$129); duck rice. $ *Average main: A$46* ⊠ *Alamanda Palm Cove by Lancemore,* *Veivers Rd.* ☎ *07/4059–1880* ⊕ *www. nunu.com.au.*

emple of Tastes

$ | **MODERN ASIAN** | Knowledgeable staff, an impressive wine and cocktail list, and torchlit waterfront terrace are among the many reasons to dine at this excellent resort restaurant that is paddock to plate dining. You can expect generous servings of fresh modern Australian food infused with Asian and South Pacific flavors. **Known for:** twice-cooked pork belly; tasting menu; gluten-free and vegetarian options. $ *Average main: A$38* ⊠ *Hotel Pullman Palm Cove Sea Temple Resort and Spa, 5 Triton St.* ☎ *07/4059–9600* ⊕ *www.pullmanhotels.com.*

ivo

$ | **MODERN AUSTRALIAN** |**FAMILY** | Enjoy Coral Sea views framed by palms and melaleucas along with Mod Oz dishes at this classy beachside eatery. Diners come for the house-made muesli and freshly baked breads at breakfast; the panini, pasta, salads, and calamari at lunch; and seafood with seasonal produce at dinner. **Known for:** a popular spot for city-strong coffee, tapas, and cocktails; open kitchen; relaxed beachside destination. $ *Average main: A$40* ⊠ *49 Williams Esplanade* ☎ *07/4059–0944* ⊕ *www.vivo.com.au.*

🛏 Hotels

★ **Alamanda Palm Cove by Lancemore**

$$$ | **RESORT** | Fine landscaping, pools, barbecues, and sunny areas for relaxation enhance this classy colonial-style vacation complex fronting a palm-shaded white-sand beach. **Pros:** terrific location; upscale restaurant; free Wi-Fi. **Cons:** no elevators; pools on the chilly side; Wi-Fi weak in some rooms. $ *Rooms from: A$418* ⊠ *1 Veivers Rd.* ☎ *07/4055–3000* ⊕ *www.lancemore.com.au/alamanda* ⤴ *67 suites* ⊘ *No meals.*

Hotel Pullman Palm Cove Sea Temple Resort and Spa

$$ | **RESORT** | The well-appointed studio rooms and apartments at Pullman's gorgeous Palm Cove property have private balcony or terrace areas, high-definition flat-screen TVs, and comfortable beds with memory-foam pillows. **Pros:** gorgeous grounds and pools; excellent on-site restaurant; five-star service. **Cons:** occasional noise from wedding parties; five-minute walk from Palm Cove's main strip and beach; busy pool area when lots of children staying. $ *Rooms from: A$278* ⊠ *5 Triton St.* ☎ *07/4059–9600* ⊕ *www.pullmanpalmcove.com.au* ⤴ *126 rooms* ⊘ *No meals.*

★ **Kewarra Beach Resort & Spa**

$$ | **RESORT** | This beachfront property just south of Palm Cove has its priorities right: Kewarra's sensitively designed bungalows and restored pioneer's cottage overlook rain forests teeming with wildlife, free-form pools, or a private white-sand beach. **Pros:** eco-friendly

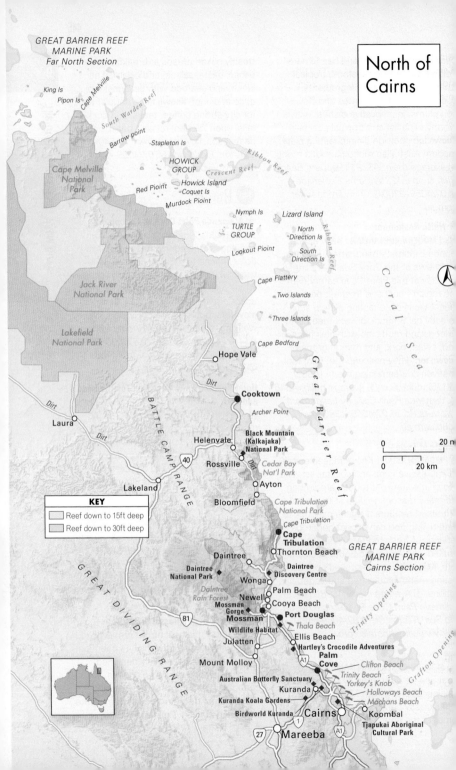

GREAT BARRIER REEF
MARINE PARK
Far North Section

North of
Cairns

King Is
Pipon Is
Cape Melville
South Warden Reef
Barrow point
Stapleton Is

Cape Melville
National
Park

HOWICK
GROUP
Crescent Reef
Ribbon Reef
Red Pioint
Howick Island
Coquet Is
Murdock Pioint

Nymph Is
Lizard Island
TURTLE
GROUP
North
Direction Is
Ribbon Reef
Lookout Pioint
South
Direction Is

Jack River
National Park

Cape Flattery

Two Islands

Three Islands

Lakefield
National
Park

Cape Bedford

○ **Hope Vale**

Dirt

● **Cooktown**

Archer Point

○ **Laura**

Dirt

Dirt

B
A
T
T
L
E
C
A
M
P
R
A
N
G
E

**Black Mountain
(Kalkajaka)
National Park**

Helenvale ○

Rossville ○

Dirt

*Cedar Bay
Nat'l Park*

○ **Lakeland**

○ **Ayton**

Bloomfield ○

*Cape Tribulation
National Park*

Cape Tribulation

KEY

Reef down to 15ft deep

Reef down to 30ft deep

**Cape
Tribulation** ●
○ **Thornton Beach**

Daintree ○

**Daintree
National Park** ◆

**Daintree
Discovery Centre** ◆

*GREAT BARRIER REEF
MARINE PARK
Cairns Section*

Wonga ○

*Daintree
Rain Forest*

Newell ○
**Mossman
Gorge** ◆
Mossman ●

○ **Palm Beach**
○ **Cooya Beach**

● **Port Douglas**
Thala Beach

Wildlife Habitat

Julatten ○

○ **Ellis Beach**

◆ **Hartley's Crocodile Adventures**

G
R
E
A
T
D
I
V
I
D
I
N
G
R
A
N
G
E

Mount Molloy ○

**Palm
Cove** ●

Clifton Beach
Trinity Beach
Yorkey's Knob

Trinity Opening

Grafton Opening

Australian Butterfly Sanctuary ◆

Holloways Beach
Machans Beach

Kuranda ●

Kuranda Koala Gardens ◆

● **Koombal**

Birdworld Kuranda ◆

Cairns ●

**Tjapukai Aboriginal
Cultural Park**

Mareeba ○

*Coral
Sea*

Great Barrier Reef

0 ———— 20 mi
0 ———— 20 km

ethos; spectacular grounds; free Wi-Fi. **Cons:** a drive from Palm Cove's cafés; no on-site gym; rain-forest environs can mean the odd critter gets into your room. [$] *Rooms from: A$299* ✉ *Kewarra Beach, 80 Kewarra St.* ☎ *07/4058–4000* 🌐 *www.kewarra.com* 🛏 *44 rooms* 🍴 *No meals.*

Peppers Beach Club & Spa

$$$ | **RESORT** | **FAMILY** | Its beachfront location, excellent on-site dining, and tropical suites make this laid-back resort popular with city dwellers seeking upscale relaxation. **Pros:** terrific on-site dining; multiple pools including a quiet pool zone and Serenity wing; well-equipped, air-conditioned gym. **Cons:** weak Wi-Fi; main pool area can be busy; may be too loud for couples looking to relax. [$] *Rooms from: A$375* ✉ *123 Williams Esplanade* ☎ *07/4059–9200 direct line, 1300/737444 toll-free in Australia, 07/5665–4426 Australia-wide reservations* 🌐 *www.peppers.com.au/beach-club-spa* 🛏 *150 rooms* 🍴 *Free Breakfast.*

The Reef House

$$ | **RESORT** | This centrally located small resort, once a private residence, feels positively quaint, and that's a good thing when you're looking for a low-key escape in this resort area. **Pros:** large, well appointed rooms; complimentary sunset punch and canapés; free Wi-Fi and movies. **Cons:** pools can be cold; Wi-Fi and phone reception patchy; grounds relatively small. [$] *Rooms from: A$249* ✉ *99 Williams Esplanade* ☎ *07/4080–2600* 🌐 *www.reefhouse.com.au* 🛏 *67 rooms* 🍴 *Free Breakfast.*

Activities

Palm Cove makes a great base for rain-forest and reef activities—hiking, biking, horseback riding, rafting, ballooning, and ATV adventures on the Atherton Tableland; snorkeling, diving, and sailing around the Low Isles and Barrier Reef; sea kayaking just offshore; and scenic flights over just about anywhere a small plane can get on a tank of gas. Though few cruise or tour companies are based in this beachside enclave, many Cairns and Port Douglas–based operators offer Palm Cove transfers.

KAYAKING

★ Palm Cove Watersports

KAYAKING | **FAMILY** | Paddling around history-rich Double Island, off Palm Cove Jetty, in a kayak or on a paddleboard is a tranquil, eco-friendly way to get close to the local marine life: you'll often spot dolphins, stingrays, turtles, and colorful fish on this local operator's terrific sunrise tours and half-day snorkeling excursions. Helpful guides impart safety briefings and labor-saving tips on technique before you set out, and there are frequent stops for refreshments, snorkeling (May through November), and wildlife-watching en route. Even if you've never paddled a kayak before you're unlikely to capsize; the single and double kayaks are super-stable. Half-day trips circumnavigate Double Island, stopping off on the fringing reef about 600 meters (½ mile) from shore and on a secluded beach. Transfers from Cairns (A$15 per person) and Port Douglas (A$30 per person) are available; bookings are essential. **■ TIP→ Safety and snorkeling gear is provided, but bring sunglasses, a hat, and sunscreen.** ✉ *149–153 Williams Esplanade* ☎ *0402/861011* 🌐 *www.palmcovewatersports.com* 🎟 *From A$50.*

Port Douglas

67½ km (42 miles) northwest of Cairns.

Known simply as "Port" to locals, Port Douglas offers almost as broad a range of outdoor adventures as Cairns, but in a more compact, laid-back setting. In this burgeoning tourist town there's a palpable buzz, despite tropical haze and humidity. Travelers from all over the world base themselves here, making excursions to the north's wild rain forests and the Great Barrier Reef. Varied lodgings, restaurants, and bars center on and around Port's main strip, Macrossan Street.

Like much of North Queensland, Port Douglas was settled after gold was discovered nearby. When local ore deposits dwindled in the 1880s, it became a port for sugar milled in nearby Mossman until the 1950s. The town's many old "Queenslander" buildings give it the feel of a simple seaside settlement, despite its modern resorts and overbuilt landscape. The rain forests and beaches that envelop the town are, for the most part, World Heritage sites—so while Port continues to grow in popularity, the extraordinary environs that draw people here are protected from development.

GETTING HERE AND AROUND

By car, it's a scenic, 75-minute drive north to Port Douglas from Cairns: take Sheridan Street to the Captain Cook Highway, following it for around 60 km (35 miles) to the Port Douglas turnoff. North of Palm Cove, along the 30-km (19-mile) Marlin Coast, the road plays hide-and-seek with an idyllic stretch of shoreline, ducking inland through tunnels of tropical coastal forest and curving back to the surf to reach Port Douglas.

Around town, most people drive, walk, or cycle. It's about 5½ km (3½ miles), or an hour's level walk from the highway to the main street. Regular shuttle buses call in at major hotels and resorts day and night, ferrying travelers to and from Cairns, the airport, and nearby towns and attractions.

◉ Sights

Port Douglas is actually an isthmus, bounded by Four Mile Beach on one side, Dickson Inlet on the other, with the town's main retail, café, and restaurant strip, Macrossan Street, running up the center. The town sprawls as far as the highway, 5½ km (3½ miles) to the west, along Port Douglas Road, which is

lined with upmarket resorts and holiday apartment complexes. At the far end of Macrossan Street, on Wharf Street, there's a busy marina.

★ Wildlife Habitat

NATURE PRESERVE | FAMILY | This world-class wildlife sanctuary just off the Captain Cook Highway is divided into "immersion" wetland, rain forest, grassland, and savanna habitats, enabling close creature encounters with everything from koalas to cassowaries and crocs. The park shelters more than 180 species of native wildlife in its 8-acre expanse, including technicolor parrots, emus, kangaroos, echidnas, and reptiles. The buffet breakfast with the birds, served daily 9–10:30 (A$56, including sanctuary entry and a guided tour) is accompanied by avian residents so tame they'll perch on your shoulders—and may steal your food if you're distracted. You can also lunch with the lorikeets from 12:30 daily (A$58), then join one of the sanctuary's free expert-guided tours, held several times daily. For something even more special book the nocturnal tour (A$42) or a two-hour animal and dining package (A$165). ⊠ *Port Douglas Rd. , at Agincourt St.* ☎ *07/4099–3235* ⊕ *www. wildlifehabitat.com.au* ⊠ *From A$36.*

🍴 Restaurants

★ Harrisons

$$ | BRITISH | A classic "Queenslander" with a lovely outdoor cocktails area shaded by century-old mango trees and fine-dining inside, Harrisons impresses with deftly executed dishes that showcase fresh seafood and small-batch ingredients, sourced locally. There's a six-course tasting menu at A$95 per person, A$135 with matched wines, and on the wine list, you'll find plenty of good mid-priced Antipodean drops and a smattering of French ones. **Known for:** has won multiple awards for its dining experience; North Queensland Cobia with soured cream, bush lemon, and pickled radish;

modern Australian menu with a British twist. $ *Average main: A$45* ✉ *22 Wharf St.* ☎ *0455 /594–011* ⊕ *www.harrisonsrestaurant.com.au.*

★ On The Inlet Seafood Restaurant

$ | SEAFOOD |FAMILY | At this much-lauded seafood restaurant, modern Australian dishes put the focus on fresh North Queensland produce and seafood, which is delivered direct from local fishing boats. You can choose your own live mud crab from holding tanks, or down the sunset special—a generous bucket of prawns and a choice of Aussie beer or wine. **Known for:** dining on the deck; terrific wine and cocktail list; family-friendly atmosphere and kids menu. $ *Average main: A$34* ✉ *18–20 Wharf St, Shop 7* ☎ *07/4099–5255* ⊕ *www.ontheinlet.com.au.*

★ Salsa Bar & Grill

$ | MODERN AUSTRALIAN |FAMILY | Rub shoulders with local foodies and enjoy intimate dining after sunset on the large wooden deck of this lively waterside institution that serves tropical Modern Australian fare. The dinner menu offers something for everyone, from kangaroo loin to herb-crusted wild barramundi, to Jambalaya loaded with yabbies (local crayfish), tiger prawns, squid, and crocodile sausage. **Known for:** great waterfront location; creative cocktail menu; linguini pepperincino with local red claw crayfish. $ *Average main: A$37* ✉ *26 Wharf St.* ☎ *07/4099–4922* ⊕ *www.salsaportdouglas.com.au.*

Watergate Restaurant & Lounge Bar

$ | MODERN AUSTRALIAN | Atmospheric indoor-outdoor dining, attentive service, and a well-stocked bar are nice, but the primary draw at this relaxed restaurant is the food, which highlights the freshest local ingredients. Enjoy reef fish and prawns straight off Port Douglas's fishing boats, and seasonal fruit, vegetables, and herbs from the Atherton Tableland. **Known for:** friendly, warm service; kangaroo loin; to-die-for dessert menu.

$ *Average main: A$37* ✉ *5/31 Macrossan St.* ☎ *07/4099–5544* ⊕ *www.watergateportdouglas.com.au.*

🛏 Hotels

Coconut Grove Port Douglas

$$$$ | RENTAL | These well-appointed luxe apartments and penthouses perched above Port Douglas's main strip have state-of-the-art furnishings and appliances, free-standing spa baths, and large entertaining spaces including big, furnished balconies or decks, some with outdoor barbecues and plunge pools. **Pros:** immaculate living areas; central location; free undercover parking. **Cons:** fees for daily housekeeping; reception closes after business hours; 10 am checkout. $ *Rooms from: A$650* ✉ *56 Macrossan St.* ☎ *07/4099–0600* ⊕ *www.coconutgroveportdouglas.com.au* ⊙ *Reception closes daily 5 pm–8 am* ⇆ *33 suites* ⊩ *No meals.*

★ Lazy Lizard Inn

$ | HOTEL |FAMILY | The clean, spacious, self-contained studios at this friendly low-rise motel just outside of town make it a practical base for those who don't mind a short walk or cycle to Port Douglas's center. **Pros:** friendly hosts; free cable TV and Wi-Fi; easy parking outside your door (or guest bikes to get around town on). **Cons:** reception closes at 6 pm; no on-site bar or restaurant; slightly out of town. $ *Rooms from: A$159* ✉ *121 Davidson St.* ☎ *07/4099–5900, 1800/995950 toll-free in Australia* ⊕ *www.lazylizardinn.com.au* ⇆ *22 studios* ⊩ *Free Breakfast.*

★ Mandalay Luxury Beachfront Apartments

$$$ | RENTAL |FAMILY | With beautiful Four-Mile Beach just outside and shops and eateries a brisk walk away, these comfortable, expansive, fully equipped apartments are in an excellent location. **Pros:** reasonable rates; plenty of space; close to the beach. **Cons:** street outside is poorly lit at night; no reception in off-peak hours; closest restaurants

are a 10-minute walk away. $ *Rooms from: A$390* ⊠ *Garrick St. at Beryl St.* ☏ *07/4099–0100* ⊕ *www.mandalay.com. au* ⌂ *41 apartments* ⦿ *No meals.*

Sheraton Grand Mirage Resort

$$$ | RESORT |FAMILY | Centered on a complex of interconnecting saltwater lagoon pools, the Sheraton Grand Mirage is a good choice for families. **Pros:** magnificent saltwater lagoon pools and steps from the beachfront; modernized rooms and suites; plenty of on-site facilities. **Cons:** it's a fair distance from Port Douglas's restaurants and shopping; cost of on-site food and other extras can add up; it can feel overwhelmingly large. $ *Rooms from: A$350* ⊠ *Davidson St.* ☏ *07/4099–5888* ⊕ *www.marriott.com* ⌂ *394 rooms* ⦿ *No meals.*

★ Thala Beach Nature Reserve

$$$ | RESORT | Set on 145 acres of private beach, coconut groves, and forest, this eco-certified nature lodge is about low-key luxury. **Pros:** 2 km (1.25 miles) of private access beaches; free activities include guided walks and wildlife and bird-watching; free Wi-Fi in the restaurant and lobby. **Cons:** no in-room Internet access; hilly property is unsuitable for guests with limited mobility; 15-minute drive to Port Douglas. $ *Rooms from: A$379* ⊠ *5078 Captain Cook Hwy.* ⊹ *Oak Beach, 38½ km (24 miles) north of Cairns, just south of Port Douglas* ☏ *07/4098–5700, 866/998–4252 toll-free from U.S.* ⊕ *www.thalabeach.com.au* ⌂ *83 suites* ⦿ *No meals.*

🛍 Shopping

★ Port Douglas markets

OUTDOOR/FLEA/GREEN MARKETS | FAMILY | Local growers and artisans gather on Sunday mornings in Port Douglas's waterfront park to sell fresh tropical produce and gourmet goodies, arts and crafts, handmade garments, precious-stone jewelry, books, and souvenirs. The atmosphere is relaxed, the crowd is colorful, and there's plenty of variety. ⊠ *Anzac Park, Wharf St., end of Macrossan St.*

🏃 Activities

Port Douglas is a great base for activities on the mainland and reef. Several tour companies conduct day trips into the rain forest and beyond in four-wheel-drive buses and vans; most include river cruises for crocodile-spotting and stops at local attractions. Various reef operators either base vessels at or pick up from Port Douglas Marina. You can also horseback ride, bungee jump, raft, go off-roading, hike, mountain-bike, and balloon on and around the Atherton Tablelands.

FISHING

MV *Norseman*

FISHING | FAMILY | Long-established MV *Norseman* is one of the best game-fishing boats on the Great Barrier Reef for novice and experienced anglers alike. Head out to the best spots on the reef's edge on a 60-foot, purpose-designed, high-tech vessel to fish for large pelagic species including Spanish mackerel, tuna, wahoo, and the elusive giant trevally. Closer in, find sea perch, mangrove Jack, red and spangeled emperor, and coral trout. It's A$280 per adult for a full day on the water (bait, equipment, instruction, lunch, and refreshments, fuel levy, rod, and reel; reef taxes included). Port Douglas accommodation transfers are free. ⊠ *Crystalbrook Superyacht Marina, 44 Wharf St., Berth E11, at Inlet Road* ☏ *0419/015–262* ⊕ *www.mvnorseman. com.au* ⊞ *From A$280 per person.*

RAIN FOREST AND REEF TOURS

★ Back Country Bliss Adventures

TOUR—SPORTS | FAMILY | Amazing wilderness locations, high-quality equipment, excellent staff, Wet Tropic World Heritage Tour Operator accreditation give the Bliss team the edge. Based in Port Douglas but ranging much farther afield, the company runs customized, culturally and eco-sensitive small-group day and multiday trips that take you to nature and adventure hot spots from the Atherton Tablelands, Mossman Gorge, and Cape Tribulation. They'll take you hiking, drift-snorkeling in rain-forest streams, and "jungle surfing" in the rain-forest canopy. ☎ *07/4099–3677* ⊕ *www. backcountrybliss.com.au* ☞ *From A$105* ☞ *Tour prices include pickups from and drop-offs to local accommodations and resorts.*

Daintree Tours

TOUR—SPORTS | FAMILY | This operator conducts daylong, well-guided trips in top-of-the-line 4WD vehicles and custom-built trucks to the Daintree rain forest and beyond, with plenty of stop-offs en route to eat, drink, swim, and explore. Visit the Mossman Gorge, the Daintree rain forest, and Cape Tribulation. You can also arrange a daylong private charter to Kuranda, the Atherton Tablelands, and the rugged track to Bloomfield Falls. Ample lunch and refreshments, included in all excursions, ensure you keep your strength up. Port Douglas pickups and drop-offs make the early-morning starts simple. ✉ *Tropical Journeys, 21–23 Warner St., Shop 3A, at Macrossan St.* ☎ *07/4099–6999, 1800/055966* ⊕ *www. daintreetours.com* ☞ *From A$199.*

Reef and Rainforest Connections

TOUR—SPORTS | FAMILY | This long-established, eco-friendly operator offers day trips exploring Kuranda's attractions and local wildlife parks; excursions to Cape Tribulation, the Daintree rain forest, and Mossman Gorge; and Great Barrier Reef cruises with Quicksilver Connections. The popular Kuranda day tour includes trips on the historic Scenic Railway and Skyrail Rainforest Cableway; a stroll around charming Kuranda Village, with its markets, curio stores, and wildlife attractions; and a visit to Tjapukai Aboriginal Cultural Park or Rainforestation. ✉ *40 Macrossan St.* ☎ *1300/780455 reservations* ⊕ *www.reefandrainforest.com.au* ☞ *From A$168.*

★ Tony's Tropical Tours

TOUR—SPORTS | FAMILY | This company gives entertaining small-group day tours in luxe Land Cruisers that take in rain forest sights and attractions as far as Cape Tribulation or, if you're prepared to get up earlier, the renowned and ruggedly beautiful Bloomfield Track. Well-informed, witty commentary from local experts, and non-rushed, well-chosen stops and activities—from interpretative rain-forest walks and Daintree River wildlife (croc) cruises, to handmade ice-cream and tropical-fruit tasting—make these trips crowd-pleasers. Refreshments, included in the cost, are a cut above the norm. Tony's also runs off-road tours through the Daintree as far as the Bloomfield Falls and terrific charter tours to the crater lakes and the Atherton Tablelands on which you might see kangaroos, birdlife, and the famed Curtain Fig tree. ✉ *Port Douglas* ☎ *07/4099–3230* ⊕ *www. tropicaltours.com.au* ☞ *From A$198.*

RIVER CRUISES

Crocodile Express

BOATING | FAMILY | Bird-watchers and photographers flock to Crocodile Express's flat-bottom boats to cruise the Daintree River on crocodile-spotting excursions; you may also see rare birds and outsize butterflies, flying foxes, snakes, and lizards en route. Sixty-minute cruises leave the Daintree Gateway, 500 meters (1,640 feet) before the ferry crossing, at regular intervals from 8:30 am to 3:30 pm; or you can board at Daintree Village Jetty and cruise the Upper Daintree regularly between 10 and 3:30. Extra cruises from both access points are scheduled in peak periods. ✉ *5 Stewart St. , end of Mossman–Daintree Rd., Daintree* ☎ *07/4098–6120* ⊕ *www.crocodileex-press.com* ☞ *From A$25.*

SNORKELING AND DIVING

Eye to Eye Marine Encounters

DIVING/SNORKELING | John Rumney, who pioneered swim-with-whales in Queensland, brings 30-plus years of experience on the Reef and extensive ecological knowledge and nautical expertise to his revered minke whale expeditions, working with highly skilled divers, scientists, and skippers to ensure each trip is as exciting as it is eco-friendly. Marine Encounters also specializes in private, curated diving trips in the region. ⊠ *10 Captain Cook Hwy.* ☎ *07/4098–5417, 0417/726622* ⊕ *www.marineencounters. com.au.*

★ Poseidon

DIVING/SNORKELING | **FAMILY** | Excellent pre-dive briefings from a marine naturalist, high safety standards, and a wide choice of dive and snorkeling sites make this advanced eco-certified operator a smart choice. Poseidon runs guided snorkeling and PADI-style diving trips to sites at three separate reef sites at the Agincourt Ribbon Reef on a small, usually uncrowded boat. A day's cruise to three Agincourt sites includes a marine biologist–guided snorkel tour, Lycra suits, masks, snorkels, fins, and flotation devices; wet suits for snorkelers can be rented at A$15 per day. For certified divers, a full day in the water includes dive gear. Morning and afternoon tea and a buffet lunch are provided for all guests. Port Douglas transfers are free; from Cairns or the Northern Beaches, it's A$32. ⊠ *Reef Marina, 44 Wharf St. , off Inlet Dr.* ☎ *07/4087–2100* ⊕ *www.poseidon-cruises.com.au* ⊠ *From A$254.*

Quicksilver Cruises

DIVING/SNORKELING | **FAMILY** | Quicksilver's fast, modern catamarans speed you from Port Douglas's marina to a large commercial activity platform on the outer Barrier Reef. There, you can dive and snorkel with the reef residents, and make leisurely sail-and-snorkel trips to Low Isle coral cays. Options at Agincourt Reef include marine-biologist-guided snorkeling tours (A$64–A$82), introductory or certified scuba dives (extra A$124–A$174), 10-minute scenic heli-tours (A$189), and "Ocean Walker"

sea-bed explorations (A$170). There's also a semisubmersible underwater observatory, included in the A$264 rate. A quieter sailing trip to a Low Isles coral cay, closer to shore (A$210), includes a biologist-guided glass-bottom-boat trip and snorkeling. The trip includes a varied lunch buffet and dive/snorkel gear. Transfers are available from Port Douglas accommodations and farther afield (A$16–A$32). ⊠ *The Reef Marina, 44 Wharf St., off Inlet Dr.* ☎ *07/4087–2100* ⊕ *www.quicksilver-cruises.com* ⊠ *From A$264.*

The Silver Series: *Silversonic*

DIVING/SNORKELING | **FAMILY** | High-end, high-speed catamaran *Silversonic* whisks visitors to three pristine dive-snorkel sites on Agincourt Reef, known for its high-visibility waters. There, you can spend five hours amid spectacular corals on the edge of the Coral Sea trench, with turtles, rays, tropical fish, large pelagic species, and, in season, the odd Minke whale. Full-day outer reef cruises run daily, weather permitting; the A$240 tariff includes a tropical buffet lunch, morning and afternoon tea, snorkeling, and gear; all scuba dives are guided at no extra cost, and everyone pays a A$6.50 reef tax. Coach transfers from local accommodations are included in the cruise fare; transfers to and from Palm Cove, the Northern Beaches, and Cairns are available for a surcharge. ⊠ *The Reef Marina, 1 Wharf St. , off Inlet Dr.* ☎ *07/4087–2100* ⊕ *www.silverseries.com.au* ⊠ *From A$240* ☞ *Need cash to purchase additional drinks on board.*

Mossman

20 km (12 miles) northwest of Port Douglas, 75 km (47 miles) north of Cairns via the Captain Cook Hwy.

This sleepy sugarcane town of just a couple of thousand residents has shops, a medical center, and gas stations, but most visitors merely pass through en route to Mossman Gorge, the Daintree, and rain-forest accommodations. There's little here to explore, but it's a good place to stop for supplies and has a few good eateries.

The spectacular wilderness around Mossman is ideal terrain for adventure sports and outdoor activities. If you have a day—or even a few hours—to spare, you can explore beaches, rain forest, and bushland trails on horseback, mountain bike, or ATV; take a scenic trek through Mossman Gorge; or drift-snorkel in the Upper Mossman River. The region's indigenous guardians, the Kuku Yalanji, run guided tours of Mossman Gorge and their coastal hunting grounds near Wonga Beach, in the World Heritage–listed Daintree rain forest.

TOURS

ABORIGINAL TOURS

★ Kuku Yalanji Cultural Habitat Tours

(*Daintree Dreaming tour*)

TOUR—SPORTS | FAMILY | On these relaxed, two-hour coastal walks, Kubirri Warra brothers Linc and Brandon Walker, members of the Kuku Yalanji *bama* (people), take turns guiding groups through three diverse ecosystems along Cooya Beach, demonstrating traditional plant use, pointing out bush tucker ingredients, recounting Dreamtime legends, and sharing their prodigious cultural and local knowledge, with plenty of jokes thrown in. Wear wading shoes, light clothing, a hat, insect repellent, and sunscreen. ⊠ *Mossman Gorge Rd.* ☎ *07/4098–3437* ⊕ *www.kycht.com.au* ☒ *From A$90.*

★ Walkabout Adventures

TOUR—SPORTS | FAMILY | Personable indigenous guide Juan Walker and his team take small groups on fascinating half- and full-day rain-forest safari and coastal hunting trips, and personalized tours on request. These excursions can include a visit to the world's oldest rain forest, Mossman Gorge, and coastal mudflats, mangroves, and beaches, with swims in rain-forest streams, foraging beach and mangrove walks, and lessons on spear-throwing. ⊠ *Daintree* ☎ *0429/478206 Juan Walker* ⊕ *www. walkaboutadventures.com.au* ☒ *From A$165, including transfers from Port Douglas, Mossman, and Daintree Village.*

ESSENTIALS

VISITOR INFORMATION Destination Daintree. ⊕ *www.destinationdaintree.com*

◉ Sights

Daintree Village, a half-hour drive north along the Mossman-Daintree Road, has restaurants, cafés, galleries, and access to croc river cruises. Drive 20 minutes northeast of Mossman to reach Wonga Beach, where you can stroll along the sand or go walkabout with indigenous guides.

★ Mossman Gorge

CANYON | FAMILY | Just 5 km (3 miles) outside Mossman are the spectacular waterfalls and swimming-hole-studded river that tumble through sheer-walled Mossman Gorge. The Kuku Yalanji–run Mossman Gorge Centre is the starting-point for various aborigine-led walks, tours, and activities. There are several boulder-studded, croc-free swimming holes within the Gorge, and a 2½-km (1½-mile) rain-forest walking track and suspension bridge. (Swimming in the river itself is hazardous, crocs or not, due to swift currents, slippery rocks, and flash flooding.) Keep your eyes peeled for tree and musky rat-kangaroos, Boyd's water dragons, scrub fowl, turtles, and big, bright butterflies—and try to avoid stinging vines (plants with serrated-edge, heart-shaped leaves, found at rain-forest edges). If you intend to hike beyond the river and rain-forest circuits, inform the information desk staff at the Mossman Gorge Centre, which also has café/ restaurant, gift shop, indigenous art gallery, restrooms, showers, and visitor parking. ⊠ *Mossman Gorge Centre, 212r*

Silky Oaks Lodge, near Daintree National Park

Mossman Gorge Rd. ☎ 07/4099–7000 🌐 www.mossmangorge.com.au ✉ Free entry to Mossman Gorge Centre; A$10 return bus trip out to gorge; tour prices vary.

🛏 Hotels

Daintree EcoLodge & Spa

$$$ | RESORT | At this 30-acre boutique eco-resort in the ancient Daintree rain forest, elevated boardwalks protect the fragile environs and link the day spa, heated pool, restaurant/bar, and 15 free-standing tree houses or "bayans." All are air-conditioned and equipped with ceiling fans, satellite TVs, and king-size canopy beds. **Pros:** alfresco spa treatments; eco-friendly; lower rates with longer stays or early bookings. **Cons:** no in-room Internet access; noise from public areas carries to proximate rooms and spa; no one at reception desk from 8 pm to 8 am. 💲 *Rooms from: A$345* ✉ *3189 Mossman-Daintree Rd.* ✛ *3 km (2 miles)*

past Daintree village, 110 km (68 miles) north of Cairns ☎ 07/4777–7377 🌐 www. daintree-ecolodge.com.au ✍ 15 suites ⭐ *Free Breakfast.*

★ Silky Oaks Lodge

$$$ | RESORT | This beautiful, retreat-like resort and Advanced Ecotourism–certified hotel in the heart of the rain forest has luxe tree houses and suites clustered around an expansive open-sided lodge, day spa, and lagoon pool. **Pros:** really special and unique property; helpful tour desk and lots of included activities; well-marked walking trails around the resort. **Cons:** no in-room Internet; steep paths to some rooms (though you can call for a buggy pickup); access road can flood after heavy rain, January through March. 💲 *Rooms from: A$440* ✉ *Finlayvale Rd.* ☎ *07/4098–1666* 🌐 *www.silkyoakslodge. com.au* ✍ *43 suites* ⭐ *No meals.*

Cape Tribulation

35 km (22 miles) north of the Daintree River crossing, 140 km (87 miles) north of Cairns.

Set dramatically at the base of Mount Sorrow, Cape Tribulation was named by Captain James Cook after a nearby reef snagged the HMS *Endeavour*, forcing him to seek refuge at the site of present-day Cooktown. Today, the tiny settlement, little more than a general store and a few lodges, is the activities and accommodations base for the surrounding national park.

GETTING HERE AND AROUND

The 140-km (86-mile) drive from Cairns to Cape Tribulation takes just under three hours. If you're renting a car, it's simplest to do so in Cairns or Port Douglas. This can be tough driving territory. The "highway" is narrow with just two lanes; many minor roads are rough and unpaved; and even major thruways in this area may be closed in the wet season due to flooding.

Mason's Cape Tribulation Tourist Information Centre, grocery store, bottle shop, and PK's Jungle Village, a little farther north on the opposite side of Cape Tribulation Road, are the last stops for food, supplies, and fuel as you head north. At PK's there's a supermarket, a bar serving meals and drinks, and an ATM.

ATMs are scarce beyond Mossman. Get cash and gas at the service station and convenience store on the Mossman-Daintree Road at Wonga Beach, or at PK's. North of the Daintree River, mobile phone coverage is limited (except in and around Mossman and Daintree Village and around Thornton Beach Kiosk), and you'll be lucky to get any signal once you get as far as Cape Tribulation.

Sun Palm Transport's daily services link Cairns airport with Cairns, Palm Cove, and Port Douglas. Charter services to Mossman, Daintree, Cow Bay, and Cape Trib can also be arranged. The journey from Cairns to Port Douglas takes around two hours, with stops at most resorts on request.

BUS TRAVEL
BUS CONTACTS Sun Palm Transport Group.
☎ *07/4099–1191* ⊕ *www.sunpalmtransport.com.au.*

FERRY TRAVEL
Daintree Ferry
The Daintree–Mossman Road winds through sugarcane plantations and towering green hills to the Daintree River, a short waterway fed by monsoonal rains that make it a favorite inland haunt for saltwater crocodiles. On the river's northerly side, a sign announces Cape Tribulation National Park. There's just one cable ferry, carrying a maximum 27 vehicles, so although the crossing takes five minutes, the wait can be 15 minutes or more, especially between 11 am and 1 pm, and all afternoon during holidays. There's no need to prebook your passage, but bring cash if you'll be crossing after dark. Return fare for a car is A$28 (one-way A$16); for a motorbike, it's A$11/A$6; a multiday car pass (five trips) is A$56; and walk-on passengers pay just A$2. ⊠ *Daintree River ferry crossing, Daintree-Mossman Rd., Daintree* ✥ *Ferry turnoff is just under 30 kms (18 miles) north of Mossman on Daintree-Mossman Rd.* ☎ *07/4099–9444 Douglas Shire Council offices* ⊕ *www.douglas.qld.gov.au/community/daintree-ferry* ✏ *Roundtrip: A$23 per car, A$9.50 motorbike, A$2 walk-on passenger/bicycle, A$46 multiday car pass (5 return trips).*

ESSENTIALS
TOURS AND VISITOR INFORMATION
Mason's Cape Tribulation Tourist Information Centre, Shop, & Mason's Tours. ⊠ *3781 Cape Tribulation Rd.* ☎ *07/4098–0070* ⊕ *www.masonstours.com.au.* **PK's Jungle Village.** ⊠ *Cape Tribulation Rd., Lot 7* ☎ *07/4098–0040* ⊕ *www.pksjunglevillage.com.au.*

Sights

Cape Tribulation Road winds through rain forest north of Cow Bay, veering east to join the coast at Thornton Beach, then skirting a string of near-deserted beaches en route to Cape Trib. Accommodations, attractions, and access points for beaches, croc cruise boats, and mangrove and rain-forest boardwalks are well signposted from the main road.

These rugged-looking yet fragile environs, Kuku Yalanji tribal lands, are best explored with experienced, culturally sensitive and eco-conscious guides. Excursions by 4WD and on horseback, bicycle, boat, and foot are offered by a few dozen local operators and resorts.

If exploring off-road on your own, arm yourself with detailed local maps, supplies, and up-to-date information. Let a reliable person know your intended route and return time, and don't underestimate the wildness of this terrain.

Daintree Discovery Centre
INFO CENTER | FAMILY | This World Heritage–accredited Wet Tropics Visitor Centre's elevated boardwalks and a high viewing tower enable you to overlook an astoundingly diverse tract of ancient rain forest. You can acquire information en route from handheld audio guides, expert talks, and the on-site interpretative center. Four audio-guided trails include a Bush Tucker Trail and a Cassowary Circuit, on which you might spot one of these large but well-camouflaged birds. Take the Aerial Walkway across part of the bush, then the stairs to the top of the 76-foot-high Canopy Tower. Keen students of botany and ecology might want to prebook a guided group tour. The shop sells books, cards, souvenirs, and clothing. There's also an on-site café. ✉ *Tulip Oak Rd., off Cape Tribulation Rd., Cow Bay* ☎ *07/4098–9171* 🌐 *www.daintree-rec.com.au* 🎫 *A$35 (includes 68-page guidebook/return entry for 7 days).*

★ **Daintree National Park**
NATIONAL/STATE PARK | The world's oldest tropical rain forest is an ecological wonderland: 85 of the 120 rarest species on earth are found here, and new ones are still being discovered. The 22,000-acre park, part of the UNESCO World Heritage–listed Wet Tropics region, stretches along the coast and west into the jungle from Cow Bay, 40 km (25 miles) or around an hour's drive northwest of Mossman. The traditional owners, the Eastern Kuku Yalanji, who live in well-honed harmony with their rain-forest environs, attribute powerful properties to many local sites—so tread sensitively. Prime hiking season here is May through September, and many local operators offer guided Daintree rain-forest walks, longer hikes, and nighttime wildlife-spotting excursions. Gather information and maps from local rangers or the Queensland Parks and Wildlife Service's **ParksQ** website before hiking unguided, and stay on marked trails and boardwalks to avoid damaging your fragile surroundings. Whatever season you go, bring insect repellent. ✉ *Daintree* ☎ *13–7468* 🌐 *www.nprsr.qld.gov.au/parks/daintree.*

Restaurants

On The Turps Bar & Restaurant
$ | MODERN AUSTRALIAN | At this open-air restaurant in the Daintree rain forest, wallabies, bandicoots, and musky rat kangaroos might join you at the table as you tuck into Mod-Oz meal that highlights local, seasonal ingredients including fresh seafood, and wines from the well-stocked bar. On The Turps also does "tropical continental" breakfasts and varied, good-value lunches, as well as leisurely morning and afternoon Devonshire teas. **Known for:** delicious local barramundi; home-style cooking ; good range of vegetarian and vegan meals. [$] *Average main: A$33* ✉ *Daintree-Cape Tribulation Heritage Lodge & Spa, Turpentine Rd., Lot 236, R36* ✣ *18 km (about 11 miles)*

north of Daintree River crossing, turn left at Turpentine Rd. ☎ *07/4098–9321* 🌐 *www.heritagelodge.net.au/restaurant.*

★ **Whet Cafe, Bar and Restaurant**

$ | **MODERN AUSTRALIAN** |**FAMILY** | Stylish and hip yet comfortable, Whet Cafe, Bar and Restaurant draws visitors and locals with its outdoor deck, perfect for long lunches, sunset cocktails, and romantic dinners. It has Modern Australian food using regional and seasonal ingredients and friendly service, and is a fully self-sustained, off-grid operation. **Known for:** jungle dining; local seafood combined in fresh, simple dishes with Asian and Mediterranean influences; melt-in your mouth steaks and delicious wild, local-caught barramundi. [$] *Average main: A$26* ✉ *Cape Tribulation Rd., Lot 1* ☎ *07/4098–0007* 🌐 *www.whet.net.au.*

Hotels

Privately run campgrounds and small resorts can be found along Daintree Road at Myall Creek and Cape Tribulation.

Cape Tribulation Farmstay B&B

$ | **B&B/INN** |**FAMILY** | A handful of simple but comfortable, solar-powered cabins sit among rambutan, mangosteen, and breadfruit trees on this 40-hectare exotic fruit farm. **Pros:** beach and rain-forest trails adjoin the property; breakfast basket of fresh tropical fruit—some of which you've probably never tasted; free Internet (but only in the central farmhouse). **Cons:** few in-room modern conveniences; no swimming pool; modest accommodations. [$] *Rooms from: A$150* ✉ *3939 Cape Tribulation Rd.* ☎ *07/4098–0042* 🌐 *www.capetribfarm.com.au* 🛏 *5 rooms* 🍴 *Free Breakfast.*

Cockatoo Hill Retreat

$$$ | **B&B/INN** | The elegant solar-powered tree houses at this impeccably run boutique retreat invite relaxation and romance. **Pros:** helpful, thoughtful host; eco-friendly; magnificent views. **Cons:** phone/Internet access only if you have Telstra service; 4WD required during or after heavy rain to get up the resort's steep driveway; no on-site food apart from breakfast. [$] *Rooms from: A$395* ✉ *2060 Cape Tribulation Rd., Diwan* ✥ *Midway between Daintree and Cape Tribulation* ☎ *07/4098–9277* 🌐 *www.cockatoohillretreat.com.au* 🛏 *4 rooms* 🍴 *Free Breakfast.*

Activities

CANOPY TOURS

Jungle Surfing Canopy Tours

TOUR—SPORTS | **FAMILY** | It's an exhilarating perspective on the rain forest and reef: suspended above the canopy on flying-fox zip lines, your speed controlled by guides as you whiz along over lush rain forest and Mason's Creek, stopping at tree platforms for killer bird's-eye views. Sessions last two hours and depart up to 12 times a day starting at 7:50 am. Nightly guided Jungle Adventures Nightwalks explore the critter-filled 45-acre grounds, departing PK's Jungle Village reception at 7:30 pm. You can also buy tickets covering zip-lining and the night tour. Transfers from most local accommodations are free, or self-drive to the central departure point. Day-tour packages from Port Douglas include lunch. Note that Jungle Surfing is unsuitable for anyone weighing more than 120 kilograms (260 pounds), and that anyone under 18 needs a medical certificate and waiver before they'll be allowed to zip-line. ✉ *Jungle Adventure Centre, Cape Tribulation Rd. , Lot 2* ✥ *Free parking at pickup point. Arrive 10 min prior to designated departure time to complete paperwork* ☎ *07/4098–0190* 🌐 *www.junglesurfing.com.au* 🎟 *From A$45.*

GREAT BARRIER REEF TOURS

★ **Ocean Safari**

TOUR—SPORTS | **FAMILY** | Eco-certified Ocean Safari runs half-day small-group tours that include snorkeling two pristine sites on the Great Barrier Reef, just half an hour's thrilling motorboat ride off Cape

Trib Beach. Well-chosen sites on magnificent Mackay and Undine reefs teem with "Nemos" (clown anemone fish), turtles, rays, barracuda, potato cod, giant clams, nudibranchs, and an astounding array of corals. A maximum of 25 passengers and a rigid inflatable boat (with covered seating area and bathroom facilities). Snorkeling equipment, expert guidance, and EMC (reef) tax are included in the price; you can rent wet suits/sunsuits (A$8) and prescription masks (A$15), and buy soft drinks, chocolate, and underwater cameras on board. Meet at Ocean Safari's office, on-site at the Turtle Rock Cafe opposite PK's; pickups from Cape Trib accommodations are free. Package deals that include safari-hut accommodation at Jungle Lodge and an Ocean Safari excursion are available. ⊠ *Ocean Safari office (at Turtle Rock Cafe), Cape Tribulation Rd., Lot 4* ✢ *Opposite PK's Jungle Village* ☎ *07/4098–0006* ⊕ *www. oceansafari.com.au* ✉ *From A$149.*

Cooktown

103 km (64 miles), around 3½-hours' drive, north of Cape Tribulation; 324 km (203-mile) or 5½-hours' drive north of Cairns.

Traveling north, Cooktown is the last major settlement on the east coast of the continent, sitting at the edge of a difficult wilderness. Its wide main street consists mainly of two-story pubs with four-wheel-drive vehicles parked out front. Despite the frontier air, Cooktown has an impressive history. It was here in 1770 that Captain James Cook beached HMS *Endeavour* to repair her hull. Any tour of Cooktown should begin at the waterfront, where a statue of Cook gazes out to sea, overlooking the spot where he landed.

GETTING HERE AND AROUND

By car from Cairns, take the inland highway, Peninsula Developmental Road, a 200-odd-mile stretch of fully paved road that barrels you through Australia's Outback—watch for errant cattle and 'roos on the drive. From Cape Tribulation, head up the Cooktown Developmental Road, or take the 4WD-only Bloomfield Track, just 97 km (60 miles), but challenging and sometimes flooded in the Wet. The Bloomfield Track journey, which roughly traces a series of indigenous story-line trails known as the Bama (People's) Way, takes around three hours, longer in wet weather; the Developmental Road is smoother but less scenic. Getting around Cooktown, a compact town, is a comparative cinch: drive, walk, or cycle.

TOURS
CULTURAL TOURS
★ **Adventure North Australia**
TOUR—SPORTS | This company's one- to three-day excursions during the dry season (April through November) offer a mix World-Heritage–listed attractions, indigenous cultural highlights, and Aussie-style adventure. Adventure North also runs short fly/fly and fly/drive tours, and a three-day rain-forest and outback 4WD tour that takes the rugged coast road from Cairns to Cooktown through the Daintree, returning through Far North Queensland's outback on the Mulligan Highway. On every tour, experienced, affable driver-guides offer a wealth of local tidbits. Rates include tours, entry fees, some meals, flights and, on multi-day trips, budget or premium accommodation. ⊠ *36 Aplin St., Cairns* ☎ *07/4028–3376,* ⊕ *www.adventurenorthaustralia. com* ✉ *From A$160* ☉ *Closed in wet season (Dec. through Mar.).*

◉ Sights

Cooktown has some lovely old buildings and a cemetery dating from the 1870s gold rush. Stroll along botanic garden trails and uncrowded beaches, check out the environment interpretative center and visitor info-hub Nature's Powerhouse, cool off in the public swimming pool, and scale Grassy Hill around sunset for stupendous views.

Black Mountain (Kalkajaka) National Park

NATIONAL/STATE PARK | Just south of Cooktown within the Wet Tropics World Heritage Area, Black Mountain (Kalkaja-ka) National Park protects a unique mix of gigantic granite boulders, wet-trop-ics species, and savanna woodland vegetation harboring abundant wildlife, including threatened species. Lucky visi-tors might spot the scanty frog, rainbow skink, Black Mountain gecko, Godman's rock-wallaby, or a rare ghost bat. Kalka-jaka means "place of the spear"; Black Mountain was a significant meeting place for the Eastern Kuku Yalanji tribe. The boulders are treacherous, so climbing and hiking is not allowed, but the lookout point provides a fairly close-up view. ✉ Mulligan Hwy., Rossville ☎ 13–7468 ParksQ hotline ⊕ www.nprsr.qld.gov.au/parks/black-mountain.

Cooktown History Centre

MUSEUM | Cooktown's historical muse-um, aptly housed in a former postal and telegraph office built in 1875, is staffed by affable volunteers and houses an extensive collection of photographs dating from 1873. The building also holds Cooktown's archives and is a research center for local history. It also houses semipermanent displays. ✉ 121 Charlotte St. ☎ 07/4069–6640 ⊕ www.cooktown-history.org.au ✍ A$5 ⊗ Closed Sun.

Cooktown School of Art Society / Elizabeth Guzsely Gallery

MUSEUM | Locally made works (includ-ing Aboriginal art) in various media line the walls of this terrific gallery, where you'll often find artists working on-site. Proceeds benefit the Cooktown School of Art Society, which also offers art classes. ✉ 125 Charlotte St., next to RSL Memorial Club ☎ 07/4069–5322 ⊕ www.cooktownart.com.au ⊗ Closed Sun.

Grassy Hill Lighthouse

LIGHTHOUSE | A strenuous, not especially scenic walk or short drive from Cook-town lie Grassy Hill and the Lighthouse, spectacular lookouts affording panoramic views of Cooktown, the Endeavour River, and the Coral Sea. Follow in the footsteps of Captain James Cook, who scaled the slope to view the reef and navigate his boat's safe passage out. The lighthouse, shipped from England in 1885, helped boats avoid the reef for a century before being rendered obsolete; it was then restored as a historical relic. ✉ Grassy Hill, at eastern end of Hope St.

James Cook Museum

MUSEUM | Cooktown, in its heyday, was a gold-mining port, with 64 pubs lining the 3-km-long (2-mile-long) main street; a significant slice of this colorful history, including mementos of Cook's voyage and Aboriginal artifacts, is preserved at this National Trust–run museum. The for-mer convent houses relics of the Palmer gold-mining and pastoral eras, including a Chinese joss house; canoes, and the anchor and one of six cannons jettisoned when the HMS Endeavour ran aground. The surprisingly good on-site shop sells books and souvenirs. It's recommend-ed that you allow at least an hour to pore over the exhibits. ✉ Helen St. at Furneaux St. ☎ 07/4069–5386 ⊕ www.nationaltrust.org.au/qld/JamesCookMu-seum ✍ A$15.

Nature's Powerhouse & Cooktown Botanic Gardens

GARDEN | This interpretive center and museum at the entrance to Cooktown's heritage-listed Botanic Gardens is home to a valuable collection of local botanical illustrations by internationally recognized artist Vera Scarth-Johnson, and impres-sive displays of Cape York Peninsula wildlife, bequeathed by local fauna expert Charlie Tanner. Take extra time to wander through the gardens, which, with its stone-pitched waterways and shady paths, include 154 acres of colorful native and exotic plants. A popular attraction in the gardens is a 7-meter python carved locally from ironwood. You can enjoy afternoon tea or a light lunch at the Vera Café; browse the shop of botanically themed gifts and souvenirs, including beautiful scarves, prints and postcards, wooden bowls, and authentic Aboriginal art; and get regional travel tips from the on-site Cooktown and Cape York Peninsula Visitor Information Centre. ✉ *Walker St.* ✥ *Follow road to end of Walker St.* ☎ *07/4069–5763* 🌐 *www.naturespowerhouse.com.au* 🎫 *Botanic Gardens free, Nature's Powerhouse free.*

Hotels

★ The Sovereign Resort Hotel
$ | HOTEL | FAMILY | This attractive, two-story colonial-style hotel in the heart of town is the best bet in Cooktown. **Pros:** furnished balconies overlooking tropical gardens or the Endeavour River; airport/wharf transfers; terrific gardens, barbecue area, and pool. **Cons:** on-site restaurant not open for dinner in wet season (November–March); furniture needs updating; front desk closes early. [$] *Rooms from: A$199* ✉ *128 Charlotte St., at Green St.* ☎ *07/4043–0500* 🌐 *www.sovereignresort.com.au* 🕓 *Café closed Sun. No dinner Sun. and Nov.–Mar.* 🛏 *38 rooms* 🍴 *No meals.*

Activities

FISHING

The closest town on the Queensland coast to the Great Barrier Reef, Cooktown offers fast, easy access to some of the reef's best fishing (and dive) sites. Boats bristling with game-fishing gear depart from the marina daily, bound for famed fishing grounds on the outer reef, and at Egret and Boulder, 10 miles offshore. The likely catch: Spanish mackerel, sailfish, coral trout, red and spangled emperor, and black marlin.

★ Gone Fishing
FISHING | FAMILY | Specializing in half- and full-day fishing charters on the Endeavour River and the estuaries and islands offshore, Gone Fishing also offers small-group, two-hour river tours and crocodile-spotting expeditions. ✉ *Wilkinson St., Lot 3* ☎ *07/4069–5980, 0427/695980* 🌐 *www.fishingcooktown.com* 🎫 *From A$115 per person.*

Airlie Beach

1,119 km (695 miles) or 13½ hours' drive north of Brisbane, 623 km (387 miles) south of Cairns via the Bruce Hwy.

Airlie Beach's balmy climate and its proximity to the Whitsunday Islands, a resort and water-sports playground, make it hugely popular with partying backpackers and holidaymakers en route to the islands and reef.

GETTING HERE AND AROUND

Whitsunday Coast Airport, near Proserpine, 36 km (23 miles) southeast of Airlie Beach, has direct flights to and from Brisbane and Sydney with Qantas, Virgin Blue, Tigerair, and Jetstar. Whitsunday Transit buses connect the airport and Proserpine Railway Station to Airlie Beach, Cannonvale, and Shute Harbour (about A$22 one-way), with services timed to meet all flights and passenger trains (drive time 30–40 minutes). It's A$14, one-way, to or from Proserpine railway station. Greyhound Australia and Oz Experience offer daily services into Airlie Beach from Sydney, Brisbane, and towns between, and from Cairns. Queensland Rail operates several long-distance trains weekly, northbound and southbound, that stop at Proserpine Railway Station, about 25 km (15 miles) from Airlie Beach.

AIRPORT Whitsunday Coast Airport. ✉ *Sir Reginald Ansett Dr., Proserpine* ☎ *07/4945–0200 airport.*

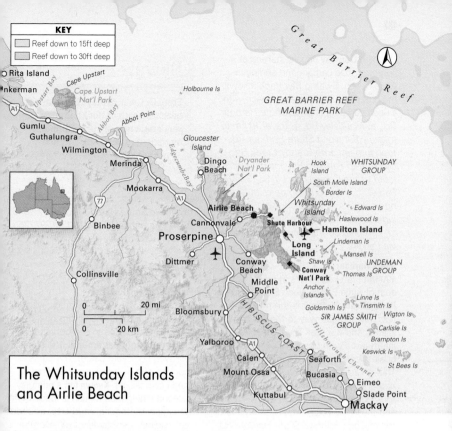

KEY

- Reef down to 15ft deep
- Reef down to 30ft deep

Rita Island
Inkerman
Cape Upstart
Upstart Bay
Cape Upstart Nat'l Park
Holbourne Is
GREAT BARRIER REEF
MARINE PARK

A1
Gumlu
Guthalungra
Wilmington
Abbot Bay
Abbot Point
Merinda
Gloucester Island
Mookarra
A1
Edgecumbe Bay
Dingo Beach
Dryander Nat'l Park
Hook Island
WHITSUNDAY GROUP
South Molle Island
Border Is
Airlie Beach
Whitsunday Island
Edward Is
Haslewood Is
Binbee
Cannonvale
Shute Harbour
Proserpine
Hamilton Island
Dittmer
Conway Beach
Long Island
Lindeman Is
Mansell Is
Collinsville
Middle Point
Shaw Is
Conway Nat'l Park
Thomas Is
LINDEMAN GROUP
0   20 mi
Anchor Islands
Linne Is
0   20 km
Bloomsbury
Goldsmith Is
Tinsmith Is
Wigton Is
SIR JAMES SMITH GROUP
Carlisle Is
Yalboroo
HIBISCUS COAST
Brampton Is
A1
Keswick Is
Calen
Seaforth
St Bees Is
Mount Ossa
Bucasia
Hillsborough Channel
Kuttabul
Eimeo
Slade Point
Mackay

Great Barrier Reef

The Whitsunday Islands and Airlie Beach

BUS CONTACTS Greyhound Australia.
☎ 1300/473946 toll-free in Australia,
07/4690–9850 ⊕ www.greyhound.com.
au. **Whitsunday Transit.** ☎ 07/4946–1800
⊕ www.whitsundaytransit.com.au.

**TRAIN CONTACTS Proserpine Railway
Station.** ✉ 6 Hinschen St., Proserpine
☎ 13–1617 in Australia ⊕ www.queens-
landrail.com.au **Queensland Rail.** ☎ 13-
1617 toll-free in Australia, 07/3072–2222
⊕ www.queenslandrail.com.au.

◉ Sights

Airlie's main street is packed with cafés,
bars, tour agencies, and hotels, with
homes and higher-end accommodations
extending up the steep hills behind it.
The waterfront Esplanade, with its boardwalk, landscaped gardens, swimming
lagoon, and weekend markets, is generally lively.

Conway National Park

NATIONAL/STATE PARK | FAMILY | Ten min-
utes' drive southeast of Airlie, Conway
National Park is a 54,000-acre expanse
of mangroves, woodlands, rocky cliffs,
and tropical lowland rain forest that
shelters the endangered Proserpine rock
wallaby and other rare species, as well
as sulphur-crested cockatoos, emerald
doves, Australian brush-turkeys, and
orange-footed scrubfowl. Most walking
trails start at the park's picnic area at the
end of Forestry Road, about 10 km (6
miles) from Airlie. Mount Rooper Walking
Track, a 5.4-km (3-mile) circuit, meanders
uphill through bushland to a lookout
with breathtaking Whitsundays views. If
time permits, and you're sufficiently fit,
you can cycle, run, or walk the 27-km

(17-mile) Conway circuit, starting at Forestry Road carpark and ending in Airlie Beach. Swamp Bay track follows the creek to a coral-strewn beach with a bush camping area. ✉ *Shute Harbour Rd., at Mandalay Rd.* ✥ *Travel 10 km (6 miles) west along Shute Harbour Rd., then turn left onto Brandy Creek Rd. Follow it to Forestry Rd. and carpark (start of the Conway circuit)* ☎ *13–7468 ParksQ hotline/camping permits* 🌐 *www.nprsr.qld.gov.au/parks/conway* 🎫 *Camping permits, A$7 per person, per night* ☞ *Camping permits must be prebooked via ParksQ.*

Shute Harbour

MARINA | Ten kilometers (6 miles) southeast of Airlie Beach along Shute Harbour Road, Shute Harbour is the main ferry terminal and gateway to the Whitsunday islands and the reef. The large, sheltered inlet teems with boats—it's one of the busiest commuter ports in Australia. Though accommodation is available, the harbor is geared toward transferring visitors. For a great view over Shute Harbour and the Whitsunday Passage, drive to the top of Coral Point. ✉ *Shute Harbour Rd., Shute Harbour.*

Beaches

★ Airlie Beach Lagoon

BEACH—SIGHT | **FAMILY** | Hugely popular with locals and visitors, especially in stinger season, this stinger-free swimming enclosure on Airlie's shorefront has dedicated lap-swimming lanes, real-sand "beaches," adjoining children's pools, and sensor-activated lighting after dark. There are toilets, showers, and change rooms nearby, and all pools are patrolled by trained lifeguards year-round. Surrounding the lagoon are a children's playground and a tropical garden, crisscrossed with walkways and dotted with public art, picnic tables, and free electric barbecues. **Amenities:** food and drink; lifeguards; showers; toilets. **Best for:** swimming.

Beware

From October to May the ocean off beaches north of Rockhampton is rendered virtually unswimmable by toxic-tentacled box jellyfish.

✉ *The Esplanade, at Broadwater Ave., parallel to Shute Harbour Rd.* ☎ *07/4945–0200 Whitsunday Council, 1300/972753* 🌐 *www.whitsunday.qld.gov.au.*

Restaurants

Fish D'Vine and Rum Bar

$ | **SEAFOOD** | The menu here showcases seafood in all its forms—from beer-battered fish-and-chips to seafood chowder and wild-caught barramundi (the chef will even cook your catch). The bar is stocked with 500-plus rums and has a mean cocktail list. **Known for:** signature seafood indulgence, which is loaded with local marine produce, mud crab, and reef fish; mojitos; beachy flavor. [$] *Average main:* ✉ *303 Shute Harbour Rd.* ☎ *07/4948–0088* 🌐 *www.fishdvine.com.au* 🕒 *No lunch.*

Northerlies Bar and Grill

$ | **MODERN AUSTRALIAN** | **FAMILY** | Overlooking a tranquil bay just outside of Airlie Beach, Northerlies has become a local favorite. A farm-to-table ethos shapes the menu, so expect fresh-from-the-boat seafood, single-farm origin steaks, and house-smoked meats paired with local produce. **Known for:** aged bone-in rib eye; quiet, waterfront location with alfresco dining; shuttle service to and from Airlie Beach. [$] *Average main:* ✉ *Pringle Rd., Lot 116* ☎ *1800/682277* 🌐 *www.northerlies.com.au.*

🛏 Hotels

Airlie Beach Hotel

$$ | **HOTEL** |**FAMILY** | With the town's small beach at its doorstep, three eateries and bars downstairs, and the main street directly behind it, this hotel makes a comfy and convenient base. **Pros:** interiors rebuilt in 2018; lots of on-site food and drink options; close to main strip, Airlie Lagoon, and waterfront. **Cons:** no room service; rooms can be noisy; basic hotel with basic facilities. $ Rooms from: A$225 ✉ 16 The Esplanade, at Coconut Grove ☎ 07/4964–1999, 1800/466233 toll-free in Australia ⊕ www.airliebeach-hotel.com.au 🛏 80 rooms ⊙| No meals.

Mantra Boathouse Apartments

$$$ | **RESORT** |**FAMILY** | Perched on the Port of Airlie Marina with enviable views of the boats swaying in the bay, the Mantra Boathouse Apartments are generously sized two- and three-bedroom apartments, ideal for those looking for self-contained accommodations. **Pros:** full-size kitchens, including full-size refrigerators/freezers, dishwashers, microwaves, and stoves; large balconies; complimentary parking. **Cons:** no room service; housekeeping only comes weekly; short walk to restaurants. $ Rooms from: A$315 ✉ 33 Port Dr. ☎ 13–1517 reservations, 07/5665–4450 international, 07/4841–4100 reception ⊕ www.mantra.com.au/queensland/whitsundays/airlie-beach/accommodation/mantra-boathouse-apartments 🛏 44 apartments ⊙| No meals.

Peppers Airlie Beach

$ | **RESORT** | The expansive one- to three-bedroom apartments at this high-end hillside resort are tailored for comfort, with spa baths the size of small cars, designer decor and appliances, high-end entertainment systems, free Wi-Fi, and big, furnished balconies with great views of the bay and yacht club. **Pros:** classy decor, food, and service; buggies to ferry you up the resort's steep driveways; free

undercover parking. **Cons:** fee for Wi-Fi use; not close to Airlie's main street; no in-room heating in winter. $ Rooms from: A$299 ✉ Mt. Whitsunday Dr. ☎ 07/4962–5100 reception, 1300/987600 toll-free in Australia ⊕ www.peppers.com.au 🛏 102 rooms ⊙| No meals.

★ Whitsunday Moorings B&B

$ | **B&B/INN** | Overlooking Abel Point Marina, this meticulously run B&B has everything you need: stupendous marina views, charming hosts, and terrific gourmet breakfasts, often accompanied by colorful chirping parrots. **Pros:** charming, knowledgeable host; fabulous breakfasts on the terrace overlooking Airlie's pretty harbor; free Wi-Fi. **Cons:** uphill walk from main street; required two-night stay for East or West rooms; reception closed between 7 pm and 6 am. $ Rooms from: A$180 ✉ 37 Airlie Crescent ☎ 07/4946–4692 ⊕ www.whitsundaymooringsbb.com.au 🛏 3 rooms ⊙| Free Breakfast.

🍸 Nightlife

Shute Harbour Road, the main strip, is where it all happens in Airlie Beach. Most main-street establishments cater to the backpacker crowd, with boisterous, college-style entertainment, live music, and a late-opening dance club. Older and more sophisticated visitors gravitate to quieter establishments with pleasant outdoor areas, such as the bars and restaurants attached to some of the hillside resorts.

🏃 Activities

BOAT TOURS

Cumberland Charter Yachts

✉ Abel Point Marina, Shingley Dr., Shop 18 ☎ 07/4946–7500, 1800/075101 ⊕ www.ccy.com.au.

Queensland Yacht Charters

(Whitsunday Yacht Charters). ✉ Abel Point Marina, Shingley Dr., Unit 9

☎ 07/4946–7400, 1800/075013 toll-free in Australia ⊕ www.yachtcharters.com.au.

Whitsunday Rent A Yacht
✉ Shute Harbour, 6 Bay Terr. ☎ 07/4946–9232, 1800/075000 toll-free in Australia ⊕ www.rentayacht.com.au.

Whitsunday Sailing Adventures
BOAT TOURS | Whitsunday Sailing Adventures runs several sailing, scuba, and snorkeling trips around the islands and Great Barrier Reef on a dozen-plus owner-operated vessels, including modern sailing cats and tall ships. Choose from sailing, diving, kayaking, and snorkeling excursions. A two-night, three-day live-aboard outer reef trip starts at A$899 per person in a private double room, A$749 in a shared room, with one scuba dive and all gear and meals included. One- and two-night performance sailing adventures start at A$389. If time is limited, there's an eco-friendly sail-and-snorkel day-trip (A$195). Book well ahead for holiday periods. ✉ 402 Shute Harbour Rd. ☎ 07/4940–2000, 1300/653100 toll-free in Australia ⊕ www.whitsundaysailingadventures.com.au ✈ From A$195.

Long Island

12 km (7 miles) west of Hamilton Island, 13 km (7½ miles) east of the mainland

Although it's 9 km (5½ miles) long and no more than 2 km (1 mile) wide—around 3,000 acres total—this aptly named island has several walking trails through tracts of dense rain forest. Most of the island is national parkland, sheltering birds, butterflies, goannas, and wallabies. Some of its beaches are picturesque; others rocky and windblown. Though its waters are less clear than those off the outer reef islands, there are some excellent snorkeling spots on the island's fringing reef, where you'll share the balmy water with soft and hard corals, tropical fish, and turtles. You may also see dolphins and migrating humpback whales July through September.

GETTING HERE AND AROUND

You can reach Long Island via water taxi from Shute Harbour or private watercraft. The trip takes around 20 minutes by water taxi, and is cheaper if you have more passengers.

Various regional operators, including Air Whitsunday and Hamilton Island Air, offer seaplane or helicopter transfers to Long Island resorts from regional airports including Great Barrier Reef (Hamilton Island), Whitsundays Airport near Airlie Beach, and Whitsunday Coast (Proserpine) Airport. Transfers are scheduled to coincide with incoming and outgoing flights. If your vacation time is limited, this is the fastest way to get here—but per-person costs can be steep. Trips require minimum passenger numbers, strict baggage limits apply, and prebooking is essential.

If you're keen to visit other resort isles from Hamilton Island, the on-island helicopter service, Hamilton Island Air, can transport you there. Helicopters take off on demand from Great Barrier Reef (Hamilton Island) Airport, flying to Long Island and to Airlie Beach on the mainland. Prebookings are essential for all charter flights; baggage is limited to 15 kg (33 pounds) per passenger, in soft-sided bags, and anyone weighing more than 110 kg (250 pounds) pays a seat surcharge.

Virgin Australia and Jetstar have direct daily flights between Hamilton Island and Melbourne, Sydney, and Brisbane.

AIR TRAVEL
Air Whitsunday
This local seaplane operator flies from Shute Harbour Airport to Palm Bay Resort on demand in a six-seater aircraft carrying two or four passengers plus luggage (A$290). Flights can be booked via Air Whitsunday or Palm Bay Resort. ✉ A Whitsunday Airport, 12 Whitsunday Rd.,

Terminal 1, Flametree ☎ *07/4946–9111 Air Whitsunday, 0477/770133 Palm Bay Resort* 🌐 *www.airwhitsunday.com.au.*

Hamilton Island Air

From Hamilton Island airport, you can take a scenic helicopter flight to Palm Bay Resort for $660 (one or two passengers, plus limited baggage). ✉ *Great Barrier Reef (Hamilton Island) Airport, Palm Valley Way, Hamilton Island* ☎ *07/4969–9599* 🌐 *www.hamiltonislandair.com.*

BOAT TRAVEL

Island Transfers

(*Shute Harbour Water Taxi*). The local water-taxi operator at Shute Harbour makes three scheduled trips a day, departing the harbor at 8:30 am, 10:30 am, 2 pm, and 5 pm and traveling directly to Palm Bay Resort on Long Island. It returns from Palm Bay at 8:30 am, 11 am, 2:30 pm, and 5:30 pm. Prebooking is essential, especially in peak periods. There is a maximum of nine people per boat. ✉ *Shute Harbour* ☎ *0488/022868* 🌐 *www.islandtransfers.com* ☞ *From A$49 per person, each way.*

Hotels

★ Elysian Retreat

$$$ | **ALL-INCLUSIVE** | Opened in early 2019, this luxurious, eco-friendly Paradise Bay retreat on the southern point of Long Island is nestled in a private cove between ocean and rain forest, and its large windows and private balconies with uninterrupted water views maximize on the setting. **Pros:** stunning setting with oceanfront villas; dedicated boat takes guests to Whitehaven Beach; magnesium pool. **Cons:** adults only; 20 guests max so limited availability; 30-minute helicopter ride to island. [$] *Rooms from: A$1100* ✉ *Long Island* ☎ *07/4939–4413* 🌐 *www.elysianretreat.com.au* 🛏 *10 villas* 🍴 *All-inclusive.*

Palm Bay Resort

$ | **RESORT** | This beachfront property houses self-catering travelers at alluringly reasonable rates. **Pros:** friendly, helpful staff; island grocery/food store and bottle shop; lovely accommodations in glorious tranquil environs. **Cons:** can be noisy at night; self-catering, though staff clean your dishes; no free Wi-Fi. [$] *Rooms from: A$269* ✉ *Long Island* ✈ *Get to and from Palm Bay Resort (one-way rates): from A$55* ☎ *1300/655126 toll-free in Australia* 🌐 *www.palmbayresort.com.au* 🛏 *25 suites* 🍴 *No meals.*

Hamilton Island

16 km (10 miles) southeast of Shute Harbour.

Though it's the most heavily populated and developed island in the Whitsunday group, more than 70% of Hamilton Island has been preserved in its natural state. The 1,482-acre island abounds in beautiful beaches (such as long, curving, palm-dotted Catseye Beach), bush trails, and spectacular lookouts. Yet for all its natural beauty, Hamilton is more an action-packed, sociable holiday isle than it is a place to get away from it all.

Around 35 minutes by ferry from Shute Harbour, Hamilton buzzes with activity. Guests of the resort, and its various types of accommodation, including hotel-style and self-catering establishments, make up most of the itinerant population, but there are private residences here—as well as throngs of day-trippers from the mainland, other islands, and cruising yachts, who wander the island's bustling marina and village each day.

For a family-friendly, one-stop Whitsundays experience, Hamilton Island is a smart choice. Many of the resort accommodations allow kids under age 12 to stay free, provided they stay with parents and use existing beds (no rollaways or cribs). Under-12s can even eat free at some island restaurants when staying at resort hotels, choosing from kids' menus.

Wind- and motor-powered water sports are popular on many Whitsunday Islands

The resort's set up like a small city, with its own school, post office, banking outlets, medical center, pharmacy, supermarket, hair and beauty salon, and DVD-rental store, plus two day spas, shops, restaurants, bars, and a nightclub. But little on Hamilton is free; prices—for food, activities, Internet use, even grocery items—can be steep. The ubiquitous golf carts that visitors rent to zip around the island are A$49 an hour, A$65 for three hours, and A$87 for 24 hours from Hamilton Island Buggy Rentals. Save a few bucks by using the free Island Shuttle service that runs around the island on two set routes at regular (15–40 minute) intervals between 6:50 am and 11 pm.

GETTING HERE AND AROUND

Virgin Australia and Jetstar fly directly to Hamilton Island from Sydney, Melbourne, and Brisbane. You can take a Cruise Whitsundays ferry to the island from Abel Point Marina, Airlie Beach, or nearby Shute Harbour (A$56), or arrange a seaplane transfer from regional mainland airports at Proserpine or Mackay, or from Airlie Beach's Whitsunday Airport with Air Whitsunday. From Hamilton Island, the "hub" of the Whitsundays, you can catch a ferry to neighboring resort isles Daydream and Hayman via fast ferry with Cruise Whitsundays Resort Connections, timed to coincide with incoming and outgoing flights from Hamilton's airport. You can get there faster by seaplane with Air Whitsunday or helicopter with Hamilton Island Air.

Sunsail Australia

This operator has various yachts available for bareboat charter at Hamilton Island's marina. You can book a five-day-minimum charter yacht and sail around the Whitsundays' sheltered waters. Optional extras include professional skipper and cook, kayaks, and dinghy. Rates vary according to the number of days, number of passengers, vessel, and season. Sunsail Whitsundays also offers certified sailing courses. ✉ *Front St.* ☎ *07/4948-8250* , *1800/803988 toll-free in Australia* ⊕ *www.sunsail.com.au.*

Castaway Cuisine

On Hamilton, the Whitsundays' largest inhabited island, guests can eat and drink at a variety of restaurants and bars. Virtually all of them are managed by the Hamilton Island consortium, whose owners, the Oatley family, made their millions out of wine. The Oatleys are keen to further the island's reputation for quality wining and dining—recruiting big-city chefs, improving supply lines, scheduling epicurean events, and adding to the island's vast central cellar and produce store. Opportunities for young guns to work their way up through Hamilton's hierarchy, training under culinary heavyweights, bring a continuing stream of fresh talent to the island. The bad news? Staff don't always stay and as a result, food and service standards can be inconsistent—and as there's a virtual monopoly on dining options, prices tend to be steep.

BUGGY RENTAL Hamilton Island Buggy Rental. ⊠ Front St. ☎ 07/9433–9444, 13–7333 toll-free in Australia, 866/209–0891 in U.S., 424/206–5274 toll-free in U.S., 07/4946–8263 buggy hire ⊕ www.hamiltonisland.com.au/ getting-around-island/buggy-hire.

FERRY Cruise Whitsundays. ⊠ 4 The Cove Rd., Airlie Beach ☎ 07/4846–7000 ⊕ www.cruisewhitsundays.com.

HELICOPTER Hamilton Island Air. ⊠ Great Barrier Reef (Hamilton Island) Airport, Palm Valley Way ☎ 07/4969–9599 ⊕ www.hamiltonislandair.com.

SEAPLANE Air Whitsunday. ⊠ Whitsunday Airport, 12 Air Whitsunday Ave., Terminal 1, Flametree ☎ 07/4946–9111 ⊕ www.airwhitsunday.com.au.

Sights

WILD LIFE Hamilton Island

NATURE PRESERVE | FAMILY | This charming wildlife sanctuary houses kangaroos, wallabies, wombats, dingoes, birds, and reptiles, including a resident croc. Guided tours run daily, and from 7:30 to 10 am, there are daily breakfasts with the koalas. ⊠ 1 Resort Dr. ☎ 07/4946–9078 sanctuary, 07/4946–8305 HI tour desk ⊕ www.wildlifehamiltonisland.com.au ⊠ From A$27.

Restaurants

Hamilton Island Resort has lots of dining options, including casual cafés and takeaway outlets, a pub serving counter meals, a dinner cruise boat, and several restaurants.

Bommie Restaurant

$$$ | MODERN AUSTRALIAN | With sail-shaped tables, chic Eames chairs, and marina views, Bommie has a sophisticated, upmarket ambience perfect for a special celebration. It's the ideal setting for fine Modern Australian cuisine, and the chef's daily tasting menus dazzle the tastebuds. **Known for:** high-end fine dining; great location; dining on the deck (book well ahead). $ Average main: A$48 ⊠ Hamilton Island Yacht Club, Front St. ☎ 07/4948–9433, 13–3777 toll-free in Australia ⊕ www.hamiltonisland.com.au/ restaurants/bommie ⊘ No lunch. Closed Sun. and Mon.

coca chu

$ | ASIAN FUSION |FAMILY | Offering hawker-style street food dining, coca chu appeals to all with its relaxed vibe, Catseye Beach views, and a varied dinner menu that showcases regional produce and Southeast Asian flavors. The twice-cooked Sichuan duck with chili, coriander, ginger, and soy black vinegar sauce is a worthy signature dish. **Known for:** casual Asian family-style dining perfect for groups; part of the Kids Stay & Eat Free offering on the island; sichuan duck with aromatics. $ Average main: A$34 ⊠ Main resort complex, Catseye Beach ☎ 07/4946–9999 resort restaurant reservations ⊕ www.hamiltonisland.com.au/restaurants/coca-chu ۞ No lunch.

Manta Ray

$ | ECLECTIC |FAMILY | This could be the island's best all-round dining establishment. It's great for breezy alfresco lunches, sunset drinks on the deck, and wood-fired pizzas. **Known for:** children (up to age 12) with adults can eat free; delicious wood-fired pizzas; well-priced menu to suit the whole family. $ Average main: A$26 ⊠ Front St. ☎ 07/4946–9999 resort restaurant reservations ⊕ www.hamiltonisland.com.au/restaurants/manta-ray.

★ Mariners

$$$ | SEAFOOD | This breezy, upscale eatery turns the local catch into fresh contemporary dishes: freshly shucked oysters, butter roasted Moreton Bay bugs, and king salmon all artfully plated. You can also get vegetarian and nonseafood options, and wine from a bar stocked mainly with mid-price Antipodean vintages. **Known for:** great views over the marina; fresh, local seafood dishes; casual fine dining. $ Average main: A$49 ⊠ Marina Village, Front St. ☎ 07/4946–9999 resort restaurant reservations ⊕ www.hamiltonisland.com.au/restaurants/mariners ۞ No lunch.

Romano's

$$ | ITALIAN | The full-frontal marina views from the broad balconies of this two-level waterfront eatery make it a favorite for family celebrations and romantic dining. The menu is loaded with traditional Italian fare like saltimbocca as well as more inventive dishes, such as squid ink spaghetti with spanner crab. **Known for:** sophisticated waterfront dining; Italian-style comfort fare; lighter alfresco dining menu available beginning at 3 pm. $ Average main: A$40 ⊠ Marina Village, Front St. ☎ 07/4946–9999 resort restaurant reservations ⊕ www.hamiltonisland.com.au/restaurants/romanos ۞ No lunch.

TAKO

$ | MODERN MEXICAN |FAMILY | Hamilton Island's latest concept restaurant, TAKO, mixes Mexican regional cuisine with Japanese and Korean flavors. The exciting menu features lots of shareable dishes that are inspired by the local cuisine and specialty dishes of various regions of Mexico. **Known for:** eclectic cuisine; lively environment; unlike anything else on Hamilton Island. $ Average main: A$20 ⊠ Front St., above general store ☎ 07/4946–8032 ⊕ www.hamiltonisland.com.au/restaurants/tako ۞ Closed Wed. and Thurs. No lunch.

🛏 Hotels

There are a variety of places to stay in Hamilton Island whether you're traveling with the family or looking for your private getaway. You also can find an apartment-style retreat. Among the accommodations options on the island are the more than 100 self-catering properties managed by Hamilton Island Holiday Homes (☎ 13–7333 ⊕ www.hamiltonislandholidayhomes.com.au). They include one- to five-bedroom vacation properties in prime locations around the island, including studio, split-level, and two-story designs. All have air-conditioning, TVs, balconies, and access to the resort's communal swimming pools and fitness center. Homes sleep between one and 12 people. Each rental comes with island airport transfers and the use of a four-seater golf buggy, nonmotorized watercraft at Catseye Beach and the Hamilton Island sports complex facilities. There is a minimum stay of four or more nights in holiday periods and a two- or three-night minimum at other times, depending on the property. Some accommodations are a bit dated and there is no housekeeping. The upsides are the privacy, the full kitchen and laundry facilities, and the complimentary use of many resort facilities.

Hamilton Island Beach Club

$$$$ | RESORT | The upscale amenities and no-kids policy mean this hotel swarms with couples, who can cool off in the infinity-edge pool, enjoy meals poolside, or admire the Catseye Beach and Coral Sea views from their private balconies or courtyards. **Pros:** beachfront location; free Wi-Fi; adults only. **Cons:** service standards vary; checkout time is 10 am; rates are quite high. [$] *Rooms from: A$710* ✉ *9 Resort Dr.* ☎ *02/9007–0009 HI accommodation, 13–7333 toll-free in Australia* 🌐 *www.hamiltonisland.com.au* 🛏 *57 rooms* 🍴 *Free Breakfast.*

Hamilton Island Palm Bungalows

$$$ | RESORT | FAMILY | Spacious, self-contained, and with a relaxed island vibe, these steep-roofed, freestanding bungalows are great for families and self-sufficient travelers. **Pros:** free use of the resort's gym/sports complex and nonmotorized watercraft; complimentary airport transfers; close to main pool, beach, and wildlife park. **Cons:** no ocean views; up a steepish hill; no Wi-Fi in rooms. [$] *Rooms from: A$400* ✉ *3 Resort Dr.* ☎ *02/9007–0009 HI accommodation, 13–7333 toll-free in Australia* 🌐 *www.hamiltonisland.com.au* 🛏 *49 rooms* 🍴 *No meals.*

Hamilton Island Reef View Hotel

$$$ | HOTEL | FAMILY | All hotel rooms here are comfortable, with private balconies, but only hotel rooms on the fifth floor and above live up to the name, with their—unbroken Coral Sea vistas. **Pros:** good buffet breakfast; some suites have private patios with barbecues, hot tubs, and private plunge pools; better-than-usual service. **Cons:** lower-level rooms can be noisy; cockatoos fly in open windows; rooms a little dated. [$] *Rooms from: A$370* ✉ *12 Resort Dr.* ☎ *02/9007–0009, 13–7333 toll-free in Australia* 🌐 *www.hamiltonisland.com.au* 🛏 *363 rooms* 🍴 *Free Breakfast.*

★ Qualia

$$$$ | RESORT | Catering to a privileged few, Hamilton Island's most exclusive resort has a tranquil and decadent ambience, private beach, infinity-edge pools, and complex of luxe, well-appointed freestanding pavilions. **Pros:** Windward Pavilions have their own plunge pools; fine food and wine; high-end everything. **Cons:** two-night minimum stay in peak periods; located well away from the main resort complex and marina; service not as polished as some may expect. [$] *Rooms from: A$1250* ✉ *20 Whitsunday Blvd. , Lot 10* ☎ *02/9007–0009, 13–7777 toll-free in Australia* 🌐 *www.qualia.com.au* 🛏 *60 suites* 🍴 *Free Breakfast.*

Shopping

Hamilton Island's Marina Village, along Front Street, houses shops selling resort and surf wear, children's clothes, souvenirs, and gifts. You'll also find an art gallery, design store, jeweler, florist, small supermarket, general store, pharmacy, newsstand, post office, pro golf shop, real-estate agent, bakery, bottle shop, and a hair salon on the island. In general, you'll pay more for goods and services here than for their equivalents on the mainland.

Activities

FISHING

Renegade Sports Fishing & Charters

FISHING | FAMILY | The outer Great Barrier Reef offers world-class fishing for species like coral trout, mackerel, and tuna—and you have a better-than-average chance of landing one off the deck of a 38-foot flybridge game boat. Take a small-group sportfishing trip with Renegade Sports Fishing & Charters, with all equipment included. A full-day excursion is A$2,900 (private charter) or A$330 per person (shared); a half-day trip (8–noon or 1–5) costs A$1,750 (private charter) or A$175 per person (shared). Full-day tours also include morning and afternoon tea and a cheese/fruit platter at lunch. If time or your budget is tight, you can hire a dinghy for puttering about closer to shore. Organize it directly or book through Hamilton Island's Tour Desk. ⊠ *Hamilton Island Marina, Front St., D Arm, DWS berth* ☏ *07/4946–8305 HI tour desk, 0429/724822 direct* ⊕ *www. renegadecharters.com.au* ✉ *From A$175 per person.*

GOLF

★ Hamilton Island Golf Club

GOLF | This Peter Thomson–designed championship course has sweeping Whitsundays views from all 18 holes. You can rent clubs, take lessons, and practice your swing on the golf driving range at the Hamilton Island–run complex, which incorporates a swanky clubhouse, pro shop, restaurant, and bar. Clubs, shoes, and lessons are also available. Ferries to Dent Island depart all day from 7 am from Hamilton Island Marina; allow five hours to play 18 holes and half that to play nine. Prices include GPS-fitted golf carts and ferry transfers. ⊠ *Main St., Dent Island* ☏ *07/4948–9760* ⊕ *www. hamiltonislandgolfclub.com.au* ✉ *A$160; A$40 club rental; A$15 shoe rental* ⚲ *18 holes, 6692 yards, par 71.*

GREAT BARRIER REEF TOURS

★ Heart Pontoon

DIVING/SNORKELING | **FAMILY** | On the outer edge of the Great Barrier Reef sits magnificent Hardy Reef Lagoon, and within it sits Heart Pontoon, a state-of-the-art pontoon around which you can snorkel and dive along easy coral trails. There's a large underwater viewing chamber, a spacious sundeck, change rooms, and fresh-water showers. There are many ways to explore the underwater environs: take a semisubmersible coral-viewing

tour, guided snorkel safari (A$55), or an introductory (A$139) or certified (A$99) dive with gear included. A scenic helicopter flight over Heart Reef starts at A$150 per person. ⊠ *Depart Hamilton Island Airport and Airport Jetty, Palm Valley Way* ☏ *07/4946–7000 Cruise Whitsundays, 07/4946–9102 Helireef Whitsunday* ⊕ *www.cruisewhitsundays.com* ⊕ *www. helireef.com.au* ✉ *From A$269.*

★ Reefsleep

TOUR—SPORTS | **FAMILY** | Stay overnight on Hardy Reef pontoon on Cruise Whitsunday's terrific two-day Reefsleep package: it includes all meals, use of the pontoon's extensive facilities, and the chance to enjoy turtles, reef sharks and colorful tropical fish without the day-tripping crowd. The cost includes fast transport to and from the pontoon, two full days on the reef, and one night sleeping in a swag under the stars. Breakfast, morning and afternoon teas, buffet lunches both days, and a barbecue are all included. Use of snorkeling gear, wet suits, bath towels, and Reefworld's many facilities, including reef presentations and semisubmersible tours, is free. Optional extras include guided "Snorkel Safari" tours (A$55); guided scuba dives for beginners (A$139), with second dives an additional A$59; night dives; and scenic heli-flights over the reef. The cost of the Reefsleep Swags Under the Stars is A$675 for a single swag or A$525 per person in a double swag (a low tent with viewing panel, mattress and bedding), with reef tax included. ⊠ *Airlie Beach* ☏ *07/4846–7062* ⊕ *www.cruisewhitsundays.com/great-barrier-reef-experiences/reefsleep* ✉ *From A$525.*

MULTISPORT OPERATORS

Hamilton Island Activities

WATER SPORTS | **FAMILY** | Hamilton Island Resort has the widest selection of activities in the Whitsundays—game fishing, snorkeling, scuba diving, waterskiing, jet skiing, wakeboarding, sea kayaking, and speedboat adventure rides are all on the agenda. Everything can be booked through the island's central tour desk. The use of nonmotorized watercraft is free to resort guests through the Beach Sports Hut on Catseye Beach, with staff ready to give assistance, tips, and—for a fee—lessons. If the Coral Sea doesn't tempt you, there are well-marked walking trails, quad-bike and ATV tours, go-karts, a nine-pin bowling center, an aquatic driving range, public-access swimming pools, and an 18-hole golf course on nearby Dent Island. The island's sports and fitness complex incorporates a state-of-the-art gym, a whirlpool spa and sauna, squash and floodlit tennis courts, and a minigolf course. You can also sign up for various tours, cruises, and special events. ✉ *Main resort complex, off Resort Dr.* ☎ *07/4946–8305 HI tour desk, 13–7333 toll-free in Australia* 🌐 *www.hamiltonisland.com.au.*

Orpheus Island

24 km (15 miles) offshore of Ingham, 80 km (50 miles) northeast of Townsville, 190 km (118 miles) south of Cairns.

Volcanic in origin, this narrow island—11 km (7 miles) long and 1 km (½ mile) wide, 3,500 acres total—uncoils like a snake in the waters between Halifax Bay and the Barrier Reef. It's part of the Palm Island Group, which consists of 10 islands, eight of which are Aboriginal reservations. Orpheus is a national park, occupied only by a marine research station and the island's resort, which has a large vegetable garden, a solar hot-water system, and a 21,134-gallon water tank, as well as an infinity-edge pool and several beachfront villas linked by a rear boardwalk.

Although there are patches of rain forest in the island's deeper gullies and around its sheltered bays, Orpheus is a true Barrier Reef island, ringed by seven unspoiled sandy beaches and superb coral reefs. Amazingly, 340 of the known 359 species of coral inhabit these waters, as do more than 1,100 types of tropical fish and the biggest giant clams in the southern hemisphere. The local marine life is easily accessed and extraordinary.

GETTING HERE AND AROUND

Nautilus Aviation helicopters depart daily at 2 pm from Townsville Airport's Domestic Gate Lounge 10, returning Orpheus guests to the mainland from 2:30 (A$295 per person, one way). You can also charter flights from other mainland ports and islands. Baggage should be soft-sided and is strictly limited to a maximum of 15 kilograms (33 pounds) per person. Excess baggage can be stored at Townsville Airport for free, and the resort offers complimentary laundry (excluding dry cleaning). Book flights with Orpheus Island Resort.

SEAPLANE Nautilus Aviation. ✉ *Townsville Airport, Gypsy Moth Court , Hangar 15, Townsville* ☎ *07/4034–9000 Nautilus Aviation, 07/4725–6056 Nautilus Aviation Townsville Airport Base* 🌐 *www.nautilusaviation.com.au.*

🛏 Hotels

★ Orpheus Island Lodge

$$$$ | **RESORT** | This unpretentious, eco-friendly resort epitomizes laid-back luxury, with sleekly appointed beachfront rooms, suites, and villas; romantic alfresco dining; boutique wines; and numerous outdoor activities included in the rate. **Pros:** the signature alfresco "Dining with the Tides" experience in which you watch fish jump from your candlelit table onto the jetty—an Orpheus must-do; free Wi-Fi in public areas; excellent underwater sites nearby. **Cons:** no in-room Internet; occasional geckos and insects indoors; no fitness center. [$] *Rooms from: A$1500* ✉ *Orpheus Island Resort* ✈ *Accessible via air from Townsville or Cairns* ☎ *07/4777–7377* 🌐 *www.orpheus.com.au* 🛏 *14 rooms* 🍴 *All-inclusive.*

Continued on page 482

WHAT LIVES ON THE REEF?

Equivalent to the Amazon Rainforest in its biodiversity, the Reef hosts the earth's most abundant collection of sea life. Resident species include (but aren't limited to):

- More than 1,500 species of fish
- 5,000 species of mollusk
- 400 species of hard and soft coral
- 30 whale and dolphin species
- More than 500 species of sea plants and grasses
- 14 sea-snake species
- Six sea-turtle species
- 200 sea-bird species
- More than 150 species of shark

DIVING THE REEF

(left) purple anthias;
(above) pink coral

To astronauts who've seen it from space, the Great Barrier Reef resembles a vast, snaking wall—like a moat running parallel to Australia's entire northeastern coast. Almost unimaginably long at 1,430-odd miles, it's one of the few organic structures that can be seen from above the earth's atmosphere without a telescope.

Up close, though, what looks (and from its name, sounds) like a barrier is in fact a labyrinthine complex with millions of points of entry. Mind-boggling in size and scope, encompassing more than 4,000 separate reefs, cays, and islands, the Reef could rightly be called its own subaqueous country.

An undersea enthusiast could spend a lifetime exploring this terrain—which ranges from dizzying chasms to sepulchral coral caves, and from lush underwater "gardens" to sandy sun-dappled shallows—without ever mapping all its resident wonders. Not only is the Reef system home to thousands upon thousands of sea-life species, the populations are changing all the time.

So how is a visitor—especially one with only a week to spend—supposed to plan a trip to this underwater Eden? How to choose among the seemingly endless spots for dropping anchor, donning fins and tanks, and plunging in?

With this many options, figuring out what you want to experience on the Reef is essential. If you've dreamed of floating among sea turtles, you'll likely need to head to a different location than if you want to swim with sharks; if you're an experienced deep-water diver with a taste for shipwrecks, you'll probably need to make separate arrangements from your friends who prefer to hover near the surface. There really is a spot for every kind of diver on the Reef; the trick is knowing where they are.

Luckily, many veteran divers agree about some of the Reef's most reliably excellent sites (and the best ways to access them). The selection compiled here should help you to—ahem—get your feet wet.

by Sarah Gold

BEST DIVING EXPERIENCES

Potato Cod and diver at Cod Hole

BEST WRECK DIVE

The coral formations of the Reef, while dazzling for divers, have proven treacherous to ship captains for centuries. More than 1,500 shipwrecks have been found on the Reef thus far—and there are almost certainly more waiting to be discovered.

S.S. *YONGALA*

The hulk of this 360-foot steamship, which sank during a cyclone in 1911, is easily the most popular wreck dive on the Reef. Part of the appeal is its easy accessibility; the Yongala lies just a half-hour's boat ride off the coast of Townsville, and though some sections are fairly deep (around 90 feet), others are just 45 feet below the surface. The entire wreck is now encrusted with coral, and swarms with a profusion of species including giant grouper, sea snakes, green sea turtles, and spotted eagle rays.

Difficulty level: Intermediate. Divers should have some previous deep-water experience before visiting this site.

How to get there: Yongala Dive (www. yongaladive.com.au), based in Alva Beach (south of Townsville), runs trips to the wreck several times per week.

BEST SITE TO GET YOUR HEART RATE UP

For some thrill-seeking divers, the wonders of the Great Barrier Reef are even better when accompanied by an extra shot of adrenaline—and a few dozen sharks.

OSPREY REEF

More than 200 miles north of Cairns (and only accessible via a live-aboard dive trip), Osprey is peerless for divers hell-bent on a rendezvous with the ocean's most famous predators. The northernmost section of the reef, where two ocean currents converge (it's known as the North Horn), is an especially thronged feeding ground for white-tipped reef, gray reef, hammerhead, and tiger sharks.

Difficulty level: Intermediate. Though the North Horn's best shark-viewing areas are only at about 60 feet, even seasoned divers may feel understandably anxious.

How to get there: Mike Ball Dive Expeditions (www.mikeball.com) offers multi-day packages to Osprey Reef from Cairns and Port Douglas.

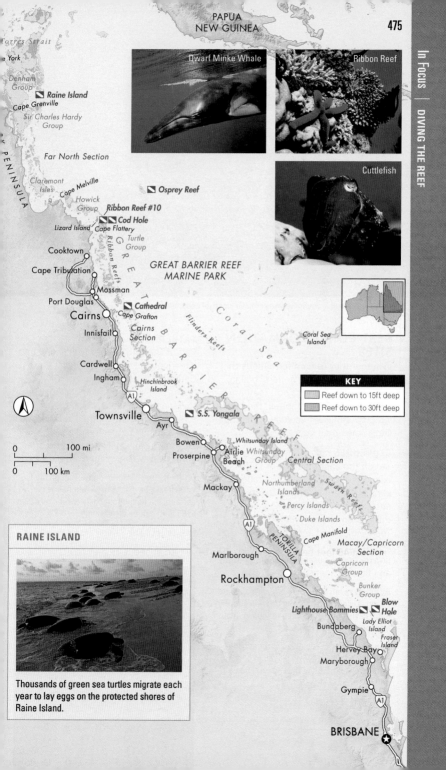

PAPUA
NEW GUINEA

Dwarf Minke Whale

Ribbon Reef

Cuttlefish

Torres Strait

e York

Denham
Group

Raine Island

Cape Grenville

Sir Charles Hardy
Group

Far North Section

PENINSULA

Claremont
Isles

Cape Melville

Howick
Group

Osprey Reef

Ribbon Reef #10

Cod Hole

Lizard Island

Cape Flattery

Turtle
Group

GREAT BARRIER REEF
MARINE PARK

Cooktown

Cape Tribulation

Mossman

Port Douglas

Cairns

Cathedral

Cape Grafton

Innisfail

Cairns
Section

Cardwell

Ingham

Hinchinbrook
Island

A1

Townsville

Ayr

Bowen

Proserpine

Airlie
Beach

Mackay

A1

Marlborough

Rockhampton

GREAT BARRIER REEF

Flinders Reefs

Coral Sea

Coral Sea
Islands

S.S. Yongala

Whitsunday Island

Whitsunday
Group

Central Section

Northumberland
Islands

Percy Islands

Duke Islands

Cape Manifold

Macay/Capricorn
Section

Capricorn
Group

Bunker
Group

Lighthouse Bommies

Blow
Hole

Bundaberg

Lady Elliot
Island

Hervey Bay

Fraser
Island

Maryborough

Gympie

A1

BRISBANE

TORILIA PENINSULA

Swain Reefs

KEY
Reef down to 15ft deep
Reef down to 30ft deep

0   100 mi
0   100 km

Thousands of green sea turtles migrate each
year to lay eggs on the protected shores of
Raine Island.

Scuba isn't the only option; snorkelers have plenty of opportunities to get up close to coral, too.

BEST CORAL-FORMATION SITES

Whether they're hard formations that mimic the shapes of antlers, brains, and stacked plates, or soft feathery Gorgonians and anemones, the building blocks of Reef ecology are compelling in their own right.

BLOW HOLE

Set off the eastern coast of Lady Elliot Island, this cavern-like coral tube is almost 60 feet in length. Divers can enter from either end, and swim through an interior festooned with Technicolor hard and soft corals—and swarming with banded coral shrimp, crayon-bright nudibranchs (sea slugs), and fluttery lionfish.

Difficulty level: Easy. Unless you're claustrophobic. Divers need only be Open-Water certified to visit this site, which ranges in depth from about 40 to 65 feet.

How to get there: The dive center at Lady Elliot Island Resort (www.ladyelliot.com.au) runs dives to the Blow Hole several times daily.

CATHEDRAL

Part of Thetford Reef, which lies within day-tripping distance of coastal Cairns, Cathedral is a wonderland of coral spires and swim-through chasms. The towering coral heads include thick forests of blue staghorn, sea fans, and sea whips; in between are sandy-bottomed canyons where shafts of sunlight play over giant clam beds.

Difficulty level: Intermediate. Though many coral peaks lie just 15 to 20 feet below the surface, the deeper channels (which go down to 85 feet) can be disorienting.

How to get there: Silverseries (www.silverseries.com.au) runs day-long trips from Cairns that visit several Thetford sites.

Divers explore a swim-through coral formation.

BEST GUARANTEED CLOSE-ENCOUNTER SITES

While just about any dive site on the Reef will bring you face-to-face with fantastic marine creatures, a few particular spots maximize your chances.

RIBBON REEF NUMBER 10

The northernmost of the Ribbon Reefs (a group that extends off the Cairns coast all the way to the Torres Strait) is home to some famously curious sea creatures. At Cod Hole, divers have been hand-feeding the enormous, 70-pound resident potato cod for decades. Ribbon Reef Number 10 is also one of the only places on earth where visitors can have breathtakingly close contact with wild dwarf minke whales. These small, playful baleen whales stop here every June and July—and they often approach within a few feet of respectful divers.

Sea turtle and diver

Difficulty level: Easy. Divers need only be Open-Water certified to dive at the 50-foot Cod Hole; dwarf minke encounters are open to snorkelers.

How to get there: Several dive operators run live-aboard trips to the Ribbon Reefs, including Mike Ball Expeditions (www.mikeball.com), Pro Dive Cairns (www.prodivecairns.com), and Eye to Eye Marine Encounters (www.marineencounters.com.au).

LIGHTHOUSE BOMMIES

Part of the southerly Whitsunday group, Lady Elliot Island is surrounded by shallow, pristine waters that teem with life. In particular, the Lighthouse Bommies—freestanding coral formations set off the island's northwest coast—host a large population of manta rays, some of which have a wingspan twelve feet across.

Difficulty level: Easy. Divers need only be Open-Water certified to visit this site; the depth averages about 50 feet.

How to get there: The dive center at Lady Elliot Island Resort (www.ladyelliot.com.au) runs dives to the Bommies daily.

RAINE ISLAND

In the far north reaches of the Coral Sea off Cape York, this coral cay is one of the Reef's greatest—and most inaccessible—treasures. Its beaches comprise the world's largest nesting ground for endangered green sea turtles; during November and December more than 20,000 turtles per week mob the shores to lay their eggs. Because Raine is a strictly protected preserve, seeing this annual phenomenon is an exceedingly rare privilege. In fact, only one dive operator, Eye to Eye Marine Encounters, is sanctioned by the Marine Park Authority to visit the site—and only twice a year.

Difficulty level: Intermediate to Expert. The dive trips involve a heavy research component; participants not only dive among the turtles, but also collect data on them and fit them with satellite tags (some also tag tiger sharks, another rare endemic species).

How to get there: The 18 spots on these ten-day trips are in high demand; learn more at www.marineencounters.com.au.

SCUBA DIVING 101

(left) ProDive is one of several great dive companies on the Reef; (right) snorkelers receive instruction.

Visiting the Reef can be a snap even if you've never dived before; most local dive operators offer Open Water (entry-level) certification courses that can be completed in just three to five days. The course involves both classroom and pool training, followed by a written test and one or more open-water dives on the Reef. Once you're certified, you'll be able to dive to depths of up to 60 feet; you'll also be eligible to rent equipment and book dive trips all over the world.

TIGHT SCHEDULE?

If time is of the essence, ask about doing your Open Water class and in-pool training near home; some Reef operators may allow you to complete your certification (and get right to the good part—the actual ocean dives) once you arrive in Australia.

Though most serious divers insist that certification is necessary for scuba safety, if you're short on time you may find yourself tempted to take advantage of what are generally called "resort courses"—single-day instruction programs that allow you to dive at limited depths under strict supervision. As long as you choose a reputable operator (like Mike Ball Dive

Expeditions, www.mikeball.com) and do exactly as your dive guides say, you'll likely be fine.

FLYING

No matter how you get yourself underwater, you'll need to make sure you don't schedule a flight and a dive in the same day. Flying too soon after diving can lead to "the bends"—an excruciating buildup of nitrogen bubbles in the bloodstream that requires a decompression chamber to alleviate. Since that's not anything you'd want to develop at the beginning of a transatlantic flight, be sure to wait 12 hours before flying after a single dive, 18 hours after multiple dives, and 24 hours if your dive(s) required decompression stops.

Regulators up! Reef visitors learn Scuba basics.

LOGISTICS

CERTIFYING ORGANIZATIONS

You'll find that all reliable dive operators—on the Reef and elsewhere—are affiliated with one of the three major international dive-training organizations: PADI (www.padi.com), NAUI (www.naui.org), or SSI (www.divessi.com). The certification requirements for all three are similar, and most dive shops and outfitters consider them interchangeable (i.e., they'll honor a certification from any of the three).

COSTS

The price for taking a full Open Water certification course (usually over four or five days of training) averages around A$500—but in many cases, rental equipment, wetsuits, and instruction manuals cost extra. Some dive shops have relationships with hotels, and offer dive/stay packages. One-day scuba resort courses usually cost around $200-$300, with all gear included.

EMERGENCIES

Before diving on the Reef, it's a good idea to purchase divers' insurance through the Divers Alert Network (DAN), an international organization that provides emergency medical assistance to divers. (Learn more about the different plans at www.diversalertnetwork.org). DAN also has a 24-hour emergency hotline staffed by doctors, emergency medical technicians, and nurses; for help with diving injuries or immediate medical advice, call (001) 919-684-4326 from Australia.

SNORKELING TIPS

Snorkelers explore Fitzroy Reef Lagoon.

■ If you're a beginner, avoid snorkeling in areas where there's chop or strong currents.

■ Every few minutes, look up and check what's floating ahead of you—you'll want to avoid boats, jellyfish, and other surface-swimmers.

■ Give corals, plants, and sea creatures a wide berth—for their protection and yours.

■ Coat every part of your back with high-SPF, waterproof sunscreen; the water's reflection greatly intensifies the sun's rays.

DIVING TIPS

■ Before heading off on a dive trip, have your doctor rule out any possible health complications.

■ Be sure your dive operator is affiliated with an internationally known training organization, such as PADI or NAUI.

■ Stick to dive trips and sites that are within your expertise level—the Reef is not the place to push safety limits.

■ Remember that in Australia, depths and weights use the metric system—so bring a conversion table if you need to.

■ Always dive with a partner, and always keep your partner in sight.

■ Never dive when you're feeling ill—especially if you're experiencing sinus congestion.

■ Never dive after consuming alcohol.

■ If you feel unwell or disoriented while diving, signal to your partner that you need to surface so she or he can accompany you.

DANGERS OF THE REEF

(left) Even the tiniest coral can serve as protective habitat; (right) divers explore a large coral formation.

Like any other wild natural habitat, the Reef is home to creatures that are capable of causing you harm—and possibly even killing you. But surprisingly, the most lethal Reef inhabitants aren't of the Shark Week variety. In fact, they're just about invisible.

THE DEADLIEST REEF DWELLER
Chironex fleckeri—better known as box jellyfish—are native to the same waters as the Reef. They also just happen to be the most poisonous sea creatures on the planet. Cube-shaped and transparent (which makes them almost impossible to see in the water), these jellies have tentacles whose stinging cells release an enormously potent venom on contact. A box-jelly sting causes excruciating pain, often followed very quickly (within three or four minutes) by death.

The good news about box jellies is that they're only rarely encountered on the outer Reef and islands (they're much more prevalent close to the mainland shore, especially in summer—which is why you may see beautiful North Queensland beaches completely empty on a hot December day). While the only

sure way to prevent a box jellyfish sting is to stay out of the sea altogether, there are measures you can take to lessen the already minimal risks. First, consider wearing a full-length Lycra "sting suit" when you dive. Second, make sure your dive operator carries a supply of Chironex antivenom onboard your dive boat, just in case.

OTHER (LESS DEADLY) DANGERS
Although box jellyfish are by far the most dangerous creatures on the Reef, there are other "biteys" and "nasties" to be aware of. In particular, you should try to stay clear of a smaller box-jelly variety called Irukandji (whose sting causes delayed but often intense pain); Millepora, or stinging coral (which causes irritation and welts when it touches bare skin); sea snakes (who seldom bite humans, but whose poison can cause paralysis); and, yes, sharks (although you'll likely only see small ones on the Reef—the much more hyped Hammerheads, Tiger Sharks, and Great Whites prefer deeper and colder waters).

PROTECTING THE REEF

(left) The Irukandji box jellyfish sting causes severe pain; (right) small sharks inhabit areas of the Reef.

Enormous though it may be, the Great Barrier Reef's ecosystem is one that requires a delicate balance. The interdependence of species here means that harming even a single food source—like a particular type of plankton—can have wide-ranging and even devastating effects.

The majority of the Reef is an official marine preserve that's managed and protected by the Great Barrier Reef Marine Park Authority. This government agency has developed a series of long-range programs to help protect the Reef—including population-monitoring of sealife species, water-temperature and salinity studies, and screening of all commercial fishing and tourism/recreational operations.

Since almost 2 million tourists visit the Reef each year, even day-trippers should be mindful of their impact on this fragile environment. Specifically, if you're planning to dive and snorkel here, you should:

■ Make sure your dive gear is secure, with no loose straps or dangling hoses that might snag on corals.

■ Swim slowly to avoid brushing against corals (and be especially mindful when wearing swim fins).

■ Avoid picking up or touching any corals, plants, or creatures (for your protection and theirs). No souvenirs, even empty shells or dead-looking coral.

■ Keep clear of all free-swimming sea creatures like sea turtles, dolphins, dugongs, or whales.

VOLUNTEERING ON THE REEF

If you'd like to do more to protect the Reef, the following organizations offer volunteer programs that allow you to help collect study data and monitor the health of reef species:

■ The Australian Marine Conservation Society: www.amcs.org.au

■ Reef Check Australia: www.reefcheckaustralia.org

■ UNESCO (United Nations Educational, Scientific, and Cultural Organization): whc.unesco.org

⚡ Activities

Orpheus Island Resort is surrounded by walking trails, and there are spectacular snorkeling and diving sites right off the beaches, with manta rays (July to early November), humpback whale migration (June to September), and the annual coral spawning (mid- to late October to late November) among the underwater highlights. Resort guests get complimentary use of snorkeling and light fishing gear, as well as kayaks, stand-up paddleboards, catamarans, and motorized dinghies in which to buzz from cove to cove. The coral around Orpheus is some of the best in the area, and cruises to the outer reef can be arranged through the resort for an additional fee. Whereas most Great Barrier Reef resort islands are more than 50 km (31 miles) from the reef, Orpheus is just 15 km (9 miles) away. Dive operators on the island provide scuba courses and various boat-diving options.

BOAT CRUISES

Hinchinbrook and Palm Islands Tours

BOATING | Orpheus Island resort guests can take helicopter flights over Hinchinbrook Island National Park, Australia's largest protected island wilderness; or cruise the Hinchinbrook-Cardwell channel, and nearby Palm Islands, with stops for wildlife-spotting, snorkeling, and bushwalks. On a daylong Hinchinbrook-Cardwell channel cruise, you'll seek out saltwater crocs in island estuaries and anchor in secluded coves for guided rain-forest treks to Zoe and Mulligan waterfalls. Or take a leisurely cruise around the Palm Islands on the resort's own vessel, the *Maree Ann*, with stops to snorkel, explore significant sites, and take guided nature walks. Sunset cruises on the *Maree Ann* include drinks and canapés on deck. ✉ *Orpheus Island* ☎ *07/4777–7377* ⊕ *www.orpheus.com. au* ✎ *From about A$300 per person depending on charter, vessel, and number of guests.*

FISHING

Orpheus Island Fishing

FISHING | The tropical waters off Orpheus Island offer prized game and reef fish species. On group trips or solo dinghy excursions via motorized dinghy (free for guests' use, as is light tackle), tasty reef fish (red emperor and coral trout, sweetlip, and giant trevally) can be caught right off the island. On excursions to the outer reef, you'll get the chance to land large pelagics including wahoo, Spanish mackerel, and dog-tooth tuna. Prebooking fishing charters is essential and all expeditions are subject to weather and tidal conditions. ✉ *Orpheus Island Jetty* ☎ *07/4777–7377* ⊕ *www.orpheus. com.au* ✎ *From A$1200 for outer reef private charter; from A$100/hour for local island private boat charter.*

GREAT BARRIER REEF EXCURSIONS

Orpheus Island Diving & Snorkeling

SCUBA DIVING | FAMILY | Orpheus Island is encircled by fringing reef, with world-class dive and snorkeling sites an easy boat or dinghy ride away; free pool scuba refresher courses and various off-island boat-diving options are available for beginner and PADI-certified divers. The resort can arrange half-day dive and snorkeling trips around the neighboring Palm Islands, and full-day charter dive and snorkeling excursions to sites on the Outer Barrier Reef teeming with turtles, colorful fish, and coral species—and, in season, massive manta rays and masses of coral spawning. Costs depend on passenger numbers and inclusions; booking ahead is essential. Resort guests can also preorder gourmet picnic hampers and use the resort's motorized dinghies to visit secluded, boulder-strewn coves and snorkeling spots on the island's fringing reef. Often, you can snorkel directly off the beach into fish-filled coral gardens. ✉ *Orpheus Island Resort Jetty* ☎ *07/4777–7377* ⊕ *www.orpheus. au* ✎ *From A$300.*

Coral Sea

Great Barrier Reef

Dunk Is
Hull Heads
ully
lly Heads
Bedarra Island
Goold Island
Brook Is
Otter Reef
Lizard Island
Fitzroy Island
Cape Sandwich
Britomart Reef
nnedy
rdwell
Girringun National Park
Hinchinbrook Island National Park
Hinchinbrook Is
Hillcock Point
Trunk Reef
Kelso Reef
Abergowrie
Wallaman Falls
Trebonne
Ingham
Lucinda
Macknade
Lucinda Point
Pelorus Is
Orpheus Island
PALM ISLANDS
Curacoa Is
Davies Reef
Upper Stone
Forrest Beach
Palm Island
Bambaroo
Halifax Bay
Havannah Is
Mutarnee
Paluma
Moongobulla
Acheron Is
Herald Is
Magnetic Island
Cape Cleveland

0   20 mi
0   20 km

Toomulla
Toolakea
Sanders Beach
Pallarenda
Deeragun
Townsville
Billabong Sanctuary
Cungulla
Alva Beach
Woodstock
Ayr
Rita Island
Home Hill
Inkerman
Bowling Green Bay
Cape Bowling Green
Cape Upstart

North Coast Islands, Townsville, and Magnetic Island

Bedarra Island

5 km (3 miles) off the coast of Mission Beach.

This tiny, 247-acre island has natural springs, dense rain-forest tracts, and eight unspoiled beaches. Bedarra Island Resort has upscale facilities, services, and dining options. It is geared for relaxation, but there's still plenty for active guests to do. You can play tennis, work out at the resort gym, sail catamarans around the coves, fish from motorized dinghies, or paddleboard with turtles off the island's main beach. You can sunbathe and picnic on rain-forest fringed beaches (gourmet hamper provided), and go bird-watching and wildlife-spotting along the island's walking trails. Deep-sea game fishing, sailing, and diving excursions on the outer Great Barrier Reef can be arranged through the resort and customized to suit. It's possible to snorkel around the island, but it's not on the reef, and the water can be cloudy during rain.

GETTING HERE AND AROUND

Bedarra Island lies about 77.3 km (48 miles) from Orpheus Island. Fast launch transfers from Mission Beach on the mainland (two hours' drive south of Cairns and about three hours' north of Townsville) depart daily on demand at 12:30 pm (A$198 per couple, one-way). Departing guests can take the daily Bedarra–Mission Beach launch at 10:30 am; launch transfers can be arranged at other times at an additional rate. If your time is more limited than your credit card, it's a 45-minute helicopter transfer from Cairns to Bedarra's beachside helipad. Prebook all transfers through the resort.

🛏 Hotels

⭐ Bedarra

$$$$ | RESORT | Billing itself as "the ultimate in barefoot luxury," the laid-back, exclusive, child-free Bedarra Island Resort hosts no more than 16 guests in modern, eco-friendly accommodations, spoiling them with fine food and service, and upscale amenities. **Pros:** relaxed but attentive service; sailing, diving, sightseeing, and game-fishing trips can be arranged; secluded, spectacular environs. **Cons:** Wi-Fi can be slow and cell phone signals intermittent; reception only open 7 am to 7 pm; no room service. 🟦 *Rooms from: A$1250* ✉ *Bedarra Island* 🕾 *07/4243–4748* ⊕ *www.bedarra.com.au* 🕘 *Closed late Jan.–late Mar.* 🛏 *10 rooms* ⊗ *All-inclusive.*

Fitzroy Island

6 km (4 miles) from Cairns.

This ruggedly picturesque, heavily forested island is 94% national park, with vegetation ranging from rain forest to heath, and an extensive fringing coral reef. Only 6 km (4 miles)—less than an hour's cruise—from Cairns, the 988-acre island, once connected to the mainland, was a hunting, gathering, and ceremonial ground for the Gungandji people, who called it Kobaburra before Cook renamed it in 1770. Today Fitzroy Island houses a modern resort and budget cabins, as well as facilities for the day-trippers who flock here year-round to snorkel, dive, and kayak with turtles and tropical fish. From June to September, migrating manta rays and humpback whales pass right by the island. We recommend it as a day trip.

GETTING HERE AND AROUND

Various ferries service Fitzroy Island daily: *Raging Thunder* and *Sunlover* cruise out of Cairns's Reef Fleet Terminal daily at 9 and 9:30 am, respectively, departing the island for the return trip at 4 and 4:20

pm. Cairns Dive Centre's *MV Sunkist* departs Marlin Marina at 7:30 am daily, dropping day-trippers at Fitzroy Island en route to the outer Great Barrier Reef (A$80) and picking them up at 3:15 on its way back to Cairns. Sunlover Reef Cruises offers Fitzroy Island transfers as part of snorkeling day-trip packages, while Raging Thunder's options include daily ferry service, island activity passes, and guided sea-kayaking snorkel excursions.

FERRY CONTACTS Cairns Dive Centre. 🕾 *07/4051–0294* ⊕ *www.cairnsdive. com.au.* **Raging Thunder Fitzroy Island Ferry.** ✉ *Departs from Cairns Reef Fleet Terminal, 1 Spence St., Cairns* 🕾 *07/4030–7990* ⊕ *www.ragingthunder. com.au* **Sunlover Reef Cruises.** ✉ *Departs from Reef Fleet Terminal, 1 Spence St., Cairns* 🕾 *07/4050–1333* ⊕ *www.sunlover. com.au*

🏃 Activities

Half a dozen marked walking trails traverse Fitzroy Island National Park; they range from half-hour rain-forest strolls to steep, challenging three-hour hikes. Take drinking water; wear sturdy closed shoes, insect repellent, sunscreen, and a hat; and watch for snakes (and in estuaries and mangroves, crocs). For maps and detailed information, visit the **Queensland Government Department of Environment and Sciences)** website (⊕ *www.nprsr.qld.gov. au*).

But most visitors to the island are keen to get on or under the water, and there are plenty of options for doing that. Day-trippers and resort guests can book guided dives and tuition, rent scuba gear at Fitzroy Island Dive & Adventure Center, and rent snorkeling and water sports equipment from Raging Thunder Adventures by the jetty on Welcome Beach. The island has some terrific snorkeling spots—some right off the beach, others accessible by sea kayak—and excellent beginner dive sites close to shore. Go sea kayaking, paddleboarding, or glass-bottom boat touring for more chances to spot turtles, rays, reef sharks, and thousands of bright-hued fish.

Cairns Dive Centre

DIVING/SNORKELING | Departing Cairns's Marlin Marina daily, dive boat MV *Sun-kist* drops day-trippers at Fitzroy Island and picks up island guests en route to the outer Great Barrier Reef. The A$80 fare includes round-trip transfers and time to snorkel, swim, and explore the island. *Sun-kist* picks you up again at 3:15 on its way back to Cairns. Daylong *Sun-kist* dive trips from Cairns include gear, lunch, and a stop at either the Milln, Briggs, Moore, or Thetford Reefs. You can also take an open-water scuba course (two days in Cairns, two on Fitzroy Island and the reef) that includes four training dives and all gear. ⊠ *Fitzroy Island Dive & Adventure Centre* ☎ *07/4051–0294, 1800/642591 toll-free in Australia* ⊕ *www.cairnsdive.com.au* ⊠ *From A$80.*

Fitzroy Island Dive & Adventure Center

DIVING/SNORKELING | FAMILY | Day-trippers, resort guests, divers, and campers can rent kayaks, paddle-skis, and stand-up paddleboards here, as well as stinger suits, diving gear and equipment, tanks, and snorkeling gear from the island's Dive and Adventure Center. Here, you can also book guided dive and snorkeling trips, sea-kayaking explorations, introductory dives, and glass-bottom boat tours. ⊠ *Fitzroy Island Resort, next to Fitzroy Island Jetty, near Welcome Bay* ☎ *07/4040–2100 bookings, 800/640–2486 in U.S.* ⊕ *www.fitzroyislandcairns.com* ⊠ *From A$15.*

Lizard Island

240 km (150 miles) off the North Queensland coast.

The small, upscale resort on secluded Lizard Island is the farthest north of any Barrier Reef hideaway. At 2,500 acres, virtually all of it protected as a national park, the island is larger than and quite different from other islands in the region. Composed mostly of granite, Lizard has a remarkable diversity of vegetation and terrain: grassy hills give way to rocky slabs interspersed with valleys of rain forest.

Ringed by two-dozen white-sand beaches, the island has some of the best fringing coral in the region. Excellent walking trails lead to lookouts with spectacular views of the coast. The island's highest point, Cook's Look (1,180 feet), is the historic spot from which, in August 1770, Captain Cook finally spotted a safe passage through the reef that had held his vessel captive for a thousand miles. Large monitor lizards, after which the island is named, often bask in this area.

GETTING HERE AND AROUND

Lizard Island has its own small airstrip. Hour-long flights to the island depart up to twice a day from Cairns, at 11 and 2, returning at 12:25 and 3:25; taking an hour and costing A$355 per person each way. Allow two and a half hours' transit time for connecting international flights, 90 minutes for domestic flight transits: check-in is 30 minutes prior to flight time at the East Air Terminal. You can also arrange charter flights to the island, with prices varying depending on the size of aircraft available (☎ *1800/837204 inside Australia, 716/276–0104 outside Australia*).

AIR CONTACTS Hinterland Aviation. ☎ *07/4040–1333 international, 1300/359428 toll-free in Australia* ⊕ *www.hinterlandaviation.com.au.*

 Sights

★ Cod Hole

REEF | For divers and snorkelers, the usually crystal clear waters off Lizard Island are a dream. Cod Hole, 20 km (12 miles) from Lizard Island, ranks among the best dive sites on Earth. Massive potato cod swim up to divers like hungry puppies; it's an awesome experience, considering that these fish can weigh 300 pounds and reach around two meters (6 feet) in length. The island lures big-game anglers from all over the world from September to December, when black marlin are running. ✉ *Lizard Island.*

Hotels

★ Lizard Island Resort

$$$$ | **RESORT** | Beloved by honeymooners, divers, and well-heeled travelers, this outer Great Barrier Reef resort ticks all the high-end tropical-island vacation boxes: luxurious beachfront accommodation, fine food and wine, and world-class diving and fishing. **Pros:** superb diving and fishing; quality food and wine (included in the rate); use of nonmotorized watercraft and dinghies. **Cons:** successive cyclones have damaged the island's vegetation; lighting inadequate for reading; no cell-phone coverage. [$] *Rooms from: A$1969* ✉ *Lizard Island* ☎ *1800/837204 bookings (toll-free in Australia), 07/4043–1999 resort, 844/887–6724 toll-free in U.S.* 🌐 *www.lizardisland.com.au* 🛏 *40 suites* 🍴 *All-inclusive.*

Activities

The lodge has catamarans, outboard dinghies, paddle-skis (including glass-bottom ones), fishing supplies, snorkeling gear, and lessons. There is superb snorkeling around the island's fringing coral, or you can cruise over it on a glass-bottom sea kayak. Self-guided bushwalking trails and nature slide shows get guests in touch with the local flora and fauna. Arrange a picnic hamper with the kitchen staff and take a dinghy out for an afternoon on your own private beach. All these activities are included in your room rate.

Other activities cost extra: inner and outer reef dive/snorkel trips, night dives, scuba courses, and game- and bottom-fishing excursions (black marlin season runs September through December). For pricing, details, and to prebook activities, contact Lizard Island Activities Desk (☎ *1800/837204* 🌐 *www.lizardisland.com.au*).

FISHING

Lizard Island is one of the big game-fishing centers in Australia, with several world records set here since the mid-1990s. Game fishing is generally best in spring and early summer, and giant black marlin weighing more than 1,000 pounds are no rarity. September through December, the folk from Lizard Island run full-day game-fishing trips to the outer reef; January through August, you can book half-day bottom-fishing excursions.

★ Lizard Island Sportfishing

FISHING | Even though fishing is banned in the waters immediately off Lizard Island, world-renowned fishing grounds lie less than an hour away. From September through December, fishing enthusiasts arrive in droves to land tuna, sailfish, mahimahi, and, if they're lucky, the legendary "Grander" black marlin. From January to August, you might nab trevally, mackerel, or queenfish. Lizard Island Resort arranges small-group, high-adrenaline trips to the outer reef and half- and full-day inner reef excursions on its 51-foot Riviera Platinum Model Flybridge cruiser, *Fascination III*. An outer-reef game-fishing day trip, including heavy tackle, lunch, and light refreshments, costs from A$3,500 for up to four people; a half-day fishing excursion, with bait, light tackle, and refreshments, begins at A$2,300. **■ TIP→ For all fishing trips, prebooking is essential.** ✉ *Lizard Island Resort Jetty* ☎ *1800/837204 toll-free in Australia, 884/833–7862 in U.S.* 🌐 *www.lizardisland.com.au* 🎟 *From A$2300.*

SCUBA DIVING

The reefs around Lizard Island have some of the best marine life and coral on the planet. The resort runs expertly guided scuba-diving and snorkeling trips on its custom-built dive boat to pristine sites on the Great Barrier Reef, including the Ribbon Reefs and globally renowned Cod Hole, as well as local dives, snorkeling excursions, and scuba courses.

★ **Lizard Island Snorkeling & Diving**

DIVING/SNORKELING | Lizard Island is a short boat ride from some of the richest, least spoiled sites on the Great Barrier Reef. Within an hour, you can dive the ribbon reefs or renowned Cod Hole, eyeballing giant potato cod, pelagic fish, turtles, rays, and sharks. You can also take guided dives to explore fish-filled coral gardens just offshore. Lizard Island Resort's 55-foot dive boat MV *Serranidae* makes reef excursions as well as dive-snorkel trips, and privately guided dives to local fringing reefs and the Cobia Hole. Need scuba skills or gear? The resort has PADI Referral courses, and a wide range of modern dive equipment for rent. Use of snorkeling masks, snorkels, and fins is complimentary. ⊠ *Lizard Island Resort* ☎ *1800/837204 toll-free in Australia, 884/833–7862 in U.S.* ⊕ *www.lizardisland.com.au* ☞ *From A$95* ☞ *All divers must bring certification card and current dive medical certificate.*

Townsville

1,358 km (844 miles) north of Brisbane, 348 km (216 mile) south of Cairns.

This coastal city has little in the way of sandy beaches or surf, but it does have shady parks, charming colonial buildings, and a boardwalk-flanked waterfront esplanade with a terrific man-made beach and picnic facilities. The historic town center has thrived in the past decade, with an influx of lively eateries and bars. There is also an excellent museum and a world-class aquarium.

Queensland Parks and Wildlife Service (ParksQ) has an office on Magnetic Island, but Tourism Townsville's information kiosk in Flinders Square and the Townsville Bulletin Square Visitor Information Centre near the Museum of Tropical Queensland (MTQ), on the mainland, are the best sources of visitor info about the island.

GETTING HERE AND AROUND

Qantas flies frequently from Townsville Airport to Brisbane, Cairns, Cloncurry, Mount Isa, and Mackay, as well as to capital cities around Australia and overseas destinations. Jetstar has services to Brisbane, Sydney, and Melbourne; Virgin Australia connects Townsville with Cairns, Brisbane, the Gold Coast, Rockhampton, Sydney, Melbourne, and Canberra. Townsville Taxis are available at the airport. The average cost of the ride to a city hotel is between A$23 and A$28, more after 7 pm.

There are no air connections to Magnetic Island; you need to take a ferry from Townsville (one-way, it's A$17 for a walk-on passenger; from A$101 each way for a vehicle with up to four passengers).

Townsville is a flat, somewhat dull 1,358-km (844-mile), 16-hour drive from Brisbane. The 348-km (216-mile), 4½-hour journey from here to Cairns, with occasional Hinchinbrook Island views, is more scenic. Greyhound Australia coaches travel regularly to Cairns, Mount Isa, Rockhampton, Brisbane, and other destinations throughout Australia from the SeaLink Terminal on Townsville's Breakwater, also the departure point for Magnetic Island ferries, day cruises, and dive trips. Regular long-distance Queensland Rail services, offering reclining seats or pod-like RailBeds, connect Townsville with Brisbane, Cairns, Mount Isa, and dozens of towns en route.

Once in town, you can flag a Townsville Taxis cab on the street, find one at taxi stands, hotels, and the island's ferry terminal, or book one online.

FERRY CONTACTS Fantasea Cruising Magnetic. ⊠ *Ross St., South Townsville, South Townsville* ☎ *07/4796–9300* ⊕ *www.fantaseacruisingmagnetic.*

com.au. **SeaLink Queensland.** ✉ Breakwater Terminal, 18 Sir Leslie Thiess Dr. ☎ 07/4726–0800 ⊕ www.sealinkqld.com.au.

TAXI CONTACTS Townsville Taxis. ✉ 11–15 Yeatman St. ☎ 13–1008 local bookings, 07/4778–9555 interstate bookings ⊕ www.tsvtaxi.com.au.

ESSENTIALS

VISITOR INFORMATION Flinders Square Visitor Information Centre. ✉ Flinders Sq., 334–336 Flinders St. ☎ 07/4721–3660 ⊕ www.townsvillenorthqueensland.com.au.

 Sights

Billabong Sanctuary

NATURE PRESERVE | FAMILY | This eco-friendly, interactive sanctuary on 22 acres of bushland shelters koalas, wombats, dingoes, wallabies, endangered bilbies, snakes, crocodiles, lizards, and numerous birds, most featuring in daily wildlife shows, presentations, and feedings. The sanctuary has daily free-flight birds of prey shows, crocodile and cassowary feedings, venomous snake presentations, and turtle racing. This is one of the few places in Australia at which you can cuddle a koala (and get your photo taken as a memento). You can also get your photo taken holding a wombat, snake, or baby croc. Thrill-seekers can book a personal croc-feeding experience, with or without souvenir photo. ✉ Bruce Hwy., Nome ✛ 17 km (11 miles) south of Townsville ☎ 07/4778–8344 ⊕ www.billabongsanctuary.com.au ➽ A$37 entry.

Castle Hill

VIEWPOINT | The summit of pink-granite monolith Castle Hill, 1 km (½ miles) from the city center, provides great views of the city and Magnetic Island. While you're perched on top, think about the proud local resident who, with the aid of several scout troops, spent years in the 1970s piling rubble onto the peak to try to add the 23 feet that would make Castle Hill a mountain, officially speaking—which means a rise of at least 1,000 feet. These days, most people trek to the top along a steep walking track that doubles as one of Queensland's most scenic jogging routes. ✉ Castle Hill Lookout, Castle Hill Rd. ☎ 07/4721–3660 Townsville visitor information.

Flinders Street

NEIGHBORHOOD | A stroll along Flinders Street from the Strand to Stanley Street takes you past some of Townsville's most impressive turn-of-the-20th-century colonial structures. **Magnetic House** and several other historic buildings along the strip have been beautifully restored. The grand old **Queens Hotel** is a fine example of the early Victorian Classical Revival style, as is the **Perc Tucker Regional Gallery,** circa 1885, originally a bank. **Tattersalls Hotel,** circa 1865, is typical of its era, with wide verandas and fancy wrought-iron balustrades; today, it houses the rambunctious **Molly Malones** Irish pub. Once the town's post office, what's now **The Brewery** had an impressive masonry clock tower when it was erected in 1889. The tower was dismantled in 1942 so it wouldn't be a target during World War II air raids, and re-erected in 1964. **The Exchange,** Townsville's oldest pub, was built in 1869, burned down in 1881, and was rebuilt the following year. ✉ Flinders St.

Museum of Tropical Queensland

MUSEUM | FAMILY | Centuries-old relics from the HMS Pandora (the ship sent by the British Admiralty to capture the mutinous Bounty crew), which sank in 1791 carrying 14 crew members of Captain Bligh's infamous ship, are among the exhibits at this repository of the region's maritime, natural, and indigenous history. There's a fun introduction to North Queensland's culture and lifestyle, a shipwreck exhibit, and the ecology-focused Enchanted Rainforest. Displays of tropical wildlife, dinosaur fossils, local corals, and deep-sea creatures round out a diverse public collection. ✉ 70–102 Flinders St.

E ☎ *07/4726–0600* ⊕ *www.mtq.qm.qld. gov.au* 🖂 *A$15.*

Queens Gardens

GARDEN | FAMILY | Offering shade and serenity less than a mile from the CBD, Townsville's colonial-era botanic gardens occupies 10 verdant acres at the base of Castle Hill. Bordered by frangipani (plumeria) and towering Moreton Bay fig trees, whose unique dangling roots veil the entry to the grounds, the gardens are a wonderful place to picnic, stroll, or amuse the kids. There are play areas, a hedge maze, formal rose garden, fountains, and a lovely rain-forest walk. A compact aviary houses bright-plumed peacocks, lorikeets, and sulfur-crested cockatoos. 🖂 *Gregory St. at Paxton St., North Ward* ☎ *1300/878001 toll-free in Australia* 🖂 *Free.*

★ Reef HQ Aquarium

ZOO | FAMILY | Come eye-to-eye with sharks, rays, giant trevally, and green sea turtles at the Reef HQ Aquarium. It houses a 200,000-gallon predator tank, a hands-on discovery lagoon, and a vast aquarium, open to the elements. The main oceanarium is populated with 120 species of hard and soft coral, as well as sea stars, spiky urchins, sponges, and more than 150 species of tropical fish. There's also a 20-meter (65-foot) Perspex underwater walkway. Time your visit to coincide with the aquarium's daily predator dive show (10:30 am), twice-daily turtle talks (noon and 3:30), guided tours, or thrice-weekly shark feeds (2:30 on Tuesday, Thursday, and Sunday). 🖂 *2–68 Flinders St.* E ☎ *07/4750–0800* ⊕ *www. reefhq.com.au* 🖂 *A$28.*

Townsville Town Common Conservation Park

NATIONAL/STATE PARK | FAMILY | Spot wallabies, echidnas, dingoes, goannas, and hundreds of bird species at this terrific wetlands conservation park crisscrossed by walking and biking trails, and dotted with bird blinds and a wildlife-viewing tower. You can take the easy, hour-long

Forest Walk to see kingfishers and honey-eaters, the Pallarenda to Tegoora Rock circuit for wetlands overviews, or several other walking and biking trails (with estimated walk times ranging from 30 minutes to five hours). The 5-km (3-mile), two-plus-hour-long trail from Bald Rock to Mount Marlowl is worth the uphill trek for the glorious regional panorama at the summit. Most trails start from Bald Rock parking lot, 7 km (4½ miles) from the park entrance on unpaved roads. 🖂 *Freshwater Lagoon Rd., off Cape Pallarenda Rd., near Rowes Bay Golf Club, Pallarenda* ☎ *07/4721–3660 Townsville tourist information, 13–7468 ParksQ infoline* ⊕ *www.nprsr.qld.gov.au/parks/ townsville.*

Wallaman Falls

NATIONAL/STATE PARK | FAMILY | Surrounding the highest sheer-drop waterfall in Australia is glorious Girringun National Park, in which ancient rain forests accessible via scenic walking trails shelter rare plants and animals that include the endangered southern cassowary, platypus, and musky rat-kangaroo. You might also spot eastern water dragons, sawshelled turtles, and crocodiles here. The park is the start of the Wet Tropics Great Walk, suitable for experienced hikers. For day-trippers, there are two spectacular lookouts and some scenic short walks, such as the 45-minute Banggurru circuit along Stony Creek's bank, or the steeper, two-hour walk to the base of the falls. 🖂 *Lava Plains Mount Fox Rd.* ✦ *From Townsville, take Bruce Hwy. (A1) north for just under 100 km (60 miles), then turn left onto Lannercost St. (signposted for Abergowrie/Wallaman Falls), taking Abergowrie-Ingham Rd. to Abergowrie, then Stone Rd. and Mount Fox Rd. to park entrance* ☎ *13–7468 ParksQ infoline* ⊕ *www.nprsr.qld.gov.au/parks.*

Beaches

Townsville is blessed with a golden, 2-km (1-mile) beach that stretches along the city's northern edge. The beach, with its associated pools, water park, and adjacent parklands, is hugely popular with the locals, especially over school holidays and summer.

★ The Strand

BEACH—SIGHT | FAMILY | Dubbed Australia's Cleanest Beach, this palm-flanked stretch of sand—lined with jogging tracks and cycleways, picnic-friendly parklands, and hip beachfront bars—has two swimming enclosures and a long pier perfect for fishing. The beach and its permanent swimming enclosure, Strand Rock Pool, are fitted with temporary nets during box-jellyfish season, November through May. There's also a free, kid-friendly Strand Water Park. All are patrolled by lifeguards daily, with hours varying seasonally. **Amenities:** food and drink; lifeguards; toilets. **Best for:** swimming. ✉ *The Strand* ☎ *13–4810 Townsville City Council* 🌐 *www.townsville.qld.gov.au.*

Restaurants

★ A Touch of Salt

$ | MODERN AUSTRALIAN | This Modern Australian eatery fits the bill: location (riverfront), service (impeccable), ambience (relaxed), food (exciting and flavorful), and wine (top-flight). The menu is a carefully curated collection of meat, seafood and vegetable creations with something to suit every palette, and there's a signature design-your-own degustation. **Known for:** perfect pick for date night; expansive waterfront deck; excellent, largely Australian wine list. [$] *Average main: A$29* ✉ *86 Ogden St.* ☎ *07/4724–4441* 🌐 *www.atouchofsalt.com.au* 🕓 *Closed Sun. and Mon. No lunch Sat.–Thurs.*

JAM Corner

$ | MODERN AUSTRALIAN | This fine-dining restaurant sources terrific organic and tropical produce for its modern Australian menus, which change seasonally, but always feature fresh seafood and premium Australian meats in artful, beautifully balanced dishes, with fine Antipodean wines to complement them. For special occasions, there's a luxurious, chandelier-lighted private dining room. **Known for:** one of the fancier restaurants in town; great breakfasts; good coffee. [$] *Average main: A$31* ✉ *1 Palmer St., South Townsville* ☎ *07/4721–4900* 🌐 *jamcorner.com.au* 🕓 *Closed Mon. No lunch or dinner Sun.*

Hotels

Grand Hotel Townsville

$ | HOTEL | With a terrific location in Townsville's liveliest bar-restaurant precinct, this stylish, secure, and spotless hotel-apartment complex has everything you need: chic, well-appointed accommodation; a clean pool and terrific gym; business center; accommodating staff; and charge-back arrangements with local eateries. **Pros:** close to many bars, eateries, and attractions; helpful, friendly staff; 24-hour room service. **Cons:** lower-floor rooms are small and lack views; Palmer Street–facing rooms can be noisy, especially on weekends; free on-site car-parking spots limited. [$] *Rooms from: A$170* ✉ *8–10 Palmer St.* ☎ *07/4753–2800* 🌐 *www.grandhoteltownsville.com.au* 🛏 *106 rooms* 🍴 *No meals.*

Oaks Metropole Hotel

$ | HOTEL | The smartly configured studios and suites at this hotel are a five-minute walk from Palmer Street's bar and dining precinct, and an easy stroll across the footbridge from Flinders Street and the ferry port. **Pros:** excellent in-room facilities; central location; discounts for longer stays. **Cons:** feels a tad clinical; service standards vary; fee for in-room Wi-Fi after first 30 minutes. [$] *Rooms from: A$129* ✉ *81 Palmer St.* ☎ *07/4753–2900 reception, 1300/559129 toll-free in Australia* 🌐 *www.theoaksgroup.com.au* 🛏 *104 rooms* 🍴 *No meals.*

Nightlife

★ The Brewery

BREWPUBS/BEER GARDENS | Townsville's historic post office now houses this sociable gastropub, which serves upmarket, bistro-style meals and boutique beers brewed on-site. The owners have combined modern finishes with the building's original design, incorporating old post-office fittings, such as the main bar, once the stamp counter, to create a venue with character and polish. ✉ *252 Flinders St.* ☎ *07/4724–2999* 🌐 *www.townsvillebrewery.com.au.*

The Ville Resort Casino

CASINOS | Dominating Townsville's waterfront, this high-rise casino-hotel complex is an entertainment hub, containing a luxury hotel, six on-site restaurants and bars, performance space featuring regular live shows, and more than 370 slot machines and 20-plus gaming tables. If you choose to stay over, the 194-room hotel has well-appointed rooms, suites, and a two-bedroom apartment. ✉ *Sir Leslie Thiess Dr.* ☎ *07/4722–2333* 🌐 *www.the-ville.com.au.*

Activities

KAYAKING

Magnetic Island Sea Kayaks

KAYAKING | **FAMILY** | On these eco-friendly kayaking trips around Magnetic Island's quieter bays, you might spot turtles, dolphins, dugongs, sea eagles, ospreys, and, mid-July through mid-September, migrating whales and their calves. The company runs two different excursions: a leisurely 4½-hour morning tour of beaches, coves, and bays (A$95) and a twilight paddle around Horseshoe Bay with a stop for drinks (A$65). Rates include the use of single or double kayaks and safety gear, expert instruction and guidance, commentary on the island's ecology, breakfast or sunset drinks, reef tax, and National Park entry fees. ✉ *Horseshoe Bay boat ramp, end of Pacific Dr., off Horseshoe Bay Rd., Magnetic Island* ☎ *07/4778–5424* 🌐 *www.seakayak.com.au* 🎫 *From A$65.*

SCUBA DIVING

Surrounded by tropical islands and warm waters, Townsville is a top-notch diving center. Diving courses, day trips, and multiday excursions tend to be less crowded than those in the hot spots of Cairns or the Whitsunday Islands.

About 16 km (10 miles) offshore, a 60-km (37-mile) boat ride southeast of Townsville, is the wreck of the mighty SS *Yongala,* a steamship that sank in 1911 and now lies 49 to 91 feet beneath the surface. It teems with marine life and is considered one of Australia's best dive sites. It can be explored on one- and two-day trips. All local dive operators conduct excursions to the wreck.

Adrenalin Dive

DIVING/SNORKELING | This local outfit runs day and live-aboard trips to diverse sites on the Great Barrier Reef, including the wreck of the SS *Yongala.* The *Yongala* trip includes weight belt, tanks, two dives, and lunch; it's an extra A$40 for dive gear and A$10 for the introductory guided dive that's compulsory for novice divers. Snorkel/dive day trips to sheltered sites on the GBR's Lodestone Reef are A$249 for snorkelers, A$289 for certified divers (A$329 with gear); for introductory divers, it's A$329 with one dive and snorkeling, A$369 with two dives. On a three-night, live-aboard eco-trip, you can make up to 10 dives, including two night dives and two dives on the *Yongala* (A$810 for a snorkeler, A$930 for a diver in a double room, including diving, gear, and meals). Cheaper twin and dorm berths are

Did You Know?

Bigeye trevally (Caranx Sexfasciatus), a type of jack, can form schools of up to 1,500 fish during the day. At night these schools break up, and individuals or small groups hunt seaborne insects, crustaceans, jelly-fish, and smaller species of fish.

available. On all dive trips, optional extras nclude PADI Adventure Dives (A$25 per dive); enriched-air nitrox (A$50 for two tanks, Nitrox-certified divers only); and camera rental (A$65). ✉ 66–70 Perkins St. W ☎ 07/4724–0600 ⊕ www.adrenalin-dive.com.au ✎ From A$249.

Magnetic Island

10 km (6 miles) from Townsville.

More than half of Magnetic Island's 52 square km (20 square miles) is national parkland, laced with miles of walking trails and rising to 1,640 feet at the Mt. Cook summit. The terrain is littered with huge granite boulders and softened by tall hoop pines, eucalyptus forest, and rain-forest gullies. A haven for wildlife, the island shelters rock wallabies, echidnas, frogs, possums, fruit bats, nonvenomous green tree snakes, and Northern Australia's largest population of wild koalas. Its beaches, mangroves, sea-grass beds, and fringing reefs support turtles nesting, fish hatching, and a significant dugong (manatee) population. You can take time out on 23 island beaches and dive nine offshore shipwrecks.

More than 2,500 people call "Maggie" home; most live on the island's eastern shore at Picnic Bay, Arcadia, Nelly Bay, and Horseshoe Bay. Many artists and craftspeople reside here, drawn by the serenity and scenic environs; you can see and buy their work at studios and galleries around the island.

GETTING HERE AND AROUND

Fantasea Cruising Magnetic
The 40-minute Fantasea Cruising Magnetic ferry service has several scheduled services daily from the mainland to Maggie's Nelly Bay Ferry Terminal, 10 km (6 miles) offshore. The first ferry leaves Townsville at 5:20 am weekdays, 7:10 on weekends, with the last return service departing the island at 6:55 pm. One-way fares are from A$110 for a vehicle

with up to six people, A$14 for a person with no vehicle (bicycles free). SeaLink Queensland has a daily 25-minute catamaran service linking Townsville and Nelly Bay on Magnetic Island. Bus and island transfers meet the ferry during daylight hours. Up to 18 SeaLink ferries a day cruise out of Townsville between 5:30 am (6:30 Sunday) and 10:30 pm (11:30 pm Friday and Saturday), returning between 6:20 am (7:10 Sunday) and 11 pm (midnight Friday and Saturday); a one-way ticket costs A$17. ✉ 22 Ross St., Townsville ☎ 07/4796–9300 ⊕ www.fantaseacruisingmagnetic.com.au.

Magnetic Island Sunbus
Get an overview of Magnetic Island riding the cheap, reliable local buses, which ply the coast road between Picnic Point, Nelly Bay, Arcadia, and Horseshoe Bay from dawn till late, and can be hailed from the roadside. Single-fare tickets (A$1.80 to A$3.60) as well as unlimited-travel day and weekly passes are available from the driver. The bus departs Picnic Bay Jetty at regular intervals throughout the week. Hail it between designated stops simply by standing at the roadside and raising your hand. ✉ Nelly Bay, 44 Mandalay Ave. ☎ 07/4778–5130 ⊕ www.sunbus.com.au.

Magnetic Island Taxi Service
This local taxi company services the entire island. Go to its website to prebook cabs and get fare estimates. ✉ Magnetic Island ☎ 13–1008 toll-free in Australia, 07/3363–2317 ⊕ www.131008.com.

TOURS

Tropicana Guided Adventure Company
The knowledgeable guides from this local tour outfit run small-group expeditions to normally inaccessible bays and beaches around Magnetic Island in a stretch jeep. The company's signature tour is its five-hour Remote Area Adventure (A$132 per person), accessing permit-only areas around Florence Bay and West Point. The excursion allows

Migaloo the Albino Whale

Migaloo was the world's only documented white humpback whale when he was first spotted in 1991, making his way up the Queensland coastline. A witty indigenous elder suggested the name Migaloo, an Aboriginal word for "white fella."

Every year, thousands eagerly watch for a glimpse of Migaloo's distinctive pure-white dorsal fin, as the 14-meter (46-foot) whale makes his annual migration from the Antarctic to tropical waters in June and July. He's been spotted as far up Australia's east coast as Port Douglas, north of Cairns—usually from the decks of dive and cruise boats (which are forbidden by law from going within 500 meters [1640 feet]of the rare cetacean). Sometimes Migaloo travels solo; on other journeys, he's accompanied by dolphins or fellow humpbacks. With humpack numbers on Australia's east coast increasing by about 10 percent each year, hopefully you will spot Migaloo with more of his friends during your visit.

Migaloo's not the only albino whale marine creature you might spot on your visit to Australia. In 2018, an adorable albino humback calf was spotted off the NSW coast.

time to explore remote beaches, hike to lookouts, photograph wildlife, and watch the sun set over the sea from West Point. The tour leaves Nelly Bay Harbour daily at 2:30, returning in time for the 7:45 SeaLink ferry to Townsville (or dropping guests off at Magnetic Island accommodations). It's A$79 per person for a three-hour eco-orientation tour, departing daily at 11 from Nelly Bay near the taxi stand (catch the 10:30 SeaLink ferry from the mainland). An 8½-hour sightseeing tour of the island, including its wildlife hot spots and remote and tourist areas, leaves daily at 11 am from Magnetic Harbour (A$198, including lunch and refreshments). ✉ *Taxi cab rank, Nelly Bay Harbour* ☎ *07/4758–1800* ☞ *From A$79.*

ESSENTIALS

VISITOR INFORMATION Queensland Parks and Wildlife Service, Magnetic Island. ✉ *22 Hurst St., Picnic Bay* ☎ *13–7468 ParksQ hotline, toll-free in Australia* 🌐 *www.nprsr.qld.gov.au/parks/magnetic-island.*

Hotels

Magnetic Island began "life" as a holiday-home getaway for Townsville residents; only in the past decade has it attracted the kind of large-scale development that has transformed other islands near the Barrier Reef. Accommodations here are a mix of functional 1970s properties; small budget lodges; and newer, upmarket but relatively small apartment complexes and resorts. Luxurious Peppers Blue on Blue Resort is one of a handful of exceptions to the rule.

Peppers Blue On Blue Resort
$$ | RESORT |FAMILY | The hotel and studio rooms, apartments, and penthouse suites at waterfront Blue on Blue are stylishly designed, with high-end entertainment systems, luxe amenities, and balconies overlooking the ferry port, pool or the island's private marina. **Pros:** fine on-site food and wine; big buffet breakfasts include eggs made to order; convenient launchpad for excursions. **Cons:** some suites lack full elevator access; lower-floor, ferry-side rooms can be noisy; limited Wi-Fi access. [$] *Rooms from:*

A$269 ✉ 123 Sooning St., adjacent to ferry terminal, Nelly Bay ☎ 07/4758–2400 reception, 1300/987600 reservations (toll-free in Australia) ⊕ www.peppers. com.au/blue-on-blue ⇆ 60 twin rooms, 127 apartment suites and penthouses ⦶ No meals.

Activities

The island has 24 km (15 miles) of hiking trails, most of which are relatively easy. The popular Forts Walk leads to World War II gun emplacements overlooking Horseshoe and Florence bays. At a leisurely pace, it takes about 45 minutes each way from the Horseshoe–Radical Bay Road. Look up en route and you may spot a sleepy koala.

Some of the island's best views are on the 5-km (3-mile) Nelly Bay to Arcadia Walk. Look out for shell middens created over thousands of years by the island's Aboriginal owners, the Wulgurukaba, or Canoe People."

Swimming and snorkeling are other popular activities, but from November to May, box jellyfish ("stingers") are a hazard: swim at Picnic and Horseshoe bays, which have stinger nets, and wear a protective suit. At other times, Alma Bay and Nelly Bay, as well as Picnic, Florence, Radical, Horseshoe, and Balding bays, are all suitable for swimming. Horseshoe has daily lifeguard patrols and a stinger-free swimming enclosure; Alma and Picnic bays are patrolled over weekends and school holiday periods, September to May.

Geoffrey Bay has a well-trafficked unofficial snorkel trail. Other good snorkeling spots include Nelly Bay, Alma Bay (which has its own snorkel trail), and the northern ends of Florence and Arthur bays. Near the northeastern corner of the island, Radical Bay has a small, idyllic beach flanked by tree-covered rock outcrops. Horseshoe Bay, the island's largest beach, is lined with boat-rental outlets and water-sports equipment.

HORSEBACK RIDING
Horseshoe Bay Ranch
HORSEBACK RIDING | FAMILY | Leaving only hoof prints on Magnetic Island's white-sand beaches, these eco-friendly horse rides offer the chance to go bareback swimming with your well-trained steed. Two-hour rides (A$130) depart Horseshoe Bay Ranch daily at 8:30 am and 2:30 pm, wending their way along bush trails to a secluded beach, where you get to unsaddle and take the horses for a Coral Sea swim. Wear a bathing suit, shirt, long pants, socks, and closed shoes, and BYO drinking water and sunscreen. Safety helmets are provided, as are stinger suits in season, and a minimum of two guides accompanies each ride. ✉ 38 Gifford St., Horseshoe Bay ☎ 07/4778–5109 ⊕ www. horseshoebayranch.com.au ⇆ From A$130.

SNORKELING AND SCUBA DIVING
Pleasure Divers
DIVING/SNORKELING | FAMILY | The local guides at Pleasure Divers run good-value dive trips to the SS Yongala shipwreck and pristine Lodestone Reef on the outer Barrier Reef as well as snorkeling and diving in the waters off Magnetic Island. Day trips include two dives and buffet lunch. Optional introductory dives, adventure diving, and guided dives (compulsory for those with fewer than 15 logged dives) cost extra. Reef dive and snorkel trips run Tuesday, Thursday, Friday, and Sunday; Yongala trips run Wednesday and Saturday, departing Nelly Bay Ferry Terminal and Townsville. Pleasure Divers run various SSI/PADI-accredited courses from the island, including refresher sessions and three-day, four-dive Open Water courses. ✉ 10 Marine Parade, Arcadia ☎ 07/4778–5788 ⊕ www.pleasuredivers. com.au ⇆ From A$50.

TOAD RACES

Arcadia Village Motel Toad Races

LOCAL SPORTS | FAMILY | A Magnetic Island institution, the Arcadia Village Motel weekly toad races offer cut-price, Aussie-style hilarity. After each race, the winners kiss their toads and collect the proceeds, with funds raised going to the Arcadia Surf Life Saving Club. The Arcadia's cane-toad races have been held every Wednesday night from 8 pm for nearly three decades, despite several changes in the hotel's ownership. Even when the toads aren't racing, the hotel is pumping, with recently-revamped accommodations, three well-patronized bars, regular live bands, pool tables, a big lagoon pool, and bistro meals. ⊠ *Arcadia Village Motel, 7 Marine Parade, Arcadia* ☎ *07/4778–5418* ⊕ *www.arcadiavillage. com.au.*

WATER SPORTS

Horseshoe Bay Watersports

WATER SPORTS | FAMILY | This outfitter can take you tube-riding, wakeboarding, waterskiing, and sailing on a Hobie cat in the translucent waters of Horseshoe Bay. All tube rides are for a minimum of two people and start from A$15 per person for an exhilarating 10 minutes; an extra person can ride for free in the ski boat to take pictures. Horseshoe Bay Watersports also rents out an array of water-sports gear and equipment. Find them beside the boat ramp at the center of Horseshoe Bay, weather permitting. ⊠ *Boat ramp, Pacific Dr., at Horseshoe Bay Rd., Horseshoe Bay* ☎ *07/4758–1336* ☎ *From A$15.*

★ Magnetic Jet Ski Tours

WATER SPORTS | FAMILY | This operator offers tours through Magnetic Island's clear waters on SeaDoo 4-stroke Jet Skis. Choose between the three-hour island circumnavigation (A$395 per ski) and the two-hour "Top End" tour (A$220 per ski), with up to two people on each ski. All equipment and instruction are included in the rate; no licenses required. ⊠ *9 Pacific Dr., Horseshoe Bay* ☎ *07/4778–5533.*

SOUTH AUSTRALIA

10

Updated by
Rachel Signer

👁 Sights   🍴 Restaurants   🛏 Hotels   🛍 Shopping   🍸 Nightlife

★★★★☆   ★★★☆☆   ★★★★★   ★★★☆☆   ★★★★☆

WELCOME TO SOUTH AUSTRALIA

TOP REASONS TO GO

★ **Arts and Music:** South Australia has fantastic events: the Adelaide Fringe Festival, DreamBIG Children's Festival, and the WOMADelaide celebration, to name a few.

★ **Bush Tucker:** The Australian palate has been reeducated in the pleasures of bush tucker: kangaroo, crocodile, and emu, are now embraced by all.

★ **Historic Homes:** Stay in the historic properties in North Adelaide and the Adelaide Hills, with easy access to the city, rustic villages, and the vineyards.

★ **Wonderful Wines:** The top-notch wines of the Barossa Region, Clare Valley, McLaren Vale, Adelaide Hills, and Coonawarra are treasured by connoisseurs.

★ **Wildlife:** Kangaroo Island is Australia's third largest island and home to colonies of fur seals, sea lions and penguins, thousands of koalas, and roughly half a million wallabies.

1 Adelaide. South Australia's lively capital.

2 Mt. Lofty. Panoramic views of Adelaide.

3 Bridgewater. Home to an historic mill.

4 Lyndoch. A perfect base for Barossa region.

5 Tanunda. Distinctly German-feeling town.

6 Angaston. Historic and alcoholic attractions.

7 Nuriootpa. Commercial center of Valley.

8 Marananga. The Valley's top wineries.

9 Sevenhill. Explore vineyards and wineries.

10 Clare. A bustling town in Clare Valley.

11 McLaren Vale. Great wineries and scenery.

12 Goolwa. Upmarket vacation destination.

13 Victor Harbor. SA's favorite seaside getaway.

14 Kingscote. Base for exploring Kangaroo Island (KI).

15 Penneshaw. A tiny ferry port on KI.

16 Seal Bay Conservation Park.

17 Flinders Chase National Park.

18 Coober Pedy. An underground town.

19 Ikara-Flinders Ranges National Park.

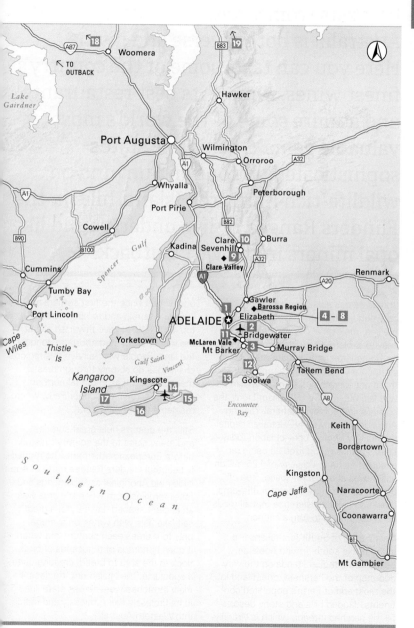

Renowned for its celebrations of the arts, its multiple cultures, and its bountiful harvests from vines, land, and sea, South Australia is both diverse and divine. Here you can taste some of the country's finest wines, sample its best restaurants, and admire some of the world's most valuable gems. Or skip the state's sophisticated options and unwind on wildlife-rich Kangaroo Island, hike in the Flinders Ranges, or live underground like opal miners in the vast Outback.

Spread across a flat saucer of land between the Mt. Lofty ranges and the sea, the capital city of Adelaide is easy to explore. The wide streets of its 1½-square-km (½-square-mile) city center are organized in a simple grid that's ringed with parklands. The plan was laid out in 1836 by William Light, the colony's first surveyor-general, making Adelaide the only early-Australian capital not built by English convict labor. Today Light's plan is recognized as being far ahead of its time. This city of 1.25 million still moves at a leisurely pace, free of the typical urban menace of traffic jams thanks to Light's insistence that all roads be wide enough to turn a cannon.

Nearly 90% of South Australians live in the fertile south around Adelaide, because the region stands on the very doorstep of the harshest, driest land in the most arid of Earth's populated continents. Jagged hills and stony deserts fill the parched interior, which is virtually unchanged since the first settlers arrived. Desolate terrain and temperatures that top 48°C (118°F) have thwarted all but the most determined efforts to conquer the land. People who survive this region's challenges do so only through drastic measures, such as in the far-northern opal-mining town of Coober Pedy, where residents live underground.

Still, the deserts hold great surprises, and many clues to the country's history before European settlement. The ruggedly beautiful Flinders Ranges north of Adelaide hold Aboriginal cave paintings and fossil remains from when the area was an ancient seabed. Lake Eyre, a great salt lake, fills with water, on average, only four times each century, but when it does hundreds of thousands of birds flock to the area to breed, creating quite a spectacle. The Nullarbor ("treeless") Plain stretches west across state lines in its tirelessly flat, ruthlessly arid march into Western Australia.

Yet South Australia is, perhaps ironically, gifted with the good life. It produces most of the nation's wine, and the sea ensures a plentiful supply of lobster and famed King George whiting. Cottages and guesthouses tucked away in the countryside around Adelaide are among the most charming and relaxing in Australia. Farther afield, unique experiences like watching seal pups cuddle with their mothers on Kangaroo Island would warm any heart. South Australia may not be grand in reputation, but its attractions are extraordinary, and after a visit you'll know you've indulged in one of Australia's best-kept secrets.

MAJOR REGIONS

Adelaide was once a rural community that now has become an urban center for this part of Australia. Sitting on Southern Australia's coast, Adelaide has museums, festivals, and more, and is an entry point to area wineries. It also is a starting point for some tours to Kangaroo Island.

With their secluded green slopes and flowery gardens, the **Adelaide Hills** are a pastoral vision in this desert state. The patchwork quilt of vast orchards, neat vineyards, and avenues of tall conifers resembles the Bavarian countryside, a likeness fashioned by the many German immigrants who settled here in the 19th century. In summer the hills are consistently cooler than the city, although the charming towns and wineries are pleasant to visit any time of year. Towns in the Adelaide Hills region include **Mt. Lofty** and **Bridgewater.**

Cultural roots set the **Barossa wine region** apart. The area, which is just over an hour's drive northeast of Adelaide, was settled by Silesian immigrants who left the German–Polish border region in the 1840s to escape religious persecution. These farmers brought traditions that you can't miss in the solid bluestone architecture, the tall slender spires of the Lutheran churches, and the *kuchen*, a cake as popular as the Devonshire tea

introduced by British settlers. It's also one of the country's best-known wine regions—more than 200 wineries across the region's two wide, shallow valleys produce celebrated wines. Most wineries in the Barossa operate sale rooms (called cellar doors) that usually have up to a dozen varieties of wine available for tasting. You are not expected to sample the entire selection; to do so would overpower your taste buds. It's far better to give the tasting-room staff some idea of your personal preferences and let them suggest wine for you to sample. Towns in the Barossa wine region include **Lyndoch, Tanunda, Angaston, Nuriootpa,** and **Marananga**.

Smaller and less well known than the Barossa, the **Clare Valley** nonetheless holds its own among Australia's wine-producing regions. Its robust reds and delicate whites are among the country's finest, and the Clare Valley is generally regarded as the best area in Australia for fragrant, flavorsome Rieslings. On the fringe of the vast inland deserts, the Clare Valley is a narrow sliver of fertile soil about 30 km (19 miles) long and 5 km (3 miles) wide, with a microclimate that makes it ideal for premium wine making. The first vines were planted here as early as 1842, but it took a century and a half for the Clare Valley to take its deserved place on the national stage. The mix of small family wineries and large-scale producers, 150-year-old settlements and grand country houses, snug valleys and dense native forests, has rare charm. As you meander through the valley, tasting as you go, enjoy some spectacular views of the Flinders Ranges. Clare Valley towns include **Sevenhill** and **Clare.**

The **Fleurieu Peninsula** has traditionally been seen as Adelaide's backyard. **McLaren Vale** wineries attract connoisseurs, and the beaches and bays bring in surfers, swimmers, and sun-seekers. Generations of local families have vacationed in the string of beachside resorts between **Victor Harbor** and **Goolwa,** near the mouth of the Murray River. The countryside, with its rolling hills and dramatic cliff scenery, is a joy to drive through. Although the region is within easy reach of Adelaide, you should consider spending the night if you want to enjoy all it has to offer. You can also easily combine a visit here with one or more nights on Kangaroo Island.

Remote, beautiful, and just verging on the right side of isolated, **Kangaroo Island** is a paradise for animal lovers and also offers some of the world's coolest accommodation. Australia's third-largest island is barely 16 km (10 miles) from the Australian mainland, yet the island belongs to another age—a folksy, friendly, less sophisticated time when you'd leave your car unlocked and knew everyone by name. The island is most beautiful along the coastline, where the land is sculpted into a series of bays and inlets teeming with bird and marine life. The stark interior has its own charm, however, with pockets of red earth between stretches of bush and farmland. Wildlife is probably the island's greatest attraction; you can stroll along a beach crowded with sea lions and watch kangaroos, koalas, pelicans, and little penguins in their native environments. You could easily spend a week here, but if you only have one day, start with the southern coast, where the standout sights are, and tour the island in a clockwise direction, leaving the north-coast beaches for the afternoon. Before heading out, fill your gas tank and pack a picnic lunch. Shops are few and far between outside the towns, and general stores are the main outlets for food and gas. The island is home to **Seal Bay Conservation Park** and **Flinders Chase National Park.** as well as towns including **Kingscote** and **Penneshaw.**

Heading north of Adelaide, a trip to South Australia's **Outback** gives visitors a glimpse into an arid and dramatic landscape that is unmistakably Australian. An expanse of desert vegetation, this land of scrubby salt bush and hardy eucalyptus trees is brightened after rain by wildflowers—including the state's floral emblem, the blood-red Sturt's desert pea, with its black, olive-like heart. The terrain is marked by geological uplifts, abrupt transitions between plateaus broken at the edges of ancient, long-inactive fault lines. Few roads track through this desert wilderness—the main highway is the Stuart, which runs all the way to Alice Springs in the Northern Territory. The people of the Outback are as hardy as their surroundings. They are also often eccentric, colorful characters who happily bend your ear over a drink in the local pub. Remote, isolated communities attract loners, adventurers, fortune-seekers, and people simply on the run. In this unyielding country, you must be tough to survive. **Ikara-Flinders Ranges National Park** is in South Australia's Outback, as is the town of **Coober Pedy.**

Planning

WHEN TO GO

Adelaide has the least rainfall of all Australian capital cities, and the midday summer heat is oppressive. The Outback in particular is too hot for comfortable touring during this time, but Outback winters are pleasantly warm. South Australia's national parks are open year-round. The best times to visit are in spring and autumn. In summer extreme fire danger may close walking tracks, and in winter heavy rain can make some roads impassable. Boating on the Murray River and Lake Alexandrina is best from October to March, when the long evenings are bathed in soft light. The ocean is warmest from December to March.

PLANNING YOUR TIME

Many of the state's attractions are an easy drive from Adelaide. However, for a taste of the real South Australia a trip to a national park or to the Outback is definitely worth the extra travel time. Short flights between destinations make any journey possible within a day or overnight, but the more time you leave yourself to explore the virtues of this underrated state, the better.

If you have limited time, spend your first day in Adelaide, enjoying the museums and historic sights as well as the bustling Central Market. Take a sunset stroll along the Torrens, then have dinner and drinks at one of the city's vibrant restaurants or wine bars, and spend the night. On Day 2 tour the Adelaide Hills, strolling the streets of 19th-century villages and taking in the panorama from atop Mt. Lofty. Stay the night in a charming bed-and-breakfast in one of the region's small towns, or come back down to North Adelaide and rest among the beautiful sandstone homes. Save Day 3 for wine tasting in the Barossa Region.

If you have more time, expand your horizons beyond Adelaide and take a tram-car ride to the beach at touristy Glenelg or its neighbors at laid back Brighton or posher Henley Beach, where you can laze on the white sands and dine at tasty outposts. Spend the night here or at a B&B on the Fleurieu Peninsula, then take Day 3 to explore the vineyards and catch the ferry to Kangaroo Island. After a night here, use Day 4 to explore and appreciate the island's wildlife and untamed beauty. Return to Adelaide in the afternoon on Day 5 and drive up to the Adelaide Hills for sunset at Mt. Lofty.

GETTING HERE AND AROUND
AIR TRAVEL
Adelaide Airport, 15 minutes from the city center, is a pleasant place to fly into and the state's main hub. The international and domestic terminals share a modern building complete with cafés, a tourist office, and free Wi-Fi.

International airlines serving Adelaide include Singapore Airlines, Malaysia Airlines, Cathay Pacific, Air New Zealand, Virgin Australia, Jetstar, and Emirates. Qantas also connects Adelaide with many international cities (usually via Melbourne or Sydney). Domestic airlines flying into Adelaide include Qantas, Jetstar, REX/Regional Express, Tigerair, and Virgin Australia. You can also fly to Coober Pedy and Kangaroo Island from here.

BUS TRAVEL
Adelaide's Central Bus Station is the state's main hub for travel across the region as well as interstate services to Melbourne and Sydney. It's difficult and time-consuming to travel by bus to the wine regions, however; we recommend either renting a car or taking a tour.

CAR TRAVEL
The best way to experience this diverse state is by road. In general, driving conditions are excellent, although minor lanes are unpaved. It's two hours from Adelaide to the Barossa and Clare, the southern coast, and most other major sights, and less than an hour to McLaren Vale's wineries. The most direct route to the Flinders Ranges is via the Princes Highway and Port Augusta, but a more interesting route takes you through the Clare Valley vineyards.

TRAIN TRAVEL
If you love train travel, you might find yourself stopping in Adelaide, as two classic train journeys also wind through this state: the *Ghan,* which runs north via Alice Springs to Darwin, and the *Indian Pacific,* which crosses the Nullarbor Plain to reach Perth. More prosaically, you can catch a train to Sydney or Melbourne, though often budget airlines are much cheaper.

RESTAURANTS

Foodies are spoiled for choice in South Australia; the region is famous throughout the country for its excellent produce. Make sure you try some of Adelaide's Mod Oz cuisine, with dishes showcasing oysters, crayfish, and King George whiting prepared with Asian and Mediterranean flavors. Bush foods are also available in some eateries; look for kangaroo, emu, and wattle seed.

Many restaurants close for a few days a week, so call ahead to check. Some upscale institutions require booking well in advance, and tables are tight during major city festivals and holidays.

HOTELS

As well as all the standard chains, South Australia is packed with delightful lodgings in contemporary studios, converted cottages, and grand mansions. Modern resorts sprawl along the coastal suburbs, the Barossa Valley, and other tourist centers, but intimate properties for 10 or fewer guests can easily be found.

There is plenty of competition in Adelaide, so shop around for great deals. Outside the city, weekday nights are usually less expensive and two-night minimum bookings often apply. *Hotel reviews have been shortened. For full information, visit Fodors.com.*

What It Costs in Australian Dollars			
$	$$	$$$	$$$$
RESTAURANTS			
under A$21	A$21–A$35	A$36–A$50	over A$50
HOTELS			
under A$151	A$151–A$200	A$201–A$300	over A$300

WINERIES

Oenophiles rejoice: in South Australia you've arrived in wine heaven. SA is the country's wine powerhouse, producing most of the nation's wine and boasting some of the oldest vineyards in the world. Thanks to its diverse geography and climate, the region produces a huge range of grape varieties—from cool-climate Rieslings in the Clare Valley to the big, full-bodied Shiraz wines of the world-famous Barossa. Less well known, McLaren Vale now punches above its weight with an exceptional variety of grapes, including Merlot, Chardonnay, and Cabernet Sauvignon, while just a 20-minute drive from Adelaide is Adelaide Hills, where temperatures are lower than the rest of the region, leading to great sparkling wines and Pinot Noir.

Although you can drive yourself to any of these regions, strict drunk driving laws mean that the unfortunate designated driver will be restricted to a few sips, if that. We highly recommend that you leave the driving to professionals.

★ A Taste of South Australia

SCENIC DRIVE | For a luxurious tour option in the region, go with Mary Anne Kennedy, the owner of A Taste of South Australia, who is one of the most knowledgeable regional food and wine guides. Her boutique tours of any region you choose with lunch included are a taste treat. ☎ 08/8371–3553, 0419/861588 ⊕ www.tastesa.com.au.

★ D'Arenburg Cube

WINERY/DISTILLERY | In South Australia's McLaren Vale wine region, the avant-garde d'Arenberg Cube recently opened its doors, offering public and private tasting rooms, wine blending workshops, virtual fermenters, master classes, and an art gallery in a multistory structure resembling a half-solved Rubik's cube. The winery itself, of course, is now its unmissable epicenter. There are multiple daytime dining options on-site, including Polly's Wine Lounge and the Verandah, the latter of which is located inside a restored 19th-century house—both open for lunch daily—and the Cube, which serves a seasonal tasting menu at lunch Thursday through Saturday. Entrance to the Cube is A$10. ⊠ *58 Osborn Rd., McLaren Vale* ☎ *8/8329–4888* ⊕ *www. darenberg.com.au.*

Adelaide

Australians think of Adelaide as a city of churches, but Adelaide has outgrown its reputation as a sleepy country town dotted with cathedrals and spires. The Adelaide of this millennium is infinitely more complex, with a large, multiethnic population and thriving urban art and music scenes supported by a "space activation program" that encourages pop-up shops, markets, performances, street food, minifestivals, art exhibitions, and other "off-the-cuff" experiences in the city's underutilized streets and public spaces.

GETTING HERE AND AROUND

Bright and clean, leafy and beautiful Adelaide is a breeze to explore, with a grid pattern of streets encircled by parkland. The heart of the greenbelt is divided by the meandering River Torrens, which passes the Festival Centre in its prettiest stretch.

A car gives you the freedom to discover the country lanes and villages in the hills region outside the city, and Adelaide also has excellent road connections with other states. But South Australia is a big place, and we recommend flying if you're looking to save time. Adelaide has an excellent bus system, including the no-cost Adelaide Free City Connector buses, which make about 30 downtown stops. Free guides to Adelaide's public bus lines are available from the Adelaide Metro Info Centre. The city's only surviving tram route now runs between the Entertainment Centre in Hindmarsh through the city to the beach at Glenelg. Ticketing is identical to that on city buses; travel between South Terrace and the Entertainment Centre on Port Road is free.

To reach the Adelaide Hills region from Adelaide, head toward the M1 Princes Highway or drive down Pulteney Street and on to Glen Osmond Road, which becomes the M1. From here signs point to Crafers and the freeway.

TAXI Suburban Taxis. ☎ *13–1008* ⊕ *www. suburbantaxis.com.au.* **Yellow Cabs.** ☎ *13–2227* ⊕ *www.yellowadelaide.com. au.*

WHEN TO GO
FESTIVALS
Adelaide Festival of Arts

ARTS FESTIVALS | Australia's oldest arts festival takes place annually for three weeks in February and March. It's a cultural smorgasbord of outdoor opera, classical music, jazz, art exhibitions, film, a writers festival, and cabaret presented by some of the world's top artists; it's held across the city at a variety of venues. ⊠ *City Center* ☎ *08/8216–4444* ⊕ *www. adelaidefestival.com.au.*

Adelaide Fringe Festival

ARTS FESTIVALS | The Fringe Festival, held over four weeks during mid-February and mid-March, is the second largest of its kind in the world. It's an open-access arts festival, featuring cabaret, street performances, comedy, circus, music, visual art, theater, puppetry, dance, and design, all across Adelaide and its surroundings. ⊠ *City Center* ☎ *08/8100–2000* ⊕ *www. adelaidefringe.com.au.*

WOMADelaide Festival

FESTIVALS | The annual four-day festival of world music, arts, and dance takes place in early March and attracts top musicians from all over the world to its multiple stages in the picturesque Botanic Park. ⊠ *Botanic Park , Hackney Rd.* ☎ *08/8271– 1488* ⊕ *www.womadelaide.com.au.*

TOURS
Adelaide Sightseeing

ORIENTATION | Adelaide Sightseeing operates pretty much every kind of tour you can think of. There's a daily city sights tour leaving each morning from

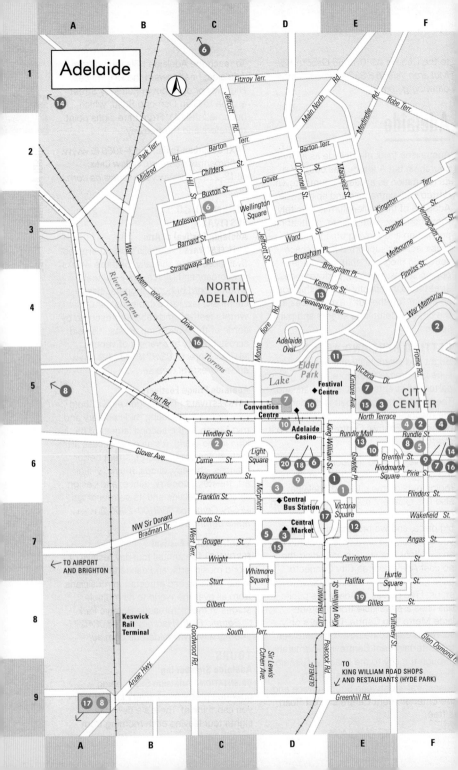

the Central Business District (CBD). The company also runs a daily afternoon bus tour of the Adelaide Hills and the German village of Hahndorf, and various other themed tours, including Nature and Wildlife Tours; Food and Wine Tours; River Cruises, and more. Prices are better if you book online. ☒ 85 Franklin St. ☏ 1300/769762 ⊕ www.adelaidesightseeing.com.au ⌨ From A$58.

Adelaide Visitor Information Centre

WALKING TOURS | Free 30- to 45-minute city orientation walking tours depart from here on weekdays at 9:30 am. No bookings needed. ☒ James Pl., just off Rundle Mall, City Center ☏ 1300/588140 ⊕ www.cityofadelaide.com.au/explore-the-city/city-information/visitor-information ⌨ Free.

Gray Line Adelaide

BUS TOURS | Gray Line Adelaide is a long-standing luxury bus tour that provides morning city tours that take in all the highlights, as well as day-long tours of nearby Barossa Valley wineries, the nature preserve center Kangaroo Island, and other attractions. ☒ 85 Franklin St. ☏ 1300/858687 ⊕ www.grayline.com.au ⌨ Tours from A$67.

★ Modernist Adelaide Walking Tour

WALKING TOURS | Architecture buffs and urban historians will love experiencing Adelaide through this walking tour, founded by mid-century modern architecture and design enthusiast Stuart Symons to celebrate Adelaide's modernist architecture. Bookings are essential for the 75-minute weekend walks; private group tours may also be arranged by appointment. See website for available dates and times. ☒ Crack Kitchen, 13 Franklin St. ☏ 421/705947 ⊕ www.eventbrite.com.au/o/modernist-adelaide-15552766578.

Tourabout Adelaide

GUIDED TOURS | **FAMILY** | Tourabout Adelaide has private tours with tailored itineraries. Prices run from around A$100 per person for a two-hour city heritage walk to A$600 for a daylong excursion to the Barossa Valley, which includes private wine tastings and lunch. ☒ Wellington Business Centre, 2 Portrush Rd., Suite 24, Payneham ☏ 08/8365–1115, 0408/809232 ⊕ www.touraboutadelaide.com.au ⌨ From A$100.

Artsy Adelaide

As soon as you pull into Adelaide you'll be greeted with the sight of tiny stone cottages aglow in morning sunshine, or august sandstone buildings gilded by nighttime floodlights. These are visual cues to the relaxed but vibrant arts and culture that emanate from here.

City Center

⊙ Sights

Adelaide Town Hall

GOVERNMENT BUILDING | An imposing building constructed in 1863 in Renaissance style, the Town Hall was modeled after buildings in Genoa and Florence. Tours, starting at 10 am each Monday, visit the Colonel Light Room, where objects used to map and plan Adelaide are exhibited, and there are frequently traveling art exhibitions. The balcony of the Town Hall is famous for the appearance of the Beatles in 1964, which attracted the venue's largest crowd to date: approximately 300,000 screaming fans. ☒ 128 King William St., City Center ☏ 08/8203–7590 ⊕ www.adelaidetownhall.com.au.

Adelaide Zoo

ZOO | **FAMILY** | Australia's second-oldest zoo still retains much of its original architecture. Enter through the 1883 cast-iron gates to see such animals as the giant pandas, Sumatran tigers,

Botanic Gardens of Adelaide

Australian rain-forest birds, and chimpanzees housed in modern, natural settings. The zoo is world renowned for its captive breeding and release programs, and rare species including the red panda and South Australia's own yellow-footed rock wallaby are among its successes. In 2008, the Australian government and Adelaide Zoo signed a cooperative agreement to help secure the long-term survival of the giant panda, and in 2009 Wang Wang and Fu Ni arrived on loan from China to become the only giant pandas in the Southern Hemisphere, and the first to live permanently in Australia. Special VIP panda tours are now also available. Free half-hour guided tours depart every half hour from 10 am to 3 pm. Ask at the ticket office about feeding times, and consult the website for opening times for specific areas of the zoo. ⊠ *Frome Rd., near War Memorial Dr., City Center* ☎ *08/8267–3255* ⊕ *www.adelaidezoo. com.au* 🎫 *A$36.*

Art Gallery of South Australia
MUSEUM | FAMILY | Many famous Australian painters, including Charles Conder, Margaret Preston, Clifford Possum Tjapaltjarri, Russell Drysdale, and Sidney Nolan, are represented in here. Extensive Renaissance and British artworks are on display, and the atrium houses Aboriginal pieces. There is usually a visiting exhibition, too. A café and bookshop are also on-site. ⊠ *North Terrace, near Pulteney St., City Center* ☎ *08/8207–7000* ⊕ *www.artgallery.sa.gov.au.*

Ayers House
HOUSE | FAMILY | Between 1855 and 1897 this sprawling colonial structure was the home of Sir Henry Ayers, South Australia's premier and the man for whom Uluru was originally named Ayers Rock. Most rooms—including the unusual Summer Sitting Room, in the cool of the basement—have been restored with period furnishings and the state's best examples of 19th-century costumes and lifestyle. Entrance is A$10 and guided tours cost an additional $5 per entry and are offered

on the hour from 10 am to 3 pm. ✉ *288 North Terr., City Center* ☎ *08/8223–1234* ⊕ *www.ayershousemuseum.org.au* ✉ *A$5* ⏱ *Closed Sun. and Mon.*

★ **Botanic Gardens of Adelaide**

GARDEN | FAMILY | These magnificent formal gardens include an international rose garden, giant water lilies, an avenue of Moreton Bay fig trees, acres of green lawns, and duck ponds. The Bicentennial Conservatory—the largest single-span glass house in the southern hemisphere—provides an environment for lowland rain-forest species such as the cassowary palm and torch ginger. Daily free guided tours leave from the Visitor Information Centre in the Schomburgk Pavilion at 10:30; or download the free app for a self-guided tour. In summer the Moonlight Cinema series (⊕ *www.moonlight.com.au*) screens new, classic, and cult films in Botanic Park, adjacent the garden at sunset; bring a picnic blanket and a bottle of wine. Tickets sell fast, so plan ahead. Check the website for workshops, events, and concerts in the Park. ✉ *Botanic Rd., North Terr., City Center* ☎ *08/8222–9311* ⊕ *www.botanicgardens. sa.gov.au* ✉ *Gardens/Conservatory Free.*

Migration Museum

MUSEUM | Chronicled in this converted 19th-century Destitute Asylum, which later in the 19th century served as a school where Aboriginal children were forced to train as servants to the British, are the origins, hopes, and fates of some of the millions of immigrants who settled in Australia during the past two centuries. The museum is starkly realistic, and the bleak welcome that awaited many migrants is graphically illustrated. ✉ *82 Kintore Ave., City Center* ☎ *08/8207– 7580* ⊕ *migration.history.sa.gov.au.*

National Wine Centre of Australia

WINERY/DISTILLERY | Timber, steel, and glass evoke the ribs of a huge wine barrel, and a soaring, open-plan concourse make this a spectacular showcase for Australian wines set in the Botanic Gardens. The free Wine Discovery Journey, offered daily at 11:30 am, takes you from neolithic pottery jars to a stainless-steel tank; you can even make your own virtual wine on a touch-screen computer. The Centre's guided tastings start at A$25 per person. In the Wined Bar, more than 120 of Australia's most iconic wines, including the famous Penfold's Grange and Henschke's Hill of Grace can be tasted in flights with their state-of-the-art enomatic servers. The Wined Bar has a good all-day menu, including a great selection of local cheeses and smoked meats. ✉ *Hackney Rd. at Botanic Rd., City Center* ☎ *08/8313–3355* ⊕ *www. wineaustralia.com.au.*

Parliament House

HISTORIC SITE | Ten Corinthian columns are the most striking features of this classical parliament building. It was completed in two stages 50 years apart: the west wing in 1889 and the east wing in 1939. Alongside is **Old Parliament House,** which dates from 1843. There's a free guided tour of both houses weekdays at 10 and 2 during nonsitting days. The viewing gallery is open to the public when parliament is sitting. ✉ *North Terr. at King William St., City Center* ☎ *08/8237–9467* ⊕ *www. parliament.sa.gov.au.*

St. Francis Xavier's Cathedral

RELIGIOUS SITE | This church faced a bitter battle over construction after the 1848 decision to build a Catholic cathedral. It's now a prominent, decorative church with a soaring nave, stone arches through to side aisles with dark-wood ceilings, and beautiful stained-glass windows. For a self-guided tour, a useful free booklet called "19 minute Cathedral Tour" is available by the entrance. ✉ *17 Wakefield St., at Victoria Sq., City Center* ☎ *08/8232– 8688* ⊕ *www.adelcathparish.org.*

St. Peter's Cathedral

RELIGIOUS SITE | The spires and towers of this cathedral dramatically contrast with the nearby city skyline. St. Peter's is the epitome of Anglican architecture n Australia, and an important example of grand Gothic Revival. Free 45-minute guided tours are available Wednesday at 11 and Sunday at 12:30. ✉ *27 King William St., North Adelaide* ☎ *08/8267–4551* 🌐 *www.stpeters-cathedral.org.au.*

South Australian Museum

COLLEGE | **FAMILY** | This museum's Australian Aboriginal Cultures Gallery houses 3,000 items, including ceremonial dress and paintings from the Pacific Islands. Old black-and-white films show traditional dancing, and touch-screens convey desert life. Also in the museum are an exhibit commemorating renowned Antarctic explorer Sir Douglas Mawson, after whom Australia's main Antarctic research station is named; an Opal-Fossils Gallery housing the fantastic opalized partial skeleton of a 19-foot-long plesiosaur; and a biodiversity gallery. There's also a café overlooking a grassy lawn. If you are traveling during local school holidays, there are fantastic interactive craft and education activities for children for a small fee. ✉ *North Terr., near Gawler Pl., City Center* ☎ *08/8207–7500* 🌐 *www.samuseum.sa.gov.au.*

★ Tandanya Aboriginal Cultural Institute

MUSEUM | A must-see, Tandanya is the first major Aboriginal cultural facility of its kind in Australia. You'll find worthwhile changing exhibitions of works by contemporary, notable Aboriginal artists, and a theater where you can watch cultural performances and shows by visiting artists from around the country and Pacific Islands. There's a great gift shop, too, where you can buy Aboriginal-designed household goods, apparel, and artwork. ✉ *253 Grenfell St., City Center* ☎ *08/8224–3200* 🌐 *www.tandanya.com.au* 🎫 *Free.*

Victoria Square/Tarntanyangga

PLAZA | The geographical center of the city, this public space is the city's focal point and a popular meeting spot. The fountain in the square, which is floodlighted at night, celebrates the three rivers that supply Adelaide's water: the Torrens, Onkaparinga, and Murray; each are represented by a stylized man or woman paired with an Australian native bird. The park hosts many events and attracts lunching office workers while shoppers and tourists come and go from the Glenelg-City Tram, which stops here on its way through the city. ✉ *King William, Grote, and Wakefield Sts., City Center* 🌐 *www.adelaidecitycouncil.com.*

🍴 Restaurants

★ Africola

$$$ | **AFRICAN** | This is one of the city's most original places both in terms of interior design (including a vibrant Technicolor bar and dining space) and the Modern Australian menu, featuring African-inspired and somewhat kitschy dishes with robust flavor such as the spicy, smoked Piri Piri Chicken and crispy chicken skin "tea sandwich," prepared by native South African executive chef Duncan Welgemoed. The wine is excellent, but the selection is fairly small; you can bring your own for $20. **Known for:** electic and lively decor and atmosphere; cooking that's way outside the box; great cocktails. [$] *Average main: A$$50* ✉ *4 East Terr.* ☎ *08/8223–3885* 🌐 *www.africola.com.au* 🕒 *Closed Sun. and Mon.*

Amalfi Pizzeria Ristorante

$$ | **ITALIAN** | This local favorite is rustic and noisy, with professionals and university students engaging in enthusiastic conversation. The terrazzo-tile dining room is furnished with bare wooden tables and paper placemat menus, which list traditional pizza and pasta dishes in two sizes—appetizer and entrée. **Known for:** spaghetti marinara; comfort food with generous portions; popular place after a show or movie because it stays open late. [$] *Average main: A$28* ✉ *29 Frome St., City Center* ☎ *08/8223–1948* 🕒 *Closed Sun. No lunch Sat.*

An exhibition at the Pacific Cultures Gallery, Adelaide

★ Big Table

$ | **CAFÉ** | Simply the best breakfast choice in Adelaide, Big Table has been at the Central Market for over 20 years, and regulars know to get there early for a chance at one of the few tables. Sitting at the counter isn't too bad an option either, especially when you have treats like fresh banana bread with rhubarb conserve and ricotta to look forward to. **Known for:** local favorite; breakfast bowls with local meats and seasonal items; good coffee. $ *Average main: A$16* ✉ *Adelaide Central Market, Southern Roadway, Stall 39/40, City Center* ☎ *08/8212–3899* 🚫 *No credit cards* 🕑 *Closed Sun. and Mon. No dinner.*

Chianti

$$$ | **ITALIAN** | Family-run since 1985, and located in one of Adelaide's iconic Victorian houses converted to commercial space, Chianti is all things to all people. Sit inside or outside and enjoy the award-winning breakfasts or, in the evenings, the traditional northern Italian trattoria cuisine. **Known for:** old-school feel; European wines including a reserve list; attentive service. $ *Average main: A$38* ✉ *160 Hutt St., City Center* ☎ *08/8232–7955* 🌐 *www.chianti.net.au.*

Concubine

$$$ | **CHINESE FUSION** | This restaurant, located in Adelaide's premier Asian dining strip, features reliably sensational food that is a fusion of modern Chinese dishes with traditional spices and fresh local produce, meat, and fish. The service is professional yet warm and friendly, with an ambience that is second to none thanks to the funky decor and trendy vibe. **Known for:** opulent space lit by colorful lanterns; good wines and cocktails; seasonal, fresh ingredients. $ *Average main: A$38* ✉ *132 Gouger St., City Center* ☎ *08/8212–8288* 🌐 *www.concubine.com.au* 🕑 *Closed Mon. No lunch Sat.*

COS

$$$ | **STEAKHOUSE** | If you're in need of a fine steak, look no further that COS on trendy Leigh Street. The simplicity of these steaks—select from a 250-gram

grain-fed yearling eye-fillet to a 500-gram rib-eye fillet—served with frites and side salad ensure even lunchers are not too gastronomically challenged. **Known for:** outdoor seating; South Australian wine; signature seafood dishes. $ *Average main: A$40* ⊠ *18 Leigh St., City Center* ☎ *08/8231–7611* ⊕ *www.18leigh.com.au* ☾ *Closed Sun.*

Exchange Coffee

| **CAFÉ** | Conveniently located on a quiet street off Rundle Mall, the cozy and friendly specialty coffee shop Exchange has what it takes to pep up customers. It sells expertly sourced, single-origin coffees from various roasters, with the option to try Aeropress preparation, and light, healthy, delicious fare for breakfast and lunch. **Known for:** fresh sandwiches; excellent Flat Whites; eggs served various ways. $ *Average main: A$20* ⊠ *1–3/12–18 Vardon Ave.* ☎ *415/966225* ⊕ *exchangecoffee.com.au.*

★ Hellbound Wine Bar

$ | **MEDITERRANEAN** | Crawl into an underground cave for wine lovers—sure, it's dark, but that makes it all the better for good conversation and wine tasting. A wine industry veteran and a winemaker partnered to open Hellbound in a Adelaide's bustling East End to offer an eclectic wine list, featuring plenty of boutique Australian producers as well as enticing finds from abroad, along with small shareable plates and imported cheeses in a lounge environment. **Known for:** edgy, very contemporary wine list; romantic night out; hospitality industry hangout. $ *Average main: A$25* ⊠ *201 Rundle St.* ☎ *0420/322715* ⊕ *www.hellboundwine-ar.com* ☾ *Closed Mon. and Tues.*

Hey Jupiter

$ | **FRENCH** | Owned by a French expat and his Australian wife, Hey Jupiter is in all aspects a Parisian brasserie transported to Adelaide—wicker seats, oyster happy hours, and all—but with better service and a wine list that goes far beyond average. Located on a quiet

street near plenty of other shops and bars, Hey Jupiter is a great place to stop for weekend breakfast, lunch, or dinner, as well as a nice place to simply grab a drink after a long afternoon of shopping on Rundle Street. **Known for:** patio dining; oyster platter; all around great, classic food. $ *Average main: A$35* ⊠ *11 Ebenezer Pl., City Center* ☎ *0416/050721* ⊕ *heyjupiter.com.au.*

★ Jasmin Indian Restaurant

$$ | **INDIAN** | Located in a basement off Hindmarsh Square, this elegant establishment is beautifully decorated with stylish timber furniture and local artwork. The dim lighting and relaxing background music really set the mood for some quality Indian cuisine, which is what you'll get in spades; in fact, you might want to try everything on the menu, and the Feed Me Menu allows for just that. **Known for:** great local wine; the Punjabi tandoori lamb and prawn sambal—perennial favorites; friendly staff offering exceptional service. $ *Average main: A$30* ⊠ *31 Hindmarsh Sq., City Center* ☎ *08/8223–7837* ⊕ *www.jasmin.com.au* ☾ *Closed Sun. and Mon. No lunch Sat.–Wed.*

Jolleys Boathouse

$$$ | **MODERN AUSTRALIAN** | Blue canvas directors' chairs and white-clothed wooden tables create a relaxed, nautical air at this mainstay—which perfectly suits the location on the south bank of the River Torrens. Sliding glass doors open onto a full-width front balcony for alfresco dining. **Known for:** its views over the River Torrens; its seasonal menu with fresh choices; the generous portions. $ *Average main: A$36* ⊠ *1 Jolleys La., Victoria Dr. at King William Rd., City Center* ☎ *08/8223–2891* ⊕ *www.jolleysboathouse.com* ☾ *No lunch Sat. No dinner Sun.*

★ Monday's

$ | **CAFÉ** | After working in Melbourne with respected roasters Market Lane and Everyday Coffee, Monday's owner Jarrad Sharrock brought his knowledge back to his hometown of Adelaide and opened his own roastery and minimalist design café in 2017, to the delight of locals. In addition to serving fantastic coffee, the shop has light fare such as sandwiches and egg dishes, and delicious pastries made fresh at a nearby bakery. **Known for:** sleek modern space; fantastic coffee including beans for sale to take home; healthy, plant-based food. $ *Average main: A$20* ✉ *7/38 Gawler Pl.* 🌐 *www.mondays.coffee* 🕒 *Closed Sun.*

Paul's Seafood on Gouger

$$ | **CAFÉ** | It may look like your run-of-the-mill fish-and-chips shop, but this Gouger Street veteran of more than 60 years is the place to get hooked on King George whiting, Australia's fabulous oysters—natural or with various preparations—or salt-and-pepper squid (an iconic Australian dish). It's been hailed as one of Adelaide's best—and best-priced—seafood restaurants. **Known for:** fresh South Australian oysters; a favorite local spot; affordable and great value. $ *Average main: A$29* ✉ *79 Gouger St., City Center* ☎ *08/8231–9778* 🌐 *www.paulsongouger.com.au.*

Red Ochre Grill

$$ | **MODERN AUSTRALIAN** | A sweeping view of Adelaide is the backdrop for contemporary workings of traditional bush meats such as kangaroo, emu, and wild boar, plus herbs, and fruits at this "floating" riverfront restaurant. The downstairs River Café, the restaurant's sister venue, is more informal, and offers a modern Italian menu for lunch weekdays. **Known for:** famous meringue dessert; beautiful setting to dine; steaks served with flair, such as with onion puree and broccolini, bush tomato chimmichurri, wattle-seeded mustard, pepper berry jam, and confit garlic. $ *Average main: A$35* ✉ *War Memorial Dr., North Adelaide* ☎ *08/8211–8555* 🌐 *www.redochre.com.au* 🕒 *Closed Sun. No lunch.*

Sibling

$ | **CAFÉ** | In 2018, Caitlin Duff and husband, Nathaniel Morse, opened this daily coffee shop, café, and coworking space next to the retail shop Ensemble, run by Caitlin's sister, Anny. They serve coffee from Monday's roastery, fresh fruit smoothies, pots of tea, cakes made by Caitlin's mother, and more, including breakfast and lunch in an airy space flooded with natural light and brightened by hanging plants. **Known for:** beautiful mood-lifting atmosphere; healthy smoothies; ideal for vegetarians and vegans. $ *Average main: A$20* ✉ *6 Gilles St.* 🌐 *www.siblingadl.com.*

Hotels

★ **Adina Adelaide Treasury**

$$ | **HOTEL** | Contemporary Italian furnishings in white, slate-gray, and ocher are juxtaposed with 19th-century Adelaide architecture in this stylish Victoria Square hotel. **Pros:** beautiful, classic building; light and airy reception rooms; short walk to Central Market. **Cons:** no on-site parking but parking station nearby; building layout can be hard to navigate; some rooms lack natural lighting. $ *Rooms from: A$195* ✉ *2 Flinders St., City Center* ☎ *08/8112–0000, 1300/633462* 🌐 *www.tfehotels.com* 🛏 *20 studio rooms, 59 apartments* 🍴 *No meals.*

BreakFree on Hindley

$ | **HOTEL** | Step out your door at this three-story redbrick complex in Adelaide's lively West End and you might think you're in the tropics—open-air walkways and palm trees suggest you're close to the beach. **Pros:** great value for money; fully equipped kitchens; complex is on the Adelaide FREE bus route. **Cons:** basic furnishings; bathrooms could do with a face-lift; pricey parking. $ *Rooms from: A$145* ✉ *255 Hindley St., City Center* ☎ *08/8217–2500* 🌐 *www.breakfree.com.au* 🛏 *142 rooms* 🍴 *No meals.*

★ The Franklin Boutique Hotel

$ | B&B/INN | Situated above the Franklin Hotel—a pub known for its relaxed but quirky atmosphere, good food, and micro beers—in the Central Business District, this hotel has seven uniquely and tastefully decorated rooms with all the amenities you'd expect, plus Nespresso machine and iPod dock in each room and original, unique artwork from local artists. **Pros:** free in-room snacks and Wi-Fi; fun boutique experience; close to Central Market. **Cons:** limited capacity; potential for noise from the downstairs pub; finding free parking can be difficult. $ *Rooms from: A$150* ⊠ *92 Franklin St., City Center* ☎ *08/8410–0036* ⊕ *www. thefranklinhotel.com.au* ⇆ *7 rooms* ⊙ *No meals.*

★ Hotel Richmond

$ | HOTEL | Situated in the center of Rundle Mall, the city's main shopping strip, the hotel is an original, 1920s art deco building and offers a boutique experience, trendy rooms, and luxurious suites. **Pros:** beautiful, classic building; undercover valet parking; free Wi-Fi. **Cons:** foot traffic in Rundle Mall and the lively Lounge Bar can be noisy; must walk through mall with luggage to reach hotel; fee for parking. $ *Rooms from: A$140* ⊠ *128 Rundle Mall, City Center* ☎ *08/8215–4444* ⊕ *www.hotelrichmond. com.au* ⇆ *30 rooms* ⊙ *All meals.*

Majestic Roof Garden Hotel

$ | HOTEL |FAMILY | Modern and stylish, each room features modern bathrooms, king-size beds, and free Wi-Fi. **Pros:** 50 meters from the restaurants, bars, and shops of Rundle Street; the rooftop garden has uninterrupted views of the famous Adelaide Hills and East End; free Wi-Fi. **Cons:** rooms are nondescript; on-site restaurant a little pricey; no pool. $ *Rooms from: A$165* ⊠ *55 Frome St., City Center* ☎ *08/8100–4400* ⊕ *www. roofgardenhotel.com.au* ⇆ *120 rooms* ⊙ *All meals.*

Oaks Embassy

$$$ | HOTEL | This hotel is ideally positioned to explore the River Torrens, visit the Adelaide Casino and Adelaide Convention Centre, or take in the many restaurants and nightlife spots along or surrounding Hindley Street. **Pros:** good city views; well serviced by public transport; minutes from River Torrens, parklands, and Hindley Street entertainment precinct. **Cons:** expensive Wi-Fi; not a lot of on-site parking; can be noisy. $ *Rooms from: A$215* ⊠ *96 North Terr., Glenelg* ☎ *08/8124–9900* ⊕ *www.oakshotelsresorts.com* ⇆ *122 apartments* ⊙ *No meals.*

★ Peppers Waymouth Hotel

$$$ | HOTEL | This ultrasleek upscale hotel sports black-tile-and-timber columns that frame the Hollywood-glamorous marble lobby, and beveled-glass elevators with marble floors, designed to resemble the interior of a diamond, whisk you to snazzy, contemporary quarters of glass, marble, and wood. **Pros:** five-star facilities; excellent wine list at the restaurant; good location. **Cons:** tiny gym; more corporate than boutique in feel; some rooms could use some updating. $ *Rooms from: A$229* ⊠ *55 Waymouth St., City Center* ☎ *08/8115–8888* ⊕ *www.peppers. com.au/waymouth* ⇆ *205 rooms* ⊙ *No meals.*

★ The Playford Adelaide

$$$ | HOTEL | Showy chandeliers illuminate a movie-set-like celebration of art nouveau in the lobby of this luxury hotel, while in the unusual loft suites, wrought-iron stairs climb to a king-size bed on the mezzanine floor. **Pros:** excellent breakfast spread; convivial bar; affordable luxury. **Cons:** expensive Internet and parking; corporate feel; in busy area, can be noisy at night. $ *Rooms from: A$210* ⊠ *120 North Terr., City Center* ☎ *08/8213–8888* ⊕ *www.accorhotels.com* ⇆ *182 rooms* ⊙ *No meals.*

The Art Gallery of South Australia

 Nightlife

BARS AND CLUBS

Austral Hotel

BARS/PUBS | From the outside, the historic lead light glass catches your eye, telling you that this is a place that's stood the test of time. The first bar in South Australia to put Coopers beer on tap, the Austral is a local favorite and a great place to drink outdoors. You can down shooters or sip cocktails from a long list while listening to a band play or a DJ spin groovy tunes. ✉ *205 Rundle St., City Center* ☎ *08/8223–4660* ⊕ *www.theaustral.com. au.*

★ Bar Torino

BARS/PUBS | The children of the owners of Chianti, a mainstay Italian restaurant in Adelaide, opened up one of the city's coolest places to hang out and enjoy great cocktails, wine, and beer (right next door to their parents' restaurant, where you may want to have dinner after a drink here). Banquettes and exposed brick walls add sophisticated touches to the chic atmosphere. Don't miss the house Vermouth, which features in many of the cocktails. There are 10 variations on the classic gin and tonic here, such as the 78°, which uses Adelaide Hills Distillery gin. Small bites include Italian specialties such as *bagna càud* (a traditional Italian vegetable dip) and there are heartier options such as lasagna and beef tartare Closed on Monday. ✉ *158 Hutt St.* ☎ *08/8155–6010* ⊕ *www.bartorino.com. au.*

Botanic Bar

BARS/PUBS | One of the oldest pubs in Adelaide, Botanic Bar has had a resurgence recently but holds onto its history thanks to nice details like branded boxes of matches. There's a well-stocked cocktail bar and an intimate back bar that features local beers. The kitchen of the attached restaurant, Golden Boy, serves high-quality Thai street food. ✉ *309 North Terr., City Center* ☎ *08/8227–0799* ⊕ *the botanicbar.com.au* ⊘ *Closed Mon.*

Casablabla

BARS/PUBS | Here you can enjoy live music ranging from Mexican mariachi bands to Samba drummers, every night at 7:45 and 8:45 pm. The bar is located on trendy Leigh Street, the first of Adelaide's lane-ways to be rejuvenated. The atmosphere and live entertainment lineup is as unique as the contemporary fusion of South East Asian and Middle Eastern decor. Wednesday night is live Latin night with free salsa lessons. A mild-mannered restaurant by day, it's a pumping club by night. ⊠ *12 Leigh St., City Center* ☎ *08/8231–3939* ⊕ *www.casablabla.com* ⊘ *Closed Sun. and Mon.*

★ Clever Little Tailor

BARS/PUBS | Adelaide has a fascination with small bars and hole-in-the-wall-style venues, and the Clever Little Tailor was one of the city's first. Named after a German fairy tale, the warmth of this place is undeniable. The bar staff is welcoming and helpful and the venue is cozy and charming with its contemporary interior, exposed red bricks, and hanging ferns. The cocktails are delicious, too, and the boutique wine and beer list is impressive. Plus, the music is soft enough to chat to your heart's content. ⊠ *19 Peel St., City Center* ⊕ *cleverlittletailor.com.au* ⊘ *Closed Sun.*

The Curious Squire

BARS/PUBS | Here you can taste freshly brewed beer from the local Australian James Squire range, which is brewed on the premises. There is also a short cocktail and wine list. The menu is full of pub snacks and bar food with a good choice of barbecue platters, pizzas, and burgers. ⊠ *10 O'Connell St., City Center* ☎ *08/7071–5767* ⊘ *Closed Mon.*

Grace Emily Hotel

BARS/PUBS | A classic old-school pub, you'll find bartenders spouting the mantra "No pokies, no TAB, no food"—pokies are the poker machines found in many pubs, and TAB, Australia's version of OTB, lets you place bets on horse races—at

this multilevel music-lover's watering hole. Instead, there's live music nightly. The beer garden is one of the city's best, with secluded spots for those wanting a quiet tipple and big round tables for groups to drink en masse and alfresco. In 2017 the pub was inducted into the South Australian Music Hall of Fame, recognizing its unique commitment to live music culture for more than a decade and a half. It's open daily from 4 pm until the wee hours. ⊠ *232 Waymouth St., City Center* ☎ *08/8231–5500*.

La Buvette Drinkery

WINE BARS—NIGHTLIFE | FAMILY | French ex-pats and locals alike gather in this relaxed yet sophisticated Parisian-inspired wine bar on a quiet lane off Rundle Street for snacks and a unique bottle of wine, whether French or South Australian. Owned by a French expat, of course, La Buvette Drinkery is more than ideal for observing the French ritual of aperitif before dinner: a local sparkling wine or well-made spritz alongside artisanal terrine to start the evening well. ⊠ *27 Gresham St.* ☎ *08/8410–8170* ⊕ *www. labuvettedrinkery.com.au* ⊘ *Closed Sun.*

Rhino Room

BARS/PUBS | This is the home of Adelaide comedy, featuring an open mic night on Thursday and live shows Friday and Saturday night. Some of Australia's best comedians as well as overseas acts grace the tiny stage; during the annual Fringe Festival you can catch a glimpse of some verified superstars. But it's also a funky little club in its own right, and DJs fill the void when the laughs take a break on other nights. ⊠ *13 Frome St., City Center* ☎ *08/8227–1611* ⊕ *www.rhinoroom.com.au* ✍ *From A$10* ⊘ *Closed Sun.–Tues.*

Udaberri

BARS/PUBS | One of the first of Adelaide's growing trend of "small bars," Udaberri is a cozy, intimate setting where some of the city's best wine and beer selection is served alongside delicious Basque-style tapas. The narrow space is reminiscent of a barn, but it's a very chic barn. DJs spin house beats, but the music is never overpowering as interaction and conversation is encouraged. If you're lucky enough to beat the crowds to the loft, you can unwind on the sofas while enjoying the view. In addition to tapas, heartier plates with Mediterranean flair, like grilled octopus, or chorizo and prawns, are served. ⊠ *11–13 Leigh St., City Center* ☎ *08/8410–5733* ⊕ *www. udaberri.com.au.*

CASINO
SKYCITY Adelaide Casino

CASINOS | Housed in the former railway station, SkyCity is the place to go for big-time casino gaming, including the highly animated Australian Two-up, in which you bet against the house on the fall of two coins. Four bars, including the elegant Chandelier Bar, and six restaurants are also within the complex. It's one of a handful of places in Adelaide that keep pumping until dawn. ⊠ *City Center* ☎ *08/8212–2811* ⊕ *www.adelaidecasino. com.au.*

Performing Arts

South Australia truly is the festival state, and with the majority of the major events running at the end of summer in "Mad March," this is the best time to visit, as cities like Adelaide take on an extra festive feel.

For a listing of performances and exhibitions, look to the entertainment pages of *The Advertiser,* Adelaide's daily newspaper. The *Adelaide Review,* a free monthly arts paper, reviews exhibitions, galleries, and performances, and lists forthcoming events.

Adelaide Entertainment Centre

ARTS CENTERS | Opened in 1991, most major concerts are held at this indoor arena, which also features a mix of everything from music, theater, and other performing arts to conventions and sporting events. ⊠ *98 Port Rd., Hindmarsh* ☎ *08/8208–2222* ⊕ *www.theaec. net.*

Adelaide Festival Centre

ARTS CENTERS | This is the city's major venue for the performing arts. The State Opera, the State Theatre Company of South Australia, and the Adelaide Symphony Orchestra perform here regularly. Performances are in the Playhouse, the Festival and Space theaters, the outdoor amphitheater, and Her Majesty's Theatre at 58 Grote St. The box office is open weekdays 9–6. ⊠ *King William St., near North Terr., City Center* ☎ *13–1246* ⊕ *www.adelaidefestivalcentre.com.au.*

BASS Ticket Agency

TICKETS | This agency sells tickets for most live performances: ballet, comedy, dance, theater, and more. ⊠ *Adelaide Festival Centre, King William St., City Center* ☎ *13–1246* ⊕ *www.bass.net.au.*

Shopping

If you are wondering where everyone in Adelaide is, you'll find them at Rundle Mall, the city's main shopping strip. Shops in the City Center are generally open Monday through Thursday 9–5:30, Friday 9–9, Saturday 9–5, and Sunday 11–5. Suburban shops are often open until 9 pm on Thursday night instead of Friday. As the center of the world's opal industry, Adelaide has many opal shops, which are around King William Street. Other good buys are South Australian regional wines, crafts, and Aboriginal artwork. The trendiest area to browse is King William Road in Hyde Park, a 20-minute walk south from Victoria Square.

Adelaide Exchange Jewellers

JEWELRY/ACCESSORIES | Located just off Rundle Mall, the exchange sells high-quality antique jewelry. They can also be found in Glenelg and Modbury. ⊠ *10 Stephens Pl., City Center* ☎ *08/8212– 2496* ⊕ *www.adelaide-exchange.com.au.*

Australian Opal and Diamond Collection

JEWELRY/ACCESSORIES | One of Australia's leading opal merchants, wholesalers, exporters, and manufacturing jewelers, Australian Opal and Diamond Collection sells superb handcrafted one-of-a-kind opal jewelry. ⊠ *14 King William St., City Center* ☎ *08/8211–9995* ⊕ *www.aodc. net.au.*

★ Central Market

OUTDOOR/FLEA/GREEN MARKETS | One of the largest produce markets in the southern hemisphere, and Adelaide's pride and joy, the Central Market is chock-full of stellar local foods, including glistening-fresh fish, meat, crusty Vietnamese and Continental breads, German baked goods, cheeses of every shape and color, and old-fashioned lollies (candy). You can also buy souvenir T-shirts, CDs, books, cut flowers, and a great cup of coffee. ⊠ *Gouger St., City Center* ☎ *08/8203– 7494* ⊕ *www.adelaidecentralmarket.com. au.*

★ Haigh's Chocolates

FOOD/CANDY | Ask anyone who no longer lives in Adelaide what they miss most about the city and chances are they'll say "Haigh's." Australia's oldest chocolate manufacturer has tempted people with corner shop displays since 1915, and although there are now Haigh's stores in several locations across the city and in other capitals, the Beehive Corner store is the original, and a local icon. The family-owned South Australian company produces exquisite truffles, pralines, and creams—as well as the chocolate bilby (an endangered Australian marsupial), Haigh's answer to the Easter bunny. No trip to Adelaide is complete without at least one chocolate indulgence. ■**TIP**→ **Free chocolate-making tours at the Haigh's Visitor Center at 154 Greenhill Road in Parkside run Monday through Saturday beginning at 9 am. Bookings are essential.** ⊠ *2 Rundle Mall , at King William St., City Center* ☎ *08/8372–7070* ⊕ *www. haighschocolates.com.*

★ Jam Factory

ART GALLERIES | A contemporary craft-and-design center at the Lion's Arts Centre, Jam Factory exhibits and sells unique Australian glassware, ceramics, wood, and metal work and you can often see the artists at work. Its fantastic gift shop is the place to pick up a unique hand-made piece of art or jewelry, including a description from the artist. ⊠ *19 Morphett St., City Center* ☎ *08/8231–0005* ⊕ *www.jamfactory.com.au.*

★ Rundle Mall

SHOPPING CENTERS/MALLS | Adelaide's main shopping area is Rundle Mall, a pedestrian plaza lined with boutiques, department stores, and arcades, including Australia's two best-known stores, Myer and David Jones, as well as some of the world's big name and luxury brands sprinkled among the local shops. People of all ages hang out on the mall, relaxing on a bench or browsing the shops. Heritage-listed Adelaide Arcade is a Victorian-era jewel, with a decorative tiled floor, skylights, and dozens of shops behind huge timber-framed windows. ⊠ *Rundle St., between King William and Pulteney Sts., City Center* ☎ *08/8203– 7611* ⊕ *www.rundlemall.com.*

Urban Cow Studio

ART GALLERIES | For quirky locally made jewelry, pottery, glass, and sculptures, visit Urban Cow Studio, which exhibits more than 150 South Australian artists and designers. ⊠ *11 Frome St., City Center* ☎ *08/8232–6126* ⊕ *www.urban-cow.com.au.*

Activities

BICYCLING

Adelaide's parks, flat terrain, and uncluttered streets make it a perfect city for two-wheel exploring.

Tour Down Under

BICYCLING | The first stop on the world cycling calendar, in January, the Tour Down Under brings in riders from all over the world as part of the UCI Pro Tour. Outside of the Tour de France, the event attracts the biggest crowds in the world for eight days, taking in metropolitan and regional South Australia. Cycling devotees may be interested in the Platinum Club Tour, which is the Santos Tour Down Under's exclusive VIP cycling society, offering to bring you up close and personal with the UCI WorldTour riders of the peloton with behind-the-scenes access. ⊠ *Victoria Sq.* ☎ *08/8463–4701* ⊕ *www. tourdownunder.com.au.*

Greater Adelaide

◉ Sights

★ Coopers Brewery
WINERY/DISTILLERY | Founded by Thomas Cooper in 1862, this is Australia's only large-scale, independent, family-owned brewery. The Coopers beer story began when Thomas tried to create a tonic for his ailing wife, Ann, but instead created his first batch of beer. Customers grew in numbers as Thomas hand-delivered his all-natural ales and stout by horse and cart; the tradition lives on with guest appearances at special events by Clydesdayles drawing the very same cart that Thomas once used. You can take guided tours (A$27.50) of the brewhouse from Tuesday through Friday at 1 pm and enjoy tastings of the award-winning signature Coopers ales, including Coopers Pale Ale, Coopers Sparkling Ale, and Coopers Stout, in the museum posttour. Proceeds from the brewery tour ticket price go to the Coopers Brewery Foundation, which then distributes funds to various charities. The museum features a display of the historic horse and cart, vintage Coopers delivery truck, and pictorials showcasing the history of the brewery. Most of the admission price goes toward charity. ⊠ *461 South Rd., Regency Park* ☎ *08/8440–1800* ⊕ *www.coopers.com. au* 🎫 *A$28* ☞ *Must be over 18 and wearing closed-toe shoes.*

National Railway Museum
MUSEUM | FAMILY | Steam-train buffs will love this collection of locomotives and rolling stock in the former Port Adelaide railway yard. The largest of its kind in Australia, the collection includes enormous "mountain"-class engines and the "Tea and Sugar" train, once the lifeline for camps scattered across the deserts of South and Western Australia. For an additional cost take a ride on the historic Semaphore to Fort Glanville Tourist Railway; it runs every Sunday and public holiday from October to end of April and daily during school holidays. There are covered outdoor eating areas with tables and chairs at the museum, where visitors may bring their own food and drink. ⊠ *76 Lipson St., Port Adelaide* ☎ *08/8341– 1690* ⊕ *nrm.org.au* 🎫 *A$12.*

★ Penfolds Magill Estate
WINERY/DISTILLERY | Founded in 1844 by immigrant English doctor Christopher Rawson Penfold, this is the birthplace of Australia's most famous wine, Penfolds Grange, and one of Australia's only city wineries. Introduced in 1951, Grange is the flagship of a huge stable of wines priced from everyday to special-occasion (collectors pay thousands of dollars to complete sets of Grange). Take the Magill Estate Heritage Tour (10 am and 1 pm daily); if you're a serious wine lover take the Ultimate Penfolds Tour and visit the original Penfold family cottage and the winery to enjoy some premium wine tastings, or go for the Iconic Penfolds Experience, which includes a three-course lunch and wine pairings in addition to the tour. ⊠ *78 Penfold Rd., Magill* ☎ *08/8301–5400* ⊕ *www.penfolds. com* 🎫 *From A$20.*

South Australian Maritime Museum
MUSEUM | FAMILY | Inside a restored stone warehouse, this museum in Port Adelaide, a 20-minute drive from central Adelaide, brings maritime history vividly to life with ships' figureheads, shipwreck relics, and intricate scale models. In

the basement you can lie in a bunk bed aboard an 1840s immigrant ship and hear passengers telling of life and death on their journeys to South Australia. In addition to the warehouse displays, the museum includes a lighthouse (worth climbing the 75 steps up to see the view), restored steam tug, and a WWII tender at the nearby wharf. Port Adelaide has decent beaches and antiques shops to visit, too. ⊠ *126 Lipson St., Port Adelaide* ☎ *08/8207–6255* ⊒ *A$15, includes lighthouse entry.*

🏖 Beaches

Adelaide's beaches offer something for everyone. From North Haven in the north to Sellicks Beach in the south, most beaches are located less than 30 minutes from the city center. Glenelg Beach is the main tourist attraction framed by restaurants, bars, and attractions. Farther south the hills meet the sea as beaches jut out from cliff faces providing great swimming, fishing, and surfing spots.

★ Glenelg Beach
BEACH—SIGHT | **FAMILY** | Located just 10 km (6 miles) from the Adelaide city center, Glenelg is a charming beachside suburb known for its sandy beach, historic jetty, serene marinas, bustling shops, hotels, restaurants, bars, and The Beachhouse entertainment complex. Trams lead the way to the beach, carrying passengers along Jetty Road from the city while pedestrians weave in and out of the various retail outlets that line the strip. A day trip to Glenelg is a must, but this seaside resort setting offers plenty of options for backpackers to more discerning travelers to make this their Adelaide base. The beach is large, sandy, and the waters are calm. But expect to see large crowds on hotter days and, depending on the season, seaweed can be a problem. **Amenities:** food and drink; lifeguards; parking; showers; toilets; water sports. **Best for:** sunrise; sunset; swimming; walking; windsurfing.

⊠ *Jetty Rd., Glenelg* ⚡ *Trams run approximately every 20 mins from downtown* ☎ *08/8294–5833 Glenelg Visitor's Centre* ⊕ *www.glenelgsa.com.au.*

Henley Beach
BEACH—SIGHT | **FAMILY** | The beach in this quiet coastal suburb offers white sand, gently lapping waves, summer entertainment, and a square known for popular dining spots. You'll find families spread out along the sand, and there are places on the grassy areas to enjoy picnics. The jetty is perfect for walking or fishing— drop a line in the water and try your luck. During summer, Henley Beach Square bordering the center of the beach itself comes alive with live music and festivals while eateries along Henley Beach Road bring the world to your plate—Asian, African, Mediterranean, and Indian mix with local cuisine. **Amenities:** food and drink; parking; toilets. **Best for:** swimming; sunrise; sunset; walking; windsurfing. ⊠ *Esplanade, Henley Beach* ☎ *08/8408– 1111 City of Charles Sturt.*

🍴 Restaurants

Magill Estate
$$$$ | **MODERN AUSTRALIAN** | Lovers of Australian wine should not miss a meal at this pavilion-style vineyard restaurant overlooking vineyards and the distant city skyline and coast. The seasonal, modern Australian cuisine is just as special as the view. **Known for:** romantic setting; a quintessential South Australian experience; 10-course tasting menu. $ *Average main: A$190* ⊠ *78 Penfold Rd., Magill* ☎ *08/8301–5551* ⊕ *www.magillestaterestaurant.com* 🕒 *Closed Sun.–Tues. No lunch Wed. and Thurs.*

★ Orana
$$$$ | **MODERN AUSTRALIAN** | One of Australia's most acclaimed chefs, Scottish-born Jock Zonfrillo, opened Adelaide's first and only fine dining restaurant Orana in 2013 with the goal of highlighting Australia's native ingredients—like

emu, kangaroo, and wattle seed—in an elevated context. It's a must-visit for anyone who swoons for creative cooking, and the wine list matches the truly inspiring cuisine in terms of elegance and breadth. **Known for:** an intellectual culinary experience; tasting menu only; hand-dived scallops. [$] *Average main: A$240* ✉ *285 Rundle St.* ☎ 🌐 *restaurantorana.com* ⏲ *Closed Mon. No lunch Sat.–Thurs.*

Sammy's on the Marina

$$$ | SEAFOOD | Adelaide is a prime spot for enjoying Australia's incredible seafood. At Sammy's on the Marina, enormous fishbowl windows frame views of million-dollar yachts at the far end of Glenelg's glitzy Holdfast Marina and are perfect for watching the setting sun, playing dolphins, or a storm rolling across Gulf St. Vincent as you tuck into a dozen freshly shucked oysters or the popular and generous hot seafood platter. **Known for:** fresh, local seafood including scallops; reliable, friendly service; classy atmosphere. [$] *Average main: A$40* ✉ *1–12 Holdfast Promenade, Glenelg* ☎ *08/8376–8211* 🌐 *www.sammys.net.au.*

★ Shobosho

$$$ | ASIAN FUSION | If you've ever turned your nose up at Asian Fusion, you may reconsider when you come to Shobosho, with its use of organic local ingredients and Korean and Japanese influences in the cooking. Everything about the space, from the approach to service to the immensely creative dishes—often cooked over coals—to the plateware and the atmosphere itself, strikes a balance between sophisticated and relaxed that is difficult to find in Adelaide. **Known for:** sake list features artisanal producers by-the-glass; yakitori (skewers) are delicious and simple; great lunch deal: imperial roast chicken ramen. [$] *Average main: A$40* ✉ *17 Leigh St.* ☎ *08/8366–2224* 🌐 *www.shobosho.com.au* ⏲ *Closed Mon.*

Sunny's Pizza

$$ | PIZZA | Sourdough pizzas topped with house-made sauces and fresh local ingredients are the first reason that locals can't stop going to Sunny's any night of the week. Then there's the Negronis so perfectly executed you'd swear you were in a piazza in Milano—plus the incredibly friendly service, the fun wine list featuring small producers from the Adelaide Hills and around Australia, DJs on weekend nights, and cold craft beers on draught. **Known for:** simple, contemporary cocktails; fun atmosphere with lively music; long waits for seating on busy nights. [$] *Average main: A$25* ✉ *17 Solomon St.* ☎ *0404/280522* 🌐 *www.sunnys.pizza* ⏲ *Closed Sun.–Tues.*

Hotels

★ North Adelaide Heritage Group

$$$ | RENTAL | In the city's leafy, oldest section, antiques dealers Rodney and Regina Twiss have converted heritage-listed mews houses, a meeting chapel, an arts-and-crafts manor house, and a fire station (complete with 1942 fire engine) into apartments and suites, and filled them with Australian antiques and contemporary furnishings. **Pros:** historic properties in Adelaide's most upscale suburb; friendly owners give helpful tips on what to do; well located for driving to Barossa Valley. **Cons:** some properties can be on the dark side; not child-friendly; setting is suburban rather than picturesque countryside. [$] *Rooms from: A$225* ✉ *82 Hill St., North Adelaide* ☎ *08/8267–2020* 🌐 *www.adelaideheritage.com* 🛏 *19 rooms* 🍴 *Free Breakfast.*

Oaks Plaza Pier

$$$ | RENTAL | Sea air wafts through open balcony doors in this all-apartment complex on Adelaide's favorite beach. **Pros:** steps from the beach; helpful reception staff who are full of advice; large rooms with views. **Cons:** corporate feel to the lobby; the bars can get noisy and messy at peak times; expensive Internet.

$ *Rooms from: A$206* ✉ *16 Holdfast Promenade, Glenelg* ☎ *08/8350–6688, 1300/551111* ⊕ *www.oakshotelsresorts. com/oaks-plaza-pier* ⤴ *191 rooms* ◯| *No meals.*

Nightlife

BARS AND CLUBS
Wellington Hotel
BARS/PUBS | First licensed in 1851, the Wellington is a hops lover's' heaven, with 20 Australian-brewed beers and ciders on tap. Line up six "pony" (sample) glasses on a taster tray, then enjoy a schooner (large glass) of your favorite while sitting outdoors or enjoying live music on DJ night. There's heart bar food, too. It's a good place to stop on the way to the nearby Adelaide Oval. ✉ *36 Wellington Sq., North Adelaide* ☎ *08/8267–1322* ⊕ *www.wellingtonhotel.com.au.*

Shopping

Harbour Town Adelaide
OUTLET/DISCOUNT STORES | For discount shopping, hop off the plane and head straight to nearby Harbourtown. You'll find Morrissey, JAG, Levi's, Esprit, Cue, RM Williams, Authentic Factory Outlet (Converse), and Woolworths among the 100 outlets. ✉ *727 Tapleys Hill Rd., West Beach* ☎ *08/8355–1144* ⊕ *www.harbourtownadelaide.com.au.*

Westfield Marion Shopping Centre
SHOPPING CENTERS/MALLS | Adelaide's largest shopping complex is easily accessible via public transport and contains more than 300 stores, including major department stores and boutiques, bars, restaurants, and the largest cinema complex in the state. ✉ *297 Diagonal Rd., Marion* ☎ *08/8298–1188* ⊕ *www.westfield.com.au.*

Activities

AUSTRALIAN RULES FOOTBALL AND CRICKET
Adelaide Oval
SPECTATOR SPORTS | **FAMILY** | The stadium received a state-of-the-art upgrade in 2013 and is now the dual home for cricket and Australian Rules Football—South Australia's most popular winter sport. The Aussie Rules season runs March through September, while cricket season is October through March. Tours of the historic stadium are led by expert volunteers and operate on nonevent days; choose between a general tour highlighting celebrated moments in the sporting, musical and civic history of this world-famous sporting arena, and a special guided tour of cricket museums. Overlooking the stadium, the elegant Hill of Grace restaurant offers modern South Australian cuisine and wines, highlighting a range of acclaimed Henschke wines, including the namesake Hill of Grace. Lunch is offered Friday only. Dinner is offered Tuesday through Saturday. ✉ *War Memorial Dr., North Adelaide* ☎ *08/8205–4700* ⊕ *www. adelaideoval.com.au* ⌁ *Tours: A$25.*

BASKETBALL
Adelaide Arena (Titanium Security Arena)
BASKETBALL | The home stadium for the Adelaide 36ers of the National Basketball League and the Adelaide Lightning of the Women's National Basketball League. Located in Findon, an inner western suburb of Adelaide, Adelaide Arena is the largest purpose-built basketball arena in Australia. The NBL season runs from October to February. ✉ *44A Crittenden Rd., Findon* ☎ *08/8268–3592* ⊕ *www. titaniumarena.com.au.*

GOLF
North Adelaide Golf Course
GOLF | A 10-minute walk outside of the city, the North Adelaide Golf Course— reputed to be one of the most picturesque golf settings in the country with game-distracting views of the city—runs

one short (par 3) and two 18-hole courses. You can rent clubs and carts from the pro shop. Playing hours are dawn to dusk daily. ✉ *Strangways Terr., North Adelaide* ☎ *08/8203–7888* ⊕ *northadelaidegolf.com.au* ✍ *North Course: from A$20 weekdays, A$25 weekends; South Course: A$30 weekdays, A$37 weekends* 🏌 *North Course: 18 holes, 4958 yards, par 69; South Course: 18 holes, 6435 yards, par 71.*

SOCCER
Coopers Stadium
SOCCER | Also known as Hindmarsh Stadium, this is a multipurpose venue and the first purpose-built soccer stadium in Australia. It's the home of the Australian A-League soccer team, Adelaide United. The national A-League season runs from October to March; finals are in April. ✉ *Holden St., Hindmarsh* ☎ *08/8241–7122* ⊕ *www.coopersstadium.com.au.*

The Dolphin Boat
WATER SPORTS | FAMILY | The Dolphin Boat, also known as *Temptation,* is the first vessel in South Australia to be given a dolphin swim license, which allows you to swim with the cute and friendly animals. The dolphins and tour guides have developed a close relationship over the years, as the company has been operating since 2002, so you're guaranteed to get up close. In fact, if you don't get into the water to swim with the dolphins, they will refund the difference between the watch and the swim. They also offer twilight and teatime cruises. The waters around Adelaide are beautiful, so these opportunities are worth considering. ✉ *Marina Pier, Holdfast Shores Marina, Glenelg* ☎ *0412/811–838* ⊕ *www.dolphinboat.com.au* ✍ *From A$24; dolphin swims from A$98.*

Mt. Lofty

16 km (10 miles) southeast of Adelaide.

There are splendid views of Adelaide from the lookout atop 2,300-foot Mt. Lofty, the coldest location in Adelaide, where snow is not uncommon in winter months. The energetic can follow some of the many trails that lead from the summit, or alternatively, have a cup of coffee in the café and enjoy the view in the warmth.

GETTING HERE AND AROUND
By car from Adelaide, take the Crafers exit off the South Eastern Freeway and follow Summit Road or from the eastern suburbs via Greenhill Road. You can get to the summit as well as the Mt. Lofty Botanic Gardens and Cleland Wildlife Park in about 40 minutes by catching Bus 842, 865, or 865F from Currie or Grenfell Street in the city center. Alight at bus stop 24A and connect to Bus 823.

A 3½-km (2-mile) round-trip walk from the Waterfall Gully parking lot in Cleland Conservation Park (15-minute drive from Adelaide) takes you along Waterfall Creek before climbing steeply to the white surveying tower on the summit; the track is closed on Total Fire Ban days.

TRANSPORTATION Adelaide Metro Info Centre. ✉ *Currie St. at King William St., Adelaide* ☎ *08/8210–1000* ⊕ *www.adelaidemetro.com.au.*

◉ Sights

★ Cleland Wildlife Park
NATURE PRESERVE | FAMILY | A short drive from Mt. Lofty Summit brings you to delightful Cleland Wildlife Park, where many animals roam free in three different forest habitats. Walking trails crisscross the park and its surroundings, and you're guaranteed to see emus and kangaroos in the grasslands and pelicans around the swampy billabongs. There are also enclosures for wombats and other less

sociable animals. Koala cuddling is a highlight of koala close-up sessions (daily 2–3:30, plus Sunday 11–noon). Two-hour night walks (A$50) let you wander among nocturnal species such as potoroos and brush-tailed bettongs: check the website for the next scheduled walk. Private guided tours can be arranged for A$120 per hour weekdays, A$180 per hour weekends. **■ TIP→ Reservations 48 hours prior are essential for tours.** The park is closed when there's a fire ban (usually between December and February). ✉ *365 Mount Lofty Summit Rd., Mount Lofty* ☎ *08/8339–2444* 🌐 *www.cleland.sa.gov.au* 🎫 *A$22.*

CRFT Wines

WINERY/DISTILLERY | Get to know one of the newer boutique wineries in the Adelaide Hills, CRFT Wines, by visiting its new cellar door, built from a converted shearing shed and horse stable, located on a beautiful country road with one vineyard after another. CRFT offers a range of unique, single vineyard wines, made by a couple of married winemakers, Candice Helbig and Frewin Ries. Their aim in forming CRFT was to champion the incredible diversity of soils and climates across South Australia's subregions. The tasting room is open to the public every weekend for wine flights (starting from $15 per person), wines by the glass or bottle, and take-home bottle sales. Complimentary olives are served with each wine flight, and there's a cheese plate you can opt for as well. The fireplace roars on chilly days. ✉ *45 Rangeview Dr.* ☎ *429/528809* 🌐 *www.crftwines.com.au* 🕒 *Closed weekdays.*

Mt. Lofty Botanic Gardens

GARDEN | With its rhododendrons, magnolias, ferns, and native and exotic trees, these gardens are glorious in fall and spring; during these seasons, free guided walks leave the lower parking lot on Thursday at 10:30 am except on days forecast above 36°C (96.8°F). ✉ *Picadilly entrance, 16 Lampert Rd., Mount Lofty* ☎ *08/8370–8370* 🌐 *www.environment.sa.gov.au/botanicgardens.*

Nice Views 👁

There is no better view of Adelaide—day or night—than the city-and-sea sweep from atop 2,300-foot Mt. Lofty. There's an appropriately named glass-front restaurant here called the Summit, though prices at both the café and restaurant are sky-high.

Ngeringa Winery

WINERY/DISTILLERY | For 20 years, this winery has practiced biodynamic farming by following lunar cycles, growing vegetables, and raising livestock, and abstaining from chemical treatments. The winery cellar door is open by appointment, and it also hosts Cellar Door Sundays on occasion, which are intimate, Paddock to Plate experiences, where Ngeringa's wine is showcased alongside the incredible produce the winery grows, which is often used by top area restaurants. Tastings by appointment. ✉ *19 Williams Rd.* ☎ *8/8398–2867* 🌐 *www.ngeringa.com.*

🍴 Restaurants

The Summit

$$$ | **ECLECTIC** | If you suffer from vertigo, think twice about dining here; this glass-front building atop Mt. Lofty is all about dining with altitude. Café by morning, the Summit also serves lunch and becomes an intimate candlelit restaurant by night, serving Modern Australian cooking (which might include kangaroo). **Known for:** local wines; excellent view; delicious breakfasts. [$] *Average main: A$39* ✉ *Mt. Lofty Lookout, Mt. Lofty Summit Rd., Mount Lofty* ☎ *08/8339–2600* 🌐 *www.mtloftysummit.com* 🕒 *No dinner Sun.–Tues in summer. No dinner Sun.–Thurs. in winter.*

Hotels

Mt. Lofty House

$$$ | **B&B/INN** | From very English garden terraces below the summit of Mt. Lofty, this refined and iconic country house overlooks a patchwork of vineyards, farms, and bushland. **Pros:** peaceful location in stunning surroundings; extensive wine cellar; incredible interior decoration. **Cons:** popular with groups, so book ahead at the restaurant; pricey; no casual dining options. *[$] Rooms from: A$299 ✉ 74 Summit Rd., Crafers ☎ 08/8339–6777 🌐 www.mtloftyhouse.com.au 🛏 36 rooms 🍴 Free Breakfast.*

Bridgewater

6 km (4 miles) north of Mylor, 22 km (14 miles) southeast of Adelaide.

Bridgewater came into existence in 1841 as a refreshment stop for bullock teams fording Cock's Creek. More English than German, with its flowing creek and flower-filled gardens, this leafy, tranquil village was officially planned in 1859 by the builder of the first Bridgewater flour mill.

GETTING HERE AND AROUND

From the city center, drive onto the Mount Barker Expressway until you see the Stirling exit. From there, travel through lush countryside following the signs to Bridgewater. The town itself is small and walkable. By public transport, take Bus 864 or 864F from Currie Street in the city to stop 46.

Restaurants

★ **Bridgewater Mill Restaurant**

$$$ | **AUSTRALIAN** | A stylish yet charmingly casual, brightly lit restaurant in a converted 1860s flour mill, this is a great spot to linger over a long lunch, which is a selection of regional platters designed to share. Using mostly local produce, Head Chef Joel Faustino creates an imaginative contemporary menu that is a mix of French, Japanese, Middle Eastern, and modern Australian. **Known for:** extensive range of local wines; à la carte dinner; dining by an open fire in the winter and nice deck in the summer. *[$] Average main: A$38 ✉ 386 Mt. Barker Rd. ☎ 08/8339–9200 🌐 thebridgewatermill.com.au 🕒 Closed Tues. and Wed.*

Lost In A Forest

$$ | **PIZZA** | Named after a song by The Cure, this "wood oven wine lounge" built into a restored old church is a cozy spot to get local wine and the best pizza in the Adelaide Hills, made with local organic ingredients. It's an ideal destination for dinner after a day of wine tasting or lunch before a short hike. **Known for:** on cold nights, the fire pit out front is lit and you can sit by it with a glass of wine; eclectic cocktail list; cool and casual vibe to match local winemaker. *[$] Average main: A$30 ✉ 1203 Greenhill Rd., Uraidla ☎ 8/8390–3444 🌐 lostinaforest.com.au 🕒 Closed Mon.–Wed. No lunch Thurs.*

Organic Market and Café

$ | **CAFÉ** | **FAMILY** | Pram-wheeling parents, hikers resting their walking poles, and friends catching up on gossip keep this red-and-blue café and adjoining organic supermarket buzzing all day. Reasons to linger include tasty focaccias and soups; rich, indulgent baked goods like home-baked muffins and cakes; free Wi-Fi; and all kinds of purportedly healthy and unquestionably delicious drinks. **Known for:** excellent coffee, chai, and tea; warm, friendly space; an attached grocery store with healthy provisions. *[$] Average main: A$16 ✉ 5 Druid Ave., Stirling ✥ 3 km (2 miles) from Bridgewater ☎ 08/8339–4835 café 🌐 www.organicmarket.com.au 🕒 No dinner.*

★ **The Summertown Aristologist**

$$$ | **MODERN AUSTRALIAN** | This is contemporary food that takes "Modern Australian" cooking to new heights. A chalkboard, listing dishes defined only by their ingredients—most of which are locally

The vineyards of the Barossa Valley

grown—greets diners who come to this casual, wine-focused, entirely seasonal restaurant, where chefs in the open kitchen work hard to deliver creatively composed dishes served on handmade ceramic dishware. **Known for:** eclectic wine list featuring small-batch organic producers; delicious, chewy house-made sourdough bread; must-have house-made "small goods," or charcuterie, and locally made cheeses. $ *Average main: A$50* ✉ *1097 Greenhill Rd.* ☎ *477/410105* ⊕ *thesummertownaristologist.com* ⊘ *Closed Mon.–Wed.*

 Hotels

Thorngrove Manor Hotel

$$$$ | **B&B/INN** | With its opulent suites set amid glorious gardens, this romantic Gothic folly of turrets and towers is *Lifestyles of the Rich and Famous* writ large. **Pros:** perfect for the archetypal romantic getaway; complete luxury; very attendant service. **Cons:** if you have to ask how expensive it is, you can't afford it; very limited room availability; no alcohol sold

(BYO welcome). $ *Rooms from: A$899* ✉ *2 Glenside La., Crafers* ☎ *08/8339–6748* ⊕ *www.thorngrove.com.au* ⇆ *6 rooms* ⦿ *Free Breakfast.*

Lyndoch

58 km (36 miles) northeast of Adelaide.

This pleasant little town surrounded by vineyards was established in 1840 and is the Barossa's oldest settlement site. It owes the spelling of its name to a draftsman's error—it was meant to be named after the British soldier Lord Lynedoch.

GETTING HERE AND AROUND

The most direct route from Adelaide to the Barossa wine region is via the town of Gawler. From Adelaide, drive north on King William Street. About 1 km (½ mile) past the Torrens River Bridge, take the right fork onto Main North Road. After 6 km (4 miles) this road forks to the right—follow signs to the Sturt Highway and the town of Gawler. At Gawler leave the highway and follow the signs to Lyndoch

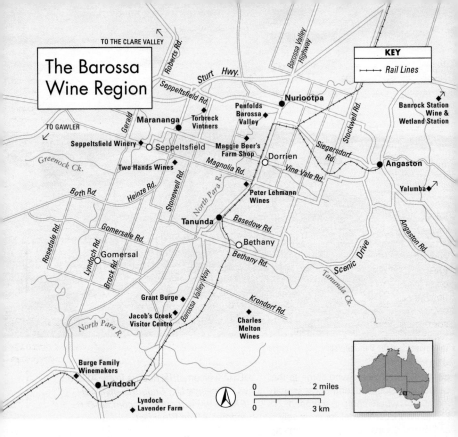

The Barossa Wine Region

on the Barossa's southern border. The 50-km (31-mile) journey should take just more than an hour. A more attractive, if circuitous, route to Lyndoch takes you through the Adelaide Hills' Chain of Ponds and Williamstown.

◉ Sights

Burge Family Winemakers

WINERY/DISTILLERY | You can drink in a leafy vineyard view while tasting from the wine barrels (if you get so lucky) at this understated cellar door. Winemaker Rick Burge's repertoire includes Semillon, Garnacha, Shiraz, and Rhone blends. An appointment is recommended. ☒ *Barossa Valley Way, near Hermann Thumm Dr.* ☎ *08/8524–4644* ⊕ *www.burgefamily. com.au.*

Lyndoch Lavender Farm

GARDEN | A family-friendly tribute to the purple flower that adorns the hills, Lyndoch Lavender Farm grows more than 90 varieties on 6 lush acres high above Lyndoch. Light café meals are available, and the farm shop sells essential oils, creams, and other products, including wine from their adjacent vineyard. ☒ *Hoffnungsthal Rd. at Tweedies Gully Rd.* ☎ *08/8524–4538* ⊕ *www.lyndochlavenderfarm.com.au* ☒ *A$2 during flowering season (Aug.–Jan.).*

🛏 Hotels

★ Abbotsford Country House

$$$$ | **B&B/INN** | Tranquillity reigns at this antiques-filled property on 50 acres of rolling beef farm with Barossa views and an 800-plant rose garden. **Pros:** a serene and luxurious place to recover from all the wine tasting; very welcoming hosts; healthy breakfast. **Cons:** dining in the restaurant is expensive; lack of gym facilities; expensive. [$] *Rooms from: A$415* ✉ *Yaldara Dr. at Fuss Rd.* ☎ *08/8524–4662* 🌐 *www.abbotsfordhouse.com* 🛏 *8 suites* 🍴 *Free Breakfast.*

Belle Cottages

$$$ | **B&B/INN** | Rose-filled gardens or sweeping rural acres surround these classic Australian accommodations, where wood-burning fireplaces in several invite you to relax with a bottle of red after a day in the Barossa region, and comfy beds tempt you to sleep late. **Pros:** great discounts available for groups; comfortable and homey accommodations; on-site therapeutic spa bath. **Cons:** not the place for an anonymous stay; some quirks to the plumbing; minimum two-night stay on weekends. [$] *Rooms from: A$240* ✉ *8 King St.* ☎ *08/8524–4825, 0411/108800* 🌐 *www.bellescapes.com* 🛏 *14 rooms* 🍴 *Free Breakfast.*

Discovery Park Glamping

$$ | **RENTAL** | **FAMILY** | Each of the 12 safari tents at the glamping park within existing Tanunda Valley caravan park features a spacious private deck for enjoying the vineyard views, en suite bathroom, kitchenette, and a large bedroom, with access to shared facilities including a private swimming pool with heated spa and premium barbecue and lounge area. **Pros:** beautiful views; heated spa; spacious. **Cons:** rustic; book in advance; no restaurant on-site. [$] *Rooms from: A$174* ✉ *Barossa Valley Way, Tanunda* ☎ *8/8563–2784* 🌐 *www.discoveryholidayparks.com.au/caravan-parks/south-australia/tanunda-barossa-valley* 🛏 *14 rooms* 🍴 *No meals.*

★ Kingsford Homestead

$$$$ | **B&B/INN** | Set in a historic 1856 homestead on a 225-acre authentic sheep station, Kingsford Homestead offers one of the Barossa Valley's most exquisite experiences and is the perfect base for exploring the surrounding wine country. **Pros:** personable hosts make you feel like family; gourmet farm-to-table seasonal menus; secluded feel yet easily accessible. **Cons:** two-night minimum; lunch not included; must rent entire property. [$] *Rooms from: A$920* ✉ *Kingsford Rd., Kingsford* ☎ *08/8524–8120* 🌐 *www.kingsfordhomestead.com.au* 🛏 *7 suites* 🍴 *Free Breakfast.*

Tanunda

13 km (8 miles) northeast of Lyndoch, 70 km (43 miles) northeast of Adelaide.

The cultural heart of the Barossa, Tanunda is its most German settlement. The four Lutheran churches in the town testify to its heritage, and dozens of shops selling German pastries, breads, and wursts (sausages)—not to mention wine—line the main street. Many of the valley's best wineries are close by.

ESSENTIALS

VISITOR INFORMATION

Barossa Visitors Centre

The Barossa Visitor Centre in Tanunda sells Barossa-inspired and-branded souvenirs and gifts, including wine glasses, accessories, clothing, and produce. It's also possible to hire a bike, use the free Wi-Fi, or ask the friendly staff to assist with booking accommodations, experiences, and tours. ✉ *66–68 Murray St.* ☎ *08/8563–0600, 1300/852982* 🌐 *www.barossa.com.*

Sights

Charles Melton Wines

WINERY/DISTILLERY | Tasting here is relaxed and casual in a brick-floor, timber-wall cellar door, which is warmed by a log fire in winter. After making sure the resident cats have vacated it first, settle into a director's chair at the long wooden table and let the staff pour. Nine Popes, a huge, decadent red blend, is the flagship wine, and the ruby-red Rose of Virginia is an iconic Australian rosé. You can enjoy a glass of either with a cheese platter or game pie on the veranda. ✉ *Krondorf Rd., near Nitschke Rd.* ☎ *08/8563–3606* 🌐 *www.charlesmeltonwines.com.au.*

Grant Burge

WINERY/DISTILLERY | This is one of the most successful of the Barossa's young, independent wine labels. Wines include impressive Chardonnays, crisp Rieslings, and powerful reds such as Meshach Shiraz. Don't miss the Holy Trinity—a highly acclaimed Rhône blend of Grenache, Shiraz, and Mourvedre. The cellar door is at Krondorf, 5 km (3 miles) south of Tanunda and has a small café overlooking the vines. ✉ *279 Krondorf Rd.* ☎ *08/8563–3700* 🌐 *www.grantburge-wines.com.au.*

Jacob's Creek Visitor Centre

WINERY/DISTILLERY | An impressive block of glass, steel, and recycled timber, Jacob's Creek Visitor Centre overlooks the creek whose name is familiar to wine drinkers around the world, as they export to more than 60 countries. It can sometimes be overrun with tour groups, but the informative staff makes the place well worth a visit—it's certainly more than your run-of-the-mill visitor center. Inside the building, plasma screens and pictorial displays tell the history of the label. Cabernet Sauvignon, Merlot, Chardonnay, and the Shiraz-rosé, served chilled, can be tasted at a 60-foot-long counter. There is a lunch-only restaurant with broad glass doors opening onto a grassy lawn edged with towering eucalyptus trees, and there are workshops and tours you can join, including food and wine matching (A$150) and behind the scenes tours (A$300). Bookings are essential. ✉ *2129 Barossa Valley Way* ✣ *Near Jacob's Creek* ☎ *08/8521–3000* 🌐 *www.jacobscreek.com.*

Peter Lehmann Wines

WINERY/DISTILLERY | This winery is owned by a larger-than-life Barossa character whose wine consistently wins international awards. Art-hung stonework and a wood-burning fireplace make the tasting room one of the most pleasant in the valley. This is the only place to find Black Queen Sparkling Shiraz. Wooden tables on a shady lawn encourage picnicking on the Weighbridge platter, a selection of local smoked meats, cheeses, and condiments. Served daily, it's big enough for two. It also offers VIP tastings in a private room with food matchings, but you must book in advance. ✉ *Para Rd., off Stelzer Rd.* ☎ *08/8565–9555* 🌐 *www.peterlehmannwines.com.*

Pace Yourself

Home-smoked meats, organic farmhouse cheeses, and mouth-filling Shiraz—the Barossa is the ultimate picnic basket. Use this fact as an excuse for a long lunch, which will give you time to recover from all that wine tasting. Remember to pace yourself as you taste, and wherever possible, make use of those spit buckets you see at each winery. You'll be glad you did.

🍴 Restaurants

★ Casa Carboni

$$ | **ITALIAN** | Local winemakers and visitors love this cozy restaurant and cooking school run by a married couple, Fiona and Matteo Carboni, united by their love for Italy. They moved to the Barossa after living in Matteo's native Italy to offer their passion for pasta and wine alike in the form of wonderful, rustic trattoria meals and classes on pasta making. **Known for:** special wine bar on Friday night; run into local winemakers having dinner with friends here; a lovely gift shop with locally made items like baskets and high-quality home items. [$] *Average main: A$30* ✉ *67 Murray St., Angaston* ☎ *415/157669*

⊕ www.casacarboni.com.au ⊗ Closed Mon.–Wed.

Die Barossa Wurst Haus & Bakery

$ | **GERMAN** | For a hearty German lunch at a reasonable price, no place in Tanunda beats this small, friendly café and shop. The wurst is fresh from local butchers, the sauerkraut is direct from Germany, and the potato salad is made on-site from a secret recipe. **Known for:** traditional German pastries; hearty breakfast plates like poached eggs; great spot for supplying your picnics. $ Average main: A$11 ⊠ 86A Murray St. ☎ 08/8563–3598 ▭ No credit cards ⊗ No dinner.

★ FermentAsian

$$$$ | **ASIAN FUSION** | Whether it's for lunch (more casual) or dinner, the creative Modern Southeast Asian cuisine works wonderfully with local and European wines alike. Vietnamese owner chef Tuoi Do incorporates local ingredients into a menu that speaks of her heritage; a tasting menu is available. **Known for:** innovative dishes with beautiful plating; enormous and world-class wine list; vegetarian friendly. $ Average main: A$60 ⊠ 90 Murray St. ⊕ fermentasian.com.au ⊗ Closed Mon. and Tues. No lunch Wed.

1918 Bistro & Grill

$$$ | **AUSTRALIAN** | This rustic and whimsical restaurant in a restored villa makes exemplary use of the Barossa's distinctive regional produce in a seasonal Oz menu flavored with tastes from Asia and the Middle East. Local olive oil and seasonal fruits and vegetables influence dishes, and the mostly Barossa wine list includes rare classics and newcomers. **Known for:** grilled fresh seafood; beautiful heritage decor; garden dining. $ Average main: A$50 ⊠ 94 Murray St. ☎ 08/8563–0405 ⊕ www.1918.com.au.

🛏 **Hotels**

Blickinstal Barossa Valley Retreat

$$ | **B&B/INN** | Its name means "view into the valley," which understates the breathtaking panoramas from this lovely B&B. **Pros:** great-value rooms in convenient location near Tanunda; complimentary port in the evening; all accommodations have air-conditioning and TV. **Cons:** don't expect corporate-style facilities or an anonymous stay; somewhat rustic feeling; no fine dining on-site. $ Rooms from: A$180 ⊠ Rifle Range Rd. ☎ 08/8563–2716 ⊕ www.blickinstal.com.au ⇄ 6 rooms ⦿ Breakfast.

Lawley Farm

$$ | **B&B/INN** | Amid 20 acres of grapes, in a courtyard shaded by gnarled peppercorn trees, these delightful stone cottage–style suites were assembled from the remains of barns dating from the Barossa's pioneering days. **Pros:** original buildings have been lovingly preserved; the breakfasts are legendary; spa and wood-fire rooms available. **Cons:** no exercise facilities for working off all the local wine and produce; not good for those with allergies to farm animals; old facility. $ Rooms from: A$175 ⊠ Krondorf Rd. at Grocke Rd. ☎ 08/8563–2141 ⊕ www.lawleyfarm.com.au ⇄ 4 suites ⦿ Free Breakfast.

Angaston

16 km (10 miles) northeast of Tanunda via Menglers Hill Road Scenic Drive, 86 km (53 miles) northeast of Adelaide.

Named after George Fife Angas, the Englishman who founded the town and sponsored many of the German and British immigrants who came here, Angaston is full of jacaranda trees, and its main street is lined with stately stone buildings and tiny shops. Schulz Butchers has been making and selling wurst since 1939; 17 varieties hang above the counter. You can buy other delicious regional produce every Saturday morning at the Barossa Farmers Market, behind Vintners Bar & Grill.

◉ Sights

★ Yalumba

WINERY/DISTILLERY | Australia's oldest family-owned winery, the iconic Yalumba sits within a hugely impressive compound resembling an Italian monastery. The cellar door is decorated with mission-style furniture, antique wine-making materials, and mementos of the Hill Smith family, who first planted vines in the Barossa in 1849. Visit the tasting room to try the award-winning Shiraz and Viognier wines. Private tours can be arranged upon request for A$35 and up. ⊠ *40 Eden Valley Rd., just south of Valley Rd.* ☎ *08/8561–3200* ⊕ *www.yalumba.com.*

🍴 Restaurants

★ Vintners Bar & Grill

$$$ | **AUSTRALIAN** | Locals flock to this sophisticated, long-standing spot, where vivid contemporary artworks adorn the walls, wide windows look out on rows of vineyards, and an upbeat jazz soundtrack and scarlet and charcoal suede chairs make it easy to relax. The menu blends Australian, Mediterranean, and Asian flavors, and features modern takes on classic seafood dishes or choice meats like locally sourced loin of lamb. **Known for:** South Australian oysters; top winemakers often come here to sample from the cellar's 160 wines; open for lunch daily. $ *Average main: A$38* ⊠ *Stockwell Rd.* ☎ *08/8564–2488* ⊕ *www.vintners. com.au* ⊘ *No dinner Sun.*

🛏 Hotels

Collingrove Homestead

$$$ | **B&B/INN** | Enjoy the evocative old-world B&B luxury at the ancestral home of the Angas family, the descendants of George Fife Angas, one of South Australia's founders. **Pros:** luxurious old-world charm; elegant interior design; breakfast served on terrace with views. **Cons:** very limited rooms available; dinner on Saturday night only and bookings essential; perhaps a bit stuffy for families with children. $ *Rooms from: A$300* ⊠ *450 Eden Valley Rd.* ☎ *08/8564–2061* ⊕ *www.collingrovehomestead.com.au* 🛏 *6 suites* ❤ *Free Breakfast* ⊟ *No credit cards.*

Nuriootpa

8 km (5 miles) northwest of Angaston, 74 km (46 miles) northeast of Adelaide.

Long before it was the Barossa's commercial center, Nuriootpa was used as a bartering place by local Aboriginal tribes, hence its name: Nuriootpa, which means "meeting place." Most locals call it Nurie.

◉ Sights

★ Maggie Beer's Farm Shop

STORE/MALL | Renowned cook and food writer Maggie Beer is an icon of Australian cuisine. Burned-fig jam, coffee, ice cream, *verjuice* (a golden liquid made from unfermented grape juice and used for flavoring), and her signature Pheasant Farm Pâté are some of the delights you can taste and buy at Maggie Beer's Farm Shop. Treat-filled picnic baskets are available all day to take out or dip into on the deck overlooking a tree-fringed pond full of turtles. Don't miss the daily cooking demonstrations at 2 pm. ⊠ *50 Pheasant Farm Rd.* ☎ *08/8562–4477* ⊕ *www. maggiebeer.com.au* ☞ *Bookings required for cooking demonstrations for groups of 10 or more.*

Penfolds Barossa Valley

WINERY/DISTILLERY | A very big brother to the 19th-century Magill Estate in Adelaide, this massive wine-making outfit in the center of Nuriootpa lets you taste Shiraz, Cabernet, Merlot, Chardonnay, and Riesling blends—but not the celebrated Grange—at the cellar door. To savor the flagship wine and other premium vintages, book a Taste of Grange Tour

Off The Beaten Path

Banrock Station Wine & Wetland Centre. The salt-scrub-patched Murray River floodplain 150 km (94 miles) east of Nuriootpa is an unlikely setting for a winery, but it is worth making the journey to this spot at Kingston-on-Murray. Within the stilted, mud-brick building perched above the vineyard and river lagoons you can select a wine to accompany an all-day grazing platter or lunch on the outdoor deck—try the pan seared Murray Cod with corn puree, braised spring onions, and beetroot chips. Afterward, you can take one of three self-guided walks (ranging from 2.5 km [1.5 miles] up to 8 km [5-mile]; trail access is by donation) to view the surrounding wetlands (which can be "drylands" during a drought), and learn about the ongoing wildlife habitat restoration and conservation work funded by Banrock Station wine sales and walkers' donations. ⊠ *Holmes Rd., just off Sturt Hwy., Kingston-on-Murray* ☎ *08/8583–0299* ⊕ *www.banrockstation.com.au.*

(A$150 per person, minimum of two, 24-hour advance notice needed). There are also 90-minute blending workshops for A$65 per person. ⊠ *30 Tanunda Rd.* ☎ *08/8568–8408* ⊕ *www.penfolds.com.*

Marananga

6 km (4 miles) west of Nuriootpa, 68 km (42 miles) northeast of Adelaide.

The tiny hamlet of Marananga inhabits one of the prettiest corners of the Barossa. This area's original name was Gnadenfrei, which means "freed by the grace of God"—a reference to the religious persecution the German settlers suffered before they emigrated to Australia. Marananga, the Aboriginal name, was adopted in 1918, when a wave of anti-German sentiment spurred many name changes in the closing days of World War I.

◉ Sights

Seppeltsfield Winery

WINERY/DISTILLERY | Joseph Seppelt was a Silesian farmer who purchased land in the Barossa after arriving in Australia in 1849. Under the control of his son, Benno, the wine-making business flourished, and today Seppelt Winery and its splendid grounds are a tribute to the family's industry and enthusiasm. Fortified wine is a Seppelt specialty; this is the only winery in the world that has ports for every year as far back as 1878. Most notable is the 100-year-old Para Liqueur Tawny. The Grenache, Chardonnay, Cabernet, and sparkling Shiraz are also worth tasting. Tours of the 19th-century distillery are run daily; you can also book 24 hours ahead for the Centenary Tour, during which you get to taste four of the six paramount wines as well a 100-year-old wine and one that was 100 years old in your birth year. There's a small café that offers delicious cakes and afternoon teas. ⊠ *Seppeltsfield Rd., 3 km (2 miles) west of Marananga, Seppeltsfield* ☎ *08/8568–6217* ⊕ *www.seppeltsfield. com.au* ⊠ *Tours from A$15.*

★ Torbreck Vintners

WINERY/DISTILLERY | This is one of Australia's top estate wineries and a good representation of classic, artfully made Barossa wine. Opened in May 2017, the modern and airy tasting room complements its original 1850s settler's cottage

Fish Tales

The Murray River is the place to head for callop (also called yellow belly or golden perch) and elusive Murray cod. In the river's backwaters you can also net a feed of yabbies, a type of freshwater crayfish, which make a wonderful appetizer before you tuck into the one that didn't get away. In the ocean King George whiting reigns supreme, but there is also excellent eating with mulloway, bream, snapper, snook, salmon, and sweep. The yellowtail kingfish, a great fighter usually found in deep water, prefers the shallower waters of Coffin Bay, off the Eyre Peninsula.

Baird Bay Ocean Eco Experience. Most well known for their Swim with Wild Sea Lions and Dolphin tours on the Eyre Peninsula—a truly awesome once-in-a-lifetime experience worth every penny of the A$150—this charter company also runs fishing charters to Coffin Bay and other top spots on request. Children are welcome. Tours are at 9:30 am and 1 pm. ✉ *Baird Bay Rd., Baird Bay* ☎ *08/8626–5017* ⊕ *www.bairdbay.com* 🖃 *A$150.*

Another popular destination is the Yorke Peninsula.

S.A. Fishing Adventures. Owners Herbie and Kirsty Glacken know just about everything there is to know about fishing the southern gulf waters and this charter takes anglers to great spots around the Yorke Peninsula, as well as Wedge, Neptune, and Kangaroo islands. Typical catches feature the delicious Nannigai, famous Whiting and lots of other Instagram-worthy big fish. ✉ *7 Gannet Crescent, Marion Bay* ☎ *08/8854–4098.*

Last, but certainly not least, is legendary Kangaroo Island.

Kangaroo Island Fishing Adventures. This tour operator has fast, clean boats and a live-aboard mother ship; the company specializes in tours along the pristine shores of Kangaroo Island. They take groups in a 30-foot cruiser out in the Western River region (the island's north coast) and into the Investigator Strait, which is rarely fished by private fishing boats. ✉ *Western River Rd., Parndana* ☎ *08/8559–3232* ⊕ *www.kangarooislandadventures.com.au.*

---

cellar door, with subtle color tones and earthy textures. Taste the iconic Shiraz wines on the deck overlooking its renowned Descendant vineyard. ✉ *348 Roennfeldt Rd.* ☎ *08/8568–8123* ⊕ *torbreck.com/pages/cellar-door.*

Two Hands Wines

WINERY/DISTILLERY | The interior of this 19th-century sandstone cottage is every bit as surprising as the wines produced here. Polished wood and glass surround the contemporary counter where the excellent staff leads you through the tasting of several "out of the box" reds,

whites, and blends. The main event is Shiraz sourced from six wine regions. Compare and contrast Shiraz from Victoria and Padthaway (South Australia); and try the Barossa-grown Bad Impersonator. On weekend mornings and by prior appointment, visitors are invited behind the scenes to see the winery. ✉ *273 Neldner Rd.* ☎ *08/8562–4566* ⊕ *www.twohandswines.com* 🖃 *General tastings A$5 (refundable with purchase).*

Hotels

The Lodge Country House

$$$$ | **B&B/INN** | Rambling and aristocratic, this bluestone homestead with period-style furniture was built in 1903 for one of the 13 children of Joseph Seppelt, founder of the showpiece winery across the road. **Pros:** beautiful gardens; informative hosts who delight in telling guests about the history of the place; views of the vineyards. **Cons:** not particularly suitable for kids; pricey; not walkable to town. [$] *Rooms from: A$360* ✉ *743 Seppeltsfield Rd., Seppeltsfield* ✣ *3 km (2 miles) south of Marananga* ☎ *08/8562–8277* 🌐 *www.thelodgecountryhouse.com.au* 🛏 *4 rooms* 🍴 *Free Breakfast.*

The Louise

$$$$ | **RESORT** | Prepare for pampering and privacy at this country estate on a quiet back road with glorious valley views and destination dining at its best. **Pros:** stunning rooms with beautiful private gardens; king-size beds; guest comfort is prized here with all sorts of luxury touches. **Cons:** pricey; no children under 10; need to book well ahead at restaurant. [$] *Rooms from: A$600* ✉ *Seppeltsfield Rd. at Stonewell Rd.* ☎ *08/8562–2722* 🌐 *www.thelouise.com.au* 🛏 *15 suites* 🍴 *Free Breakfast.*

Sevenhill

126 km (78 miles) north of Adelaide.

Sevenhill is the Clare Valley's geographic center, and the location of the region's first winery, established by Jesuit priests in 1851 to produce altar wine. The area had been settled three years earlier by Austrian Jesuits who named their seminary after the seven hills of Rome.

The Riesling Trail, a walking and cycling track that follows an old Clare Valley railway line, runs through Sevenhill. The 36-km (22-mile) trail passes wineries and villages in gently rolling country between Auburn and Clare, and three loop trails take you to vineyards off the main track.

Sights

Kilikanoon Wines

WINERY/DISTILLERY | Award-winning and internationally known Kilikanoon produces multilayered reds, such as the dense, richly colored Oracle Shiraz (occasionally available for tasting); Prodigal Grenache is another beauty. Tastings are $5 for five wines, $10 for 10, refundable on any purchase. Or opt for the Asset Collection composed of the small production Reserve wines that showcase regional and varietal diversity. Call ahead for a produce platter or cheese board, or to bring a large group. ✉ *Penna La., 2 km (1 mile) off Main North Rd., Penwortham* ☎ *08/8843–4206* 🌐 *www.kilikanoon.com.au.*

★ **Sevenhill Cellars**

WINERY/DISTILLERY | **FAMILY** | The area's first winery, Sevenhill Cellars was created by the Jesuits, and they still run the show, with any profits going to education, mission work, and the needy within Australia. In the 1940s the winery branched out from sacramental wine to commercial production, and today 21 wine varieties, including Riesling (try the St. Aloysius label), Verdelho, Grenache, and fortified wines, account for 75% of its business. Book a guided tour with the charming Brother John May, Jesuit winemaker emeritus, who takes you to the cellars, the cemetery, and the church crypt where Jesuits have been interred since 1865. You can also rent bicycles here to explore the rolling hills and vineyards, and there are toys for the kids. ✉ *College Rd., just off Main North Rd.* ☎ *08/8843–4222* 🌐 *www.sevenhill.com.au* 🎟 *Tours A$10.*

Skillogalee Winery

WINERY/DISTILLERY | Known for its excellent Riesling, Gewürztraminer, and Shiraz, this boutique, family-owned winery is

Off The Beaten Path

Martindale Hall. Just outside the slate-mining hamlet of Mintaro, 10 km (6 miles) southeast of Sevenhill, wealthy bachelor Edmund Bowman built this gracious manor house in 1879—as legend has it, to lure his fiancée from England to the colonies. He failed, but continued to spend lavishly. In 1891 a near-bankrupt Bowman sold the grand house to the Mortlock family, who in 1965 willed it—and its contents—to the University of Adelaide. Now privately leased, Martindale Hall is a museum of late-19th- and early-20th-century rural life, filled with the Mortlocks' books, beds, furniture, crockery, glassware, and billiard table. The house, which is open for self-guided tours, was featured in director Peter Weir's first film, *Picnic at Hanging Rock.* ✉ *1 Manoora Rd., 2 km (1¼ miles) south of Mintaro, Mintaro* ☎ *08/8843–9088* 🌐 *www.martindalehall-mintaro.com.au* 🎟 *A$12* 🕒 *Closed Tues.*

also known for its wonderful restaurant. Wine tasting takes place in a small room in the 1850s cottage. Don't miss the sparkling Riesling. ■ **TIP→ There's also an on-site, self-contained cottage for rent.** ✉ *Trevarrick Rd.* ☎ *08/8843–4311* 🌐 *www.skillogalee.com.*

🍴 Restaurants

The Rising Sun Hotel

$$ | MODERN AUSTRALIAN | People have watched the world go by from the veranda of this landmark hotel in Auburn, 16 km (10 miles) south of Sevenhill, since it was built in 1849. Pull up a chair overlooking the street and partake of the delicious modern Australian food, perhaps kangaroo fillet with quandong (a native fruit) and sweet-potato mash, or butterfish in a batter of Coopers Pale Ale (Adelaide's own beer). **Known for:** Clare Valley wines, including old vintages; historical atmosphere; large list of Australian and international beers and ciders. [$] *Average main: A$30* ✉ *19 Main North Rd., Auburn* ☎ *08/8849–2015* 🌐 *www.therisingsunhotel.com.au.*

Skillogalee Winery

$$$ | AUSTRALIAN | The dining area at this local favorite spills from a 1850s cottage onto a beautiful veranda overlooking a flower-filled garden and rows of grapevines. The menu changes seasonally, but entrées might include fish tagine with olives, apricots, and Skillogalee figs with saffron and lemon couscous or dukkah-crusted chicken breast. **Known for:** lovely morning and afternoon teas; fireplace in cozy dining room; house wines available by the glass. [$] *Average main: A$40* ✉ *Trevarrick Rd.* ☎ *08/8843–4311* 🌐 *www.skillogalee.com.au* 🕒 *No dinner.*

🏃 Activities

BICYCLING

Clare Valley Cycle Hire

SPORTS—SIGHT | Riding the Riesling Trail from Clare to Auburn is one of the best ways to explore the valley—it takes around 2½ hours to cycle the whole thing (one way), unless, of course, you get distracted by the wineries along the way. This 35-km-long (22-mile-long) cycling track follows the path of the old rail line that sliced through the hills until it was irreparably damaged by the

1983 Ash Wednesday bushfires. Bikes (including helmets, which are mandatory in Australia) for both adults and kids (and baby seats) can be rented from Clare Valley Cycle Hire. ⊠ *32 Victoria Rd., Clare* ☎ *0418/802077* ⊕ *www.clarevalleycyclehire.com.au* ✉ *From A$20.*

Clare

10 km (6 miles) north of Sevenhill, 136 km (84 miles) north of Adelaide.

The bustling town of Clare is the Clare Valley's commercial center. Unusual for ultra-English South Australia, many of its early settlers were Irish—hence the valley's name, after the Irish county Clare, and place-names such as Armagh and Donnybrook.

GETTING HERE AND AROUND

The Clare Valley is about a 90-minute drive from Adelaide via Main North Road. From the center of Adelaide, head north on King William Street through the heart of North Adelaide. King William becomes O'Connell Street. After crossing Barton Terrace, look for Main North Road signs on the right. The road passes through the satellite town of Elizabeth, by-passes the center of Gawler, and then runs due north to Auburn, the first town of the Clare Valley when approaching from the capital. Main North Road continues down the middle of the valley to Clare.

As with the Barossa wine region, a car is essential for exploring the Clare Valley in any depth. Taste wine in moderation if you're driving; as well as keeping yourself and others safe, you'll avoid paying the extremely high penalties for driving while intoxicated.

TOURS

Clare Valley Experiences

SPECIAL-INTEREST | Clare Valley Experiences combines wine and beer tasting with food, culture, and cycling on its tour of the region's major wineries and sites

(A$250 each for two people, including lunch), departing from Clare. ⊠ *29 Hope St.* ☎ *08/8842–1880* ⊕ *www.clarevalleyexperiences.com* ✉ *A$215 each for 2 people, including lunch.*

ESSENTIALS
VISITOR INFORMATION
Clare Valley Visitor Information Centre

Located within the Clare Valley Wine, Food and Tourism Centre, the staff here can provide information about upcoming events, exhibitions, and workshops in the Clare Valley. ⊠ *8 Spring Gully Rd., 6 km (4 miles) south of Clare* ☎ *1800/242131, 08/8842–2131* ⊕ *www.clarevalley.com. au.*

⊙ Sights

Knappstein Enterprise Winery & Brewery

WINERY/DISTILLERY | One of the most recognizable and popular wineries in the Clare Valley, Knappstein is located in the original 19th-century Enterprise Brewery, a heritage-listed building and a well-known landmark of a township that's oozing with history. Knappstein Hand Picked Riesling is consistently rated among Australia's finest, though the same could be said for any of the wines lovingly handcrafted here. There's also an on-site microbrewery that produces the award-winning Knappstein Reserve Lager, a premium Bavarian-style lager. ⊠ *2 Pioneer Ave.* ☎ *08/8841–2100* ⊕ *www.knappstein.com.au.*

Tim Adams Wines

WINERY/DISTILLERY | The small, no-frills tasting room means there is nothing to distract you from discovering why Tim Adams Wines has a big reputation. The standout in an impressive collection of reds and whites, which includes a celebrated Riesling and delicious Pinot Gris, is the purple-red Aberfeldy Shiraz, made from 100-year-old vines. You can buy wine by the glass and bottle to enjoy with a bring-your-own-picnic on the veranda. ⊠ *Warenda Rd. just off Main North Rd.,*

Off The Beaten Path

Burra. This town full of character—and characters—about 44 km (27 miles) northeast of Clare is worth a detour. The discovery of copper in 1845 made Burra the country's largest inland town but the ore ran out quickly (the biggest mine closed after just 32 years) and Burra settled into a quiet existence. Today the 11 km (7 miles) Heritage Trail leads you to 49 sites related to Burra's rich mining past: the A$30 Heritage Passport (available from the visitor information center) includes a booklet with information about each of the sites on the trail and free entry to eight locked sites and museums—these include the massive open-cut Monster Mine; two "homes" dug into the banks of Burra Creek, where some 2,000 people lived before a flood in 1851; and colonial Redruth Gaol, which appeared in Australian film *Breaker Morant*. It includes a guidebook, map, and a key to eight locked historic sites and four museums. ✉ *2 Market Sq., Burra* ☎ *1300/775540* ⊕ *www.visitburra.com.*

5 km (3 miles) south of Clare ☎ 08/8842–2429 ⊕ www.timadamswines.com.au.

🛏 Hotels

Bungaree Station

$$ | B&B/INN |FAMILY | Journey back to colonial Australia at this family-owned farm, where outlying cottages and the heritage-listed stables beside the stone homestead have been converted into family-friendly, self contained accommodations and the reception area and a farm shop is in the original station store. **Pros:** fascinating insight into a working homestead; local produce, as well as fresh coffee and free Wi-Fi, is available at the farm shop; great option for groups, with some cottages sleeping up to 10. **Cons:** city types might find it too rustic; food options are limited; no exercise facilities on-site. $ *Rooms from: A$168* ✉ *Main North Rd., 12 km (7 miles) north of Clare* ☎ *08/8842–2677* ⊕ *www.bungareestation.com.au* 🛏 *10 rooms* ⧚ *Free Breakfast.*

McLaren Vale

39 km (24 miles) south of Adelaide.

The nearest wine region to Adelaide, the McLaren Vale and the Fleurieu Peninsula area has a distinctly modern, upscale look, even though many of the more than 80 wineries in and around town are as old as their Barossa peers. The first vines were planted in 1838 at northern Reynella by Englishman John Reynell, who had collected them en route from the Cape of Good Hope. The McLaren Vale region has always been known for its big—and softer—reds, including Shiraz, as well as a few white varietals. Local microbrewed beer is also becoming an increasingly popular attraction in the region.

GETTING HERE AND AROUND

The Fleurieu Peninsula is an easy drive south from Adelaide. Renting a car in Adelaide and driving south is the best way to visit the area, especially if you wish to tour the wineries, which aren't served by public transportation. McLaren Vale itself is less than an hour away. Leave central Adelaide along South Terrace or West Terrace, linking with the

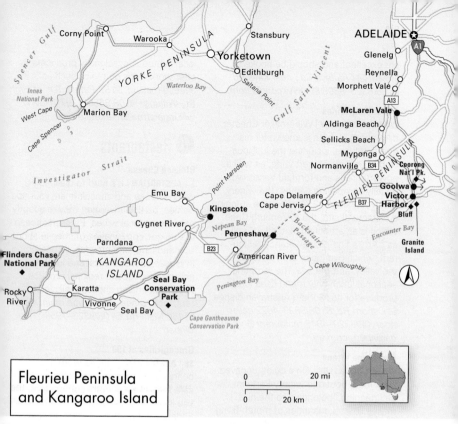

Fleurieu Peninsula and Kangaroo Island

Anzac Highway, which heads toward Glenelg. At the Gallipoli Underpass intersection with Main South Road, turn left. This road takes you almost to McLaren Vale. After a detour to visit the wineries, watch for signs for Victor Harbor Road. About 20 km (12 miles) south the highway splits. One road heads for Victor Harbor, the other for Goolwa. Those two places are connected by a major road that follows the coastline. Drivers heading to Cape Jervis and the Kangaroo Island ferries should stay on Main South Road.

ESSENTIALS
VISITOR INFORMATION
McLaren Vale and Fleurieu Visitor Centre
Conveniently located on a main road, the visitor center offers a free accommodation and tour booking service, a café, public toilets, and a shop featuring a wide range of local produce, souvenirs, gifts, and maps. ⊠ *796 Main Rd.* ☎ *08/8323–9944* ⊕ *www.mclarenvale.info.*

◉ Sights

Coriole Vineyards
WINERY/DISTILLERY | The 1860s stone cellar door at Coriole Vineyards sits among nasturtiums and hollyhocks on a hill with stunning St. Vincent Gulf views. From the surrounding vines, winemakers Simon White and Mark Lloyd make some of Australia's most exciting Italian varietal wines, such as Sangiovese and Nebbiolo. Coriole makes olive oils, as well, which you can taste along with their wine. Enjoy a platter of estate-grown and local produce—cheese, smoked kangaroo, roasted vegetables, and chutney—in the flagstone courtyard (lunch Thursday to Monday). The hosted tastings

are excellent and should be booked ahead. ✉ *Chaffeys Rd., near Kays Rd.* ☎ *08/8323–8305* 🌐 *www.coriole.com.*

d'Arenberg Wines

WINERY/DISTILLERY | Winemaker Chester d'Arenberg Osborn is known for his quality whites, including the luscious Noble Riesling dessert wine, as well as powerful reds and fortified wines with equally compelling names. The winery, family-run since 1912, offers the stunning architectural site, the d'Arenburg Cube, which is an attraction in itself as well as d'Arry's fine-dining veranda restaurant, which overlooks the vineyards, the valley, and the sea. The tempting seasonal lunch-only menu uses local produce for its Modern Australian dishes. ✉ *Osborn Rd.* ☎ *08/8829–4822 cellar door, 08/8329–4848 restaurant* 🌐 *www.darenberg.com.au.*

Pertaringa Wines

WINERY/DISTILLERY | On a quiet, unpaved back road, boutique winery Pertaringa (meaning "belonging to the hills") makes limited quantities of mouth-filling reds and several whites. At the cellar door, facing the vines, you can sip Two Gentlemen's Grenache and Scarecrow Sauvignon Blanc, a great accompaniment to a bring-your-own picnic, or make up a platter from the selection of cheese and other goodies sold at the cellar door. Opt for the premium varietal tasting for A$10 per person, redeemable upon purchase. ✉ *Hunt Rd. at Rifle Range Rd.* ☎ *08/8383–2700* 🌐 *www.pertaringa.com.au.*

★ **Wilunga Farmer's Market**

MARKET | **FAMILY** | At South Australia's first farmers' market—and arguably its best in terms of the quality of the products and the overall experience—there are more than 60 stalls showcasing local cheese, meat, and produce as well as famous bakeries. There family-friendly, Saturday-morning-only market also has excellent freshly brewed coffee. Visiting here is a wonderful way to get to know local culture. Occasionally producers offer workshops on topics such as cheese-making. ✉ *St. Peter's Terr. at High St., Willunga* ☎ *08/8556–4297* 🌐 *www.willungafarmersmarket.com.au.*

🍴 Restaurants

Blessed Cheese

$ | **AUSTRALIAN** | It's hard to disappoint when cheese and chocolate are your specialties, particularly when they're adeptly paired with local wines. Blessed cheese is a unique combination of cheese shop, licensed café, and provedore specializing in artisan cheeses, local and imported gourmet foods, and regional produce. **Known for:** artisan cheeses; picnic platters; local wines. [$] *Average main: A$15* ✉ *150 Main Rd.* ☎ *08/8323–7958* ⏲ *No dinner.*

Bracegirdles at 190

$$ | **AUSTRALIAN** | With its worn floorboards and pressed-metal ceilings, this café feels like a country corner store, but you'll also find a large alfresco area and undercover courtyard, perfect in spring. Come early for a cup of coffee, a piece of chocolate, and the best breakfast outside Adelaide. **Known for:** delicious artisanal chocolate; open every day; fresh coffee made by trained baristas. [$] *Average main: A$25* ✉ *190 Main Rd.* ☎ *08/8323–8558* 🌐 *bracegirdles.com.au* ⏲ *No dinner Sun.–Thurs.*

★ **Salopian Inn**

$$$ | **MODERN AUSTRALIAN** | Opened in 2014, the Salopian Inn sources its food from a home garden as well as pasture-fed, locally sourced beef and lamb, free-range poultry and pork, as well as Australian-caught seafood. The A$80 per person tasting menu showcases the dishes the kitchen most loves cooking. **Known for:** enjoy a long lunch here any day of the week; focus on sustainability in sourcing ingredients; several fantastic dessert options. [$] *Average main: A$50* ✉ *Main Rd. at McMurtrie Rd.*

☎ *08/8323–8769* ⊕ *salopian.com.au* ⊙ *No lunch. No dinner Sun.–Wed.*

★ Star of Greece

$$ | AUSTRALIAN | More for the linen-slacks-and-deck-shoes set than the board-shorts-and-sunscreen crowd, this extended weatherboard kiosk on the cliffs at Port Willunga, 10 km (6 miles) southwest of McLaren Vale, is beach-ball bright and extremely popular. Wooden chairs painted in mandarin, lime, and sky-blue stripes sit at paper-draped tables, and windows frame the aqua sea. (The offshore buoy marks where the three-masted *Star of Greece* foundered in 1888.) Reading the menu nets mostly seafood, and depending on the season, you might find seared scallops wrapped in octopus bacon, or crispy skinned ocean trout on prawn salsa. **Known for:** stunning beach views; fresh seafood; popular site for events, such as weddings. ⓢ *Average main: A$34* ⊠ *1 Esplanade, Port Willunga* ☎ *08/8557–7420* ⊕ *www.starofgreece.com.au* ⊙ *No dinner Sun.–Wed. No lunch Mon. and Tues.*

★ The Victory Hotel

$$$ | MODERN AUSTRALIAN |FAMILY | Local families, winemakers, and travelers convene here for great seafood and a stellar wine list, all in a relaxed, comfortable setting. There are daily specials not to miss, and the menu ranges from fresh oysters to excellent bar food like classic shnitzel and and salt-and-pepper squid, and also includes more composed Modern Australian dishes with fresh seafood and seasonal vegetables. **Known for:** excellent wine cellar featuring top European and local producers; patio has views of the gulf; weekend lunch spot. ⓢ *Average main: A$40* ⊠ *Old Sellicks Hill Rd.* ☎ *08/8556–3083* ⊕ *victoryhotel.com.au.*

🛏 Hotels

Wine and Roses B&B

$$$ | B&B/INN | It may look like a regular residential house from the outside, but this luxury B&B five minutes from the main McLaren Vale road has an interior that's far from ordinary and pampering that includes a pillow menu at bedtime. **Pros:** perfect for a romantic getaway; the complimentary port is delicious; on-site bike hire available for guests. **Cons:** if all four suites are booked it's a little cramped; not child-friendly; not beachside. ⓢ *Rooms from: A$249* ⊠ *39 Caffrey St.* ☎ *08/8323–7654* ⊕ *www.wineandroses.com.au* ⇄ *4 suites* �|◎| *Free Breakfast.*

Goolwa

44 km (27 miles) southeast of McLaren Vale, 83 km (51 miles) south of Adelaide.

Beautifully situated near the mouth of the mighty Murray River, which travels some 2,415 km (1,594 miles) from its source in New South Wales, Goolwa grew fat on the 19th-century river paddle-steamer trade. Today, with its enviable position close to the sea and the combined attractions of Lake Alexandrina and Coorong National Park, tourism has replaced river trade as the main source of income.

👁 Sights

Goolwa Wharf

MARINA | FAMILY | Set sail from here for daily tour cruises upon the *Spirit of the Coorong,* a fully equipped motorboat that offers a 4½-hour (A$95) or 6-hour cruise (A$115) to Coorong National Park. Both include guided walks, lunch, and afternoon tea. Visitors can also enjoy locally brewed craft beer at the Steam Exchange Brewery located in the old railway goods shed on the wharf or go shopping at the Goolwa Wharf Markets on the first and third Sunday of each month. ⊠ *Goolwa Wharf* ☎ *08/8555–2203, 1800/442203 tour cruises* ⊕ *www.coorongcruises.com.au.*

Oscar W

LOCAL INTEREST | FAMILY | Goolwa is the home port of paddle-steamer *Oscar W.* Built in 1908, it's one of the few remaining wood-fired boiler ships. This boat holds the record for bringing the most bales of wool (2,500) along the Darling River, which flows into the Murray River. When not participating in commemorative cruises and paddleboat races, the boat is open for inspection and, in warmer weather, one-hour cruises, which depart from the Goolwa Wharf Precinct on weekends and the occasional Friday ($20). ⊠ *Goolwa Wharf* ☎ *1300/466592* ⊕ *www.oscar-w.info* ✉ *Donation requested to inspect boat.*

Victor Harbor

18 km (11 miles) west of Goolwa, 83 km (51 miles) south of Adelaide.

As famous for its natural beauty and wildlife as for its resorts, Victor Harbor is South Australia's favorite seaside getaway. In 1802 English and French explorers Matthew Flinders and Nicolas Baudin met here at Encounter Bay, and by 1830 the harbor was a major whaling center. Pods of southern right whales came here to breed in winter, and they made for a profitable trade through the mid-1800s. By 1878 the whales were hunted nearly to extinction, but the return of these majestic creatures to Victor Harbor in recent decades has established the city as a premier source of information on whales and whaling history.

ESSENTIALS
VISITOR INFORMATION
Victor Harbor Visitor Information Centre
This visitor center offers a wide range of free brochures, maps, and event

guides, plus plenty of suggestions and friendly advice on what to see and do in Victor Harbor and the Fleurieu Peninsula. ⊠ *The Causeway* ☎ *08/8557–0777, 1800/557094* ⊕ *holidayatvictorharbor.com.au.*

⊙ Sights

Bluff

VIEWPOINT | Seven kilometers (4½ miles) west of Victor Harbor, the Bluff is where whalers once stood lookout for their prey. Today the granite outcrop, also known as Rosetta Head, serves the same purpose in very different circumstances. It's a steep, 1,400-foot climb to the top, on a formed trail, to enjoy the bluff views. ⊠ *The Bluff.*

Cockle Train

TRANSPORTATION SITE (AIRPORT/BUS/FERRY/TRAIN) | FAMILY | Traveling the route of South Australia's first railway line—originally laid between Goolwa and Port Elliot, and extended to Victor Harbor in 1864—the line traces the lovely Southern Ocean beaches on its 16-km (10-mile), half-hour journey. The train runs by steam power, subject to availability and weather conditions, daily during summer school holidays (late December to late January), on Easter weekend, and on the third Sunday of each month from June to November. A diesel locomotive pulls the heritage passenger cars (or a diesel railcar operates) on other Sundays and public holidays, and days of Total Fire Ban. ⊠ *Railway Terr., near Coral St.* ☎ *08/8263–5621 on days train operates, 1300/655991* ⊕ *www.steamrangerheritagerailway.org* ✉ *A$29 round-trip.*

Granite Island

ISLAND | FAMILY | This island is linked to the mainland by a 650-yard causeway, along which Clydesdales pull a double-decker tram. Within Granite Island Nature Park a self-guided walk leads around the island, and guided two-hour walking tours to view the colony of abou

500 fairy penguins are run each night at dusk; book at the Victor Harbor Visitor Centre before 4 pm (A$25). ■TIP→ **Look out for seals in the shallows.** ☒ *Granite Island* ☎ *1800/557094* ⊕ *www.graniteisland.com.au* ⊠ *A$9 round-trip tram; A$25 guided nature tours and penguin tours.*

South Australian Whale Centre

INFO CENTER | FAMILY | The center tells the often graphic story of the whaling industry along South Australia's coast, particularly in Encounter Bay. Excellent interpretive displays spread over three floors focus on dolphins, seals, penguins, and whales—all of which can be seen in these waters. In whale-watching season the center has a 24-hour information hotline on sightings. There's a Discovery Trail and craft area for children. ☒ *2 Railway Terr.* ☎ *08/8551–0750, 1900/942537 whale information* ⊕ *www.sawhalecentre.com* ⊠ *From A$9.*

Beaches

Boomer Beach

BEACH—SIGHT | The surf here is very big thanks to the exposed reef break. Most waves are dumpers, hence the name Boomer, and can get up to 15 feet high. As a result, this is a beach for surfers and strong swimmers. Waves decrease toward Victor Harbor, providing lower surf and usually calm conditions. In summer the surf tends to be mostly flat, but you need to be vigilant of rocks, rips, and sharks year-round. There is an excellent view down the entire beach from the headland at Port Elliot; from here you can spot the southern right whale, which in winter claims this area as its territory. **Amenities:** lifeguards; parking; toilets. **Best for:** fishing; surfing; swimming. ☒ *Port Elliot.*

Horseshoe Bay, Port Elliot

BEACH—SIGHT | This 2,300-foot-long beach faces east at the jetty and swings round to face south against Commodore Point. Thanks to the protection on either side,

the waves are relatively low, making this a great swimming destination. However, the waves can be heavy during a high swell and surge up the steep beach. The safest swimming is at the western surf club end, where waves are always smallest. Fishing is popular around jetty and boundary rocks. **Amenities:** parking; toilets. **Best for:** swimming; walking. ☒ *Basham Parade, Port Elliot.*

Middleton

BEACH—SIGHT | One of South Australia's most popular surfing beaches is also one of its most hazardous due to the persistent high waves. The entire beach is composed of fine sand and waves averaging more than 2 meters (6½ feet) breaking across a 500-meter-wide (1,640-feet-wide) double bar surf zone. Numerous spilling breakers, substantial wave setup and set-down at the shoreline, and widely spaced rips during lower wave conditions are common characteristics here. Thanks to the very wide surf zone, it is moderately safe to swim in the inner surf zone on the bar, but it is advised that swimmers do not venture

The effects of the sea are visible in oddly shaped rocks at Remarkable Rocks National Park

beyond the first line of breakers as strong currents occupy the trough between the sand bars. **Amenities:** parking; toilets. **Best for:** surfing; walking. ⊠ *Esplanade, Middleton.*

🏃 Activities

BICYCLING
Encounter Bikeway

BICYCLING | For cycling enthusiasts, there's Encounter Bikeway, a paved track that runs 30 km (19 miles) from the Bluff along a scenic coastal route to Laffin Point (east of Goolwa). Almost flat, the bikeway is suitable for riders of most ages and experience levels. ■TIP→ **When the Cockle Train is operating the Encounter Bikeway users can combine their trip with a journey on the train, traveling one-way on the bike path and returning on the train.** ⊠ *Encounter Bikeway* ⊕ *holidayatvictorharbor.com.au.*

Kingscote

121 km (75 miles) southwest of Adelaide

Kangaroo Island's largest town, Kingscote is a good base for exploring. Reeves Point, at the town's northern end is where South Australia's colonial history began. Settlers landed here in 1836 and established the first official town in the new colony. Little remains of the original settlement except Hope Cottage, now a small museum, several graves, and a huge, twisted mulberry tree that grew from a cutting the settlers brought from England—locals still use the fruit to make jam. Today American River, about halfway between Kingscote and Penneshaw, the island's second-largest town, is another accommodation and restaurant hub.

ESSENTIALS
VISITOR INFORMATION
Department of Environment, Water and Natural Resources Office
The Kangaroo Island Pass (A$74.50, A$197 families) is available from any

National Parks and Wildlife Park Pass agent, including various visitors centers and resource centers, or from the Department of Environment, Water and Natural Resources Office. The pass covers a selection of guided tours and park entry fees and is valid for a year. ⊠ *Natural Resources Centre Kangaroo Island, 37 Dauncey St.* ☎ *08/8553–4444* ⊕ *www.parks.sa.gov.au/book-and-pay/ parks-passes/kangaroo-island-tour-pass.*

🛏 Hotels

Kangaroo Island Bayview Villas

$$ | **RENTAL** | **FAMILY** | Located on a hillside overlooking Nepean Bay and the town of Kingscote, these bayview villas are fully equipped, self-contained-style accommodations with a private patio and barbecue facilities. **Pros:** panoramic views; modern and spacious; good for groups and/or families. **Cons:** single-night surcharge is included for one-night stays; no on-site dining; lacks the assistance of a hotel concierge. $ *Rooms from: A$199* ⊠ *20 Reeves St.* ☎ *08/8553–0149* ⊕ *www.bayview-villas. com.au* ⊋ *4 rooms* ⦿ *No meals.*

Mercure Kangaroo Island Lodge

$$$ | **RESORT** | Facing beautiful Eastern Cove at American River, the island's oldest resort, located 39 km (24 miles) southeast of Kingscote, has rooms that overlook open water or the salt-water pool; the most attractive are the "waterview" rooms, which have mud-brick walls, warm terra-cotta tones, and king-size beds. **Pros:** set in beautiful and peaceful surroundings; pool on-site; chic bar/lounge area for sipping cocktails and wine. **Cons:** dated rooms and basic breakfast; part of a hotel chain, so not as much local charm; not many rooms equipped for families. $ *Rooms from: A$225* ⊠ *Scenic Dr., American River* ☎ *08/8553– 7053, 1800/355581* ⊕ *www.kilodge.com. au* ⊋ *38 rooms* ⦿ *No meals.*

Ozone Hotel

$ | **HOTEL** | The original Victorian facade on this two-story 1920s hotel is contrasted

by modern and spacious rooms that overlook Nepean Bay, and lots of windows, flat-screen TVs, vibrant modern artworks, and some in-room whirlpool tubs make the suites, town houses, and Penthouse Apartments among the island's best. **Pros:** across the street from the waterfront; friendly staff; hot and cold buffet breakfast served seven days a week. **Cons:** older rooms are old-fashioned, as is the breakfast; modern design lacks charisma; gambling on premises might be a no-go for some people. $ *Rooms from: A$159* ⊠ *Commercial St.* ☎ *08/8553–2011, 1800/083133* ⊕ *www. auroraresorts.com.au* ⊋ *75 rooms* ⦿ *All meals.*

Wanderers Rest

$$$ | **B&B/INN** | Delightful local artworks dot the walls in this country inn's stylish units, all of which have king-size beds. **Pros:** simple, high-quality accommodations with stunning views; wake up to birdsong; wood fire in the restaurant on cool evenings. **Cons:** kids under 10 aren't allowed; tours and extras quickly add up; rooms aren't particularly unique in design. $ *Rooms from: A$246* ⊠ *Bayview Rd. , Lot 2, American River* ☎ *08/8553–7140* ⊕ *www.wanderersrest. com.au* ⊋ *8 suites* ⦿ *Free Breakfast.*

Penneshaw

62 km (39 miles) east of Kingscote.

This tiny ferry port once had a huge population of penguins—locals would complain about the birds burrowing in their gardens, and you'd often see them around town after dark—but sadly, the colony's numbers have decreased in recent years due to an increased number of seals (and domestic cats and dogs) who prey on the flightless birds. You can still see some on nocturnal tours, but other reasons to visit Penneshaw include a gorgeous shoreline, views of spectacularly blue water, and rolling green hills.

Exploring Kangaroo Island

Because Kangaroo Island's main attractions are widely scattered, you can see them best on a guided tour or by car. The main roads form a paved loop, which branches off to such major sites as Seal Bay and Admirals Arch and Remarkable Rocks in Flinders Chase National Park. Stretches of unpaved road lead to lighthouses at Cape Borda and Cape Willoughby, South Australia's oldest. Roads to the island's northern beaches, bays, and camping areas are also unpaved.

Getting to Kangaroo Island

REX/Regional Express (☎ 13–1713 ⊕ www.regionalexpress.com.au) flies two times daily between Adelaide and Kingscote, Kangaroo Island's main airport. Flights to the island take about 30 minutes.

SeaLink ferries (☎ 13–1301 ⊕ www.sealink.com.au) allow access for cars through Penneshaw from Cape Jervis, at the tip of the Fleurieu Peninsula, a two-hour drive from Adelaide. There are four daily sailings each way, with additional crossings at peak times. SeaLink operates the vehicular passenger ferry *Sea Lion 2000* and *Spirit of Kangaroo Island*, a designated freight boat with passenger facilities. Ferries are the favored means of transportation between the island and the mainland, and reservations are necessary.

Kangaroo Island Tours

Adelaide Sightseeing. Expert local guides will bring you to all the wonderful Kangaroo Island attractions including unique highlights like Remarkable Rocks, Admirals Arch, and Little Sahara. One- and two-day tours with various themes are offered, from A$296 per person and up. ⊠ 85 *Franklin St., City Center* ☎ 1300/769762 ⊕ *www.adelaidesightseeing.com.au/kangaroo-island.*

Exceptional Kangaroo Island. Quality four-wheel-drive and bushwalking tours with a focus on sustainable wildlife encounters in the wild and featuring local food served picnic style. Guides lead guests in conversation on Kangaroo Island's rich history, unique ecology and contemporary lifestyle. Tailor-made itineraries can also be arranged. ☎ 08/8553–9119 ⊕ *www.exceptionalkangarooisland.com* 🖃 *From A$425.*

Kangaroo Island Odysseys. Luxury four-wheel-drive nature tours from one to three days: expect lots of wildlife and great food. Tours enter normally restricted areas of the island's national parks for undisturbed nature. ☎ 08/8553–0386 ⊕ *www.kangarooislandodysseys.com.au* 🖃 *From A$440.*

Kangaroo Island Wilderness Tours. Personalized four-wheel-drive wilderness tours from one to four days, helmed by local guides. Think: spectacular scenery, penguin feedings, and memorable meals and lodgings. ☎ 08/8559–5033 ⊕ *www.wilderness-tours.com.au* 🖃 *From A$451.*

SeaLink Kangaroo Island. SeaLink Kangaroo Island operates one-day (A$269) bus tours of the island, departing from Adelaide, in conjunction with the ferry service from Cape Jervis. They also can arrange fishing and self-drive tours and extended packages. ⊠ 440 *King William St., Adelaide* ☎ 13–1301 ⊕ *www.sealink.com.au* 🖃 *From A$157.*

ESSENTIALS

VISITOR INFORMATION Kangaroo Island Gateway Visitor Information Centre. ✉ *Howard Dr.* ☎ *1800/8553–1185* 🌐 *www.tourkangarooisland.com.au.*

Sights

Penneshaw Penguin Centre

NATURE PRESERVE | FAMILY | There are now only around 15 pairs of the delightful little (formally called fairy) penguins in the colony here at Penneshaw. From the indoor interpretive center, where you can read about bird activity—including mating, nesting, and feeding—a boardwalk leads to a viewing platform above rocks and sand riddled with burrows. Because the penguins spend most of the day fishing at sea or inside their burrows, the best viewing is after sunset. The informative guided tour starts with a talk and video at the center. Tours currently leave from the center at 6:30 pm and 7:30 pm daily except Wednesday and Thursday. You might see penguins waddling ashore, chicks emerging from their burrows to feed, or scruffy adults molting. Although sometimes you may not see any at all. Bookings essential. ✉ *Middle Terr. at Bay Terr.* ☎ *08/8553–7407* 🌐 *www.users.on.net/~nickpike/penguins.html* 🎟 *Guided tours A$13* ⏰ *Closed Feb. 1–21.*

Sunset Winery

WINERY/DISTILLERY | Sip smooth Chardonnay while overlooking Eastern Cove at this calm, cool, and pristine place among Kangaroo Island's thriving wine industry. You can sample wines at the cellar door, and opt for the shareable Savoury Platter: a selection of Kangaroo Island and regional cheeses, KI Source Relish, South Rock Salami, local olives, crackers, and more. Alternately, try a Dukkah Plate from the Fleurieu, served with local Wild olive oil and delicious local bread. ✉ *4564 Hog Bay Rd.* ☎ *08/8553–1378.*

Beaches

Island Beach

BEACH—SIGHT | Known locally as Millionaires' Row for its fabulous real estate, Island Beach is the quintessential beach holiday location. Framed by dense bushland, the sandy beach is secluded, stretches almost as far as the eye can see, and provides very safe swimming. Walking along the coast toward American River yields plenty of bird-watching opportunities. **Amenities:** food and drink; parking. **Best for:** solitude; swimming; walking. ✉ *Island Beach* ✥ *Off Island Beach Rd.*

Restaurants

Fish of Penneshaw

$$ | SEAFOOD | At this tiny shop renowned for its fish-and-chips and other affordable local seafood dishes, you can get your food to go, eat it at the counter, or enjoy it with a glass of wine in the seating area next door. Choose your fish—whiting, John Dory, garfish—from the blackboard menu and have it beer-battered, crumbed, or grilled, or get a paper-wrapped parcel of scallops, prawns, lobster, and oysters (in season) shucked to order. **Known for:** elevated fish and chips; parcel of scallops; soothing views. [$] *Average main: A$25* ✉ *43 North Terr.* ☎ *08/8553–1177 Fish of Penneshaw, 08/8553–7406 2 Birds & A Squid* 🌐 *www.2birds1squid.com/fish-of-penneshaw* 💳 *No credit cards* ⏰ *Closed May–mid-Oct. No lunch.*

Hotels

Kangaroo Island Seafront Resort

$$ | HOTEL | This hotel has an ideal position near the ferry terminal and overlooking Penneshaw Bay. You can choose an ocean-view room or stay amid tropical gardens in freestanding chalets. **Pros:** steps away from ferry terminal and penguin viewing; free Wi-Fi; nice views. **Cons:**

"Naptime on the beach at Kangaroo Island" —photo by lstarr, Fodors.com member

older parts of the hotel are showing their age; no air-conditioning in rooms; quite no-frills in terms of design and decor. [$] *Rooms from: A$187* ✉ *49 North Terr.* ☎ *08/8553–1028, 1800/624624* 🌐 *www.seafront.com.au* 🛏 *18 rooms* 🍴 *Free Breakfast.*

Seal Bay Conservation Park

60 km (37 miles) southwest of Kingscote via South Coast Rd.

There are no seals in Seal Bay, but a visit to Seal Bay is a highlight of most people's time on Kangaroo Island—it's one of the only places in the world where you can walk along a beach crowded with wild sea lions. The endangered Australian sea lion is one of the rarest species in the world, Seal Bay is home to around 1,000—the misleading name is thanks to whalers who couldn't tell the difference between seals and sea lions (the latter have ear flaps and can use their back flippers to "walk" on land, unlike seals). The tours here are some of the best close-up animal encounters of their kind.

Sights

★ Seal Bay Conservation Park

NATURE PRESERVE | FAMILY | This top Kangaroo Island attraction gives you the chance to visit one of the state's largest Australian sea lion colonies. About 300 animals usually lounge on the beach, except on stormy days, when they shelter in the dunes. You can only visit the beach, and get surprisingly close to females, pups, and bulls, on a 45-minute tour with an interpretive officer; otherwise, you can follow the self-guided boardwalk to a lookout over the sand. **■ TIP→ Two-hour twilight tours are only available during South Australian daylight saving times and visitors must call ahead.** The park visitor center has fun and educational displays, and a touch table covered in sea-lion skins and bones. There is also a souvenir shop. ✉ *Seal Bay Conservation Park*

✢ *End of Seal Bay Rd.* ☎ *08/8553–4463* ⊕ *www.environment.sa.gov.au/sealbay/ home* ✉ *From A\$16.*

 Beaches

Hanson Bay

BEACH—SIGHT | This beach is off the beaten path. A narrow, winding, unsealed road off South Coast Road, 46 km (29 miles) west of Seal Bay Road, ends at this perfect little sandy cove. Rocky head-lands on either side protect the gently sloping beach so swimming is safe. To the east are several secluded beaches; these are more exposed, though, and riptides make swimming dangerous. **Amenities:** parking; toilets. **Best for:** surf-ing; swimming; walking. ✉ *West River Rd., off South Coast Rd., Karatta.*

Flinders Chase National Park

102 km (64 miles) west of Kingscote.

Some of Australia's most beautiful coast-al scenery is in Flinders Chase National Park on Kangaroo Island.

⊙ Sights

★ **Flinders Chase National Park**

NATIONAL/STATE PARK | The effects of seas crashing mercilessly onto Australia's southern coast are visible in the oddly shaped rocks on the island's shores. A limestone promontory was carved from beneath at Cape du Couedic on the southwestern coast, producing what is known as **Admiral's Arch.** From the board-walk you can see the New Zealand fur seals that have colonized the area around the rock formation. About 4 km (2½ miles) farther east are the aptly named **Remark-able Rocks,** huge, fantastically shaped boulders balanced precariously on the promontory of Kirkpatrick Point. This is a great place to watch the sun set or rise.

How Remarkable ⊙

Balanced precariously on the promontory of Kirkpatrick Point in Flinders Chase National Park, the Remarkable Rocks are aptly named. Sitting with your back against one of these fantastically shaped boulders is the best way to view sunset or sunrise on Kangaroo Island.

Much of Kangaroo Island has been cul-tivated since settlement, but after being declared a national treasure in 1919, a huge area of original vegetation has been protected in Flinders Chase and the park has several 1½-km to 9-km (1-mile to 5½-mile) loop walking trails, which take one to three hours to complete. The trails meander along the rivers to the coast, passing mallee scrub and sugar gum for-ests, and explore the rugged shoreline. The 4-km (2½-mile) Snake Lagoon Hike follows Rocky River over and through a series of broad rocky terraces to the remote sandy beach where it meets the sea. The sign warning of freak waves is not just for show.

The park is on the island's western end, bounded by the Playford and West End highways. The state-of-the-art visitor center, open daily 9–5, is the largest National Parks and Wildlife office. Displays and touch screens explore the park's history and the different habitats and wildlife in Flinders Chase. The center provides park entry tickets and camping permits, and books stays at the Heritage cabins. A shop sells souvenirs and provi-sions, and there is also a café. ✉ *South Coast Rd.* ⊕ *www.environment.sa.gov.au* ✉ *From A\$11.*

Lots of Remarkable Rocks, Flinders Chase National Park

Hotels

Kangaroo Island Wilderness Retreat
$$ | **RESORT** | With wallabies and possums treating the grounds as their own domain, this eco-friendly retreat is everything a wildlife-loving traveler could want. **Pros:** wonderful experience for animal lovers; free Internet access and DVDs; breakfast included. **Cons:** only two time slots for dinner; basic rooms might disappoint city slickers; restaurant stocks only Kangaroo Island wines. [$] *Rooms from: A$190* ✉ *1 South Coast Rd.* ☎ *08/8559–7275* 🌐 *www.kiwr.com* 🛏 *31 rooms* 🍴 *All meals.*

★ Southern Ocean Lodge
$$$$ | **HOTEL** | This truly remarkable hotel near the water might be the highlight of your trip—if money is no object. **Pros:** superb fine dining restaurant; simple but stunning decor exudes luxury and class; lounge and dining with panoramic view. **Cons:** if you have to ask the price, you can't afford this place; sophisticated surroundings are not really suitable for children, though kids over six years are welcome; not close to any town. [$] *Rooms from: A$1100* ✉ *Hanson Bay Rd., Kingscote* ☎ *08/8559–7347* 🌐 *www.southernoceanlodge.com.au* 🛏 *21 suites* 🍴 *All-inclusive.*

Activities

FISHING

Fishing is excellent on Kangaroo Island's beaches, bays, and rivers. The island's deep-sea fishing fleet holds several world records for tuna. No permit is required for recreational fishing, but minimum lengths and bag limits apply. You can pick up a fishing guide from the information center in Penneshaw.

Turner Fuel
FISHING | This spot sells fishing tackle and bait. ✉ *26 Telegraph Rd., Kingscote* ☎ *08/8553–2725.*

Coober Pedy

850 km (527 miles) northwest of Adelaide.

Known as much for the way most of its 1,700 inhabitants live—underground in dugouts gouged into the hills to escape the relentless heat—as for its opal riches, Coober Pedy is arguably Australia's most singular place. The town is ringed by mullock heaps, pyramids of rock, and sand left over after mine shafts are dug.

Opals are Coober Pedy's reason for existence. Australia has 95% of the world's opal deposits, and Coober Pedy has the bulk of that wealth; this is the world's richest opal field.

Coober Pedy is a brick-and-corrugated-iron settlement propped unceremoniously on a scarred desert landscape. It's a town built for efficiency, not beauty. However, its ugliness has a kind of bizarre appeal. There's a feeling that you're in the last lawless outpost in the modern world, helped in no small part by the local film lore—*Priscilla Queen of the Desert, Pitch Black, Kangaroo Jack,* and *Mad Max 3* were filmed here. Once you go off the main street, you get an immediate sense of the apocalyptic.

GETTING HERE AND AROUND

REX/Regional Express Airlines flies direct to Coober Pedy from Adelaide Sunday through Friday. Because it's the only public carrier flying to Coober Pedy, prices are sometimes steep. The airport is open only when a flight is arriving or departing. At other times, contact the Desert Cave Hotel (⇨ *see Hotels*).

Greyhound Australia buses leave Adelaide's Central Bus Station for Coober Pedy daily. Tickets for the 12-hour overnight ride can cost A$148–A$180 each way.

The main road to Coober Pedy is the Sturt Highway from Adelaide, 850 km (527 miles) to the south. Alice Springs is 700 km (434 miles) north of Coober Pedy. The drive from Adelaide to Coober Pedy takes about nine hours. From Alice Springs it's about seven hours.

A rental car enables you to see what lies beyond Hutchison Street, but an organized tour is a better way to do so. Thrifty and Budget have rental-car outlets in Coober Pedy. Although some roads are unpaved—those to the Breakaways and the Dog Fence, for example—surfaces are generally suitable for conventional vehicles. Check on road conditions with the police if there has been substantial rain.

The most interesting route to Flinders Ranges National Park from Adelaide takes you north through the Clare Valley vineyards and Burra's copper-mining villages. For a more direct journey to Wilpena Pound, follow the Princes Highway (A1) north to Port Augusta, and then head east toward Quorn and Hawker. A four-wheel-drive vehicle is highly recommended for traveling on the many gravel roads around the national park.

TRANSPORTATION Coober Pedy Airport. ⊠ *Airport Rd., off Stuart Hwy., 2 km (1 mile) north of town* ☎ *08/8672–5688* **Greyhound Australia.** ⊠ *Hutchinson St.* ☎ *1800/801294, 1300/4739–46863* ⊕ *www.greyhound.com.au* **REX/Regional Express.** ☎ *13–1713* ⊕ *www.rex.com.au.*

ESSENTIALS
VISITOR INFORMATION Coober Pedy Tourist Information Centre. ⊠ *Coober Pedy District Council Bldg., Hutchison St., Lot 773* ☎ *1800/637076* ⊕ *www.cooberpedy. sa.gov.au.*

◉ Sights

Fossicking or searching for opal gemstones—locally called noodling—requires no permit at the Jewellers Shop mining area at the edge of town. ⚠ **Take care in unmarked areas, and always watch your step, as the area is littered with abandoned** opal mines down which you might fall. (Working mines are off-limits to visitors.)

Although most of Coober Pedy's devotions are decidedly material in nature, the town does have its share of spiritual houses of worship. In keeping with the town's layout, they, too, are underground. **St. Peter and St. Paul's Catholic Church** is a National Heritage–listed building, and the Anglican **Catacomb Church** is notable for its altar fashioned from a windlass (a winch) and lectern made from a log of mulga wood. The **Serbian Orthodox Church** is striking, with its scalloped ceiling, rock-carved icons, and brilliant stained-glass windows.

Breakaways

SCENIC DRIVE | A striking series of buttes and jagged hills centered on the Moon Plain is reminiscent of the American West. There are fossils and patches of petrified forest in this strange landscape, which has appealed to makers of apocalyptic films. *Mad Max 3—Beyond Thunderdome* was filmed here, as was *Ground Zero.* The scenery is especially evocative early in the morning or at sunset. The area is home to almost 60 native flora species and a variety of wildlife, including red kangaroos, euro, echidna, numerous bird species, and the fat-tailed dunnart (a mouselike marsupial). The Breakaways area is 30 km (19 miles) northeast of Coober Pedy. ■TIP→ Permits to explore the area cost A$10 per vehicle and can be purchased at the Coober Pedy Tourist Information Centre in the District Council Office on Hutchinson Street. ⊠ *Coober Pedy* ✛ *Off Stuart Hwy. 33 km (20 miles) north of Coober Pedy* ⛁ *Permits A$10 per vehicle.*

★ Mail Run Tour

TOUR—SIGHT | This 12-hour, 600-km (372-mile) tour through the Outback (A$195) is one of the most unusual experiences anywhere, with stops at outback cattle stations, bush pubs, and the world's longest man-made structure, the Dingo Fence. Tours (maximum of four people

per tour; price is per person) depart Monday and Thursday at 8:45 am from Underground Books on Post Office Hill Road. ⊠ *Post Office Hill Rd., Lot 374* ☎ *08/8672–5226, 1800/069911* ⊕ *www. mailruntour.com* ⛁ *A$295.*

Old Timers Mine

MUSEUM | FAMILY | This is a genuine opal mine turned into a museum. Two underground houses, furnished in 1920s and 1980s styles, are part of the complex, where mining memorabilia is exhibited in an extensive network of hand-dug tunnels and shafts. You can also watch demonstrations of opal-mining machines several times throughout the day. Tours are self-guided. ⊠ *Crowders Gully Rd., near Umoona Rd.* ☎ *08/8672–5555* ⛁ *A$15.*

★ Umoona Opal Mine & Museum

MUSEUM | This is an enormous underground complex with an original mine, a noteworthy video on the history of opal mining, an Aboriginal Interpretive Center, and replications of underground bunk camping and cooking facilities. Learn about the story of opal, different types and qualities of opal, examples of hand-dug and modern dugouts, and the experience of living underground. Guided tours of the mine are available at 10, 2, and 4 daily. There is also an opal shop. ⊠ *14 Hutchison St.* ☎ *08/8672–5288* ⊕ *www. umoonaopalmine.com.au* ⛁ *$12.*

🍴 Restaurants

Italo-Australian Miners Club

$ | ITALIAN | Adorned with photographs from a bygone era, this casual eatery opened in 1964 during the height of opal mining and is a popular spot for viewing the sunset, watching a rugby game on TV, and unwinding at the end of a day of sightseeing. Comforting dishes like lasagna are served as are beer and Australian wine. **Known for:** historical feeling; no-frills and affordable drinking and eating; generous portions. ⑨ *Average main:*

A$20 ✉ Italian Club Rd. ☎ 08/8672–5101 🕙 Closed Sun.

Nostimo Pizza

$$ | **PIZZA** | Locals swear that the pizzas at the popular Stuart Range outback resort and caravan park are among Australia's best—maybe, maybe not, but they are certainly the best in Coober Pedy. The toppings combinations can be classic, creative, or gourmet, such as the Noon (with tomato, mushrooms, and onions) and the Garlic Prawn (with basil pesto and semidried tomatoes). **Known for:** local social hub; gluten-free pizza option; Wednesday happy hour. 💲 *Average main: A$25 ✉ Stuart Hwy. at Hutchison St. ☎ 08/8672–5179, 1800/067787 ⊕ www.stuartrangeoutbackresort.com.au/nostimo-pizza 🕙 No lunch.*

🛏 Hotels

★ Desert Cave Hotel

$$$ | **HOTEL** | This underground hotel presents a contemporary, blocky face to the desert town. **Pros:** unique place to stay; pool is welcome relief in the heat; peaceful underground rooms. **Cons:** not for the claustrophobic; overpriced for the novelty; can be pushy with various tour offerings. 💲 *Rooms from: A$259 ✉ Hutchison St. at Post Office Hill Rd., Lot 1 ☎ 08/8672–5688 ⊕ www.desertcave.com.au 🛏 50 rooms 🍴 No meals.*

The Underground Motel

$ | **HOTEL** | The Breakaways sometimes seem close enough to touch at this hilltop motel, where you can lounge on a veranda watching the sun set on the rock formations 30 km (19 miles) across the desert. **Pros:** lovely patio to sit out on and watch the stars; very helpful owners; complimentary continental breakfast. **Cons:** slightly out of town, which in the heat is a disadvantage; rooms are a little dated; can be noisy on windy days on account of the air shaft. 💲 *Rooms from: A$135 ✉ 1185 Catacomb*

Rd. ☎ 08/8672–5324 ⊕ www.theundergroundmotel.com.au 🛏 8 rooms 🍴 Free Breakfast.

🛍 Shopping

Underground Books

BOOKS/STATIONERY | There's an excellent selection of reading material, maps, arts, and crafts, but the best buy is a postcard by local photographer Peter Caust, who captures the essence of the desert landscape. This is also the booking office for the Coober Pedy–Oodnadatta Mail Run Tour. ✉ *Post Office Hill Rd., Lot 374 ☎ 08/8672–5558.*

Ikara-Flinders Ranges National Park

690 km (430 miles) southeast of Coober Pedy, 460 km (285 miles) northeast of Adelaide.

Extending north from Spencer Gulf, the Flinders Ranges mountain chain includes one of Australia's most impressive Outback parks—the 367-square-mile Ikara–Flinders Ranges National Park. Once the bed of an ancient sea, these dry, folded, and cracked mountains and deep valleys today are covered by cypress pine and casuarina, and the creeks are lined with river red gums. The area is utterly fascinating—for geologists, for bird-watchers, for photographers, and for anyone else who revels in wild, raw scenery and exotic plant and animal life.

ESSENTIALS

VISITOR INFORMATION

Wilpena Pound Visitor Centre

A mud-brick visitor center, part of the Wilpena Pound Resort, has information about hiking trails and campsites within the park. ✉ *1 Wilpena Rd., Hawker ☎ 08/8648–0048 ⊕ www.environment.sa.gov.au.*

Sights

Ikara-Flinders Ranges National Park

NATIONAL/STATE PARK | The numerous steep trails make the Flinders Ranges ideal for bushwalking, even though the park has few amenities. Water in this region is scarce, and should be carried at all times. The best time for walking is during the relatively cool months between April and October. This is also the wettest time of year, so you should be prepared for rain. Wildflowers, including the spectacular Sturt's desert pea, are abundant between September and late October.

The park's most spectacular walking trail leads to the summit of 3,840-foot **St. Mary's Peak,** the highest point on the Pound's rim and South Australia's second-tallest peak. The more scenic of the two routes to the top is the outside trail (15-km [9-mile] return); give yourself a full day to get up and back. The midsection of the ascent is steep and strenuous, but views from the summit—including the distant white glitter of the salt flats on Lake Frome—make the climb worthwhile. ✉ *Hawker* ✥ *End of Wilpena Rd.* ☎ *08/8648–0048* 🎟 *A$10 entry fee per vehicle.*

Wilpena Pound

NATURE SITE | The scenic center of the Flinders Ranges is the crater-like Wilpena Pound, an 80-square-km (31-square-mile) bowl ringed by hills that curve gently upward, only to fall away from the rims of sheer cliffs. The only entrance to the Pound is a narrow cleft through which Wilpena Creek sometimes runs. The best way to see it is from above—scenic flights are available at Wilpena Pound Resort (from A$169) and are well worth the splurge. ✉ *Wilpena Rd., Hawker* 🌐 *www.wilpenapound.com.au.*

Hotels

★ **Wilpena Pound Resort**

$$$ | **RESORT** | You couldn't ask for a more idyllic and civilized nature outpost than this popular resort at the entrance to Wilpena Pound. **Pros:** quiet and peaceful rooms; perfect for animal lovers; glamping done right. **Cons:** campsites can be overrun with school groups; permanent tents are overpriced; necessities are a drive away. [$] *Rooms from: A$227* ✉ *1 Wilpena Rd., Hawker* ✥ *156 km (97 miles) off Princes Hwy. via town of Hawker* ☎ *08/8648–0004* 🌐 *www.wilpenapound.com.au* 🛏 *121 rooms* 🍴 *No meals.*

Chapter 11

THE OUTBACK

Updated by
Kaeli Conforti

◉ Sights	🍴 Restaurants	🛏 Hotels	💼 Shopping	🍸 Nightlife
★★★★★	★★★☆☆	★★★☆☆	★☆☆☆☆	★★☆☆☆

WELCOME TO THE OUTBACK

TOP REASONS TO GO

★ **Red Heart:** Watching the sun rise and set at Uluru (Ayers Rock) is an unforgettable, once-in-a-lifetime experience.

★ **Old Culture:** The Red Centre, Top End, and the Kimberley are the best places to encounter and learn about one of the oldest cultures in the world, that of Australia's Aboriginal people.

★ **National Parks:** With spectacular terrain and one-of-a-kind plant and animal species, rugged national parks tell the story of Australia's age-old landforms, especially across the gorge-pocked Kimberley region.

★ **Wild Rivers:** The waterways and billabongs of the Top End teem with wildlife, including saltwater crocodiles and a multitude of birdlife.

★ **Cable Beach:** It may be touristy, but riding a camel into the sunset on one of Australia's most beautiful beaches is hard to resist.

Big, vast, expansive, huge—whichever way you cut it, the Outback is daunting. This, in many respects, is the "real Australia" as you imagine it—remote, mostly uninhabited, the landscape ground down over millennia.

Getting around by road will absorb days, if not weeks, but fortunately air services can cut the travel times between the gems of this vast area—the Red Centre, the Top End, and the Kimberley—to hours not days.

1 Alice Springs. Tourist center in the middle of the desert.

2 East and West MacDonnell Ranges. Eye-catching scenery and Aboriginal rock art.

3 Watarrka National Park (Kings Canyon). Home to Kings Canyon.

4 Uluru–Kata Tjuta National Park. Iconic and sacred rock formations.

5 Darwin. City base to explore Top End.

6 Kakadu National Park. Unspoiled wilderness and ancient Aboriginal art.

7 Katherine Gorge. Thirteen gorges best explored by canoe.

8 Kununurra. Gateway to East Kimberley.

9 Purnululu (Bungle Bungle) National Park. One of the most striking geological landmarks in W.A.

10 Danggu Geikie Gorge National Park. Spectacular waterway with weathered cliffs.

11 Broome. Home to Cable Beach and pearl farms.

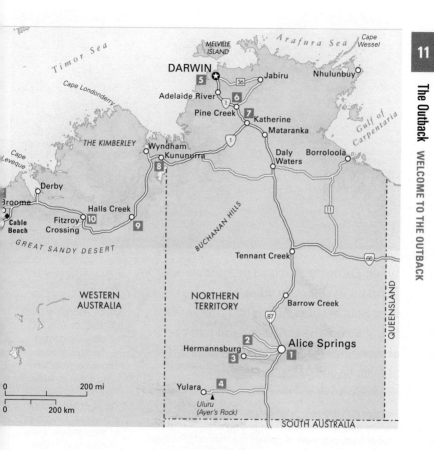

ABORIGINAL CULTURE

When Europeans arrived to establish a permanent colony in what was to become New South Wales, Aboriginal people were living across the continent and had been, archaeologists and geneticists believe, for at least 60,000 years.

Perhaps 600 different "clan groups" or "nations"—each with its own distinctive culture and beliefs—greeted the new settlers in a clash of civilizations that remains largely unresolved today. Despite the efforts of governments of all persuasions and society at large, Aboriginal people by all measures—economic, health, social, education— remain an underprivileged group.

But Aboriginal culture as expressed in oral tradition, art, and lifestyle and by sacred sites such as Uluru, is of growing interest to travelers. Experiences range from taking organized tours to viewing dance performances, and from shopping for traditional artifacts and art, to visiting Aboriginal land to see what the daily lives are like for the people who live there. Tourism here represents an important source of income, ensuring that local communities prosper and that their heritage is preserved.

COMMUNITY VALUES

On an Aboriginal-guided tour, you may be officially welcomed to the land by an Aboriginal elder via a ritual that is called Welcome to Country. Pay attention and join in if asked; it is a sign of good manners and respect to your local hosts.

There were once strict rules about eye contact so you may find that some people won't make eye contact with you. This, or lowering the eyes, are two actions that are a show of respect toward older people.

SACRED SITES

Uluru's (Ayers Rock) traditional owners, the Anangu people, believe they are direct descendants of the beings—which include a python, an emu, a blue-tongue lizard, and a poisonous snake—who formed the land and its physical features during the Tjukurpa (the "Dreamtime," or creation period). Uluru is one of the world's largest monoliths, though such a classification belies the otherworldly, spiritual energy surrounding it.

Kakadu National Park contains some of the best ancient rock art accessible to visitors in Australia. The Anbangbang Gallery features a frieze of Aboriginal rock painting dating back thousands of years, and among the six galleries at Ubirr there is a 49-foot frieze of X-ray paintings depicting animals, birds, and fish. Warradjan Aboriginal Cultural Centre's large display, developed by the local Bininj/Mungguy people, provides detailed information about culture in Kakadu.

Purnululu National Park Although the Bungle Bungle Range was extensively used by Aboriginal people during the wet season, when plant and animal life was abundant, few Europeans knew of its existence until the mid-1980s. The area is rich in Aboriginal rock art, and is home to many burial sites, although these are not typically open to visitors.

Farther west in the **Kimberley Region** the pearling town of **Broome** is the starting point for many adventure tours into the most remote sections of the Outback along the legendary Gibb River Road, as well as for visits to Aboriginal communities like Bardi Creek, Biridu Community, and One Arm Point Community with local Aboriginal guides. Danggu Geikie Gorge, Windjana Gorge, and Tunnel Creek combine wilderness scenery with indigenous rock art, lifestyles, and stories from the Dreamtime.

11

The Outback ABORIGINAL CULTURE

TOP SIGHTS

By far the best way to experience Aboriginal culture is on foot with an experienced guide, though at some national parks, interpretive centers, signage, and—occasionally—self-guided audio equipment mean you can visit on your own. Going about it on foot generally requires a level of fitness and surefootedness for trails and pathways; even the best locations are uneven and stony, and can include steep climbs. Boats provide an easier alternative—at Danggu Geikie Gorge and Kakadu guided tours offered along the waterways include information about Aboriginal culture.

From Broome, four-wheel-drive safaris can get you into remote Aboriginal communities where you can meet the locals and listen to campfire stories.

If mobility is an issue, there are easily accessible interpretive centers at Uluru and Kakadu national parks with extensive displays describing traditional and contemporary Aboriginal life.

Few visitors who explore Australia's remote Red Centre and wild Top End are left unmoved by the stark, expansive beauty of the landscape. The Outback's amazing World Heritage national parks, many on the ancestral homelands of the traditional indigenous owners, are home to some of Australia's most fascinating and iconic natural attractions, such as Uluru (Ayers Rock), the magnificent Bungle Bungles, and the vast bird-filled wetlands and raging waterfalls of Kakadu. The Outback contains deeply carved rock canyons, deserts with unending horizons, and prolific wildlife. It is Australia at its wildest, rawest, and most sublime, and it's a landscape that will sear itself onto your memory forever.

The Top End of Australia is a geographic description—but it's also a state of mind. Isolated from the rest of Australia by thousands of miles of desert and lonely scrubland, Top Enders are different and proud of it, making the most of their isolation with a strongly independent and individualistic attitude. The region is a melting pot of cultures and traditions. Darwin and Broome—closer geographically to the cities of Southeast Asia than to any Australian counterparts—host the nation's most racially diverse populations with a multicultural cast of charaters sharing a relaxed, tropical lifestyle.

In the west, the Kimberley offers some of the most dramatic landscapes in Australia. A land of rugged ranges and vast cattle stations, this is still the frontier, a place even few Australians get to see. Like Top Enders, the people of the region see themselves as living in a land apart from the rest of the nation, and it's easy to see why: climate extremes, inaccessibility of the landscape, and great distances combine to make the Kimberley one of the world's few uniquely unpeopled spaces.

For thousands of years, this area of northern and central Australia has been home to Aboriginal communities that have undiminished ties to the land. Stunning examples of ancient rock art remain—on cliffs, in hidden valleys, and in city art galleries and cooperative art centers in remote communities. Aboriginal artwork has now moved into Australia's mainstream art movement, and some expensive canvases by local artists decorate galleries, homes, and corporate boardrooms around the world. But there is more to Aboriginal culture than art, and there is no better place to try and understand it than here, on a guided tour of some of the country's most spiritually significant sites.

MAJOR REGIONS

Red Centre has as its primary areas of interest **Alice Springs,** which is flanked by the intriguing **East and West MacDonnell Ranges,** with their cliffs and gorges; **Watarrka National Park (Kings Canyon)**; and **Uluru–Kata Tjuta National Park**, home to Uluru (pronounced *oo*-loo- *roo* and also called Ayers Rock) and Kata Tjuta (*ka*-ta *tchoo*-ta and also known as The Olgas). Uluru, that magnificent stone monolith rising from the plains, is one of Australia's iconic images and is the main reason people visit the Red Centre. Unless you have more than three days, focus on only one of these Red Centre areas.

The **Top End** of Australia packs in some of the world's great natural environments, and with few people to crowd the views. From **Arnhem Land** in the east—home to remote Aboriginal people—to the lush tropical city of **Darwin,** the Top End offers some of the most dramatic landscapes in Australia, along with modern and ancient Aboriginal art and locals with a definite individualistic attitude. It's a land of rugged ranges and tropical wetlands, of vast cattle stations and wonderful national parks, including **Kakadu National Park,** a wilderness area that is one of Australia's natural jewels and the reason many people come to this part of Australia. The **Katherine Gorge** is also here.

Look no further than the **Kimberley** for a genuine Outback experience. Perched on the northwestern hump of Western Australia only half as far from Indonesia as it is from Sydney, the Kimberley remains a frontier of sorts, remote and with few facilities and people (only 45,000 people living in an area of 423,517 square km [163,521 square miles]). The region contains such spectacular national parks as **Kununurra,** a good base for exploring Mirima National Park; **Purnululu (Bungle Bungle) National Park,** a vast area of bizarrely shaped and colored rock formations; and **Danggu Geikie Gorge National Park,** an ancient flooded reef with red walls from iron oxide—as well as numerous tropical forests, croc-infested rivers, and soaring cliffs, and the town of **Broome,** rich in pearl history. The region is also dotted with cattle stations. The first European explorers, dubbed by one of their descendants as "cattle kings in grass castles," ventured into the heart of the region in 1879 to establish cattle stations. They subsequently became embroiled in one of the country's longest-lasting conflicts between white settlers and Aboriginals, led by Jandamarra of the Bunuba people.

Planning

WHEN TO GO

May to October are the best months to visit the Red Centre and the Top End; nights are crisp and cold, while days are pleasantly warm. Summer temperatures in the Centre—which can rise above 43°C (109°F)—are oppressive, while the wet season (November through April) means Darwin and surroundings are hot, humid, and, well, wet. In the Kimberley,

June through August is the preferred season, with usually clear skies and balmy days and nights.

In the Top End, the year is divided into the wet season (the Wet; November through April) and the dry season (the Dry; May through October). The Dry is a period of idyllic weather with warm days and cool nights, while the Wet brings extreme humidity and monsoonal storms that dump an average of 59 inches of rain in a few months, resulting in widespread road closures. You can also catch spectacular electrical storms, particularly over the ocean. The "Build Up," usually sometime between late-September and mid-November, is the Top End's most oppressive weather period in terms of humidity, so be warned.

The Kimberley has a similar wet season; however, the rainfall is less and generally comes in short, heavy storms. Cyclones also occur during this period and can disrupt travel arrangements. Each August in Broome there's a 10-day festival celebrating the town's pearl history.

PLANNING YOUR TIME

The sheer size of the Outback, which includes the entire Northern Territory and parts of Western Australia, means it is impossible to cover it all on a short visit. You will need to be selective.

If you choose one of Australia's great icons—Uluru, for instance—you could fly directly to Ayers Rock Airport and spend two days there, taking a hike around the rock followed by a look at the Uluru–Kata Tjuta Cultural Centre near its base. The next day, take a sightseeing flight by helicopter or fixed-wing aircraft, then visit Kata Tjuta (the Olgas) to explore its extraordinary domes, and end the day with sunset at the rock. A short flight will get you to Alice Springs, where you can easily take a day trip to either the Eastern or Western MacDonnell Ranges to explore the gorges and take a dip in a waterhole.

If you make Darwin your starting point, head east early on the Arnhem Highway to Fogg Dam to view the birdlife. Continue into Kakadu National Park and picnic at the rock-art site at Ubirr. Take a scenic flight in the afternoon, then a trip to the Bowali Visitors Centre, and overnight in Jabiru. On the second day, head to Nourlangie Rock; then continue to the Yellow Water Billabong cruise at Cooinda and stay there for the night. The next day, drive to Litchfield National Park and take a dip in Florence, Tjaynera (Sandy Creek), or Wangi Falls—be sure to heed the warning signs if crocs have been spotted in the area.

The easiest way to see Purnululu's amazing "beehive" rock formations is from the air. To do this, you'll need to fly to Kununurra from Darwin or Broome, then take a sightseeing flight. If you want to drive from Darwin to Broome, it's 1,162 miles. Ideally, take a week to do the drive, as there is much to see and do along the way.

In the Red Centre region, the primary areas of interest are Alice Springs and the Eastern and Western MacDonnell Ranges, Kings Canyon, and Uluru–Kata Tjuta National Park, with neighboring Ayers Rock Resort. Unless you have more than three days for this region, focus on only one of these areas.

GETTING HERE AND AROUND
AIR TRAVEL

Darwin is the main international arrival point. Qantas and Virgin Australia are Australia's main domestic airlines, and both operate an extensive network and regular services criss-crossing the country from all the major cities to smaller regional centers like Alice Springs and Broome. Both airlines also have budget subsidiaries—Jetstar (Qantas) and Tigerair (Virgin Australia)—while Air North has an extensive network throughout the Top End and covers some Western Australia legs.

CAR AND BUS TRAVEL

Driving around the Outback is relatively easy, with sealed (paved) two-lane roads and light traffic outside Darwin—several popular unsealed (sand or dirt) roads can certainly make the journey more interesting but are considered unsafe without a proper four-wheel-drive vehicle. Distances can be daunting; for example, Adelaide to Alice Springs via the Stuart Highway is 952 miles, and can take 16 hours. From Darwin to Broome is 1,162 miles, a tiring 21-hour drive (you really want to take a week for it, with many stops along the way). Greyhound Australia operates an extensive network of long-distance coaches. Although major highways usually remain open, many regional roads are closed during the wet season due to flooding—or occasionally for bush fires if conditions are especially dry and windy.

TRAIN TRAVEL

Great Southern Railways operates *The Ghan* from Adelaide north to Alice Springs, then on to Darwin (and also in the reverse) once or twice a week depending on the time of year.

RESTAURANTS

Restaurants and cafés in the Northern Territory are largely reflective of their location: in the Red Centre, you'll find "bush tucker" menus with crocodile, kangaroo, camel, and native fruits, berries, and plants; in Darwin and Broome, locally caught seafood is prepared with flavor influences from Asia. Many restaurants and cafés offer alfresco dining. Tips aren't expected, but an extra 10% for exceptional service is welcome.

HOTELS

From five-star to basic, you'll find suitable accommodations throughout the region. The well-known international chains are largely in Darwin, but there are also sublime boutique accommodations set in wilderness or natural settings outside these centers, especially in the Kimberley. You can also experience Outback

Australia at homesteads and working cattle stations, while owner-run bed-and-breakfasts provide comfort, charm, and a glimpse of local life. In the cities and the Outback there are plenty of less-than-memorable motels where you can at least get a clean bed for the night. Popular options—especially for families and small groups—are self-contained apartments, villas, and chalets. With two or three bedrooms, living areas, and fully stocked kitchens, they allow you to save on dining costs by cooking your own meals and are best if you're staying more than one night. *Hotel reviews have been shortened. For full information, visit Fodors.com.*

What It Costs in Australian Dollars			
$	**$$**	**$$$**	**$$$$**
RESTAURANTS			
under A$21	A$21–A$35	A$36–A$50	over A$50
HOTELS			
under A$151	A$151–A$200	A$201–A$300	over A$300

HEALTH AND SAFETY

If you are self-driving—especially in remote areas—make sure you have enough fuel, water, and food, and carry a first-aid kit. Let others know where you are going and for how long. If you go off bushwalking or hiking, bring adequate supplies and directions, and let others know your plan.

There are "critters" to avoid—snakes, crocodiles, and box jellyfish, for example. Mosquitoes are prevalent, so cover up and use a good insect repellent; the worst times for mosquitoes are dawn and dusk.

Respect the Australian sun, especially in summer. Sunburn is a real danger if you don't do what the Australians are urged to do: slip, slap, slop—that is, slip on a hat, slap on sunglasses, and slop on sunscreen. On popular beaches around major cities and towns, lifesavers (lifeguards) are usually on duty and put up flags to swim between, but generally most beaches are unguarded. Take extra care, especially where there are strong currents.

⚠ **Crocodiles are active in many of the Outback's waterways, so obey warning signs and check before swimming.**

The emergency contact number for police, fire, and ambulance is ☎ *000*. From a GSM mobile (cell) phone you can also dial ☎ *112*, although triple zero will still get through. Telstra is the only service provider that has reliable network coverage outside of major cities; however, be aware that mobile phone coverage outside of town limits is almost nonexistent in the Outback. If traveling in remote areas by car, consider renting a satellite phone, which you can find at many Outback tourist information centers.

TOURS

If you want to avoid the hassles of getting yourself around this vast region, a tour group is certainly an option. Hundreds of tours and tour operators cover Western Australia and the Northern Territory, and can introduce you to the many experiences on offer here: four-wheel-drive treks, helicopter flights, bush-tucker-gathering expeditions, Aboriginal-guided walks, fishing safaris, and national park tours to name a few.

You can also take a day tour or shorter overnight tours up to, say, five days, most of which operate from Darwin, Broome, Perth, and Alice Springs. The benefit is that all your transport, accommodations, meals, and sightseeing arrangements are preset, and you will get to see and do things you may otherwise miss if you try to organize them yourself.

★ Bill Peach Journeys

AIR EXCURSIONS | This agency runs the small airline Aircruising Australia, uses private aircraft to fly you to the iconic attractions of central Australia, and includes overnights in best-available hotels and motels. The 12-day Great Australian Aircruise departs from and returns to Sydney, with stops at Longreach in Queensland; Katherine, Kakadu, and Darwin in the Northern Territory; Kununurra and Broome in Western Australia; and finally Uluru and Alice Springs in the Northern Territory. ✉ *1753 Botany Rd., Suite 4.04* ☎ *1800/252053 within Australia, 02/8336–2990 international* ⊕ *www.billpeachjourneys.com.au* ✈ *From A$17,750.*

Kimberley Wild Adventure Tours

ADVENTURE TOURS | This company offers a variety of multiple-day camping safaris, from one and two days up to 22 days, through the Kimberley using four-wheel-drive vehicles. Highlights of the 10-day Broome to Darwin Adventure Tour are Western Australia's legendary Gibb River Road, Cable Beach, Broome, Windjana Gorge, Tunnel Creek, Echidna Chasm, Cathedral Gorge, Purnululu National Park (the Bungle Bungles), El Questro Wilderness Park, Kununurra, Lake Argyle, Katherine, and Darwin. There are plenty of chances to see wildlife and Aboriginal rock art along the way. ✉ *9 Bagot St., Broome* ☎ *1300/738870* ⊕ *kimberleywild.com.au* ✈ *From A$1995.*

North Star Cruises

BOAT TOURS | North Star Cruises operates the small luxury expedition cruise ship *True North*, which takes just 36 passengers on 7-, 10-, and 13-night sailings between Broome and Wyndham along the otherwise inaccessible Kimberley coastline. Trips are adventure oriented, with daily activities including scenic walks, fishing, diving, snorkeling, and on-shore picnics. The ship also has six expedition craft and its own helicopter for scenic flights. ✉ *The Port of Broome, Broome* ☎ *08/9192–1829* ⊕ *www.northstarcruises.com.au* ✈ *From A$13,595.*

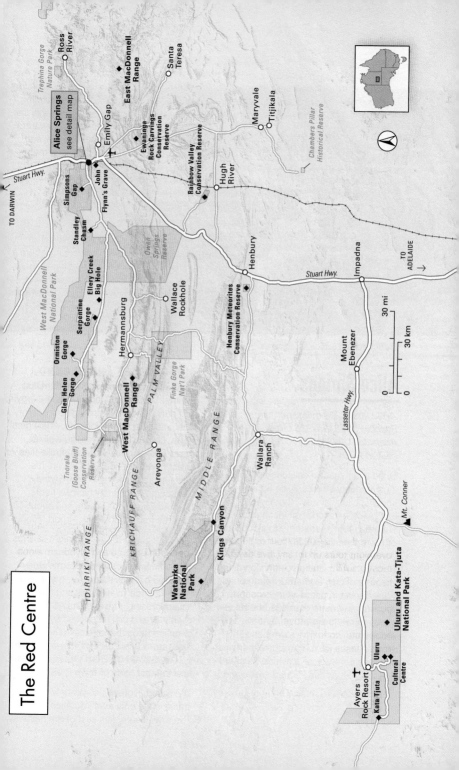

The Red Centre

Ross River

Trephina Gorge Nature Park

East MacDonnell Range

Santa Teresa

Alice Springs — see detail map

Emily Gap

Maryvale

Titjikala

Ewaninga Rock Carvings Conservation Reserve

Chambers Pillar Historical Reserve

Stuart Hwy.

TO DARWIN

Simpsons Gap

John Flynn's Grave

Rainbow Valley Conservation Reserve

Hugh River

Standley Chasm

Owen Springs Reserve

Henbury

Impadna

TO ADELAIDE

West MacDonnell National Park

Ellery Creek Big Hole

Serpentine Gorge

Hermannsburg

Wallace Rockhole

Henbury Meteorites Conservation Reserve

Stuart Hwy.

30 mi

Mount Ebenezer

30 km

Ormiston Gorge

Glen Helen Gorge

West MacDonnell Range

PALM VALLEY

Finke Gorge Nat'l Park

Tnorala (Goose Bluff) Conservation Reserve

Areyonga

MIDDLE RANGE

Wallara Ranch

Lasseter Hwy.

IDIRRIKI RANGE

KRICHAUFF RANGE

Kings Canyon

Watarrka National Park

Mt. Conner

Uluru and Kata-Tjuta National Park

Ayers Rock Resort

Uluru

Kata Tjuta

Cultural Centre

The Outback just outside Alice Springs

Alice Springs

2,028 km (1,260 miles) northwest of Sydney, 1,329 km (826 miles) north of Adelaide, 1,992 km (1,237 miles) northeast of Perth

Once a ramshackle collection of buildings on dusty streets, Alice Springs—known colloquially as "the Alice" or just "Alice"—is today an incongruously suburban tourist center with a population of more than 29,000 in the middle of the desert, dominated by the MacDonnell Ranges, which change color according to the time of day, from brick red to purple. Alice derives most of its income from tourism, and more than 459,000 people visit annually from within Australia and around the world. The town's ancient sites, a focus for the Arrernte Aboriginal people's ceremonial activities, lie cheek-by-jowl with air-conditioned shops and hotels.

GETTING HERE AND AROUND

Alice Springs Airport is 15 km (9 miles) southeast of town. Qantas flies in and out daily with direct flights from Brisbane, Sydney, Melbourne, Adelaide, Perth, Darwin, and Cairns, as well as Ayers Rock Airport. Virgin Australia flies direct from Adelaide and Darwin. It's three hours' flying time from Sydney, Melbourne, and Brisbane; two hours from Adelaide and Darwin; and about 40 minutes from Ayers Rock Airport. Flights run less frequently in the "Wet" summer months.

The Alice Springs Airport Shuttle Bus, operated by Alice Wanderer, meets every flight. The ride to all hotels and residential addresses in town costs A$16.50 each way and can be booked by phone or online through the Alice Wanderer website, ⊕ *www.alicewanderer.com.au* (☎ *08/8952–2111*). From the airport, taxi fare to most parts of town is about A$30.

The Stuart Highway, commonly called the Track, is the only road into Alice Springs. The town center lies east of the highway.

The 1,532-km (952-mile) drive from Adelaide takes about 16 hours, while the drive from Darwin is about 1,496 km (930 miles), and takes about 16½ hours. Bus tours run between all Red Centre sites, as well as between Alice Springs and Ayers Rock Resort, a journey that can take six hours. Note that Kings Canyon is a further four-hour drive from Ayers Rock Resort—in turn, its own six-hour drive from Alice Springs—so plan accordingly and fly directly into Ayers Rock Airport instead of Alice Springs if you're especially short on time.

Traveling by car will give you the most flexible itinerary—although the trade-off is that you'll travel many long, lonely stretches of one-lane highway through the red-dust desert. Vehicles can be rented at Alice Springs and Ayers Rock Resort. The Central Australian Tourism Industry Association in Alice Springs books tours and rental cars, and provides motoring information.

TRAIN TRAVEL
The Ghan

If you're looking for a unique, relaxing, and memorable way to see the Outback, this is it. *The Ghan* train travels from Adelaide up to Alice Springs and Darwin on a three-day ride through the wilds of Central Australia, giving you a chance to get out and explore Katherine, Alice Springs, and certain South Australia towns along the way. Trains generally run twice a week from Adelaide on Sunday and Wednesday, while there are slight variations in the schedule between June and August, and in November and February. The Ghan Expedition series also runs from April to October 2019 and again in March 2020, offering a four-day, three-night journey with full-day excursions of Katherine, Alice Springs, and Coober Pedy as you travel from Darwin to Adelaide. ⊠ *Adelaide Parklands Terminal* ☎ *1800/703357 within Australia, 08/8213–4401 outside Australia* ⊕ *www. greatsouthernrail.com.au* ☞ *From*

A$1529; the Ghan does not run in Dec. and Jan.

TAXIS
CONTACT Alice Springs Taxis. ⊠ *1/13 Whittaker St.* ☎ *08/8952–1877, 13–1008 for taxis Australia-wide* ⊕ *www.131008. com.*

SAFETY AND PRECAUTIONS
Please note that many Aboriginal people living in or around Alice Springs have been asked to leave their native villages by tribal elders because of their problems with alcohol. As a result, crime and violence stemming from alcohol abuse can make Alice unsafe at night, and it's recommended you travel only by taxi after dark. Sections of the dry Todd riverbed function as makeshift campsites for some folks, so caution is advised when traversing it. Remember to lock up your rental car and hide any interesting looking belongings—like Eskys (coolers)—in the trunk to help discourage theft.

TIMING
The best time to visit is between May and September, when the weather is mild during the day, although often freezing at night; the summer months can be blisteringly hot, and some tourism services are less frequent or stop altogether. Alice Springs is pleasant enough, but note that most of the Red Centre's main attractions are at least a four- to six-hour drive outside the town. If visiting Uluru is the main reason for your visit to the Red Centre, you can skip Alice Springs and fly directly to Ayers Rock Airport to position yourself closer to Uluru–Kata Tjuta National Park and Kings Canyon.

TOURS
AAT Kings
BUS TOURS | This well-known bus company operates half-day tours that include visits to the Royal Flying Doctor Service headquarters, School of the Air, Alice Springs Reptile Centre, Telegraph Station, and the Anzac Hill scenic lookout. Full-day tours to Palm Valley via four-wheel-drive

vehicles and highlights of the West MacDonnell Ranges—including Standley Chasm, Ellery Creek Big Hole, the Ochre Pits, Simpsons Gap, Ormiston Gorge, and lunch at Glen Helen Lodge—are also available. ⊠ *48 Priest St.* ☎ *08/8953–5187, 1300/228546* ⊕ *www.aatkings. com.au* ✆ *From A$110.*

ESSENTIALS

VISITOR INFORMATION Alice Springs Visitor Information Centre. ⊠ *Todd Mall at Parsons St.* ☎ *08/8952–5800, 1800/645199* ⊕ *www.discovercentralaustralia.com.*

◉ Sights

★ Alice Springs Desert Park

NATIONAL/STATE PARK | FAMILY | Focusing on the desert, which makes up 70% of the Australian landmass, this 128-acre site contains 92 types of plants and 37 animal species in several Australian ecosystems—including the largest nocturnal-animal house in the southern hemisphere. An open-air habitat is also open at night, when animals are most active. At daily presentations, Aboriginal guides discuss the different plants and animals that have helped people traditionally survive and thrive in such an arid desert environment. Don't miss the twice-daily birds of prey presentation at 10 am and 3:30 pm from June 1 to August 31, or the once-daily presentation at 10 am from November 1 to February 28. Allow about four hours to explore the park, which is located about 7 km (4 miles) west of downtown Alice Springs. ⊠ *871 Larapinta Dr.* ☎ *08/8951–8788* ⊕ *www.alicespringsdesertpark.com.au* ✆ *A$32.*

Alice Springs Reptile Centre

ZOO | FAMILY | Thorny devils, frill-neck lizards, some of the world's deadliest snakes, and "Terry" the saltwater crocodile inhabit this park in the heart of town, opposite the Royal Flying Doctor Service. From May to August, viewing is best from 11 to 3, when reptiles are most active. There's also a gecko cave and free talks conducted daily at 11, 1, and 3:30, during which you can handle small critters and pick up pythons. ⊠ *9 Stuart Terr.* ☎ *08/8952–8900* ⊕ *www.reptilecentre. com.au* ✆ *A$18.*

Alice Springs School of the Air Visitor Centre

COLLEGE | FAMILY | What do children who live hundreds of miles from the nearest school do for education? Find out at this informative visitor center, which harbors a working school within its walls. Discover how distance education has been delivered to the country's most remote parts since 1951; from pedal-operated radio systems to interactive online classes, it's come a long way. Visit before 3 pm on a school day so you can watch a live lesson; outside school hours, you can see a recorded lesson. ⊠ *80 Head St.* ☎ *08/8951–6834* ⊕ *www.assoa.nt.edu. au* ✆ *A$11.*

Araluen Cultural Precinct

MUSEUM | The most distinctive building in this complex is the Museum of Central Australia ($8 entry), which charts the evolution of the land and its inhabitants—human and animal—around central Australia. Exhibits include a skeleton of the 10½-foot-tall *Dromornis stirtoni,* the largest bird to walk on earth, which was found northeast of Alice. Also in the precinct are the Aviation Museum (free), Central Craft (free, prices for workshops vary), and Araluen Arts Centre, home to the Araluen Art Galleries and the Namatjira Gallery ($8 entry), a collection of renowned Aboriginal landscapes, and the Yeperenye Scuplture—a 3-meter-high caterpillar that you can walk through, representing the sacred Dreamtime creator of the country around Alice Springs. The precinct is located 2.4 km (1½ miles) southwest of town, and is on most tourist bus itineraries. ⊠ *61 Larapinta Dr.* ☎ *08/8951–1122* ⊕ *araluenartscentre. nt.gov.au* ✆ *A$8.*

★ The Kangaroo Sanctuary

NATURE PRESERVE | FAMILY | Arguably the must-do attraction here in Alice Springs, The Kangaroo Sanctuary is the passion project of Chris "Brolga" Barns, whose life's mission is to rescue and rehabilitate orphaned kangaroos and education people about how they can easily do the same—all you need to do is pay attention while you're driving, and if you spot a deceased kangaroo on the side of the road, check to see if there's still a living joey in its pouch, since they'll often survive the impact of a vehicle and can live for up to four more days after it. Your ticket includes door-to-door transfers (no one is allowed to drive straight to the property), a 2½–3-hour tour, and gives you a chance to take turns holding baby kangaroos and feed Roger, Brolga's marsupial co-star in the popular BBC documentary series *Kangaroo Dundee*, who started it all. ✉ *Alice Springs* ☎ *08/8965–0038* 🌐 *kangaroosanctuary.com* 🎟 *A$85* 🕒 *Closed Sat.–Mon.* ☞ *The tour picks you up and drops you off at your Alice Springs accommodations.*

National Pioneer Women's Hall of Fame and Old Alice Springs Gaol

HISTORIC SITE | There's no denying it, the women who helped make Australian history by raising their families on remote cattle stations back in the day were tough. This fascinating museum—which happens to be housed in the Old Alice Springs Gaol simply because it's a historic building—tells the stories of these brave souls, with exhibits showing the important role women played during WWII, and how women of all races helped shape Australian politics, education, medicine, aviation, sports, and pretty much every aspect of today's society. You'll also be able to tour the old jail, which began as a prison for both sexes but became an all-male prison in the 1980s, and hear the stories of its former inhabitants through an interactive audio display. ✉ *2 Stuart Terr.* ☎ *08/8952–9006* 🌐 *pioneerwomen.com.au* 🎟 *A$15.*

Royal Flying Doctor Service (RFDS) Alice Springs Tourist Facility

MUSEUM | This much-visited tourist attraction in Alice Springs has a theater, interactive displays, and a full-scale replica of the fuselage of the service's current Pilatus PC-12 aircraft. The site has long been the radio base for the Royal Flying Doctor Service, which directs doctors (using aircraft) on their house calls to remote settlements and homes hundreds of miles apart, making it a vital part of Outback life. The center features historical displays, a holographic audiovisual show portraying RFDS founder Reverend John Flynn, tours that run every half hour throughout the year, and a lovely café at the back. ✉ *8–10 Stuart Terr.* ☎ *08/8958–8411* 🌐 *www.rfdsalicesprings.com.au* 🎟 *A$17.*

🍴 Restaurants

Barra on Todd

$$ | AUSTRALIAN | Barramundi is the name of the game at this venerable and popular restaurant on the banks of the dry Todd River, part of the Mercure Alice Springs Resort. Don't leave without trying the distinctly Australian dessert of banana Mars bar—a Mars candy bar and a banana wrapped in pastry, deep fried, and served with macadamia nut ice cream and chocolate sauce. **Known for:** Thai-style barramundi spring rolls; saltbush dukkah-crusted barramundi; herb and macadamia nut over roasted barramundi. [$] *Average main: A$30* ✉ *34 Stott Terr.* ☎ *08/8951–4545.*

Bojangles Saloon and Restaurant

$$ | AUSTRALIAN | Cowhide seats, tables made from old *Ghan* railway benches, and a life-size replica of bushranger Ned Kelly give this lively restaurant true Outback flavor. It's a touristy watering hole but well worth dropping by for a drink or two and taking a few snaps of the Aussie decor. **Known for:** classic Northern Territory tucker; great beer; a lively, kitschy atmosphere. [$] *Average main: A$30*

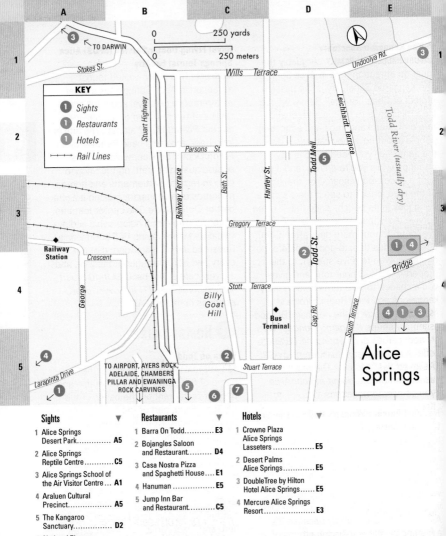

Alice Springs

KEY

- ① Sights
- ① Restaurants
- ① Hotels
- ┼━┼ Rail Lines

Sights ▼

1. Alice Springs Desert Park.............. **A5**
2. Alice Springs Reptile Centre............**C5**
3. Alice Springs School of the Air Visitor Centre ... **A1**
4. Araluen Cultural Precinct..................**A5**
5. The Kangaroo Sanctuary................ **D2**
6. National Pioneer Women's Hall of Fame and Old Alice Springs Gaol..............**C5**
9. Royal Flying Doctor Service (RFDS) Alice Springs Tourist Facility............**C5**

Restaurants ▼

1. Barra On Todd............ **E3**
2. Bojangles Saloon and Restaurant......... **D4**
3. Casa Nostra Pizza and Spaghetti House.... **E1**
4. Hanuman **E5**
5. Jump Inn Bar and Restaurant............**C5**

Hotels ▼

1. Crowne Plaza Alice Springs Lasseters **E5**
2. Desert Palms Alice Springs.............**E5**
3. DoubleTree by Hilton Hotel Alice Springs......**E5**
4. Mercure Alice Springs Resort....................**E3**

✉ *80 Todd St.* ☎ *04/6975–0550* 🌐 *www.boslivesaloon.com.au.*

Casa Nostra Pizza and Spaghetti House
$$ | **ITALIAN** | Red-and-white checkered tablecloths, Chianti bottles, and plastic grapes festoon this family-run Alice Springs classic spot that continues to draw in locals with traditional Italian meat dishes, pizza, and pasta. Take a tip from the regulars and preorder a serving of vanilla slice for dessert, or you might miss out on this scrumptious cake of layered papery pastry and custard cream. **Known for:** Al's Special; cream-and-black-pepper sauce that the chef took 15 years to perfect; BYO beer and wine. [$] *Average main: A$29* ✉ *1 Undoolya Rd., at Sturt Terr.* ☎ *08/8952–6749.*

★ **Hanuman**
$$ | **ASIAN** | With its Thai, Nonya (Malaysian), and Indian-flavored menu, this lovely spot is the only place in the desert to offer a range of big-city-quality southeast Asian food. It's as popular with the locals as it is with the tourists, which means you should book a day or two ahead. **Known for:** trumpet mushrooms topped with prawn and pork mince; barramundi poached in coconut sauce; desserts like black-rice brûlée and banana spring rolls with butterscotch sauce. [$] *Average main: A$30* ✉ *DoubleTree by Hilton Hotel Alice Springs, 82 Barrett Dr.* ☎ *08/8953–7188* 🌐 *www.hanuman.com.au* 🕒 *No lunch weekends.*

★ **Jump Inn Bar and Restaurant**
$ | **TAIWANESE** | This bar and restaurant of popular poshtel Jump Inn Alice opened to the general public in spring 2018, and its comfy chairs, cozy atmosphere, and spacious outdoor beer garden instantly became a hit with locals and visitors alike. Don't miss the Tuesday night Jam Sessions, where there's always live music and anyone can take the stage to share their own. **Known for:** an enormous selection of craft beer; a twist on pad Thai; Taiwanese street food gua bao. [$] *Average main: A$18* ✉ *4 Traeger Ave.* ☎ *08/8929–1609* 🌐 *jumpinnalice.com/bar-restaurant* 🕒 *No lunch Mon.–Wed.*

Hotels

Desert Palms Alice Springs
$ | **RESORT** | **FAMILY** | Accommodations at Desert Palms are in self-contained, free-standing A-frame units set up as double, triple, quad, and family villas, each with a private balcony and access to a lovely island pool with a waterfall to help you take your mind off the dry desert heat. **Pros:** private, comfortable villas with fully stocked kitchenettes; golf course adjacent; free Wi-Fi. **Cons:** no-frills bathrooms; villas have thin walls; taxi or car needed to reach town center. [$] *Rooms from: A$130* ✉ *74 Barrett Dr.* ☎ *08/8952–5977, 1800/678037 reservations* 🌐 *www.desertpalms.com.au* 🛏 *80 apartments* 🍴 *No meals.*

DoubleTree by Hilton Hotel Alice Springs
$$ | **HOTEL** | **FAMILY** | Landscaped lawns with elegant eucalyptus and palm trees greet you at this upscale international chain about a mile outside town. **Pros:** many rooms have views of the MacDonnell Ranges; excellent on-site restaurants; Wi-Fi is free in the lobby and in rooms if you join Hilton Honors. **Cons:** taxi or car is needed to reach the town center; no shopping nearby; Wi-Fi is pricey if you're not a Hilton Honors member. [$] *Rooms from: A$159* ✉ *82 Barrett Dr.* ☎ *08/8950–8000* 🌐 *doubletree3.hilton.com* 🛏 *236 rooms* 🍴 *Free Breakfast.*

★ **Crowne Plaza Alice Springs Lasseters**
$$ | **HOTEL** | **FAMILY** | A popular place thanks to great views of the MacDonnell Ranges from guest rooms and the nightlife provided by the casino, the Crowne Plaza is the most luxurious resort in Alice Springs. **Pros:** on-site gym facilities; complimentary in-room Wi-Fi; casino and nightlife on the property. **Cons:** adjacent convention center attracts big groups; 30-minute walk to town center;

restaurants are on the pricey side. [$] *Rooms from: A$159* ✉ *93 Barrett Dr.* ☎ *08/8950–7777* 🌐 *www.ihg.com* 🛏 *205 rooms* 🍴 *No meals.*

Mercure Alice Springs Resort

$$ | HOTEL | FAMILY | Many of the rooms at this new addition to Accor Hotels' portfolio open directly onto lawns or gardens where dozens of native birds chatter, making you forget you're in the middle of the desert and instead, perhaps inside a tropical garden. **Pros:** 10-minute walk to Todd Mall shops; soft pillows and comfortable beds; free Wi-Fi. **Cons:** convention facilities attract tour groups; no views; small parking lot for hotel and restaurant. [$] *Rooms from: A$165* ✉ *34 Stott Terr.* ☎ *08/8951–4545* 🌐 *www.accorhotels.com* 🛏 *139 rooms* 🍴 *Free Breakfast.*

Nightlife

Lasseters Casino

CASINOS | Entry is free at Lasseters Casino, where the action goes late into the night with more than 300 slot machines, plus blackjack, roulette, craps, and baccarat tables. Choose from six restaurants and bars, each with its own style ranging from exotic eats at Tali to tapas at Tempo. The Juicy Rump is known for live music, Stadium 93 for its sports bar atmosphere. The Goat & Bucket is a beer lover's paradise, while Casbah is perfectly positioned should you need a break from betting. ✉ *93 Barrett Dr.* ☎ *08/8950–7777, 1800/808975* 🌐 *www.lasseters.com.au/casino.*

Maxim's Bar at Todd Tavern

BARS/PUBS | Maxim's Bar, located inside Todd Tavern, the only traditional Australian pub in town, has something going on every night. The property also includes a restaurant, bottle shop (liquor store), and gambling facilities. You can bet on horse races across the country with TAB (the Australian equivalent of OTB) or try your luck at Keno—but keep some change aside to lose in the slot machines. Shoot some pool, be a pinball wizard, or catch some sports on the TVs. ✉ *1 Todd Mall* ☎ *08/8952–1255* 🌐 *www.toddtavern.com.au.*

Shopping

Shopping in Alice Springs is all about Aboriginal artwork. Central Australian Aboriginal paintings are characterized by intricate patterns of dots—and are commonly called sand paintings because they were originally drawn on sand as ceremonial devices.

Mbantua Aboriginal Art Gallery

ART GALLERIES | Supporters of the Aboriginal artists of Central Australia since 1987, the Mbantua Art Gallery's Todd Mall shop houses some of the best samples of indigenous art in Alice Springs. Learn more about this fascinating culture at the Gallery's Cultural Museum, where you can see boomerangs, spears, and other artifacts and objects collected around the Northern Territory. ✉ *64 Todd St.* ☎ *08/8952–5571* 🌐 *www.mbantua.com.au/alice-springs* ☞ *Free.*

Papunya Tula Artists

ART GALLERIES | Encouraged to paint a mural on a blank building wall by a local school teacher in 1971, the Papunya Tula artists were the founders of the modern western and central desert art movement. This gallery showcases the work of some of the area's best. ✉ *63 Todd St.* ☎ *08/8952–4731* ☞ *Free.*

★ **Red Kangaroo Books**

BOOKS/STATIONERY | From bush poetry and traditional bush tucker recipes to anthropological texts on Aboriginal people and their culture, Red Kangaroo Books has an outstanding collection of literature pertaining to all things Australian. ✉ *79 Todd St.* ☎ *08/8953–2137* 🌐 *www.redkangaroobooks.com* ☞ *Free.*

This Is Aboriginal Art
ART GALLERIES | Stop by the gallery to explore two floors full of artwork by local painters, who typically work from the on-site studio. Finished pieces can also be purchased online through the website. ✉ *87 Todd St.* ☎ *08/8952–1544* ⊕ *www.thisisaboriginalart.com.au* ☞ *Free.*

Todd Mall Markets
OUTDOOR/FLEA/GREEN MARKETS | **FAMILY** | Held every other Sunday morning from 9 am until around 1 pm, mid-February to December, the markets feature more than 100 stalls of local arts, crafts, and food, which are displayed while musicians entertain. ✉ *Todd St.* ☎ *04/5855–5506* ⊕ *www.toddmallmarkets.com.au.*

Activities

CAMEL RIDING
Pyndan Camel Tracks
LOCAL SPORTS | Daily one-hour camel rides are offered three times a day at noon, 2:30, and sunset, during which you'll explore a valley of diverse habitat of Iron Bark and Mulga trees, and, of course, take in views of the ancient MacDonnell Ranges. While it's located about 15 km (9 miles) from the town center, the company offers free rides from your Alice Springs accommodation so you can spend some quality time with your new furry friend. ✉ *21259 Jane Rd.* ☎ *04/1617–0164* ⊕ *www.cameltracks.com* ☞ *From A$79.*

HOT-AIR BALLOONING
★ Outback Ballooning
BALLOONING | Floating over the desert spinifex in a hot-air balloon while the sun comes up is a once-in-a-lifetime experience. Outback Ballooning makes hotel pickups about an hour before dawn and returns you between 8 am and 9 am depending on the time of year. The A$295 fee gives you 30 minutes of flying time, mandatory Civil Aviation Safety Authority insurance, and a Champagne breakfast; a 60-minute flight will cost you A$390. Those who still want to participate but are sensitive to heights can pay A$40 for what the company calls a Balloon Chase, allowing you to see how the balloons are set up pre-flight, watch them take off, and follow along with them through the desert alongside crewmembers before meeting back up with your group for celebratory snacks and bubbles. ■**TIP→ Take warm clothes to beat the predawn chill.** ✉ *35 Kennett Ct.* ☎ *08/8952–8723* ⊕ *www.outbackballooning.com.au* ☞ *From A$295.*

East and West MacDonnell Ranges

Alice Springs is flanked by the MacDonnell Ranges. Those to the east of Alice Springs are known as the East MacDonnell Ranges and those to the West are known as the West MacDonnell Ranges.

Art Hunt

The essence of this ancient land is epitomized in the paintings of the renowned Aboriginal landscape artist Albert Namatjira and his followers. Viewed away from the desert, these artists' images of the MacDonnell Ranges may appear at first to be garish and unreal in their depiction of purple-and-red mountain ranges and stark-white ghost gum trees. However, seeing the real thing makes it difficult to imagine executing the paintings in any other way. Galleries abound along Todd Mall (the main shopping street); they're filled with canvas and bark paintings, as well as handcrafted didgeridoos and other artifacts.

Eye-catching scenery and Aboriginal rock art in the MacDonnell Ranges east of the Alice are well worth a day or more of exploration. Emily Gap (a sacred Aboriginal site), Jessie Gap, and Corroboree Rock, once a setting for important male-only Aboriginal ceremonies, are within the first 50 km (31 miles) east of Alice Springs. Beyond these are Trephina Gorge, John Hayes Rockhole, and N'Dhala Gorge Nature Park (home to numerous Aboriginal rock carvings).

The West MacDonnell Ranges, which stretch westward from just a few kilometers outside Alice Springs to around 200 km (125 miles) farther away, are a spectacular series of red-rock mountains interspersed by canyons and narrow gorges. Each of the chasms and gorges has its own unique character, and in many, there are waterholes where you can swim. Black-footed rock wallabies are among the wildlife to be spotted. The 223-km (139-mile) Larapinta Trail in the park, the showpiece of central Australian bushwalking, is broken into 12 sections, each a one- to two-day walk.

GETTING HERE AND AROUND

To reach all the major sights of the West MacDonnell Ranges, the Red Centre Way follows Larapinta Drive (the western continuation of Stott Terrace) from Alice Springs and Namatjira Drive westward to Glen Helen, about 130 km (81 miles) from Alice Springs. Roads leading off it access the highlights. To reach key attractions in the East MacDonnell Ranges such as Emily Gap and Jessie Gap, take Ross Highway east from Alice Springs.

SAFETY AND PRECAUTIONS

Take care when bushwalking or hiking, as paths are usually rocky and uneven. Snakes inhabit most areas, so be especially cautious when walking through tall grass. You should always carry and drink plenty of water; at least one liter of water for every hour of walking in hot weather.

TOURS

Emu Run Experience

BUS TOURS | One-day tours are offered by air-conditioned bus to all the major West MacDonnell sights, including Simpsons Gap, Standley Chasm, the Ochre Pits, Ormiston Gorge, and Glen Helen, and there's a chance to take a dip in the Ellery Creek Big Hole, a picturesque waterhole popular with the locals. You'll also get morning tea, lunch, afternoon snacks, and door-to-door pickup and drop-off service. ✉ *12 Power St., Alice Springs* ☎ *08/8953–7057* ⊕ *www.emurun.com.au* 🖭 *From A$132.*

Trek Larapinta

ADVENTURE TOURS | Whether you're looking for a short three-day excursion into the wilderness (from A$1,495), a six-day trek (from A$2,895), a nine-day journey (from A$3,395), or an epic 16-day adventure covering the entire Larapinta Trail (from A$4,695), this company gives you plenty of options based on how much time you have and how much hiking you really want to do. ✉ *Box 9043, Alice Springs* ☎ *1300/133278* ⊕ *www.treklarapinta. com.au* 🖭 *From A$1495.*

ESSENTIALS

VISITOR INFORMATION Emily and Jessie Gaps Nature Park Information. ✛ *10 km (6 miles) east of Alice Springs* ☎ *08/8952– 1013* ⊕ *nt.gov.au/leisure/parks-reserves/ find-a-park-to-visit/yeperenye-emily-jes- sie-gaps-nature-park* Simpsons Gap Visitor Information Centre. ☎ *08/8951–8250.*

◉ Sights

These sights are organized by distance— from closest to farthest—from Alice Springs.

John Flynn's Grave Historic Reserve

CEMETERY | John Flynn, the Royal Flying Doctor Service founder, is memorialized at this spot along Larapinta Drive just 6½ km (4 miles) west of Alice Springs in view of the majestic West MacDonnell

The Australian Heartland

For most Australians, the Red Centre is the mystical and legendary core of the continent and Uluru is its beautiful focal point. Whether they have been there or not, locals believe its image symbolizes a steady pulse that radiates deep through the red earth, through the heartland, and all the way to the coasts.

Little more than a thumbprint within the vast Australian continent, the Red Centre is harsh and isolated. Its hard, relentless topography (and lack of conveniences) makes this one of the most difficult areas of the country to survive in, much less explore. But the early pioneers—some foolish, some hardy—managed to set up bases that thrived. They created cattle stations, introduced electricity, and implemented telegraph services, enabling them to maintain a lifestyle that, if not luxurious, was at least reasonably comfortable.

The people who now sparsely populate the Red Centre are a breed of their own. Many were born and grew up here, but others were "blow-ins"—immigrants from far-flung countries and folks from other Australian states who fell in love with the area, took up the challenge to make a life in the desert, and stayed on as they succeeded. Either way, the people out here have a few common characteristics. They're laconic and down-to-earth, canny and astute, and likely to try to pull your leg when you least expect it.

No one could survive the isolation without a good sense of humor: Where else in the world would you hold a bottomless-boat race in a dry river-bed? The Henley-on-Todd Regatta, as it is known, is a sight to behold in Alice Springs each August, with dozens of would-be skippers bumbling along within the bottomless-boat frames.

As the small towns grew and businesses quietly prospered in the mid-1800s, a rail link between Alice Springs and Adelaide was planned. However, the undercurrent of challenge and humor that touches all life here ran through this project as well. Construction began in 1877, but things went wrong from the start. No one had seen rain for ages, and no one expected it; hence, the track was laid right across a floodplain. It wasn't long before locals realized their mistake, when intermittent heavy floods regularly washed the tracks away. The railway is still in operation today, and all works well, but its history is one of many local jokes here.

The Red Centre is a special place where you will meet people whose generous and sincere hospitality may move you. The land and all its riches offer some of the most spectacular and unique sights on the planet, along with a sense of timelessness that will slow you down and fill your spirit. Take a moment to shade your eyes from the sun and pick up on the subtleties that nature has carefully protected and camouflaged here, and you will soon discover that the Red Centre is not the dead center.

range. ✉ *623 Larapinta Dr., Alice Springs*
⊕ *www.discovercentralaustralia.com*
💲 *Free.*

Simpsons Gap

NATIONAL/STATE PARK | The closest gorge
to Alice Springs—there's even a bicycle
and walking track from the city center—
greets you with views of stark-white
ghost gums (Australian evergreen trees),
red rocks, and gorgeous, purple-haze
mountains that provide a taste of scenery
to be seen farther into the ranges. Heed
the "No Swimming" signs, as freshwater crocodiles may be present if there's
enough water, and come in the morning
and late afternoon for a chance to catch
a glimpse of rock wallabies. ✉ *Larapinta
Dr., Alice Springs ✛ 18 km (11 miles)
west of Alice Springs, then 6 km (4
miles) on side road* ☎ *08/8951–8250*
⊕ *nt.gov.au/leisure/parks-reserves*
💲 *Free.*

Standley Chasm

NATURE SITE | At midday, when the sun
is directly overhead, the 10-yard-wide
canyon glows red from the reflected
light, a phenomenon that lasts for just
15 minutes. The walk from the parking
lot takes about 20 minutes and is rocky
toward the end. For a greater challenge,
climb to the top via the steep trail that
branches off to the left at the end of the
gorge; the views are spectacular. There's
also a kiosk selling snacks and drinks at
the park entrance. ✉ *Larapinta Dr., Alice
Springs ✛ 40 km (25 miles) west of Alice
Springs, then 9 km (5½ miles) on Standley Chasm Rd.* ☎ *08/8956–7440* ⊕ *www.
standleychasm.com.au* 💲 *A$12.*

★ Ellery Creek Big Hole

NATURE SITE | This is one of the prettiest
(and coldest) swimming holes in the Red
Centre, so it's quite popular with locals
and visitors alike—it's also the deepest
and most permanent waterhole in the
area, so you may glimpse wild creatures
like wallabies or goannas (monitor lizards)
quenching their thirst. Take the 3-km

(2-mile) Dolomite Walk for a close-up
look at this fascinating geological site.
✉ *Namatjira Dr., Alice Springs ✛ 88
km (55 miles) west of Alice Springs*
☎ *08/8951–8250* ⊕ *northernterritory.com/
alice-springs-and-surrounds* 💲 *Free.*

Serpentine Gorge

NATURE SITE | Accessible only by four-
wheel-drive vehicle, this site is best
experienced by taking a refreshing swim
through the narrow, winding gorge.
According to an Aboriginal myth, a fierce
serpent makes its home in the pool,
hence the name. ✉ *Namatjira Dr., Alice
Springs ✛ 99 km (61 miles) west of Alice
Springs* ☎ *08/8951–8250* ⊕ *www.discov-
ercentralaustralia.com/serpentine-gorge*
💲 *Free.*

Glen Helen Gorge

NATURE SITE | This gorge, cut by the spo-
radic Finke River, often described as the
oldest river in the world, slices through
the MacDonnell Ranges, revealing
dramatic rock layering and tilting. Here
the river forms a broad, cold, permanent
waterhole that's great for a bracing swim.
✉ *Namatjira Dr., Alice Springs ✛ 132
km (82 miles) west of Alice Springs*
☎ *08/8951–8250* ⊕ *northernterritory.com/
alice-springs-and-surrounds* 💲 *Free.*

★ Ormiston Gorge

NATURE SITE | This beautiful gorge has
something for everyone, whether you're
interested in swimming in the waterhole,
taking a short hike to Gum Tree Lookout
for fantastic views of the 820-foot-high
gorge walls rising from the pool below, or
experiencing the best of both worlds on
the 90-minute, 7 km (4½-mile) Ormiston Pound Walk. ✉ *Namatjira Dr., Alice
Springs ✛ 135 km (84 miles) west of
Alice Springs* ☎ *08/8956–7799* ⊕ *north-
ernterritory.com/alice-springs-and-sur-
rounds* 💲 *Free.*

Hotels

Glen Helen Lodge

$$ | HOTEL | FAMILY | Choose from motel, dorm, or campsite accommodations and enjoy views of Glen Helen Gorge and its wildlife, including many bird species, rock wallabies, dingoes, and lizards. **Pros:** traditional Outback Australia atmosphere; easy access to the Larapinta Walking Trail and Glen Helen Gorge; plenty of opportunities to see local fauna. **Cons:** no swimming pool; limited Wi-Fi in the restaurant and at reception; rooms 10–17 are next to the generator and can be noisy. $ *Rooms from: A$160* ✉ *1 Namatjira Dr., Alice Springs* ⊹ *135 km (84 miles) west of Alice Springs* ☎ *08/8956–7208* ⊕ *www.glenhelenlodge.com.au* ⤴ *25 rooms* ◯ *Free Breakfast.*

Activities

HIKING

The **Larapinta Trail,** a 223-km-long (139-mile-long) walking track that runs from Alice Springs into the Western MacDonnell Ranges, is a spectacular, though challenging, track that takes hikers through classically rugged and dry central Australian landscapes. Hikers are encouraged to participate in the voluntary Overnight Walker Registration Scheme, designed to ensure that all trekkers on the trail can be tracked and accounted for in case of an emergency. Contact the **Northern Territory Parks & Wildlife Service** (☎ *08/8951–8250*) for more information. **Tourism Central Australia** in Alice Springs (☎ *08/8952–5800*) can also advise you if you're interested in planning bushwalking itineraries. **World Expeditions** runs guided and self-guided, multiday hikes on the best sections of the trail, ranging from three to 14 days, with accommodation in permanent campsites and all meals. Prices start at A$920 for a three-day self-guided trek. ⊕ *www.worldexpeditions.com*

Watarrka National Park (Kings Canyon)

Several impressive geological sights lie along the route from Alice Springs to Watarrka National Park along the Stuart and Lasseter highways, with the finale being Kings Canyon, the must-see attraction for this area.

GETTING HERE AND AROUND

Watarrka National Park is 450 km (280 miles) southwest of Alice Springs via the Stuart and Lasseter highways and Luritja Road. You also can reach the park from Alice Springs by taking Larapinta Drive through the mountains (the West MacDonnell Ranges); however, if you take this route, you need a four-wheel drive and also a Mereenie Loop Pass, which you can purchase at the Alice Springs Visitor Information Centre (☎ *08/8952–5800*). If you're coming from Uluru or Yulara, take Lasseter Highway and Luritja Road to the park's entrance. Within the park, Luritja Road takes you northwest through the park from Kings Creek Station to Kings Canyon, while Larapinta Drive heads south into the park toward Kings Canyon.

TOURS

Karrke Aboriginal Cultural Experience

SPECIAL-INTEREST | FAMILY | Within the Wanmarra Aboriginal community just a few minutes' drive from Kings Creek Station, this one-hour cultural tour gives visitors an up-close look at some of the bush tucker, plants, and other artifacts still important to indigenous culture today. Let Peter and Christine introduce you to the all-important grinding stone, weapons made from Mulga wood, and traditional dot painting techniques—you might even get to sample a witchetty grub, which tastes remarkably like buttered popcorn when cooked on the fire. Tours take place four times a day, Wednesday through Sunday at 9, 10:30,

2, and 4, and operate from mid-January to mid-November. ⊠ *Wanmara, Petermann NT 0872, Kings Canyon ⊹ 3 km (2 miles) northwest of Kings Creek Station. Look for signs and take dirt road just off Luritja Dr.* ☎ *08/8956–7620* ⊕ *www.karrke.com.au* ✉ *A$65, cash only on-site or can be booked with a credit card through Kings Canyon accommodations.*

ESSENTIALS
VISITOR INFORMATION Watarrka National Park (Kings Canyon) Visitor Information. ☎ *08/8956–7460 Watarrka Ranger Station* ⊕ *nt.gov.au/leisure/parks-reserves.*

 Sights

Henbury Meteorites Conservation Reserve
NATURE SITE | The Henbury Meteorites craters, 12 depressions between 6 feet and 600 feet across, are believed to have been formed by a meteorite shower 4,700 years ago—the largest one measures roughly 590 feet wide by 50 feet deep! To get here, you must travel 15 km (9 miles) off the highway on an unpaved road—conventional 2WD sedans will be fine, but be aware that some rental car companies don't cover you if you break down on unsealed roads. ⊠ *Ernest Giles Rd. ⊹ 119 km (74 miles) south of Alice Springs and 15 km (9 miles) west of Stuart Hwy.* ☎ *08/8952–1013* ⊕ *nt.gov.au/leisure/parks-reserves* ✉ *Free.*

★ Kings Canyon
NATIONAL/STATE PARK | Inside Watarrka National Park, Kings Canyon is one of the most spectacular sights in central Australia. Sprawling in scope, the canyon's sheer cliff walls shelter a world of ferns and woodlands, permanent springs, and rock pools. The main path is the 6-km (4-mile) Kings Canyon Rim Walk, which starts with a short but steep 15-minute climb straight up from the parking lot to the top of the escarpment; the view 886 feet down to the base of the canyon is amazing. Steep stairs mark your arrival into the scenic Garden of Eden—the only

way out along the main trail is via another round of intense stair-climbing back up to the top of the canyon wall, so make sure you're carrying plenty of water for the hike. An easier walk, called the Creek Walk, which starts at the parking lot and winds through the base of the canyon, is just as worthwhile. Alternatively, Kings Canyon Resort offers 8-, 15-, and 30-minute helicopter rides so you can view it all from above (from A$95, A$150, and A$285, respectively). ⊠ *Luritja Rd., Alice Springs ⊹ 450 km (280 miles) southwest of Alice Springs (167 km [104 miles] from Lasseter Hwy. turnoff)* ☎ *08/8956–7460* ⊕ *nt.gov.au/leisure/parks-reserves* ✉ *Free.*

Napwerte / Ewaninga Rock Carvings Conservation Reserve
NATURE SITE | More than 3,000 ancient Aboriginal rock engravings (petroglyphs) are etched into sandstone outcrops in Napwerte/Ewaninga Rock Carvings Conservation Reserve, 35 km (22 miles) south of Alice on the road to Chamber's Pillar. Early morning and late-afternoon light are best for photographing the lines, circles, and animal tracks. A 2-km (1-mile) trail leads to several art sites. The reserve is open all day year-round and is accessible by regular (rather than four-wheel-drive) cars; technically, however, the road is unsealed, so check with your rental car company to make sure it's not against their rules to drive on it. ⊠ *Old South Rd. ⊹ 35 km (22 miles) south of Alice Springs* ☎ *08/8952–1013* ⊕ *nt.gov.au/leisure/parks-reserves* ✉ *Free.*

Rainbow Valley Conservation Reserve
NATIONAL/STATE PARK | Amazing formations in the sandstone cliffs of the James Range take on rainbow colors in the early-morning and late-afternoon light; the colors are caused by water dissolving the red iron in the sandstone and further erosion that has created dramatic rock faces and squared towers. To reach the reserve, turn left off the Stuart Highway 75 km (46 miles) south of Alice. The

next 22 km (13 miles) are on a dirt track, requiring a four-wheel-drive vehicle. ✉ *Stuart Hwy., Alice Springs* ✥ *75 km (46 miles) south of Alice Springs, then 22 km (13 miles) east via an unsealed road* ☎ *08/8952–1013* 🌐 *nt.gov.au/leisure/parks-reserves* 🎟 *Free.*

Hotels

★ Kings Canyon Resort

$$$$ | RESORT | FAMILY | The best place to stay near Watarrka National Park, this resort is 9 km (6 miles) from Kings Canyon and offers accommodations ranging from budget-friendly rooms with shared bathrooms and campsites to deluxe cabins with luxurious spa tubs overlooking rugged rock formations. **Pros:** dining options for every budget; complimentary activities and tour bookings available at reception; game and trivia nights are offered several times a week. **Cons:** unless you opt for a guided tour, you'll need your own transport to get to the actual canyon; Wi-Fi is only available for purchase and works best in The Thirsty Dingo Bar; it's about four hours from Uluru and five hours from Alice Springs. [$] *Rooms from: A$459* ✉ *Luritja Rd., Watarrka National Park* ☎ *1800/837168* 🌐 *www.kingscanyonresort.com.au* 🛏 *177 rooms* 🍴 *No meals.*

Kings Creek Station

$$$ | RESORT | FAMILY | This working cattle and camel station just 36 km (22 miles) from Kings Canyon offers affordable, rustic accommodation options ranging from campgrounds and twin-share Safari Cabins to a $1,100-a-night luxury glamping experience. **Pros:** cabin rate includes an impressive bushman's-style breakfast; children five and under stay free; complimentary microwave, fridge, and gas barbecues so you can self-cater. **Cons:** all Safari Cabins have twin beds and shared bathroom facilities; it's a 35-minute drive from Kings Canyon; accommodations basic but pricey. [$] *Rooms from: A$202* ✉ *Luritja Rd., Kings Canyon* ✥ *Luritja Rd. via Lasseter Hwy. (from Alice Springs or Uluru), 36 km (22 miles) before you reach Kings Canyon* ☎ *08/8956–7474* 🌐 *www.kingscreekstation.com.au* 🛏 *28 rooms* 🍴 *Free Breakfast.*

Uluru and Kata Tjuta National Park

It's easy to see why Aboriginal people attach such spiritual significance to Uluru (Ayers Rock). It rises magnificently above the plain and dramatically changes color throughout the day. At 2,831 feet, Uluru is one of the world's largest monoliths, though such a classification belies the otherworldly, spiritual energy surrounding it. The Anangu people are the traditional owners of the land around Uluru and Kata Tjuta. They believe they are direct descendants of the beings—which include a python, an emu, a blue-tongue lizard, and a poisonous snake—who formed the land and its physical features during the Tjukurpa (the "Dreamtime," or creation period).

Kata Tjuta (the Olgas), 58 km (36 miles) west of Uluru, is a series of 36 gigantic rock domes hiding a maze of fascinating gorges and crevasses. The names Ayers Rock and the Olgas are used out of familiarity alone; at the sites themselves, the Aboriginal Uluru and Kata Tjuta are the respective names of preference. The entire area is called Yulara, though the airport is still known as Ayers Rock.

Uluru and Kata Tjuta have very different compositions. Monolithic Uluru is made up of a type of sandstone called arkose, while the rock domes at Kata Tjuta are composed of conglomerate. Both of these intriguing sights lie within Uluru–Kata Tjuta National Park, which is protected as a UNESCO World Heritage site. The whole experience is a bit like seeing the Grand Canyon turned inside out, and a visit here will be remembered for a lifetime.

In terms of where to eat and stay, Ayers Rock Resort, officially known as the township of Yulara, is essentially a complex of lodgings, restaurants, and facilities, and is base camp for exploring Uluru and Kata Tjuta. Note that the accommodations and services here are the only ones in the vicinity of the national park. Uluru is about a 20-minute drive from the resort area (there's a sunset-viewing area on the way); driving to Kata Tjuta will take another 30 minutes. The park entrance fee of A$25 is valid for three days but can be extended to five days free of charge.

The resort "village" includes a bank, newsstand, supermarket, several souvenir shops and restaurants, an Aboriginal art gallery, hair salon, and child-care center.

The accommodations at the resort, which range from luxury hotels to a campground and hostel, are all run by Voyages Indigenous Tourism Australia and share many of the same facilities. Indoor dining is limited to each hotel's restaurants and the less-expensive eateries in the Town Centre, all of which can be charged back to your room. All reservations can be made through Voyages Indigenous Tourism Australia (⊕ *www. voyages.com.au*) on-site, or through their central reservations service in Sydney.

GETTING HERE AND AROUND

Qantas's budget subsidiary, Jetstar, operates nonstop flights from Sydney, Brisbane, and Melbourne, while Qantas offers nonstop hops from Cairns and Alice Springs; and Virgin Australia flies nonstop from Sydney. Passengers from other capital cities fly to Alice Springs to connect with flights to Ayers Rock Airport, which is 9 km (6 miles) north of the resort complex.

AAT Kings runs a complimentary shuttle bus between the airport and Yulara, which meets every flight. If you have

Watch the Sky ⊙

More stars and other astronomical sights, such as the fascinating Magellanic Clouds, are visible in the southern hemisphere than in the northern, and the desert night sky shows off their glory with diamond-like clarity. Look out for the Southern Cross, the constellation that navigators used for many centuries to find their way—most Australians will proudly point it out for you.

reservations at the resort, representatives wait outside the baggage-claim area of the airport to whisk you and other guests away on the 10-minute drive.

If you're driving from Alice Springs, it's a five-hour-plus, 440-km (273-mile) trip to Ayers Rock Resort. Like every major Australian highway, the road is paved, but lacks a shoulder and is one lane in each direction for the duration, making it challenging and risky to overtake the four-trailer-long road trains, although the drivers will sometimes flash their blinker, indicating when it's safe for you to pass. The route, long and straight with monotonous desert scenery, often induces fatigue; avoid driving at night, sunrise, and sunset, as wildlife is prolific and you've a good chance of colliding with a kangaroo—they typically sleep all day but wake up just before sunset, thus making nighttime driving a lot more complicated.

From the resort it's 19 km (12 miles) to Uluru or 53 km (33 miles) to Kata Tjuta on winding, sealed roads.

If you prefer to explore Uluru and Kata Tjuta on your own schedule, renting your own car is a good idea; the only other ways to get to the national park are on group bus tours or by chauffeured taxi or coach. Avis, Hertz, and Thrifty all rent cars at Ayers Rock Resort as well as Ayers Rock Airport. Arrange for your rental early, since cars are limited.

TRANSPORTATION CONTACTS
AAT Kings
From complimentary airport transfers to and from Ayers Rock Resort to a multitude of tour packages, AAT Kings is the one tour bus you'll see everywhere in these parts. ⊠ *167 Yulara Dr., Yulara* ☎ *08/8956–2171, 1300/228546* ⊕ *www. aatkings.com.*

Automobile Association of the Northern Territory
Roadside assistance anywhere in the Northern Territory once you sign up for a membership. ⊠ *2/14 Knuckey St., Darwin* ☎ *08/8925–5901, 131111 emergency road assistance* ⊕ *www.aant.com.au.*

NT Road Report
Check conditions before you head out in case of road closures due to flooding or bushfires. ☎ *1800/246199* ⊕ *roadreport. nt.gov.au.*

Uluru Hop On Hop Off
This nifty hop-on, hop-off shuttle service offers round-trip transfers from Ayers Rock Resort to Uluru (from A$49), Kata-Tjuta (from A$95) or one-, two-, and three-day passes to both (from A$120, A$160, and A$210, respectively). ⊠ *118 Kali Ct., Yulara* ☎ *08/8956–2019* ⊕ *uluru-hoponhopoff.com.au.*

SAFETY AND PRECAUTIONS
Water is vital in the Red Centre. It is easy to forget, but the dry atmosphere and the temperatures can make you prone to dehydration. If you are walking or climbing, you will need to consume additional water at regular intervals. You should carry at least one liter of water for every hour. Regardless of where you plan to travel, it is essential to carry plenty of water, which means 10 liters minimum if you're driving into the desert.

TIMING
If seeing Uluru is your reason for visiting the Red Centre, there are tours that fly in and out, stopping just long enough to watch the rock at sunset. However, for a more leisurely visit, allow two days so you can also visit Kata Tjuta (The Olgas) nearby.

TOURS
AIR TOURS
Ayers Rock Helicopters
AIR EXCURSIONS | Helicopter flights are A$150 per person for 15 minutes over Uluru, or A$285 for 30 minutes over both Kata Tjuta and Uluru. A slightly longer 36-minute flight for A$310 offers a different angle view of the two sites from the back. ⊠ *149 Yulara Dr., Yulara* ☎ *08/8956–2077* ⊕ *www.flyuluru.com.au* ✈ *From A$150.*

Ayers Rock Scenic Flights
AIR EXCURSIONS | The best views of Uluru and Kata Tjuta are from the air. Light-plane tours, with courtesy door-to-door pickup from Ayers Rock Resort hotels, include 24-minute flights over Uluru (from A$120), 40-minute flights over both sites (from A$240), as well as day tours to Kings Canyon (from A$575) and a huge meteorite crater known as Gosses Bluff (from A$675). For more information and options, visit the tourism information office at Ayers Rock Resort's Town Square. ⊠ *149 Yulara Dr., Yulara* ☎ *08/8956–2345* ⊕ *www.flyuluru.com.au* ✈ *From A$120.*

ABORIGINAL TOURS
Small group tour company SEIT Outback Australia (☎ *08/8956–3156*) organizes trips through the Uluru and Kata Tjuta region, with two of them led by local Aboriginal guides. These tours, which leave from Ayers Rock Resort and cost A$280 for a full-day experience, include a trip to Cave Hill and into the desert of the Pitjantjatjara Lands of Central Australia, as well as a special trip to traditional homelands to meet the locals and learn firsthand how they fought to establish

land rights and make Uluru-Kata Tjuta National Park what it is today. Aboriginal art aficionados can also attend 90-minute dot-painting workshops held twice daily by Maruku Arts and Crafts in Yulara Town Square for a chance to learn about this ancient art form and create your own souvenir (A$69).

CAMEL TOURS
★ Uluru Camel Tours
SPECIAL-INTEREST | FAMILY | A great way to get out in the open and see the sights is from the back of one of the desert's creatures. Uluru Camel Tours has sunrise and sunset tours that last for 2½ hours and include breakfast or Champagne, beer, wine, and snacks depending on which one you do (A$132); 45-minute "express" rides for A$80 and even quicker 10-minute jaunts around the paddock for A$15 offer a brief introduction to this incredible animal. ⊠ *Box 25, Yulara* ☎ *08/8956–3333* ⊕ *ulurucameltours.com.au* ⊠ *From A$80.*

ESSENTIALS
VISITOR INFORMATION
The Uluru–Kata Tjuta Cultural Centre is on the park road just before you reach the rock. It also contains the park's ranger station. The Cultural Centre is open daily from 7 am to 6 pm. The Tours and Information Centre at Yulara Town Square is open daily from 8 am to 7 am.

CONTACTS Ayers Rock Resort Central Reservations Service. ⊠ *Voyages Indigenous Tourism Australia, 179 Elizabeth St., Sydney* ☎ *1300/134044* ⊕ *www.ayersrockresort.com.au.* **Tours and Information Centre.** ⊠ *127 Yulara Dr., Yulara* ☎ *08/8957–7324* ⊕ *www.ayersrockresort.com.au.* **Uluru–Kata Tjuta Cultural Centre.** ⊠ *Uluru Rd., Yulara* ☎ *08/8956–1128* ⊕ *www.parksaustralia.gov.au.*

 Sights

★ Kata Tjuta
NATURE SITE | There are three main walks at Kata Tjuta, the first from the parking lot into Walpa Gorge, a 2.6-km (1.6-mile)

hike to the deepest valley between the rocks. The round-trip journey takes about one hour. The gorge is a desert refuge for plants and animals and the rocky track gently rises along a moisture-rich gully, passing inconspicuous rare plants and ending at a grove of flourishing spearwood. More rewarding, but also more difficult, is the Valley of the Winds Walk, which takes you along a stony track to two spectacular lookouts, Karu (2.2 km or 1.3 miles return; allow an hour) and Karingana (5.4 km or 3.3 miles; allow 2½ hours). Experienced walkers can also complete the full 7.4-km (4.6-mile) circuit in about four hours. ■ **TIP→ Note that the Valley of the Winds Walk closes when temperatures rise above 36°C (97°F), which is usually after 11 am in summer.** The Kata Tjuta Viewing Area, 25 km (16 miles) along Kata Tjuta Road is 600 meters (1,970 feet) from the car park, and interpretive panels explain the natural life around you. It's also where tour buses line up for sunrise photos about a half hour before dawn. Be prepared for crowds—and amazing views of Kata Tjuta and Uluru in the distance. ⊠ *Lasseter Hwy., Yulara* ✛ *53 km (33 miles) west of Yulara* ⊕ *www.parksaustralia.gov.au* ⊠ *A$25.*

★ Uluru
NATURE SITE | Rising like an enormous red mountain in the middle of an otherwise completely flat desert, Uluru (formerly called Ayers Rock) is a marvel to behold. Two car parks—Mala and Kuniya—provide access for several short walks, or you can choose to do the full 10-km (6-mile) circuit on the Uluru Base Walk, which takes about four hours. Some places are Aboriginal sacred sites and cannot be entered, nor can they be photographed or captured on video—these are clearly signposted—while signs around the base explain the significance of what you're looking at and recount traditional myths and legends.

The Mala Walk is 2 km (1 mile) in length and almost all on flat land, taking you

The monumental Uluru as seen from the air

to Kanju Gorge from the car park; park rangers provide free tours daily at 8 am from October through April and at 10 am from May through September.

The Liru Walk starts at the cultural center and takes you to the base Uluru. Along the way are stands of mulga trees and, after rain, wildflowers. The track is wheelchair accessible and the walk is an easy 1½ hours.

On the southern side of Uluru, the Kuniya Walk and Mutitjulu Waterhole trail starts at the Kuniya car park and is an easy 45-minute walk along a wheelchair-accessible trail to the water hole, home of Wanampi, an ancestral snake. A rock shelter once used by Aboriginal people houses rock art.

Another popular way to experience Uluru is to watch the natural light reflect on it from one of the two sunset-viewing areas. As the last rays of daylight strike, the rock positively glows as if lit from within. Just as quickly, the light is extinguished and the color changes to a somber mauve and finally to black. ✉ *Lasseter Hwy., Yulara* ⊕ *www.parksaustralia.gov. au* ✉ *A$25.*

Uluru–Kata Tjuta Cultural Centre

MUSEUM | The cultural center is the first thing you'll see after entering the park through a tollgate. The two buildings are built in a serpentine style, reflecting the Kuniya and Liru stories about two ancestral snakes who fought a long-ago battle on the southern side of Uluru. Inside, you can learn about Aboriginal history and the return of the park to its traditional owners on October 26, 1985. There's also an excellent park ranger's station where you can get maps and hiking guides, as well as two art shops, Maruku and Walkatjara, where you'll likely see indigenous artists at work. Pick up a souvenir or grab refreshments at the Ininti Cafe, or rent a bicycle for another fun way to explore this beautiful Outback landscape (from A$90). ✉ *Uluru Rd., Yulara* ☎ *08/8956–1128* ⊕ *www.parksaustralia.gov.au/uluru* ✉ *Free.*

🍴 Restaurants

Gecko's Cafe

$$ | **MEDITERRANEAN** | In the center of the Yulara Town Centre, this casual eatery has reasonably priced options, including affordable appetizers, salads, burgers, pastas, pizzas, and sweet treats. Open every day for lunch and dinner, it's one of the most budget-friendly spots in Ayers Rock Resort. **Known for:** beer-battered barramundi served with desert lime aioli; crocodile ribs marinated in lemon myrtle; kangaroo and Wagyu beef burgers. [$] *Average main: A$26* ✉ *Yulara Town Sq., 1/127 Yulara Dr., Yulara* ☎ *02/8296–8010* 🌐 *www.ayersrockresort.com.au.*

Ilkari Restaurant

$$$$ | **AUSTRALIAN** | Situated inside the Sails in the Desert hotel, Ilkari Restaurant serves specialties like lamb cutlets and kangaroo skewers at live cooking stations, giving you a sort of dinner-and-a-show experience compared to that of the usual hotel buffet. The buffet items change nightly and the decor reflects local legends with a Kuniya Dreaming mural covering the rear wall. **Known for:** the perennially popular chocolate fountain; South Australian oysters and King Prawns; cooked-to-order dishes made with flair. [$] *Average main: A$75* ✉ *1/163 Yulara Dr., Yulara* ✣ *Located inside Sails in the Desert Hotel* ☎ *02/8296–8010* 🌐 *www.ayersrockresort.com.au.*

Pioneer BBQ and Bar

$$ | **AUSTRALIAN** | Order steaks, barramundi, emu sausages, crocodile tails, or kangaroo loins from the server, then cook it to your liking Aussie-style on large barbecues. This DIY-dining option and its adjacent bar with live music is one of the most popular in the resort, and with barbecue being practically a national sport here, it's easy to see why. **Known for:** vegetarian options such as tofu and vegetable stir fry plus salad bar; chicken breast marinated in locally sourced lemon myrtle; trio of chilli cheese kransky, Italian, and chicken sausages. [$] *Average main: A$25* ✉ *Outback Pioneer Hotel, 2/1 Yulara Dr., Yulara* ☎ *08/8957–7605* 🌐 *www.ayersrockresort.com.au.*

Pira Pool Bar

$$ | **ECLECTIC** | A lovely spot for a late-afternoon cocktail or mocktail, this casual poolside bar at Sails in the Desert offers an all-day menu of light bites from 11 am to 7 pm. A variety of wines, beers, ciders, soft drinks, coffees, teas, and juices are also available. **Known for:** curry of the day; James Squire 150 Lashes beer-battered barramundi; tandoori chicken sliders. [$] *Average main: A$26* ✉ *Sails in the Desert Hotel, 163 Yulara Dr., Yulara* ☎ *08/8957–7417* 🌐 *www.ayersrockresort.com.au.*

★ **Sounds of Silence**

$$$ | **AUSTRALIAN** | Australian wines and Northern Territory specialty dishes like bush salads and Australian game are served at a lookout here before you dine on your buffet meal in the middle of the desert and enjoy an astronomer-led stargazing tour of the southern sky. A more intimate and pricier small-group table d'hôte four-course dinner called Tali Wiru is also available for a maximum of 20 diners at a different vantage point. **Known for:** complimentary transfers and open bar are included in the price; bush tucker–inspired buffet items; canapés made with locally sourced indigenous ingredients. [$] *Average main: A$210* ✉ *171 Yulara Dr., Yulara* ☎ *02/8296–8010* 🌐 *www.ayersrockresort.com.au/experiences/detail/sounds-of-silence.*

🛏 Hotels

Desert Gardens Hotel

$$$$ | **HOTEL** | Blond-wood furniture complements desert hues in this hotel's small, neat rooms, which are named after different Australian flora, have a balcony or courtyard, and are surrounded by lovely native gardens. **Pros:** views of Uluru; free in-room Wi-Fi; shady gardens

An Official End to Climbing Uluru

While the topic of climbing Uluru is a heated subject in Central Australia these days, it was decided in 2017 by the park's management board that the climbing trail will be closed as of October 26, 2019, the 34th anniversary of the handover of the parklands to the Anangu traditional owners. Besides being a strenuous, even dangerous hike—the 1.5-km (1-mile) hike takes about three hours round-trip in extreme heat without a real trail, just a single chain to cling to for folks traveling in both directions—it's considered extremely disrespectful to climb such a sacred Aboriginal site. Several signs posted at the base of the trail remind visitors of the many cultural, environmental, and safety reasons to admire this amazing monolith from the ground level.

With climbing Uluru no longer an option, it's important to remember that there are many other ways to experience it from below—or above. You can rent a bike, ride a Segway, take a motorcycle tour, go on an Aboriginal cultural tour, take a helicopter ride to see it from above, sky dive next to it, view it from a blimp, enjoy a fancy dinner under the stars or view a fabulous art and light exhibit (Field of Light, through December 2020) near it, see it at sunrise and sunset from one of the viewing areas, or just take a drive or walk around the base to view it from all possible angles.

among gum trees. **Cons:** busy resort entrance road passes hotel; the property looks a little dated; a 10- to 15-minutes walk or shuttle ride (free) to Yulara Town Centre. $ *Rooms from: A$550* ⊠ *1 Yulara Dr., Yulara* ☎ *02/8296–8010* ⊕ *www. ayersrockresort.com.au/accommodation/ desert-gardens-hotel* ⤳ *218 rooms* ❍ *No meals.*

Emu Walk Apartments

$$$$ | **HOTEL** | **FAMILY** | Perfect for families, large groups, or folks who otherwise just like to cook while they're on the road, Emu Walk Apartments is the only accommodation at Ayers Rock Resort that offers an in-room self-catering option, complete with full kitchens. **Pros:** extra beds ideal for families or traveling companions; within walking distance to shops and supermarket; adjacent to resort dining options. **Cons:** room rates are pricey; limited amenities in rooms; you may hear some noise from folks walking to and from Yulara Town Centre next door. $ *Rooms from: A$575* ⊠ *3 Yulara Dr., Yulara* ☎ *02/8296–8010* ⊕ *www.ayersrockresort.com.au/accommodation/emu-walk-apartments* ⤳ *60 apartments* ❍ *No meals.*

★ Longitude 131°

$$$$ | **RESORT** | With 15 elevated, hard-floored "tents" offering king-size beds and uninterrupted, panoramic views of Uluru thanks to the floor-to-ceiling sliding-glass doors, this desert oasis about 3 km (2 miles) from the Ayers Rock Resort provides the ultimate Outback luxury experience. **Pros:** luxury tented accommodation, some convertible to twin share; dinner under the stars; touring included. **Cons:** children younger than 13 not allowed; no bathtubs; minimum two-night stay requirement. $ *Rooms from: A$1500* ⊠ *Yulara Dr., Yulara* ☎ *02/9918–4355* ⊕ *longitude131.com.au* ⤳ *15 suites* ❍ *All-inclusive.*

The Lost Camel

$$$$ | **HOTEL** | This boutique-hotel-style property is built around a blue-tile, rivet-and-glass-paneled, reverse infinity pool, arguably the fanciest in Ayers Rock

Resort. **Pros:** brightly colored decor; the prettiest, most stylish swimming pool in the resort; Aboriginal-themed photographs on walls. **Cons:** unusual bathroom layout; rooms can be pricey; it's next to Yulara Town Square, so can be busy. $ *Rooms from: A$460* ✉ *Yulara Dr., Yulara* ☎ *02/8296–8010* 🌐 *www.ayersrockresort.com.au/accommodation/the-lost-camel-hotel* 🛏 *99 rooms* 🍴 *No meals.*

Outback Pioneer Hotel and Lodge

$$$ | HOTEL | FAMILY | The theme at this affordable and popular hotel is the 1860s Outback, complete with corrugated iron, timber beams, and camel saddles. **Pros:** lodge rooms are cheapest in the resort; free shuttle bus; tennis courts. **Cons:** some of the budget-style rooms require the use of communal bathroom and shower facilities, which are cleaned regularly; hotel rooms are basic for the price; rooms closer to Pioneer BBQ will hear live music and DJs until about 11 pm, with people talking outside for another hour or so. $ *Rooms from: A$280* ✉ *Yulara Dr., Yulara* ☎ *02/8296–8010* 🌐 *www.ayersrockresort.com.au/accommodation/outback-pioneer-lodge* 🛏 *167 rooms* 🍴 *No meals.*

★ **Sails in the Desert**

$$$$ | RESORT | FAMILY | Architectural shade sails, ghost-gum-fringed lawns, Aboriginal art, and numerous facilities distinguish this upscale hotel with rooms in three-tiered blocks that frame a gorgeous white-tiled pool. **Pros:** Aboriginal artworks featured throughout; kids under 12 stay free; complimentary in-room Wi-Fi. **Cons:** rooms and dining options are the priciest at Ayers Rock Resort; this hotel is popular with families and well-to-do tour groups; you must walk 5–10 minutes or take the free shuttle to get to Yulara Town Square. $ *Rooms from: A$680* ✉ *163 Yulara Dr., Yulara* ☎ *02/8296–8010* 🌐 *www.ayersrockresort.com.au/accommodation/sails-in-the-desert* 🛏 *228 rooms* 🍴 *No meals.*

Shopping

Uluru–Kata Tjuta Cultural Centre

GIFTS/SOUVENIRS | FAMILY | The cultural center not only has information about the Anangu people and their culture, it also houses beautiful art for purchase. The Ininti Cafe carries souvenirs and light food, while Maruku and Walkatjara Art Uluru sell Aboriginal paintings and handicrafts. The Cultural Centre itself is open daily from 7 am to 6 pm (information desk from 8 am to 5 pm); Ininti Cafe is open daily from 7 am to 5 pm; Maruku Arts is open daily 7:30 am to 5:30 pm; Walkatjara Art Uluru is open daily from 8 am to 4 pm. ✉ *Uluru–Kata Tjuta National Park, Uluru Rd., Yulara* ☎ *08/8956–1128.*

Darwin

3,149 km (1,956 miles) northwest of Sydney, 2,618 km (1,626 miles) north of Adelaide.

Darwin is Australia's most colorful and exotic capital city. Surrounded on three sides by the turquoise waters of the Timor Sea, the streets are lined with tropical frangipani flowers and palm trees. Warm and dry in winter, hot and steamy in summer, it's a relaxed and casual place, as well as a beguiling blend of tropical frontier outpost and Outback hardiness. Thanks to the humidity levels, its close proximity to Southeast Asia, and its multicultural population, it almost seems more like Asia than the rest of Australia.

Darwin is a city that has always had to fight for its survival. Its history of failed attempts date from 1824, when Europeans attempted to establish an enclave in this harsh, unyielding climate. The original 1869 settlement, called Palmerston, was built on a parcel of mangrove wetlands and scrub forest. It was not until 1911, after it had already weathered the disastrous cyclones of 1878, 1881,

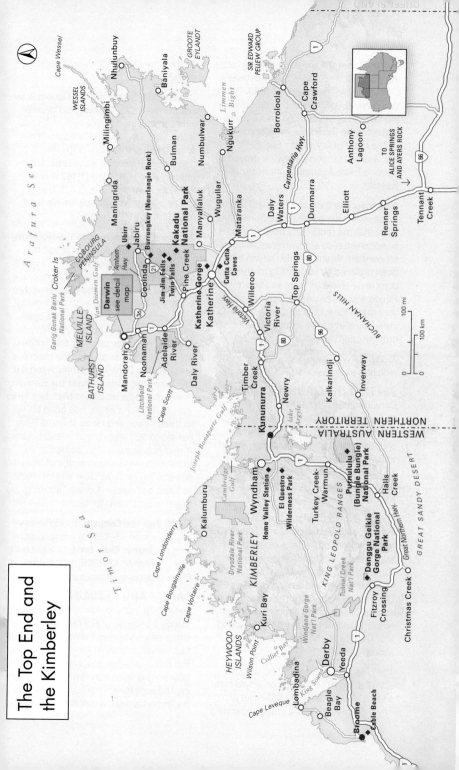

The Top End and the Kimberley

and 1897, that the town was named after the scientist who had visited Australia's shores aboard the *Beagle* in 1839. During World War II, it was bombed 64 times, as the harbor full of warships was a prime target for the Japanese war planes. Then, on the night of Christmas Eve 1974, the city was almost completely destroyed by Cyclone Tracy, Australia's greatest natural disaster.

It's a tribute to those who stayed and to those who have come to live here after Tracy that the rebuilt city now thrives as an administrative and commercial center for northern Australia. Old Darwin has been replaced by something of an edifice complex—such buildings as Parliament House and the Supreme Court all seem very grand for such a small city, especially one that prides itself on its casual, outdoor-centric lifestyle.

Today, Darwin is the best place from which to explore Australia's Top End.

GETTING HERE AND AROUND

Darwin's International Airport is serviced from overseas by Qantas, Jetstar (and Jetstar Asia), Donghai Airlines, SilkAir, and Air North. Jetstar flies from Darwin to Bali several times a week, while SilkAir and Jetstar Asia connect Darwin with Singapore, and Air North flies to Dili in East Timor.

Qantas, Air North, Virgin Australia, Tigerair, and Jetstar all fly into Darwin regularly from other parts of Australia and operate regional flights within the Top End. Air North flies west to Kununurra and Broome, and east to Gove. The Darwin City Airport Shuttle offers regular service between the airport and the city's hotels for A$18 one-way or A$36 round-trip. The taxi journey downtown costs about A$25–A$30.

The *Ghan* train connects Darwin with Adelaide via Alice Springs on a two-night all-inclusive 2,979-km (1,851-mile) journey a couple of times a week depending on the time of year (⊕ *www.greatsouthernrail.com.au*).

The best way to get around Darwin is by car and the Stuart Highway is Darwin's land connection with the rest of Australia. By road, Darwin is 16½ hours from Alice Springs (1,497 km [930 miles]), 21 hours from Broome via the Great Northern Highway (1,871 km [1,162 miles]), 38 hours from Brisbane (3,425 km [2,128 miles]), and 44 hours from Perth (4,041km [2,510 miles]).

For drivers headed outside the Northern Territory, note that one-way drop-off fees for rental vehicles are often twice as much as a weekly rentals. If you don't feel like driving, the bus network in Darwin links the city with its far-flung suburbs, and a choice of minibus operators, including the 24-hour Metro mini buses, run all over town for fixed prices starting at A$4 per person. The main bus terminal (the Darwin Bus Interchange) is on Harry Chan Avenue, near the Bennett Street end of Smith Street Mall; bus fares start at A$3 for a single ride good for up to three hours, and range from A$7 day passes to $20 weekly and 10-trip tickets. A mini bus stand is also located at the front of Darwin's airport terminal. Popular ride-sharing services Uber and Hi Oscar can also be found in Darwin, allowing you to get around town for less.

TAXIS Blue Taxi Company. ⊠ *15 Finniss St., Darwin* ☎ *13–8294* ⊕ *www.bluetaxi. com.au.* **Darwin Radio Taxis.** ⊠ *315 Larkin Ave., Darwin* ☎ *13–1008 in local area* ⊕ *www.darwinradiotaxis.com.au.*

SAFETY AND PRECAUTIONS

Swimming in the ocean is not recommended because of the box jellyfish, commonly known as "stingers." Salt and freshwater crocodiles are found in most Top End billabongs and rivers, and are occasionally seen even on Darwin beaches. The accessible rivers and billabongs are generally signposted if saltwater crocodiles are known to inhabit the area, but if you are not sure, don't swim.

Avoid driving outside towns after dark due to the dangers presented by roaming buffalo, cattle, horses, donkeys, and kangaroos. If your vehicle breaks down, stay with it; it is easier to find a missing car than missing people. If you are going for a bushwalk, always tell someone your plan and when you expect to return.

TIMING

Although Darwin has some attractions, many people view the city as the entry point to the Top End's national parks, in particular Kakadu and Litchfield. Two days in the city will be enough to see the main attractions, after which you will want to head to Kakadu.

TOURS

AAT Kings Darwin Day Tours

GUIDED TOURS | AAT Kings offers afternoon tours to several popular sights around the city, including the Darwin Aviation Museum, Museum and Art Gallery of the Northern Territory, and George Brown Botanic Gardens, all while guides discuss the culture of the area's Larrakia traditional owners, the city's role in World War II, and how it came to be such a multicultural locale today (A$99). Those in a more adventurous mood should check out the company's Jumping Crocs and Nature Adventure tour, which includes a cruise down the Adelaide River about 90-minutes outside of town that also happens to be home to more than 1,600 crocodiles. You'll also visit the Window on the Wetlands and Fogg Dam Conservation Reserve on this half-day trip (A$115). ⊠ 6/52 Mitchell St., City Center ☎ 1300/228546 ⊕ www.aatkings.com/tours/?q=darwin 🖾 A$99.

Darwin City Explorer (Tour Tub)

BUS TOURS | Known in these parts as the "Tour Tub," the Darwin City Explorer takes you on a half-day guided trip to some of the area's biggest attractions, including the WWII Oil Storage Tunnels,

the Defence of Darwin Experience & Darwin Military Museum, the Museum and Art Gallery of the Northern Territory, Fannie Bay Gaol, the Aviation Heritage Centre, and on certain days, the Parap Markets (Saturday) and the Qantas Hanger (Monday through Friday). Your ticket also gives you complimentary transfers from your hotel and covers entrance fees to all listed attractions. ⊠ 50 Mitchell St., City Center ☎ 08/8985–6322 ⊕ northernterritory.com/tours/darwin-city-explorer-tour-tub 🖾 From A$120.

Spirit of Darwin Sunset Cruises

BOAT TOURS | Embark on a 2½-hour cruise around scenic Darwin Harbour, with a complimentary drink and canapés as you take in views of one of the best sunsets in the Top End. For A$30 more, you can add the dinner option, which includes your choice of main dish, salad, and dessert. ⊠ Dock, 2 Stokes Hill Rd., City Center ☎ 0417/381977 ⊕ spiritofdarwin.com.au 🖾 From A$70.

ESSENTIALS

VISITOR INFORMATION Top End Tourism.
⊠ 6 Bennett St., City Center ☎ 08/8980–6000, 1300/138886 ⊕ www.tourism-topend.com.au.

◉ Sights

Crocosaurus Cove

ZOO | FAMILY | Right in the heart of Darwin City, this is the place to go swimming with saltwater crocodiles and live to tell the tale. Feeding times for the big crocs (daily at 11:30 am, 2:30 pm, and 4:30 pm) and the Cage of Death, a not-for-the-faint-of-heart attraction where visitors are lowered into croc-infested pools in a clear perspex container (A$170), are not to be missed. Bring your swimsuit along and take a photo of you swimming alongside these impressive creatures (again, you're in a completely separate pool). Feedings and presentations happen at different times throughout the day in the four main sections—fish, big crocs, turtles,

Sights ▼

1 Crocosaurus Cove......... **C7**

2 Crocodylus Park **D3**

3 Darwin Aviation Museum **D3**

4 Defence of Darwin Experience at the Darwin Military Museum **A1**

5 The Darwin Waterfront Precinct and Stokes Hill Wharf **D8**

6 George Brown Darwin Botanic Gardens..... **C5**

7 Indo Pacific Marine **D8**

8 Museum and Art Gallery of the Northern Territory..... **B4**

9 Territory Wildlife Park **D5**

Restaurants ▼

1 Crustaceans on the Wharf **D8**

2 Hanuman ... **B7**

3 il lido BARpizza.... **C8**

4 Lola's Pergola...... **A6**

5 Manoli's Greek Taverna **C7**

6 Pee Wee's at the Point **A2**

Hotels ▼

1 DoubleTree by Hilton Hotel Esplanade Darwin **B7**

2 Novotel Darwin CBD Hotel... **B7**

3 Sky City Darwin **B6**

4 Vibe Hotel Darwin Waterfront.. **C8**

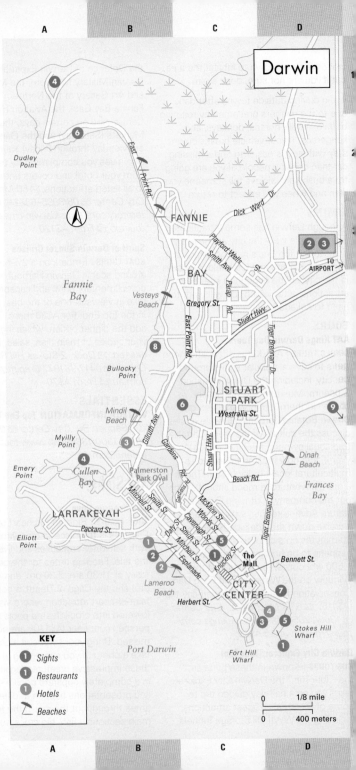

Darwin

KEY

1 Sights

1 Restaurants

1 Hotels

⌐ Beaches

0 ____ 1/8 mile

0 ____ 400 meters

and nocturnal reptiles—during which you can take your turn feeding young crocs and holding a variety of reptiles. ⊠ *58 Mitchell St., Darwin* ☎ *08/8981–7522* ⊕ *www.crocosauruscove.com* ✉ *A$35*.

Crocodylus Park

ZOO | FAMILY | This research facility has an excellent air-conditioned crocodile museum and education center. There are more than 1,200 crocodiles here, from babies to giants up to 5 meters (16 feet) long. The saurian section of the zoo includes the croc-infested Bellairs Lagoon and pens for breeding and raising. The park also has enclosures with lions, tigers, American alligators, cassowaries, primates, turtles, an emu, and a dingo, among other animals, and holds one of the biggest snakes in Australia: a Burmese python weighing 140 kg (308 lbs). Tours and feedings are at 10 am, 12 pm, and 2 pm, while a croc boat cruise gets you a little closer to these magnificent creatures twice a day at 11 am and 1 pm. ⊠ *815 McMillans Rd., Berrimah* ☎ *08/8922–4500* ⊕ *www.crocodyluspark. com.au* ✉ *A$40*.

Darwin Aviation Museum

MUSEUM | Due to its isolation and sparse population, the Northern Territory played an important role in the expansion of aviation in Australia, and this impressive museum traces the history of flight Down Under. Planes on display include a massive B-52 bomber on permanent loan from the United States and a recently retired RAAF F-111 fighter jet, as well as a Japanese Zero shot down on the first day of bombing raids in 1942. There's also a great exhibition on female aviators, including Amy Johnson, the first to fly solo from the U.K. to Australia in 1930. ⊠ *557 Stuart Hwy., Winnellie* ☎ *08/8947–2145* ⊕ *www.darwinaviationmuseum. com.au* ✉ *A$15*.

The Darwin Waterfront Precinct and Stokes Hill Wharf

MARINA | FAMILY | The best views of Darwin Harbour are from Stokes Hill Wharf,

Be Croc Smart ◉

The crocodile has long been a dominant predator in the wetland regions of Australia. Powerful and stealthy, the saltwater (estuarine) crocodile has little to fear—and that includes humans. More than 150,000 "salties" and another 100,000 freshwater crocs ("freshies") make their home in the coastal and tidal areas of rivers, as well as floodplains and freshwater reaches of rivers of northern Australia. Attacks on people are rare and deaths few (about one a year), but you should observe all no-swimming and warning signs and treat crocs with respect.

11

The Outback DARWIN

a working pier that receives cargo ships, trawlers, defense vessels, and, occasionally, huge cruise liners. It's also a favorite spot for Darwinites to fish, and when the mackerel are running, you can join scores of locals over a few beers. The cluster of cafés becomes crowded on weekends and when cruise ships arrive. On the city side, in the Waterfront Precinct, is the Wave Lagoon (entry is $7; open daily 10 am to 6 pm) and a free, stinger-free (safe from jellyfish) swimming lagoon. Both are popular on hot days. The Waterfront is also home to some of the city's best restaurants and cafés, and is where free festivals and movie nights are held during the dry season. ⊠ *19B Kitchener Dr., Darwin Harbour* ☎ *08/8999–5155* ⊕ *www. waterfront.nt.gov.au*.

Defence of Darwin Experience at the Darwin Military Museum

MUSEUM | WWII came to Australia when 188 Japanese planes bombed Darwin on February 19, 1942, killing 235 people and injuring an additional 400. This high-tech, newer section of the museum at East Point—opened in 2012 to commemorate the 70th anniversary of the attack—tells the story of the people who were there that day, the events that led up to and followed it, and Darwin's role in the war. The Defence of Darwin Experience is the highlight—when you hear the air raid siren, head to the back of the museum and enter the theater to view an intense, multi-sensory telling of what happened that day, complete with loud explosive sounds, strobe lights, and flash effects. It's part of the Darwin Military Museum, which has lots of guns and other military equipment on display, as well as some original buildings that were there during World War II. ⊠ *5434 Alec Fong Lim Dr., East Point* ☎ *08/8981–9702* ⊕ *www.darwinmilitarymuseum.com.au* ✉ *A$20.*

George Brown Darwin Botanic Gardens
GARDEN | FAMILY | First planted in 1886 and largely destroyed by Cyclone Tracy, the 103-acre site today displays rain forest, mangroves, and open woodland environments. There are more than 450 species of palms growing in the gardens. A popular walk takes visitors on a self-guided tour of plants that Aboriginal people have used for medicinal purposes for centuries. The Children's Evolutionary Playground traces the changes in plant groups through time, while the plant display house has tropical ferns, orchids, and other exotic plants to check out. Head to Eva's, a lovely café nestled in a heritage listed church within the gardens—it's open from 7 am to 3 pm for breakfast, lunch, and offers a variety of tasty baked goods, coffee, and tea in case you need a break. ⊠ *Gilruth Ave. at Gardens Rd., Mindil Beach* ☎ *08/8999–4418* ⊕ *www.nt.gov.au* ✉ *Free.*

Indo Pacific Marine
ZOO | This marine interpretative center houses a large open tank with one of the few self-contained coral-reef ecosystems in the southern hemisphere—and it's been growing on its own for more than 20 years. Other exhibits include a static display of rare, deepwater coral skeletons and an exhibit explaining the effects

A Tropical Summer

Darwin's wet season—when the humidity rises and monsoonal rains dump around 68 inches—runs from November to April. The days offer a predictable mix of sunshine and afternoon showers, along with some spectacular thunder and lightning storms. There are fewer visitors at this time of the year, and Darwin slows to an even more relaxed pace. Across the Top End, waterfalls increase in size, floodplains rejuvenate to a lush green, and flowers bloom.

of global warming on the planet. Night tours, which begin at 6:30 on Wednesday, Friday, and Sunday, take you by ultraviolet flashlight to view the biodiversity of the fluorescing reef and live venomous animals; the colors the coral produce are astounding. You'll also get a four-course seafood dinner, followed by a nocturnal coral reef tour of the exhibitions. Bookings are essential. ⊠ *29 Stokes Hill Rd., Wharf Precinct* ☎ *08/8981–1294* ⊕ *www.indopacificmarine.com.au* ✉ *From A$27.*

★ **Museum and Art Gallery of the Northern Territory**
MUSEUM | Collections at this excellent—and free—museum and art gallery encompass Aboriginal art and culture, maritime archaeology, Northern Territory history, and natural sciences. One gallery is devoted to Cyclone Tracy, where you can listen to a terrifying recording of the howling winds. You can also see "Sweetheart," a 16-foot, 10-inch stuffed saltwater crocodile that was known for attacking fishing boats on the Finniss River in the 1970s. ⊠ *19 Conacher St., Fannie Bay* ☎ *08/8999–8264* ⊕ *www.magnt.net.au* ✉ *Free.*

Off The Beaten Path

Litchfield National Park. This beautiful park lies just 120 km (75 miles) southwest of Darwin off the Stuart Highway. Its 1,500 square km (579 square miles) are an untouched wilderness of monsoonal rain forests, rivers, and striking rock formations. The highlights include four separate, spectacular waterfalls—**Florence, Tjaynera (Sandy Creek), Wangi, and Tolmer Falls**—all of which have secluded plunge pools. ⚠ **The pools are suitable for swimming but occasionally there are crocs here, so observe any "no swimming" signs.** There is also a dramatic group of large, freestanding sandstone pillars known as the **Lost City** (accessible only by four-wheel-drive track), and **Magnetic Termite Mounds,** which have an eerie resemblance to eroded grave markers, which dot the black-soiled plains of the park's northern area. You'll need to camp if you want to stay in the park; campgrounds and RV sites are located near several of the major sights (call the Parks and Wildlife Service of the Northern Territory at ☎ *08/8976–0282* for more information on the facilities, as they vary by campsite). There are also a few restaurants and modest hotels in the nearby town of Batchelor, though most folks just visit Litchfield as a day-trip from Darwin, about a 90-minute drive away. ✉ *Litchfield Park Rd., Litchfield Park* ✣ *120 km (75 miles) southwest of Darwin* 🌐 *nt.gov.au* 🎫 *Free.*

Territory Wildlife Park

NATURE PRESERVE | **FAMILY** | With 1,544 acres of natural bushland, this impressive park is dedicated to the Northern Territory's native fauna and flora. In addition to saltwater crocodiles, dingoes, olive pythons, and waterbirds, among other animals, the park also has an underwater viewing area for observing freshwater fish and a nocturnal house kept dark for late-night creatures. The treetop-level walkway through the huge aviary allows you to watch native birds from the swamps and forests at close range. Daily events include feedings, guided walks, and a birds of prey display: see the website for daily schedules. There's also a nifty tram to help you get around. ✉ *Cox Peninsula Rd., Berry Springs* ✣ *50 km (31 miles) or about 45 mins south of Darwin* ☎ *08/8988–7200* 🌐 *www.territorywildlifepark.com.au* 🎫 *A$32.*

🍴 Restaurants

Crustaceans on the Wharf

$$ | **SEAFOOD** | **FAMILY** | Located at the end of Stokes Hill Wharf, and in a great spot to catch the sunset, this casual restaurant specializes in all things seafood, with dishes like local wild-caught barramundi, lobster mornay, and crumbled calamari on the menu. Kids ages 10 and under eat free for every adult main meal purchased. **Known for:** Moreton Bay bugs (similar to small lobsters); chilli prawns; Thai Massaman beef curry. [$] *Average main: A$30* ✉ *Stokes Hill Wharf, Darwin Wharf Precinct, Wharf Precinct* ☎ *08/8981–8658* 🌐 *www.crustaceans.net.au.*

★ **Hanuman**

$$ | **THAI** | By drawing on Thai, Nonya (Malaysian), and Indian tandoori culinary traditions, Hanuman's chefs turn local herbs, vegetables, and seafood into sumptuous and innovative dishes. Excellent food and a wine list that includes the best from every grape-growing region in Australia are served against a backdrop of furnishings, tableware, and artwork from around the world in Hanuman's indoor and alfresco dining areas. **Known for:** lightly cooked oysters in a spicy coriander-and-lemongrass sauce; prawns cooked in coconut with wild ginger and curry sauce; creative curries–green curry of chicken, jungle curry beef, and red curry of duck. [$] *Average main: A$30* ✉ *93 Mitchell St., City Center* ☎ *08/8941–3500* 🌐 *www.hanuman.com.au* 🕓 *No lunch weekends.*

il lido BARpizza

$$ | **ITALIAN** | This polished pizzeria and bar in Darwin's vibrant Waterfront Precinct provides reflective views as you drink and dine in the open air. With toppings like truffled mushrooms and roast pork belly with smoked bacon, toffee apple jam, and crackling, this isn't your average pizzeria. **Known for:** European-style pizza, with tarte flambée, crème fraîche, bacon, and onion; burgers, braised lamb shank, and barbecue beef short ribs; outrageous cocktails. [$] *Average main: A$25* ✉ *3/19 Kitchener Dr., Darwin Harbour* ☎ *08/8941–0900* 🌐 *www.illidodarwin.com.au.*

Lola's Pergola

$ | **AUSTRALIAN** | Named for the owner's daughter, this whimsical waterfront spot along the Cullen Bay Marina serves pub grub favorites like burgers, pizzas, and, of course, chips, in a circus-inspired setting complete with carousel horses (some which can be used) and other retro-style, nostalgia-inducing decor. It's a great place to take the kids and your young-at-heart friends. **Known for:** an excellent craft beer selection; family-friendly atmosphere; mango chicken burgers. [$] *Average main: A$20* ✉ *48 Marina Blvd., Cullen Bay* ☎ *08/8941–5711* 🕓 *Closed Mon.*

Manoli's Greek Taverna

$$ | **GREEK** | Darwin's got a vast Greek community and this foodie hot spot is a celebration of Kalymnian cooking traditions handed down from generation to generation. With a simple white and blue decor, the focus here is on the food, and the approach is Mezethes-style dining, or having plates of food to share with your friends and family. **Known for:** live bouzouki music on Friday and Saturday nights; tender fried calamari (kalamaraki); classic Greek sweets like baklava and galatobouriko. [$] *Average main: A$28* ✉ *4/64 Smith St., Darwin* ☎ *08/8981–9120* 🌐 *www.manolisgreektaverna.com.au* 🕓 *Closed Sun. and Mon. No lunch Sat.*

Pee Wee's at the Point

$$$ | **MODERN AUSTRALIAN** | Uninterrupted views of Darwin Harbour at East Point Reserve, modern Australian fare, and a carefully considered wine list make this restaurant a favorite with locals and visitors wanting a special night out. Dine inside with views of the harbor through large glass doors, or site out on the tiered timber decks beneath the stars. **Known for:** oven-baked, wild-caught NT saltwater barramundi; spicy threadfin salmon wings; a deliciously decadent dessert called Fifty Shades of Chocolate. [$] *Average main: A$45* ✉ *East Point Reserve , Alec Fong Ling Dr., Fannie Bay* ☎ *08/8981–6868* 🌐 *www.peewees.com.au* 🕓 *Closed Sun. and Mon. Closed during the wet season (late Jan.–mid-Mar.).*

Hotels

DoubleTree by Hilton Hotel Esplanade Darwin

$$$ | **HOTEL** | Located at the edge of the CBD next to another completely separate DoubleTree property, this hotel is an easy five-minute walk from all the popular pubs, restaurants, and shopping on Mitchell Street. **Pros:** great location in the city center; large swimming pool with pool floats and noodles; free parking. **Cons:** nearby convention center attracts tour groups; Wi-Fi costs A$9.95 for 24 hours if you're not a Hilton Honors member; room temperature is set and controlled outside the room, so it can be too warm or too cold sometimes. [$] *Rooms from: A$275* ✉ *116 The Esplanade,*

Tiwi Islands sculptures at a gallery in Darwin

Darwin ☎ 08/8980–0800 🌐 doubletree3.
ʰilton.com 🛏 197 rooms 🍴 No meals.

★ **Novotel Darwin CBD Hotel**
$$$ | **HOTEL** | Situated along Darwin's magnificent Esplanade, just one block from all the action on Mitchell Street, this hotel offers a green tropical oasis in its lobby, a charming bar and restaurant in the vine-filled atrium, and rooms that overlook the park and the bright blue waters below. **Pros:** tropical garden in the atrium; some rooms have views overlooking Darwin Harbour; close to restaurants, pubs, and shopping. **Cons:** rooms absorb noise from the central atrium and bar, breakfast area; bathrooms are a little on the small side; parking is not free. [$] *Rooms from: A$239* ✉ *100 The Esplanade, Darwin* ☎ *08/8963–5000* 🌐 *www.accorhotels.com* 🛏 *141 rooms* 🍴 *No meals.*

★ **Sky City Darwin**
$ | **RESORT** | **FAMILY** | The most luxurious place to stay in Darwin, the three-story hotel adjacent to the SkyCity Darwin casino offers oceanfront accommodations set amid lush lawns and gardens plus 32 resort rooms and suites surrounding a huge lagoon-style swimming pool. **Pros:** Darwin's only swim-up bar; award-winning restaurants on-site; next door to Mindil Markets (open mid-April to mid-October during the dry season). **Cons:** casino operates 24 hours, so nights can be noisy; convention center attracts big groups; parking is not free ($15 a night). [$] *Rooms from: A$189* ✉ *Gilruth Ave., Mindil Beach* ☎ *08/8943–8888* 🌐 *www.skycitydarwin.com.au* 🛏 *152 rooms* 🍴 *No meals.*

Vibe Hotel Darwin Waterfront
$$$ | **HOTEL** | This good-value hotel overlooks the Darwin Wave Pool and Lagoon and puts you right in the heart of the busy Waterfront precinct. **Pros:** great location; nice views of Darwin Waterfront; surrounded by great pubs and restaurants. **Cons:** 10-minute walk to city center; parking on-site but not free (A$15 per day); Wi-Fi is free but slow at 1 MBPS. [$] *Rooms from: A$252* ✉ *7 Kitchener Dr., Waterfront* ☎ *13–8423* 🌐 *vibehotels.com/*

hotel/darwin-waterfront ⤴ *121 rooms*
|○| *No meals.*

🍸 Nightlife

★ The Darwin Ski Club

BARS/PUBS | This favorite local spot is *the* place to go for a sunset beer in the tropics, and it's right next to the Museum and Art Gallery of the Northern Territory. Its plastic white chairs and tables add to the laid back, "old Darwin" vibe. There's live music on Friday and Saturday night, too. ⊠ *20 Conacher St., Fannie Bay* ☎ *08/8981–6630* ⊕ *www.darwinskiclub. com.au.*

Hotel Darwin

BARS/PUBS | Built as an iconic hotel in the 1940s, the original structure survived the bombing of Darwin and Cyclone Tracy only to be torn down in 1999 and rebuilt as the popular bar and restaurant you see today. Stop by for daily lunch specials between 11:30 am and 2:30 pm (or daily dinner specials between 6 pm and 9 pm), catch a game inside the sports bar, try your luck with with the Keno and UBET machines, or grab a drink and listen to live music in the spacious outdoor beer garden. ⊠ *39 Mitchell St., City Center* ☎ *08/8941–7947* ⊕ *www.thehoteldarwin. com.au.*

★ Shenannigans

BARS/PUBS | You'll likely hear it before you see it—there's live music nearly every night of the week, and folks are singing or dancing along with it outside on the terrace. This lively and local favorite Irish pub and restaurant offers traditional pub grub as well as a special Sunday roast, with Guinness, Kilkenny, and Harp on tap, among other popular beer selections. Join in on trivia night or karaoke night, held once a week, or dance the night away with everyone else. ⊠ *69 Mitchell St., City Center* ☎ *08/8981–2100* ⊕ *www. shenannigans.com.au.*

The Indigenous 🛍 Arts Scene

Start at the Museum and Art Gallery of the Northern Territory for a comprehensive understanding of indigenous art and artifacts, then head to one of many arts and crafts outlets in and around Darwin to purchase an authentic and unique piece of art. In many indigenous communities throughout the tropical Outback—including Maningrida, Oenpelli, the Tiwi islands, and Yirrikala—you can buy direct from the artist.

SkyCity Darwin Casino

CASINOS | SkyCity Casino is one of Darwin's most popular evening spots. The more than 700 gaming machines are open 24 hours, while gaming tables are open from noon until 4 am Thursday and Sunday and until 6 am Friday and Saturday. Fancy a break from the betting? Choose from one of four restaurants—Cove (steak house), Dragon Court (Asian-fusion), il Piatto (Italian), or The Vue (bistro dining). SkyCity's bars—Sandbar, The Sportsbar, Lagoon Bar, and Infinity, a new beach club–themed bar beside the casino's infinity pool—are just as fabulous. ⊠ *Mindil Beach, Gilruth Ave., Mindil Beach* ☎ *08/8943–8888* ⊕ *www. skycitydarwin.com.au.*

🎭 Performing Arts

Darwin Entertainment Centre

DANCE | Following a five-month hiatus and a $7.2-million renovation, the Darwin Entertainment Centre reopened in May 2018 with the Tony and Grammy award-winning show *American Idiot*, the first of many Broadway-level productions to pay a visit. Tickets generally start around A$35 and go up to A$100 depending on the show. ⊠ *93 Mitchell St., City Center* ☎ *08/8980–3333* ⊕ *www.yourcentre.com.au* ⊡ *Ticket prices vary.*

★ **Deckchair Cinema**

FILM | Watching a movie beneath the stars while relaxing on canvas deck chairs with a glass of wine at this outdoor, 400-seat movie theater is one of Darwin's quintessential experiences. Australian, foreign, art house, or classic films are screened every night from April through November. Gates open nightly at 6 pm, and picnic baskets (no BYO alcohol) are permitted, although there is a hot food kiosk and a bar. The first movie usually screens at 7:30 pm, with a second showing at 9 or 9:30 pm on Friday and Saturday nights offered for A$10 instead of the usual A$16. Make sure you hold onto your belongings—especially your food!—while you're watching the movie, as there are possums that roam the grounds and love to rummage through things. ⊠ *Jervois Rd., off Kitchener Dr., Wharf Precinct* ☎ *08/8981–0700* ⊕ *www.deckchaircinema.com* ⊡ *A$16.*

🛍 Shopping

★ **Mindil Beach Sunset Market**

OUTDOOR/FLEA/GREEN MARKETS | **FAMILY** | The Mindil Beach Sunset Market is an extravaganza that takes place every Thursday from 5 pm to 10 pm and every Sunday from 4 pm to 9 pm from April through October. Come in the late afternoon to snack at one of more than 60 stalls offering food from more than 25 different countries. You can shop at more than 200 local artisans' booths; enjoy performances by singers, dancers, fire artists, and musicians; catch a whip-cracking demonstration, or join the other Darwinites with a bottle of wine to watch the sun plunge into the sea. ⊠ *Beach Rd., Mindil Beach* ☎ *08/8981–3454* ⊕ *www.mindil.com.au.*

Nightcliff Market

OUTDOOR/FLEA/GREEN MARKETS | One of the few markets here open year-round, Nightcliff Market takes place on Sunday morning and lasts until around 2 pm in Nightcliff Village, with craft and food stalls and performances by musicians, dancers, and other entertainers; it's a great spot for breakfast. ⊠ *Pavonia Way, Nightcliff* ☎ *04/1436–8773.*

Parap Markets

OUTDOOR/FLEA/GREEN MARKETS | Located north of the city center, the Parap Markets is where the locals shop. The stalls are open every Saturday rain or shine from 8 am to 2 pm and have a terrific selection of ethnic Asian food, including some of the best laksa in the country. Complimentary shuttles are available from several Darwin City accommodations, so check the website for current times and pickup locations. ⊠ *3/3 Vickers St., Parap* ☎ *04/3888–2373* ⊕ *parapvillagemarkets.com.au.*

Rapid Creek Markets

OUTDOOR/FLEA/GREEN MARKETS | Open Sunday morning until about 1:30 pm, the Rapid Creek Markets are Darwin's oldest and have fresh organic produce, as well as flowers, seafood, and locally made handicrafts. Shop 'til you drop alongside the locals just 20 minutes north of the city center while you listen to live music and stock up on fresh groceries at one of more than 60 stalls. ⊠ *Rapid Creek Shopping Centre, 48 Trower Rd., Rapid Creek* ☎ *08/8948–4866* ⊕ *rapidcreekmarkets.com.au/markets.*

🏃 Activities

FISHING

Barramundi, the best-known fish of the Top End, can weigh up to 110 pounds and are excellent fighting fish that taste great on the barbecue afterward.

Department of Primary Industry and Resources Fisheries Division

FISHING | The office has information on licenses and catch limits. ✉ *Goff Letts Bldg., Berrimah Farm, Makagon Rd., Berrimah* ☎ *08/8999–2144* ⊕ *nt.gov.au/marine.*

Equinox Fishing Charters

FISHING | Equinox Fishing Charters has half-day, full-day, and extended fishing trips using the 38-foot *Tsar,* which is licensed to carry 12 passengers and two crew, and *Equinox II,* which can carry 18–20 people. Full-day fishing charters with all meals and tackle provided are from A$270 per person; shorter five- and seven-hour trips are also available, from A$170 and A$210, respectively. ✉ *64 Marina Blvd., Shop 2, Cullen Bay* ☎ *08/8942–2199* ⊕ *www.equinoxcharters.com.au* 🖾 *From A$170.*

Kakadu National Park

Begins 151 km (94 miles) southeast of Darwin.

This national park—almost the size of West Virginia—is a jewel among the Top End parks, and many visitors come to the region just to experience this tropical wilderness. The ancient landform has wetlands, gorges, waterfalls, and rugged escarpments. Beginning southeast of Darwin and covering some 19,800 square km (7,645 square miles), the park protects a large system of unspoiled rivers and creeks, as well as one of the highest concentrations of accessible Aboriginal rock-art sites in the world.

GETTING HERE AND AROUND

From Darwin it's a 90-minute drive south along the Stuart Highway, then east along the Arnhem Highway to the entrance to the park, then another hour or so to the Bowali Visitor Center, located near Jabiru. Although four-wheel-drive vehicles are not necessary to travel to the park, they are required for many of the unpaved

Gone Fishing 🏃

Joining a local tour guide is the best way to hook a big one. Locals know the best spots and techniques, and the guides' in-depth knowledge can make an enjoyable experience even better. In the estuaries, you can catch (among others) threadfin and blue salmon, cod, queenfish, black jewfish, cobia, coral trout, golden snapper, mud crabs, and the Top End's most famous fighting fish, the barramundi—barra in the local parlance. And you don't have to go far—Darwin's harbor teems with fish.

roads within, including the track to Jim Jim Falls. Entry is free, but you must buy a A$40 National Park permit, which is good for seven days.

SAFETY AND PRECAUTIONS

If you are driving, watch out for road trains—large trucks up to 160 feet in length with up to four trailers behind a prime mover. They are common on Northern Territory roads, and you should give them plenty of room. Avoid driving after dark outside towns because of the high likelihood of straying animals—kangaroos and cattle in particular. It is a good idea to always tell someone of your plans if you intend to travel to remote places; the same applies when bushwalking. Always make sure you have adequate water and food.

TIMING

The best time to visit is between May and September during the dry season. The shortest time you should allow is a three-day, two-night itinerary from Darwin, which will provide opportunities to visit the major sights—a cruise on the East Alligator River; Ubirr, a major Aboriginal rock-art site; a flight-seeing journey from Jabiru Airport; Nourlangie

Rock, another impressive Aboriginal rock-art site; the Warradjan Aboriginal Cultural Centre; and a sunset cruise on Yellow Water Billabong to see birds, crocodiles, and other wildlife up close. On the way into the park from Darwin, you can visit the Mamukala Wetlands to view an abundance of birds and wildlife. A five-day itinerary will give you time to visit Jim Jim Falls and Twin Fallson, a four-wheel-drive excursion.

TOURS

During the dry season, park rangers conduct free walks and tours at several popular locations. Pick up a program at the entry station or at either of the visitor centers to see what's on offer.

Far Out Adventures

ADVENTURE TOURS | Far Out Adventures runs private, customized tours of Kakadu, as well as other regions of the Top End, ideally suited for small groups. Trips are on the pricey side, with a three-day adventure for two starting around A$4,000, but you'll get to visit off-the-beaten-path places via four-wheel-drive vehicle and have a truly personalized itinerary. ⊠ Box 518, Humpty Doo ☎ 04/2715–2288 ⊕ www.farout.com.au ⌖ From A$4000.

★ Kakadu Air

AIR EXCURSIONS | The best way to see Kakadu's famous waterfalls is from the air during the wet season or early in the dry season around April. This company's flights out of Jabiru—a scenic hour (A$250) and a scenic half-hour (A$150) are well worth the splurge. In the dry season, the flight encompasses the northern region, including Arnhem Land escarpment, Nourlangie Rock, Mamakala Wetlands, East Alligator River, and Jabiru Township. Helicopter flights are also available for 20-minute (A$275) and 30-minute (A$345) hops. During the wet season only, helicopter flights take in Jim Jim and Twin Falls, when they are most spectacular, though prices go up to A$660 per person for the one-hour experience. ⊠ Jabiru Dr., Jabiru ☎ 1800/089113, 08/8941–9611 ⊕ www.kakaduair.com.au ⌖ From A$150.

Kakadu Tourism

SPECIAL-INTEREST | The Cooinda Lodge arranges magical boat tours of Yellow Water Billabong, one of the major water-holes in Kakadu, where innumerable birds and crocodiles gather. There are five tours that run throughout the day at 6:45 am, 9 am, 11:30 am, 1:15 pm, and 4:30 pm; the sunrise and sunset cruises are best, both in terms of temperature and animal activity. Note that the 9 am and 1:15 pm cruises only operate May to October, and the sunrise one also includes a buffet breakfast after your two-hour tour. Feeling more adventurous? Book a Spirit of Kakadu Adventure Tour if you're there from early April to mid-October, for a chance to visit two scenic waterholes via four-wheel-drive vehicle (from A$219). ⊠ Kakadu Hwy. ☎ 08/8979–1500 ⊕ www.kakadutourism.com ⌖ From A$72.

ESSENTIALS

VISITOR INFORMATION

Bowali Visitor Centre

The visitor center has state-of-the-art audiovisual displays and traditional exhibits that give an introduction to the park's ecosystems and its bird population, the world's most diverse. Kids love the giant crocodile skeleton. It's open daily from 8 am to 5 pm and its Anmak An-me Cafe and Marrawuddi Gallery make a great spot for a break between the Arnhem Highway and Jabiru side of the park on your way south to Cooinda. ⊠ Kakadu Hwy. ☎ 08/8938–1120 ⊕ parksaustralia.gov.au/kakadu/plan/visitor-centres ⌖ Free.

Warradjan Cultural Centre

Named after the pig-nosed turtle unique to the Top End, Warradjan Aboriginal Cultural Centre provides an excellent experience of local Bininj (pronounced bin-ing) tribal culture. Displays take you through the Aboriginal Creation period, following the path of the creation ancestor Rainbow Serpent through the ancient landscape of Kakadu. ⊠ *Kakadu Hwy.* ⊹ *1 km (0.6 mile) from Cooinda Lodge* ☎ *08/8979–0525* ⊕ *www.kakadutourism. com/tours-activities/warradjan-cultural-centre* ☞ *Free.*

CONTACTS Kakadu National Park. ⊠ *Kakadu Hwy., Jabiru* ☎ *08/8938–1120* ⊕ *parksaustralia.gov.au/kakadu.* **Tourism Top End.** ⊠ *6 Bennett St., Darwin* ☎ *1300/138886, 08/8980–6000* ⊕ *www. tourismtopend.com.au.*

⊙ Sights

★ Burrungkuy (Nourlangie Rock)
NATURE SITE | Like the main Kakadu escarpment, Burrungkuy, also known as Nourlangie Rock, is a remnant of an ancient plateau that is slowly eroding, leaving sheer cliffs rising high above the floodplains. The main attraction is the **Anbangbang Gallery,** an excellent frieze of Aboriginal rock paintings. ⊠ *Kakadu Hwy.* ⊹ *19 km (12 miles) from Bowalk Visitor Centre on Kakadu Hwy.; turn left toward Nourlangie Rock, then follow paved road, accessible year-round, 11 km (7 miles) to parking area* ⊕ *parksaustralia.gov.au/ kakadu/discover/regions/burrungkuy.*

Jim Jim Falls
BODY OF WATER | The best way to gain a true appreciation of the natural beauty of Kakadu is to visit the waterfalls running off the escarpment. Some 39 km (24 miles) south of the park headquarters along the Kakadu Highway, a track leads off to the left toward Jim Jim Falls, 60 km (37 miles) or about a two-hour drive away. The track is rough and unpaved, and you'll need a four-wheel-drive vehicle to navigate it. From the parking lot, you have to scramble 1 km (½ mile) over boulders to reach the falls and the plunge pools they have created at the base of the escarpment. Note that after May, the water flow over the falls may cease, and the unpaved road is closed in the Wet.

Local Language ⊙

The name Kakadu comes from an Aboriginal floodplain language called Gagudju, which was one of the languages spoken in the north of the park at the beginning of the 20th century. Although languages such as Gagudju and Limilngan are no longer regularly spoken, descendants of these language groups are still living in Kakadu.

■ TIP→ The best way to see these falls at their best is on a scenic flight from Jabiru during the wet season (from $660 per person for an unforgettable one-hour trip). ⊠ *Jim Jim Falls Track, Kakadu Hwy.* ⊕ *parksaustralia.gov.au/kakadu/discover/regions/ jim-jim-and-twin-falls.*

★ Kakadu National Park
NATIONAL/STATE PARK | The superb gathering of Aboriginal rock art is one of Kakadu National Park's major highlights. Two main types of artwork can be seen here—the Mimi style, which is the oldest, is believed to be up to 20,000 years old. Aboriginal people believe that Mimi spirits created the red-ochre stick figures to depict hunting scenes and other pictures of life at the time. The more recent artwork, known as X-ray painting, dates back fewer than 9,000 years and depicts freshwater animals—especially fish, turtles, and geese—living in floodplains created after the last ice age.

As the dry season progresses, billabongs (waterholes) become increasingly important to the more than 280 species of birds that inhabit the park. Huge flocks often gather at Yellow Water, South Alligator River, and Magela Creek. Scenic flights over the wetlands and Arnhem Land escarpment provide unforgettable moments in the wet season. ⊠ *Kakadu*

Gunlom Falls in Kakadu National Park

Hwy., Jabiru ⊕ *parksaustralia.gov.au/ kakadu* ⌧ *A$40 for up to 7 days.*

Twin Falls

BODY OF WATER | As you approach Twin Falls Gorge, the ravine opens up dramatically to reveal a beautiful sandy beach scattered with palm trees, as well as the crystal waters of the falls spilling onto the end of the beach. This spot is a bit difficult to reach, but the trip is rewarding. Take the four-wheel-drive-only road to Jim Jim Falls, turn off just before the parking lot, and travel 10 km (6 miles) farther to the Twin Falls parking lot. A regular boat shuttle (A$12.50; buy your tickets before you go at Bowali Visitor Centre) operates a return service up the Twin Falls Gorge, and then you need to walk over boulders, sand, and a boardwalk to the falls. Note that saltwater crocodiles may be in the gorge, so visitors are urged not to enter the water. The round-trip journey, including the boat shuttle, takes around two hours. ⌧ *Off Jim Jim Rd.* ⊕ *parksaustralia.gov.au/kakadu/do/ waterfalls/twin-falls-gorge.*

Ubirr

LOCAL INTEREST | Ubirr has an impressive display of Aboriginal paintings scattered through six shelters in the rock. The main gallery contains a 49-foot frieze of X-ray paintings depicting animals, birds, and fish. A 1-km (½-mile) path around the rock leads to all the galleries. It's just a short 250-meter (820-foot) clamber to the top for wonderful views over the surrounding wetlands, particularly at sunset. ■**TIP→ Take a flashlight to help you get down after sunset.** For lunch or a post-sunset Thai dinner, or to puruse arts and crafts for sale, stop by the Border Store and Cafe on your way in, if you're visiting during the dry season May through October. ⚠ **Beware of wildlife on the roads if driving after dark.** ⌧ *Kakadu National Park* ⊹ *43 km (27 miles) north of Bowali Visitor Centre along paved road* ☎ *08/8979–2474 Border Store and Cafe* ⊕ *parksaustralia. gov.au/kakadu/do/walks/ubirr-walk.*

🛏 Hotels

There are several lodges in the park, and basic campgrounds at Merl, Djarradjin Billabong (Muirella Park), Mardugal, and Gunlom have toilets, showers, and water for A$15 per campsite per night. Alcohol is not available in Jabiru, but you can buy it in Darwin.

Aurora Kakadu

$$ | HOTEL | Located about a two-hour drive from Darwin, Aurora Kakadu is the first accommodation you'll hit upon entering Kakadu National Park, a welcome sight with its comfortable double and family rooms—which sleep up to five—amid lush tropical gardens. **Pros:** location within Kakadu National Park; beautiful grounds with an on-site restaurant, bar, and pool; free bottled water in rooms. **Cons:** some distance from park attractions, so having your own transport is essential; thin walls; Wi-Fi is expensive and only works in certain parts of the resort. $ *Rooms from: A$195* ✉ *Arnhem Hwy., South Alligator, Kakadu National Park* ✛ *2½ km (1½ miles) before highwy crosses South Alligator River* ☎ *08/8979–0166, 1800/818845* ⊕ *www. auroraresorts.com.au* ⤳ *66 rooms plus campsites* ⓘ◯ⓘ *No meals.*

★ Cooinda Lodge

$$$ | RESORT |FAMILY | With plenty of accommodation options—all of which are managed by Accor Hotels—Cooinda Lodge offers standard rooms, superi-or-style Pandanus Rooms, and a campground. **Pros:** bus pickup available from the lodge to nearby Yellow River Cruises; close to Warradjan Aboriginal Cultural Center; on-site fuel station and access to Telstra pay phones. **Cons:** 30-minute drive from Jabiru shops; limited amenities in rooms; no Wi-Fi or cell phone service if you don't have Telstra. $ *Rooms from: A$288* ✉ *Kakadu National Park, Kakadu Hwy., Cooinda* ✛ *2 km (1 mile) toward Yellow Water Wetlands* ☎ *08/8979–1500* ⊕ *www.accorhotels.com* ⤳ *48 rooms* ⓘ◯ⓘ *No meals.*

Mercure Kakadu Crocodile Hotel

$$$$ | HOTEL | Shaped like a crocodile, this unusual hotel is situated deep in the heart of Kakadu National Park in the tiny town of Jabiru and is one of the area's best accommodation options. **Pros:** great on-site restaurant; local Aboriginal artwork on sale; Jabiru town is within walking distance. **Cons:** pool area is small; large tour groups stay here, so it can feel a little touristy; ground-floor rooms can have "critters". $ *Rooms from: A$329* ✉ *1 Flinders St., Jabiru* ☎ *08/8979–9000* ⊕ *www.accorhotels.com* ⤳ *110 rooms* ⓘ◯ⓘ *Free Breakfast.*

Katherine Gorge

30 km (18 miles) east of Katherine, 346 km (215 miles) southeast of Darwin, 543 km (337 miles) northeast of Kununurra.

Officially called Nitmiluk, the Aboriginal or Jawoyn name for the cicadas associated with the creation stories of the area, this stunning canyon formed by the Katherine River in Nitmiluk National Park is actually a series of 13 gorges, each separated by a jumble of boulders. The gorge is 12 km (7½ miles) long, and in many places the red rocky walls are almost 230 feet high. During the wet season (November through April), the gorges are full of raging water and saltwater crocodiles, but during the dry season you can hire canoes or take a cruise to explore them up close. Rangers clear the river of dangerous crocodiles at the start of each season so you can also swim, if the harmless freshwater crocodiles don't bother you, that is.

GETTING HERE AND AROUND

There are no commercial flight services that fly direct into Katherine; the closest airport is Darwin, which is about a three-hour drive.

TOURS

Nitmiluk Tours

BOAT TOURS | Although you can explore Katherine Gorge on foot on one of the many bushwalking trails, the best way to see it is to hit the water. Jawoyn-owned Nitmiluk Tours offer a range of cruises, starting at A$92 for a two-hour trip that departs several times each day. Wear comfortable walking shoes as there is some walking involved between gorges. **■TIP→ The best time to go is during the late afternoon, when you'll get the best photo opportunities, as the walls of the gorge glow a deep red.** Canoe adventure tours start at A$69 for a half-day tour and A$89 for a full-day journey, or you can view it all from above in a helicopter (from A$99). ✉ *Nitmiluk National Park, Gorge Rd., Katherine* ☎ *1300/146743* 🌐 *www.nitmiluktours.com.au* 🎫 *From A$92.*

Hotels

Cicada Lodge

$$$$ | **RESORT** | Each of the stylish air-conditioned rooms at Cicada Lodge has a private balcony overlooking Katherine Gorge, is decorated with Aboriginal artwork, and comes with breakfast as well as complimentary canapés and cocktails at sunset. **Pros:** great location close to walking trails, cruises, and other Katherine Gorge activities; excellent food and service; complimentary drinks and snacks each evening. **Cons:** quite expensive; tours and meals other than breakfast cost extra; views of the gorge can vary greatly depending on the time of year. [$] *Rooms from: A$660* ✉ *Nitmiluk National Park , Gorge Rd., Katherine* ☎ *1300/146743* 🌐 *cicadalodge.com.au* 🕒 *Closed for 1 month during wet season, usually mid-Feb.–mid-Mar.* 🛏 *18 rooms* 🍴 *Free Breakfast.*

Kununurra

516 km (321 miles) west of Katherine, 840 km (522 miles) southwest of Darwin.

Kununurra is the eastern gateway to the Kimberley. With a population of around 6,000, it's a modern, planned town that was developed in the 1960s for the nearby Lake Argyle and Ord River irrigation scheme. Today, it's a convenient base from which to explore local attractions such as Mirima National Park (a mini–Bungle Bungle on the edge of town), Lake Argyle, the River Ord, and some lovely countryside attractions just north of the city center. The town is also one starting point for adventure tours of the Kimberley; the other option is to start from Broome.

GETTING HERE AND AROUND

Distances in this part of the continent are colossal, and flying is the fastest and easiest way to get to and around the Kimberley. Both Virgin Australia and Air North have extensive air networks throughout the Top End, linking Kununurra to Broome, Perth, and Darwin.

From Darwin to Kununurra and the eastern extent of the Kimberley, it's 840 km (522 miles). The route runs from Darwin to Katherine along the Stuart Highway, and then along the Victoria Highway to Kununurra. The entire road is paved but narrow in parts—especially so, it may seem, when a road train (a long truck towing three or four trailers) is coming the other way. Drive with care and keep an eye on the speed limit, which is 110 km (68 miles) here instead of the usual 130 km (80 miles) in the Northern Territory. If you're driving from the Northern Territory into Western Australia, you'll have to make a brief but mandatory stop at the quarantine checkpoint at the border before you can continue, so get rid of any fruit, honey, plants, or seeds before you head out or else you may be fined (visit *www.agric.wa.gov.au* for more info), Fuel and supplies can be bought at small settlements along the way, but you should always keep supplies in abundance and expect to pay a pretty penny.

TAXIS Bert's Taxi Service. ✉ *18 Pointceta Way* ☎ *08/9168–2553*. **Taxi Services Kununurra.** ✉ *12 Riverfig Ave.* ☎ *13–1008, 08/9168–1521.*

SAFETY AND PRECAUTIONS

Driving long distances through the Kimberley can be an adventure, but it also carries risks. For drivers not used to the conditions, and not taking adequate rest breaks, the combination of warm sun through the windshield, long sections of road, and lack of traffic can have a hypnotic effect. Take regular breaks every two hours to walk and have a stretch, and get plenty of sleep the night before. If you are feeling sleepy, stop immediately and take a break. Many vehicle crashes in this area are vehicle versus animal, often a kangaroo or straying cattle. Dusk and dawn are when animals are most active. If you see an animal on the road in front of you, brake firmly in a straight line and sound your horn. Do not swerve: it is safer to stay on the road.

TIMING

You should allow at least five days to see Kununurra and the Kimberley, including your arrival and departure days. That will allow enough time to visit the Ord River and cruise Lake Argyle, take a scenic flight to the Bungle Bungles and hike the area with a guide, and take a four-wheel-drive excursion to El Questro Wilderness Park. Winter—May through September—is the dry season here, and June and July are the most popular times to visit, as days are warm and there is little rain. November through March is the wet season and temperatures can be a lot higher—up to 45°C (113°F).

TOURS

APT Kimberley Wilderness Adventures

ADVENTURE TOURS | This agency conducts tours from Broome and Kununurra, which include excursions along the legendary Gibb River Road and into Purnululu National Park. Two-day guided trips from Kununurra to the Bungle Bungles include a scenic flight (from A$1,495) while a four-day tour from Broome includes a trip to a popular pearl farm and an iconic camel ride on Cable Beach (from A$1,695). See the website for additional touring options. ✉ *1230 Nepean Hwy., Level 4* ☎ *1300/336–932* ⊕ *www.aptouring.com.au* ✇ *From A$1495.*

Aviair

AIR EXCURSIONS | This company conducts both fixed-wing and helicopter flights from Kununurra and Purnululu National Park. A two-hour fixed-wing flight over the Bungle Bungles and Lake Argyle is A$399. ✉ *319 Laine Jones Dr.* ☎ *1800/095500* ⊕ *www.aviair.com.au* ✇ *From A$399.*

Bungle Bungle Savannah Lodge

AIR EXCURSIONS | If you're looking to spend some quality time in Purnululu National Park, Bungle Bungle Savannah Lodge offers several fly-in, fly-out packages from Kununurra that include scenic flights over Lake Argyle, guided tours of Cathedral Gorge, and overnight accommodations at the lodge (from A$1,390). Others offer an additional guided hike at Echidna Chasm before you head back to Kununurra by plane (from A$1,638) or give you two nights in the park with extra hikes (from A$1,935). ✉ *Bungle Bungle Savannah Lodge, Campsite B Bellburn Camp, Purnululu National Park* ☎ *08/9168–2213* ⊕ *www.bunglebunglesavannahlodge.com.au* ✇ *From A$1390.*

★ Kingfisher Tours

AIR EXCURSIONS | This company operates scenic flights from Kununurra Airport, starting at A$375 for a trip over Purnululu National Park from Kununurra. For A$780, you can take a full-day tour that includes a flight into the remote park, sightseeing via four-wheel-drive, and guided treks to Cathedral Gorge and The Lookout. Check the website for additional touring options that include overnight accommodations, fishing trips, sunset dinner cruises, and heli-trekking through even more remote parts of the Kimberley region. ✉ *306 Victoria Hwy.* ☎ *08/9148–2630* ⊕ *kingfishertours.net* ✈ *From A$780.*

★ Lake Argyle Cruises

BOAT TOURS | Excellent trips on Australia's largest expanse of freshwater are offered from Lake Argyle and Kununurra if you're staying in town 70 km (43 miles) or about an hour's drive away. Treat yourself to a morning cruise (A$70 from Lake Argyle, no transfers from Kununurra) or a full-day tour of the lake and nearby Durack Family Homestead (A$160 from Lake Argyle, A$190 including return transfers from Kununurra). Sunset cruises, which start at 2:30 pm, give you a chance to see this remarkable landscape by twilight, as well as complimentary drinks and snacks (A$95 from Lake Argyle, A$125 from Kununurra). If you'd rather not schlep all the way back to Kununurra, Lake Argyle Resort offers accommodations ranging from four-bedroom Lake View Grand Villas (A$959 for up to eight people), one- and two-bedroom Lake View Villas (from A$359); standard cabins (from A$259); and a caravan park (unpowered sites from A$17.50 a night). Day passes are also available for A$10 for anyone wanting to drop by and check out the resort's legendary infinity pool. ✉ *3001B Lake Argyle Rd.* ☎ *08/9168–7687* ⊕ *www. lakeargylecruises.com* ✈ *From A$70.*

ESSENTIALS

VISITOR INFORMATION Kununurra Visitor Centre. ✉ *75 Coolibah Dr.* ☎ *08/9168– 1177, 1800/586868* ⊕ *www.visitkununurra.com.*

 Sights

Hoochery Distillery

WINERY/DISTILLERY | Located just 16 km (10 miles) north of downtown Kununurra on Weaber Plain Road, Hoochery Distillery offers tours at 11 am and 2 pm (A$14) so you can get behind the scenes and learn all about the longest-running rum operation in Western Australia. Pick up some homemade Ord River rum cake and a cup of coffee at the on-site Hoochery Cafe, or treat yourself to a rum flight and sample some of the ones you just heard about on the tour. ✉ *300 Weaber Plain Rd.* ☎ *08/9168–2467* ⊕ *www. hoochery.com.au* ⊘ *Closed Sun.*

The Sandalwood Factory and Cafe

STORE/MALL | More shop and café than actual factory—the real one is far to the south in Mt. Romance, Western Australia—this popular spot, about a 15-minute drive north of Kununurra, is dedicated to all things sandalwood. Learn how it starts out basically as a parasitic tree and is eventually turned into any number of products ranging from lotions and bath soaps to perfumes and incense, all of which can be purchased at the shop. The on-site café offers a wide range of delicious breakfast and lunch items, and smoothies, all of which are made fresh using local produce from the surrounding farms you'll pass on the way there. ✉ *Weaber Plains Rd., Lot 51* ☎ *08/9169–1987* ⊕ *mtromance.com.au/ visit-us/the-sandalwood-factory-kununurra* ⊘ *Closed mid-Dec.–late-Mar.*

🍴 Restaurants

★ Pumphouse Restaurant

$$ | **AUSTRALIAN** | Located on an old fishing dock jutting out into Lake Kununurra, this local favorite is the place to have dinner while watching the sunset, with live music most nights, great food and cocktails, and the chance to view local wildlife (yes, we mean birds and freshwater crocodiles) doing their thing. The fare is contemporary Australian, so you can expect to see steaks, pan seared salmon, and risotto on the menu, while Sunday night is dedicated strictly to wood-fire pizza and tapas specials. **Known for:** wood-fire pizza and tapas night with a special menu on Sunday; eight-hour,

Off The Beaten Path

El Questro Wilderness Park. This 700,000-acre property features some of the most ruggedly beautiful country in the Kimberley. El Questro has a full complement of recreational activities like fishing, swimming, horseback riding, and helicopter rides, and offers individually tailored walking and four-wheel-drive tours. Four independent accommodation facilities are on-site, each different in style and budget: the luxury Homestead (from A$2,029 per night with a two-night minimum-stay requirement and a policy that guests must be ages 16 and up); the safari-style tented cabins at Emma Gorge Resort (from A$316); air-conditioned Riverside Bungalows (from A$175); and Riverside Campgrounds (from A$20 per person per night) at El Questro Station. Each has a restaurant, and rates at the Homestead include drinks and food, laundry, and activities. Alternatively, you can choose to take a full-day tour of El Questro with included trips to Emma Gorge, Zebedee Springs, lunch at The Station, a Chamberlain River Cruise, and round-trip transport from Kununurra (A$268). Not renting a four-wheel-drive vehicle? Take a shuttle from Kununurra starting at A$110 each way to Emma Gorge Resort, A$135 each way to El Questro Station, and A$140 each way to El Questro Homestead. ✉ *El Questro Rd.* ✛ *110 km (68 miles) west of Kununurra; 58 km (36 miles) on Great Northern Hwy., 36 km (22 miles) on Gibb River Rd., and 16 km (10 miles) on El Questro Rd. on gravel road* ☎ *1800/837168* ⊕ *www.elquestro.com.au* ⛺ *An El Questro Wilderness Park permit (required) is A$20 and valid for 7 days with access to gorge walks, thermal springs, fishing holes, rivers, and use of the Emma Gorge Resort swimming pool* ⊙ *Closed Nov.–Apr.*

Home Valley Station. If you've ever fancied being a cowboy or cowgirl, this massive 3½-million-acre working cattle farm at the foot of the majestic Cockburn (pronounced *co-burn*) range is the place to do it. Owned and operated by the traditional owners of the land, the Balanggarra people through the Indigenous Land Corporation, you can join a cattle muster or just take a half-day horse trek. Other activities include Barramundi fishing and four-wheel-drive trips. There's a bar and restaurant on-site and a range of accommodations from stylish "Grass Castle" bungalows complete with cow-skin rugs, air-conditioning, fully stocked minibar, flat-screen cable TV, huge walk-in rain shower, and resident tree frogs (from A$330) to motel-style guesthouse rooms (from A$240), eco-tents with a raised wooden floor and queen-size bed (from A$155), and remote bush camping beside the Pentecost River, 4 km (2½ miles) from the homestead (from A$21 per person per night). Note that a four-wheel-drive vehicle is required to reach Home Valley Station and these can be rented in Kununurra via Avis, Budget, Hertz, Thrifty, and Europcar. Air transfers and charter flights can also be arranged from Kununurra Airport. ✉ *Gibb River Rd.* ✛ *120 km (75 miles) from Kununurra via Great Northern Hwy. and Gibb River Rd.* ☎ *1300/134044, 02/8296–8010* ⊕ *www.hvstation.com.au* ⊙ *Closed mid-Oct.–May.*

slow-roasted lamb shoulder; Ord Valley crème brûlée dessert made with rum butterscotch sauce from nearby Hoochery Distillery. [$] *Average main: A$35* ✉ *Lakeview Dr.* ☎ *08/9169–3222* 🌐 *www.thepumphouserestaurant.com* 🕓 *Closed Mon. No breakfast weekdays.*

Hotels

★ Freshwater East Kimberley Apartments

$$$ | **RESORT** | **FAMILY** | Just a two-minute drive from downtown Kununurra, these fully self-contained one-, two-, and three-bedroom apartments are the perfect place to unwind before or after a thrilling tour through the Kimberley, with stocked kitchens, sandalwood products provided by Mt. Romance, and luxurious outdoor showers (in some apartments). **Pros:** local Mt. Romance Sandalwood bath products; beautiful swimming pool area; complimentary airport transfers. **Cons:** it's about a 15-minute walk to the city center; no on-site restaurants; a security deposit of up to A$500 may be required for group bookings. [$] *Rooms from: A$228* ✉ *Victoria Hwy.* ✥ *Across from Celebrity Tree Park* ☎ *08/9169–2010, 1300/729267* 🌐 *www.freshwaterapartments.net.au* 🛏 *60 rooms* 🍴 *No meals.*

Ibis Styles Kununurra Hotel

$ | **HOTEL** | Set amid tropical gardens, the familiar and brightly furnished rooms here provide a comfortable base from which to explore Kununurra and the eastern Kimberley region. **Pros:** walking distance to downtown; everything you've come to expect from this budget-friendly brand; nice swimming pool in a relaxing tropical garden setting. **Cons:** limited amenities in rooms; limited dining options; reception isn't always attended and there's a phone number to call if you need them. [$] *Rooms from: A$149* ✉ *Victoria Hwy. at Messmate Way* ☎ *08/9168–4000* 🌐 *www.accorhotels.com.au* 🛏 *60 rooms* 🍴 *Free Breakfast.*

Kununurra Country Club Resort

$$ | **HOTEL** | **FAMILY** | Located in the center of town, this hotel with smartly furnished apartments is encircled by its own little rain forest of tropical gardens. **Pros:** complimentary airport shuttle; poolside dining and bars; easy walk to downtown. **Cons:** tour groups stay here; Wi-Fi is free but slow; you may hear the outdoor cinema next door on Saturday night but the noise dies down once the movie is over. [$] *Rooms from: A$185* ✉ *47 Coolibah Dr.* ☎ *08/9168–1024* 🌐 *www.kununurracountryclub.com.au* 🕓 *Closed Christmas–New Year's Eve weekend* 🛏 *88 rooms* 🍴 *No meals.*

Lakeside Resort

$$$ | **RESORT** | On the shores of Lake Kununurra sits this understated, tranquil resort, where you can see stunning sunsets over the water and watch for fruit bats flying overhead. **Pros:** lakeside location; courtesy bus available; crocodile spotting on the lake at night. **Cons:** rooms are basic; Wi-Fi is only available in public areas near the pool and bar; not within walking distance of downtown Kununurra. [$] *Rooms from: A$205* ✉ *50 Casuarina Way, off Victoria Hwy.* ☎ *08/9169–1092, 1800/786692* 🌐 *www.lakeside.com.au* 🛏 *50 rooms* 🍴 *No meals.*

Wunan House

$$ | **B&B/INN** | If you're looking for a chance to give back to the local community when you travel, stay at Wunan House, a charming Aboriginal-owned and -operated B&B just a few blocks from downtown Kununurra. **Pros:** complimentary breakfast and Wi-Fi; comfortable beds and memory foam pillows; shared kitchen space and lovely continental breakfast spread in the morning. **Cons:** no pool; no on-site restaurants; about a 10-minute walk from downtown Kununurra shops. [$] *Rooms from: A$155* ✉ *167 Coolibah Dr.* ☎ *08/9168–2436* 🌐 *wunanhouse.com* 🛏 *10 rooms* 🍴 *Free Breakfast.*

Purnululu (Bungle Bungle) National Park

291 km (181 miles) southwest of Kununurra.

Wind and water have savaged the rocks of Purnululu National Park, creating one of the most unusual landscapes in the world. All around, the conically weathered formations cluster together like a meeting of some metamorphic executives. Traveling into the area is a remarkable experience—and young and old can delight in the fantasy landscape.

This park covers more than half a million acres in the southeast corner of the Kimberley. While Australians of European descent first "discovered" its great beehive-shape domes—their English name is the Bungle Bungles—in 1983, the local Kidja Aboriginals, who knew about these scenic wonders long ago, called the area Purnululu, meaning sandstone.

The striking, black-and-orange-stripe mounds seem to bubble up from the landscape. Climbing on them is not permitted, because the sandstone layer beneath their thin crust of lichen and silica is fragile and would quickly erode without protection. Walking tracks follow rocky, dry creek beds. One popular walk leads hikers along **Piccaninny Creek** to **Piccaninny Gorge,** passing through gorges with towering 328-foot cliffs to which slender fan palms cling.

GETTING HERE AND AROUND

The Bungle Bungles are 291 km (181 miles) south of Kununurra along the Great Northern Highway. A very rough, 53-km (32-mile) unsealed road, negotiable only in a four-wheel-drive vehicle, makes up the last stretch of road leading to the park from the turnoff near the Turkey Creek–Warmun Community. That part of the drive can take two to three hours depending on the condition of the road. The most-visited section of the park is in the south, where there are rough walking trails to the main sights.

SAFETY AND PRECAUTIONS

The park is usually open from April through December (depending on whether the road is passable after the wet season); however, temperatures in April, October, November, and December can be blisteringly hot. If you travel in these months, make sure you have plenty of water and be sun-smart.

TIMING

Purnululu National Park can be visited in a day from Kununurra, but only with a flight and safari package. There are also tours available that include overnight camping, but the road trip from Kununurra takes the best part of a day. Driving yourself to the park is not recommended, as the last 53-km (32-mile) section is a very rough unsealed track suitable only for four-wheel-drive vehicles; it has been kept deliberately so to limit visitation and those driving anything else will be turned away. If you do decide to drive in yourself, be aware that there are few facilities in the park's public campgrounds so you need to take in all your own food and camping equipment.

ESSENTIALS

VISITOR INFORMATION Purnululu Visitor Centre. ⊠ *Purnululu National Park, Purnululu National Park* ⊹ *300 km (186 miles) south of Kununurra, in Purnululu National Park* ☎ *08/9168–7300* ⊕ *parks.dpaw. wa.gov.au/park/purnululu.*

⊙ Sights

The most popular walking trails are in the southern end of the park, where the famous "beehives" are located. From the Piccaninny Creek car park, you can hike to Cathedral Gorge in about an hour. Take a 20-minute detour on the Domes Walk to see more of the famous sandstone "beehives." If you have more time, follow the Piccaninny Creek walk into Piccaninny Gorge, following an eroded riverbed and sandstone ledges to the Lookout point. On the northern side of the park, there are walks to Echidna Gorge, which takes about one hour—where dino-saur-era livistona palms cling to the cliffs and the gorge narrows to about three feet across—and Mini Palms Gorge, a rock-strewn gorge filled with livistona palms. At the end, there is a viewing platform overlooking the valley. Allow an hour for this walk as well.

🛏 Hotels

Once you make it past that last bumpy stretch of unsealed road you have three options: two campgrounds, Walardi and Kurrajong, both of which cost $13 per person per night and offer basic facilities like bush toilets (read: there are no showers and you need to boil water here before you drink it or bring your own); or Bungle Bungle Savannah Lodge, which offers a dinner bed and breakfast deal from A$297 per adult per night and provides en suite cabins with hot show-ers, flushing toilets, and other creature comforts (☎ 08 9168–7300).

Danggu Geikie Gorge National Park

458 km (284 miles) southwest of Pur-nululu National Park, 416 km (258 miles) east of Broome.

Halfway between Purnululu National Park and Broome, just outside the little Outback town of Fitzroy Crossing, Geikie Gorge, an ancient flooded reef, is one of the highlights of a trip through the Kimberley.

TOURS

⭐ **National Park Ranger Station Boat Tours**
BOAT TOURS | FAMILY | The best way to see the gorge is aboard one of the one-hour boat tours led by a ranger from the National Park Ranger Station, departing at 8 am, 9:30 am, 2:30 pm, and 4 pm from May to mid-October. The knowledgeable rangers are helpful in pointing out the vegetation, strange limestone forma-tions, and many freshwater crocodiles along the way. You may also see part of the noisy fruit-bat colony that inhabits the region. The park is open for day visits daily from 6:30 am to 6:30 pm between April and November. Entry is restricted during the wet season, from December through March, when the Fitzroy River floods. ✉ *Geikie Gorge Rd., King Leopold Ranges* ✛ *20 km (12 miles) northeast of Fitzroy Crossing via Geikie Gorge Rd.* ☎ *08/9191–5112* ⊕ *parks.dpaw.wa.gov. au/park/danggu-geikie-gorge* 🖃 *From A$45.*

👁 Sights

Danggu Geikie Gorge National Park
NATIONAL/STATE PARK | Geologists believe the mighty Fitzroy River cut and shaped the limestone walls you see today at Danggu Geikie Gorge, and during the wet season, the normally placid waters roar through the region. The walls of the gorge are stained red from iron oxide, except where they have been leached of the mineral and turned white by the floods, which have washed as high as 52 feet from the bottom of the gorge.

The gorge is one of the few places in the world where freshwater barramundi, mussels, stingrays, and prawns swim. The park is also home to the freshwater archerfish, which can spit water as far as a yard to knock insects out of the air. Aboriginal people call this place Dang-gu, meaning "big fishing hole." ✉ *Geikie Gorge Rd., King Leopold Ranges* ✛ *20 km (12 miles) northeast of township of Fitzroy Crossing via Geikie Gorge Rd.* ⊕ *parks.dpaw.wa.gov.au/park/dang-gu-geikie-gorge* ☉ *Closed during the wet season.*

🛏 Hotels

Fitzroy River Lodge

$$$ | HOTEL | With Broome being four hours from Danggu Geikie Gorge, you're better off staying in nearby Fitzroy Crossing, and with accommodations ranging from motel-style lodge rooms and private studios to single rooms and campgrounds, the Fitzroy River Lodge is your best bet. **Pros:** accommodation options for every budget and type of traveler; motel is on stilts so it can stay open all year long despite wet season floods; watch the wallabies and kangaroos graze the grounds from your doorstep. **Cons:** limited food options; reliable yet outdated; Wi-Fi outages take a long time to fix due to lodge's remote location. ⓢ *Rooms from: A$265* ✉ *277 Great Northern Hwy.* ☎ *08/9191–5141* ⊕ *www.fitzroyriver-lodge.com.au* ⤳ *102 rooms* ⦿ *No meals.*

Broome

1,044 km (649 miles) southwest of Kununurra via Halls Creek, 1,558 km (968 miles) southwest of Katherine, 1,871 km (1,163 miles) southwest of Darwin.

Some say Broome is the holiday capital of the Kimberley. It's the only town in the region with sandy beaches, and is the base from which most strike out to see more of the region. Chinatown is charming while the rest of the area, especially Cable Beach, is becoming noticeably upscale.

Long ago, Broome depended on pearling for its livelihood. By the early 20th century 300 to 400 sailing boats employing 3,000 men provided most of the world's mother-of-pearl shell. Many of the pearlers were Japanese, Malay, and Filipino, and the town is still a wonderful multicultural center today with the modern pearling industry very much at its heart. Each August during the famous Shinju Matsuri (Festival of the Pearl),

Broome commemorates its early pearling years and heritage with a 10-day festival featuring many traditional Japanese ceremonies. Because of its popularity, advance bookings for accommodations are highly recommended.

Several tour operators have multiday cruises out of Broome along the magnificent Kimberley coast. The myriad deserted islands and beaches, with 35-foot tides that create horizontal waterfalls and whirlpools, make it an adventurer's delight.

Broome marks the western extent of the Kimberley. From here it's another 2,240 km (1,392 miles) south to Perth, or 1,871 km (1,163 miles) back to Darwin.

GETTING HERE AND AROUND

Qantas and its subsidiaries fly to Broome seasonally from Brisbane, Sydney, and Melbourne via Perth. Direct flights from Sydney and Melbourne happen twice a week during the dry season. Air North has an extensive air network throughout the Top End, linking Broome to Kununurra and Darwin. Virgin Australia also services Broome from Perth. Broome's airport is right next to the center of town, on the northern side. Note that though it's called Broome International Airport, there are no scheduled overseas flights; charter flights and private flights do arrive there.

SAFETY AND PRECAUTIONS

From November to April there is a possibility of cyclones off the Kimberley coast. It is important that visitors are aware of the procedures to follow in the event of a cyclone alert, which are provided in all accommodations as well as the Broome Visitor Centre or the Shire of Broome office. Call ☎ *1300/659210* for cyclone watch and warning messages, or check the Australian Government Bureau of Meteorology website at ⊕ *www.bom. gov.au.* Certain times of the year also mean bush fires are more likely to occur, often caused by lightning strikes or when a controlled suddenly becomes an out-of-control burn due to drier-than-anticipated conditions or high winds. Follow signs and advice by authorities if roads are closed or rerouted, and should you encounter smoke on the road, turn your lights on so other cars can see you and drive slowly if deemed safe to do so.

November to April is also when mosquitoes are at their most prevalent. To avoid the discomfort of mosquito bites and any risk of infection, it is advisable to cover up at dawn and dusk and apply insect repellent, which is supplied in most hotels. Sand flies become more active in Broome on high tides; use the same prevention methods.

Tropical waters can also contain various stingers. The two to watch out for are the chironex fleckeri box jellyfish (a large but almost transparent jellyfish up to 12 inches across with ribbonlike tentacles from each of its four corners) and the Irukandji (a tiny transparent jellyfish less than one inch across with four thin tentacles). Both are found during the summer months of November to May. Take care when swimming—wear protective clothing like a wet suit or Lycra stinger suit to reduce exposure to potential stings—and obey signs displayed on the beaches at all times. Medical attention should be sought if someone is stung—pour vinegar onto the sting and call ☎ 000 for an ambulance.

Saltwater crocodiles live in estuaries throughout the Kimberley, while freshwater Johnsons crocodiles hang out in freshwater gorges and lakes. Look for warning signs. Even if not signposted, advice from a reliable local authority should always be sought before swimming in rivers and waterholes.

TIMING

Ideally, you need at least five days in Broome and the West Kimberley, including your arrival and departure days. This will give you time to go swimming and sunbathing on Cable Beach, take

a camel ride, and cruise on a restored pearl lugger. A scenic flight will show you the pristine Kimberley coastline and the horizontal waterfalls of the Buccaneer Archipelago. A day tour will get you to Cape Leveque or Windjana Gorge. To go farther afield, join a four-wheel-drive safari; a two-day tour will show you the gorges of the area, including Danggu Geikie Gorge.

The most popular time to visit is from May to October during the dry season, but especially June and July when the weather is ideal.

TOURS

Astro Tours

SPECIAL-INTEREST | Astro Tours organizes entertaining, informative night-sky tours of the Broome area from April to mid-October. Two-hour educational star shows offered one to three nights a week depending on the cosmos cost A$75 if you self-drive to the site 20 minutes outside town (or A$95, including transfers from your hotel), comfy stargazing chairs, hot beverages, and cookies. Wear warm clothing if visiting in June, July, and August, as temperatures can drop below 10°C (50°F). ⊠ *Broome Rd. ⊕ A 20-minute drive from downtown Broome on Broome Rd., next door to Malcolm Douglas Crocodile Park* ☎ *04/1794–9958* ⊕ *www.astrotours.net* ⊡ *From A$75* ↻ *Closed Nov.–Apr.*

★ Kimberley Quest

EXCURSIONS | Much of the Kimberley coast is inaccessible by land and can be visited only by boat. Kimberley Quest offers multiday Kimberley adventures along the region's magnificent coastline in their luxury *Kimberley Quest II* cruiser. All meals and excursions (including fishing trips) are included in the cost of A$10,900 for 8 days; A$9,500 for 10 days, A$16,900 for 14 days, or A$14,900 for an epic 21-day sailing. There's also a four-day Taste of the Kimberley cruise available from A$3,500 as well as a fishing expedition from A$6,390. Cruising

Broome By Camelback

Though not native to Australia, camels played a large part in exploring and opening up the country's big, dry, and empty interior. In the 1800s, around 20,000 camels were imported from the Middle East to use for cross-country travel—along with the handlers (many from Afghanistan) who cared for them.

When railways and roads became the prime methods of transport in the early 20th century, many camels were simply set free in the desert. A steady population of wild camels—some 1,000,000 of them—now roams across the Australian Outback.

Broome has for many years been a place where people enjoy camel rides—especially along the broad, desertlike sands of Cable Beach. Two tour companies in town now offer camel "adventures" on a daily basis; yes, it's touristy, but it's great fun and a wonderful way to see the coast while getting a taste of history.

Broome Camel Safaris. Open Monday through Saturday, Broome Camel Safaris offers 30-minute presunset rides (A$40), 45-minute morning rides (A$65), or one-hour sunset rides (A$90). As a special treat, ladies on tour receive a complimentary pair of freshwater pearl sterling-silver earrings by Dahlia Designs, a local jewelry company. ⊠ *Lot 303 Fairway Dr.* ⊹ *Meet above rocks on Cable Beach and look for camels in blue* ☎ *04/1991–6101* ⊕ *www.broomecamelsafaris.com.au* ✉ *From A$40* ⊙ *Closed Sun.*

Red Sun Camels. Morning, pre-sunset, and sunset rides are available every day on Cable Beach north of the rocks. The morning ride lasts for 40 minutes and costs A$70; the presunset ride runs for 30 minutes and costs A$45; the sunset ride takes an hour and costs A$95. ⊠ *Cable Beach* ⊹ *Meet above rocks on Cable Beach and look for camels in red* ☎ *08/9193–7423* ⊕ *www.redsuncamels.com.au* ✉ *From A$45.*

season runs from March to September, so check the website to see which ones run during which months. ⊠ *15 Dampier Terr.* ☎ *08/9193–6131* ⊕ *www.kimberleyquest.com.au* ✉ *From A$9639.*

ESSENTIALS

VISITOR INFORMATION Broome Visitor Centre. ⊠ *1 Hamersley St.* ☎ *08/9195–2200* ⊕ *www.visitbroome.com.au.*

 Sights

Broome is a small, compact town that's easy to explore on foot—you can even walk to the airport on the northern edge of town. You will need transportation to get to and from Cable Beach, which is around 7 km (4½ miles) from the

city center. Chinatown, with its historic buildings, pearl showrooms, and art galleries, is in the middle of the main street shopping strip, while Roebuck Bay is only a few blocks to the south.

Broome Bird Observatory

NATURE PRESERVE | A nonprofit research, education, and accommodation facility, the Broome Bird Observatory provides the perfect opportunity to see the Kimberley's numerous bird species, some of which migrate annually from Siberia or China. On the shores of Roebuck Bay, 25 km (15 miles) east of Broome, the observatory has a prolific number of migratory waders. The observatory offers a variety of daily guided tours in the dry season (from May to around

September), including some focused around the native shorebirds, mangroves, bush and plains—each are 2½ hours and cost A$70—as well as a full-day tour of the lakes that includes morning tea (A$150). Pickup from Broome can also be arranged for A$60 for the first person and A$15 for each additional person in your group. Start times depend on the day of the week and the tides and season, but are typically between 8 am and 3 pm, with the exception of the bush and plains tour, which starts at 3 pm or 3:30 pm and returns after sunset. ⊠ *Crab Creek Rd.* ✛ *15 km (9 miles) from Broome Hwy.* ☎ *08/9193–5600* ⊕ *www.broomebirdob-servatory.com* ✉ *From A$70.*

Japanese Cemetery

CEMETERY | More than 900 pearl divers are buried in the Japanese Cemetery, located on the road out to Broome's deepwater port. The graves testify to the contribution of the Japanese people to the development of the industry in Broome, as well as to the perils of pearl gathering in its early days. ⊠ *1 Port Dr.* ✉ *Free.*

Malcolm Douglas Crocodile Park

NATURE PRESERVE | FAMILY | Entering through the jaws of a giant crocodile, this huge wildlife park opens up each day from 2 pm to 5 pm to reveal the Kimberley's native species in a variety of habitats. You'll get to see dingoes, cassowaries, barking owls, several types of kangaroo, a litany of bird species, American alligators, and, of course, hundreds of saltwater and freshwater crocodiles. Don't miss the famous croc feeding tour at 3 pm daily, a one-hour guided walk through the vast property where you get to watch the guide feed salties, freshies, and American alligators, and meet several problem crocs who were brought to the park after wreaking havoc in some of the surrounding estuaries. ⊠ *Broome Rd.* ✛ *Go 16 km (10 miles) out of Broome on Broome Rd. and*

look for sign ☎ *08/9193–6580* ⊕ *www.malcolmdouglas.com.au* ✉ *A$35.*

★ Pearl Luggers

MUSEUM | This historical display sheds light on the difficulties and immense skill involved in pearl harvesting. You'll have a chance to check out one of the restored luggers on a replica jetty along with other such pearling equipment as diving suits and a A$100,000 pearl you can hold. Get an insight into the risky lives of pearl divers, who spent years aboard pearling luggers and diving for pearl shells, on the regular 90-minute tours. This is a must-see for those interested in Broome's history, and for anyone who wants to sample pearl meat, a true delicacy worth A$120 a kilo. ⊠ *31 Dampier Terr.* ☎ *08/9192–0022* ⊕ *www.williecreek-pearls.com.au/pages/visit-pearl-luggers* ✉ *A$30.*

★ Sun Pictures

ARTS VENUE | FAMILY | Opened in 1916, Sun Pictures is the world's oldest operating outdoor movie theater. Here, silent movies—accompanied by a pianist—were once shown to the public while these days, current releases are presented in the very pleasant outdoors. Drop in and have a look during the day for free or stick around for a charming movie-viewing experience that hearkens back to another era. ⊠ *Carnarvon St.* ☎ *08/9192–1077* ⊕ *www.broomemovies.com.au* ✉ *From A$18.*

Willie Creek Pearl Farm

FARM/RANCH | You can watch demonstrations of the cultured pearling process—including the seeding of a live oyster and a boat ride to the marine farm—at Willie Creek Pearl Farm, located about 38 km (23½ miles) north of Broome. Drive out to the farm yourself (you must make reservations first and a four-wheel-drive vehicle is recommended on this unsealed road), or join a five-hour bus tour that'll pick you up and bring you back to your in-town accommodation. There's also the option of taking a scenic helicopter ride

Camel riding on Cable Beach, Broome

while on the property for an additional fee, and tours offer breakfast (A$25 more per person) and lunch add-ons (A$30 more per person) depending on the time of day you visit. At the end of the your, you'll have a chance to view and try on gorgeous pearl necklaces worth more than A$20,000 and peruse the gift shop. ✉ *Willie Creek Rd.* ⊹ *Drive 9 km (5½ miles) east from Broome on Broome Hwy., turn left onto Cape Leveque Rd. for 15 km (9 miles), turn left onto Manari Rd. for 5 km (3 miles), turn left and follow signs for 2½ km (1½ miles); allow about 1 hr* ☎ *08/9192–0000* ⊕ *www.williecreek-pearls.com.au* ✆ *From A$75.*

🌀 Beaches

★ Cable Beach

BEACH—SIGHT | Watching the sun sink into the sea on Cable Beach is a nightly ritual for almost all visitors to Broome, who flock to the 22-km (14-mile) stretch of dazzling white sand lapped by turquoise water 7 km (4½ miles) from the center of town. The most popular way to watch the sunset is from the back of a swaying camel, but you can also unpack a picnic at the beachside park, drive a four-wheel-drive vehicle onto the sand, or sip a cocktail from the beachside bar at Cable Beach Resort & Spa. By day it's a lot less crowded, and about 500 meters (1,640 feet) north of the vehicle access ramp is a declared nude beach. It's good for swimming, but low tide can mean a long walk across sand to get to the water. Beware of marine stingers (deadly Box and Irukandji jellyfish) in the water from December through to April. **Amenities:** lifeguard; parking (free); toilets. **Best for:** sunset; swimming; walking. ✉ *Cable Beach Rd. W.*

🍴 Restaurants

★ Matso's Broome Brewery

$$ | AUSTRALIAN | One of the most popular spots to eat and drink in Broome, this microbrewery in an old bank building overlooking Roebuck Bay serves bar snacks, burgers, steaks, and fish-and-chips. The fan-cooled bar is full of pearling memorabilia and historic photographs, although most people choose to sit on the breezy veranda or shady beer garden. **Known for:** a very refreshing alcoholic ginger beer; one-hour brewery tours on Wednesday and Friday at 11 am (A$35); authentic Indian curry dinners. *[$] Average main: A$35 ✉ 60 Hammersley St. ☎ 08/9193–5811 🌐 matsos.com.au.*

★ The Zookeeper's Store

$$ | **AUSTRALIAN** | Housed in what was formerly Lord Alistair McAlpine's zoo, this gourmet deli of sorts serves homemade specialties using locally sourced produce, perfect whether you're in the mood for coffee, breakfast, lunch, or dinner after a long day of sightseeing. The breakfasts here are legendary and you're sure to find the place packed with locals first thing in the morning. **Known for:** deliciously fresh baked goods; pindan and pearl, an appetizer at dinner made of pearl meat from the Willie Creek Pearl Farm; chili scrambled eggs, served with chorizo, fried shallots, buffalo mozzarella, and house-made ciabatta bread. *[$] Average main: A$30 ✉ 2 Challenor Dr. ☎ 08/9192–0015 🌐 www.zks.com.au ⏲ Closed Tues. and Wed. No lunch weekdays.*

Hotels

★ Cable Beach Club Resort and Spa

$$$$ | **RESORT** | **FAMILY** | An institution in Cable Beach, this family-friendly resort caters to guests of all ages with multiple pools, a water park, playground, minigolf course, tennis courts, a luxury day spa, meditation garden, and five seasonal restaurants featuring everything from Italian, Southeast Asian, and Japanese food, bistro fare, and a beachfront sunset bar and grill. **Pros:** easy walk to Cable Beach; peaceful, tropical atmosphere; separate swimming pool area just for adults. **Cons:** no shopping nearby; need transport to get into town; property is huge and it's easy to get lost. *[$] Rooms from: A$469 ✉ Cable Beach Rd. ☎ 08/9192–0400 🌐 www.cablebeachclub.com 🛏 189 rooms 🍴 Free Breakfast.*

Kimberley Sands Resort and Spa

$$$ | **RESORT** | One of the Cable Beach area's best accommodation options, this glam, adults-only resort seduces with its stunning pool, spa facilities, and chic bar that sit at the heart of its luxurious rooms and suites, which, by the way, provide you with your own private balcony or courtyard. **Pros:** great resort-style lap pool; free Wi-Fi; all rooms have a private balcony or courtyard. **Cons:** you'll need a car or a cab to get to and from downtown Broome and the airport; parking-lot-facing rooms are noisy; an adults-only property as of July 2019. *[$] Rooms from: A$299 ✉ Cable Beach, 10 Murray Rd. ☎ 08/9193–8300 🌐 www.kimberleysands.com.au 🛏 72 rooms 🍴 No meals.*

★ Mantra Frangipani

$$$$ | **HOTEL** | In lush, tropical gardens, these one-, two-, three-bedroom self-contained villas offer a wonderful escape from hustle and bustle of downtown Broome and Cable Beach, with private garden courtyards, barbecues, and luxurious outdoor showers. **Pros:** luxurious Balinese-style outdoor showers; lovely gardens throughout the grounds, mango trees you can pick from (seasonally); ability to self-cater and use private barbecues. **Cons:** small pool; pull the shades or close the bedroom door or else the whole place can see you in the outdoor shower; it's a 20-minute walk to the nearest beach. *[$] Rooms from: 339 ✉ 15 Millington Rd. ☎ 08/9195–5000 reception, 131517 reservations 🌐 www.mantra.com.au 🛏 60 rooms 🍴 No meals.*

Moonlight Bay Suites

$$$ | **HOTEL** | Home to 49 charming self-contained one- and two-bedroom suites, complete with fully loaded kitchens, spa tubs, a separate lounge room, and views overlooking grand gardens or scenic Roebuck Bay, Moonlight Bay

Suites is a great place to rest up before or after an epic Kimberley adventure. **Pros:** across the street from Matso's Broome Brewery; family-friendly, with an extra twin bed in the lounge room with a couch that opens up into a bed; fully stocked kitchens so you can self-cater. **Cons:** limited gym amenities; need a car to get to Cable Beach; no on-site restaurant. $ *Rooms from: A$239* ⊠ *51 Carnarvon St.* ☎ *08/9195–5200* ⊕ *www. moonlightbaysuites.com.au* ⊰ *49 suites* ⊠ *No meals.*

Pinctada McAlpine House
$$$ | B&B/INN | With an inviting pool, a library, personalized service, and heaps of Javanese teak furniture, this B&B, originally built in 1910 for a local pearling master, is a good place to unwind while giving you a chance to swap travel tales with your fellow guests at breakfast. **Pros:** highly personalized service; luxurious suites; complimentary airport transfers, breakfast, and Wi-Fi. **Cons:** limited leisure facilities; no children under 16 allowed; 30-minute walk to downtown Broome and you'll need a car to get to Cable Beach. $ *Rooms from: A$259* ⊠ *55 Herbert St., at Louis St.* ☎ *08/9192–0588* ⊕ *mcalpinehouse.com.au* ⊙ *Closed mid-Dec.–Mar.* ⊰ *8 rooms* ⊠ *Free Breakfast.*

Ramada Eco Beach Resort
$$$ | RESORT | Luxury villas and safari eco-tents dot the red dirt landscape, connected by environmentally friendly boardwalks and edged with herb and vegetable gardens at this wilderness retreat, which, with its cliff-side ocean-front location, gives the impression it's incredibly remote despite being just a 90-minute drive south of Broome. **Pros:** lots of on-site activities, including day spa services, yoga classes, and cave tours; beautiful waterfront location; you can self-cater. **Cons:** no shopping nearby; restaurant is a big pricey; the last 12 km (7 miles) into the resort is along an unsealed dirt road suitable for four-wheel-drive vehicles. $ *Rooms from: A$225*

⊠ *Great Northern Hwy., Lot 323* ⊕ *134 km (83 miles) south of Broome along the Great Northern Hwy.; look for signs and take the dirt road for the last 12 km (7 miles)* ☎ *08/9193–8015* ⊕ *www.ecobeach.com.au* ⊙ *Closed Mon.–Thurs. from Nov.–Apr.* ⊰ *57 rooms* ⊠ *No meals.*

🔒 Shopping

Given its pearly history, it's no surprise that Broome has an abundance of jewelry stores.

Allure South Sea Pearls
JEWELRY/ACCESSORIES | This store sells high-end jewelry. It also has an outlet at Cable Beach Club Resort and Spa. ⊠ *25 Dampier Terr.* ☎ *08/9192–2430* ⊕ *www. alluresouthseapearls.com.au.*

Kailis Australian Pearls
JEWELRY/ACCESSORIES | This shop specializes in high-quality, expensive pearls and jewelry. ⊠ *23 Dampier Terr., Shop 3* ☎ *08/9192–2061* ⊕ *www.kailisjewellery. com.au.*

Paspaley Pearling
JEWELRY/ACCESSORIES | Family-owned Paspaley Pearling, located in Chinatown, sells pearls and stylish local jewelry. ⊠ *2 Short St.* ☎ *08/9195–1600* ⊕ *www. paspaley.com.*

Chapter 12

WESTERN AUSTRALIA

12

Updated by
Jennifer Morton

⊙ Sights	🍴 Restaurants	🛏 Hotels	🛍 Shopping	🍸 Nightlife
★★★★☆	★★★★★	★★★★★	★★★☆☆	★★★☆☆

WELCOME TO WESTERN AUSTRALIA

TOP REASONS TO GO

★ **Beach Heaven:** Some of Australia's finest beaches are in Western Australia. Hundreds of miles of virtually deserted sandy stretches and bays invite you to swim, surf, snorkel, or laze about.

★ **National Parks:** With spectacular terrain and one-of-a-kind plant and animal species, rugged national parks tell the story of Australia's age-old landforms, especially across the gorge-pocked Kimberley region.

★ **Slick Eats:** Perth's modern food revolution has made way for a smorgasbord of small bars and edgy restaurants excelling at local, seasonal fare.

★ **Wine Trails:** Follow the beautiful wine trails from Perth to the south coast to enjoy free tastings of internationally renowned drops at the cellar doors.

★ **Art and Culture:** Perth's public art scene is thriving throughout the city with larger-than-life sculptures, bronze statues, colorful murals, urban furniture, and unique street art in abundance.

Glance at a map of Australia and you'll see that the state of Western Australia (aka WA) encompasses one-third of the country. It's a massive slab, all 1 million square miles of it, so it may take longer than you expect to reach your destination. But efforts are rewarded with fewer tourists and unadulterated nature.

The state's glamour girl is undoubtedly the Margaret River wine region, as rich in native forests and rugged beaches as it is vineyards. The once sleepy capital city of Perth is now a vibrant eating and drinking scene. Fremantle and Rottnest Island are mere day trips away. Journeying up the sparsely populated but beautiful northern coast is made easier with air travel—only tackle the roads if you have ample time.

1 Perth. Western Australia's capital, highlights in this easygoing city include Cottesloe Beach and Kings Park.

2 Fremantle. Perth's "Brooklyn," Fremantle is a cool port city with a lively market and harbor area.

3 Rottnest Island. A short ferry-ride from Freemantle or Perth, this car-free island is home to parks, beaches, and the most adorable creatures in Australia – Quokkas!.

4 Bunbury. A small and cute seaside town with a great beach and Dolphin Discovery Centre.

5 Busselton. Home to the longest timber jetty in the Southern Hemisphere and a great base for your Margaret River plans.

6 Dunsborough. A seaside town with access to great diving and the spectacular coastline of Leeuwin-Naturaliste National Park.

7 Margaret River. The center of the South West's wine region with more than 200 wineries.

8 Nannup. A small town with beautiful, scenic drives.

9 Augusta. Home to the tallest lighthouse on mainland Australia and a few great trails.

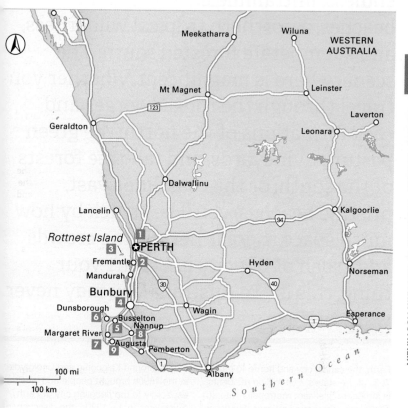

Meekatharra
Wiluna
WESTERN
AUSTRALIA
Mt Magnet
Leinster
123
Laverton
Geraldton
Leonara
Dalwallinu
Lancelin
Kalgoorlie
34
Rottnest Island
1
3
PERTH
Fremantle
2
Hyden
Mandurah
Norseman
Bunbury
30
40
Dunsborough
4
Wagin
6
Busselton
Esperance
Margaret River
5
Nannup
1
7
8
Augusta
9
Pemberton
1
Albany
Southern Ocean

100 mi
100 km

Western Australia is a stunningly diverse place, with rugged interior deserts, endless, untrammeled white-sand beaches, a northern tropical wilderness, and a temperate forested south. The scenery here is magnificent, whether you travel through the rugged gorges and rock formations of the north; the green pastures, vineyards, and tall-tree forests of the south; or the coastline's vast, pristine beaches, you'll be struck by how much space there is here. If the crowds and crush of big-city life aren't your thing, this is the Australia you may never want to leave.

Perth, the capital city and home to nearly 70% of the state's 2.64 million residents, is a modern, pleasant metropolis with an easygoing, welcoming attitude. However, at almost 3,000 km (1,864 miles) from any other major city in the world, it has fondly been dubbed "the most isolated city on Earth." Its remoteness is part of what makes Western Australia so awe-inspiring.

It took more than 200 years after Dutch seafarer Dirk Hartog first landed on the coast of "New Holland" in 1616 in today's Shark Bay before British colonists arrived to establish the Swan River Colony (now Perth) in 1829. Progress was slow for half a century, but the discovery

of gold around Kalgoorlie and Coolgardie in the 1890s brought people and wealth, especially to the fledgling city of Perth; much later, in the 1970s, the discovery of massive mineral deposits throughout the state began an economic upswing that still continues.

Western Australia produces much of Australia's mineral, energy, and agricultural wealth, though recent falls in resources prices have slowed development, curbed employment figures, and reduced the population flow to WA, with fewer people chasing the highs of its boom-and-bust cycle. Nonetheless, development continues: a number of the state's airports are being expanded; central train lines are being sunk, linking the city's divided heart; and the long-term riverside development known as Elizabeth Quay continues to evolve (expect road delays). The cooling economy has delivered a boon for travelers: hotel prices have fallen, making for a more affordable experience in this land of oft-inflated prices.

MAJOR REGIONS

Perth and Environs encompasses Western Australia's capital, **Perth,** a once-quiet town that now matches the wow-factor of its Caribbean-style coastline; the port town of **Fremantle,** charming for its curving, colonial streets and the quirky vibe of its residents; and **Rottnest Island,** the ultimate escape, with no cars (bikes are the dominant mode of transport), no pretension, and no cares in the world. The promise of 63 beaches just 19 km (12 miles) from Perth has people flocking here.

Internationally known and loved as one of Australia's top wine regions—Chardonnay and Cabernet Sauvignon are the standout varieties—and producers of paddock-to-plate cuisine, **the Margaret River region** is Western Australia's most popular destination, with 2.4 million visitors annually. Perth residents flock here year-round for the wines, beaches, surfing, marine wildlife, forests, locally produced crafts and artisan products, and the country vistas. Most towns in this don't-miss region are on the coast with easy beach access. The best surfing beaches are on the coast between Cape Naturaliste and Cape Leeuwin. Also called the South West and "Down South," this region stretches from the port city of **Bunbury**—about two hours south of Perth by freeway and highway—through **Busselton,** on the shores of Geographe Bay and considered the region's main gateway, to **Dunsborough,** **Margaret River,** and on to Augusta, a coastal village in the far south where the Indian and Southern Oceans meet, at the tip of Cape Leeuwin. There's also the town of **Nannup,** an easy jaunt from Margaret River for a day trip.

Planning

WHEN TO GO

You can visit Western Australia year-round, though the weather will influence your activities and sightseeing. Perth enjoys more sunny days than any other Australian capital city. Summer (December through February) in Perth is *hot* and temperatures can rise to 40°C (100°F), but the locals love it and flock to the beaches. Be aware major school and university holidays occur at this time, so expect crowds and higher prices. The Perth Festival in February is an excellent reason to visit. Weather-wise, March, April, November, and December are most pleasant, with sunny days and warm, comfortable temperatures. July and August are traditionally cool and wet, which is why Broome and the state's northwest is the favorite place to be during these months

FESTIVALS

★ Perth Festival

FESTIVALS | With music, fireworks, indigenous performances, and world-famous artists, this energetic, big-name summer festival brings the city to life. The highly anticipated festival is held February and March in venues throughout the city, and its more highbrow shows are tempered with the raucousness of the Perth Fringe World Festival, which runs in January and February. While most shows for both festivals are ticketed, there are also plenty of free outdoor performances. PF is Australia's oldest and biggest annual arts festival, running for more than 50 years. ⊠ *Perth* ☎ *08/6488–5555 bookings* ⊕ *www.perthfestival.com.au.*

PLANNING YOUR TIME

Fly into Perth and spend most of the first day exploring the city center, especially Kings Park and, by night, the restaurants and small bars of the CBD and Northbridge. The following day, take the train to Cottesloe Beach and gaze at the translucent water. As the sun's rays strengthen, continue along the tracks to charmingly preserved Fremantle and stroll through the heritage precinct, stopping for breaks at sidewalk cafés and the bustling markets. On day three, take a ferry to Rottnest Island and rent a bike or walk around to the lovely beaches—keep an eye open for small local marsupials called quokkas. For the following days, take a wine-touring excursion to the glamorous Margaret River region.

GETTING HERE AND AROUND
AIR TRAVEL

Perth is the main international arrival point on this side of the country and is serviced by more than 30 airlines. Qantas is Australia's main domestic airline; its budget subsidiary, Jetstar, operates an extensive network and regular services crisscrossing the country, from all the major cities to regional centers like Exmouth and Broome. Virgin Australia competes with Qantas in major cities, and, after purchasing local carrier Skywest, now covers many regional centers such as Albany, Kununurra, Esperance, and Broome. Airnorth has an extensive network throughout the Top End and covers some WA legs in the north. Perth City Shuttle (☎ 0427/438533 ⊕ perthcityshuttle.com.au) operates minivan services from the terminals to the CBD, Cottesloe, or Fremantle hotels (call or book online).

BUS TRAVEL

Integrity Coach Lines operate an extensive network of long-distance coaches. Greyhound operates from Broome, going north only. From Perth to Adelaide, there are no bus options; when driving, expect to be on the road for 36 hours.

South West Coachlines

Daily services depart Perth Elizabeth Quay Busport on Mounts Bay Road—as well as from Perth domestic and international airports—to South West towns, including Bunbury, Busselton, Dunsborough, Margaret River township, Collie, and Manjimup. Services may vary according to season. ☎ 08/9753–7700 ⊕ www.southwestcoachlines.com.au.

CAR TRAVEL

Driving around Western Australia is relatively easy, with mostly good paved roads and light traffic outside Perth. While the distances in the Outback are daunting (Perth to Broome is 2,240 km [1,386 miles]), Perth to the Margaret River region in the South West is just over three hours along good roads; mostly dual-lane highway. Always be aware of wildlife on the roadsides, particularly at dawn and dusk.

TAXI TRAVEL

Taxis are at the airport around the clock, and there is a rideshare pickup point for Uber and Ola customers. Trips to Perth city cost about A$45 and take around a half hour. The cost to or from downtown Perth starts at A$25.

CONTACTS Black & White. ☎ 13–1222 ⊕ www.blackandwhitecabs.com.au. **Swan Taxis.** ☎ 13–1330 ⊕ www.swantaxis.com.au.

TRAIN TRAVEL

Crossing the Nullarbor Plain from the eastern states is one of the great rail journeys of the world. You traverse an entire continent, going 4345 km (2,700 miles) from Sydney to Perth on the longest stretch of straight track in the world. Great Southern Railways' *Indian Pacific* links Sydney and Perth via Kalgoorlie and Adelaide, with once-weekly services each way. The trip takes around four days.

From Perth, TransWA operates train services to Bunbury twice daily and to Northam and Kalgoorlie, with coaches linking to other destinations, including Geraldton, Kalbarri, Albany, and Esperance.

Getting around Perth by train is quick and easy, with lines to Armadale/Thornlie, Midland, Butler, Fremantle, Mandurah, and Rockingham.

HEALTH AND SAFETY

If you are self-driving—especially in remote areas—make sure you have enough fuel, water, and food, and carry a first-aid kit. Let others know where you are going and for how long. Mosquitoes are prevalent, so cover up and use a good insect repellent; the worst times for mosquitoes are dawn and dusk.

Respect the Australian sun, especially in summer. Sunburn is a real danger if you don't follow the Australian mantra: slip, slap, slop—that is, slip on a hat, slap on sunglasses, and slop on sunscreen. On popular beaches around major cities and towns, lifesavers (lifeguards) are usually on duty and put up flags to swim between, but generally most beaches are unguarded. Take extra care, especially where there are strong currents.

The emergency contact number for police, fire, and ambulance is ☏ *000*. From a GSM mobile (cell) phone the number is ☏ *112*.

RESTAURANTS

A number of talented chefs have returned to Perth from overseas, bringing international trends, abilities, and standards with them. This influence, coupled with a healthy push for seasonal, local produce, has given the Perth dining scene an exciting shot in the arm. Throughout the young city's history, waves of immigrants from Italy, the former Yugoslavia, and Asia have also delivered cultural authenticity to the more traditional eateries. A British handover, fish-and-chips, remains one of the beach-going state's favorite picnic meals.

Expect to find Western Australian wines on the wine list when dining in most licensed restaurants in Perth and, of course, in the Margaret River wine region, where first-class food is matched with highly regarded vino.

Many restaurants and cafés have alfresco dining. Perth suffers from a sometimes justified reputation for below-par service. Tips aren't expected, but when you experience exceptional service, an extra 10% is welcome. Expect added surcharges of up to 20% on public holidays.

HOTELS

From five-star to basic, you'll find suitable accommodations throughout the region. The well-known international chains are all in Perth but there are also sublime boutique accommodations. Perth once had some of the highest occupancy rates in Australia, largely due to business travelers, but a cooling of this has reduced room rates. Ideally, book ahead, though last-minute bargains can be had, especially for weekends. Other popular options—especially for families and small groups—are self-contained apartments or villas. With two or three bedrooms, living areas, and kitchens, they allow you to save on dining costs by cooking your own meals; these are best if staying more than one night. *Hotel reviews have been shortened. For full information, visit Fodors.com.*

What It Costs in Australian Dollars			
$	**$$**	**$$$**	**$$$$**
RESTAURANTS			
under A$21	A$21– A$35	A$36– A$50	over A$50
HOTELS			
under A$151	A$151– A$200	A$201– A$300	over A$300

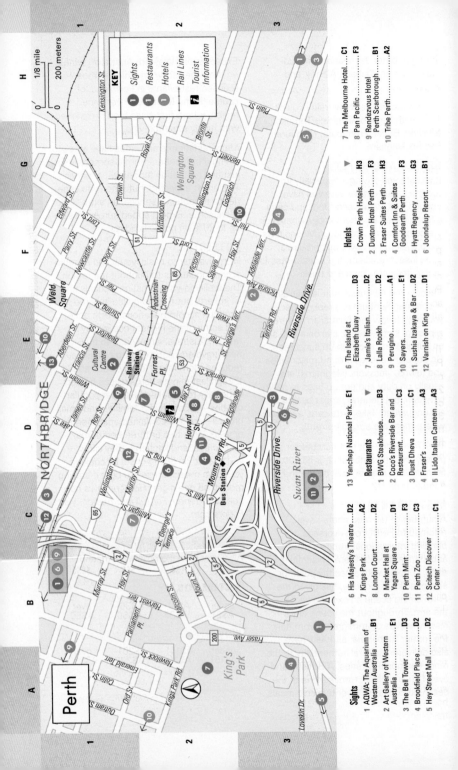

Perth

KEY
- Sights
- Restaurants
- Hotels
- → Rail Lines
- **i** Tourist Information

0 1/8 mile
0 200 meters

Sights
- ▶
1 AQWA: The Aquarium of Western Australia.....B1
2 Art Gallery of Western Australia.....E1
3 The Bell Tower.....D3
4 Brookfield Place.....D2
5 Hay Street Mall.....D2
6 His Majesty's Theatre.....D2
7 Kings Park.....A2
8 London Court.....D2
9 Market Hall at Yagan Square.....D1
10 Perth Mint.....F3
11 Perth Zoo.....C3
12 Scitech Discover Center.....C1
13 Yanchep National Park.....E1

Restaurants
- ▶
1 BWG Steakhouse.....B3
2 Coco's Riverside Bar and Restaurant.....C3
3 Dusit Dheva.....C1
4 Fraser's.....A3
5 Il Lido Italian Canteen.....A3
6 The Island at Elizabeth Quay.....D3
7 Jamie's Italian.....D2
8 Lalla Rookh.....D2
9 Perugino.....A1
10 Sayers.....E1
11 Sushia Izakaya & Bar.....D2
12 Varnish on King.....D1

Hotels
- ▶
1 Crown Perth Hotels.....H3
2 Duxton Hotel Perth.....F3
3 Fraser Suites Perth.....H3
4 Comfort Inn & Suites Goodearth Perth.....F3
5 Hyatt Regency.....G3
6 Joondalup Resort.....B1
7 The Melbourne Hotel.....C1
8 Pan Pacific.....F3
9 Rendezvous Hotel Perth Scarborough.....B1
10 Tribe Perth.....A2

NORTHBRIDGE

King's Park

Weld Square

Wellington Square

Swan River

Riverside Drive.

Railway Station

Bus Station

Cultural Centre

Perth

Buoyed by a history of mineral wealth and foreign investment, Perth has high-rise buildings dotting the skyline, and an influx of immigrants gives the city a healthy diversity. Within 15 minutes' drive of the city are some of Australia's finest sandy beaches and seaside villages; the best postcard beaches lie just north of bohemian Fremantle. The main business thoroughfare is St. Georges Terrace, an elegant street lined with skyscrapers and an excellent set-back entertainment precinct, while urban villages such as Leederville and Mt. Lawley deliver chic-yet-welcoming community vibes. Perth's literal highlight is Kings Park, 990 acres of greenery atop Mt. Eliza, which affords panoramic city views.

GETTING HERE AND AROUND

The main gateway to Western Australia is Perth's busy airport. It has four terminals: T1, T2, T3, and T4. Terminals 1 and 2 (about 16 km [10 miles] from Perth's central business district), and terminals 3 and 4 (about 13 km [8 miles] away), host a mix of domestic and international flights, so always check with your airline before heading to the airport. A free shuttle bus connects the terminals 24 hours a day.

Perth and its environs are well connected by Transperth buses. The main terminals are at the Elizabeth Quay Bus Station on Mounts Bay Road and Perth Station on Wellington Street. Buses run daily 6 am–11:30 pm, with reduced service on weekends and holidays. Rides within the city center are free. CAT (Central Area Transit) buses circle the city center, running frequently on weekdays 6 am–6:45 pm, and weekends and most public holidays 8:30 am–6 pm. Routes and timetables are available from Transperth (☎ 13–6213 ⊕ www.transperth.wa.gov. au). Transperth tickets are valid for two hours and can be used on Transperth trains and ferries. The ferries make daily runs from 6:30 am to 6:45 pm between Elizabeth Quay in Perth to Mends Street, across the Swan River in South Perth. Reduced services run on weekends and holidays.

Transperth trains also provide a quick way to get around the city. Most attractions are accessed via the Fremantle line, which traces the coast via Perth's most affluent suburbs. Other lines run east to Midland, north to Butler, southeast to Armadale/Thornlie, and south to Mandurah. Central-city trains depart from Wellington Street and Perth Underground at the corner of William and Murray streets. Tickets must be purchased at vending machines before boarding.

SAFETY AND PRECAUTIONS

A safe city to visit, Perth doesn't have any "no-go" neighborhoods, and a strong police presence—on foot, bike, and horse—usually ensures that late-night hot spots like Northbridge and Fremantle—are safe. Still, for your personal safety, avoid walking alone, especially late at night. Also, pickpocketing isn't a particular risk, but as with visiting any city, it's best to keep your personal belongings close, especially in busy shopping areas, and don't leave valuables—such as cameras—in the car when parked overnight, or when visiting attractions.

ESSENTIALS

BANKS AND CURRENCY EXCHANGE

Banks with dependable check-cashing and money-changing services include ANZ, Westpac, Commonwealth, and National Australia Bank. ATMs—which accept Cirrus, Plus, Visa, and Master-Card—are ubiquitous. A number of exchange booths with better rates can be found in Perth's malls, in London Court and on St. George's Terrace.

VISITOR INFORMATION

CONTACT Western Australia Visitor Centre. ✉ 55 William St., CBD ☎ 08/9483–1111 outside Australia, 1800/812808 ⊕ www. westernaustralia.com.

12

Western Australia PERTH

TOURS

ADAMS Pinnacle Tours

GUIDED TOURS | This local outfit conducts day tours of Perth and its major attractions. You can also take a day or multiday trip of outer sights like Nambung National Park—with its weird limestone formations—Rottnest Island to see the quokkas, Margaret River and its wineries, or, with more time, Monkey Mia, Wave Rock near Hyden, and the Treetop Walk near Walpole (be aware that this is a long 14½-hour tour). Perth hotel pickup is available. ✉ *Barrack St. Jetty, Shop 1, CBD* ☎ *08/6270–6060 outside Australia, 1300/551687* ⊕ *www.adamspinnacle-tours.com.au* ◱ *From A$65.*

Australian Pacific Touring

ADVENTURE TOURS | Commonly known as APT, this national group runs extended 4WD adventure coach trips around Western Australia for groups of 20, and one very special cruise. Comfortable, multiday tours travel from Perth to Monkey Mia, via wildflower country and Shark Bay, and from Broome to Perth, stopping in at Ningaloo Reef and the Pinnacles. APT specializes in the Kimberley, crossing the fabled Gibb River Road, and staying in their own wilderness lodges at numerous locations including Purnululu National Park. The most popular tour is the 15-day Kimberley Complete. You can also cruise the Kimberley coastline by boat. Tours run from six days and up. ✉ *Perth* ☎ *1300/336932 call center, 1300/278278 reservations* ⊕ *www.aptouring.com.au* ◱ *From A$9995.*

★ Captain Cook Cruises

BOAT TOURS | A scenic glide on the flat water of the Swan River with this tour company makes for an excellent afternoon, especially if you want to travel from Perth to the Indian Ocean at Fremantle. Enjoy the captain's commentary and free tea and coffee. Optional 1½-hour stopovers are included. There are lunch options and tours upriver to the Swan Valley vineyards, too. ✉ *Pier 3, Barrack St. Jetty,* *CBD* ☎ *08/9325–3341* ⊕ *www.captain-cookcruises.com.au* ◱ *From A$30.*

Casey Australia Tours

ADVENTURE TOURS | Created with the mature traveler in mind, a range of extended tours departing from Perth covers nearly every inch of the state, including a 14-day four-wheel-drive tour that traverses the iconic Gibb River Road and covers the Bungle Bungle Range in Purnululu National Park, plus an optional flight over Mitchell Falls. Some accommodation is in motels, but it's mostly camping—this is an Outback tour, after all! Day tours and shorter tours are available, including a visit to the South West's apple and truffle growing region. ✉ *63 Birdwood Circus W, Bicton* ☎ *08/9339–4291, 1800/999677* ⊕ *www.caseytours.com.au* ◱ *Day trips from A$109.*

★ d'Vine Wine Tours

EXCURSIONS | Take a guided day trip to the Swan Valley—one of the state's favorite wine and food regions—with d'Vine Wine Tours and discover fine wines, hoppy beers, gourmet cuisine, chocolates, and French pastries that will make you want to relocate. The company has van pickups from Perth CBD; it's a 25-minute drive to the valley. ■ **TIP→ Expect to shop at each of the places visited—it's hard not to.** ☎ *08/9244–5323* ⊕ *www.dvinetours.com.au* ◱ *From A$110.*

Perth Explorer

BUS TOURS | This open-top bus company runs informative hop-on, hop-off trips around central Perth and to Kings Park on a typical red double-decker. Tickets are valid for 48 hours, and you can get on and off as you choose, or stay on for the full two-hour tour. Book online for discounts or upgrade your ticket to a Triple Tour, which includes a Swan River cruise and tour of Fremantle in a wooden replica tram. ☎ *08/9370–1000* ⊕ *www.perthexplorer.com.au* ◱ *From A$40.*

★ Rottnest Express

BOAT TOURS | Rottnest Express runs excursions to Rottnest Island once daily from Perth and six to 12 times daily from Fremantle, depending on the season. It also runs marine life adventure tours between September and April. There are several package options available, including some with bike rentals. ⊠ *Pier 2, Barrack St. Jetty, CBD* ☎ *1300/467688* ⊕ *www.rottnestexpress.com.au* ⊠ *From $A64.*

★ Two Feet and a Heartbeat

GUIDED TOURS | These guys are award-winning for several reasons: their walking tours are fun and informative, and they wrap in elements that reveal the personality of a city, such as street art, small bars, sculptures, history, and hidden relics. There are several food and drink-themed tours in Perth city and Fremantle; art and culture tours; convicts and crimes tours; and even nature- and wildlife-focused walking tours. A tour is a great way to get to know the city's history and top spots. ⊠ *CBD* ☎ *08/7007–0492 outside Australia, 1800/459388* ⊕ *www.twofeet.com.au* ⊠ *From A$40.*

◉ Sights

Because of its relative colonial youth, Perth has an advantage over most other capital cities in that it was laid out with foresight. Streets were planned so that pedestrian traffic could flow smoothly from one avenue to the next, and this compact city remains easy to negotiate on foot. Many points of interest are in the downtown area close to the banks of the Swan River, while shopping arcades and pedestrian malls are a short stroll away.

The city center (CBD, or Central Business District), a pleasant blend of old and new, runs along Perth's major business thoroughfare, St. Georges Terrace, as well as on parallel Hay and Murray streets.

AQWA: Aquarium of Western Australia

ZOO | **FAMILY** | Huge, colorful aquariums filled with some 400 different species of local sea creatures—including sharks that are 13 feet long—from along the 12,000 km (7,456 miles) of Western Australia's variable coastline are the fascinating draws of this boutique aquarium in northern Perth. Sharp-toothed sharks, stingrays, turtles, and schools of fish swim overhead as you take the moving walkway beneath a transparent acrylic tunnel. You can even do a guided snorkel or scuba dive with the sharks for 30–45 minutes; bookings are essential. Perhaps most interesting is the change in habitats and species as you move from colder, southern waters to the tropics of Western Australia's north—AQWA boasts one of the largest living coral reef displays in the world. Check it out from above and then below in the underwater gallery. Other highlights include the rare seadragons and DANGERzone, featuring a deadly lineup of sea creatures. ■ **TIP→ Age minimums apply for some activities.** ⊠ *Hillarys Boat Harbour, 91 Southside Dr., Hillarys* ⊹ *AQWA is a 20-min drive north of Perth's CBD via Mitchell Freeway, turn left at Hepburn Ave. and continue to Hillarys Boat Harbour. Or, take northern Joondalup train line. Get off at Warwick station and take bus No. 423* ☎ *08/9447–7500* ⊕ *www.aqwa.com.au* ⊠ *From A$30.*

Art Gallery of Western Australia

MUSEUM | Founded in 1895, the Art Gallery of Western Australia is home to more than 17,500 treasures and numerous free exhibitions of Indigenous and modern art, which makes it worth an afternoon's devotion. The collection of Indigenous art is impressive, while other works include Australian and international paintings, sculpture, prints, crafts, and decorative arts. Free guided tours run regularly, though times vary. An entry charge usually applies to special exhibitions. ⊠ *Perth Cultural Centre, James St., at Beaufort and Roe Sts., CBD* ☎ *08/9492–6600,*

08/9492–6622 24-hr information ⊕ *www.artgallery.wa.gov.au* ✉ *Free* ⊙ *Closed Tues.*

The Bell Tower

LOCAL INTEREST | The spiral-like Bell Tower is home to one of the world's largest musical instruments, the 12 antique Swan Bells, which have surprising historical links. Originally from St. Martin-in-the-Fields Church of London, England, these same bells were rung to celebrate the destruction of the Spanish Armada in 1588, the homecoming of Captain James Cook in 1771, and the coronation of every British monarch. The tower contains fascinating displays on the history of the bells and bell ringing, and provides views of the Perth skyline and the nearby Swan River. Flat, closed shoes must be worn for access to the observation deck; stroller and wheelchair access are available via the elevator. ■TIP➔ **Purchase a heart-shape love lock to leave on the chain fence to secure forever-love.** ✉ *Barrack St., at Riverside Dr., CBD* ☎ *08/6210–0444* ⊕ *www.thebelltower.com.au* ✉ *A$18.*

★ Brookfield Place

PLAZA | See where corporate suits de-stress after a long day at the office. Once the clock hits 5 pm, like bees swarming a hive, punters flood Perth's CBD's main thoroughfare, St. Georges Terrace, and its strip of hip new venues. Swanky Print Hall serves some of the city's best modern Australian fare, while Bob's Bar is a happening rooftop venue focusing on simple, tasty, Mexican-inspired eats. There's also the Heritage Wine Bar for contemporary eats and fine wine. ✉ *123–137 St. Georges Terr., CBD* ☎ *08/9428–6400 general number* ⊕ *brookfieldplaceperth.com.*

★ Hay Street Mall

PEDESTRIAN MALL | Running parallel to Murray Street and linked by numerous arcades, the Hay Street Mall is an extensive, mainstream shopping area teeming with intriguing places. The mall is also a brilliant place to people-watch. Make

The View from Kings Park ◉

The best spot is the manicured eastern edge of the park, past the border of tall, white-bark trees and overlooking Perth's Central Business District and the Swan River. While it's a jubilant place buzzing with friends and families picnicking, it also has a somber edge, home to the State War Memorial and its eternal flame, as well as the memorial to local victims of the 2002 terrorist bombing in Bali.

sure you wander through the arcades that connect Hay and Murray streets, such as the **Carillion** and **Piccadilly Arcades,** which have many more shops. Also, look for the monument dedicated to Percy Button, Perth's original street performer. ✉ *Hay St., CBD.*

★ His Majesty's Theatre

ARTS VENUE | The opulent Edwardian His Majesty's Theatre, which opened in 1904, is admired by those who step inside. His Maj, as it's locally known, is home to the West Australian Opera company and the West Australian Ballet, and hosts most theatrical productions in Perth; there's also a comedy lounge downstairs. ■TIP➔ **Tardiness is frowned upon—you will not be permitted inside until a break in the performance.** ✉ *825 Hay St., CBD* ☎ *08/6212–9292 tickets* ⊕ *www.ptt.wa.gov.au.*

★ Kings Park

CITY PARK | FAMILY | Locals boast that this is one of the few inner-city parks to dwarf New York City's Central Park; it covers 1,000 acres and grants eye-popping views of downtown Perth and its riverfront at sunrise, sunset, and all times in between. Once a gathering place for

King's Park with downtown Perth in the distance

Aboriginal people, and established as a public space in 1890, it's favored for picnics, parties, and weddings, as well as regular musical and theater presentations, plus the excellent summer Moonlight Cinema (in Synergy Parkland, on the western side). Each September, when spring arrives, the park holds a wildflower festival and the gardens blaze with orchids, kangaroo paw, banksias, and other native wildflowers, making it ideal for a walk in the curated bushland. The steel-and-glass **Lotterywest Federation Walkway** takes you into the treetops and the 17-acre botanic garden of Australian flora. The **Lotterywest Family Area** has a shaded playground for youngsters ages 1–5, and a café for parents. The Rio Tinto Naturescape is fun for bigger kids who enjoy climbing and exploring in nature. Free walking tours depart daily from Aspects Gift Shop on Fraser Avenue at 10 am, noon, and 2 pm. ⊠ *Fraser Ave., at Kings Park Rd., West Perth* ☎ *08/9480–3634* ⊕ *www.bgpa.wa.gov.au* ⊠ *Free.*

London Court

PEDESTRIAN MALL | Gold-mining entrepreneur Claude de Bernales built this quaint outdoor shopping arcade in 1937. Today it's a magnet for anyone with a camera wanting to recapture the atmosphere and architecture of Tudor England, and for those looking for Australian souvenirs. Along its length are statues of Sir Walter Raleigh and Dick Whittington, the legendary lord mayor of London. Above the arcade entry, costumed mechanical knights joust with one another when the clock strikes the quarter hour. ■ **TIP→ The Genuine UGG boot store is popular with tourists; Aboriginal Art has many Australia-themed gifts and souvenirs.** ⊠ *St. Georges Terr. at Hay St., CBD* ☎ *08/9261–6666* ⊕ *www.londoncourt.com.au.*

★ **Market Hall at Yagan Square**

PLAZA | FAMILY | With its quintessential Western Australia design, color, and flora, Yagan Square opened in March 2018 as a community space and the gateway to Northbridge. It's become a central meeting spot for both locals and tourists. Market Hall, its high-end food court, draws a daily lunch crowd with its variety of local and international flavors. Wheat Street (think pasta and bruschetta) is licensed to serve alcohol, and you are welcome to take it to any seat within the open-plan dining area. Pop into Sue Lewis Chocolatier for handmade chocolate. ⊠ *Wellington St. at William St., near Perth Station.*

Perth Mint

BANK | All that glitters is gold at the Perth Mint, one of the oldest mints in the world still operating from its original premises, and a reminder of the great gold rush days at the turn of the century. Established in 1899, it first refined gold from Western Australia's newly discovered goldfields, striking gold sovereigns for the British Empire. Today it still produces Australia's legal tender in pure gold, silver, and platinum bullion and commemorative coins for investors and collectors. Visitors can have a hands-on experience at the Mint—watch 200 ounces of molten gold being poured in time-honored fashion to form a gold bar; marvel at the biggest coin ever made, weighing 1 ton; get close to more than A$50 million worth of gold bullion; see Australia's best collection of natural gold nuggets, including the 369-ounce Golden Beauty, one of the largest natural nuggets in the world; and discover your own weight in gold. There's an on-site gift shop and café. ⊠ *310 Hay St., East Perth* ☎ *08/9421–7222* ⊕ *www.perthmint.com. au* ⊠ *A$19.*

Perth Zoo

ZOO | **FAMILY** | From kangaroos to crocodiles and venomous Aussie snakes to Asian sun bears and orangutans, this expansive, more than century-old zoo is an easy 10-minute drive from Perth's CBD. Expect lush gardens—perfect for a BYO picnic—and different native habitats of various animals from around the world. Walk among Australian animals in an environment depicting the diversity of Australia's native landscape, including a bird-filled wetland. Discover the Reptile Encounter, Rainforest Retreat, and the Australian Bushwalk. For something a little more exotic, there's the African Savannah, with rhinoceroses, giraffes, lions, cheetahs, and baboons; and the Asian Rainforest, with elephants, tigers, otters, gibbons, and a Komodo dragon. A number of special encounters are available, such as joining a keeper as they feed the lions, which is best booked and paid for in advance. Free guided walks depart daily at 11 am and 1pm, and there are more than a dozen free talks and presentations each day. A one-hour guided tour around the zoo on an electric Zebra Car, seating seven passengers, is also available. ⊠ *20 Labouchere Rd., South Perth* ✛ *Catch No. 30 or 31 bus at Esplanade Busport or take ferry ride across Swan River from Elizabeth Quay and then walk 10 mins, following signs* ☎ *08/9474–0444, 08/9474–3551 24-hr info* ⊕ *www.perthzoo.wa.gov.au* ⊠ *A$32.*

Scitech Discovery Centre

MUSEUM | **FAMILY** | Interactive science and technology displays educate and entertain visitors of all ages—particularly the younger ones—in this excellent facility. There are more than 100 hands-on general science exhibits, as well as in-depth feature exhibitions. Daily science and puppet shows present science in an entertaining way, and the space shows in the half dome planetarium will stretch your imagination as they take you to the far edges of the known Universe. Minimum age restrictions apply to the planetarium. ■TIP→ **Keep an eye out for the quirky facts that dot the space, including the fact that the heart of a giraffe is two feet long.** ⊠ *City West Centre, Sutherland St., West Perth* ☎ *08/9215–0700* ⊕ *scitech. org.au* ⊠ *A$19.*

The Pinnacles of Nambung National Park, Western Australia

Yanchep National Park

NATIONAL/STATE PARK | Sure, it's nice to cuddle a koala in an enclosure, but it's far more exciting to see them in the wild, just above your head. Take the 240-meter (787-foot) Koala Board Walk through native bush with your eyes raised skyward to see one of the state's largest populations of koalas. Watch for western grey kangaroos on the 2-km (1.2-mile) wetland walking trail around Loch McNess lake and then escape summer's heat by joining one of several daily underground tours of Crystal Cave, where cooling caverns open up to impressive stalactite galleries and clear water pools. The park is also a lovely picnic spot, and there's a hotel and café within the grounds. ■TIP→ **Yanchep National Park is a 45-minute drive north of Perth and is open every day of the year; book tours and get walk trail information at McNess House Visitor Centre.** ✉ *1 Indian Ocean Dr., Yanchep* ☎ *08/9303–7759 McNess House Visitor Centre* ⊕ *www.dpaw. wa.gov.au* ⌸ *A$13 per vehicle.*

☂ Beaches

Perth's beaches and waterways are among the city's greatest attractions. Traveling north from Fremantle, the first beach you come to is **Leighton,** where windsurfers and astonishing wave-jumpers ride boards against the surf and hurl themselves airborne. **Cottesloe** is Perth's glamour puss—don't miss it—home to lithe, tanned bodies, sun-hungry backpackers, and excited youngsters. It becomes a shoulder-to-shoulder picnic ground on Sundays, while **North Cottesloe** attracts families and locals. Farther north, **Trigg,** a top surf site, overlooks an emerald-green bay. **Scarborough** is favored by teenagers and young adults. Be aware of its sometimes strong waves. **Swanbourne** (between North Cottesloe and City Beach) is a "clothing-optional" beach. Fremantle's town beach is great for kids and a local secret.

Off The Beaten Path

Batavia Coast. A drive along this part of the coast, which starts at Green Head, 285 km (178 miles) north of Perth, and runs up to Kalbarri, takes you past white sands and emerald seas, and some lovely small towns. Among them are the fig-shaded, seaside village of **Dongara** and the more northerly **Central Greenough Historical Settlement,** whose restored colonial buildings—including a jail with original leg irons—date from 1858. A few miles north is **Geraldton,** whose skyline is dominated by the beautiful Byzantine St. Francis Xavier Cathedral. Its foreshore playground is great for kids; also worth a visit is the haunting HMAS Sydney II Memorial, which is the only recognized national war memorial outside of Canberra and has expansive views. The huge Batavia Coast Marina has a pedestrian plaza, shopping arcades, and the fascinating Western Australian Museum, which houses a collection of artifacts from the *Batavia,* a Dutch vessel shipwrecked in 1629. ✉ *Batavia Coast.*

Nambung National Park. Imagine an eerie moonscape where pale yellow limestone formations loom as high as 15 feet. Now see the image in your head displayed before you at Nambung National Park, set on the Swan coastal plain 200 km (125 miles) north of Perth, along the scenic Indian Ocean Drive. At the park you can walk among those other-worldly formations in the **Pinnacles Desert,** home to one of the world's most spectacular karst landscapes. Geologists believe the pinnacles were created by the dissolving action of water on exposed limestone beds that formed under wind-blown sand dunes. Only a tiny proportion of them have been uncovered. The 1.2-km (0.7-mile) return walk starts at the parking area. There's also a 4-km (2½-mile) one-way Pinnacles Desert Loop scenic drive (not suitable for large RVs or buses). Stop in to the Pinnacles Desert Discovery Centre to see interpretative displays focused on the region's unique geology, flora, and fauna. August through October the heath blazes with wildflowers. Note the rules: no pinnacle climbing, no dogs, no littering (no receptacles are provided, so take your trash with you), and no camping. There is no drinking water available throughout the park, although water is available to purchase at the interpretative center and gift shop. ⚠ **Indian Ocean Drive is a frequent crash zone; please take care and avoid driving at dawn, dusk, and dark.** ✉ *Nambung National Park* ☏ *08/9652–7913 Pinnacles Desert Discovery Centre* ⊕ *parks.dpaw.wa.gov. au* 🎫 *$13 per vehicle.*

★ **Cottesloe**

BEACH—SIGHT | FAMILY | Perth's poster beach is as beguiling as it is relaxing, what with its soft cream sand, transparent blue waters, and strip of beachy pubs and restaurants. Naturally, it's very popular, particularly on Sunday, when people of all ages picnic on grass beneath the row of Norfolk pines that also hosts masses of squawking birds.

The water is fairly calm, though punchy waves can roll through, crashing mainly in shallow depths. "Sunday sessions"— afternoon beer drinking in two local pubs at the Ocean Beach Hotel and the swanky Cottesloe Beach Hotel, both of which have good, ocean-facing accommodations—are also held here. South of the Cottesloe groyne is a reasonable reef surf break, but it's often crowded. ■TIP→ **Time your visit for the annual**

Sculptures by the Sea event, a shoreside exhibition of huge sculptures each March. **Amenities:** food and drink; lifeguards; parking (free); showers; toilets. **Best for:** swimming; surfing; snorkeling; sunset; walking. ✉ *Marine Parade, Cottesloe* ⊕ *beachsafe.org.au* ☞ *Parking is free but don't overstay the time limits—inspectors are vigilant, and fines are high.*

North Cottesloe

BEACH—SIGHT | FAMILY | This is the quieter end of Cottesloe, where local residents go to walk their dogs (a section by Grant Street is a designated dog beach), dive in for an early morning dip, or share a sunset wine on the sand. The concrete walking path looks over the sandy beach and affords impressive views of the coastal mansions that look out to sea. Coastal reef fans out to the right of Grant Street and makes for good snorkeling in summer, but take caution in high waves as stronger currents form near the reef. ⚠ **Beware invisible jellyfish, known as stingers, which cause pain but pose little other threat. Amenities:** lifeguards; showers. **Best for:** snorkeling; solitude; sunset; swimming; walking. ✉ *365 Marine Parade, North Cottesloe* ⊕ *beachsafe. org.au.*

Scarborough

BEACH—SIGHT | After the West Australian Premier described the Scarborough precinct as "tired and old," the state government pledged A$30 million to pretty-up the beachfront, and things have markedly improved. The beach was always beautiful and the waves surfable, but now there are a number of busy cafés, including the Wild Fig, the Local Shack, and the Squire's Fortune. There's also the long-standing takeout spot, Peters by the Sea. Kids love to run wild on the beachfront playground and the Snake Pit skate park, while holidaymakers come and go from the towering Rendezvous Hotel. The more enviable locales of Cottesloe, Fremantle, and Perth CBD are all a 15- to 20-minute cab ride away; Scarborough is not on the train line. ⚠ **Waves can be strong at times. Amenities:** food and drink; lifeguards; parking; showers; toilets. **Best for:** kitesurfing; partiers; sunset; walking. ✉ *The Esplanade, Scarborough* ⊕ *beachsafe.org.au.*

Trigg

BEACH—SIGHT | Surfers and body boarders favor this beach, riding the transparent blue waves from Trigg Point and Trigg Island, sometimes crashing into the sandy bottom. Swimmers don masks and paddle to the snorkeling spot of Mettams Pool that is lovely on calm days but should be avoided when the swell is up. The hip, surfer-themed coffee haunt, Yelo, is the best café in the area. Across the road away from the ocean, the Trigg Bushland Reserve makes for interesting, paved bush walking—just follow the trail and its interpretive signage. ⚠ **There is a strong undertow off this beach, and swimmers have struck trouble. Amenities:** food and drink; lifeguards; parking; toilets. **Best for:** snorkeling; sunset; surfing. ✉ *West Coast Dr., Trigg* ⊕ *beachsafe.org.au.*

🍴 Restaurants

Northbridge, northwest of the railway station, used to be *the* dining, barhopping, and nightclubbing center of Perth, but since the city has grown in size and reputation, you can find a myriad of great restaurants throughout the central business district (CBD) and neighboring suburbs, particularly in Mount Lawley, Subiaco, Leederville, and Fremantle (*see* Fremantle). Seafood and international restaurants, some with stunning views over the Swan River, beachside, or city, and cantilevered windows make for a seamless transition between indoor and alfresco dining.

For those on a budget, the noisy fun of a dim sum lunch at one of Perth's many traditional Asian teahouses (especially in Northbridge) is cheap and delicious; expect long lines on Sunday morning.

Along with a cup of green tea, you can enjoy steamed pork buns, fried chicken feet, and dumplings served at your table from a trolley. Food halls in Perth, Northbridge, and Fremantle are other budget options. For more upscale food courts, *see* Brookfield Place and Market Hall at Yagan Square in Sights.

BWG Steakhouse
$$$ | MODERN AUSTRALIAN | Bustling with locals, BWG Steakhouse serves modern Australian cuisine with an emphasis on top-quality meats cooked to perfection and local seafood. Just 7 km (4 miles) from Perth CBD, in the affluent suburb of Applecross—once home to actor Heath Ledger—the heritage restaurant commands a skyline view across a marina full of palatial leisure boats. **Known for:** weekend breakfast menu; grass-fed local beef; gourmet shared boards. $ *Average main: A$42* ✉ *58 Duncraig Rd., Applecross* ☎ *08/9315–7700* ⊕ *bwgsteakhouse. com.au* ⊘ *No dinner Sun.*

Coco's Riverside Bar and Restaurant
$$$ | AUSTRALIAN | Appealing to the glitzy, moneyed, cosmetically conscious crowd in Perth, this is the it spot on Friday, when rollicking long lunches can extend well past sunset, making it challenging to get a table—unless you book in advance. The views are as good as the people-watching, and though the classic food is expensive, it's beautifully executed. **Known for:** a diverse menu featuring aged-beef, fresh fish, and seafood; handmade pasta; prix-fixe for lunch from 11:30 am to 5 pm. $ *Average main: A$45* ✉ *Southshore Centre, 85 The Esplanade, South Perth* ☎ *08/9474–3030* ⊕ *www. westvalley.com.au.*

Dusit Dheva
$$ | THAI | A renovation, a name change, a menu update, and an award-winning head chef has put Dusit Dheva Thai Cusine on the map as Perth's best Thai restaurant. Come to this delightful, contemporary, Asian-inspired dining room for authentic Thai food, creatively prepared by Chef Mhee and his team. **Known for:** attentive service; the best green curry outside of Thailand; spicy, full-flavored dishes. $ *Average main: A$30* ✉ *249 James St., Northbridge* ☎ *08/9228–8311* ⊕ *www.dusitdheva.com.au* ⊘ *Closed Mon.*

Fraser's
$$$ | MODERN AUSTRALIAN | The large outdoor area at this Kings Park restaurant fills with people eyeing views of the city and Swan River (spectacular in the evening) while enjoying chef favorites such as pork belly with confit fennel, chargrilled steaks, and handcut chips with aioli. The ever-changing menu of share plates or larger dishes highlights fresh Western Australian produce. **Known for:** a sophisticate and elegant dining experience; an elaborate wine and cocktail menu; located next to its casual cousin, the Botanical Cafe. $ *Average main: A$45* ✉ *Kings Park, 60 Fraser Ave., West Perth* ☎ *08/9482–0103* ⊕ *www. frasersrestaurant.com.au.*

Il Lido Italian Canteen
$$$ | MODERN AUSTRALIAN | This whitewashed canteen scores with simple, seasonal food delivered with finesse plus window seats overlooking iconic Cottesloe Beach. The convivial alfresco area looks out to a coastal conga line of walkers, joggers, and cyclists, while at night, candles deliver a romantic feel. **Known for:** authentic Italian meals made from family recipes; favorite breakfast spot for locals; communal tables. $ *Average main: A$36* ✉ *88 Marine Parade, Cottesloe* ☎ *08/9286–1111* ⊕ *illido.com. au.*

★ The Island at Elizabeth Quay
$$ | AUSTRALIAN | Few eateries have a backstory that includes a brick-by-brick relocation of its heritage-listed Federation-style building, but The Island has just such a story and honors it with framed photos of the 1920s building throughout

the restaurant. This ideally located Perth icon has character, charm, and a contemporary menu, as well as several dining options, including a 110-seat dockside alfresco bar selling wood-fired pizza. **Known for:** Sunday sessions with live music and cold beer from the on-site microbrewery; incredible views of the CBD; inspired-by-nature kids' play areas. $ *Average main: A$27* ✉ *Elizabeth Quay, 1 Valdura Pl.* ☎ *08/9243–2711* ⊕ *www. islandbrewhouse.com.au.*

Jamie's Italian

$$ | ITALIAN |FAMILY | The British celebrity chef and good food crusader Jamie Oliver has a long-established relationship with Australia, so it's no wonder he opened a restaurant in Perth. Fun, fresh, and fabulous, Jamie's Italian serves fantastic value with every dish. **Known for:** simple, home-cooked style meals; fresh, house-made pasta; share planks of mixed cured meats, cheese, olives, and bread. $ *Average main: A$28* ✉ *140 William St., CBD* ☎ *08/9363–8600* ⊕ *www.jamieoliver.com.*

Lalla Rookh

$$$ | MODERN AUSTRALIAN | Any place that takes its name from a Kalgoorlie showgirl has got to have spunk, and Lalla Rookh has it in spades. The below-street-level venue on Perth's business strip is a real find, and combines a slick restaurant with dishes inspired by Italy with a tiny wine bar that introduces quaffers to local and "untampered with grape" varieties. **Known for:** il capo share plate featuring six seasonal tasters; a cozy atmosphere; an extensive wine list. $ *Average main: A$36* ✉ *77 St. Georges Terr., lower level, CBD* ☎ *08/9325–7077* ⊕ *www.lallarookh. com.au* ☾ *Closed Sun.*

Perugino

$$$ | ITALIAN | Since 1986, chef and owner Giuseppe Pagliaricci has taken an imaginative yet simple approach to the cuisine of his native Umbria, serving elegant, homemade Italian dishes to his loyal customers. Popular in old-school business and political circles, the restaurant has prix-fixe lunches, and a fine dining atmosphere. **Known for:** traditional service and values; game meat, such as rabbit and quail, on the menu; seven-course customized degustation menu (must be prebooked). $ *Average main: A$38* ✉ *77 Outram St., West Perth* ☎ *08/9321–5420* ⊕ *perugino.com.au* ☾ *Closed Sun. and Mon. No lunch Sat.*

Sayers

$$ | MODERN AUSTRALIAN | Ask any Perthite where to go for breakfast, and chances are the response will be Sayers, where the simple chocolate and banana bread has achieved cult status, and the poached eggs and potato rosti are not far behind. Crowds line up for the flavor-rich breakfast dishes, which are created with primo local/free-range/organic/seasonal ingredients. **Known for:** Sunday brunch; bespoke coffee blend by Five Senses Coffee; hearty breakfasts. $ *Average main: A$24* ✉ *224 Carr Pl., Leederville* ☎ *08/9227–0429* ⊕ *sayersfood.com.au* ☾ *No dinner.*

Sushia Izakaya & Bar

$$ | JAPANESE | Hidden within Brookfield Place's cluster of lower ground venues, Sushia is one of the city's best Japanese restaurants. The sashimi is as fresh as it gets, artfully carved within an open kitchen, and staff helpfully explain Japanese cooking methods such as kushiyaki, robata, and teppanyaki. **Known for:** elegant atmosphere with communal-style seating; artful and eye-pleasing portions; the city's best Bento Box. $ *Average main: A$35* ✉ *Brookfield Pl., 129 St. Georges Terr., CBD* ☎ *08/9322–7771* ⊕ *www. sushia.com.au* ☾ *Closed Sun.*

Varnish on King

$$ | MODERN AUSTRALIAN | Since American whiskey is the specialty at this hard-to-find basement bar, you might expect the food to play second fiddle, but it gets just as much love. This venue with an artisan

12

Western Australia PERTH

grunge theme and the scent of bacon in the air could in fact be called a foodie heaven—come with a huge appetite or a group to share plates. **Known for:** the bacon flight: four pieces of bacon coupled with four shots of American whiskey; more than 150 varieties of whiskey; chef's hookup for the indecisive: five menu items for $50 per person. [$] *Average main: A$30* ✉ *75 King St., downstairs, Northbridge* ☎ *08/9324–2237* 🌐 *varnishonking.com* ⏲ *Closed Sun. No lunch Sat.*

Hotels

During the week, businesspeople from eastern Australia and all parts of Asia flock to Western Australia, and consequently hotel rooms in Perth are often full. But the flow is slowing, and several new hotels have been built—with more on the way—so prices are coming down. Weekends provide the best rates. **■ TIP→ The wise will book early.**

Comfort Inn & Suites Goodearth Perth
$ | **HOTEL** | **FAMILY** | Tourist accommodation for the budget-minded can be hard to find close to Perth's central business district, which is why this full-service apartment-style hotel just minutes from the river, is favored not only by regional Western Australians and their families, but also by dollar-conscious tourists. **Pros:** on-site bar and restaurant; free parking (first-come, first-served basis); free Wi-Fi. **Cons:** room decor is dated; small bathrooms; rooms near elevators can be noisy. [$] *Rooms from: A$139* ✉ *195 Adelaide Terr., CBD* ☎ *08/9492–7777, 1800/098863* 🌐 *goodearthhotel.com.au* 🛏 *180 rooms* 🍴 *No meals.*

Crown Perth Hotels
$$$ | **RESORT** | Across the river from the city center, Crown Perth is like an island where everything is self-contained, and the rooms are spacious and tastefully decorated. **Pros:** impressive lobby at Crown Towers rises the full height of the building; high-end Crown Spa adds luxury; free Wi-Fi. **Cons:** adjacent casino and nightclub attracts a boisterous crowd; some rooms overlook the parking lot; hotel parking is not included in the room rates. [$] *Rooms from: A$228* ✉ *Great Eastern Hwy., at Bolton Ave., Burswood* ☎ *08/9362–8888, 1800/999667* 🌐 *crownperth.com.au* 🛏 *1188 rooms* 🍴 *No meals.*

Duxton Hotel Perth
$$ | **HOTEL** | Facing the Swan River and adjacent to the Perth Concert Hall, this elegant hotel sits at the eastern end of the business district, within easy walking distance of the city center. **Pros:** free Wi-Fi; easy access to free bus; popular restaurant with alfresco terrace. **Cons:** valet parking fee of A$48 applies; some rooms are dated; minimal menu selection for vegetarian diners. [$] *Rooms from: A$199* ✉ *1 St. Georges Terr., CBD* ☎ *08/9261–8000, 1800/681118* 🌐 *duxtonhotels.com* 🛏 *306 rooms* 🍴 *No meals.*

Fraser Suites Perth
$$ | **HOTEL** | This flashy, executive-style hotel impresses guests with its good value, modern design, corporate standards, and the fact that every room is a self-contained suite. **Pros:** free Wi-Fi; indoor swimming pool and gym; popular contemporary restaurant Heirloom on-site. **Cons:** far eastern end of the CBD; perfunctory reception; parking costs $30 per night. [$] *Rooms from: A$151* ✉ *10 Adelaide Terr., East Perth* ☎ *08/9261–0000* 🌐 *perth.frasershospitality.com* 🛏 *236 suites* 🍴 *No meals.*

Hyatt Regency
$$$ | **HOTEL** | Big stylish rooms, great river views, and an easy walk to the nearby Swan River make this glamorous hotel a worthy choice, particularly if you score a weekend deal. **Pros:** undercover (paid) parking; complimentary morning shuttle (weekdays); free Wi-Fi. **Cons:** primarily a business market hotel with corporate design; 15-minute walk into the CBD;

few dining options nearby. $ *Rooms from: A$215* ✉ *99 Adelaide Terr., CBD* ☎ *08/9225–1234* ⊕ *perth.regency.hyatt. com* ⇌ *399 rooms* ❑ *No meals.*

Joondalup Resort

$$$ | **RESORT** |**FAMILY** | This resort-style, palm-shaded building shares its location with a pro-standard, 27-hole Robert Trent Jones Jr.–designed golf course and handful of resident kangaroos. Spacious rooms, decorated in subdued pastels and warm tones, have views of the lake or garden. **Pros:** pool access until 3 pm on departure day; on-site restaurant, bar, and café; free Wi-Fi and parking. **Cons:** in suburban area 25 minutes (28 km [17 miles]) from Perth's business district; conventions can make venues crowded; rooms accessible by external corridor. $ *Rooms from: A$275* ✉ *Country Club Blvd., Connolly* ☎ *08/9400–8888* ⊕ *joondalupresort.com.au* ⇌ *70 rooms* ❑ *Free Breakfast.*

The Melbourne Hotel

$$$ | **HOTEL** | A restored 1890s building listed on the National Heritage Register houses this stylish boutique hotel that sits in the heart of the city, across from some excellent restaurants and fantastic shopping. **Pros:** option for a noon checkout; 24-hour fitness center; five on-site dining options, including a rooftop bar. **Cons:** no swimming pool or spa; parking is off-site and costs extra; only seven (highly sought-after) rooms with balconies. $ *Rooms from: A$229* ✉ *33 Milligan St., CBD* ☎ *08/9320–3333* ⊕ *melbournehotel.com.au* ⇌ *73 rooms* ❑ *No meals.*

Pan Pacific

$$ | **HOTEL** | It's high-class glitz and glamour in the city when you stay at the Pan Pacific in East Perth, a place where the rooms are spacious, immaculate, and offer sweeping views of the Swan River or the busy business district below. **Pros:** valet parking available; heated outdoor pool; 24-hour gym with steam rooms.

Cons: hotel is in an office area; parking costs extra; 15-minute walk to Elizabeth Quay. $ *Rooms from: A$200* ✉ *207 Adelaide Terr., CBD* ☎ *08/9224–7777, 1877/324–4856 toll-free from U.S.* ⊕ *pan-pacific.com* ⇌ *486 rooms* ❑ *No meals.*

Rendezvous Hotel Perth Scarborough

$$$ | **HOTEL** |**FAMILY** | For a beachfront holiday in a towering, iconic hotel with a wide variety of stylish rooms and suites with ocean views and all the amenties you could ever need, look no further than Rendezvous Hotel Perth Scarborough. **Pros:** all rooms have balconies; walk straight on to Scarborough Beach; shuttle to the city (weekdays only). **Cons:** limited attractions in the area; breakfast and parking cost extra; 20-minute drive to the city. $ *Rooms from: A$209* ✉ *148 The Esplanade, Scarborough Beach* ☎ *08/9245–1000* ⊕ *rendezvoushotels. com* ⇌ *336 rooms* ❑ *No meals.*

★ Tribe Perth

$$ | **HOTEL** | When hip and trendy meets luxury, creativity, and affordability, you're faced with Tribe Perth, a fabulous boutique hotel on the fringes of Kings Park. **Pros:** delicious grazing-style breakfast; free on-demand movies; in-room USB ports. **Cons:** very limited parking; nearest off-site parking lot is a 10-minute walk away; only one queen bed per room. $ *Rooms from: A$159* ✉ *4 Walker Ave., West Perth* ☎ *08/6247–3333* ⊕ *tribe-hotels.com.au* ⇌ *123 rooms* ❑ *Free Breakfast.*

🍸 Nightlife

Perth's inner city has gone through a significant revitalization; it's now a hotbed of classy small bars that buzz until midnight and later. Twenty- and thirtysomethings also flock to Northbridge, Leederville, Mount Lawley, Subiaco, and Fremantle. Pubs generally close by midnight, which is when the crowds start arriving at the nightclubs; these tend to stay open until 5 am.

The London Court shopping mall facade at Hay Walking Street, Perth

Details on cultural events in Perth are published in *Weekend West Australian, The Sunday Times, X-Press Magazine,* and ⊕ *xpressmag.com.au,* listing music, concerts, movies, entertainment reviews, and who's playing at pubs, clubs, and hotels. Additionally, *SCOOP* digital magazine (⊕ *www.scoop.com.au*) is an excellent guide to the essential Western Australian lifestyle.

BARS

Mechanics Institute

BREWPUBS/BEER GARDENS | Perched above a gourmet burger bistro called Flip Side—yes, they deliver upstairs—this rooftop haunt is furnished with market umbrellas, upcycled bench tables, and retro couches, which make it both welcoming and hip. Access to the cocktail, wine, and craft beer bar is via a rear lane coated in street art, adding to the intrigue. Owners of both top and bottom businesses—a husband-and-wife team—aimed to create a neighborhood atmosphere when they moved into the gritty urban suburb of Northbridge, and they have.

⊠ *222 William St., at rear, Northbridge* ☎ *08/9228–4189* ⊕ *mechanicsinstitute-bar.com.au.*

The Queens Tavern

BREWPUBS/BEER GARDENS | The Queens, as it's known locally, resides in an attention-grabbing colonial-style property that was built in 1899 and offers an excellent, thriving outdoor beer garden that features plenty of local and international craft brews. The upstairs bar has a relaxed lounge vibe, with DJs on Friday and Saturday. There is also free Wi-Fi throughout. ⊠ *520 Beaufort St., Highgate* ☎ *08/9328–7267* ⊕ *thequeens.com.au.*

Subiaco Hotel

BARS/PUBS | Known as the Subi, this gastropub attracts a lively after-work crowd during the week—especially on Friday—and has an excellent, busy restaurant that serves sophisticated pub-grub from the bar menu and elegant cuisine at the bistro. Built in 1897, this much-loved establishment is rich in history and drenched in true blue Aussie vibes. ■ TIP→ The Subi burger is delish. ✉ *465 Hay St., Subiaco* ☎ *08/9381–3069* ⊕ *subiacohotel.com.au.*

JAZZ AND BLUES

The Ellington Jazz Club

MUSIC CLUBS | Inspired by the New York jazz scene, the Ellington is *the* place for jazz in Perth. For an entry fee, you can catch live music seven nights a week in an intimate and sophisticated setting. A low-key tapas menu is available; be prepared to share a table with other patrons for sold-out performances. ✉ *191 Beaufort St., Northbridge* ☎ *08/9228–1088* ⊕ *ellingtonjazz.com.au.*

The Laneway Lounge

MUSIC CLUBS | This sexy little number is as sultry as the jazzy tunes that fill the discreet laneway space each night. A number of the cocktails use smoked ice cubes—not to be confused with tacky dry ice—giving the liquor a heavenly, charred dimension. There are live jazz performances most nights. ■ TIP→ The bar is accessed down a laneway off Murray Street—look out for the "red carpet" painted on the pavement. ✉ *414A Murray St., Northbridge* ☎ *08/9321–2508* ⊕ *thelanewaylounge.com.au* ⊙ *Closed Sun. and Mon.*

Eve

DANCE CLUBS | Eve is a glitzy, two-story venue done up with stainless steel and retro fittings. Thursday through Sunday, the five bars, cozy lounge areas, stage, and dance floor with sound-and-light show reverberate to the sounds of renowned DJs spinning the latest dance tunes. Doors open at 9 pm. There's free entry Friday through Sunday before 10 pm. ✉ *Crown Perth, Great Eastern Hwy. at Bolton Ave., Burswood* ☎ *08/9362–7699* ⊕ *www.crownperth.com.au.*

Rockin' in Perth

Thanks to pop, rock, and metal bands like Eskimo Joe, the John Butler Trio, the Waifs, Karnivool, Little Birdy, San Cisco, and the Sleepy Jackson—who all started in Perth—the music scene here is thriving. Despite—or perhaps because of—their isolation from the rest of Australia, Western Australian musicians are turning out some top-notch material. Music commentators claim there isn't a "Perth sound" as such, just a talented bunch of artists writing and performing original music. Check out ⊕ *xpressmag.com.au* for an up-to-date guide on live shows.

ⓝ Performing Arts

Ticketek

TICKETS | This is the main booking agent in Perth for the performing arts. It operates solely online, though there are several physical box offices at arts venues such as the Perth Convention Exhibition Centre, the State Theatre, and His Majesty's Theatre in the CBD. ✉ *Perth* ⊕ *premier. ticketek.com.au.*

BALLET

West Australian Ballet Company

DANCE | This world-class ballet company has earned an international reputation for excellence due to its overall innovation and creativity. Its diverse repertoire includes new, full-length story ballets, cutting-edge contemporary dance, and classical and neoclassical ballets. Performances are held throughout Perth, including at His Majesty's Theatre, the atmospheric Quarry Amphitheatre, and the State Theatre Centre. ✉ *134 Whatley Crescent, Maylands* ☎ *08/9214–0707* ⊕ *waballet.com.au.*

CINEMA
Rooftop Movies

FILM | Perth's first—and only—rooftop cinema opened after a summer trial run sold out night after night. It's now one of the city's anticipated seasonal venues. Crowning a seven-story car park, it shows mainstream blockbusters—with the odd cult or classic film thrown in for good measure—on a giant movie screen. It's the perfect date night, complete with a romantic sunset. There's a booze, food, and candy bar, but self-packed picnic baskets are welcome. ■ TIP→ **Movies run each night, except Monday, during the warmer months of November through March, weather permitting.** ⊠ *Roe St. car park, access off 129 James St., Northbridge* ✛ *Drive in at 68 Roe St., Northbridge; walk in off James St., opposite Northbridge Piazza, and take elevator to top* ☎ *08/9227–6288* ⊕ *www.rooftopmovies.com.au* ⊠ *From A$16.*

CONCERTS
Perth Concert Hall

CONCERTS | A starkly rectangular building overlooking the Swan River in the city center, the Perth Concert Hall stages regular plays, comedy acts, musicals, and recitals by the excellent West Australian Symphony Orchestra, as well as Australian and international performers. It's particularly busy during the Perth Festival. Adding to the appeal of the fine auditorium is the 3,000-pipe organ surrounded by a 160-person choir gallery. ■ TIP→ **The hall is said to have the best acoustics in Australia.** ⊠ *5 St. Georges Terr., CBD* ☎ *08/9231–9900* ⊕ *perthconcerthall.com.au.*

OPERA
West Australian Opera Company

OPERA | The West Australian Opera Company presents three seasons annually—generally in February, July, and October, though this may change each year—at His Majesty's Theatre. It also performs the free Opera in the Park in Perth's Supreme Court Gardens each February.

The company's repertoire includes classic opera and operettas. ⊠ *His Majesty's Theatre, 825 Hay St., CBD* ☎ *08/9278–8999 information* ⊕ *www.waopera.asn.au.*

🛍 Shopping

Shopping in Perth, with its pedestrian-friendly central business district, vehicle-free malls, and many covered arcades, is a delight. Hay Street Mall and Murray Street Mall are the main city shopping areas with large department stores, linked by numerous arcades with small shops; up the far western end is King Street and its glitzy international stores including Louis Vuitton, Tiffany & Co., and Gucci. Head to Northbridge's William Street for hipster and local designer boutiques. In the suburbs, top retail strips include Napoleon Street in Cottesloe for classic, beachy clothing, and homewares; Claremont Quarter in Claremont for fashion-forward garments; Oxford Street in Leederville for edgy threads and unique knickknacks; and Beaufort Street in Mount Lawley for idiosyncratic finds.

Australian souvenirs and iconic buys are on sale at small shops throughout the city and suburbs.

ART AND CRAFT GALLERIES
Creative Native

CRAFTS | You can find authentic Aboriginal artifacts at Creative Native with an extensive selection of Aboriginal art. Each piece of original artwork comes with a certificate of authenticity and you simply cannot leave WA without a didgeridoo lesson. Once you learn to play, buy one to take back home and show off your skills ■ TIP→ **Worldwide shipping is available.** ⊠ *Forrest Chase, 158 Murray St., Shop 58, CBD* ☎ *0466/401977* ⊕ *creativenative.com.au.*

★ Maalinup Aboriginal Gallery

LOCAL SPECIALTIES | FAMILY | Find true
Aboriginal art here, as well as gifts and
souvenirs, including soaps, bath, and
beauty products, featuring Australian
native plants. Oils and clays are made
on-site and native Australian foods and
flavors known as bush tucker is available
to sample and buy. The gallery is owned
and operated by local Aboriginal people.
You can find their smaller outlet in
Market Hall at Yagan Square in Perth city,
too. ⊠ *10070 W. Swan Rd., Henley Brook*
☎ *041/111–2450* ⊕ *maalinup.com.au.*

Mossenson Galleries

ART GALLERIES | Get your fill of authentic
Aboriginal art—far more than just dot
paintings—by viewing one of the solo or
group-curated exhibitions by emerging
and established artists and communities
at the Mossenson Galleries, which has
been one of Australia's leading Indigenous commercial galleries since 1993.
⊠ *115 Hay St., Subiaco* ☎ *08/9388–2899*
⊕ *mossensongalleries.com.au.*

CLOTHING
R. M. Williams

CLOTHING | This shop sells everything for
the Australian bushman—and wom-
an—including moleskin pants, hand-
tooled leather boots, Akubra hats, and
their characteristic cobalt blue shirts.
■ **TIP→ Design your own boots with their
bespoke footwear service.** ⊠ *Carillon
City Centre , Hay St., Shop 38, CBD*
☎ *08/9321–7786* ⊕ *rmwilliams.com.au.*

DEPARTMENT STORES AND SHOPPING CENTERS
Claremont Quarter

SHOPPING CENTERS/MALLS | For a mix of
designer threads, high fashion, and com-
fy staples, head to this shiny enclosed
shopping center. You'll find gorgeous
Australian beauty products by Aesop and
Jurlique; classic garments at Country
Road; mature but glam women's wear at
Carla Zampatti; cosmetics at Napoleon
Perdis; and electrical goods and gadgets
at Dick Smith—they're all Australian.

For international brands, seek out Calvin
Klein, French Connection, Karren Millen,
and Mecca Cosmetica. There are half
a dozen chic cafés, too—get a chocolate hit at Koko Black and great yum
cha at Yamato Sushi. ⊠ *9 Bayview Terr.,
Claremont* ☎ *08/286–5888* ⊕ *www.
claremontquarter.com.au.*

David Jones

SHOPPING CENTERS/MALLS | This classy
department store opens onto the Murray
Street pedestrian mall. ⊠ *Murray St.
Mall, CBD* ☎ *08/9210–4000.*

Myer

SHOPPING CENTERS/MALLS | This popular
upmarket department store, Australia's
largest, carries all manner of goods and
sundries, along with Australian brands.
⊠ *Murray St. Mall, at Forrest Pl., CBD*
☎ *08/9265–5600* ⊕ *www.myer.com.au.*

Watertown Brand Outlet Centre

SHOPPING CENTERS/MALLS | FAMILY | If
you feel the need for retail therapy,
here's a great spot to let loose, as every
store—and there are a lot of them—sells
discounted goods here. There are clothes
for all ages and styles, shoes, sneakers,
gifts, books, sporting gear, beauty products, and more. There are cafés to refuel
in, but the food is nothing special. ⊠ *840
Wellington St., West Perth* ☎ *08/9321–
2282* ⊕ *watertownbrandoutlet.com.au.*

⚡ Activities

BICYCLING

Perth's climate and its network of excellent trails make cycling a safe and enjoyable way to discover the city. But beware:
summer temperatures can exceed 40°C
(100°F) in the shade. A bicycle helmet
is required by law, and carrying water is
prudent. Free brochures detailing trails,
including stops at historic spots, are available from the Western Australia Visitor
Centre.

12

Western Australia PERTH

About Bike Hire

BICYCLING | Rent everything from regular bicycles to tandems, family quads, and caboose carriers for the kids and discover Perth by bike. Kayaks and SUP boards can be rented, too. The company does drop-offs and pickups for those wanting to trail ride or venture further afield, and it also offers a bike repair service. ✉ *Point Fraser Reserve, 305 Riverside Dr., East Perth* ☎ *08/9221–2665* ⊕ *aboutbikehire. com.au* ☞ *From $A10.*

SURFING

Western Australians take to the surf from a young age—and with world-famous surfing beaches right on the city's doorstep, it's no wonder. The most popular year-round beaches for body and board surfing are Scarborough and Trigg, where waves can reach 6 to 9 feet. There are also more than a dozen beaches heading north from Leighton (near Fremantle), including the Cables Artificial Reef (near Leighton) and Watermans (in the northern suburbs of Perth). Cottesloe Beach is favored by novice surfers and children; south of the groyne (a man-made breakwater or jetty) is popular with stand-up paddleboard riders.

Outside the city, Rottnest Island's west end has a powerful surf, and south of the mainland coast are more than 30 surf locations from Cape Naturaliste to Cape Leeuwin. Main Break at Surfer's Point in the Margaret River region is the best known, where waves often roll in at more than 12 feet.

Wet suits are de rigueur for the colder months (May through September), when the surf is usually at its best. ⚠ **Great White sharks frequent this coastline.**

Big Wave Surf School

SURFING | Big Wave Surf School has a range of classes available, starting at A$30 for a one-hour casual class, Saturday only at 11:45. Two day courses start at $99. ☎ *08/97588315* ⊕ *www. surfingschool.com.au.*

Catching Waves

Western Australians adore the beach. During the summer months you'll find thousands of them lazing on sandy beaches, swimming, and surfing. Serious board surfers head to the rugged coastline from Cape Naturaliste to Cape Leeuwin. Favorite big surf breaks are Surfer's Point, Lefthanders, Three Bears, Grunters, Cow Bombie, Bunker Bay Bombie, Moses Rock, the Guillotine, the Farm, Boneyards, and Supertubes. Check ⊕ *www.seabreeze.com. au* for up-to-date wind and wave reports.

★ **Scarborough Beach Surf School**

SURFING | These surfer dudes have been pushing beginners out into the white water since 1986. They specialize in adult lessons at Scarborough Beach in summer and Leighton Beach (*see* Fremantle) in winter but also provide separate kiddy lessons, or family groups, too. If you want to get serious, there are several levels you can complete, and when you do, you'll be able to call yourself a real surfer. Courses run daily; participant conditions and minimum age restrictions apply (see website). ■**TIP**➔ **Courses sell out one week in advance so book ahead.** ✉ *The Esplanade, Scarborough* ☎ *08/9448–9937* ⊕ *www.surfschool.com* ☞ *From A$70.*

WATER SPORTS

Funcats Watersports

WATER SPORTS | **FAMILY** | If you want to enjoy the Swan River at a leisurely pace and possibly spot its resident dolphins, rent a 14-foot catamaran, kayak, or a stand-up paddle (SUP) board from Funcats Watersports. Funcats has been hiring out water-sport equipment since 1976; it operates from the end of September through April; instruction and life jackets are included. Cash only. ⊠ *Coode St. Jetty, South Perth* ☎ *0408/926003,* ⊕ *www.funcats.com.au* ☞ *From A$25.*

WA Surf

SURFING | Perth has consistent winds, particularly in the afternoons, so it's one of the best places to learn to kite surf. WA Surf gives lessons in kitesurfing year-round on the shores of Safety Bay, just south of Perth, where the water is flat and calm. As people improve, kites increase in size, adding more power to their ride, so it can be as extreme or as mellow as you like. Safety systems are built-in, so you can be detached from your kite in a couple of seconds if you get into trouble. Most people opt for a series of three, two-hour lessons, but tricks can be taught to old hands, too. Closed May through August. ⊠ *Safety Bay Yacht Club, Safety Bay Rd. at Arcadia Dr., Safety Bay* ☎ *08/9592–1657* ⊕ *www.wasurf.com.au* 🖃 *From A$195* ⊘ *Closed May.–Aug.*

Fremantle

About 19 km (12 miles) southwest of Perth.

The port city of Fremantle is a jewel in Western Australia's crown, largely because of its colonial architectural heritage and hippy vibe. Freo (as the locals call it) is a city of largely friendly, interesting, and sometimes eccentric residents supportive of busking, street art, and alfresco dining. Like all great port cities, Freo is cosmopolitan, with mariners from all parts of the world strolling the streets—including thousands of U.S. Navy personnel on rest and recreation throughout the year. It's also a good jumping-off point for a day trip to Rottnest Island, where lovely beaches, rocky coves, and unique wallaby-like inhabitants called quokkas set the scene. These cute little marsupials have become world-famous for their picture-posing abilities and antics.

Modern Fremantle is a far cry from the barren, sandy plain that greeted the first wave of English settlers back in 1829 at the newly constituted Swan River Colony. Most were city dwellers, and after five months at sea in sailing ships they landed on salt-marsh flats that sorely tested their fortitude. Living in tents with packing cases for chairs, they found no edible crops, and the nearest freshwater was a distant 51 km (32 miles)—and a tortuous trip up the waters of the Swan. As a result they soon moved the settlement upriver to the vicinity of present-day Perth.

Fremantle remained the principal port, and many attractive limestone buildings were built to service the port traders. Australia's 1987 defense of the America's Cup—held in waters off Fremantle—triggered a major restoration of the colonial streetscapes. In the leafy suburbs nearly every other house is a restored 19th-century gem.

GETTING HERE AND AROUND

Bus information for service from Perth is available from Transperth (☎ *13–6213* ⊕ *www.transperth.wa.gov.au*). The Central Area Bus Service (CAT) provides free transportation around Fremantle in orange buses. The route begins and ends outside the Fremantle Bus/Train Station, and stops include the Arts Centre, the cappuccino strip, and the Fremantle Market. CAT buses run every 10 minutes weekdays 7:30–6:30, and 10–6:30 on weekends and public holidays.

Trains bound for Fremantle depart from Perth approximately every 15–30 minutes from the Perth Station on Wellington Street. You can travel from Perth to Fremantle (or vice versa) in about 30 minutes. Tickets must be purchased at the ticket vending machines prior to travel.

If you are driving from downtown Perth, the most direct route is via Stirling Highway, from the foot of Kings Park; it will take about 35 minutes, depending on traffic.

TAXI CONTACTS Black & White. ☎ *13–3222.* **Swan Taxis.** ☎ *13–1330.*

SAFETY AND PRECAUTIONS

Fremantle is a safe destination and popular with families, particularly on weekends and during the school holidays. It also has a lively nightlife, and late-night crowds leaving pubs and clubs can—and do—cause problems. Taxis are in high demand late at night when other public transport stops operating.

TIMING

Fremantle can easily be visited in a day from Perth, though if you want to head over to Rottnest Island you will have to add an extra day. Most of the sights are clustered in a relatively small area along Market Street and South Terrace, and close to the Fishing Boat Harbour, and you can take a walking tour or take a hop-on, hop-off tour tram.

TOURS

Fremantle Tram Tours

BUS TOURS | This company runs hop-on, hop-off tours around the city daily from 9:45 am to approximately 3:30 pm, with six stops all close to the major sights. The bus driver does a running commentary along the way, so this tour around Fremantle is a great way to get to know each area of the port city and its history. A full-day tour is the Triple Tour, which includes a guided tour of Fremantle, a cruise on the Swan River to Perth, and a sightseeing tour in Perth. The tour finishes in Perth, but you can catch a train or bus back to Fremantle. ⊠ *Fremantle* ☎ *08/9473–0331* ⊕ *fremantletrams.com* 🖰 *From A$30.*

ESSENTIALS

VISITOR INFORMATION Fremantle

Visitor Centre. ⊠ *Kings Sq., 8 Williams St.* ☎ *08/9431–7878* ⊕ *visitfremantle.com. au.*

◉ Sights

An ideal place to start a leisurely stroll is South Terrace, known as the Fremantle cappuccino strip. Wander alongside locals through sidewalk cafés or browse in bookstores, art galleries, and souvenir shops until you reach the Fremantle Markets. From South Terrace walk down to the Fishing Boat Harbour, where there's always activity—commercial and pleasure craft bob about, and along the timber boardwalk is a cluster of outdoor eateries and a microbrewery.

Between Phillimore Street and Marine Terrace in the West End is a collection of some of the best-preserved heritage buildings in the state. The Fremantle Railway Station on Elder Place is another good spot to start a walk. Maps and details for 11 different self-guided walks are available at the Fremantle Visitor Center; a popular heritage walk is the Convict Trail, passing by 18 different sights and locations from Fremantle's convict past.

Fremantle Arts Centre

ARTS VENUE | **FAMILY** | Like most of Fremantle, the fine, Gothic Revival Fremantle Arts Centre (FAC) was built by convicts in the 19th century. First used as a lunatic asylum, by 1900 it was overcrowded and nearly shut down. It became a home for elderly women until 1942, when the U.S. Navy turned it into its local submarine base in WWII.

As one of Australia's leading arts organizations, FAC has an engaging, year-round cultural program. There are also dynamic exhibitions, a gift shop, and an expansive live music and special events program, which includes free live music on Sunday afternoons from October to March; people like to bring picnics and blankets but there's also an on-site bar/café. ⊠ *1 Finnerty St.* ☎ *08/9432–9555* ⊕ *fac.org. au* 🖰 *Free.*

★ Fremantle Market

MARKET | FAMILY | The eclectic, artsy, and always bustling Fremantle Market has been housed in this huge Victorian building since 1897 and sells everything from WA landscape photographs to incense, freshly roasted coffee, toys, clothing, and fruit and vegetables. You can also get a delicious array of street food, such as Turkish gözleme, German sausages, doughnuts, chocolate cake, and fresh-squeezed orange juice. Around 150 stalls attract a colorful mix of locals and tourists. ■ **TIP→ Allow a couple hours.** ⊠ *South Terr., at Henderson St.* ☎ *08/9335–2515* ⊕ *fremantlemarkets. com.au* ☉ *Closed Mon.–Thurs.*

★ Fremantle Prison

JAIL | FAMILY | One of the most popular tourist attractions in the state, prison day tours illustrate convict and prison life—including (successful) escapes and the art cell, where a superb collection of drawings by prisoner James Walsh decorates his former quarters. The jail was built by convicts in the 1850s and is an important part of the region's history. Choose from a variety of tours, including a goosebump-inducing one by flashlight or a thrilling underground tour for which visitors are provided with hard hats, overalls, boots, and headlamps before descending 65 feet into the labyrinthine tunnels. ⊠ *1 The Terrace* ☎ *08/9336–9200* ⊕ *fremantleprison.com.au* ☎ *From A$22.*

★ Little Creatures Brewery

WINERY/DISTILLERY | Little Creatures has got a lot going for it—including its harborside location and fun-loving, artsy vibe. Regarded as the founders of craft beer in WA, a tour of this iconic brewery is a must for all hoppy beer lovers. The tours leave daily at 12, 1, 2, and 3 pm and include a beer-making 101 session, a jaunt around the brewhouse, and a sample of the current brews and ciders on tap. Factor in time to stay for some contemporary pub grub or grab a table in the lively Great Hall for an evening meal. ⊠ *40 Mews Rd.* ☎ *08/6215–1000* ⊕ *littlecreatures.com.au* ☎ *A$15 brewery tour.*

Roundhouse

BUILDING | FAMILY | An eye-catching landmark of early Fremantle atop an ocean-facing cliff, the Roundhouse was built in 1831 by convicts to house other convicts. This curious, 12-sided building is the state's oldest surviving public structure. Its ramparts have great vistas spanning from High Street to the Indian Ocean. Underneath, a tunnel was carved through the cliffs in the mid-1800s to give ships lying at anchor easy access from town. From the tunnel you can walk to the calm and quiet Bathers Beach, where there used to be a whaling station, and listen for the firing of the cannon at 1 pm daily. Volunteer guides are on duty during opening hours. ⊠ *West end of High St.* ☎ *08/9336–6897* ⊕ *fremantleroundhouse.com.au* ☎ *Free; donation suggested.*

★ Western Australian Maritime Museum

MUSEUM | FAMILY | Resembling an upside-down boat, the Western Australian Maritime Museum sits at the edge of Fremantle Harbour. It houses *Australia II,* winner of the 1983 America's Cup, and has hands-on, rotating exhibits that are great fun for children. You can also take one-hour guided tours of the *Ovens,* a former Royal Australian Navy World War II submarine. Another attraction is the Welcome Walls, a record of all those who immigrated to WA via ship during the major postwar migration. A five-minute walk away on Cliff Street in a separate, heritage building, is the Shipwreck Galleries, home to more fascinating maritime history. ⊠ *West end of Victoria Quay* ☎ *1300/134081* ⊕ *museum.wa.gov.au/ maritime* ☎ *From A$15.*

🏖 Beaches

Bathers Beach

BEACH—SIGHT | **FAMILY** | Sometimes, good things come in small packages. This flat, soft-sand beach sits hidden between the Fishing Boat Harbour and the Round-house and is an ideal spot to picnic, with takeout fish-and-chips, or to enjoy a sunset cocktail from Bathers Beachhouse, the only restaurant licensed to serve drinks on the beach. **Amenities:** food and drink. **Best for:** solitude; sunset; swimming; walking. ⊠ *Behind Roundhouse, accessed via Fleet St. or Mews Rd.*

Leighton Beach

BEACH—SIGHT | **FAMILY** | South of busy Cottesloe and about 30 minutes from central Perth, Leighton is a relatively quiet beach loved for its sugarlike sand and flat, calm water, which is perfect for those who like to paddle. It's equally loved by wind- and kite-surfers on windy days, who tear across the tabletop surface. At the northern end of the beach, dogs are allowed to be off-leash, so expect to see lots of happy pooches running around. ■**TIP**➔ **It's close to the North Fremantle train station. Amenities:** lifeguards; parking; toilets. **Best for:** snorkeling; swimming; sunset; walking; windsurfing. ⊠ *Leighton Beach Blvd., North Fremantle* ⊕ *beachsafe.org.au.*

Port Beach

BEACH—SIGHT | **FAMILY** | A local favorite, wide Port Beach has small, gentle waves; water the color of a Bombay Sapphire bottle; and pale white sand. It butts up against Fremantle Harbour's North Quay wharf and stretches towards Leighton. Like most of the western-facing coast, the sunsets are epic and the views of Rottnest charming. **Amenities:** food and drink; lifeguards; parking. **Best for:** snorkeling; sunset; swimming; walking; windsurfing. ⊠ *Port Beach Rd., North Fremantle* ⊕ *beachsafe.org.au.*

🍽 Restaurants

Bread in Common

$$ | **MODERN AUSTRALIAN** | This industrial-chic bakery-cum-restaurant wins the gong for hottest interior in town, with dozens of vintage-style globes streaming from the warehouse ceiling or looping in red electrical cord over suspended beams. Herb boxes line the 1890s heritage facade, while out back the wood-fired oven that pumps out organic bread and an open kitchen that creates modern Australian meals that go well with, you guessed it, bread. **Known for:** delicious smells wafting from the bakery; noisy, lively atmosphere, especially on weekends; comfort food like crispy duck fat roasted potatoes. $ *Average main: A$26* ⊠ *43 Pakenham St.* ☎ *08/9336–1032* ⊕ *breadincommon.com.au.*

Capri Restaurant

$$ | **ITALIAN** |**FAMILY** | You'll get a warm welcome from the Pizzale family, who have owned and run this Freo restaurant for more than 50 years, before you sit down to an old-style Italian meal with a BYO bottle of wine (small corkage fee applies). It's first in, first served here. **Known for:** complimentary soup and bread; a favorite among longtime locals; rich and tasty spaghetti marinara. $ *Average main: A$30* ⊠ *21 South Terr.* ☎ *08/9335–1399* ⊕ *caprirestaurantfremantle.com* ◷ *No lunch Mon.*

Char Char Bull

$$$ | **STEAKHOUSE** | Waterfront Fremantle is renowned for its seafood restaurants, so going to a harborside venue for steak seems almost irreverent, but meat lovers revel in the juicy steak selection at Char Char Bull. This lively restaurant, with full table service, specializes in chargrilled prime beef selected from year-old, grass-fed Murray Grey cattle. **Known for:** epic harbor views from floor-to-ceiling windows; beef carpaccio with mustard créme; tables on the deck. $ *Average* main: A$42 ⊠ Fishing Boat Harbour, 44b Mews Rd. ☎ 08/9335–7666 ⊕ charchar-bull.com.au.

Cicerello's

$$ | SEAFOOD |FAMILY | No visit to Fremantle is complete without a stop at this locally famous fish-and-chippery that was once featured on a postage stamp. Housed in a boathouse-style building fronting Fremantle's lovely Fishing Boat Harbour, this joint serves the real thing: fresh oysters, mussels, crabs, fish, lobsters, and crispy chips. **Known for:** massive aquariums with more than 100 species of marine life; large portions; long lines most lunch hours. $ Average main: A$25 ⊠ Fisherman's Wharf, 44 Mews Rd. ☎ 08/9335–1911 ⊕ cicerellos. com.au.

Gino's Café

$$ | ITALIAN |FAMILY | The original owner, the late Gino Saccone, was so passionate about coffee that he closed his tailor shop to open this cappuccino-strip property with a busy alfresco terrace. Now, the iconic café insists it serves the best coffee in Perth, and let's face it, it's pretty good—plus you can get a bowl of soul-comforting pasta or an authentic cannoli. **Known for:** Gino's Blend coffee beans, available to take home; handmade pasta; old-school service. $ Average main: A$27 ⊠ 1–5 South Terr. , at Collie St. ☎ 08/9336–1464 ⊕ ginoscafe.com.au.

Joe's Fish Shack

$$ | SEAFOOD |FAMILY | Fremantle's quirkiest restaurant looks like everyone's vision of a run-down, weather-beaten Maine diner. With uninterrupted harbor views, authentic nautical bric-a-brac, and great food, you can't go wrong. **Known for:** popular local spot; harbor views; stuffed tiger prawns. $ Average main: A$32 ⊠ 42 Mews Rd. ☎ 08/9336–7161 ⊕ joes-fishshack.com.au.

The Cup

In 1848, Britain's Queen Victoria authorized the creation of a solid silver cup for a yacht race that would be "open to all nations." In 1851, the New York Yacht Club challenged 16 English yachts and won with the boat *America*. The United States continued to win for 132 years straight until the upstart *Australia 11* won 4–3 in sensational style, and the Cup came to Fremantle. Australia was euphoric. Fremantle spruced up for the defense of the Cup in 1987, but the fairy tale ended in a 4–0 loss to the San Diego Yacht Club entrant. Today *Australia 11* is a centerpiece display at the WA Maritime Museum.

★ Moore and Moore Café

$$ | MODERN AUSTRALIAN | You'll know this clean-living café by the retro bike stacked out front next to the potted garden, the eclectic mix of people, and live music that often streams from the doorway. The health-conscious food here is as tasty as the vibe is charming, and you can expect organic eggs, nitrate-free bacon with sides of chickpeas or spinach, and coffee-alternatives like beetroot lattes and chai tea. **Known for:** an all-day breakfast menu; no-scrambled-eggs policy; delicious vegetarian and vegan options. $ Average main: A$21 ⊠ 46 Henry St. ☎ 08/9335–8825 ⊕ mooreandmoorecafe. com.

Ootong & Lincoln

$ | MODERN AUSTRALIAN |FAMILY | You'll recognize this place by its giant, multicolor zebra mural on the external wall, which was commissioned by a local artist. Inside, take a seat at one of the colorful communal tables that are surrounded by dividers made from plumbing pipes and then enjoy classic and healthy café eats like Bircher Muesli, free-range eggs, burgers, or Ootong & Lincoln's ever-popular coffee-and-cake special. **Known for:** made-from-scratch meals; potato cake, served with poached eggs and hollandaise; smushed avocado on quinoa or linseed toast (an Aussie favorite). [$] *Average main: A$17* ✉ *258 South Terr., South Fremantle* ☎ *08/9335–6109* 🌐 *ootongandlincoln.com.au.*

The Raw Kitchen
$$ | **VEGETARIAN** | A large, open space, exposed brick, timber beams, high ceilings, and funky booth seating give way to a warehouse feel at this plant-based, dairy-free, gluten-free, refined-sugar-free, vegetarian, and vegan eatery. If you commonly say *yes* to meals like pumpkin mash, ramen noodles, and coconut curry and *no* to bottled water, plastic straws, and excess waste, then you'll surely love this bohemian-vibe restaurant. **Known for:** amazing raw peanut butter; preservative organic wines; sustainable living practices. [$] *Average main: A$25* ✉ *181 High St.* ☎ *08/9433–4647* 🌐 *therawkitchen.com.au* 🕓 *No dinner Mon. and Tues.*

Hotels

★ Be. Fremantle
$$$ | **HOTEL** | **FAMILY** | Immerse yourself in Fremantle's boat-loving history with a stay at this marina-side apartment-style accommodation with studios to three-bedroom flats. **Pros:** all rooms have water views; fully self-contained; located in a quiet area. **Cons:** limited paid parking; no on-site restaurant or pool; walls are thin in old section. [$] *Rooms from: A$250* ✉ *43 Mews Rd.* ☎ *08/9430–3888* 🌐 *befremantle.com.au* 🛏 *74 apartments* 🍴 *No meals.*

Esplanade Hotel Fremantle—By Rydges
$$ | **HOTEL** | Part of a colonial-era hotel, this huge, conveniently located establishment has balconies facing the park and nearby harbor, Essex Street, or the pool. **Pros:** central to Fremantle attractions; two heated swimming pools; ample dining and shopping options nearby. **Cons:** sea views are limited to some rooms; functions can make venues crowded; parking costs extra. [$] *Rooms from: A$159* ✉ *Marine Terr., at Essex St.* ☎ *08/9432–4000* 🌐 *rydges.com* 🛏 *300 rooms* 🍴 *No meals.*

Fothergills of Fremantle
$$ | **B&B/INN** | Antiques, pottery, sculptures, bronzes, and paintings adorn these popular, two-story, 1892 limestone terrace houses opposite the old Fremantle prison. **Pros:** complimentary in-room snacks and afternoon tea in dining room; personalized service; free Wi-Fi and parking. **Cons:** cooked breakfast with direct bookings only; continental breakfast if via a booking agent; no communal lounge room; small bathrooms. [$] *Rooms from: A$175* ✉ *18–22 Ord St.* ☎ *08/9335–6784* 🌐 *fothergills.net.au* 🛏 *7 rooms* 🍴 *Free Breakfast.*

Norfolk Hotel
$ | **HOTEL** | With an excellent location, leafy beer garden, and a basement live music bar all part of its assets, this central accommodation is popular with the outgoing, fun-loving crowd. **Pros:** free parking in central location; free Wi-Fi; free CAT bus nearby. **Cons:** shared facilities in some rooms; potential noise from pub; 10-minute walk to waterfront. [$] *Rooms from: A$150* ✉ *47 South Terr.* ☎ *08/9335–5405* 🌐 *norfolkhotel.com.au* 🛏 *9 rooms* 🍴 *No meals.*

Port Mill Bed & Breakfast
$$ | **B&B/INN** | Discreetly concealed in a picture-postcard courtyard reminiscent of Provence, this flour mill-turned-bed-and-breakfast contains four sunny, individually decorated suites, all named after ships—Batavia, Leeuwin, Zuytdorp, and Duyfken—and each with its own Juliette balcony. **Pros:** heritage-listed accommodation; free Wi-Fi; close to shopping, dining, and tourist attractions. **Cons:** parking nearby for A$11 per day;

two-story building has winding stairs and no elevator; no pool or restaurant. [$] *Rooms from: A$180* ✉ *3/17 Essex St.* ☎ *08/9433–3832* 🌐 *portmillbb.com.au* 🛏 *4 suites* 🍴 *Free Breakfast.*

★ Seashells Fremantle

$$ | **HOTEL** | Although aimed at the corporate traveler, this apartment-style accommodation offers a delightful base for vacationers, too. **Pros:** free secure parking and Wi-Fi; luxury Australian-made bathroom amenities; apartments are clean and tastefully decorated. **Cons:** about a mile away from central Fremantle; residential building with no facilities or 24-hour front desk; upper floor may hear noise from the rooftop bar. [$] *Rooms from: A$219* ✉ *1 Silas St., East Fremantle* ☎ *08/9387–0800* 🌐 *seashells.com.au* 🛏 *24 apartments* 🍴 *No meals.*

Nightlife

There's nothing more pleasant than relaxing in the evening at one of the sidewalk tables on the cappuccino strip. This area, along South Terrace, opens at 6 am and closes around 3 am, but be sure to check out the side streets for the area's small bar scene, too

★ Holy Smokes

BARS/PUBS | This American-themed whiskey bar may be small, but it's packed with pizzazz and down-to-earth vibes. The owners, a brother-and-sister team, were motivated to re-create some of the flavors and feels of a "back to roots" road trip to Missouri to visit Grandma. Now, with more than 100 bourbons, and other very American drops (think Moonshine) at the ready, this boutique bar is the place for a quiet drink and some USA-inspired eats. **■ TIP→ Try the chicken-fried steak.** ✉ *Collie St.* ✣ *between Marine Terrace and South Terrace* ☎ *0414/839823* 🌐 *holysmokesfreo.com.au* ☞ *Closed Mon.*

Sail and Anchor Pub

BREWPUBS/BEER GARDENS | Thanks to its selection of craft beers—40 on tap—and right-in-the-middle-of-it location, the heritage-listed Sail and Anchor Pub is one of Australia's most popular watering holes. You can watch buskers from the balcony, enjoy live music (often) in the front bar, and partake of no-nonsense pub grub at the bistro. There are comfy couches upstairs. ✉ *64 South Terr.* ☎ *08/9431–1666* 🌐 *sailandanchor.com.au.*

Who's Your Mumma

WINE BARS—NIGHTLIFE | This city-style venue is on one of boho Fremantle's loveliest streets. Who's Your Mumma really comes alive at night. Its industrial globes put out warm light, and its wooden tables and chairs are packed with hip, fashionable, but friendly locals sipping on quirky cocktails and craft beers. **■ TIP→ If you're peckish, the pork buns are divine.** ✉ *142 South Terr.* 🌐 *whosyourmumma.com.au.*

Shopping

★ Japingka Gallery

ART GALLERIES | For more than 30 years, the owners of this gallery have been dedicated to the fair work trade of Aboriginal artists, so rest assured, when you purchase a piece of local art here, you are giving back to a community. You'll find traditional dot painting, as well as contemporary creatives here. Worldwide shipping is available. ✉ *47 High St.* ☎ *08/9335–8265* 🌐 *japingka.com.au.*

Key Sole Fremantle

SHOES/LUGGAGE/LEATHER GOODS | **FAMILY** | There's no better or practical Aussie souvenir than a pair of warm and wooly, genuine Ugg boots, and Key Sole Fremantle sells them at its three locations around Fremantle. It also stocks famed Australian brands like Crocs and Emu. ✉ *103 High St.* ☎ *08/9433–3714* 🌐 *keysole.com.*

Snorkeling at the Basin on Rottnest Island, Western Australia

Rottnest Island

19 km (12 miles) west of Fremantle.

An easy 30-minute cruise from Fremantle, or about one hour down the Swan River from Perth, sunny, quirky Rottnest Island makes an ideal day trip. Known to locals as "Rotto," the former penal colony, boys' reformatory, and war base is as much a part of Western Australia as mine sites, colorful entrepreneurs, and untouched beaches. Its strange moniker—translated to mean rat's nest—can be attributed to 17th-century Dutch explorers who mistook the native marsupials called quokkas for cat-size rats.

Much of the island's charm lies in the fact it's largely car free—so rent a bike to make the most of it. The island has an interesting past, which is evident in its historic buildings. Though records of human occupation date back six thousand-some years, European settlement only dates back to 1829. Since then the island has been used for a variety of purposes, including attempts at agriculture and for military purposes in both the Great War and World War II. The Rottnest Museum is a great place to get the history, further enhanced by the many free daily tours run by volunteers. You can also take a train trip and tour to Oliver Hill to see gun emplacements from World War II.

Of course, most West Australians go to the island for the beaches, the swimming, and the laid-back atmosphere on Perth's doorstep. A warm ocean current passes by Rottnest, allowing it to host an unusual mix of tropical and temperate marine life. In fact, it's home to 135 species of tropical fish and 20 species of coral, and even the air temperature is warmer than on the mainland.

GETTING HERE AND AROUND

A number of operators run light plane and helicopter flights to Rottnest Island, but most people take the ferry. Check the Rottnest Island Visitor Information Centre website for other options.

There are no taxis on Rottnest Island. Almost everyone rides bikes, which can either be rented when booking your ferry ticket, or once you arrive, at Rottnest Bike Hire.

CONTACTS
Charter1 Catamaran

Cuddle up on board a 43-foot, island-circling catamaran for snorkeling and seal- and dolphin-spotting adventures to Rottnest Island's isolated bays by day, and gently rocking accommodation complete with stargazing by night. The day tours head to a small rocky island where Australian fur seals like to loll about—once they see you, they splash into the ocean, as they're keen to swim around you and play in the water. From September to November, spot dolphins and humpback whales frolicking in the ocean. All-day snorkel tours depart from Fremantle and head to Rottnest October through March. Two relaxing options are half-day tours sail to Carnac Island and twilight sails along the coast. There are minimum passenger requirements, so bookings are essential. ■TIP→ **Snorkeling gear is included.** ✉ *Rottnest Island* ☎ *0499/444796* ⊕ *charter1.com.au* ☞ *From A$98.*

Rottnest Air Taxi

This speedy, on-demand air service to Rottnest Island flies from Perth's Jandakot airport and offers amazing views of Perth's holiday jewel sitting pretty in the Indian Ocean. Flights are around 12 minutes, are weather-dependent, and the price depends on how many passengers are on board. Joy flights over Rottnest or Perth and its surrounding beaches are also available. Bookings are essential. ☎ *0421/389831* ⊕ *rottnestairtaxi.com.au* ☞ *From A$130.*

★ Rottnest Express

Rottnest Express is the main operator running ferries to Rottnest Island from two locations in Fremantle and from central Perth, which includes a scenic cruise of the Swan River. ■TIP→ **As biking is a popular way to get around the island, consider the ferry and bike combo.** ✉ *Pier 2, Barrack St. Jetty, Perth* ☎ *1300/467688* ⊕ *rottnestexpress.com.au* ☞ *From $A64.*

Rottnest Fast Ferries

Rottnest Fast Ferries runs boats from Hillarys Boat Harbour. The ferries take approximately 45 minutes from Hillarys to Rottnest, with hotel pickups from Perth available. Round-trip prices include Rottnest entry fee. Bike and snorkel packages are available at extra costs. Whale-watching tours, which are cheapest on weekdays, run from early September to late November. ☎ *08/9246–1039* ⊕ *rottnestfastferries.com.au* ⊗ *Closed June, July (except school holidays), and Aug.* ☞ *From A$87.*

SAFETY AND PRECAUTIONS

Be sun-smart, especially from October through April. Even on cloudy days people unused to being outdoors for any length of time can suffer severe sunburn. Wear a hat, long-sleeved shirt, and high-strength sunscreen. If you are a weak or novice swimmer, always swim with a friend; lifesavers (lifeguards) patrol certain beaches during peak holiday periods.

TIMING

Rottnest Island can be visited in a day. An early ferry gets you to the island with plenty of time to tour the main attractions or beaches, returning to Fremantle or Perth in the late afternoon. Staying an extra day or two gives you time to laze at a beach or go surfing or diving. Avoid mid- to late-November, when the island is overrun with Australian school leavers known as "schoolies."

TOURS

There's a narrated 90-minute coach tour of the island's highlights, including convict-built cottages, World War II gun emplacements, salt lakes, and the remote West End. Tours depart daily from Main Bus Stop. The Oliver Hill Railway made its debut in the mid-1990s, utilizing 6 km (4 miles) of reconstructed railway line to reach the island's World War II gun batteries. Information is available from the Rottnest Island Visitor Centre.

Discovery Tour

BUS TOURS | FAMILY | For those not keen on biking or hop-on, hop-off buses, Rottnest Express runs a popular Discovery Tour that gives an overview of the island's activities, history, environment, and wildlife as it circumnavigates the island in about 90 minutes. Highlights of the tour are the salt lakes, Wadjemup Lighthouse, convict-built cottages, World War II gun emplacements, and the remote West End. Tours depart daily from the Main Bus Stop at 11:20 am and 1:50 pm; tickets are available online. ⊠ Thomson Bay ☎ 1300/467688 ⊕ rottnestexpress.com.au ☞ A$49.

★ Island Explorer

BUS TOURS | FAMILY | This service, which runs on a continuous hop-on, hop-off island circuit, picks up and drops off passengers at the most beautiful bays and beaches. Day tickets can be purchased from the Rottnest Island Visitor Centre, online, at ticket machines on the Island, or through bus operator, Adams. Timetables are published on bus stops around the island. ■TIP➔ The Island Explorer is free from Geordie Bay to the Main Bus Stop in Thomson Bay. ⊠ Thomson Bay, Henderson Ave. ☎ 08/6270–6060 local or outside Australia, 1300/551687 within Australia only ⊕ rottnestisland.com ☞ A$20.

The Oliver Hill Train

TRAIN TOURS | FAMILY | Known as the *Captain Hussey*, the Oliver Hill train is an ideal way to see the island. The route from the Main Settlement to Oliver Hill runs daily at 12:30, 1:30, and 2:30 and the first two departures connect with a guided tour of the historic Oliver Hill gun battery. Tickets are available at the visitor information center. ⊠ Thomson Bay ☎ 08/9372–9732 ⊕ rottnestisland.com ☞ A$29.

★ Skydive Geronimo

AIR EXCURSIONS | If you think Rottnest is beautiful from the water's edge, you should see it from 14,000 feet above while the wind rushes through your hair and adrenaline pumps through your bloodstream. Skydive Geronimo sells a boutique tandem skydiving experience that will catapult your island holiday to "Awesome!" status. ■TIP➔ It also operates seasonal drop zones in Busselton (October through May) and Broome (June through September). ⊠ Rottnest Island Airport, Brand Way ☎ 1300/449669 ⊕ skydivegeronimo.com.au ☞ From A$329.

ESSENTIALS

VISITOR INFORMATION Rottnest Island Visitor Centre. ⊠ Thomson Bay beachfront ☎ 08/9432–9300 ⊕ rottnestisland.com.

◉ Sights

The most convenient way to get around Rottnest is by bicycle, as private cars are not allowed on the island. A self-guided bicycle tour of the island covers 26 km (16 miles) and can take as little as three hours, although you really need an entire day to enjoy the beautiful surroundings.

Heading south from Thomson Bay, between Government House and Herschell Lakes, you'll find the Quokka Walk and a man-made causeway, where you'll find a few quokka colonies. Continue south and to Oliver Hill and the Wadjemup Lighthouse, where tours are run every half hour from 10 am until 2:30 pm. As you continue to Bickley Bay you can spot the wreckage of ships—the oldest dates from 1842—that came to rest on Rottnest's rocky coastline.

Follow the main road past Porpoise, Salmon, Strickland, and Wilson bays to West End, the windiest point on the island and home to a harem of seals at Cathedral Rocks. Heading back to Thomson Bay, the road passes a dozen rocky inlets and bays. Parakeet Bay, the prettiest, is at the northernmost tip of the island.

Rottnest Museum

MUSEUM | FAMILY | At the Thomson Bay settlement, don't miss the Rottnest Museum, which includes mementos of the island's sometimes turbulent past. Staying true to local history, displays are housed in an old mill and hay store built in 1857, showing local geology, natural and social history, and maritime lore with a bunch of surprising facts. It's open daily 10:45–3:30. **Wadjemup Lighthouse Tours**—find out what goes on within the confines of a working lighthouse and climb to the top of this Heritage structure for fabulous 360-degree views. Tours depart daily at 10 am and every half hour until 2:30 pm. Book at the visitor center. ⊠ Thomson Bay, Digby Dr., at Kitson St. ☎ 08/9372–9732 ⊕ rottnestisland.com ☒ Donation suggested.

🏖 Beaches

There are some 63 beaches on Rottnest Island, suitable for swimming, surfing, snorkeling, and diving. The most popular include Geordie Bay, Little Parakeet, Parker Point, Little Salmon Bay, and the Basin.

Surfers and body-boarders will head for Stark Bay, Strickland Bay (closed during fairy tern nesting season), and West End, while swimmers love the sandy-white beaches at Pinky Beach and the Basin. Beach spots for snorkeling and diving include Little Salmon Bay (it has underwater markers) and Parker Point.

The Basin

BEACH—SIGHT | FAMILY | This pool-like bay is one of Rottnest's most popular, both for its safe, shallow waters and proximity to the main settlement. Protected by an outer reef, the ocean is crystal clear, the waves are gentle, and little fish dart about. **Amenities:** lifeguards; showers; toilets. **Best for:** snorkeling; swimming.

Marsupial Selfie Stars 👁

Quokkas were among the first Australian mammals ever seen by Europeans. In 1658, the Dutch Captain Willem De Vlamingh described them as rats, but in fact they are marsupials, carrying their young in a pouch. Once common around Perth, quokkas are now confined to isolated pockets on the mainland, but they still thrive on their namesake Rottnest Island, where they are safe from predators, most of which have now been eradicated. Their cute, furry faces and inquisitive nature make them very photogenic.

⊠ Northwest of Thomson Bay ⊕ rottnestisland.com.

Geordie Bay

BEACH—SIGHT | FAMILY | Over the dunes is the whitest of white sand and the most azure waters of Geordie Bay. Photographed by many, this beach abuts a flat, motionless ocean that makes for safe swimming. A confetti of yachts spreads across the bay in summer months (there are protected, boat-free swimming zones), and beachside accommodation mirrors the cove. Nearby, next to a mini-mart, find Geordie's Cafe and Art Gallery (☎ 08/9292–5411), one of the best foodie options on the island. Open for breakfast, lunch, and dinner, it also serves many gluten-free dishes. Expect to see furry quokkas looking for scraps. **Amenities:** food and drink; showers; toilets. **Best for:** swimming. ⊠ Geordie Bay Rd. ⊕ rottnestisland.com.

★ Little Salmon Bay

BEACH—SIGHT | FAMILY | Make sure you pack your snorkeling gear for this one—due to Rottnest's warmer waters, created by the passing Leeuwin Current, there's a fascinating mix of tropical and temperate fish species in the clear waters. Aim to go at low tide and look out for bream, red-lipped morwong, zebrafish, and king wrasse, plus plenty of little colored fish. There are underwater plaques that guide you along a great snorkel trail and the waters are calm so you can enjoy flipping about. Coral reefs are about 330 feet out but worth checking out if you're a confident swimmer. **■ TIP→ If it's overcrowded, head to the next, bigger beach, Salmon Bay. Amenities:** none. **Best for:** snorkeling; swimming. ✉ *Little Salmon Bay, southwest of Thomson Bay, off Parker Point Rd.* 🌐 *rottnestisland.com.*

🍴 Restaurants

★ Rottnest Bakery

$ | BAKERY | FAMILY | Locally famous for freshly made pastries and decent coffee, this central bakery does a roaring trade every day of the week. It may be the tasty treats that gets people through the door, but it's the cute little quokkas on the deck who encourage patrons to stay awhile. **Known for:** delicious jam doughnuts; traditional Aussie meat pies; cheeky seagulls who will snatch your food when you're not looking. [$] *Average main: A$6* ✉ *Maley St.* ☎ *08/9292–5023.*

★ Thomsons Rottnest

$$ | MODERN AUSTRALIAN | FAMILY | Named in honor of Robert Thomson, an island salt farmer from the mid-1800s, this nautical-themed, seaside restaurant specializes in seafood, naturally. Think calamari, octopus, snapper, and massive WA prawns, served either with hand-cut chips or on a wood-fired pizza. **Known for:** locally sourced produce, when possible; sharable seafood platters, featuring crayfish; playground for kids. [$] *Average main: A$27* ✉ *Thomson Bay , Colebatch Ave.* ☎ *08/9292–5171* 🌐 *thomsonsrottnest.com.au* 🕒 *Closed Wed. and Thurs. in winter.*

🛏 Hotels

Accommodation on the island ranges from basic camping sites to self-contained holiday villas and hotels. Space is at a premium during the summer months, Easter, and school holidays. November can be busy because of the so-called schoolies week, when high-school leavers celebrate the end of senior school. This time is best avoided. Outside these times, accommodation is easier to find. Check 🌐 *www.rottnestisland.com* for details.

Hotel Rottnest

$$$ | HOTEL | This blindingly white, fort-like property was once the official summer residence for the governors of Western Australia but today it's decked out in Astroturf and bench seats as the island's social hub. **Pros:** some rooms have ocean views; complimentary snacks in room; casual atmosphere. **Cons:** courtyard rooms are small; can be noisy due to day-trippers and formal events; reception closes once ferry stops for the day. [$] *Rooms from: A$275* ✉ *Thomson Bay, 1 Bedford Ave.* ☎ *08/9292–5011* 🌐 *hotelrottnest.com.au* 🛏 *18 rooms* 🍽 *No meals.*

Karma Rottnest Lodge

$$$ | HOTEL | FAMILY | The largest hotel on Rottnest and the only one with leisure facilities, this sturdy structure reveals an interesting past as a colonial barracks and a prison. **Pros:** close to ferry; free Wi-Fi; some rooms ideal for families. **Cons:** not on beachfront; no outside food or drink allowed in rooms; some design is dated. [$] *Rooms from: A$295* ✉ *Kitson St.* ☎ *08/9292–5161* 🌐 *rottnestlodge.com.au* 🛏 *60 rooms* 🍽 *Free Breakfast.*

🏃 Activities

BIKING

Rottnest Island Pedal and Flipper

BICYCLING | FAMILY | Rent one of 1,650 bikes—the island's must-have item—from Pedal & Flipper, the island's only

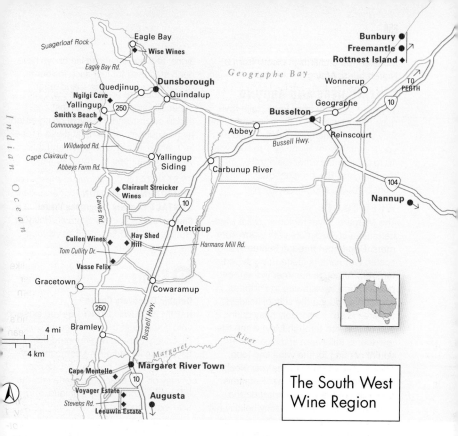

bicycle rental shop. Also for rent are tandem bikes and attachable buggies for children, plus snorkel sets, paddleboards, surfboards, bodyboards, wet suits, scooters, and beach cricket and soccer essentials. The store is open daily, though hours vary according to the season and the ferry schedule. Expect lines at ferry arrival times. ⊠ *Thomson Bay* ☎ *08/9292–5105* ⊕ *rottnestisland. com* ⌕ *From A$30.*

Bunbury

154 km (96 miles) south of Perth.

Bunbury is more of a place to stop en route to Busselton and other towns in the Margaret River region than a destination in itself, but it *is* worth a stop along the way. In fact, we recommend you make the Bunbury area your first port of call on your journey "down south" (a local term for the region below Perth, which includes all of the Margaret River region)—especially if you love dolphins.

In the city of Bunbury you can swim with wild dolphins (in season) or wade in shallow waters with them under the watchful eye of center volunteers and biologists. About 100 bottlenose dolphins make their permanent home in and around the waters of Koombana Bay off Bunbury, making your chances of seeing them in their natural habitat very high. Next, head inland to meet the community of 5,000 garden gnomes at Gnomesville in the Ferguson Valley. If you travel farther along the South Western Highway, you come to the picturesque town of Donnybrook, where there are rolling landscapes and miles of fruit orchards in bloom from November to May

GETTING HERE AND AROUND

To get to Bunbury from Perth, take Kwinana Freeway south; it joins Forrest Highway and then Highway 1. After Bunbury, you'll switch from Highway 1 to Highway 10 to explore the other main towns in the Margaret River region: Busselton, Dunsborough, and Margaret River.

WHEN TO GO

The Margaret River region enjoys a Mediterranean-style climate with warm summers (December through February) and cooler, wet winters (June through September). Although summer is the most popular time to visit, due to Perthites vacationing during the school holidays, the area is still reasonably busy during autumn (March through May) when the weather is still warm and pleasant. If you're coming for the wine and food, plan to visit any time of the year (keeping in mind the famed Gourmet Escape is held in November, ⊕ gourmetescape. com.au). If you want a beachy holiday full of swimming and barbecues, visit from November through Easter. Note that in November is "schoolies week," a time when teenage students boisterously celebrate the end of their high school days and take over Dunsborough in droves.

SAFETY AND PRECAUTIONS

You are unlikely to have any personal safety concerns in the Margaret River area, except, perhaps, on the roads. Many of the roads leading to the wineries, the beaches, and accommodations are narrow and winding, though traffic is usually light. Caves Road in particular is known for car accidents.

The coastline provides a natural, and beautiful, playground, and although the temptation is to climb all over the rocky outcrops, such as Canal Rocks, Sugarloaf Rock, and Skippy Rock, be aware of "king waves" that rise up with little warning from the ocean. Take note of the warning signs; at a few locations life buoys have been stationed for just such incidents.

Mosquitoes are prevalent in summer, especially along the South West coast and in swamplands. To avoid being bitten by mosquitoes, cover up and use a repellent, especially around dawn and dusk, when mosquitoes are most active.

ESSENTIALS
VISITOR INFORMATION
CONTACT Bunbury Geographe Visitor Centre. ⊠ Old Railway Station , Haley St., Bunbury ☎ 08/9792–7205, ⊕ visitbunburygeographe.com.au.

◉ Sights

Dolphin Discovery Centre
NATURE PRESERVE | FAMILY | Get up close to wild dolphins at the not-for-profit Dolphin Discovery Centre. Two-hundred dolphins have been identified in Koombana Bay— swim with them, book an eco-cruise, or stay on the beach and wade into the interaction zone. Enjoy a unique, immersive experience at the discovery center, which enjoyed a A$2-million refurbishment in 2018, with its digital 360-degree dolphinarium, interpretive panels, theater, aquariums, dolphin displays, and on-site café and gift shop. ■ TIP→ **Call first to book the weather-dependent swim and eco-cruises. Dolphin encounters are not guaranteed, but the chances are higher in the warmer months.** ⊠ 830 Koombana Dr., Bunbury ☎ 08/9791–3088 ⊕ dolphindiscovery.com.au ⧉ From A$18.

Busselton

222 km (138 miles) south of Perth.

Busselton is the largest city in the Margaret River region and is considered the gateway to the region. The seaside municipality is rapidly increasing in population as more people relocate to the area in search of the laid-back, coastal lifestyle that is so coveted. Busselton draws a crowd for its 1.84-km (1¼ mile) wharf that jets into the Indian Ocean, its family-friendly foreshore, and the myriad of sporting events, such as the annual Jetty Swim in February, the Chevron City to Surf fun run in July, and the world-famous Ironman triathlon every December. It's no wonder Busselton is called the Event Capital of Western Australia. The city of around 37,000 people is a great base for your Margaret River region vacation.

GETTING HERE AND AROUND

From Bunbury, take Highway 10 to Busselton. Public transport is available in Busselton, but your best option is to rent a car in Perth to explore Busselton and other Margaret River locales. Alternatively, **South West Coachlines** (☎ 08/9261–7600 ⊕ www.southwestcoachlines.com.au) does have daily South West Express coach service from Perth Central Bus Station at the Elizabeth Quay Bus Port on Mounts Bay Road to Busselton, Dunsborough, and Margaret River. However, note that many accommodations—farmstays, bushland chalets, and boutique hotels— as well as the wineries, the beaches, and other attractions, are outside of towns, and you'll need your own transportation to reach them.

TRANSPORTATION INFORMATION
Busselton Taxis

⊠ Busselton ☎ 13–1008 ⊕ busseltontaxis.com.au.

Rent A Car Busselton and South West
From budget, sedans, and four-wheel-drive trucks to mini buses and boats, all your transportation needs and wants are here. This place also rents bikes, kayaks, fishing rods, and camping gear. ⊠ 16 Queen St., Busselton ☎ 0437/791691 ⊕ busseltonswrentacar.com.au.

SAFETY AND PRECAUTIONS

The calm waters of Geographe Bay are home to a jellyfish with a nasty sting— colloquially named "stingers." They are not deadly, so don't panic, but they are painful and hard to spot. The main body of the stinger is translucent and only about 2 inches across, and the hard-to-see tentacles trailing are the cause for concern. The jellyfish like warm, very calm water, so still days in summer are when you are most likely to encounter them as they drift close to shore. Rubbing a sting is *not* recommended. The best thing to do is rinse the area in a very hot shower, or apply ice for a numbing effect.

TOURS

★ Busselton Jetty and Underwater Observatory
SPECIAL-INTEREST | FAMILY | At almost 2-km (1¼-miles) long, the Busselton Jetty is the longest timber jetty in the southern hemisphere. You can visit the Interpretive Center and Heritage Museum at the start of the jetty, then either catch the miniature train (45-minute ride) or walk to the fascinating Underwater Observatory— one of only seven in the world—where you'll spy all manner of soft, colorful coral as you descend the cylindrical, windowed observatory. Tours for up to 40 people run every hour, taking you 26 feet below the water. The warm Leeuwin Current and the sheltering effect of the jetty above have created a unique microclimate rich with colorful tropical and subtropical corals, sponges, fish, and invertebrates— there are 300 marine species in all.
■ TIP➜ The jetty is open 24 hours for fishing and walking. ⊠ Busselton Beachfront, end of Queen St., Busselton ☎ 08/9754–0900 ⊕ busseltonjetty.com.au ⊡ A$4.

★ Cellar d'Or Winery Tours
DRIVING TOURS | This small group wine-and-gourmet food tour of the Margaret River region takes you on an all-day journey to some of the best boutique cellar doors, breweries, and all-time favorite snack producers (chocolate and cheese, anyone?) of the area. The tours include pickup from your hotel in Busselton, Dunsborough, Margaret River town, or anywhere in between. ⊠ Busselton

☎ 0428/179729 🌐 cellardortours.com.au 🎟 From A$105.

ESSENTIALS

VISITOR INFORMATION Busselton Visitor Centre. ✉ *Busselton Beach, 17 Foreshore Parade, Busselton* ☎ *08/9780–5911 option 2* 🌐 *www.margaretriver.com/services/visitor-centres.*

Beaches

★ Busselton Beach

BEACH—SIGHT | FAMILY | This is the beach for loads of family fun in the sun. The calm, translucent, and turquoise waters of Geographe Bay are perfect for swimming, stand-up paddling, kayaking, fishing, and relaxing. From mid-December until the end of January, an inflatable waterpark (🌐 *aquatastic.net*) is set up and available to the public for an hourly or daily fee. The City of Busselton has invested millions of development dollars into foreshore infrastructure that includes an amazing kids adventure park, skate park, amphitheater, and plenty of bench seating and free-to-use barbecues—a favorite Aussie dinner is fish-and-chips on the beach at sunset. **Amenities:** food and drink; parking; showers; toilets; water sports. **Best for:** sunset; swimming; walking. ✉ *Busselton Foreshore, Busselton* 🌐 *beachsafe.org.au.*

Restaurants

★ Al Forno

$$ | EUROPEAN |FAMILY | Tucked away on the fringes of the Busselton central business district, this popular family-owned Mediterranean-inspired eatery is much loved for its rich pasta dishes, thin-crust pizzas, and soul-comforting, slow-cooked favorites like beef bourguignon and cog au vin. Before you get overexcited and order everything off the menu, remember to leave room for dessert—like dream-worthy chocolate mousse and tiramasu. **Known for:** $20 pizza of the month—add a Margherita pizza for only $5 extra; consistently good home-style cooking; friendly, attentive service. [$] *Average main: A$25* ✉ *19 Bussell Hwy., Busselton* ☎ *08/9751–3775* 🌐 *al-forno.com.au* 🕓 *Closed Mon.*

★ The Fire Station

$$ | AUSTRALIAN | This boutique bar in the heart of Busselton is a favorite spot among locals for its stylish reinvention of the town's former fire station, and, of course, its more-ish menu and flowing taps and wine barrels. Dine in beside the buzzing bar, under the low-hanging mood lighting, or outside in the garden courtyard where you'll be closer to the sounds of the solo singers and small bands who perform regularly. **Known for:** Happy Hour at 5 pm weekdays (except during peak season and public holidays); rotating taps of craft beer and popular food and drink specials on Tuesday, Thursday, and Sunday; unique toppings on wood-fired pizza. [$] *Average main: A$25* ✉ *68 Queen St., Busselton* ☎ *08/9752–3113* 🌐 *firestation.bar* 🕓 *No dinner Sun. in winter.*

The Goose Cafe

$$ | AUSTRALIAN |FAMILY | No doubt about it, The Goose Cafe has the best views of the Busselton Jetty and Geographe Bay—It's so close, you could chuck one of their crispy French fries and hit the start of the famed timber wharf (of course, a hungry seagull would get it before it hits the ground). In peak season, the café opens daily at 7 am for breakfast and then it's game-on all day until after the dinner crowd leaves well beyond sunset. **Known for:** great spot for people-watching and postsunset drinks; quick-bite takeaway classics like mac-and-cheese and pork ribs; wood-fired foods: pizzas, breads, meats, fish. [$] *Average main: A$28* ✉ *Geographe Bay Rd./Foreshore Parade, Busselton* ☎ *08/9754–7700* 🌐 *thegoose.com.au* 🕓 *No dinner Sun.–Tues. in winter.*

Hotels

Gale Street Motel and Villas

$ | **HOTEL** | Just a five-minute walk to the beach, this delightful, family-owned and -run accommodation is the perfect base for a Busselton getaway. **Pros:** free Wi-Fi and secure parking; complimentary coffee and tea; built-in UBS ports. **Cons:** no swimming pool; no restaurant; no views. [$] *Rooms from: A$130* ✉ *40 Gale St., Busselton* ☎ *08/9754–1200* 🌐 *galestvillas.com.au* 🛏 *16 rooms* 🍴 *No meals.*

★ **The Observatory Guesthouse**

$$ | **B&B/INN** | Settle into this charming bed-and-breakfast just a block away from the Busselton beach—so close that the waves crashing on the shore may lull you to sleep at night. **Pros:** plush Sheridan brand bath towels; free Wi-Fi; blackout curtains. **Cons:** not suitable for persons under 18; no pool; maximum two guests per room. [$] *Rooms from: A$160* ✉ *7 Brown St., Busselton* ☎ *08/9751–3336* 🌐 *observatoryguesthouse.com* 🛏 *5 rooms* 🍴 *Free Breakfast.*

The Sebel Bussleton

$$ | **HOTEL** |**FAMILY** | An easy eight-minute drive from Busselton's city center, and a hop, skip, and a jump to the beach, this collection of self-contained apartments are set on a sprawling property and attract fun-loving families and leisure-seeking holidaymakers. **Pros:** shopping complex within walking distance; every apartment has a bathtub; path from resort to the beach. **Cons:** free Wi-Fi is for Accor members only; only one car park per room; no restaurant or café. [$] *Rooms from: A$199* ✉ *553 Bussell Hwy., Busselton* ☎ *08/9754–9800* 🌐 *thesebel.com* 🛏 *73 rooms* 🍴 *No meals.*

Dunsborough

252 km (157 miles) south of Perth and 26.2 km (16.3 miles) from Busselton.

The attractive and fashionable seaside town of Dunsborough is perfect for a few days of swimming, sunning, and fishing—which is why it's become a popular holiday destination for many Perth families. Onshore attractions include Meelup Beach, a protected cove encircled by native bush with calm swimming water, and several nearby wineries and breweries. Offshore, you can dive on the wreck of the HMAS *Swan*, the former Royal Australian Navy ship deliberately sunk in Geographe Bay (🌐 *capedive.com*), or take a cruise to see migrating humpback and southern right whales September through December. Attractions in nearby Yallingup, about 15 minutes away from Dunsborough via Caves Road, are included in this section.

GETTING HERE AND AROUND

From Busselton, take Highway 10 to Dunsborough. Public transport is available in Dunsborough, but we recommend a car for ease and cost-efficiency in getting around while here.

TAXI CONTACTS Dunsborough Taxis. ☎ *08/9756–8688* 🌐 *dunsboroughtaxis.com.au.*

TOURS

Naturaliste Charters

SPECIAL-INTEREST | **FAMILY** | This company runs eco-conscious whale-watching tours along the southwestern coastline. The tours follow the whale migration from Augusta to Dunsborough to Bussleton as the mammals travel north from late May to early December. You can expect to see playful humpbacks and surfacing southern right whales, and if you're lucky, rare blue and minke whales too. For something really special, join a Bremer Canyon expedition from January through April, to see a killer whale and shark feeding ground in a remote and deep part of ocean off the Albany coast. ⊠ *Shop 1 Bayview Centro , 25–27 Dunn Bay Rd.* ☎ *08/9750–5500* ⊕ *whales-australia.com. au* ⧐ *From $80.*

★ Ngilgi Cave

GUIDED TOURS | FAMILY | While crawling through tight spots, sliding down smooth rock surfaces, and gazing at stalactites lit with a rainbow of lights, you'll learn about the fascinating history of this special cave, once explored by candlelight in the early 1900s. Semiguided cave tours take about one hour and run every half hour from 9:30 am to 4 pm. Highly recommended adventure caving tours are also available for families with older children. ■**TIP→ Multicave passes are available and recommended if you want to explore the other main tourist caves in the Margaret River region.** ⊠ *76 Yallingup Caves Rd., Yallingup* ☎ *08/9755–2152 information* ⧐ *A$23.*

VISITOR INFORMATION

CONTACTS Dunsborough Visitor Centre. ⊠ *Dunn Bay Centre, 31 Dunn Bay Rd., Shop 1* ☎ *08/9755–3517* ⊕ *margaretriver. com.*

◉ Sights

Cape Naturaliste Lighthouse

LIGHTHOUSE | FAMILY | At the northern end of Leeuwin-Naturaliste National Park, a 13-minute drive from Dunsborough, stands Cape Naturaliste Lighthouse. From the lighthouse keeper's cottages (now a gift shop, tour desk, information center, and café) take a 15-minute walk to the whale lookout, a purpose-built deck that overlooks the Indian Ocean. If you want to go inside the 23-meter (75-foot) tall lighthouse, you'll need to book a guided tour (every half hour from 9:30 am to 4:30 pm), where you learn everything there is to know about the history and operations of the lighthouse. You'll also get to climb the stairs to the top and stand on the outside balcony to take in the spectacular seascapes of this rugged coastline. Migrating whales are often spotted along this stretch from September through December. This is also the start of the coast-hugging 135-km (86-mile) Cape-to-Cape Track. ⊠ *Leeuwin Naturaliste National Park, 1267 Cape Naturaliste Rd.* ☎ *08/9157–7411* ⊙ *A$15.*

Clairault Streicker Wines

WINERY/DISTILLERY | This winery is known for its award-winning Chardonnay, Cabernet Sauvignon, and Cabernet Merlot, and loved for its natural bushland setting, about 18 km (11 miles) south of Dunsborough. The contemporary-style cellar door offers free wine tastings and the spacious café has glass doors that open on to a large timber deck that overlooks a picturesque vineyard in warm weather, while two huge stone fireplaces warm the tables in winter. ■**TIP→ Borrow one of the café's picnic blankets and relax in the garden.** ⊠ *3277 Caves Rd., Wilyabrup* ☎ *08/9755–6225 cellar door café* ⊕ *clairaultstreickerwines.com.au.*

★ Leeuwin-Naturaliste National Park

NATIONAL/STATE PARK | This national park clutches one of Western Australia's most spectacular coastlines, from Cape Naturaliste in the north, to Cape Leeuwin, near Augusta, in the south. The park is not a composite destination, rather a narrow patchwork of protected areas along the coast, intersected by beach access roads and small beachside villages, and traced by the Cape to Cape Track.

The mostly unspoiled coastal vistas are as awe-inspiring as any in the world—on a calm day the view northwards from Yallingup past Sugarloaf Rock towards Cape Naturaliste is nature at its best and it's often sprinkled with surfing dolphins. Farther south, between Cowaramup Bay and Karridale, scenic lookouts allow you to access coastal cliffs and rocky shoreline that bear the brunt of giant ocean swells generated across thousands of miles of Indian Ocean. ⚠ **Use extreme**

Canal Rocks near Yallingup, Leeuwin-Naturaliste National Park, Western Australia

care when hiking or fishing cliffside.
✉ *Leeuwin-Naturaliste National Park*
☎ *08/9752–5555* ⊕ *parks.dpaw.wa.gov.au.*

Wise Wines

WINERY/DISTILLERY | The view from the hilltop overlooking Geographe Bay is almost as good as the wines at this northernmost winery in the region, about a 15-minute drive from Dunsborough towards Cape Naturaliste. This family-owned boutique vineyard has a history of producing award-winning Chardonnay, though its collection of more than 20 wines are all worth a try (especially the Prosecco and Fiano) at the cellar door. If you fancy the wine, pair it with something from the seasonal menu at the adjoining Wise Vineyard Restaurant. ✉ *80 Eagle Bay Rd.* ☎ *08/9750–3103 cellar door* ⊕ *wisewine.com.au.*

⊙ Beaches

★ Bunker Bay

BEACH—SIGHT | FAMILY | When you turn off Bunker Bay Road onto Farm Break Lane, the wow-worthy vista of the bay takes one's breath away with its eye-popping turquoise waters. Pack the beach bag and a picnic, and prepare for a day lazing on white sand and swimming in see-through water. **Amenities:** food and drink; parking; showers; toilets. **Best for:** solitude; swimming; walking. ✉ *Dunsborough* ⊕ *beachsafe.org.au.*

Meelup Beach

BEACH—SIGHT | FAMILY | Sheltered from wind, this soft-sand haven makes for a gorgeous coastal escape. Its aquamarine-blue waters attract visitors and locals alike. You can bring food with you if you like and use the barbecue facilities and picnic tables. Meelup Beach Hire (⊕ *meelupbeachhire.com*) offers heaps of beach and water-play rentals, including stand-up paddleboards, kayaks, body-boards, umbrellas, and snorkel sets.

Amenities: showers; toilets. **Best for:** solitude; swimming; walking. ⊠ *Meelup Beach Rd.* ⊕ *meelupbeachhire.com.*

Smiths Beach

BEACH—SIGHT | In a state of extraordinary beaches, this one rates high on the list. Bookended by rounded granite boulders, the caramel-hued sand sinks beneath your feet and the gentle, rolling waves beckon, daring you to cool off in the clean ocean. Edged by native bush, this beach that is 12 km (7 miles) from Dunsborough is quiet and secluded. Smiths Beach Resort and Lamont's Restaurant (at resort) are nearby. **Amenities:** food and drink; parking; toilets. **Best for:** solitude; sunset; surfing; walking. ⚠ **North of the creek has strong waves and rips (undertows) and can be hazardous.** ⊠ *Smiths Beach Rd., Yallingup* ⊕ *beachsafe.org.au.*

★ Yallingup Beach

BEACH—SIGHT | **FAMILY** | What's not to love about this 1.3-km (1-mile) beach at the hillside town of Yallingup? Picture-perfect views; transparent water; clean, sun-baked sand; and a gentle pool of ocean at the southern end that protects you from the waves beyond. On any given day you'll see a tribe of surfers riding the waves, while wannabes and newbies take lessons (⊕ *yallingupsurfschool.com*) in the lagoon. There are limited food and drink options nearby, so come prepared. **Amenities:** lifeguards; parking; showers; toilets. **Best for:** snorkeling; surfing; sunset; swimming; walking. ⚠ **High waves and rips increase north of the parking lot.** ⊠ *Yallingup Beach Rd., Yallingup* ⊕ *beachsafe.org.au.*

 **Restaurants**

Arimia Estate

$$$$ | **MODERN AUSTRALIAN** |**FAMILY** | If you're keen to get off the beaten path and discover how one winery restaurant is striving to create garden and farm-fresh dishes that pair well with wine in an elegant, alfresco setting, follow the 2-km (1-mile) dirt road to Arimia's charming timber cottage set among the forest. Make a beeline for the deck, and stay for a light lunch after sampling the award-winning wines (fee for tastings), and if you absolutely can't fathom leaving, consider staying at their on-site guesthouse. **Known for:** creative sustainability; raising their own pigs; ever-changing set price menu of local flavors like char siu kangaroo, barbecue squid, and lilly pilly. ⓢ *Average main: A$85* ⊠ *242 Quininup Rd., Yallingup* ☎ *08/9755–2528* ⊕ *arimia.com.au* ⊘ *Closed Wed.*

★ Eagle Bay Brewing Co

$$ | **MODERN AUSTRALIAN** | After a day at the beach, stop at the Eagle Bay Brewing Co. to grab a six-beer tasting flight so you can sample the company's many craft creations, then have a ball seeing which ones best complement your lunch. The food is pure gastropub in a casual yet upscale setting with an alfresco dining area that overlooks rolling, green pastures that stretch towards the sea. **Known for:** cold, frothy pale ale; hearty beef burger with bacon and cheddar cheese; crispy wood-fired pizzas with gourmet toppings. ⓢ *Average main: A$26* ⊠ *236 Eagle Bay Rd.* ☎ *08/9755–3554* ⊕ *eaglebaybrewing.com.au* ⊘ *No dinner.*

★ Lot 80

$$ | **EUROPEAN** |**FAMILY** | Housed in a former farmhouse on the expansive grounds of Wise Wine, this quirky, rustic restaurant is having a love affair with Mediterrarean flavors, and gin—there are more than 100 gins on the menu. There's certainly a welcoming vibe when you step through the front door, and the often-changing menu is so tasty that it's common for patrons to come for lunch and stay for dinner, too. **Known for:** Sunday paella made on the back deck; kid and dog-friendly grounds; dangerously delicious gin cocktails. ⓢ *Average main: A$28* ⊠ *54 Sheens Rd., Eagle Bay* ☎ *08/9756–8937* ⊕ *lot80.com.au* ⊘ *Closed Mon. and Tues.*

Simmos Ice Creamery and Fun Park

$ | **IRISH** | **FAMILY** | Simmos has been delighting locals and visitors since 1993 when a father and son teamed up to put their Irish ice cream recipe to the test. Some people thought they'd gone mad, but now this ice creamery and fun park is popular excursion for families and sweet tooths. **Known for:** 60 flavors of ice cream and sorbet; mango macadamia ice cream; mini-golf course. $ *Average main: A$5* ⌧ *161 Commonage Rd.* ☎ *08/9755–3745* ⊕ *simmos.com.au* ▭ *No credit cards.*

The Studio Bistro

$$$ | **MODERN AUSTRALIAN** | This is fancy pants food at its best as the meals are not only palatable to the taste buds, but also to the eyes. Choose from light, hearty, or share plates that feature an abundance of Thai-spiced duck, WA seafood, or grass-fed beef, and remember to always leave room for dessert. **Known for:** willingness to split bills; the whole duck share pan; the bistro hosts regularly changing art exhibitions with art coating the walls. $ *Average main: A$36* ⌧ *7 Marrinup Dr., Yallingup* ☎ *08/9756–6164* ⊕ *thestudiobistro.com.au* ☙ *Closed Tues. and Wed. No dinner Sun.–Fri.*

Hotels

Cape Lodge

$$$$ | **RESORT** | Regarded as the grandest boutique property in Margaret River wine country, the award-winning lodge's five-bedroom residence and 22 luxury suites deliver in service, space, and views of an 8-acre vineyard that produces Sauvignon Blanc and Shiraz exclusively for guests. **Pros:** large, luxurious rooms, some with spas; swimming pool; exclusive cooking classes (check website for calendar). **Cons:** no shopping nearby; limited evening dining options nearby; own transport essential. $ *Rooms from: A$385* ⌧ *3341 Caves Rd., Yallingup* ☎ *08/9756–6311* ⊕ *www.capelodge.com.au* ↪ *23 rooms* ⅋O⅋ *Free Breakfast.*

Dunsborough Central Motel

$ | **HOTEL** | Smack-bang in the middle of Dunsborough, this motel serves as a nice little base for the budget-conscious traveler. **Pros:** good-value beds for the area; guest laundry; free Wi-Fi. **Cons:** not beachfront; no on-site restaurant; room decor is dated. $ *Rooms from: A$140* ⌧ *50 Dunn Bay Rd.* ☎ *08/9756–7711* ⊕ *dunsboroughmotel.com.au* ☙ *Closed during school leavers (schoolies) wk each Nov.* ↪ *52 rooms* ⅋O⅋ *No meals.*

★ Forest Rise Eco Retreat

$$$ | **RENTAL** | This getaway in the peaceful bushland of the Margaret River wine region is eco-friendly but also semi-indulgent, with amenities including king-size beds, fluffy robes, fireplaces, dreamy candlelit spas with overhead windows looking up to the forest canopy, and oh-so-private verandas. **Pros:** two mountain bikes per chalet; private chef and massage therapist on request; barbecues available. **Cons:** free Wi-Fi in office area only; no shopping, dining, or market nearby; not suitable for children. $ *Rooms from: A$259* ⌧ *231 Yelverton Rd., Yelverton* ☎ *08/9755–7110* ⊕ *www.forestrise.com.au* ↪ *11 rooms* ⅋O⅋ *No meals.*

★ Pullman Bunker Bay Resort

$$$$ | **RESORT** | **FAMILY** | Sprawling down the hillside of the Cape Naturaliste Ridge, this resort woos with its sexy infinity pool, swanky villas, and easy access to one of the area's most beautiful beaches. **Pros:** on-site restaurant, bar, and spa; quiet, nature-infused environment; trusted brand. **Cons:** limited sea views from rooms; own transport essential; no shopping nearby. $ *Rooms from: A$379* ⌧ *42 Bunker Bay Rd., off Cape Naturaliste Rd.* ☎ *08/9756–9100* ⊕ *accorhotels.com* ↪ *150 villas* ⅋O⅋ *No meals.*

Smiths Beach Resort

$$$$ | **RESORT** | **FAMILY** | Perched above the sand dunes of Smiths Beach in Yallingup, this luxury resort offers a variety of self-contained shacks, apartments, villas, and holiday homes perfect for an

Australian beach vacation. **Pros:** tennis courts; infinity edge swimming pool; separate kids pool. **Cons:** Wi-Fi can be inconsistent; car needed to access; limited dining options within walking distance. ⓢ *Rooms from: A$350* ✉ *67 Smiths Beach Rd., Yallingup* ☎ *08/9750–1200* ⊕ *smithsbeachresort.com.au* ⤳ *60 rooms* ❏ *No meals.*

★ Wildwood Valley Cottages

$$$ | **RENTAL** | **FAMILY** | Discover what it's like to wake up to birdsong echoing from the trees, and kangaroos greedily grazing outside your bedroom window at this stunning rural holiday property. **Pros:** pod-style coffeemaker; claw-foot bathtub; free Wi-Fi. **Cons:** no on-site restaurant; own vehicle is essential; nearest shop is a 15-minute drive away. ⓢ *Rooms from: A$250* ✉ *1481 Wildwood Rd., Yallingup* ☎ *08 /9755–2120* ⊕ *wildwoodvalley.com. au* ⤳ *4 rooms* ❏ *No meals.*

Margaret River Town

181 km (112 miles) south of Perth, 38 km (24 miles) south of Cape Naturaliste.

The lovely town of Margaret River is considered the center of the South West's wine region, though vineyards and wineries stretch well beyond its pretty surroundings. Nevertheless, there are more than 200 wineries in the region and more than 100 cellar doors that offer tastings and sales of some of the world's best wines. The region is often compared to France's Bordeaux for its similar climate and soils; it's gaining huge national and international acclaim for its exceptional red and white vintages, the most notable labels touting Chardonnay, Sauvignon Blanc, Shiraz, as well as Cabernet-Sauvignon and Cabernet-Merlot blends.

GETTING HERE AND AROUND

From Dunsborough, take Highway 10 to Margaret River. There is no public transport available in Margaret River town; it's taxis only, and that will soon blow the budget, so again we recommend you rent a car in Perth for exploring this town and region.

TAXI CONTACTS Margaret River Taxis. ☎ *08/9757–3444* ⊕ *www.margaretrivertaxis.com.*

TOURS

Margaret River Visitor Centre is the best starting point if you want to do a tour. They will find the right tour for you, make the booking, and arrange pickup at your accommodation if appropriate (many tours provide this service). Tour operators in the area run tours as diverse as wineries and food tasting, horseback riding, surfing, bushwalks, whale-watching, kayaking, scenic flights, mountain biking, stand-up paddleboarding, rock climbing, and abseiling.

★ Bushtucker River and Wine Tours

ADVENTURE TOURS | No visit to the Margaret Rier region is complete without a guided tour of the area's famous wineries, breweries, and cultural sites. This company provides a variety of options, including canoe and cave tours, and wine tours that include a "bush-tucker" lunch. The tours give you an opportunity to see inaccessible parts of the river, Aboriginal sites, and caves while canoeing sections of the river down to the mouth at Surfers Point. A short walk shows you the rich variety of "bush tucker" Aboriginal people would have eaten, while lunch includes a selection of authentic foods. The canoe and cave tours take about four hours, while the wine and beer tours are all day with pickups from Busselton, Dunsborough, Margaret River town, and even Bunbury by special request. ✉ *20 Auger Way* ☎ *08/9757–9084* ⊕ *bushtuckertours.com* ⤳ *From A$95.*

Cape to Cape Tours

ADVENTURE TOURS | Gene Hardy, a born-and-raised Margaret River local, is a hands-on ambassador for the Maragaret River region, and his Cape to Cape Tours show off this great land and the spectacular Cape to Cape Track. He offers a range of guided tours with the End to End eight-day hikes being the most popular. ■ TIP→ **Day trips are available; see website for all options.** ☒ *24 Auger Way W, Unit 1* ☎ *0459/452038* ⊕ *www. capetocapetours.com.au.*

Lake Cave

GUIDED TOURS | **FAMILY** | Centered on a tranquil, eerie-looking underground lake, Lake Cave is the deepest of all the open caves in the region, and requires navigating 130 stairs to the first platform; then it's 62 meters (203 feet) down, and back up again, all under the care of a professional tour guide. ■ TIP→ **A drop of water on the head is said to be lucky.** ☒ *40 Conto Rd., Forest Grove* ☎ *08/9757–7411* 💲 *A$23.*

Mammoth Cave

ADVENTURE TOURS | Discover ancient fossil remains of extinct animals and a tannin-stained stream as you self-guide yourself through this ground-level-entry cave system. Opt for an audio experience, which will give you a history lesson and various interesting facts about the giant cave. Wheelchair access is possible to the first chamber. ☒ *Caves Rd.* ☎ *08/9757–7411.*

McLeod Tours

DRIVING TOURS | Every visitor to Australia wants to see the country's famous fauna and kangaroos top the list. And although roos (that's what the locals call them) are everywhere, a tourist may not know when or where to get a good look at one. That's why the McLeod family offer a seasonal (mid-October through May only) Kangaroo Safari that will take you onto the family farm in Margaret River for a slow ride in Neil McLeod's restored 1962 Bedford truck to see roos in the wild. The 2½-hour trip includes a stop for a cup of tea and a piece of freshly baked cake, made by Mrs. McLeod. You may also get to feed carrots to the family's horses, which will come up to the open-back

truck. ■ TIP→ **McLeods also offer popular wine tours of the region.** ☒ *Margaret River* ☎ *08/9757–2747* ⊕ *mcleodtours.com.au* 💲 *A$60.*

ESSENTIALS
VISITOR INFORMATION
Margaret River Visitor Centre

Margaret River Visitor Centre has extensive information on the region. The friendly staff will answer all your questions, and can book accommodation, tours, and activities at no additional cost. ☒ *100 Bussell Hwy.* ☎ *08/9780–5911* ⊕ *www. margaretriver.com.*

 Sights

Cape Mentelle Vineyards

WINERY/DISTILLERY | One of the "founding five" wineries in the area, Cape Mentelle planted its first vines in 1970 on a 16-hectare block just outside Margaret River. Today, it's still one of the most notable wineries, not only for its delectable drops, but also for its seasonal movie nights. From mid-December until the end of March, you can enjoy a balmy evening of food, wine, and film at the winery's outdoor cinema. To learn more about the vineyard, take the one-hour Behind the Scenes tours; there's also a food and wine pairing experience Monday through Wednesday, and Friday and Saturday at 11:30 am (less frequent May through October). ☒ *331 Wallcliffe Rd., 4 km (2 miles) west of Margaret River* ☎ *08/9757–0812 cellar door* ⊕ *capementelle.com.au.*

Cullen Wines

WINERY/DISTILLERY | Biodynamic? Tick. Homegrown produce? Tick. Gorgeous vineyard setting? Tick. Stellar wines. Tick, tick, tick. Cullen isn't the flashiest winery in Margaret River, but its rustic, cottage feel is a strong part of the allure. Family-owned since it began, it has long followed an ethos to care for the planet and exist sustainably, and it seems Mother Nature is returning the favor. The cellar door serves crispy, clean wines, while the on-site restaurant uses fresh, flavorsome ingredients from the organic kitchen garden (visit for free independently) to give considerable sparkle to the dishes. **■ TIP→ Traveling in a group of seven or more? Make a booking for wine tastings.** ✉ *4323 Caves Rd., Wilyabrup* ☎ *08/9755–5277 cellar door, 08/9755–5656 restaurant* 🌐 *www.cullenwines.com.au.*

Hay Shed Hill

WINERY/DISTILLERY | Winemaker and owner Michael Kerrigan—once chief winemaker at neighboring Howard Park and Madfish Wines—is on a mission to produce "modern wines from old vines" under several different labels. His hands-on approach, using the best grapes from the 30-something-year-old plantings, has won show awards and five-star endorsements by wine writers. The tasting room breaks from the usual Margaret River architecture—no rammed earth, timber, and stone here, rather a lovely white-painted clapboard building, polished concrete floors, and pitched ceiling. As the name suggests, the building is the original hay shed on what was a dairy farm. Rustico Restaurant serves tapas from 11 to 5 daily. ✉ *511 Harmans Mill Rd., Wilyabrup* ☎ *08/9755–6046* 🌐 *hayshedhill.com.au.*

★ Leeuwin Estate

WINERY/DISTILLERY | This winery's Art Series wines—especially the Chardonnay and Cabernet Sauvignon—have a deserved reputation as some of the best in the country, and feature on Australia's "most collected" list. Complimentary tastings (for some wines) and guided tours (for a fee) are conducted on the property daily, introducing you to the extensive art gallery in the cellar. Setting aside the entire afternoon is the way to go at Leeuwin's restaurant, open daily for lunch and for Saturday dinner. **■ TIP→ In January the estate holds its iconic Leeuwin Concert Series; many international superstars—including Tom Jones, Diana Ross, Sting, and the late Ray Charles—have performed here against a backdrop of tall, floodlit karri trees.** ✉ *Stevens Rd., off Gnarawary Rd.* ☎ *08/9759–0000* 🌐 *leeuwinestate.com.au.*

Vasse Felix

WINERY/DISTILLERY | The first vines planted in the region were here at Vasse Felix in 1967. Today, its ground-level cellar door provides free wine samples, while the upstairs restaurant offers fine dining and sweeping views of the vineyards and landscaped grounds. In the winery, Virginia Willcock, who was awarded Australian Winemaker of the Year in 2012, is at the helm, perfecting the region's strong suits of Chardonnay and Cabernet Sauvignon, as well as developing clean, flavorsome Sauvignon Blanc, Semillon, and Shiraz. **■ TIP→ An on-site art gallery houses regular exhibitions from prominent Australian artists.** ✉ *Tom Cullity Dr., at Caves Rd., Cowaramup* ☎ *08/9756–5000 cellar door, 08/9756–5050 restaurant* 🌐 *www.vassefelix.com.au.*

🍴 Restaurants

The Berry Farm Cottage Cafe

$ | **CAFÉ** | Nestled in the hills of Rosa Glen, a scenic 16-minute drive from Margaret River town, is this quaint and enchanting café, famous for its fruit-infused ciders, wines, and desserts. You can while away an afternoon over lunch and also enjoy tea, wine tastings, shopping for homemade jams (and more) at the cellar door, and in season, a walk through the "berry circle," where you can pick and munch wild berries. **Known for:** homemade scones with cream and delicious jam; famous boysenberry pie; playground for kids. [$] *Average main: A$18* ✉ *43 Bessell Rd.* ☎ *08/9757–5054* 🌐 *www.theberryfarm.com.au.*

Flutes Restaurant

$$$ | **MODERN AUSTRALIAN** | The pastoral setting over the dammed waters of Wilyabrup Brook, encircled by olive groves in the midst of the Brookland Valley Vineyard, is almost as compelling as the cuisine—French bistro fare mixed with tropical influences from the northern Australian town of Broome. Executive chef and restaurant owner François Morvan makes use of prime local produce, creating a variety of mouthwatering dishes. **Known for:** picturesque setting; three-course set menu; local produce. $ *Average main: A$42* ⊠ *Brookland Valley Vineyard, 4070 Caves Rd., 5 km (3 miles) south of Metricup Rd., Wilyabrup* ☎ *08/9755–6250* ⊕ *www.flutes.com.au.*

Settler's Tavern

$$ | **MODERN AUSTRALIAN** |**FAMILY** | Sometimes you don't need to dab foams or spread purees across a plate to impress; sometimes you just have to serve up consistently good, hearty fare that fills the belly and doesn't burn a hole in the pocket. The crowds at this pub are testament to the fact that Settler's got the formula right, be it a thick scotch fillet cooked to perfection or a sweet and spicy Malaysian laksa jammed with prawns and herbs. **Known for:** live music, including national and international acts; locally sourced ingredients; American barbecue and chargrilled steak. $ *Average main: A$28* ⊠ *114 Bussell Hwy.* ☎ *08/9757–2398* ⊕ *www.settlerstavern.com.*

Voyager Estate

$$$$ | **CONTEMPORARY** | One of the appellation's grande dames, with its expansive, manicured gardens—featuring more than 1,000 roses—this splendid winery has a restaurant that takes you on a gastronomic journey via a seven-course Discovery Menu that is, naturally, inspired by the wine as well as local, seasonal ingredients. The decor features antique wooden furniture, comfortable wing-back armchairs, and soaring cathedral ceilings. **Known for:** seated wine tastings, which can include aged wines; an often-changing, seasonal menu; a tour that takes you into the winery. $ *Average main: A$180* ⊠ *Stevens Rd.* ☎ *08/9757–6354* ⊕ *www.voyagerestate.com.au* ☾ *No dinner.*

Watershed Winery

$$$ | **AUSTRALIAN** | This upscale restaurant has impressive modern architecture, from big windows to a wraparound deck that offers uninterrupted views of the vineyard. The seasonal menu, inspired by local produce, may include favorites like local marron and slow-braised lamb shoulder. **Known for:** award-winning wines; chef's selection three-course set menu; full-flavored, elegant dishes. $ *Average main: A$38* ⊠ *Bussell Hwy. at Darch Rd.* ☎ *08/9758–8633* ⊕ *www.watershedwines.com.au* ☾ *Closed Mon. and Tues. No dinner.*

🛏 Hotels

Grand Mercure Basildene Manor

$$$ | **RESORT** | Each of the rooms in this grand, circa-1912 house has been lovingly refurbished to reflect modern comforts, though history still looms large in the main homestead, and due to its big-name chain ownership (Accor), it has loads of extras on offer. **Pros:** heritage rooms with new design; lavish breakfast; horse riding, tennis, bushwalking, and beach nearby. **Cons:** own transport essential; no lunch or dinner; dining options 1½ km (1 mile) away. $ *Rooms from: A$279* ⊠ *187 Wallcliffe Rd.* ☎ *08/9757–3140* ⊕ *www.basildenemanor.com.au* ⤙ *19 rooms* ⦿ *Free Breakfast.*

Heritage Trail Lodge

$$$ | **HOTEL** | Nestled among towering karri trees, this luxury retreat is only about ½ km (¼ mile) from Margaret River township and its spacious suites have hot tubs, king-size beds, and private balconies overlooking the forest. **Pros:** free Wi-Fi and parking; 10-minute walk to shops and restaurants; lush garden setting. **Cons:** no leisure facilities; children discouraged; two rooms face highway, meaning traffic noise. $ *Rooms from: A$249* ⊠ *31 Bussell Hwy.*

☎ *08/9757–9595* 🌐 *heritage-trail-lodge.com.au* 🛏 *10 suites* 🍴 *Free Breakfast.*

★ Island Brook Estate Vineyard Chalets
$$ | **RENTAL** | Located halfway between Busselton and Margaret River, this family-owned and-operated option lets you stay at a working vineyard, enjoying an authenetic Margaret River region experience. **Pros:** forest views; guests receive 20% off wine sales; wildlife, including kangaroos. **Cons:** no oven in cabins; shower over spa bath is not suitable for mobility-challenged persons; secluded, with closest major supermarket a 12-minute drive away. [$] *Rooms from: A$180* ✉ *7388 Bussell Hwy.* ☎ *0409/577580* 🌐 *www.islandbrook.com.au* 🛏 *3 cabins* 🍴 *No meals.*

Riverglen Chalets
$$ | **RENTAL** | In a magical woodland setting, Riverglen Chalets consists of modest, self-contained timber cabins interspersed among 7 acres of forest and gardens just a 10-minute stroll along the river into Margaret River township. **Pros:** breakfast hampers supplied on request; some outdoor spas; communal games room. **Cons:** some road noise during the day; cabins may be drafty in cooler months; this property may attract partygoers, especially during "school leavers" week in November. [$] *Rooms from: A$190* ✉ *321 Carters Rd.* ☎ *08/9757–2101* 🌐 *www.riverglenchalets.com.au* 🛏 *14 cabins* 🍴 *No meals.*

Shopping

Howard Park Wines
WINE/SPIRITS | One of the big pluses of stopping in at WA's largest boutique family-owned winery is that there are a number of labels you can taste, all fixed at different quality and price points. Beneath high ceilings and with views of vineyard rows, compare the Howard Park branded wines against the simpler Mad-Fish and the elegant drops under their super premium offering, Marchand & Burch. Interestingly, feng shui principles were used to design the spacious tastings room. Floor-to-ceiling windows allow in plenty of light as well as giving views over the property, and even the door has specific measurements to allow good luck to flow through. Wines produced under the Howard Park label include Riesling, Chardonnay, Sauvignon Blanc, and Cabernet Sauvignon. ✉ *543 Miamup Rd., Cowaramup* ☎ *08/9756–5200* 🌐 *www.howardparkwines.com.au.*

★ Vasse Virgin
LOCAL SPECIALTIES | This award-winning artisanal producer smack-dab in the middle of vineyards and olive trees is an aromatherapy feast for the senses. Inside a converted machinery shed (the soap factory), there are a chemical-free range of soaps and body care products hand blended with natural organic ingredients, as well as yummy olives, tapenades, dukkahs, and pestos all without preservatives or artificial additives. This is a place for gastronomes and purists. Sniff, rub, scrub, pamper, and taste to your heart's content. **■TIP→ Check website for the shop's "make your own" classes.** ✉ *135 Puzey Rd., Wilyabrup* ☎ *08/9755–6111* 🌐 *www.vassevirgin.com.au.*

Activities

HIKING

There's no better way to see and experience the beautifully wild coastline of the Margaret River region than by hiking the Cape to Cape Track, a 135 km (84 miles) long rugged path that runs along the coast of the Leeuwin-Naturaliste National Park from Cape Naturaliste Lighthouse near Dunsborough to Cape Leeuwin Lighthouse in Augusta. It can be completed as one long trek, or short day treks. You will find the start points generally at beachside parking lots. A number of tour companies have guided walks (⇨ *see* Cape to Cape Tours *in Tours*) of varying duration, or drop-off and pickup services (as do some accommodations).

Canal Rocks to Wyadup is a two-hour return walk from the car park on Canal Rocks Road.

Away from the coast, a popular short walk is from the historic homestead of Ellensbrook (Ellensbrook Road off Caves Road, 13 km [8 miles] from Margaret River). The walk takes about 40 minutes to the Meekadarabee Falls, known to Aboriginal people as the "bathing place of the moon," and is best in winter and spring.

Nannup

100 km (62 miles) east of Margaret River.

Rustic timber cottages and historic buildings characterize the small town of Nannup, which makes a nice day-trip from Margaret River. Several scenic drives wind through the area, including the Blackwood River Tourist Drive, a 113-km (70-mile) ride through some of WA's most spectacular scenery. You can also canoe on the Blackwood River or bush-walk through Kondil Park. A map of the buildings used in the 2013 surf movie, *Drift,* is available from the Nannup Visitor Centre. At various times of the year look out for Nannup's popular festivals: music, flower and garden, and art and photography. The Festival of Country Gardens displays an artist's palette of WA's spring and autumn colors.

ESSENTIALS

VISITOR INFORMATION Nannup Visitor Centre. ⊠, *16 Warren Rd., Nannup* ⊕ *Warren St. at Forrest St.* ☎ *08/9756–1901* ⊕ *www.everythingnannup.com.au.*

👁 Sights

★ Cambray Cheese
FARM/RANCH | FAMILY | Calling all cheese lovers and connoisseurs to this family-operated sheep and dairy farm located on the outskirts of Nannup. Stop in to the farmhouse and sample the

award-winning sheep cheese (in season) and flavor-punching dairy cheeses that are skillfully handmade on-site by the clever Wilde family. ■**TIP→ Bring a picnic blanket and a bottle of wine to enjoy with a cheese platter near the grazing sheep.** ⊠ *4573 Vasse Hwy., Nannup* ☎ *08/9756–2037* ⊕ *cambraysheepcheese.com.au.*

Holberry House
HOTEL—SIGHT | Overlooking Blackwood Valley, Holberry House is a charming colonial B&B with exposed beams and stone fireplaces. The gardens are peppered with statues and sculptures set among a woodland of jarrah trees through which Mount Folly Creek flows, and for a small donation at the main gate, the general public is welcome to explore the extensive gardens without overnighting here. ■**TIP→ Ask about the facts and myths surrounding the legend of the Nannup Tiger.** ⊠ *14 Grange Rd., Nannup* ☎ *08 /9756–1276* ⊕ *www.holberryhouse.com. au* ⊠ *A$4* ⊗ *Closed after dark.*

Augusta

40 km (25 miles) south of Margaret River.

Augusta is probably most known for the Cape Leeuwin lighthouse, which is at the end of the Cape to Cape trail. It also is a great spot for whale-watching, and spelunking at Jewel Cave.

TOURS
Jewel Cave
ADVENTURE TOURS | The southernmost, and largest, cave of the WA underground system, Jewel has one of the longest straw stalactites in any tourist cave in the world. Prepare to delve 40 meters (131 feet) below ground to witness the natural beauty of this impressive grotto that is accessible by guided tour only. There's also an interpretive center and on-site café. ⊠ *Jewel Caves Rd., Augusta* ☎ *08 /9757–7411* ⊠ *A$23.*

Sights

★ **Cape Leeuwin Lighthouse**

LIGHTHOUSE | The view from the top of the Cape Leeuwin Lighthouse, the tallest lighthouse on mainland Australia and only a 10-minute drive south of Augusta, allows you to witness the meeting of the Southern and the Indian oceans. In some places this alliance results in giant swells that crash against the rocks; in others, you'll spot whales surfacing (May through September). The lighthouse precinct is open daily and offers guided tours, which includes climbing 176 stairs to the top and a trek around the outside balcony. Bring your camera, and wear a windproof jacket—gusts of 156 kmph (97 mph) have been recorded at ground level here. ■**TIP→ Order lunch from the café and watch the rock parrots graze on the grass.** ✉ *Leeuwin Rd., Augusta* ☎ *08/9758–1920* 🎟 *A$20 for tour.*

Restaurants

★ **Augusta Bakery and Cafe**

$$ | **BAKERY** | Since 1948, the bakers at the Augusta Bakery have been seducing unsuspecting visitors with its sweetness in the way of tasty breads, cakes, cookies, pastries, pies, and sausage rolls. You can grab a premade sandwich and treat to go, or sit in the café's modest dining room with lovely views of the Blackwood River and daily lunch specials. **Known for:** to-die-for apple and custard strudel; flaky-crust fruit pies; meat pies with gravy and peas. [$] *Average main: A$22* ✉ *121 Blackwood Ave., Augusta* ☎ *08/9758–1664.*

Blue Ocean Fish and Chips

$ | **SEAFOOD** | When you visit a sleepy seaside village like Augusta, you'd expect a decent feed of fresh, local fish and seafood, and that's exactly what you'll get at Blue Ocean Fish and Chips. The small haunt serves Dhu fish, bronze whaler, and yellow-fin whiting, and is decorated in a nautical theme, complete with fish decals and mini seagulls, deck chairs, shells, and sand. **Known for:** deep-fried Snickers bars; daily lunch specials; fisherman's basket with a variety of seafood. [$] *Average main: A$15* ✉ *73 Blackwood Ave., Augusta* ☎ *08/9758–1748.*

Activities

The 135-km (84-mile) Cape to Cape Track that begins at the Cape Naturaliste Lighthouse near Dunsborough ends at Cape Leeuwin Lighthouse in Augusta. A one-hour walk via beach, rocks, and bushland begins at the Leeuwin Waterwheel, near Cape Leeuwin Lighthouse in Augusta; and a four-hour walk with expansive coastal views starts at the Hamelin Bay boat ramp and heads to Cosy Corner.

Index

682

Photo Credits

Photo Credits

PRAISE FOR

THE EPIC CRUSH
OF GENIE LO

★ "In this dazzlingly fun debut, Yee mixes humor, Chinese folklore, and action to deliver a rousing, irreverent adventure packed with sharp-edged banter." —*Publishers Weekly*, starred review

★ "A tough, self-disciplined Chinese-American teen deals with the supernatural derailing of her college-prep activities in this speculative fiction novel that draws on the folklore of the Chinese Monkey King . . . An exciting, engaging, and humorous debut that will appeal widely, this wraps up neatly enough but leaves an opening for further installments—here's hoping." —*Kirkus*, starred review

★ "Genie's perspective on the strange turn her life has taken will have readers laughing out loud . . . Hilarious and action-packed, this fantastically executed tale of the Monkey King in modern-day California introduces a great new character in Genie Lo." —*School Library Journal*, starred review

★ "Pulling ancient mythology into the modern world . . . Yee ensures his book will find a solid fan base . . . Yee builds a world filled with characters that carry the page-turning plot." —*VOYA*, Perfect Ten

"Genie is a unique and uniquely funny heroine, a trove of biting cultural commentary, insight on life as an Asian-American teen, and compelling interpretations of ancient Eastern legends." —*Chicago Tribune*

"It's refreshing to see the Chinese pantheon steal some of the literary attention lavished on the Greek, Roman, and Nordic gods, and Lee handily gets Western readers up to speed on requisite backstories and proclivities." —*Bulletin of the Center for Children's Books*

AMULET BOOKS
NEW YORK

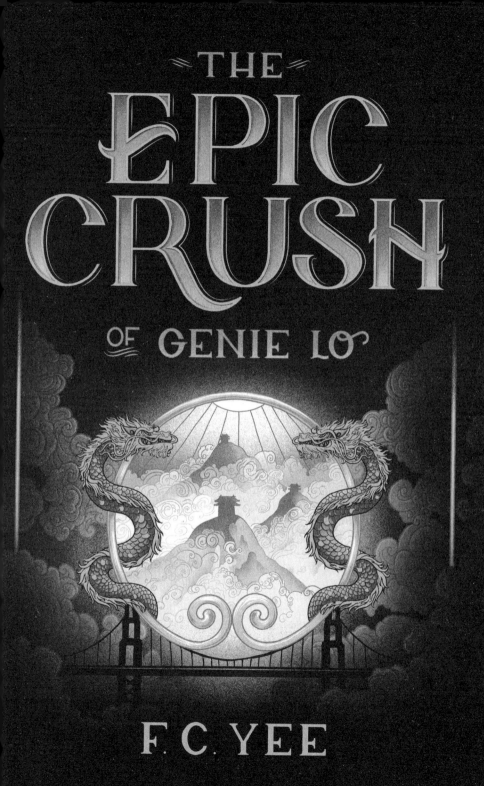

Cataloging-in-Publication Data has been applied for and may be obtained from the Library of Congress.

Paperback ISBN 978-1-4197-3209-6

ABRAMS The Art of Books
195 Broadway, New York, NY 10007
abramsbooks.com

for
ABIGAIL

1

SO I DIDN'T HANDLE THE MUGGING AS WELL AS I COULD HAVE.

I would have known what do to if I'd been the victim. Hand over everything quietly. Run away as fast as possible. Go for the eyes if I was cornered. I'd passed the optional SafeStrong girl's defense seminar at school with flying colors.

But we'd never covered what to do when you see six grown men stomping the utter hell out of a boy your age in broad daylight. It was a Tuesday morning, for god's sake. I was on my way to school, the kid was down on the ground, and the muggers were kicking him like their lives depended on it. They weren't even trying to take his money.

"*Get away from him!*" I screamed. I swung my backpack around by the strap like an Olympic hammer thrower and flung it at the group.

The result wasn't exactly gold medal-worthy. The pack, heavy with my schoolbooks, fell short and came to rest at one of the assailants' heels. They all turned to look at me.

Crap.

I should have made a break for it, but something froze me in place.

It was the boy's eyes. Even though he'd taken a beating that should have knocked him senseless, his eyes were perfectly clear as they locked on to mine. He stared at me like I was the only important thing in the world.

One of the men threw his cigarette on the ground and took a step in my direction, adjusting his trucker cap in a particularly menacing fashion. *Crap, crap, crap.*

That was as far as he got. The boy said something, his words lost in the distance. The man flinched like he couldn't believe what he was hearing, and then turned back to resume the brutal pounding.

Finally my legs remembered what they were good for. I ran away.

I should have been worried that the assault and battery would turn into outright homicide, but I kept going without looking back. I was too freaked out.

The last sight I had of that kid was his gleaming white teeth.

. . .

"You shouldn't have bothered in the first place," Yunie told me in homeroom. "He was with them."

I lifted my head up from the desk. "Huh?"

"It was a gang initiation. The older members induct the new ones by beating the snot out of them. If he was smiling at you the whole time, it was because he was happy about getting 'jumped in.'"

"I don't think there are gangs that hang out in the Johnson Square dog run, Yunie."

"You'd be surprised," she said as she thumbed through her messages. "Some areas past the Walgreens are pretty sketch."

Maybe she was right. It was easy to forget in the bubble of Santa Firenza Prep that our town wasn't affluent. A competitive school was really the only thing it had going for it. We were hardly Anderton or Edison Park or any of the other pockets of Bay Area wealth where the venture capital and tech exec families lived.

On the other hand, that kid couldn't have been a gang member. It wasn't the kind of detail you focus on in the heat of the moment, but looking back on it, he was wearing rags. Like a beggar.

Ugh. I'd run across a group of assholes beating a homeless person for kicks and wasn't able to do anything to stop them. I groaned and dropped my forehead to the desk again.

"Flog yourself some more," Yunie said. "You told a teacher as soon as you got to school and spent all morning giving the police report, didn't you?"

"Yeah," I muttered into the veneer. "But if I wasn't such an idiot, I could have called the cops right there." The skirts on our uniforms didn't have pockets. So of course I was carrying my phone in my backpack. That is to say, I'd *been* carrying it.

It was going to be a long haul, re-creating the notes from my AP classes. My secret weapons—all of the practice exams that I'd hounded my teachers into giving me—were gone. Studying by any method other than active recall was for chumps.

And my textbooks. I wasn't sure what the school policy on replacements was. If the cost fell on me, I'd probably have to sell my blood plasma.

But while I'd never admit it, not even to Yunie, what hurt most wasn't losing my phone or my notes. It was the fake-gold earrings I'd pinned to the canvas straps. The ones my dad had bought me at Disneyland, even though I'd been too young for piercings back then—too young to remember much of the trip at all.

I'd never see them again.

The bell rang. Something heavy fell past my head to the floor, and I bolted upright.

"Hey, jerk!" I yelped. "That could have hit me in the—*whuh?*"

It was my backpack. With all my stuff still in it. Minnie Mouses unharmed.

Mrs. Nanda, our homeroom teacher, stood by her desk and rapped her EDUCATOR OF THE YEAR paperweight to get our attention, punctuating the air like a judge's gavel. Her round, pleasant face was even more chipper and sprightly than usual.

"Class, I'd like to introduce a new student," she said. "Please welcome Quentin Sun."

Holy crap. It was *him*.

2

"GREETINGS," HE SAID, HIS ACCENT THICK BUT HIS VOICE LOUD and clear. "I have arrived."

Now, I'd done my best to describe this guy to the police. They pressed me hard for details, as apparently this wasn't the first group mugging in recent weeks.

But I'd let Officers Davis and Rodriguez down. Nice eyes and a winning smile weren't much to go by. I was too frazzled to notice anything before, which meant this was my first decent look at the boy without the influence of adrenaline.

So a couple of things.

One: He was short. Like, really short for a guy. I felt bad that my brain went there first, but he wasn't even as tall as Mrs. Nanda.

Two: He was totally okay, physically. I didn't see how anyone could be up and about after that beating, but here he was, unbruised and unblemished. I felt relieved and disturbed at the same time to see there wasn't a scratch on him.

And his mint condition just made Point Three even more obvious. He was . . . *yeesh*.

Nothing good could come of our new classmate being that handsome. It was destructive. Twisted. Weaponized. He had the cheekbones and sharp jawline of a pop star, but his thick eyebrows and wild, unkempt hair lent him an air of natural ruggedness that some pampered singer could never achieve in a million years of makeup.

"Argh, my ovaries," Yunie mumbled. She wasn't alone, judging by the soft intakes of breath coming from around the room.

"Arrived from where?" said Mrs. Nanda.

Quentin looked at her in amusement. "China?"

"Yes, but where in, though?" said Mrs. Nanda, trying her best to convey that she was sensitive to the regional differences. Fujianese, Taishanese, Beijingren—she'd taught them all.

He just shrugged. "The stones," he said.

"You mean the mountains, sweetie?" said Rachel Li, batting her eyelashes at him from the front row.

"No! I don't misspeak."

The class giggled at his English. But none of it was incorrect, technically speaking.

"Tell us a little about yourself," Mrs. Nanda said.

Quentin puffed out his chest. The white button-down shirt and black pants of our school's uniform for boys made most of them look like limo drivers. But on him, the cheap stitching just made it clearer that he was extremely well-muscled underneath.

"I am the greatest of my kind," he said. "In this world I have no equal. I am known to thousands in faraway lands, and everyone I meet can't help but declare me king!"

There was a moment of silence and sputtering before guffaws broke out.

"Well . . . um . . . we are all high achievers here at SF Prep," said Mrs. Nanda as politely as she could. "I'm sure you'll fit right in?"

Quentin surveyed the cramped beige classroom with a cool

squint. To him, the other twenty-two laughing students were merely peons on whom his important message had been lost.

"Enough wasting of time," he snapped. "I came to these petty halls only to reclaim what is mine."

Before anyone could stop him, he hopped onto Rachel's desk and stepped over her to the next one, like she wasn't even there.

"Hey! Quentin!" Mrs. Nanda said, frantically waving her hands. "Get down now!"

The new student ignored her, stalking down the column of desks. Toward mine.

Everyone in his way leaned to the side to avoid getting kicked. They were all too flabbergasted to do anything but serve as his counterweights.

He stopped on my desk and crouched down, looking me in the eye. His gaze pinned me to my seat.

I couldn't turn away. He was so close our noses were almost touching. He smelled like wine and peaches.

"You!" he said.

"What?" I squeaked.

Quentin gave me a grin that was utterly feral. He tilted his head as if to whisper, but spoke loud enough for everyone to hear.

"You belong to *me*."

3

"HE'S GOING TO SUE YOU, GENIE," JENNY ROLSTON SAID WHILE we were changing in the locker room. "Once he learns that's how we do things in America, he's going to find a lawyer."

I slammed my locker shut. It immediately bounced back open, more than a year of my rough handling having misaligned the latch. It took the weight of my shoulder to close the dented gray door for good.

"Hey, *he* got in *my* face," I said, my head still buried under my jersey.

"Yeah, he was rude. And crazy. But you totally overreacted. He's probably blind now."

"Big Joe from SafeStrong would have approved of my reflexes. And my use of thumbs."

Jenny sighed. "If they suspend you for gouging out the eyes of a transfer student and I have to use a sub during regionals, I'm going to murder you."

I let the team captain have the last word. After today's double-dose of unpleasantness I just wanted to focus on practice. I had better things to worry about than a wackjob new student who'd latched on to me like a newborn duck. I laced up my sneakers, tied my hair back, and joined the rest of the girls on the court.

Jenny's death threat had been a compliment, sort of. I'd been pretty instrumental to the SF Lady Sharks' sudden surge of victories in the last year and a half. But it's not because I'm the greatest athlete in the world. I have no illusions as to why I've been on varsity volleyball since I was a freshman.

It's because I'm tall.

Ridiculously tall. Grossly tall. Monstrously tall.

Tall like a model, Yunie says. She's allowed to lie to me.

Jenny had her eye on me from day one. She didn't have to twist my arm to recruit me; it's safe to say this has been a mutually beneficial arrangement. I lead the league in career stuffs despite only having half a career, and I can probably get the attention of a college coach for a few minutes come admissions time. At least until he or she realizes I have the jump serve of a walrus.

The one thing I'm not too keen on is being nicknamed "The Great Wall of China." But then again, there are too many Asian students here to make it a minority slur. I'm pretty sure one of them came up with it in the first place.

My feet squeaked against the hardwood as I took my position in middle blocker. The time flew by as I sweated and grunted and spiked out the minutes in the echoing gym. Our only audience besides Coach Daniels were the shoddily painted murals of fall and spring sports athletes covering the walls.

At first I'd only joined this team to look well-rounded. I didn't have Yunie's gift for music, and I needed some extracurriculars. But over time I really came to love the game. When people asked why, I told them I thrived on the camaraderie.

In reality, though, I liked destroying people. Single-handedly.

I liked ruining the carefully crafted offensive schemes of the other team simply by existing. For five sets a week, the world was unfair in my favor. That didn't happen very often.

I was in the zone today, carrying the rookies that had been intentionally loaded on my side. Until I saw *him* standing in the bleachers.

"What the hell?" I said. "Get him out of here!"

"Can't," said Jenny. "Practice is over and we're in extra time. We don't have claim on the gym anymore. Just finish the scrim."

I grunted angrily and turned back to match point. I could still feel his eyes burning into the back of my head.

"Someone's got an admirer," Maxine Wong said from the other side of the net.

"Shut up."

"I heard all about it from Rachel," said the girl whose starter spot I'd taken. "You wigged out because he wanted to have an arranged marriage right there in class? I thought FOBs were into that kind of thing."

My eyes widened. The serve from my side was bumped and set for her.

"Shut UP!" I screamed as I went for the block.

Maxine wasn't beyond playing mind games. She was the same year as Jenny, but she crossed the line way too often with the sophomores and freshmen, at least in my opinion. I didn't like her at all.

Her taunts worked this time. She was better at playing while trash-talking than I was. I was off-balance and didn't have enough off the jump. She was going to get the winning kill—

"Gah!" Maxine yelped, landing hard on her butt. The ball bopped her on the head and rolled over the sideline.

"Dang, girl!" Jenny shouted from behind. "I wanna see that come game time!"

I looked at my hands, puzzled. I could have sworn I didn't have that block.

"Freak," Maxine said, as she got to her feet.

I glanced toward the bleachers. Quentin was gone.

Damn it. That scumbag was throwing me off so much that he was throwing me on.

. . .

"All right, this has gone too far," I said. "You crossed the border into stalker territory a long time ago. I don't mind talking to the police twice in one day."

Quentin was "walking me home." Or at least that's what he'd asked to do as I left school. I should have told him off right away instead of giving him the silent treatment. Now any uninitiated observers would think we were hashing out a misunderstanding like civilized people.

"Go ahead and call them," he said. "I'm told it's a free country."

Wait, had his English gotten better?

"I don't know what kind of game you're playing," I said, picking up the pace so that he fell behind and hopefully stayed there. "But it stops now. I don't know you. I don't want to know you. Just because I found you getting your ass kicked doesn't mean a thing. And you're welcome, by the way."

He snorted. "A lot of help you were. You didn't even tell anyone at school it was me you saw getting beat up, did you?"

I growled in frustration. There were actually a bunch of things I wanted to ask—like how he'd healed up so quickly, or what had happened to his old raggedy clothes, or how his speech seemed to randomly fluctuate between a Bay Area teenager and a Confucian bard—but I didn't want to encourage him.

"You dream of a mountain," Quentin said.

I stopped in my tracks and turned around. We were completely alone on the block, a splintery picket fence hemming us in on one side, and an empty lot with more abandoned bicycles than grass across the street.

"You dream of a mountain," he repeated. "Green and full of flowers. Every night when you fall asleep, you can smell the jasmine blossoms and hear the running streams."

He said this with real drama. Like it was supposed to hit home for me. Forge some kind of a connection between us.

I smirked. Because it didn't.

"Last night I dreamed I was floating in space and watching the stars," I said, feeling smug. "But you should keep trying that pickup line. I know at least a couple of girls at school like cheese."

Quentin didn't respond for a second. Apparently I was the one who'd floored him.

He broke out into a gigantic, ear-to-ear smile. Under better circumstances it would have been gorgeous.

"That's it!" he said, hopping in excitement. "That proves it! You really *are* mine!"

Okay. That kind of talk had to stop right here and right now. I inhaled deeply to unleash both a torrent of verbal abuse and a refresher in women's history over the last century.

But before I could give him what he asked for, Quentin jumped onto the neighboring fence, taking five feet in one smooth leap as easily as you'd take the escalator. He laughed and hooted and *cartwheeled* back and forth on the uprights, balancing on a surface that must have been narrower than a row of quarters.

My head began to spin. Something about his uninhibited display made it feel like there was a light shining behind my eyes, or like I was breathing in too much oxygen. I felt all the nausea that he should have, flipping around like that.

He wasn't normal. He must have been a gymnast or parkourista or whatever from online videos. Maybe a Shaolin.

I didn't care. I kicked the fence in the hope that he would fall and crotch himself, and I ran straight home.

■ ■ ■

A few minutes later I crossed the finish line into my driveway, gasping for breath.

I hurried with the keys to my house, my hands clumsier than usual. The click of the lock never sounded sweeter. Finally, finally, I slipped inside and sighed.

Only to find Quentin sitting at the kitchen table with my mom.

4

I CHECKED BEHIND ME AS A REFLEX AND BANGED MY FACE against the door in the process.

"Genie," Mom said, beaming like we'd won the lottery. "You have a visitor. A friend from school."

I pointed at Quentin while holding my nose. "How did you get inside?"

He looked puzzled. "I knocked on the door and introduced myself to your mother? We've been chatting for a while now."

I had taken the shortest route home and hadn't seen him pass me. Given that I was a decent runner, he must have sprinted here like a bat out of hell. How was he not winded in the slightest?

"Quentin is so nice," Mom said. "He explained how you rescued him this morning. He came over to say thank-you in person." She pointed to a fancy-wrapped box of chocolates on the kitchen counter.

"I had to ask around for your address," Quentin said. "In case you were wondering."

I rubbed my eyes. I felt like I was going crazy. But I could figure out his little magic trick later, once he was gone.

"I don't know how you got here before me," I said to Quentin. "But get the hell out."

"Pei-Yi! Rude!" Mom snapped.

Quentin made eye contact with me. Maybe he thought I'd stay quiet in front of my mother for the sake of decorum. That a boy's good name was more important than a girl's safety. If so, he was dead effin' wrong.

"Mother," I said slowly. "While this person seems like a nice young man on the surface, he threatened me during class this morning. He's not my friend."

My mother looked at him.

"I'm so sorry!" Quentin cried out, his face stricken. He shot to his feet and lowered his head. "I came here to apologize. And to explain my horrendous behavior."

"I'd love an explanation," I said. "Starting with what happened in the park."

"That was a misunderstanding that got out of hand," he said. "Those men weren't even bad people, just ordinary folk I tried to make conversation with. But I accidentally insulted them to such a degree that they sought to teach me a lesson. I can barely even blame them."

I frowned. At the time, the beating had seemed a bit extreme for a misunderstanding. But then again, I hadn't turned the other cheek in class myself. I guess he had a knack for pissing people off to the point of violence.

"After they left I picked up your bag, cleaned myself off, and brought it to school," Quentin said. "I knew you went to the same one as me because I recognized your uniform.

"It was just a fortunate coincidence I was assigned to your class on my first day," he went on. "I was so happy when I saw the person who saved my life this morning that I lost my head and made the same error all over again. My English is from a book, and I still don't know how things really work in America."

Mom sniffled like she was watching a soap finale.

"I'm sorry to have spoken to you so personally," Quentin said, his voice cracking.

I bit the inside of my cheek. I wasn't inclined to believe any of his BS, but he said it in such a heartfelt way that I was actually considering giving him the benefit of the doubt. Maybe he was just a really, really awkward transplant with no sense of personal space.

That's when the bastard winked at me.

Fine. Two could play at this game.

"You know what would be great?" I said, putting on a coy expression. "If we could have you and your parents over for dinner. Let us welcome you to the States."

Quentin raised a black, regal eyebrow.

Got you, jerk. Let's see if you can handle me blowing your creepstory to the real *authorities.* If I let his parents know about his behavior, there'd be no way he'd get off scot-free.

"Oh, how lovely," Mom said, clapping her hands. "That's a wonderful idea."

"Uh . . . okay," said Quentin, looking unsure of himself for the first time ever. "They would also want to give their thanks . . . I guess."

"But for now you must be going," I said. "You promised the chess club you'd go out with them to try your first real American hamburger."

"Yes!" he said. "I am most interested in this thing that you're talking about."

As Quentin laced his shoes up in the hallway, Mom pulled me aside.

"Be nice to him," she said. "Not so harsh, like you always are."

Ugh. My mom is of the generation that believes the male can do no wrong.

"I should be nice like you were?" I said. "You took his side over your own daughter's pretty quickly. Did he tell you exactly what he did at school?"

She looked up at me sadly. "It's hard, coming to this country," she said. "You were born here; you never had to experience that. Of course he's going to make some mistakes."

Then her eyes gleamed. "Plus he's so handsome. And rich, too, probably. Like a prince. I can tell these things."

Ugggghhhhhh.

I showed Quentin out, mostly because I wanted to make sure he walked the hell away and didn't sneak into our bushes or something. Once I'd closed the door behind us, I stared him down.

"You picked the wrong girl to bully, asshat."

"I said I was sorry!"

"No, you lied about being sorry to my mother! There's a difference!"

"What, do you want me to grovel in front of your dad, too? Where is he? Still at work?"

At the mention of my father my teeth clenched so hard they almost turned to shrapnel.

"You don't have the right to talk to any of my family!" I said. "You have no right to anything of mine!"

"I don't understand why you're so upset!"

I poked him hard in his chest. It was like tapping granite.

"That doesn't matter," I hissed. "You are not entitled to my thoughts, emotions, or any other part of my life unless I say so.

What you get from me is jack and squat, regardless of whether or not you understand. *Ming bai le ma*, dickhead?"

Quentin opened his mouth to retort but nothing came out. He stood there, failing to turn over, like a car with a faulty ignition. I could read his face as plain as day. He just couldn't believe that I, an actual human being, was talking to him like this.

Finally he just scowled and stomped away.

I watched him go. I waited till he was out of sight.

The tension in my body left with him. I nearly toppled over with relief. He'd been banished, out of sight and out of mind. Hopefully for all time.

Then I remembered he was in my homeroom, where I'd see him every day.

5

A LITTLE MORE THAN A DECADE AGO THERE WAS SOME KIND of brainwave, some kind of collective spasm, some bug in the water, that induced every single Asian couple with a newborn daughter in America to name her Eugenia. Or Eunice. Something with an E-U. Seriously, these two vowels together had a base rate of next to nothing in the broader population and then BAM! An epidemic of Eumonia.

Eugenia Park has been my best friend ever since we made a deal in second grade to split the name we both hated like a turkey. She got the front end and was forevermore "Yunie." I got the back, "Genie." There was even a third girl in our class to whom we'd hopefully offered "Eugie," but we turned out not to like her, so she's not part of the treaty.

"You're gonna hate me," Yunie said during our study hall in the computer lab. "But I have to bail on the Read-a-Thon."

I made a face. "Your children will serve me in hell for this."

"I'll find a replacement. I'm sure there's someone else who wants to wake up extra early on Saturday and wrangle twenty screaming kindergartners. I'll tell them—"

"Hold on a second."

I glanced behind me across the room. Michael and his posse

were at it again, crowding around the workstation that Rutsuo was using.

Rutsuo Huang was one of the ultrageniuses at our school, a programming prodigy who was miles ahead of everyone else. I mean, I've only been able to wrap my head around introductory JavaScript. But Rutsuo had blown through our school's electives in a semester and could probably work at a startup right now if he wanted to. He was also painfully awkward and shy, and at SF Prep that's saying a lot.

He was working on what must have been a personal project, as there weren't any assignments left for him. But every so often while he was typing, Mike Wen or one of his two gym-rat flunkies would reach over his shoulder and press a random bunch of keys on the keyboard.

"*Boop,*" Mike said as a series of complex statements turned to gibberish.

It was perhaps the nerdiest form of harassment ever invented, but still. Rutsuo kept plugging away without telling them to stop, fixing his code over and over. I could tell he was bothered, but he wouldn't say anything. And the teacher on duty was in the bathroom.

"Anyway, it's because we're celebrating my cousin's MCAT results," Yunie explained. "Apparently she did well enough that my aunt needs to force the entire bloodline to stop and congratulate her."

"*Boop,*" said one of the other guys around Rutsuo.

"I think the only reason my parents are going is so they can pull the same move if I win my *concours,*" Yunie went on. "It's like, gee, thanks for the additional pressure."

"Boop."

I wasn't listening. I slammed my palms down hard on the table as I stood up to put an end to this.

But someone else beat me to it.

"This game looks like fun," Quentin said, his fingers tight around Mike's wrist. "How do I play?"

Mike tried to yank his hand away, but he was caught fast in Quentin's grip. There was an audible balloon-rubbing sound that promised the mother of all friction burns on Mike's forearm when this was over.

"Back off, shrimp," he said, his face turning red. But even with both arms he couldn't get Quentin to let go.

"Am I winning yet?" Quentin wondered.

One of Mike's friends, John or something, threw a sucker punch at Quentin's head. I saw it coming but couldn't say anything fast enough.

Quentin turned his head just enough to let the punch slide by and clasped John's fist under his chin. I didn't see how it was possible, but he had the other boy held just as tight as Mike, using only his *neck*.

The third one whose name I couldn't remember also tried to hit him, but Quentin swung his leg up like a contortionist and clamped the guy's fingers in the crook of his knee, squeezing hard enough to make him howl in pain. All four of them were wrapped up together like a human octopus. The way he was stretched out it should have been Quentin screaming, but he just laughed at the writhing, shrieking goons he'd trapped.

"Boop," he said, pressing Mike's nose hard with the heel of his free hand.

"The hell is going on here?" Androu bellowed as he stormed into the room.

It wasn't a teacher intervening. But it was the next best thing. The whole school, even the punks like Mike and his crew, respected Androu Glaros.

Androu was a senior, but it wasn't like he was the student council president or the captain of anything. He just had a natural charisma that made people listen to him. Admire him. Nurse a secret crush on him ever since he gave me the new student's tour on my first day of school.

Hey, it's not my fault. He's one of the few guys around who's actually taller than me.

Androu was naturally an imposing presence, his impeccable posture and steely eyes giving him the air of a poorly-disguised reporter who was always ducking in and out of phone booths when disaster struck. But Quentin looked up at him, nonchalant as can be.

"We are having the fun times together," said Quentin, regressing his English in a manner I now knew was more intentional than not. "Would you like to also?"

"Oh, drop the newcomer act, Quentin," Androu snapped. "This isn't acceptable anywhere."

Quentin's grin held but became a little more rigid. He unwound his limbs from his victims, who ran off while spewing a bunch of curses. No one paid them any mind. They didn't even qualify as a sideshow to the epic staredown going on.

"You are late to the scene," said Quentin. "But somehow still early to judgment."

"I know what I saw," said Androu. "And I heard what you did to Genie."

I nearly jumped at my name. While the whole school knew about Quentin's first day, and had spent a good week pointing fingers at me and laughing, I didn't think Androu cared enough to get upset about it.

"It doesn't matter whether you're 'adjusting,'" he said. "Pull this crap again, and we're gonna have a talk with the faculty."

With the last word firmly in hand, he exited stage left, continuing his journey onward to wherever it is heroic hot guys go during Sixth Period.

Quentin rolled his eyes and turned to Rutsuo, who'd been curled up in his chair the whole time. He whispered something in the quiet boy's ear and then punched him jovially in the arm. It was way too hard and nearly knocked him off his seat, but Rutsuo just blushed and smiled.

Yunie eyed Quentin, and then me.

"You two are a lot alike," she said.

"Don't even."

"I'm going over there," she said.

"I said *don't* even!"

Very little could prevent Yunie from doing what she wanted to. She marched right up to Quentin and tapped him on the shoulder.

"That was very good of you," she said.

Quentin shrugged. "I have always hated people like that."

"Yeah, Mike and his friends are assholes."

"No," said Quentin. "I mean the big one with curly hair."

"Huh? Androu?"

"Yes." Quentin's face darkened. "*Bai chi* like him care only for order, not justice. They'll let banditry run free right under their nose so long as no one raises a fuss."

23

Even Yunie had a hard time keeping a straight face at that. Calling our school douchebags a pack of bandits seemed like an upgrade they didn't deserve. She fought back a giggle and glanced across the room at me.

"Good thing we have one more fuss-maker around now," she said.

I gave her both middle fingers.

WAKING UP THIS EARLY ON SATURDAY WOULD HAVE SUCKED any time of the year, but today was a high-pollen-count day. My eyes burned at the beautiful weather outside, even though the window was shut tight. Lush green foliage, crisp breezes, chirping birds: Allergy apocalypse.

I sat up and rubbed my face until my room came into focus. It had been tiny for a very long time. Even though I kept it clean, it was covered in a thick layer of grade-school knickknacks that I never bothered to clear out—art projects that were mostly glue, dolls with bad haircuts, works of fiction that spanned from *Dick and Jane* to *Great Expectations*.

You could have dug a glacial core in my room and pinpointed the exact moment I stopped caring about anything but escaping it. That was where the textbooks and extra study materials and supplementary lessons took over the fossil record. That was when the comet had struck my family. My personal Chicxulub.

The news from the shower radio promised no respite from the assault on my eyes. The wildfires raging unchecked in the hills on the other side of the Bay could be sending us a welcoming embrace of particulate at any time. The governor was calling for a state of emergency due to drought conditions. California! What a paradise.

After I dressed, I made myself a pot of coffee and downed the whole thing while packing my lunch. I knew some of my classmates didn't drink it, but I could replace my blood with the stuff. It wasn't like it was going to stunt my growth at this point. Plus any magical liquid that makes you study harder was A-OK by my mom.

As lame as it sounds, this was no different from my weekday routine. I just left my house in a different direction, for the center of town instead of toward school.

It wouldn't have made a difference in the scenery. The houses in this part of the neighborhood had a chronic case of sameface. Garage-less brick boxes with lawns too small to make snow angels. And this was the "more livable" part of town. The rest of Santa Firenza by the office parks was a prairie of concrete and asphalt that grilled your optic nerves from reflected glare. Sure there were a few trees, but they didn't commit. This was a land that was hot, flat, and almost entirely without shade.

A far cry from the glorious playground of gleaming aluminum and primary colors that everyone thinks of when they imagine Silicon Valley. That image only holds up in the campuses of the two or three truly giant tech companies, the lone islands drifting in a sea of reality. The rest of the Bay Area is, unfortunately, the Bay Area.

The one thing we do have down here, more so than green spaces or the changing of the seasons, is education. We gobble up as much of it as we can, in forms both cheap and expensive, from bank-breaking Montessori preschools to flannel-wearing college kids paid under the table for tutoring. Whatever each of us can afford, really. Call it a side effect of our Asian-ness, whether genetic or absorbed through proximity.

Today I was doing my part to perpetuate the cycle of violence to the next generation. Every so often the library closes to the general public and holds an all-day event for children where older students read aloud to them. The kids get points for how long they last and how many books they sit through, with the winner at the end of the year receiving I don't remember what. A trip to Great United amusement park maybe.

The readers, on the other hand, get a big ol' badge of VOLUNTEERS and GIVES BACK TO THE COMMUNITY.

Yunie and I have been doing the Read-a-Thon ever since Ketki Pathpati graduated and unofficially passed the torch to us. Technically anyone can help, but it's sort of our thing now. I only wish we had invented it ourselves—the colleges would have given us a lot more points.

Mrs. Thompson, the town librarian, was waiting outside the building for me. "You didn't get my email?" she said. "We had to start half an hour earlier than normal."

"I don't have anything from you," I said. I'd checked my messages during breakfast.

Mrs. Thompson smacked her forehead. "I must have sent it to just Yunie."

"I'm going to kill that girl. I'm so sorry, Mrs. Thompson. The kids must be bored out of their minds . . ."

"Actually, they're doing fine," she said brightly as we walked inside. "She found a wonderful replacement."

"Replacement?" I thought Yunie had been joking before, so I assumed I'd be alone.

"Right in here," said Mrs. Thompson.

I'M GOING TO KILL THAT GIRL, I thought.

"Ready?" Quentin shouted from underneath the pile of laughing, squealing children. "One, two, three!"

He rose to his feet, kids clinging to his back, hanging off his biceps, sitting on his shoulders and using his hair as a grip. He made a slight bounce as if to throw them off, but they just shrieked with delight and hung on tighter. He was even stronger than he looked.

"*Raargh!*" he play-screamed, slowly spinning around underneath the toddler mountain until he faced me. "*Raaaaa . . .* oh . . . hello."

"He's been a treasure," Mrs. Thompson said adoringly. "I've never seen them take to anyone so quickly."

"Teacher's here, you little apes," said Quentin. "Quiet down and get to your spots. Or else I'll smash your heads open and eat your brains."

I thought someone would have an objection to that, but the kids all laughed and scrambled into neat rows at his behest. They plopped down onto musty blankets and cushions on the floor. Some were still talking and shoving each other.

"Change to stone!" Quentin shouted, wiggling his fingers like he was casting a spell. The children immediately straightened up and closed their mouths in intense concentration, sucking in their cheeks and biting their lips.

Call me a hypocrite, but I genuinely didn't want to make a scene here, of all places. I decided to just power through it. Plus the kids really did seem to like him. Kids could smell evil like dogs, right?

"How did you get them to behave like that?" I whispered as I slid onto the reader's bench. Yunie and I had never been able to rein them in so quickly.

"Mind control," he said. He sat next to me and handed me a book. "You can begin any time now, *laoshi*."

That was a little more respectful than necessary, but whatever. "*Father was eating his egg,*" I read. "*Mother was eating her egg. Gloria was sitting in a high chair and eating her egg, too. Frances was eating bread and jam.*"

"*Omnomnom slurp slurp gulp,*" said Quentin. "*Burp.*"

I was about to glare at him for going off message, but the kids giggled and rolled in their seats.

"*'What a lovely egg,' said Father.*" I read on. "*'It is just the thing to start the day off right,' said Mother. Frances . . . did not eat her egg.*"

Quentin gasped as if the fate of the world rested on that little badger eating that egg. The kids did the same.

He was like a goofy morning show puppet. I smiled in spite of myself and went on. "*Frances sang a little song to it . . .*"

We settled into that rhythm, where I did the word-for-word reading, and Quentin made sound effects, spot-on animal noises, and embellishments that kept everyone awake.

"HOW hungry was that caterpillar?" he'd shout.

"VERY!" twenty young voices would respond.

It worked. It was a lot more raucous than normal, but a lot more fun. We almost didn't want to break for lunch.

The librarians herded the kids toward the pizzas that served as the bribe to get them here in the first place. The picnic tables outside the library were reserved for the readers, to give them a moment's peace.

Quentin sat down at the far end of the table from me as I took out my lunch. He glanced at the distance between us as if to say, *See? What you wanted.*

"Your friend asked me to help her, and her alone," he said. "She didn't tell me you'd be here."

I believed him. Only because I knew how much Yunie delighted in trolling me at every possible opportunity.

I noticed he was empty-handed. "You didn't bring any food? This is an all-day thing."

"I didn't think to. I'll be fine."

Yeah, right. He could play tough all he wanted, but I saw him give a long look at the fruit I'd packed.

"Here," I said, handing it over. "Just take it."

"Thanks!" He held up the gift for a brief moment with both hands like a monk accepting alms. "Peaches are my favorite food in the universe. But this one looks different?"

He took a nibble and his eyes grew as big as plates.

"It's a peach hybrid," I said. "Crossed with a plum or apricot or something. You like it?"

"It's amazing!" he mumbled through massive bites, trying to keep the juice from dribbling far and wide.

I watched him eat, completely absorbed in his treat. It was cute. If he had a tail, it would've been wagging like a puppy's.

I decided that small talk was acceptable. "You handled Mike and his gang pretty well," I said. "Where did you learn wushu?"

"Didn't," said Quentin. "Never took a single lesson in fighting."

"Oh? What about babysitting? You're a natural at that, too?"

"I've got a lot of little cousins and nieces and nephews back home that I used to take care of. I like kids. I was happy to volunteer for this."

He shifted the peach stone into his cheek like a gumball and stared accusingly at me. "From what I could gather from your friend, however, the two of you are only doing this to gain access to a magical kingdom called Harvard."

"*Pfft.* Yale would also suffice."

He didn't appreciate the joke. In fact, he grew downright serious.

"It seems to me that you are jumping through many hoops to please some petty bureaucratic gatekeepers," he said.

I laughed. I'd never heard the admissions process described like that before.

"That's how the system works," I said. "You think I care about my grades just because? You think I enjoy working on my essays for their own sake?"

His naïveté was strange. A transfer student from the mainland shouldn't have been this clueless. Most of them were only here in the first place to improve their shot at a top-tier school.

"I'm doing this because I don't want to be poor," I said. "I don't want to stay in this town. I want to move forward in life, and that means college. The more prestigious the better."

I wadded up my paper bag and chucked it into the recycling bin. "If you're a *taizidang* like my mother thinks you are, then you wouldn't understand. You probably had everything handed to you."

He looked disappointed in my response.

"I hope you have better luck with the system than I did," he said.

Quentin had a troubled, faraway look on his face, like he was remembering his own long-ago ordeal in academia. He must have gone to one of those cram-factories where they spanked you with abacuses. Maybe that was how his English seemed to be improving at an exponential rate.

I sighed. "You want half of my sandwich? It's ham and Swiss."

"Thanks," he said. "But I'm a vegetarian."

■ ■ ■

We went way over our allotted time. At the close of the Read-a-Thon, there was a whole crowd of parents just as enthralled as the kids they'd come to pick up.

"*George didn't say a word,*" I read. "*He felt quite trembly. He knew something tremendous had taken place that morning. For a few brief moments, he had touched with the very tips of his fingers the edge of a magic world.*"

"*The End,*" said Quentin. Somehow the difficulty level of the books had risen over the course of the day. The two of us got up and took a bow at Mrs. Thompson's insistence while everyone clapped.

The room began to clear out slowly, the adults lingering to chit-chat with each other and the children running around to enjoy their last moments of freedom.

"How soon can we have you two back?" Mrs. Thompson said with a smile. "After today's performance, I'd be willing to make this an every week thing."

An adorable little cherub tugged at Quentin's trouser leg.

"Where's the pretty girl?" the kid said to him. "You should read with the pretty girl instead of *her.*"

"Beth!" Mrs. Thompson gasped. "Your mother's calling. Get along now." She shooed the towheaded child away from the awkward-bomb she'd just dropped.

Yunie and I spent so much time together it was only natural that people would refer to us as a pair. And no one thinks she's gorgeous more so than me. She's petite, slender—the natural beauty.

Which means I'm the . . . *not.*

If she's the small one then I'm the big one. If she's the friendly one who's on good terms with everyone, then I'm the rough one with a sharp tongue and bad temper. If she's the attractive one, then, well, it's pretty obvious what's left over.

"Yeah . . . so, uh . . . this was a one-time arrangement," said Quentin.

"Aw," Mrs. Thompson said. "But the two of you have such good . . ." She waved her index fingers crisscross at him and me.

"Comedic contrast?" There was way too much edge in my voice. "Yeah, we're a regular Laurel and Hardy. I'll see you next month."

I spun on my heel and went out the back of the library, avoiding the crush of parents and children in the front lobby.

7

I DIDN'T HEAR FOOTSTEPS AS I BEGAN THE WALK BACK TO MY house, or see a shadow trailing mine, but I spoke anyway.

"Are you going to tell me I was rude?" I said. "That I shouldn't have spoken to an adult like that?"

Inside I was kicking myself. I *was* rude. Mrs. Thompson didn't deserve any guff from me. She was like Mrs. Claus and Maria von Trapp put together.

"I'm not going to tell you anything," Quentin said from behind. "Except that you're going the long way."

I turned to face him. "Okay, how much of a stalker are you that you know more than one way to my—"

Standing behind Quentin, perfectly and unnaturally stock still, was a huge man.

The hugest one I'd ever seen. He had to have been at least eight feet tall.

He was wearing a suit made out of silk so black it looked like human hair. His bulging eyes didn't seem to point in the same direction, and there was something crooked about his massive arms, almost as if they had an extra joint he was hiding.

Quentin noticed my surprise and glanced behind him. In the blink of an eye he was by my side, shoving me away from the stranger.

"Ho, little one," the giant said to him. "You've gone soft to let me sneak up on you. What happened to that famous vision of yours?"

"Hunshimowang!" Quentin shouted. "So it was *you* I sensed lurking about this town! How did your sorry ass get out of Hell?"

"Oh, wouldn't you like to find out?" the man in black said with a laugh. "Let's call it 'good behavior.' What really matters is that I, Hunshimowang, the Demon King of Confusion, am finally back in the world of the living." He fanned the air toward his egg-size nostrils and breathed in appreciatively.

Oh god oh god. Yunie was right. Quentin was a gangster and this was some Tong friend of his from prison. I fumbled for my phone to call someone, anyone, but the sweat pouring out of my palms cost me crucial seconds.

"Mmm, is that the smell of human child?" said the man. "After I kill you I'm going to have to follow the trail back and have myself a celebratory meal. It's been ages since I've tasted flesh of any kind."

"You make one move toward her and I'll feed you your own liver!" Quentin snapped.

"Always such concern for mortals." One of the man's eyes, just the one, swiveled toward me, and he licked a strand of drool off his lips with a tongue as thick and knotted as a two-by-four. His nauseating appearance and bizarre threats robbed me of the ability to respond quickly. Maybe I could have gotten over my confusion, and maybe I could have powered through my fear, but not both together.

"I notice you haven't told the girl to run yet," he said to Quentin. "Could it be that you're scared to face me without her? Surely you haven't become that weak?"

Quentin bristled. "You don't know who she is! And I don't need anybody's help to beat you to death a second time!"

He snatched my phone out of my grasp before I could hit the second 1 of 911.

"I'm sorry, Genie," Quentin said, crushing it to glass and metal splinters with a single squeeze. "But we can't involve anyone else."

The man in black grinned. And grinned. And kept grinning. His smile parted his face and sliced toward his ears, exposing a mouth that went nearly all the way around his head like a crocodile's.

Quentin snarled, his flawless looks contorting into a mask of rage. I could see his canines bared, much longer than they should have been. He gave me a hard push to the side, sending me through the air. I landed on the grass as he launched himself at the giant.

The force from their collision nearly popped my eardrums. Quentin was telling the truth before. Whatever he and the man in black were doing, it wasn't wushu. They attacked each other like rabid animals, clawing and biting as much as they punched and kicked.

I scrabbled backward on my heels and hands, trying to get away from the radius of their malice. My heart hadn't beat in the last minute. I was looking at two people trying to kill each other. The sight was an infection that I couldn't allow to reach me.

I heard a sharp wooden *crack* across the street like a tree had split and fallen, and suddenly Quentin was gone from sight. He must have been thrown off into the distance.

The giant yawned in pain and rolled his shoulders before turning his attention to me. He walked over and crouched down, slamming his hands against the ground on either side of me, blotting out the sun above.

"It's strange, meeting you for the first time under these circumstances," he said, his foul, raw-meat breath descending over me.

"Let's see if I can get a taste of you without cracking my teeth."

His saliva spattered against my cheek. I shut my eyes, screamed my lungs out, and kicked him as hard as I could.

It felt like I completely whiffed, which should have been impossible given how big he was. But the stench abated. I looked up to see an expression of complete shock on the man's face as he back-pedaled away, a foot-size chunk missing from his flank. Black goo dripped from the wound onto the sidewalk.

He and I must have shared the same bewilderment at that moment. *Look buddy, I'm as confused as you.*

"Don't touch her!" Quentin roared, taking advantage of his opponent's distraction to make his flying reentry. He dropped from the sky onto the man's platform-like shoulders and the two of them spiraled away into the street.

Despite their injuries, the fight wasn't over by a long shot. The giant managed to get Quentin at both arms' length and smashed him into the ground repeatedly like he was trying to open a coconut. I thought Quentin was dead from the first impact alone, but his legs snaked out and wrapped around the man's neck. He pulled the man's head into his abdomen and began strangling him with his whole body, all while being bounced against the pavement so hard I could see an outline of his shoulders on the ground where they blew away the dust.

The giant kept ramming Quentin into the earth, but his strength started to flag, especially since he was still bleeding heavily from his side. His knees buckled and he fell to the ground like a chain-sawed oak. Quentin maintained the chokehold until the man in black stopped moving, and then some.

Finally he scooted out from under his opponent. Then, without hesitating, Quentin clambered onto the man's back and grasped his chin and the top of his head.

"Wait, no!" I shrieked once I realized what he was going to do.

With a twist of his arms, he broke the man's neck.

．　．　．

Quentin looked up at me, breathing heavily.

"Are you okay?" he said.

"No," I whispered. "No no *no*."

"Genie, please," he said, reaching toward me. "I can explain—"

I wasn't listening. I was too busy staring at what was happening to the giant's corpse.

It was dissolving. Into the air. The dead man's body suddenly resembled a still-wet painting dunked into a tank of water, the colors and hues that made up his existence bleeding away into a surrounding liquid.

His body silently burst into a great splash of ink. Spouting swirls of his former mass chased each other in all directions like calligraphy strokes until they faded into invisibility.

Nothing remained of him. Even his blood, including the half that had been splattered all over Quentin, was gone.

Quentin waved his hand over where the body had been. "I, uh, can explain that, too."

No he couldn't.

I didn't waste another word. I just ran, and ran, and ran.

8

I ARRIVED HOME IN A DAZE, TRYING TO FIGURE OUT WHAT to do.

Mom wasn't going to be any help in this situation. I passed her in the kitchen without a word. That little slight would probably snowball into a future screaming match between us at a time yet to be determined.

I climbed the stairs to my room. Once I got there I sank into my desk chair, my head in my hands.

Taptaptap.

I could have tried to call the cops again on our landline, but what was I going to say? That my classmate fought with some kind of runaway circus experiment, *killed* him in cold blood, and that I helped? That I had no evidence any of this happened, because the victim self-liquefied somehow?

Taptaptaptap.

The bigger problem was Quentin. I didn't know if I was next on his list of people to murder, or if he had a list, or if he was trying to initiate me into his gang. I mean, if he'd just stop knocking on my window for one second, I could think straight—

Taptaptaptaptaptap.

I fell out of my chair. Quentin hovered outside the glass with a

39

pleading look on his face. The worst part was that in my current state I couldn't even remember if we had a tree there for him to stand on.

He slid the window up and clambered inside. *"Silence,"* he said.

"Mom!" I shouted, crawling backward on my butt. "Help!"

"This isn't what you think! Let me explain." He got down on his knees to look at me on my level. It was more terrifying than reassuring.

"Mom!" She was just downstairs. Why wasn't she answering?

Quentin began kowtowing in submission, knocking his skull against the floor. It only added to the commotion in my room.

"Please," he said. "I'm not a danger to you, and I can prove it. Give me a chance. If you don't like what you hear, you can do as you will. You can even take my head if you wish."

"I don't want your head!" I said. "What is it with you and murder? You killed a man back there!"

"That wasn't a human being. That was a demon. A *yaoguai.* If the two of us weren't there to stop him, he could have slain this entire town!"

I was going to tell him that was stupid, but remembering the man in black's hulking form and monstrous visage made me seize up in post-traumatic fear. He could very well have been right on that point.

Quentin sensed my hesitation. "And I didn't kill him in the sense you're thinking of. I only sent his evil spirit back to *Diyu,* where it belonged."

"Diyu? You mean Chinese Hell? That doesn't make any sense!"

"It will once I tell you my real name!"

So he'd been operating under a false identity this whole time to boot? Wonderful. I couldn't wait to see how much deeper he was going to dig this hole.

"Go ahead," I said, groping behind me for any heavy, hard object I could find to clock him with. "Tell me your real name and we'll see if that makes it all better."

Quentin took a deep breath.

"My true name," he said, " . . . is SUN WUKONG."

A cold wind passed through the open window, rustling my loose papers like tumbleweed.

"I have no idea who that is," I said.

. . .

Quentin was still trying to cement his "look at me being serious" face. It took him a few seconds to realize I wasn't flipping out over whoever he was.

"*The* Sun Wukong," he said, scooping the air with his fingers. "Sun Wukong the Monkey King."

"I said, I don't know who that is."

His jaw dropped. Thankfully his teeth were still normal-size.

"You're Chinese and you don't know me?" he sputtered. "That's like an American child not knowing Batman!"

"You're Chinese Batman?"

"No! I'm stronger than Batman, and more important, like—like. *Tian na*, how do you not know who I am!?"

I didn't know why he expected me to recognize him. He couldn't have been a big-time actor or singer from overseas. I never followed mainland pop culture, but a lot of the other people at school did; word would have gotten around if we had a celebrity in our midst.

Plus that was a weird stage name. Monkey King? Was that what passed for sexy among the kids these days?

Quentin let go of his temples and began unbuttoning his shirt.

"What are you doing, you perv?" I shut my eyes and bicycle-kicked the empty air between us.

When he didn't say anything I glanced between my fingers to make sure he was keeping his distance, and *oh my god* I shouldn't have looked.

I wasn't sure how anyone could get muscles like that without eating meat. He had the kind of body-fat percentage where he could have done it for a living.

"See?" he said, brandishing his tanned, professional-grade torso at me.

"Like that means anything!" I said, throwing my elbow back over my face. "So you've got abs. Big deal. I've got abs."

"Not my body, you dolt! My tail! Look at my tail!"

With great reluctance, *great reluctance I tell you*, I ran my gaze down his stomach. The last two cans of his rippling eight-pack were partly covered by a fur belt running around his waist. I thought it was just a weird fashion statement until it twitched and pulled away from his body, unraveling behind him.

Quentin, it would appear, had a monkey's tail.

■ ■ ■

I gaped at the fuzzy appendage dancing in the air.

"Go see a doctor," I said, holding out my finger between us. "Have your weird mutation somewhere other than my room. Somewhere other than my life."

Quentin seemed moderately disappointed with the way this conversation had gone, like he had the right to expect better than a raging dumpster fire. He got up and put his shirt back on but neglected to button it up.

"You've been through a lot today," he said, using the same tone as a country gentleman who recognized that his lady's corset was too tight. "I suppose I shouldn't have sprung this on you all at once."

"Get out."

He smiled gravely at me. "Take some time to think. We can pick up where we left off tomorrow."

I found a stapler and threw it at his head.

"Pei-Yi!" shouted my mother. She clomped up the stairs. "Where are you?"

Dear god, finally. I didn't care how bad it would look to have an undressed boy with an abnormal pelvis in my room. I just needed not to be alone with him anymore.

My mom threw open the door to my room without knocking, her usual practice. She stood over me, judgment raining down from her birdlike frame. Her square, ageless face was a carved-in-marble ode to perpetual indignation.

"What are you doing on the floor?" she said to me. "You look like a city bum."

I glanced back to see Quentin gone.

He must have jumped out the window. I popped up and stepped to the sill, leaning into the air to look around. Not a trace of him anywhere.

"What's the matter?" my mother snapped. "You sick?"

I pulled my body back inside and bumped my head against the window hard enough to make the glass rattle, but the pain was inconsequential right now. "No, I . . . I just needed some fresh air."

She squinted at me. "Are you pregnant?"

"*What!?* No! Why would you even think that?"

"Well then if you're not sick and you're not pregnant then ANSWER ME WHEN I CALL YOUR NAME!"

Mom began screaming at me since she'd apparently been telling me to come down for the last five minutes and not ignoring me asking her to come up. This kind of crazy I could take. I almost sobbed with relief, her banshee song as soothing and familiar as a lullaby.

9

I HAD A WHOLE SLEEPLESS NIGHT TO FIGURE OUT WHAT TO DO.
I couldn't talk to anyone without proof. But at the same time, I needed to protect myself. I would have to take matters into my own hands.

I was ready when Quentin approached me after school the following day.

"Genie," he said. "Please. Let me expl—*moomph!*"

"Stay away," I said, mashing the bulb of garlic into his face as hard as I could. I didn't have any crosses or holy water at home. I had to work with what was available.

Quentin slowly picked the cloves out of my hand before popping them into his mouth.

"That's white vampires," he said, chewing and swallowing the raw garlic like a bite of fruit. "If I was a *jiangshi* you should have brought a mirror."

I wrinkled my nose. "You're going to stink now."

"What, like a Chinese?" He pursed his lips and blew a kiss at me.

Instead of being pungent, his breath was sweet with plum blossoms and coconut. Like his body magically refused to be anything but intensely appealing to me, even on a molecular level.

I tried to swat away his scent before it made me drunk.

"Stop it with the tricks," I said. "I don't know why you and your giant buddy needed to stage a magic show in front of me yesterday, but your act sucks and I never want to see it again."

"Genie, I am telling you, that was a yaoguai."

"Yaoguai don't exist!" I was firm in my conviction, but that hadn't stopped me from looking them up online last night. "They're folk demons, and I bet no one has believed in them for hundreds of years!"

"That's because no one has seen them in hundreds of years. They're not supposed to be walking the earth anymore. Especially not *that* one." Quentin looked chagrined, as if his disposing of another living being were akin to being caught double-dipping at a party.

"I came to this town because I felt a demonic presence stirring in the human world for the first time in centuries," he said. "I knew modern people weren't equipped to deal with yaoguai, so I hunted down the source myself. I didn't expect to find *you* of all people here as well."

There were many things I was not okay with in this explanation. The way he said *human world* like he had been hanging out somewhere else. His loose use of time signifiers. The way he still talked to me as if he knew me intimately.

"So you're only stalking me as an afterthought," I said.

"Yes. I mean no!" Quentin closed his eyes and pinched invisible threads from the air, trying to figure out which ones were connected to the end he wanted.

"Look," he said. "What happened yesterday was impossible."

I was about to violently agree with him in a general sense, but he kept going down a weird path.

"The Demon King of Confusion should not have been up and about," he said, seemingly more concerned about *which* monster we'd seen, like a fanatic who believed in Bigfoot but was shocked by the Abominable Snowman. "I personally rid the mortal world of him a very long time ago. The fact that he showed up alive means that there's something funny going on here, and until we find out what it is, the two of us have to stick together."

"*You* are the funny thing that's going on," I said. "You and your . . . demons, yaoguai, whatevers. I don't want any part of it. In fact, if you ever trot this horse crap out in front of me or my family again I will make it my life's mission to see you regret it."

I turned away and walked halfway down the block before stopping.

"That wasn't a cue to follow me!" I screamed at Quentin, who was trailing only a few steps behind.

"Well, tough. We're heading to the same place, regardless of whether or not you believe me about yaoguai."

"Oh you have got to be kidding me."

"Yup." He grimaced like a man condemned. "Tonight is when I promised your mother we'd have dinner."

■ ■ ■

One of the reasons I didn't have friends over for meals very often was because of how seriously my mother took the occasions. Eating at our table was like some kind of blood pact for her. If the get-together went well, you were *in*. For life. You could sleep in our cupboard if you wanted to and she wouldn't bat an eye.

If you did not hold up your end of the bargain in terms of being good company, or if, god forbid, you *flaked*, then you were cast into the lake of fire for eternity. Quentin, who must have picked up on Mom's peculiarities in this regard, was right in that we were locked in for one last dance. The Apocalypse couldn't have prevented this dinner.

I could smell food even before entering our driveway—a deep, savory promise of good things to come. My mother must have been at the stove all day. For someone who gives me such a hard time about my weight, you'd think she wouldn't cook so goddamn much.

"Remember," Quentin said as we went inside. "This was your idea."

His parents were already there, sitting at our table. "Pei-Yi," Mom said. "Come and meet the Suns."

Mr. Sun was tall and reedy with wiry hair, most of the resemblance to his son coming from the mischief in his eyes that his banker's suit failed to tamp down. Mrs. Sun was the picture-perfect image of a young *taitai*. She was a straight-backed beauty resplendent in tasteful fashions, the kind of woman Yunie would turn out to be in a decade or two if she dropped the punk-rock look in favor of European couture.

"Eugenia," said Mr. Sun. "We've heard so much about you."

To their credit, they didn't flinch at my height. Quentin must have warned them that I was a *kaiju*.

"We're forever in your debt," Mrs. Sun said. "Our boy can be so careless. It was a miracle you were there to save him."

Having seen what I'd seen, I seriously doubted Quentin was in any sort of trouble when I'd first run into him at the park. I wondered if his parents were in on his weirdness. They had to have been aware of his extra limb at least.

"You two are just in time," Mom said. "Dinner's ready."

The table was decked out with more food than my entire volleyball team could have eaten in two sittings. Red wine chicken. Steamed white radish with *conpoy*. *Misua* swimming in broth.

"Wait a sec," I said, tilting my head at Quentin. "He's a vegetarian."

"It's all mock meat," my mother said proudly. "It took me a few tries."

Of course she would kill herself over an attempt to impress. The Suns were everything she wanted our family to be. Rich. Refined. Whole. Quentin's parents even had British accents when they spoke in English, like they'd learned in an overseas grammar school or owned property in London. If there was one group of people my mother idolized more than the wealthy, it was the British.

"This looks absolutely delicious," said Mr. Sun.

He was not wrong. Mom was a spectacular cook. But I already knew that very little of this dinner was going to be touched. Mr. and Mrs. Sun were too genteel to finish the massive quantities that had been prepared, and if I had anything more than a "ladylike" serving in front of guests, my mother would have lasered me to death with her eyes.

Quentin alone had license to eat. He began chowing down with delight, scarfing the mouthwatering grub as fast as he could.

Over the course of the conversation I learned that his dad worked in international shipping and logistics, coming up with new route calculations based on incidents like storms and pirates. And his mom ran her family's charitable foundation, which spread basic technology like flashlights and cell phones to undeveloped areas around the world.

Now both of those jobs were actually really, really cool. I'd gone into this dinner eager to harness my class resentment and write Quentin's parents off as useless gentry, but both of them were genuinely interesting. I could have coasted on them talking shop all night.

Instead of going on about themselves, though, his parents kept turning the conversation back to me. I hated talking about myself to other people. It was why I had such a difficult time with my application essays.

But what really caused my gears to lock up was the way, whether through prior research or on-the-fly Holmesian deduction, they continually managed to avoid bringing up my dad. Not even a question about where I got my height from, since it clearly wasn't maternal. Their collective inquiries left a father-shaped hole in the conversation, like snow falling around a hot spot. I would have felt less on edge and defensive had they not been going out of their way to be tactful.

"So Genie," said Mr. Sun. "What are your plans for the future? What do you want to do with your life?"

"I don't know yet," I said, with what I hoped was a demure smile. "I guess one of the reasons why I study as much as I do is to keep my options open."

There. A better answer than screaming *I just wanna be somebody!* like a chorus member from a forties musical.

"Do you have a favorite subject?" Mrs. Sun asked. "Sometimes that can be a big life hint."

Jeez, let it go already. "I like them all about the same."

"Really?" said Quentin. "Rutsuo told me you once got pretty excited about computer science."

"That was an elective that didn't count for credit," I said. "And I only jumped on the table to celebrate because my code for a binomial heap finally compiled after fifteen tries."

"Passion's passion," said Mr. Sun. "Ever thought about being a programmer?"

I had. And no.

We lived in the epicenter of the tech industry. I'd paid enough attention to the news to know that all the good programming careers were concentrated right here in the Bay Area, not even fifty miles from where we were sitting. I wasn't going to work my ass off only to end up right back where I started in life, within shouting distance of my mother.

I racked my brain for a more polite way of saying that I felt zero obligations to the place where I grew up. Santa Firenza wasn't a quaint bucolic suburb where happy families were grown from the rich earth. Santa Firenza was a blacktopped hellscape of bubble tea shops and strip-mall nail salons, where feral children worshipped professional video-game streamers. The major cultural contribution of this part of the country was recording yourself dancing alongside your car while it rolled forward with no one driving it.

"Well, I'm sure that once you decide what you want, you'll get it," Mrs. Sun said in response to my silence. "You have so much determination for someone so young."

"She's always been like that, even as a baby," said Mom. "She used to watch the educational shows with the puppets and get the questions for the kids right. But then there would be a joke for the adults that she couldn't have possibly understood, and she'd get so *angry* that she'd missed something. That she didn't get a 'perfect score.' She was such an angry little girl."

"It's not like you got the *Masterpiece Theatre* references inside *Sesame Street* either," I snapped. "I remember asking you to explain them, and you never could."

The only person to smell the change in the wind was Quentin, who glanced up at me while chewing a mouthful of noodles.

"There was also the time you cracked that boy's rib for pushing Yunie into a tree," Mom said. "The only reason you didn't get suspended was because he was so embarrassed he wouldn't admit the two of you got into a fight. You should have seen yourself standing up to the principal, saying over and over that you *did* hit him and you *deserved* your proper punishment. The teachers didn't know what to make of it."

"Ah, so she has a sense of justice," Mrs. Sun said admiringly. "If only our boy were the same way. He was such a little delinquent when he was young."

"Now look at him," said Mr. Sun. "He pretends to be good but it's all an act. He thinks he has us fooled."

I did look at Quentin, who was busy slurping the last of his soup. He didn't seem at all bothered by his parents' put-downs. In fact, he gave me a little wink over the edge of his bowl.

"I also hear that you're the star of the volleyball team," Mrs. Sun said to me. "Their secret weapon. Have you always been stronger than other people?"

"Yes," said my mother. "She's always been big."

Oh boy. The gates were open.

"Oh, I meant in an athletic sense," said Mrs. Sun. "Skill-wise. Good *gongfu* at sports."

The distinction was lost on my mother. All those words meant the same thing to her. Masculine. Ungirly. Wrong.

"She's always towered over the other girls," Mom said. "The boys, too. I don't know where she got it from."

"Oh yeah, like my height is under my control," I responded. "There was a button you press to grow taller and I got greedy and hit it too many times."

"Maybe it was my fault," she added, turning martyr mode on. "Maybe I fed you too much."

"Okay, the implications of that are horrifying." I raised my voice like I'd done a thousand times before. "You're going to say you should have done the reverse and starved me into a proper size?"

"Why are you getting so upset?" Mom said. "I'm just saying life would be easier for you if you weren't . . ." She waved her hand.

"Thank you!" I practically shouted. Okay, I was flat-out shouting. "I well and truly did not know that before you said it this very moment!"

"I think Genie's beautiful," Quentin said.

The air went out of the room before I could use it to finish exploding. Everyone turned to look at him.

"I think Genie is beautiful," he repeated. "Glorious. Perfection incarnate. Sometimes all I can think about is getting my hands on her."

. . .

"*Quentin!*" shouted Mrs. Sun. "You awful, horrible boy!"

Mr. Sun smacked Quentin in the back of the head so hard his nose hit the bottom of his empty bowl. "Apologize to Genie and her mother right now!" he demanded.

"No," said Quentin. "I meant it."

His parents each grabbed an ear of his and did their best to twist it off.

"Ow! Okay! Sorry! I meant that I like her! Not in the bad sense! I mean I want to become her friend! I used the wrong words!"

"Sure you did, you terrible brat," Mrs. Sun hissed. She turned to us, crimson. "I am so, so sorry."

My mother was stunned. Torn. While that display by Quentin was definitely improper by her delicate standards, she also had wedding bells chiming in her ears. The sum of all her fears had just been lifted from her shoulders.

"Oh, it's all right," she murmured. "Boys."

I could only stare. At everything and everyone. This was a car accident, and now burning clowns were spilling out of the wreckage.

"Who's Sun Wukong?" I blurted out.

I had absolutely no idea why I said that. But *that* was anything but *this*, and therefore preferable.

"Sun Wukong," I said again, talking as fast as I could. "Quentin mentioned him earlier at school and I didn't get the reference. Everyone knows I hate it when I don't get a reference. Who is he?"

My mother frowned at me and my one-wheeled segue. "You want to know? Now?"

"Yes," I insisted. "Let me go to the bathroom first, and then when I come back I want to hear the whole story."

My outburst was bizarre enough to kill the momentum of the other competing outbursts. While everyone was still confused, I stood up and marched out of the room.

■ ■ ■

I hadn't even filled my hands with water to splash my face when Quentin appeared behind me in the mirror.

"Gah!" The running faucet masked my strangled scream. "What is wrong with you? This is a bathroom!"

"You left the door open," he said.

I could have sworn I heard his voice twice, the second time coming faintly from the dining table. It must have been my mind deciding to peace out of this dinner, because if not, Quentin was casually violating time and space again.

"*Who's Sun Wukong?*" he repeated in a mocking tone. "Smooth."

"You don't get to criticize after what you did!"

"I was trying to . . . how does it go? 'Have your back?' "

"Your English is perfectly fine," I snapped. "Or at least good enough to make your point without being lewd."

"I'll work on it. Anyway, the situation is turning out perfectly."

That was in contention for the dumbest comment made tonight. "In what *possible* way?"

Quentin reached behind me and turned the faucet off. "You'll hear the story of Sun Wukong from someone else, so you'll know I'm not making it up."

Before I could question his logic, he slipped out the bathroom door.

■ ■ ■

When I came back to the table, Mr. Sun was unwrapping a gift. It was a huge urn of horridly expensive *baijiu*, big enough to toast the entire Communist Party. It probably cost more than our car.

"The legend of Sun Wukong can get pretty long," he said. "We should hear it over a drink." He winked at me, willing to run with the diversion I'd handed him. Bless his heart.

Mr. Sun poured us all a bit, even me and Quentin after getting a nod from my mom. I took a single tiny sip and felt it etch a trail down my throat like battery acid.

"All right, so Sun Wukong," I said. "What gives?"

"I tried telling you these stories at bedtime when you were young," said Mom. "You never wanted to listen back then. But here goes . . ."

10

SO TO PARAPHRASE MY MOTHER'S STORY . . .

A long time ago, in a galaxy far, far away, there was China. Ancient China.

Here, in a long-lost place called the Mountain of Flowers and Fruit, all the wisdom and splendor of the sun and the moon poured into a stone until—crack!—out popped a monkey.

When the monkey was born, a light shone from his eyes all the way up to the Heavens. But the Jade Emperor who ruled the universe from atop the celestial pantheon ignored the obvious sign of greatness, and the monkey was left to fend for himself on the lowly Earth.

It didn't go so badly. The monkey was much stronger and braver than the other apes of the mountain, and he became their king. But he wanted more than to feast and frolic with his subjects until he died. He wanted to keep the party going forever. He wanted to become immortal.

He left the Mountain of Flowers and Fruit and searched the lands of the humans until he found the Patriarch Subodai, an enlightened master who had transcended death. Subodai was so impressed with the monkey's grasp of the Way (the Way being one of the many things that Asian culture refuses to explain but vigorously condemns you for not understanding) that he taught him the Seventy-Two Earthly Transformations, spells of kickass power that allowed one to change shape, split into multiple bodies, and leap across the world in a single somersault.

Subodai also gave his star pupil a name. Sun Wukong. It meant Monkey Aware of Emptiness.

Once he achieved these new abilities, Sun Wukong wasted no time in getting kicked out of school for bad behavior. He left Subodai and went home to his mountain, only to find that it had been taken over by a monster known as Hunshimowang, the Demon King of Confusion—

I nearly dropped my glass when my mother got to that part. I whipped around to look at Quentin. He just tilted his head and motioned me to keep listening.

The Demon King of Confusion had been terrorizing the other monkeys in their king's absence. Sun Wukong defeated the hulking monster with his bare hands, but he was dissatisfied that demons should think of him and his kin as easy targets.

What he really needed was a weapon. A big, threatening, FU kind of weapon that would show everyone the Monkey King meant business.

He paid a visit to Ao Guang, the Dragon King of the Eastern Sea. Ao Guang was willing to let Sun Wukong take a gift from the armory, but what the Monkey King really wanted was the great pillar from the old dragon's underwater palace.

This beam of black iron, end-capped with bands of gold, had once been used to measure the depths of the celestial ocean and anchor the Milky Way. It glowed with heavenly light as Sun Wukong approached, much as his own eyes had when he was born. Ao Guang thought the pillar couldn't be lifted and was unusable as a weapon, but at Sun Wukong's command it shrank until it became the perfect staff. That was how the Monkey King got his famous weapon, the Ruyi Jingu Bang. The As-You-Will Cudgel.

The first thing that Sun Wukong did with the Ruyi Jingu Bang was to march straight into Hell. It turned out that Subodai hadn't actually taught him immortality, and that his name was still in the big book of people scheduled to die. Sun Wukong threatened the horse-faced and ox-headed guardians of Hell with the Ruyi Jingu Bang, and out of fear they let him strike his name from the ledger.

So that was how Sun Wukong became immortal. Not through mastery of enlightenment. But by carrying the biggest, baddest stick in the valley.

The Jade Emperor didn't take kindly to monkeys subverting the laws of life and death willy-nilly. On the advice of his officials, he invited Sun Wukong into the celestial pantheon in order to keep an eye on him. And hopefully a tighter leash.

The Monkey King was pleased to be in Heaven at first, rubbing elbows with noble gods and exalted spirits. But he was repeatedly humiliated with low-status assignments in the Thunder Palace, like grooming the divine horses in the stables, and kept from attending the great Peach Banquets. Sun Wukong got fed up with his treatment and went AWOL from Heaven after trashing the joint like a rock star on a bender.

The Jade Emperor sent a whole army of martial gods to Earth after him. And Sun Wukong beat the tar out of them all. The only one who could take him down was the Jade Emperor's nephew, Erlang Shen, Master of Rain and Floods.

The duel between the two powerhouses shattered the scales. Erlang Shen chased Sun Wukong down through many forms as they fought and shapeshifted all over the Earth. The rain god finally got the upper hand, but even then securing the win took the combined effort of Erlang Shen's six sworn brothers, a pack of divine hunting hounds, and an assist from Lao Tze, the founder of Daoism.

The celestial pantheon dragged Sun Wukong to Heaven and tried to execute the Monkey King by throwing him in the furnace used to create elixirs of longevity. It didn't work. The dunking only gave Sun Wukong even more strength, plus the ability to see through any deception. Sure, his now-golden eyes also developed a lame Kryptonite-like weakness to smoke, but that didn't matter. He broke free from the furnace, grabbed his Ruyi Jingu Bang, and began laying waste to the heart of Heaven.

All the gods hid from Sun Wukong's rage. He was actually close to seizing the Dragon Throne of Heaven for himself, deposing the Jade Emperor to become ruler of the cosmos, but at the last minute a ringer, an outsider, was called in to help.

Buddha. Sakyamuni Buddha. *The* Buddha.

Even Sun Wukong would spare a moment to listen to the Venerable One. Buddha proposed a challenge—if the Monkey King could leap out of the Buddha's outstretched hand, then he was free to overthrow Heaven. If not, he'd have to chill the eff out.

Sun Wukong took the bet and sprang forth from the Buddha's palm. He leaped to what looked like the End of the Universe where five pillars marked the boundary. But those were nothing more than the fingers of Buddha's hand. Buddha grabbed Sun Wukong, slammed him to the Earth, and dropped an entire mountain on top of him. The prison was sealed with the binding chant *Om Mani Padme Om*.

Sun Wukong, who had struck fear into Heaven itself, was trapped. . . .

11

AFTER DESCRIBING THE MONKEY KING'S IMPRISONMENT BY the Buddha, my mother leaned back into her chair.

"I don't get it," I said. "Is Sun Wukong a good guy or a bad guy?"

"He's an anti-hero," said Quentin. "He doesn't play by anyone else's rules."

"He sounds like a tool," I said.

Quentin gave me an angry squint. My mother didn't know that particular phrase, so she didn't yell at me for being vulgar.

"He redeems himself later by becoming the enemy of evil spirits and protecting the innocent," she said. "That was only the first part, and the story is really long. I mean *really* long. A lot of English translations leave out whole chunks."

"So then what happens after he gets stuck under the rock?" I said. "How does he get out?"

"I'm not telling anymore," she said, making a face. "You have this book somewhere in your room. Go read it."

"How long ago did all of this happen?" I said without thinking.

It's not often that I'm the one making the verbal blunder in a conversation with my mom.

"Genie," she said, looking at me like there was something growing out of my forehead. "It's a folk tale."

"But it's one that's very important to our culture," said Mrs. Sun. "If you live in Asia, there's probably some TV show or movie playing any given time of day that either tells the story of Sun Wukong or is based off it in some form."

"It was always Quentin's favorite," said Mr. Sun. "I'm sure our last name helped. It would be like an American child being named Bruce Wayne. You bet he'd love Batman."

Quentin gave me a look. *See? They know Batman, but you don't know Sun Wukong?*

He yawned and stretched his arms, sending thick bundles of trapezius muscle skyward. "Genie, before I forget, can I take a look at your bio notes from today? I mean, I did mine, but I zoned out in class and missed a section."

"They're in my room." I waited, and watched.

He glanced toward our parents. Mr. and Mrs. Sun gave him threatening glares, but my mother shooed at him with her hands.

"It's okay," she said. "You two can go upstairs."

■　■　■

I led Quentin to my room. It felt way too intimate, doing that. His footsteps were heavier than mine up the stairs, a mismatched thump-thump that I could feel in my bones.

He closed the door behind us, shutting out our parents' laughter, and looked into my eyes. I don't know what he thought of mine, but his felt like they went all the way down to the bottom of the universe.

Dark brown, I thought to myself. Not shining gold. Just a very dark, drinkable chocolate.

"Yo, so those notes?" he said.

Ugh. The baijiu must have gotten to my head.

"Very funny. So that's the story of Sun Wukong? You're that guy?"

"More or less."

"Well, I don't believe it," I said. "Any of it. You're crazy and you've latched on to a story because you happen to bear a resemblance to the main character."

Quentin gave me a dry stare like he was puzzling something out. What to say next.

"Your mom's a great cook," he offered. "I can tell how much she cares about you. I'm jealous."

"Huh?" I was thrown off guard. "Why? Your parents are awesome. They're smart and they're rich and they're relevant!"

"They're not real," said Quentin.

"Wait, what?"

"Didn't you hear your mom's story? I came from a rock. I don't have a mother or father. Never did."

"Then who are those people downstairs? Actors? Con artists?" I was starting to get indignant at being lied to again.

"They're no one."

He reached into his hair and yanked a couple of strands out of his scalp. He tossed them into the air where they poofed into a white cloud like road flares.

"Goddamnit Quentin!" I waved my arms and prayed the smoke detector wouldn't go off.

"Look."

Once I finished coughing and fanning the vapors away, there, in my room, were Mr. and Mrs. Sun. They beamed at me as if we were meeting for the first time.

Downstairs, Mr. and Mrs. Sun and my mother laughed raucously at some joke, probably at my expense.

"Wha—what *the hell IS THIS?*" I half-yelled through clenched teeth.

"Transformation," he said. "I can turn my hairs into anything. I needed parents to bring over for dinner, so I made a couple."

He gestured at his mother and father and they disappeared with another puff of smoke.

■　■　■

This was . . . this was . . .

"Hoo," I said without knowing what I meant. "Hoooo."

I sank to the floor and began to furiously rub my eyes. Partly out of disbelief and partly because the faint white dust the Suns left behind was making my tear ducts itch. When my fingers wouldn't cut it, I began scraping my face against my knees.

"Sorry," said Quentin. "But I did promise to explain everything."

I took a couple of Lamaze breaths.

"What," I said as steadily as I could, *"do you want with me?"*

Quentin scanned my room before walking up to my shelves and plucking a book out. He took a seat on the floor in front of me, cross-legged. He could pull a full lotus with ease.

"Do you believe in reincarnation?" he asked.

"No," I said flatly. That was the truth. Compared to some of the girls at school, I was about as spiritual as a Chicken McNugget.

"Well, it doesn't matter," he said. "It's something that just happens. All creatures live their lives, and then they die. If they've built up enough merit through good deeds and conduct, they're reborn in another time and place, in more fortunate circumstances. If they've done evil then they'll suffer in their next life. They might even end up in Hell."

"What about you?"

"I'm immortal," he said. "I freed myself of the Wheel of Rebirth because I liked being who I was. I didn't want to have to struggle through who knows how many different versions of myself just to gain standing in the cosmos. I accumulated enough power within my first life to become unstuck in time, like a god."

I could hear his words but couldn't bring myself to allow them any quarter inside my head. How could any of this be true?

"I've seen people come and go over the ages," said Quentin. "And rarely, very rarely, I see them come back. I knew you in your past life, Genie."

He handed me the book. It was the one my mother was talking about. *Journey to the West*, it said, the big black letters covered by a thick layer of dust. If I had ever read it, it had been ages ago.

"Here," he said. "This is the second half of my story."

I took it with an air of suspicion even though it had come from my own shelf. "Why is this important?" I said.

"Because you're in it."

I swallowed my jitters and attempted to pry open the book, but the glossy, child-friendly covers were stuck from years of compression. The sudden crack as they pulled apart rattled me like a gunshot, and I slammed it back shut before any of its contents could leap off the page and melt my face.

I frisbeed the book to the side. The stiff cardboard backing allowed it to sail through the air and land on my bed.

"No," I said. "Nope. All the nope. I'm done. I'm done with tonight."

"Genie, you can't ignore what you've seen with your own eyes."

Sure I could. "If your parents are fake, then your demon could be fake, and I bet your tail is fake, too," I said. "Animatronic or something."

Quentin looked personally insulted by that last accusation. "You *saw* my tail. It's as real as can be."

"Prove it."

He scowled and untucked his shirt, wiggling on his butt to free up some room around the waist of his pants. I caught a brief glimpse of the muscled crease running down his hip before the smooth skin was blocked by fur. The thick brown rope came loose and stood up behind him.

"There," he said. "See?"

Not good enough. I held my hand out and wagged my fingers, demanding. He looked hesitant but brought it forward anyway, gingerly laying it across my palm.

This was beyond weird.

His tail was alive and warm. It wasn't too gross. In fact, it was strangely comforting to hold. An elongated Tribble. I rubbed the soft, silky fur into crisscross patterns with my thumb.

I must have squeezed too hard at some point because Quentin made a strangled noise from deep in his larynx. At the exact same time his mother entered my room.

"Quentin," Mrs. Sun said. "It's getting late. We should be lea—"

We scrambled to our knees. Quentin wrapped up his tail again, quick as a whip. But the lingering image was still him with part of his shirt undone, and me pulling my hands away from his lap. Not the most innocent diorama.

"QUENTIN! *NI ZAI GAN MA?!?*" Mrs. Sun shouted.

"What has he done now?" roared Mr. Sun from downstairs. "You're dead once we get home, you hear? Dead!"

"Whatever it is, it's okay," Mom called out.

Quentin's mother stormed in and hauled him downstairs like a milk crate while apologizing to me all the while. She was stronger than her delicate build suggested.

The Suns gave their hurried, mortified thanks to my mother and left, yelling at Quentin all the way. Only the slamming of their car doors silenced the smacks, slaps, and scoldings heaped upon his head. It made me smile to hear such familiar sounds, to the extent that it wasn't until after they were long gone that I remembered Mr. and Mrs. Sun weren't real.

Quentin's trick must have endowed them with some kind of independent AI, to better serve the illusion. If there was a flaw in their behavior, it was that they hadn't blamed me for the compromising situation and accused me of corrupting their precious little emperor, like actual Asian parents would have. Or Western ones, for that matter.

∎ ∎ ∎

My mother stood next to me in the doorway, looking out into the street.

"I haven't had that much fun in a while," she said quietly. "I was so worried they'd look down on us. But they're lovely people. Some folks are just good in everything. Luck, character, everything."

She looked so relieved that I thought she might cry. I was struck by the fact that she hadn't talked to anyone besides me in a meaningful way for a very long time. She had no family in California, and her adult connections had been mostly Dad's friends.

I put my arm around her shoulders, and we went back inside.

12

"SO HAVE YOU TAPPED THAT SWEET ASS YET OR WHAT?" YUNIE asked me the next day in the school library.

"Oh come on! We could be talking about literally anything else. Didn't you win your *concours*? Doesn't that make you the best violinist in the state now?"

"It was only a qualification round," my best friend said as she doodled over my oxidation-reduction equations. "But yes, I crushed everyone so hard even the woodwinds went home crying. And as my victory prize, I want a full report on whether you're getting any."

"First of all, there is nothing between us. *Nothing.* Second of all, do you know how ridiculous Quentin and I would look as a couple? It'd be like Boris and Natasha chasing moose and squirrel."

A massive grin spread across Yunie's face. "So he's bite-size. Doesn't mean he's not tasty. Rachel made a run at him. So did Charlotte, Nita, Hyejeong, both Vivians, and Other Eugenia. Greg and Philip, just to touch all the bases. Even Maxine, though that was probably an attempt to screw with you. That girl is a psycho, by the way."

"And you?"

I wasn't asking her seriously, but she totally took it seriously, putting her hands up. "Sister Code," she said. "I don't have dibs. You should have seen the way the two of you looked at each other the first day you met. I could swear you were both glowing like a pair of heat lamps."

Yunie got up to go to her next class. I was the only one of us who was supposed to be in the library for study hall; she was just habitually late for everything.

"By the way," she whispered into my ear. "I was talking about Androu at first. You're the one who brought up Quentin."

I pushed the lead in on my mechanical pencil so it was less pointy. Then I hurled it at her as she retreated through the door, laughing all the way down the hall.

As much as I loved her, I was glad to be alone. I needed the peace and quiet to continue my study-bender.

Tearing through my homework put me at ease like nothing else. It got me ready—or at least readier—to think about what I'd seen recently. By crushing my assignments, it felt like I was putting deposits into the First National Bank of Sanity. Confronting Quentin's craziness was going to require one gigantic withdrawal.

I pushed aside my chem papers once I was finished and pulled out a book from my bag without stopping for a break. It was the one from my room. The continued legend of Sun Wukong.

It felt safer to read it here, in the light of day, away from my home. Just to be sure, though, I moved to the table in the back alcove, near the last row of shelves. The library may have already been empty, but I still wanted to isolate myself like a responsible bomb technician.

I was able to get the book all the way open this time. There had to be something in it that would make my life fall back into place . . .

. . .

The Tang Emperor of China, as emperors are wont to do, looked around him one day and decided that everything sucked. His lands were filled with greed, hedonism, and sin. What he needed, he reasoned, was for an ambassador to travel to the West and retrieve the holy scriptures that would bring his people back to right-mindedness.

The man he found for the task was a pure-hearted monk named Xuanzang. Xuanzang was a learned and earnest man, beautiful and dignified of appearance, talented in both preaching and the arts. He was eager for the monumental task. Unfortunately he was also weak and hopelessly naïve.

Xuanzang needed a bodyguard. Someone who could handle the vicious bandits and flesh-eating demons that lay in wait on his journey. Someone who needed a difficult quest to atone for defying Heaven.

It wasn't a difficult search. The gods had the perfect candidate lying under a rock.

The Bodhisattva Guanyin made the introductions. She freed Sun Wukong from his mountain prison and ordered him to serve Xuanzang on his trip. The Monkey King refused, forcing Guanyin to place a magic band around his head that would tighten whenever Xuanzang said the words *Om Mani Padme Om*. If Sun Wukong didn't want to suffer excruciating pain, he would have to obey his new master to the letter.

Because it wasn't enough to be accompanied by the beast who scared the crap out of every god in Heaven, Xuanzang was assigned a few more traveling companions. The gluttonous pig-man Zhu Baijie. Sha Wujing, the repentant sand demon. And the Dragon Prince of the West Sea, who took the form of a horse for Xuanzang to ride. The five adventurers, thusly gathered, set off on their—

"Holy ballsacks!" I yelped. I dropped the book like I'd been bitten.

"How far did you get?" Quentin said.

He was leaning against the end of the nearest shelf, as casually as if he'd been there the whole time, waiting for this moment.

I ignored that he'd snuck up on me again, just this once. There was a bigger issue at play.

In the book was an illustration of the group done up in bold lines and bright colors. There was Sun Wukong at the front, dressed in a beggar's cassock, holding his Ruyi Jingu Bang in one hand and the reins of the Dragon Horse in the other. A scary-looking pig-faced man and a wide-eyed demon monk followed, carrying the luggage. And perched on top of the horse was . . . me.

The artist had tried to give Xuanzang delicate, beatific features and ended up with a rather girly face. By whatever coincidence, the drawing of Sun Wukong's old master could have been a rough caricature of sixteen-year-old Eugenia Lo from Santa Firenza, California.

■ ■ ■

"That's who you think I am?" I said to Quentin.

"That's who I know you are," he answered. "My dearest friend. My boon companion. You've reincarnated into such a different

73

form, but I'd recognize you anywhere. Your spiritual energies are unmistakable."

"Are you sure? If you're from a long time ago, maybe your memory's a little fuzzy."

"The realms beyond Earth exist on a different time scale," Quentin said. "Only one day among the gods passes for every human year. To me, you haven't been gone long. Months, not centuries."

"This is just . . . I don't know." I took a moment to assemble my words. "You can't walk up to me and expect me to believe right away that I'm the reincarnation of some legendary monk from a folk tale."

"Wait, what?" Quentin squinted at me in confusion.

"I said you can't expect me to go, 'okay, I'm Xuanzang,' just because you tell me so."

Quentin's mouth opened slowly like the dawning of the sun. His face went from confusion to understanding to horror and then finally to laughter.

"*mmmmphhhhghAHAHAHAHA!*" he roared. He nearly toppled over, trying to hold his sides in. "HAHAHAHA!"

"What the hell is so funny?"

"You," Quentin said through his giggles. "You're not Xuanzang. Xuanzang was meek and mild. A friend to all living things. You think that sounds like you?"

It did not. But then again I wasn't the one trying to make a case here.

"Xuanzang was delicate like a chrysanthemum." Quentin was getting a kick out of this. "*You* are so tough you snapped the battle-axe of the Mighty Miracle God like a twig. Xuanzang cried over squashing a mosquito. *You*, on the other hand, have killed more demons than the Catholic Church."

I was starting to get annoyed. "Okay, then who the hell am I supposed to be?" If he thought I was the pig, then this whole deal was off.

"You're my weapon," he said. "You're the Ruyi Jingu Bang."

I punched Quentin as hard as I could in the face.

13

I WILL ADMIT TO BEING AN ANGRY PERSON. CERTAIN THINGS I get upset about. Certain things are worth getting upset about.

But never in my life had I felt as furious as when Quentin called me the Ruyi Jingu Bang.

The volcanic surge of bile rising in my throat collided with a skull-cleaving headache going in the opposite direction. I was bisected by the pain of my anger. Blinded by it. My vision went.

The best way I could describe it was like my life's work had been doused with gasoline and set on fire. I didn't have a life's work yet, but that's how I felt.

"Genie," Quentin said from a million miles away. I could barely hear him.

"Genie," he said again, tapping me on my wrists. "Let up a bit."

He was coming in garbled, on helium. The lights gradually turned back on.

I had bodily thrown him onto the table. My hands were wrapped around his neck. I was strangling him so hard that I could feel my fingernails beginning to bend.

"Please stop doing that," he coughed. "You're one of the few things in the universe that can hurt me."

"Good." I squeezed harder.

I couldn't explain why I was behaving this way. Calling me the Ruyi Jingu Bang should have meant nothing. It should have been a non sequitur, like walking up to a stranger and saying, "Hello my good fellow, did you know you are a 1976 Volkswagen Beetle?" I was overreacting in a way that lent credence to a zero-percent scenario.

Quentin managed to loosen my grip on his throat enough for his face to return to its normal color. "Can we talk about this?"

He slid off the table and got back to his feet. I only let him go because I didn't want to give my impending speech to a corpse. He wanted to talk? Sure. I was going to go Supreme Court on his ass and hammer home an articulate, lengthy, and logical rebuttal to his claim of me being the reincarnated Ruyi Jingu Bang.

"I hate you," I said instead.

I poked my finger into his chest as hard as my joints would take.

"I hate you," I said again. That was all I was capable of, it seemed.

He slowly put his hands up and began backing away. "Why?"

I wouldn't let him get away so easily. "Because," I said. "I don't need a reason. People don't need a reason to hate things. And I am *people*."

I kept jabbing him over and over as he retreated, trying to drive home the message like a spear point.

"I am a human person," I snarled. "I am not the Ruyi Jingu Bang. I am not a freaking stick, do you hear me?"

"Um, Genie," Quentin said, looking down awkwardly.

I hadn't noticed that I'd been continuously poking Quentin in the chest from where I stood, even though he'd now backed all the way across the room.

My arm had stretched out to follow him. My arm was twenty feet long.

. . .

There's a moment when you realize that you've never been truly scared before. It wasn't when I'd met Quentin, and it wasn't when I'd been introduced to the Demon King of Confusion. Those times were apparently just practice.

"AAAAAAAAA!" I screamed. "WHAT DID YOU DO TO ME?!"

"I didn't do anything!" Quentin screamed back. "Put it back before someone sees us!"

I was too terrified to move my elongated arm for fear that it would shatter under its own ridiculous proportions. "It's too big!" I said, waving at it with my other hand. "Make it smaller! Make it go down!"

"I can't! You have to do it yourself!"

"I don't know how!"

By now footsteps were coming down the hall toward us. I could hear teachers' voices. If they sounded upset now, they hadn't seen anything yet.

Quentin realized I wasn't going to do much other than hyperventilate. He ran over and grabbed me by the waist. Then he rolled up the window behind us and jumped straight out of it. I could feel my arm accommodating his trajectory by bending in places where I didn't have joints.

I saw nothing but cloudless blue sky as Quentin hauled me up the sheer brick side of the building. It didn't fully register that he was dangling me two stories off the ground as he scampered up the school walls. I had, believe it or not, even worse things to worry about.

The ascent was over in a split second. Quentin reached the roof and unceremoniously dumped me onto the asphalt. We were safely out of sight for the moment.

I squeezed my eyes shut so I wouldn't have to look at my arm trailing away like the streamer on a bike handle.

"I can't be stuck like this!" I wailed. Visions of having to gnaw it off like a jackal in a trap flooded my brain.

Quentin knelt before me and put his hands on my trembling shoulders.

"You're not going to be stuck," he said, his voice low and reassuring in my ears. "You are the most powerful thing on Earth short of a god. You can do absolutely anything. So believe me when I say you can certainly change your arm back to normal."

He held me firmly, the way you'd brace someone trying to pop a dislocated joint back into place. "Just relax and breathe," he said. "It'll happen as you will it."

I took his advice and focused on calming down. Focused on nothing. Focused on him.

I couldn't really feel my arm retracting. And I certainly didn't want to look at it happening. I just . . . remembered how I was supposed to be. I kept quiet, kept at it for what must have been a good ten minutes, until I could feel both of my hands firmly on Quentin's broad back.

"There you go," he said.

I opened my eyes. My arm was normal again. I was aware that we were sort of hugging.

I buried my face in his chest and blew my nose on his shirt. "I'm a human being," I muttered.

"I never said you weren't."

I raised my head. Quentin looked at me with a smile that was free of any smugness. He didn't even mind my snot on his lapel.

"Reincarnation as a human is practically the highest goal any spirit can achieve," he said. "It's considered the next best thing to enlightenment. If anything, I'm proud of you for what you've accomplished."

I'm not sure why, but the rage that had been so palpable before seemed to float away at his words. Like I could have been angry with him forever had he said anything different.

I was mildly relieved. It was a hell of a one-eighty on my part, but right now I didn't think I wanted to hate Quentin until the end of time.

"Genie Lo, you are unquestionably, undeniably human," he said. "You just . . . have a whole bunch of other stuff going on as well."

"Tell me about it."

14

"WAS THERE EVER ANYTHING WEIRD ABOUT ME AS A BABY?"
I asked my mother at the breakfast table.

The soles of her cheap slippers scraped against the linoleum of our kitchen as she put a steaming bowl of porridge in front of me. Only then did she consider my question.

I was all ready for her to say, *What, besides the fact that you weren't a boy? Besides your size?* There was always a certain amount of thorny jungle I had to pass through in order to arrive at a straight answer.

But today was different, for reasons unknown. She shuffled around the table and sat down even though she hadn't prepared any food for herself.

"No," she said.

She pulled her legs up into one side of her chair, the kind of thing that young girls did. I'd yelled at her in the past for it, afraid she'd risk hurting her back.

"You were perfect," she said matter-of-factly. "We'd had such a hard time having you that I didn't know what to expect when you were born. But the doctors told me you were the healthiest child they'd ever seen. They showed me the chart of your vitals. It was the first perfect score you ever earned."

"There was nothing out of the ordinary at all? What about coincidences? Full moons? Solar eclipses?"

She shrugged. "There could have been an earthquake and I wouldn't have noticed. I only had eyes for you at the time. After the labor I was just so . . ."

"Exhausted?"

She smiled at me. "Grateful."

I looked away. It was best not to think of all the times in the past few years that she and I had proved incapable of a simple conversation like this—where one person spoke and the other listened. It would have been a difficult thing to tally the waste.

"Come on," she said, nudging the bowl toward me. "It'll get cold."

. . .

It was a good thing the route to Johnson Square, where I first met Quentin, was so ingrained into my memory. I nearly sleepwalked there, not having gotten any rest last night. I had been too busy reading *that* book.

It was a bizarre story, Sun Wukong's journey to the west. As I got further and further into it, the only lesson I could take away was that everyone in Ancient China was a gigantic asshole. Xuanzang's traveling circus was constantly beset by yaoguai who wanted to eat him.

In addition to monk flesh apparently being the filet mignon of human beings, nearly every demon thought it would gain Xuanzang's spiritual powers by consuming his body. They were so desperate for this leapfrog in personal growth that even when their schemes were caught by Sun Wukong, they'd resort to open combat instead of running away.

The Monkey King managed to outsmart or defeat most of these adversaries, but what came afterward was rather galling. If the demon at hand wasn't killed and sent back to Hell immediately, it was often revealed to be an animal spirit from Heaven who had gained magic powers and used them to terrorize people on Earth. After Sun Wukong's victory, a Chinese god would show up and be like, "Sorry, bruh, that ogre was actually my goldfish. I'll take him back now."

And then that would be that. No mention of all the little farmer children said goldfish-ogre had eaten before being defeated by Sun Wukong. No retribution for any damages. Not even a slap on the wrist for trying to chow down on Xuanzang.

Compared to the "regular" evil demons that Sun Wukong killed, the fallen animal spirits suffered the same punishment as a rich kid on a DUI charge. None. Having a god in your corner was the ultimate get-out-of-jail-free card. Nor did anyone ever call out the various divinities on their negligence. You would think that after the fifteenth time their pet ferret or whatever escaped and caused a whole mess of human suffering they'd accept some responsibility.

And Xuanzang himself. Woof. Dude did nothing but cry all the time. Like he'd literally cry at having to cross a stream. I kept hoping he might be able to pull out some badass exorcisms, being a holy man and all, but spirits seemed to be able to tie him up at will. And he kept using the band-tightening spell on Sun Wukong in ways that were exceptionally cruel. If Sun Wukong attacked a demon disguised as a human, Xuanzang would torture him instead of, you know, trusting the member of the party who has all-seeing golden eyes of Detect Evil.

Maybe I was missing a deeper message. I could ask the guy who supposedly had been there.

■　■　■

I found him in the square in a secluded little spot masked from the surrounding huddle of commercial properties by a row of shrubs. The smell of cut grass and gasoline still lingered from a dawn mowing. It was still early enough that I'd arrived before the old-timers who used the space to practice tai chi.

Quentin, however, had me beat. I caught him checking me out as I approached, his eyes roaming up and down my legs.

I was surprised he'd even bother. "Stop that, you skeez," I said.

He blinked and shook his head. "I'm not used to the way people dress these days."

"This is yoga gear," I said. "And it's perfectly acceptable for outdoors."

"I'll take your word for it."

Quentin might not have been kidding about lacking a sartorial sense. He was still in his school uniform, the only concession being his sleeves rolled up for our "training" session.

Guh. His forearms were like bridge cables. My spine twitched at the sight of them flexing in the breeze.

I blinked and shook my head. "You said you were going to teach me how to manage my limbs so they don't go wonky again."

"It would be a crime if that were the only thing I taught you," he said. "You have abilities that most people couldn't begin to imagine. Sit."

I lowered myself down, cringing at the dew on the grass. "I don't want superpowers," I said. "I want control."

"You'll get it, trust me." Quentin took the spot in front of me, the guru before his disciple. I had to admit it wasn't a bad look on him.

"Do you remember when we first laid eyes on each other?" he asked.

I nodded. "You were just about where we are now."

"And *you* were all the way over *there*," he said, pointing over my shoulder far down the park. "You were more than three hundred feet away from me, Genie. You threw your bag farther than an entire American football field."

"That's impossible. I could see you right nearby, plain as day. And there's no way I'm that strong."

"Your sight works beyond human limits," he countered. "Your strength is enough to challenge the gods. And, as you've clearly seen, your true reach knows no bounds."

I looked at my hands and clenched my fingers. That time when I blocked Maxine into next week. Had I accidentally stretched myself without anyone noticing?

"Close your eyes," Quentin said. He shut his own and rolled his shoulders a few times.

"Are we meditating?"

"Yes. Close your eyes."

"Is this the single step that the journey of a thousand miles begins with?"

"*Close your eyes.*"

I did as he told. And then I cheated. I kept one lid open a crack so I could watch Quentin breathe deeply in and out. Watch him settle his mind. I was only doing it so I could crib his technique.

But damn it if he wasn't beautiful right then.

This was a completely different side to him. I mean, Monkey King or not, most times he acted like the worst kind of bro. But here, I was looking at a master of the universe. He radiated calm and tranquility, becoming so still that the Earth seemed to rotate behind him like a time-lapse video.

"Truth and spells, revealing all," Quentin chanted, his voice echoing off I'm not sure what.

"They come from vapor, essence, and spirit.

Stored in the body, never to be revealed

A radiant moon shining on a tower of quicksilver

The snake and the tortoise are twisted together

Then life will bear golden lotuses

Turn the Five Elements upside down

And you may become a Buddha or an Immortal."

■ ■ ■

Quentin opened his eyes and smiled serenely at me.

"What the hell was that?" I asked.

"Huh?"

"That made no sense. You just zoned out and spouted a bunch of gibberish. What do snakes and turtles have to do with anything?"

He made an expression like I'd hocked a loogie on the *Mona Lisa*. "Did you not experience the Way of Heaven and Earth ensorcelling you just now?"

I scratched my head. " . . . Sort of? I think I felt something. The air around us got a little warm and fuzzy."

Quentin buried his face in his palms. "Those were the first words of true wisdom Master Subodai ever expounded to me, and all you have to say is that they make you warm and fuzzy, *sort of*?"

"Look," I said. "I don't learn well with vague instructions. Can't you lay out all the steps from start to finish, so I can see what I'm supposed to be working toward?"

"Lay out!? These aren't differential equations we're talking about!"

"Well if they were, I'd pick them up faster! That's how I do things! I arrange my curriculum into manageable chunks and then I destroy them piece by piece. You told me I had abilities far beyond those of mortal men. Now, what are they?"

Quentin jumped to his feet and paced around, swearing up and down. I sat there unyielding as he glanced at me, which set him off into a fresh round of expletives each time. He couldn't *believe* me right now.

Finally he threw in the towel and plopped back down, abandoning a proper cross-legged position for a don't-give-a-crap-anymore slouch. The guru image had popped like a soap bubble.

"You have the ability to keep up with me as I perform my Seventy-Two Earthly Transformations," he said, staring up at the sky.

"That sounds lame."

"Says the girl who doesn't want superpowers. Don't you realize what that implies? You can split into as many copies as I can. Each one as strong as the original, and capable of acting independently."

I thought about that for a bit. Having extra mes to go around would be useful in the extreme. One copy for school, one doing extra plyos in the gym, one racking up more volunteer work in the city. Assuming that recombining let you keep all of the good you did.

"Okay, okay." I was starting to get vaguely excited. "What else?"

"You can grow as tall as a mountain. You can be like a Pillar of Heaven. As I change, you change."

Yeah, less interested in that one. The view from my current altitude already wasn't kind. Stomping around downtown like a '50s sci-fi monster was far from an appealing prospect.

"What else?" I asked. "Something good."

"You weigh a whole lot," Quentin said.

"Excuse me?"

"You're supernaturally heavy," he explained. "It's what makes you such a fearsome weapon."

In his defense, he wasn't trying to needle me. In his mind he was rattling off a fact. Obliviously.

"Your true weight is seventeen thousand five hundred American pounds," he said, not noticing that my cheeks were turning red hot. "You can hit like a ten-ton truck because you weigh nearly ten tons. It's demonic, how much you weigh—*OOF!*"

I tested out the truth of his claims. On his chest. With my fist.

Just checking to see which one of us was denser.

15

"YOU NEED TO CONTROL YOUR TEMPER," QUENTIN SAID. HE winced as he rubbed the spot where I'd clocked him.

We'd hit a roadblock in my training earlier than expected. Meditating wasn't optional for this project, it was required. And I absolutely sucked at it.

The two of us had spent the entire morning in the park trying to get me to relax and focus. I had no idea why I wasn't catching on. Discipline, self-governance—those were supposed to be my strong points. Failure got me more and more annoyed until finally Quentin insisted we take a break at a nearby bubble tea shop.

I *hate* bubble tea. So now I was cranky about two things.

I kicked a rhythm into the steel wire table we were sitting at. The feet of my chair scraped the sidewalk concrete inch by inch. It sounded as if I was abusing a metal songbird that chirped in pain with each impact.

"Get in line," I muttered. "People have been calling me a hothead my whole life."

Quentin slurped his pearls. "I didn't mean it like there's something wrong with you, I mean you only need to reach the point of tranquility where you can absorb my teachings. After that I don't care what you do with your emotions."

"That doesn't make sense. I thought achieving gongfu requires maintaining a calm, virtuous character?"

"It does, but only while you're still learning. Think of it this way. At one point you had no volleyball skills at all, right? So you were probably open-minded and humble toward your coaches and seniors. Otherwise it would have been impossible for them to teach you. But now that you have a certain amount of gongfu, there's nothing preventing you from getting pissed off at an inferior opponent and running up the score in a display of poor sportsmanship. You're not going to suddenly lose the ability to play volleyball just from that."

"But I'm not actually that good yet. Jenny and Coach Daniels keep telling me that I'm relying too much on my height and not enough on technique."

"And yet you don't seem to be upset about that," Quentin said. "You have room to develop. Just like you have room to develop as the Ruyi Jingu Bang."

He swirled the ice around his cup. "If you want another example, most of the enemies I fought on my journeys were animals or demons who trained their bodies and minds in the exact same way that holy men did. They cultivated their conduct and performed austerities. If they can do it, you can do it."

"Evil beings can also become stronger by being disciplined and working out? They're not barred from the wizard club? Chinese magic is jacked up."

"The Way is there for anyone to grasp," Quentin clarified. "If an evil person trains harder than you, they will be stronger than you, and that's that. Spiritual power isn't just or merciful. It's *fair*. That's what makes it so dangerous."

Hearing him say that actually cheered me up a bit. If learning special abilities required a kind heart or a pure soul, I'd be screwed. This system was like climbing the corporate ladder. Or getting tenure.

"I mean, look at me," Quentin said. "I achieved spiritual mastery and immortality. And *then* I made war on Heaven."

"Which basically makes you Chinese Satan."

He drained the last of his drink. "Two sides to every story."

I watched him for a bit. There was nothing about Quentin that betrayed any sort of legendary origin. In the short time I'd known him, his behavior had smoothed out into that of a regular teenager. Albeit the cockiest one I'd ever seen.

"If you're not from these parts, how did you acclimate so fast? Clothes aside, you picked up modern culture pretty fast. You even ordered the small boba without anyone telling you."

"I only need to pick up the tiniest part of something in order to understand the whole," he said. "I simply watched your classmates until I absorbed how to act. Same thing with our schoolwork. It's all pretty easy stuff; I don't know why you spend so much time on academics."

Overpowered bastard. "Is that how you got into my school? You dazzled them with your standardized test scores?"

"No, I just used a harmless spell. All the adults think I go there, but there's no Quentin Sun Wukong in the records."

"So then where do you go after school? When you're not with me?"

He grinned. "I interact with other people. I explore the area. Not everything is about *you*, you know."

"Oh, bite me. You were the one who was all, '*waaah you were my dearest companion, waaah.'* If the Ruyi Jingu Bang was so important to you, how did you lose it in the first place?"

He pretended not to hear me. I never let anyone pull that move on me if I could help it.

"It would have had to die in order to reincarnate," I said. "So what gives? Did a demon break it? Did you try to crack a magic Walnut of Invincibility?"

"I don't want to talk about it!"

I was going to tell him that given he'd insinuated himself into my life on the basis that we were once a demon-slaying tag-team in the distant past, I had a goddamn right to know how the partnership broke up to begin with. But my words exploded into a coughing fit.

I turned around in my chair.

"Excuse me," I said to the man smoking a cigarette at the table behind me. "You're not supposed to do that so close to the shop entrance."

He said nothing. And blew another deliberate plume of smoke into the air.

The metal of Quentin's chair screeched as he stood up. "The lady is asking you to put it out."

Ugh. There wasn't a need to escalate like that. But the man got up, too.

Friggin' dudes and their pissing matches. Fine. I got to my feet as well. *Ace card played, buddy, tallest person right here.*

The man turned around and looked up at me. I nearly jumped backward onto the table.

"Something on my face?" he said with a grin.

He looked to be a middle-aged construction worker, judging by

THE EPIC CRUSH OF GENIE LO

how much blue denim he was wearing. There were tons of guys like him in the surrounding towns, tearing down and putting up houses at the behest of newly minted tech families.

But that was only from the neck down. His face was a Halloween mask, a really good one. Black-ringed eyes, a long muzzle, and facial hair that went all the way round like a mane. A big cat straight out of the savannah.

The bipedal lion exhaled more smoke, and suddenly his face fritzed back to a human's. His entire appearance was a broken TV unable to decide which channel to land on.

Quentin obviously wasn't seeing what I was seeing or else he would have immediately flipped out into rage mode. But he could tell something was wrong.

"Genie," he said, his voice full of suspicion. "Does that guy look normal to you?"

"Probably not," the man answered for me. "Given that I'm a demon."

16

"SO," THE MAN SAID TO QUENTIN IN A CATCHY-UPPY TONE. "How have you been?"

I wanted to smack myself for being so stupid. Quentin and I had spent the entire morning cozying up over which member of the X-Men I wanted to be, when what really mattered was the two of us had killed a monster only three days ago. I should have pressed him about whether the Demon King of Confusion was some kind of onetime incident or not.

Because the answer was most decidedly *not*.

From the look of it, though, Quentin was as much on his back foot as I was. He frowned like he was at a party where he didn't know anyone.

"Something wrong with your eyes?" the man asked. He pointed to himself. "Huangshijing? No?"

The name finally rang a bell for Quentin. "Tawny Lion," he said. "I didn't recognize you without your trash brothers around."

"That's rude of you. Especially since they're right here."

Six more men filed around the corner to back up the first. They had human faces, but they were dressed identically to the smoker, down to the last stitch. The costume department somewhere had gotten lazy.

They made a semicircle around us, hemming us in against the building. I'd always thought the shots of the criminal gang pouring in to attack the hero in martial arts films were silly. But in real life, from the hero's perspective, being outnumbered? It was actually rather terrifying.

Quentin tensed up for another knock-down, drag-out fight. His muscles snapped into readiness hard enough to be audible. My stomach lurched at the prospect of more bloodshed and violence on the level of our previous encounter.

"Oh come on," said the leader of the gang. "Have you no decorum?"

A young couple pushed their baby stroller right by us. The street was filling up. Whatever we did outside was sure to be noticed.

The man tossed his cigarette butt aside and motioned to the inside of the tea shop. "Let's talk. The girl, too. I wouldn't want to be rude to your guest."

Possibly as a show of good faith, he went in first. His brothers began to trickle in after him.

"When you said you sensed a demonic presence in my town, did that include *these guys*?" I hissed at Quentin under my breath.

"No! These assholes are supposed to be dead!"

"According to you, a lot of assholes are supposed to be dead, and yet we keep running into them!"

Only one member of the gang remained outside. This was our last chance to book it. None of this demon business, dead or undead, had anything to do with me.

As if he knew what I was thinking, Quentin tapped the back of his hand against the back of mine.

"Stay," he said.

"Because it'll be safer?"

"Because I might need your help if this gets ugly."

It was jarring how gravely serious he sounded. I could tell he really was at a disadvantage here. But somehow *I* leveled the playing field?

The last man held the door and whipped his hand in a circle, telling us to get a move on.

Following Quentin inside was less of a struggle than I expected. My better instincts were failing me.

■ ■ ■

The shop was empty except for one person. "Something else I can get you folks?" asked the piercing-riddled college student who was working the register.

"*Sleep,*" Quentin told her.

I knew Quentin had mentioned it, but I never would have believed he could bewitch people with a single command. Not without seeing it here. The girl's eyes fluttered shut and she sank to the floor, disappearing behind the ice cream counter.

"*Conceal,*" said Tawny Lion, gesturing at the front of the store.

The glass windows and doors turned into a hazy amber. People moved about outside, but they were vague shadows. Not one tried to enter the shop.

The six men, the ones who'd arrived later, settled in around the biggest table toward the back. The way they watched like attentive students made it clear their leader was to do all the talking. Tawny Lion remained in the three-way standoff with Quentin and me.

"First things first," he said. "You should apologize for calling my brothers trash. One of the very first things we do with our newfound freedom from Hell is to seek you out so we can make amends, and you insult us? You haven't changed a bit."

"A pack of thieves like you *is* trash, and you should still be rotting in the pits!" Quentin snapped. "Did the Jade Emperor install a revolving door since last I checked?"

"Hmmm, I suppose I could tell you how we got out," Tawny Lion said, tapping at his bottom lip with his finger. "But then again, the first rule you learn in prison is 'no snitching.'"

Quentin looked ready to break the cease-fire and give him stitches anyway. I motioned for him to calm down. The situation was still negotiable.

"He's only miffed because we pulled off the same feat he did, breaking free from Diyu," Tawny Lion said to me, tilting his head at Quentin. "He's also the one who sent us there in the first place, which makes it even more embarrassing for him."

If the demon was going to speak to me like a familiar fellow conspirator, then maybe I could play along.

"Well," I said nervously. "You sure showed his dumb ass."

Quentin stared at me like I'd laid an egg right there on the floor, but Tawny Lion beamed.

"It's really impressive that you've managed to escape Hell itself," I said, remembering how satisfied the Demon King of Confusion was with himself for the feat. "The mystery makes it all the more mysterious. I mean intriguing. Fascinating."

The demon pointed both hands at me, palms up. "See?" he said to Quentin happily. "Someone gets it. This is a feat that only you accomplished before. In many ways this makes me your equal."

"Yes!" I said before Quentin could protest at being compared to the demon. "But now that you two have made your peace, I'm sure you'll be on your way. Back to your home, wherever it is. Probably some place far from here."

LEAVE this mortal realm! I wanted to shout. I would have sounded like a reality-show medium dealing with an invisible poltergeist in the rafters.

The very solid, tangible demon in front of me laughed.

"On the contrary," Tawny Lion said. "Confronting the specters of our past is only the first item on our to-do list. If we want to make any headway toward the rest of our goals, we're going to have to settle in right here on Earth."

Dammit. So much for the "weaseling out of small talk" strategy.

"What, uh, are your goals exactly?" I felt like a Super Bowl sideline reporter forced to interview her least-favorite team. "Because maybe you don't have to be here to accomplish them."

"Eh, you know, a bit of this, a bit of that," Tawny Lion said to me. "Mostly they revolve around becoming stronger. You may not believe it, but for a yaoguai, self-improvement is the greatest goal imaginable. To have ultimate control over your body and mind is to move closer to enlightenment. All demons want to attain the Way."

He winked at me. "And the wealth of powers that come along with it aren't so bad."

I yielded to his explanation with a slight nod-shrug. Quentin had only just been saying that a lot of his enemies trained themselves to level up as much as possible. And from what I'd read so far in the book of Sun Wukong's journeys, the bulk of the demons attacked the party because they wanted Xuanzang's flesh as a spiritual steroid boost.

"Earth is like one big nature retreat, ideal for discovering your inner strength," Tawny Lion said. "Slim chance of getting anything done in Hell with so many distractions. Now that we're alive again, my brothers and I are going to continue our personal development and pick up where we left off back in the days of Xuanzang."

Quentin did not like the name of his old master crossing the demon's lips. "You mean you're going to cheat your way to power by eating any human being that suits your needs!"

"Whaaat? Nooo," Tawny Lion said, teasing. "That's not our plan at all. Maybe that's what the other yaoguai are going to do once they get here, but not us."

■ ■ ■

The bottom had just dropped out of this conversation. Not that it was a sparkler to begin with, but now it was fully pear-shaped.

"*Other* yaoguai?" Quentin said slowly. "*What* other yaoguai? You mean the Demon King of Confusion?"

"That weakling? I guess he's around somewhere, too, but I meant the other yaoguai coming to Earth," Tawny Lion said, as if it were common knowledge. "I'm talking about your old friends from your little road trip."

The look on Quentin's face told me I could start freaking out any time now. I was way ahead of him. The sinking feeling that had been in my stomach since the beginning of this encounter was now the size of an iceberg.

"Oh dear," Tawny Lion said. "I thought you knew. Because there are some real bad characters in that bunch. I wouldn't want to be a human caught in their path. Can you say *bloodbath*?" The demon chuckled at the thought.

"Quentin?" I said, unsure of what to do.

He didn't answer. He was lost in thought, moving his lips silently over a number of possible futures, all of which appeared to be very, very bad.

"See, that's what I'm talking about," Tawny Lion said to me. "Check out the monkey's face! That's how you can tell I'm an okay guy. Most other demons take shortcuts on the path to power by eating anyone they think will give them the slightest leg up.

"I've got a different strategy," he went on, obviously fishing for the follow-up question.

I fell for the bait. "Which is?"

Tawny Lion smiled. "*My* shortcut is that I'm going to steal the Ruyi Jingu Bang."

■ ■ ■

He made a quick signal, and the six men in the back pounced on Quentin.

"*Barrier,*" Tawny Lion said, spreading his hands out.

The shop snapped in two. Not physically. But I could feel a wall slam down, separating me and Tawny Lion from Quentin and the others. I could still see them, but the sound of their scuffle was muted by half.

"*Bind,*" Tawny Lion added.

My legs and arms jerked together, and I stood up so straight it hurt, a fresh recruit ordered to attention by a drill sergeant. I couldn't move.

"Genie!" Quentin shouted. The other men weren't brawling with him; they were focusing solely on containment. Three of them were grappling him physically, and the others were standing back to channel a similar binding spell, muttering the command over and over to hold him down. Between all six, they were succeeding.

The invisible constriction around me tightened, and I cried out in pain.

"Don't be so dramatic," Tawny Lion said. "I know who you are, and that's not even close to causing you harm."

He leaned in, secretive. "I didn't track down the monkey's aura, you know. I followed yours. The original feud between me and Sun Wukong started because I tried to take the Ruyi Jingu Bang once before. Why do you think he hates me beyond all proportion?"

I strained against the bindings, hoping to find more room to breathe. "I thought—it was because—you're a pompous piece of trash."

Tawny Lion laughed. "Well get used to it. This pompous piece of trash is going to be your new master now. Whoever controls the staff of the Monkey King controls enough power to take Heaven by force. Once I figure out a way to strip that pesky human form from you, I'll have the gods kissing my feet."

The demon's attention turned away from me to someone I'd forgotten about the whole time.

"You know what?" Tawny Lion said. He walked over to the counter and bent down behind it. "Given how much I have to cele-brate, I think I'm going to cheat on my diet a little."

He reappeared holding the girl who had been working the regis-ter. She dangled limply in his arms. Her bandana had fallen off and tresses of wavy red hair covered her face.

I expended the last of my air. "But you said you didn't eat—"

"I lied. I'm a lion, you fool. Did you think I was a frugivore?"

Tawny Lion cha-cha'ed with the girl's unconscious body out to the center of the room, swaying his hips to the radio song trickling through the barrier's muting effect. He dipped her toward me and her head lolled back, her pupils dilated and unseeing.

"Ah," he said, "This one has a surprising amount of spiritual energy. I'd bet she has excellent gongfu. A talented artist, maybe? She looks like the type."

He sniffed her exposed neck. "Great bouquet, too. Xuanzang-esque, you might say."

I thrashed back and forth, desperately hoping that I could wriggle free by sheer oscillating force.

Come on! I shrieked inwardly at myself, wishing more than anything that I hadn't treated Quentin's catalog of powers so lightly before. *Strength, magic, kick in! PLEASE!*

The demon grasped the girl by her shoulders. He opened his jaws wide, exposing a pink, ridged throat and rows of pointed carnivore's teeth. His mouth kept impossibly distending, reaching an angle so obtuse he resembled a lamprey more than a cat. He drew her head into his bite radius, working his lips forward as if he meant to crunch the top half of her skull off in one try, like a child impatient to get at the bubblegum in the center of a lollipop.

■ ■ ■

"*Da ge!*" shouted one of the men in the back. "The monkey!"

Quentin had slipped free. He hurled himself at the invisible wall between us. A loud *whump* rattled the store as his shoulder made contact—a hockey player crashing into the Plexiglas.

The barrier held, but Tawny Lion stumbled. I felt the constriction around me loosen.

The demon quickly drew his mouth away, unraveling his jaws from the girl's head with the insulted air of someone whose phone had rung during dinner. He threw her into the nearest chair, where she sprawled out, unharmed for the moment. I squeezed my elbows outward with all my might and felt the magic give.

"One thing, you idiots!" he yelled, his words distorted and jowly from speaking before his mouth shrunk fully back to normal. "I ask for just one thing!"

He took a stance and raised his hands like he was going to recast the spell that was keeping Quentin away. But right now he had something bigger than the Monkey King to worry about.

Me.

17

I'D TRIED GYMNASTICS AS A CHILD. THIS WAS WHEN I STILL HAD a chance of fitting between the uneven bars, so that tells you how long ago it was.

The coach explained to us that when you weren't used to doing a sudden move like a handspring or flip, it was common to lose your vision for a second or two in the middle of it. Your eyes wouldn't be able to process the motion without practice, so you could be watching your own limbs the whole time without really seeing them.

That's what happened to me. I couldn't visualize my surroundings clearly.

But I was doing *something*.

And then suddenly, there I was. Out of breath. Panting and sweating in the middle of the room with no one around.

The men who'd been fighting with Quentin now littered the corners of the café, crumpled and discarded like straw wrappers. They hadn't been beaten. They'd been caved in, wrecked to the point where they weren't even twitching.

The remnants of a broken chair lay at my feet instead of theirs, and there were splinters in my hair. If I didn't know any better, I would think someone had smashed the heavy piece of furniture over my head. But I didn't feel a thing. No lumps, no bruises.

Given the demons' identical dress, it took me a second to locate Tawny Lion. I used deduction to find him—seeing who'd gotten the worst of it. There he was.

The leader of the demons had been hammered face-first into the wall so hard he was partially embedded like a nail. It would have been comical—Sunday morning–cartoonish—if not for the blood leaking out of the cracks. I watched it drip to the floors, wondering when I would start to feel sick or scared or anything but hugely satisfied with the carnage.

I heard a whistle. "Damn," said Quentin. "Remind me never to piss you off."

"I did this? It wasn't you?"

"Nope. I just got out of your way. I was afraid you wouldn't be able to tell us apart."

An awkward silence passed. It probably should have been filled with me vigorously denying everything. *There was no way I could have done any of this! I'm not that strong! I'm not that violent!*

But instead, nothing.

Ah dang it. I kept forgetting the girl in the shop. I ran over to her and laid her on the ground. She was breathing, deep and slow enough to give me pause, but breathing nonetheless.

"You saved her life," Quentin said. "I didn't get through the barrier in time. She'd be dead if it weren't for you."

It had been such a close call that a drop of blood trickled down her forehead from where one of Tawny Lion's fangs had pricked the skin. I dabbed it away with my sleeve, a brief motherly instinct overtaking me even though I was younger than her.

"I thought from reading the book of your stories that consuming spiritual power might be like a ritual, or a vague kind of energy vampirism," I said.

"Nope. Straight-up chewing and swallowing."

The sound of tapping on glass startled me out of my reverie. I looked over to see the opaque shield that Tawny Lion had put up over the front of the store beginning to fade. There were people outside, some of whom looked like they wanted in.

Oh god.

What was I *doing*? There were bodies in this store. Dead ones, maybe. We couldn't be caught like this.

Oh god oh god.

I ran over to the door and locked it before anyone could come in, but once the veil disappeared completely we'd still be visible to bystanders. "Quentin!" I shouted. "What the hell are we going to do about this?"

"About what?"

I waved my arms around. "This!"

"Oh!" he said. "Right. Wow. This is not good for you, is it? Not a thing that happens to people these days. Hrm."

He began pacing about like we had all the time in the world for him to think. I wanted to scream.

"Can't you hide them with magic?" I pleaded.

"I could, but the next people to walk in here might, oh, I don't know, notice tripping over invisible bodies? You know this would have been a lot easier if you had killed them."

"What!?"

"Yaoguai disappear back to Hell once they're dead. These guys are still alive, even Tawny Lion. You want me to, uh . . ." He made a clicking noise with his teeth and a twisting motion with his hands.

"No!" Fighting was one thing, but straight-up killing a downed enemy was a line I couldn't cross yet.

Quentin rolled his eyes at me like I was being the unreasonable one.

"Then the only other option is to have a member of the celestial pantheon come and take them into custody," he said. "But Tawny Lion and his brothers were never associated with any gods. There's no one who'd be willing to pay bail. Except for maybe—"

"No maybes! Get help now or else the two of us will be seeking enlightenment from the inside of a juvenile detention facility!"

He scrunched his nose. Whoever it was I was making him call upon, he really didn't want to owe them one. He sat down in the middle of the floor and pulled his legs underneath him.

"What the hell are you doing?"

"Praying." He took a deep breath, inhaling for what seemed an eternity, and lowered his head.

A vibration like a brewing storm emanated from his throat. It hardened into syllables. He was chanting, not like a monk but like a whole choir of monks in an echoing stone abbey that doubled and redoubled their voices. The air tingled with a sense of urgency.

"Na mo guan shi yin pu sa," Quentin droned.

"NamoguanshiyinpusanamoguanshiyinpusaNamoguanshiyinpusa."

I could have sworn the ground was shaking under our feet. Quentin grew louder and louder until it seemed like all the glass inside the shop would crack.

"Na mo guan shi yin pu sa," Quentin continued. *"Salutations to the most compassionate and merciful Bodhisattva."*

A burst of light came from the window, startling the bejeezus out of me. Quentin, however, appeared to be expecting it. He got up, opened the door, and motioned for me to come outside with him.

I was so worried at what I might see that I shielded my eyes, a bomb shelter refugee stepping out of the hatch. But the scene in the street was fairly normal. Sunshine, people, cars.

Everything was just frozen in time, was all.

Pedestrians had stopped mid-stride. Anyone who had been talking had their mouths open. A driver checked her mirror for a turn that had been paused indefinitely. The entirety of Johnson Square, as far as the eye could see, had been turned into a snowglobe without any white flakes.

There was no sound anywhere. I snapped my fingers to see if my ears still worked. Thankfully they did.

"Did you do this?" I asked Quentin.

He shook his head. "I'm not that powerful."

I tried not to touch anything. I'd read enough sci-fi to be unsure of what time manipulation rules applied here. Maybe I could have posed everyone's bodies in amusing positions, or maybe any contact with them would have triggered a quantum wave collapse or something.

Quentin led me to one person who turned out not to be frozen, just standing still across the street. I probably should have noticed her earlier. She was only the most gorgeous woman I had ever seen in my whole life.

She was as tall as I was. But she wore her height with such grace and poise that it made me feel unworthy to share that trait with her. Her elegant face was the kind that needed to be painted and housed in a museum, just to be fair to everyone born in the next century. She smiled at Quentin, and then at me.

"Genie Lo," Quentin said. "This is the Bodhisattva Guanyin,

the Goddess of Mercy, She Who Hears the Cries of the World. Benefactor to Xuanzang and my friend from the old days."

"Hey girl!" Guanyin threw her arms around me in a fierce hug.

Huh. I thought the deified personification of kindness and compassion would have touched down on Earth in flowing robes and a crown of jewels. Not jeans and a pixie cut.

"Nice to meet you," I said, my chin stuck on her shoulder. "Who's that guy?"

There was another person who was free to move about. He was dressed like a cross between a Secret Service agent and a GQ model. He was as handsome as Guanyin was pretty, his facial features sharper than his five-figure suit. But his air of cold disdain made it clear he wasn't in the business of handing out hugs. Quentin tensed up when he saw him.

"Erlang Shen," he hissed with more vitriol than he spent on the Demon King of Confusion. "What the hell are you doing here?"

Erlang Shen pulled off his sunglasses and scanned the block with an imperial, unblinking gaze.

"Escorting the Lady Guanyin," he said while completely overlooking Quentin. "Aren't you going to introduce me as well, Keeper of the Horses?"

That had to have been some kind of insult, because Quentin looked as if he'd rather Erlang Shen's face get acquainted with his fist. All I knew of the other god was that he was the only person who'd ever bested Sun Wukong in a fight. The grudge must have run deep.

"Of course not," said Erlang Shen. He smirked as if getting under Quentin's skin was the sport of kings. Then he turned to me and bowed slightly.

"You're . . . the nephew of the Jade Emperor, right?" I asked.

"Among other things. I prefer to be known for mastering the torrents and bringing life to the fields."

"He's basically a glorified ditch-digger," Quentin said.

"Be nice," said Guanyin. "I heard you two needed some help."

"Yes!" I chimed in. "We do. We need to get rid of some demons, quickly."

Erlang Shen made a move like the bodyguard he resembled, stepping forward and reaching inside his jacket, but Guanyin held him off. "Where are they?" she asked.

"Inside the shop. We need someone to take them away, or else I'm going to be in trouble. A lot of trouble."

"Okay, sure." Guanyin wiggled her fingers vaguely in that direction. "Done. Bibbity bobbity boo."

"What?" I said. "Just like that?"

She smiled. "Sometimes it's just like that."

The door to the shop swung open and lions filed out. Not men in lion masks, like what had briefly appeared to me before. Full-on lions with lion bodies, walking on all fours. I had to do a double take to make sure it wasn't a group of oversize housecats or possums or any other more plausible animal. But no, seven lions limping meekly on parade.

They picked their way through the forest of frozen humans and went up to Guanyin, pushing me aside. The wounded beasts flocked around her and nuzzled at her outstretched hands. She looked like a Disney princess befriending the local wildlife, her munificence taming even the most vicious of creatures.

One of them was in way worse shape than the others. That must have been Tawny Lion. It cringed when I looked at it and tried to keep to the opposite side of Guanyin.

It was a lot harder not to feel bad when they were in this form. I wasn't big on animal cruelty.

He nearly killed someone, I reminded myself. *He's lucky he's not a rug by now.*

Guanyin stepped back and made a face of slight concentration. The pride of lions began to quiver. Not like they were afraid or cold, but like they couldn't decide whether they wanted to exist or not. In a final small flash of light, only the strength of a disposable camera maybe, they were gone.

I stared at the space where they'd been, trying to wrap my head around the last ten minutes.

"I'm having a hard time believing what I'm seeing," I said. "The lions, the people in the street, all of it."

"Do not doubt the Lady Guanyin's abilities," said Erlang Shen. "She once pacified Hell itself by giving away her own good karma. There was so much overflowing from her that Yanluo, King of Death, had to beg her to leave before her virtuous aura quenched the fires of suffering and allowed the guilty demons to escape their sentences."

"I'll . . . take your word for it?" I said.

Guanyin turned to me. "That's that. I put them in one of my divine sanctuaries, where they can do penance for their crimes. It's not as harsh as sending them to Hell, but at least you won't have any trouble from Tawny Lion again. I took care of that poor girl, too; she'll be fine. Won't remember a thing."

"Thank you," I said. "Is there, uh, anything I can do for you? Light some joss? Recommend a restaurant?"

"You could give me the pleasure of your company for a while," Guanyin said. "We really need to talk."

She raised her hand as if to cast another spell. "Let's do it some-where more private. Your place, if you don't mind?"

I flinched. "You're not going to zap us there, are you?"

Guanyin smiled. She swirled her finger and suddenly the street came back to life. People resumed what they were doing, unaware that anything had happened.

"Actually, it's such a nice day that I was thinking we could walk."

18

I'D NEVER POURED TEA FOR A GOD BEFORE. AND NOW THERE were two of them in my house. Mom was missing out on the biggest guests of her life.

The composition of the scene in my kitchen was disjointed in a way that was hard to describe. Guanyin and Erlang Shen didn't quite fit in the frame. They were larger than life. Or a lot better looking than it, anyhow. To have them casually and patiently wait for me while I played host was like those moments where your favorite celebrities proved how down-to-earth they were on camera.

Quentin ruined the divine triptych by refusing to sit at the same table as Erlang Shen. He skulked off to the side, pacing back and forth.

I brought the tray over and poured for everyone. I was glad that we had jasmine instead of oolong. I didn't want Guanyin thinking I was being cute, serving her a drink named after her.

She took a sip to be polite and set her cup aside.

"So you're her," Guanyin said with a warm smile. "I never would have guessed. You look a little like Xuanzang."

I knew I looked like that drawing of him, but hearing someone else compare me to a guy made me hitch a little. "Xuanzang was prettier than the Four Great Beauties," Guanyin said, sensing my discomfort. "It's a compliment."

"Thanks, I guess? You know who I am?"

"We know you're the Ruyi Jingu Bang," Erlang Shen said, eyeing me side-to-side like a vase that he would have been upset to find any cracks in. "Any spiritual being who has been in the As-You-Will Cudgel's aura would recognize it if they got near enough. The Lady Guanyin and I have both seen your original form many times."

It was unsettling to hear the two of them talk like that. Like meeting a distant aunt and uncle who only remembered you in diapers. "The two of you are really gods?"

"Yes," said Guanyin. "We're members of the celestial pantheon of immortal spirits, over which the Jade Emperor presides."

Oookay. "And you're from . . . Heaven?"

She nodded. "A different plane of existence than the one that contains Earth, if that helps you think about it."

It really didn't. My skeptical side was taking an absolute beating right now. *But science!* I wanted to shout. *Empirical thought! Magnets!*

"I know you might be a bit confused," Guanyin went on. "But by and large, there's no need to be. Earth is still Earth. Your universe is still your universe. It's just that sometimes there's bleed-over from other spiritual dimensions. Like today, for instance."

I wasn't sure what other kind of explanation would have kept my head from spinning, so I decided I'd have to roll with this one. Gods in Heaven. Check.

"To preserve order and stability, we retain dominion over the mortal realm in many areas," Erlang Shen said, interjecting in case I'd gotten the wrong idea about the power balance. "Such as those involving yaoguai."

Quentin slapped the nearest wall at the end of his lap around my kitchen. "Yes!" he said, his not-great patience already running thin. "Can we talk about that for a moment? Why a bunch of demons I personally dispatched a long time ago suddenly show up out of the blue?"

I cared more about the broader issue than the particulars of whom Quentin killed or didn't kill once upon a time. "Why are there *any* demons walking around my town in the first place?" I asked, raising my voice above his. "These aren't ye olden days of legend!"

"And why did Tawny Lion claim that more are coming!?" Quentin shouted, topping me with one last demand.

Erlang Shen met our agitation with stoicism. He picked up his tea, quaffed it, and set his cup down before speaking.

"The answer to all of your questions is that there's been a jailbreak," he replied.

Quentin couldn't believe what he was hearing. "A jailbreak? From Diyu?"

"Yes. A number of yaoguai have escaped the plane of Hell, and we have good reason to believe they're headed to Earth, if they're not here already."

Quentin didn't respond, either a minor miracle in itself or a sign of impending disaster. He rubbed his face up and down.

"You would have learned about this had you not run off to Earth, itching for a fight, at the first sign of demonic presence," Guanyin said to him gently.

"Hold up," I said. "That doesn't explain why a bunch of these escaped demons showed up in my hometown. There's nothing special about Santa Firenza."

"Of course there is," Erlang Shen said. "You."

It was my turn to go mute.

Erlang Shen saw that he needed to elaborate. He took the lid off the teapot and pushed it to the center of the table. This explanation needed props, apparently.

"Imagine the tea leaves are yaoguai," he said.

"Okay," I said. I had chosen the glass set, so I could see the loose tea scattered across the bottom of the broad, round pot.

Erlang Shen held up his index finger. "And this is you. The Ruyi Jingu Bang, former axis of the Milky Way."

He dipped his finger into the vessel. The pale green liquid began swirling around it in a miniature vortex. The tea leaves were whisked along by the flow, rising and falling in a tightening loop, faster and faster until Erlang Shen ceased the water's motion. Once everything had settled, there was a tight pile of tea debris gathered right under the spot he was pointing at.

He withdrew his finger and flicked the moisture away.

"Every otherworldly being has its own spiritual gravity," he said. "That's why they aggregate in the same general locations instead of dispersing to the four corners of the Earth. They're drawn to existing supernatural masses like moons around a planet. *You* are what's pulling them to this location."

I looked at Quentin. He looked at me.

"Technically, the Monkey King also being here makes it even worse," Erlang Shen said. "It's not fate or destiny that has you running into your old enemies. Sun Wukong and the Ruyi Jingu Bang are each the equivalent of a black hole. Any yaoguai that come to Earth are going to get sucked into your orbits, without fail. It's just a matter of how close and how fast."

"Oh my god," I said. "You're telling me a horde of demons is going to show up on my doorstep?"

"If only," Erlang Shen said, insensitive to how that sounded. "Then it would be a lot easier to track them down. I'd say they could show up anywhere within a couple hundred miles around your physical location, give or take."

That wasn't a whole lot better. I mean, it was, but still not great.

"Please tell me you're going to do something about this," I said. "You can't let demons from Hell wander freely over the entire Bay Area."

"Heaven has a plan to deal with the situation." Erlang Shen stretched in his chair with the litheness of a panther, hinting at a wiry martial artist's build under his suit. "My uncle the Jade Emperor has decreed that the fugitive yaoguai will be apprehended by a pair of champions who are well-tailored to facing this particular menace."

"Okay then." I breathed a little easier. "I'm glad you and Guanyin are on the job."

The god returned to his normal posture and fixed me with a pointed stare. "I wasn't talking about us."

I didn't get it. Were there other divine beings nearby I didn't know about?

Quentin coughed and kicked the back of my seat.

Oh.

Ohhh.

Oh *fu—*

19

I DON'T THINK I COULD BE BLAMED FOR BEING SLOW ON THE uptake. It isn't like one gets conscripted as a demon hunter on the reg.

"Whoa," I said. "Whoa, whoa, whoa. That is a bad idea. A very bad idea."

"I wish I could say that the circumstances were different, and that the two of us could take charge," Guanyin said. "But for better or worse, the Jade Emperor's policies adhere strictly to the philosophy of *wu wei*."

"*Without action?*" I asked, translating the words directly.

"Yes. The belief that doing nothing is the best, most natural way to behave. That everything will play out as it should, as long as you don't interfere. This is why he's ordered the rest of the pantheon to stand by as Sun Wukong and the Ruyi Jingu Bang take care of the problem. The two of you are not true gods, so you don't represent a commitment of Heavenly resources."

I glanced at Quentin. His face said, *I told you so.* This must have been why he was so reluctant to call upon divine help in the first place. The favor they'd done for us today was snowballing out of control.

"It is the Way of Heaven to act on Earth through lesser

intermediaries," Erlang Shen said. "This is how it's been through the centuries, from the first dynastic kings to Xuanzang to now."

"But I'm not the intermediary you want doing this!" I said. "I don't know anything about monsters and magic. You want some kind of sorcerer with a cage full of gremlins. Or a wushu master who's been training his whole life for this sort of thing."

"Did you not just wipe the floor with several yaoguai at once today?" Erlang Shen asked.

"I don't . . . I can't do that on command."

"Then I suggest you learn how. And quickly."

"What happens if I say no?"

"Look, I don't think you understand," he said. "You don't have any choice in the matter."

"What do you mean? Xuanzang chose to go on his journey to get the sutras. The gods didn't make him."

"That was different. Xuanzang had a say because he was a human. You, however, are not."

Clank.

My fist hitting the table sloshed the contents of the cup in front of me over the sides. Tepid water dripped on the floor but I made no motion to clean it up. Quentin shifted uncomfortably. He'd gotten pretty good at telling when I was primed to go off.

"Would you like to say that again? I don't think I heard you right."

Erlang Shen was unfazed by how long I'd dragged out the sentence through my teeth.

"Yes, you have a human form," he said. "Yes, you're mortal. But humans don't have the essence of a celestial body inside them. Humans aren't walking weapons so powerful they're strategic assets in their own right. My uncle's stance is that you're still the lost property of Heaven and thus beholden to his will."

I flexed my fingers open and closed a few times.

"From what little I understand of reincarnation," I enunciated very carefully, "any person, spirit, or whatever can become human. So long as they work hard enough at it in their past life. I thought those were the rules. That everyone gets their chance to spin the Wheel of Life and Rebirth in the hopes of bettering themselves."

"I'm sorry, Genie," Guanyin said. "But there aren't rules for what's happened to you. A weapon reincarnating is completely unprecedented. Not in the history of gods and men has this ever happened. When you were the Ruyi Jingu Bang, no one even guessed you had a soul."

Welp. Nothing like having your personhood denied in the morning to start the day off right.

I finally understood the piercing, migraine-y anger that shot through my core the first time Quentin had called me the Ruyi Jingu Bang. If there was any of my past self in me right now, it hated being thought of as an object. It hated not being acknowledged for what it accomplished by turning human. It valued Genie.

Even if no one else did.

"What a pile of crap," said Quentin.

I turned to find him giving me a hard stare.

Most people probably would have thought from his facial expression that he was agreeing with the Jade Emperor. After all, he was the one who'd lost his most valuable possession as a result of my very existence.

Except that he glanced at the gods, and then back at me. I had a sense of what he was thinking.

"You come here to Earth to tell us how it's going to be," Quentin said to Erlang Shen. "Let me tell *you* how it's going to be. If Genie refused, the Jade Emperor would be up the creek without a paddle. Your uncle has made the biggest gaffe of his career, letting these demons escape, and he's so afraid of losing face over it that he needs to beg for her help without appearing to do so. Meanwhile you're too much of a kiss-ass to go against his orders and pitch in the effort, you *goutuizi*."

Erlang Shen didn't change expressions, but I could have sworn the room got several degrees colder and draftier as he bristled at Quentin. A duel might have broken out in my kitchen right then and there, but Guanyin put her hand on the rain god's forearm.

"Enough," she commanded.

The thunderclouds slowly rolled back. Erlang Shen calmed himself under her grasp, but Quentin eyed the contact between him and Guanyin, not liking it one bit. Interesting.

Guanyin faced me with a wince of sadness and right then I knew I was in trouble. She wasn't throwing in the towel with her long-suffering air. She was powering up.

"Genie, I know none of this seems fair," she said. "But if demons are returning to the mortal world, this no longer becomes solely about you."

I knew that. And I'm sure she knew I knew that. But we were going down this road anyway.

"These particular fugitives—they're ambitious," Guanyin said. "They'll stop at nothing to gain more power. And their go-to strategy is to consume humans with strong spirits.

"It doesn't have to be a holy man like Xuanzang. There are plenty of laypeople in this day and age who have the essence they're looking for, like that girl in the shop. Once the demons arrive, they'll begin hunting, picking off innocents from the shadows."

Guanyin motioned at Quentin. "Tell her. Am I exaggerating?"

Quentin let out a deep sigh.

"She's right, Genie," he said. "If this is the bunch that I'm thinking of, then the common folk are in trouble. Obtaining human energies was an obsession for some of these demons. A madness. They won't stop, not even in the face of death."

I squeezed my nose between my palms. Partly out of frustration and partly to keep the stench of the Demon King of Confusion from flooding back into my nostrils. Closing my eyes only brought the image of Tawny Lion's gaping, distended jaws back to the forefront of my mind. Monsters like these couldn't be left alone.

Guanyin sensed her victory was near. "I can tell deep down that you want to help," she said. "You're the type of person who takes matters into her own hands. You're like me in that regard."

I remembered some of Guanyin's legend. The story went that she was once a mortal girl who was so pure, kind, and enlightened that she easily attained Buddhahood in her youth. Just like that, in a relative snap, she accomplished what some holy men couldn't in lifetimes of training.

But as she was about to leave the planes of Heaven and Earth entirely for the ultimate nirvana, she looked back and heard the cries of the suffering and downtrodden. Her compassion led her to stay behind as a Bodhisattva, a lesser divine being, so that she could do her best to relieve the pain of humanity and guide it to its own enlightenment. She was a figure of self-sacrifice and humility. I couldn't see how we compared.

This sucked.

This sucked so goddamn much.

"Fine," I said, in a grouchy harrumph that was very un-Bodhisattva-like. "I'll do what I can."

20

GUANYIN'S EYES SPARKLED AT ME. IT WAS TOO PRETTY TO look at, and I wanted to sneeze.

The sunbeams of her countenance traveled around my kitchen until they found Quentin, still the only one of us who hadn't taken a seat at my table.

"What about you, dear?" she asked.

"Sure," he replied with a shrug. "I have my reputation to think about. Sun Wukong doesn't shy away from a fight."

Maybe I was reading into it too much, but that was a pretty weaksauce reason to go along with everything, even for someone as prideful as Quentin. Which meant he was taking up this burden to protect the little people, like in the old stories. Or he was doing it simply to have my back.

It was a nice feeling either way. The cockles of my heart and such.

"So do you have names?" Quentin asked. "Or do we have to wait until every yaoguai shakes our hands and reintroduces themselves?"

"Baigujing," Erlang Shen answered. "The Immortals of Tiger, Deer, and Goat. Linggandaiwang. The Hundred-Eyed Demon Lord. Huangpaogui. General Yin. The Wolf of the Twentieth Mansion . . ."

He went on. And on.

And on.

Quentin's frown grew more and more profound with each successive name until finally he threw his hands into the air.

"*Tamade!*" he shouted, interrupting the roll call. "What's the point of having a Hell in the first place if you're going to let every asshole walk free?"

"What's the total count of escapees?" I said. "Or do you not know how many?"

"We know how many." Erlang Shen squared his shoulders like an accountant about to report to his boss that the whole company was insolvent. "It's one hundred and eight."

"A HUNDRED AND EIGHT?"

"Well a hundred now, after today's events," Erlang Shen said. "If it gives you any reassurance, I can almost guarantee you won't have to fight them all at once."

I could certainly guarantee him that it did not. A wedding guest list's worth of demons. A Roman centuria. Enough demons to create a half a professional soccer league, without substitutions.

While my fretting brain coped by forming worse and worse analogies, Quentin laughed bitterly.

"A hundred and eight," he said, shaking his head. "A hundred and eight! If it had been a handful of the small fry slipping through the cracks, I could have chalked this up to your uncle's usual negligence! You want to tell me how every demon from Chang'an to Vulture Peak managed to parade through the gate?"

"We think Red Boy broke them out," Guanyin said.

Quentin immediately went silent. He stood where he was for a brief second, and then stormed over to her. He grabbed her arm.

Erlang Shen and I both started to say something about him being too rough, but Guanyin didn't pull away. Quentin shoved her unseasonably long sleeve up to her elbow, exposing her wrist and forearm. It was covered in burns.

The wounds had healed, but they'd been bad. Really bad. The vicious, blood-colored splotches shone under the ceiling light. Against the rest of Guanyin's beautiful skin the injuries looked like an act of vandalism.

Without a word Quentin led Guanyin out of the kitchen, never letting go of her hand. The goddess followed him into the hallway, where she gestured over their heads. I could feel something come down around them, similar to Tawny Lion's spell of concealment, only the two of them were still visible.

Quentin's wild-eyed screaming, however, was completely muted. He and Guanyin began noiselessly going at each other.

"So, uh, what's going on?" I asked Erlang Shen.

"During his journey with Xuanzang to recover the sutras, the monkey faced an exceptionally powerful demon named Red Boy," Erlang Shen said. He watched the proceedings with an unreadable look on his face. "Red Boy had the ability to breathe True Samadhi Fire, which no substance, mortal or divine, could resist. The monkey tried to defeat him several times but could not."

I didn't know there was anyone Sun Wukong flat-out couldn't beat in a fight. I'd assumed even Erlang Shen was a coin flip.

"He asked the Lady Guanyin for assistance. With her magic, she captured Red Boy and bound his limbs. The monkey wanted to slay him, but Guanyin pushed for mercy."

"Well that sort of makes sense, given she's the Goddess of—"

"Three times," Erlang Shen interrupted. "Three times Guanyin released Red Boy after he swore to give up fighting. Three times he went back on his word and attacked her."

"Wait, he attacked *her*? After she took his side?"

"Yes." Erlang Shen's mask of dispassion slipped a little, and I could see how upset he was underneath. "Guanyin finally subdued Red Boy for good. In order to receive the clemency he'd thrown away so carelessly before, he promised to become her disciple. Instead of being thrown into Hell, he was given an acolyte's position on a small island shrine in the middle of a Heavenly ocean— isolated from other spirits, but still a paradise compared to what he deserved.

"Over the years he served faithfully. He appeared to have reformed. But the last time Guanyin was with him, he attacked her yet again and fled. That was when she suffered those wounds."

No wonder they were screaming up a storm. Nothing to light a fire under an argument like an "*I told you so*."

"Red Boy wants revenge against everyone that he believes wronged him," Erlang Shen said. "Springing the other demons from Hell is his return stroke against Guanyin and Sun Wukong. A personal message. All the events that have transpired so far are his doing, ultimately."

"You're certain of this?"

Erlang Shen nodded. "There aren't that many ways out of Hell before your sentence is up. You can either get out on borrowed karma from someone like Guanyin, or you can make an escape route if you're powerful enough. Red Boy is that powerful."

"But if that's the case, why'd he wait until now to make his move?"

"He must have caught word that the Ruyi Jingu Bang was no

longer the fearsome weapon of the Monkey King," he said, making a valiant attempt to keep the irony levels in his voice from reaching critical mass. "The fighting power of his enemies has been reduced immeasurably. Now is the perfect time for him to exact his vengeance."

Erlang Shen didn't go so far as to say this whole deal was my fault. Which was good, because if he had I would have blown my stack from here all the way to Canada. The god seemed to be learning where to toe the line with me much faster than Quentin had.

"How strong is he exactly?" I asked. I had a tough time placing supernatural beings on a relative power scale. "Like if the Demon King of Confusion is a 'one' then Red Boy—"

"Red Boy once burned a country to the ground," Erlang Shen said curtly, without a trace of exaggeration.

I hesitated. "Wouldn't that have been noticed in history somewhere?"

Erlang Shen shook his head. "He *really* burned it to the ground."

"Holy crap. You know, this is the kind of news you should lead with. Seems a little important not to mention right away."

His response was to gesture at Guanyin and Quentin tearing each other apart. "If I had, there would have been no chance whatsoever of a reasonable conversation afterward."

Touché, I guess.

Quentin and Guanyin must have reached a tipping point in their monumental argument, because the goddess left the zone of silence and came back to the kitchen. On the way she ran her hand over my backpack, which had been lying on the countertop.

"Mind if I borrow these?" she asked. I didn't know what she was referring to until she opened her hands. My earrings rested in her palm.

"Those are actually kind of important to me," I said.

"This won't work unless they are." Without waiting for my permission she went over to Quentin, who was fuming in the corner. Before he could resume shouting, she leaned over and pulled him into a kiss.

Quentin was so surprised that he went completely rigid as her hands caressed the back of his neck. Erlang Shen grunted in protest. But I was at the right angle to see that it was a total fakeout. She stopped just short of his lips, needing only for him to hold still while her fingers brushed his ears like a pickpocket.

Guanyin straightened up and waved the silencing spell away. My souvenirs from the Happiest Place on Earth were now fastened to Quentin's earlobes. He realized he was involuntarily wearing jewelry and began pawing helplessly at the clasps. They were probably stuck on there with magic, but it could also have been that he was a boy and didn't know how to undo them.

"What was that?" I asked her.

"A bit of forbidden help," she said. "Those earrings will let the wearer know every time a demon gets too close to a human."

"Okay," I said. "How close are we talking about? Like restraining order distance or county lines distance?"

She gave me a look that said I was examining her gift horse in the mouth. "Far enough away that you should be able to react accordingly. The magic in them will provide a general sense of what direction the demon is in, but beyond that you'll have to do the searching yourselves. Once you receive the alarm, you must strike as soon as you can, Genie. A yaoguai that has fed will be exponentially more dangerous."

The human tragedy inherent in that statement was probably implied. "But what about Red Boy?"

A shade of agony passed over Guanyin's face. "For now we have no choice but to wait until he shows himself. There will undoubtedly be a confrontation with Red Boy at some point, but until then you have to minimize the damage caused by the other demons."

She gestured behind her at Quentin. "The earrings will also help if he gets out of control. Just say the magic words. You know which ones."

She swept past Erlang Shen and motioned for him to follow, in no mood for any departing pleasantries. The mighty nephew of the Jade Emperor got up without a peep. He nodded to me before closing the door.

Another flash of light streamed through the windows and then faded. I didn't feel the need to go outside and check that they were gone. Guanyin really did not screw around when it came to making an exit.

I turned to Quentin. "How much of a dick do you have to be to upset the Goddess of Compassion into leaving without saying goodbye?"

He glowered at me, hands still on his ears.

"I'm joking," I said. "I understand how you feel, honestly. It's maddening to see those you care about get hurt, even if it's their own fault."

"It was my fault," said Quentin. "If I could have defeated Red Boy on my own she never would have come near that son of a bitch. I shouldn't have gotten her involved."

I took a closer look at the side of his head. "What did she do to you?"

"I'm assuming she put the Band-Tightening Spell back on, only with a different focus item. It'll trigger if you say the chant that kept me imprisoned under the Five Elements Mountain."

"What, you mean, Om Mani Padme Om?"

The words left my mouth before I realized what I'd done.

. . .

Quentin's back snapped into a crescent. His scream of pain was shut off by the closure of his airways. He toppled over to the ground, hitting his head hard on the floor.

"No!" I shouted. "Stop! I didn't mean it!"

He was having a seizure. I raced to his side and put my hand under the back of his skull as it slammed into the floor over and over. I had to hug him to my body to keep him from smashing into the base of the counter.

I could feel Quentin wail into my shoulder, his teeth caught in the weave of my shirt. "I'm sorry!" I cried, even though he was in no condition to hear me. "I'm sorry! Please stop!"

The spell must have been on a timer. After a few more eternal seconds, Quentin's body slowed to a halt. I realized I was smothering him and sat up so he could breathe.

His skin was burning up like a fever that hadn't broken. When his eyelids fluttered open they were mostly whites.

" . . . hot," he mumbled.

I let his head down as gently as I could before grabbing a towel and wetting it under the cold tap. I slid my lap back under him and patted his face and neck until he shivered and relaxed.

Quentin opened his mouth to speak. I wiped my eyes and nose so I wouldn't drip on him when I leaned in to hear.

"So anyway . . ." he whispered. "That's what that spell does."

I could have killed him for joking after what just happened. Instead I held him while he laid his head back and rested.

■ ■ ■

The microwave clock said that ten minutes had passed. It was getting late in the day, the shadows in my house growing longer across the kitchen floor where we lay. My mother would be home at some point.

"Genie," Quentin said, his voice back to its normal strength. "I think I'm okay now. Thank you—*urk!*"

I shook him by the neck. "*That's* the Band-Tightening Spell? That's what happened to you every time Xuanzang said those words?"

Quentin was either nodding or his head was just flopping back and forth. "Pretty much."

"Jesus Christ!" I shouted. "How was that okay with anyone? That's screwed up! What kind of holy man just tortures another person? What kind of human being?"

I tried to pry the earrings off Quentin without success. "If I ever meet Xuanzang I'm going to knock his teeth down his throat," I said, my fingernails jamming against the clasps. "And I'm not too happy with Guanyin either, right now."

"Genie, stop! Ow! You're pulling my earlobes off!"

He tried to fend me off but I didn't let him. We struggled against each other, using our hips for leverage. He flipped over on top of me and managed to pin my wrists to the floor before we realized what we were doing.

Quentin picked up on the sudden flush in my cheeks and slowly pulled his hands away as if I might be upset by any sudden moves. But he didn't unlock his eyes from mine.

"I should go," he said, sitting back on his heels. "Before your mom finds us like this."

"Wait."

I reached up and buttoned the top of his shirt. I'd undone it part of the way when I was toweling him off. The damp fabric clung to his skin. I could see his muscles twitch like live wires as I slowly popped each button through its hole.

"Thanks." He let me fix and smooth his collar before we finally got up. Benefits of having a long reach.

I walked him to the door and he lingered on the steps. "So I'll see you at school then," he said, giving me a drawn-out, hungry look.

"I guess so."

"Or if you want to meet elsewhere, I have a phone now. It could be any time, any place."

My breathing picked up at the hint.

"That's good," I said. "You should have one."

I could feel where this was leading. And as glorious and satisfying as it would be to dive headlong into it, to drink deeply from the river, I wasn't quite ready yet.

"Thanks for introducing me to your ex," I said.

Quentin's face went scandalized, a rarity that was particularly delicious. "The Lady of Mercy is above any sordid entanglement!" he said. "Her virtue is unquestioned! How could you even imply such blasphemy?"

"Way to put your ex on a pedestal."

"God, I hate you," he muttered.

That was more like it. The moment successfully ruined, I laughed and shut the door in his face.

21

"OH MY GOD," SAID YUNIE. "I KNEW THERE WAS A DIRTY GIRL waiting to come out of that shell of yours."

"What are you talking about?"

"You *marked* him," she said, pointing at Quentin, who sat across the library reading by himself. "That is the hottest thing I've ever seen happen at this school."

Aw, hell. I should have remembered that Yunie, sharp-eyed as ever, would recognize my earrings on Quentin. They weren't exactly small. They weren't exactly meant for anyone but a ten-year-old girl, either.

"Is he like your toy now? Does he have to obey your every command?"

I racked my brain for a feasible explanation and couldn't.

"Just . . . just don't tell anyone they're mine, okay?"

Yunie grinned so wide I thought her face might split. "Sure," she said. "I'll keep your twisted little game a secret. Oh wait, look."

Rachel Li had sauntered up to Quentin. I couldn't hear what she was saying, but the way she nearly brushed his hair with her fingers, it was obvious she was asking about his ears.

Quentin was completely oblivious to her flirting. He said

something and pointed at me. Rachel frowned and glared daggers in my direction before stomping away.

"Oops," Yunie giggled. I slammed my forehead into my open textbook.

As if on cue, a note fell out of the pages and fluttered to the floor. I picked it up and held it to the light. It was in Chinese, a messy cursive written with as much forcefulness as lack of convention.

Meet me after your practice is over. Where I first showed you my true self.

He must have meant the park again. I looked up to see Quentin giving me an intense stare. He really couldn't do anything with subtlety.

Over my shoulder, Yunie squealed with glee as she read the overdramatic note.

Crap. I forgot she understood traditional characters as well as I did, if not better. I wadded up the paper and shoved it as far down as I could in my backpack.

· · ·

I cornered Quentin in the hallway the very next break.

"I thought we were meeting after school," he said. "Didn't you get my note?"

"You can just come over and talk to me, you dingus. Instead of skulking around like Batman."

"It's not safe to have our conversations out in the open."

"I think we could tell if there were demons lurking around the corners of our school," I said. "We have those earrings, remember? You're being paranoid."

Quentin grimaced. "You don't understand. Tawny Lion got the drop on me. In the old days he wouldn't have been able to come within a dozen miles without me spotting him."

"What about the Demon King of Confusion? I thought you came to Earth because you sensed his presence."

"I did, but I should have been able to pick him out immediately instead of bumbling across him like an idiot. The fact that he and Tawny Lion got so near means that something is incredibly wrong with my senses, earrings or no."

He glanced around uncomfortably, as if the admission were a sign of weakness the hall monitors would just pounce on. "My true sight hasn't worked since I came to Earth," he said. "In fact, I think when you left my side to become human, you took a lot of my power with you."

"So you're weaker than you were in the stories?"

"*Shh!*" he hissed. "Do you know how many people would kill to know that?"

I pinched the bridge of my nose. "Okay, so what does this mean for us?"

"It means you have to develop your abilities, and fast. Especially your vision. Or else we'll be running around picking fights with random mailmen and lawyers and skateboarders who turn out *not* to be yaoguai."

"Oh my god. That's what happened the first day we met, wasn't it? You weren't being mugged. You just got aggro with a bunch of strangers thinking they were demons in disguise."

"Yes, and I could have killed them by accident. We need another training date. Soon."

"I'm busy this weekend."

Quentin shook his head like he couldn't hear me. "You're busy?"

"I have plans on Saturday. We could meet on Sunday. Given how crappy our last session went, we're not going to lose out on a ton of progress if we postpone a single day."

"You can't postpone the secrets of the universe!" he seethed. "Cancel whatever you're doing. It's not important now."

"Don't tell me what is and isn't important! I told you when I was free, and if you don't like it you can take a hike!"

I turned around and nearly bumped into Androu.

"Is there a problem here?" he asked, peering over me at Quentin.

Quentin was right—we did need to be more discreet in our conversations. The whole hallway could have heard me deliver that last line.

"No problem," I said to Androu. "We were just talking about . . ."

Quentin didn't help me fill in the blanks. He left me swinging in the breeze. I bared my teeth at him and then turned it into a smile for Androu.

"Dinner," I said. "I had his parents over for dinner and they want to return the favor at their house."

Androu was still standing very close, so I patted him on the chest reassuringly. "You should come over for dinner someday, too. My house, I mean. Not Quentin's. Not that his parents don't want you in his house. They just never met you. That would be sort of weird."

"Yeeeah," Androu replied. "Genie, can we talk for a minute?"

He pulled me around the corner and behind a locker.

. . .

Now, I had fantasized about this moment—sneaking off somewhere private with Androu—a bunch of times before. So in theory

I should have known how to play it smooth, from the flirting to the intensifying conversation, all the way up to the halting but tender first kiss.

But the gesture was less exciting than I'd imagined. Turns out I didn't like being dragged by the arm.

Androu checked to see that we weren't followed.

"Hey, so, what's up with you and Quentin these days?" he asked. "I thought you two didn't get along."

"We've . . . come to an understanding," I said. "Why do you ask?"

"You seem different lately."

"Different how?" I got ready to panic in case he said "stretchier."

"I can't put my finger on it, but it's like ever since Quentin came to this school you've been . . . I don't know. Distracted. You've always been such a focused person, but not around him."

This was a big letdown. I hadn't seriously been expecting a romantic conversation, but I thought at the very least Androu would want to talk about me and him in some regard. Not me and Quentin.

"That's what you wanted to ask about? There's nothing else you wanted to say?"

He shook his head. "Just concerned about you. I'm your friend, you know."

Aaand down went the Hindenburg. Blown up by a heat-seeking F-bomb. I held back a sigh.

"Quentin and I are working on an extra-credit project," I said. "Actually, it's more like we got stuck with one against our will. That's all there is to it. Work."

Androu opened his mouth to say something, but I cut him off. "Also, I appreciate you looking out for me, but honestly, what he and I do together is kind of our business, you know?"

I knew that wasn't what you were supposed to say to a guy to assure him you were still available, but that was the truth. I didn't owe anyone a reason for spending time with Quentin, regardless of what we were doing.

Androu seemed ambivalent about my response, but if there was one signal I did know how to give off, it was *I don't want to talk anymore.* He smiled and clapped me on the shoulder.

"As long as it's strictly professional," he said. "I'm always here if you need me, in case things get weird."

Well, too late for that. If things got weirder than they already were, I would need a lot more than the support of a platonic *friend* to cope.

After Androu left, I went back to Quentin. He was waiting patiently, leaning against the wall. He was also giving me god-level side eye.

"Really?" he said. "You and Mr. Straightlaces?"

"Oh shut up."

"Hey, you can do whatever you want. Though you might as well go out with Erlang Shen if that's your type."

"Maybe I should," I snapped. "Erlang Shen's as good-looking as you and he's a better dresser to boot."

Quentin waved his fists rudely at me and walked away down the hall.

"He probably wouldn't show up for a date in our school uniform!" I called out.

22

SATURDAY MORNING, THE LADY OF THE CASTLE AWAITED HER chariot to the ball.

Only her castle was a parking lot so barren that not even fast-food franchises wanted to risk planting a flag nearby. The only building at this train station was a little barnlike wooden depot with padlocked doors and a dark, shadowed interior. I had been coming to this place my entire life and had never once been inside or seen the lights on.

Santa Firenza in a nutshell, folks.

I sweated under the sun, my exposed arms browning in the heat. Because of my general hawkishness on time, I ended up with a lot of moments like this, where I had nothing to do but wait for the rest of the world to catch up.

After about fifteen minutes or so, the clang of bells and an air horn announced that I was done. The northbound train was here, ready to whisk me away. A magical journey redolent with the odors of bicycle grease and blue porta-potty liquid.

Sometimes the cars could be full of rowdy pregamers rocking orange and black, gripping paper-bagged tallboys and *woo*-ing at each other. Today it was less crowded. I watched a man who was much shorter than me splay his legs into the aisle, putting his feet up on an opposing strut even though he could have fit perfectly well into his chair.

We stopped at every station along the way, letting me take in the landscape as it became stripmalls, then regular malls, and then stripmalls again. I could tell I was getting closer as freestanding offices bearing signage for various unicorn startups began appearing.

It took an hour and a half for the train to reach the end of the line in the city. I stepped out onto the platform and shivered. I untied my spare jacket from my waist and put it on properly. This was a different climate system entirely. Different rules.

I looked around, orienting myself under the gray sky of the city. If I strayed to the south I would be in the SoMa district, which if I understood correctly was composed entirely of loft condos and coworking offices. Following the avenues too far to the east would take me to the water's edge, where I might find the Ferry Building disgorging tourists out of its maw.

There were too many buses heading in the same direction, and I never remembered the numbered routes. Eventually I gave in and did what I always did. Follow the old Chinese people. I hopped on the line that had the most passengers carrying plastic bags and settled in for more waiting.

Public transportation among my kind is its own special hell. No bus has ever moved so slowly as it does through a Chinatown. I was pretty sure that if you needed to decelerate a photon for a physics experiment, all you had to do was throw some cardboard boxes full of dark leafy greens in the laser beam's path and let nature take over.

Eventually, the bus I was on burst through the stasis field of budget realtors, dry goods stores, and oddly terrible dim sum shops.

Upon reaching a petite, bright-green park, we swung a westward turn, both literally and figuratively.

Instead of bubble tea shops, you now had cafés that served lattes in a bowl so you could dunk your Viennoiseries easier. You had eyewear galleries that displayed three, four different frames, tops. Tiny dogs. Double strollers. "Hallelujah" (the song—the new one).

Most of all you had space. Personal space, breathing room, everywhere. On the sidewalks and in the two-bedroom apartments and in the career tracks. I didn't know if I needed that much space, but I was damn sure I'd work my ass off for it first, and then decide.

Speaking of which, my stop. I got off the bus at a plush little walkup, the brass plate reading SILVERLINE ADMISSIONS COUNSELING.

Inside the second-floor lobby I sat waiting in a pod chair surrounded by pots of bamboo. The furniture was eggshell white. The walls were eggshell white. I tried to ignore the tasteful indie rock and R&B, played low and targeted at my generation more precisely than a payload from a stealth bomber.

The door opened and it wasn't Anna who stepped out. It was a girl my age—another client.

I could tell immediately she was more put together than me. I didn't mean my appearance, though that, too. It was the way she carried herself with enough confidence and quirk and receptiveness that it could have been a sign plastered over her head: I AM WHO EVERYONE WANTS.

Her session had run to the end and might have gone over had someone not graciously noticed the clock. That's how much raw material Anna had to work with. My sessions were always punctuated by five minutes of awkward chitchat.

"Hi," the girl offered, blushing cutely. She swung her backpack over her shoulder, revealing patches from both Habitat for Humanity and Amnesty International. I was severely outclassed. What kind of scrub game had I been playing?

"Man, talking with Anna's fun but terrifying," she said, trying to start a conversation. She didn't even have the decency to be catty with me. I just wanted her to tuck her charmingly wispy curls under her beret and go, before I had to get out of my chair.

"Genie," Anna said as she bustled into the room. "So sorry, dear. Come in, come in, we're not late yet."

I sighed and stood up. The decor in the room always made me look more like a skyscraper than usual. I glanced down at the other girl. She made a cowed squeak, waved politely to Anna, and then scurried away.

■ ■ ■

Anna Barinov had never reacted that way to me, not even the first day we met. She was a certain kind of unflappable, a scion of old money who had forged a successful small business of her own. Insured against disaster at either end of the economic spectrum. I envied that.

I chose her from the kajillions of admissions consultants in the area because out of the ones I could afford, she had the best background. Lengthy stints as an admissions officer for several top-tier universities decorated her resume. She knew better than anyone what colleges looked for in applicants, because she had done the looking herself. Anna would provide valuable feedback as to how I could present myself as a better candidate.

That's what my Western sensibilities believed. The Chinese running through my veins said *come on.* COME ONNNN.

All those years working for the Ivy League had to have meant she'd stockpiled a nuclear arsenal of inside connections. Friends back in Cambridge and New Haven. People she could drop hints to over lunch about this one really impressive young lady she'd crossed paths with.

If that idea sounded corrupt, it was. It was *guanxi*—exerting social influence to get the outcome you needed. The grease in the gears of Asian culture. The need for networking was why so many overseas students crashed like waves against the doors of American universities in the first place—so they could make powerful, long-lasting connections.

Granted, I had little reason to believe Anna operated in this manner. But she had the power to. I told myself that maybe once I impressed her enough, she'd pull out a big red phone that went straight to Princeton.

Anna settled into her chair behind her desk, and then settled again like a falcon adjusting its wings.

"Practice essays," she said. "I believe we were looking at first revisions."

"Right," I said. I fumbled with my bag trying to get at the papers I should have already been holding. I handed them over with only a few extra creases.

Anna began scanning the first of my essays, and already I was starting to get uncomfortable with how fast her eyes were moving. Was she even reading the sentences? Couldn't she at least *pretend* not to skim?

And then she was done. A month's worth of work consumed in

thirty seconds. Maybe that was what the supposed time difference between Heaven and Earth felt like.

"Well, given that your initial draft was you listing your statistical performance at various activities, I'd be lying if I said this version wasn't an improvement."

"But it's still not good enough," I said.

"Genie, we talked about this. You only have one chance to tell the admissions board who you really are."

"I didn't do that? I thought I did that."

"What you've done is address the prompts directly, word for word," she said. "But there has to be an underlying current of your personality. A cohesive story of who you are."

These conversations always left me frustrated. I didn't know how to do this kind of doublespeak in real life, and I sure as hell didn't understand how to do it in six hundred fifty words or fewer.

It didn't help that this portion of the application infuriated me on a fundamental level. The message that I got from these drills was that I wasn't a real person. Not by default. My humanity had to be proved with a vague test where "getting it" meant everything and hard work meant nothing. It was the Way, and I couldn't see past the tortoises and snakes to grasp it.

"I could write about the time I fought a demon," I said out of sheer frustration.

"A personal demon?" said Anna.

"No, a Chinese demon. An actual monster. Yaoguai, they call them."

Anna pursed her lips. "I didn't know those still existed."

"They do, and they're back in a big way. The first one I saw was this big ugly SOB who tried to eat me alive. I kicked his ass pretty bad."

"Hmmm. There could be some traction there."

This was the first hint of excitement I'd gotten out of Anna. I leaned back in my chair and put my feet up on her desk, buoyed by my newfound confidence.

"I've fought other demons, too," I boasted. "Just recently I beat up a bunch of shape-shifting lions. It was easy once I started using my magic powers."

Anna was so pleased with me she began grinning like a maniac. "Well, there's your angle. In fact, I'm pretty sure Brown offers a guaranteed full scholarship for their new demon-slaying track."

"*Pfft.* We can do better than Brown." I picked a tropical umbrella drink off her bar cart and sipped it through the crazy straw. "That's like the caboose of the Ivy train."

"You're right, Genie. What you deserve is some kind of joint program along with some merit fellowship grant money to do with as you please. All the grant money in fact. You deserve it all."

"Aw, let's leave a few bucks on the table for the other meritorious fellows."

"You're so kind, Genie. Genie? Genie?"

■ ■ ■

"Genie?" Anna said. "Are you okay?"

I blinked. Someone calling me kind was too much to believe, even for a daydream.

"The story of me," I parroted.

"Try this exercise," Anna said. "Completely ignore the essay prompts and word limits for now. Write about yourself however you can, with your thoughts, your feelings, some personal anecdotes. Get something down on paper first, and then we'll refine it from there.

"Who is Genie Lo?" she said, wiggling her fingers. "That's what the admissions board wants to know."

There is no Genie Lo, I wanted to shout. Not the kind that lived prettily in air-quotes. There was a sixteen-year-old girl from the Bay who answered to that name, but there wasn't some sparkling magic nugget underneath that I could dig up, polish, and put on display.

I swallowed my pride and smiled.

"I think I get it," I said. "I'll have a better draft next time."

■ ■ ■

I left Anna's completely fried, but that wasn't anything new. I bought two coffees from the café next door that was too fancy to sell a "large" and chugged one immediately. The other I took into the cab with me.

The taxi was a waste of money, but in my current state I couldn't handle getting back on a bus. The driver took a different route downtown through the financial district, which was mostly empty on the weekend. We pulled up to a building that only looked like a bank. The second half of today's trip.

I opened the door to the gym and was immediately greeted by the latest remix of the latest EDM hit. The girl behind the counter who tagged members' badges with a bar code reader smiled and waved me on by.

It wasn't crowded, not on a weekend afternoon. The gym was

gigantic—an orchard of pulleys and benches—but I found him in the corner wiping chalk off the barbell grips. I tapped him on the shoulder and he turned.

"Hi, Dad."

My father beamed and gave me a big hug.

Then, without so much as a word, he held up his hands. I grabbed them and we began trying to twist each other's arms off, laughing the whole time.

I don't know when playing Mercy became our standard greeting, but I did know that he hadn't won in a very long time. Dad wasn't much bigger than Mom.

As soon as I'd bent his wrists beyond ninety degrees, he squawked, "I give, I give!" I let go and he shook his hands out. "I don't remember you being that strong last month."

"Coach Daniels has us doing grip training now," I said. "We squeeze tennis balls."

"They've got a class here like that for the rock climbers. You should see the new wall they're planning. *Shhoop.* Goes all the way to the top."

I listened to him enthusiastically describe the various improvements going on at the gym as if he were an owner and not part of the cleaning staff. Business must have surged again recently, the energy rubbing off on him. It was good to see him like this.

My father was born the same year as my mother, but you wouldn't have known it from looking at him. He was the portrait of Dorian Gray that took all the slings and arrows of Time bouncing off Mom's youthful skin. Only his still-dark hair kept his weathered face from looking painfully old for his age.

Dad was a specimen that not many people saw out in the open, or at least admitted to seeing. He was a failure. An abysmal, no-bones-about-it failure. One of the worst things you could be in this era.

My family used to be slightly more prosperous. That's not saying much, but it was a meaningful difference, a trip to Disneyland's worth, perhaps. Dad used to work at an insurance company when I was very little. He had a modest, nondescript career, but a career nonetheless.

Until one day, to hear Mom tell the story, he decided he was too good to work for someone else. He quit his job, took out a loan, and opened a furniture store, like an idiot.

In Dad's version it was a calculated risk, an attempt to get the better life that his wife had always passive-aggressively demanded. He'd carry cheap inventory in parts and assemble it with the help of cheap employees and sell it to cheap customers. A foolproof plan.

I have memories of the store. The desks that smelled like dust no matter how much they'd been spritzed with lemon. A whole series of glass coffee tables that only came in octagons. I used to run between the aisles of the showroom, before I learned not to by way of a splinter the size of a toothpick buried in my cheek.

There's nothing worse than just enough success. The store was a slow death that took years to metastasize, sucking in more and more of Dad's money and soul. He tried everything, including going upscale in a brief, costly branding experiment. All he learned was that reinventing yourself was not something people allowed you to do very often.

Once the writing was on the wall, Mom refused to work the

register anymore. She had to get a job somewhere else to make ends meet, or so she said. Dad thought it was a betrayal. They grew heated and icy with each other in ways that didn't cancel out.

After the store was liquidated at great loss—after we were thoroughly ruined—he left the house. Or was kicked out. It didn't matter. His ability to interact with other people in a professional environment had deteriorated to the point where it was even worse than Mom's. He wasn't getting any kind of old job back.

Especially given that he had no higher education. My father had never gone to college.

· · ·

When Mom told me he was living in the city on his own, I'd imagined the worst. A squalid apartment in a bad neighborhood. Unable to make ends meet. Drinking.

When I finally saw him after the split, he told me that I'd been spot-on. But only for the first few months or so of his exile.

At his lowest point, after he'd given up all hope for his continued existence, he'd taken a walk that brought him past this gym. The door had been open, blaring *untz-untz* beats into the sidewalk. He'd peered inside, confused by the sculpted bodies and clanging iron.

The one thing he understood was the Now Hiring sign. On impulse he asked about it. Perhaps also on impulse, the young things on duty at the time took him onboard as the newest member of the CleanUp PowerDown Crew.

It probably saved his life. He was a middle-aged person doing an entry-level job, sure, but no one asked questions, no one wondered how it came to this for him. Perhaps that was due to condescension, everyone assuming that a minority sweeping up was the natural state of affairs.

But the trainers and therapists treated him with kindness, and he found he'd missed that very much. He had a wage and people to talk to. The elements of sanity.

And thus it was, up to this day. I liked visiting him here, where he was happy. And truthfully, he looked better each time. The employees had a good health plan and were allowed to use the equipment during off hours. He'd put on a little muscle for his age.

"How's Mom?" he asked.

"Same." I couldn't think of a whole lot of news. About her, at least. "She entertained for some school friends. Got really into it, too."

"Good. No better medicine when it comes to your mother."

That reminded me that I had to have Quentin and his "parents" over again sometime. For Mom's sake. I could stomach the embarrassment to see her cheered again.

"And how about you?" he asked.

"Honestly? Not good. I feel very . . . put upon these days. You ever get people telling you to do things you don't want to do? Ordering you around?"

I realized that was a dumb question right after I asked it. I'd forgotten where we were, and thought I'd set him up to complain about the downsides of his current job. But he surprised me.

"I remember back at the insurance company I had a chain of

bosses who were pretty awful," Dad said. "They wouldn't give you a reason for their decisions, and everything that went wrong was your fault, not theirs. It's hard to work for those kinds of folks.

"I know you're capable of handling anything life throws at you," he went on. "But you shouldn't feel forced into a situation. Nothing good will come of it."

He didn't press me on who or what was bothering me, which was exactly what I was counting on.

I never had to get into specifics with Dad. He and I could have whole conversations without proper nouns. I mean, sure, his disregard for details probably contributed heavily to the shattering of our household, but for the moment I was grateful to not have to go deeper than I needed about gods. Or college.

"In this case, I should probably go along with it," I said. "It's actually pretty important that I do."

"Then it's an easy decision, right?" Dad said. "You have to pick and choose your battles. Fight too much and you'll wear yourself out."

Dad smiled at me. "You take everything so seriously. You're still young, you know? I feel like I have to remind you every so often or you'd forget. Your future's not going to be set in stone because of what happens today."

His certainty, the same certainty that had gotten him into so much trouble, flowed out to me like a balm. He couldn't conceive of my failure, of my unhappiness. All my faults lay buried deep within his mile-wide blind spots, where I could pretend they didn't exist.

I didn't love my dad more than my mom. But it was hard not to think of him as my favorite person in the world sometimes.

"Is that who I think it is?" said a booming voice behind us.

I turned to see two of the gym's trainers—Brian and K-Song—quickstep over.

"Miss Loooo!" Brian hooted. "Whaddup whaddup?"

I traded high fives with the two bros like we were three bros. They knew me from previous visits.

"Hot damn, girl, you're even taller than I remember!" K-Song said.

"She's a beanpole!" Brian roared. "We got to get you in the cage! Strong is the new skinny! A lady with your length could be putting up two plates!"

I laughed. Brian always said the same thing every time I visited. He was a great proponent of women lifting heavy, but he had a hard time convincing the clientele. His biker beard and tattooed cannonball shoulders probably scared them off. Sleek, hairless K-Song was more trusted by the ladies.

These two random coworkers of my dad's were oddly the only people I didn't get pissed at for commenting on my body. They were meatheads, sure, but they were the most well-meaning, least snarky meatheads I knew. They thought of my flesh purely in terms of its output and potential.

"I got your pops pulling one-thirty," K-Song bragged. He slapped Dad on the shoulder. "New PR."

"*Pfft.* One-thirty *sumo*," Brian said, rolling his eyes.

"IPF legal, dickbag!" K-Song shouted back. "Get with the times!"

The two started arguing viciously about the merits of different deadlift techniques. It would be resolved around the same time as the heat death of the universe.

I turned to my dad. "I'm gonna go."

"Give my best to Mom," he said, his eyes shining at me.

I rushed forward and gave my father one last hug. I would see him again soon. In the meantime, it would be back to trying my hardest not to turn out anything like him.

23

I LEFT THE GYM AND WENT AROUND THE CORNER TO WHERE
Quentin was waiting. It wasn't him stalking me—in a moment of
weakness, I'd called him during the cab ride after leaving Anna's
and he promised he could meet me soon, regardless of the distance. Better to think about demons than my future.

I laughed as I walked up to him. He'd taken some of my advice to
heart. He was still wearing his school uniform, but with a gigantic
chunky candy-cane-striped scarf around his neck and shoulders.

"What?" he said. "It was cold."

The look actually worked, in a Tokyo-street-fashion sort of way.
Another instance of beautiful people looking beautiful, no matter
what.

"I was waiting at Viscount and Second," Quentin groused. "You
told me the wrong address."

"This is *New* Viscount and Second, and no I didn't. Anyway, I've
been thinking. I have a theory about you and where you come from."

"Which is?"

"Scientists say once it becomes possible to create computer sim-
ulations of reality, simulated universes will vastly outnumber real
ones," I said. "Heaven and Earth are both virtual realities. Beings
like you and Guanyin use different number values for things like

gravity and light, so when you're inserted into the Earth simulation, you bring your own laws of physics into localized surroundings. That's how you do magic."

Quentin raised an eyebrow.

"It explains everything," I argued. "Earth time passes faster because our clock speed is faster. Reincarnation is when the source code for a person is pasted into a different era."

"That is the nerdiest thing I have ever heard," Quentin said. "Even coming from you."

I shrugged. He wasn't wrong.

"I have a theory about you, too." He brought his hands out from behind his back. In one he held a cup of bubble tea he'd already finished drinking, and in the other was a coffee.

"Thanks, but I've already had some."

"Have more. I want your heart racing."

I took the still-hot cup from him and sniffed it gingerly. It smelled divine. "This is for your theory?"

"Yes. I may have taken the wrong approach with your training by asking you to attain stillness."

The coffee tasted like rainy mountains and toasted honey. I'd have to ask him where he got it.

"Yours is a power born of battle," Quentin said as I drank. "Rage. Bloodlust."

"Way to make me sound like a monster."

"You're as much of a monster as I am. The only times your power has manifested so far have been when you were absolutely furious. We shouldn't run away from that. We should embrace it."

"That is the complete opposite of everything you've told me, and everything I've read about gongfu."

"That's because most teachers and disciples are focused on the aspects of soft power. Wavy, flowing soft power that redirects instead of confronts. There's hard power, too. The kind that moves in straight lines and overcomes instead of giving way. It's just as valid and just as essential.

"In my hands you were the living embodiment of hard power," Quentin continued. He looked nostalgic. "We'll double down on that instead of trying to suppress it."

"Won't that throw my *yin* and *yang* energies off balance? I thought balance was an important concept."

"Screw balance," he said. "What are you, old?"

I grinned and banked our empty cups into a nearby recycling can. No I was not.

Quentin motioned me into the alleyway where no one could see us. He held out his arms.

"Hop on."

"What?"

"I'm going to hold you for a moment, as an exercise. Carry you."

I shook my head. He was acting like he wanted me draped across his arms bridal-style but wasn't considering our relative proportions. I would have dangled all the way down past his knees.

"Will you stop fighting me on every single little thing and get in my arms?" he hissed. "I have to lift you up completely for this to work! Just trust me for once!"

Well fine, if he was going to be pouty about it. I spun him around, ignoring his protests, and made him lean over so I could get on top of him piggyback.

This wasn't much better. I had to straighten my legs out to the side and hold them there or else my soles would've touched the ground. I felt like I was riding a child's tricycle downhill.

Quentin shifted me around for a better grip as easily as if I were a sack of feathers. Unfortunately his hands landed where they weren't supposed to.

"Hey!" I yelped. "You're grabbing my aaaaAAAAAAAAAHHHH!"

Then we disappeared into the sky.

24

"**AAAAAAAAHAHAHAHA!**"

The ground shot away from Quentin's feet. It looked like that footage from NASA launches where the camera's mounted at the top, pointed downward, and you can see the coils of fire and thrust pushing you higher and higher. Only this was a million times faster, and there was no smoke to obscure the view of the rapidly shrinking Earth.

Street, block, district, peninsula. I screamed as each gave way to the next. The wind stung the tears right out of my eyes. I probably should have died of fright right there on his back. It would have served him right if I voided myself on top of him.

But somewhere, probably right around the time I recognized we were passing over Fisherman's Wharf, the terror turned to joy. The first plunge of the roller coaster wasn't going to kill me, and I was free to whoop and holler to my heart's content.

We were doing a slow turn as we traveled. The world gradually flipped upside down and then right side up in an astronaut's sunrise. Quentin was doing one big somersault.

That meant we were going to descend now. I clutched him tighter as a thrill went through my body. Maybe we would die after all, smashed against the Earth so hard there wouldn't be anything left. We were about to find out.

I thought Quentin was going for some kind of water landing before the rusty red towers of the bridge came into view. I braced for impact, but he did not.

His feet slammed into the painted iron and stuck without moving an inch, a perfect 10.0 landing. The sudden stop should have liquefied my internal organs. The impact should have sent a bell-like clang throughout the platform. But neither happened.

Localized laws of physics, I told myself.

"We're here," said Quentin.

I didn't get off him. Instead I clapped his chest excitedly.

"Again!" I shouted. "Again! Let's go to Wine Country!"

He dumped me on my feet. "This isn't a joyride. We're here to train."

"Nerd." I flicked his ear, making a little clack against what used to be my jewelry.

We were alone high up in the gray sky. I knew they let people go to the top of the bridge on occasion, so the platform wasn't without the trappings of safety. But I was still heady from the way we'd arrived, making the red tower feel like uncharted alien territory. Olympus Mons.

"Look around and tell me what you see," he said.

"I see the city. The Bay."

"Good. Now open your eyes and tell me again."

I did as told before realizing the incongruity.

. . .

The landscape suddenly became a painting, full of bright brushstrokes and swirling pigments. I could see the details of the world in thick outlines of color and black. My sense of scale was limitless, unconfined. The daubed-on windows of the smallest building were as visible to me as the tallest spires of the city.

"Oh wow," I murmured.

Cars in motion danced across the bridge like flipbook animations. I could see inside to the passengers, their faces zoetroping between emotions. That man was hungry. That woman was bored. That child held a secret.

I felt as if I could touch things on the far side of the Bay. Farther. I was hemmed in only by the Sierra Nevada and the western horizon.

I glanced at Quentin, and then stared. He blazed like a golden bonfire.

Energy poured off him in licking waves, an act of inefficient combustion that leaked so much power into the air I could hear the atmosphere whine and sizzle. There was a scorching heat at his core, and I was immune to it.

Around his shoulders was the faintest palimpsest overlay of another form. Skin as hard as diamonds. Fur as soft as velvet. A face of becalmed savagery. He was magnificent. Godlike. A Buddha victorious in battle.

"Well," he said in two voices, one his normal classroom baritone and the other a bass that could crack the sky. "Do you have anything to say?"

"Yeah. Did you put something in my coffee?"

Quentin laughed, and I could have sworn they heard him in New York.

"No. The only magic there is that it was expensive. You have true sight now, Genie. Technically you have *my* true sight. I used to be able to see the world like you can right now, but that's mostly gone. My guess is that our powers had become so intertwined in the old days that when you became human, you ripped this one from me like dirt clinging to a stump."

"I am genuinely sorry then," I said. It would have felt like a tragedy if I had to give this experience up to someone else, and I'd only had it for seconds.

"Try the lie detection," Quentin said. "It's pretty neat."

"Well, you have to tell me a lie then."

He blanked for a bit, one of those understandable moments where you have too many options to choose from.

"I hate you," he finally settled on.

As Quentin said it a dark, metallic bubble popped out from his lips, like he'd blown it from mercury. It pulsed in the air, a tiny opaque jellyfish, before floating away and dissipating.

"That's freaky," I said. "I don't think I'd want to know all the time if people were lying to me."

"It'll come in handy at some point, trust me."

I went back to drinking in the view. It was moving artwork, zooming and flattening where I wanted it to for my inspection. I watched a container ship full of almonds and canned tomatoes steam away into the distant Pacific. One of the crew members was bluffing his ass off in a poker game, holding nothing but unsuited low cards.

I turned toward land, drawn by a column of smoke. The wildfires in the scrubby hills north of the city were no closer to being put out than when I'd first heard about them on the news. The black whorls looked more like a series of opaque screens than vapor, blocking out anything behind them.

"You should try looking at yourself," Quentin said.

My eyes were starting to get tired, but I held my hands up in front of my face. As I wiggled my fingers, rippling lines of pressure played out in the air, almost like a topographical map or an artist's rendition of sound waves.

"That's how I recognized you," Quentin said. "Guanyin and Erlang Shen, too. Out of the billions of humans that have come and gone since the old days, only you have an aura as steady and unshakable as that. Just like the Ruyi Jingu Bang."

I watched one of the bigger pulses travel from my skin across the distance until it made contact with Quentin's erratic inner fire. Rather than clashing, the two energy signatures meshed with each other to become brighter. Stronger. On some fundamental level, Quentin and I harmonized.

Then the waves vanished. My vision reverted back to normal.

"Ow," I said, fighting back the ache in my corneas. "Is there a time limit on this thing?"

"Sort of. It's extremely difficult to sustain if you're not used to it. You'll have to build up your endurance through practice."

"Oh my god, everything is always practice, practice, practice with you Asians."

Quentin laughed, and then suddenly hiccuped. His whole body began shaking like a phone on vibrate. He dropped to one knee and clamped his hands to the platform we were standing on in order to steady himself.

"Jeez, it wasn't that funny," I said. "Is there something wrong?"

Quentin wriggled his shoulders back and forth to clear the spasms. "The magic in the earrings is going off. There must be a yaoguai within striking distance of a human."

"Where?"

He pointed to the south. "Somewhere over there. The feeling is stronger on that side of my body."

"That's as much resolution as you get from those things? That's barely better than a grandpa saying it'll rain because his trick knee's gone all a-tingly."

"Well, Guanyin said they're meant to be an early warning signal, not a map with GPS."

I leaned on top of Quentin, using him like a tripod over his protests. Turning true sight back on was surprisingly easy, merely a matter of knowing there was an extra level of vision available to me and then concentrating until I got there. I didn't know how I was supposed to pick out a demon from the rest of the visual noise, but once I started looking in the direction Quentin was pointing, the answer made itself pretty clear.

A blip appeared that was both brighter and darker than anything else around it—a smear of white ash on top of black soot. I was able to zoom in farther by instinctively squinting.

The flare was coming from inside an industrial building. What industry I didn't know; something that involved large gray tanks and a jungle of pipes next to a broad warehouse. Judging from its state of disrepair and the long weeds growing around the entrance, the facility should have been completely abandoned. But the eerie, colorless light moved from room to room in the pattern of something alive.

I realized why I was having such a hard time making out the source's silhouette. It didn't have one. It was a translucent skeleton, completely fleshless. My eyes kept passing through the spaces between its ribs.

"Quentin," I said, thoroughly weirded out by the apparition.

"Do you have any friends who are skeletons?"

"Skeletons? Is that what you're seeing?"

"I see one skeleton," I said. "Kind of floating around, pacing back and forth. It's giving off light like you do, except without any color or brightness. Am I even making sense?"

Quentin's grim expression alone told me yes, unfortunately I was. "Baigujing. The White Bone Demon. Don't let her out of your sight."

Watching the yaoguai waltz to and fro unnerved me beyond the fact that its appearance was firmly lodged at the bottom of the uncanny valley. I felt like a vulnerable Peeping Tom. In horror movies, the person trying to watch the monster through a telescope is usually moments away from biting it.

"What do we do now?" I asked. "Do we . . . do we go get her?"

"*Hell* no. We sit our asses down and think of a plan."

I was so surprised at his tone, I nearly looked away from Baigujing, but he reached up and propped my chin back into place.

"I'm serious," he said. "She's bad news—extremely bad. I don't think we're ready for her yet. Find whatever human she's lurking too close to and then we can make sure their paths don't cross."

I looked around the edges of the factory for a night watchman or a delinquent tagger sneaking onto the property. Nothing. The demon didn't look like she was hunting down any intruders.

Wait.

She wasn't pacing back and forth. She was walking around in a circle, her eyeless gaze fixed on a small shape on the center of the floor.

A little girl of five, looking too scared to cry.

. . .

"Damn it!" I screamed. "Damn it damn it damn it! There's a kid with her! Like *with* her!"

"What?" Quentin sprang to his feet and nearly clocked me in the jaw with his skull. "How did she get her hands on a human so fast?"

"I don't know, but we have to get there now!"

"I don't know where 'there' is!" You're the only one who can see her from this distance!"

I grabbed Quentin's shoulders and pointed him toward the derelict building. "I'll guide you! Just start jumping!"

Quentin made a handhold for me to climb on his back. "You have to give me some indication of where I'm trying to land!"

"About half the distance to my house, but in this direction! Go, damn it!"

Quentin and I took to the sky. The natural curve of his leap made it easy to fixate on our target while we sped through the air. The skeleton had stopped wandering and was now crouching directly in front of the catatonic child, contemplating. Any number of thoughts bounced inside its empty, polished skull.

"Hurry up!" I shouted into Quentin's ear.

"We're not flying! I can't change direction or speed in midair!"

I cursed, and then cursed again even louder as we overshot. "That factory we just passed!" I yelled. "Second floor, the biggest room!"

"I saw it," Quentin grunted. "Hold on."

We came down in an empty municipal baseball diamond that might have been in the same town as the factory. Quentin took the landing much harder than on the bridge. We slammed into the ground, gouging up fountains of dirt and grass. Before the debris even settled, Quentin had us back in the air, on a smaller arc in the opposite direction.

This leg of our journey took much less time. As the building loomed near, Quentin stuck out an arm to act as a battering ram. I buried my face in his shoulder as we made impact with one of the huge glass windows.

I heard us burst through and land on the other side as easily as if it were a pane of sugar. Quentin held my head down while shards tinkled around us, to make sure I didn't catch an eyeful.

Once it was safe he patted my knee. I got up and took a measure of our surroundings.

The hall we were in had been stripped of equipment a long time ago. Exposed I-beams buttressed walls of cinderblock that had never been painted. The dust under our feet was thick enough to pass for light snowfall.

I found the child in the center of the open space. She looked scared out of her wits, but whole.

Standing over her in a flowing evening gown was a beautiful, shapely woman. With no lips. They were simply missing. Her teeth, otherwise perfect, lay bare to the world, giving her the same insouciant smirk as a poison bottle.

She reached out and brushed a nail down the little girl's cheek. A razor line of blood followed it, and the girl cried out in pain.

"Get away from her!" I shrieked.

"Or what?" said the demon. "I'm not afraid of either of you."

Her voice was like nothing so much as a pepper grinder. She compensated for her liplessness by rolling her tongue to make certain sounds, the same way a ventriloquist did.

"Now or never," Quentin said to me.

"Now."

I ran straight at Baigujing. Whatever magical toughness had protected me from being cut to ribbons by a plate-glass window would have to do. Quentin got clever and flickered off to the side, rounding the demon to hit her in the flank.

Unfortunately for us, I got there first. My wild, untrained punch met Baigujing right in the center of her chest, but she went limp and weightless the split second before, offering no resistance. She and I tumbled together a few steps before disentangling.

Quentin had the wherewithal to change his target. He scooped up the kid and wrapped her in his scarf. Then he leapt out of the window.

"Looks like you've been abandoned," Baigujing said.

I nearly smiled; Quentin had only done exactly what he should have. I just needed to stall until he got back from putting the child somewhere safe. I raised my hands like I knew how to fight, hoping that Big Joe's "don't mess with me" stance from the self-defense class was a good enough bluff.

This was it. I was facing off against a demon. For real this time, with no blind rage to act as a crutch. There was a clarity to every second that passed while I was guarding a life other than my own. I felt pure. Unassailable.

Not in the literal sense, though, because Baigujing advanced upon me steadily. She was either being unnecessarily wary or she was toying with me.

"We can wait until the monkey gets back," she said. "If you'd like."

"Sure." I jabbed at her eyes and missed. That must only work when they aren't expecting it.

The demon tutted. "You've got to put your weight behind it, or else there's no point. I've taken blows from you and the monkey at full strength."

"Here's another." Quentin reappeared and delivered a flying knee to the side of her head.

Baigujing's body rumpled and pinwheeled away. She righted herself, hardly any worse for wear.

"*Displace,*" she intoned, making the motions for a spell.

"Oh no, you don't." Quentin lunged at her to interrupt it.

But he didn't succeed. In fact, he didn't even come close to Baigujing. He dove in the wrong direction by more than ninety degrees.

"What the hell?" Quentin was unable to believe the extent to which he'd whiffed. He flailed in the empty air and tried to lay hands on her again, but he ended up running in a new angle that was equally bonkers.

Baigujing hadn't moved at all, from my perspective. She must have screwed with Quentin's eyes. There was no telling what kind of illusion he was seeing at the moment.

"Can you hear me?" I asked him. "I can see her but I'm not sure if she's real or—"

The demon crossed the distance between us in one step and backhanded me all the way into the wall.

Okay, I thought through the smear of pain that was my spine hitting the bricks. *Guess she's real.*

I keeled over on my hands and knees, gasping for breath. I saw Baigujing's bare feet stop in front of me.

She nudged me in the chin with her toe. "Your turn," she said.

I planted myself, a sprinter in a starting block, and slugged her as hard as I could in the stomach. I could feel her flesh wrap around my fist without taking any of the punch. It was like trying to fight a plastic bag floating in the breeze.

Baigujing smiled at me. She had to use her eyes to do it. She grabbed me by the jaw and bent me backward, squeezing hard enough that I couldn't speak.

"You're not going to get anywhere like that," she said. "I met the monkey for the first time while disguised as a human. He knew I was up to no good, though, and struck me with the Ruyi Jingu Bang with all his might. I survived unharmed. Do you know how rare that is, to be able to shrug off direct hits from the Monkey King? I feel like I'm not appreciated enough for that."

I glanced over at Quentin, who was still chasing shadows.

"The funny thing is, after he struck me I left behind a body of flesh to make it look like he'd murdered an innocent girl," Baigujing giggled. "You should have seen how Xuanzang punished him for that one! The beast that threatened Heaven, rolling in the dust, clutching his head and pleading for mercy. I laughed for weeks!"

I didn't know how I had any nerves left to touch, but she found them. I took her by the hair with one hand. She merely grinned, figuring I was going to punch her with the other.

But instead I used my grip to swing my legs around and wrap up her neck and shoulders. My ankles found each other and I squeezed Baigujing with every ounce of strength I had left.

I was ripping a page from Quentin's playbook. Judging from the demon's howl, it was a good one.

She clawed frantically at my face but couldn't reach. My body was simply too long. I had her locked up with all the time in the world.

What did Quentin do next to the Demon King of Confusion? I wondered, my thoughts surprisingly cold-blooded. *Oh yeah. This.* I took hold of Baigujing's skull with impunity and began cranking her neck.

"Aaagh!" she hissed. "Ugly girl! Ugly, ugly girl!"

Really? We were going to do that now?

"Yeah, well . . . you're overdressed," I said. I squeezed tighter and heard something crack.

Through the cloud of adrenaline fogging my brain, an idea slipped through like a ray of light. I closed my eyes and reopened them with true sight on. Baigujing was a skeleton once more, her muscle and skin invisible under my X-ray vision.

"Where's Red Boy?" I bellowed. "Tell me, and I'll spare your life!" I didn't know if I was strong enough to dictate either way; but it sounded like the type of thing you said when you had a monster in a headlock.

Baigujing froze. But only for an instant. She began trembling in my grasp and making the most hideous noise. I almost let go out of fear before I realized she was simply laughing.

"I'll never tell you," she said. "Nothing you can do will ever make me tell you."

There were no lie bubbles. Either she didn't know or she really wasn't going to say. So much for my idea.

"*Spare my life?*" she sneered. "You don't have what it takes to end me. The instant you slip, I'll find that child and rip the meat from her *bones!*"

Still no bubbles. "Come again?" I said.

"I'll kill her and every other miserable human I get my hands on! I will turn this town into a sea of *corpses!* You will *swim* to me in dead flesh!"

The air was clear. If I let her go she'd do her best to make good on her threat.

"I can't be killed by the likes of you!" Baigujing roared. "Do you hear me? You can't kill me!"

Bubble.

"Don't tell me what I can't do," I said. I arched back and snapped her in two.

Unlike the Demon King of Confusion's slow melt, Baigujing burst into ink and nothingness like a popped balloon. I nearly hit my head on the floor as a result of her body's vanishing act. I flailed and spat away the black inky liquid that I thought would be covering me, only to find that it was already gone.

I closed my eyes and shook the true sight out of my head. With it went all the rush that had been keeping me afloat.

It felt as if I'd been run over by a dozen trucks. My body hurt where I'd been hit, sure, but I also seemed to have self-torn every muscle fiber I had.

One down, ninety-nine to go, I thought to myself. If the remaining bottles of beer on the wall were going to be similarly hard, then I did not like my chances of emerging unscathed from this mess.

I staggered over to Quentin, who was only now coming out of his daze.

"Way to be useful, chief," I deadpanned, slapping my hand on his shoulder. I kept it there for support, so I didn't topple over in the next breeze.

Quentin scrunched his eyes. "I could see you two, but you were always just out of reach."

He draped my arm over his neck and dragged me to the stairs. We took each step slowly.

"To think you beat her completely on your own," he said. "You were amazing."

"I was lucky. You have got to teach me wushu. I can't handle not knowing what to do in these situations."

"I keep telling you, I don't know any formal martial arts. If you want these fights to get any easier, we should work on shape-changing you back into a staff so I can wield you like I used to."

I smacked him on the chest with my load-bearing arm.

"That's gross," I said. "*Wield* me? No."

"We did it all the time back in the day! It would only be temporary."

"I'm not transforming into anything else. If everything you've told me is true, then I must have worked my ass off as the Ruyi Jingu Bang in order to get a human body. I'm not throwing it away just so you have a blunt object to beat on people with."

Quentin grumbled but gave up the argument. At least for the moment. He took me to the first floor, a much smaller room. The little girl sat in the corner on a pile of rubber hose, nervously chewing on his scarf.

She saw us and burst into tears. I kneeled in front of her and tried to pat her head soothingly. The cut on her cheek was clean and not too deep. Other than that she wasn't injured.

"*La llorona,*" the girl sobbed. "*La llorona.*"

Crud. "*Uh, todo bien,*" I said. "*Nosotros . . . ganamos? Todo bien, todo bien.*"

Quentin picked the girl up and hushed her, swinging gently back and forth. She calmed down immediately. I'd forgotten how much of a wizard he was with children.

"La mala mujer se ha ido," he murmured. *"Ella ha sido derro-tado. Vamos a traer a tu mama. Duerme ahora, preciosa."*

The girl nodded into his shoulder and fell asleep.

I gave Quentin a look. He shot one back.

"What?" he said. "I talk to non-Chinese people too, you know."

25

I DON'T REMEMBER HOW I GOT HOME AFTER WE SNUCK THE girl into the fire station. I don't remember how we did that without getting caught, either. Events were lost in a haze of exhaustion.

Mom usually gave me some wiggle room on when I returned from the city due to the vagaries of public transportation, but this evening was pushing it. I was only able to end her angry harangue by telling her I had run into Quentin on the walk back through town and stopped to chat. Her hypocrisy between me hanging out with "boys" as a vague concept versus an individual boy she knew and liked was astounding.

I ate a reheated dinner, showered any remaining demon residue off my skin, and collapsed in bed. I would never leave my mattress again.

But I couldn't sleep.

I slipped my hand out from the mound of covers and groped around for the replacement clamshell phone I'd been forced to use after Quentin crushed my real one. There was a message from my dad, just his usual ping about how glad he was to see me. There were status updates from Yunie trailing into a long, one-sided thread that made me laugh. She knew that I went into the city for these appointments and wasn't always online.

I scrolled past all of the messages and dialed Quentin while lying on my side. We were going full middle-school.

"What's up?" he said.

It was noisy on his end. "Why is it noisy on your end?"

"I'm at a casino off the highway."

"What?" I had to stop myself from speaking at full volume so as not to wake up Mom. "Why?"

"I'm earning money. I need cash to fit in and move around human society. Plus I don't need as much sleep as you do, and it's a decent way to kill time."

It shouldn't have been weird that he was blowing off steam by gambling; there were more ads for the local casinos written in Chinese than in English. But his teasing from before had been on point. It did feel strange, knowing that he did things without me.

"Did you just want to talk?" he asked.

I didn't have an answer. As cheesy as it was, maybe I simply wanted to know that I could hear him and that he could hear me, for a while.

"What's Heaven like?" I said to break the silence. "Is it nice?"

"It's very nice. Everything about Heaven is nice. There is nothing ugly, sick, or out of place in Heaven."

Whoops. From the shift in his voice I could tell we had started off heavy for a simple chitchat.

"Being allowed inside was everything I wanted for a very long time," he said. "When they let me through the door, I thought I would finally become content. At peace with myself. And then . . . well, you know what happened. Technically you were there, even if you don't remember it."

If the legend was true, then I'd been the instrument of the

Monkey King's wrath in Heaven after he realized he was nothing but a second-class citizen among the gods. The moral of the tale was probably supposed to be that patience and good manners were more important than power. But what I took from it was that the people in charge could withhold respect from you, and there wasn't a damn thing you could do about it.

"Can I see Heaven? Can you take me there?"

"Absolutely not," Quentin said sharply. "It's too dangerous for a normal person born of Earth. Your base humanity would be scorched away by the excess of *qi* energies, leaving only your spiritual essence behind. Genie Lo would be gone, and only the Ruyi Jingu Bang would remain. Forever."

"That's not what you would prefer? You'd get to fight with your stick like you used to, without any backtalk."

"Don't twist my words. Even if I took you to Heaven now, any powers you haven't recovered in your current human form would be lost forever. You've got strength and true sight, sure, but there are still a few tricks you haven't remembered yet."

"Well, if you didn't want your magic iron staff back immediately when we first met, what exactly were you hoping for when you came to my school?"

Quentin sighed and took a sip of some unknown drink, the ice cubes clinking against his glass.

"I was hoping you'd recognize an old friend," he said. "I assumed the memories would come rushing back and you'd be so happy to see me that you'd take my hand right there in class and I don't know . . . we'd run off and have an adventure or something. Go exploring, like back in the day."

"Ha! You wanted to sweep me off my feet. Dork."

I could practically hear him blush through the receiver.

"I'm going." His voice was adorably gruff. "You're distracting me. I'm down seven thousand bucks because of you."

I bolted upright. "You're fooling around with *that* kind of money?"

Quentin laughed in my ear and hung up on me.

■ ■ ■

School felt a little weird the next day. People stared at me like they knew something.

I wandered around from class to class until I caught up with Yunie at lunch. When she saw me she covered her mouth trying not to laugh.

"What is it?"

"Are you trying out a new look?" she asked.

The answer was no. I'd slept like the dead, and ended up having to run to make it on time without washing up. But half the school came in looking like slobs. I couldn't have been much worse.

Yunie pulled out her compact mirror and held it up. I peered into it until I found what didn't belong.

My irises were gold. Shimmering gold.

"You shouldn't leave those in overnight and forget," Yunie said. "It's bad for your eyes. But I like the color."

Shining, 24-karat eyes. Ten-year-old me would have been thrilled beyond belief.

Sixteen-year-old me had to go find Quentin.

■ ■ ■

179

"Well, of course," Quentin said. "My eyes turned gold when I gained true sight in Lao Tze's furnace. I'd be worried if yours *weren't* gold."

We were outside, near the away team's end of the soccer field. Quentin sat on a tree branch, eating a nectarine from a bag that was full of them. He really liked his drupes.

"People think I'm wearing contacts," I complained. "They're ridiculous."

He raised his hand solemnly. "One should never feel ashamed about their true self."

I picked up a rock and threw it at him. Yunie was still waiting for me back in the cafeteria.

"All right, all right." He hopped down to the ground and dusted himself off. Then he reached for my face.

I batted his hands away. "What are you doing?"

"Genie, you're asking me to conceal the mark of one of the greatest powers in the known universe, an ability that the gods themselves would envy. I need a little more contact with you than for a normal spell. This is going to take a moment."

Fine, whatever. I presented myself for a harsh grip as clinical as the Vulcan mind-meld.

But instead Quentin's touch was feather-soft. He grazed the back of his nails over my skin and brushed gently at my hair, tucking the loose strands behind my ears. I couldn't tell what he was whispering in his hushed tones, but it felt like poetry.

It was intensely soothing. Our faces drew closer as he chanted. The cadence of his voice seemed to be pulling me toward his lips.

God, he smelled good.

"There," Quentin said, suddenly stepping back. "They're brown again. Happy?"

No. Yes. Wait.

I collected the bits of myself I'd dropped on the ground and stacked them back in more or less the right order.

"You know you could have done that last night, before you left," I said.

He shrugged. "I forgot. Plus, I like the color. They're your real eyes, you know. The brown is just an illusion. I'll have to recast the spell every time you use true sight."

Great. I was permanently stuck as a Fae Princess from Emotionland.

"I don't get how 'spells' work," I said. "I've seen you and the demons perform them, but not Guanyin or Erlang Shen."

"A spell is just an application of a person's spiritual power to alter their surroundings," Quentin said. "The smaller and more generic the effect, the easier it is to do, which is why we normally stick to one-word commands. You need sufficient internal energies to power a spell, but you also need sufficiently refined technique.

"It's like throwing a punch," he went on. "You could throw a crisp jab that has no power behind it, or a wild haymaker that has no chance to connect. Spells are tools, not guarantees."

"Then what is Guanyin doing when she, you know, does her stuff?" I made jazz hands in a poor imitation of the goddess' awesome abilities.

"That's more of an innate thing. She's still using her spiritual power, but she has so much of it that an individual domain of reality is hers to control. She doesn't need to focus through words or hand motions."

"So I could learn spells too?"

Quentin scoffed. "You could if you weren't so ass at meditating.

We've been relying on your raw power to force your talents to the surface like a high-pressure boiler."

I glared at him but he simply shrugged. "Harsh truths. Red Boy's domain is fire. Erlang Shen's is water. *Your* domain is hitting stuff really hard."

I tried to come up with a different specialty that could have applied to me, but he pretty much had me in a corner.

"I've been thinking more about what happened with Baigujing, though," he said. "Did any of that seem strange to you?"

That was a dumb question. Besides the parts where we fought an evil skeleton and sent it back to Hell?

"She didn't say anything unusual," I offered. "For a demon trying to kill me."

"That's exactly what I'm talking about. She didn't say anything. She was just there, in the factory. It was all such a . . . set piece."

"Well, we could always deduce her motives by cross-checking police reports with eyewitness accounts of the security footage following the paper trail of blah blah-blah blah blah. Quentin, she was going to eat a baby."

"In an abandoned factory?"

"She probably took the kid back to her lair like a jaguar dragging its prey into a tree. People have eating habits. I've seen you bury your peach pits because you have some idea in your head that they'll magically grow into trees and you'll get a second helping of peaches. I hate to break it to you but the soil here probably isn't as fertile as the mystical mountain where you're from."

"I know that," he said with a scowl. "All I'm saying is that something doesn't add up."

"And I'm saying that if we waste time on recaps, we'll never get through this—this quest or geas, or whatever it is we agreed to. Quentin, that was *one* demon. One, and it nearly ended us! We have ninety-nine more to catch. Let's focus on them instead of fights we already won.

"We put the bad guy in the dirt and saved a baby," I concluded. "That's perfect math to me."

Quentin snorted. "Someone's taking to the demon slaying lifestyle rather comfortably."

26

YUNIE SLAMMED HER HAND DOWN IN THE MIDDLE OF THE textbook I was reading. She was the only person who could do that without pulling back a stump.

"*This* is the final round of the *concours*," she announced. "The last stage of the competition. The performance that counts."

I looked at the four concert tickets underneath her fingers, dated for a couple weeks out. One was for me.

I knew that two were for my parents. Both of them loved her like a second daughter. Mom had gotten all the "why-can't-you-be-more-like-Yunie" out of her system by fourth grade, and Dad was resigned to the fact that most of his family photos of me past a certain age also had Yunie in them.

It was unspoken that those two tickets were for me to decide a suitable arrangement. She wasn't *not* going to invite them to the most important event in her musical career to date. Nor would she ever show a favorite. But I could freely pick one or none or both of my parents to come, and feel guilty about whatever combination I chose in order to keep the peace.

It was the fourth ticket that confused me. "What's this for?"

"That one's for you to give to Androu as your plus one."

"Why would I take Androu and not Quentin?"

Yunie rolled her eyes at me like I was trying to play checkers at a chess match. "To make Quentin jealous. You really have to get with the program here, because your lack of game is disturbing."

She slid the ticket back and forth with her pinky. "And way to incriminate yourself. You didn't even hesitate there."

I prickled all the way up the back of my neck. My mind had only gone to Quentin because it'd be easier to explain his presence to my mother. And I'd talked to him most recently. And because demons.

"You didn't tell me the two of you were that far along," Yunie continued.

Anyone else would have thought she was teasing me. And she was. But my Yunie-sense, the only superpower that I truly believed in, indicated that she also sounded slightly hurt.

"We're not," I said. "I mean, we're not anywhere along. Of course I would tell you if we were anywhere. There's nothing to tell, really. Really."

I couldn't keep track of what I was embarrassed about at this point. I only wanted to make sure she knew that I wasn't trying to hide something as important as a relationship from her. While at the same time hiding a massive supernatural conspiracy that she could never know about.

"I'm sorry," she said. "I should lay off. I just like seeing you without that line of concentration running down your forehead all the time. Sometimes you get so stressed out from studying that you could hold a playing card between your eyebrows."

I looked at my friend. She was brimming with nervous energy, almost bouncing on her toes. Which meant for once she wasn't convinced she would win this competition. Yunie showed fear by turning even more radiant and pretty. Judging by the glow on her face, this one was for all the marbles.

I handed her back the fourth ticket.

"I won't need this," I said. "I'm going without distractions. You're the only person who matters."

She threw her arms around me and squeezed. "Well, yeah, duh."

. . .

"What's the need for secrecy?" I asked.

"Huh?"

Quentin and I were on the school roof again, giving meditation training another shot. I'd bought us this window of time by telling my mother that all team workouts had been changed to doubles, so I'd be home late every day. She wasn't happy about it, and I couldn't help imagining the gross liquid metal escaping my lips as I lied to her, but this was for the greater good.

The roof had become our own private spot, mostly because we could get there without tripping the stairwell alarms. The thrum of the ventilation units provided white noise that I had hoped would drown out my thoughts. That obviously hadn't worked, but at the very least I found this a relaxing way to cool down after practice.

"Every supernatural being I've met so far has been in disguise, or hiding," I said. "Or concerned to some degree with not being found out by a normal human. Why do they care whether people on Earth know about gods and demons?"

Quentin scowled at how quickly I'd given up trying to sit still, but he kept his eyes closed as if he could still salvage the session for himself. "In the case of yaoguai, the simple answer is because it's easier for them to hunt if no one knows about their existence."

"And the complex answer?"

He drew a deep breath. Either because his exercise required it or he was about to say something serious.

"At their core, every demon desperately wants to become human," he said. "Even if they're in denial about it."

"What? That doesn't make any sense."

"Are you sure? You are what you eat. There's a psychological drive behind a demon's hunger, besides the powers they might gain. The yaoguai who wanted to consume Xuanzang's flesh also wanted to become more like him, in a way."

I shuddered. That was the logic of cannibal serial killers.

"That's also why they wear disguises even if they can't really pull them off," said Quentin. "Back in the old days, the few demons who could successfully pass for human sometimes built entire lives inside monasteries and villages without being discovered. The really disciplined elite were able to manage it without eating anyone."

"Sounds like it would take a lot of willpower, fasting right next to your food source."

Quentin nodded. "Those demons tended to be either relatively decent beings, or the most dangerous monsters of all."

"Okay—but why would the gods bother with hiding? Why not reveal themselves in a big, glitzy display across the sky? The world would get pious in a hurry."

"More worshippers equals more work. More prayers to answer, more dynasties to support. The Jade Emperor got sick of it at some point and withdrew his direct influence from Earth. Now he can spout 'wu wei' as an excuse for not interfering with human matters, while laying back and enjoying the endless bounties of Heaven."

"Ugh, that's privileged BS if I ever heard it. 'Hey, I'm personally doing fine so let's not rock the boat, okay? You people who have nothing just need to wait and it'll all work out somehow.' "

Quentin's laugh petered out. "If you don't like it, you can wait a couple hundred eons until the Jade Emperor steps down and another god becomes Supreme Ruler of Heaven."

Huh. That got me thinking.

"Does that mean Guanyin could be in charge?" I asked. "I can't imagine she'd be so passive if she were the leader of the celestial pantheon."

Quentin frowned and opened his eyes at the mention of Guanyin.

"I asked her about it once," he said quietly. "She refused to think about leading the gods. She said it would keep her from tending to the suffering of ordinary humans."

"Too busy doing actual work." I replied with a sigh. Verily, on Earth as it was in Heaven with some people. I went back to my poor excuse for meditating and focused on my—

"Aaagh!"

Quentin suddenly leaned across the small gap between us and seized me by the shoulders. The shaking traveled from his body into mine, rattling my teeth. There was nothing I could do except hold him steady until the tremors passed.

"Sorry," he said once he'd settled down. "I didn't mean to grab you like that. The yaoguai alert doesn't hurt like the Band-Tightening Spell, but it hits me deep down in my body the same way."

I didn't mind. Mostly because his aftershocks resembled a dog twitching adorably from a vigorous petting session. I had the over-whelming urge to rub his belly and ask him who the good boy was.

But as enjoyable as that would be, it would have to wait. "All right," I said, getting to my feet. "We've got an hour and a half at most before I have to be home. Dial me in."

Quentin gave me a funny look, but if he thought I was being too cocky he didn't say so.

■　■　■

The two of us stood on the sidewalk, craning our necks upward to look at the grand stone residence framed by the evening sky. It was much smaller and older than the glass towers in the financial district of the city, but also much more elegant. The exterior was styled in fanciful Art Deco, as if to say, *Have fun in your liquefaction zones, losers—we're on bedrock.*

"Is he still there?" Quentin asked.

I touched my temple like a mutant with eyebeams; I'd found that the gesture helped me manage my newfound supernatural vision. The floors of the building dissolved away until only the penthouse remained. Sitting on a couch in the living room was a glowing green man with a face as blank and smooth as an eggshell. He had no eyes, no nose, no mouth. Nothing.

"He's still there," I said. "I think he's watching TV."

Despite not having any sensory orifices to speak of, the yao-guai was channel-surfing on a huge wall-mounted screen. Each time he clicked the remote, the surface of his face rippled like a pond with a pebble thrown into it. I had the distinct feeling that he was absorbing something from the experience, the way hit men in movies practiced different accents while looking into mirrors.

I couldn't see any signs of the apartment's original occupants. Maybe they were still at work. Maybe the demon had swallowed them whole. We had to move now.

"So the plan is we go in through the main entrance on the ground floor to cut off his escape," Quentin said. "I get us past any security on the way up, and we confront him once we're sure that no one's around to get caught in the cross fire."

A strange well of confidence filled my chest. "Let's do it."

We strode into the lobby like we owned the place. I approached the blazer-wearing man at the front desk and put on a cheery smile.

"Excuse me sir," I said, Quentin winding up for a spell behind me. "Can you tell me if the folks on the top floor have—"

The doorman leaped over the desk and clamped his jaws around my windpipe.

27

I LET OUT A SHRIEK OF SURPRISE. THE MAN'S TEETH SLID OFF my skin without drawing blood as I frantically pulled away. But the fury in his eyes was terrifying in its complete mindlessness. He would kill himself trying to kill me.

I reared back to clock him in the head.

"No!" Quentin snagged my arm from behind and brought me down, allowing the man to pummel me with impunity.

"What's wrong with you?" I screamed at him. My attacker was doing his best to cram more of my face into his mouth.

"He's a human!" Quentin said, pinned under us both. "You'll kill him if you hit him that hard!"

I was going to snap at Quentin for not giving me any options, but then I remembered how many I really had. The doorman was a massive, bulky guy, and only my head thought that I lacked the strength to throw him off. That wasn't the case anymore.

With a form that would have made Brian and K-Song proud, I grabbed the rabid human by the collar and belt and hoisted him bodily over my head. He continued to thrash and flail in the air, but he wasn't as frightening once I held him like an overgrown toddler.

"Okay, so what's his deal then?" I said to Quentin, craning my neck to avoid a frothy wad of spit dangling from the man's mouth.

"He's under some kind of frenzy spell. If you put him down he's liable to tear his own skin off."

"I can't hold him like this forever. We still have the yao-guai on the top floor to deal with. Do you think it noticed us by now?"

Ding!

All three elevators reached the lobby at the same time. The doors opened to reveal they were packed sardine-tight with people bubbling at the mouth with pure hatred for no one but Genie Lo and Quentin Sun. They barreled out the doors at us like horses at the Kentucky Derby.

"I would say yeah," Quentin called out before disappearing under a pile of rage zombies.

▪ ▪ ▪

I got tackled to the floor and landed with my face in someone's armpit. As gently as I could under the circumstances, I shoved at the mass, hoping to get some breathing room. A few of the people went flying across the lobby hard enough to crack the full-length mirrors they landed on. Whoops.

"Cast Dispel Magic on them or something!" I shouted at Quentin.

"That's not a thing!" he said scornfully. "The effects have to wear off over time!"

A woman in hair curlers with a good left hook busted her knuckles wide open on my nose. "Then put them to sleep! For however long it takes!"

Quentin spun around, throwing attackers off his back with

centrifugal force. I acted as a human chain-link fence, keeping back anyone who would have interfered with his hand motions.

"*Sleep,*" he declared. "*Sleep!*"

"Why isn't it working?"

"This spell is really strong! Whoever cast it is nearly as good as I am!"

"Then you have to do one better! Now!"

Quentin inhaled so deeply that he could have snuffed out a campfire. "*SLEEP!*" he bellowed.

The shock wave of his voice expanded throughout the lobby, knocking people aside. The formerly berserking apartment-dwellers slumped against the walls and sank unconscious to the floor.

The room, littered with limply stirring bodies, looked like the aftermath of some devastating party. There wasn't time to deal with these people, though. We got in one of the elevators and slammed the button for the top floor.

The sudden acceleration pulled at my stomach, as if my own dread wasn't heavy enough. Each bell chime of the floors we passed was a countdown to a fight with a yaoguai that was smart enough and evil enough to use humans as expendable pawns. I'd known that demons were dangerous on an individual, starving-predator type of level, but this was different. Even Quentin was steeling himself, wringing the cricks out of his neck and knuckles.

The penthouse hallway only had one door. I didn't want to let my fear catch up to the rest of me, so I walked up to it straight away and kicked it off its hinges. Quentin and I filed in and took a position in sight of the yaoguai that stood in the living room, his back turned to us as he gazed through the window over the landscape. Sunbeams filtered in through a large skylight overhead, casting dramatic shadows over our gathering.

"Okay asshole," I said. "Time to dance."

The demon turned to face us. *Face* being a relative term. The front of its skull had a slight taper to it, the way illustrators might draw a head by starting with an oval and a cross as a placeholder for the eyes. It looked at Quentin, rippled once, and then raised its hand into the air.

"Spell! Spell!" I shouted like a Secret Service agent spotting a gun.

Only it wasn't. The wiggling of the yaoguai's fingers didn't do anything. It was the toodle-oo gesture.

He set his feet and then jumped straight up through the skylight. Glass shards rained down on us. It was like one of Quentin's takeoffs, only more destructive.

"Track him!" Quentin said.

I tried to keep my eye on him with true sight, but it was much harder than I thought—the equivalent of trying to watch a jet plane with a telescope. The yaoguai kept slipping out of my narrow field of view. It didn't help that right before I had a lock, I was hit in the back of the head with an upright vacuum cleaner, knocking me over.

I looked up to see Quentin with a rampaging cleaning lady wrapped up in a full nelson.

"Sorry," he said. "She was quicker than she looks."

I collapsed back to the floor and groaned.

■ ■ ■

Rearranging the hulking doorman back into his chair without making it look like he'd died mid-nap was an exercise in futility. I had to leave him slumped over, sleeping with the unnatural stillness that came with Quentin's knockout spell.

I'd lost patience with the rest of the people in the lobby and stuffed them in the hallway of the first floor. They'd sort themselves out once they woke up.

Quentin emerged from an unmarked room holding a bunch of tapes and computer equipment.

"We're lucky they had an old system," he said. "The newer security cameras upload recordings to the Internet automatically."

"How do you even know that?" I said. "Did you break into fancy apartment buildings all the time back in ancient China?"

He shrugged off the question and gave his armful of electronics a squeeze over the nearest trash can. The broken bits filtered through his fingers, shades of my annihilated phone.

My self-imposed deadline had been blown, and my mother would be furious with me once I got home. But that wasn't what I was worried about right now.

"This is bad," I said, chewing my fingernails. "This is so bad. We effed up, Quentin. He got away. The demon got away. There's a hole in the roof of this building."

A middle-aged man in running shorts with a Yorkie on a leash entered the lobby as I was speaking.

"What hole in the building?" the man asked. He saw the doorman spread-eagled behind the desk. "What did you do to Lucius? Who are you two?"

"*Sleep.*" Quentin tossed the spell over his shoulder without looking. The man crumpled to the carpet. His dog began licking his passed-out face.

I rubbed my arms and paced back and forth, suddenly cold. This was the first time we tried to apprehend a demon with full knowledge and preparation of what we were doing, and we'd borked it.

"Look, I'm not gonna lie and call this the best demon hunt I've ever been on," Quentin said. "But look on the bright side. All of these people are . . . roughly okay. We scared off the yaoguai before it caused any real damage."

His words weren't much of a comfort. I kicked at the floor hard enough that it startled the dog into whimpering.

"We'll talk to Guanyin," Quentin said. "It'll be okay. You'll see."

28

"YOU LET HIM GET AWAY?"

It was the first weekend after our debacle with the faceless man, and our first debriefing with Guanyin and Erlang Shen. For our meeting spot we were in a dim sum restaurant near the train station two towns over from mine. The clanking, cackling, brunchtime chatter formed a cone of deafness around us as good as any silencing spell.

Which was good, because Quentin had severely misrepresented what Guanyin's reaction to our little escapade would be. The Goddess of Mercy was more upset than anyone I'd ever seen capable of, outside of me and my mother.

"You let him get away," she repeated incredulously.

"This one wasn't an eater," Quentin said. "I'm sure of it."

"And how do you know that?" Erlang Shen asked.

"He was too powerful. You can't reach that level of manipulation ability if you still crave human flesh. Also he had no mouth."

Guanyin looked at Quentin like his answer physically hurt her brain. "So it's okay that this particular yaoguai is running free, *because* he's strong enough to bewitch any human into doing his bidding. *Yau mou gaau cho ah . . .*"

I'd thought maybe being in public would have lessened our

gloom, but instead the restaurant mirrored it back on us tenfold. It might have been the sheen of grease on the floors, or the glass of the fish tanks lining the wall. Either way, it felt like a spotlight of unfestiveness was being aimed at us.

We ignored most of the carts that passed by. The two gods didn't bother with human food, and I couldn't muster an appetite in a situation like this. Even Quentin toned down his consumption to normal levels, having long finished his vegetable dumplings out of a sense of obligation rather than enjoyment.

"We searched the building after scaring him off, and we didn't find any remains," I said.

"Well that's nice," Guanyin said. "But that's not the only issue here. Having a ravenous yaoguai on the loose would have meant that the two of you were only on the hook for every missing person report until it was caught. Now that we know it likes controlling people against their will, you can also add every act of violence, depravity, and self-harm to your list as well."

Quentin shot to his feet. *"A word outside,"* he barked.

The goddess locked eyes with him for a long second, but eventually she stood and followed him out of the restaurant.

I could barely look up from the table. I felt like garbage.

I wasn't used to failing in ways that I couldn't make up for with sheer brute effort. I could usually cover my normal-world short-comings by hitting the books or the gym harder, but Guanyin was right. There was no way to spin this.

In the interim silence my phone vibrated, a period on the end of the sentence. Probably Yunie. I let it go until it stopped.

Erlang Shen took the moment to speak up.

"She takes her job very seriously," he explained. "When you first meet her she's all sweetness and favors. But if you ever disappoint her . . ."

"Yeah, she's got layers," I muttered.

"Don't take it too hard. In my opinion, you're holding up your end of the bargain as well as can be expected. The two of you have looked for this faceless man since then, right?"

"Yeah. For hours. And miles. But I couldn't find anything. I don't know if it's because my version of true sight is weaker than Quentin's, or what."

Erlang Shen looked gobsmacked at my admission. "*Your* version?"

Crap. "I . . . uh . . . yes. I'm the one who's got true sight now, not Quentin. Is that a problem?"

"No," he said. "Not at all. But it's a pretty big deal, the Ruyi Jingu Bang having that ability tacked on to the rest of its portfolio. You're more powerful than you ever were before."

"Even though I can't size change or make clones of myself yet?"

He waved dismissively. "Those are party tricks. They'll come to you eventually. But the strength of the Ruyi Jingu Bang combined with the all-seeing vision of the Monkey King? With those two powers alone you could conquer Heaven. I'm very impressed."

Flattery was nice. Especially when delivered with Erlang Shen's genuine, cloud-parting smile. But given my recent missteps, I would have preferred he lend me a hand instead of moral support.

"Are you sure you can't help?" I asked. "Being a warrior god and all?"

He seemed to appreciate that I'd remembered his stature, but he shook his head all the same. "Very sure. My hands are tied because of that idiotic *laotouzi*."

"What old man? You mean Quentin? I don't think he'd be so petty as to reject your help in this case."

"No," he said. "I meant my uncle. The Jade Dunderhead."

Whoa. I wasn't expecting that kind of talk from the god everyone understood to be the poster boy for filial piety. I nudged my chair away from him in case the ground cracked open and swallowed him whole.

"You look surprised. Did you think I liked my uncle's decisions? That I approved of his methods? That do-nothing is responsible for this world going to the dogs, in my opinion.

"Only the Goddess of Mercy stretches the limits of what we're allowed to do on Earth," he said. "If someone as active and strong as her were in charge, we would never have ended up in this scenario to begin with."

Huh. I approved of this outspoken version of Erlang Shen. We were aligned on a surprising number of levels. It was too bad I only got to see him while our counterparts were having it out.

"A word of wisdom, on both the demon-hunting front and on sharpening your powers," he said. "Don't let the setbacks mess with your overall progress. I know that Guanyin is going to hound you over every outcome, but what's done is done. Focus on becoming stronger, which you *can* control, over possible failures, which you can't always."

That was pretty decent advice. Anna-like, in a way. "Got any suggestions on getting into a good college?" I asked.

"Yeah. Bribe the hell out of everyone you can."

I laughed out loud. Erlang Shen pretended to look insulted, but he couldn't prevent his grin from peeking out.

"What?" he said. "It's the truest Way, if there ever was one."

. . .

Quentin and Guanyin came back in and sat down, each wearing the sourest, most ex-boyfriend and ex-girlfriend-y faces I'd ever seen. Seriously, after that display nothing was going to convince me that they hadn't broken up with each other at least three times.

"You're doing well," Guanyin said. She was clearly not the Goddess of Lying to Make You Feel Better. "And I know that it seems unfair that I hold you to account for a perfect record like some overzealous schoolteacher. But a slipup like this, so early on in your endeavors, has consequences."

She waved at Erlang Shen. "Remember his thing with the tea, and the swirling, and the whatnot? If you don't, he can do it again."

Erlang Shen raised his eyebrows at her dismissive tone. "I remember," I said. "No need."

"Then if you'll recall, yaoguai are attracted to masses of spiritual energy," Guanyin said. "And that includes *other* yaoguai. Especially powerful ones. Previously it was just you and Sun Wukong involuntarily broadcasting your signals throughout the cosmos, but now this faceless man is doing it as well. The demons will be coming faster and in greater numbers now. You've made this job significantly harder on yourselves."

God.

Friggin'.

Damn it.

I *knew* there was going to be blowback. Erlang Shen and Quentin might have thought from their lofty, dude-tinted perspectives that everything was cool, but Guanyin's simple truth threw that idea right out the window.

"I don't let yaoguai get the best of me," Quentin said, falling back to platitudes. "We'll manage."

"I sincerely hope so," Guanyin said. "Once Red Boy makes his move, you two will need your undivided attention to stop him. If he comes to Earth while you're still chasing your tails, then there is no limit to the damage he could do."

She gave a brief, flat chuckle. "In fact, that's undoubtedly his plan, now that I say it out loud. To strike us at our lowest point, while we're distracted. It makes sense, don't you think?"

There was a long beat in the conversation.

"Come on now," Guanyin said. "I didn't mean to depress everyone. Sometimes I get worked up because, well . . ." She sucked in her lips as she searched for the right explanation.

"I think of us like a family right now," she said. "Strange as it is to say."

Huh. There were two other confused frowns besides mine on that one.

Guanyin reached out to either side of her, grabbing Quentin and Erlang Shen by the hand, hard enough to make them both wince. Since I was sitting across from her out of reach, I got the full force of her withering gaze.

"What's going on right now?" she went on. "It's like family business, when you look at it from a certain angle. Our little divine family is responsible for this awful mess, letting yaoguai run loose on Earth. But we're going to clean it up."

Now I knew where Guanyin was going with the metaphor. These weren't words of comfort. These were twists of the knife.

"And the reason why we're going to succeed is because we know what's important." She wagged Quentin and Erlang Shen's hands up and down for emphasis. "What's important is that we don't let anyone else get dragged into our family garbage. If someone who isn't family suffers because of our failings, then there isn't a word for the kind of shame we should feel. Does everyone get me?"

No one spoke. My phone started vibrating again, loud and insistent, until I finally yanked it out and put it on silent.

"I'm so glad you all understand," Guanyin said.

29

I LOOKED AT MYSELF IN THE MIRROR AND SMOOTHED DOWN the front of my dress. "I can do this," I said. "I can do this."

Mom poked her head into my room. "Do you remember when I last wore my pearls?" she asked.

"Huh? Why?"

She grunted at my inability to follow her logic with the precision of a mind reader. "Because if it was at Auntie Helen's gathering, then they're in a different jewelry box, not the normal one."

I was so confounded that I forgot what I had been preparing the last few minutes to tell her. "Then just check the other jewelry box!" I said instead.

"Don't raise your voice at me," she muttered before sweeping back down the hallway.

I couldn't really blame her for being scatterbrained at the moment. Yunie's competition performance tonight had her excited beyond measure. She reveled in any opportunity to show that her in-group was better than someone else's. And since volleyball was definitely not as prestigious as classical music on the Asian Parent Scale, I rarely scratched that itch for my mother in the right way.

She'd been looking forward to this night. It was too bad I'd have to ruin it for her.

. . .

I approached her in the kitchen as she was busy unwrapping hard candy so as not to make sounds during the performance if she needed a throat lozenge. She'd read that advice in an opera program once and had been fascinated with the idea ever since. Like it was the fanciest way possible to stifle a cough.

"Mom," I said. This was it. "I invited Dad."

She stopped what she was doing and looked up at me.

"He's got a seat at the opposite wing of the hall. I'm not trying to trick you into talking to each other or anything. It's just that it wouldn't be fair if only one of you got to come."

Somewhere in my head, the idea of telling her last minute so that she wouldn't back out had played out better than it was doing right now.

Because right now was the part of the action film where she dipped her finger in the wound I'd opened on her, tasted her own blood, and sneered disdainfully at me. The juggernaut had been unleashed. The human era had ended. The language of man could not begin to describe what would happen next.

The doorbell rang.

"That's not him," I said quickly. Then I ran, because whoever the hell it was, they'd given me the timeliest of outs.

I opened the door. It was Quentin.

"Is that also proper gear for outdoor exercise?" he said, eyebrow raised.

I didn't understand what he was referencing until I remembered that we normally snuck off to train at this hour. With everything that had been going on, I'd forgotten to cancel on him.

I closed the door behind me as silently as I could. "I can't tonight," I said. "I should have told you sooner. I'm sorry."

"I'm not." A roguish smirk spread over his face as he drank me in.

"Oh knock it off. Just because this is the first time I've worn something with bare shoulders around you doesn't mean you need to be all 'hurr, she cleans up real good.' I know you think you're being nice, but it's condescending."

"Turn true sight on," Quentin said.

"What? Why?"

He shrugged. "Humor me."

I didn't know how much longer Mom was going to stay inside without bothering to check on me, so I did. Whatever would make him leave sooner.

"Are you looking at me?" he asked.

"Yes, and hurry up. It's like staring into a light bulb."

Quentin cleared his throat. "Genie Lo, you are definitely . . . NOT the most gorgeous human being I've ever laid eyes on."

A metal bubble bigger than our heads spewed out of his lips and rose into the air. It could have taken out a power line. It looked revolting.

How it felt was another matter entirely.

I couldn't keep an uncontrollable, dizzy grin off my face. And I started to get self-conscious about my neckline. I didn't need Quentin seeing how far down I blushed.

"That's messed up," I said. I reached out and poked him in the chest, but my touch lingered longer than it meant to. "Everyone keeps saying I look like your former master who used to torture you."

Quentin laced his fingers between mine and pulled me closer to him. "Maybe I have some issues I need to work through. You might be able to help with that."

I couldn't think straight. The look in his eyes was out of hand. This was first-day Quentin. Quentin standing on my desk, not caring who or what anyone else thought. A demigod who knew exactly what he wanted.

Whom he wanted.

The door opened behind me and I nearly tumbled backward into my mother.

"Pei-Yi, if you think for one minute you can—oh, hello dear," she said once she saw Quentin. "Are you coming to the concert too? Genie didn't tell me. Because *why would she tell me anything?*"

Quentin snapped back into propriety and raised his hands. "Just paying a visit. Sadly, I don't think I'm invited to whatever's going on tonight."

"Oh, such a pity," Mom said. Her voice was the tonal equivalent of a public assassination. "Who knows how she chooses which people to bring and who to exclude. I thought for certain that you'd be on the list."

I wheeled around. "I'm not the sole arbiter of who gets access to Vivaldi in the Bay Area!"

"Oh please! Don't pretend you don't know what I'm talking about!"

"I'd better go," Quentin said. "You ladies have fun. Try not to get into any trouble." He tucked his hands into his pockets and sauntered away, whistling into the evening air. The tune might have been the "Spring" concerto from *The Four Seasons.*

Mom let out a snort. "See? That's what happens when you act like that. You scare the good ones away."

■ ■ ■

It was not a pleasant car ride across the bridge and up the highway, but at least it was a silent one. The two of us knew that we needed not to show our asses this evening.

The performance was being held at the auditorium of a nearby state school. A good one too—one that would have been at the top of my list had I not been so desperate to gain some distance from Santa Firenza.

We pulled into a lot in front of the hall. It was a weird building, ugly concrete bones on the outside harboring a beautiful, creamy wood interior. People mingled throughout the upper and lower levels, mites inside a larger see-through organism.

"You should find him before the performance," Mom said softly. "You don't get the chance to talk to him much."

I tried to do what I should have done earlier and apologize, but she shushed me. "Go on," she said. "It'll take me a while to find a parking space. It's okay."

There was nothing I could do but get out of the car and go inside. I only prayed she wouldn't ditch the performance and drive off into the night.

The hallways of the auditorium were filled with older folks dressed to the nines, grim-lipped parents and grandparents readying themselves for battle by proxy. The stakes of this competition must have been even higher than I thought. The Tiger Mom Olympics.

Yunie and the other performers were in the back getting ready. I knew I wouldn't see her before she went on stage. Nor did I want to. The two of us never interrupted each other's warm-up routine before big events.

Instead I looked for Mr. and Mrs. Park and found them in the corner, avoiding the game of conversational one-upsmanship breaking out over the foyer. ("Oh, so your Guadagnini's a rental? How sensible of you.")

They looked relieved to see me. Yunie's parents were square, honest, open people, unsuited for this shark tank. Both were podiatrists who met each other at a podiatrists' convention. It was extremely difficult to figure out where Yunie got her sharper edges from, in both looks and attitude.

"Genie!" They got on their tiptoes to give me a barrage of kisses on the cheek. "We haven't seen you in so long. When was the last time you came over for dinner?"

"I'm sorry, I've been really busy lately." *With demons. And gods. I'm in over my head. Send help.*

Mrs. Park nodded solemnly. "It's a tough time for everyone in your grade. SATs are coming up, college apps are around the corner. I don't know how you kids these days handle so much pressure. It was easier for us when we were young."

Mr. Park clapped me on the shoulder. "We're just glad you could make it. And so is Yunie. She was getting really lonely without you."

I winced upon hearing that. Then I did a mental backtrack to confirm exactly how much time I had been spending with my best friend in recent weeks, and I winced much harder at the result.

Compared to how entwined we normally were, I'd basically cut her off. And she hadn't said a word. She'd picked up that I had something else going on and left me to it.

I was a terrible friend. Or at the very least, acting like one.

I'd make it up to her after the performance. Right now I had to focus on being a terrible daughter.

"My dad should be here somewhere," I said. "Have you seen him?"

Mr. Park arced his arm to mimic the curve of the hallway. "He's around the corner. I saw him talking to another student from your school."

I said goodbye to Yunie's parents with a big smile on my face that vanished instantly the moment I turned around. *Quentin*, I thought with murder on my mind. Whatever had passed between us on my doorstep didn't give him the right to sneak in here with magic. To introduce himself to my father without me being there. I stomped around the hallway to the other side of the auditorium and found Dad talking to . . .

Androu?

"Oh hey," he said.

I blinked a couple of times. "I didn't invite you," I blurted out.

Androu took my rudeness in stride—as if he had girls greeting him with insults all the time. "My cousin who lives in the city is performing tonight. He's a timpanist. Holds a beat like superglue."

"Androu here was filling me in on your volleyball season," Dad said. "He's a big fan of yours." Then he made the most obvious, over-the-top wink possible.

I stood there, catching flies with my mouth. The silence emanating from my throat was so thick that Androu coughed and excused himself to go to the bathroom.

Once he was gone, Dad turned to me with a twinkle in his eye. "I knew there was a boy," he said. "Given how mopey you were at the gym? There had to be a boy."

This . . . this wasn't so bad. Of all the misunderstandings.

"You should tell me about these things," Dad said. "You know I don't judge like your mother. I'm okay with you dating."

I could triage this. The patient was stable.

"We have to have 'the talk' though; I won't have you making irresponsible choices." He tried to say it sternly but couldn't hide his glee at getting to check off one of those American-style parenting milestones he'd read so much about in magazines. I wasn't sure if he fully understood what "the talk" entailed.

Androu came back. "We'll save it for later," Dad whispered.

"So yeah," Androu said, doing his best to ignore my father's blatant winking again. "I didn't know Yunie was performing tonight. Wild, huh? We should plan to go to more concerts together. It'd be fun."

Dad was about to joyously agree, but then he suddenly deflated, his high spirits gone with the wind. There was only one person who could make him go one-hundred-to-zero just like that. And she was right behind me.

My mother didn't say anything in greeting. She glanced at me. Then my father. Then up at Androu.

EKG flatline. Code Blue.

"I found a space," she announced.

She hadn't bumbled into us. She could have easily avoided this encounter. Every previous indication she'd given said that was her preference. And yet here she was, claiming this patch of land for Spain. I abandoned all hope of understanding this woman for what must have been the fiftieth time.

Mom craned her head forward. None of us knew what she was doing until the gesture stirred something deep and lost in my father. He pecked her on the cheek and then they both returned to their stations.

211

"Androu, this is Genie's mother," Dad said. He meant to gently prod my classmate forward, but the motion resembled a Spartan raising his shield against a hail of stones.

Androu gallantly bent at the waist to shake her hand. "Hello Mrs. Lo. It's a pleasure to finally meet you."

Mom was mildly placated in the sense that the new person she had to greet was at least polite and handsome. But then Androu, that sweet summer child, ruined all hope of a clean escape.

"I'd love to take you and Genie up on that offer for dinner at your place," he said. "I hear your cooking is legendary."

In his mind he was only continuing the last conversational thread we had. He had no idea what boundaries he was stepping over.

"Oh, so she's making invitations to people I've never met now," Mom said. She turned to me like a doll in a horror movie. "I suppose I can't decline, can I?"

Dad rushed in to try and douse the flames, but he was holding a jug of gasoline, not water. "Androu is Genie's very good friend," he said. With emphasis on the *very good*.

This did not compute with Mom. According to her programming, there was only ever supposed to be one boy at a time holding the Most Favored Nation spot. Preferably the same boy throughout my entire life.

"I thought Quentin was your *very good* friend," she said.

This was new. Tonight I got to discover the face Mom made when she thought I was being a hussy. Never mind the fact that her idea of promiscuity would be outdated in Victorian England.

"Quentin?" Dad said. "Who's Quentin?"

"I see now why you didn't want to invite him," Mom said. "It would expose the double life you've been leading."

Androu, still out of sync, postured up valiantly at the mention of Quentin's name. "Don't worry, Mr. and Mrs. Lo. If that guy's still bothering Genie at school, I'll put a stop to it. She can count on me. Right?" He nudged me with his elbow.

He was prodding a corpse. My soul had left my body a long time ago. It had flown to the top of Mount Can't Even, planted its flag, and dissipated into the stratosphere.

An usher came over and told us it was time for the performance to start. We all made shows of pulling out our tickets, as if they contained our queue spots for a kidney. Androu smiled and bumped my stub with his.

"Oh hey," he said. "I think we're sitting together!"

■ ■ ■

Androu and I went in first while Mom made her last-minute hellos to Yunie's parents. We picked our way through the narrow aisles like cranes in the mud until we found our seats.

The chair backs in front of us were too close, and they jammed our knees to the side. Tall people problems. He and I had that in common at least.

Androu chuckled to himself.

"What is it?" I asked.

"Oh, it's just—sorry if I'm being offensive, but that whole thing with your Mom and Dad out there. It felt like the stereotype was true. Asian parents not really showing a lot of affection in public."

I thought of the way Mr. and Mrs. Park clutched each other for comfort tonight, the way they loved to gross out Yunie whenever possible by cuddling and kissing in front of me when I visited.

I remembered a fleeting dream in a fairyland tale, where my dad had chased my mom around a fountain trying to put a mouse-eared hat on top of her head while I watched and laughed and laughed.

Maybe I had been subconsciously trying to *Parent Trap* them into speaking again. Who knew.

"Yeah," I mumbled, the vowels stuck in my throat. "You know what they say."

Mom came in and immediately made a disapproving click. There was no way for me and Androu to avoid our legs touching each other. We were leg-making-out right next to her. Had we no shame?

Androu tried to help her settle in. "Where's Mr. Lo—"

"Seating accident; not enough spaces together," she snapped.

We all suddenly found our programs very, very interesting. Luckily we didn't have to wait long for the curtain.

I tuned out the bespectacled, tweeded man explaining the history of the competition and how we could all get involved with the arts by making small donations. The pain was over for now. I could relax for as long as it took to determine who would emerge unscathed from musical thunderdome.

"Because they've already worked so hard to get here, we're going to do something a little different tonight," said the emcee. "Could our finalists please come on stage to take a bow? No matter who wins tonight, you all deserve a big hand."

The majority of the audience believed that was patently false. There could be only one. But we clapped anyway as the contestants lined up on stage.

I spotted Yunie. She looked like a star in the night sky. Mom,

Androu, and I mashed our hands together when she emerged, all prior conflicts forgotten.

And then someone flicked me in the back of my neck.

I turned around, ready to yell at the jerk who did it, but the little old grandmother behind me was busy trying to work up enough saliva to whistle for the brass section. It wasn't her.

The same flick hit me from the same direction. I peered down the aisle until I saw where it was coming from.

Quentin. Hovering in the shadows by the fire exit.

He raised his fist to his lips and blew. The little bullet of air that shot out from the tunnel formed by his fingers smacked me in the face. It would have been the most annoying sensation in the world under any circumstances. Right now I was livid beyond belief.

Quentin waved his hands once he saw that he had my attention.

I slid my finger across my throat at him.

He widened his eyes and tugged frantically on his own earlobes, hopping up and down to exaggerate the motion.

Oh god no. Not now.

I surreptitiously glanced at my phone, which had been on silent all evening. Forty-six notifications. Quentin had been trying to contact me for more than an hour.

More than an hour of a yaoguai doing whatever it wanted on Earth, with no one to stop it.

I tried to unwedge myself from the chair and kneed the man in front of me in the shoulder. He frowned at me but decided I wasn't worth it.

"Genie, what are you doing?" Mom hissed.

"I—I feel sick," I stuttered. "Light-headed. I . . . have to go outside."

"Now!?"

I was able to creep halfway down the aisle before I froze. On stage, Yunie was watching me. Watching me leave.

Of course I stuck out too much to make a clean getaway. Yunie's eyes followed my path and flickered at its end. She'd seen Quentin.

My universe was reduced to a handful of silent, screaming voices. The distress on my mother's face. The urgency of Quentin's. Androu's guileless concern.

And loudest of all was the confused heartbreak coming from my best friend on the biggest night of her life.

"I'm sorry," I whispered to anyone who would have it. I ran out the side door to where Quentin was waiting.

■　■　■

"We need to make up for lost time," he said in the bushes behind the auditorium. "What's the point of me having a phone if you're not going to answer my—"

"Quentin," I said, my voice as quiet as the eye of a hurricane. "I know what happened isn't your fault, but before this night is through, I *will* kill someone. I would rather that person not be you."

He shut up and pointed at where I should start searching. "There's barely any towns in that direction, thankfully. I don't think it'll be as close to the population as the other demons were."

I pressed the side of my head and swept over the landscape.

Quentin was right; the area around the dancing light was mostly empty grassland, dotted with sleeping bovines. Guanyin's alarm had given us a decent head start this time, for once.

"It's in a farm," I said.

■ ■ ■

Quentin plowed through the barn roof feet-first. I disembarked from his back and called out to the shadows.

"I'm not really in the mood," I said. "So I'd appreciate it if we made this quick."

A stream of sticky, gooey threads shot out of a dark corner with the volume of a garden hose. It methodically swept over Quentin and me, covering us in a thickening, hardening cocoon of webs. It didn't stop until we were encased from the neck down, our legs glued to the floor of the barn.

A man stepped into the moonlight in front of us and wiped his mouth. His face was bearded with fingers—human fingers. They sprouted from his skin and wriggled as he spoke.

"Ha!" the yaoguai cackled. "You've fallen into my trap! Vengeance is mine!"

"Who are you?" said Quentin.

"The Hundred-Eyed Demon Lord!" The fingers coating his face pointed in unison on certain words for emphasis. "Master of webs and venom!"

The yaoguai opened his jaws wide to flash a set of dripping fangs at us. "I've been distilling my poisons in the fires of Diyu for more than a thousand years, waiting for this moment! You cannot escape my bite, for the silk that imprisons you is stronger than the hardest steel—*bu hui ba, what are you doing!?*"

I tore my way out of the cocoon with a few thrashes of my arms. The strands of silk twanged like overtuned guitars as I snapped them. Looking down, I found that the one nice dress that I owned was completely ruined. There wasn't going to be a way back into the performance tonight.

Quentin shook his head, not bothering to try and free himself.

"Oh buddy," he said to the yaoguai with genuine sorrow for a fellow sentient being. "Oh, buddy, I couldn't do anything for you now, even if you begged me. This is the end of the line."

The Hundred-Eyed Demon Lord looked at my face. Whatever he saw there made him give off a high-pitched *skreee* in alarm. He fell to all fours and scuttled away from me like an insect. The yaoguai backed into the barn's wall and went straight up it, reaching as far as the rafters in his attempt to get some distance between us.

I didn't feel like chasing him. Looking around the floor, I found the nearest object I could, picked it up, and winged it hard at the demon with all my might.

The metal horseshoe zipped from my hand. It flew so fast I couldn't see its arc, but I did spot the hole it left behind in the roof after it punched straight through. The edges of the wood glowed red hot like a cigarette burn in a sheet of paper.

"Holy crap," Quentin blurted out.

"You—you missed!" the Hundred-Eyed Demon Lord said in nervous triumph.

"Good thing horses have four feet," I said, waving three more horseshoes in the air.

30

IT WAS THREE WEEKS AFTER THE NIGHT OF THE CONCERT WHEN finally I could take no more. We'd just finished a yaoguai hunt. A successful one, but somewhat of a Pyrrhic victory.

"Call them," I said to Quentin.

"Why?"

The demon had been aquatic. Hence the reason we were currently standing waist-deep in freezing ocean water, still in our school uniforms.

We'd cut class for the second time. A third strike would go on my permanent record and earn me an in-person parent-teacher conference. There was a piece of seaweed stuck in my ear.

"I feel the need to talk," I said. "Right now. Call them."

Quentin gazed over the coastline. This section of the beach was normally open for people to bring their dogs to play in the surf, but right now it was vacant. The picnickers up on the cliff who'd triggered the earring alarm hadn't seen our thrashing and flailing in the shallows on their behalf.

"In case you haven't noticed, I'm trying to keep our interactions with those two down to a minimum," he said. "They never end well."

"Quentin, we just spent the last hour beating up a fish. This can't go on. *Call them.*"

He closed his eyes, put his palms together, and grumbled under his breath for about a minute. It looked like he was throwing a tantrum instead of praying.

Nothing happened.

"Okay," I said. I waved my hands at the general lack of gods in the vicinity.

"What, you think they're going to plop down in the middle of the water? They're somewhere on shore. Go find them and talk to them."

I couldn't believe how much attitude he was giving me. "You're not coming?"

Quentin responded by leaning back and floating on top of the water, arms crossed behind his head like he was relaxing in a lounge chair. The tide began carrying him slowly out to sea.

"Fine!" I waded back to shore by myself. My clothes were soaked through and the wind made me shiver down to the bone. If I was magically resistant to cold, it was only to the point of not letting me collapse of hypothermia.

There were no gods on the beach, which meant I had to continue up the low cliff using a sandy ramp that gave way under my steps. Grit got into my shoes. Probably dog poop as well.

Once I got to the top, I saw a lone figure standing by the roadside. It was Erlang Shen, sans Guanyin. He eyed my wet, bedraggled state.

If he had said one smartass sentence, even something as innocuous as "Rough day, huh?" then I might have committed deicide on the spot. Instead he silently raised his hand and made a "come hither" gesture.

It wasn't me he was speaking to. It was the water. The dampness in my clothes wicked away, flying off my body and gathering into a sphere of liquid that hovered in the air before me. It grew and grew until I was completely dry. Not even the salt remained on my skin.

Erlang Shen flung the skinless water balloon back toward the ocean. Then he said the magic words that made me want to marry him right then and there.

"Let's get you some coffee."

■　■　■

"Hold on, hold on," he said, trying to keep his laughter contained. "You destroyed the Hundred-Eyed Demon Lord, the Guardian of Thousand Flowers Cave at Purple Clouds Mountain, by chucking horseshoes at him?"

"What can I say." I gulped from my cup of burnt water. Non-dairy creamer had never tasted so good. "I was out of lawn darts."

It would have been generous to call the shack we were sitting in a diner. The surly, rotund man behind the counter had a hot plate to cook on but nothing else. This particular eating establishment was more of a hedge maze made out of single-serving potato chip bags.

Our conversation, if anyone could even hear beyond the sports radio blaring the scores, probably sounded like we were talking about a video game.

"It sounds like you could have also grown to giant proportions and swatted him down," Erlang Shen said.

"I still haven't figured that one out. I must have some kind of mental block against it."

"Like I said before, it's nifty but not essential." Erlang Shen leaned back in his chair and gave me an appraising look up and down. "Is there something else you want to talk about? I don't need true sight to see that something's bothering you."

My fingers trembled around my paper cup.

"Yeah, there is actually," I said. "So we beat the Hundred-Eyed Demon Lord, right?"

"Yes. A while ago, if I followed your story correctly."

"You did. And since then we've also taken down the Yellow Brows Great King, Tuolong, the Pipa Scorpion, Jiutouchong, and some generic-looking guy with bells whose name I didn't catch. Today out there in the ocean was the King of Spiritual Touch. What kind of name is that for an aquatic fish-demon?"

"An unfortunate one."

If I wasn't so tired I would have laughed. "And then there's Baigujing. Also the two others from before you and I met. Eight if you count Tawny Lion's brothers."

Erlang Shen nodded. "You've been productive to say the least. I know the faceless man still hasn't been found, but other than that your success rate has been flawless. Heaven has no problem with the pace you've been keeping recently."

"Yeah but what if *I* do?"

I was a little louder then I meant to be. Another customer glanced over at us before tilting the rest of his corn chips into his mouth and walking out the door.

The last three weeks had taught me that I wasn't a machine, as much as I liked to pretend I was when it came to doing work. Trying to act like a heroic yaoguai-slayer of old had left me with my gears bruised and my fuel tank bleeding.

"This is hard," I said to Erlang Shen. "This is really hard. I know that's an idiotic thing to say, but it's hard in a way I wasn't expecting. The demons keep popping up here and there and everywhere. They don't stop coming. It's a giant game of whack-a-mole."

My carnival game analogy may have been a little bit off. The pace of the demon incursions reminded me more of wind sprints, where Coach D would have us run end-to-end on the volleyball court until she decided we were done. It was supposed to improve our cardio, but without knowing when the whole thing would be over, it felt like pointless punishment.

"I don't feel like we're making any progress," I said. "None of the other demons will give up Red Boy's whereabouts, even under pain of death. Stamping them out while we wait for him is like having a sword hanging over our heads while we rearrange deck chairs on the Titanic."

I was mixing my references but Erlang Shen appeared to follow well enough.

"We've only found sixteen so far, and already the grind is getting to me," I said. "I can hardly believe it. What has happened to me since meeting Quentin and you and Guanyin has been the wildest mindbender imaginable and yet it *still* somehow turned into a grind like every other part of my life. At the current rate we're pushing, I'm going to break down long before we catch the other eighty-two demons."

"Ninety-two," Erlang Shen corrected.

"See? I'm so burned out I can't do basic math in my head. If you knew me, that would be a really worrying sign."

I put my face in my hands. It stayed there long enough to trouble him.

"Genie?" he said tentatively.

"I haven't talked to my best friend in a long time."

It was the safety of my rabbit hollow that let me finally talk about what was truly wrong with this whole deal.

"I screwed things up with her really badly because of this demon business," I said. "And I can't even tell her why. She'll never know what I've been doing, running around without her."

Erlang Shen tiptoed around the cracks appearing in my voice, an arctic explorer suddenly finding himself on thin ice. "If she's your friend, she'll forgive you, no?"

"I don't *want* her to forgive me. I'd rather she be angry at me forever."

An outside observer would have assumed I was being illogical. And overdramatic. They'd tell me that Yunie and I could hash things out easily. Such a close friend would understand that I had good reasons for shutting her out recently and might even be okay with me not explaining them fully. She'd trust me when I told her I hadn't ditched her for a boy.

Of course that was the case. I didn't actually believe our eight-year relationship was completely over because of a single spate of neglectfulness on my part.

But that wasn't the point. The looming monster here was the future, bearing down and unstoppable. Yunie and I were destined for different colleges, her to a specialized music program and me to any snob-factory that would have me. We knew this even before we entered high school.

We didn't have much time left together. Our little routines were precious to me, and our big events even more so. The day when the two of us would have to buckle up and accept our inevitable drift apart was coming, and I didn't want it to happen prematurely.

Reckoning with Yunie would be pulling up the anchor just a little bit farther. That was probably why I'd put it off for so long.

Erlang Shen, perhaps using some magical water-detecting sense, pushed the stack of flimsy brown napkins on the table over to me. I snatched them up and wadded them against my nose and eyes so that he couldn't see my face.

Great, now I was blubbering in front of a god. Go me.

"I think of my family when things get rough," Erlang Shen said. "When my resolve wavers."

"The situation with them is even worse," I said, muffled by the scratchy paper. "My parents think I'm a hot mess right now."

"Not my point. What I'm trying to say is that the people we care about make the grind worthwhile. Even if the two never meet."

He stared out the window, his fingers playing lightly against the table.

"The Jade Emperor doesn't know about half of what I do in Heaven on his behalf," Erlang Shen said. "And yet I put up with his incompetence, his passivity, his constant rejection. Because one day he'll see me for my abilities. I want to show my uncle what I'm capable of more than anything else in the universe. Your friend. She means a lot to you?"

"I'd do anything for her."

I surprised myself how easily and without embarrassment I said those words. Heartfelt declarations weren't my strong suit.

"Then keep up the good fight, for her sake." Erlang Shen smiled at me. "You know, when I originally fought back the waters of the

Great Flood, I was trying to impress my uncle and the rest of the celestial pantheon. Not invent agriculture."

I laughed in spite of myself.

"Genie," Erlang Shen said. "I'll talk to the Jade Emperor and convince him to let me help you."

"I wasn't trying to guilt you into—"

"No." He shook his head. "I should have been right beside you from the start. It was a mistake not to be more hands-on."

The weight in my chest lifted significantly. Sure, none of my problems had gone away. But given how few people with the full story were actively assisting me, my support network had risen by fifty percent.

"Thank you," I said. "I really mean it. Thank you."

The god shrugged. "Don't worry about it. In the meantime, remember that Red Boy's plan to keep you distracted has a chance to backfire on him. Each time you catch a lesser demon, you're training your true sight muscle, not to mention your combat skills. Eventually you'll get to the point where he can't hide from you anymore, in this world or the next. When that happens, I'll be right there with you for the showdown."

"Red Boy wouldn't stand a chance with you in our corner," I said. "He's a fire-type, right? If you're the master of water, you can just put him out."

Erlang Shen laughed as he got up and pushed in his chair. "It doesn't work exactly like that." Then he cocked his head, pursing his lips. "It works a little like that?"

. . .

I let the divine being leave first and gave him a few minutes to do whatever it was he needed to do to get back to Heaven. It seemed polite, though I'd only made that rule up in my head.

When I stepped out of the shack, Quentin was there by the roadside, waiting for me.

"Have a nice chat?"

I knew his peevish tone was his usual allergic reaction to Erlang Shen, but for some reason I didn't field it well today.

"Yeah, we really connected on an emotional level," I snapped. "I promised to turn into a stick for him."

That was perhaps the weirdest, most hyper-targeted dig I'd ever leveled at someone, but boy did it work. Quentin looked like I'd broken him in half and left him on the curb for pickup. He was completely silent the entire trip back to civilization.

He didn't call or text me that night either. It had become a little ritual for us to debrief and unwind over the phone after every yaoguai hunt ever since Baigujing but instead, radio silence.

While I could have reached out first to tell him I was extremely sorry he was being such a baby about this particular subject, I figured I had time to do it when I saw him at school. So I went to bed and thought little of it.

But I was wrong. Quentin wasn't the type to stew in anger by his lonesome. He preferred action to waiting.

Which was likely why the very next day at school, I came upon him in the hallway making out with Rachel Li.

31

WELL, THIS CERTAINLY ESCALATED MORE THAN I WAS expecting.

"Sorry to interrupt," I said. He and Rachel pulled away from each other, but not very far.

"Is this important?" she asked, her lips still wet.

"It is, or I wouldn't be interrupting."

Once Rachel saw I wasn't going to back down, she peeled herself off Quentin and walked away, trailing her finger across his jaw all the way up to his earlobe as she left. He gazed at her wistfully before turning to me.

"What is it?" he asked, as if nothing different had happened.

"It's Friday. We were going to try high-altitude training this weekend." My voice came out like a text-to-speech simulator, devoid of human emotion and jaunty in all the wrong places. "You know, to see if that would unlock more of my powers. You never picked a mountaintop. You said the feng shui had to be just right."

"Oh. Yeah. Whatever's fine." He glanced around, as if searching for more interesting people to sidle up to at a party.

"All right then, I'll pick a spot," I said. Focusing on logistics, appointment-keeping, the squeezing of blood through my veins would keep my roiling guts on the inside. Or so I hoped. "When I text you, you'll be ready to go?"

"Sure."

"Is there something you want to talk about?" I asked, on the odd chance that he wanted to explain his behavior. But he was already shoving past me, done with this conversation.

"I'll text *you*," he said, waving me off with the back of his hand.

I nearly put my fist through a locker.

■ ■ ■

Quentin didn't make good on his promise to text me. Instead, he found me in the cafeteria at lunch.

His personality had changed from spacey to grumpy. He must have been suffering withdrawal symptoms from Rachel's saliva.

"I forgot that the lunar cycle's not right," he groused. "Mountaintop meditation's not going to be the best for this weekend. We have to shift our whole calendar around."

"So now you want to make a plan? I thought we were winging it."

Quentin tilted his head. "You . . . don't want to make a plan? That's weird. I've seen you write to-do lists with only one item on them. You even put a number one on them with nothing underneath."

"Well, maybe it's time to loosen up," I said. "Act differently for a change. Improvise."

Quentin reached over and put his hand on my forehead to check my temperature.

I smacked his arm away only to see Rachel watching us and

laughing. She obviously wasn't threatened by her new boyfriend flirting with someone else. She knew there was no comparison.

Quentin returned a fake smile and a wave to her. "I don't know how I feel about that girl," he said. "We've only been spending time together because I'm bored. But I think she's imagining something that doesn't exist."

Okay, so that irked me to the core. Rachel was annoying, but she was genuinely into Quentin. He could at least have the decency not to use her as a stress reliever.

"Congrats on completing your assimilation into modern life," I said. "You've become something that's unique to this era."

"What's that?"

"A douchebag." I got up with my tray. "When you figure out how to stop being one, you can come and talk to me. Otherwise don't bother."

■ ■ ■

"I'm going to kill him," Yunie said once she found me in the library at my usual spot. "I'm going to rip his balls off and shove them in his eye sockets."

Gossip about Quentin and Rachel's hookup had gotten sufficiently around. Anatomical impossibilities aside, Yunie's first words to me since the concert fiasco were bittersweet.

On one hand, we were speaking again. That was a victory I'd crawl through salt and broken glass for. On the other hand, I could see the narrative playing out in her head, and it hurt my soul.

I'd done the crazy threatening friend routine on one of Yunie's terrible exes in the past, and the reason she could have been itching so badly to return the favor was because it was a perfect way to erase the cloud between us. There was more hopefulness than violence in her anger toward Quentin—hope that with this show of force, *I* might forgive *her* for whatever part she played in our rift.

My friend thought she needed to earn her way back into my good graces, which utterly destroyed me. This was our version of fighting. We were incapable of getting truly angry with each other, so instead we tore our hearts out and handed them over on silver platters.

I swallowed all the things I desperately needed to tell her and responded the way I knew she wanted. Like nothing had ever happened.

"For the last time, Quentin and I are not together," I said. Each word was leaden in my mouth, for multiple reasons. "He can do what he feels like."

The flash of relief in Yunie's shoulders was palpable. Once it finished circulating through her veins, it was back to business for her. Getting to cut someone for me, purely for the fun of it now.

"Of course he can," she said airily, the last couple of weeks gone with the wind. "He just needs to accept the consequences. Which in this case is having to see through his own testicles."

Normally I would have moved on right alongside her. Cracked a few jokes about nuts. Pushed and pulled in our familiar pattern. But this time, the burning lump of coal remained stuck in my throat. It didn't go away.

Quentin entered the library to return a stack of books. Yunie locked on to him like a planet-destroying laser.

"The bastard didn't even take off your earrings," she hissed. "That's the last straw. I'm going to get them back."

"They don't open. We tried once but they're stuck."

She grinned at me.

"Yunie, wait!"

My best friend, drunk on righteous anger, marched across the library. In her head Quentin wasn't only a two-timer; he was also responsible for making me miss her concert. She went up and gave him a ringing slap across the face that could have knocked Baigujing's teeth loose.

"*Pbthbdth!* What the hell!?" Quentin shouted.

"You creep!" Yunie roared. "Take them off or I'm going to rip them off!"

She lunged at his face and he caught her by the wrists. It gave me enough time to wrap my arms around her waist and lift her away. The good cop/bad cop routine worked better when bad cop wasn't smaller than most freshmen.

Of course the room had to be packed today. Everyone was laughing at us. Even without the boost from our half-assed making up, this was the kind of drama that could power Yunie for weeks. She'd be queen of the school by the end of it.

I, on the other hand, needed to shut this down. I put down my friend, grabbed my whatever-Quentin-was, and hauled ass out the door.

"What the hell was that?" Quentin asked once we were safe from prying eyes. "Did you tell her to do that?"

"No," I said. "She's upset about you and Rachel."

Quentin furrowed his brow. "Why would she be upset about that?"

"I have no idea," I said. The benefit of time had given me the ability to speak to Quentin in monotone, rather than whatever bird language I was yelping this morning. "I'm certainly fine with it. All I ask is that you not carry on with her right in front of me."

He frowned again. "*Everywhere* is right in front of you, you know that?"

Ahem.

I knew Quentin was referring to my true sight. If I ever turned it on at school, I'd be able to see him no matter where he was. Deep down, way deep down, I knew that was what he meant. No question.

But.

There was also the slightest chance that he was either A) making a comment about my height like he'd never done before, in a "yo' momma sits AROUND the house" sort of joke, or B) accusing me of being clingy and a tagalong, which honestly felt a lot worse.

I didn't want to play interpreter in my current mood. I shut my eyes and walked past him.

■ ■ ■

With nothing going the way it was supposed to, I did what I always did. I threw myself under the mountain. Schoolwork.

That afternoon in study hall I was so deep in a paper that it took me a minute to notice the fire alarm ringing.

Someone shook me gently by the shoulders.

"Genie," Androu said. "We've got to get out of here."

I blinked and looked around the classroom. Everyone else had left.

I swatted off his attempt to take me by the hand and ran into the hallway to see what was going on.

The air was hazy, like someone had smeared Vaseline on a camera lens. I got that there was a fire in the building somewhere, but this was too much smoke, too fast. SF Prep wasn't made out of dried pine needles.

Red Boy, I thought to myself in a panic. We spoke the devil's name too many times and now he was here. I turned on true sight.

And instantly regretted it. The irritating smoke became full-blown acid. It felt like I'd just scrubbed my pupils with sandpaper. I couldn't keep the vision going for more than a second before doubling over in tears.

But it was enough to catch a quick glimpse of blue-black light. A yaoguai, in my school.

I started pushing in that direction.

"Genie!" Androu shouted. "You're going the wrong way!"

I hadn't made it much closer to the source of the demonic energy when I noticed a teacher slumped over in his classroom, passed out. My first thought was that someone had cast sleep on him, but it could have also been a regular old fainting spell. Mr. Yates wasn't exactly a spring chicken.

Androu came running up behind me.

"I don't know how you saw him, but thank god you did." He scrambled past the student chairs and wrapped his arms around our AP calculus teacher's sandbagging weight, hoisting him away from his desk.

"He's still breathing," Androu grunted. "You should have stuck to that Paleo diet, Mr. Yates."

I bit my lip. I could help him carry the body out. But in that time the yaoguai . . . there was no way to tell how many people the demon had its hands on right now. I made the same choice as I did when I bailed on Yunie and my family at the auditorium.

"I saw someone else who needs help," I lied.

"Go," Androu said. "I'll be fine."

I left the classroom and ran down the hallway at a speed that would have made him or any other witnesses do a spit-take. The smoke tore and stripped at my face until I had to slow down.

Right when I thought I'd have to crawl on my hands and knees to get any farther, I heard a violent crash in one of the classrooms. I pressed myself against the wall outside and tilted my head around the door to take a peek.

There were two people fighting in the back, rolling around behind the lab tables. The air in the classroom was soupy with grit. There was no way normal people could have exerted themselves in it.

"Quentin!" I shouted. Just the one word made me want to hack up a lung.

"Genie! Stay back!"

The brawl spilled over the table into view. Quentin had his opponent in a headlock. The struggling figure in his grasp was . . . also Quentin.

There were two Monkey Kings.

"It's the Six-Eared Macaque!" said the one who was getting his trachea squeezed. "He's a shape shifter! He copied my form to infiltrate the school!"

"You're the fake, you bastard!" said the other. "You set this fire so she wouldn't be able to see through your disguise!"

A wave of anger washed over me. I'd been expecting the king of all monsters and instead I got two clowns playing grab-ass with each other.

I ran into the room, gathering all my frustration into my fist, and punched the one on top in the face. He went sprawling back over the table.

"Thanks," the other Quentin said. He rubbed his throat. "I knew you could tell the real—"

I kicked that one in the stomach. He curled up and gasped on the floor.

I backed away to block the exit and tried true sight again. Not a good idea. The smoke in the room flat-out blinded me. By the time I recovered so had the two Quentins, and we were now in a three-way standoff.

"He knows everything I know when he copies my form," said the one on the left. "Secret questions won't work."

"Then how did you beat him last time, back in the old days?" I said.

"The Buddha intervened," said the one on the right.

The Buddha. Oy vey. I dug the heels of my hands into my eyeballs.

Wait a sec, I thought. The Buddha could help me after all. I raised my head and put on my best ultra-pissed-off face, which wasn't too hard given the circumstances.

"OM MANI PADME!" I shouted, leaving off the last syllable.

The two Quentins were identical down to the last hair. And they were both wearing my earrings. But only one of them involuntarily cringed in fear for a split second like a whipped dog, his body flooding with whatever the monkey god version of cortisol and stress hormones were. Knowing of great pain was not the same thing as having actually suffered great pain.

I turned to the other Quentin. The Six-Eared Macaque, whatever the hell kind of yaoguai that was, realized his mistake in the face of my aborted spell. It threw him off to the point where his disguise briefly slipped, Quentin's eyes and mouth rippling away into a smooth, featureless surface.

"Psych," I said to the faceless man.

. . .

Quentin and I crawled outside the building and flopped onto the grass. I was bleeding from a gash across my forehead that he promised would seal itself and disappear within minutes, as long as I didn't die first. With the way I felt, we'd have to wait and see.

Quentin grabbed his own fingers and pulled, relocating his joints. The popping noise made me want to vomit.

"Dear god," I croaked. "How did . . . why was that . . . so hard?"

"He was an identical copy of me," Quentin said. He spat a bloody tooth out to the side. "What were you expecting, a pushover?"

I watched his blood sink into the ground and sprout a little daisy with perfect white petals. Whatever. I was beyond surprise when it came to Quentin at this point.

"He seemed so eager to get away from us before that I thought he'd be weaker," I said. "But he fought like a prison inmate from Krypton. He nearly killed the both of us just now!"

"You know we would have had a bigger edge if you ever let me use you as a weapon."

The bad atmosphere between Quentin and me must have also passed if he was bringing up this topic again. Hooray for a return to normalcy. "I told you no already."

Quentin pouted. "Think of it as a deeper, more intimate form of teamwork," he said. "There's no shame in it. If anything, you're the dominant one when we couple ourselves like that."

"Okay, so part of why I will never fight with you as a staff is your inability to describe the process without sounding like a total pervert," I said. "Besides, I can't imagine a worse opponent than your evil doppelganger. As long as you don't get your ass copied like a brand-name handbag again, we'll be fine in the future."

"I don't know," Quentin said. "There's Red Boy . . ."

"When I saw the fire I thought this *was* Red Boy."

He winced. "If it had been Red Boy, there wouldn't be any school left."

We lay on the lawn for a good while, gulping the clean air and prodding our bruises for deeper breaks.

"I need to apologize," I said.

"For what?"

"Making you think I was ever going to say that spell."

Quentin smiled. "I'm sorry, too. For believing that you actually might."

I hesitated.

"Where were you after Third Period?" I said. "Before we saw each other at lunch?" I felt pretty stupid asking; there were more important things to talk about.

"In the computer lab with Rutsuo," he said. "Why?"

That was all the way on the other side of the school from where I saw him playing tonsil hockey. "Really? You weren't with Rachel?"

Guilt dawned over Quentin's face. He ran a hand through his hair.

"I'm sorry for what happened earlier," he said. "I know you don't like her much but I didn't realize helping her with her Spanish homework would upset you. I'll stop."

I thought about turning on true sight to verify his statements, but decided to simply trust him instead. "That's all the two of you do together?"

He looked genuinely confused. "Yeah. What else would I be doing with one of your classmates? I have to fit into this school if I want to be near you, and everyone just studies all the time. You're a bunch of gigantic nerds."

Well there was my answer. It was the Six-Eared Macaque that had gotten to first base with Rachel. I cringed on her behalf and felt supremely glad that I'd sent the asshole who'd duped her to Hell.

It was going to be pretty awkward for Quentin though, the next time they ran into each other. In a lingering fit of pettiness I declined to warn him, even though the real Quentin had done nothing wrong.

"You can hang out with whoever you want." I closed my eyes and leaned back against the nearest tree. "It's not like I own you or anything."

. . .

Once Quentin and I were able to make ourselves presentable enough, we circled around the building to join the rest of our class.

The trail of smoke leading into the sky only made it seem bluer and clearer by contrast. The grass under our feet was as crisp and green as money. Even the plain, redbrick façade of the school looked handsomer than most days. Good old SF Prep! Dinged up a bit by today's events, but still standing proud.

I could feel my wounds melting away like Quentin said they

would. The tingling sensation was mildly euphoric. But even better than the mutant healing factor was the sense of closure. We'd found the faceless man, sewn up the loose thread. We'd corrected our mistake and could close the book on this case.

We ran into Mrs. Nanda coming the other way around the building. She was wearing a bright-orange safety vest over her dress and carrying a walkie-talkie.

"Genie! Quentin! Where *were* you two?" she cried out, angry and relieved at the same time. "You know our class's rendezvous point is by the baseball diamond! I was worried sick!"

"I'm sorry, Mrs. Nanda," I said. "The, uh, smoke got too thick and we had to use the opposite exit. We're fine."

"Well get over there right now and stay put!" She pressed the button on her handset and it squawked to life. "I found Lo and Sun," she said. "Repeat. Lo and Sun are with me."

The walkie-talkie beeped back. "Affirmative. What about Park and Glaros?"

Quentin and I stopped walking at the mention of Yunie's and Androu's last names.

Mrs. Nanda's voice wavered as she spoke. "Still no sign."

"I don't understand," said the person on the other end. "We've done a full sweep. A bunch of the kids said they saw them before the alarm went off. Where'd they go?"

"I'll check back in the East wing again, including the locked areas," Mrs. Nanda said. "Maybe they got past the doors somehow. Do another head count just to be sure, and call their parents."

Our teacher hurried off, concern for her missing students quickening her pace.

■ ■ ■

The siren of a fire engine wailed louder. Approaching. Imminent. My words echoed in my head.

An evil copy of Quentin.

A copy of Quentin.

According to the book, Quentin could make copies of himself.

"What are the signs of spiritual power in a layperson?" I asked, swaying where I stood, a palm tree buffeted by a storm. "How do demons choose their prey?"

"If you're not a monk like Xuanzang, then the biggest indicators are . . ." Quentin's eyes widened. "Unyielding moral character. Or exceptional talent."

I began to tremble.

"Genie." Quentin gripped me by the arms. "Genie, breathe."

I couldn't feel his hands on me. I couldn't feel anything. I would never feel anything again.

Quentin guided me across the school lawn to a side street where no one would see us. It took a long time. I was deteriorating rapidly.

He set me gently down on the curb. I squeezed my knees to my chest. I wanted to be small, to shrink myself until I died.

"We won't find her," I choked out over the tightness in my throat. "If the earrings aren't going off then they're not working for some reason. I won't know where to look."

"Genie, don't give up."

Quentin was doing his best to be resolute, but even he couldn't keep the act going. I could tell he thought the odds of getting her back were slim to none.

He began walking in a circle. "Think," he said out loud to himself, rubbing his temples. "Think."

I had never seen him do this before. He must have been truly desperate.

"We don't know where he is," Quentin muttered. "We only defeated a copy of him before. But if he took two humans for whatever purpose, he would have done it himself."

I choked back a sob. Yunie and Androu didn't even have names anymore in Quentin's clinical triage.

"There's only so far they could have gone," he said. "The farthest away they could be is . . . as far as I could have taken them."

He stopped pacing. A glimmer of hope poked through in his voice. "The Macaque's not an ordinary demon. He's not setting off the demon alarm . . . because he's me. He's me, down to the last hair on my head. He has my looks, my smell, my aura. My aura that reacts to your aura."

Quentin kneeled down in front of me. "Genie," he said. "I might be able to find them using *you* as a signal. But you have to be in a state of complete disconnection for your aura to be strong enough. This is a long shot and I know it's never worked in the past, but I need you to calm yourself and—and—"

I knew what he was asking. He needed me to meditate.

"You can do it," he said. "Just empty your mind and think of nothing. Nothing at all."

I didn't protest. This would be easy.

I took one last look around. The street was still empty and silent, the din of the emergency vehicles having ended. The firemen were probably making their way through the halls of the school right now, searching for two students who fit Mrs. Nanda's description.

I closed my eyes and found only hollowness inside me. I didn't want to continue anymore. I wanted to sever myself from the Earth completely.

■ ■ ■

A deep chime erupted from my core.

It was as if someone had struck a giant iron bell with a sledge-hammer. Concentric rings of energy shot out from me in every direction. I could sightlessly feel them carry over the landscape, like I had joined the ranks of whales and bats and other creatures with echolocation.

"Stay here," I heard Quentin say. "I'll come back for you once I find them."

He ran away so fast that a small dust cloud blew into my face. I opened my eyes. They were blurry with tears, so I could have been seeing things, but it looked like there was a geometrically increasing number of Quentins speeding off into the distance, chasing the invisible sonar waves of my aura.

■ ■ ■

I had no idea how long I had been sitting there in the street when Quentin returned. Even the position of the sun failed to register for me.

He came in hot. I felt the impact of his landing, a small quake in the ground under my feet, and then he was by my side again. Like he'd never left.

"Get on!" he shouted in my ear. "Hurry!"

He wouldn't have motored like this if the situation were either irrevocably lost or saved. But I couldn't share in his hope. I was still numb.

I wasn't moving fast enough, so he swept me onto his back, and we were airborne.

■ ■ ■

We landed in the middle of a tree grove. We'd traveled all the way to the city in one leap, touching down in the forested park that drivers had to pass before crossing the landmark bridge where Quentin first taught me how to use true sight.

The eucalyptus trees reached to the sky, forming bar codes against the waning daylight. There was no beaten path anywhere near us. The woods were silent, strained free of man-made noise.

This was the site of a showdown. Handpicked for maximum effect. The director of the scene stepped out from behind a thick tree trunk, still wearing Quentin's face.

"You made good time," the Six-Eared Macaque said, using Quentin's voice but in a slightly higher register, as if he was doing me a favor to tell them apart.

"So are you a copy, too?" Quentin said.

The Macaque grinned. "Nope. You're looking at the head vampire right here."

He was telling the truth.

"If you're relieved that you only have to kill me one more time, I wouldn't be," the Macaque said. "After all, I have your friends. They're still alive, but they won't be unless you do exactly as I say."

He spread his hands out like he'd arranged a delicious feast. "Let's play a little game. One that requires you to use every power of the Ruyi—"

I was upon him before either of us knew how.

I pinned the demon to the ground by the neck with one hand and punched him with all of my might.

My knucklebones broke with the first impact, but so did part of his face. I punched him again, hard enough to indent the soil underneath his head.

The Macaque's expression was one of total shock. "But—"

But nothing. The worldly detachment, the meditative calmness that had allowed me to harness my aura, was gone. Pitch-black hatred poured into my fist. I punched the demon again, knocking the Quentin out of him. The blank eggshell of the faceless man rippled into being and somehow under the smooth surface, he looked scared.

He was supposed to look dead. I smashed him again, over and over, and found enough rhythm to speak.

"DON'T YOU! EVER! TOUCH HER! YOU SON OF A BITCH!" I screamed, hammering him with each word. "I'LL KILL YOU! I'LL FOLLOW YOU TO HELL AND I'LL KILL YOU THERE!"

On second thought, I was glad the Macaque was tough. I didn't want him to die easily. My blows struck growing cracks into his skull. I ignored the equivalent injuries to my hand.

The demon screamed and writhed in my grip. Like a threatened animal with camouflage, he changed color and shape, trying to find a form that would relieve the assault. His face cycled through random people, including the doorman and the maid from the apartment building we'd first found him in. He even tried switching to Yunie and Androu in turn, but by that point I'd done so much damage that only half of his face was capable of changing, ruining the illusion.

I didn't stop. I hit him even harder. I needed to hit him so hard that my message would be stamped across the bones of the universe. There needed to be more of me just to hit him forever, until the end of time.

Suddenly the Macaque lost his solidness, my fist embedding in the ground up to my elbow. I would have kept going into the cloud of ink that indicated he was finally no more, but Quentin tackled me.

"Genie, stop!"

I flung Quentin away and looked around for something else to hit. My eyes still weren't functioning properly, because all of a sudden there were Yunie and Androu, lying unconscious under a tree. I'd completely missed how they'd gotten here.

At the sight of my friend I fell to my hands and knees and dry heaved all over the ground underneath me.

"What is wrong with you?" Quentin said. "The Macaque had spells rigged up like a dead man's switch in case you attacked him! I almost couldn't save them in time! You put her in the most danger she's been in today!"

I sat back down and clutched my ribs until they stopped fighting me. Quentin's accusation wasn't the half of it.

The Six-Eared Macaque had the Monkey King's strength and knew how to neutralize my true sight. Which made him the perfect infiltrator. Someone had sent him to hurt me personally.

How could I have been so stupid as to think the demons would be content to wait in their lairs until I showed up to fight them? That they wouldn't go on the offensive, hunting down me and my loved ones in kind? Yunie had been in danger ever since I took on this role—the instant I'd accepted that I was the Ruyi Jingu Bang. My first and biggest mistake.

I looked up to see Quentin angling his fingers for a spell. He put his hands on Yunie's head.

"Wait!" I screamed.

A pulse of energy bounced between his palms, and Yunie's eyes rolled around under her lids like she was dreaming. The whole effect was too close to a person in an electric chair and I panicked, throwing myself between them.

"It's just a *forget* spell!" Quentin said as I shoved him away. "She saw too much! If I don't keep recasting it on her, she'll remember the Macaque taking her, me using magic, all of it!"

"Don't do that!" After everything that happened today, hexing Yunie was another intolerable violation. I was terrified by the notion that when she woke up, she wouldn't recognize me, or even worse, herself. "Undo it! Take it back!"

"Genie, we don't have time for this!" Quentin turned to Androu and scooped up the much larger boy with surprising tenderness. "He's dying from smoke inhalation! We have to get him to a hospital right now, or he's done for!"

32

I CAME HOME EARLY FROM SCHOOL FOR THE FIFTH DAY IN A
row. But that would be it—volleyball practice was going to resume
a normal schedule on Monday.

I tossed my bag on the counter. Mom stood over the stove. I'd
been trying to talk to her more in general, and I could tell she liked
having the few extra hours with me even if they ended up being
filled with more of our usual squabbling.

"What's for dinner?" I asked.

She didn't answer.

"Are you mad about something?" I couldn't think of anything I'd
done. I leaned over to look at her face.

It was perfectly still. The pinch of salt she was adding to the
pot arced from her fingers, stuck in the air. The pot itself probably
would've burned over hours before, but the bubbles hovered under
the surface, never bursting, never moving.

"What the hell do you want?" I snapped. I turned around to see
Guanyin sitting on the stairs.

"To talk."

I looked around the house to see how much space had been
affected. "I don't want you doing this to my mother," I snapped.
"Don't cast anything on her ever again."

"You know she's not being harmed in any way."

"I said don't screw with my mother!"

Guanyin frowned. "Then we should take a walk."

. . .

I could have pretended we were headed to the town library. This was the long way, the same path Quentin and I had been walking when the Demon King of Confusion had shown up. Reality was an infinite loop.

"Quentin says you won't speak to him," Guanyin said.

I stepped on fallen leaves that were drying in the heat. Crushing their delicate, fractal forms felt good. I was ruining configurations that would never exist again.

"Perhaps you've decided you'll cover more ground if you hunt separately. I don't advise that. The two of you have always made a good team."

I said nothing.

Guanyin closed her eyes, trusting that I wouldn't take her into a ditch. "I'm sorry about what happened to your friends."

"Yeah?" I stopped where I was. "Then maybe you should have led with that."

"Forgive me my preoccupation with the bigger picture," she said, a little testier than before. "I understood that Yunie was ultimately unharmed. And that Androu made a miraculous, complete recovery in the hospital. Which I may have had something to do with, by the way."

"Gee, thanks!" I shouted. "It was the least you could do after nearly killing them both!"

"Genie, I didn't consider that a yaoguai with the right skills could have copied Quentin so completely as to bypass detection. Are you angry at me for being fallible?"

"No, I'm angry at you for being a liar! You and Erlang Shen told me I was going to be hunting demons. But that wasn't true, was it? The Demon King of Confusion and Tawny Lion took Quentin and me completely by surprise. Baigujing and the Hundred-Eyed Demon Lord were laying traps. Red Boy is probably watching me right now, laughing!"

These were all clues I should have pieced together myself, but this is what I did when I was upset. Shift blame.

"I'm not the hunter here!" I said. "I never was. The demons are hunting *me*. And you *let* them!"

Guanyin didn't deny my accusation. She stood there with the practiced air of a punching bag, waiting for me to finish. I didn't have much left anyway.

"I'm out," I said. "I'm done. You know what the Macaque proved? That I'm an awful person who doesn't care about everyone equally. I have a hierarchy of people I care about, and random strangers who might end up as demon food don't make the cut. Not when my friends and family are at risk."

What I didn't say aloud was that I was even worse than that. My loved ones also had their own ranks. Throughout the whole encounter with the Macaque, beginning with the fire in my school, I hadn't given a single thought to Androu. If I had helped him carry our teacher, if I had given him just an ounce of consideration in the forest, he might not have come so close to dying.

I could claim distraction and panic over Yunie all I wanted as an excuse, but the fact of the matter was that I *chose*, even if it was by omission. I disgusted myself.

"I'm not like you," I said to Guanyin. My anger was a burned-out husk at this point, exhaustion seeping in to claim the void. "I can't be the world's protector. I can't even protect my hometown, let alone the entire friggin' Bay Area. You have to find a different champion. Maybe Xuanzang's reincarnation is hanging around somewhere, wondering why you haven't shown up."

Guanyin crossed her arms and went silent for a while, tapping her foot slowly. I watched her ruminate, a gentle worry creasing her brow. She looked all the more beautiful and heavenly for it, an angel wondering what she could do to shepherd her charge back onto the right path.

When she finally opened her mouth, I braced for the inevitable speech about how wrong I was, how only *I* could do this. A stronger, better rehash of the talk she used to convince me in the first place.

"Wow, Genie," she said. "I never realized you were such a pathetic coward."

Meanness did not suit the goddess's lovely voice. It made her words creaky and rough. A muscle she hadn't used in a long time.

"So you had a close call," she said. "Big deal. You know what you learn after a few centuries of bearing the world's suffering? They're *all* close calls. The only victories you get are by the skin of your teeth."

I couldn't believe what I was hearing.

"When things break their way, most people call themselves lucky and move on," Guanyin said. "Instead you wallow in self-pity. How dare you."

"Are you *serious*?" I shouted. "Do you know what could have happened that day!?"

"I hear the torment of billions of souls hammering on my ears every second of every day of every year. I know exactly what could have happened, in every permutation of death and suffering there is to know. I'm not impressed by your guilt, Genie. Or your love for your friends. I get that you want to peacock in front of me how much they mean to you. But I don't care. I simply don't."

"You know what this is to me?" she said. "A numbers game. Perhaps I should have been more up front about that from the beginning. This is about head count. Not feelings."

Guanyin stepped closer, and it was all I could do not to crumple into a ball from her presence.

"I sacrificed the chance to leave Heaven and Earth behind me," she said. "I gave up *Enlightenment*. Can you imagine? The greatest personal accomplishment one can possibly achieve in existence. And I gave it up because *one* is not a very big number, is it?"

She was nearly toe-to-toe with me at this point. "I keep going because there's a chance I can help a few more people out of the billions. But you! Getting spooked because it's finally sunk in for you that stoves are hot, scissors are sharp, and someone could get hurt! If I were as weak as you I wouldn't have lasted a minute as a Bodhisattva."

The goddess finally looked off to the side, too disgusted with me to make eye contact anymore. Her jaw flexed angrily like a heartbeat.

I wasn't prepared for this line of attack. I had thought that somewhere deep down, Guanyin would have given me the same consideration she gave her other supplicants. I thought it was her job to do that, to cradle my hopes and fears. Instead she'd done the math of human suffering and figured I was merely the end of the lever she could pull for maximum results.

It took me a few swallows to force the lumps down my throat. "You ever give Xuanzang this kind of pep talk?"

Guanyin scoffed. "I didn't have to. Xuanzang was an incompetent boob who had nothing better to do than go on a journey where he faced zero hard choices. He never had to make any real trade-offs in the first place."

She'd said it with the sureness and momentum of someone treading on familiar ground. If she hadn't spoken those words out loud before, she'd certainly thought them countless times before.

"Don't you dare try to compare yourself to Xuanzang," Guanyin pressed on. "People like Xuanzang and the Jade Emperor are free to do as they please. People like you and me are not."

"What do you mean?"

"I mean that Xuanzang was free to bumble across a continent and fail upward into sainthood. The Jade Emperor is free to sit on his ass and ignore the world screaming for his help. You and I are not free. You and I have a duty."

"As what?" I could only spot one glaring difference between figures like the Jade Emperor and Xuanzang in one hand, and me and Guanyin in the other. "You and I have duties as what?"

She raised her palms up, letting her generosity flow out. It was the posture she was worshipped in. It was also a shrug.

"As beings of great power," she said.

We stared at each other for what could either have been an eternity or a time freeze. Maybe the problem wasn't that Guanyin didn't understand. It could have been that she understood too well.

The goddess broke the silence first.

"In the off-chance that it gives you enough spine to resume the hunt, I've put your entire town under my direct protection," she said. "You have no idea what that act cost me among the other gods, and you never will. But at least that's one less concern for *you*."

I didn't let on how much of a relief it was to hear that. Instead I decided to ask a question that I'd been holding in my head for a while. It wasn't as if there was going to be a better moment.

"Did Red Boy actually break out those other demons? Or did you make a mistake giving out your karma again, to the point where they could leave Hell on their own?" It would have explained why she was so dead set on me finishing this quest. She might have needed me to right her wrong.

"Please," Guanyin said. "That's the first thing everyone in Heaven accused me of. I made one error long ago, thinking that a general amnesty for those sentenced to Hell might be a good experiment, and I'm still dealing with the fallout to this day."

"Well it is kind of your M.O."

"Any powerful being can give away their karma. Erlang Shen can do it. The Jade Emperor can do it. I happened to be the only one who was willing to take the risk."

The corner of her lip hiked upward in amusement.

"But you're right in that the rest of the celestial pantheon thinks this whole mess is my fault anyway," Guanyin said. "'That stupid woman was too soft on Red Boy! What was she thinking, putting a fearsome demon on a blessed island instead of sending him to Hell where he belonged?'"

"You were thinking that imprisoning Red Boy in Hell would be pointless if he could break in and out so easily," I answered for her. "You cared more about minimizing the harm he could do than making sure he was punished. You put him on an island in the middle of a Heavenly ocean because that's as good a jail as any for a fire demon. You took the burden of watching him upon yourself because everyone else was too afraid."

Guanyin smiled, proud that I'd figured it out. "There's my smart girl."

It seemed like our talk was coming to a close. I didn't want to let her get away completely unscathed.

"You know, you wouldn't have to put up with crap from the other gods if you took over from the Jade Emperor," I said. "If you were sitting on the Dragon Throne of Heaven."

She looked at me incredulously. I could tell I was speaking treason.

"But that's me saying crazy things," I went on. "After all, you know your place, don't you?"

Guanyin blinked, and then burst out into laughter. Surprisingly deep, side-clutching laughter. It was as rusty on her as her cruel voice was.

"Oh man," she said when she was finally done. "If you ever try to provoke me like that again, I'll slap the taste out of your mouth."

She wiped a tear from her eye and smiled, her face put back to its normal serenity.

"And then I'll turn you into a goddamn cricket."

33

I MAY HAVE ACTED TOUGH, STANDING UP TO GUANYIN, BUT IN reality I felt as if I'd barely escaped that conversation with my life. I could finally see why Quentin was so hesitant to get on her bad side.

In what I considered a massive reprieve, she didn't show up again for a while. I assumed the goddess was plotting her next move now that her best piece was proving wayward.

Despite what I'd told her, though, I hadn't left the game entirely. After what happened to Yunie and Androu, I'd simply switched my priorities to defense. Guanyin might have put wards of some kind around Santa Firenza, but like she said, she wasn't infallible. There were still more than ninety demons out there, and I'd be damned if I let one get too close again.

I used true sight preemptively at school until the brink of exhaustion, trying to act like an early warning radar for the entire building in case a yaoguai came back for more. Eventually I had to settle for only looking during class breaks, or I wouldn't have had the stamina to extend the search at night.

I stayed awake in my room until my eyes nearly fell out of my head, scanning as far and wide as I could. Without the height advantage that Quentin's leaping provided, it took a lot longer to get a decent area covered. I began to feel like a human lighthouse, casting high beams into the endless sea.

With nothing better to do in between sweeps, I worked on my college application essays. If guilt and fear weren't going to let me sleep, I could at least be productive.

I wrote in a pensive, dreamlike state in the wee hours of the night. Hopefully that introduced a touch of whatever magic was missing, because I sure as hell didn't know how to add it on purpose.

I made so many revisions I might have created a wormhole in space-time. On the advice of some admissions blog, I interviewed myself in my head, using posh Oxbridge voices reserved for world leaders. I even tried staring at the page with true sight, and I felt pretty dumb when all it did was show me the raccoons eating our garbage in the yard.

The sheer amount of effort I was putting into these essays had to add up to something. It would be a violation of thermodynamics if it didn't.

■   ■   ■

The end of the month arrived. I bounded down the stairs to make my pilgrimage to Anna's.

"Wait." Mom pounced as I passed her. "You're going to let her see you wearing those?"

I patted myself down, confused. My clothes should have been fine. She'd never objected to how I looked on any of my city trips before.

Then it hit me. I hadn't seen Quentin in a while, which meant the spell that kept my (ugh) golden eyes hidden was long expired.

I'd been going out every day "wearing contacts," often right in front of my mother.

"I'll, uh, take them out," I said. "Why didn't you say anything about them earlier?"

"You're at that age." She made a face of intense bitterness where another woman might have been pleasantly wistful. "I can't stop you from doing everything. Even if you want to look like a cheap Internet girl."

I stared at my mother for a second, and then I wrapped her in a big hug.

"But if you dye your hair I swear I'll throw you out of this house," she muttered into my shoulder.

■ ■ ■

My knee was bouncing up and down so much, I was afraid Anna could feel it all the way through her thick, solid floors. I couldn't stop it. I was too nervous.

She had already blown past the amount of time she'd ever spent reading my essays before. A new PR. K-Song would have been proud.

Anna opened her mouth. I hitched in anticipation, fearing the worst.

Then she chuckled.

"Genie, this is a hoot," she said. "I had no idea you could be this funny."

Huh. My hope sprouted like the first daisy of spring. Ready to be obliterated by the slightest breeze, but present regardless.

"I, um, did what you said and focused on my own thoughts. I wasn't too familiar in my tone?"

"Not at all. I can't get enough of this bit about your parents. This is a major improvement in your writing, by leaps and bounds. Any reader would be happy to get this in their pile."

My god.

I'd done it. I'd gotten past the barrier of "If you have to ask, you'll never know." I was seeing the inside of their secret club, even if they'd only let me in through a case of mistaken identity.

I resisted the urge to run into the street and fist-bump the oncoming traffic in celebration. "Thank you," I said. "I guess once I get to Harvard I'll go out for the *Lampoon*."

My joke fell flat with Anna. She looked disappointed, like she wanted to stay in the happy place a little longer.

"We . . . should talk about that," she said, putting my papers to the side.

I didn't like how far she'd put them to the side. Had she kept them a little closer to her elbow, I could have pretended all was well.

"Genie, I played a little loose with the rules the other day. I called up a contact at . . . I won't say where exactly, but I talked to a relevant decision maker, let's put it."

Oh damn. She'd gone to bat for me. She'd gone. To bat. She really did have guanxi. And here I was thinking all I'd get from her was advice on how to articulate my inner nature.

"Now I didn't mention you or anyone else specifically," she said, "but I was able to talk about your scenario in a fair amount of detail because it applies to many applicants. And therein lies the problem. Based on how the conversation went, I think we need to adjust our expectations."

She was pulling a reality show host move. There would be

dramatic music leading to a commercial break, after which she would complete her sentence. *Higher!* she'd say brightly. *We need to be aiming even higher, with how strong you are! There's a secret exclusive university on the moon!*

"I—I don't understand. What problem are we talking about? My grades? I have perfect grades."

"You do," she said. "But so do a huge number of students, from great schools just like yours. Your writing is great, and so is theirs. This is the point I'm trying to make, Genie. The very reason why I could get away with talking about you anonymously is the fact that there are a lot of applicants with your exact candidacy profile."

I could feel the floor spinning away from me. I was being ensorcelled.

"Colleges care about geographic diversity as much as any other kind, and right now you're swimming in one of the biggest, most competitive pools," Anna said. "That's going to have a material effect on your application experience."

"I think I get it," I said. "Your contacts told you there's only so many Bay Area Chinese they're willing to take."

Anna looked pained. "Genie, that's not what I'm saying."

Yes it was, even if she didn't know it.

I didn't blame Anna. Hell, I didn't even blame the colleges. SF Prep was full of people like me. Grasping, thirsting, dying to get ahead. We were like roaches, and only multiplying by the day. I didn't want to be around my kind any more than the admissions boards did.

I had done everything I could to declare myself a real person. But it didn't matter. It still boiled down to a numbers game, and not one that tilted in my favor.

"I wish I had better news," Anna said. "I called my old office up because I can see how hungry you are. But my duty as your advisor is to help you make the right call in the long term, not just that one moment when you tear open the envelope. Your financial aid needs—they're not trivial. None of your top choices give athletic or merit-based scholarships. We have to consider what to do if they end up out of reach."

I closed my eyes.

"Out of reach," I said. "That's ironic, given that I've made my arms longer than this room."

"This room's not very big," she responded.

I stood up from my chair. "Colleges like well-traveled applicants, right? I'm well-traveled. I went from Chang'an to Vulture Peak to recover the sutras. It only took me a couple of years."

"That was a long time ago. A million tourists have completed the same trip since then. With selfies."

"Let's talk about volunteer work then!" I leaped onto Anna's desk and thumped my chest with my fists. "I've fought pure evil! Do you understand? Cannibalistic boogeymen! Nearly twenty and counting!"

Anna looked up at me and sucked in air through her teeth. "I'm sorry. The minimum requirement for a Van Helsing Grant is thirty demons."

■　■　■

It took me a while to come back. I opened my eyes.

Once I did, I was treated to the sight of Anna reaching across her desk and patting my hand in sympathy.

"I know it's hard to hear, but we should talk about what to do if we need to pivot. Consider local schools, maybe lean more on sports. There are plenty of colleges that could be a great fit. Many of them right here in the Bay."

Have a life just like the one I had right now. Stop all forward movement. Be pinned under the Milky Way.

"I could live at home instead of a dorm," I said, my voice cracking. "I'd save on boarding fees with my mother as my roommate."

Anna nearly said "that's the spirit" before she saw my eyes. She squeezed my hand. I couldn't believe how wrong I was about her before—how utterly kind she was underneath her imposing exterior.

"I think I should go for today," I said, suddenly short of breath. "Even if the session's not over. I have a . . . thing."

"Of course, hon. We'll prorate the time and I'll clear up an extra half-hour next month to make up for it."

I nodded and stumbled out her door.

Hon. That's how pathetic I was. I was a *hon.*

. . .

Quentin was outside Anna's office, waiting for me. I hadn't asked him to come, but here he was. People passed around us on the busy sidewalk like we were stones in a river.

"Back when I was storming Heaven," he said, as if it were the most normal thing in the world to start a sentence like that, "when you were in my hands, and together we were smashing the door to the throne room of the Thunder Palace—the most powerful barrier in the known universe, turning bit by bit to splinters and dust—a funny thought occurred to me then."

A funny thing happened on the way to the Dragon Throne. There was an epic punch line coming.

"Gatekeepers decide within a few seconds whether or not they're going to open the gate for you," he said. "And then once they decide to keep you out, you're out forever. All it takes is a few seconds."

"Once they make their snap judgment, they can't be swayed. They will *never* open the gate. You could be on fire and they could have water and they won't open the gate. They could be starving and you could be made of food, and they still won't open the gate."

Quentin scratched the back of his head, embarrassed to reveal he wasn't the insensate berserker the story made him out to be.

"I stopped swinging, one blow away from breaking through the doors to the other side and becoming King of Heaven," he said. "I sat down on the floor and waited for the Buddha to show up. I patiently waited for a very long time. Then once he arrived, I climbed into his hand, and he did his whole thing with the mountain."

It was a good story. But I wanted a different one right now.

"How did I die?" I said.

"Huh?"

"How did I die? When I was the Ruyi Jingu Bang?"

Quentin hadn't been willing to tell me before, but he knew better than to deny me now. He took a deep breath, as if he were the one who needed steadying.

"You didn't die," he said. "You moved on. I woke up one day and you were gone from my side. You'd taken all the karma you'd earned from hundreds of years of fighting evil and saving lives and expended it in one risky attempt to become human.

"I can't tell you how because I don't know. There was no guarantee it would work. You could have stepped into the Void and ended up in Hell, or worse. You could have disappeared entirely. But that's how badly you wanted to keep moving forward. That's how much you hated being told to stay in your place."

I felt my eyes burn in a way that they wouldn't for anyone else in the world. I'd let the old me down, more than I ever thought possible. After epic toil and hardship, the Ruyi Jingu Bang had erased herself from existence to become something new, and I'd failed her by hitting the wall within one lifetime.

"You should go back to Heaven," I said to Quentin.

"Why?"

"To sit there and wait eighty, ninety days."

"But if I did that you'd—"

"I know. If you did that, I would age out and die. For every day in Heaven, a year passes on Earth, right? So wait three months in Heaven. A fiscal quarter. After I pass away as a human being, maybe I'll come back as a stick.

"That should have been your plan all along," I continued. "You should never have come to Earth in the first place. The two of us are demon magnets, and being together makes it worse. Get out of here and let me run out my life span."

I knew exactly how much hurt would be in Quentin's eyes when I said it. So all the worse on me for letting him walk away without a word.

34

I WATCHED MY DAD FROM OUTSIDE THE GYM'S GLASS
windows, whistling to himself as he sanitized the incline benches.
He didn't know I was there. A few weeks ago I would have said
he was the fish in the fishbowl, but now I knew that wasn't true.

He'd earned the right to a peaceful existence like this one.
He'd taken the kind of risk that the extreme sportsmen he wiped
up after would never understand. My father had given the finger
to the system and sure, maybe that finger had been bitten off,
but hey. The breaks. He understood thems.

And meanwhile his daughter, who'd gone to school on his
meager dimes, and worn the clothes he'd put on her back, had
thought she'd float into the sky and ascend gracefully into
Heaven, buoyed by a cloud of rules followed and boxes checked.

I always faulted him for overconfidence. Thought I was better than him. But he'd at least put his blind faith in his own two
fists instead of letting the fight go to the judges. I'd never been
so brave.

For a moment, Dad looked up as if he'd sensed I was late. But
a client entering the gym, a young banker type in Lycra knitwear,
came over to say hi to him. The two of them, as different a pair of

human beings as could possibly be, became engrossed in a conversation that involved pantomiming shoulder injuries.

I turned around and left.

■ ■ ■

I had a lot of time to kill after flaking on both Anna and Dad. I went to the park.

The weather was good, and it was packed sidewalk to sidewalk with sunbathing, wine-drinking yuppies. They formed a carpet of trim, attractive bodies over the grass that would occasionally bunch up as people rolled on their elbows to check each other out.

I sat against a tree in the back. The shade was cold and the knobs on the roots were hurting my thighs. I didn't deserve comfort.

I felt old. Older than everyone around me, even though that wasn't true. They came in different flavors of twentysomething. Unless they'd been trucked in from far away, they were uniformly well-to-do. Only people with large salaries could afford the rent nearby. Most of the accents I heard wafting on the breeze weren't local.

This, if I had to be honest, was exactly what I'd been fighting for. I was after a good school and a good job, wasn't I? Well, these people went to good schools and had good jobs. Chilling here on a sunny Saturday was what people who went to good schools and had good jobs did in these parts. Somewhere on one of these blankets was my spot. My eternal reward.

"None of you have ever fought what I've fought," I said out loud. "You can't see what I see."

I could have said the word *demons*. No one was listening, and even if they were, it didn't matter a lick.

My eye caught on a tall, starkly handsome man picking his way toward me through the crowd. He was wearing an athletic top and sandals like half the people lying on the grass, but he was in much better shape than all of them. When he got close enough he lowered his shades.

"I thought it was you," Erlang Shen said.

The last person I was expecting. "What are you doing here?"

He produced a can wrapped in a brown bag and wiggled it. "I'm getting drunk."

The last thing I was expecting him to say. He must have seen the confusion on my face because he laughed as he sat down next to me.

"There's a Peach Banquet going on in Heaven," he said. "Lots of wine flowing freely. But I can't stand celebrations, and I don't like indulging in front of the other gods. So in times like these I find various watering holes on Earth and drink human drinks. I was at a bar down the street but I felt your presence nearby."

"Do you need three hundred and sixty-five human cocktails to match one Heaven serving?"

"Actually the exchange rate for alcohol is a binary logarithm, so it's one thousand twenty-eight," he said. "Right now I'm on six hundred thirteen."

I snorted. He was as big of a dork as I was.

"By the way," he said, waving the can. "I have completely failed on every promise I gave you before."

"There was just the one promise. Your uncle won't let you help round up the remaining demons?"

"Nope. He refused to entertain the subject during the celebration and told me that bringing it up further would be a sign of disrespect. That I would be displaying to the other gods a lack of filial piety."

Erlang Shen raised his drink in a toast.

"Here's to the delicate sensibilities of our elders," he said. "The most important and fragile treasures in the universe. May we break our backs protecting them."

"Hear, hear."

We watched the newly minted adults frolic on the green. Most of them probably only called their parents once a month on average.

"I didn't ask what you were doing here," he said. "You don't live in this city. And when I first saw you, your face looked like death itself."

"Gee, thanks," I answered. "I was gazing into my future."

"What did you see?"

"That the only way to keep my loved ones safe forever is to self-immolate," I said. "I have it all planned out. I'm going to sit on top of Half Dome and send a golden light into the sky like I did when I was still in Ao Guang's treasure hoard. It'll be a beacon for every yaoguai to come and get it. A dinner bell.

"I'll fight them all in one big battle," I went on. "King-of-the-hill style. If I can't defeat them all, I'll take down as many as I can."

"It's not a bad plan. Do you know how to glow with Heavenly light?"

"Nope. I'll have to figure that out first. And I notice you're not trying to talk me out of it."

"There's nothing wrong with grand gestures sometimes. I will say this, though, if you're planning to go down in flames . . ."

He leaned back on his elbows. "I, as an immortal with infinite eternities to enjoy, advise you, a pathetic insect whose life span is but a candle flicker, to at least have some fun before you die."

I could only laugh at his brutal honesty.

"That's partly why I chose the nearest national park," I said. "I've never been."

"What else do you want to do?"

"It'd be cool to stop a crime in progress. Like a superhero. It'd have to be a regular, human crime. I don't know why, but yaoguai wouldn't count."

"Of course not. You'd need the change of pace. Anything else?"

"I want to destroy something."

He was taken aback at how quickly I said it. And perhaps at how much I meant it.

"I want to lose control and utterly wreck something," I said. "I don't know what. Probably not anything anyone cares about, like a building. But maybe a boulder. Although some people would be angry if certain landmark boulders were destroyed, so I can't do it in the park. I'd have to go to a quarry."

"You've . . . given this some thought, haven't you?"

"Yeah, that's not a Ruyi Jingu Bang desire. That one's pure Genie."

"You know where you could really go nuts with your powers?" he pitched. "Heaven."

"I'm sure that would go over well with the other gods, seeing as how I wrecked the place the last time I was there."

"I'm serious," he said. "There are so many holy mountains that no one uses. The place is infinitely big; it won't matter if one tiny part gets leveled."

He sat up and faced me.

"Tell you what. Why don't you come with me to Heaven for a bit? As my guest? We can check out the Peach Banquet together.

With you there, it might be tolerable. And if you don't like it, we can go break stuff. It'll be fun."

"Isn't there that time difference thing? If I'm in Heaven for a day, I'm gone for a year on Earth."

"So?" said Erlang Shen. "Maybe you deserve a vacation. A semester abroad. What people never tell you is that a day in Heaven is worth more than a hundred years on Earth. Earth sucks."

It was awfully tempting, I had to admit. Earth did often suck. Walking away from everything might have been just what I needed.

I sighed. But still.

"Not happening," I said. "My mother would—"

"To hell with your mother," Erlang Shen snapped.

It was an uncharacteristic flash of temper. When I looked at him, he withdrew immediately and shrugged.

"Thanks for the offer," I said. "But I think I'll pass."

I got up to leave. It was a long train ride back, and I was already late. Mom would be furious. "I'm gonna do a quick yaoguai check here before going home."

"Wait, wait," he said, suddenly alarmed. "You're just using true sight randomly now? Without Guanyin's warning?"

"It's my new paranoia in action," I said as I pressed my temple.

The park was all clear. Maybe demons preferred to sunbathe in less-trendy spots. I glanced at Erlang Shen, who seemed a little embarrassed at being laid out in all his godly glory.

He needn't have been. The pulsing waves of energy radiating off him would have knocked me to the ground, but I was used to the effect from Quentin. I gave him a reassuring smile.

"That reminds me," I said. "Quentin told me it'd be dangerous if I went to Heaven. Did you have a spell or something that would protect me?"

Erlang Shen said nothing.

"Or was he lying about it being dangerous? He said my humanity would be burned away, but he could have been making up an excuse to get out of taking me there."

Erlang Shen still said nothing. Not even a mumble.

I frowned.

I had only been speaking in a by-the-way manner, but something wasn't right. I gave Erlang Shen a closer look. There was an odd cold spot on his flank where the spiritual heat was completely missing, like he'd donated a kidney to someone. Given part of his godliness away.

"Hey," I said, ignoring the blistering sensation on my eyeballs. "I asked a question. How were you planning to bring me to Heaven without killing me? I'm talking about me as in Genie Lo, not the Ruyi Jingu Bang."

Erlang Shen puttered his lips in frustration. "You know it's really rude to ask someone a question with true sight on. Don't you want to turn it off before I answer? For the sake of good manners?"

"I don't."

"Then I suppose I have no choice but to tell the truth," said Erlang Shen. "I was planning on you dying."

. . .

No.

It couldn't have been.

I didn't want it to be.

"You really should have come with me when I offered," Erlang Shen said, his voice suddenly laced with venom. "Instead of being such an unpleasant girl. Humans can only be taken to Heaven if they're willing to go. There was no need for a fuss."

I tried to put the pieces together in my head as fast as possible. Why. How. Where. As if solving the greater mystery would make the immediate danger in front of me stand still.

But of course it wouldn't.

I slowly clenched my hands into fists. "Sorry to disappoint," I said. "Apparently I'm a well-known fuss-maker."

"You really think you're going to fight me?"

"I'm guessing I have a fair shot."

"You misunderstand. There was a reason why I approached you here, in a crowd."

He waved his arm across the field of sunbathers as if to wipe them all away. "Are you willing to sacrifice these people to deny me my prize?"

I didn't answer. I hadn't yet seen a god or demon perform deadly, offensive magic, but now was not the time to test whether Erlang Shen could throw lightning bolts.

I took a deep breath.

"Scream if you want," he said. "I don't care about the Jade Emperor's secrecy anymore. There's really nothing you can say at this point that will do you any good."

Sure there was.

"NA MO GUAN SHI YIN PU SA!" I shouted, dropping to my knees. "Salutations to the most compassionate and merciful Bodhisattva!"

Erlang Shen's eyes went wide.

Only a few people looked our way. This was the city after all; people screaming unintelligibly in public spaces were as common as pigeons.

But even still, there were some witnesses to Erlang Shen fritzing into thin air where he stood, his tail between his legs.

Their shocked expressions became their portraits. Every Frisbee stopped its journey through the air and decided to hover over the lawn like a UFO. A dog was caught mid-bound, a happy smile frozen on its face.

It occurred to me that I'd never seen Guanyin arrive with my naked eyes. A glowing fireball grew out of the air twenty feet up, like the way a child would paint the sun in the corner of the paper. It was like the brightness of a welding torch with none of the discomfort of looking at it. The sphere reached the limits of its containment and burst into a nova ring that spread over the entire field.

Guanyin stepped down onto the Earth as if she'd taken the stairs. She looked at me in my supplicant's pose, puzzled over why I'd summoned her. Especially after how poorly our last conversation went.

"I know where the remaining yaoguai are!" I shouted at her. "And I know who's responsible for setting them free! I need to talk to Quentin, *right now!*"

The goddess frowned, then reached into her back pocket.

"You know you could have just called him yourself," she said, putting her cell phone to her ear.

35

"I TOLD YOU HE WAS A PRICK!" QUENTIN SAID. "WHAT DID YOU think, I was saying it for funsies?"

He was shouting partly because he was still mad at me and partly because the wind rushing by this high up in the air made it hard to hear.

"I thought you were jealous or something!" I said. I felt my grip on him loosening as he made the turn on his somersault and clutched his warm body tighter to mine. I'd missed that feeling.

"Why would I be jealous? That'd be like you getting jealous of Guanyin!"

"Wait, you think I'm in the same league as Guanyin? Quentin! That's the sweetest thing I've ever heard!"

His skin flushed all the way up to his neck. "Focus! What are we doing here?"

"It'll make more sense once we land. Trust me."

The demons hadn't been appearing randomly. They'd been dealt out like cards from a pack. And to do that required a home base nearby, one that could keep them hidden if I swept over it with true sight. There was only one place in the entire Bay where my vision was blocked, ever since that first day on top of the bridge.

The wildfires burning in the remote headlands north of the city. They created shrouds of smoke—the only substance that Sun Wukong's golden eyes couldn't penetrate.

Quentin landed us on a hill upwind of the blaze. The scrubby ground, brittle from the drought, crunched beneath our feet. The greenery on the surrounding slopes was fighting a losing battle against the brown.

Pillows of smoke nestled over the peaks, only ascending with great reluctance. I couldn't use true sight in a place like this, which was exactly what Erlang Shen had been counting on.

Quentin and I rounded a bend and saw the flames. They weren't sprawling, but more like a patchy film of flickering orange over the landscape. Had they been any bigger the fire department would have attacked them in force.

As they were, it was a controlled burn. And the person in control was the shirtless, bright red man sitting on the ground cross-legged, with his back to us.

We flanked him as quietly as we could, ducking behind shrubs and rocks. The gentle roar and crackling of the flames masked our footfalls.

His skin was the same color as an artificially ripened tomato. I thought he might have been meditating, but it turned out he was engrossed in a handheld video game. Every so often he would inhale deeply and then blow out through his mouth. The entire fire-line glowed brighter when he exhaled, like one giant tinder puff he was keeping stoked with his breath.

He did this absentmindedly, without looking up from his screen. It was a chore he'd been assigned.

Quentin and I hunkered down behind a boulder.

"That's Red Boy," he whispered. "How did you know he would be here?"

"Process of elimination," I said. The way Erlang Shen had clammed up in the park under the influence of true sight made it clear—this was about what I *couldn't* see rather than what I could.

"You think there's more?"

I nodded. "I'm pretty sure the other demons who escaped Hell are hiding somewhere close by, using the smoke as cover."

"Why would they be doing that?"

"Because I told them to," Erlang Shen said.

We floundered around looking for him but couldn't spot him. We needed to look up. He was hovering gently in the air behind us, two stories off the ground.

Quentin lunged deep. I didn't hold him back. I'd learned my lesson with Tawny Lion to fight first and ask questions later. The Monkey King shot forth like a bullet, his big traveling jump weaponized.

Erlang Shen seemed to have expected this. He banked to the side, Quentin's wild charge clipping him in the foot. The impact spun him around in the air like a top, but that was it. He came to a halt as purposefully as a figure skater.

Quentin's arc was much less graceful. He went careening off at an angle, unable to control his motion once he was off the ground. He landed on the hillside, throwing up a puff of dust like a cartoon coyote.

The advantage that Erlang Shen had, being able to truly fly, was embarrassingly obvious. But to drive home the point, he swooped over to Quentin, grabbed him by the ankle, and flew back to me, using his speed to slam Quentin into the boulder. There was an awful cracking sound, a billiards break. It all happened before I could even move.

"Oh don't look so horrified," Erlang Shen said. "It takes more than that to put the ape down."

Quentin staggered to his feet. The wind had been knocked out of him, but hopefully nothing else along with it.

"What are you up to, you *hundan*?" Quentin spat.

"He wants the Throne of Heaven," I said. "He's sick of being under his uncle's thumb, so he's going to take it by force. And to do that, he needs the weapon that nearly conquered the gods once before. A full-power Ruyi Jingu Bang."

"The real version," Erlang Shen said. He bobbed on the air currents above us as if he were a buoy in a harbor. "The staff, that is. Not this human you're pretending to be."

"That's why you freed the demons from Hell and sent them after us, one by one," I said. "This was some kind of sick training regimen."

"Active recall combined with progressive overload," he replied. "The best way to remember old skills and develop new ones. I even took care to send yaoguai you'd beaten in the past, so that your body would 'remember.' Hence why I needed the jailbreak."

He'd been challenging me, ramping up the difficulty of my opponents bit by bit. I couldn't have come up with a better study plan myself.

"Granted, I didn't do a perfect job, since you don't have all of your abilities back. You seemed particularly determined not to change size or split into copies. But you've baked long enough. I'm done waiting."

"Oh, and speaking of baking," he said. "Shenyingdawang! Could you spare a moment?"

I didn't know who he was talking to until a voice rang out. "One sec. I'm almost at a save."

Quentin's face took on an expression I'd never seen on him before. Absolute fear. In one swift, fluid motion he threw me over his shoulder and started sprinting away. Fleeing.

Erlang Shen laughed at us instead of giving chase.

"What are you doing?" I shouted at Quentin.

He didn't even take the time to respond. He zeroed in on a ditch and threw me into it, hard. Then he dove on top of me.

The sky above turned into plasma. It felt as if we were trapped in one of those Tesla globes, blanketed by neon filaments that reached for human contact. Quentin pressed me down, away from the colorful display like my life depended on it.

The heat was so intense that it overloaded my nerves. The scale went all the way around again to cold, a frost-burn numbness that my brain had to take as a joke. There was no fire like this on Earth, ha-ha.

Then it stopped. I could see blue again.

"We have fifty-eight seconds before he can do that again," Quentin said into my ear. "Fighting a god *and* Red Boy—we're not prepared. We should run."

We should have. We should have fled and come up with a plan. We should have fled to the other side of the world and retired from the demon-fighting business.

But what rooted me in place, of all the random images that had to come to my mind unbidden right now, was that stupid book sitting in my room. The book of Sun Wukong's tales.

I couldn't shake the thought of how many unnamed villagers and peasants in those stories had to die just so that Xuanzang's deeds would look greater for it. Were they like the babbling, happy people in the park, completely oblivious to the end? Or did they see the demons coming for them, their last moments full of terror and pain?

Genie Lo, caring about strangers, bearing the weight of the world? No one was more surprised than me.

"We can't run," I said. "Erlang Shen's willing to blow his cover and start killing anyone he can get his hands on. We have to stop them here and now."

Quentin smiled at me. "Then we have forty-seven seconds to do it."

Maybe it was because we were in mortal danger, but he'd never looked more beautiful. I craned my neck upward and gave him a peck on the lips. "Let's go."

We sprang out of the ditch and ran straight at the source of the unholy flames. Red Boy greeted our attack with mild interest.

"Forty!" Quentin shouted. "Thirty-five!"

"Zero," Red Boy said. He inhaled through his nose, opened his mouth, and another vortex of color came out.

I wasn't fast enough to react. Quentin elbowed me to the side. I fell just in time to see the sun itself wash over him. He was completely engulfed in flame.

The pain from the True Samadhi Fire this close was a crisis of faith. It felt like my organs would never speak to each other again. The blood stopped in my veins.

Red Boy closed his mouth and the storm cleared.

"I've been training, too," he said. "I don't take as long to recharge now. I got a lot stronger on that island without anyone knowing."

I tried to crawl back to Quentin, my eyes barely working, the gravel stinging my skin. A rock formation with his shape stood where he should have been. I put my hands on it without worrying about the residual heat searing me to the bone.

He'd been tempered. His body didn't even feel like tissue anymore. This was a gray stone cast of Quentin, a mineral replacement.

And it had a crack running across the body from shoulder to hip.

"No," I said, trying to figure out how deep it went with my fingernails. *"No!"*

Quentin didn't move or speak. The expression that had been frozen on his face wasn't shock or anger. It was resignation. His eyes were closed, his mouth calm. It was too much of a goodbye, and I screamed.

36

ERLANG SHEN SWOOPED IN AND GRABBED ME BY THE BACK OF the neck. He flew up, up, and away, taking me into the sky.

I thrashed in his vise grip, but he kept me at arm's length. I tried to say that I'd kill him, but it came out as an unintelligible shriek of rage.

Quentin should have been invulnerable. Immortal. Always by my side. Maybe I was destined to lose, but I was never supposed to lose Quentin, not even in the most tragic of possible outcomes. I had been cheated down to my very soul. This was an abomination.

I screamed and screamed again, so hard that I tasted blood.

"It upsets me to see you mourn him," Erlang Shen said. "Wasn't the whole point of your reincarnation to get away from Sun Wukong and find a better owner? One who wasn't such a brute? One who treated you with more dignity and respect, like a gentleman?"

"Shut up!" I howled. "Shut up shut up shut up!"

"I found your new human form first, you know. By all rights you're mine, not the monkey's. The only reason I didn't reveal myself was because I needed his unwitting assistance to draw out your powers. Talent as big as yours can require multiple coaches, you know."

He kept flying higher, but he turned us around to face the city.

"I have the feeling you didn't take my threat in the park seriously," he said. "So I'm going to take as many lives as the Great Fire of 1906 did, and make you watch. We'll see how willing you are to come with me to Heaven after that."

"Shenyingdawang!" He had to shout to be heard over my screaming. "I'd like a couple of blocks removed from the city."

"Which ones?" the demon asked, a contractor sizing up his quote.

"Any. Just make sure you get—"

Erlang Shen glanced at me and made a coy little face of trying to remember something.

"Make sure you include New Viscount Street and Second," he said.

My father.

Guanyin had put my town under her protection. But it didn't extend to the city, and I hadn't remembered to ask. I'd neglected my father. I'd shelved him outside my conception of "home."

I'd killed him.

"You know what?" Red Boy shouted back from the ground. "I think I'm just gonna level all of downtown entirely. I don't feel like going through the effort to be picky."

Erlang Shen laughed his consent.

Red Boy made two fists and began rubbing his knuckles together. His bright color became incandescent, the heat inside him forcing its way through his skin into the surrounding air.

"It's really quite fascinating, what you're about to see," Erlang Shen said to me. "The best way to describe it would be a human missile. A demon missile, rather."

Red Boy drew his legs up into the air, encased in a thick layer of energy, his pose a mockery of an abbot in meditation. He began skimming silently over the ground toward the heart of the city in a straight line, slowly at first but accelerating, doubling and redoubling in speed. He wasn't a missile; he was the bullet in a railgun.

The demon reached the velocity where I knew there was no stopping him. The trigger had been pulled—the button had been pressed on my father and thousands of other innocent people.

I couldn't bring myself to look. I shut my eyes, shut my true sight down, shut everything down except for the tears streaming over my face.

■ ■ ■

"What are you doing?" Erlang Shen asked.

I didn't answer him. Then I realized he wasn't talking to me. I came back to the world of the living, steadied my sobs, and looked around.

Red Boy was no longer moving toward the city. He hovered where he was, the nucleus in a hot streak of light. A snapshot of a shooting star.

"Red Boy!" said Erlang Shen.

"He can't hear you," I said, sniffling. "He's trapped in a time bubble."

Erlang Shen had forgotten about the other divine being in my corner and smashed his head into a great big ceiling of impenetrable nothing. I could see the giant barrier spell hovering over us only because the wildfire smoke had stopped rising at that point. He dropped me, and I fell.

The air whistled past my ears. Erlang Shen shook off his daze and flew straight down to catch me, but he only made it a dozen yards before he hit another wall. He was caught in a smaller barrier, forced to play an angry mime in a real invisible box. The Goddess of Mercy had the aim of a cold-blooded sniper.

I plunged toward the ground. The wind stung my eyes, but the Earth taking over my view filled me with a sudden calm.

It's okay, I said to myself, a moment before impact. *I'm made of iron.*

The noise was greater than any Quentin and I had ever made upon landing. It was meteoric. Cataclysmic. But I'd absorbed none of the shock. The shock was heaped upon the rest of the world, and the planet would have to deal with it.

I stood up in the middle of a smoking crater. I was untouched. My lack of injury made perfect sense.

I saw Guanyin kneeling over Quentin's body, and I clambered out of the depression to their side. She was checking him with her hands, much as I'd done, but this time it meant something.

Guanyin looked up at Erlang Shen and then gave me a bitter smile.

"I sure can pick 'em, huh?" she said wryly.

"He had us all fooled. Can you heal Quentin?"

"I can try to restore Quentin, or I can help you end this," she answered. "But not both. It's taking most of what I've got to hold the two of them back, and I don't have enough karmic juice to go around. I'm already bewitching too many people right now to keep this fight a secret."

That she didn't talk about Quentin like he was dead gave me a thump of hope in my chest. "Fix him," I said. "Please."

"The two of you will be on your own afterward. You're asking me to put my faith in you."

"We can do it." I was ready to lie to her to get Quentin back, but this felt like the truth.

"Very well." She cleared a space around him and put her hands on the sides of his face.

A sphere of energy encircled them both. Quentin and Guanyin began twitching. Their movements weren't voluntary, especially not his. The little settlings of his stony form and her breathing were being played at higher than normal speed. And, I soon noticed, in reverse.

Dust around them that had risen sank back down to the ground. Errant stalks of dry grass cartwheeled backward, cleaning up their tracks as they went. A tiny beetle caught in the bubble moonwalked away.

A rocky splitting noise sent fear through my spine, but it was only the seam on Quentin's body sealing up. The gray pallor of his skin dissolved, and it became warm and touchable once more.

Guanyin was winding back causality itself. Undoing the passage of time.

She was so *powerful*. I had to fight the urge to fall to my knees and clasp my hands together in awe.

Quentin awoke with a gasp. He scrambled back from Guanyin in surprise. She staggered to her feet, breathing heavily.

"Well," she said, "that's everything I've got left in the tank."

"Are you okay?" I asked. The goddess looked pale and bloodless, as if she'd traded her very life for Quentin's.

"I'll recover once I'm back in Heaven, but I won't be doing that particular trick again for another century or three," she said, her voice already wavering like a ghost's. "Which means it's all on you to clean up properly. I don't even have the energy to maintain my grip on Earth right now."

She sounded like we were about to lose connection for who knew how long. I had to choose my remaining words to her carefully.

"Thank you," I said. *"Thank you!"*

"You can thank me by winning," she answered. "I'm not supposed to condone physical violence, but when it comes to those two *laan zai* . . ."

I raised my palms upward and then clenched my fists. "I promise to serve as your mortal intermediary."

Guanyin smiled. She fritzed once, twice. And then she was gone.

I couldn't escape the feeling that I'd been dropped off at the world's coolest party by the world's coolest older cousin.

"What just happened?" Quentin asked.

"You died and came back to life," I said. "Get with the program."

Even after all that, Guanyin had given us one last gift. Her spells were wearing off gradually instead of blinking out with her. In the sky, Erlang Shen pounded on the barrier, which looked to be on the verge of shattering, and Red Boy was only now picking up speed again.

I pointed Quentin upward. "Body block him," I said. "Don't let him near me for a minute."

Quentin glanced at Red Boy, his eyes full of worry for me. But he nodded.

The barrier above us broke. Quentin jumped straight up and met Erlang Shen halfway. This time he got a good grip. I could hear him whoop with glee at finally being able to lay his hands on that bastard. The two of them tussled in the sky, zigzagging over the hills.

I ran in front of Red Boy, placing myself right in his path. Even through the time bubble I could detect the spark of recognition in his eyes. He knew that in seconds I'd be taking the full impact of his speed.

I slammed my right foot down, embedding it six inches deep into the solid ground.

The smug air around Red Boy's face disappeared. Now he saw, like I did, that the next few seconds also meant that he was a sitting duck. A nice fat pitch hovering over the plate, and me with plenty of time to tee up.

It was time for drastic measures. Something I'd never done before.

Scratch that. I'd done it once before.

I thrust my arm at Red Boy, reaching out five feet, ten feet, twenty feet. Just like in the library with Quentin. I could feel my limb rubber banding, but it was merely reaching states that were perfectly natural to it. My arm was remembering.

I kept stretching it out, picking up more and more speed to the point where my hand was now a projectile. My palm strike smashed into Red Boy's torso, knocking the wind out of his lungs, and my long fingers wrapped around his body, hog-tying him.

The time bubble popped. I screamed from the pain of the True Samadhi Fires surrounding my prey, but I held my grip, and I kept flinging my arm forward. There were no brakes on this train.

Red Boy's aura hit critical mass and flared outward. Only it didn't reach me. I was carrying him away far enough and fast enough that I was safe. My arm was a pair of tongs, and the faster I stretched the less it hurt. My growing limb distributed the heat over a wider area.

Localized laws of physics are still laws of physics, I thought as I clenched my teeth. *Dickhead.*

I slammed his back into the hillside, squashing the remaining air out of him. But I wasn't done, not by a mile.

My arm went on, diagonally down, plowing Red Boy deeper and deeper into the base of the hill. Bedrock and boulders gave way to me as easily as the crumbling foundations of a sand castle. If he'd said anything or done anything before he disappeared under the rubble, I'd missed it completely.

Once it felt like I'd gone deep enough, I unclenched my hand and withdrew it. The impromptu mineshaft I left behind glowed orange, then red, then white. I threw myself to the side just in time to dodge a knot of flame so concentrated it looked like a giant worm escaping the molten core of the Earth. Fire in the hole.

Once Red Boy's detonation subsided, the mineshaft collapsed, bringing the surrounding earth down with a mighty *whump*. Some seismologist was going to have a confusing time working out what had happened.

As far as I was concerned, it was okay to leave Red Boy where he was. If he wasn't dead, he couldn't be sent to Hell where he might escape. And with an entire mountain crushing him, he wouldn't have any air to power his fire breath. If this kind of prison was good enough for the Monkey King, it was good enough for him.

My dust-covered arm slurped back into my body like a strand of extra-long linguini. The sight was nauseating. I should have kept my eyes closed like back when I was on the school roof.

Quentin slammed into the ground beside me, landing on his back. He scrambled to his feet.

"Son of a bitch keeps running away from me," he grumbled.

I looked up, visoring my eyes from the sun. Erlang Shen was

conjuring up something big, gesturing at us with his hands, and I finally remembered that he was a rain god.

"I, uh, think he only wanted a clear shot," I said.

Two manhole-diameter jets of water stomped us flat like elephant's feet. The Hoover Dam had opened a valve above our heads.

I knew how dangerous high-pressure water was. It was how they cut titanium. But still, I was surprised how hard the impact was. On a scale of one to Baigujing, this was like eating a dozen of her haymakers all over my body at once.

Quentin might have shouted after me but his words were lost amid the roar of the water. He was a flat blur. Neither of us could lift ourselves off the ground.

The downpour continued unabated. If we didn't do something fast, we were going to drown eight hundred feet above sea level.

My body screamed at me as I ran out of oxygen. It was screaming a message I'd been doing my best to ignore since I was young, if not little.

Grow.

I finally gave in to it.

37

THE ONLY SENSATION WAS THAT OF THE WATER STREAM getting smaller. My head was freed of the river, and I could breathe again. I put my hand up as a shield; it wasn't a completely ineffective gesture.

The view was like Quentin's skyward jump, slowed down to the extreme. Trees became smaller and smaller. The ground got farther and farther away. If we were in the city I might have been able to use the ascending floors of a nearby skyscraper like backdrop markers on a police lineup. As it was, I could only guess how big I was getting.

I got to my feet, unhindered by the square-cube law. I grew taller. And taller. Erlang Shen tried to shoot me down, and he even let up on Quentin to concentrate his efforts, but it was pointless. We were operating at different scales now.

I knew how big I needed to be. There was no need to go overboard. I just needed to grow to the size where the god hovering in midair was a little larger than the palm of my hand, relatively speaking.

Roughly the size of a volleyball.

I recognized the look on Erlang Shen's face. I'd seen it on my opponents so many times, up close, masked only by the loose weave of a net. The look that said, *Oh god, she can't be that tall. Who paired me against her?*

He turned to flee but caught a mouthful of Quentin's shoulder. His collision with the Monkey King kept him spinning in the air. Quentin had given me the perfect set.

"MINE!" I screamed out of habit. My voice thundered over the mountain, warning anyone and everyone not to take my kill.

I spiked Erlang Shen into the ground with so much heat that I could have made the dinosaurs go extinct all over again. I highlight-reeled him. It made me sad that scouts for the national team weren't watching.

And gods bounced, apparently. Who knew?

Erlang Shen dribbled away from my feet like a ball without enough air in it. Before he even came to a stop, he imploded around an infinitesimal point, some kind of gravity sucking his body inward into nothing, like a black hole. It happened without a sound.

Maybe when you were giant, everything seemed anticlimactic.

"Is he dead?" I asked. I winced after I spoke. I hated how loud I was.

"No," answered Quentin, who managed not to come across as tinny. "Gods get a sweeter deal when their physical body is busted. It's straight back to Heaven for him."

"That's BS."

"Not this time. He's committed blood treason against the Jade Emperor. There will be a quick hearing before he's punished. There's literally a special place in Hell for that crime."

Of course—the only thing the Jade Emperor would act quickly upon was a threat to his rule. If it meant Erlang Shen getting what he deserved, though, I wouldn't complain.

"Are you going to stay up there all day?" Quentin asked.

Shrinking down was easier and much less disturbing than drawing back an extended limb. Quentin and the ground came closer as if I were on a helicopter touching down. My body stopped naturally where it was supposed to. I could have tried to keep going and see what life would have been like as a size small, but there was no way I was ready to unpack all of that baggage right now. Regular, tall-ass Genie would suffice.

We were both still soaking wet. I figured watching Quentin shake the water from his hair like he'd emerged from the pool in a cologne ad was my reward for a job well done. His now-transparent shirt lapped at the muscles on his torso.

His eyes caught mine before doing a double take. "Holy crap," he said. "Look at your arm."

I yelped. The limb that Red Boy burned had been washed clean of rock dust. Now it was shiny black from my fingers up to my elbow. The color of polished iron.

My nails were as golden as my true sight eyes. They glittered expensively in the sun, like unburied treasure.

I wiggled my fingers. There was no loss of motion or sensation. The transition between the iron and flesh was a fine ombré.

Hoo boy.

Rather than process this like I needed to, I let my mind slip away. It might return to me later. Right now my thoughts were as free as a bird.

"Hey, tell me something," I said. "I never made it to the end of your book. What did your traveling group get for completing their quest?"

Quentin rubbed his chin. "Xuanzang was given Buddhahood.

Sandy became an arhat. Pigsy got to be a shrine cleaner, which meant he could eat all the offerings of food people left for the gods. He couldn't have been happier. Why?"

Xuanzang might have gone all the way to the West and back purely out of noble intentions, with no expectation of a reward. But it sounded like everyone still got what they wanted at the end.

That settled it then. I happened to want *this*.

I grabbed Quentin by the collar, leaned down, and kissed him.

He was a little startled at first, but then he kissed me back, hard. Like real hard. Like he'd been waiting for this moment since the day we met.

I felt his strong arms circle my waist and cinch tight, lifting me off the ground. I grabbed fistfuls of his hair, which I'd always secretly dreamed about doing, and crushed his lips to mine. Kissing Quentin was as rough and as confrontational as any of our other interactions, and I loved it.

"This is so wrong," he said, his words slightly muffled as I bit him in the mouth. "It's like King Arthur having feelings for Excalibur."

Eh. From my perspective it was more like Jane Goodall hooking up with King Kong. You know, if King Kong were hot and infuriating and oddly supportive of Jane's feelings over time.

Quentin went for my neck in a way I was highly looking forward to, but then he suddenly stopped.

"Uh, Genie," he said, pulling away. He peered over my shoulder at something.

"Do not give me bad news right now," I snapped. "Don't you dare."

"All right," said Quentin. "Good news, then. We found what we were looking for."

"What do you mean?"

"You know how there were one hundred and eight escapees from Hell? And we only took care of a handful at most?"

I groaned. "And I said that the rest were probably hiding here under the cover of the smoke, waiting for Erlang Shen to call upon them as needed."

"Yeah," said Quentin. "The good news is that you were right, as usual. Yaaay."

The wildfires had receded without Red Boy there to sustain them. They mostly just disappeared instead of burning out, leaving behind brush that didn't even appear scorched. The smoke that had been clogging my true sight rolled up and left, drawing back the curtain on . . .

Demons. Lots and lots of demons.

"There's the Black Wind Demon," said Quentin. "Lingxuzi as well. The Golden Horned King. Xiong Shanjun. The Scholar in a White Robe—"

"Quentin, I get it."

They could have been a crowd sitting around an outdoor concert waiting for the band to appear. The smoke clearing up got them on their feet. Maybe the show was about to start.

A few of them tapped tentatively at the air, expecting there to be a barrier of some sort. If Erlang Shen had been using one to contain them, it was gone now.

I could tell the figures were all yaoguai without true sight. They fit the profile—human forms, with one or more monstrous aspects. Clothes that were just slightly off-kilter somehow. An expression of intense hatred once they spotted Quentin.

I seethed right back at them.

"This is bull crap!" I shouted. "I'm tired! I don't have the energy for this!"

"Genie," Quentin said. "Please stop telling the swarm of yaoguai how weak you are right now."

"I don't want to deal with you!" I hollered at the demons from afar. "Screw everything! Evil wins, are you happy?"

"You know, if you're not up for another fight, you could let me take care of it. Like in the old days."

And here I thought our make-out session had signaled progress.

"Oh my god *fine*," I shouted, throwing my hands in the air. "I will let you use me as a stick. I'll be the Ruyi Jingu Bang again. Get it out of your system just this once, and then shut up forever about it."

I was even more disappointed than I was letting on. Getting closer to Quentin didn't mean much if he'd been simply playing the long, long game to get his staff back. I didn't know what the process was for turning into the iron staff of yore, so I shut my eyes and held out my arms angrily as if I was demanding a hug.

"That's not what I'm asking for!" Quentin said. "I was talking about something else! I know how much you hate that idea!" He looked deeply hurt that I would even imply that.

I opened my eyes so I could roll them at him. "Okay, then what *is* your plan?"

"This." He reached around my back and grabbed the end of my ponytail, which had miraculously held together throughout the whole ordeal.

"Ow!"

"Relax, I'm using my hair, too." He showed me the two dark strands in his fingers, one plucked from his head and one plucked from mine. Long and short, just like us.

Then he did something gross and popped them into his mouth.

The action meant something to the yaoguai, beyond being disgusting. Their eyes grew wide and they stopped in their tracks, afraid to come any closer.

He chewed the hairs with the front of his mouth instead of his molars, chopping them into little bits. Then he stepped forward and spat an army into the air.

. . .

I assumed that the pieces of hair were turning into clones. Like the trick he'd pulled with his parents. That was the only way I could explain the horde of Genie Los and Quentin Suns that spilled out of his mouth onto the hillside.

The doppelgangers started out small but then grew to full size as they scrambled to their feet and blinked in the sunlight. They were like baby foals, able to walk and see only moments after being born. They looked exactly like us, right down to the burns and tears on our clothing.

Once he was done hocking the world's weirdest loogie, Quentin wiped his mouth and pointed toward the assembled yaoguai.

"Sic 'em," he commanded.

The assembled legion of us took off for the yaoguai with a delighted roar. The demons were outnumbered, a clone-Genie and clone-Quentin for every one.

"See?" the real Quentin said to me. "We're on perfectly equal footing, technically. Full partners."

"I . . . uh . . . sure?"

The brawl that ensued once the two sides made contact was ugly, lopsided, and quick. The yaoguai had no chance, and some of them even tried to preemptively flee, only to get tackled from behind.

But despite the savage beatdown our side was raining upon them, there were no telltale whorls of ink that indicated the demons were being slain. In fact, you could have argued that the little clone army was being relatively merciful. They grabbed and pinned their enemies, forcing the demons to look at Quentin and me.

Real Quentin leaped onto a boulder.

"Hear this!" he bellowed. "If any of you even look funny at the human world again, I swear on every god who ever sits upon the Dragon Throne that you will regret it. Harm a human and I will turn you into *puppets* of suffering and regret. Do you understand?"

I saw a few demons nod as much as their captors would allow them to. The general look of terror on their faces told me that this bunch wasn't quite as nasty as Red Boy or Baigujing. They might have been rounded up by Erlang Shen to fill out the B-squad.

"Swear it!" Quentin shouted. "Swear on your very spirits!"

The demons bowed as hard as they could before the clones let them go. They scattered into the hillsides, leaving with some kicks on the backside for good measure.

"That was lenient of you," I said.

"My earrings still work. If they threaten humanity, we'll stop them. Like we always do."

Once the demons were gone, Quentin let out a pinky whistle with the proficiency of a football coach.

"Okay," he said. "Let's pack it up."

The clones began poofing into white smoke. I watched, dumbfounded. I was wrong about Quentin before. Somehow, even after everything that we'd been through, he could still show me things that screwed with my head.

Quentin plopped back down next to me and sighed. "Man, that trick takes a lot out of me."

"Probably for the best that you don't do it too often. It's kind of unsettling and . . . hey! *Hey! You two!*"

A delinquent Genie-clone and Quentin-clone had ignored the order to self-destruct and were instead getting busy with each other, right there on the ground. Sure, Quentin and I had kissed, but this was escalating to a higher MPAA rating.

I couldn't believe I needed to chaperone my own clone. "THAT'S OFF LIMITS!" I shouted at them. "NOT UNTIL YOU'RE NINETEEN!"

"Aw, come on," Quentin said with pure dismay on his face. "Nineteen?"

"Go wait it out in Heaven if you don't like it."

■ ■ ■

We were almost home before I remembered I'd forgotten something.

"Crap!" I said. "My arm!"

I wasn't *too* worried, because I figured Quentin had a spell to hide it. But his face told me otherwise. It said I should worry.

"I'm not sure what I can do about that," he said. "The True Samadhi Fire burned away anything that masked your inner nature."

"Well, you better friggin' try."

Quentin grumbled and took my iron hand. His skin felt extra-warm against the metal. He hummed to himself and swayed with the effort.

Slowly but surely the iron color receded, leaving my skin behind. It drew out of my fingertips, removing the gold from my nails.

"There," Quentin said. "Done."

"Uh, no. Not done."

Most of the metallic hues had disappeared, but there was still a halo around my wrist. A swirl of gold pinpoints on a black background circled my arm. It looked like a beautiful tattoo of the Milky Way, the kind that I would see shared in an online photo feed.

"Get rid of it," I said.

"I can't. This is the most I could reduce the perception of your inner self. Like how I can't hide my tail."

"Get. Rid. Of. It."

"It's fetching," he said.

"It's a *tattoo*. Do you know what my mother will do when she sees it?"

Quentin gave a helpless shrug. I started panicking more than I ever had in any of the demon battles. Forget my mom. Not even my dad would be cool with this, and he couldn't get worked up over anything. Disowning me would be their first agreement in years.

"Quentin!" I shouted.

He threw his hands in the air. "I could always bewitch your mother so she permanently overlooks whatever's on your wrist?"

"Do it!"

He frowned. "I wasn't being serious."

I was, despite the hypocrisy of it, after having told Guanyin not to magic my mom.

"Trust me," I said, gripping him by the shoulders. "This is the lesser of two evils."

38

I WAS TAKING A BREAK FROM STUDYING IN MY ROOM WHEN I first saw the video on the evening news.

Some hiker had caught distant snippets of our rumble with Erlang Shen. There I was, growing taller and taller until I swatted something that couldn't be seen out of the air. That's when the clip ended. A freeze-frame of me in all my titanic glory.

I looked like a giant robot in a skirt. In what I could only assume was yet another favor from Guanyin, an unnaturally cloudy mist obscured my face from view.

"Witnesses are calling it a CGI marketing stunt, most likely for an unannounced reboot of *Attack of the 50 Foot Woman*," the news anchor said. "Which begs the important question—*is Hollywood out of ideas?*"

I groaned into my palms. I would have to burn that outfit and pray Yunie didn't have my wardrobe catalogued in her head. I didn't want her suddenly remembering the magical crap she'd been exposed to.

Not before I could tell her about it.

I had decided. Yunie was going learn everything that had happened to me regarding gods and demons, down to the last tooth and claw, and she was going to hear it from me, face-to-face. Quentin's long-lasting forgetfulness spell had given me the chance to make a proper confession to my friend, and I wasn't going to waste it.

There was a tapping at my window. I ignored it. Quentin could let himself in.

"The Colossus of the Headlands," he said. "You have so many likes."

"You're going to have to cast another spell on my mother. Being online famous is her worst nightmare for me. More so than being eaten by demons."

"How's your arm?" he asked. "No one else thinks you have a new tattoo?"

I raised my wrist. "I haven't taken off this sweatband in three days," I said. "I'm going to be known as Sweatband Girl. You've cursed me to that existence. I hope you're happy."

I heard Quentin sit on my bed, the springs creaking up and down. The pages of a book riffled open. He'd probably helped himself to the contents of my shelves.

"What are you going to do now?" I asked.

"What do you mean?"

"You cleaned up the worst of the demonic incursion. You beat your oldest enemy. There's no reason for you to stick around."

"Of course there's a reason. The yaoguai could always go back on their promise to stay out of trouble. New ones might arrive. I'll have to remain on Earth to keep watch over the whole situation."

I'd been biting my lip the entire time in anticipation of his response. But he said he was staying. I could stop chewing on myself now.

"I'll flesh out my background," he said. "Set up clones for my parents on a long-term basis. I sort of miss having them around. Even if they were overly strict."

"Don't change their personalities," I said. "I like your parents. In fact, I have them penciled in for dinner with my mom next week."

"Sure," Quentin said. "What about you, though? What are your plans now that Heaven and Hell are out of your hair?"

"It's back to the grind. I'll be a junior soon. Application season is going to start for real."

"Still aiming for the promised land, huh?"

"I've got no reason not to. I don't care what Anna said. I'm gunning for every top-tier school out there. If they want to say no to me, I'll make them go through the effort."

"Bash on the gates and see what happens," Quentin concurred. "I can't argue with that logic."

"And in the meantime, I'm hitting the programming books. I'll learn what I can on my own, and Rutsuo offered to mentor me for the rest. My goal is to make my own app by the end of the year."

"I thought you weren't into computers."

"I've recently learned that what I *am* into is having skills," I said. "Skills that no one can deny or take away from me. People can always say I don't look impressive enough, but they can't argue over how strong I am once I punch them in the face."

Quentin chuckled.

"With an app," I corrected. "Once I metaphorically punch them in the face with a really slick, well-made app."

"You should be careful," Quentin said. "If you go too far down that route, you could end up making a life in the Bay Area."

I let the statement hang as I went back to my notes. Sometimes you just had to accept that you might never change as much as you want to.

Quentin smiled, flipped a page, and began reading.

■ ■ ■

Half an hour passed before he got bored and stood up.

"Want to go make out while flying through the air?" he asked. "We can land in Wine Country."

I spun around in my chair to face him. "I don't know. Any higher than a thousand feet up and I only kiss the ancient legends I'm in a proper relationship with."

Quentin immediately dropped to one knee. "Eugenia Lo Pei-Yi, will you—"

I knocked him over with a kick before he could finish the sentence.

"Okay, too fast." He sprang back up and grinned, undaunted. "How about a date then?"

That was acceptable. I took Quentin's hand and left all my plans, all my fears, all my worries behind me. They'd be there when I got back.

■ ■ ■

"This looks like the stuff that comes with bubble tea." Quentin prodded the tapioca pearls that garnished his oyster.

"That's because it is," I said. "Give me that if you're not going to eat it."

I wasn't going to let the food go to waste. We were sitting at a table inside the best restaurant in the country.

We'd lost track of time during our jaunt to Wine Country and gotten hungry. Quentin had asked me where I wanted to eat, and I'd said the name of this place as a joke. But after a quick search on his phone, he'd jumped us to the unassuming, renovated saloon that served as the premier culinary destination in the western half of the United States.

The inside of the restaurant was pretty unassuming for a fancy place, mostly white wallpaper and white tablecloths and dark wooden leather chairs. But the other diners had the nervous air of competitive high-divers on the ledge, about to take their last shot at the gold.

Magic and hexes must have gotten us past the door and into our seats. That, or Quentin bribed the crap out of the staff with more gambling winnings than I could have hidden under my mattress. I let the details slide. I deserved a nice meal after everything I'd been through.

A waiter set down the next course as gracefully as a ninja in early retirement. It was something made out of cucumbers, which was much more Quentin's speed. We both wolfed it down in an instant.

Quentin swallowed his portion first, which gave him time to laugh at me.

"What?"

"You're the only human being here who isn't taking pictures of the food before eating it," he said.

"You mean *we're* the only human beings. As far as I'm concerned, you're one of us. Help as many people of Earth as you have, and you're part of the club. Past the gate."

Quentin's eyes softened. "I don't think it works like that. I haven't been reborn as a human. I didn't earn it like you did."

"You did in my book. Besides, I'm not open-minded enough to have a boyfriend who isn't at least part human."

He grinned and shook his head at me. "You're crazy, you know—"

BONGGGGG.

Quentin was interrupted by the sound of a gong. A big brass gong. A big brass Chinese gong, right here in a French restaurant.

Dozens of pairs of feet tromped over the wooden floors. Two columns of hatted, robed men shuffled into the room, making use of all the space in between the tables. Someone who was better than me at being Asian could have said what dynasty their colorful silken dress was from.

Judging by their subservient posture, they weren't a threat. Quentin hadn't leaped out of his seat, ready to fight. In fact, he was leaning back and slumping over like he did when he was bored in class.

The men all took a knee simultaneously, forming a human walkway that led straight to our table. A sedan chair entered from the other end. The golden, lacquered palanquin was borne by silent armored guardians who coordinated their steps like ballet dancers so as not to jostle the occupant.

Ever so slowly the chair made its way across the room to our table. Once it finally arrived, a servant pulled the embroidered silk curtain aside.

Out stepped a fuming, red-faced bank manager. Or a summer camp director. That was the impression I got of the man, even though he was decked out in fineries that could have stocked the Met's exhibition halls for ten seasons straight.

A servant cleared his throat. *"All hail His Imperial Majesty, August Ruler of Heaven and Divine Master of—"*

The Jade Emperor waved off the announcer so violently that he backhanded the poor schlub in the mouth. I hadn't expected to meet the king of the gods under these circumstances.

"*You,*" he hissed at me.

"*Moi?*" I said as innocently as I could. Quentin snickered. This was going to go poorly if he kept egging me on.

"Yes, you! Flaunting your powers where any human can see them! How dare you!"

I looked around the room. The other diners were frozen mid-bite. Guanyin stepped out from behind the palanquin, being her gorgeous self in a plain *qipao*. She gave me a smile and a finger wave behind the Jade Emperor's back.

"Look, nothing stays hidden for very long these days," I said. "Everyone's got a smartphone. Your big masquerade was going to fail at some point. You might even have to—and I know this is a big shock—manage your own affairs in the mortal realm."

"*Ooooh,*" Quentin mooned.

"Shut up, you damned ape!" the Jade Emperor shrieked. He apparently had as little control over Quentin as Mrs. Nanda did. "You're part of the reason this mess is spiraling out of control! The two of you have let yaoguai run free on Earth for the first time in more than a thousand years!"

"Okay, that is on us," I said. "But what did you want me to do, slaughter them all?"

"Yes!"

I narrowed my eyes. Killing every single yaoguai would have meant a convenient cleanup of Erlang Shen's misdeeds, and a lot of face saved for his uncle. The Jade Emperor would have wu wei'ed himself into another moral victory.

"They were living beings that hadn't done anything wrong yet," I said. "They deserved a chance to do better. Who knows, maybe with enough time they'll become human."

"Of course *you* would think that the scum of the universe could ever improve their lot," the Jade Emperor scoffed. "Just because the Ruyi Jingu Bang managed to worm its way around its karmic betters doesn't mean the rest of the gutter trash—"

I interrupted him by draining my glass and slamming it on the table upside down. I'd read somewhere that in Australia, it was a signal that I could beat up anyone in the room.

"What are the odds that you want to finish that sentence?" I asked.

It took a little while for the Jade Emperor to gather that I was threatening him, probably out of sheer unfamiliarity with the sensation. But the payoff was worth it. His eyes goggled out, and he spat into the air like a trumpet player with no trumpet.

"No, please, continue," I said. "You were in the middle of insulting the living weapon your nephew wanted to use to destroy you."

Quentin hooted and clapped his hands together. There was no popcorn, so he took a big chunk of bread and tore into it with glee as he watched us.

The Jade Emperor tried to recover from his tailspin. "You impudent—wretched—disrespectful . . ."

This was getting sad. "You didn't come here solely to wag your finger at us. Say what you really wanted to say."

The King of Heaven huffed and puffed until he calmed himself down. I waited patiently for him to compose himself.

"I am here to make a proclamation," he said, finally. "Because you have so thoroughly violated my policies of discretion, an official Judgment of Heaven is necessary to handle the fallout."

"Well hey—haven't seen one of those in a thousand years," Quentin chimed in.

The Jade Emperor shot him a dirty look before continuing.

"This region of Earth has degraded to the point where it requires more direct management than the celestial pantheon can provide. Therefore, the great Kingdom of California will be cut loose from our jurisdiction."

I mashed my nose into my palm. "California's not a—never mind. Go on."

"Any spirit or yaoguai may henceforth set foot in these borders, enjoying the *freedom* you value so much," he said with a sneer. "Accountability for what happens will fall squarely on the shoulders of a specially appointed Divine Guardian, who will manage all non-terrestrial interactions inside the protectorate."

Guanyin came up to the table and lowered her eyes.

Finally. The Goddess of Mercy and Gettin' Stuff Done deserved to be in charge for once. Governing a chunk of Earth would be right in her wheelhouse.

But something about the situation didn't sit right. The smugness in the Jade Emperor's tone made it sound less like he was giving Guanyin a promotion worth celebrating and more like he was washing his hands of an impossible task. The lengths to which he'd go not to do any dirty work astounded me.

"Non-terrestrial interactions," I said. "Let me guess. What you really mean is demon fights, rogue gods, and magic spells exploding in people's faces. Pure chaos. California is going to turn into a big hot mess of spiritual shenanigans that nobody in their right mind would want on their plate."

The Jade Emperor smiled and then bent his head.

Quentin and I shared a confused glance at the gesture. Surely he couldn't—

No. No way.

The ruler of Heaven was bowing. To me.

I thought maybe he'd fallen asleep on his feet, or suddenly lost the tendons in his neck.

But Guanyin had dipped even further, fixing me with a pointed stare. And all the other attendants kneeling on the floor had pivoted toward me, kowtowing.

No way no way no way . . .

"Well stated, Madame Divine Guardian," the Jade Emperor said. "Your very own big hot mess indeed."

ACKNOWLEDGMENTS

I'd like to thank my entire family, especially my sisters Melissa and Blythe. I'd like to thank my wonderful editor, Anne Heltzel, for giving my work a home, and my fantastic agent, Stephen Barr, for showing me the way. I'd like to thank Nancy Sondel for putting me in the right place at the right time. And I'd like to thank Karen. She knows what she did.

Turn the page for an exclusive first look at

THE RISE OF

coming in July 2019 from F. C. Yee.

降若神通

AVATAR
THE LAST AIRBENDER.

THE RISE OF
KYOSHI

F.C. YEE
with AVATAR CO-CREATOR
MICHAEL DANTE DiMARTINO

The sages did their best to keep the missing Avatar a secret, but it was no use. The cruel, the power-hungry, the lawless—people who normally had the most to fear from the Avatar—were starting to feel that the scales had shifted in their favor, even if they didn't know it for certain. Like sand sharks, responding to the slightest vibrations on pure instinct, they tested their limits. Probed new grounds.

Time was running out.

Kelsang barely finished setting up the Avatar test when the noon gongs struck. The sun was high enough to melt snow off the roof, and the dripping flow of water pattered on the ground like light rain. The silhouettes of villagers and their children queuing up could be seen outside through the paper screen windows. The air was full of excited chatter.

No more waiting, Jianzhu thought. This happens, now.

"For the last time, I can't negotiate a salary with you!" Jianzhu shouted in the face of a particularly blunt farmer. "Being the Avatar is not a paid position!"

The stocky man shrugged. "Sounds like a waste of time then. I'll take my child and go."

Out of the corner of his eye, Jianzhu caught Kelsang frantically waving his hands, making a cutoff sign at the neck. The little girl had wandered over to the whirly flying toy that had once entertained an ancient Avatar and was staring at it intently.

Huh. They weren't intending to get a genuine result today. But picking the first item correctly was already improbable. Too improbable to risk stopping now.

"Okay," Jianzhu said. This would have to come out of his own pocket. "Fifty silvers a year if she's the Avatar."

"Sixty-five silvers a year if she's the Avatar and ten if she's not."

"WHY WOULD I PAY YOU IF SHE'S NOT THE AVATAR?" Jianzhu roared.

Kelsang coughed and thumped loudly on the floor. The girl had picked up the whirligig and was eying the drum. Two out of four correct. Out of thousands.

Holy Shu.

"I mean, of course," Jianzhu said quickly. "Deal."

They shook hands. He nearly laughed out loud. It would be ironic, a prank worthy of previous Avatar's sense of humor, to have his reincarnation pop up as a result of a peasant's greed. And the very last child in line for testing, to boot! Kuruk, you son of a . . .

Now the girl had the drum in her arms as well. She walked over to a stuffed hog monkey. Kelsang was beside himself with excitement, his neck threatening to burst through the wooden beads wrapped around it. Jianzhu felt light-headed. Hope bashed against his rib cage, begging to be let out after so many years trapped inside.

The girl wound up her foot and stomped on the stuffed animal as hard as she could.

"Die!" she screamed in her tiny little treble. She ground it under her heel, the stiches audibly ripping.

The light went out of Kelsang's face. He looked like he'd witnessed a murder.

"Ten silvers," the farmer said.

"Get out," Jianzhu snapped.

"Come on, Suzu," the farmer called. "Let's get."

After wresting the other toys away from the Butcher of Hog Monkeys, he scooped the girl up and walked out the door, the whole escapade nothing but a business transaction. In doing so he nearly bowled over another child who'd been spying on the proceedings from the outside.

"Hey!" Jianzhu said. "You forgot your other daughter!"

"That one ain't mine," the farmer said as he thumped down the steps into the street. "That one ain't anyone's."

An orphan then? Jianzhu hadn't spotted the unchaperoned girl around town in the days before, but maybe he'd glossed over her, thinking she was too old to be a candidate. She was much, much taller than any of the other children who'd been brought in by their parents.

As Jianzhu walked over to examine what he'd missed, the girl quavered, threatening to flee, but her curiosity won over her fright. She remained where she was.

Underfed, Jianzhu thought with a frown as he looked over the girl's hollow cheeks and cracked lips. And definitely an orphan. He'd seen hundreds, if not thousands of children like her in the inner provinces where daofei outlaws ran unchecked, parents slain by whatever organized bandit group was ascendant in the territory. She must have wandered far, into the relatively peaceable area of Yokoya.

Upon hearing about the Avatar test, the families of the village had uniformly dressed their eligible children in their finest garments, like the town was hosting a festival. But this child was wearing a threadbare coat with her elbows poking through the holes in the sleeves. Her oversized feet threatened to burst the straps of her too-small sandals. None of the local farmers were feeding or clothing her.

Kelsang, who was always better with children despite his fearsome appearance, joined them. Stooping down, he transformed from an intimidating orange mountain into an oversized version of the stuffed toys behind him.

"Why hello there," he said, putting an extra layer of friendliness into his booming rumble. "What's your name?"

The girl took a long, guarded moment, possibly sizing them up.

"Kyoshi," she whispered. Her eyebrows knotted as if revealing her name was a painful concession.

Kelsang's instincts must have told him to avoid asking about her parents. "Kyoshi, would you like a toy?"

"Are you sure she isn't too old?" Jianzhu said. "She's bigger than some of the teenagers."

"Hush, you." Kelsang made a sweeping gesture at the hall festooned with relics.

The unveiling of so many toys at once had an entrancing effect on most of the children they'd seen today. But Kyoshi didn't gasp, or smile, or move a muscle. Instead she maintained eye contact with Kelsang until he blinked.

As quick as a whip, she scampered by him, snagged an object off the floor and ran back to where she was standing on the porch. She gauged Kelsang and Jianzhu for their responses as intently as they watched her.

Kelsang glanced at Jianzhu and tilted his head at the clay turtle Kyoshi clutched to her chest. One of the four true relics.

They should have been as excited for her as they were for evil little Suzu, but Jianzhu's heart was clouded with doubt. It was hard to believe they'd be so lucky after that previous head-fake.

Still, though.

"Good choice," Kelsang said. "But I've got a surprise for you. You can have three more! Four whole toys, to yourself! Wouldn't you like that?"

Jianzhu sensed a shift in the girl's stance, a tremor in her foundation that was obvious even through the wooden floorboards.

Yes, she would like three more toys very much. What child wouldn't? But in her mind, the promise of more was dangerous. A lie designed to hurt her. If she loosened her grip on the single prize she held right now, she would end up with nothing. Punished for her desire.

Kyoshi shook her head. Her knuckles whitened around the clay turtle.

"It's okay," Kelsang said. "You don't have to put that down. That's the whole point; you can choose different—hey!"

The girl took a step back, and then another, and then before they could react, she was sprinting down the hill with the one-of-a-kind, centuries-old Avatar relic in her hands. Halfway along the street, she took a sharp turn like an experienced fugitive throwing off a pursuer and disappeared in the space between two houses.

Nine Years Later

To Kyoshi, it was very clear—this was a hostage situation.

Silence was the key to making it through to the other side. Complete and total passivity. Neutral jing.

Kyoshi walked calmly down the path through the fallow field, ignoring the covergrass that leaned over and tickled her ankles, the sweat beading on her forehead that stung her eyes. She kept quiet and pretended that the three people who'd fallen in beside her like muggers in an alley weren't a threat.

"So like I was telling the others, my mom and dad think we'll have to dredge the peakside canals earlier this year," Aoma said, drawing out the mom and dad intentionally, dangling more of what Kyoshi lacked in front of her. She crooked her hands into the Crowding Bridge position while slamming her feet into the ground with solid whumps. "One of the terraces collapsed in the last storm."

Above them, floating high out of reach, was the last, precious jar of pickled spicy kelp that the entire village would see this year. The one that Kyoshi had been charged with delivering to Jianzhu's mansion. The one that Aoma had earthbent out of Kyoshi's hands and was now promising to drop at any second. The large clay vessel bobbed up and down, sloshing the brine against the waxed paper seal.

Kyoshi had to stifle a yelp every time the jar lurched against the limits of Aoma's control. No noise. Wait it out. Don't give them anything to latch on to. Talking will only make it worse.

"Of course, she doesn't care," Suzu said. "Precious servant girl doesn't give a lick about farming matters. She's got her cushy job in the fancy house. She's too good to get her hands dirty."

"Won't step in a boat, neither," Jae said. In lieu of elaborating further, he spat on the ground, nearly missing Kyoshi's heels.

Aoma never needed a reason to torment Kyoshi, but as for the others, genuine resentment worked just fine. It was true that Kyoshi spent her days under the roof of a powerful sage instead of breaking her nails against fieldstones. She'd certainly never risked the choppy waters of the Strait in pursuit of a catch.

But what Jae and Suzu conveniently neglected was that every plot of arable land near the village and every seaworthy boat down at the docks belonged to a family. Mothers and fathers, as Aoma was so fond of saying, passed along their trade to daughters and sons in an unbroken bloodline, which meant there was no room for an outsider to inherit any means to survive. If it hadn't been for Kelsang and Jianzhu, Kyoshi would have starved in the streets, right in front of everyone's nose.

Hypocrites.

Kyoshi pressed her tongue against the roof of her mouth as hard as she could. Today was not going to be the day. Someday, maybe, but not today.

"Lay off her," Aoma said, shifting her stance into Dividing Bridge. "I hear that being a serving girl is hard work. That's why we're helping with the deliveries. Isn't that right, Kyoshi?"

For emphasis, she threaded the jar through a narrow gap in the branches of an overhanging tree. A reminder of who was in control here.

Kyoshi shuddered as the vessel dove toward the ground like a hawk before being swooped back up to safety. Just a little further, she thought as the path took a sharp around the hillside. A few more silent, wordless steps until—

There. They'd arrived at last. The Avatar's estate, in all its glory.

The mansion that Jianzhu built to house the savior of the world was designed in the image of a miniature city. A high wall ran in a perfect square around the grounds, with a division in the middle to separate the austere training grounds from the vibrant living quarters. Each section had its own imposing, south-facing gatehouse that was larger than the Yokoya meeting hall. The massive iron-studded doors of the residential gate were flung open, offering a small windowed glimpse of the elaborate topiary inside. A herd of placid goatdogs grazed over the lawn, cropping the grass to an even length.

Foreign elements had been carefully integrated into the design of the complex, which meant that gilded dragons chased carved polar orcas around the edges of the walls. The placement of the Earth Kingdom–style roof tiles cleverly matched Air Nomad numerology principles. Authentic dyes and paints from around the world had been imported at great expense, ensuring that the colors of all four nations were on full, equitable display.

The consensus around the village was that the manor was an eyesore, an alien creature that had sprouted overnight from the native soil, but to Kyoshi it was the most beautiful sight she could ever imagine.

It was a home.

Behind her, Suzu sniffed in disdain. "I don't know what our parents were thinking, selling these fields to a filthy Ganjinese."

Kyoshi's veins flooded with heat. Jianzhu was indeed from the Gan Jin tribe up in the north, but it was the way she'd said it.

"Maybe they knew the land was as worthless and unproductive as their children," Kyoshi muttered under her breath.

The others stopped walking and stared at her.

Whoops. She'd said that a bit too loud, hadn't she?

Jae and Suzu balled their fists. It dawned on them, what they could do while Aoma had Kyoshi helpless. It had been years since any of the village kids could get within arm's reach of her, but today was a special occasion, wasn't it? Maybe a few bruises, in remembrance of old times.

Kyoshi steeled herself for the first blow, rising on her toes in the hope that she could at least keep her face out of the fray, so Auntie Mui wouldn't notice. A few punches and kicks and they'd leave her in peace. Really, it was her own fault for letting her mask slip . . .

"What do you think you're doing?" a familiar voice snarled.

Kyoshi grimaced, even before she opened her eyes.

Peace was no longer an option. Because now Rangi was here.

Rangi must have seen them from afar and stalked across the entire great lawn unnoticed. Or lain in ambush for them all night. Or dropped out of a tree like a webbed leopard. Kyoshi wouldn't have put any of those feats past the military-trained firebender.

Jae and Suzu backed away, trying to swallow their hostile intent like children stuffing stolen candy into their mouths. It occurred to Kyoshi that this might have been the first time they'd ever seen a member of the Fire Nation up close, let alone one as intimidating as Rangi. In her form-fitting armor the color of onyx and dried blood, she could have been a vengeful spirit come to cleanse a battlefield of the living.

Aoma, rather impressively, held her ground. "The Avatar's bodyguard," she said with a faint smile. "I thought you weren't supposed to leave his side. Aren't you slacking off?"

She glanced to the left and right. "Or is he here, somewhere?"

Rangi looked at Aoma like a wad of foulness she'd stepped in during the walk over.

"You're not authorized to be on these grounds," she said in her charred rasp. She pointed upward at the jar of kelp without breaking eye contact. "Nor to lay your hands on the Avatar's property. Or accost his household staff, for that matter."

Kyoshi noticed she personally landed a distant third in that list of considerations.

Aoma tried to play it cool. "This container weighs a ton," she said, shrugging to emphasize her still-ongoing feat of earthbending. "It would take two grown men to lift it without bending. Kyoshi asked us to help her bring it inside the house. Right?"

She gave Kyoshi a radiant smile. One that said tell on me and I'll kill you. Kyoshi had seen that expression before countless times when they were younger, whenever a hapless adult blundered into the two of them "playing" around town, Kyoshi badly scraped up and Aoma with a rock in her hand.

But today she was off her game. Her normally flawless acting had a plaintive, genuine tone to it. Kyoshi suddenly understood what was going on.

Aoma really did want to help her with her delivery. She wanted to be invited inside the mansion and see the Avatar up close, like Kyoshi got to every day. She was jealous.

A feeling akin to pity settled in Kyoshi's throat. Not close enough to hold Rangi back from doing her thing, though.

The firebender stepped forward, the air around her body rippling like a living mirage. "Put the jar down, walk away, and don't come back," she said. "Unless you want to know what the ashes of your eyebrows smell like."

Aoma's expression crumbled. She'd blundered into the predator with much larger fangs. And unlike the adults of the village, no amount of charm or misdirection would work on Rangi. But that didn't mean a parting shot was out of the question.

"Sure," she said. "Thought you'd never ask." With a fling of her hands, the jar rocketed straight up into the air, past the tree line.

"You'd better find someone who's authorized to catch that." She bolted down the path with Suzu and Jae close behind.

"You little—" Rangi made to go after them, fingers of one hand reflexively winding into a cradle for a dose of flaming pain, but she checked herself, thinking better of it. Fiery vengeance would have to wait.

She shook her hand out and clasped it to her forehead, peering up at the rapidly shrinking jar. Aoma had thrown it really, really hard. No one could claim the girl wasn't talented.

Rangi elbowed Kyoshi sharply in the side. "Catch it," she said. "Use earthbending and catch it."

"I— I can't," Kyoshi said, wracked with dismay. Her poor doomed charge reached the apex of its flight. Auntie Mui was going to be furious. A disaster of this magnitude might even get back to Jianzhu. Her pay would get cut.

Rangi still hadn't given up on her. "What do you mean you can't? The staff ledgers have you listed as an earthbender! Catch it!"

"It's not that simple!" Yes, Kyoshi was technically a bender but Rangi didn't know about her "little problem."

"Do the thing with your hands like she did!" Rangi formed the dual claws of Crowding Bridge as if a crude visual reminder by a person who wielded a different element entirely were the missing component.

"Look out!" Kyoshi screamed. She threw herself over Rangi, shielding the smaller girl with her body from the plummeting missile.

No impact came. No deadly shards of ceramic, or explosion of pickling liquid.

"Get off of me, you oaf," Rangi muttered. She shoved against Kyoshi's protective embrace, a bird beating its wings against a cage. Her face and ears were bright red.

The jar floated next to them waist-high above the ground. Under Aoma's control it had wavered and trembled, following her natural patterns of breathing and involuntary motion. But now it was completely still in the air, as if it had been placed on a sturdy iron pedestal.

The pebbles in the dusty path trembled. They began to move and bounce in front of Kyoshi's feet, directed by unseen power from below like they'd been scattered across the surface of a beating drum. They marched in seemingly random directions, little drunken soldiers, until they came to rest in a formation that spelled a message.

You're welcome.

Kyoshi's head snapped up and she squinted at the distant mansion. There was only one person she knew who could have managed this feat. The pebbles began their dance again, settling into words much faster this time.

This is Yun by the way. You know, Avatar Yun.

As if it could have been anyone else in the entire world. Kyoshi couldn't spot where Yun was watching them from, but she could imagine his handsome face and playful, teasing smirk as he performed yet another astounding act of bending like it was no big deal, charming the rocks into complete submission.

She'd never heard of anyone using earth to communicate legibly at a distance. Yun was lucky he wasn't an Air Nomad or else the stunt would have gotten him tattooed in celebration for inventing a new technique.

What are my two favorite ladles doing today?

Kyoshi giggled. Okay, so not perfectly legibly.

Sounds like fun. Wish I could join you.

"He knows we can't reply, right?" Rangi said.

Dumplings, please. Any kind but leeks.

"Enough!" Rangi shouted. "We're distracting him from his training! And you're late for work!" She swept away the pebbles with her foot, less concerned with blazing new trails in the world of bending and more with maintaining the daily schedule.

Kyoshi plucked the jar off the invisible platform and followed Rangi back to the mansion, stepping slowly through the grass so as not to outpace her. If household duties were all that mattered to the firebender, then that would be the end of it, and nothing more would need to be said. Instead she could feel Rangi's silence compacting into a denser form inside her slender frame.

They were halfway to the gate once it became too much to bear.

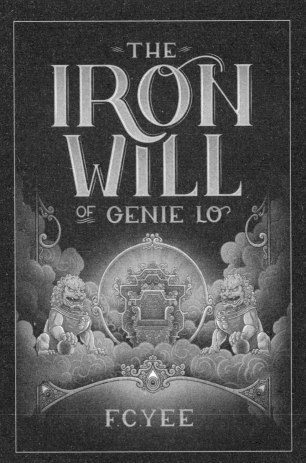